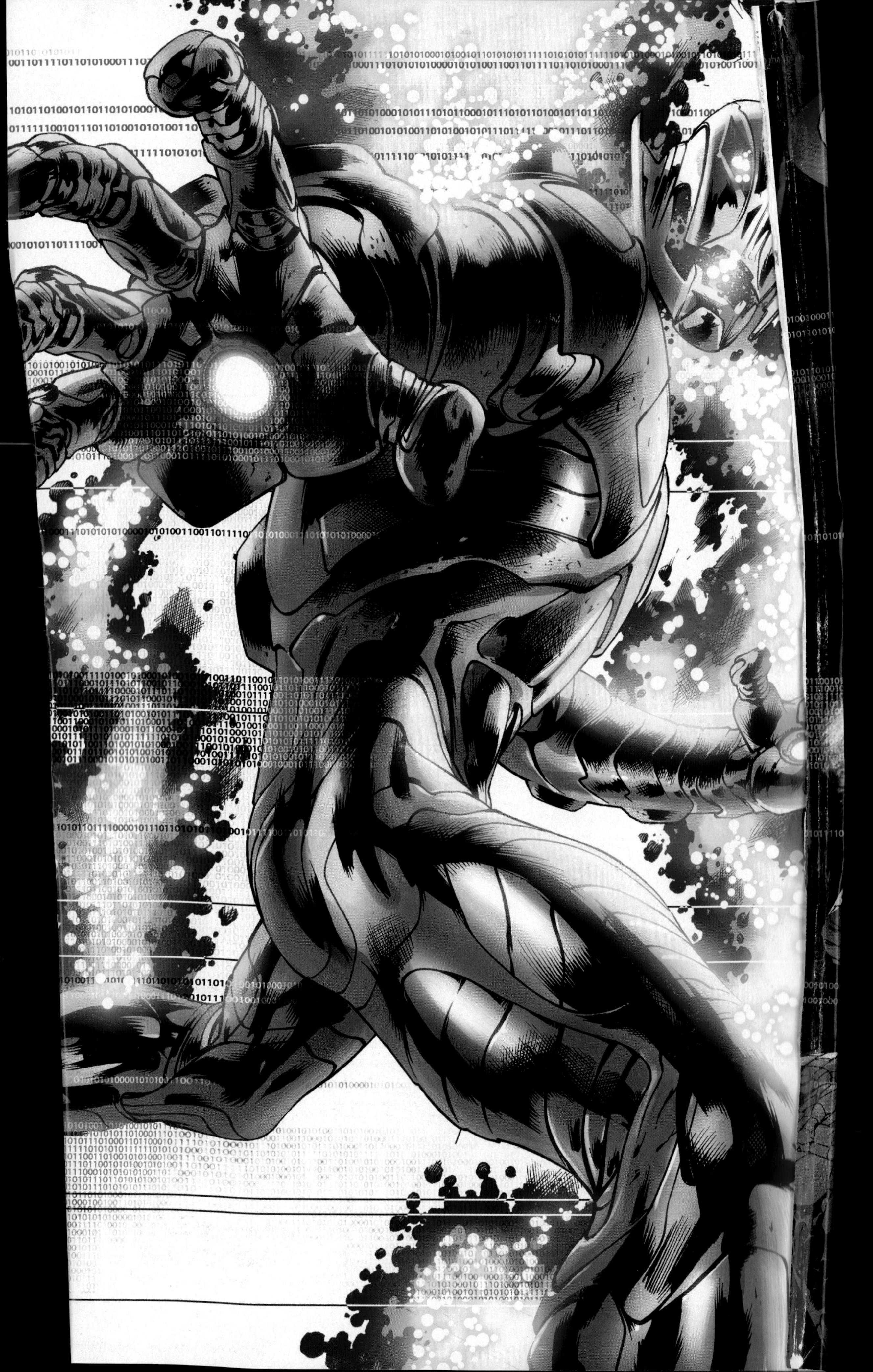

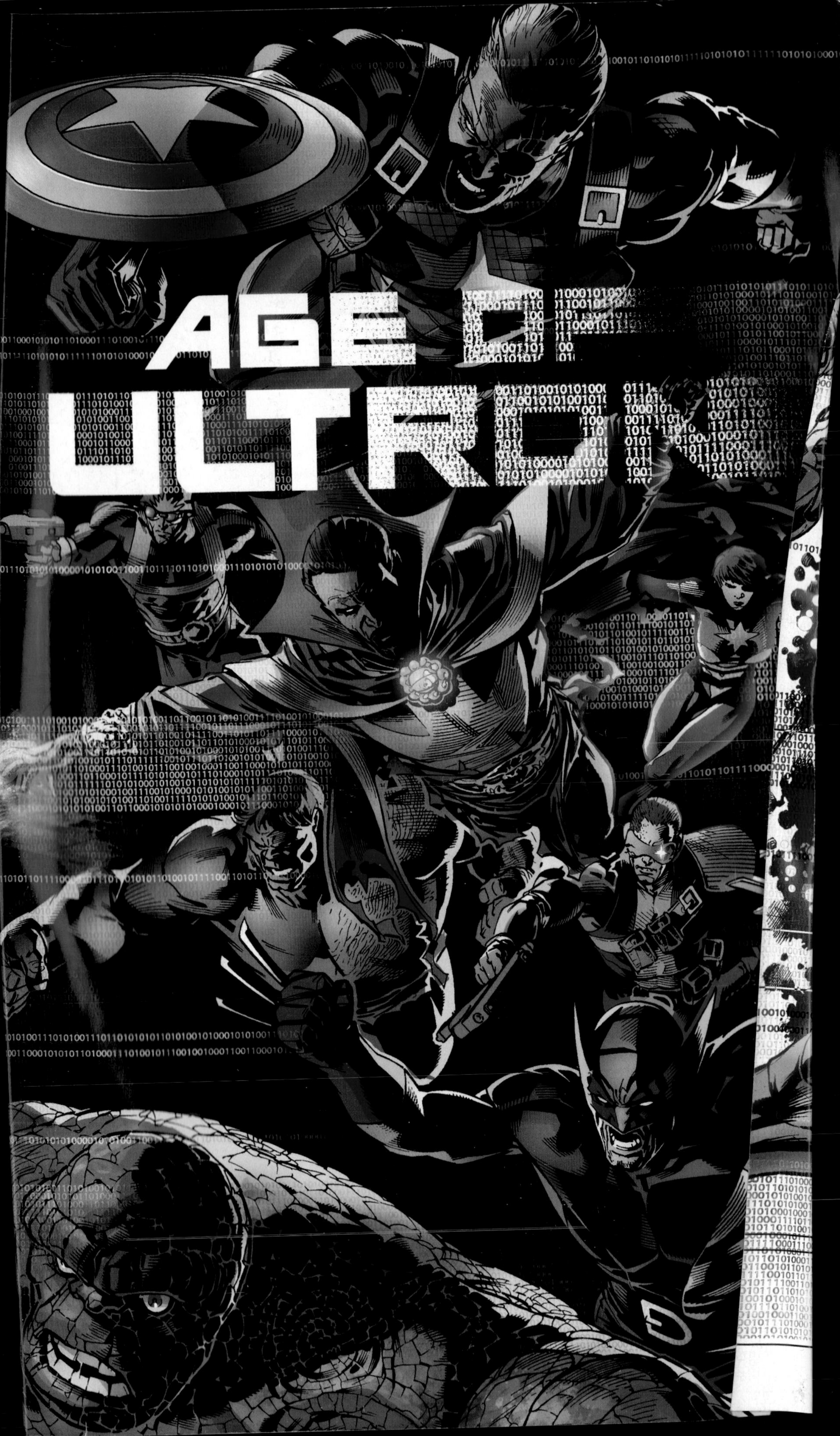
AGE OF
ULTRON

AGE OF ULTRON

WRITER:
BRIAN MICHAEL BENDIS

ISSUES #1-5 & AVENGERS #12.1
PENCILER: **BRYAN HITCH** INKER: **PAUL NEARY**
COLOR ARTIST: **PAUL MOUNTS** LETTERER: **VC'S CORY PETIT**
COVER ART: **BRYAN HITCH, PAUL NEARY** & **PAUL MOUNTS**

ISSUES #6-9
PRESENT/FUTURE, ARTIST: **BRANDON PETERSON**
PRESENT/FUTURE, COLOR ARTIST: **PAUL MOUNTS**
PAST, PENCILER: **CARLOS PACHECO**
PAST, INKER: **ROGER BONET**
PAST, COLOR ARTIST: **JOSE VILLARRUBIA**
COVER ART: **BRANDON PETERSON** (#6-8) WITH **PAUL MOUNTS** (#6) AND
CARLOS PACHECO & **JOSE VILLARRUBIA** (#9)

ISSUE #10
ARTISTS: **ALEX MALEEV;**
BRYAN HITCH & **PAUL NEARY;**
BUTCH GUICE; BRANDON PETERSON;
CARLOS PACHECO & **ROGER BONET**
WITH **TOM PALMER; DAVID MARQUEZ;**
AND **JOE QUESADA**
COLOR ARTISTS: **PAUL MOUNTS** & **RICHARD ISANOVE**
COVER ART: **BRANDON PETERSON**

ASSISTANT EDITORS: **JAKE THOMAS** & **JOHN DENNING**
EDITORS: **TOM BREVOORT** WITH **LAUREN SANKOVITCH**

AVENGERS ASSEMBLE
#14AU & #15AU
WRITER: **AL EWING**
PENCILER: **BUTCH GUICE**
INKERS: **TOM PALMER** WITH
RICK MAGYAR (#15AU)
COLORIST: **FRANK D'ARMATA**
LETTERER: **VC'S CLAYTON COWLES**
COVER ART: **NIC KLEIN**
ASSISTANT EDITOR: **JAKE THOMAS**
EDITOR: **LAUREN SANKOVITCH**
EXECUTIVE EDITOR: **TOM BREVOORT**

FANTASTIC FOUR #5AU
WRITER: **MATT FRACTION**
ARTIST: **ANDRÉ ARAÚJO**
COLOR ARTIST: **JOSE VILLARRUBIA**
LETTERER: **VC'S CLAYTON COWLES**
COVER ART: **MARK BAGLEY,**
SCOTT HANNA & **RAIN BEREDO**
ASSISTANT EDITOR: **JAKE THOMAS**
EDITOR: **TOM BREVOORT**

SUPERIOR SPIDER-MAN #6AU
WRITER: **CHRISTOS GAGE**
ARTIST: **DEXTER SOY**
COVER ART: **MARCO CHECCHETTO**
LETTERER: **VC'S JOE CARAMAGNA**
EDITOR: **ELLIE PYLE**
SENIOR EDITOR: **STEPHEN WACKER**
EXECUTIVE EDITOR: **TOM BREVOORT**

ULTRON #1AU
WRITER: **KATHRYN IMMONEN**
ARTIST: **AMILCAR PINNA**
LETTERER: **VC'S JOE CARAMAGNA**
COVER ART:
KALMAN ANDRASOFSZKY
ASSISTANT EDITOR: **JAKE THOMAS**
EDITOR: **LAUREN SANKOVITCH**
EXECUTIVE EDITOR: **TOM BREVOORT**

WOLVERINE &
THE X-MEN #27AU
WRITER: **MATT KINDT**
PENCILER: **PACO MEDINA**
INKER: **JUAN VLASCO**
COLORISTS: **DAVID CURIEL** WITH
RACHELLE ROSENBERG
LETTERER: **VC'S CLAYTON COWLES**
COVER ART: **MIKE DEODATO**
& **RAIN BEREDO**
1967 TECHNICAL SUPPORT:
IDETTE WINECOOR
ADDITIONAL ART BY
JACK KIRBY & **JOE SINNOTT**
AND **JOHN BUSCEMA**
& **GEORGE ROUSSOS**
EDITOR: **JEANINE SCHAEFER**
GROUP EDITOR: **NICK LOWE**

UNCANNY AVENGERS #8AU
WRITERS: **RICK REMENDER**
& **GERRY DUGGAN**
ARTIST: **ADAM KUBERT**
COLOR ARTIST: **FRANK MARTIN**
LETTERER: **VC'S CORY PETIT**
COVER ART: **JIM CHEUNG,**
MARK MORALES &
JUSTIN PONSOR
EDITORS: **TOM BREVOORT**
WITH **DANIEL KETCHUM**

FEARLESS DEFENDERS #4AU
WRITER: **CULLEN BUNN**
PENCILER: **PHIL JIMENEZ**
INKERS: **KARL KESEL** WITH
AARON MCCONNELL
(BACKGROUND INKS)
COLORIST: **ANTONIO FABELA**
LETTERER: **VC'S CLAYTON COWLES**
COVER ART: **PHIL JIMENEZ**
& **ANTONIO FABELA**
EDITOR: **ELLIE PYLE**
EXECUTIVE EDITOR: **TOM BREVOORT**

AGE OF ULTRON #10AI
WRITER: **MARK WAID**
ARTIST: **ANDRÉ ARAÚJO**
COLOR ARTIST: **FRANK D'ARMATA**
LETTERER: **VC'S CLAYTON COWLES**
COVER ART: **SARA PICHELLI**
& **MARTE GRACIA**
ASSISTANT EDITOR: **JAKE THOMAS**
EDITOR: **LAUREN SANKOVITCH**
EXECUTIVE EDITOR: **TOM BREVOORT**

COLLECTION EDITOR: **JENNIFER GRÜNWALD**   ASSISTANT EDITORS: **ALEX STARBUCK** & **NELSON RIBEIRO**
EDITOR, SPECIAL PROJECTS: **MARK D. BEAZLEY**   SENIOR EDITOR, SPECIAL PROJECTS: **JEFF YOUNGQUIST**
SVP OF PRINT & DIGITAL PUBLISHING SALES: **DAVID GABRIEL**   BOOK DESIGNER: **RODOLFO MURAGUCHI**

EDITOR IN CHIEF: **AXEL ALONSO**   CHIEF CREATIVE OFFICER: **JOE QUESADA**
PUBLISHER: **DAN BUCKLEY**   EXECUTIVE PRODUCER: **ALAN FINE**

AGE OF ULTRON. Contains material originally published in magazine form as AVENGERS #12.1, AGE OF ULTRON #1-10, AVENGERS ASSEMBLE #14AU-15AU, FANTASTIC FOUR #5AU, FEARLESS DEFENDERS #4AU, SUPERIOR SPIDER-MAN #6AU, ULTRON #1AU, UNCANNY AVENGERS #8AU, WOLVERINE & THE X-MEN #27AU AND AGE OF ULTRON #10AI. First printing 2013. ISBN# 978-0-7851-5565-2. Published by MARVEL WORLDWIDE, INC., a subsidiary of MARVEL ENTERTAINMENT, LLC. OFFICE OF PUBLICATION: 135 West 50th Street, New York, NY 10020. Copyright © 2011 and 2013 Marvel Characters, Inc. All rights reserved. All characters featured in this issue and the distinctive names and likenesses thereof, and all related indicia are trademarks of Marvel Characters, Inc. No similarity between any of the names, characters, persons, and/or institutions in this magazine with those of any living or dead person or institution is intended, and any such similarity which may exist is purely coincidental. **Printed in the U.S.A.** ALAN FINE, EVP - Office of the President, Marvel Worldwide, Inc. and EVP & CMO Marvel Characters B.V.; DAN BUCKLEY, Publisher & President - Print, Animation & Digital Divisions; JOE QUESADA, Chief Creative Officer; TOM BREVOORT, SVP of Publishing; DAVID BOGART, SVP of Operations & Procurement, Publishing; C.B. CEBULSKI, SVP of Creator & Content Development; DAVID GABRIEL, SVP of Print & Digital Publishing Sales; JIM O'KEEFE, VP of Operations & Logistics; DAN CARR, Executive Director of Publishing Technology; SUSAN CRESPI, Editorial Operations Manager; ALEX MORALES, Publishing Operations Manager; STAN LEE, Chairman Emeritus. For information regarding advertising in Marvel Comics or on Marvel.com, please contact Niza Disla, Director of Marvel Partnerships, at ndisla@marvel.com. For Marvel subscription inquiries, please call 800-217-9158. **Manufactured between 7/12/2013 and 8/19/2013 by WORZALLA PUBLISHING CO., STEVENS POINT, WI, USA.**

10 9 8 7 6 5 4 3 2 1

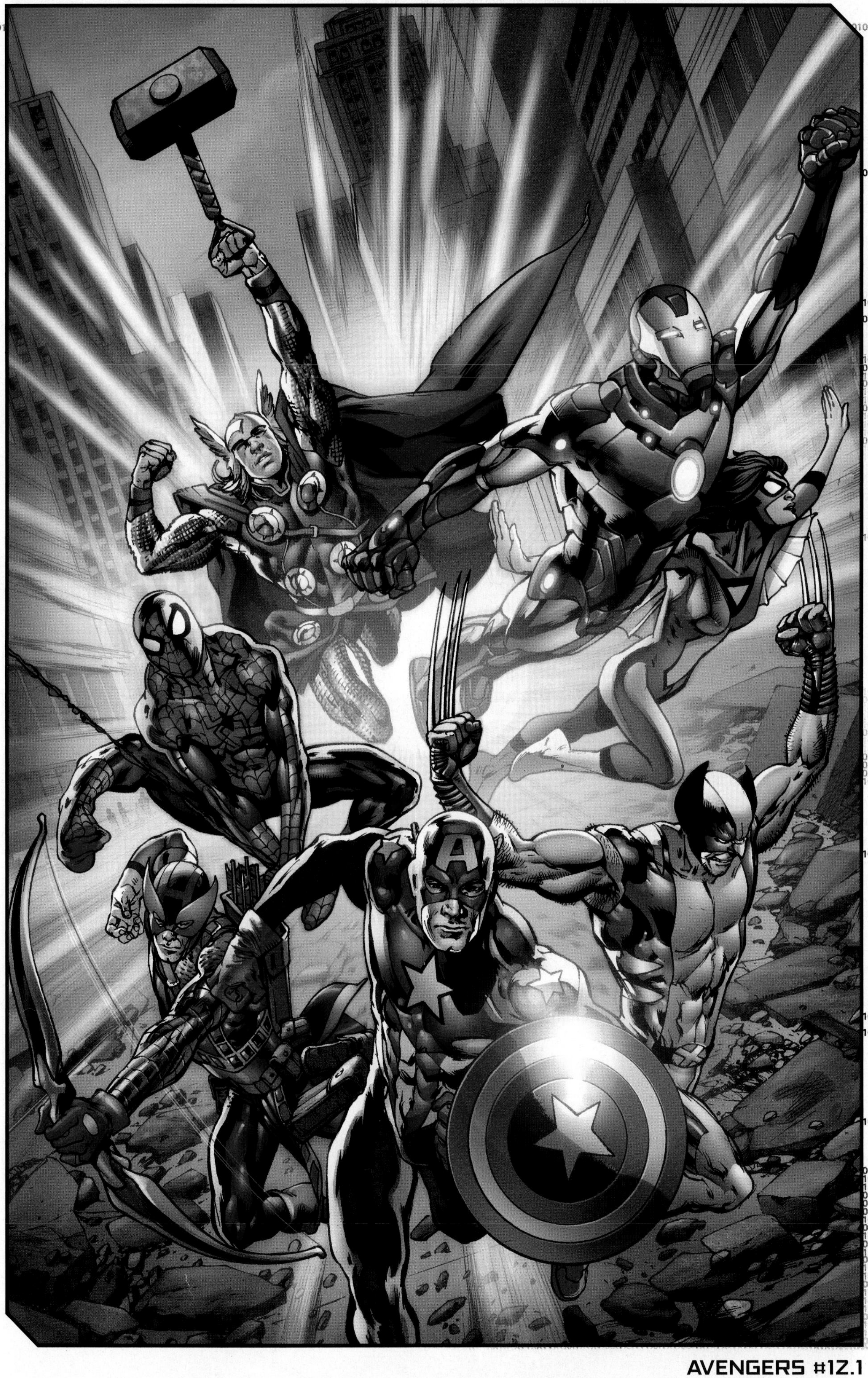

AVENGERS #12.1

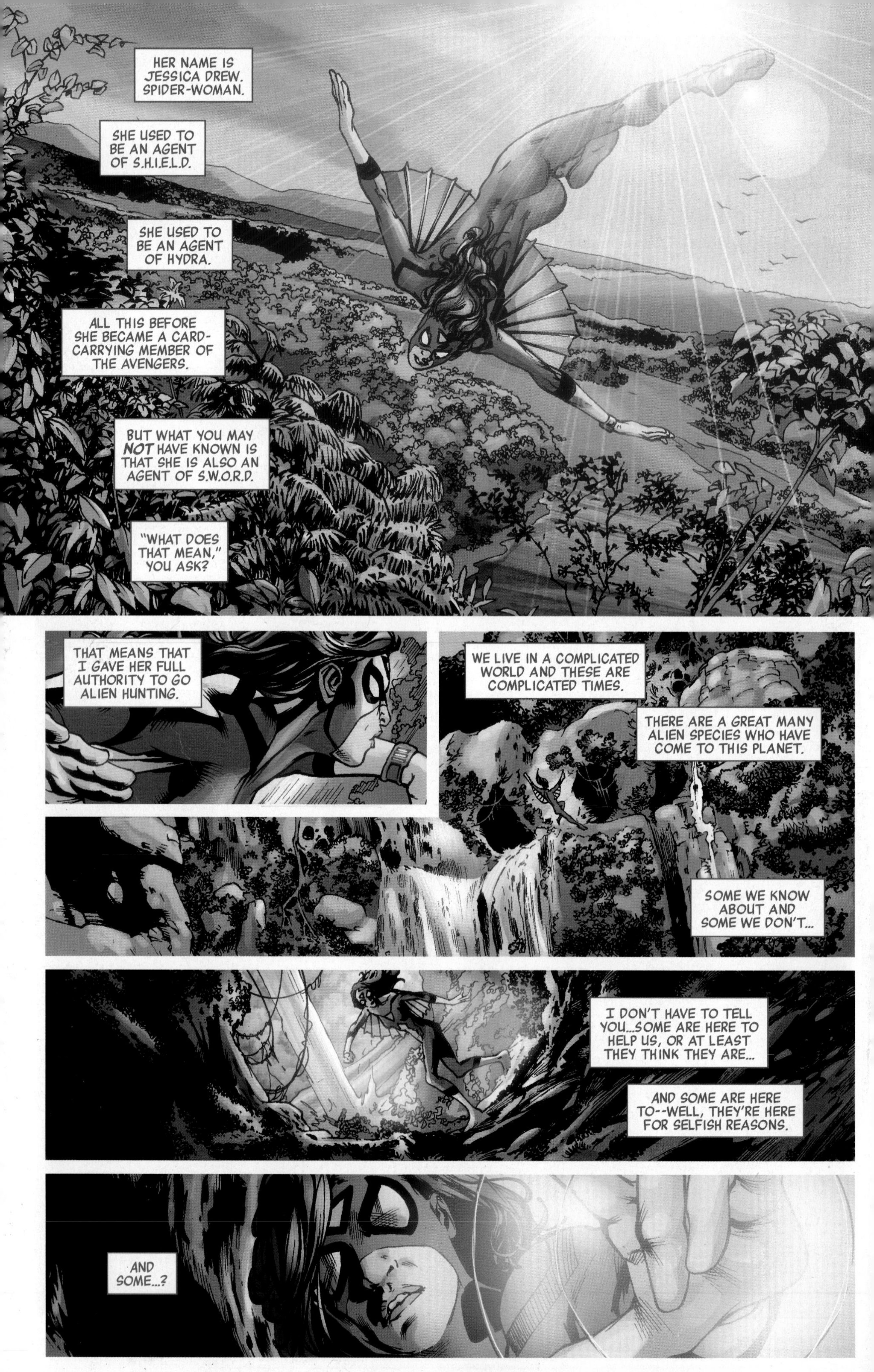
HER NAME IS JESSICA DREW. SPIDER-WOMAN.
SHE USED TO BE AN AGENT OF S.H.I.E.L.D.
SHE USED TO BE AN AGENT OF HYDRA.
ALL THIS BEFORE SHE BECAME A CARD-CARRYING MEMBER OF THE AVENGERS.
BUT WHAT YOU MAY **NOT** HAVE KNOWN IS THAT SHE IS ALSO AN AGENT OF S.W.O.R.D.
"WHAT DOES THAT MEAN," YOU ASK?
THAT MEANS THAT I GAVE HER FULL AUTHORITY TO GO ALIEN HUNTING.
WE LIVE IN A COMPLICATED WORLD AND THESE ARE COMPLICATED TIMES.
THERE ARE A GREAT MANY ALIEN SPECIES WHO HAVE COME TO THIS PLANET.
SOME WE KNOW ABOUT AND SOME WE DON'T...
I DON'T HAVE TO TELL YOU...SOME ARE HERE TO HELP US, OR AT LEAST THEY THINK THEY ARE...
AND SOME ARE HERE TO--WELL, THEY'RE HERE FOR SELFISH REASONS.
AND SOME...?

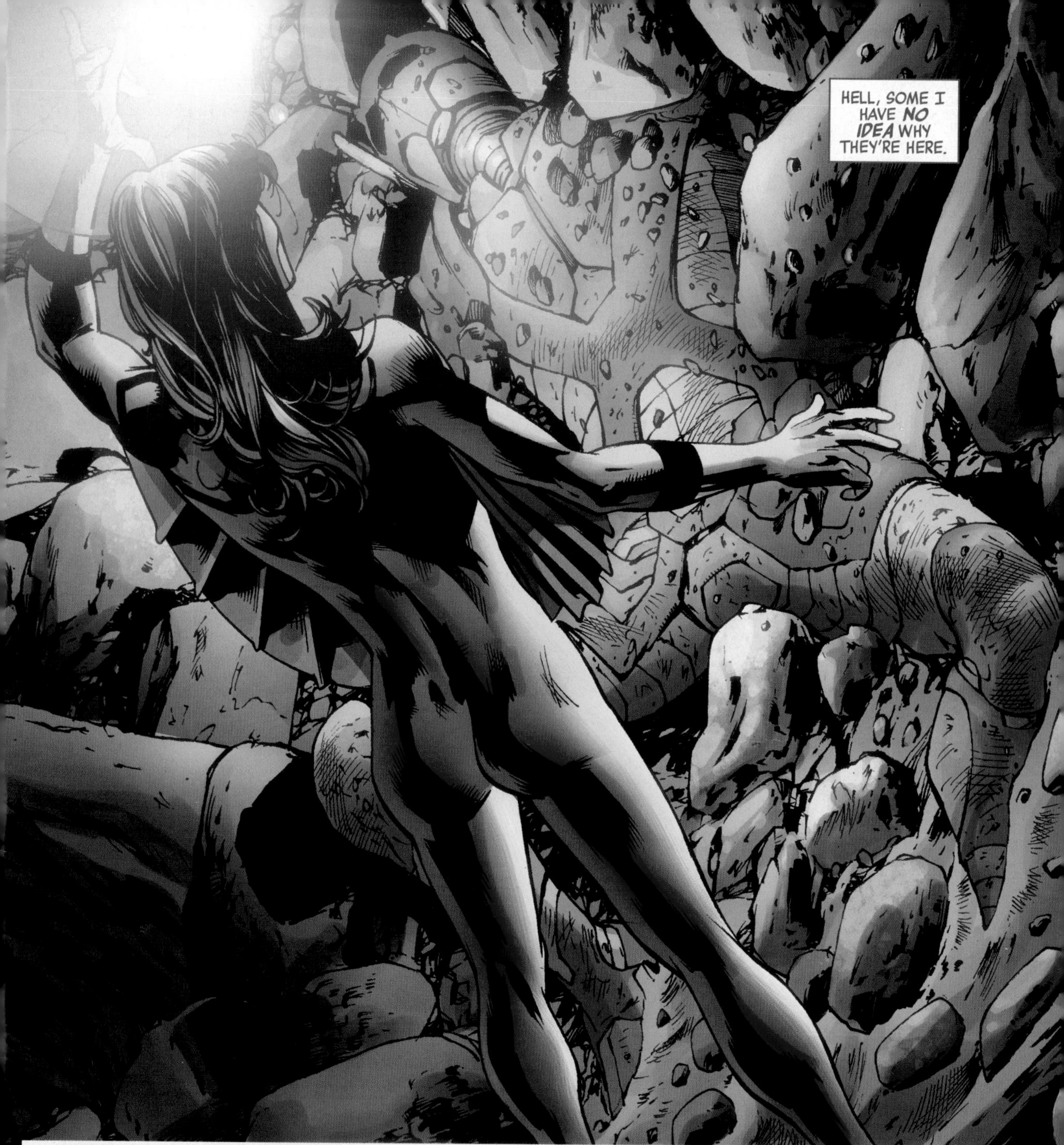
HELL, SOME I HAVE NO IDEA WHY THEY'RE HERE.
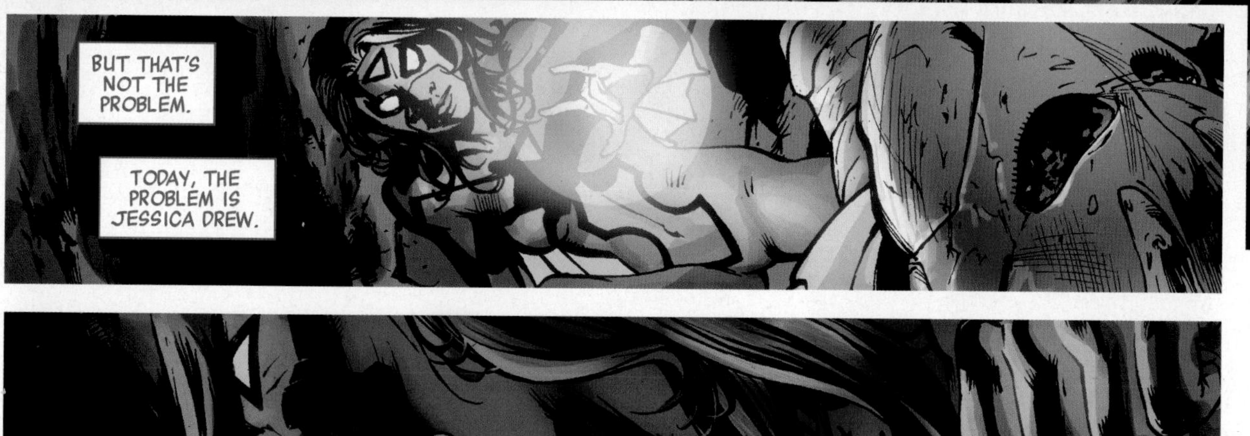
BUT THAT'S NOT THE PROBLEM.
TODAY, THE PROBLEM IS JESSICA DREW.
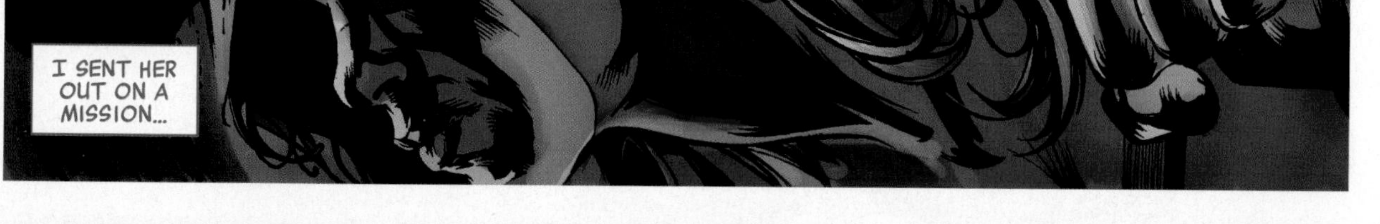
I SENT HER OUT ON A MISSION...

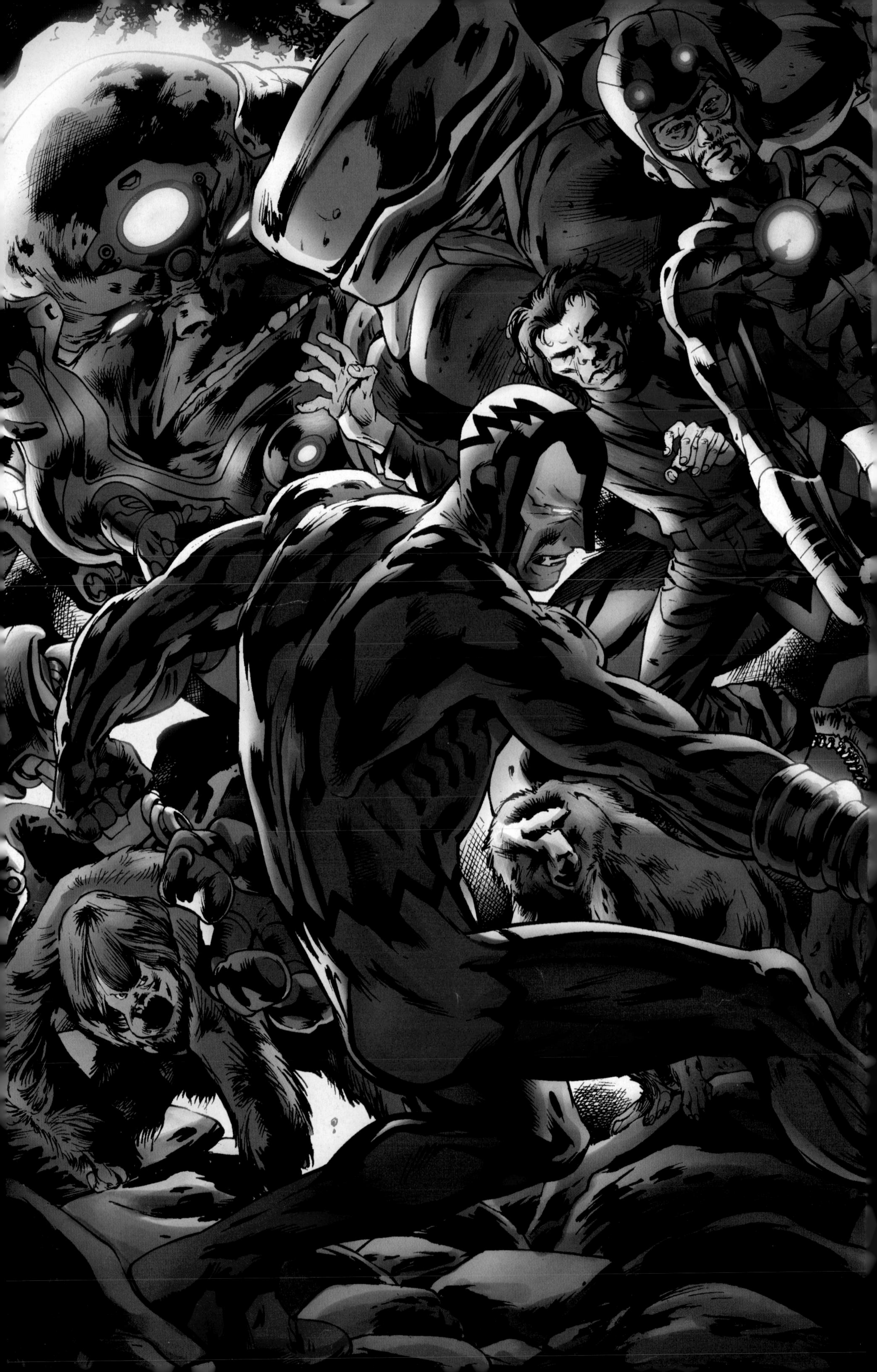

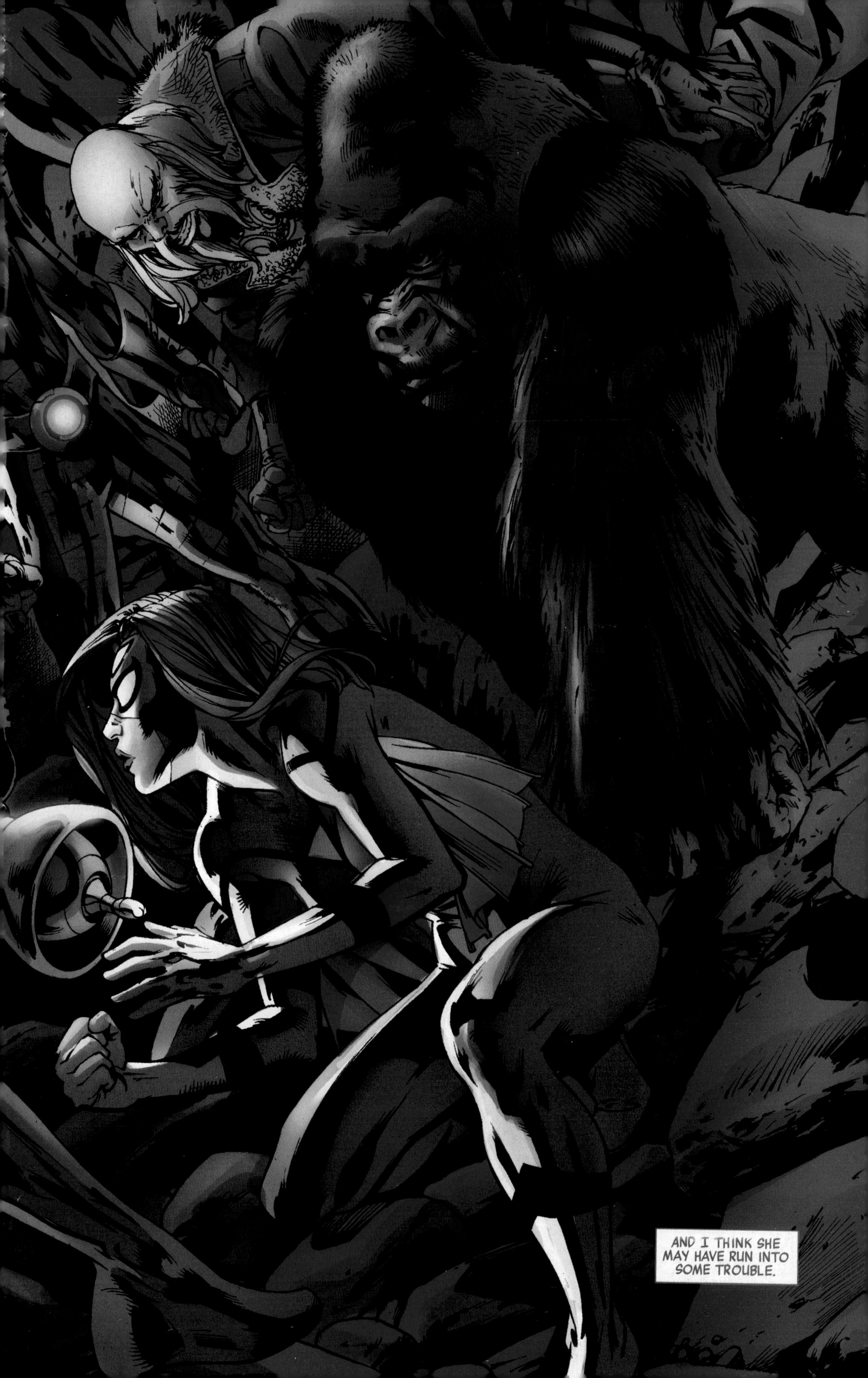
AND I THINK SHE MAY HAVE RUN INTO SOME TROUBLE.

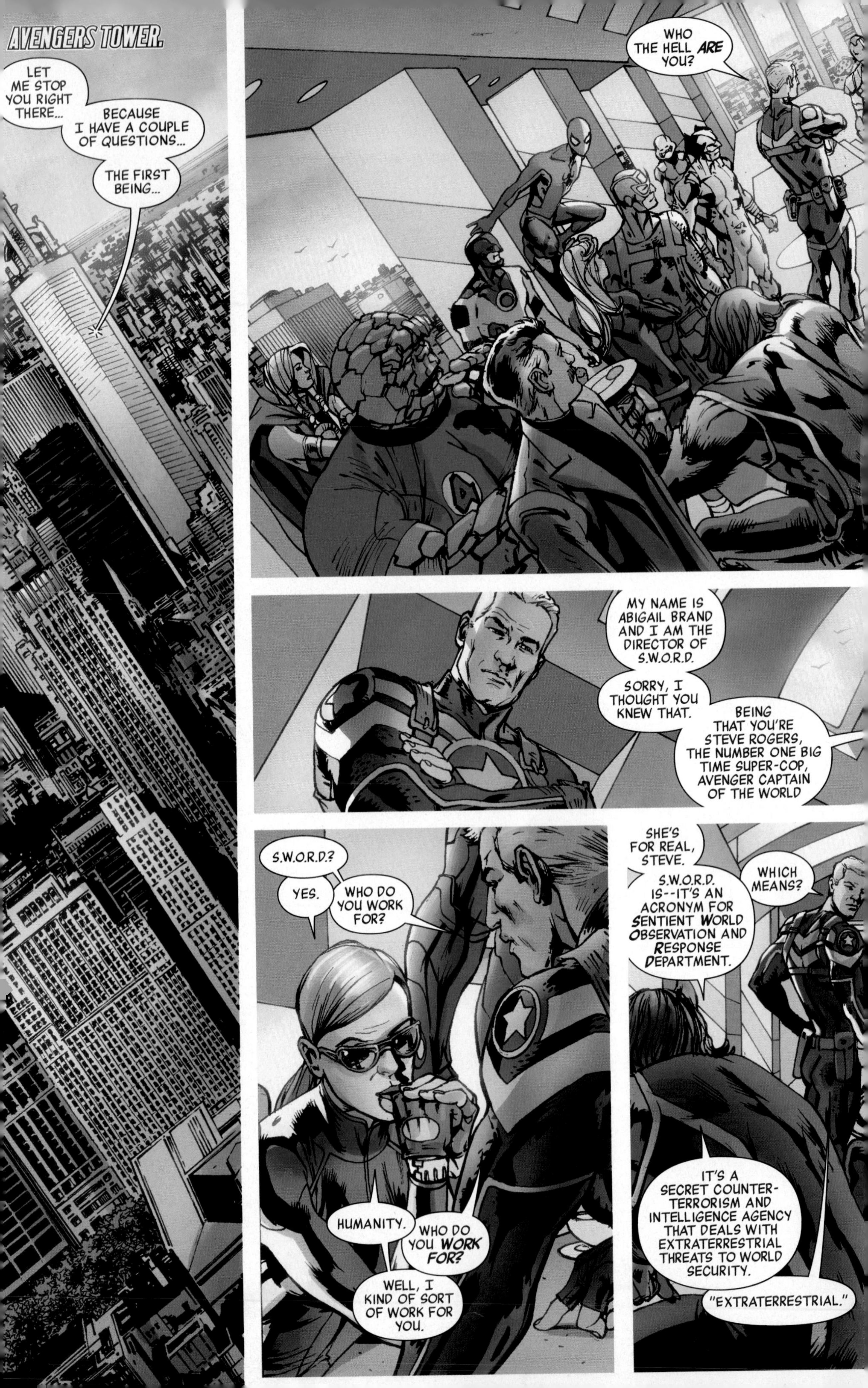
AVENGERS TOWER.
LET ME STOP YOU RIGHT THERE...
BECAUSE I HAVE A COUPLE OF QUESTIONS...
THE FIRST BEING...
WHO THE HELL ARE YOU?
MY NAME IS ABIGAIL BRAND AND I AM THE DIRECTOR OF S.W.O.R.D.
SORRY, I THOUGHT YOU KNEW THAT.
BEING THAT YOU'RE STEVE ROGERS, THE NUMBER ONE BIG TIME SUPER-COP, AVENGER CAPTAIN OF THE WORLD
S.W.O.R.D.?
YES.
WHO DO YOU WORK FOR?
HUMANITY.
WHO DO YOU WORK FOR?
WELL, I KIND OF SORT OF WORK FOR YOU.
SHE'S FOR REAL, STEVE.
S.W.O.R.D. IS--IT'S AN ACRONYM FOR SENTIENT WORLD OBSERVATION AND RESPONSE DEPARTMENT.
WHICH MEANS?
IT'S A SECRET COUNTER-TERRORISM AND INTELLIGENCE AGENCY THAT DEALS WITH EXTRATERRESTRIAL THREATS TO WORLD SECURITY.
"EXTRATERRESTRIAL."

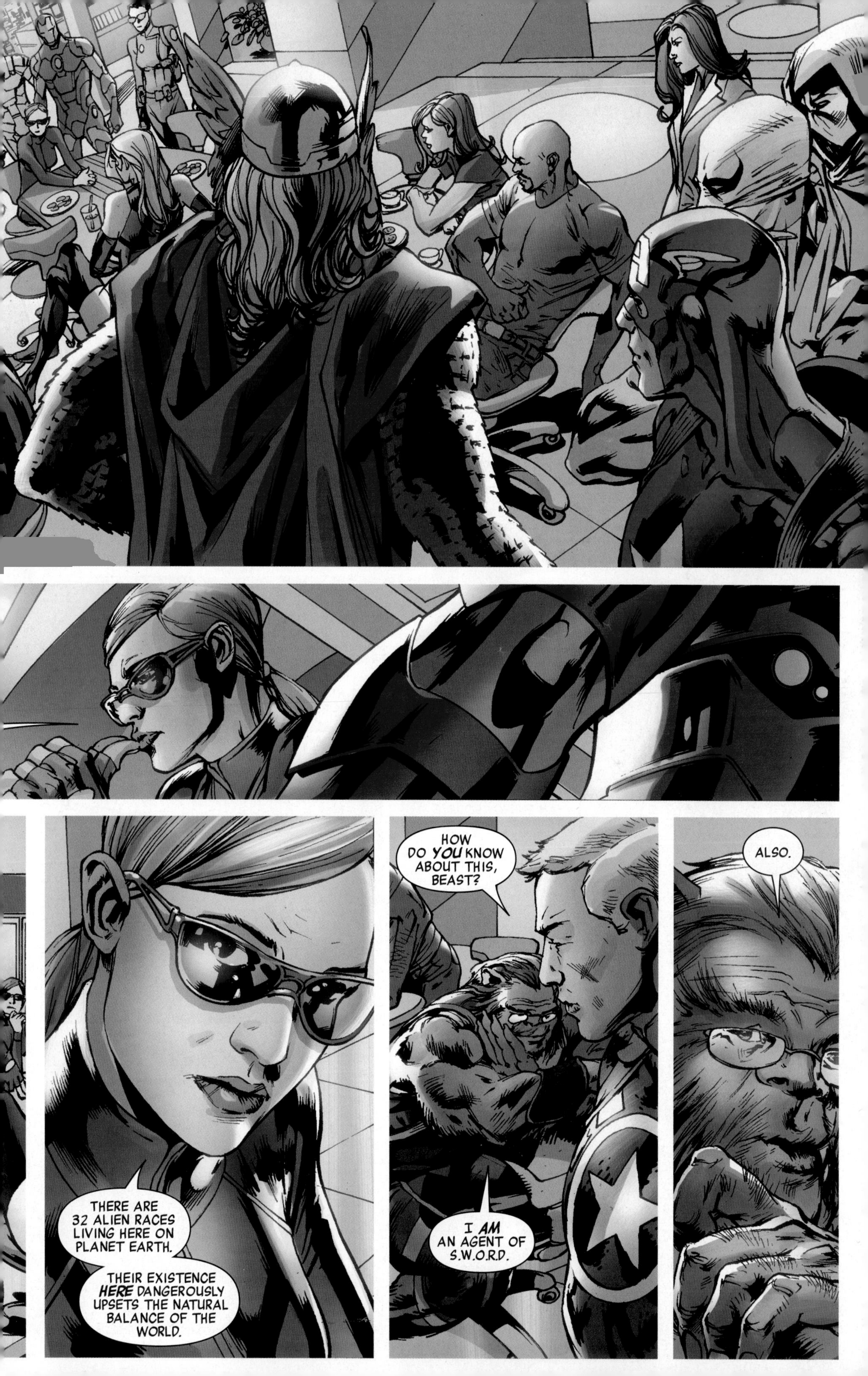
THERE ARE 32 ALIEN RACES LIVING HERE ON PLANET EARTH.
THEIR EXISTENCE HERE DANGEROUSLY UPSETS THE NATURAL BALANCE OF THE WORLD.
HOW DO YOU KNOW ABOUT THIS, BEAST?
I AM AN AGENT OF S.W.O.R.D.
ALSO.

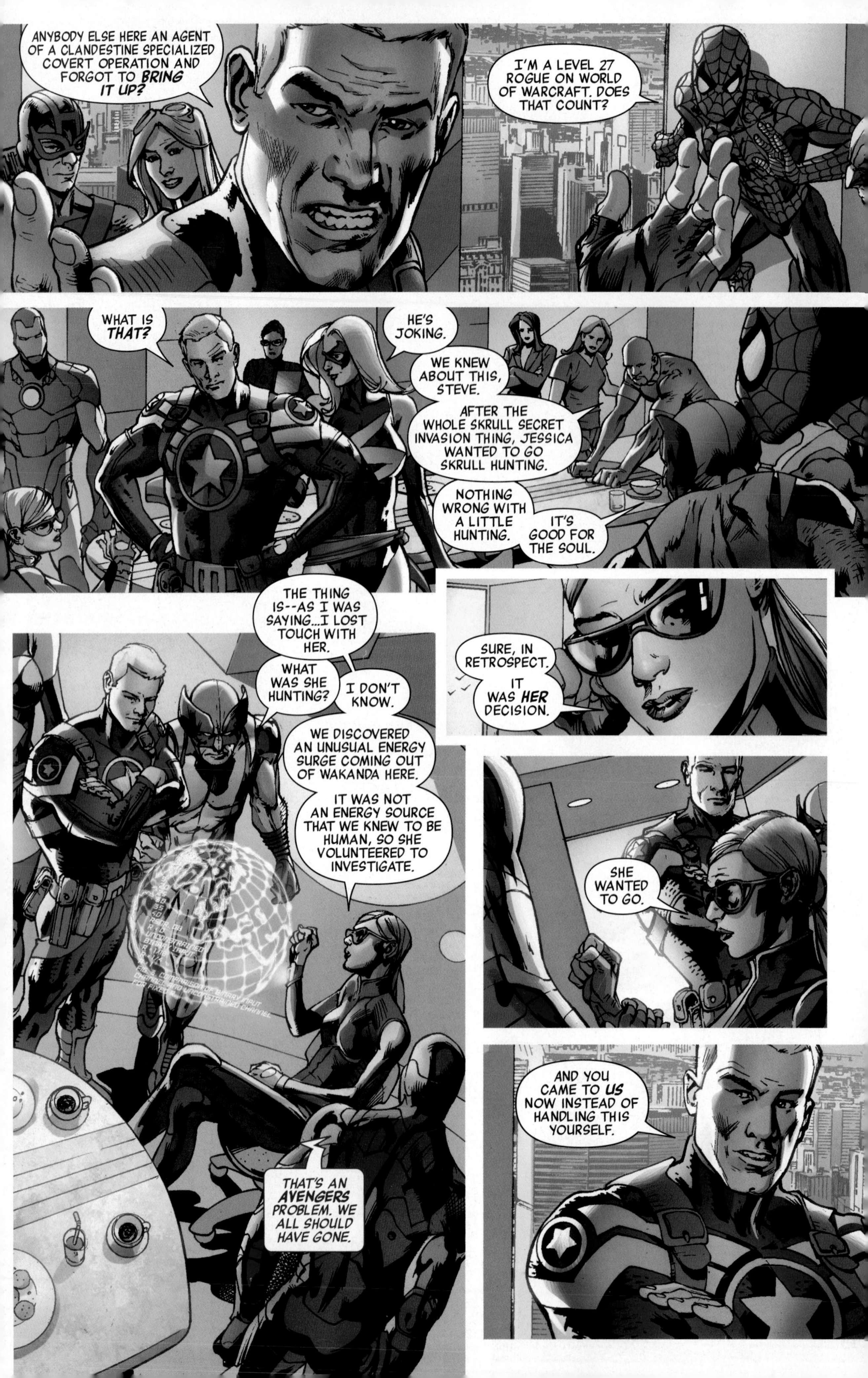
ANYBODY ELSE HERE AN AGENT OF A CLANDESTINE SPECIALIZED COVERT OPERATION AND FORGOT TO BRING IT UP?
I'M A LEVEL 27 ROGUE ON WORLD OF WARCRAFT. DOES THAT COUNT?
WHAT IS THAT?
HE'S JOKING.
WE KNEW ABOUT THIS, STEVE.
AFTER THE WHOLE SKRULL SECRET INVASION THING, JESSICA WANTED TO GO SKRULL HUNTING.
NOTHING WRONG WITH A LITTLE HUNTING.
IT'S GOOD FOR THE SOUL.
THE THING IS--AS I WAS SAYING...I LOST TOUCH WITH HER.
WHAT WAS SHE HUNTING?
I DON'T KNOW.
WE DISCOVERED AN UNUSUAL ENERGY SURGE COMING OUT OF WAKANDA HERE.
IT WAS NOT AN ENERGY SOURCE THAT WE KNEW TO BE HUMAN, SO SHE VOLUNTEERED TO INVESTIGATE.
THAT'S AN AVENGERS PROBLEM. WE ALL SHOULD HAVE GONE.
SURE, IN RETROSPECT.
IT WAS HER DECISION.
SHE WANTED TO GO.
AND YOU CAME TO US NOW INSTEAD OF HANDLING THIS YOURSELF.

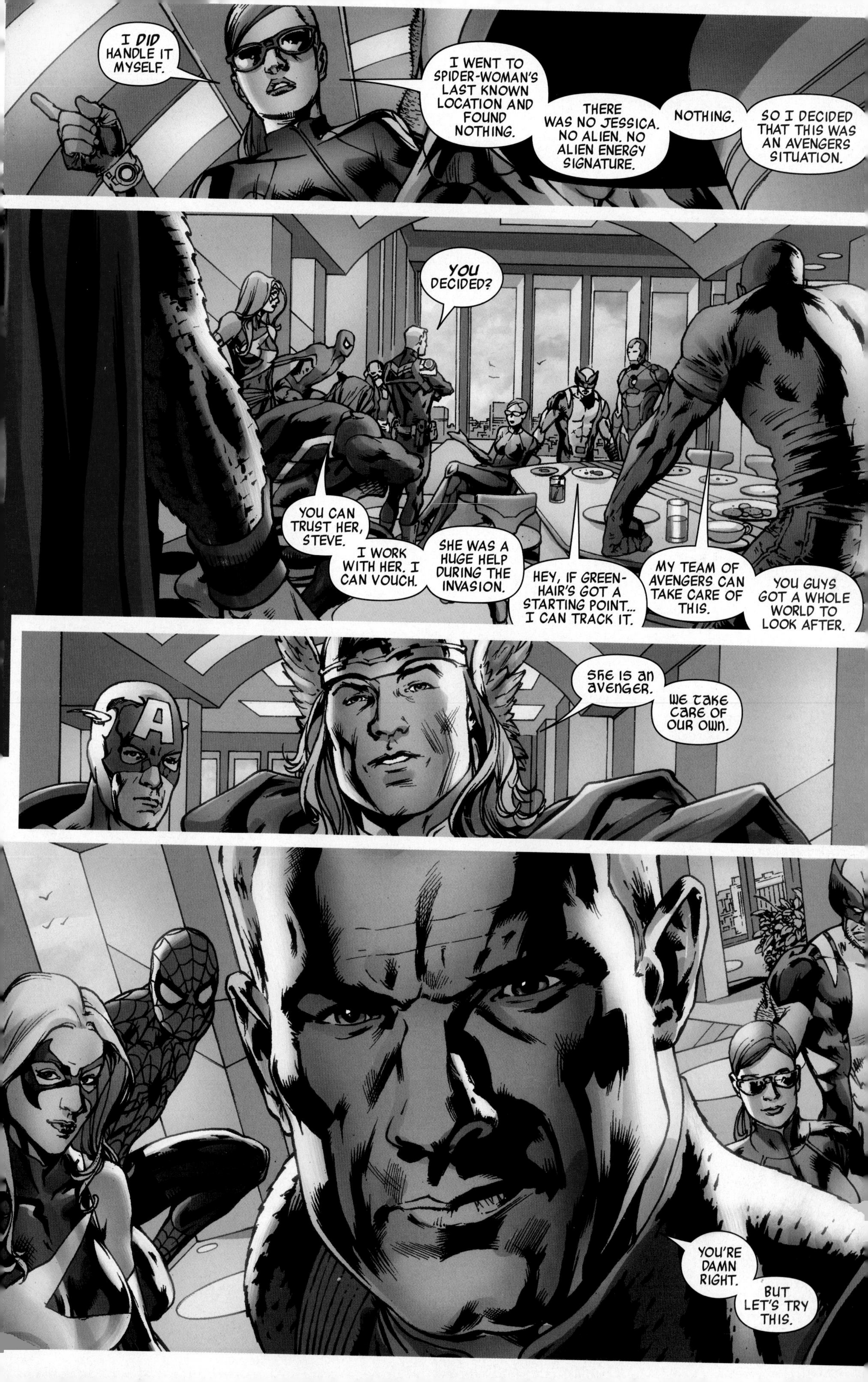
I *DID* HANDLE IT MYSELF.
I WENT TO SPIDER-WOMAN'S LAST KNOWN LOCATION AND FOUND NOTHING.
THERE WAS NO JESSICA. NO ALIEN. NO ALIEN ENERGY SIGNATURE.
NOTHING.
SO I DECIDED THAT THIS WAS AN AVENGERS SITUATION.
YOU DECIDED?
YOU CAN TRUST HER, STEVE.
I WORK WITH HER. I CAN VOUCH.
SHE WAS A HUGE HELP DURING THE INVASION.
HEY, IF GREEN-HAIR'S GOT A STARTING POINT... I CAN TRACK IT.
MY TEAM OF AVENGERS CAN TAKE CARE OF THIS.
YOU GUYS GOT A WHOLE WORLD TO LOOK AFTER.
SHE IS AN AVENGER.
WE TAKE CARE OF OUR OWN.
YOU'RE DAMN RIGHT.
BUT LET'S TRY THIS.

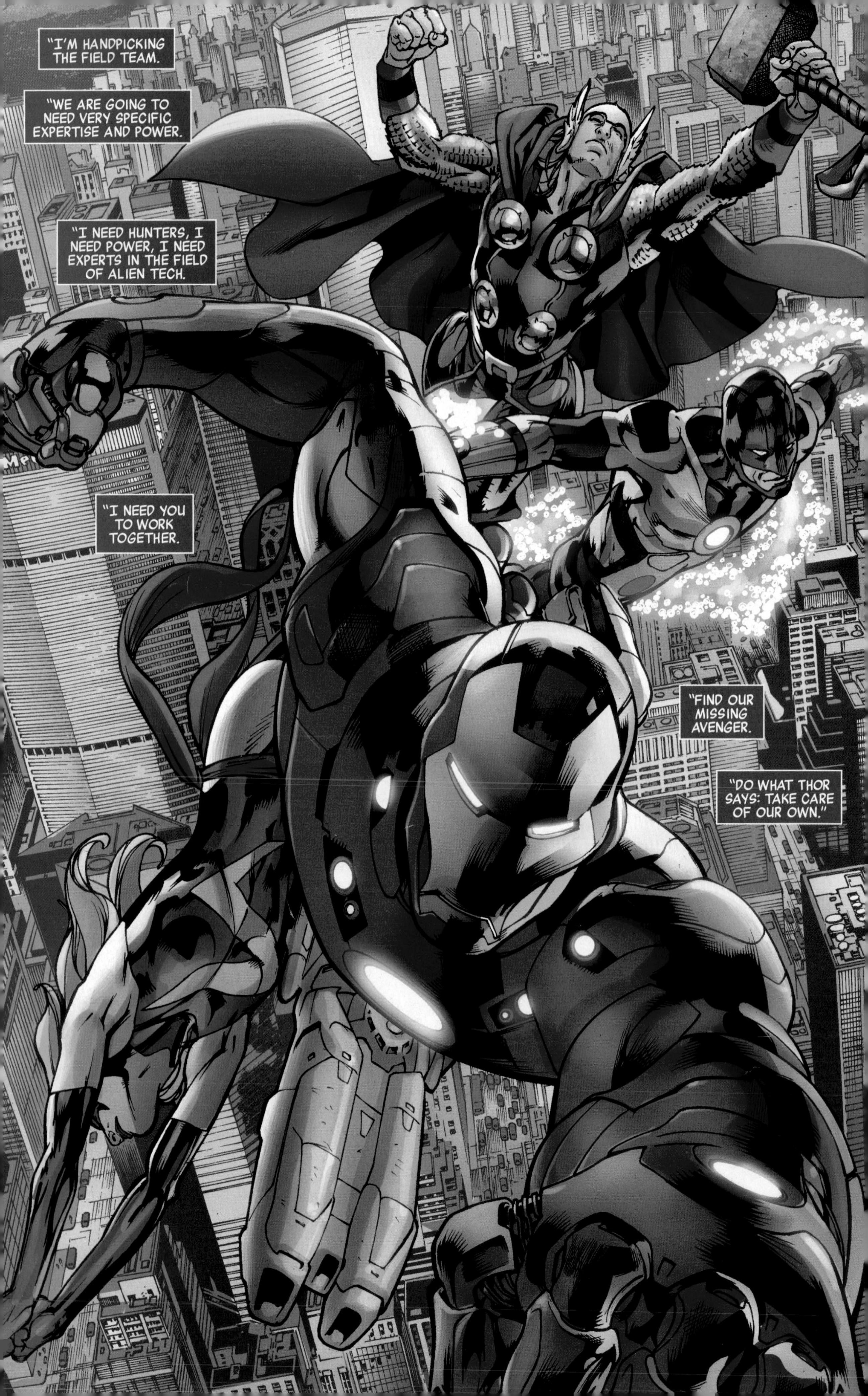
"I'M HANDPICKING THE FIELD TEAM.
"WE ARE GOING TO NEED VERY SPECIFIC EXPERTISE AND POWER.
"I NEED HUNTERS, I NEED POWER, I NEED EXPERTS IN THE FIELD OF ALIEN TECH.
"I NEED YOU TO WORK TOGETHER.
"FIND OUR MISSING AVENGER.
"DO WHAT THOR SAYS: TAKE CARE OF OUR OWN."

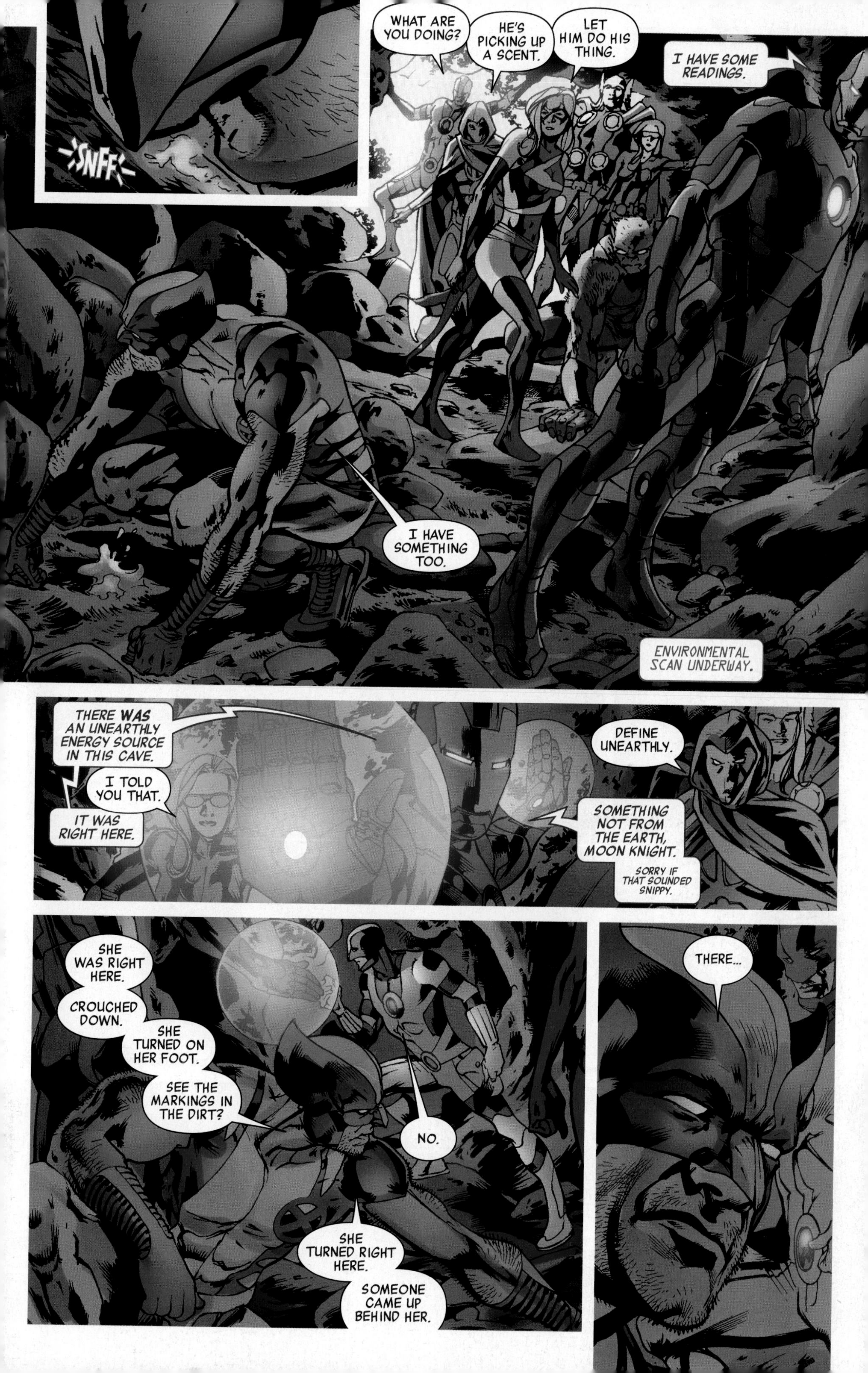
SNFF
WHAT ARE YOU DOING?
HE'S PICKING UP A SCENT.
LET HIM DO HIS THING.
I HAVE SOME READINGS.
I HAVE SOMETHING TOO.
ENVIRONMENTAL SCAN UNDERWAY.
THERE WAS AN UNEARTHLY ENERGY SOURCE IN THIS CAVE.
I TOLD YOU THAT.
IT WAS RIGHT HERE.
DEFINE UNEARTHLY.
SOMETHING NOT FROM THE EARTH, MOON KNIGHT.
SORRY IF THAT SOUNDED SNIPPY.
SHE WAS RIGHT HERE.
CROUCHED DOWN.
SHE TURNED ON HER FOOT.
SEE THE MARKINGS IN THE DIRT?
NO.
SHE TURNED RIGHT HERE.
SOMEONE CAME UP BEHIND HER.
THERE...

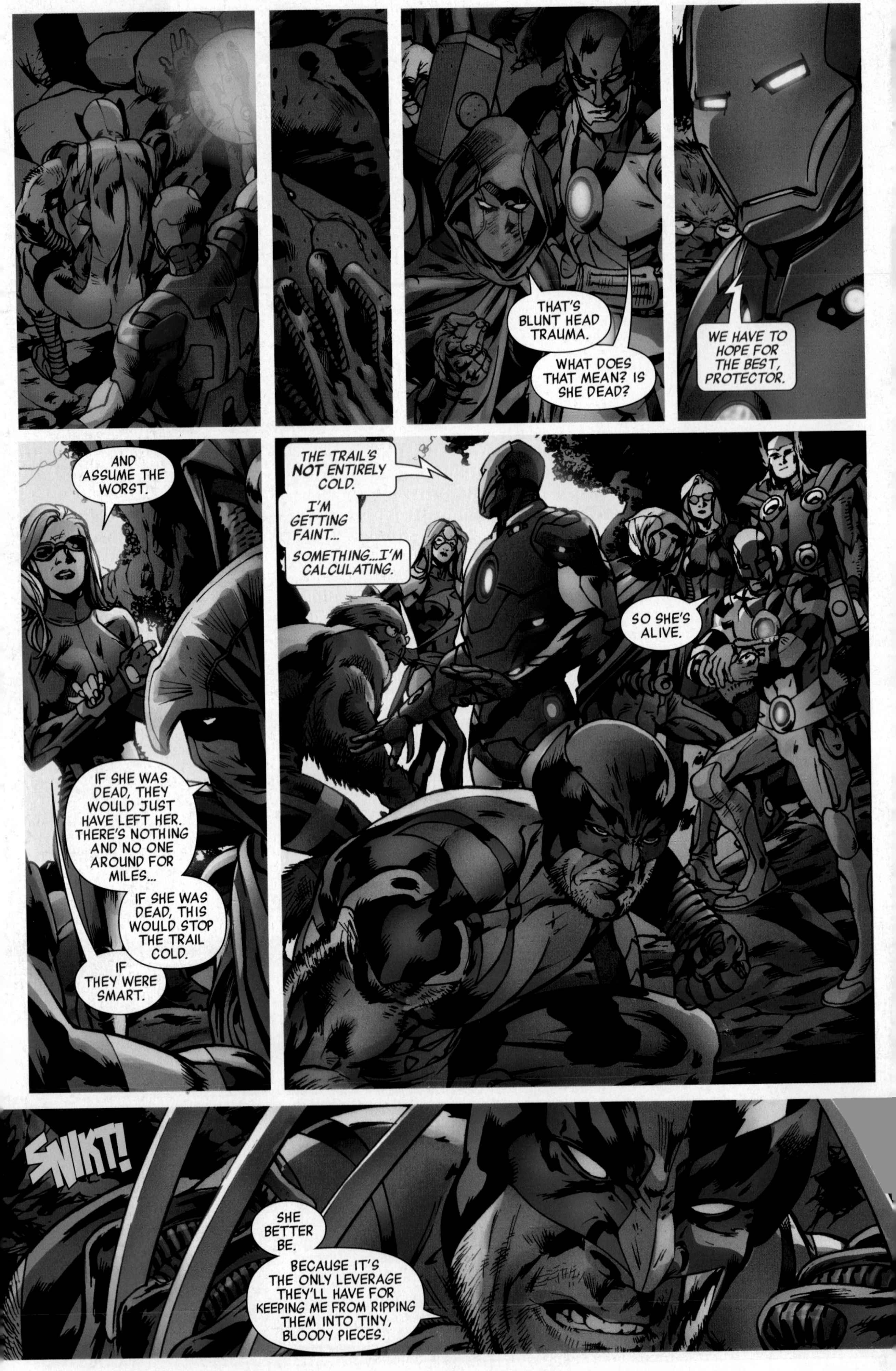
THAT'S BLUNT HEAD TRAUMA.
WHAT DOES THAT MEAN? IS SHE DEAD?
WE HAVE TO HOPE FOR THE BEST, PROTECTOR.
AND ASSUME THE WORST.
THE TRAIL'S **NOT** ENTIRELY COLD.
I'M GETTING FAINT...
SOMETHING...I'M CALCULATING.
SO SHE'S ALIVE.
IF SHE WAS DEAD, THEY WOULD JUST HAVE LEFT HER. THERE'S NOTHING AND NO ONE AROUND FOR MILES...
IF SHE WAS DEAD, THIS WOULD STOP THE TRAIL COLD.
IF THEY WERE SMART.
SNIKT!
SHE BETTER BE.
BECAUSE IT'S THE ONLY LEVERAGE THEY'LL HAVE FOR KEEPING ME FROM RIPPING THEM INTO TINY, BLOODY PIECES.

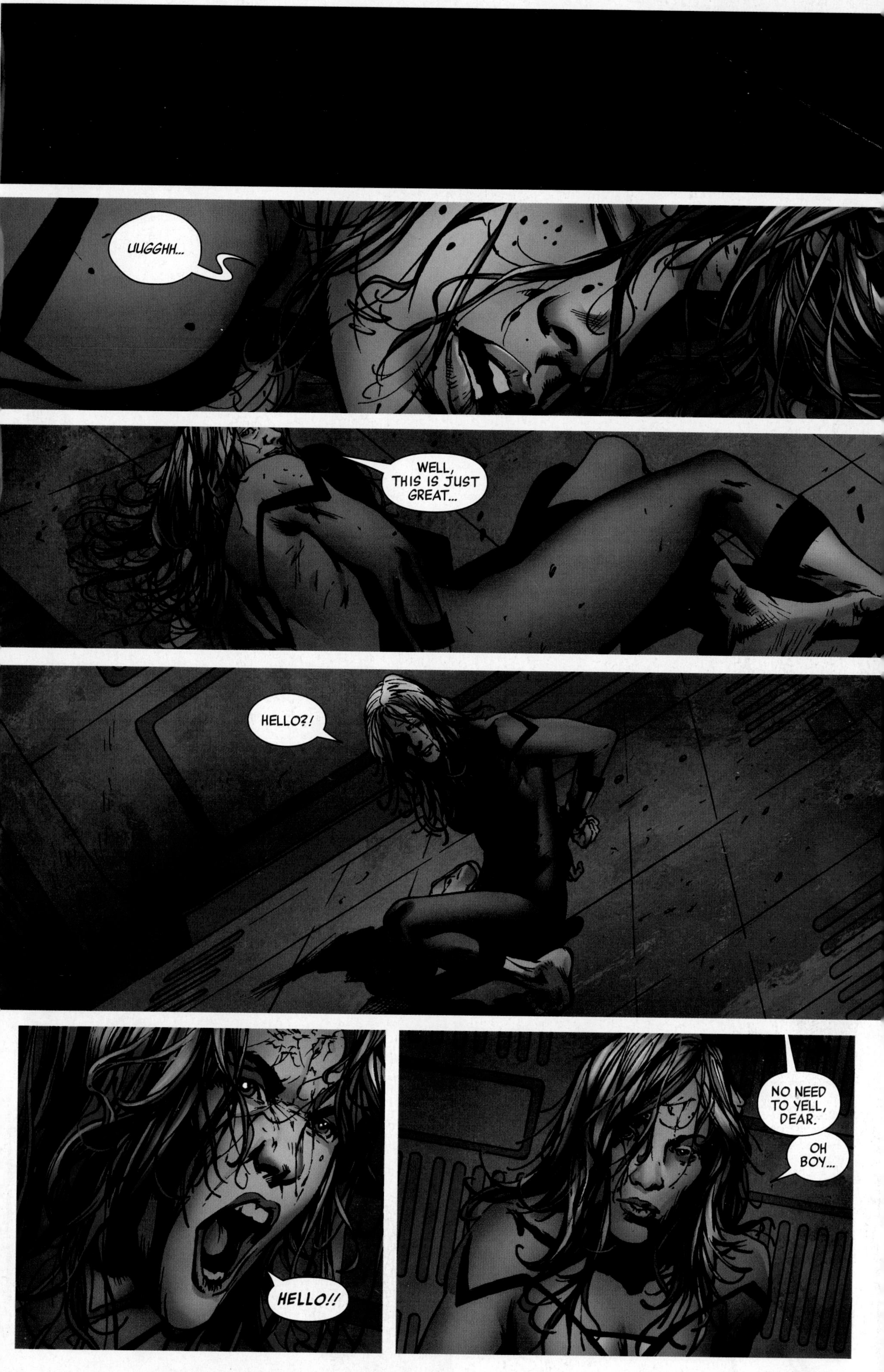
UUGGHH...
WELL, THIS IS JUST GREAT...
HELLO?!
HELLO!!
NO NEED TO YELL, DEAR.
OH BOY...

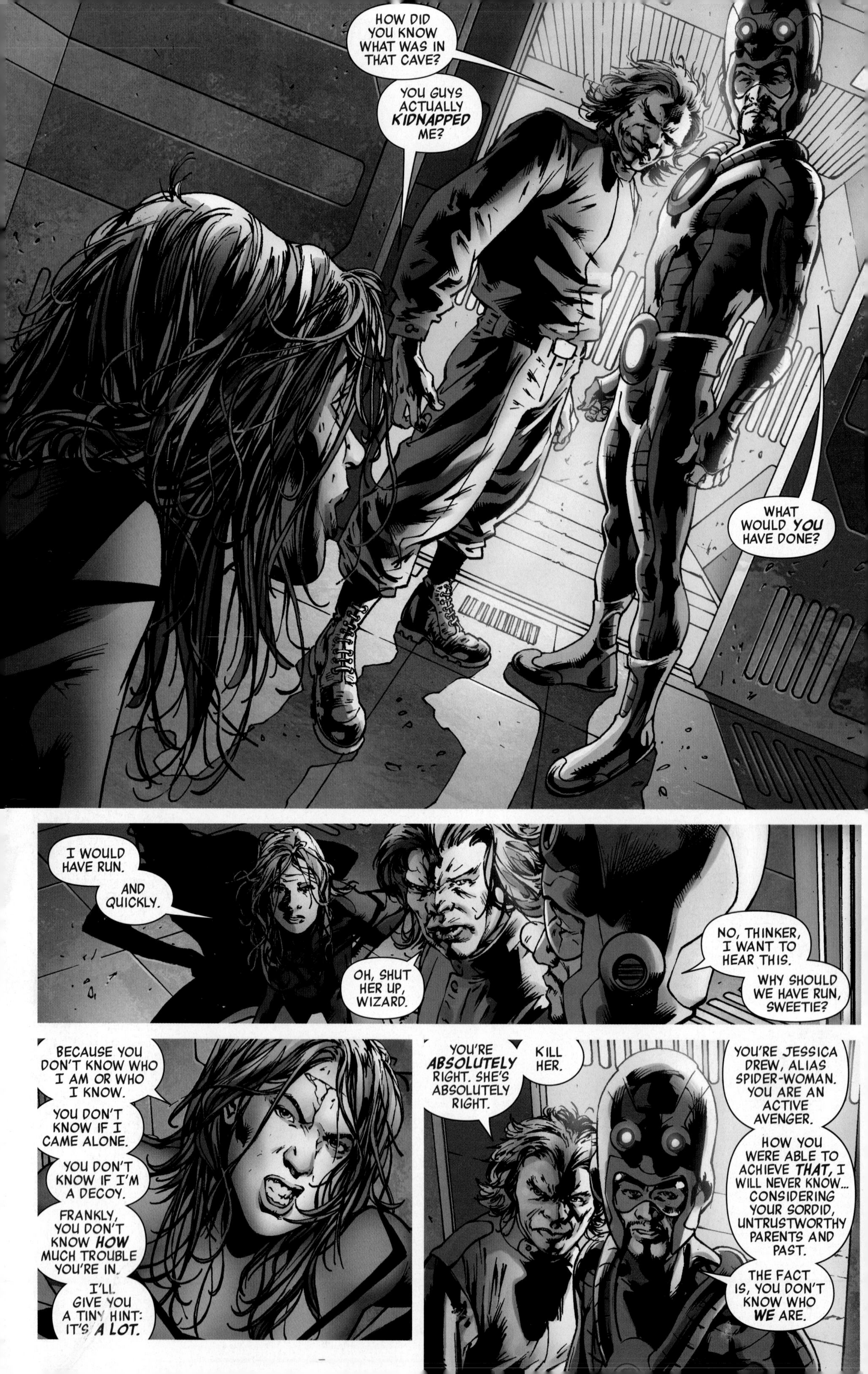
HOW DID YOU KNOW WHAT WAS IN THAT CAVE?
YOU GUYS ACTUALLY KIDNAPPED ME?
WHAT WOULD YOU HAVE DONE?
I WOULD HAVE RUN.
AND QUICKLY.
OH, SHUT HER UP, WIZARD.
NO, THINKER, I WANT TO HEAR THIS.
WHY SHOULD WE HAVE RUN, SWEETIE?
BECAUSE YOU DON'T KNOW WHO I AM OR WHO I KNOW.
YOU DON'T KNOW IF I CAME ALONE.
YOU DON'T KNOW IF I'M A DECOY.
FRANKLY, YOU DON'T KNOW HOW MUCH TROUBLE YOU'RE IN.
I'LL GIVE YOU A TINY HINT: IT'S A LOT.
YOU'RE ABSOLUTELY RIGHT. SHE'S ABSOLUTELY RIGHT.
KILL HER.
YOU'RE JESSICA DREW, ALIAS SPIDER-WOMAN. YOU ARE AN ACTIVE AVENGER.
HOW YOU WERE ABLE TO ACHIEVE THAT, I WILL NEVER KNOW... CONSIDERING YOUR SORDID, UNTRUSTWORTHY PARENTS AND PAST.
THE FACT IS, YOU DON'T KNOW WHO WE ARE.

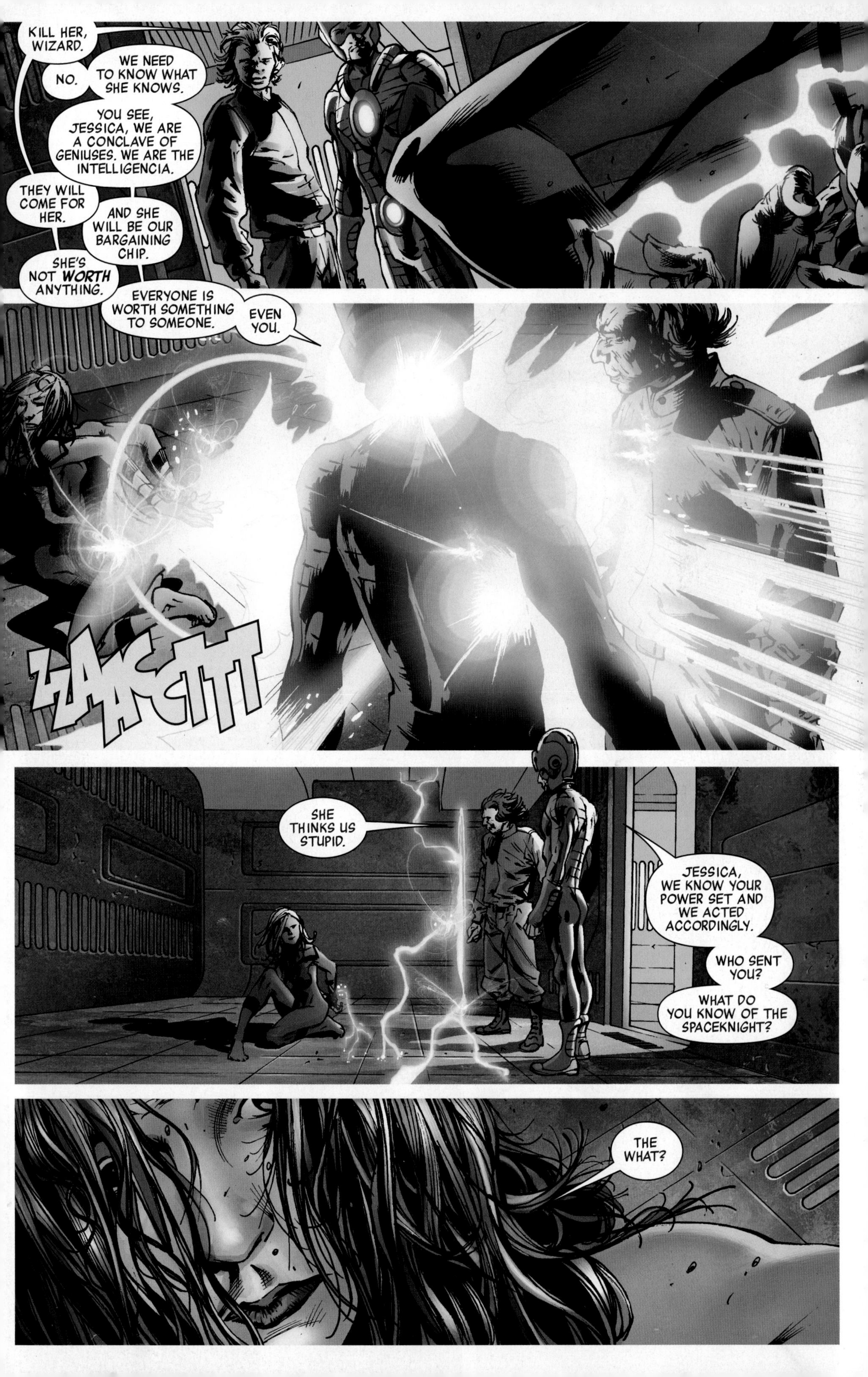

KILL HER, WIZARD.
NO.
WE NEED TO KNOW WHAT SHE KNOWS.
YOU SEE, JESSICA, WE ARE A CONCLAVE OF GENIUSES. WE ARE THE INTELLIGENCIA.
THEY WILL COME FOR HER.
AND SHE WILL BE OUR BARGAINING CHIP.
SHE'S NOT **WORTH** ANYTHING.
EVERYONE IS WORTH SOMETHING TO SOMEONE.
EVEN YOU.
ZZAACTTT
SHE THINKS US STUPID.
JESSICA, WE KNOW YOUR POWER SET AND WE ACTED ACCORDINGLY.
WHO SENT YOU?
WHAT DO YOU KNOW OF THE SPACEKNIGHT?
THE WHAT?

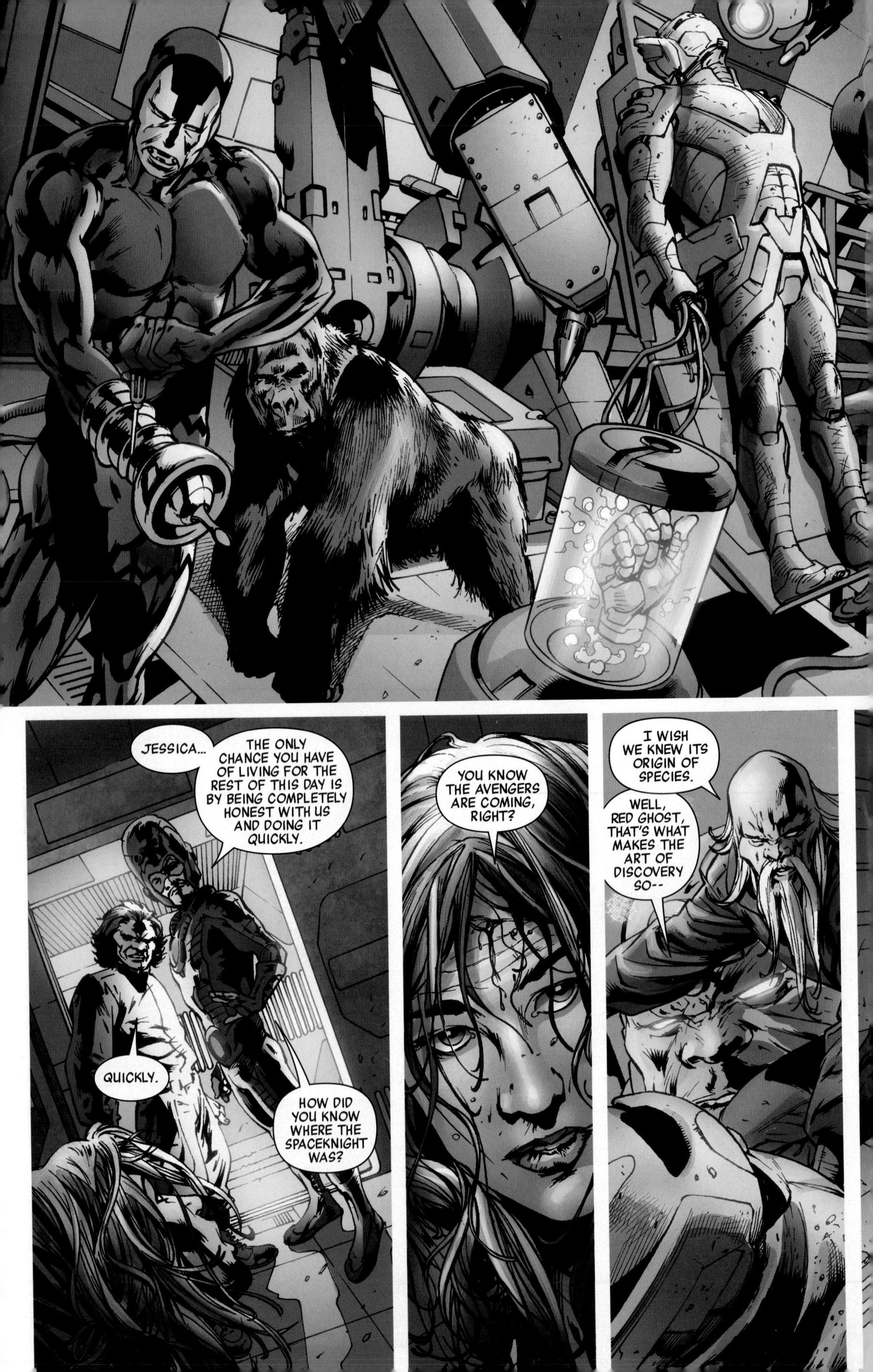
JESSICA...
THE ONLY CHANCE YOU HAVE OF LIVING FOR THE REST OF THIS DAY IS BY BEING COMPLETELY HONEST WITH US AND DOING IT QUICKLY.
QUICKLY.
HOW DID YOU KNOW WHERE THE SPACEKNIGHT WAS?
YOU KNOW THE AVENGERS ARE COMING, RIGHT?
I WISH WE KNEW ITS ORIGIN OF SPECIES.
WELL, RED GHOST, THAT'S WHAT MAKES THE ART OF DISCOVERY SO--

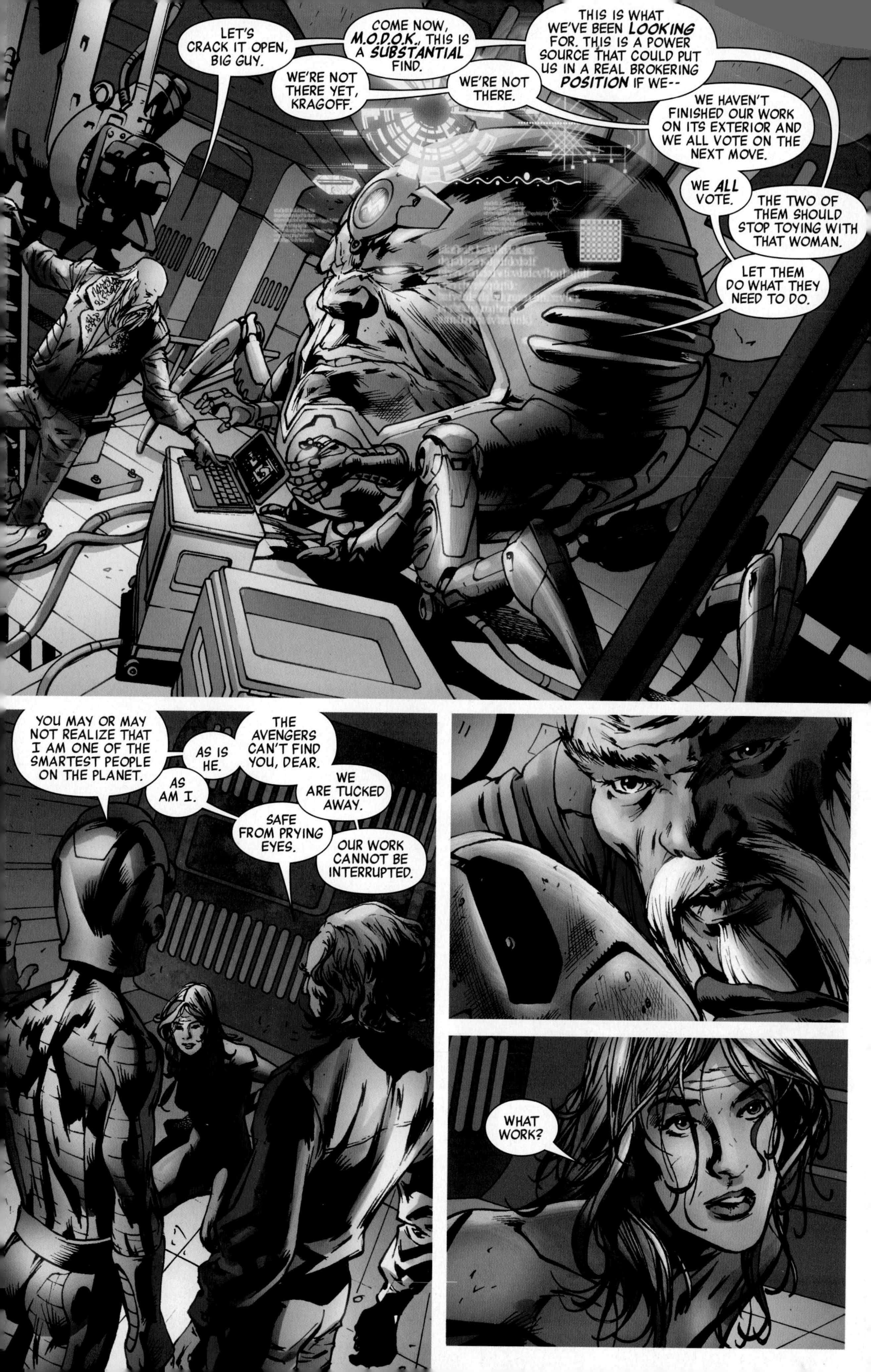
LET'S CRACK IT OPEN, BIG GUY.
COME NOW, M.O.D.O.K., THIS IS A SUBSTANTIAL FIND.
THIS IS WHAT WE'VE BEEN LOOKING FOR. THIS IS A POWER SOURCE THAT COULD PUT US IN A REAL BROKERING POSITION IF WE--
WE'RE NOT THERE YET, KRAGOFF.
WE'RE NOT THERE.
WE HAVEN'T FINISHED OUR WORK ON ITS EXTERIOR AND WE ALL VOTE ON THE NEXT MOVE.
WE ALL VOTE.
THE TWO OF THEM SHOULD STOP TOYING WITH THAT WOMAN.
LET THEM DO WHAT THEY NEED TO DO.
YOU MAY OR MAY NOT REALIZE THAT I AM ONE OF THE SMARTEST PEOPLE ON THE PLANET.
AS IS HE.
AS AM I.
THE AVENGERS CAN'T FIND YOU, DEAR.
WE ARE TUCKED AWAY.
SAFE FROM PRYING EYES.
OUR WORK CANNOT BE INTERRUPTED.
WHAT WORK?

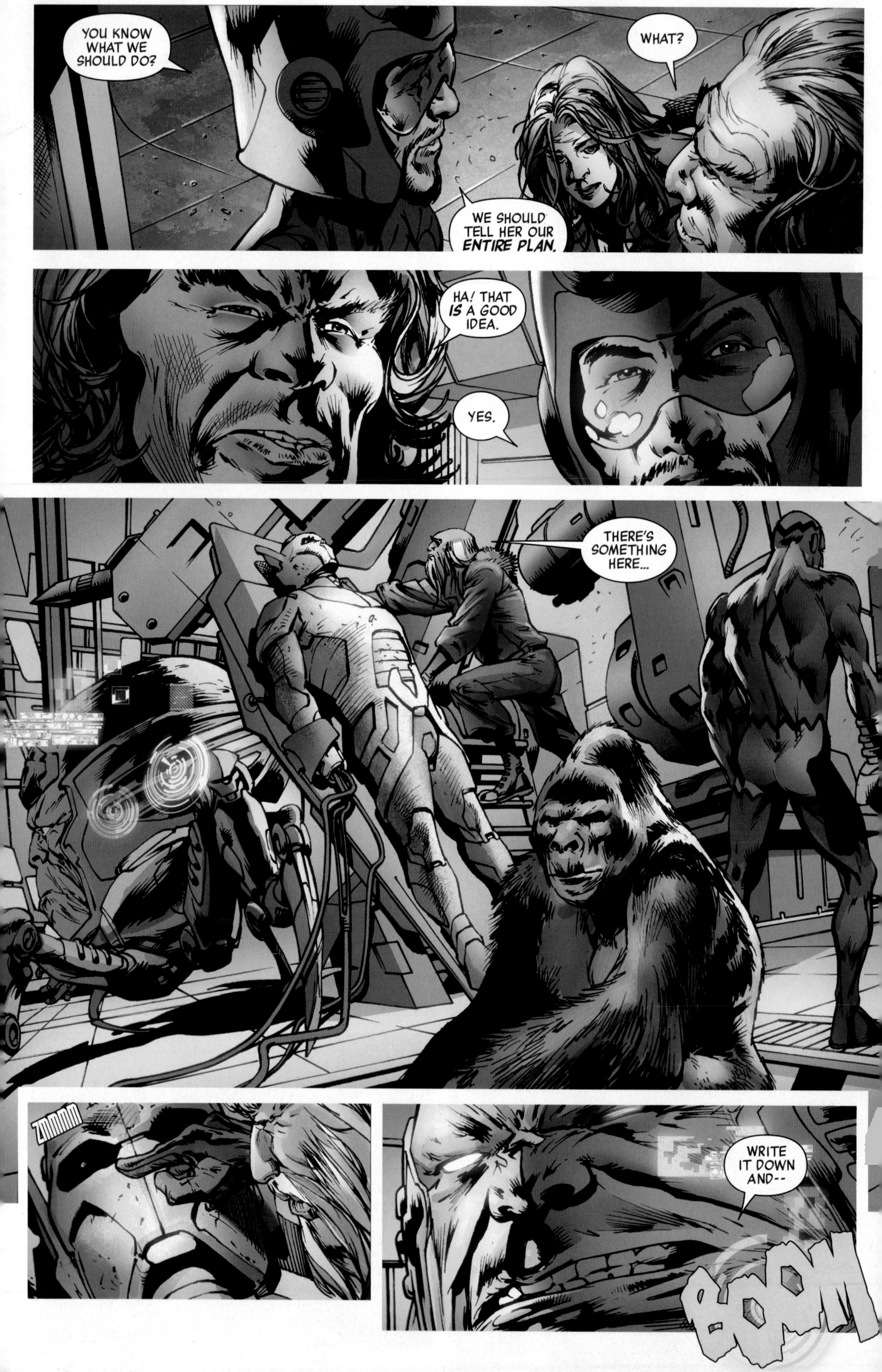
YOU KNOW WHAT WE SHOULD DO?
WHAT?
WE SHOULD TELL HER OUR ENTIRE PLAN.
HA! THAT IS A GOOD IDEA.
YES.
THERE'S SOMETHING HERE...
ZMMM
WRITE IT DOWN AND--
BOOM

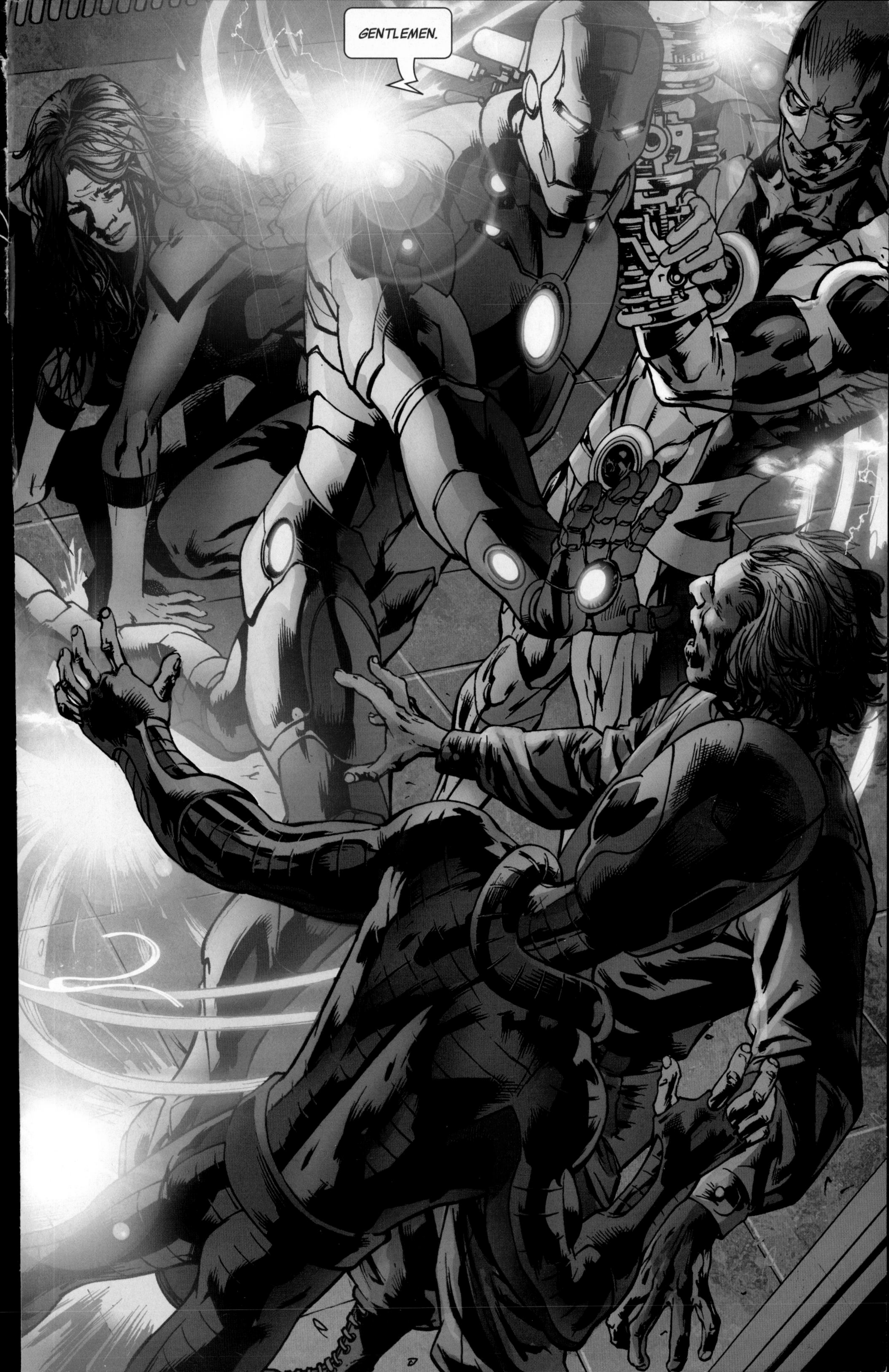
GENTLEMEN.

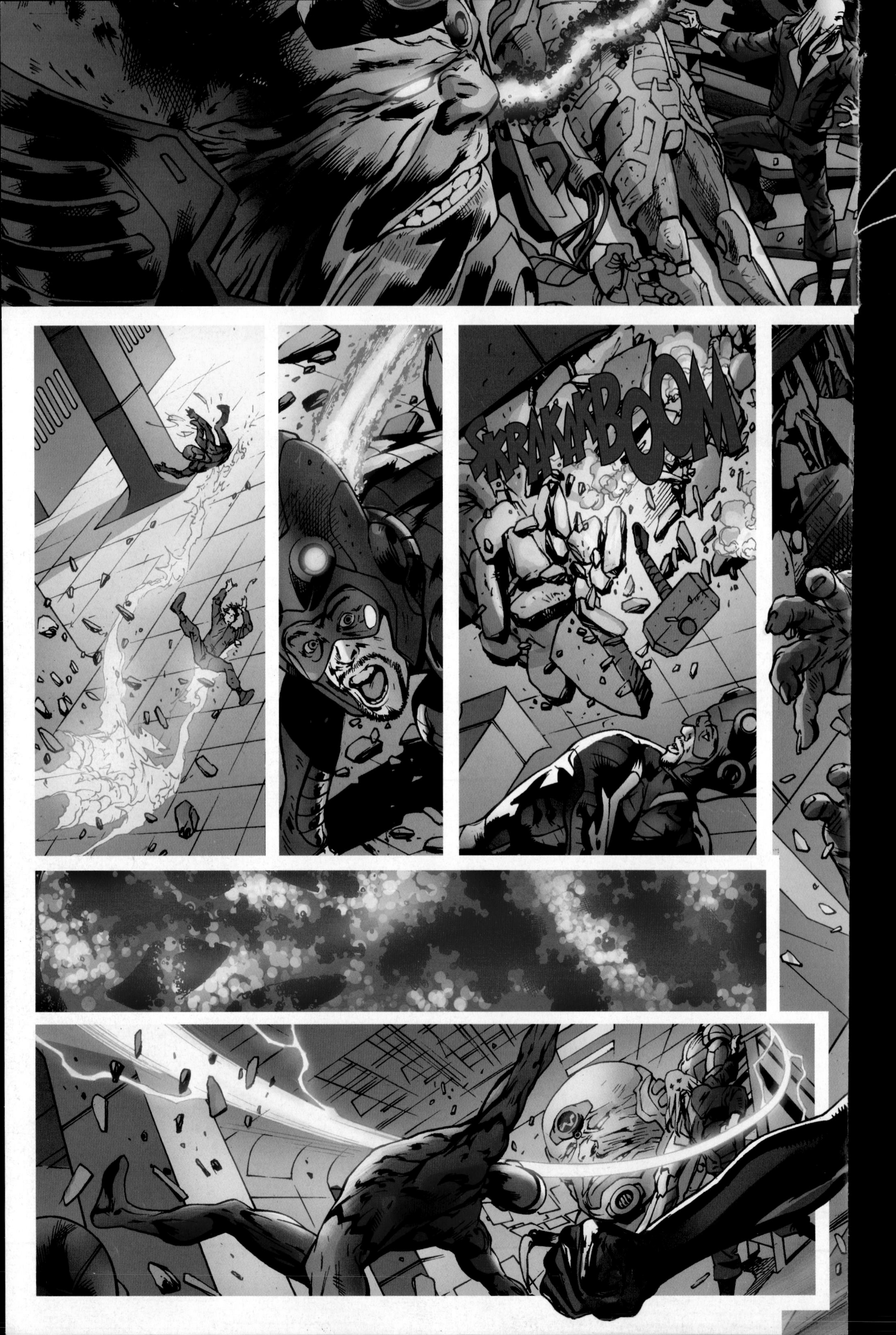
SKRAKAKBOOM

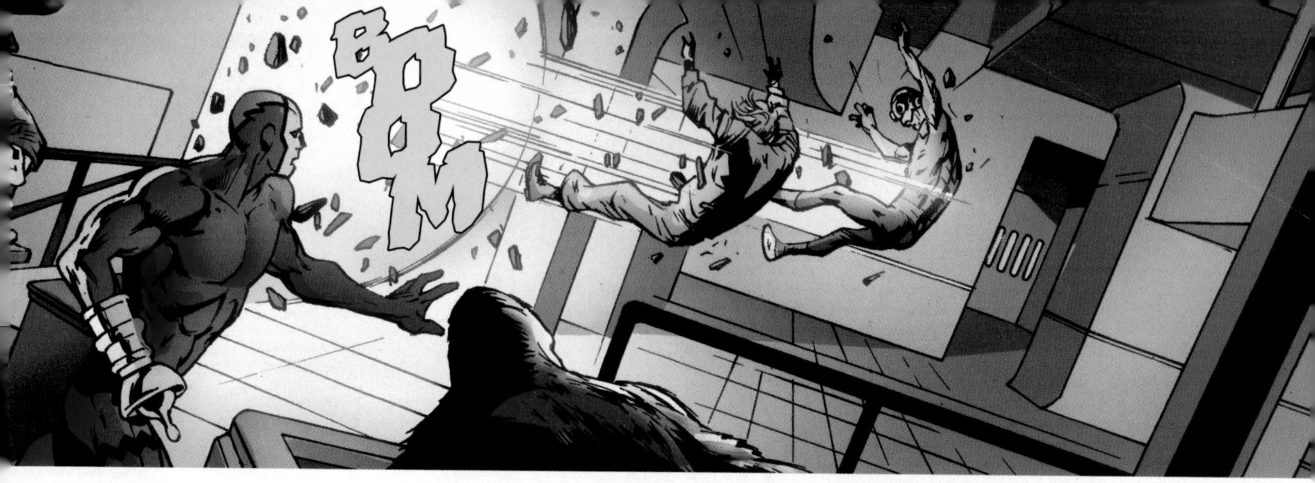
BOOM

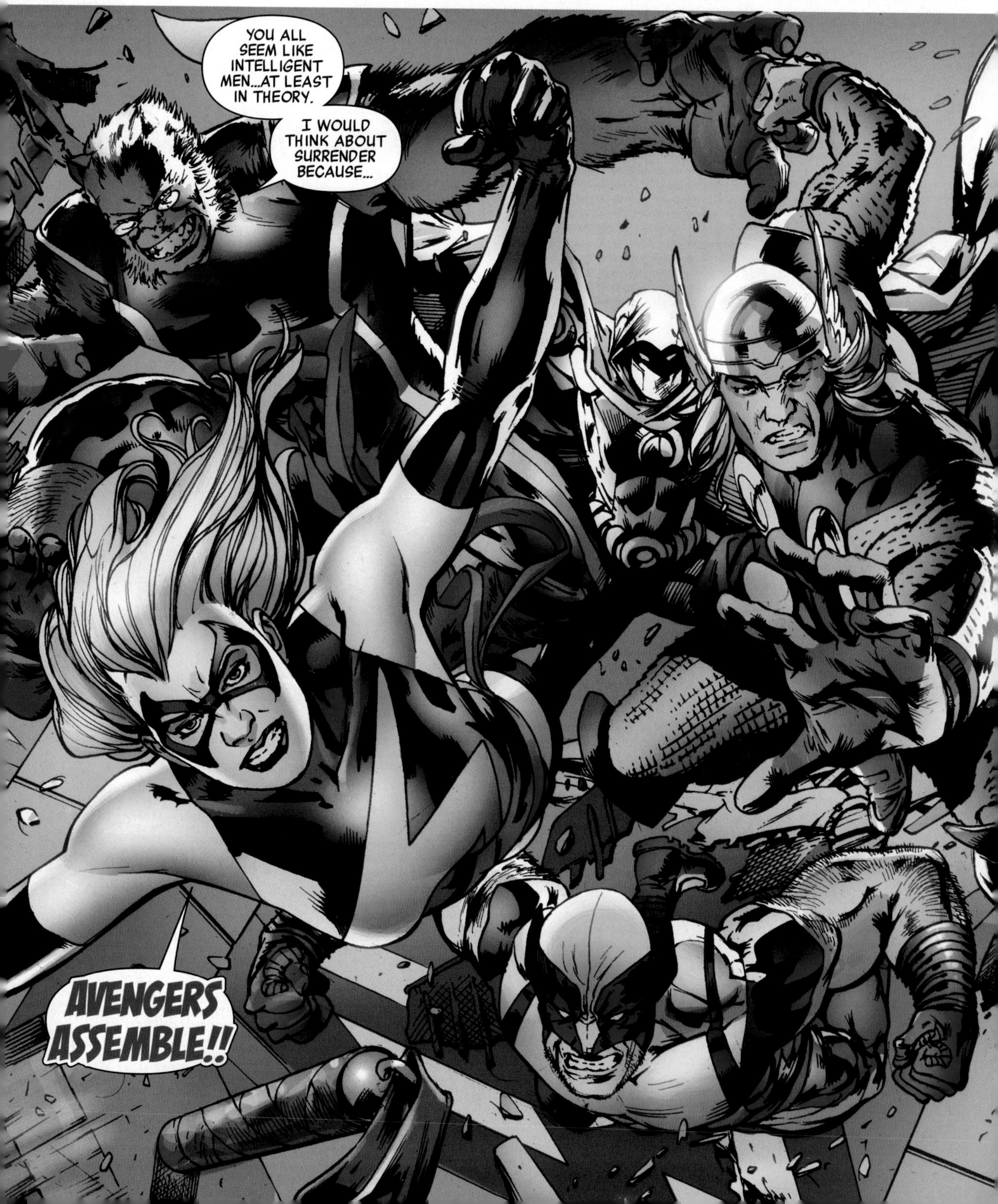
YOU ALL SEEM LIKE INTELLIGENT MEN...AT LEAST IN THEORY.
I WOULD THINK ABOUT SURRENDER BECAUSE...
AVENGERS ASSEMBLE!!

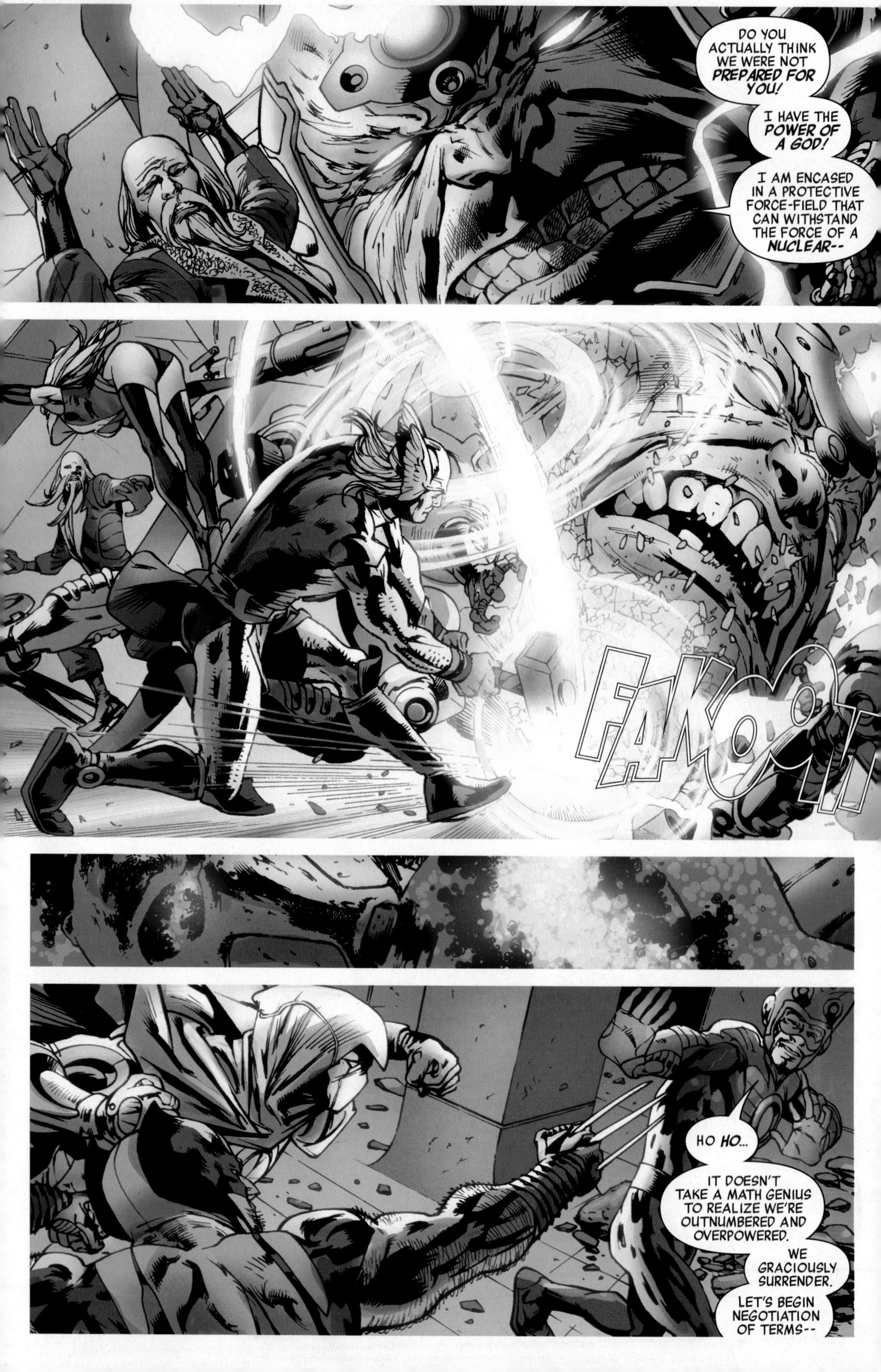

DO YOU ACTUALLY THINK WE WERE NOT *PREPARED FOR YOU!*
I HAVE THE *POWER OF A GOD!*
I AM ENCASED IN A PROTECTIVE FORCE-FIELD THAT CAN WITHSTAND THE FORCE OF A *NUCLEAR--*
FAKOOM
HO *HO*...
IT DOESN'T TAKE A MATH GENIUS TO REALIZE WE'RE OUTNUMBERED AND OVERPOWERED.
WE GRACIOUSLY SURRENDER.
LET'S BEGIN NEGOTIATION OF TERMS--

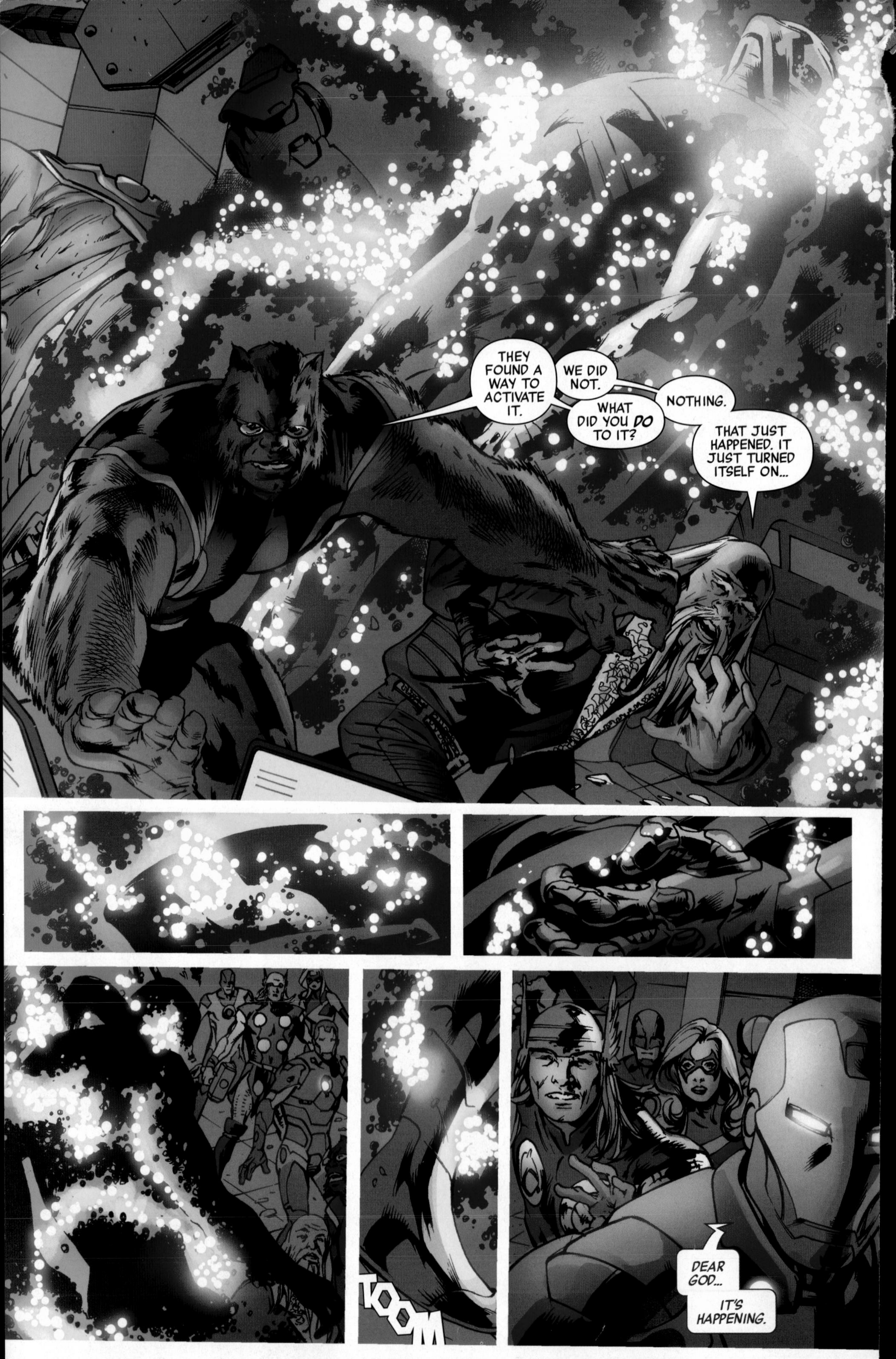
THEY FOUND A WAY TO ACTIVATE IT.
WE DID NOT.
WHAT DID YOU *DO* TO IT?
NOTHING.
THAT JUST HAPPENED. IT JUST TURNED ITSELF ON...
TOOM
DEAR GOD...
IT'S HAPPENING.

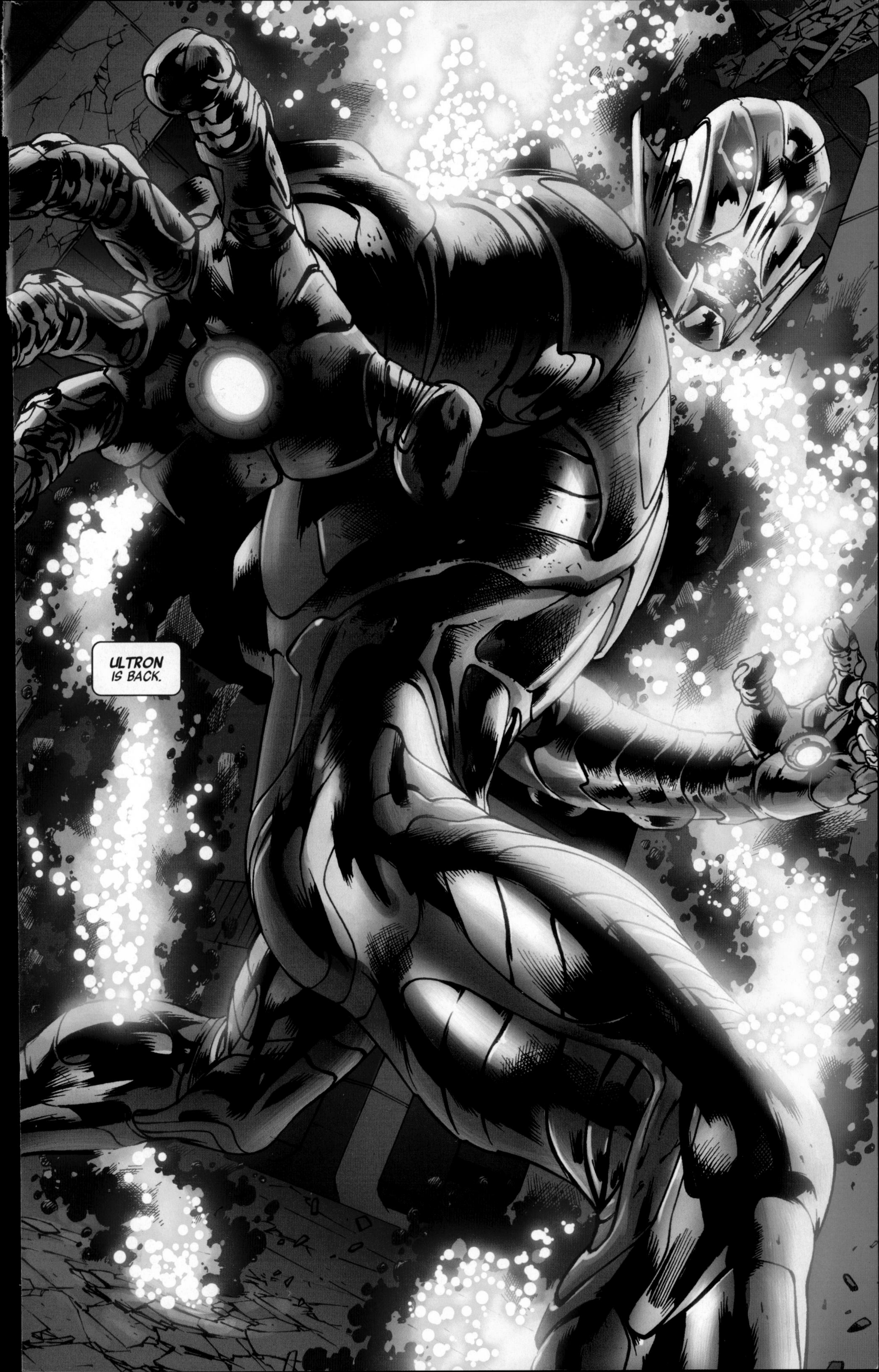
ULTRON IS BACK.

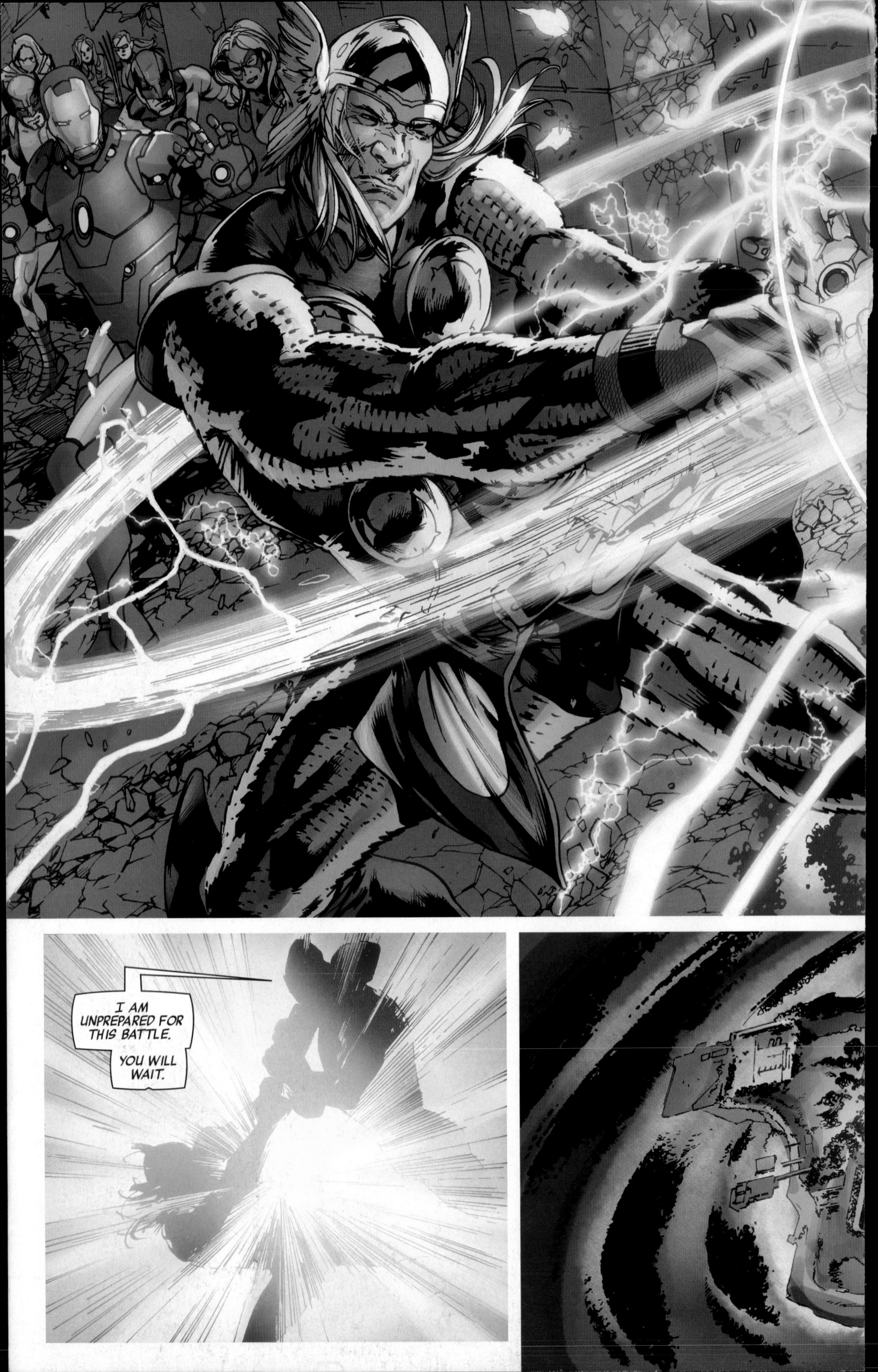
I AM UNPREPARED FOR THIS BATTLE.
YOU WILL WAIT.

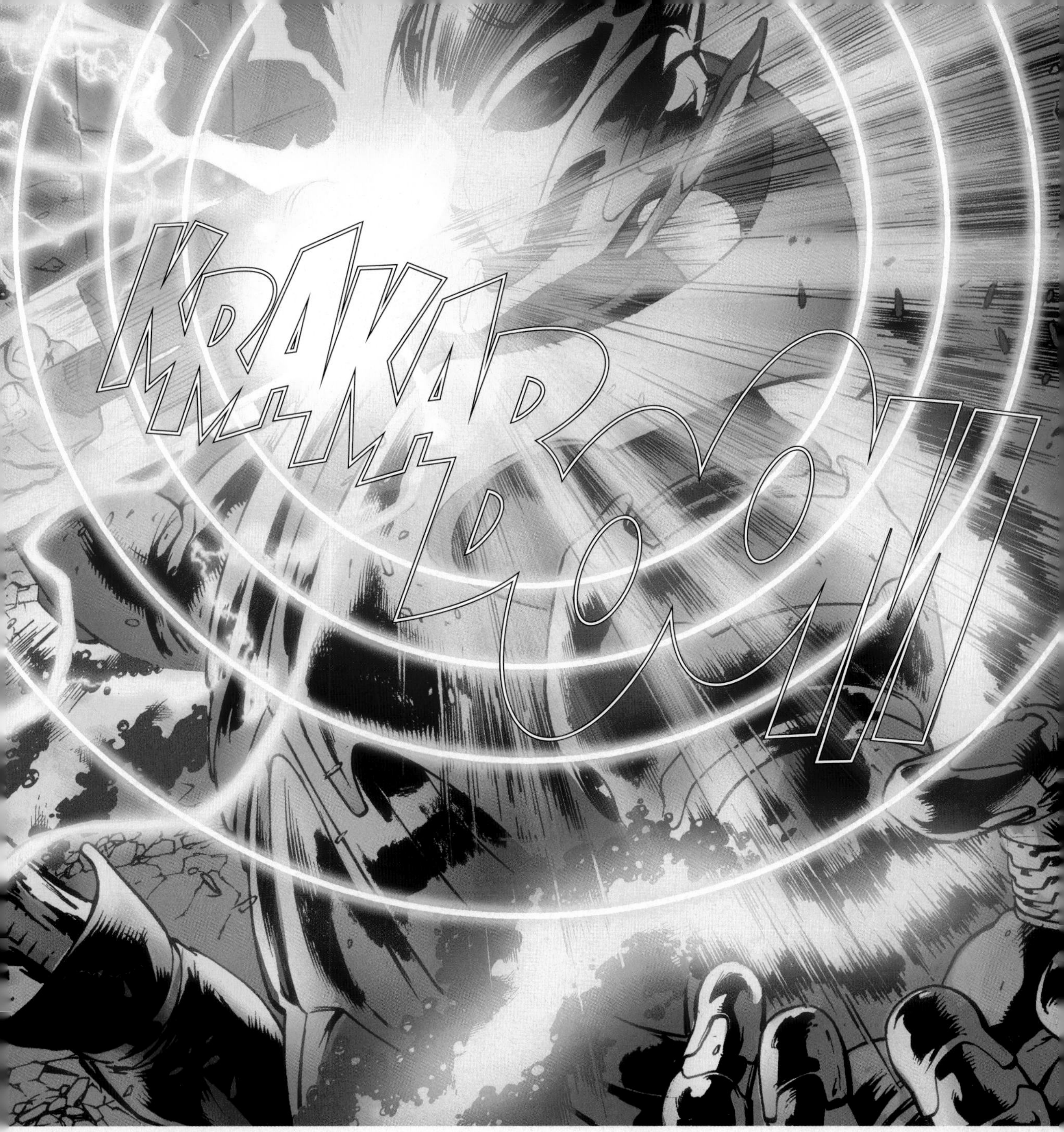
KRAKADOOM!!

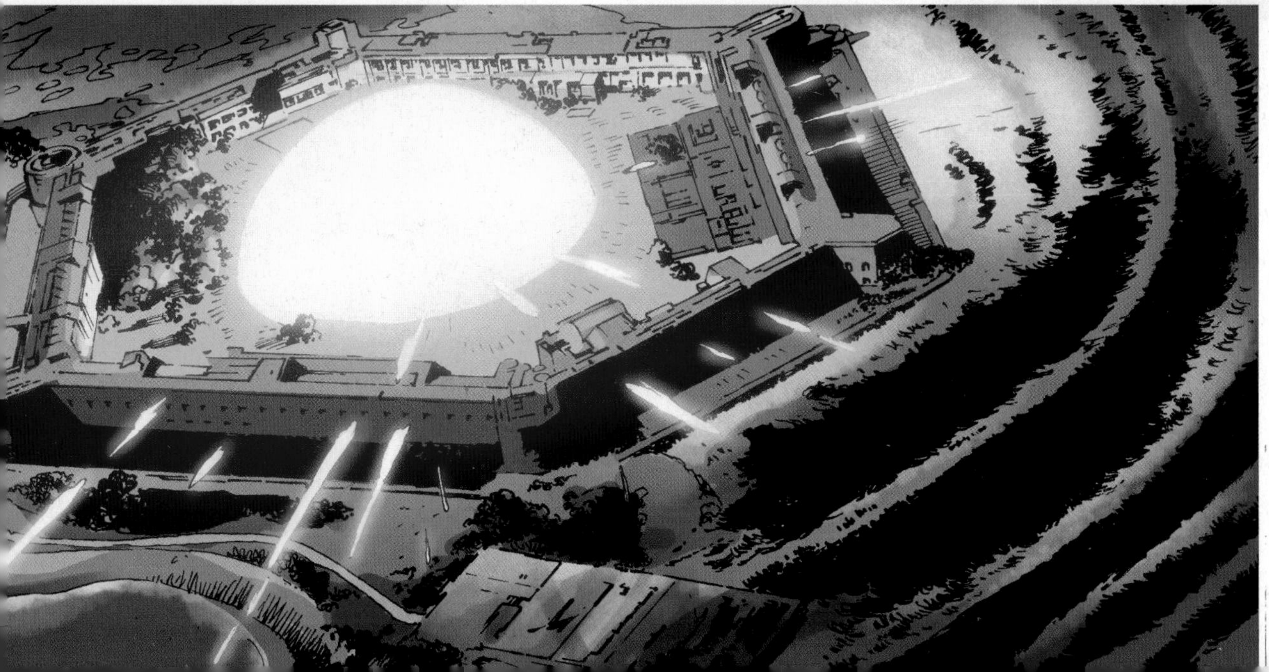

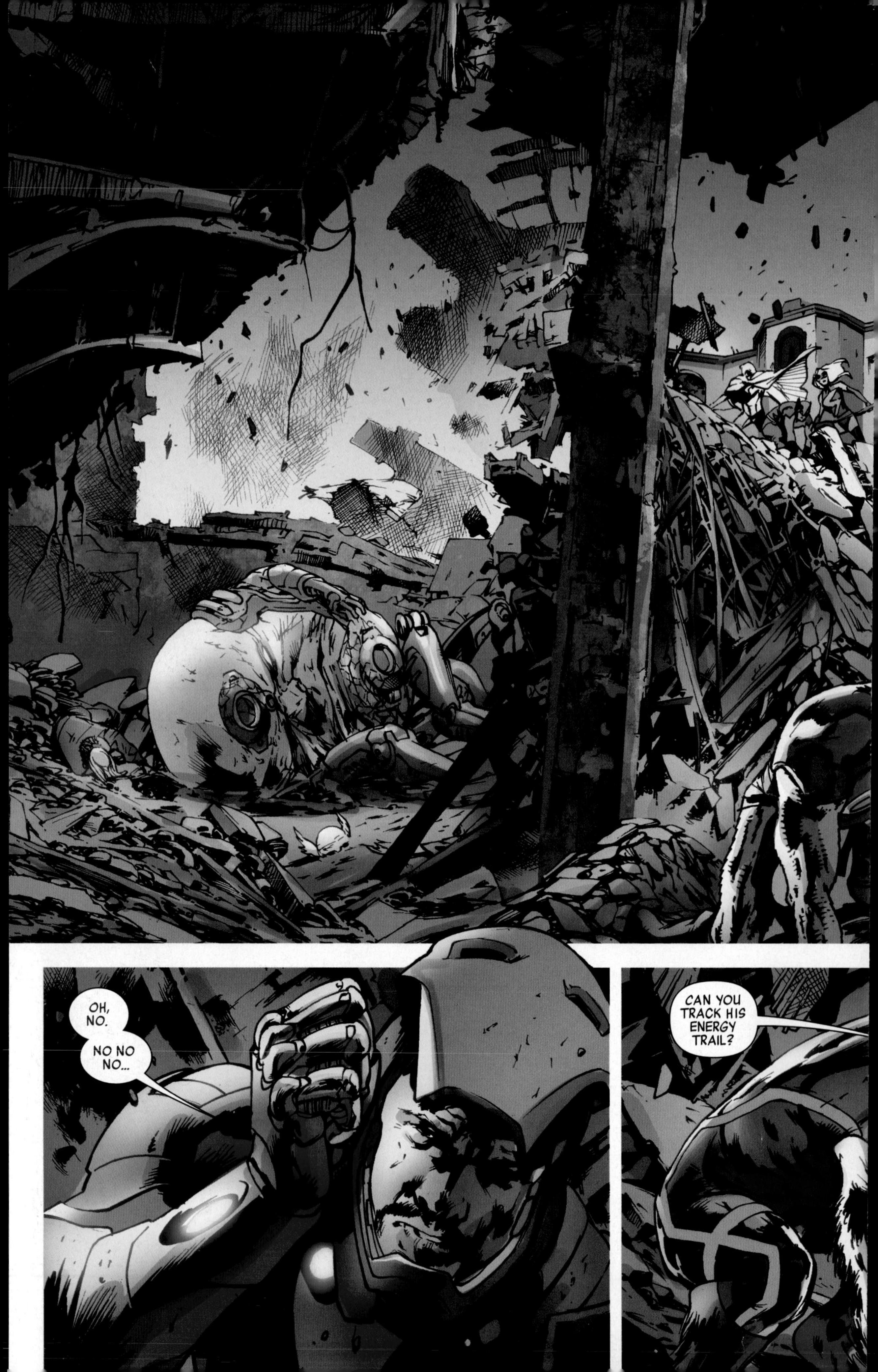
OH, NO.
NO NO NO...
CAN YOU TRACK HIS ENERGY TRAIL?

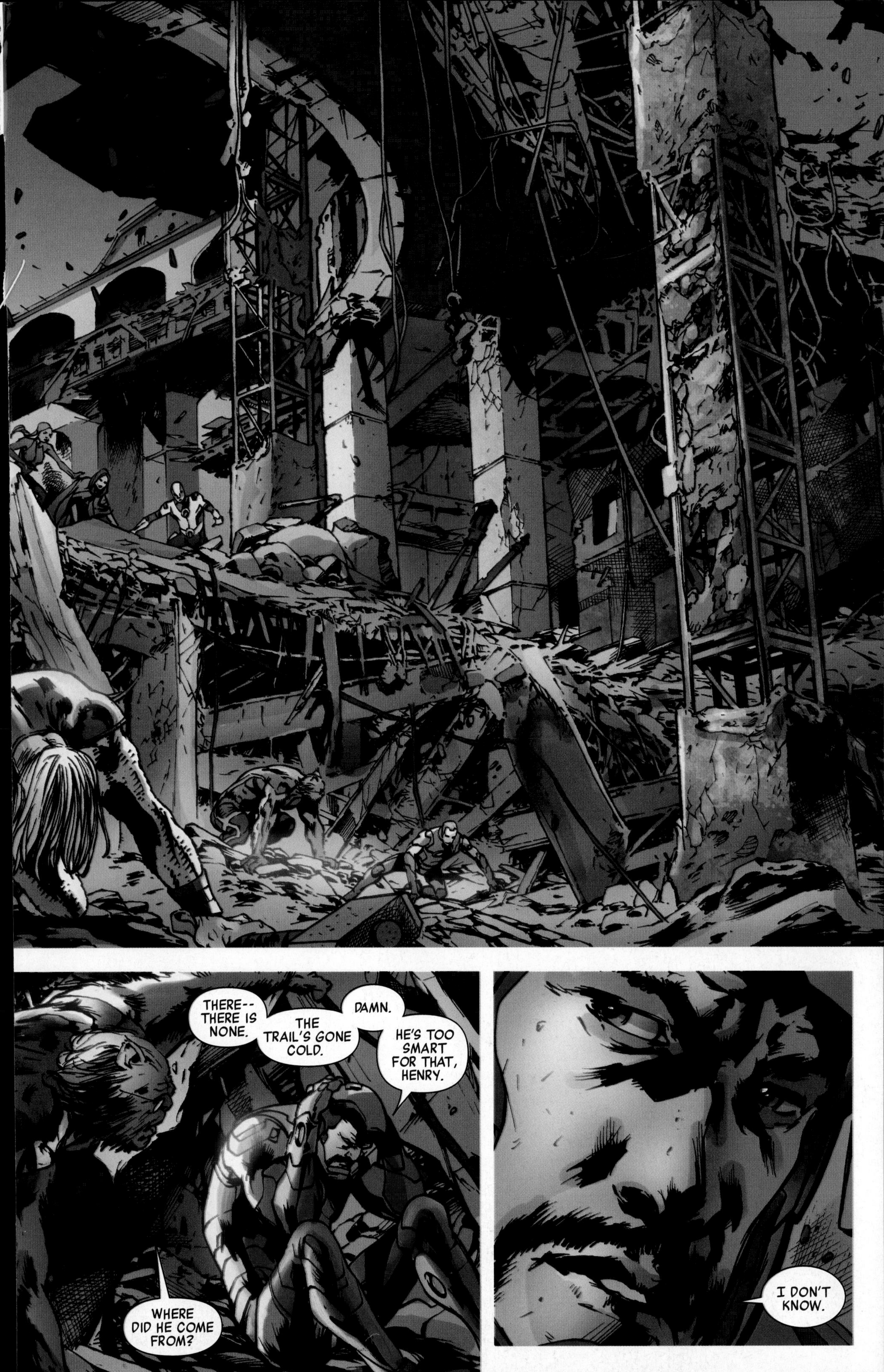
THERE-- THERE IS NONE.
THE TRAIL'S GONE COLD.
DAMN.
HE'S TOO SMART FOR THAT, HENRY.
WHERE DID HE COME FROM?
I DON'T KNOW.

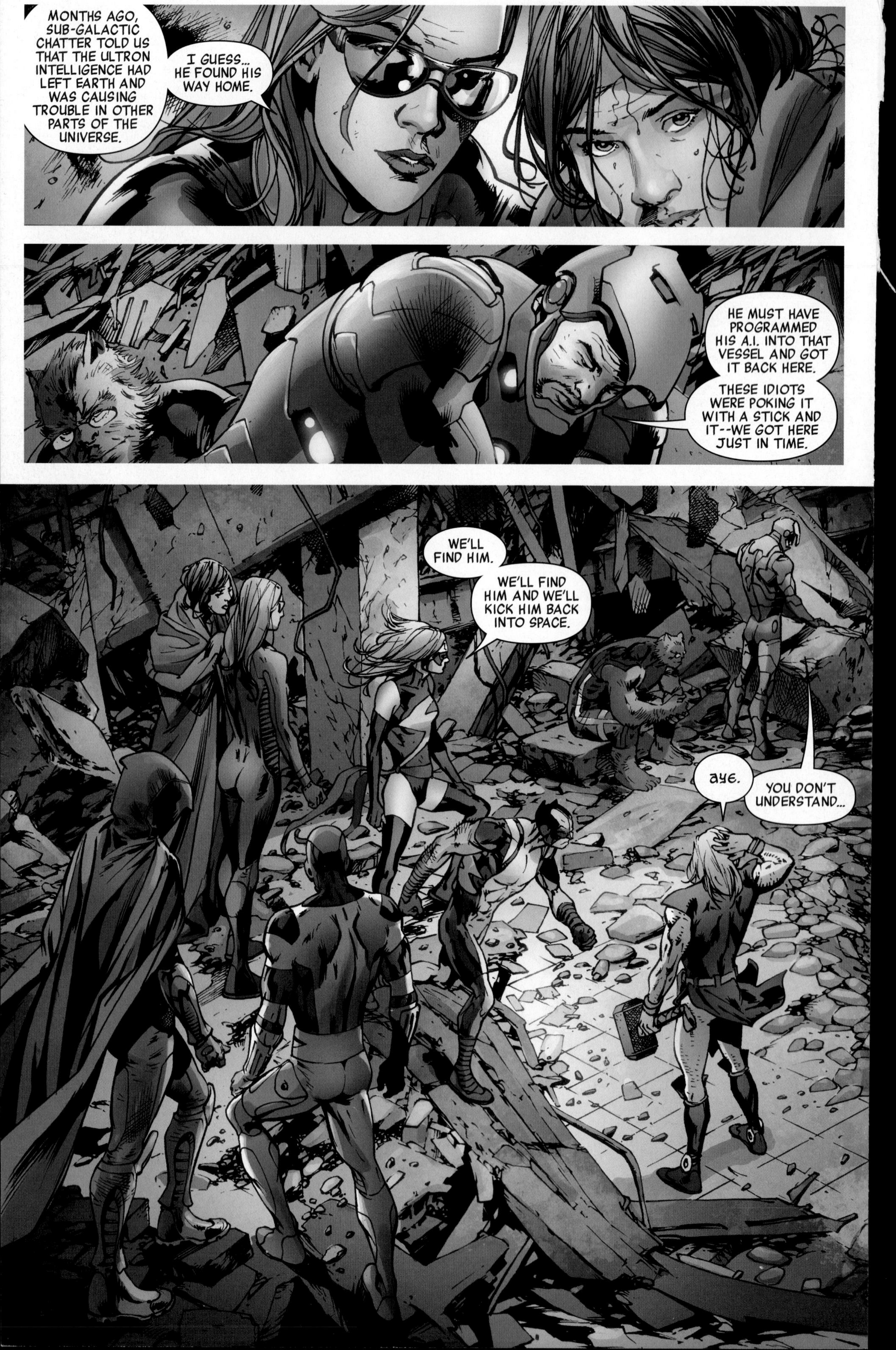
MONTHS AGO, SUB-GALACTIC CHATTER TOLD US THAT THE ULTRON INTELLIGENCE HAD LEFT EARTH AND WAS CAUSING TROUBLE IN OTHER PARTS OF THE UNIVERSE.
I GUESS... HE FOUND HIS WAY HOME.
HE MUST HAVE PROGRAMMED HIS A.I. INTO THAT VESSEL AND GOT IT BACK HERE.
THESE IDIOTS WERE POKING IT WITH A STICK AND IT--WE GOT HERE JUST IN TIME.
WE'LL FIND HIM.
WE'LL FIND HIM AND WE'LL KICK HIM BACK INTO SPACE.
aye.
YOU DON'T UNDERSTAND...

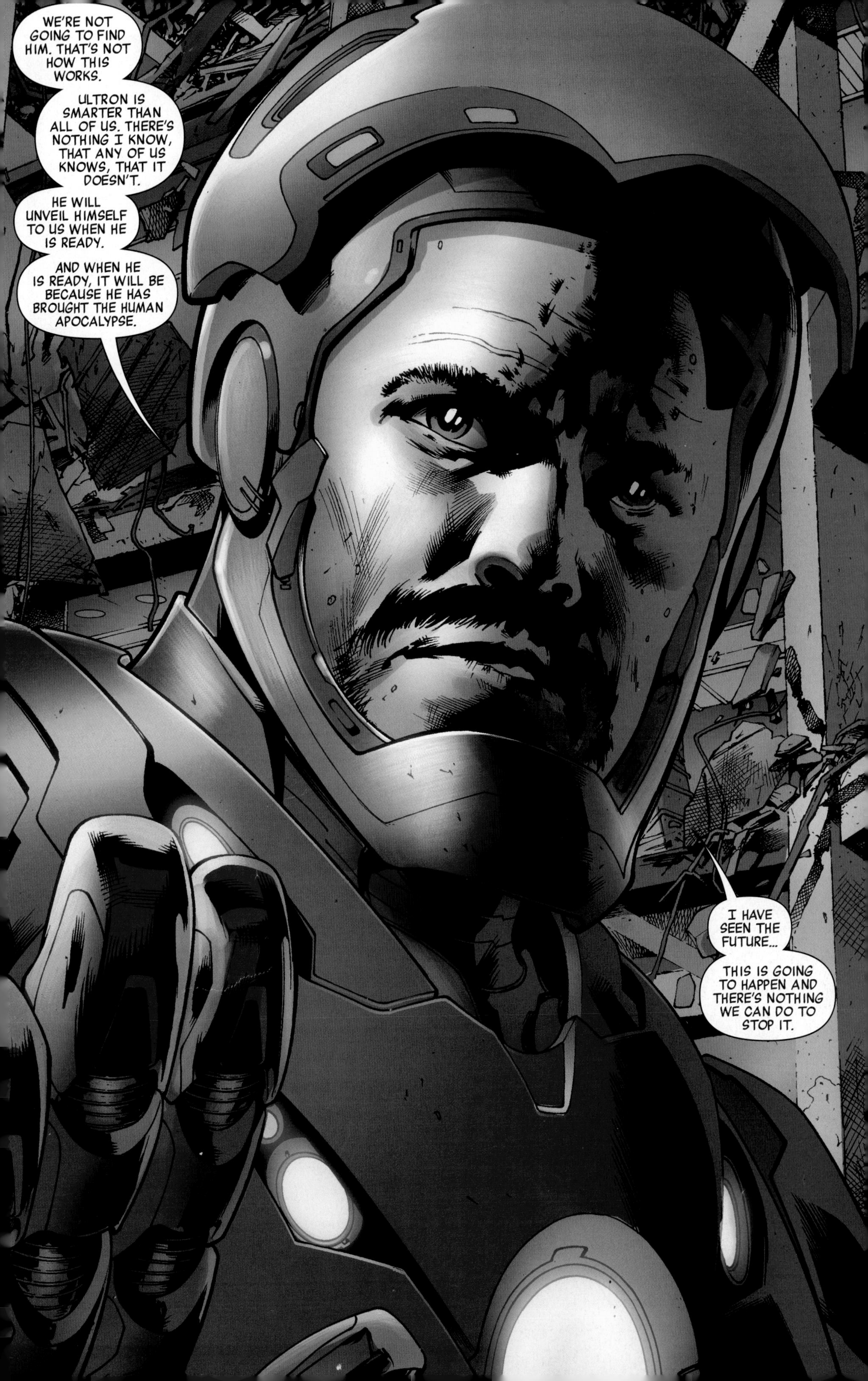
WE'RE NOT GOING TO FIND HIM. THAT'S NOT HOW THIS WORKS.
ULTRON IS SMARTER THAN ALL OF US. THERE'S NOTHING I KNOW, THAT ANY OF US KNOWS, THAT IT DOESN'T.
HE WILL UNVEIL HIMSELF TO US WHEN HE IS READY.
AND WHEN HE IS READY, IT WILL BE BECAUSE HE HAS BROUGHT THE HUMAN APOCALYPSE.
I HAVE SEEN THE FUTURE...
THIS IS GOING TO HAPPEN AND THERE'S NOTHING WE CAN DO TO STOP IT.

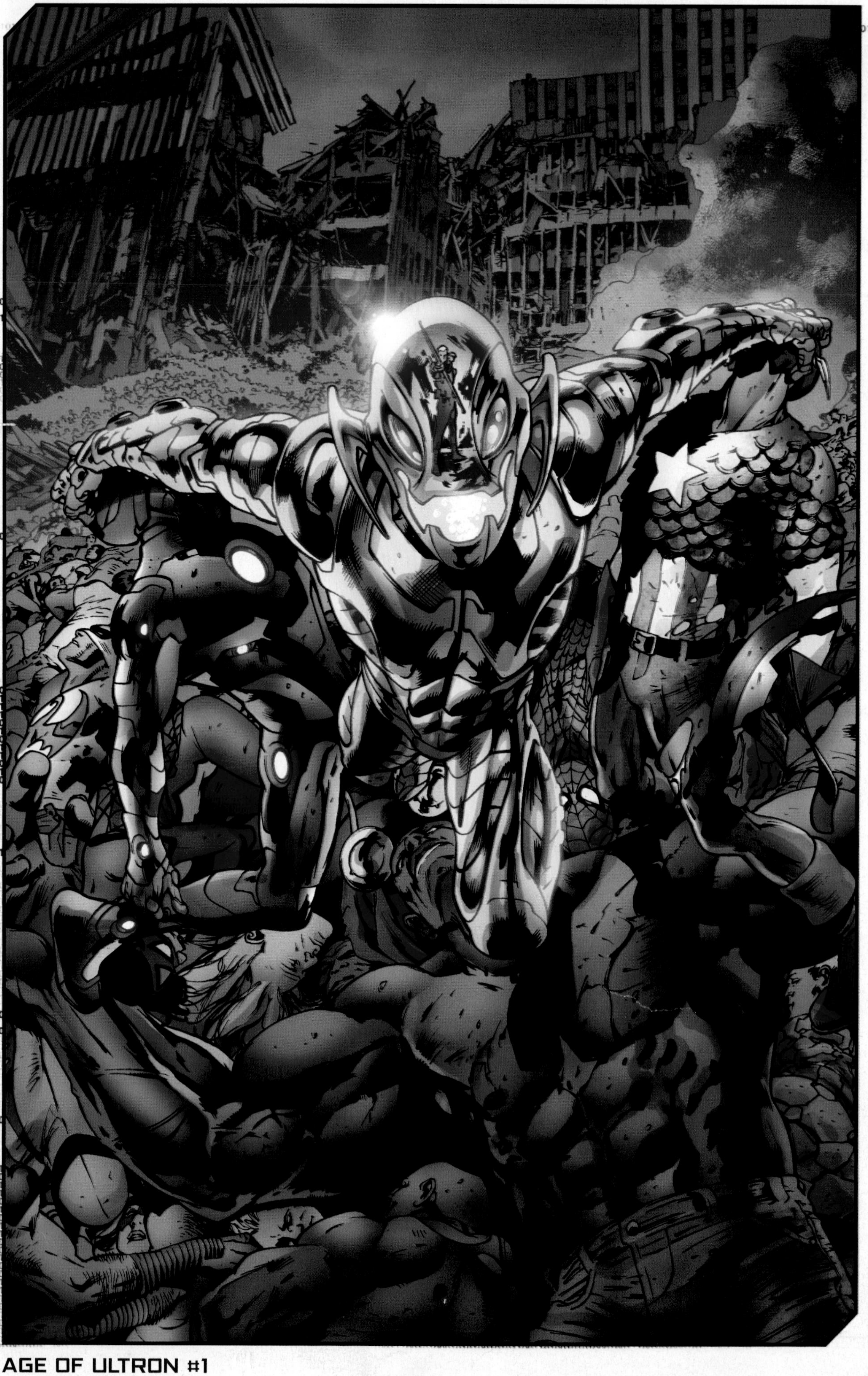

AGE OF ULTRON #1

AGE OF ULTRON

HANK PYM OF THE AVENGERS CREATED THE ARTIFICIAL INTELLIGENCE KNOWN AS ULTRON.

IT HATES HUMANITY...AND IT HAS RETURNED...

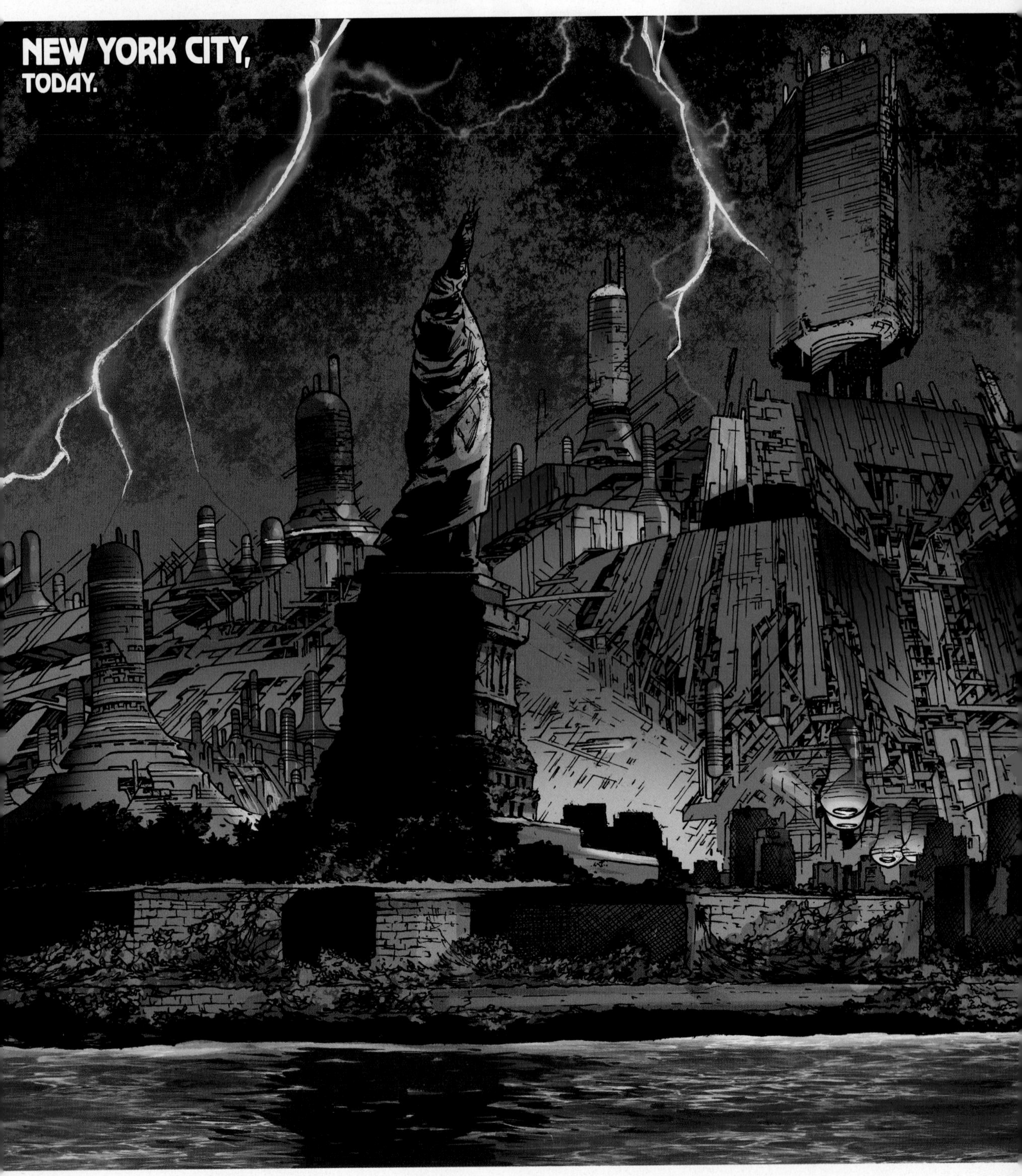
NEW YORK CITY,
TODAY.

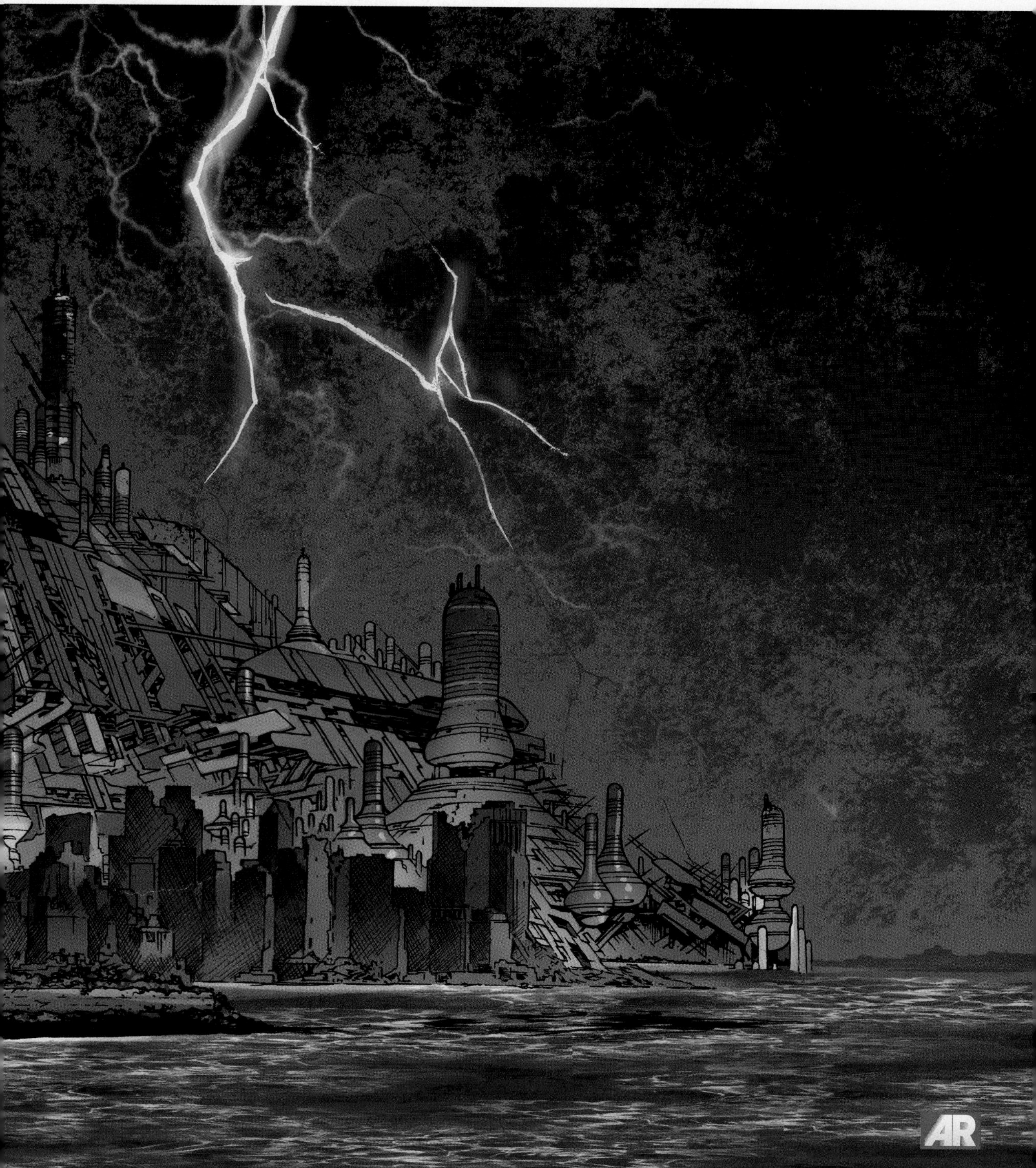

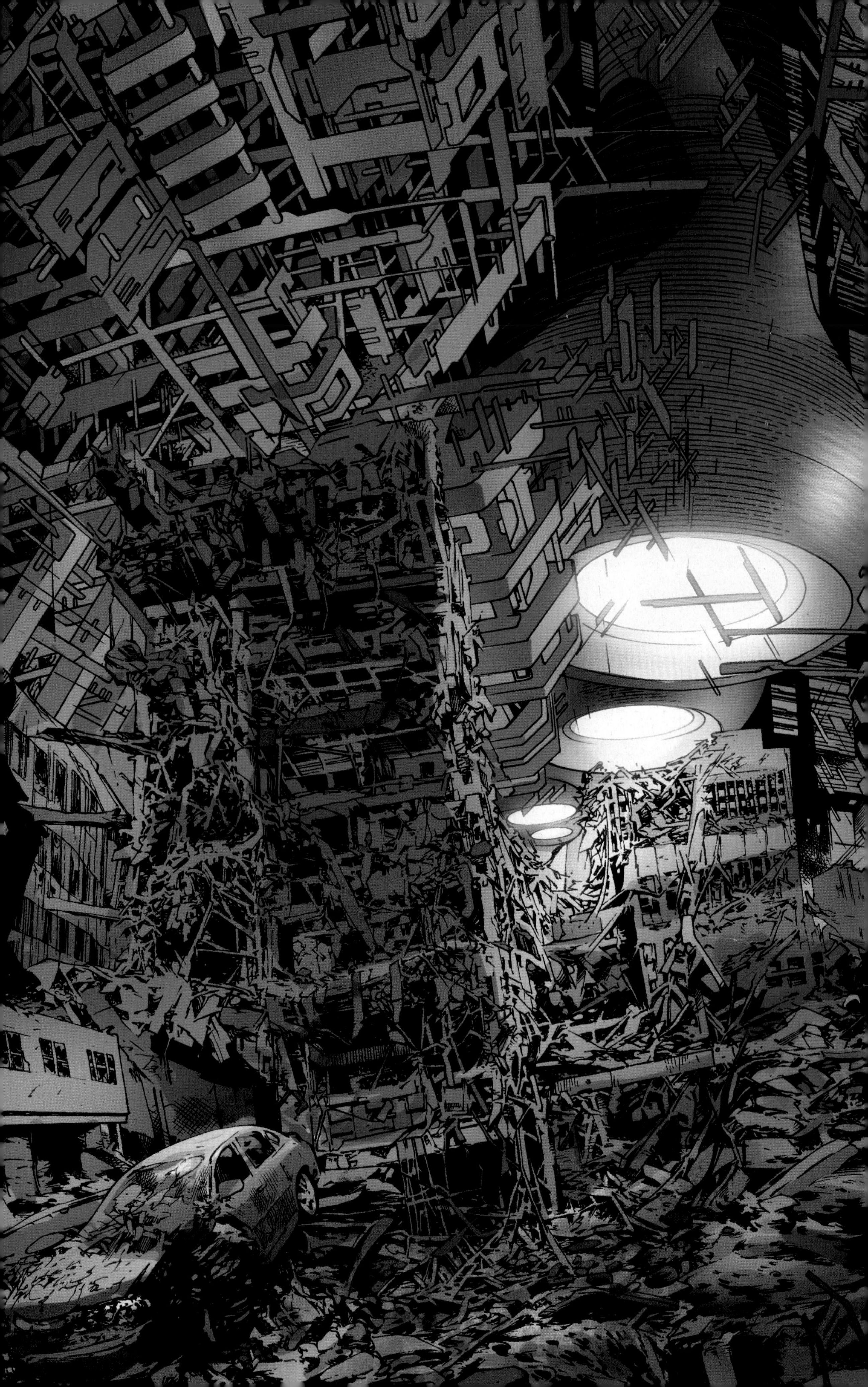

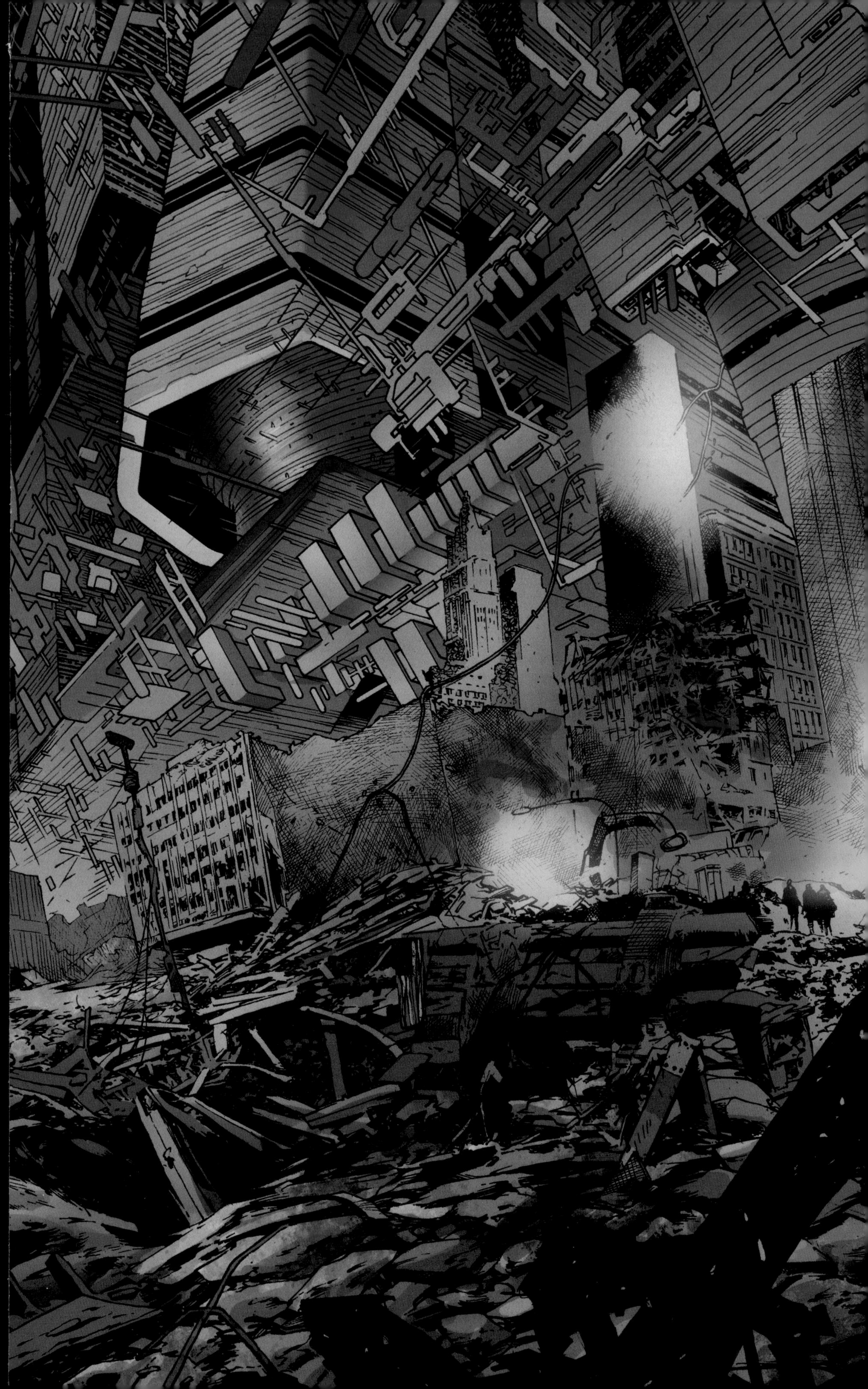

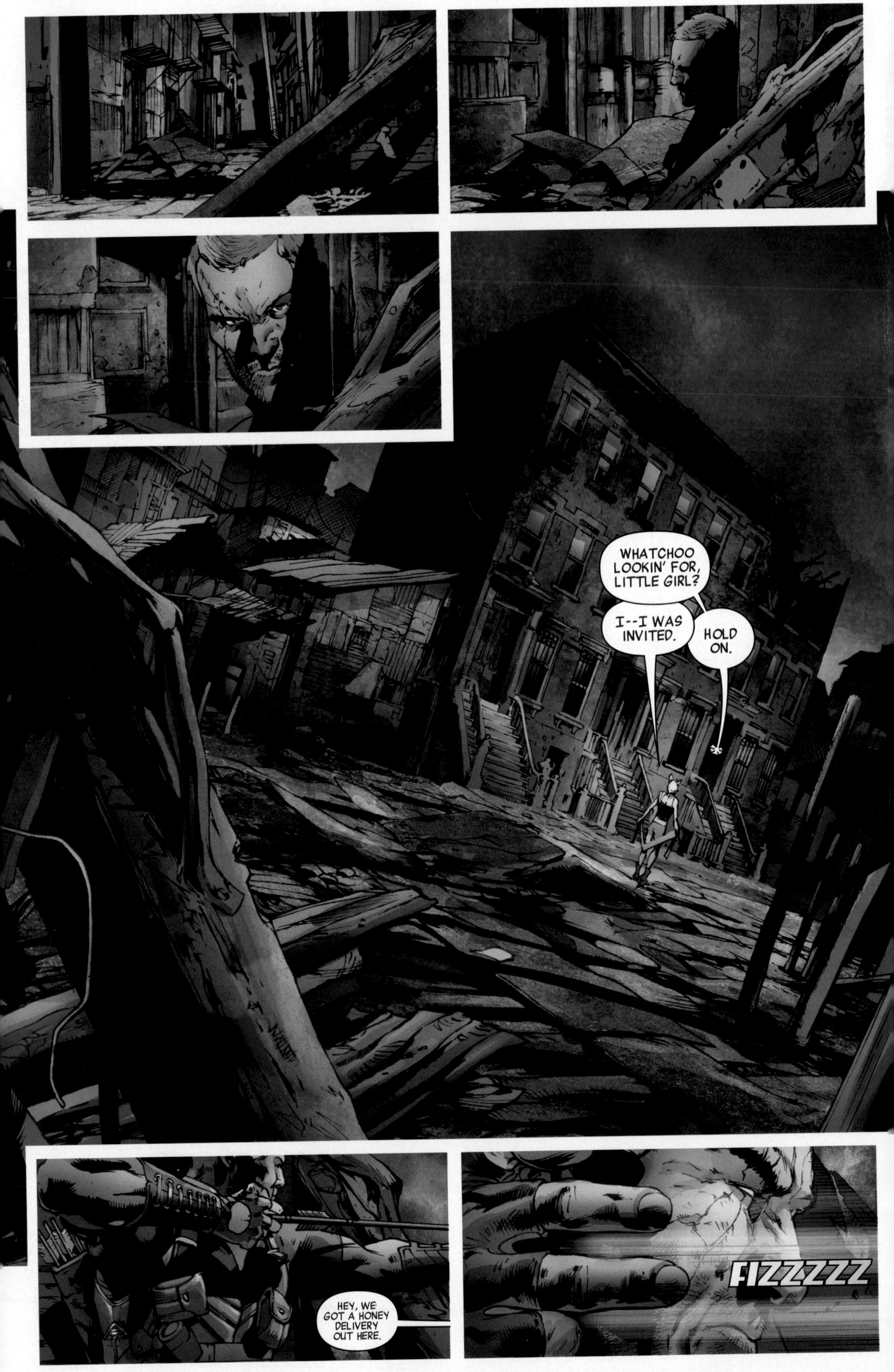
WHATCHOO LOOKIN' FOR, LITTLE GIRL?
I--I WAS INVITED.
HOLD ON.
HEY, WE GOT A HONEY DELIVERY OUT HERE.
FIZZZZZ

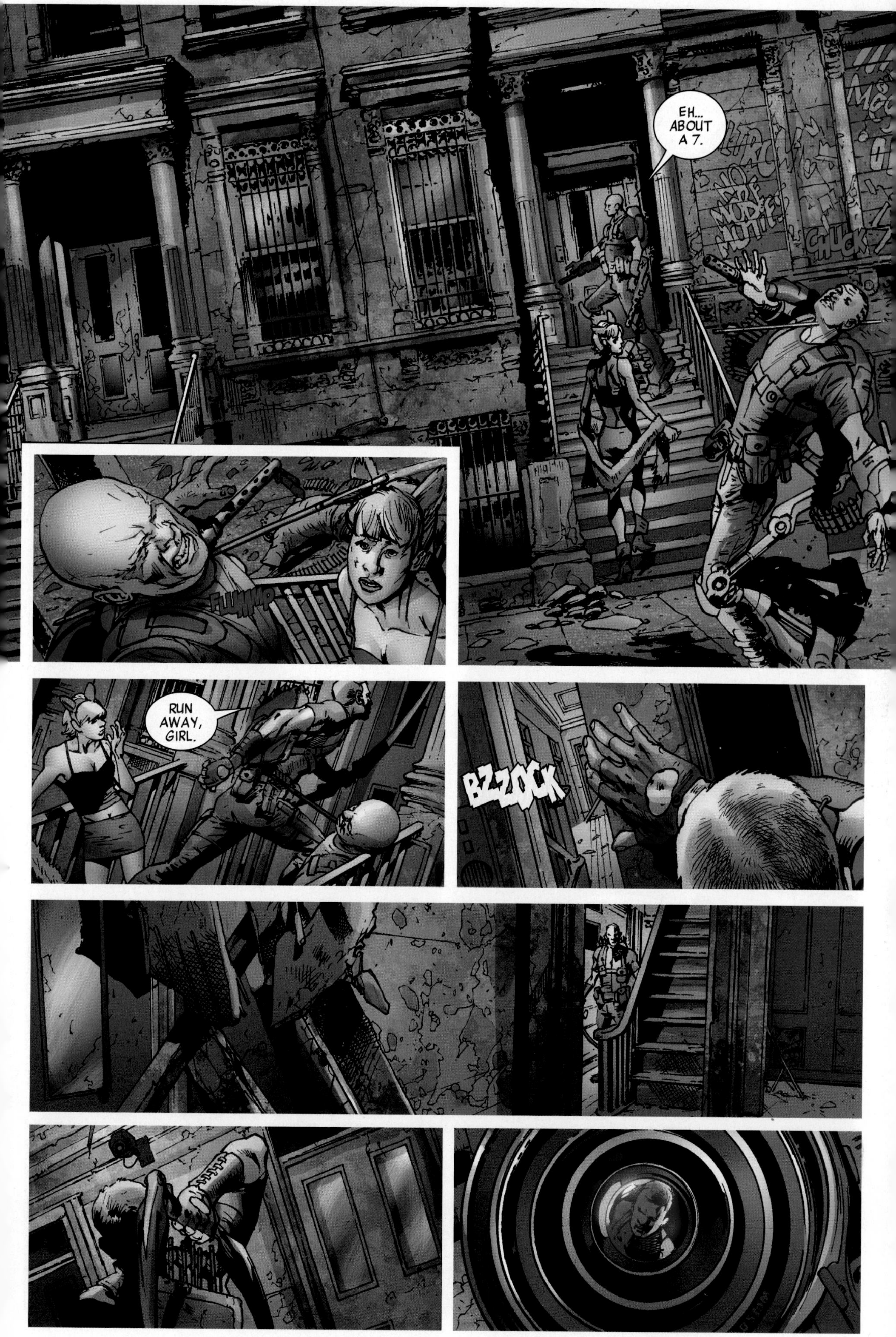
EH... ABOUT A 7.
FLUMMP
RUN AWAY, GIRL.
BZZOCK

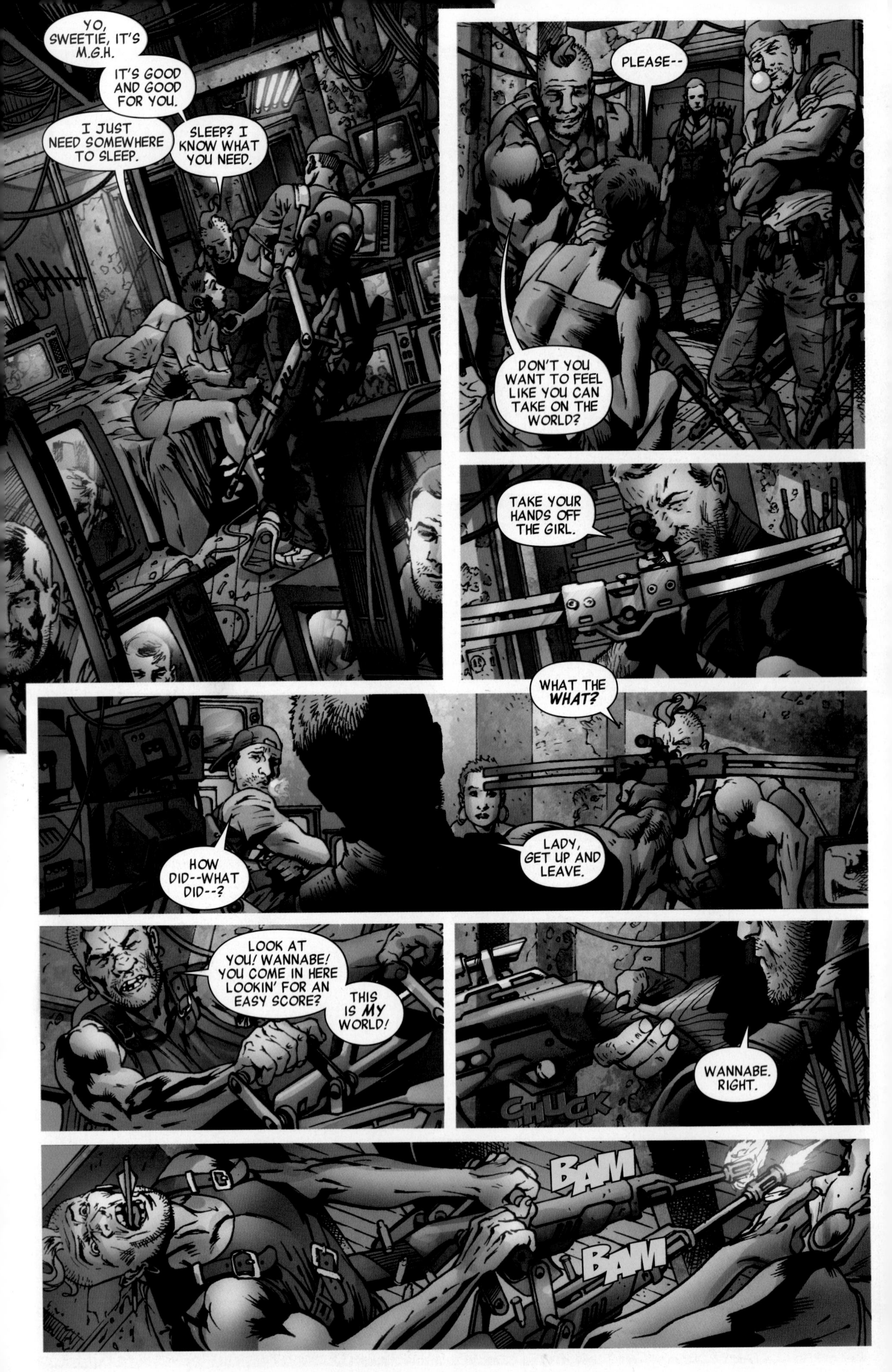
YO, SWEETIE, IT'S M.G.H.
IT'S GOOD AND GOOD FOR YOU.
I JUST NEED SOMEWHERE TO SLEEP.
SLEEP? I KNOW WHAT YOU NEED.
PLEASE--
DON'T YOU WANT TO FEEL LIKE YOU CAN TAKE ON THE WORLD?
TAKE YOUR HANDS OFF THE GIRL.
WHAT THE WHAT?
HOW DID--WHAT DID--?
LADY, GET UP AND LEAVE.
LOOK AT YOU! WANNABE! YOU COME IN HERE LOOKIN' FOR AN EASY SCORE?
THIS IS MY WORLD!
CHUCK
WANNABE. RIGHT.
BAM
BAM

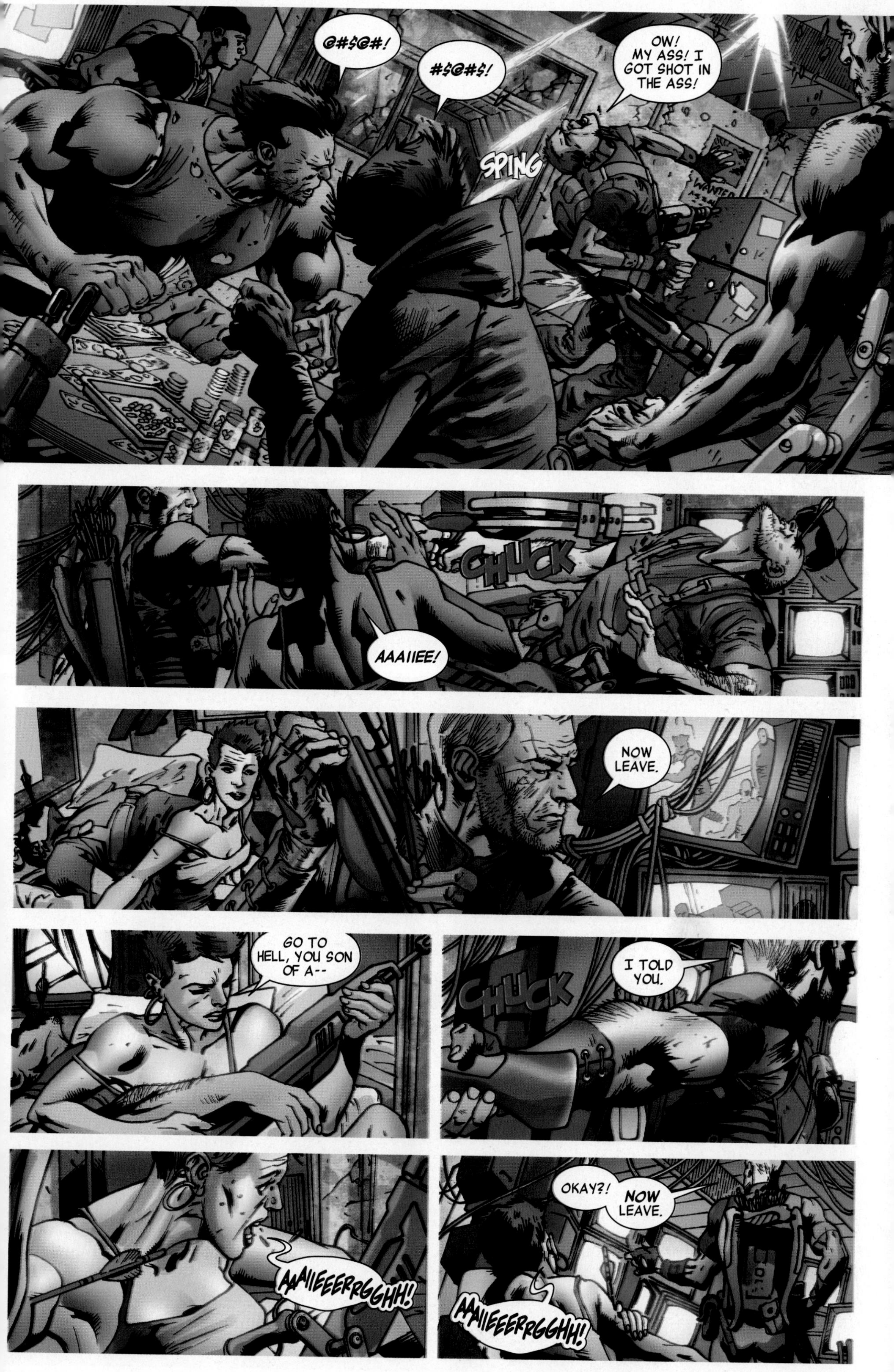
@#$@#!
#$@#$!
OW! MY ASS! I GOT SHOT IN THE ASS!
SPING
CHUCK
AAAIIEE!
NOW LEAVE.
GO TO HELL, YOU SON OF A--
CHUCK
I TOLD YOU.
AAAIIEEERRGGHH!
OKAY?! NOW LEAVE.
AAAIIEEERRGGHH!

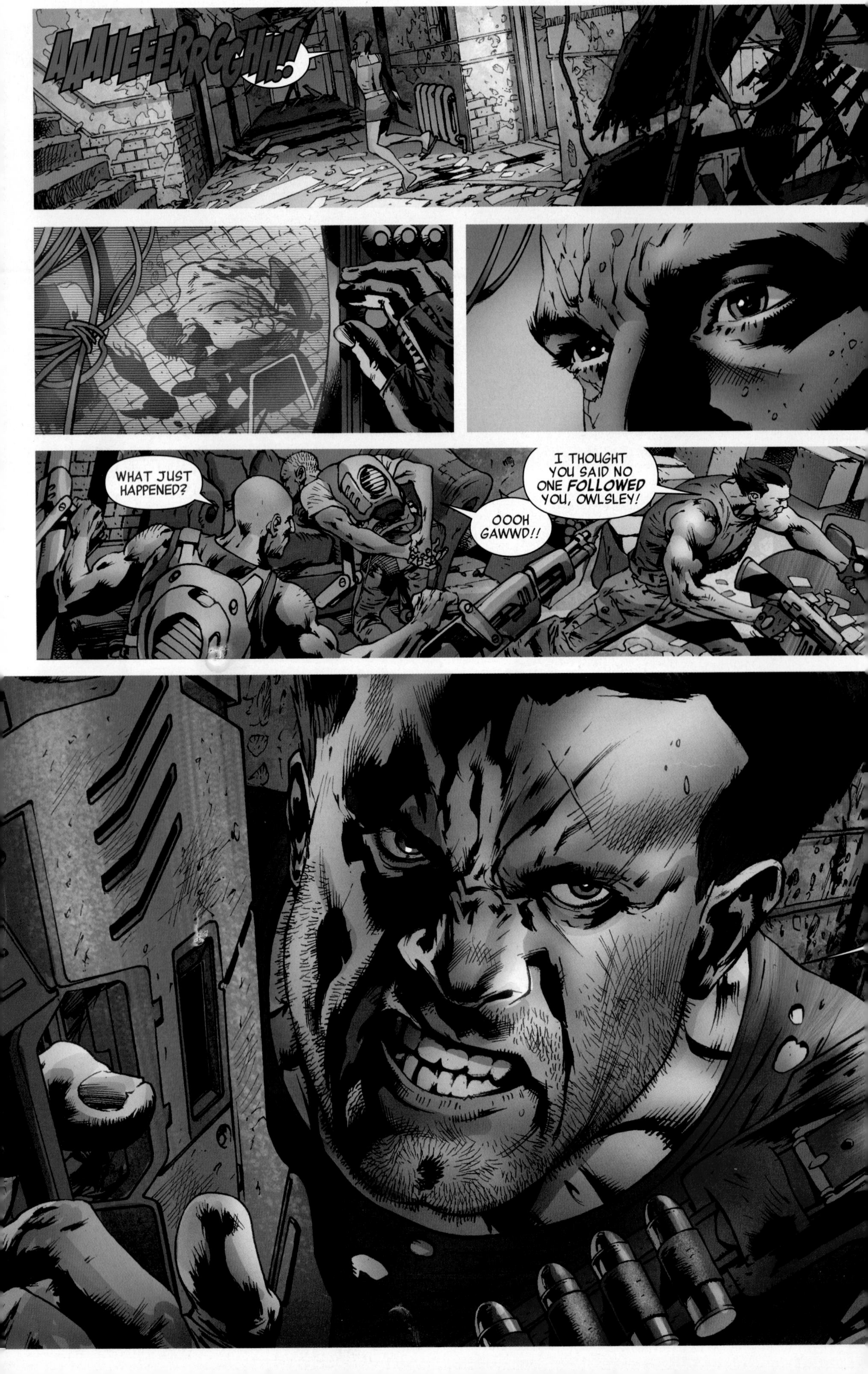
AAAIIEEEERRGGHH!!
WHAT JUST HAPPENED?
OOOH GAWWD!!
I THOUGHT YOU SAID NO ONE FOLLOWED YOU, OWLSLEY!

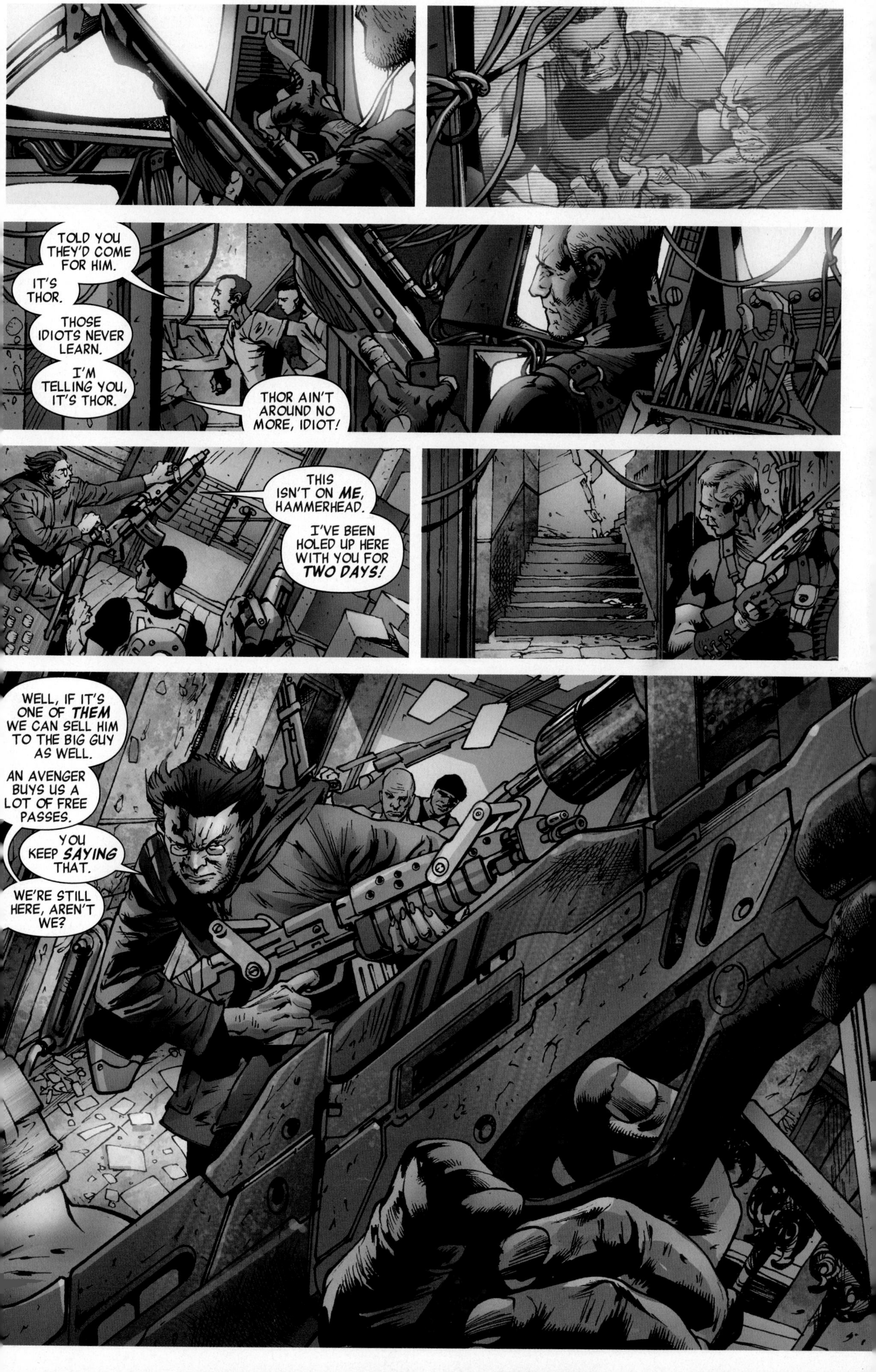
TOLD YOU THEY'D COME FOR HIM.
IT'S THOR.
THOSE IDIOTS NEVER LEARN.
I'M TELLING YOU, IT'S THOR.
THOR AIN'T AROUND NO MORE, IDIOT!
THIS ISN'T ON ME, HAMMERHEAD.
I'VE BEEN HOLED UP HERE WITH YOU FOR TWO DAYS!
WELL, IF IT'S ONE OF THEM WE CAN SELL HIM TO THE BIG GUY AS WELL.
AN AVENGER BUYS US A LOT OF FREE PASSES.
YOU KEEP SAYING THAT.
WE'RE STILL HERE, AREN'T WE?

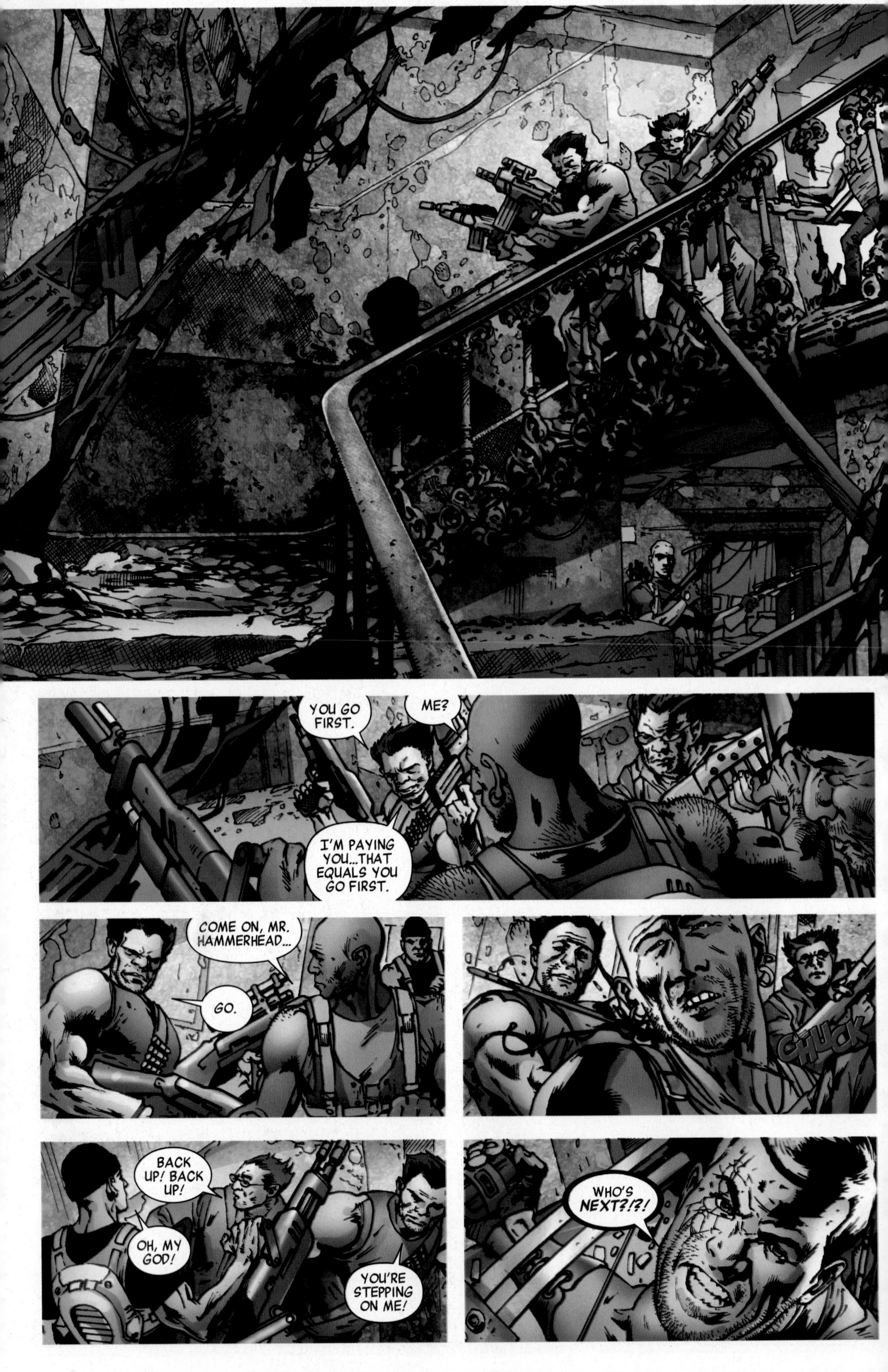
YOU GO FIRST.
ME?
I'M PAYING YOU...THAT EQUALS YOU GO FIRST.
COME ON, MR. HAMMERHEAD...
GO.
CHUCK
BACK UP! BACK UP!
OH, MY GOD!
YOU'RE STEPPING ON ME!
WHO'S NEXT?!?!

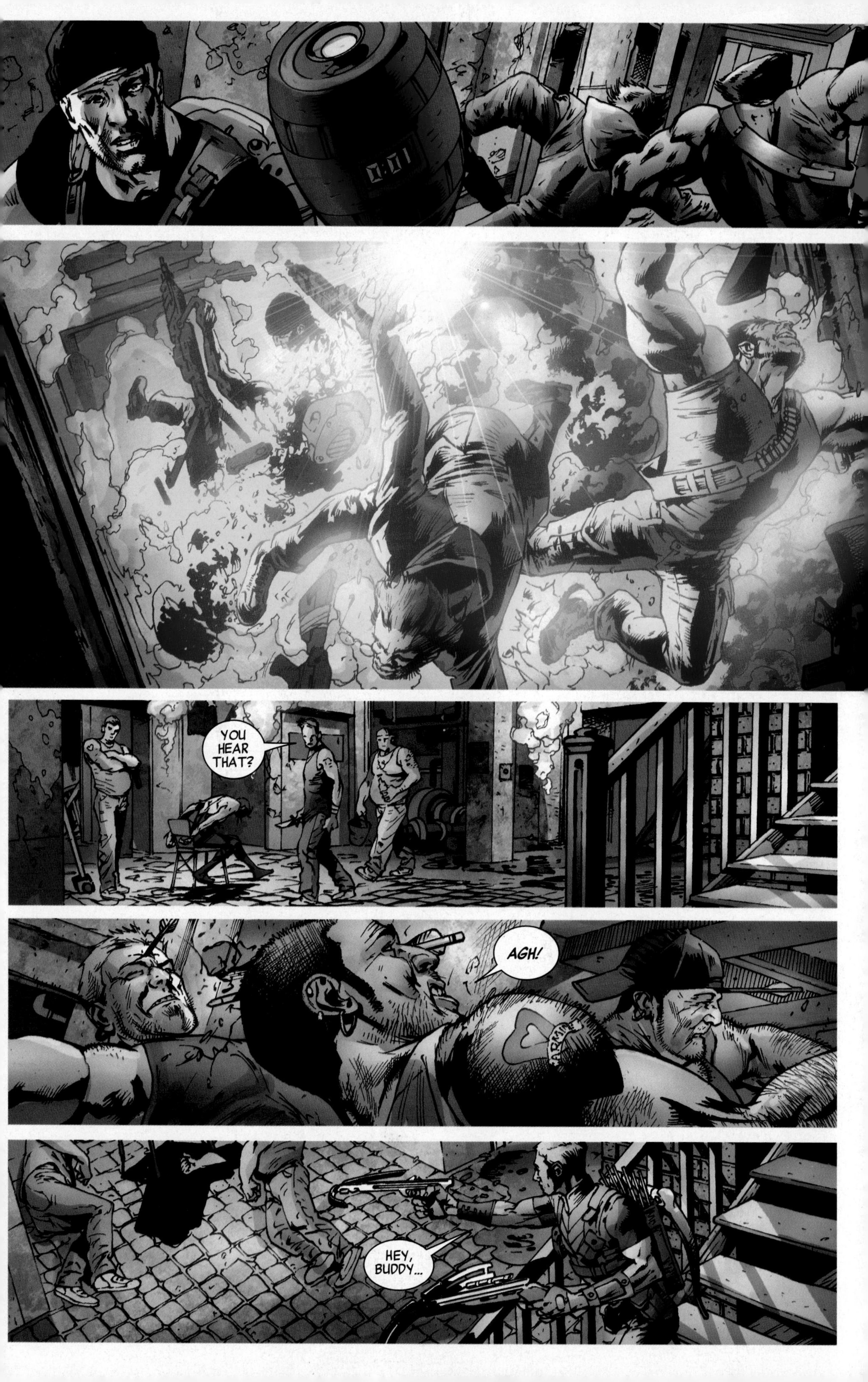
YOU HEAR THAT?
AGH!
HEY, BUDDY...

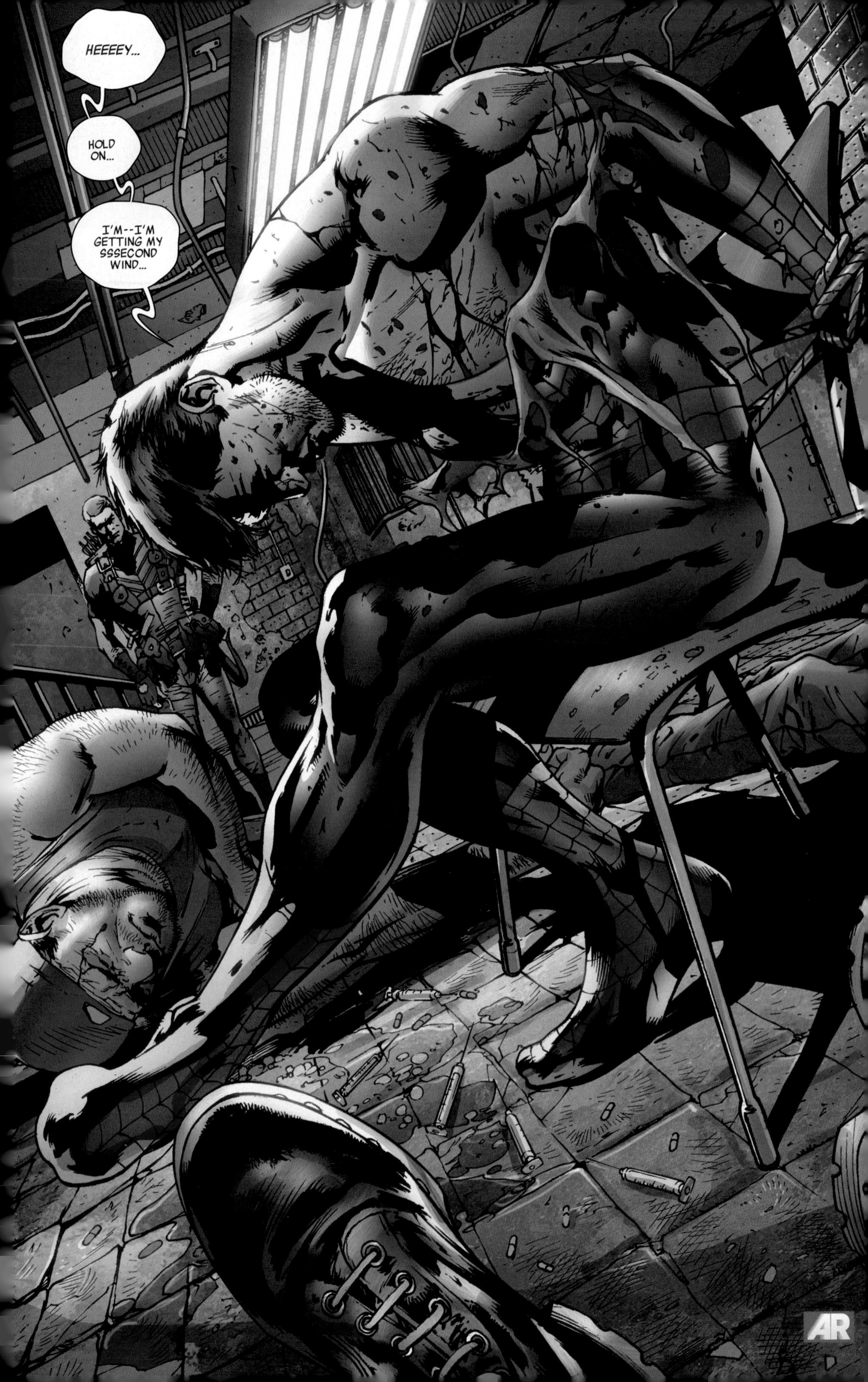
HEEEEY...
HOLD ON...
I'M--I'M GETTING MY SSSECOND WIND...

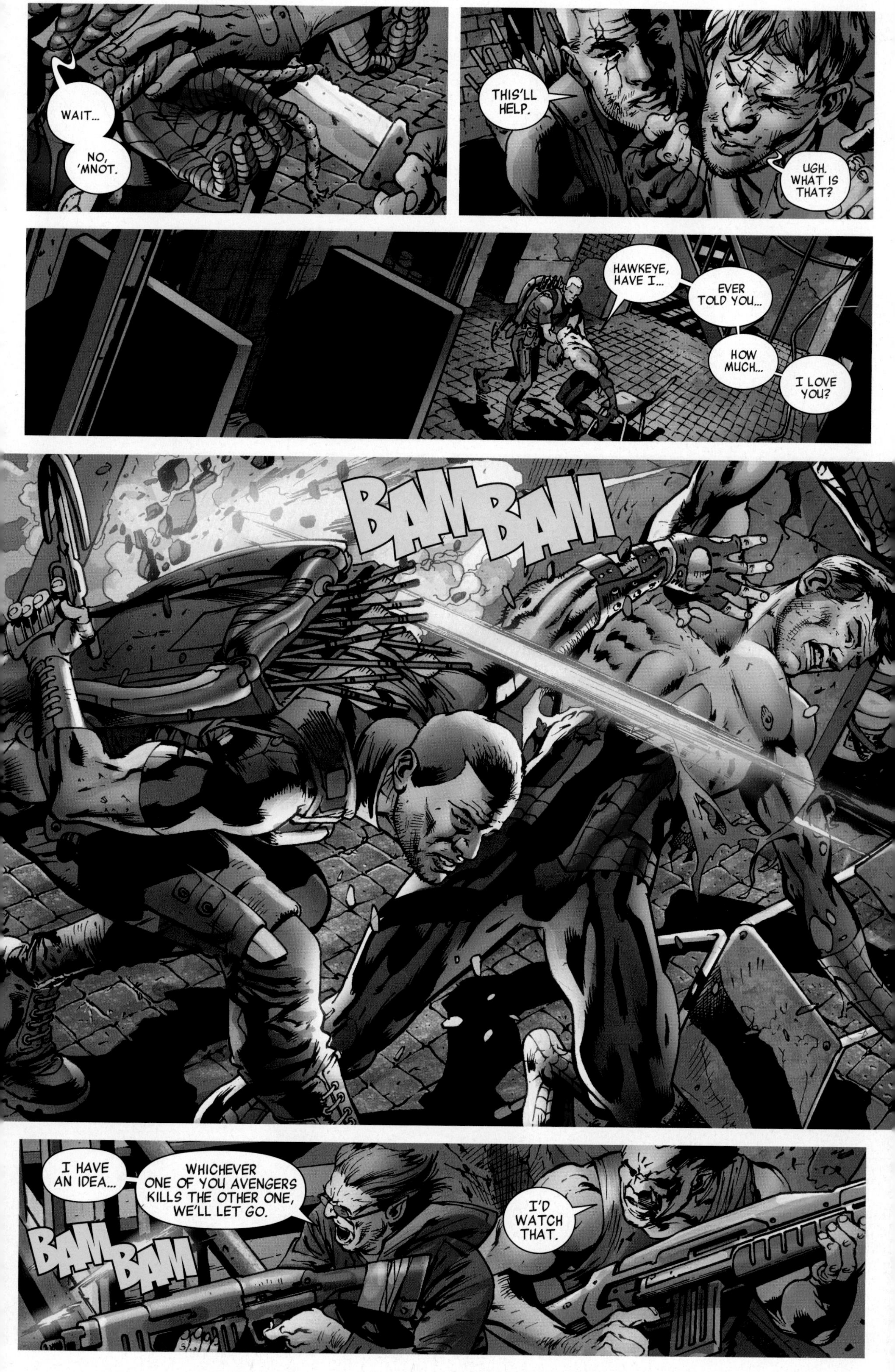
WAIT...
NO, 'MNOT.
THIS'LL HELP.
UGH. WHAT IS THAT?
HAWKEYE, HAVE I...
EVER TOLD YOU...
HOW MUCH...
I LOVE YOU?
BAM BAM
I HAVE AN IDEA...
WHICHEVER ONE OF YOU AVENGERS KILLS THE OTHER ONE, WE'LL LET GO.
BAM BAM
I'D WATCH THAT.

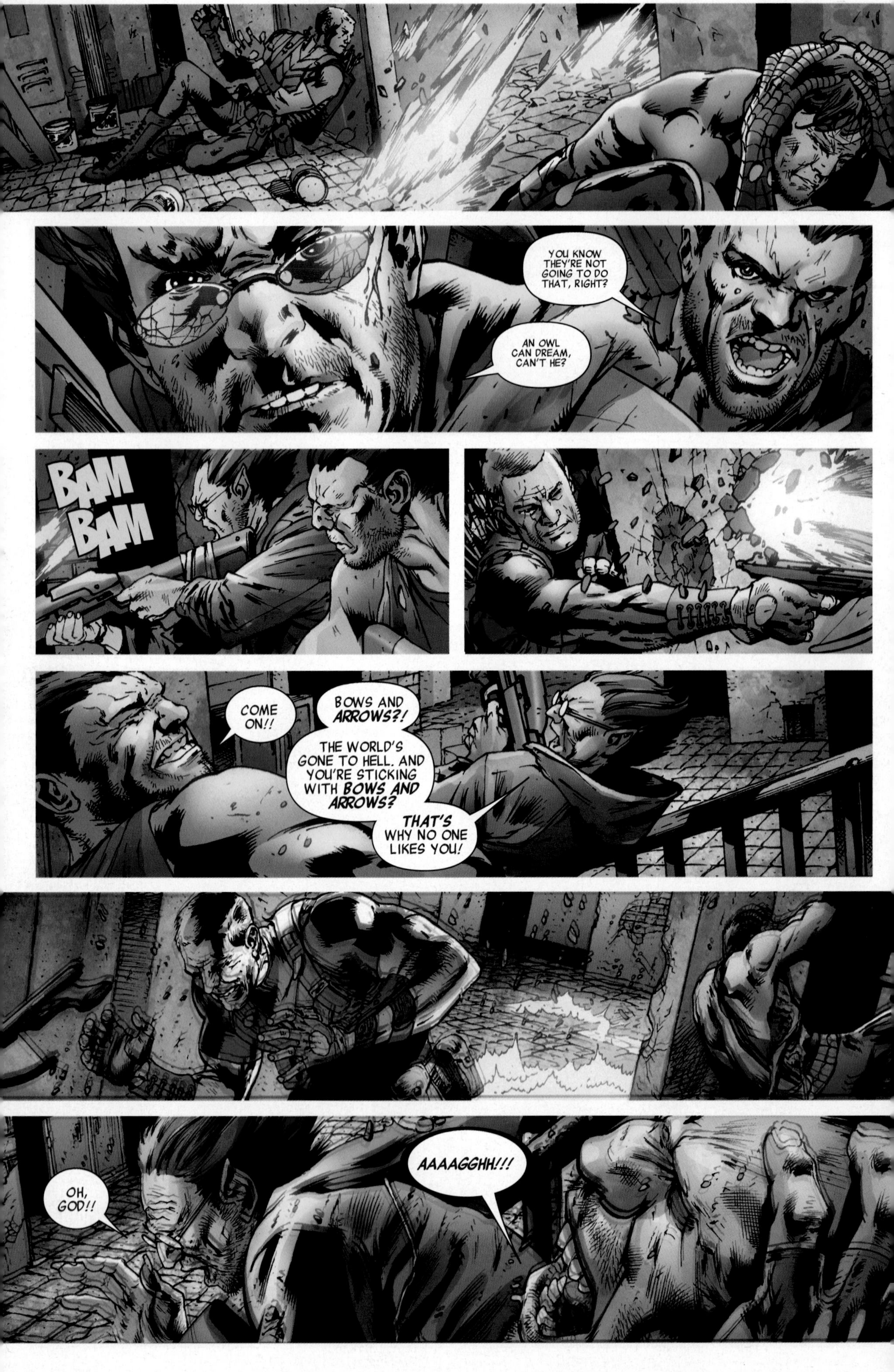
YOU KNOW THEY'RE NOT GOING TO DO THAT, RIGHT?
AN OWL CAN DREAM, CAN'T HE?
BAM BAM
COME ON!!
BOWS AND ARROWS?!
THE WORLD'S GONE TO HELL. AND YOU'RE STICKING WITH BOWS AND ARROWS?
THAT'S WHY NO ONE LIKES YOU!
OH, GOD!!
AAAAGGHH!!!

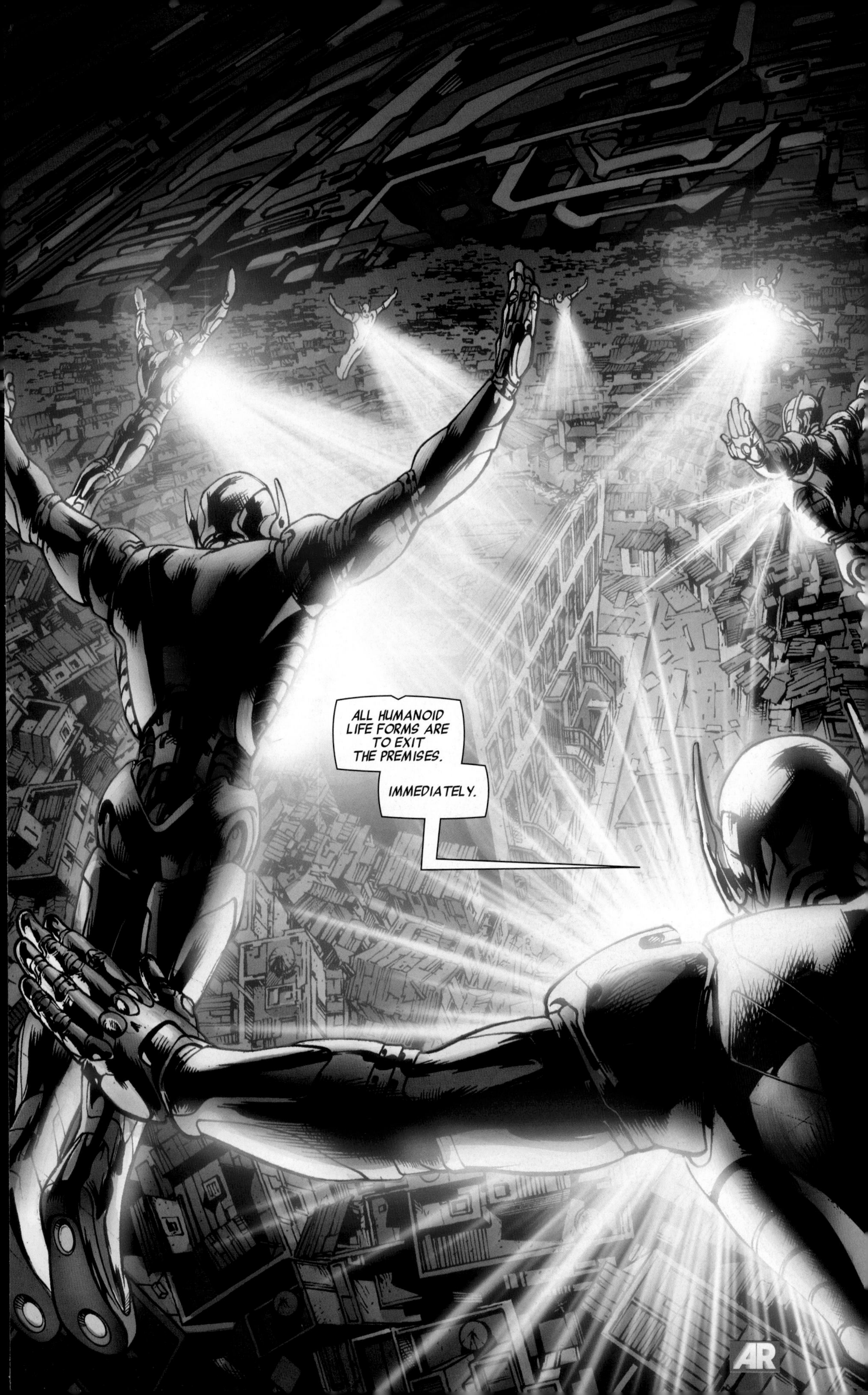
ALL HUMANOID LIFE FORMS ARE TO EXIT THE PREMISES.
IMMEDIATELY.
AR

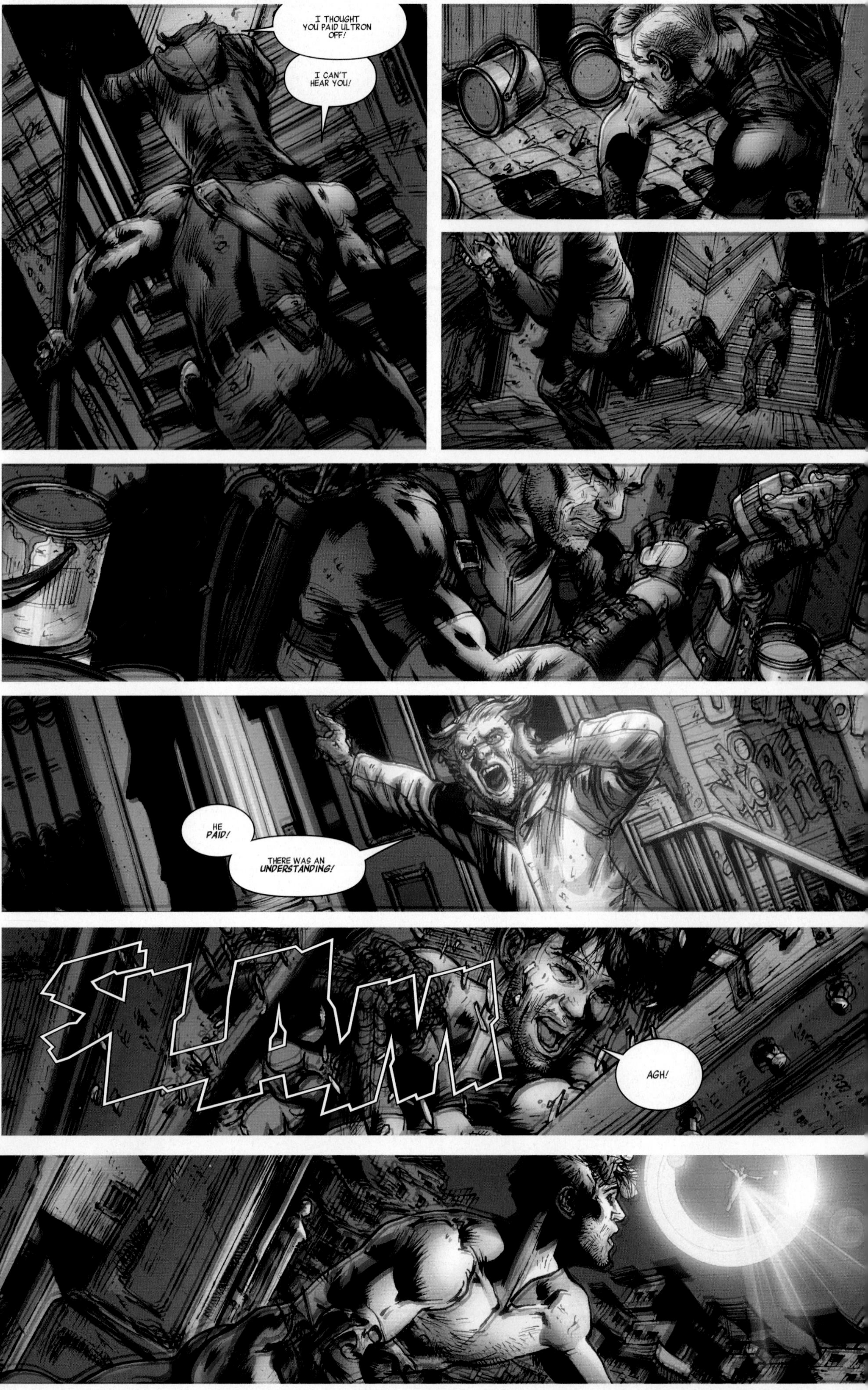
I THOUGHT YOU PAID ULTRON OFF!
I CAN'T HEAR YOU!
HE PAID!
THERE WAS AN UNDERSTANDING!
SLAM
AGH!

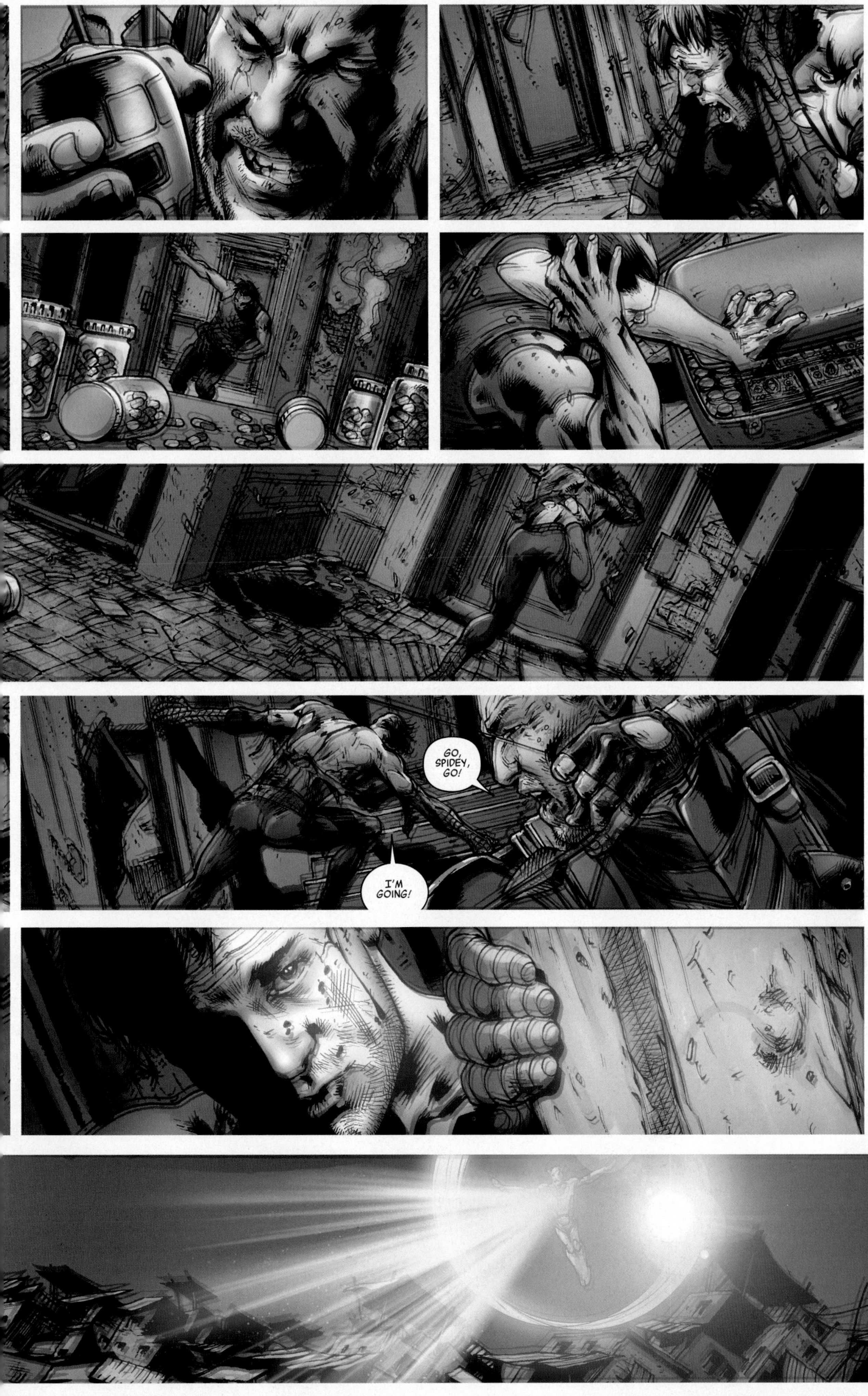
GO, SPIDEY, GO!
I'M GOING!

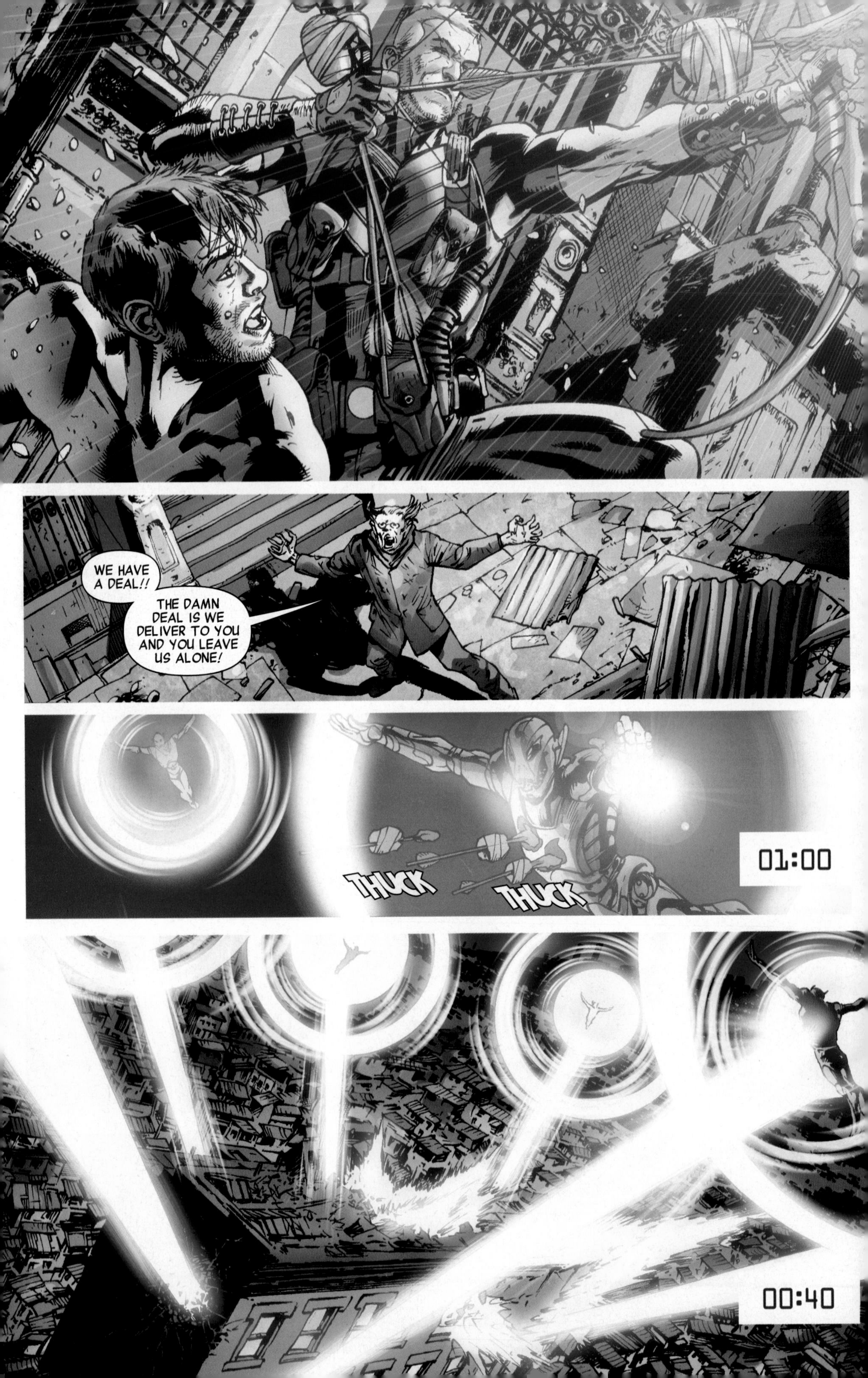
WE HAVE A DEAL!!
THE DAMN DEAL IS WE DELIVER TO YOU AND YOU LEAVE US ALONE!
01:00
THUCK
THUCK
00:40

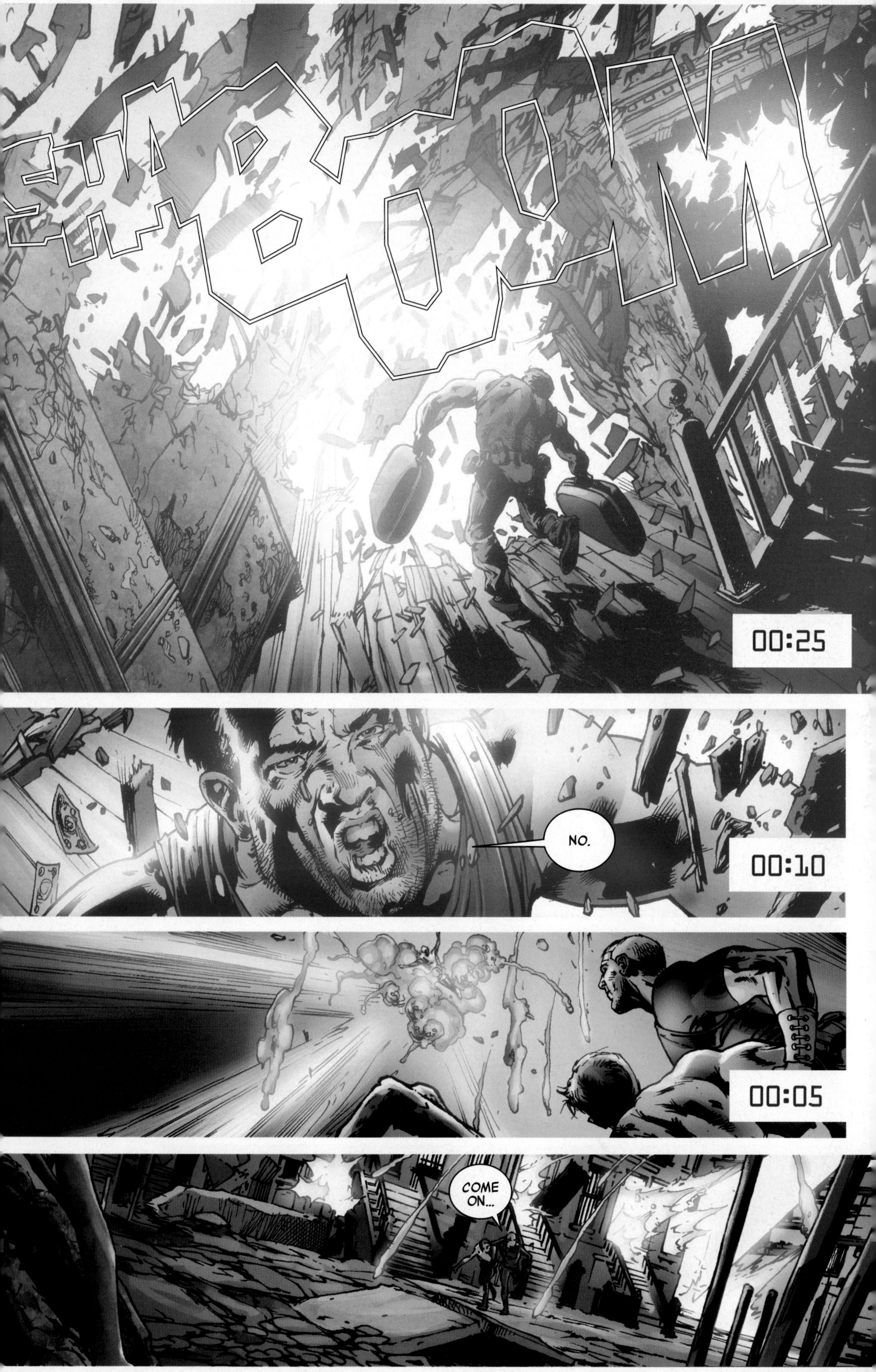
SHABOOM
00:25
NO.
00:10
00:05
COME ON...

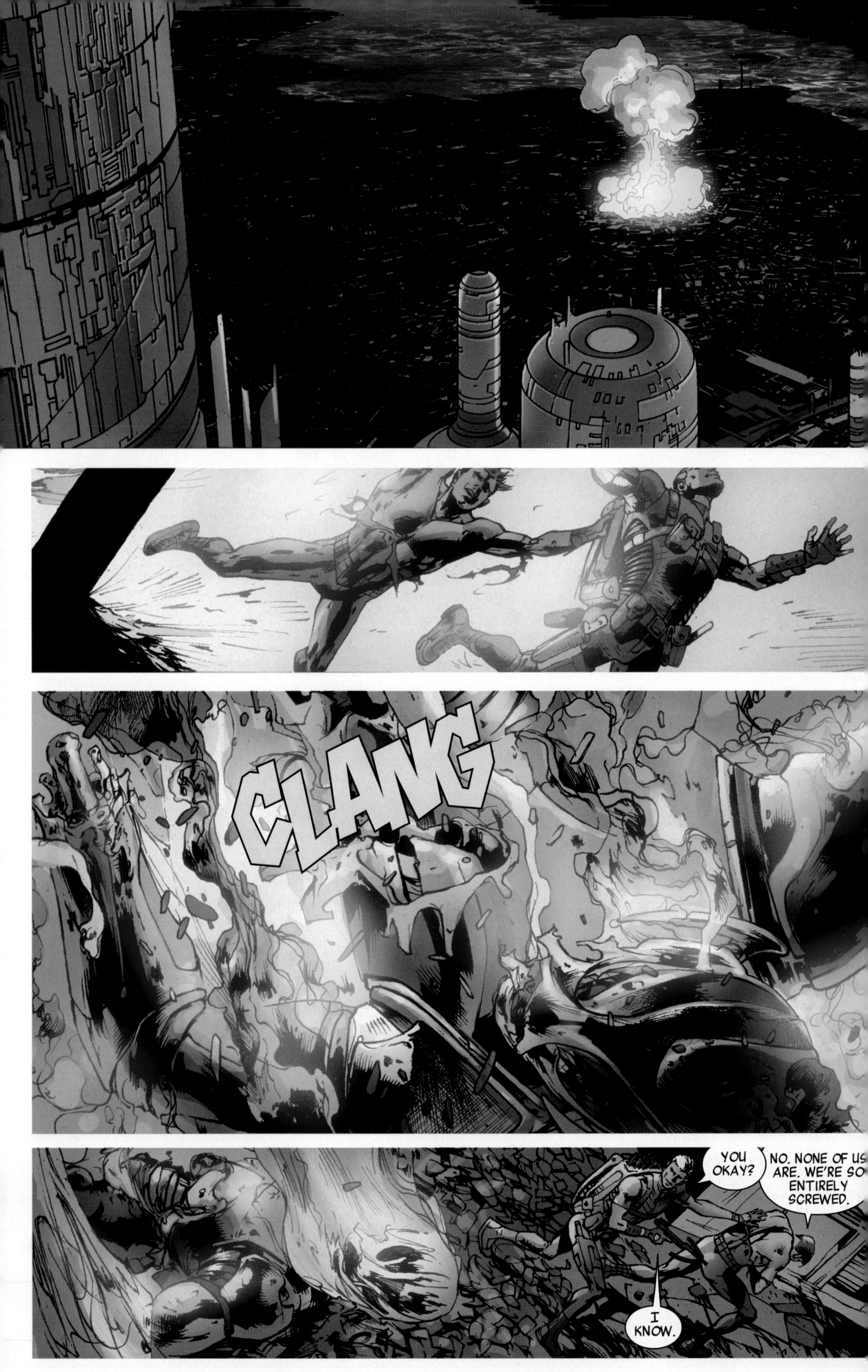
CLANG
YOU OKAY?
NO. NONE OF US ARE. WE'RE SO ENTIRELY SCREWED.
I KNOW.

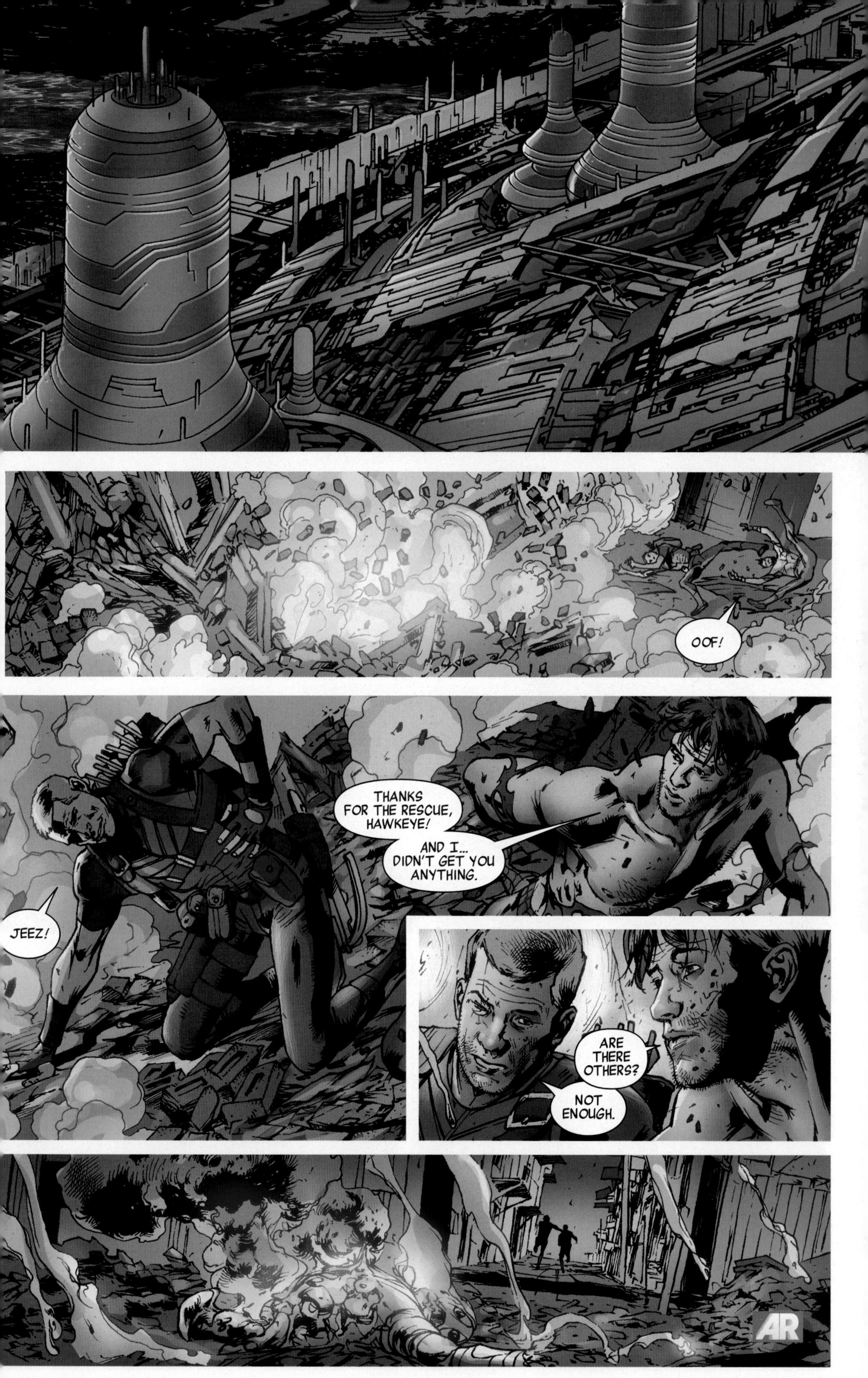
OOF!
THANKS FOR THE RESCUE, HAWKEYE!
AND I... DIDN'T GET YOU ANYTHING.
JEEZ!
ARE THERE OTHERS?
NOT ENOUGH.
AR

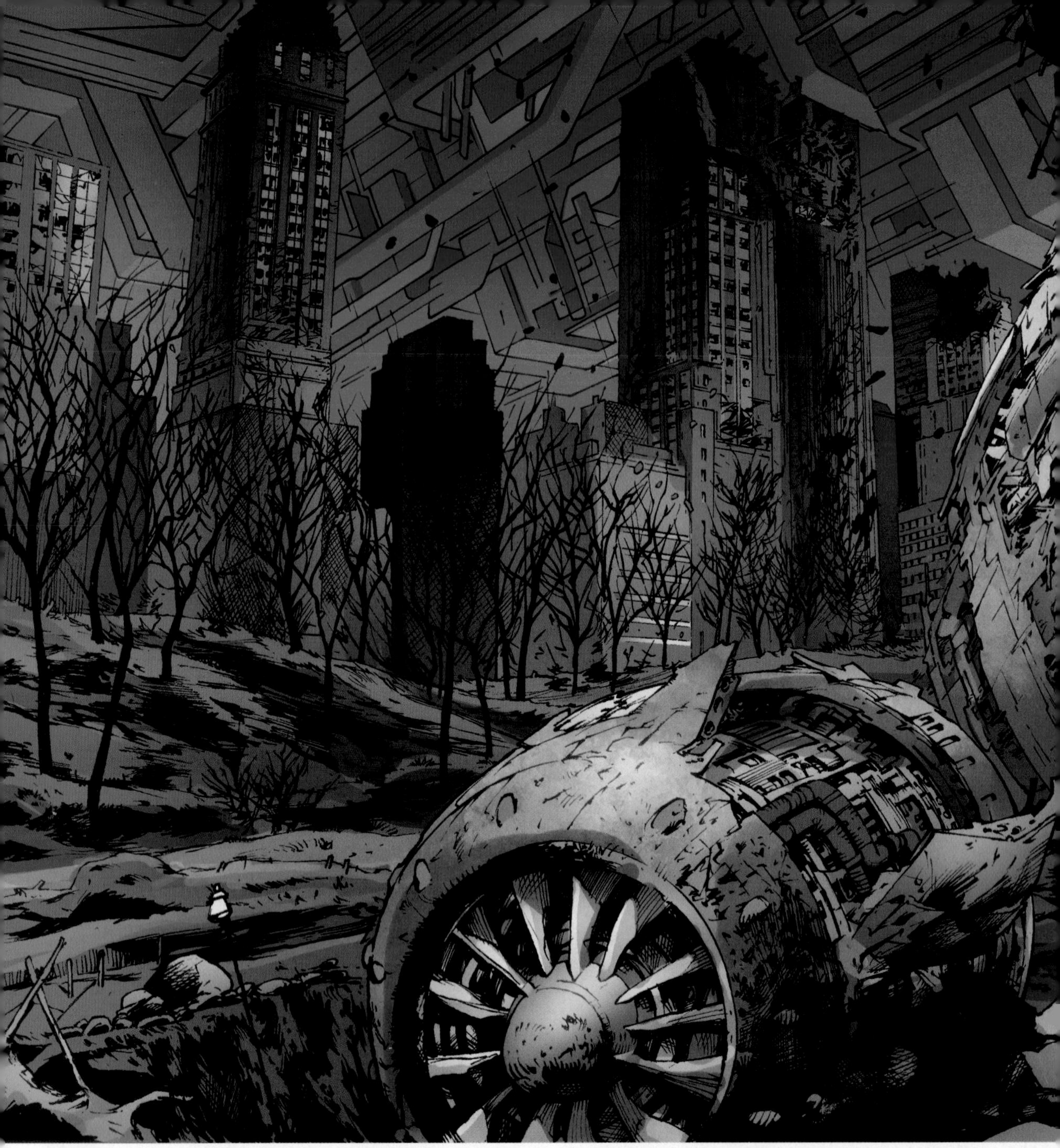

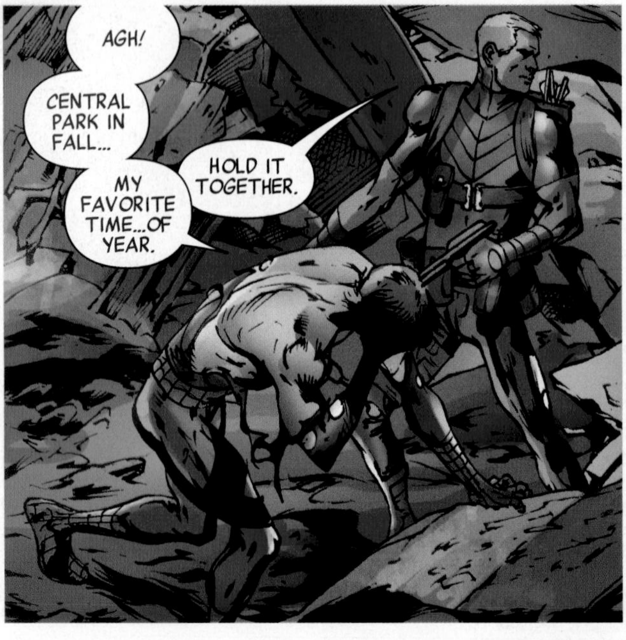
AGH!
CENTRAL PARK IN FALL...
MY FAVORITE TIME...OF YEAR.
HOLD IT TOGETHER.

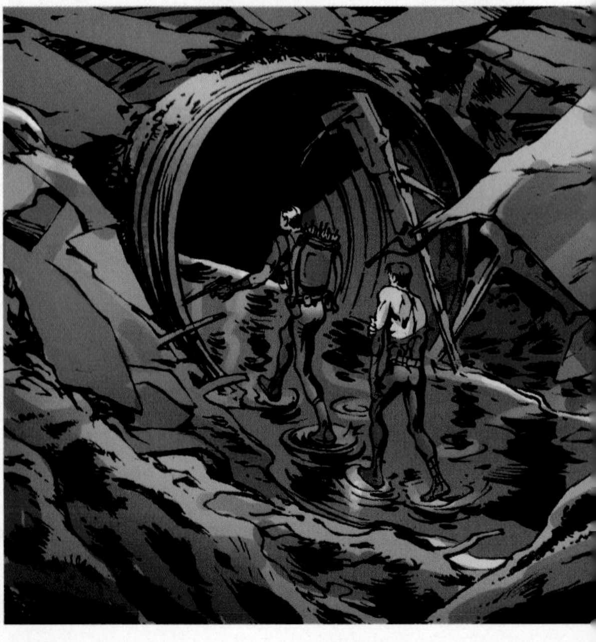

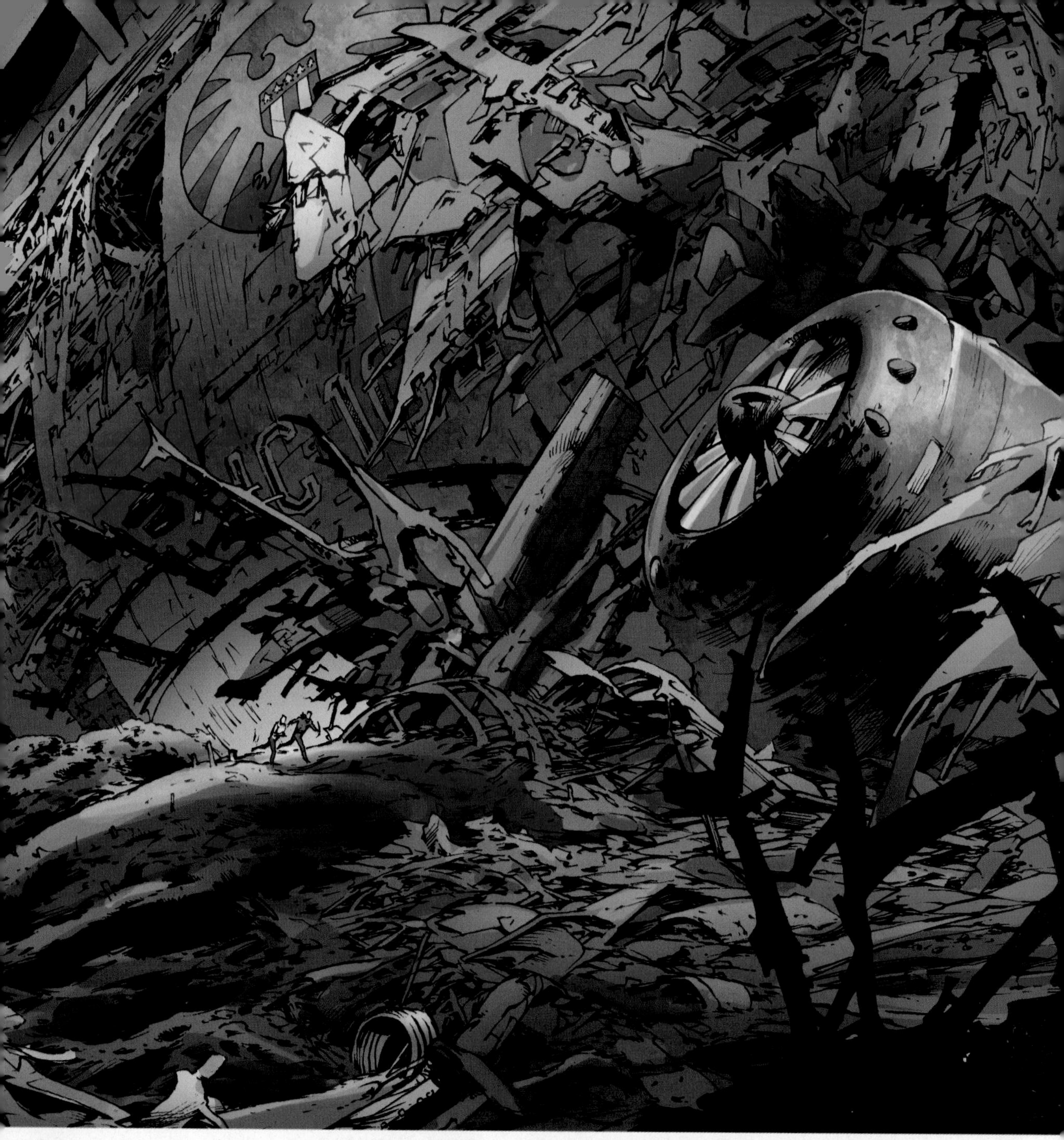

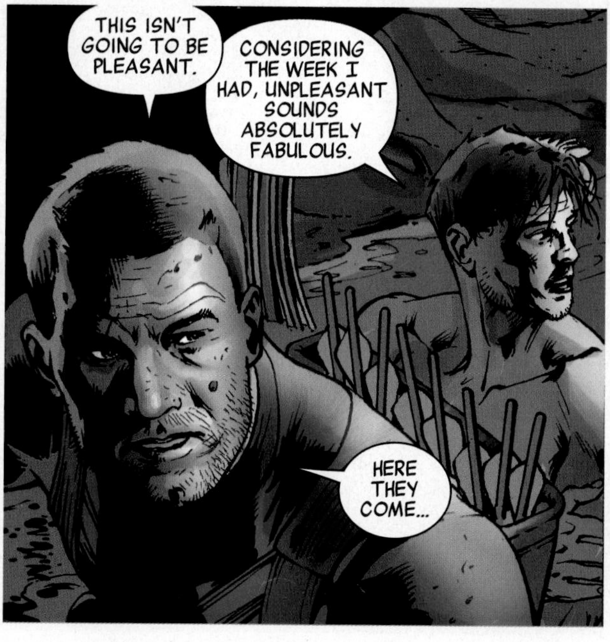
THIS ISN'T GOING TO BE PLEASANT.
CONSIDERING THE WEEK I HAD, UNPLEASANT SOUNDS ABSOLUTELY FABULOUS.
HERE THEY COME...

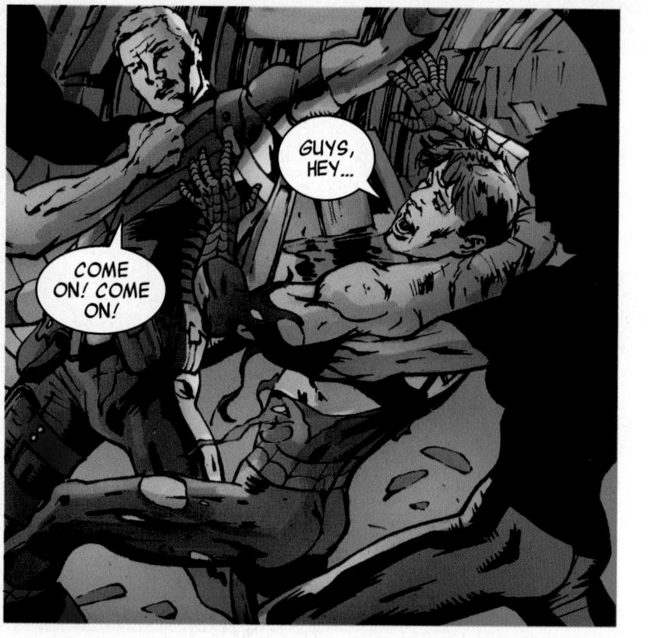
GUYS, HEY...
COME ON! COME ON!

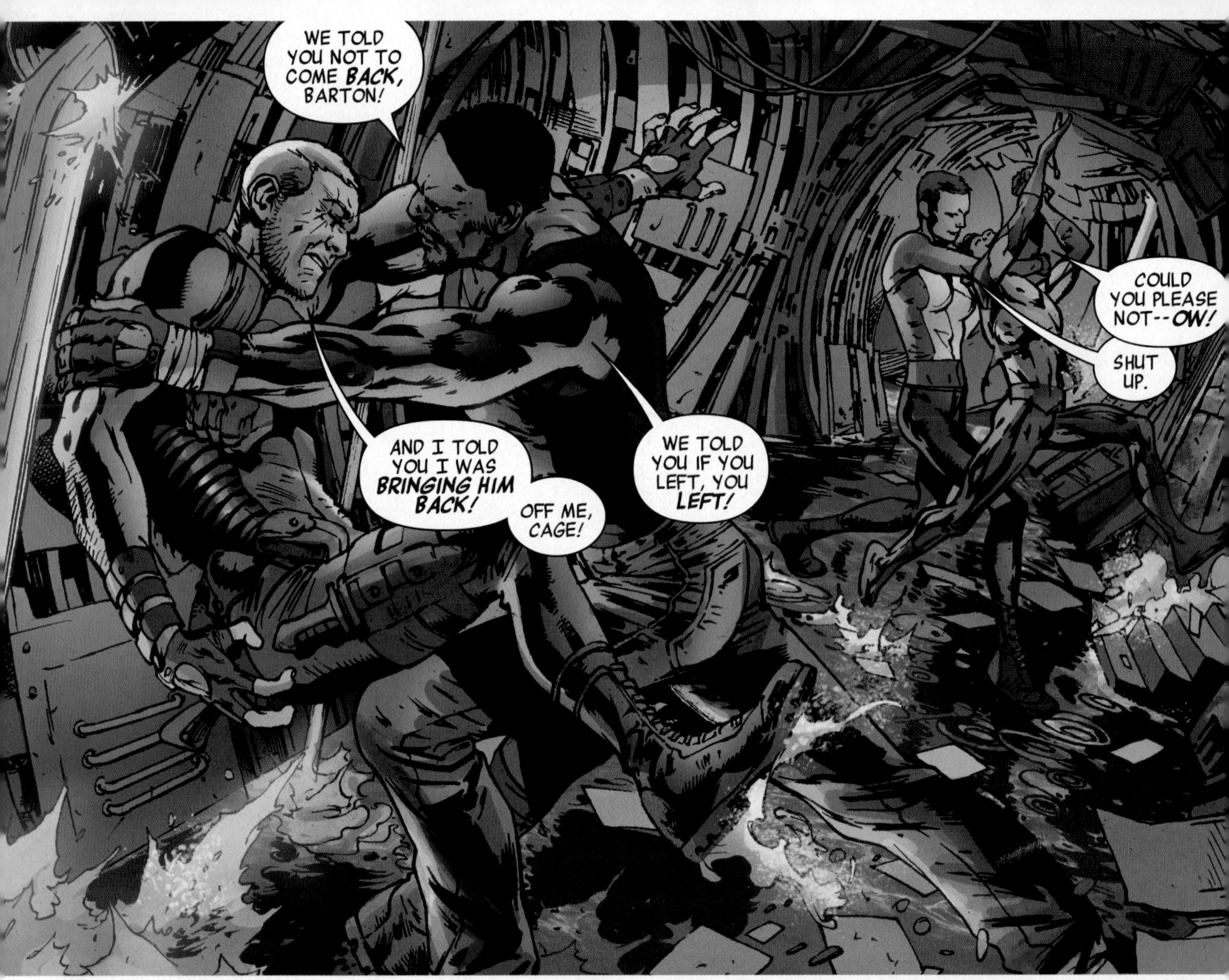
WE TOLD YOU NOT TO COME BACK, BARTON!
AND I TOLD YOU I WAS BRINGING HIM BACK!
OFF ME, CAGE!
WE TOLD YOU IF YOU LEFT, YOU LEFT!
COULD YOU PLEASE NOT--OW!
SHUT UP.

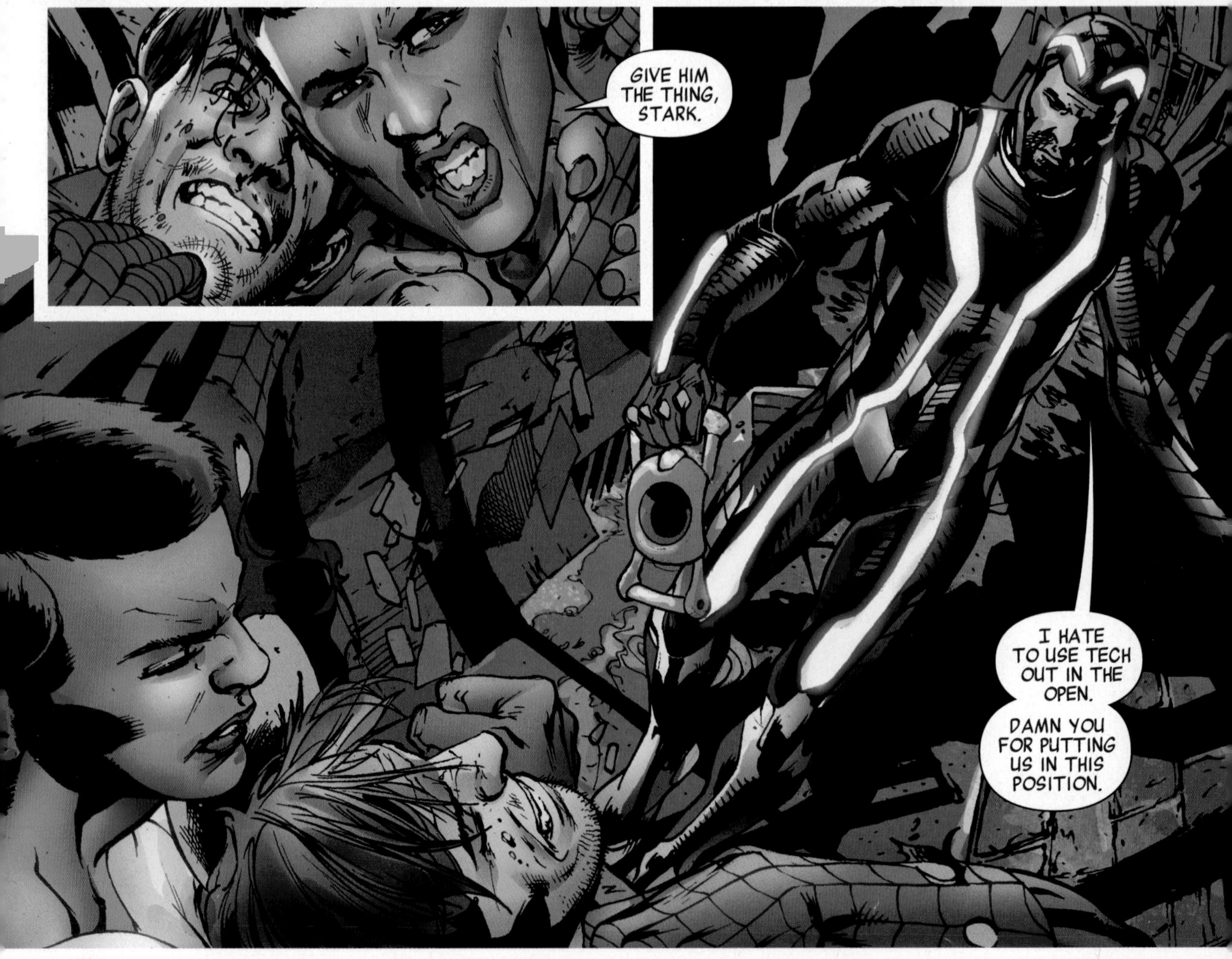
GIVE HIM THE THING, STARK.
I HATE TO USE TECH OUT IN THE OPEN.
DAMN YOU FOR PUTTING US IN THIS POSITION.

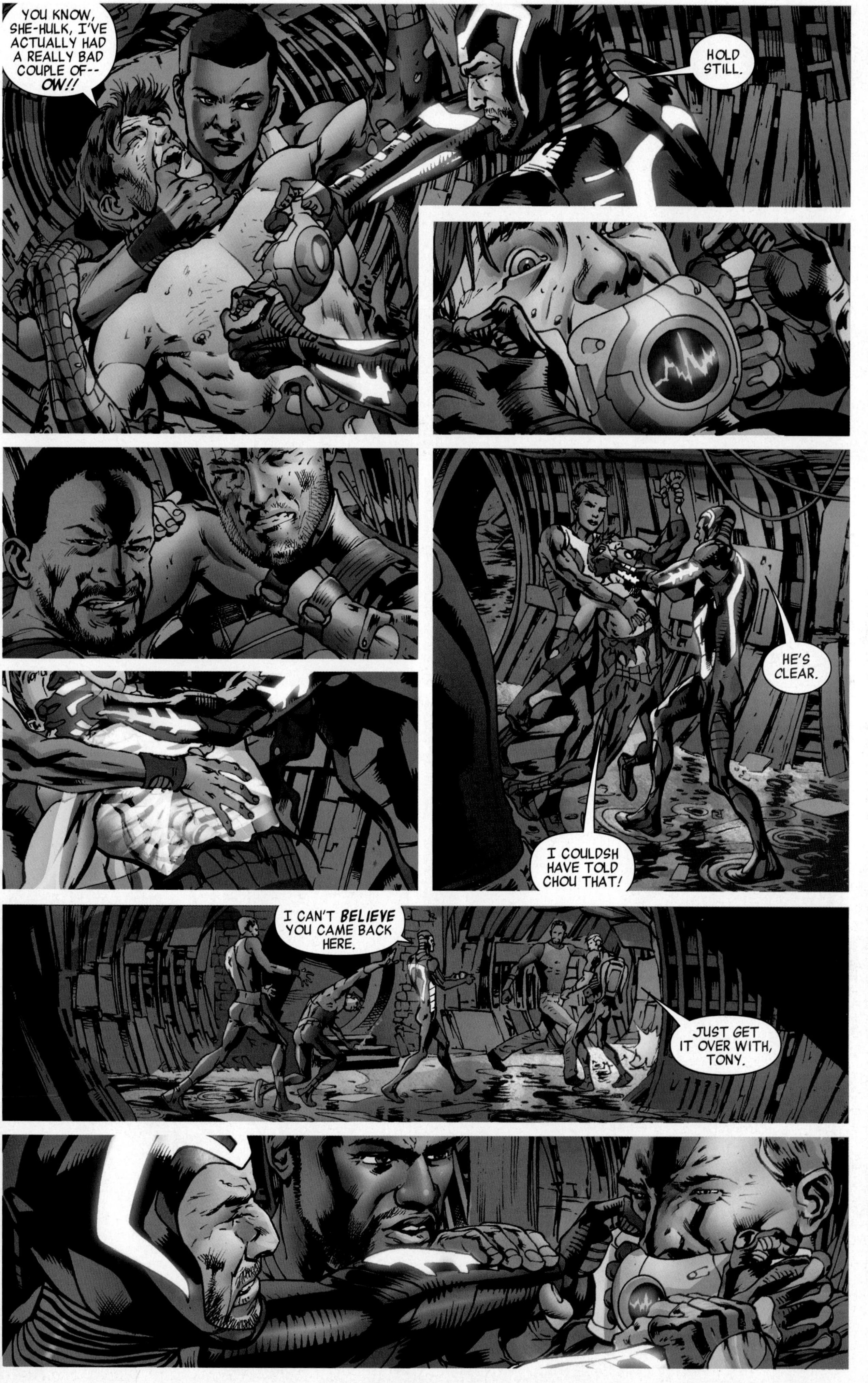

YOU KNOW, SHE-HULK, I'VE ACTUALLY HAD A REALLY BAD COUPLE OF-- OW!!
HOLD STILL.
HE'S CLEAR.
I COULDSH HAVE TOLD CHOU THAT!
I CAN'T BELIEVE YOU CAME BACK HERE.
JUST GET IT OVER WITH, TONY.

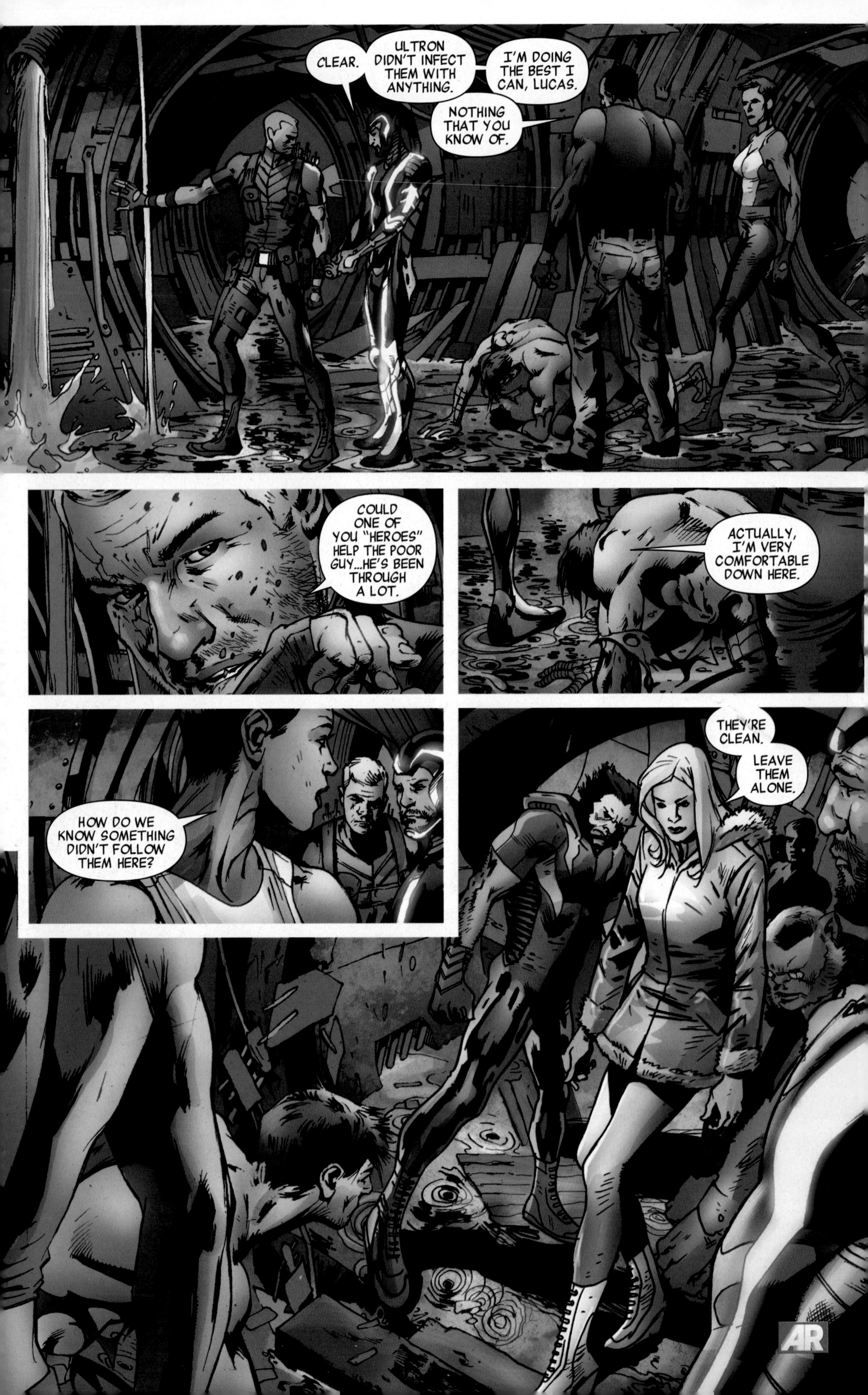
CLEAR.
ULTRON DIDN'T INFECT THEM WITH ANYTHING.
I'M DOING THE BEST I CAN, LUCAS.
NOTHING THAT YOU KNOW OF.
COULD ONE OF YOU "HEROES" HELP THE POOR GUY...HE'S BEEN THROUGH A LOT.
ACTUALLY, I'M VERY COMFORTABLE DOWN HERE.
HOW DO WE KNOW SOMETHING DIDN'T FOLLOW THEM HERE?
THEY'RE CLEAN.
LEAVE THEM ALONE.

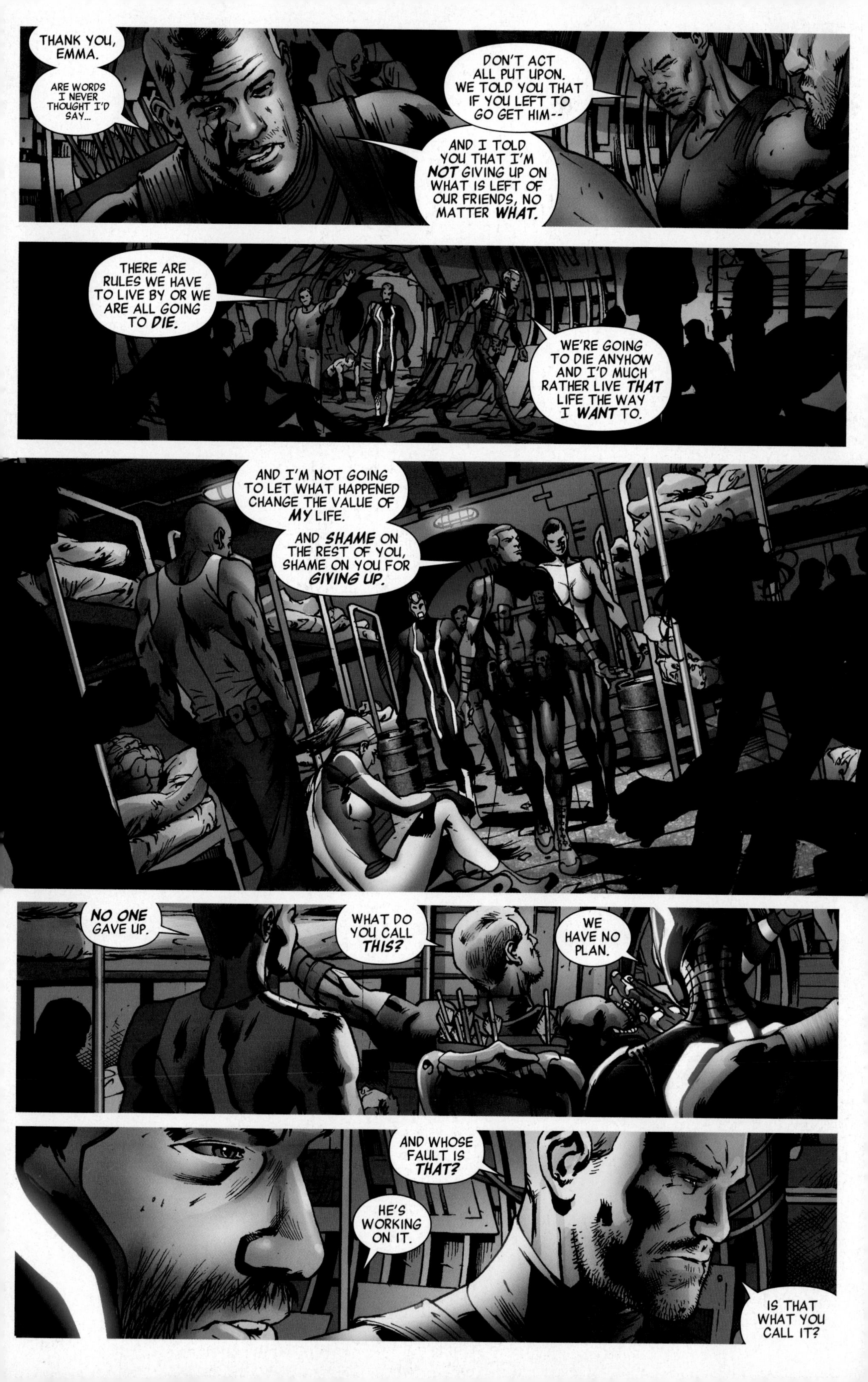
THANK YOU, EMMA.
ARE WORDS I NEVER THOUGHT I'D SAY...
DON'T ACT ALL PUT UPON. WE TOLD YOU THAT IF YOU LEFT TO GO GET HIM--
AND I TOLD YOU THAT I'M NOT GIVING UP ON WHAT IS LEFT OF OUR FRIENDS, NO MATTER WHAT.
THERE ARE RULES WE HAVE TO LIVE BY OR WE ARE ALL GOING TO DIE.
WE'RE GOING TO DIE ANYHOW AND I'D MUCH RATHER LIVE THAT LIFE THE WAY I WANT TO.
AND I'M NOT GOING TO LET WHAT HAPPENED CHANGE THE VALUE OF MY LIFE.
AND SHAME ON THE REST OF YOU, SHAME ON YOU FOR GIVING UP.
NO ONE GAVE UP.
WHAT DO YOU CALL THIS?
WE HAVE NO PLAN.
AND WHOSE FAULT IS THAT?
HE'S WORKING ON IT.
IS THAT WHAT YOU CALL IT?

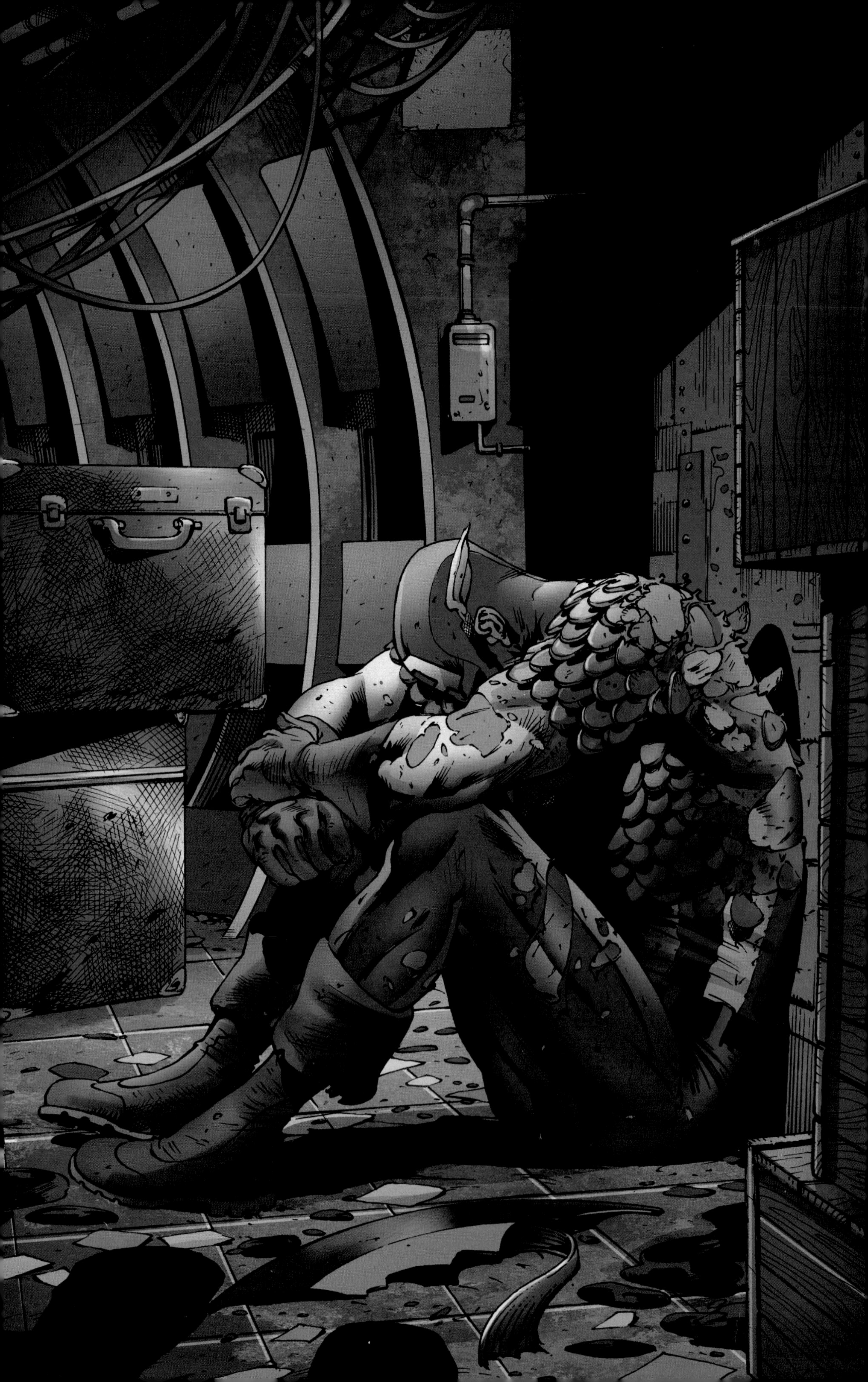

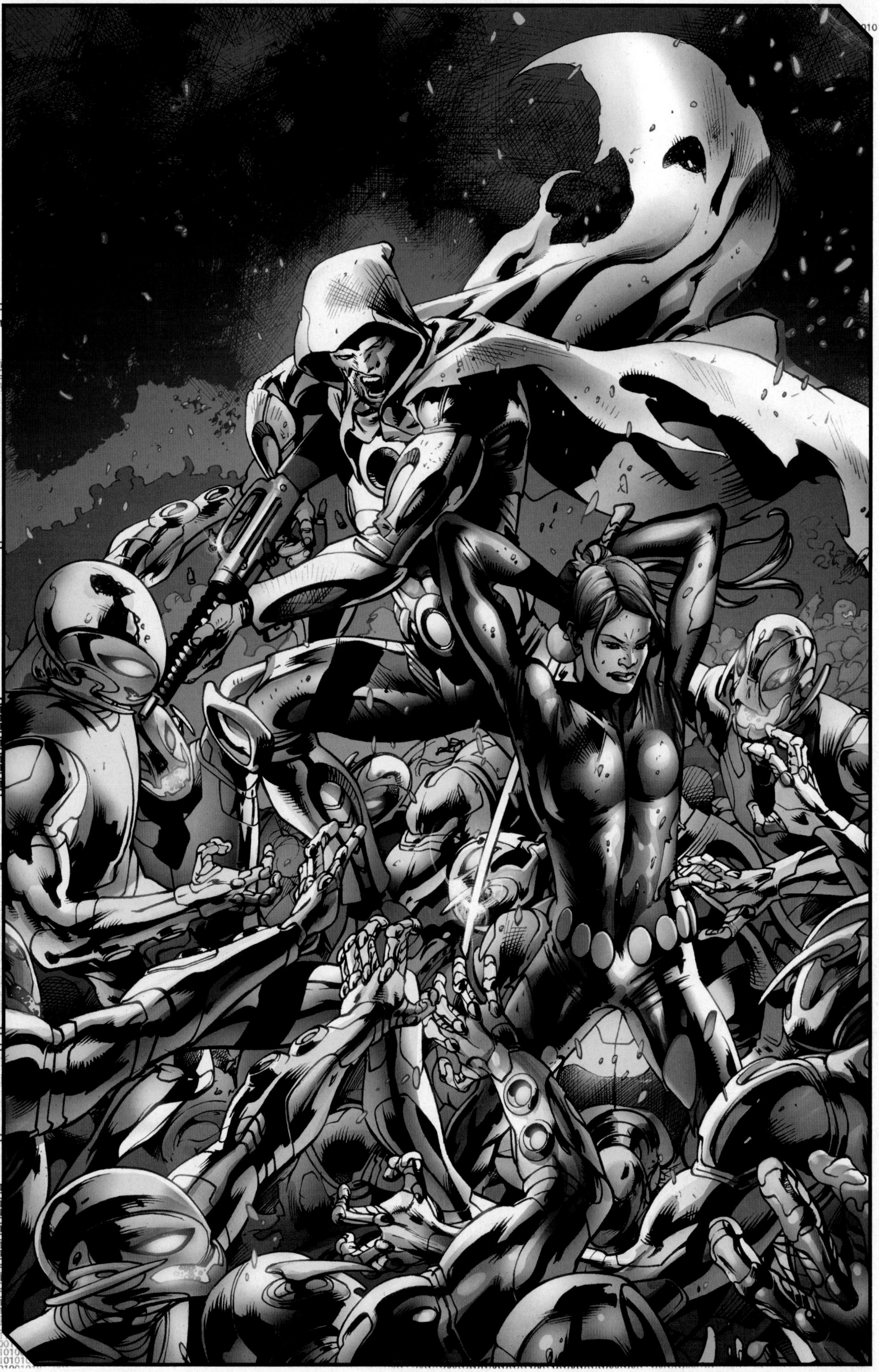

AGE OF ULTRON #2

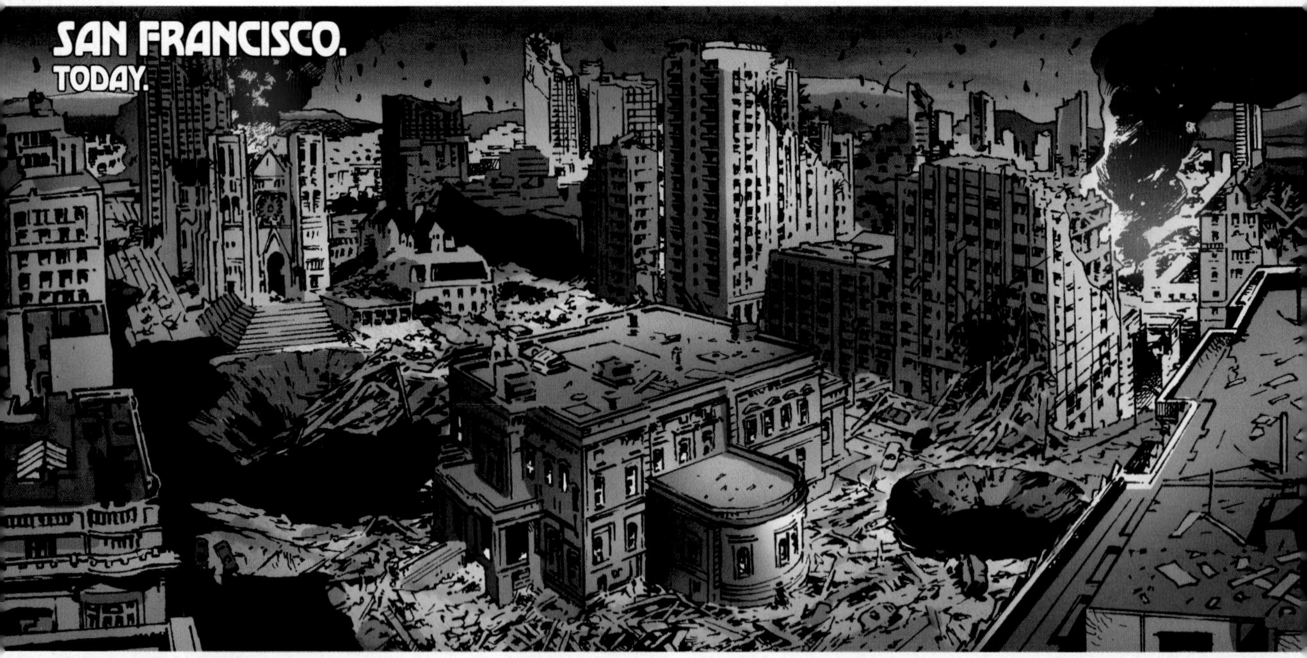
SAN FRANCISCO.
TODAY.

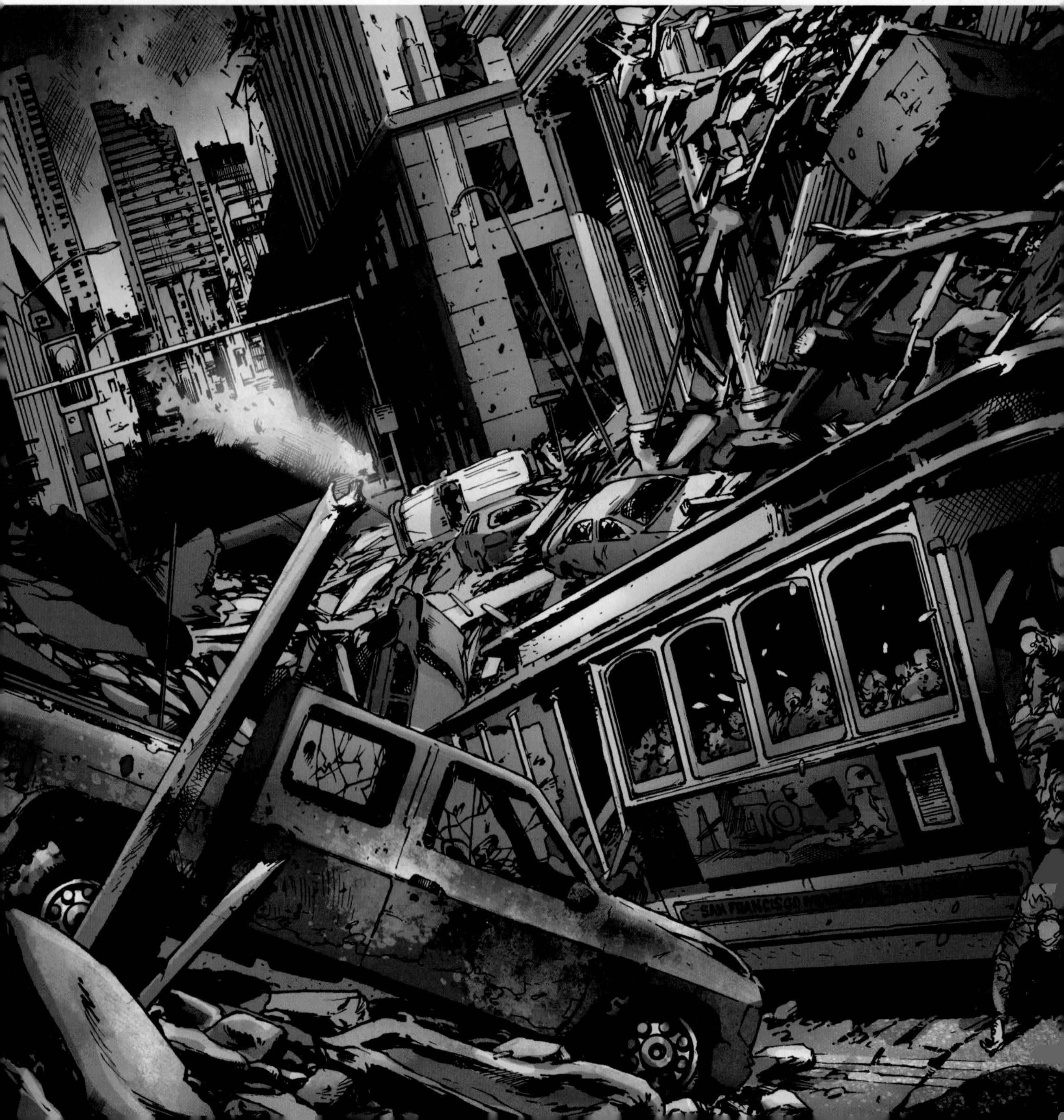
SAN FRANCISCO

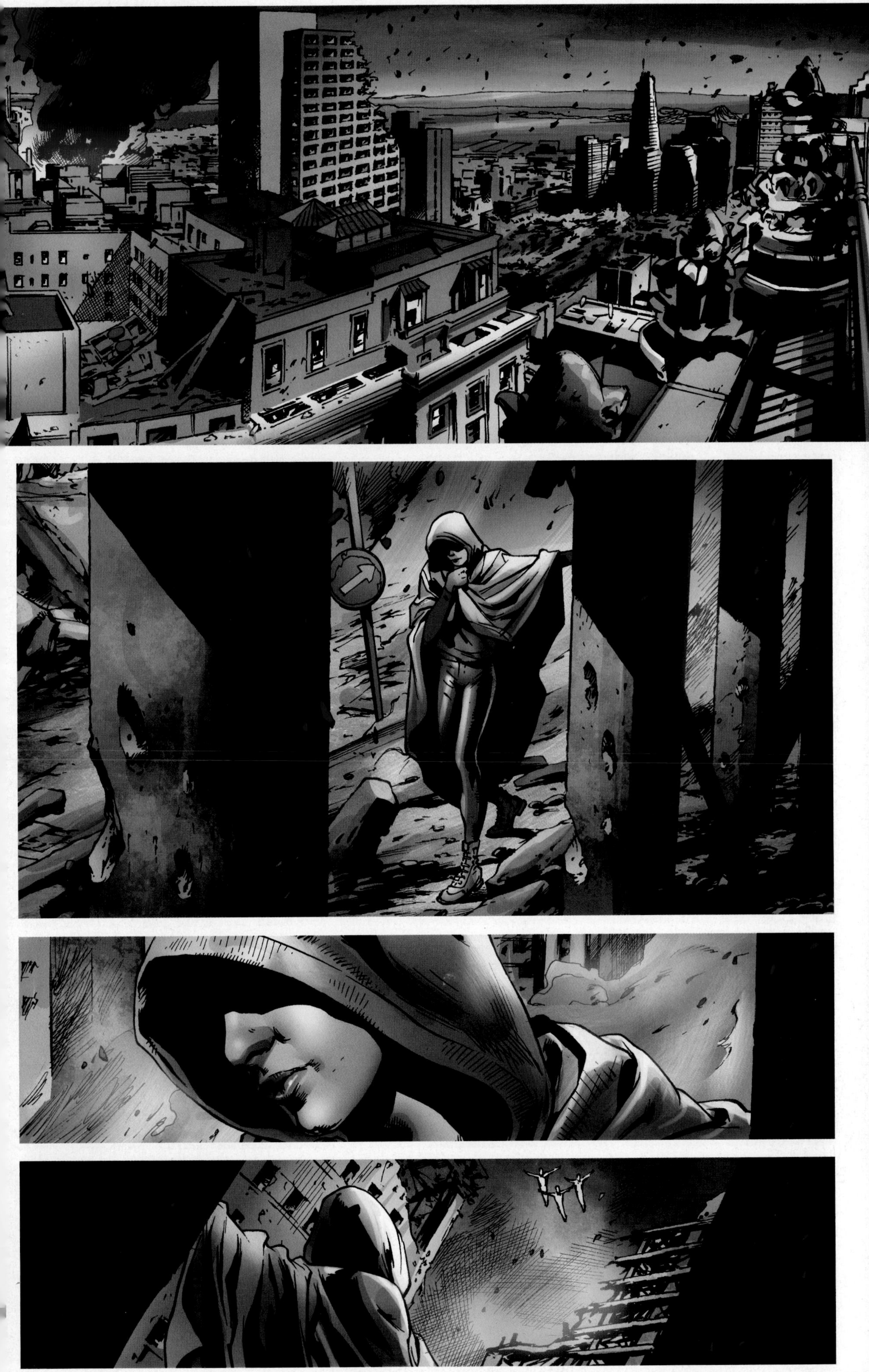

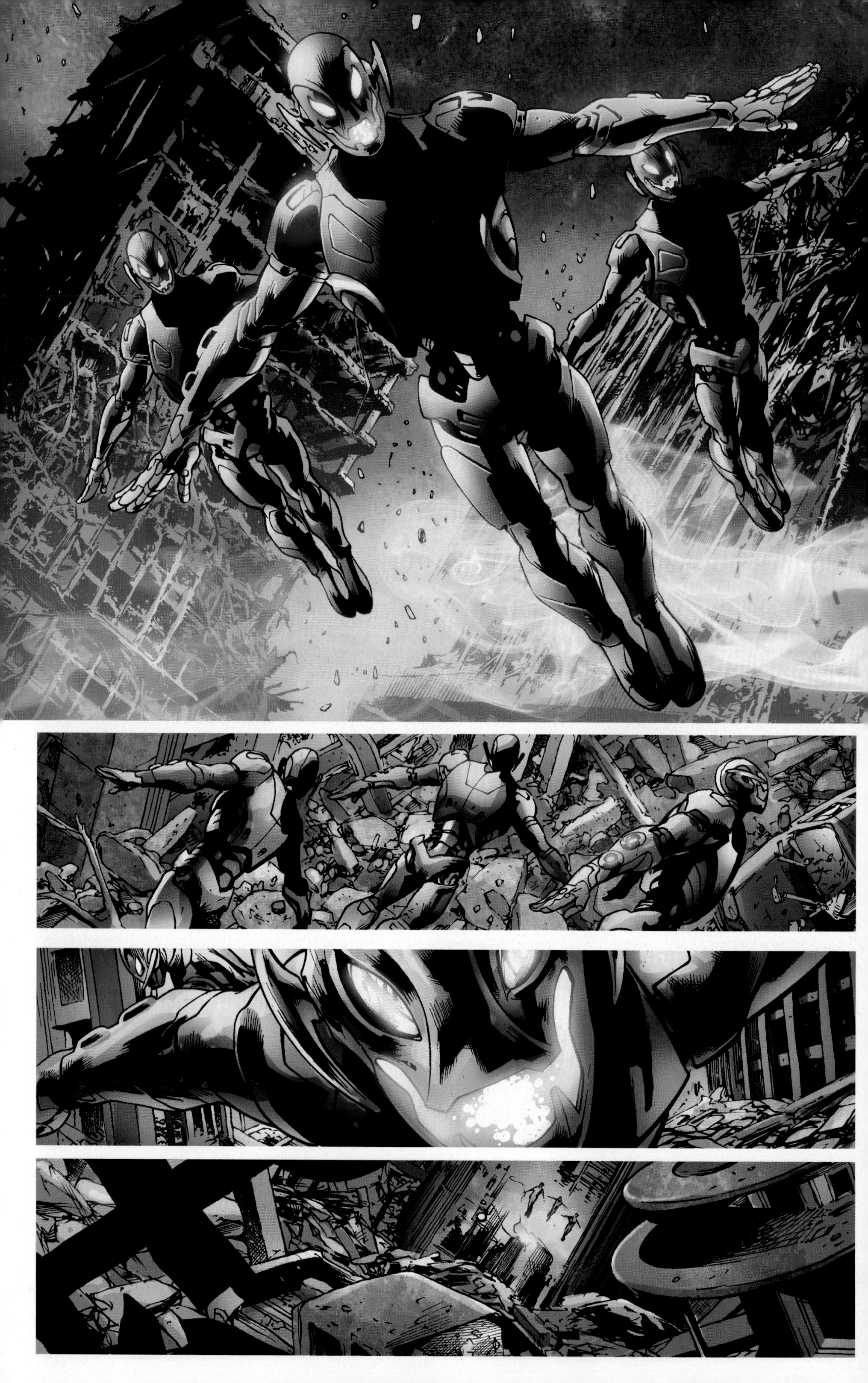

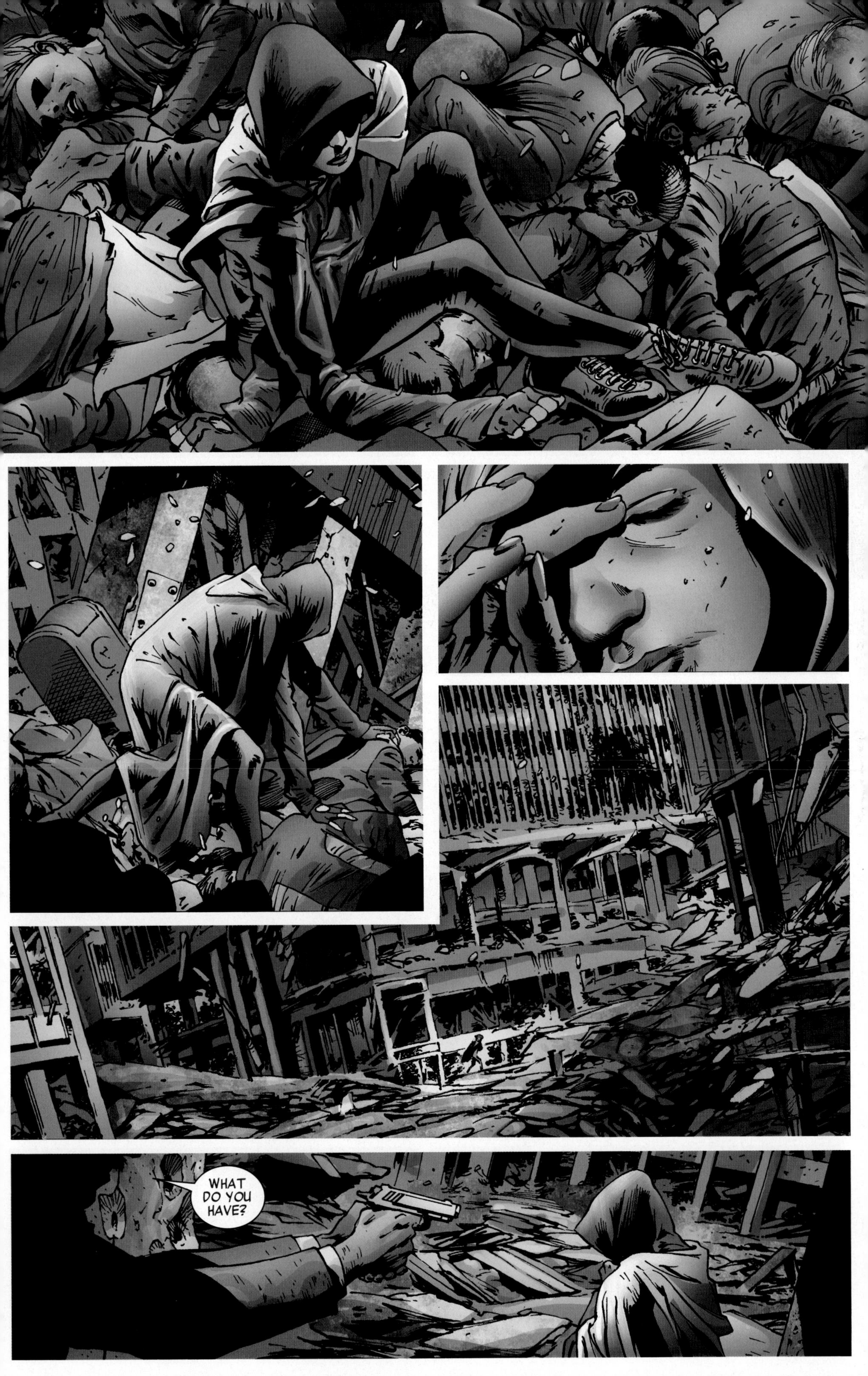
WHAT DO YOU HAVE?

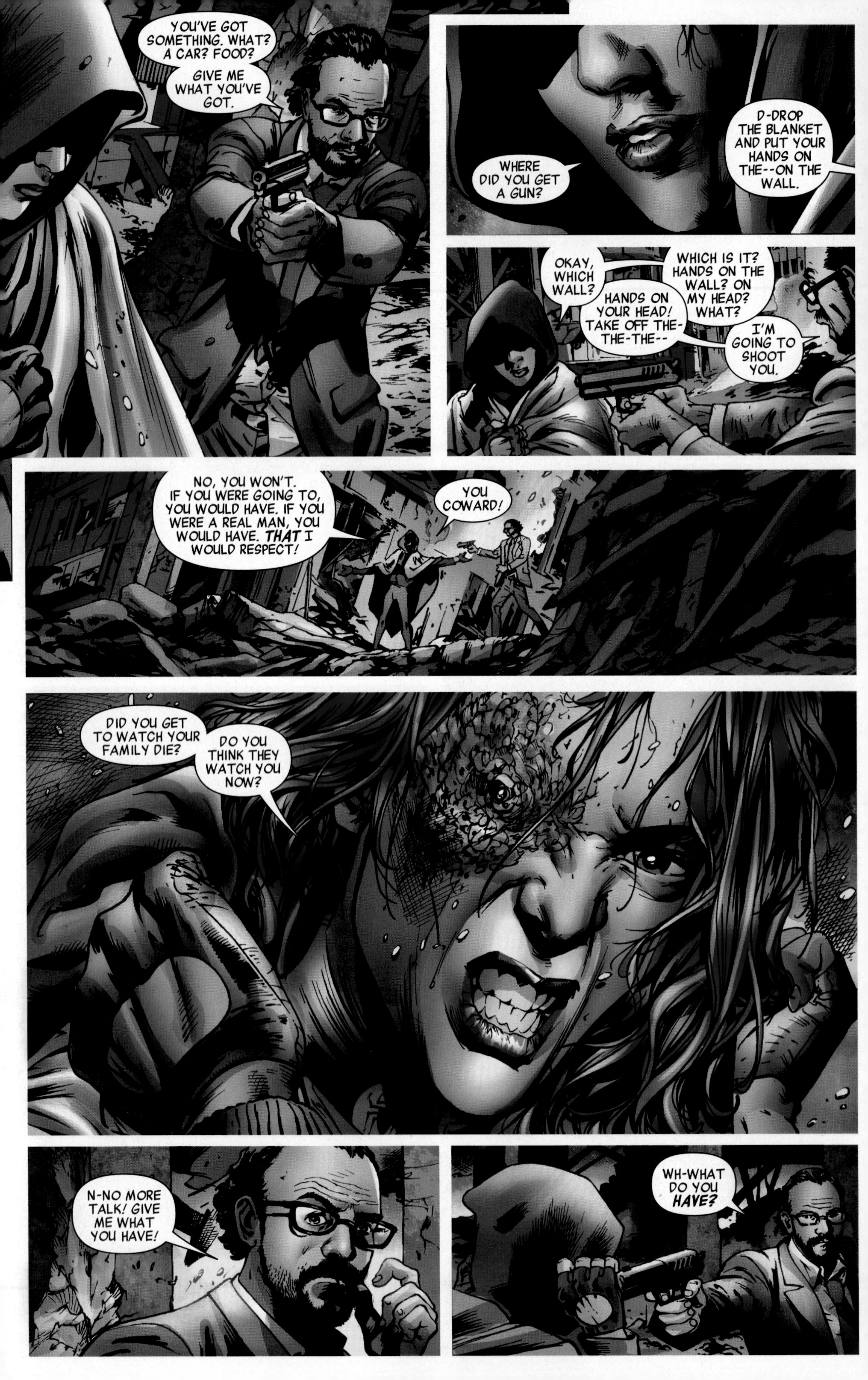
YOU'VE GOT SOMETHING. WHAT? A CAR? FOOD?
GIVE ME WHAT YOU'VE GOT.
WHERE DID YOU GET A GUN?
D-DROP THE BLANKET AND PUT YOUR HANDS ON THE--ON THE WALL.
OKAY, WHICH WALL?
HANDS ON YOUR HEAD! TAKE OFF THE-THE-THE--
WHICH IS IT? HANDS ON THE WALL? ON MY HEAD? WHAT?
I'M GOING TO SHOOT YOU.
NO, YOU WON'T. IF YOU WERE GOING TO, YOU WOULD HAVE. IF YOU WERE A REAL MAN, YOU WOULD HAVE. THAT I WOULD RESPECT!
YOU COWARD!
DID YOU GET TO WATCH YOUR FAMILY DIE?
DO YOU THINK THEY WATCH YOU NOW?
N-NO MORE TALK! GIVE ME WHAT YOU HAVE!
WH-WHAT DO YOU HAVE?

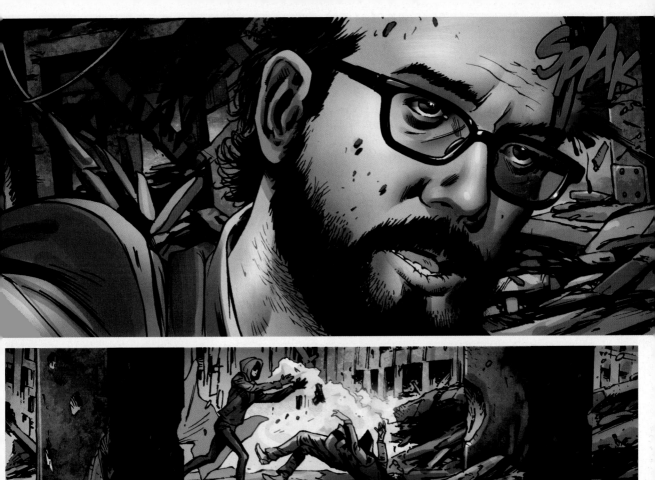

SPAK

SIGN LANGUAGE:
I HAD IT.

SIGN LANGUAGE:
SURE YOU DID.

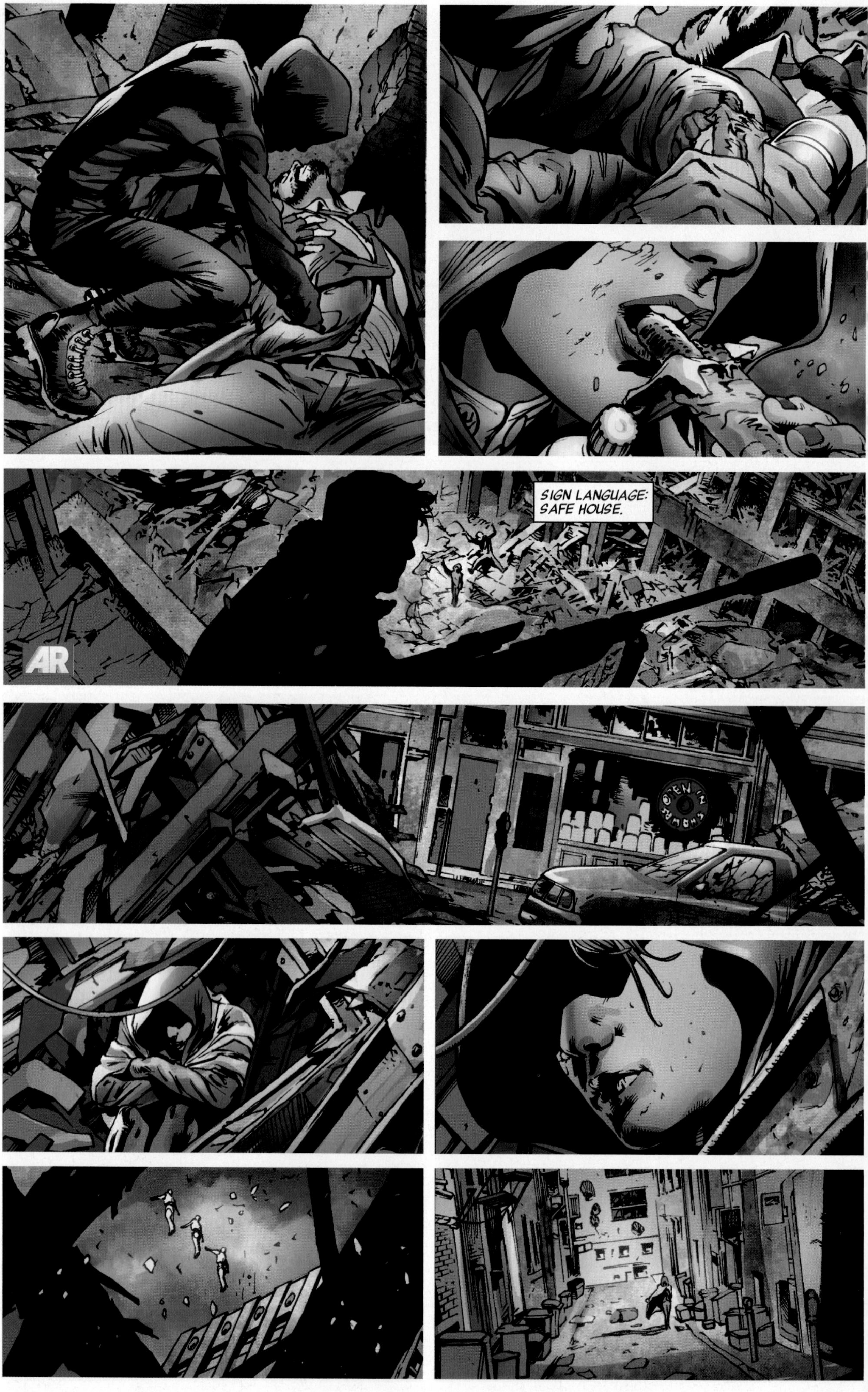
SIGN LANGUAGE:
SAFE HOUSE.

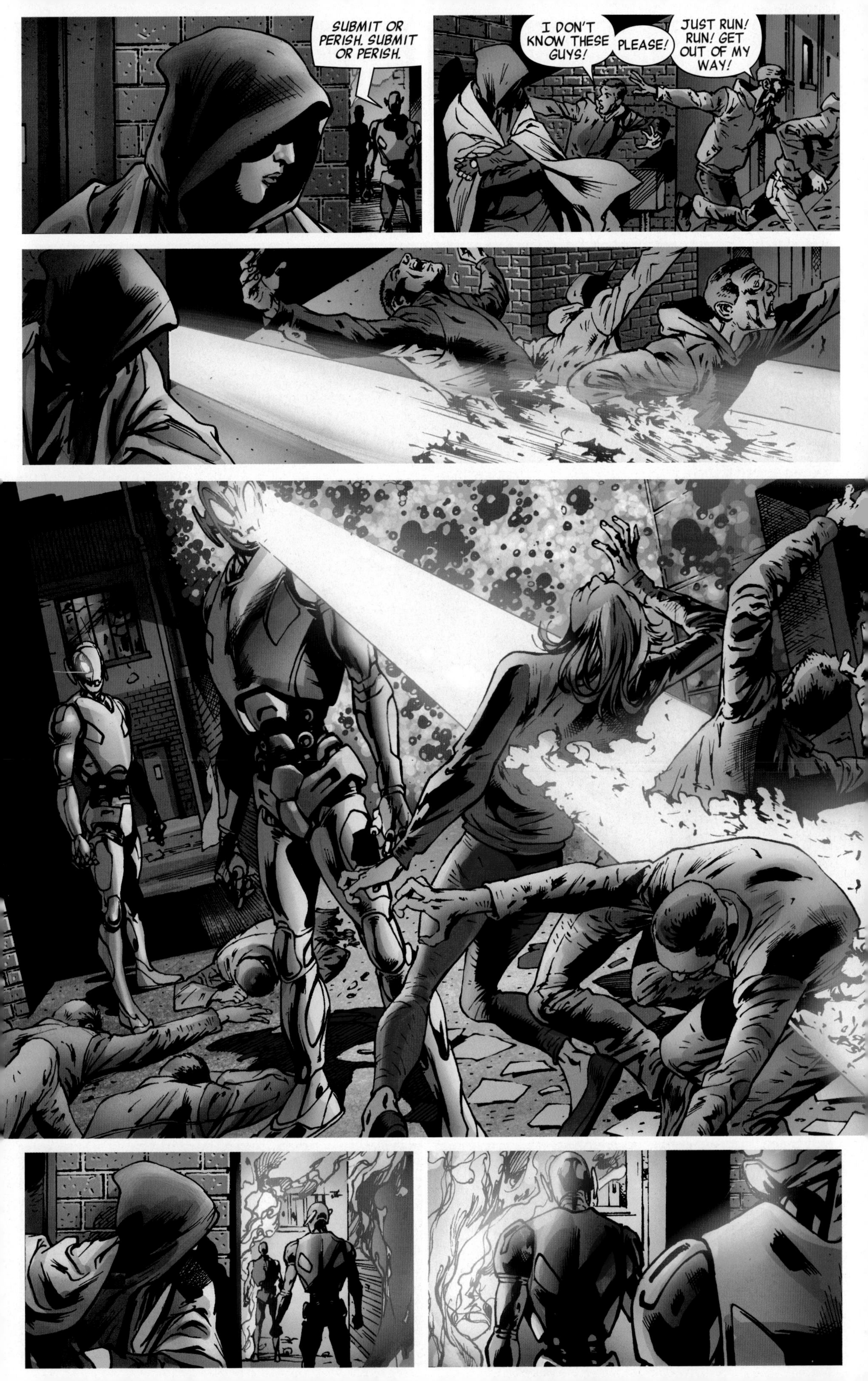
SUBMIT OR PERISH. SUBMIT OR PERISH.
I DON'T KNOW THESE GUYS!
PLEASE!
JUST RUN! RUN! GET OUT OF MY WAY!

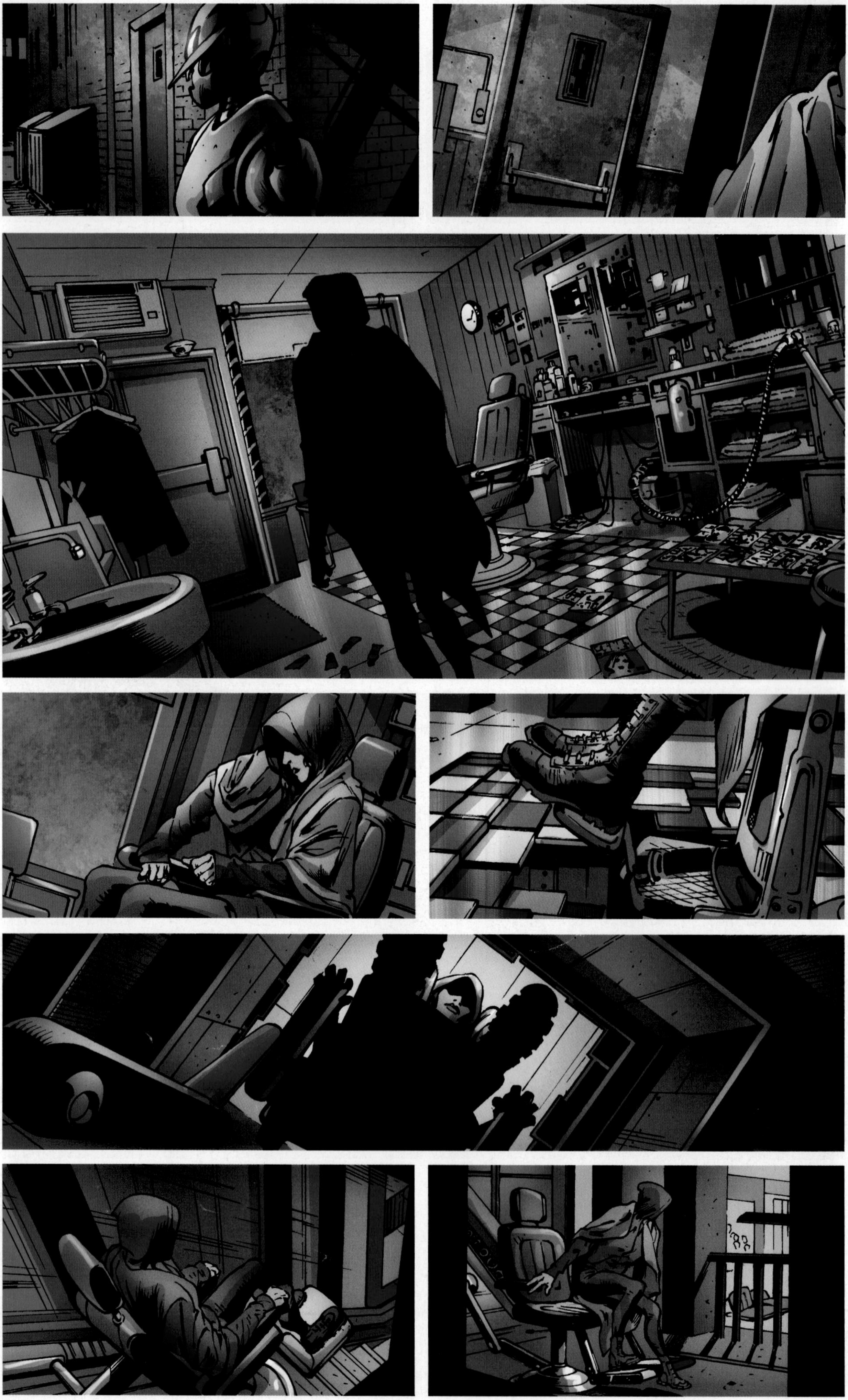

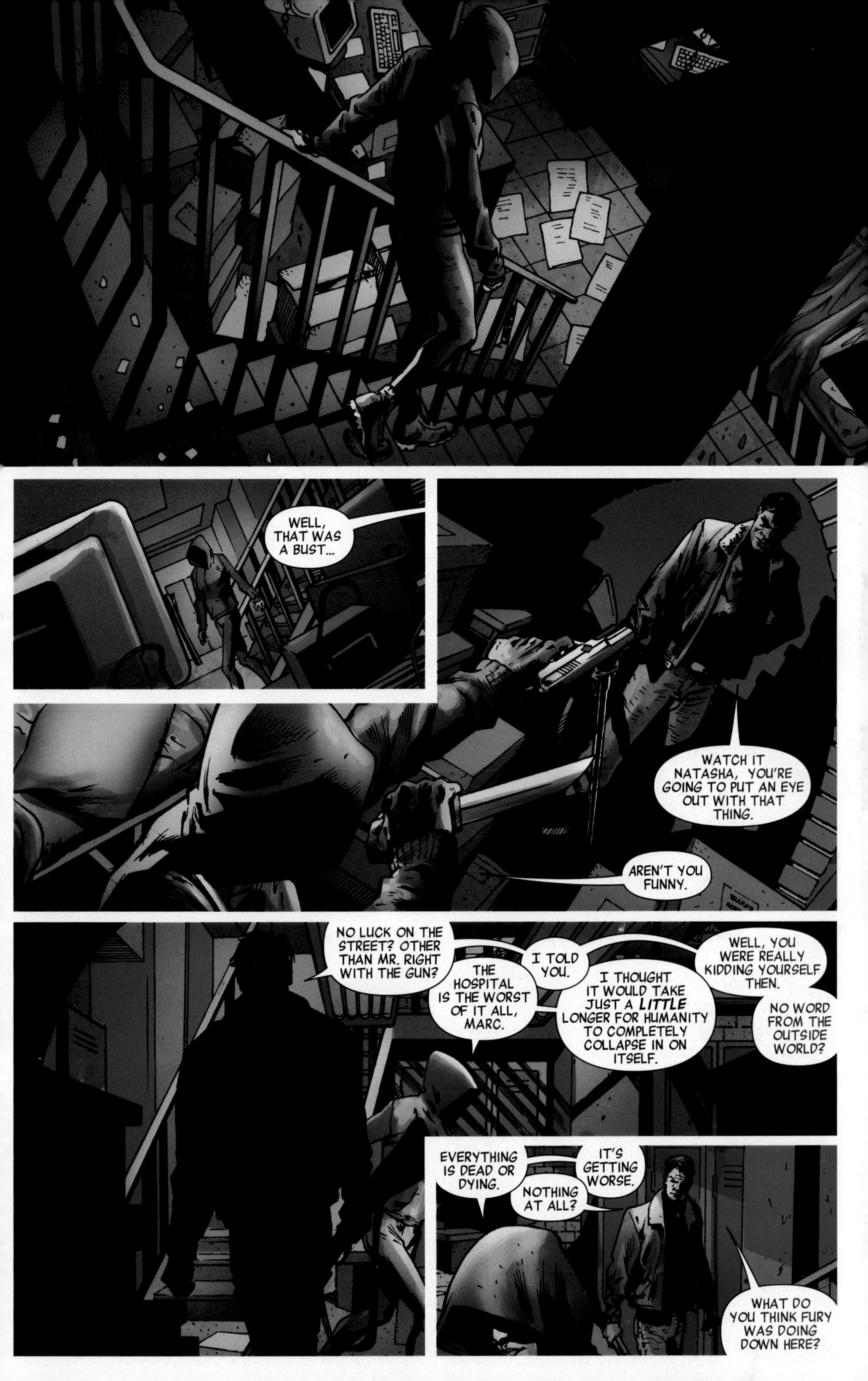
WELL, THAT WAS A BUST...
WATCH IT NATASHA, YOU'RE GOING TO PUT AN EYE OUT WITH THAT THING.
AREN'T YOU FUNNY.
NO LUCK ON THE STREET? OTHER THAN MR. RIGHT WITH THE GUN?
THE HOSPITAL IS THE WORST OF IT ALL, MARC.
I TOLD YOU.
I THOUGHT IT WOULD TAKE JUST A LITTLE LONGER FOR HUMANITY TO COMPLETELY COLLAPSE IN ON ITSELF.
WELL, YOU WERE REALLY KIDDING YOURSELF THEN.
NO WORD FROM THE OUTSIDE WORLD?
EVERYTHING IS DEAD OR DYING.
IT'S GETTING WORSE.
NOTHING AT ALL?
WHAT DO YOU THINK FURY WAS DOING DOWN HERE?

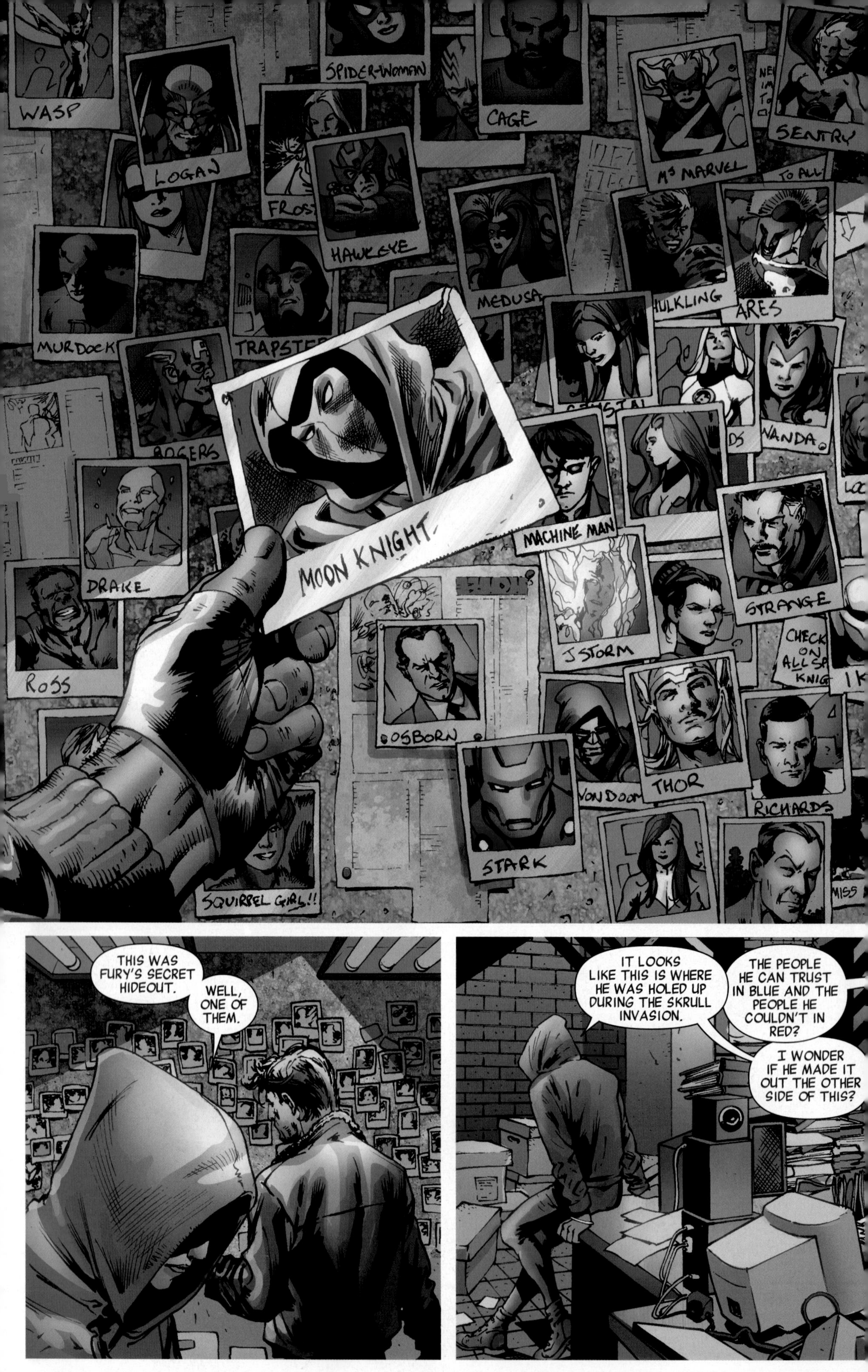
WASP
SPIDER-WOMAN
CAGE
SENTRY
LOGAN
FROST
Ms MARVEL
TO ALL
HAWKEYE
MEDUSA
HULKLING
ARES
MURDOCK
TRAPSTER
WANDA
ROGERS
MOON KNIGHT
MACHINE MAN
DRAKE
STRANGE
ROSS
J STORM
CHECK ON ALL SP KNIG
OSBORN
THOR
RICHARDS
VON DOOM
STARK
SQUIRREL GIRL!!
MISS
THIS WAS FURY'S SECRET HIDEOUT.
WELL, ONE OF THEM.
IT LOOKS LIKE THIS IS WHERE HE WAS HOLED UP DURING THE SKRULL INVASION.
THE PEOPLE HE CAN TRUST IN BLUE AND THE PEOPLE HE COULDN'T IN RED?
I WONDER IF HE MADE IT OUT THE OTHER SIDE OF THIS?

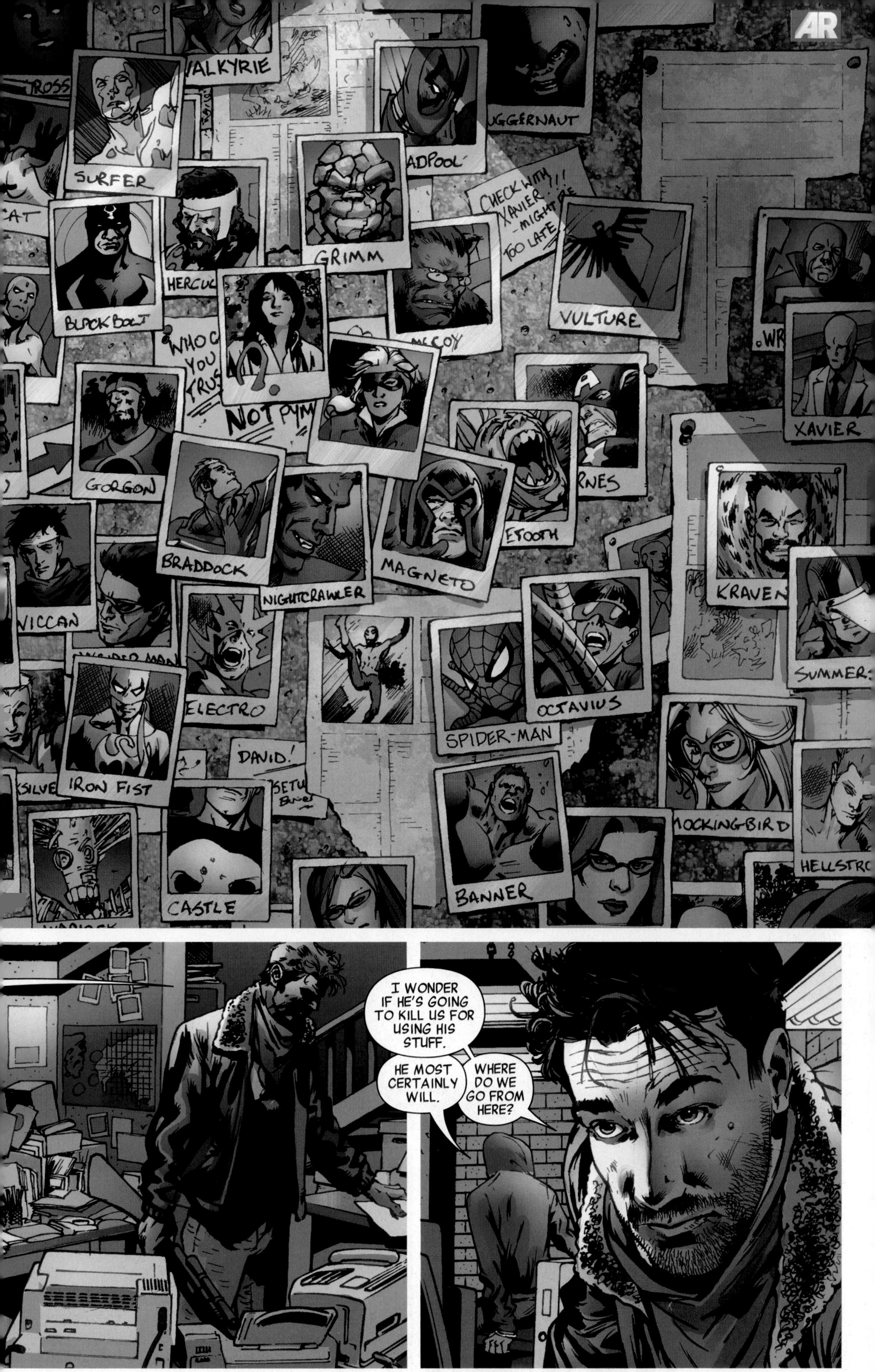

VALKYRIE
SURFER
UGGERNAUT
ADPOOL
CHECK WITH XAVIER - MIGHT BE TOO LATE!!!
GRIMM
HERCUL
BLACK BOLT
VULTURE
WHO C YOU TRUS
NOT PYM
MCCOY
XAVIER
GORGON
RNES
BRADDOCK
ETOOTH
MAGNETO
NIGHTCRAWLER
KRAVEN
WICCAN
ELECTRO
OCTAVIUS
SUMMERS
SPIDER-MAN
IRON FIST
DAVID!
KSILVE
MOCKINGBIRD
CASTLE
BANNER
HELLSTRO
I WONDER IF HE'S GOING TO KILL US FOR USING HIS STUFF.
HE MOST CERTAINLY WILL.
WHERE DO WE GO FROM HERE?

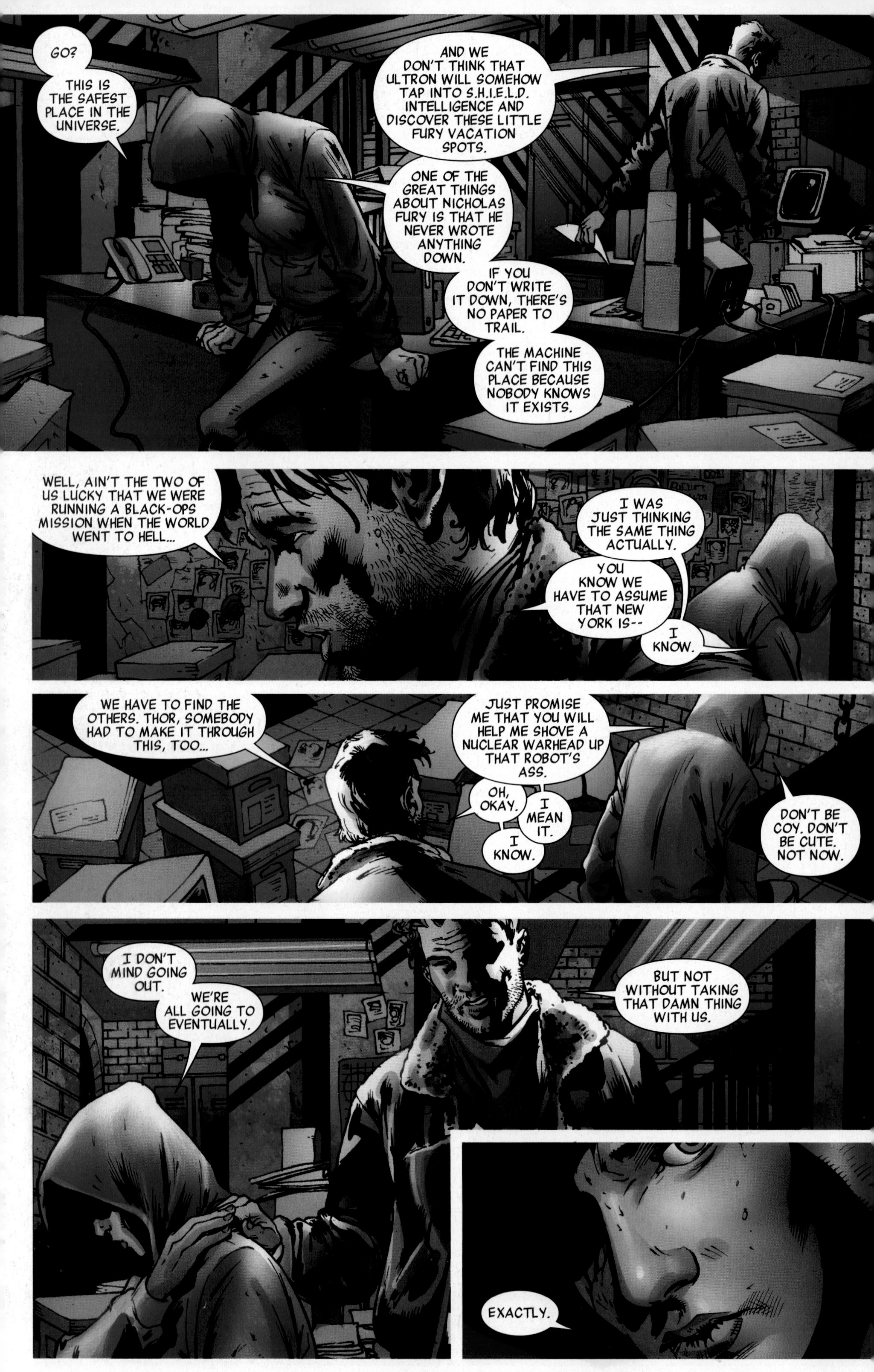
GO?
THIS IS THE SAFEST PLACE IN THE UNIVERSE.
AND WE DON'T THINK THAT ULTRON WILL SOMEHOW TAP INTO S.H.I.E.L.D. INTELLIGENCE AND DISCOVER THESE LITTLE FURY VACATION SPOTS.
ONE OF THE GREAT THINGS ABOUT NICHOLAS FURY IS THAT HE NEVER WROTE ANYTHING DOWN.
IF YOU DON'T WRITE IT DOWN, THERE'S NO PAPER TO TRAIL.
THE MACHINE CAN'T FIND THIS PLACE BECAUSE NOBODY KNOWS IT EXISTS.
WELL, AIN'T THE TWO OF US LUCKY THAT WE WERE RUNNING A BLACK-OPS MISSION WHEN THE WORLD WENT TO HELL...
I WAS JUST THINKING THE SAME THING ACTUALLY.
YOU KNOW WE HAVE TO ASSUME THAT NEW YORK IS--
I KNOW.
WE HAVE TO FIND THE OTHERS. THOR, SOMEBODY HAD TO MAKE IT THROUGH THIS, TOO...
JUST PROMISE ME THAT YOU WILL HELP ME SHOVE A NUCLEAR WARHEAD UP THAT ROBOT'S ASS.
OH, OKAY.
I MEAN IT.
I KNOW.
DON'T BE COY. DON'T BE CUTE. NOT NOW.
I DON'T MIND GOING OUT.
WE'RE ALL GOING TO EVENTUALLY.
BUT NOT WITHOUT TAKING THAT DAMN THING WITH US.
EXACTLY.

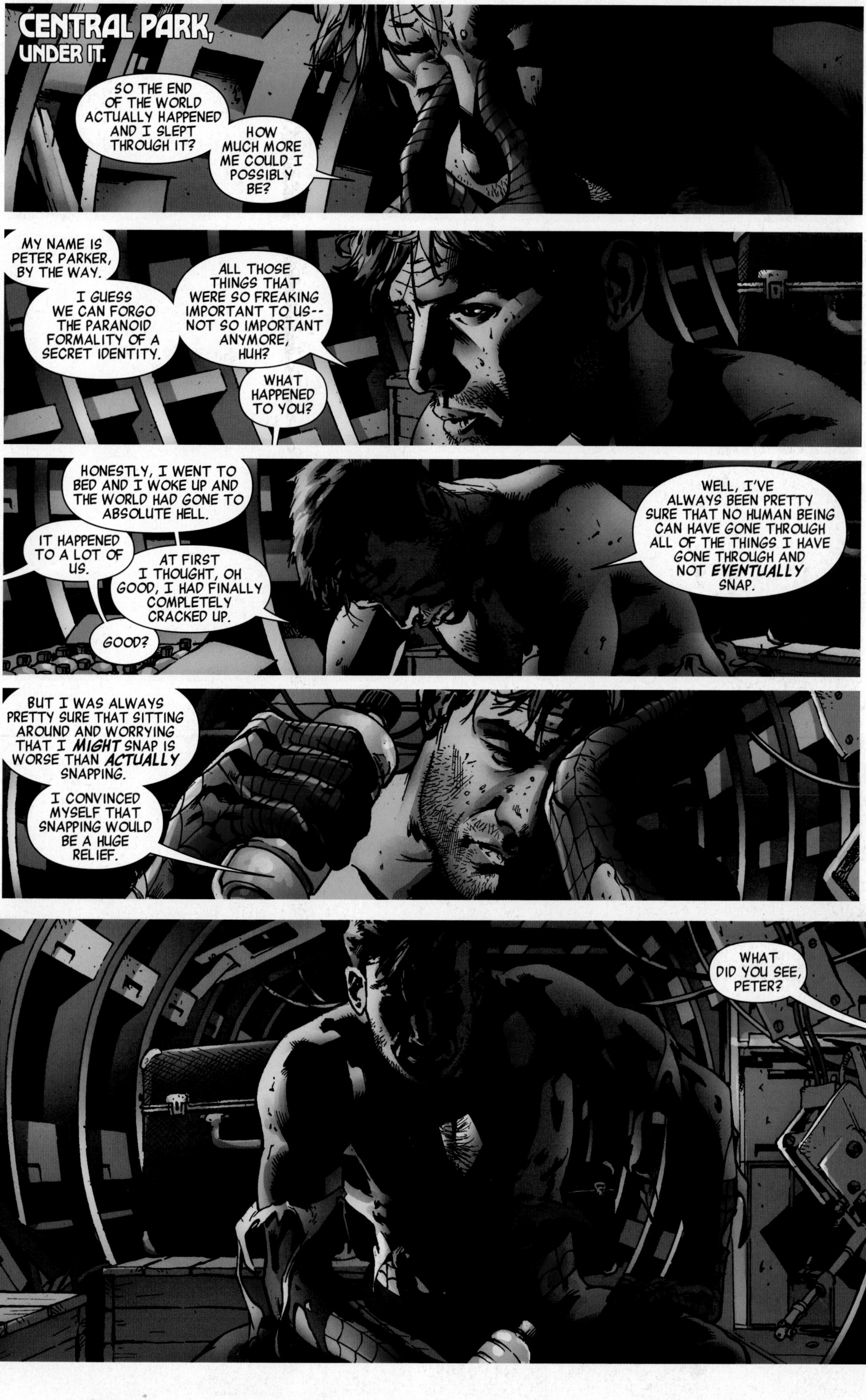
CENTRAL PARK, UNDER IT.
SO THE END OF THE WORLD ACTUALLY HAPPENED AND I SLEPT THROUGH IT?
HOW MUCH MORE ME COULD I POSSIBLY BE?
MY NAME IS PETER PARKER, BY THE WAY.
I GUESS WE CAN FORGO THE PARANOID FORMALITY OF A SECRET IDENTITY.
ALL THOSE THINGS THAT WERE SO FREAKING IMPORTANT TO US-- NOT SO IMPORTANT ANYMORE, HUH?
WHAT HAPPENED TO YOU?
HONESTLY, I WENT TO BED AND I WOKE UP AND THE WORLD HAD GONE TO ABSOLUTE HELL.
IT HAPPENED TO A LOT OF US.
AT FIRST I THOUGHT, OH GOOD, I HAD FINALLY COMPLETELY CRACKED UP.
GOOD?
WELL, I'VE ALWAYS BEEN PRETTY SURE THAT NO HUMAN BEING CAN HAVE GONE THROUGH ALL OF THE THINGS I HAVE GONE THROUGH AND NOT EVENTUALLY SNAP.
BUT I WAS ALWAYS PRETTY SURE THAT SITTING AROUND AND WORRYING THAT I MIGHT SNAP IS WORSE THAN ACTUALLY SNAPPING.
I CONVINCED MYSELF THAT SNAPPING WOULD BE A HUGE RELIEF.
WHAT DID YOU SEE, PETER?

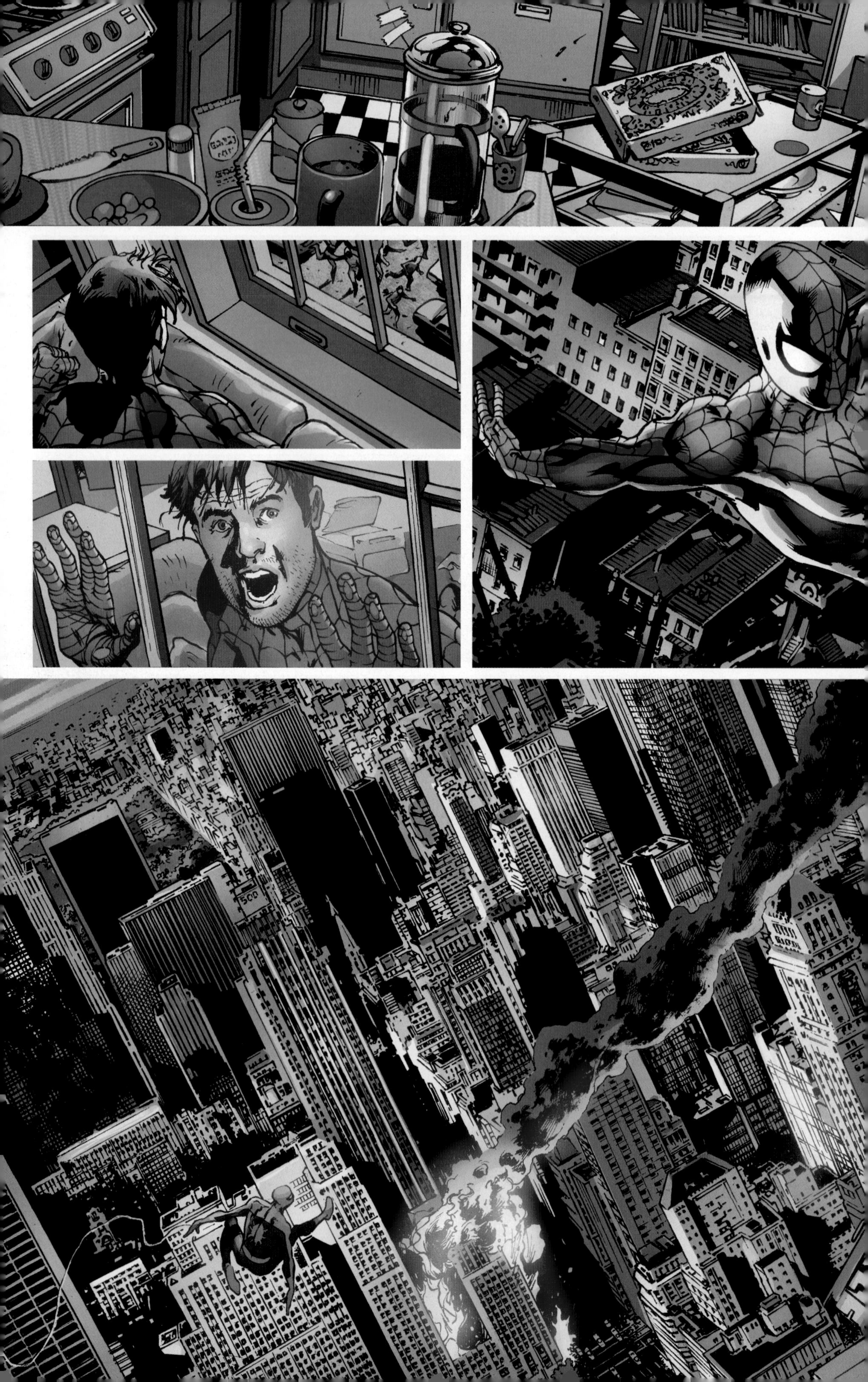

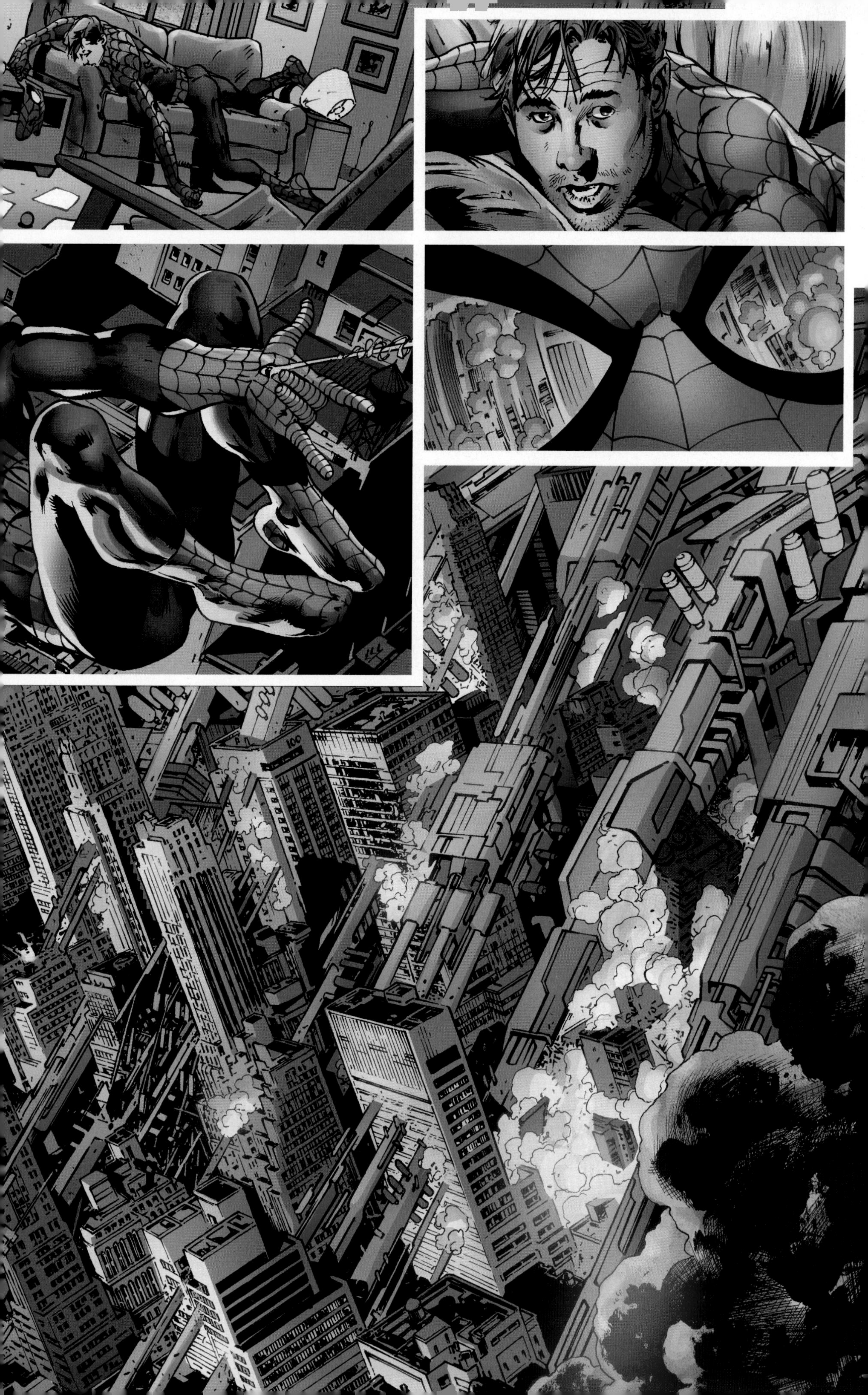

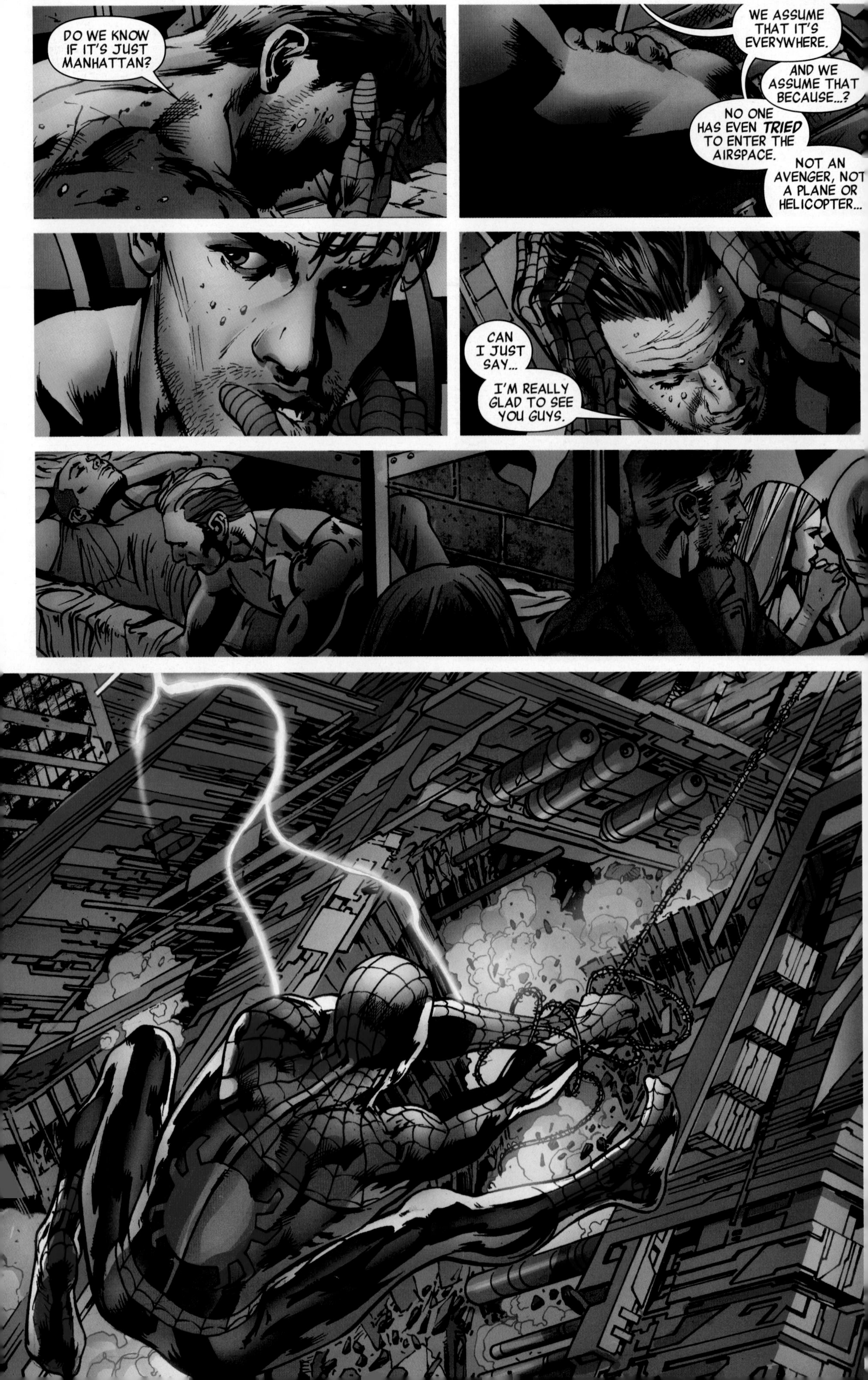
DO WE KNOW IF IT'S JUST MANHATTAN?
WE ASSUME THAT IT'S EVERYWHERE.
AND WE ASSUME THAT BECAUSE...?
NO ONE HAS EVEN **TRIED** TO ENTER THE AIRSPACE.
NOT AN AVENGER, NOT A PLANE OR HELICOPTER...
CAN I JUST SAY...
I'M REALLY GLAD TO SEE YOU GUYS.

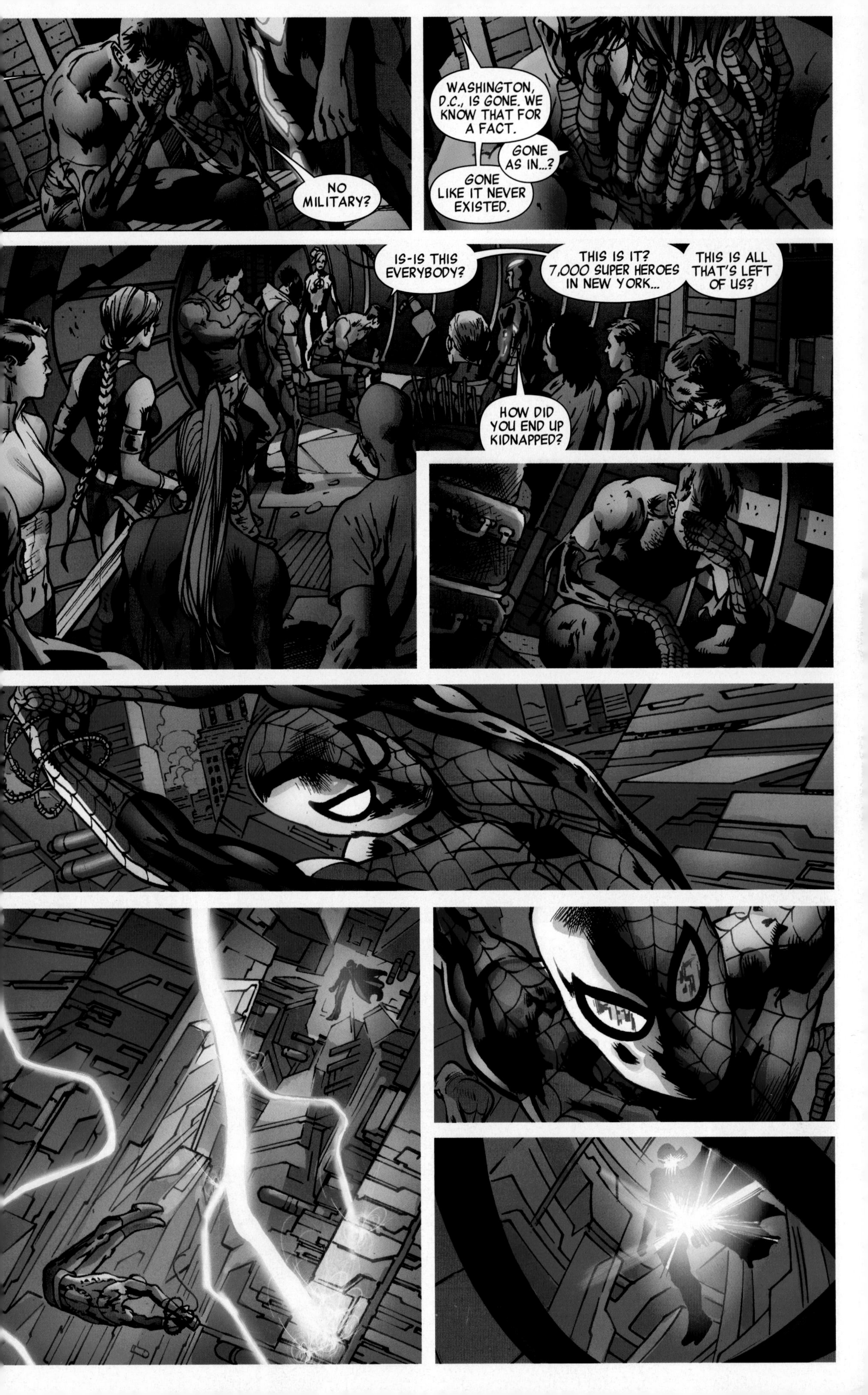
NO MILITARY?
WASHINGTON, D.C., IS GONE. WE KNOW THAT FOR A FACT.
GONE AS IN...?
GONE LIKE IT NEVER EXISTED.
IS-IS THIS EVERYBODY?
THIS IS IT? 7,000 SUPER HEROES IN NEW YORK...
THIS IS ALL THAT'S LEFT OF US?
HOW DID YOU END UP KIDNAPPED?

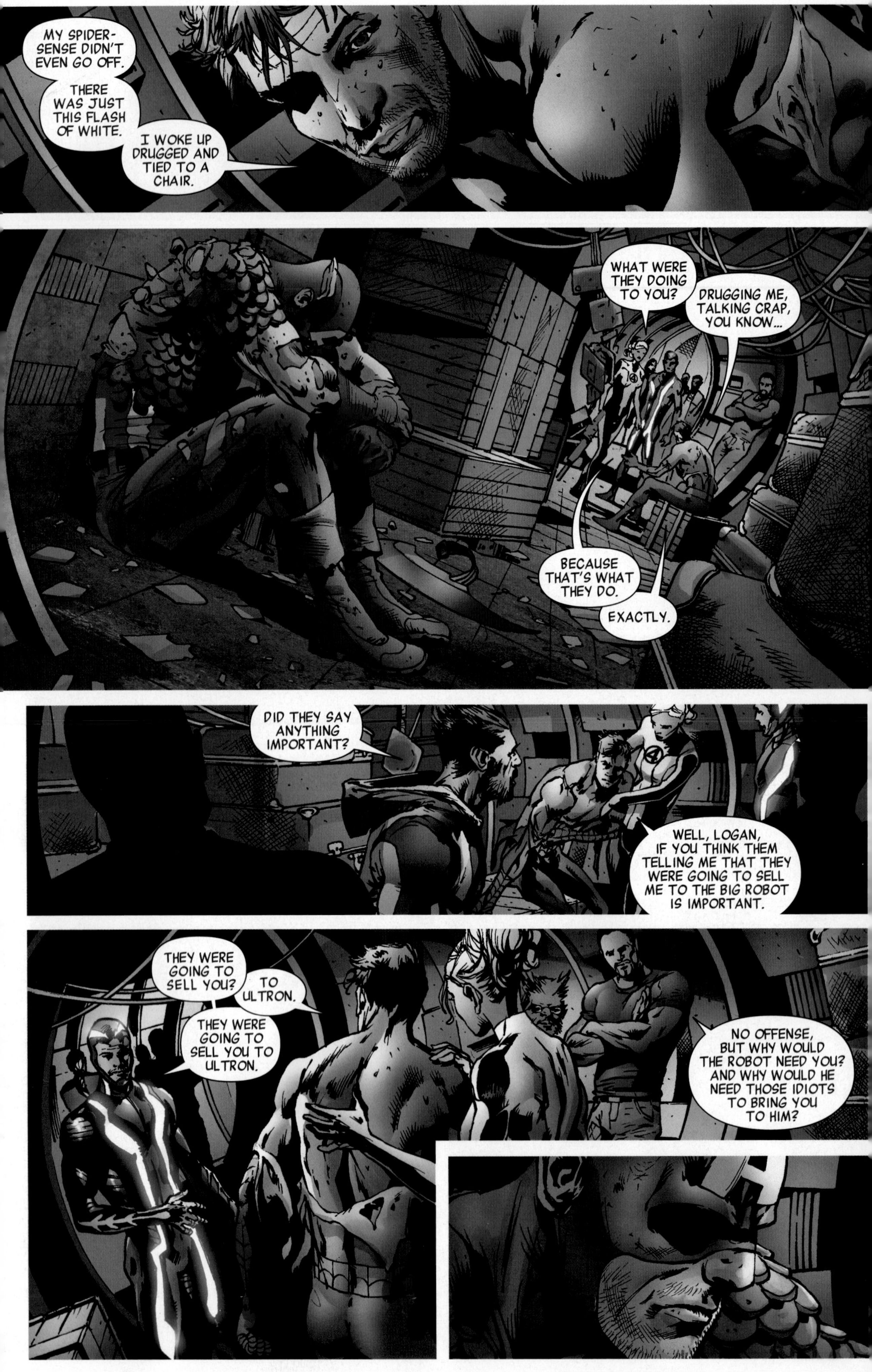
MY SPIDER-SENSE DIDN'T EVEN GO OFF.
THERE WAS JUST THIS FLASH OF WHITE.
I WOKE UP DRUGGED AND TIED TO A CHAIR.
WHAT WERE THEY DOING TO YOU?
DRUGGING ME, TALKING CRAP, YOU KNOW...
BECAUSE THAT'S WHAT THEY DO.
EXACTLY.
DID THEY SAY ANYTHING IMPORTANT?
WELL, LOGAN, IF YOU THINK THEM TELLING ME THAT THEY WERE GOING TO SELL ME TO THE BIG ROBOT IS IMPORTANT.
THEY WERE GOING TO SELL YOU?
TO ULTRON.
THEY WERE GOING TO SELL YOU TO ULTRON.
NO OFFENSE, BUT WHY WOULD THE ROBOT NEED YOU? AND WHY WOULD HE NEED THOSE IDIOTS TO BRING YOU TO HIM?

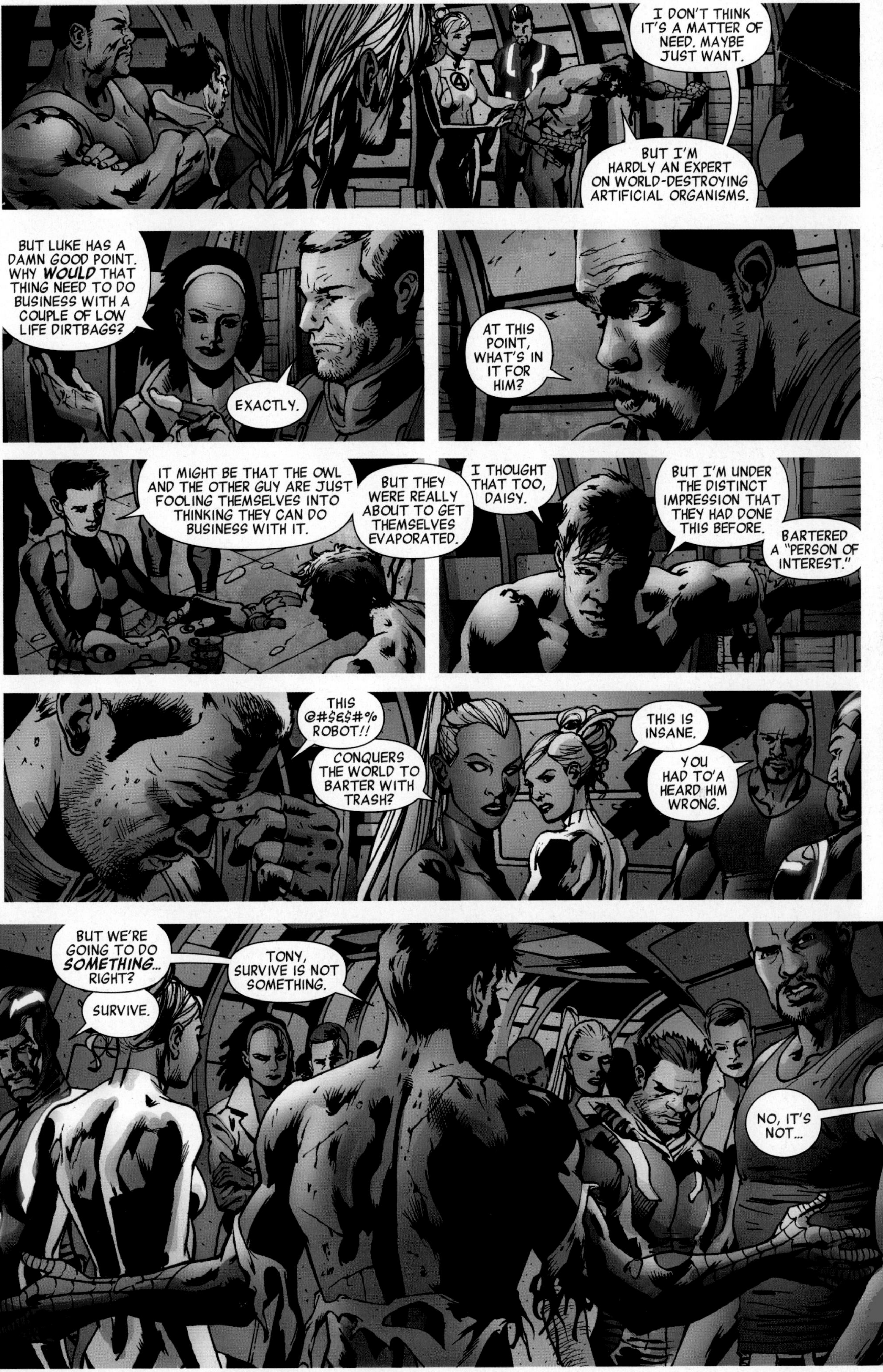
I DON'T THINK IT'S A MATTER OF NEED. MAYBE JUST WANT.
BUT I'M HARDLY AN EXPERT ON WORLD-DESTROYING ARTIFICIAL ORGANISMS.
BUT LUKE HAS A DAMN GOOD POINT. WHY WOULD THAT THING NEED TO DO BUSINESS WITH A COUPLE OF LOW LIFE DIRTBAGS?
EXACTLY.
AT THIS POINT, WHAT'S IN IT FOR HIM?
IT MIGHT BE THAT THE OWL AND THE OTHER GUY ARE JUST FOOLING THEMSELVES INTO THINKING THEY CAN DO BUSINESS WITH IT.
BUT THEY WERE REALLY ABOUT TO GET THEMSELVES EVAPORATED.
I THOUGHT THAT TOO, DAISY.
BUT I'M UNDER THE DISTINCT IMPRESSION THAT THEY HAD DONE THIS BEFORE.
BARTERED A "PERSON OF INTEREST."
THIS @#$£$#% ROBOT!!
CONQUERS THE WORLD TO BARTER WITH TRASH?
THIS IS INSANE.
YOU HAD TO'A HEARD HIM WRONG.
BUT WE'RE GOING TO DO SOMETHING... RIGHT?
SURVIVE.
TONY, SURVIVE IS NOT SOMETHING.
NO, IT'S NOT...

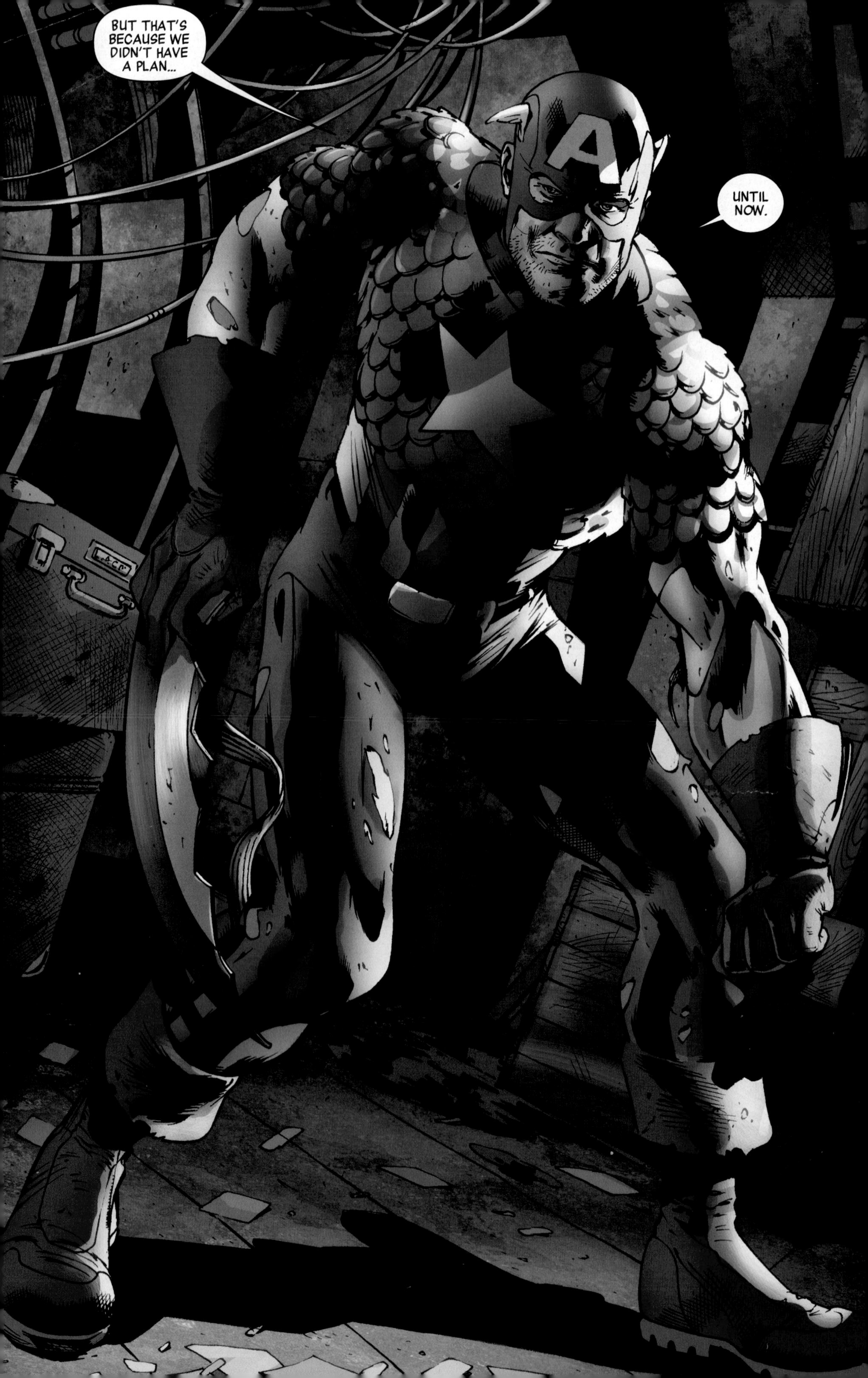
BUT THAT'S BECAUSE WE DIDN'T HAVE A PLAN...
UNTIL NOW.

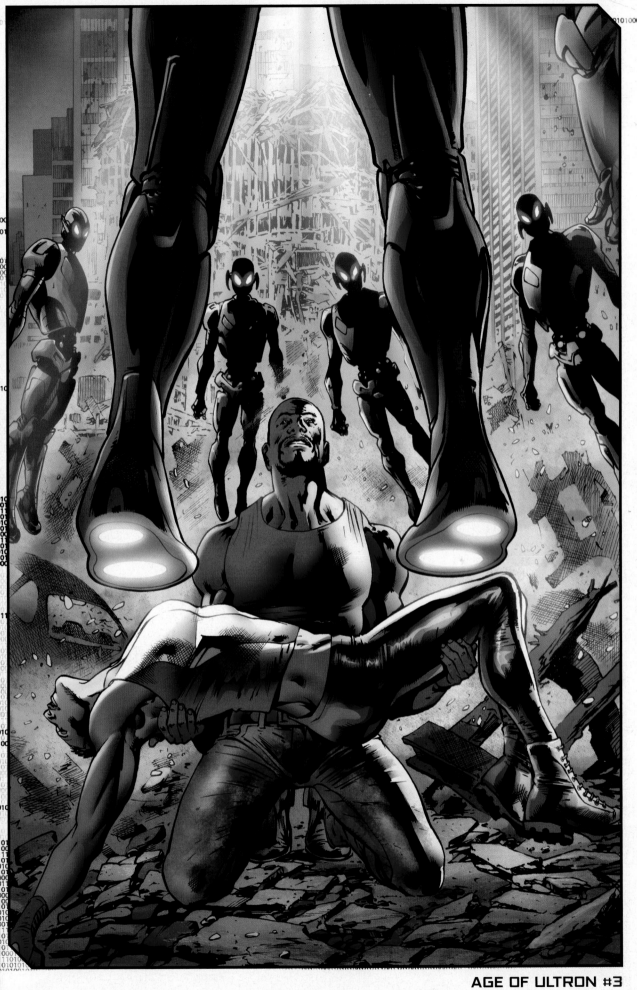

AGE OF ULTRON #3

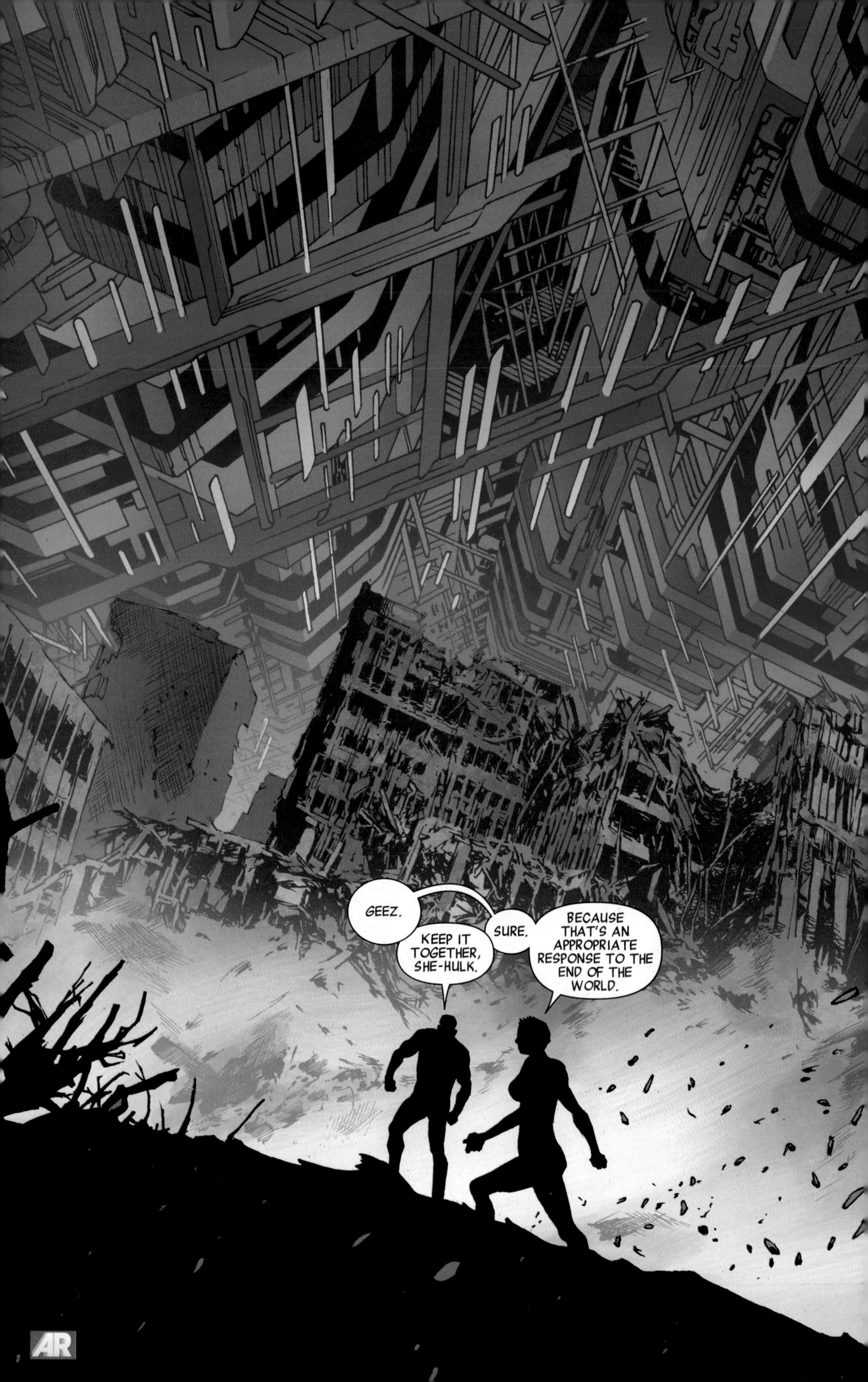
GEEZ.
KEEP IT TOGETHER, SHE-HULK.
SURE.
BECAUSE THAT'S AN APPROPRIATE RESPONSE TO THE END OF THE WORLD.

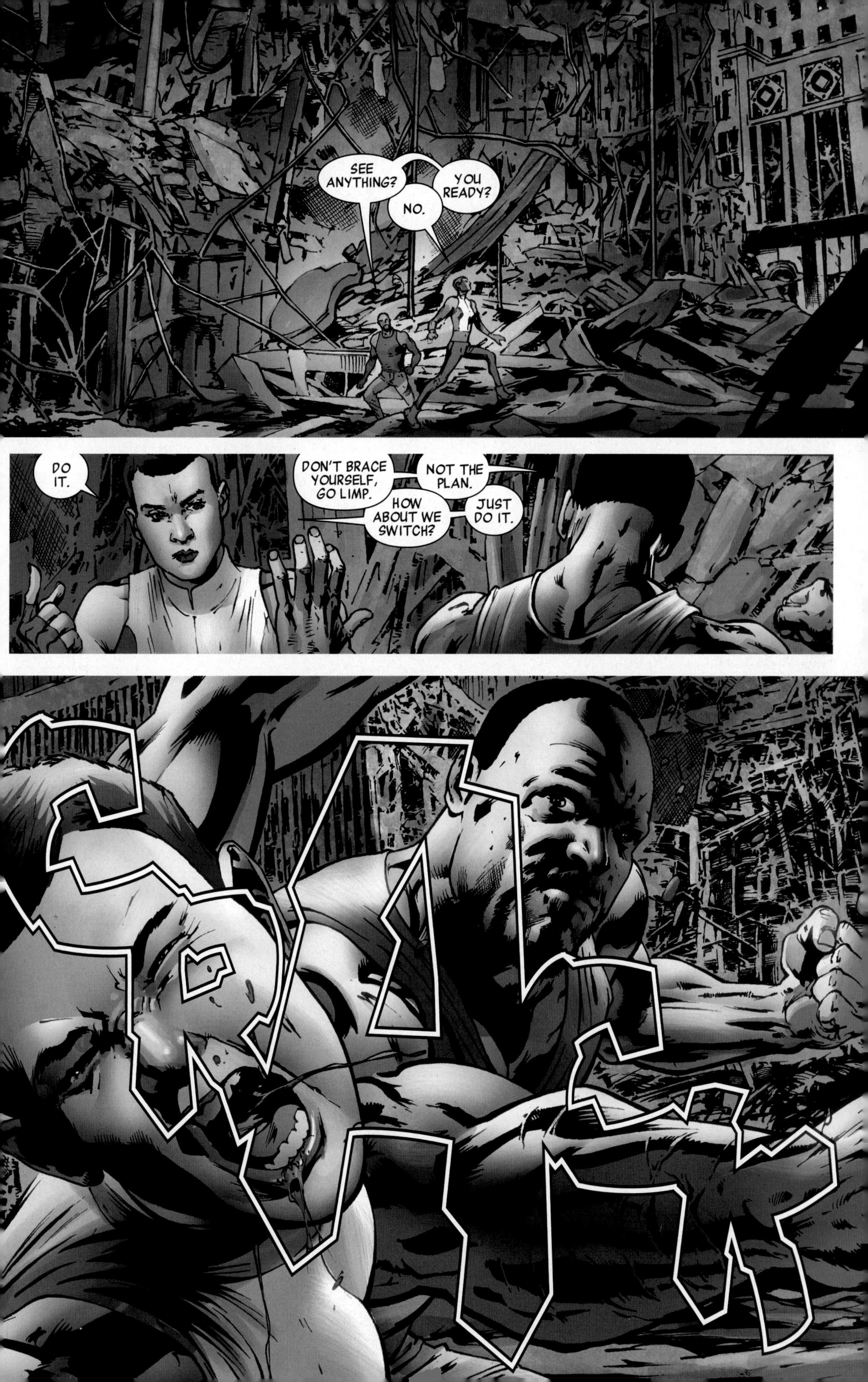
SEE ANYTHING?
NO.
YOU READY?
DO IT.
DON'T BRACE YOURSELF, GO LIMP.
NOT THE PLAN.
HOW ABOUT WE SWITCH?
JUST DO IT.

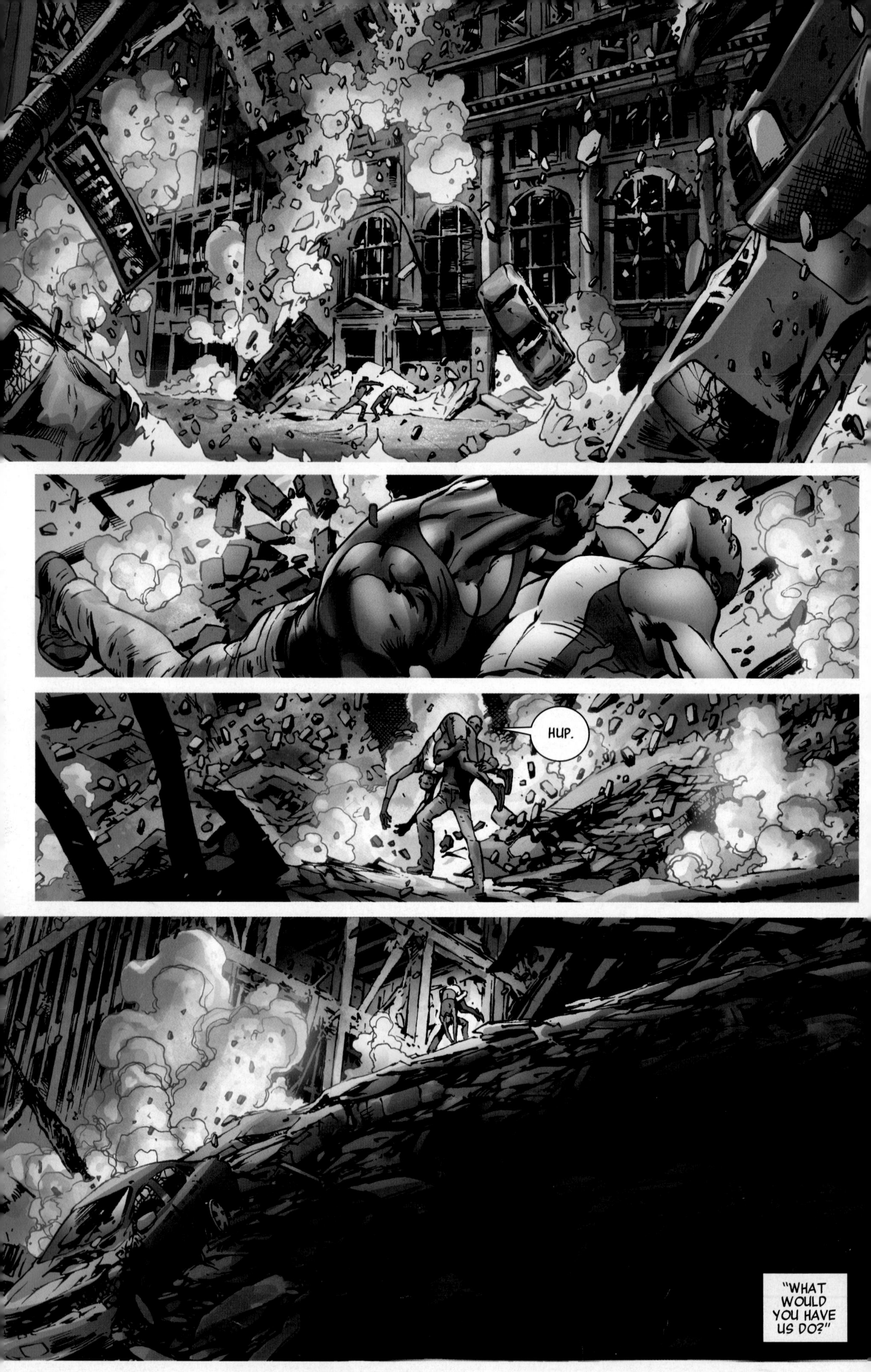
HUP.
"WHAT WOULD YOU HAVE US DO?"

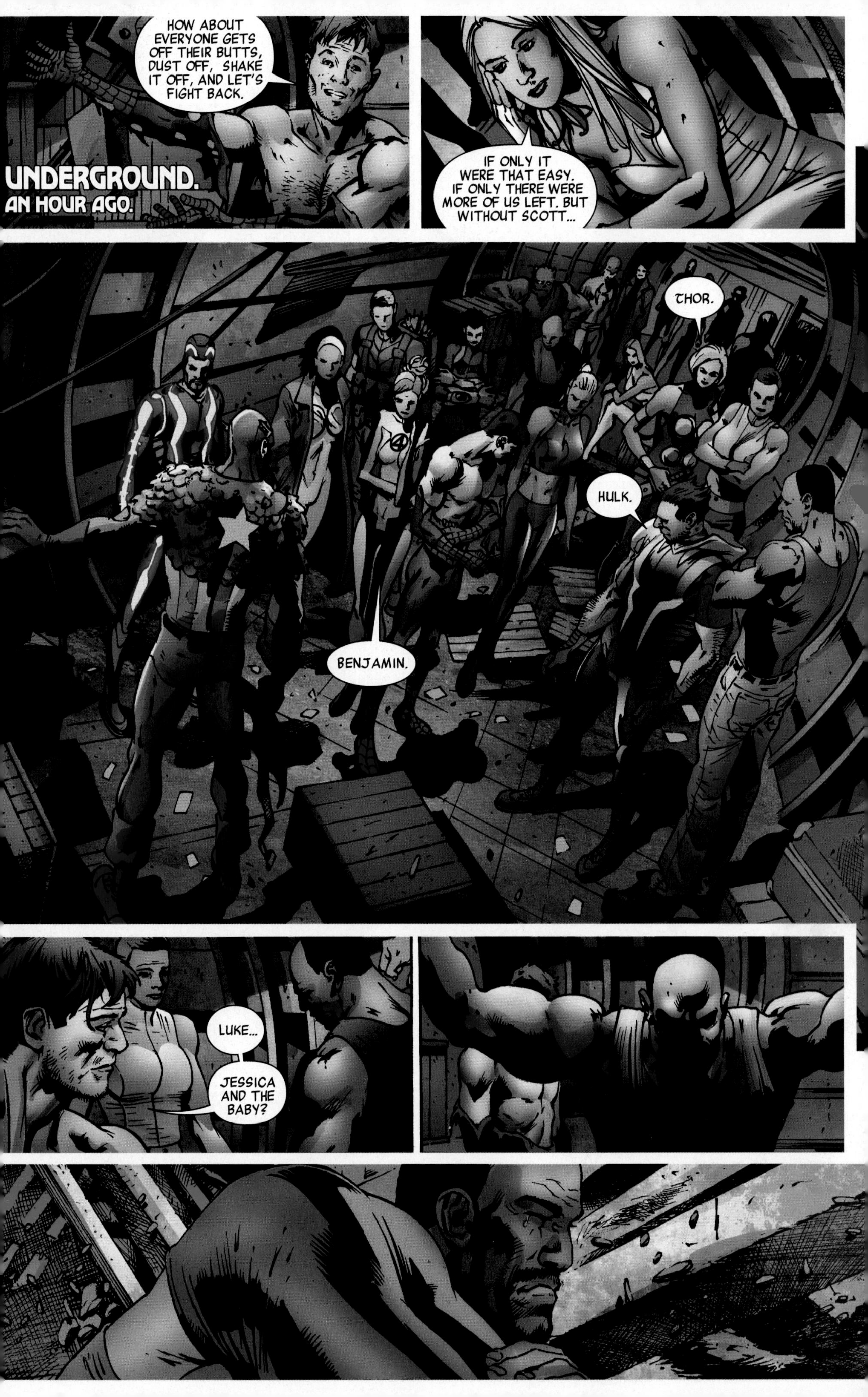
HOW ABOUT EVERYONE GETS OFF THEIR BUTTS, DUST OFF, SHAKE IT OFF, AND LET'S FIGHT BACK.
UNDERGROUND. AN HOUR AGO.
IF ONLY IT WERE THAT EASY. IF ONLY THERE WERE MORE OF US LEFT. BUT WITHOUT SCOTT...
THOR.
HULK.
BENJAMIN.
LUKE...
JESSICA AND THE BABY?

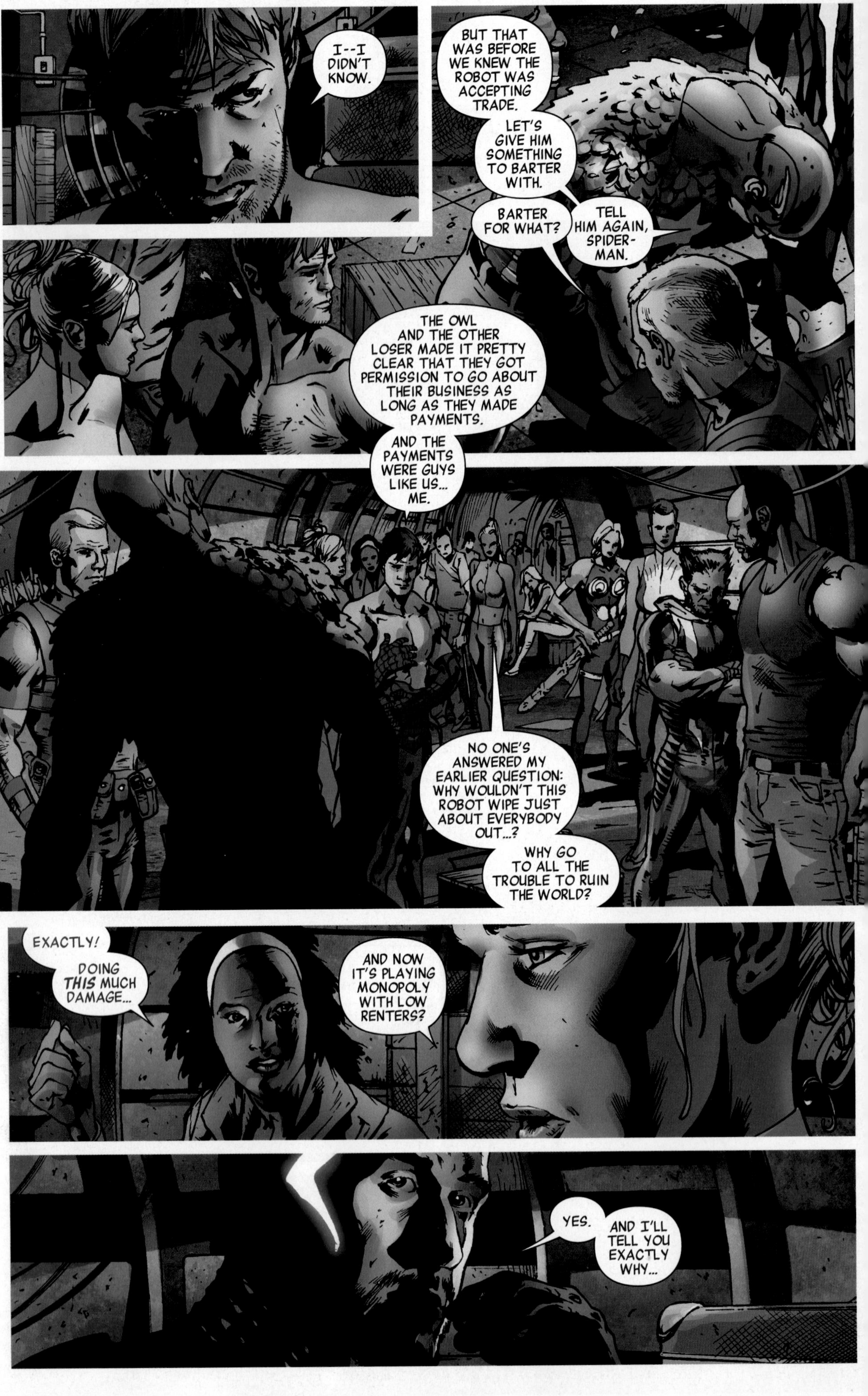
I--I DIDN'T KNOW.
BUT THAT WAS BEFORE WE KNEW THE ROBOT WAS ACCEPTING TRADE.
LET'S GIVE HIM SOMETHING TO BARTER WITH.
BARTER FOR WHAT?
TELL HIM AGAIN, SPIDER-MAN.
THE OWL AND THE OTHER LOSER MADE IT PRETTY CLEAR THAT THEY GOT PERMISSION TO GO ABOUT THEIR BUSINESS AS LONG AS THEY MADE PAYMENTS.
AND THE PAYMENTS WERE GUYS LIKE US... ME.
NO ONE'S ANSWERED MY EARLIER QUESTION: WHY WOULDN'T THIS ROBOT WIPE JUST ABOUT EVERYBODY OUT...?
WHY GO TO ALL THE TROUBLE TO RUIN THE WORLD?
EXACTLY!
DOING *THIS* MUCH DAMAGE...
AND NOW IT'S PLAYING MONOPOLY WITH LOW RENTERS?
YES.
AND I'LL TELL YOU EXACTLY WHY...

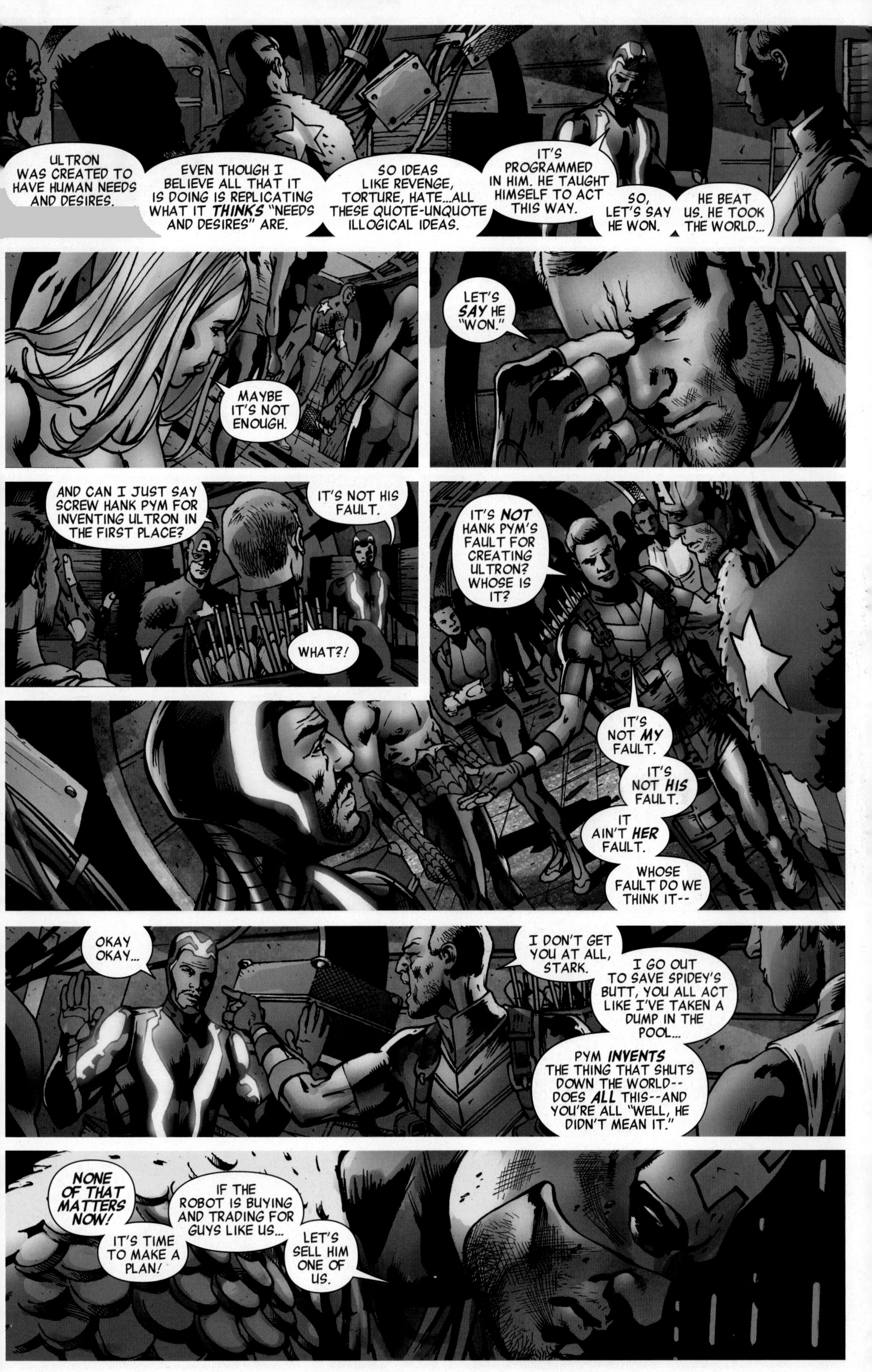

ULTRON WAS CREATED TO HAVE HUMAN NEEDS AND DESIRES.
EVEN THOUGH I BELIEVE ALL THAT IT IS DOING IS REPLICATING WHAT IT THINKS "NEEDS AND DESIRES" ARE.
SO IDEAS LIKE REVENGE, TORTURE, HATE...ALL THESE QUOTE-UNQUOTE ILLOGICAL IDEAS.
IT'S PROGRAMMED IN HIM. HE TAUGHT HIMSELF TO ACT THIS WAY.
SO, LET'S SAY HE WON.
HE BEAT US. HE TOOK THE WORLD...
MAYBE IT'S NOT ENOUGH.
LET'S SAY HE "WON."
AND CAN I JUST SAY SCREW HANK PYM FOR INVENTING ULTRON IN THE FIRST PLACE?
IT'S NOT HIS FAULT.
WHAT?!
IT'S NOT HANK PYM'S FAULT FOR CREATING ULTRON? WHOSE IS IT?
IT'S NOT MY FAULT.
IT'S NOT HIS FAULT.
IT AIN'T HER FAULT.
WHOSE FAULT DO WE THINK IT--
OKAY OKAY...
I DON'T GET YOU AT ALL, STARK.
I GO OUT TO SAVE SPIDEY'S BUTT, YOU ALL ACT LIKE I'VE TAKEN A DUMP IN THE POOL...
PYM INVENTS THE THING THAT SHUTS DOWN THE WORLD--DOES ALL THIS--AND YOU'RE ALL "WELL, HE DIDN'T MEAN IT."
NONE OF THAT MATTERS NOW!
IT'S TIME TO MAKE A PLAN!
IF THE ROBOT IS BUYING AND TRADING FOR GUYS LIKE US...
LET'S SELL HIM ONE OF US.

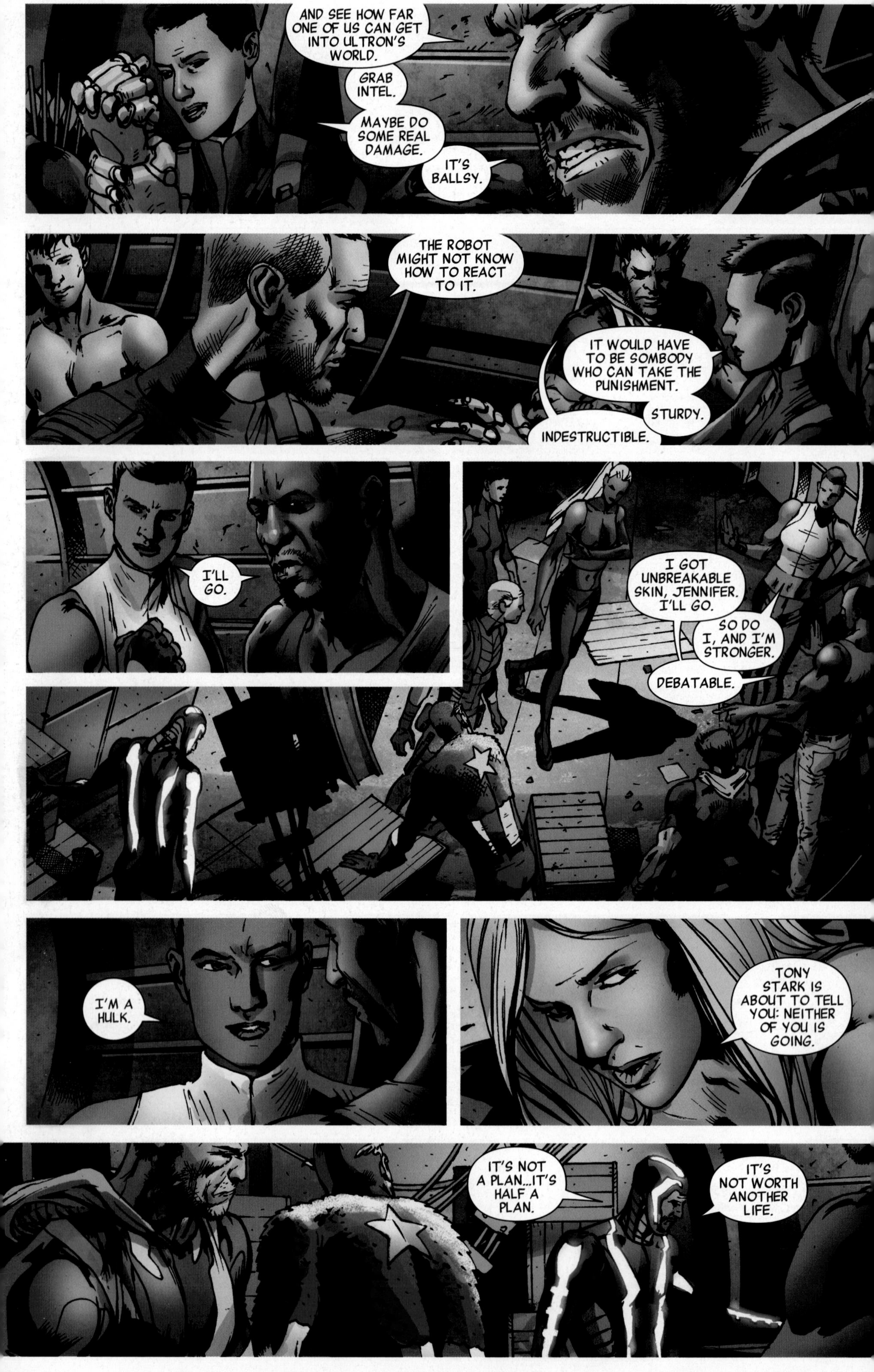
AND SEE HOW FAR ONE OF US CAN GET INTO ULTRON'S WORLD.
GRAB INTEL.
MAYBE DO SOME REAL DAMAGE.
IT'S BALLSY.
THE ROBOT MIGHT NOT KNOW HOW TO REACT TO IT.
IT WOULD HAVE TO BE SOMBODY WHO CAN TAKE THE PUNISHMENT.
STURDY.
INDESTRUCTIBLE.
I'LL GO.
I GOT UNBREAKABLE SKIN, JENNIFER. I'LL GO.
SO DO I, AND I'M STRONGER.
DEBATABLE.
I'M A HULK.
TONY STARK IS ABOUT TO TELL YOU: NEITHER OF YOU IS GOING.
IT'S NOT A PLAN...IT'S HALF A PLAN.
IT'S NOT WORTH ANOTHER LIFE.

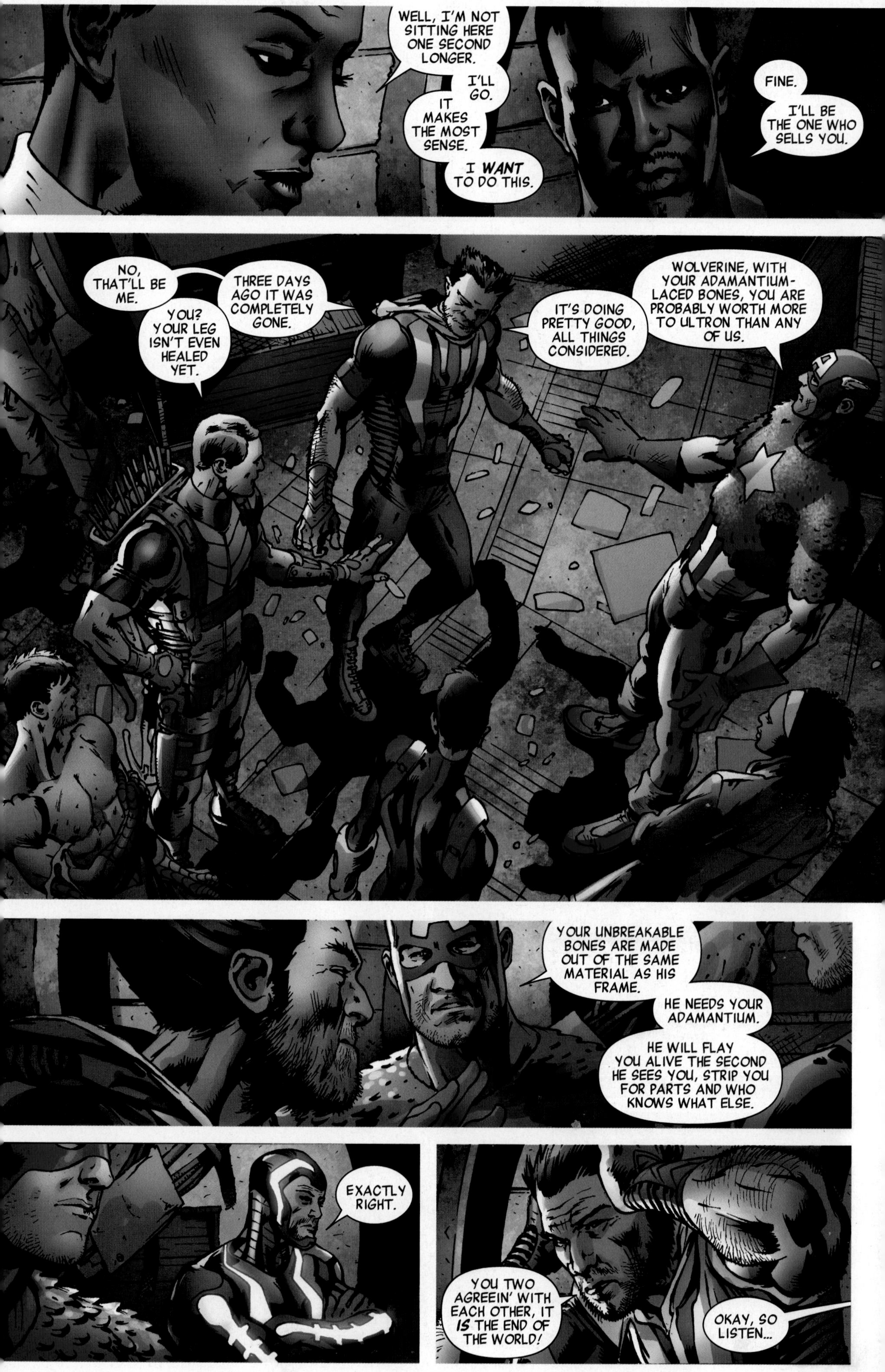
WELL, I'M NOT SITTING HERE ONE SECOND LONGER.
I'LL GO.
IT MAKES THE MOST SENSE.
I **WANT** TO DO THIS.
FINE.
I'LL BE THE ONE WHO SELLS YOU.
NO, THAT'LL BE ME.
YOU? YOUR LEG ISN'T EVEN HEALED YET.
THREE DAYS AGO IT WAS COMPLETELY GONE.
IT'S DOING PRETTY GOOD, ALL THINGS CONSIDERED.
WOLVERINE, WITH YOUR ADAMANTIUM-LACED BONES, YOU ARE PROBABLY WORTH MORE TO ULTRON THAN ANY OF US.
YOUR UNBREAKABLE BONES ARE MADE OUT OF THE SAME MATERIAL AS HIS FRAME.
HE NEEDS YOUR ADAMANTIUM.
HE WILL FLAY YOU ALIVE THE SECOND HE SEES YOU, STRIP YOU FOR PARTS AND WHO KNOWS WHAT ELSE.
EXACTLY RIGHT.
YOU TWO AGREEIN' WITH EACH OTHER, IT ***IS*** THE END OF THE WORLD!
OKAY, SO LISTEN...

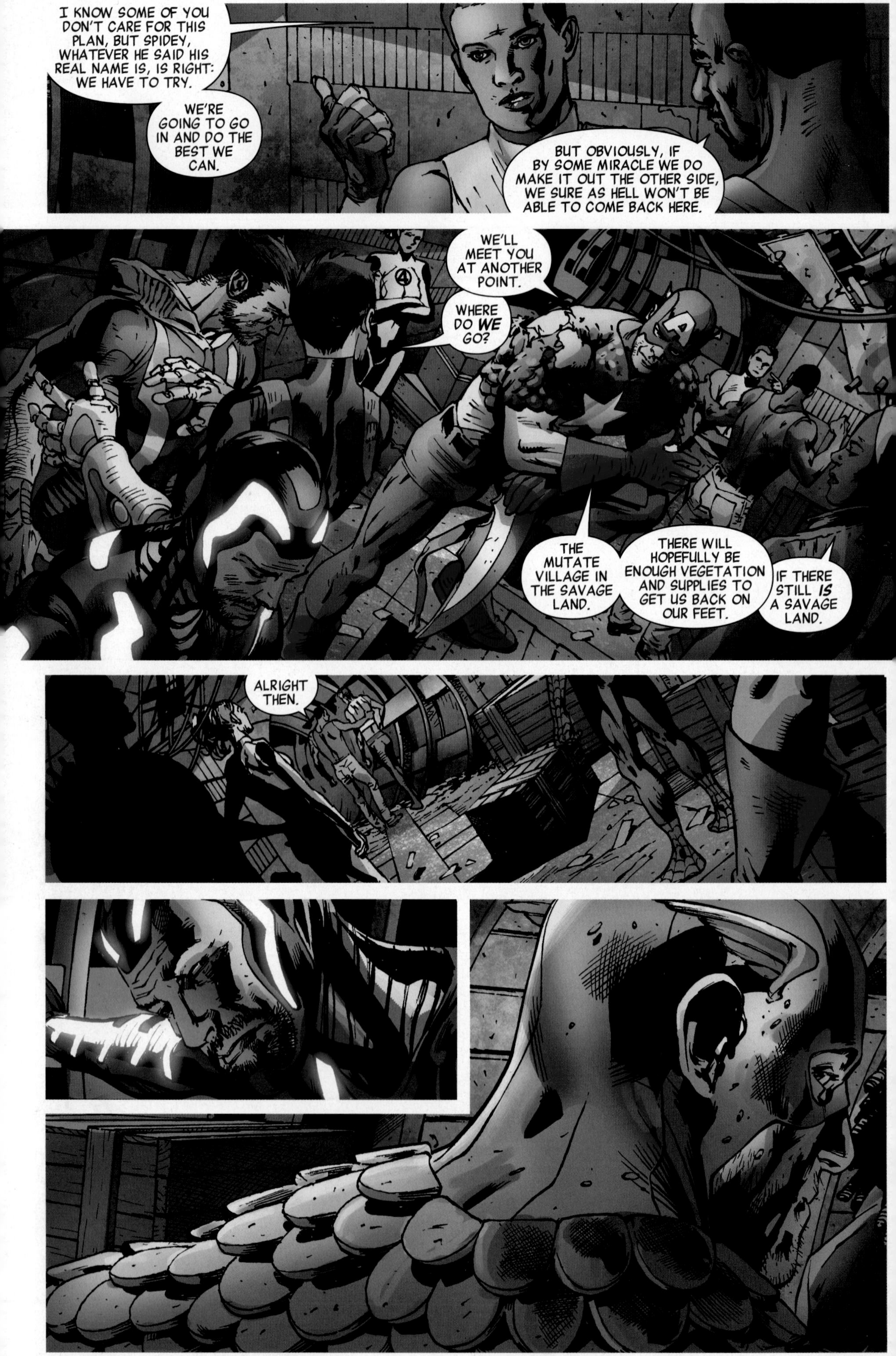
I KNOW SOME OF YOU DON'T CARE FOR THIS PLAN, BUT SPIDEY, WHATEVER HE SAID HIS REAL NAME IS, IS RIGHT: WE HAVE TO TRY.
WE'RE GOING TO GO IN AND DO THE BEST WE CAN.
BUT OBVIOUSLY, IF BY SOME MIRACLE WE DO MAKE IT OUT THE OTHER SIDE, WE SURE AS HELL WON'T BE ABLE TO COME BACK HERE.
WE'LL MEET YOU AT ANOTHER POINT.
WHERE DO WE GO?
THE MUTATE VILLAGE IN THE SAVAGE LAND.
THERE WILL HOPEFULLY BE ENOUGH VEGETATION AND SUPPLIES TO GET US BACK ON OUR FEET.
IF THERE STILL IS A SAVAGE LAND.
ALRIGHT THEN.

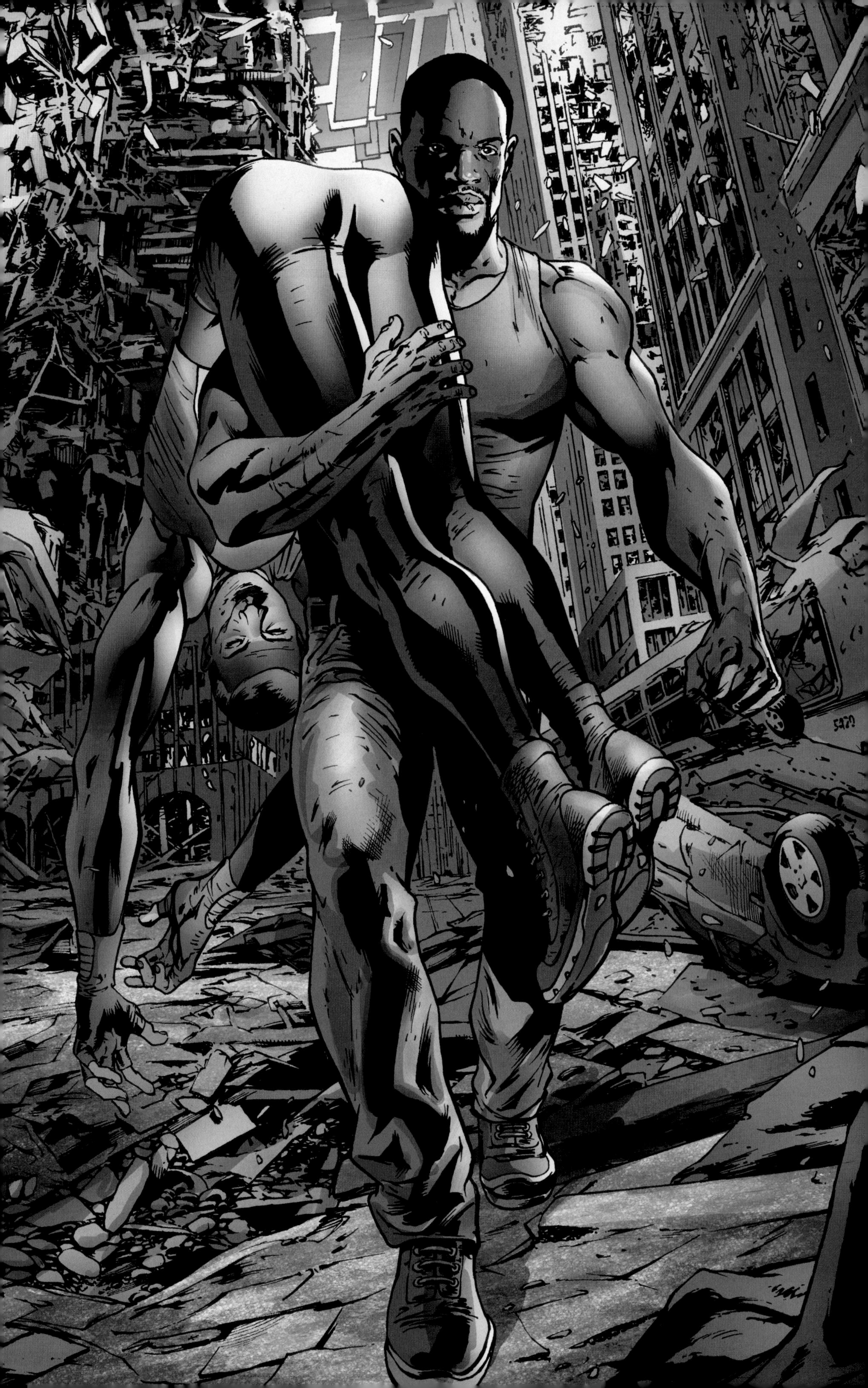

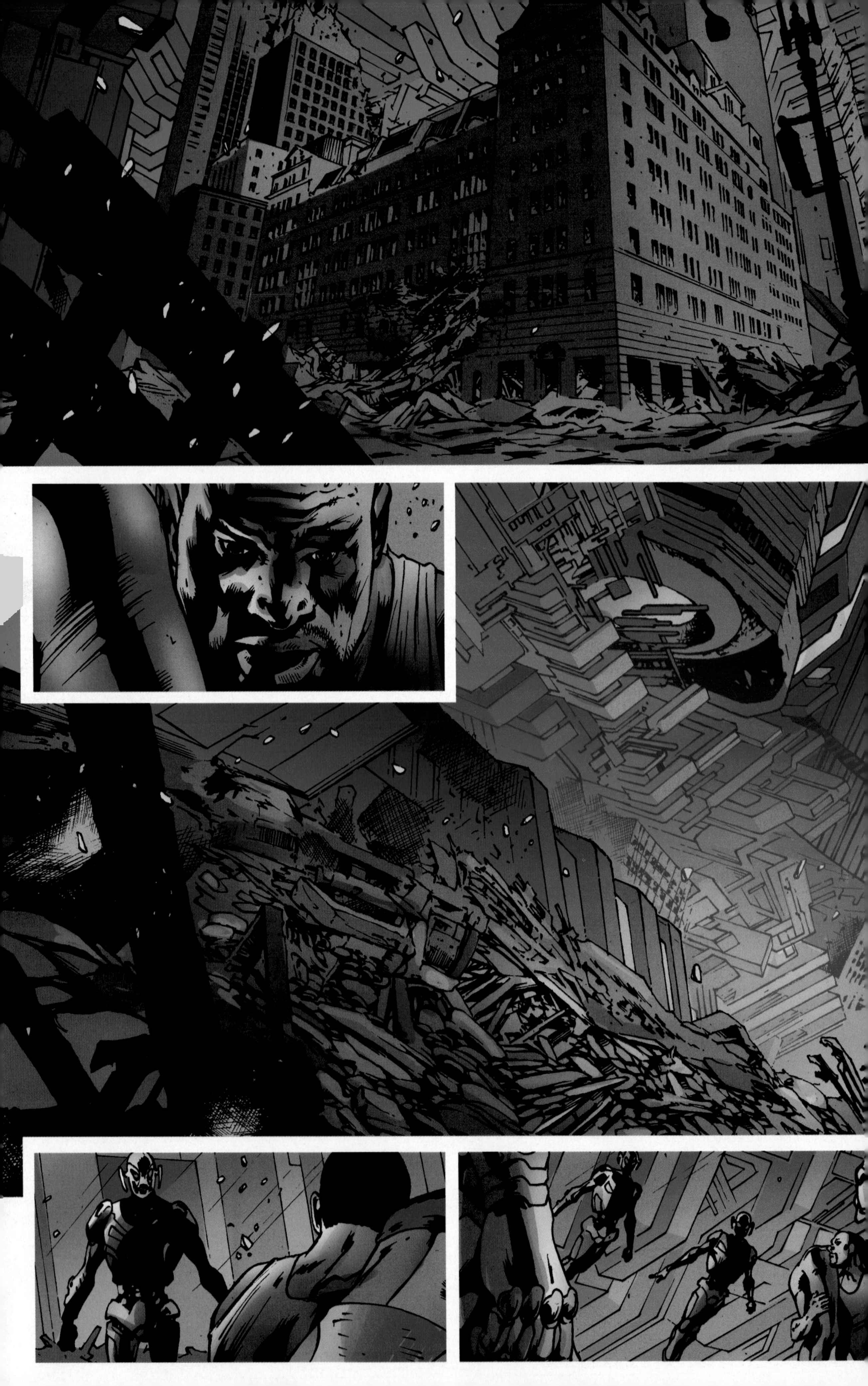

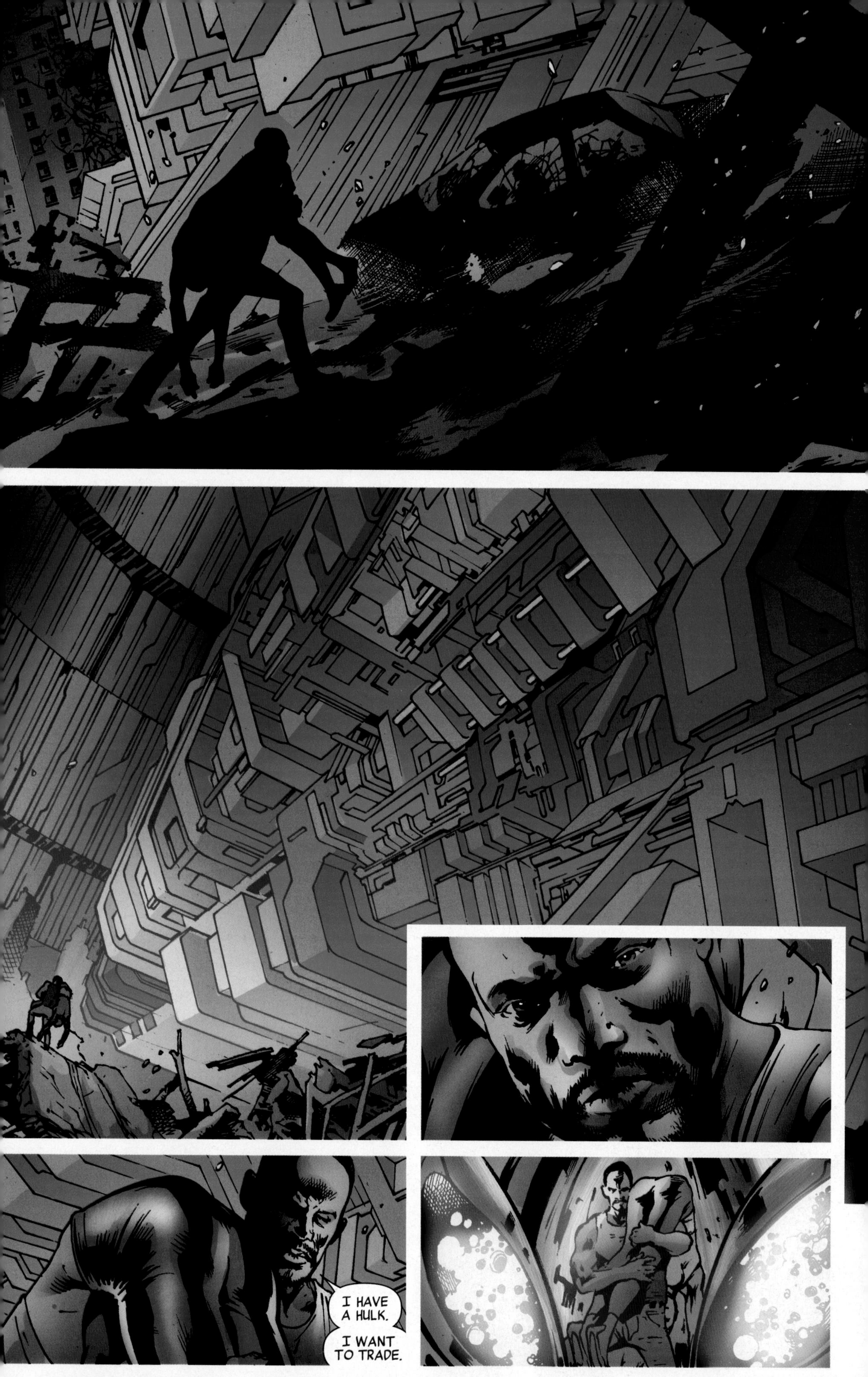
I HAVE A HULK.
I WANT TO TRADE.

CHICAGO.

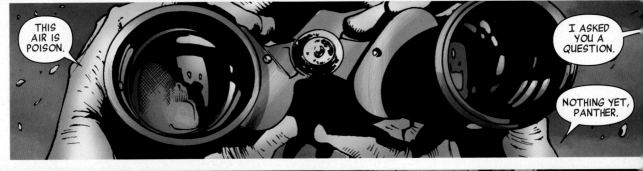

THIS AIR IS POISON.

I ASKED YOU A QUESTION.

NOTHING YET, PANTHER.

WE CAN'T BE EXPOSED THIS LONG.

I'M DOING THE BEST I CAN, DAVE.

MY NAME ISN'T DAVE, TASKMASTER.

WELL, I'M NOT CALLING YOU RED HULK, SO I'VE DECIDED TO CALL YOU DAVE.

HURRY UP.

HOLD ON...

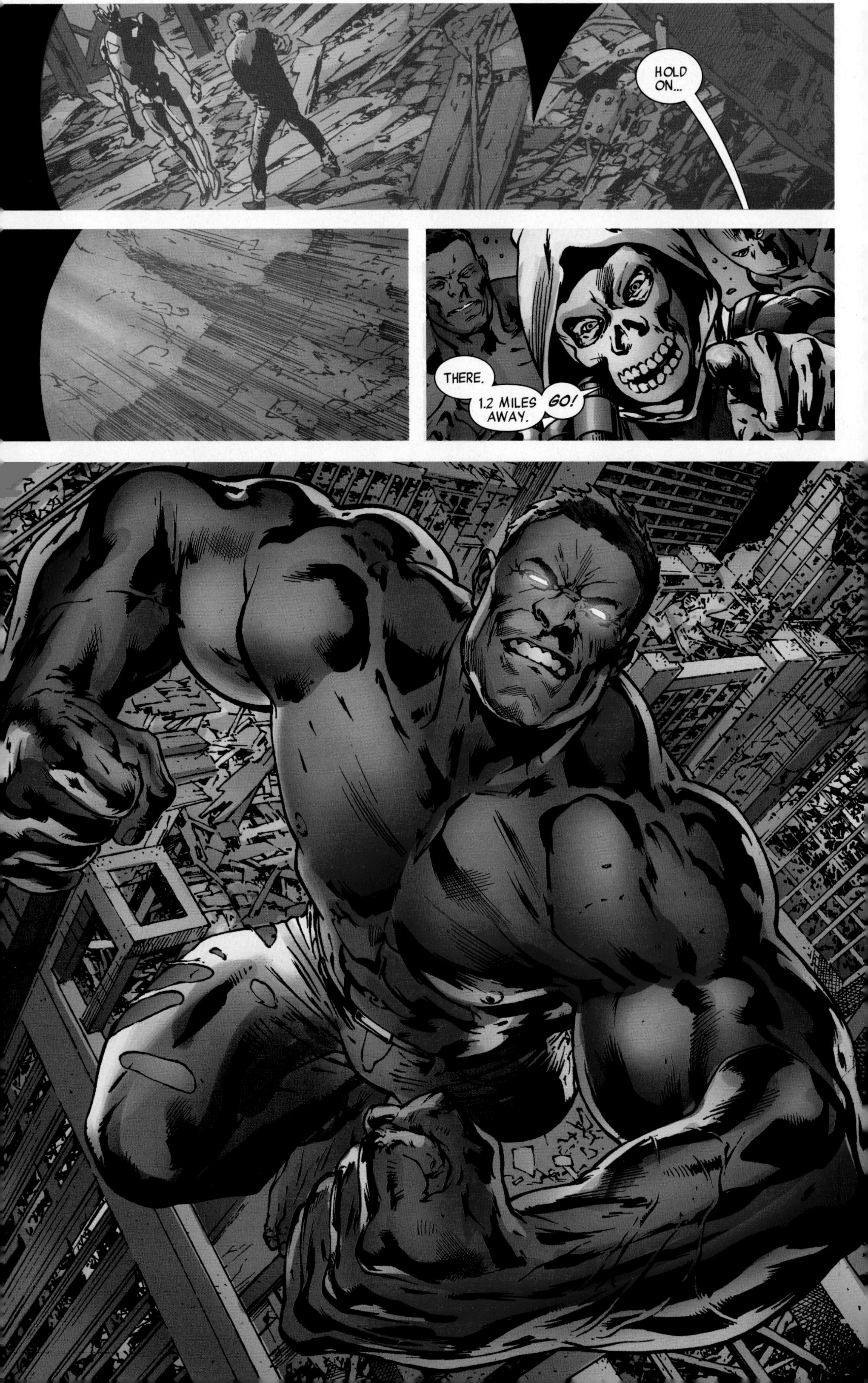
HOLD ON...
THERE.
1.2 MILES AWAY.
GO!

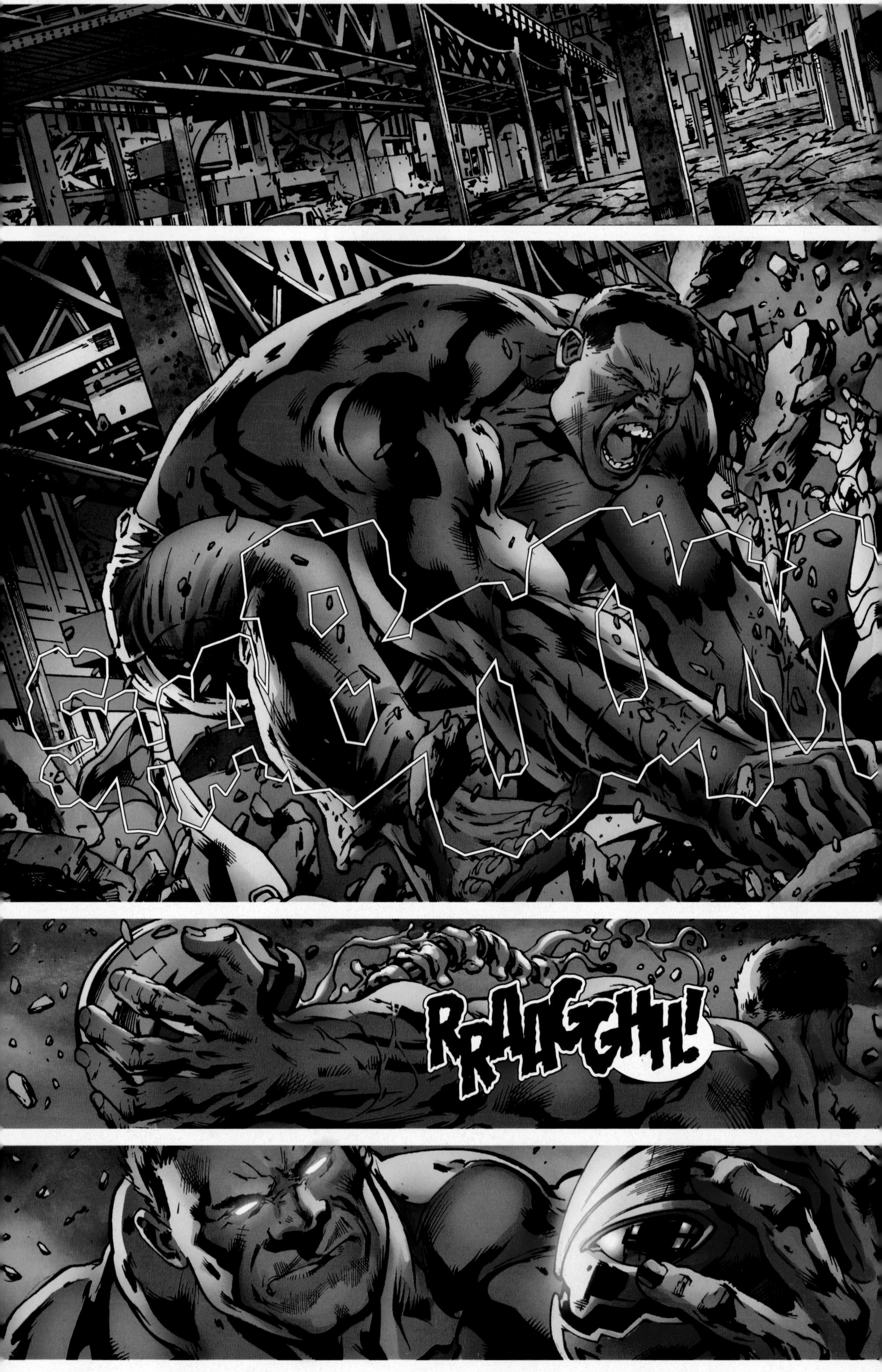
RRAUGHH!

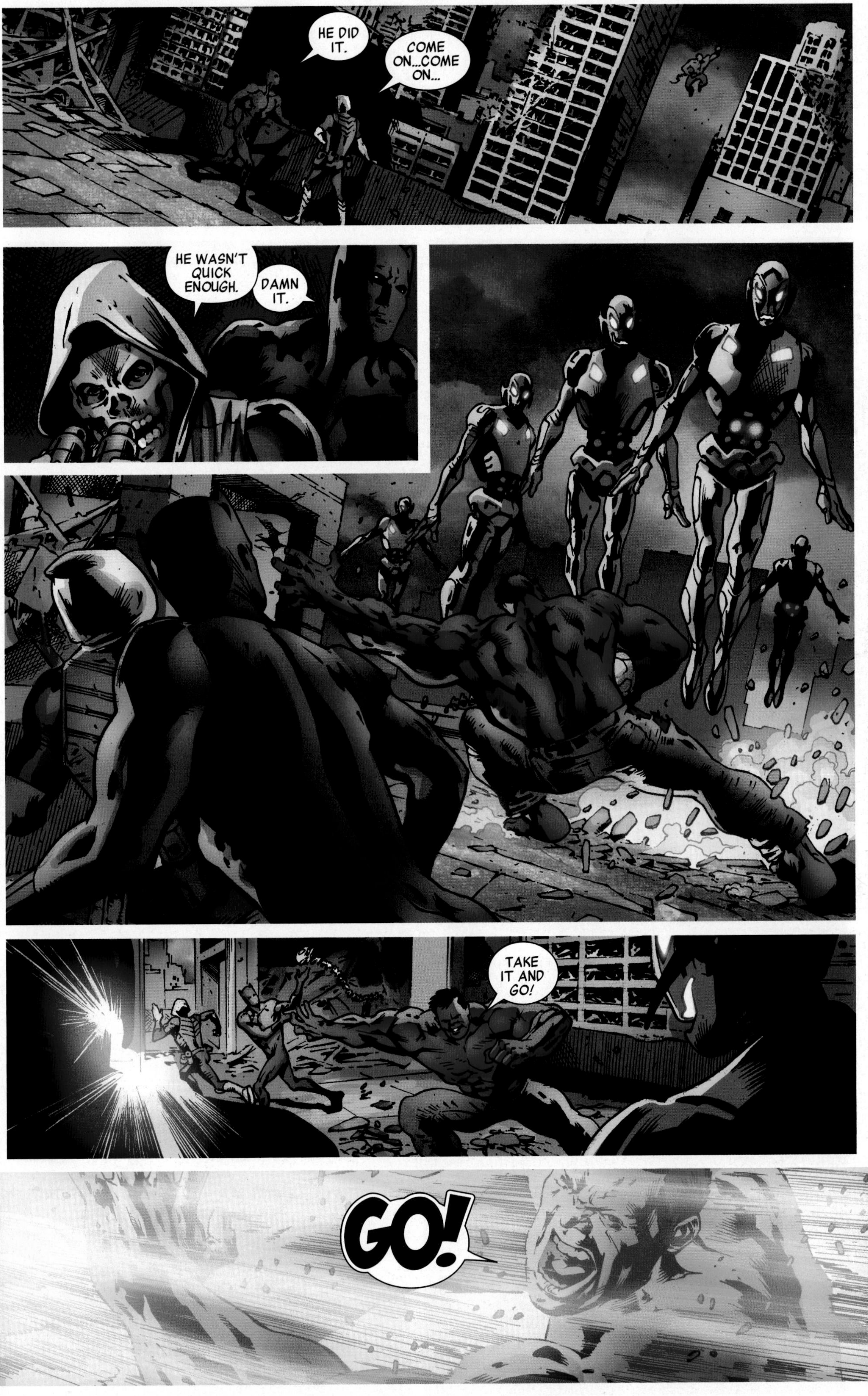
HE DID IT.
COME ON...COME ON...
HE WASN'T QUICK ENOUGH.
DAMN IT.
TAKE IT AND GO!
GO!

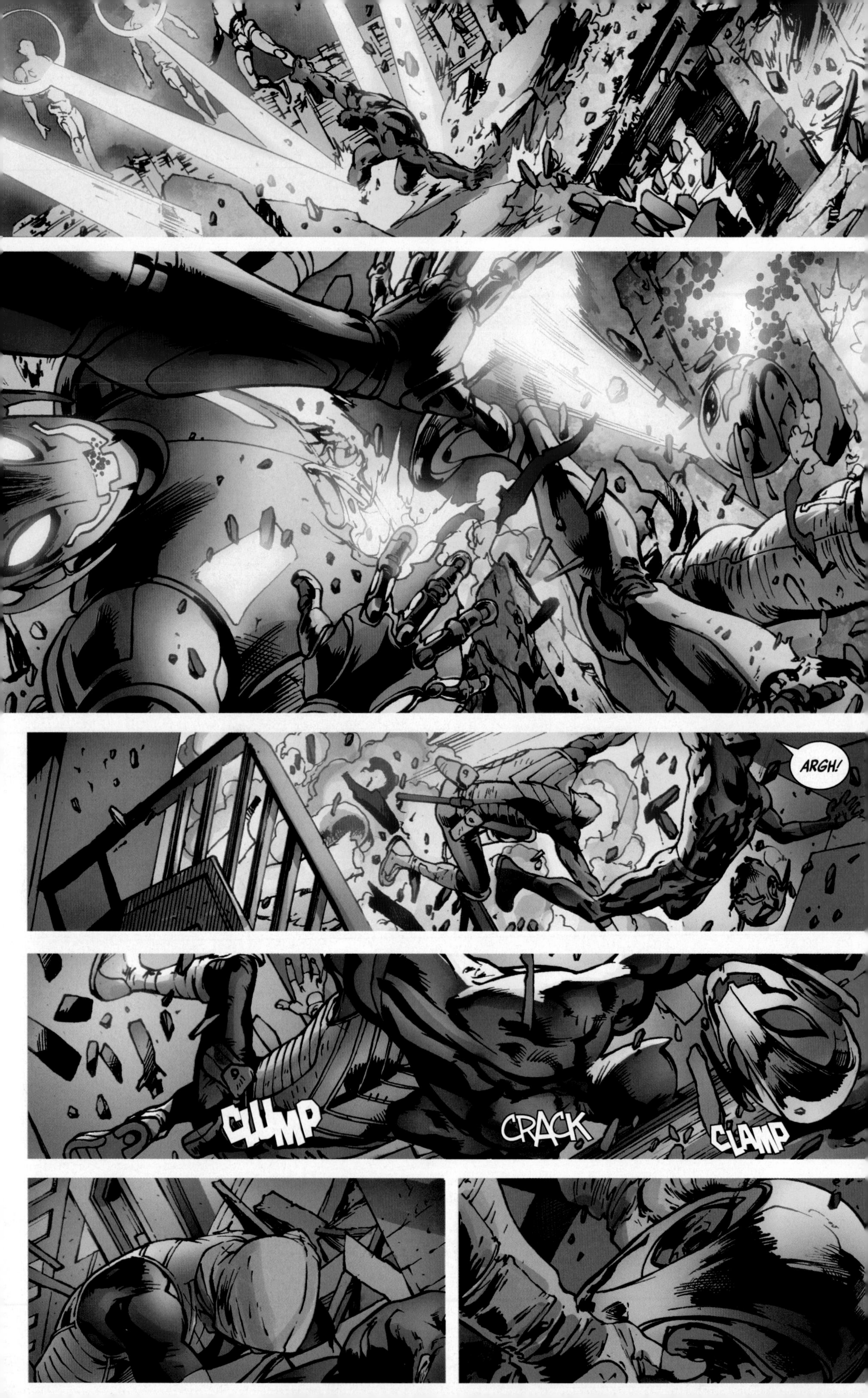
ARGH!
CLUMP
CRACK
CLAMP

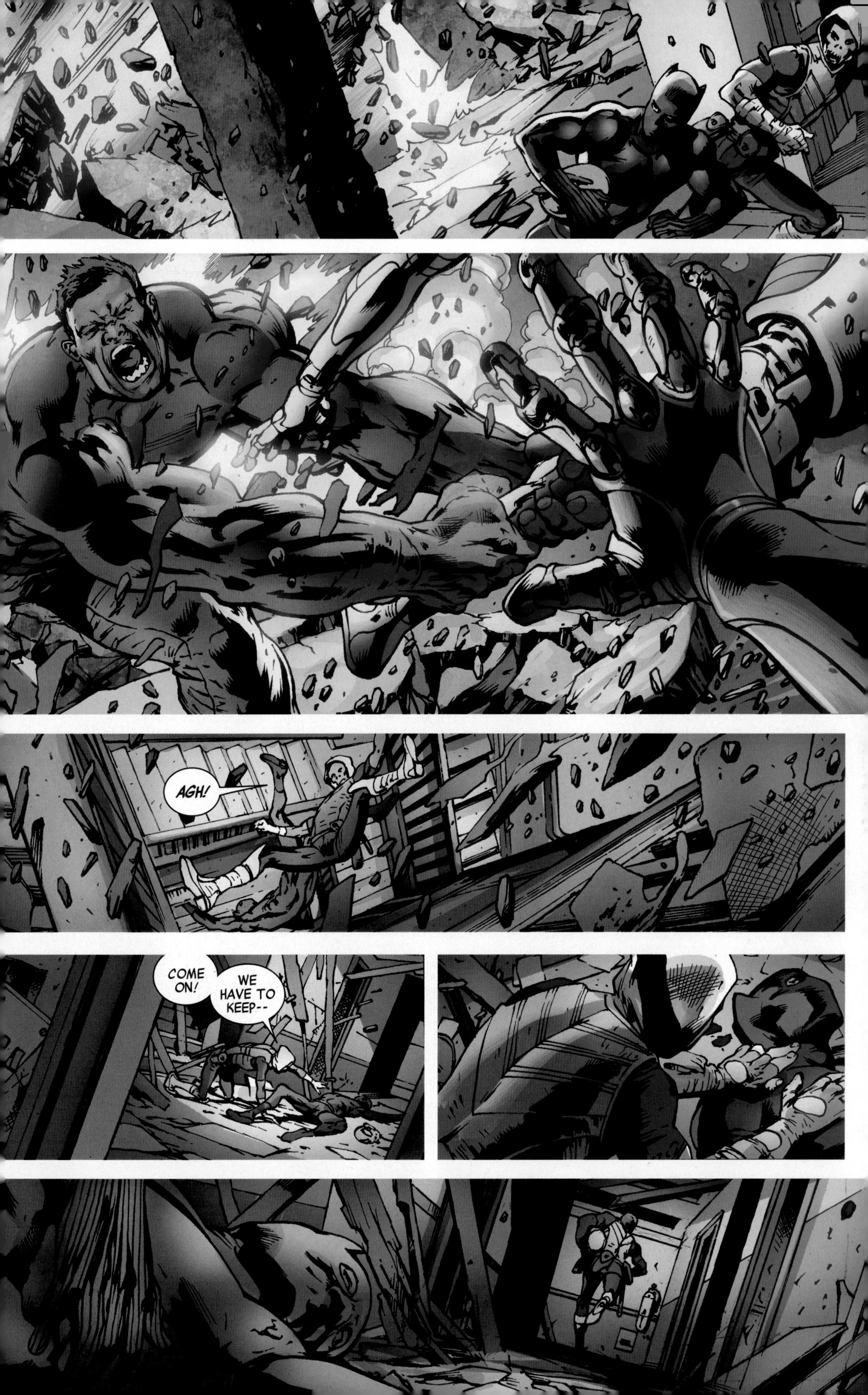
AGH!
COME ON!
WE HAVE TO KEEP--

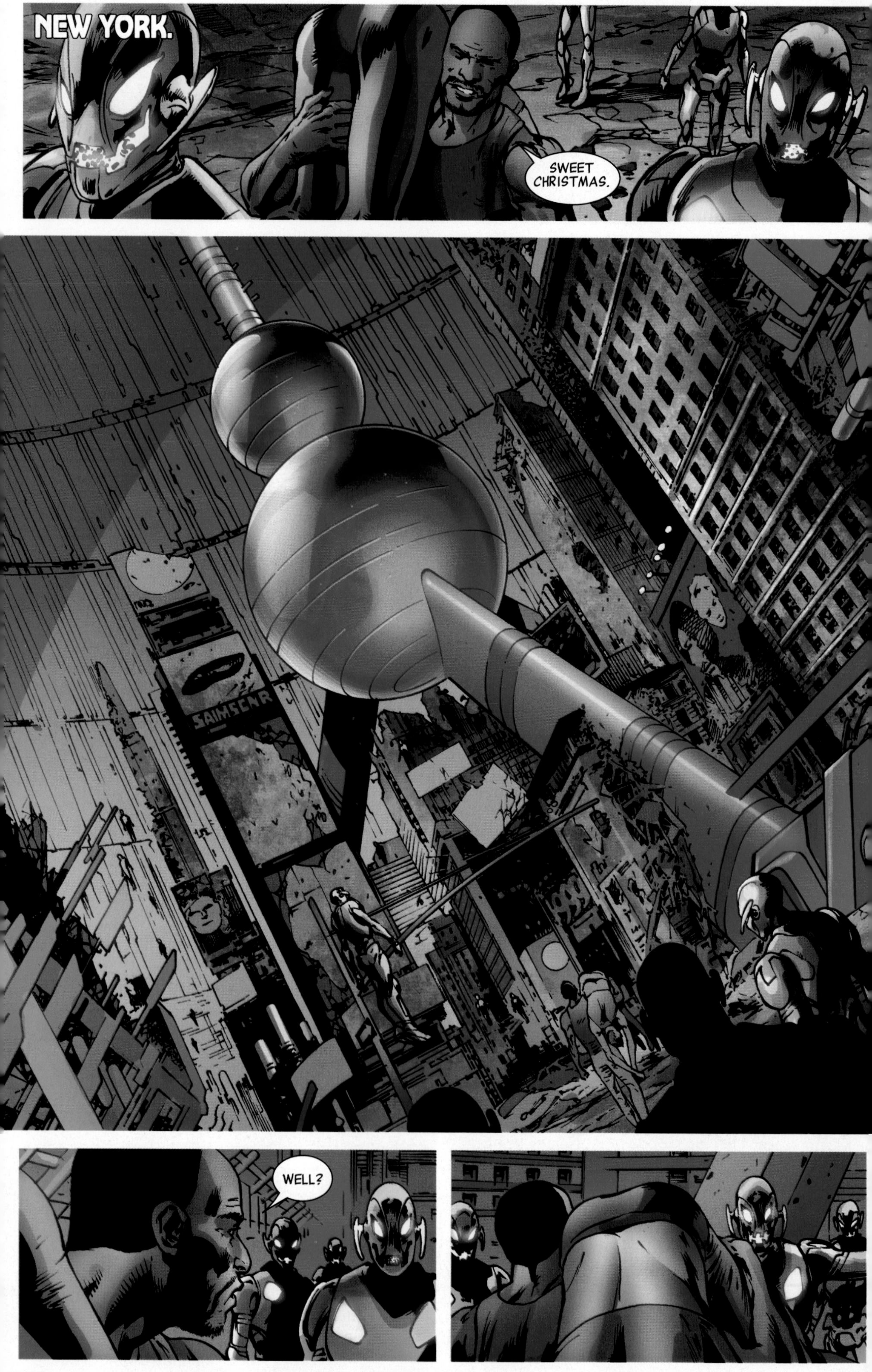
NEW YORK.
SWEET CHRISTMAS.
WELL?

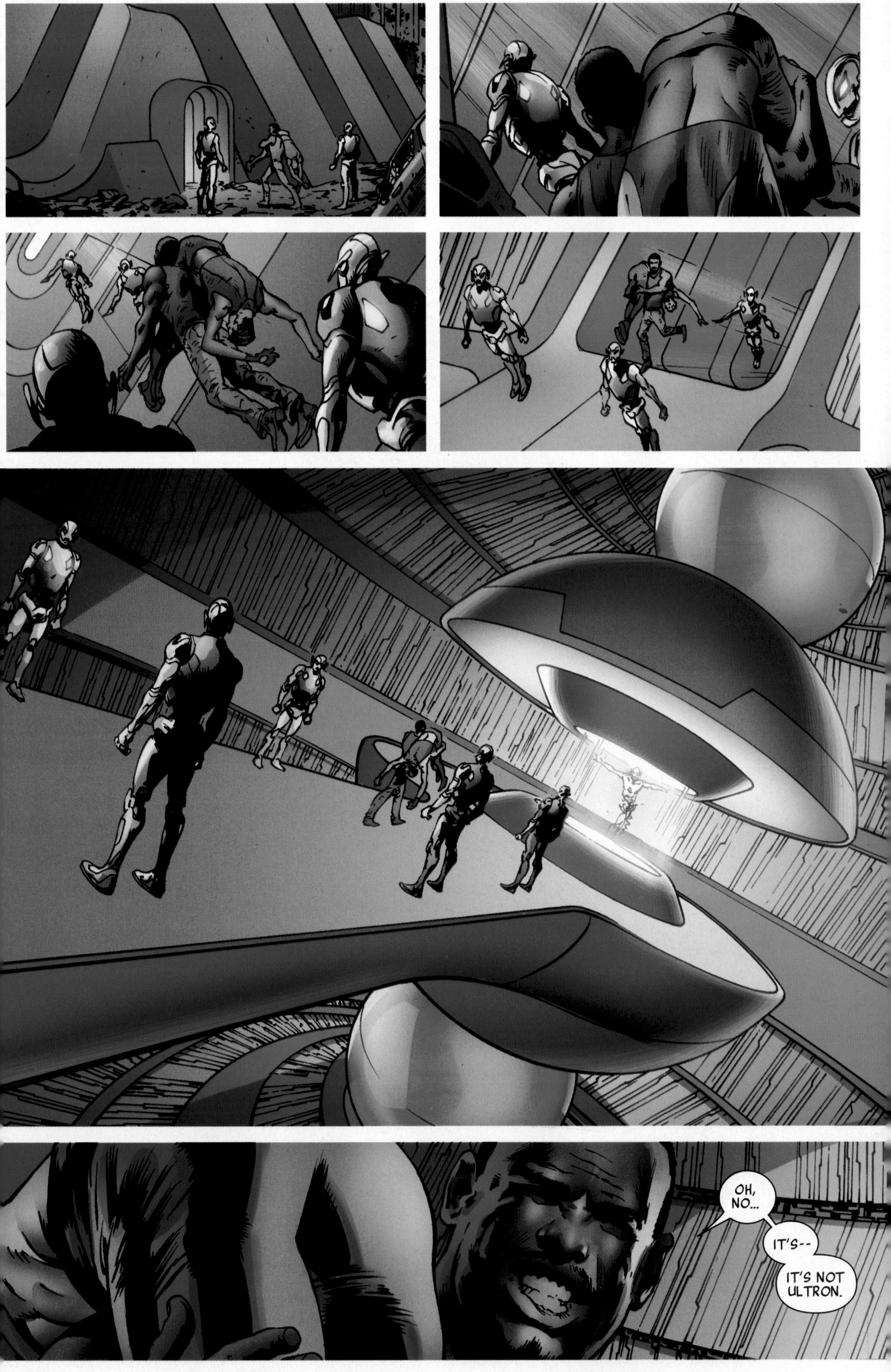
OH, NO...
IT'S--
IT'S NOT ULTRON.

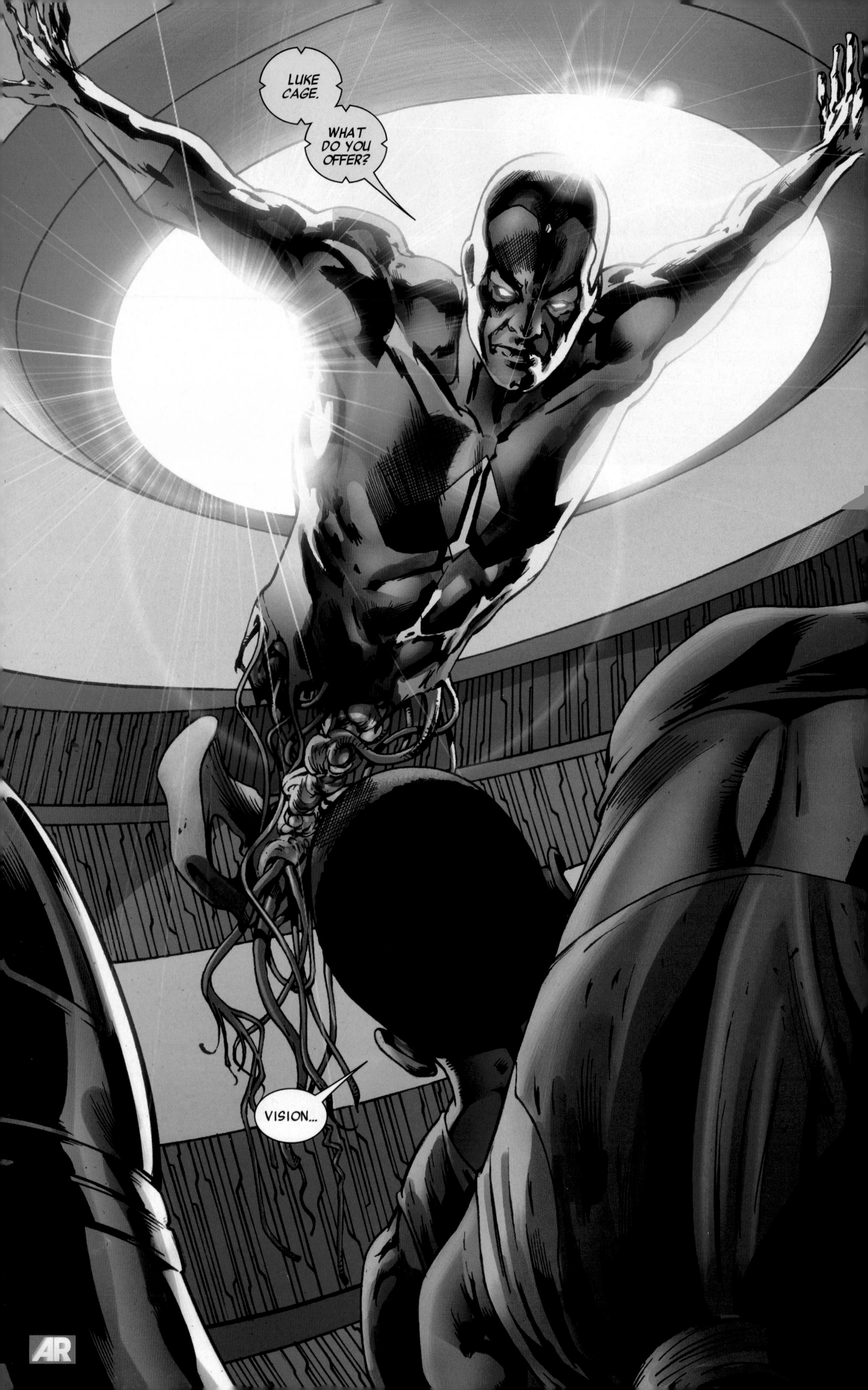
LUKE CAGE.
WHAT DO YOU OFFER?
VISION...
AR

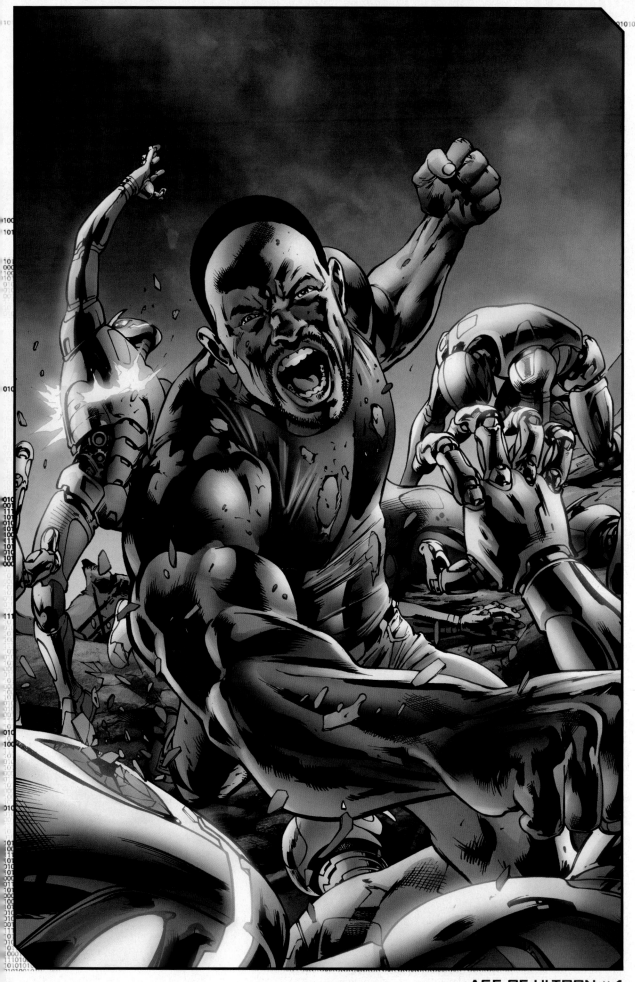

AGE OF ULTRON #4

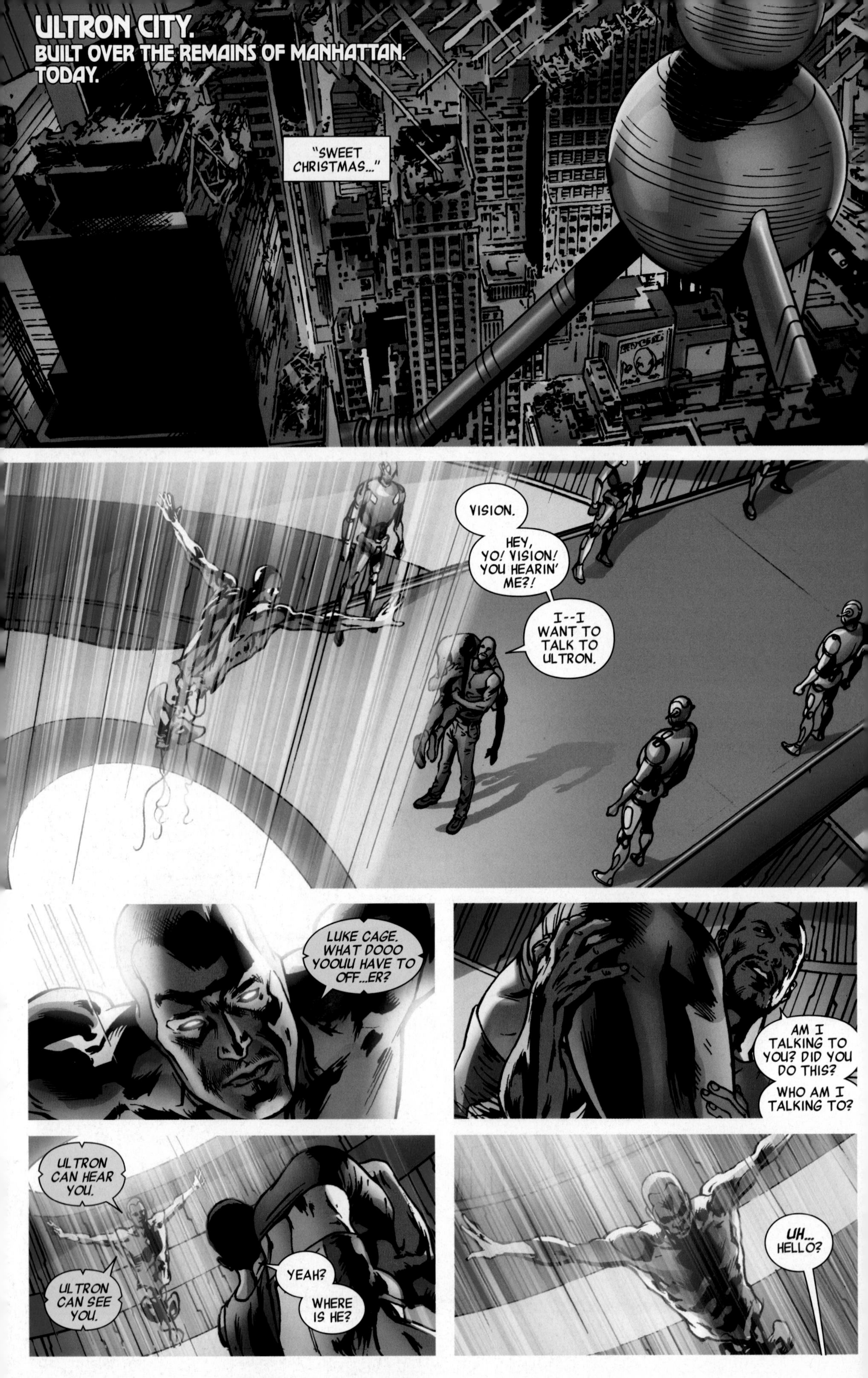
ULTRON CITY.
BUILT OVER THE REMAINS OF MANHATTAN.
TODAY.
"SWEET CHRISTMAS..."
VISION.
HEY, YO! VISION! YOU HEARIN' ME?!
I--I WANT TO TALK TO ULTRON.
LUKE CAGE. WHAT DOOO YOOUU HAVE TO OFF...ER?
AM I TALKING TO YOU? DID YOU DO THIS?
WHO AM I TALKING TO?
ULTRON CAN HEAR YOU.
ULTRON CAN SEE YOU.
YEAH?
WHERE IS HE?
UH... HELLO?

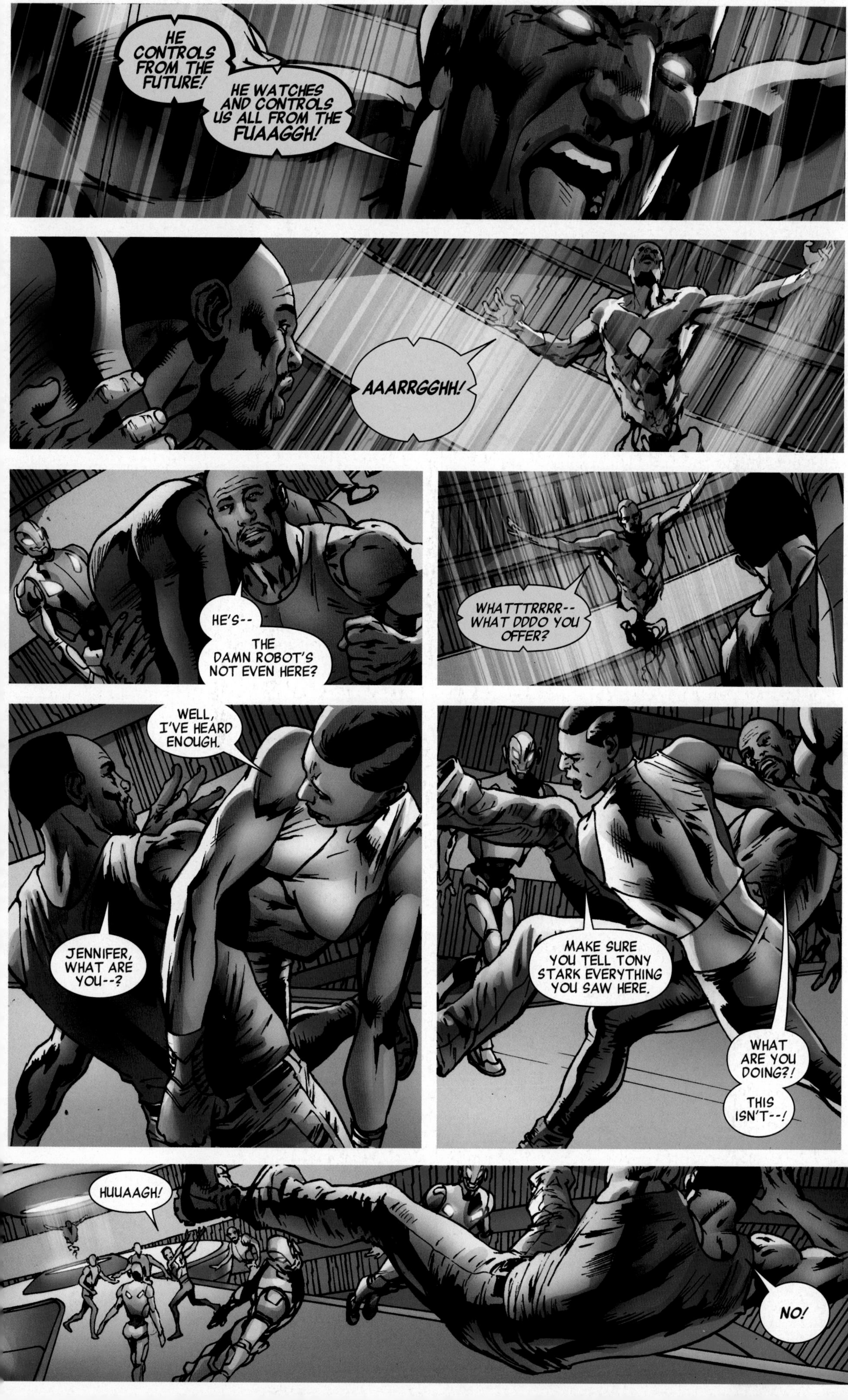

HE CONTROLS FROM THE FUTURE!
HE WATCHES AND CONTROLS US ALL FROM THE FUAAGGH!
AAARRGGHH!
HE'S--
THE DAMN ROBOT'S NOT EVEN HERE?
WHATTTRRRR-- WHAT DDDO YOU OFFER?
WELL, I'VE HEARD ENOUGH.
JENNIFER, WHAT ARE YOU--?
MAKE SURE YOU TELL TONY STARK EVERYTHING YOU SAW HERE.
WHAT ARE YOU DOING?!
THIS ISN'T--!
HUUAAGH!
NO!

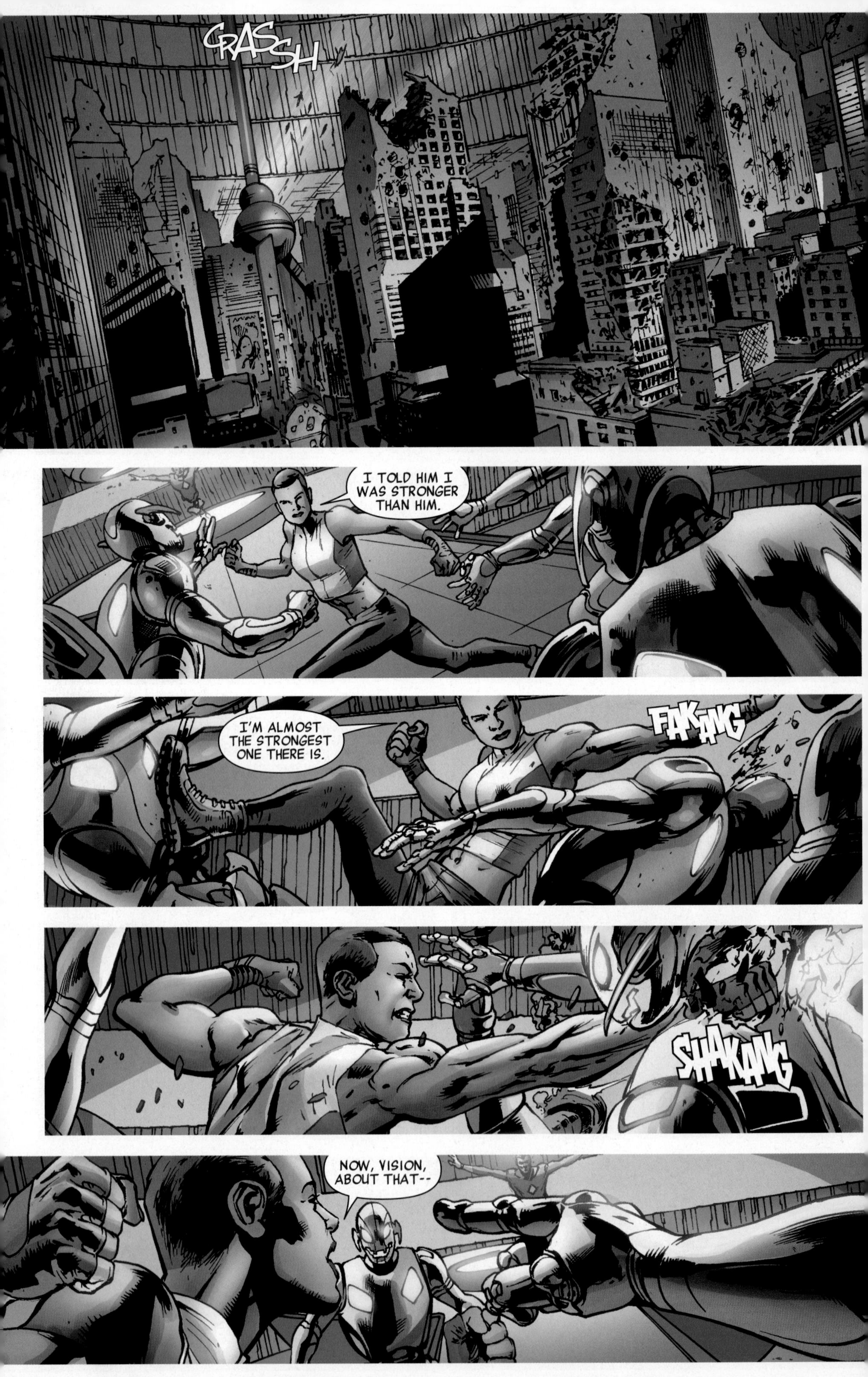
CRASSH
I TOLD HIM I WAS STRONGER THAN HIM.
I'M ALMOST THE STRONGEST ONE THERE IS.
FAKANG
SHAKANG
NOW, VISION, ABOUT THAT--

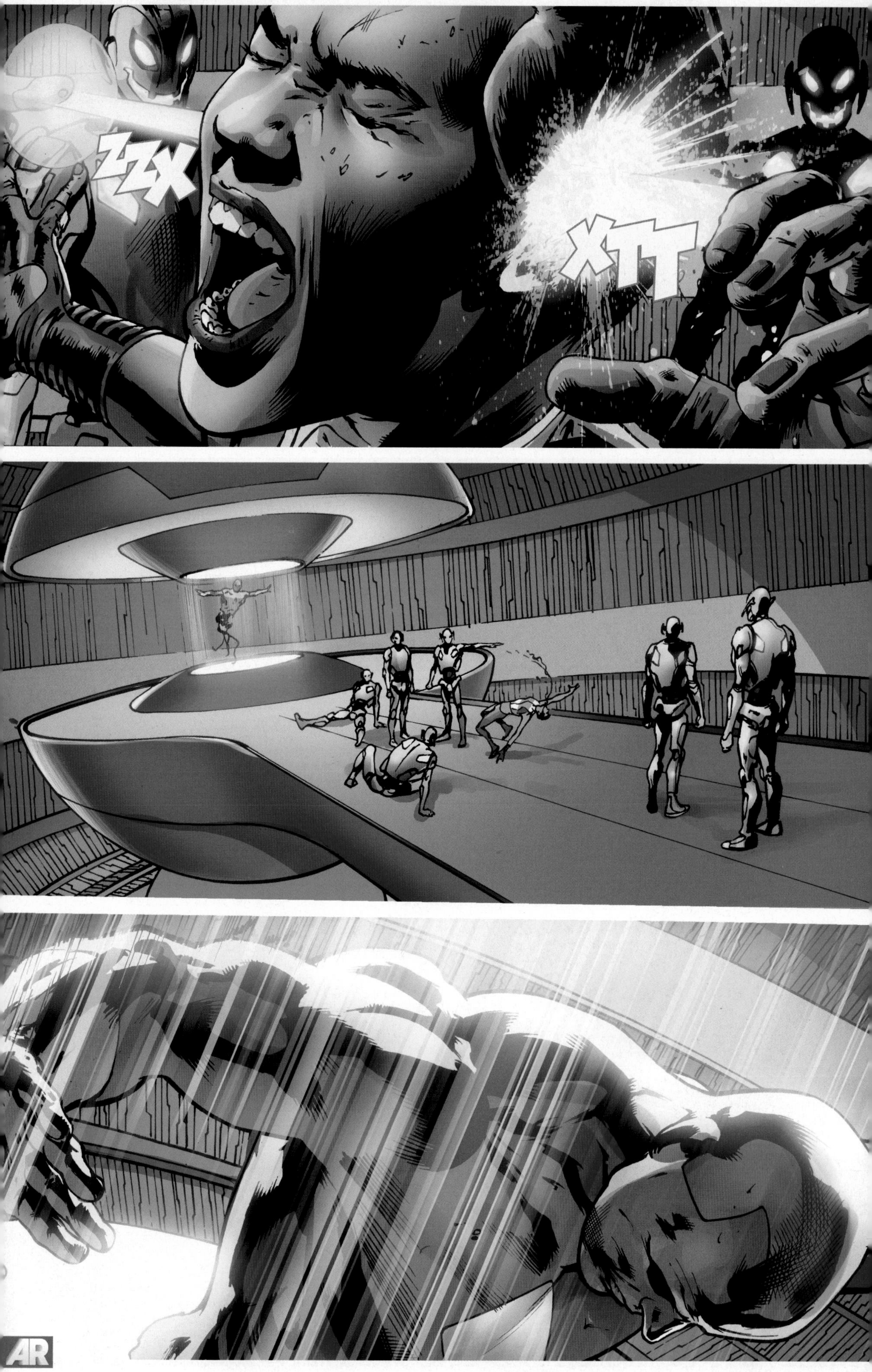
ZZX
XTT

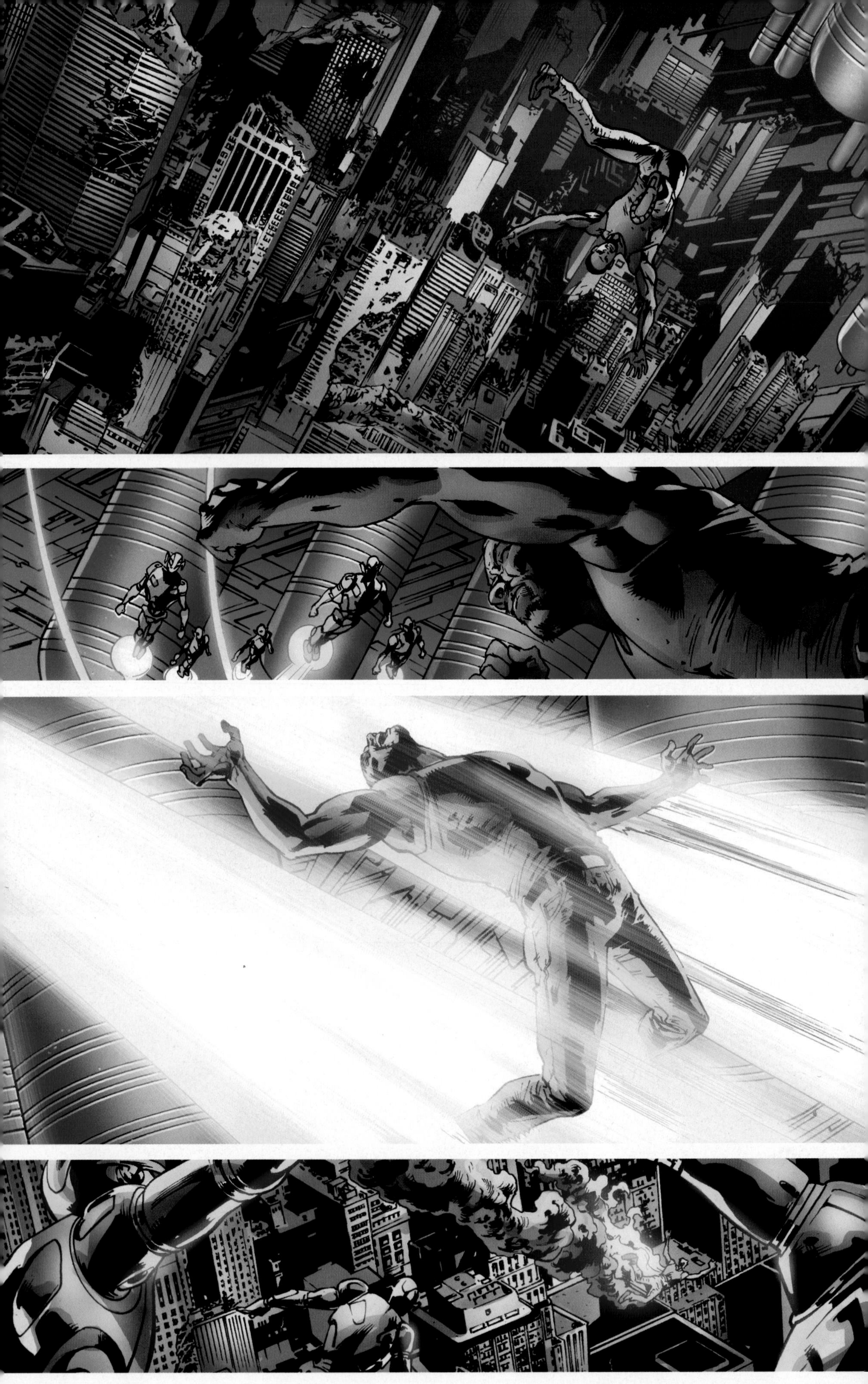

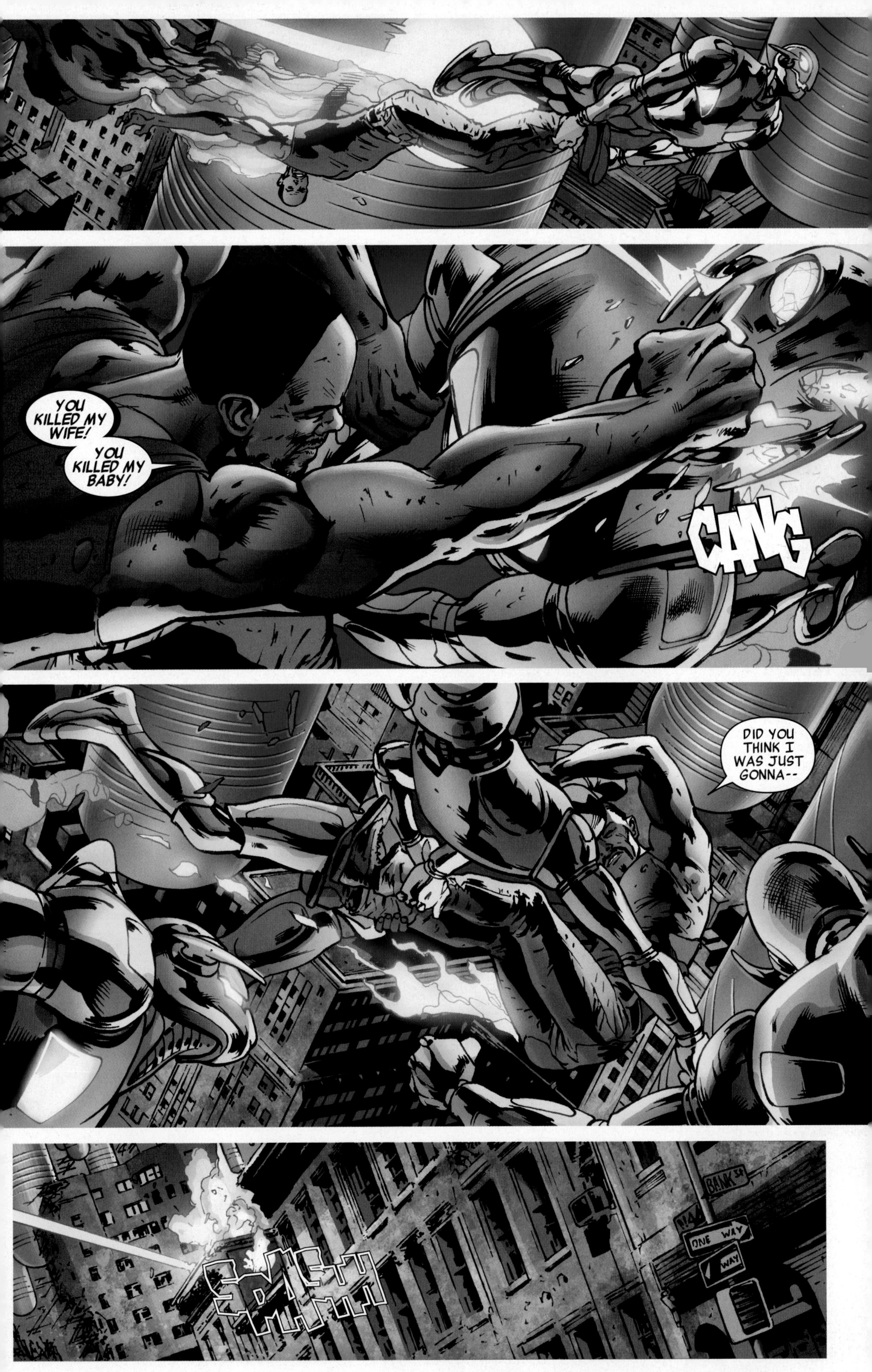
YOU KILLED MY WIFE!
YOU KILLED MY BABY!
CANG
DID YOU THINK I WAS JUST GONNA--
BANK ST
ONE WAY
WAY

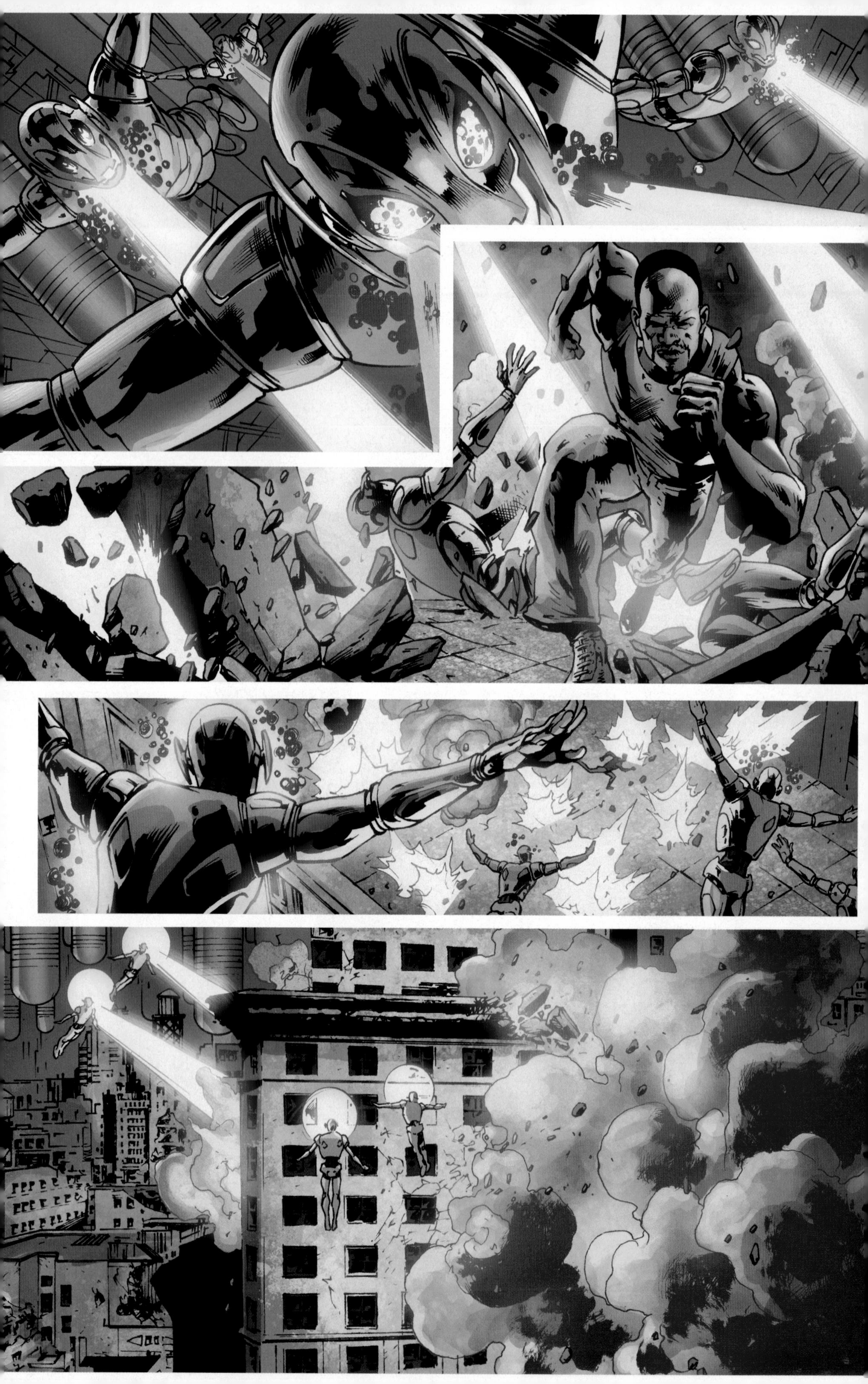

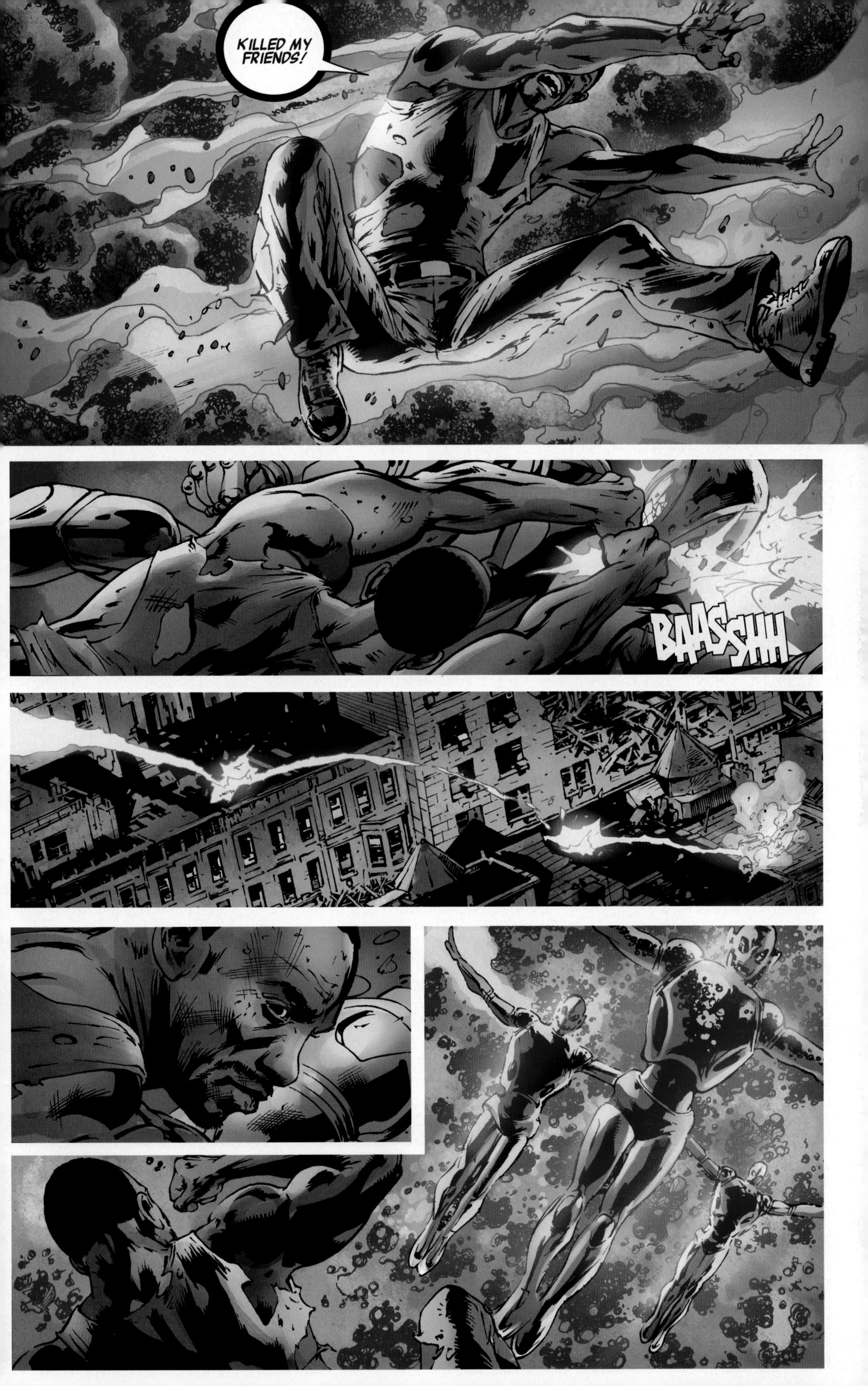
KILLED MY FRIENDS!
BAASHH

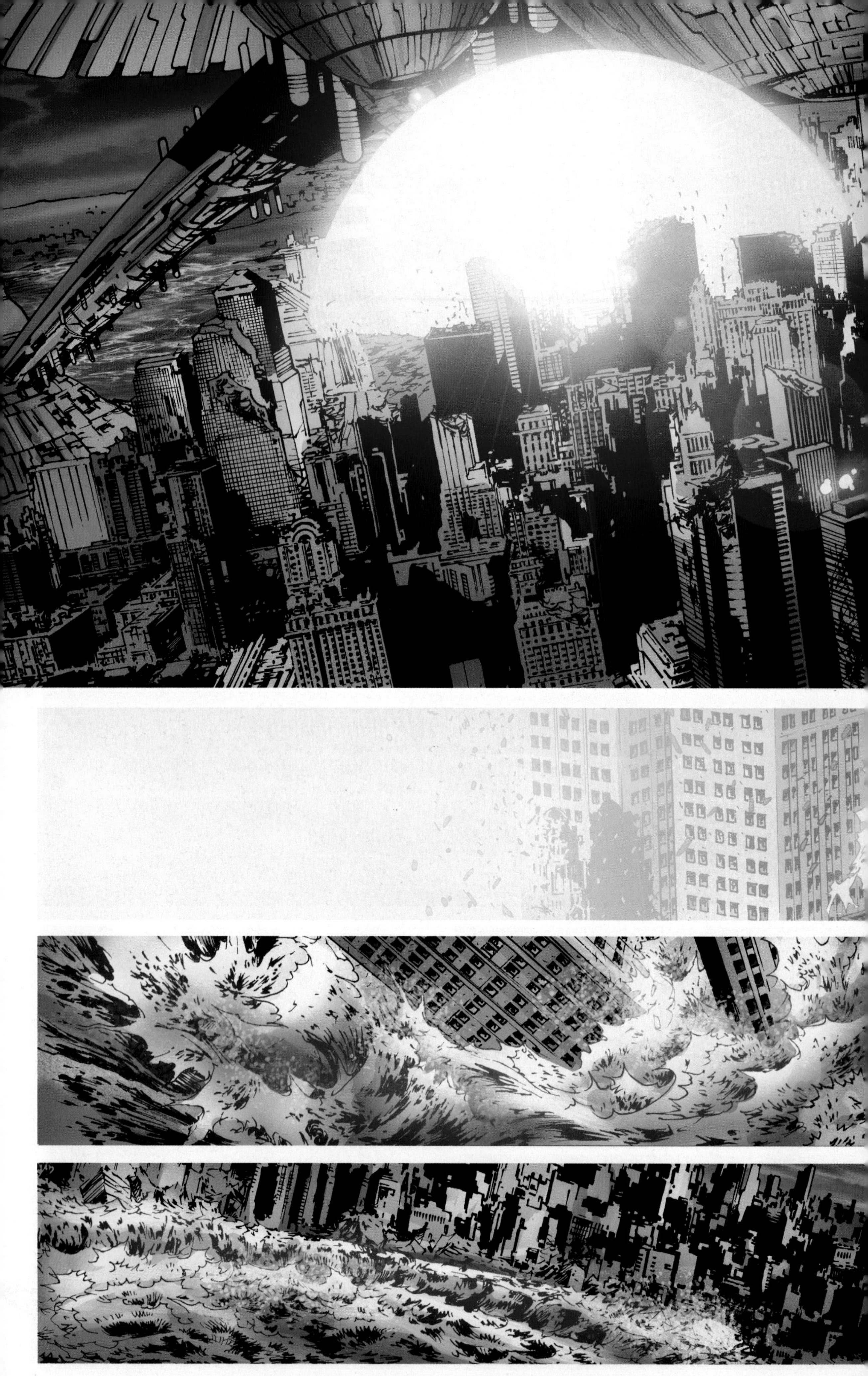

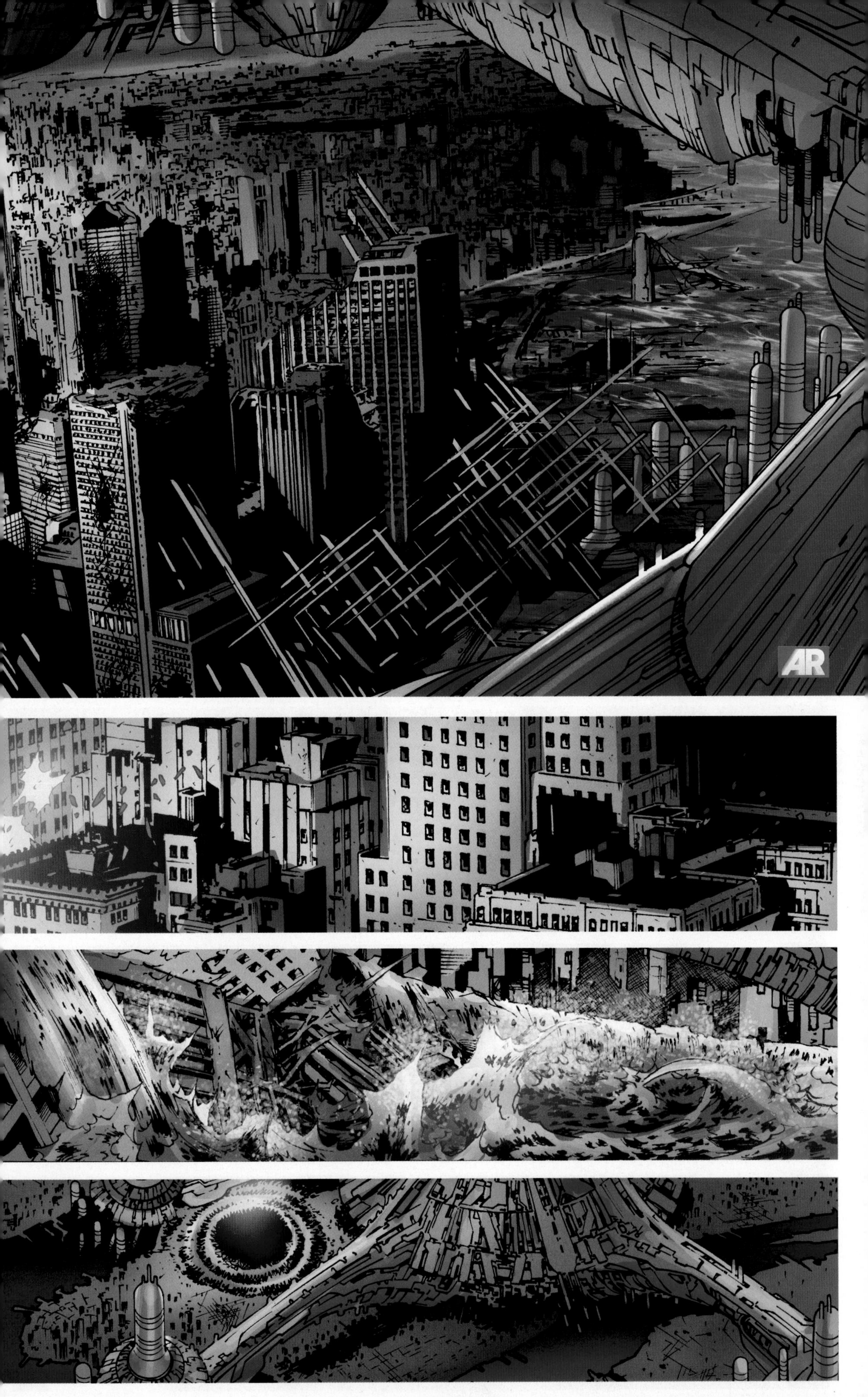

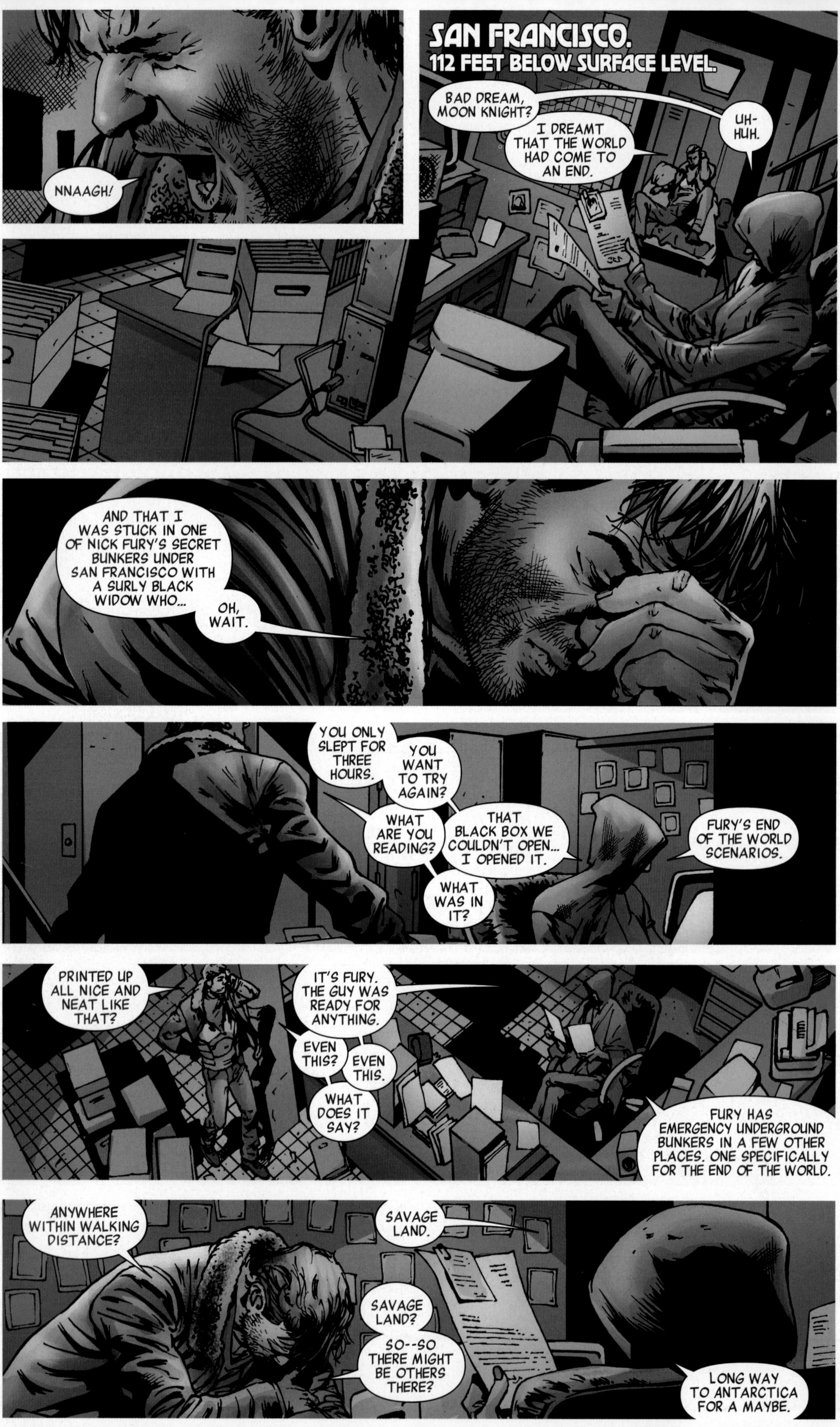
NNAAGH!
SAN FRANCISCO.
112 FEET BELOW SURFACE LEVEL.
BAD DREAM, MOON KNIGHT?
UH-HUH.
I DREAMT THAT THE WORLD HAD COME TO AN END.
AND THAT I WAS STUCK IN ONE OF NICK FURY'S SECRET BUNKERS UNDER SAN FRANCISCO WITH A SURLY BLACK WIDOW WHO...
OH, WAIT.
YOU ONLY SLEPT FOR THREE HOURS.
YOU WANT TO TRY AGAIN?
WHAT ARE YOU READING?
THAT BLACK BOX WE COULDN'T OPEN... I OPENED IT.
WHAT WAS IN IT?
FURY'S END OF THE WORLD SCENARIOS.
PRINTED UP ALL NICE AND NEAT LIKE THAT?
IT'S FURY. THE GUY WAS READY FOR ANYTHING.
EVEN THIS?
EVEN THIS.
WHAT DOES IT SAY?
FURY HAS EMERGENCY UNDERGROUND BUNKERS IN A FEW OTHER PLACES. ONE SPECIFICALLY FOR THE END OF THE WORLD.
ANYWHERE WITHIN WALKING DISTANCE?
SAVAGE LAND.
SAVAGE LAND?
SO--SO THERE MIGHT BE OTHERS THERE?
LONG WAY TO ANTARCTICA FOR A MAYBE.

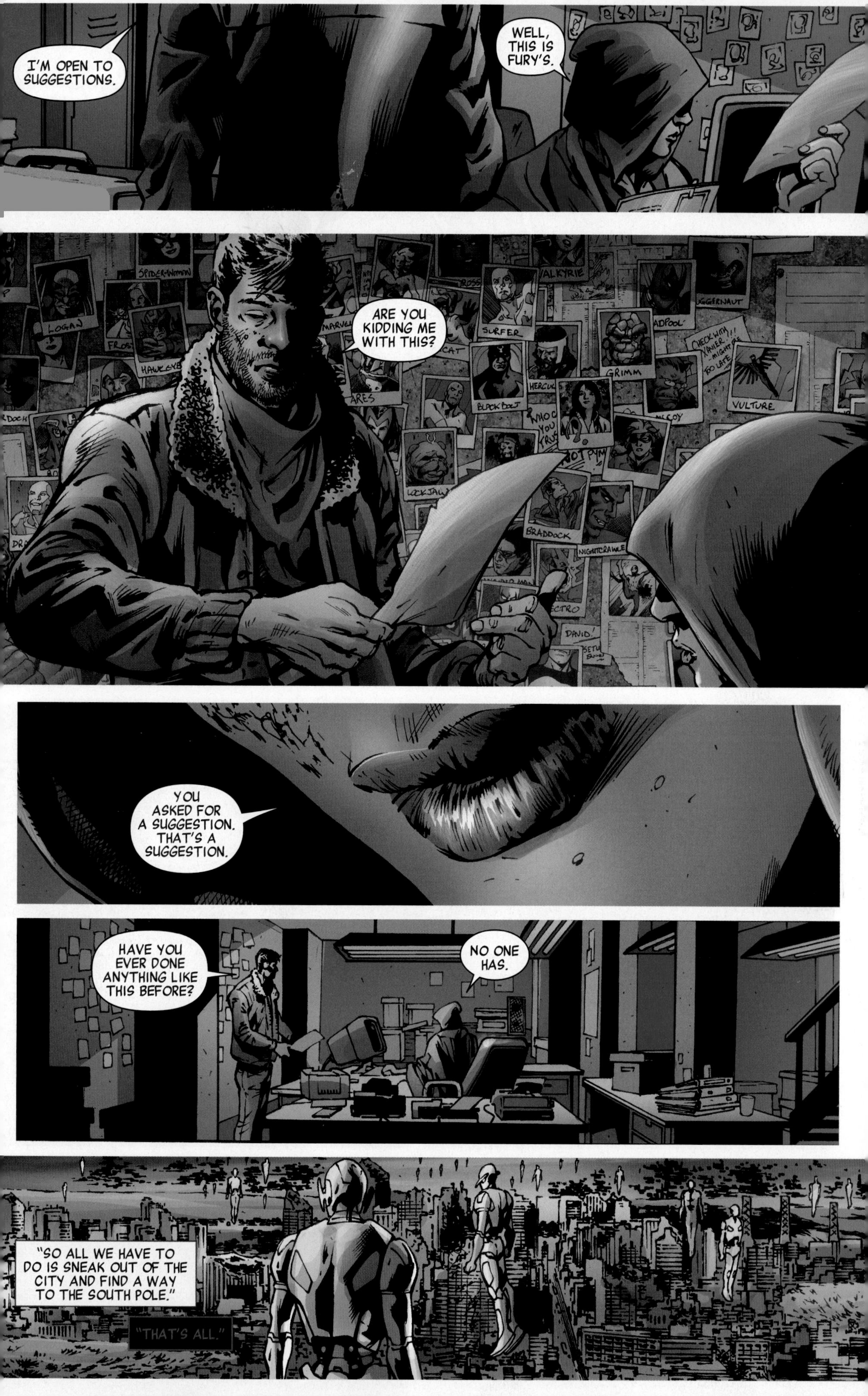
I'M OPEN TO SUGGESTIONS.
WELL, THIS IS FURY'S.
ARE YOU KIDDING ME WITH THIS?
YOU ASKED FOR A SUGGESTION. THAT'S A SUGGESTION.
HAVE YOU EVER DONE ANYTHING LIKE THIS BEFORE?
NO ONE HAS.
"SO ALL WE HAVE TO DO IS SNEAK OUT OF THE CITY AND FIND A WAY TO THE SOUTH POLE."
"THAT'S ALL."

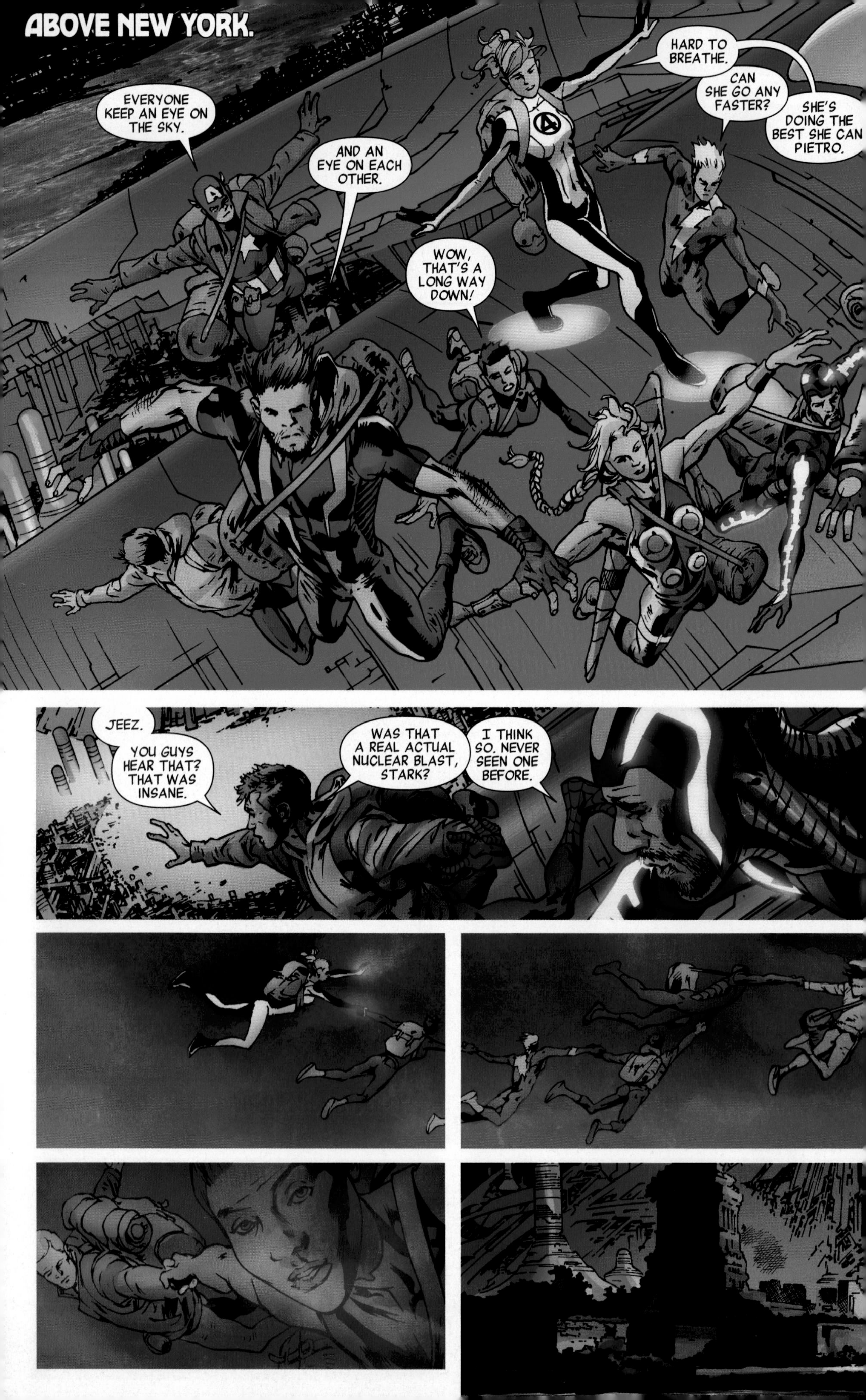
ABOVE NEW YORK.
EVERYONE KEEP AN EYE ON THE SKY.
AND AN EYE ON EACH OTHER.
HARD TO BREATHE.
CAN SHE GO ANY FASTER?
SHE'S DOING THE BEST SHE CAN PIETRO.
WOW, THAT'S A LONG WAY DOWN!
JEEZ.
YOU GUYS HEAR THAT? THAT WAS INSANE.
WAS THAT A REAL ACTUAL NUCLEAR BLAST, STARK?
I THINK SO. NEVER SEEN ONE BEFORE.

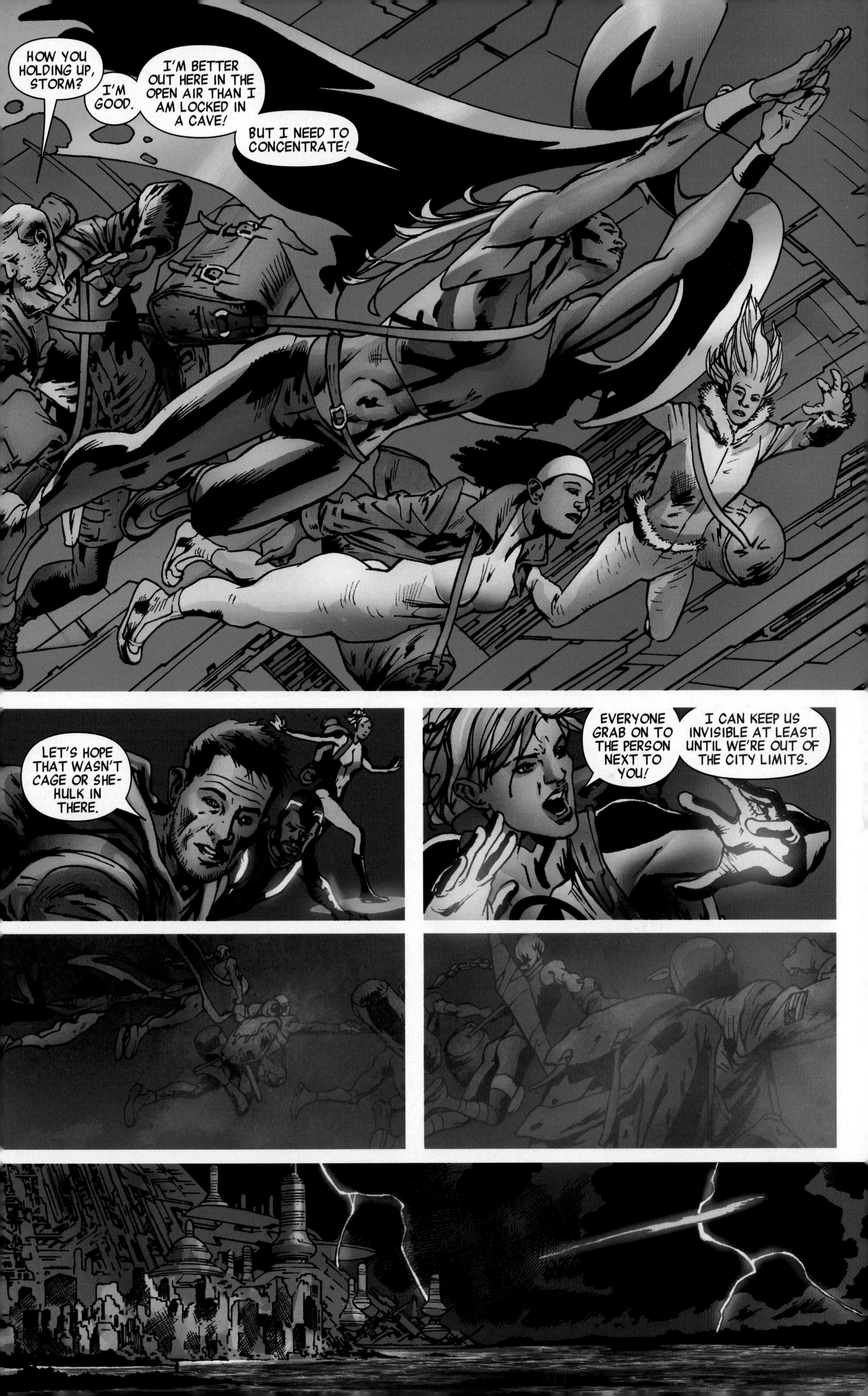
HOW YOU HOLDING UP, STORM?
I'M GOOD.
I'M BETTER OUT HERE IN THE OPEN AIR THAN I AM LOCKED IN A CAVE!
BUT I NEED TO CONCENTRATE!
LET'S HOPE THAT WASN'T CAGE OR SHE-HULK IN THERE.
EVERYONE GRAB ON TO THE PERSON NEXT TO YOU!
I CAN KEEP US INVISIBLE AT LEAST UNTIL WE'RE OUT OF THE CITY LIMITS.

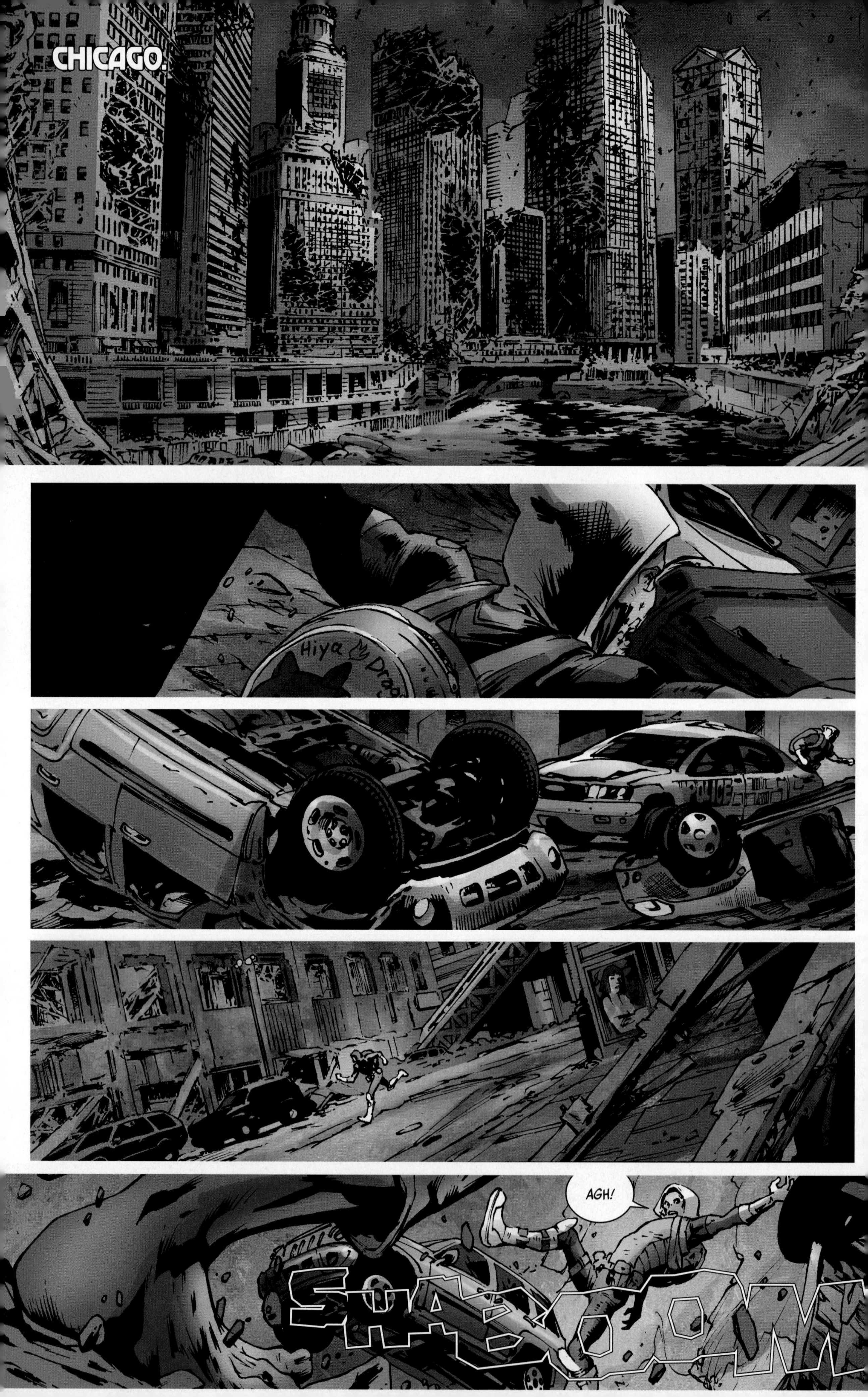
CHICAGO.
Hiya
POLICE
AGH!
SHABOOM

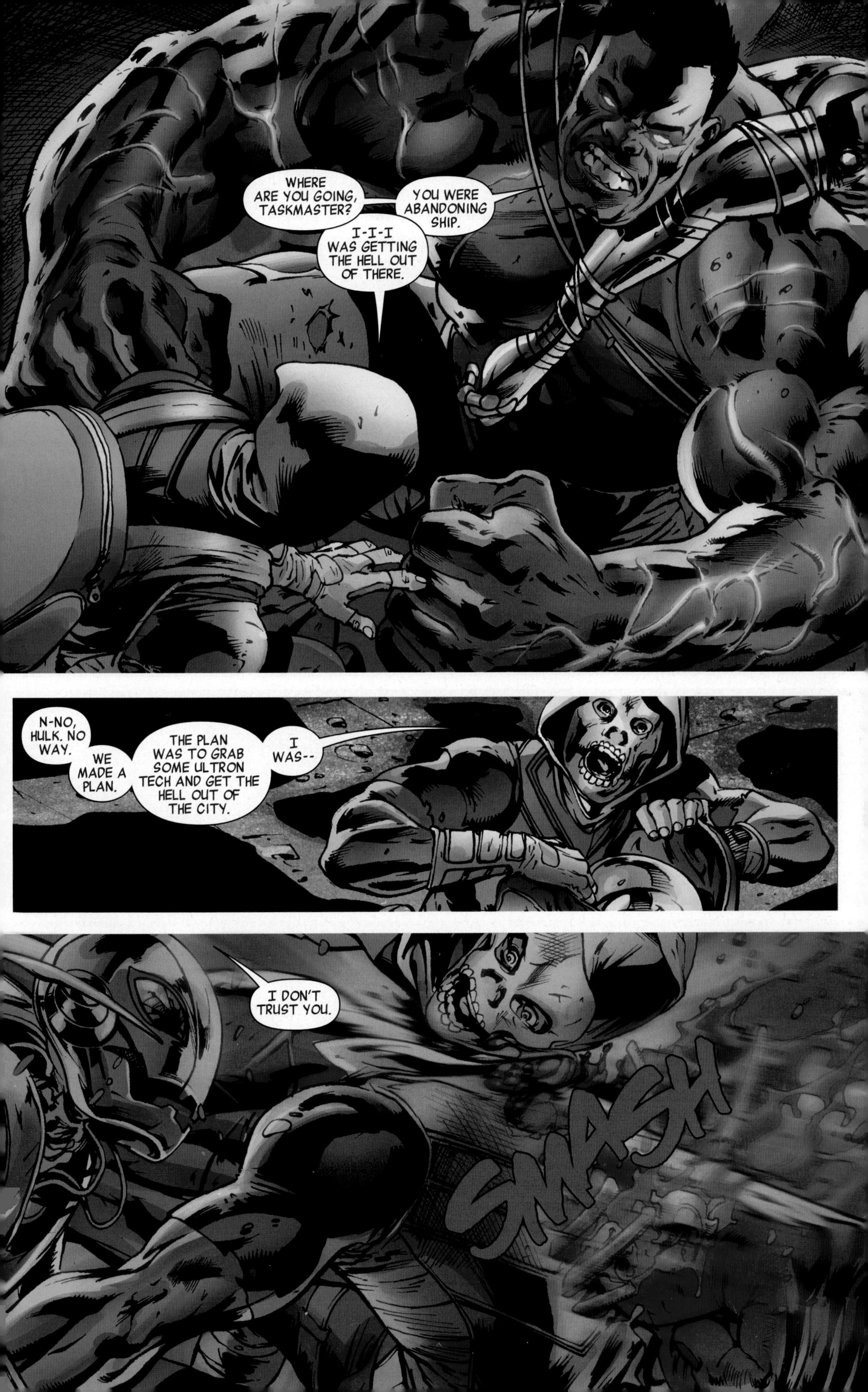
WHERE ARE YOU GOING, TASKMASTER?
YOU WERE ABANDONING SHIP.
I-I-I WAS GETTING THE HELL OUT OF THERE.
N-NO, HULK. NO WAY.
WE MADE A PLAN.
THE PLAN WAS TO GRAB SOME ULTRON TECH AND GET THE HELL OUT OF THE CITY.
I WAS--
I DON'T TRUST YOU.
SMASH

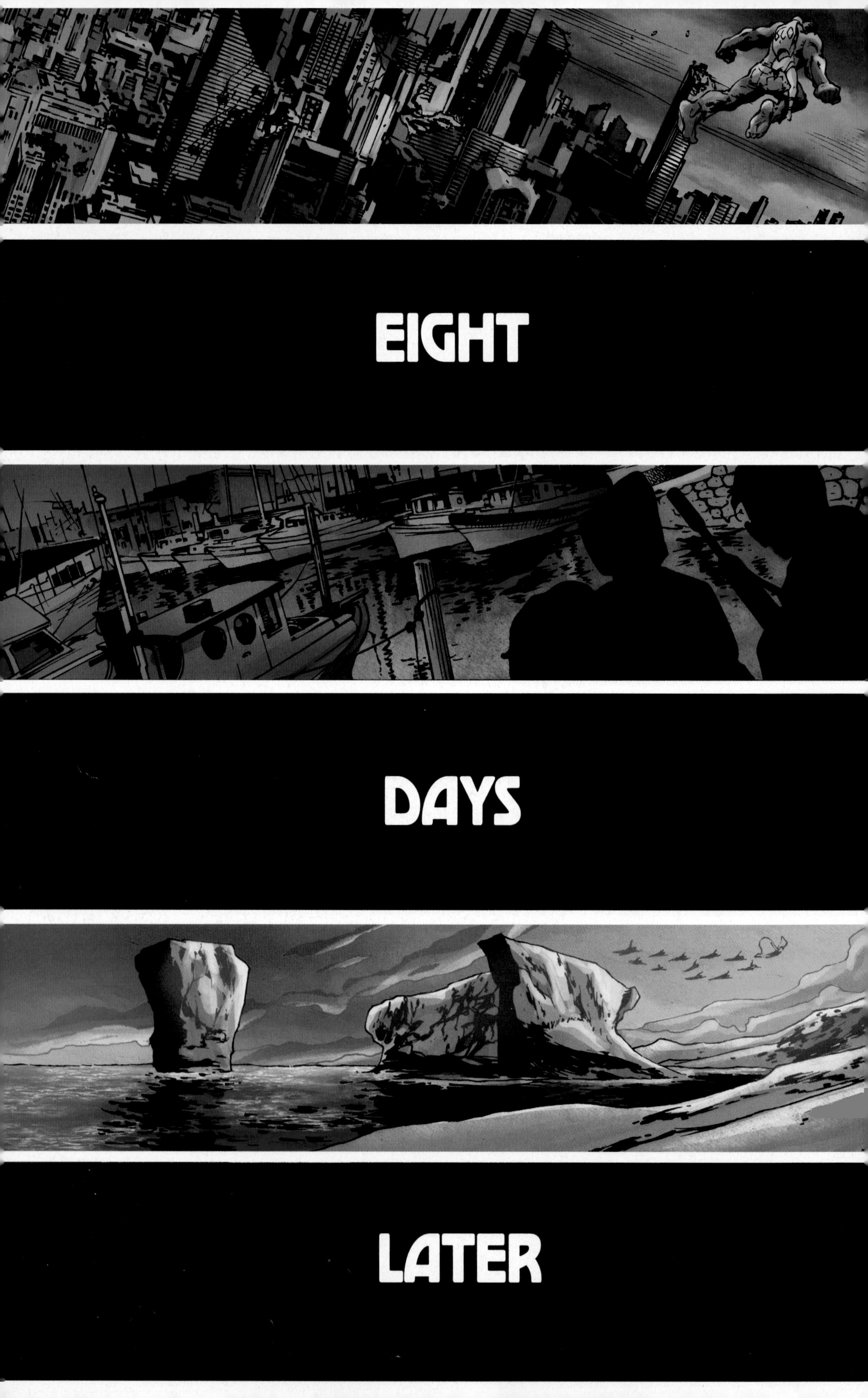
EIGHT
DAYS
LATER

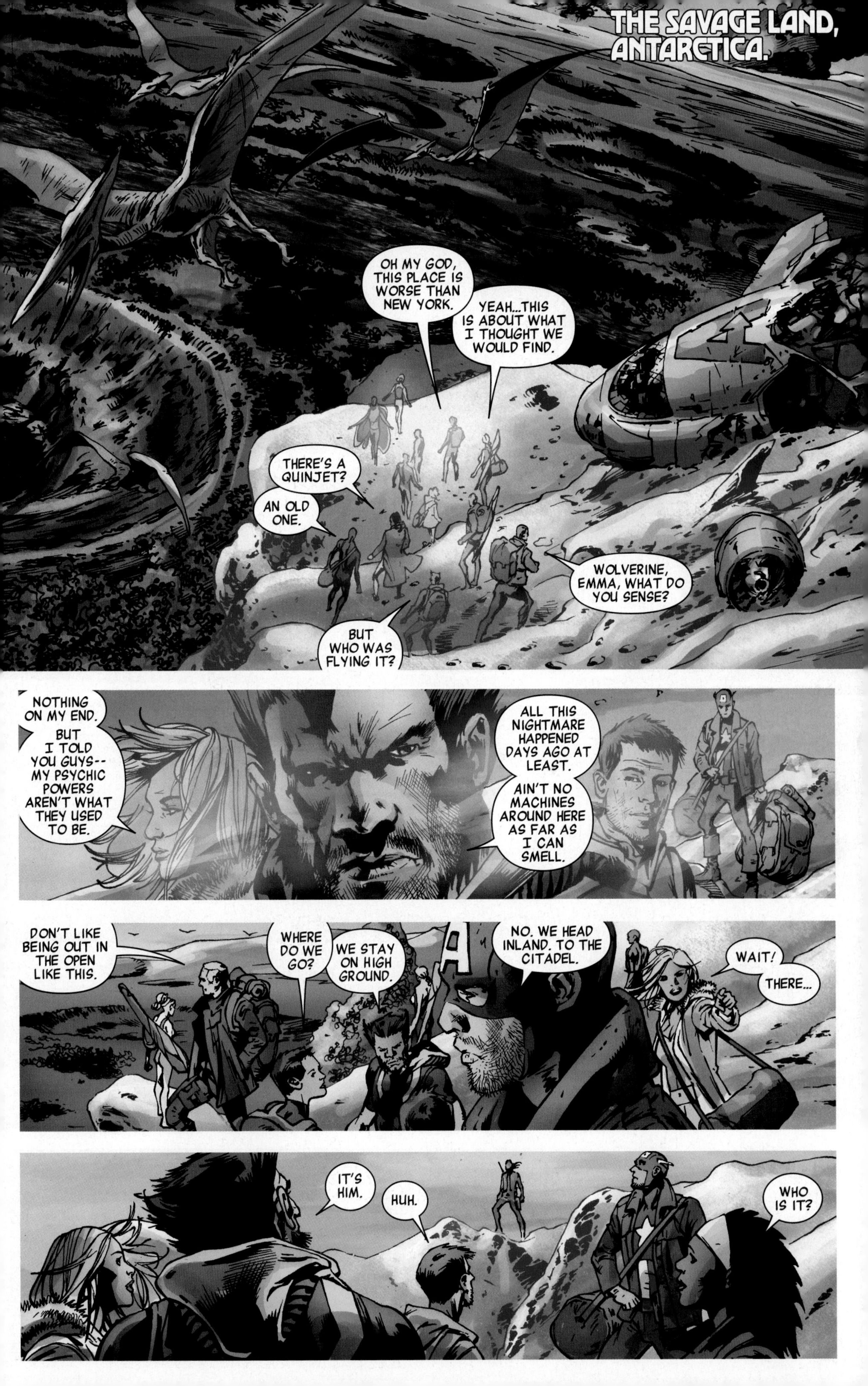
THE SAVAGE LAND, ANTARCTICA.
OH MY GOD, THIS PLACE IS WORSE THAN NEW YORK.
YEAH...THIS IS ABOUT WHAT I THOUGHT WE WOULD FIND.
THERE'S A QUINJET?
AN OLD ONE.
BUT WHO WAS FLYING IT?
WOLVERINE, EMMA, WHAT DO YOU SENSE?
NOTHING ON MY END.
BUT I TOLD YOU GUYS-- MY PSYCHIC POWERS AREN'T WHAT THEY USED TO BE.
ALL THIS NIGHTMARE HAPPENED DAYS AGO AT LEAST.
AIN'T NO MACHINES AROUND HERE AS FAR AS I CAN SMELL.
DON'T LIKE BEING OUT IN THE OPEN LIKE THIS.
WHERE DO WE GO?
WE STAY ON HIGH GROUND.
NO. WE HEAD INLAND. TO THE CITADEL.
WAIT!
THERE...
IT'S HIM.
HUH.
WHO IS IT?

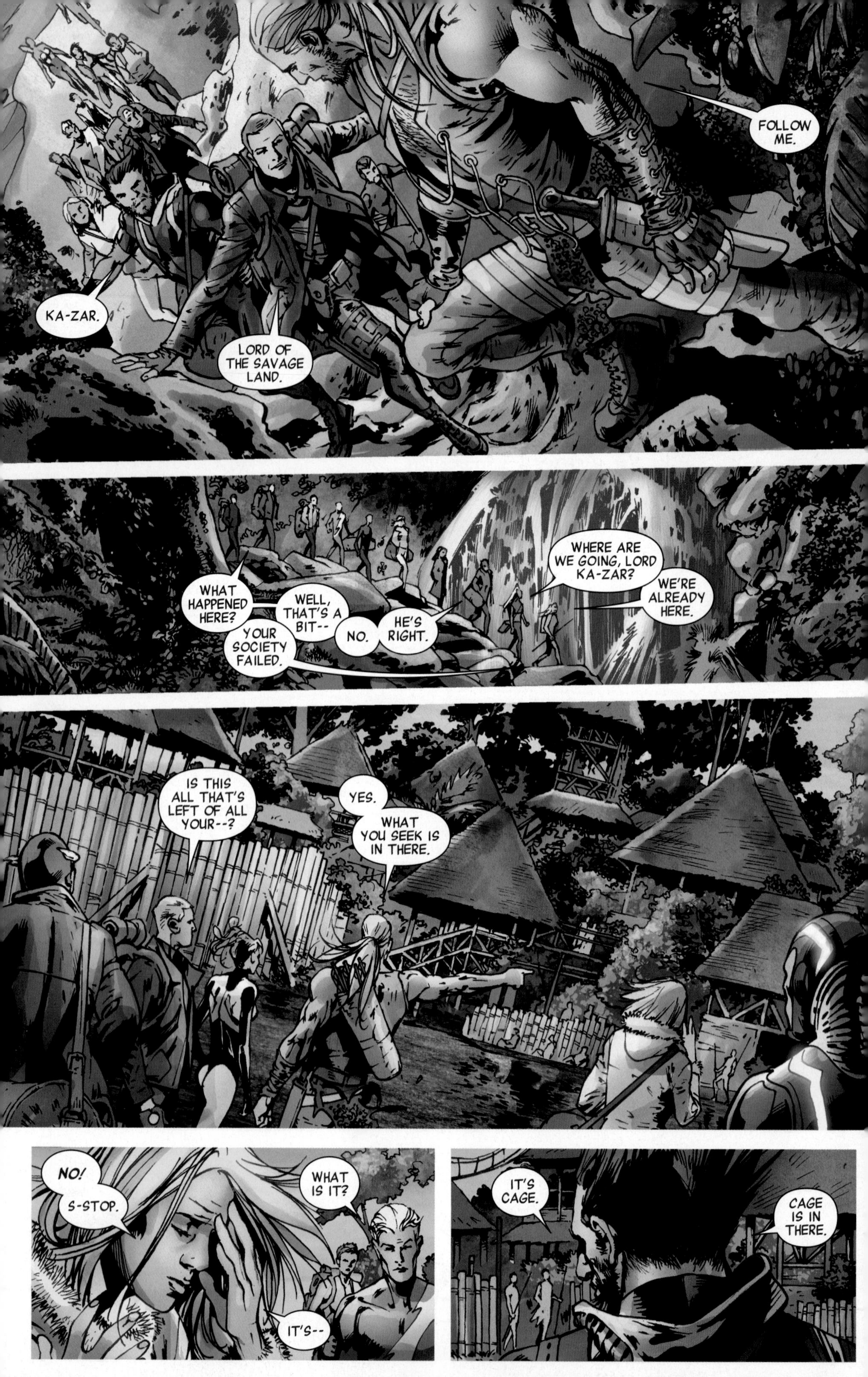

FOLLOW ME.
KA-ZAR.
LORD OF THE SAVAGE LAND.
WHAT HAPPENED HERE?
WELL, THAT'S A BIT--
YOUR SOCIETY FAILED.
NO.
HE'S RIGHT.
WHERE ARE WE GOING, LORD KA-ZAR?
WE'RE ALREADY HERE.
IS THIS ALL THAT'S LEFT OF ALL YOUR--?
YES.
WHAT YOU SEEK IS IN THERE.
NO!
S-STOP.
WHAT IS IT?
IT'S--
IT'S CAGE.
CAGE IS IN THERE.

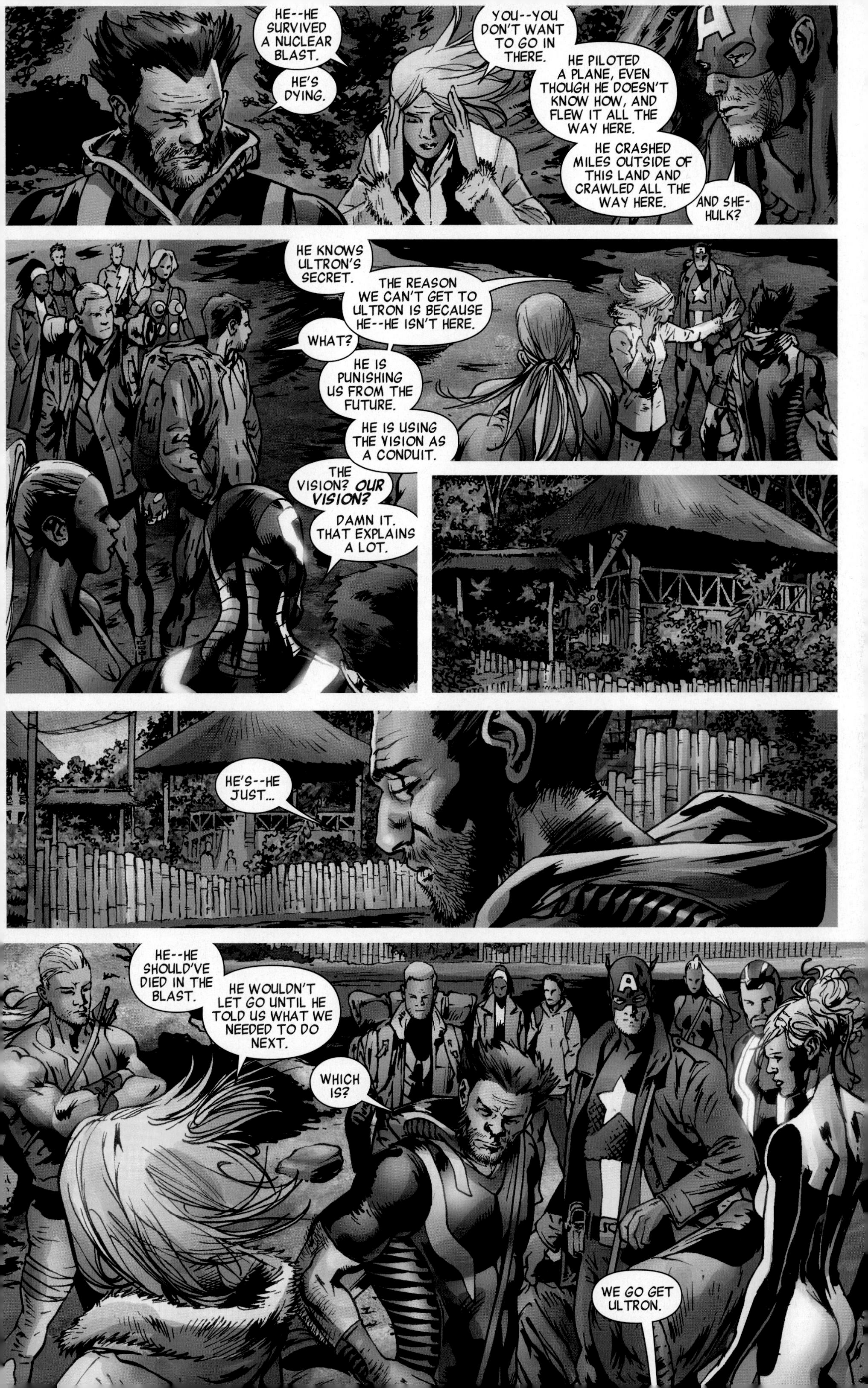
HE--HE SURVIVED A NUCLEAR BLAST.
HE'S DYING.
YOU--YOU DON'T WANT TO GO IN THERE.
HE PILOTED A PLANE, EVEN THOUGH HE DOESN'T KNOW HOW, AND FLEW IT ALL THE WAY HERE.
HE CRASHED MILES OUTSIDE OF THIS LAND AND CRAWLED ALL THE WAY HERE.
AND SHE-HULK?
HE KNOWS ULTRON'S SECRET.
THE REASON WE CAN'T GET TO ULTRON IS BECAUSE HE--HE ISN'T HERE.
WHAT?
HE IS PUNISHING US FROM THE FUTURE.
HE IS USING THE VISION AS A CONDUIT.
THE VISION? **OUR VISION?**
DAMN IT. THAT EXPLAINS A LOT.
HE'S--HE JUST...
HE--HE SHOULD'VE DIED IN THE BLAST.
HE WOULDN'T LET GO UNTIL HE TOLD US WHAT WE NEEDED TO DO NEXT.
WHICH IS?
WE GO GET ULTRON.

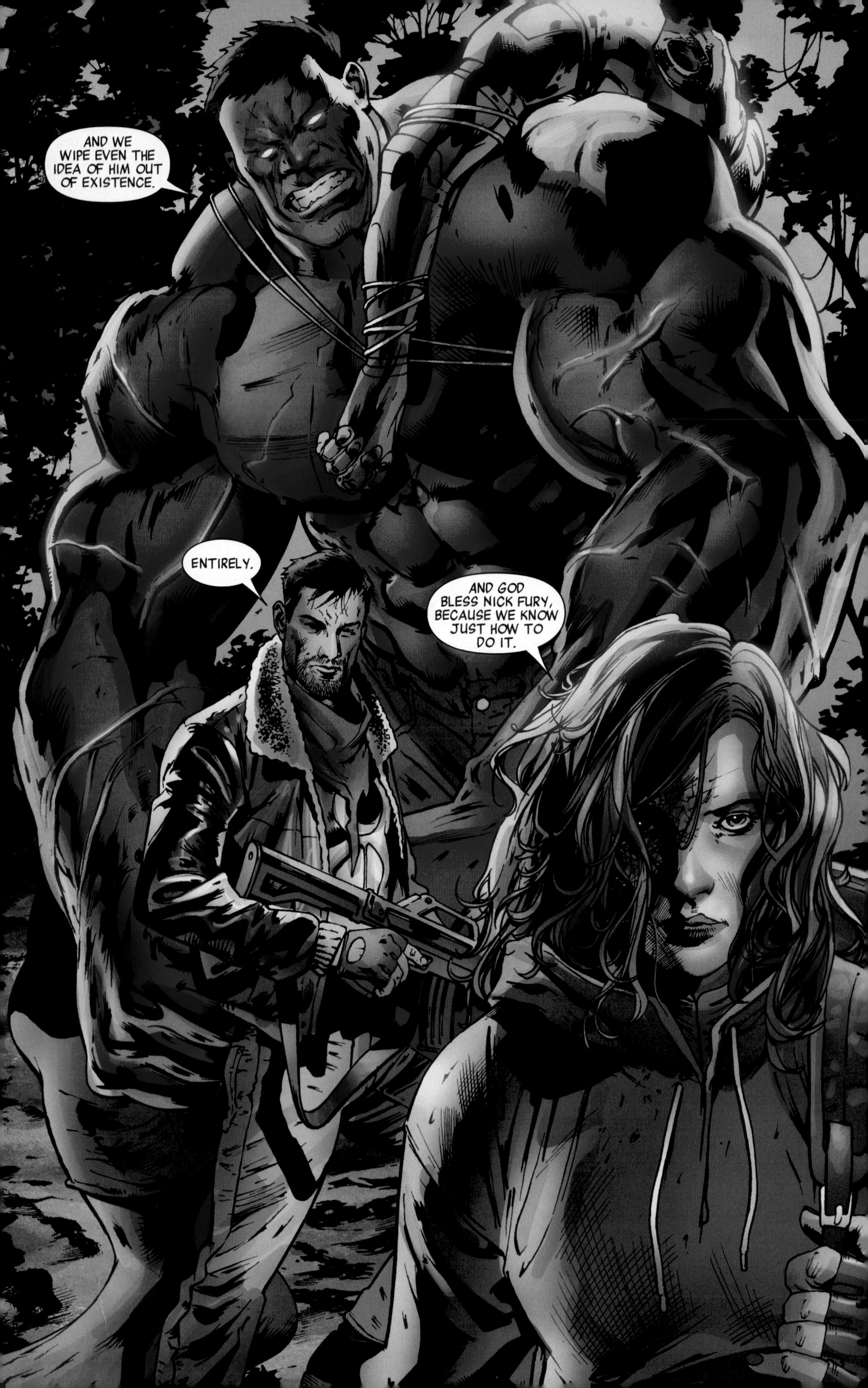
AND WE WIPE EVEN THE IDEA OF HIM OUT OF EXISTENCE.
ENTIRELY.
AND GOD BLESS NICK FURY, BECAUSE WE KNOW JUST HOW TO DO IT.

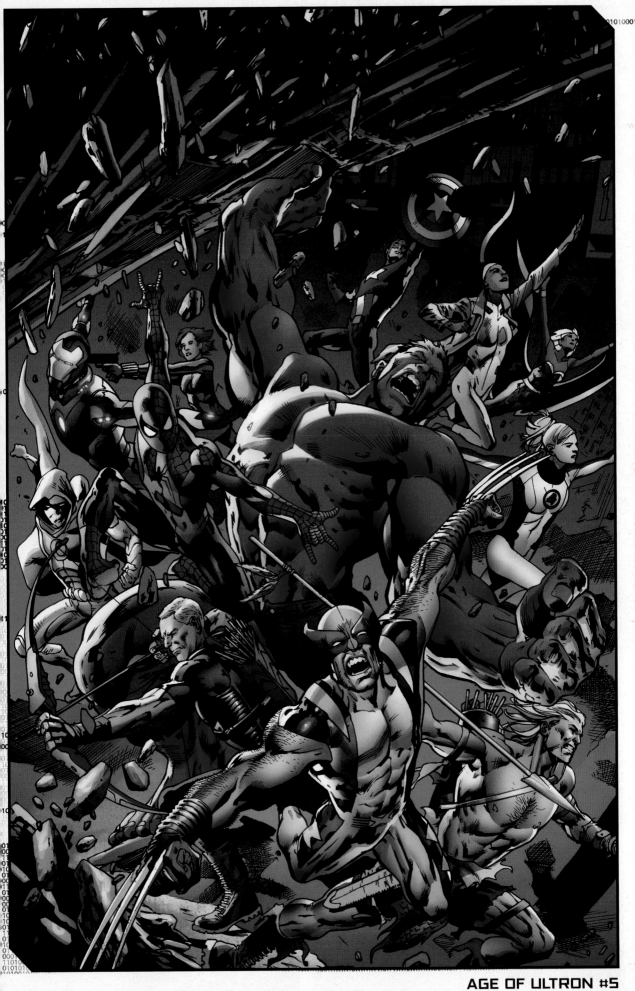

AGE OF ULTRON #5

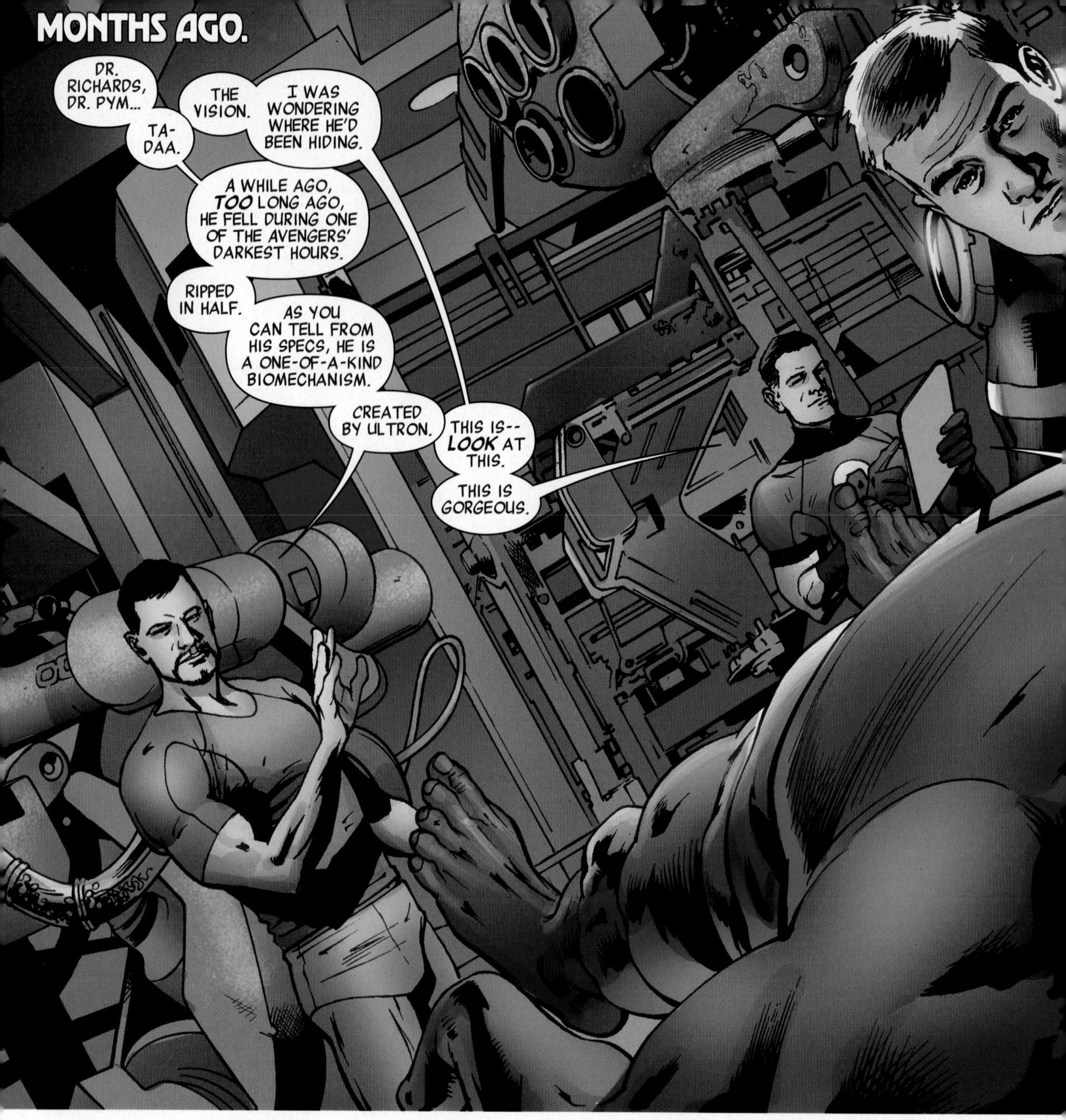
MONTHS AGO.
DR. RICHARDS, DR. PYM...
TA-DAA.
THE VISION.
I WAS WONDERING WHERE HE'D BEEN HIDING.
A WHILE AGO, TOO LONG AGO, HE FELL DURING ONE OF THE AVENGERS' DARKEST HOURS.
RIPPED IN HALF.
AS YOU CAN TELL FROM HIS SPECS, HE IS A ONE-OF-A-KIND BIOMECHANISM.
CREATED BY ULTRON.
THIS IS-- LOOK AT THIS.
THIS IS GORGEOUS.

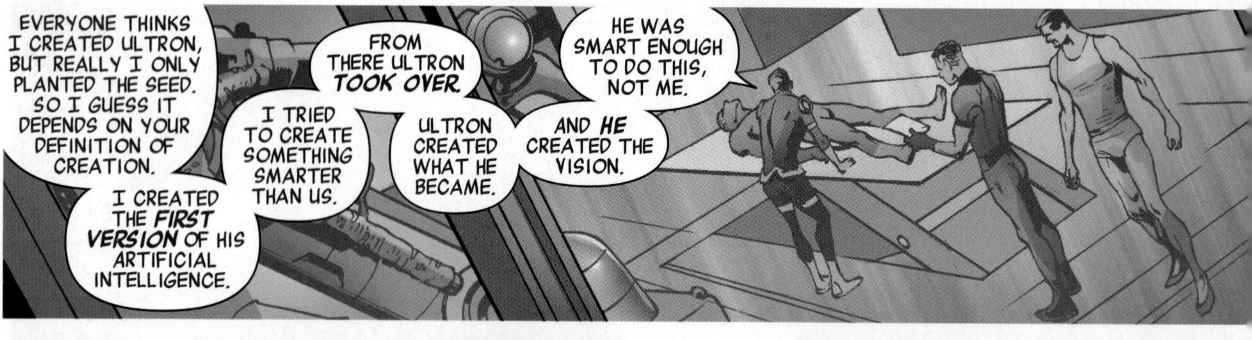
EVERYONE THINKS I CREATED ULTRON, BUT REALLY I ONLY PLANTED THE SEED. SO I GUESS IT DEPENDS ON YOUR DEFINITION OF CREATION.
I CREATED THE FIRST VERSION OF HIS ARTIFICIAL INTELLIGENCE.
I TRIED TO CREATE SOMETHING SMARTER THAN US.
FROM THERE ULTRON TOOK OVER.
ULTRON CREATED WHAT HE BECAME.
HE WAS SMART ENOUGH TO DO THIS, NOT ME.
AND HE CREATED THE VISION.

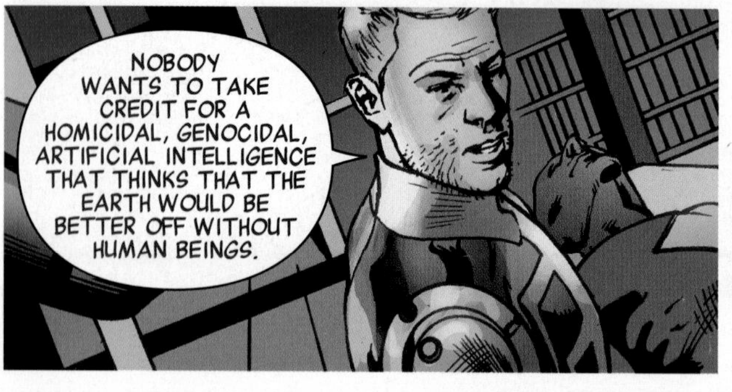
NOBODY WANTS TO TAKE CREDIT FOR A HOMICIDAL, GENOCIDAL, ARTIFICIAL INTELLIGENCE THAT THINKS THAT THE EARTH WOULD BE BETTER OFF WITHOUT HUMAN BEINGS.

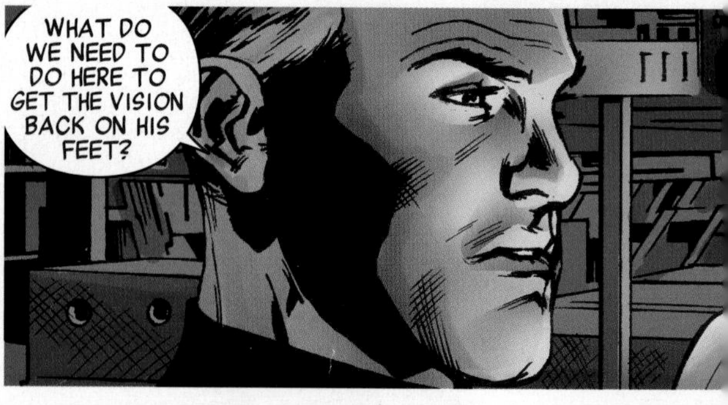
WHAT DO WE NEED TO DO HERE TO GET THE VISION BACK ON HIS FEET?

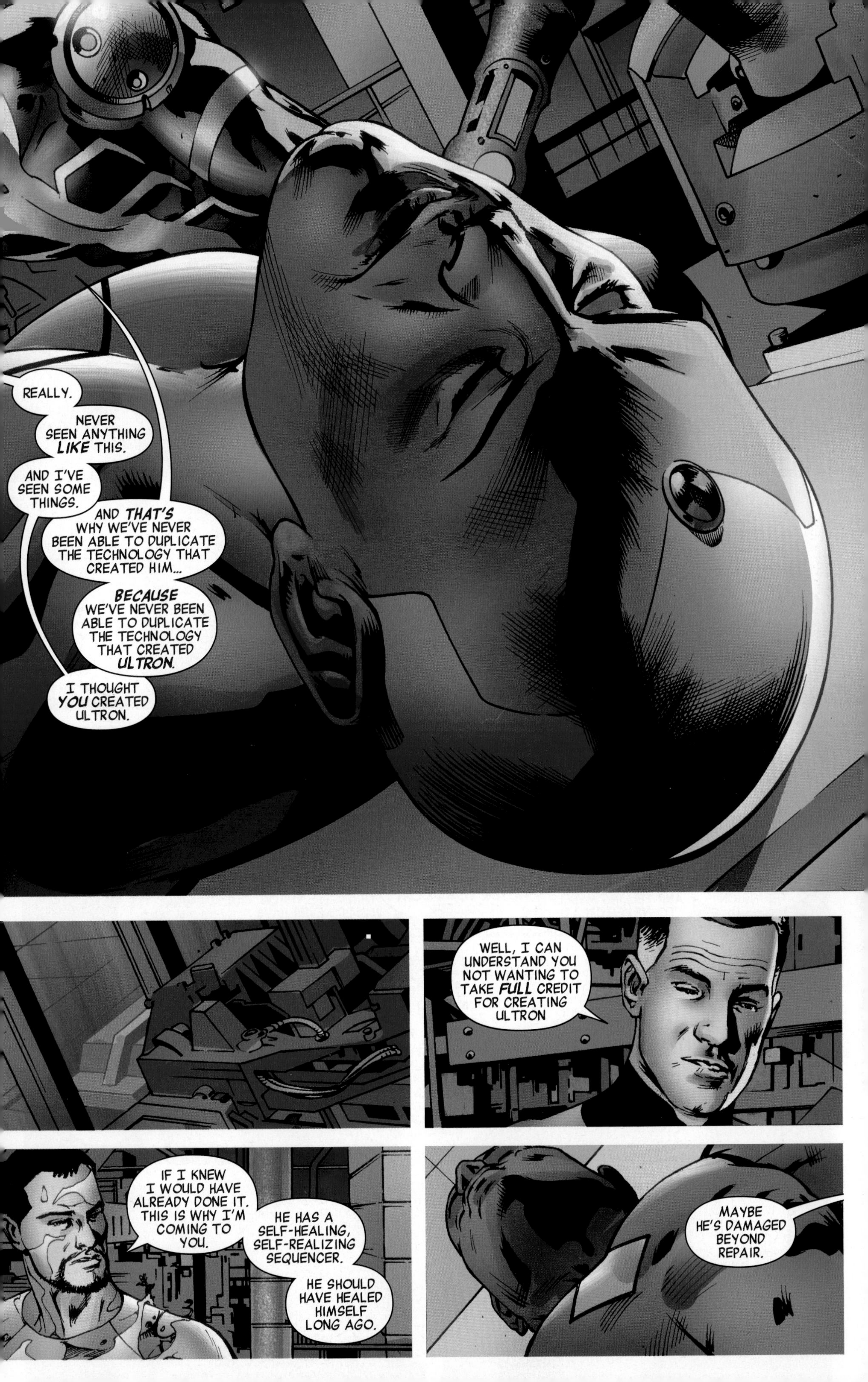
REALLY.
NEVER SEEN ANYTHING *LIKE* THIS.
AND I'VE SEEN SOME THINGS.
AND *THAT'S* WHY WE'VE NEVER BEEN ABLE TO DUPLICATE THE TECHNOLOGY THAT CREATED HIM...
BECAUSE WE'VE NEVER BEEN ABLE TO DUPLICATE THE TECHNOLOGY THAT CREATED *ULTRON*.
I THOUGHT *YOU* CREATED ULTRON.
WELL, I CAN UNDERSTAND YOU NOT WANTING TO TAKE *FULL* CREDIT FOR CREATING ULTRON
IF I KNEW I WOULD HAVE ALREADY DONE IT. THIS IS WHY I'M COMING TO YOU.
HE HAS A SELF-HEALING, SELF-REALIZING SEQUENCER.
HE SHOULD HAVE HEALED HIMSELF LONG AGO.
MAYBE HE'S DAMAGED BEYOND REPAIR.

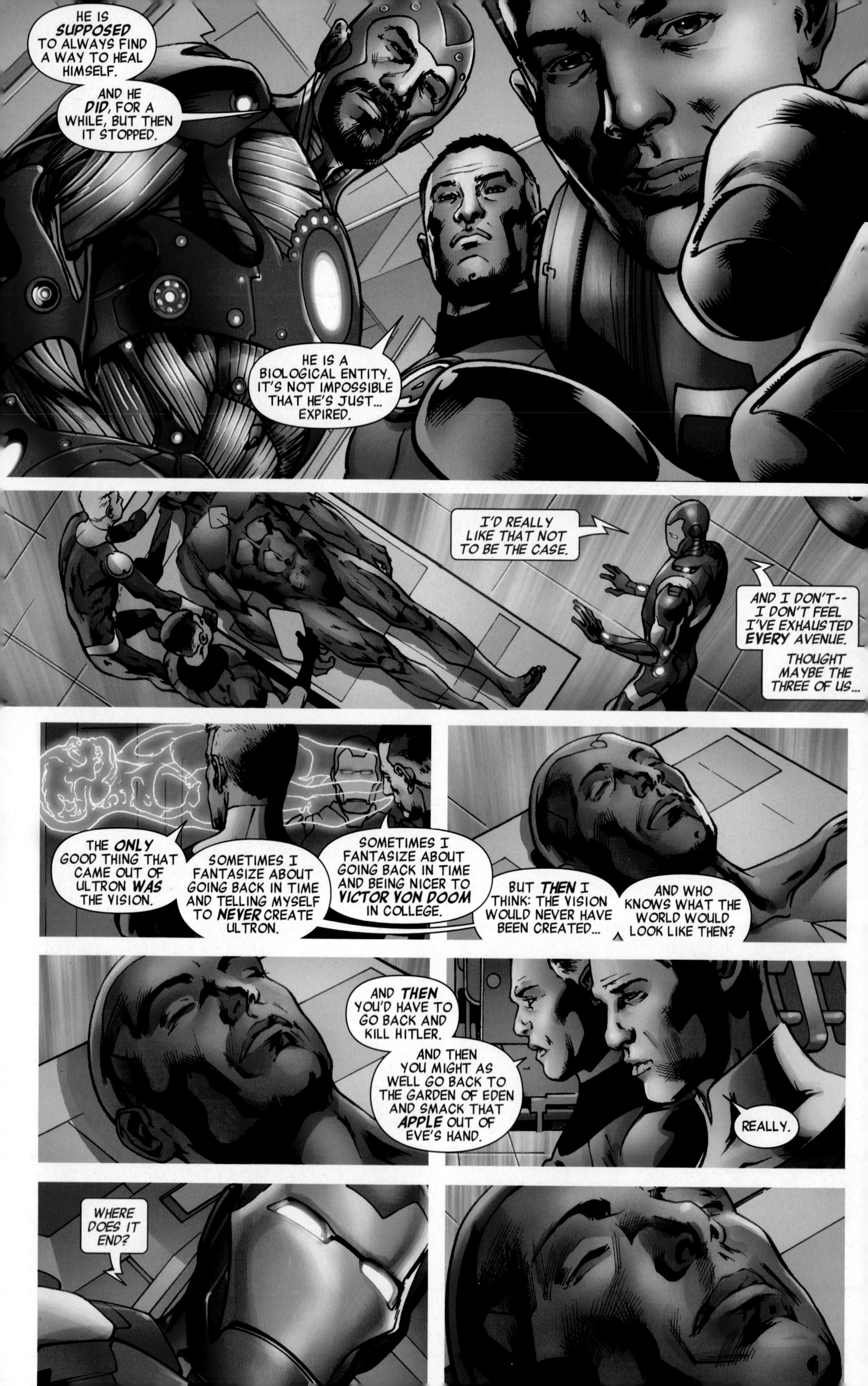

HE IS SUPPOSED TO ALWAYS FIND A WAY TO HEAL HIMSELF.
AND HE DID, FOR A WHILE, BUT THEN IT STOPPED.
HE IS A BIOLOGICAL ENTITY. IT'S NOT IMPOSSIBLE THAT HE'S JUST... EXPIRED.
I'D REALLY LIKE THAT NOT TO BE THE CASE.
AND I DON'T-- I DON'T FEEL I'VE EXHAUSTED EVERY AVENUE.
THOUGHT MAYBE THE THREE OF US...
THE ONLY GOOD THING THAT CAME OUT OF ULTRON WAS THE VISION.
SOMETIMES I FANTASIZE ABOUT GOING BACK IN TIME AND TELLING MYSELF TO NEVER CREATE ULTRON.
SOMETIMES I FANTASIZE ABOUT GOING BACK IN TIME AND BEING NICER TO VICTOR VON DOOM IN COLLEGE.
BUT THEN I THINK: THE VISION WOULD NEVER HAVE BEEN CREATED...
AND WHO KNOWS WHAT THE WORLD WOULD LOOK LIKE THEN?
AND THEN YOU'D HAVE TO GO BACK AND KILL HITLER.
AND THEN YOU MIGHT AS WELL GO BACK TO THE GARDEN OF EDEN AND SMACK THAT APPLE OUT OF EVE'S HAND.
REALLY.
WHERE DOES IT END?

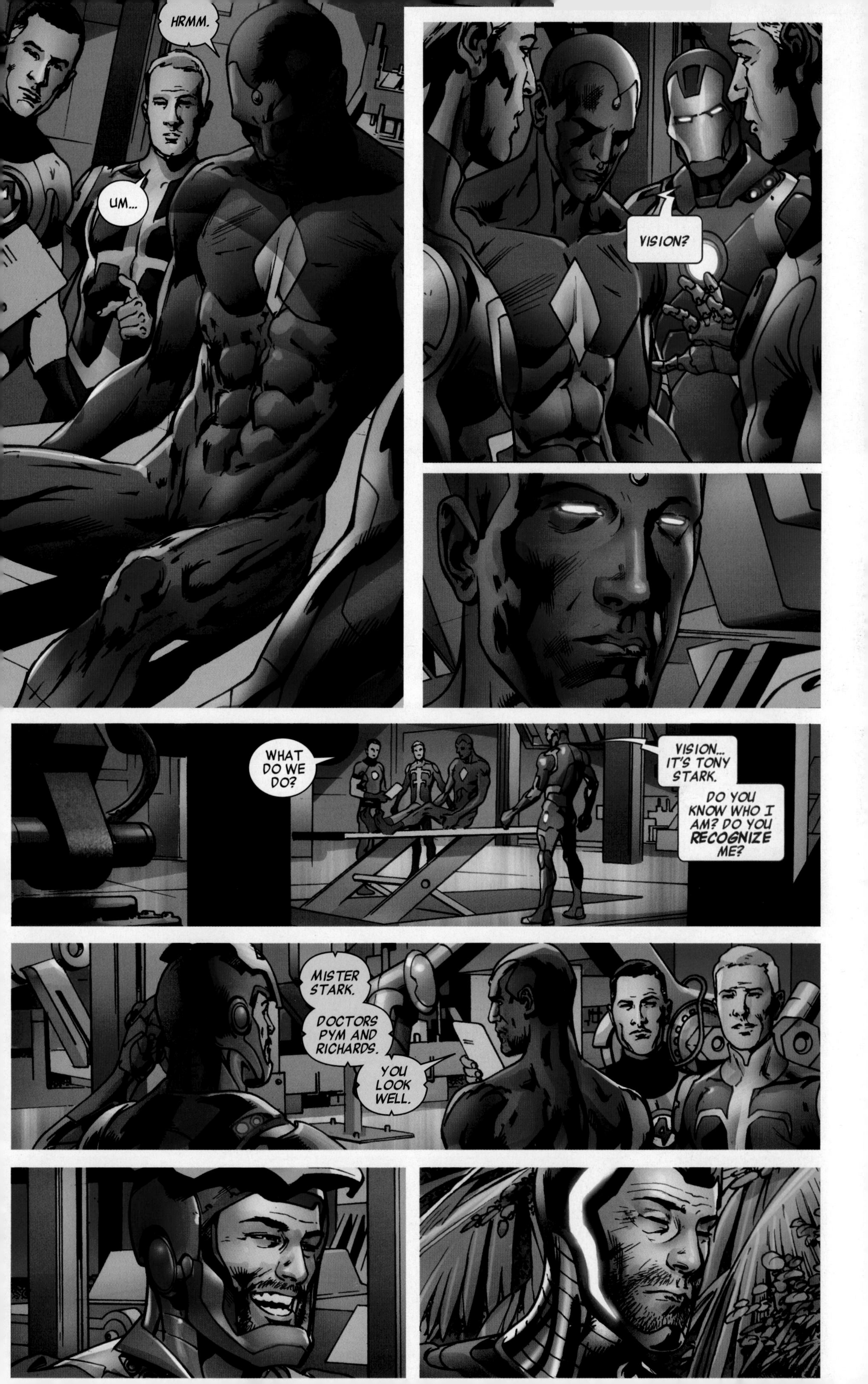
HRMM.
UM...
VISION?
WHAT DO WE DO?
VISION... IT'S TONY STARK.
DO YOU KNOW WHO I AM? DO YOU RECOGNIZE ME?
MISTER STARK.
DOCTORS PYM AND RICHARDS.
YOU LOOK WELL.

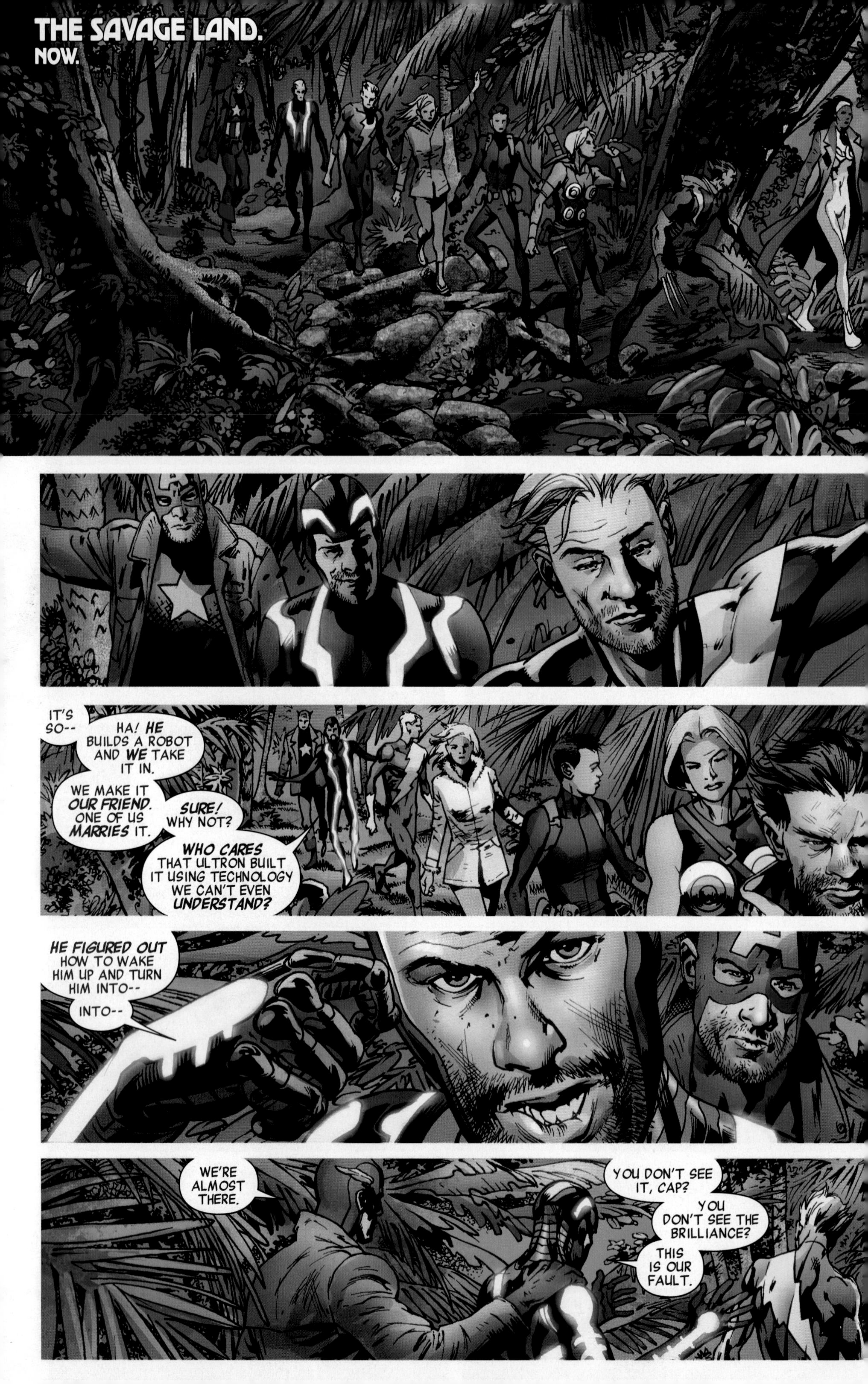
THE SAVAGE LAND.
NOW.
IT'S SO--
HA! HE BUILDS A ROBOT AND WE TAKE IT IN.
WE MAKE IT OUR FRIEND. ONE OF US MARRIES IT.
SURE! WHY NOT?
WHO CARES THAT ULTRON BUILT IT USING TECHNOLOGY WE CAN'T EVEN UNDERSTAND?
HE FIGURED OUT HOW TO WAKE HIM UP AND TURN HIM INTO--
INTO--
WE'RE ALMOST THERE.
YOU DON'T SEE IT, CAP?
YOU DON'T SEE THE BRILLIANCE?
THIS IS OUR FAULT.

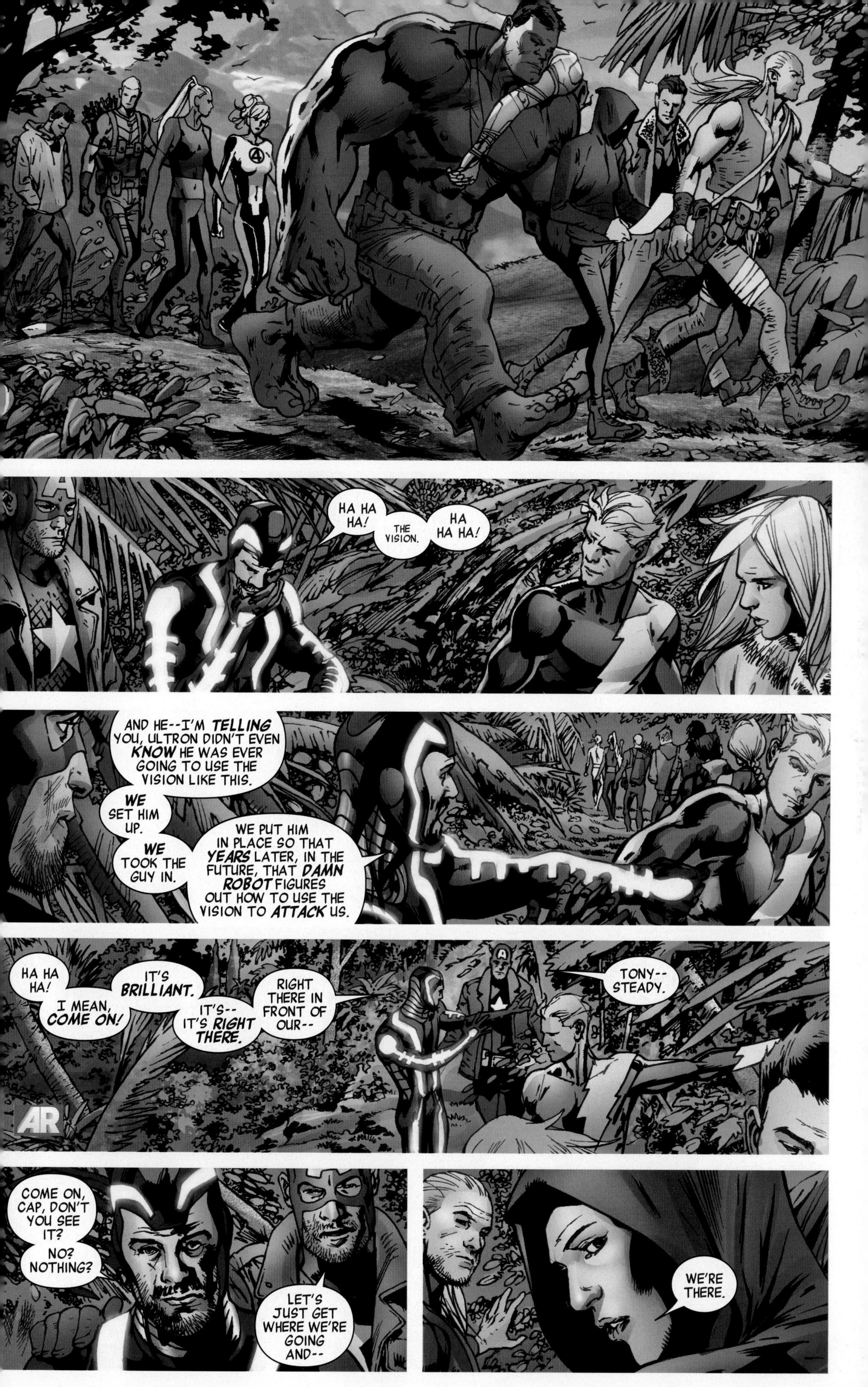
HA HA HA!
THE VISION.
HA HA HA!
AND HE--I'M TELLING YOU, ULTRON DIDN'T EVEN KNOW HE WAS EVER GOING TO USE THE VISION LIKE THIS.
WE SET HIM UP.
WE TOOK THE GUY IN.
WE PUT HIM IN PLACE SO THAT YEARS LATER, IN THE FUTURE, THAT DAMN ROBOT FIGURES OUT HOW TO USE THE VISION TO ATTACK US.
HA HA HA!
I MEAN, COME ON!
IT'S BRILLIANT.
IT'S-- IT'S RIGHT THERE.
RIGHT THERE IN FRONT OF OUR--
TONY-- STEADY.
COME ON, CAP, DON'T YOU SEE IT?
NO? NOTHING?
LET'S JUST GET WHERE WE'RE GOING AND--
WE'RE THERE.

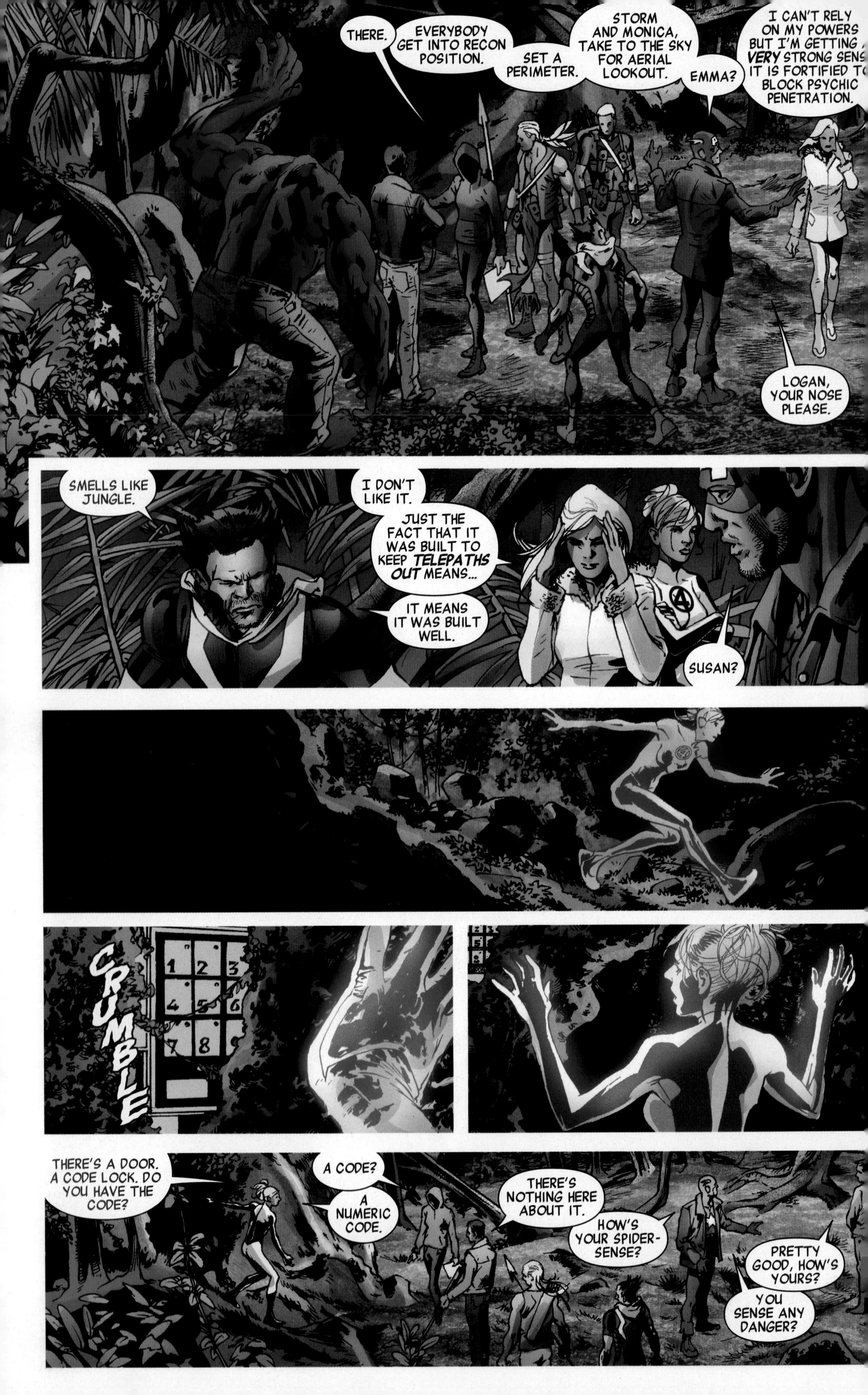
THERE.
EVERYBODY GET INTO RECON POSITION.
SET A PERIMETER.
STORM AND MONICA, TAKE TO THE SKY FOR AERIAL LOOKOUT.
EMMA?
I CAN'T RELY ON MY POWERS BUT I'M GETTING A VERY STRONG SENS IT IS FORTIFIED TO BLOCK PSYCHIC PENETRATION.
LOGAN, YOUR NOSE PLEASE.
SMELLS LIKE JUNGLE.
I DON'T LIKE IT.
JUST THE FACT THAT IT WAS BUILT TO KEEP TELEPATHS OUT MEANS...
IT MEANS IT WAS BUILT WELL.
SUSAN?
CRUMBLE
THERE'S A DOOR. A CODE LOCK. DO YOU HAVE THE CODE?
A CODE?
A NUMERIC CODE.
THERE'S NOTHING HERE ABOUT IT.
HOW'S YOUR SPIDER-SENSE?
PRETTY GOOD, HOW'S YOURS?
YOU SENSE ANY DANGER?

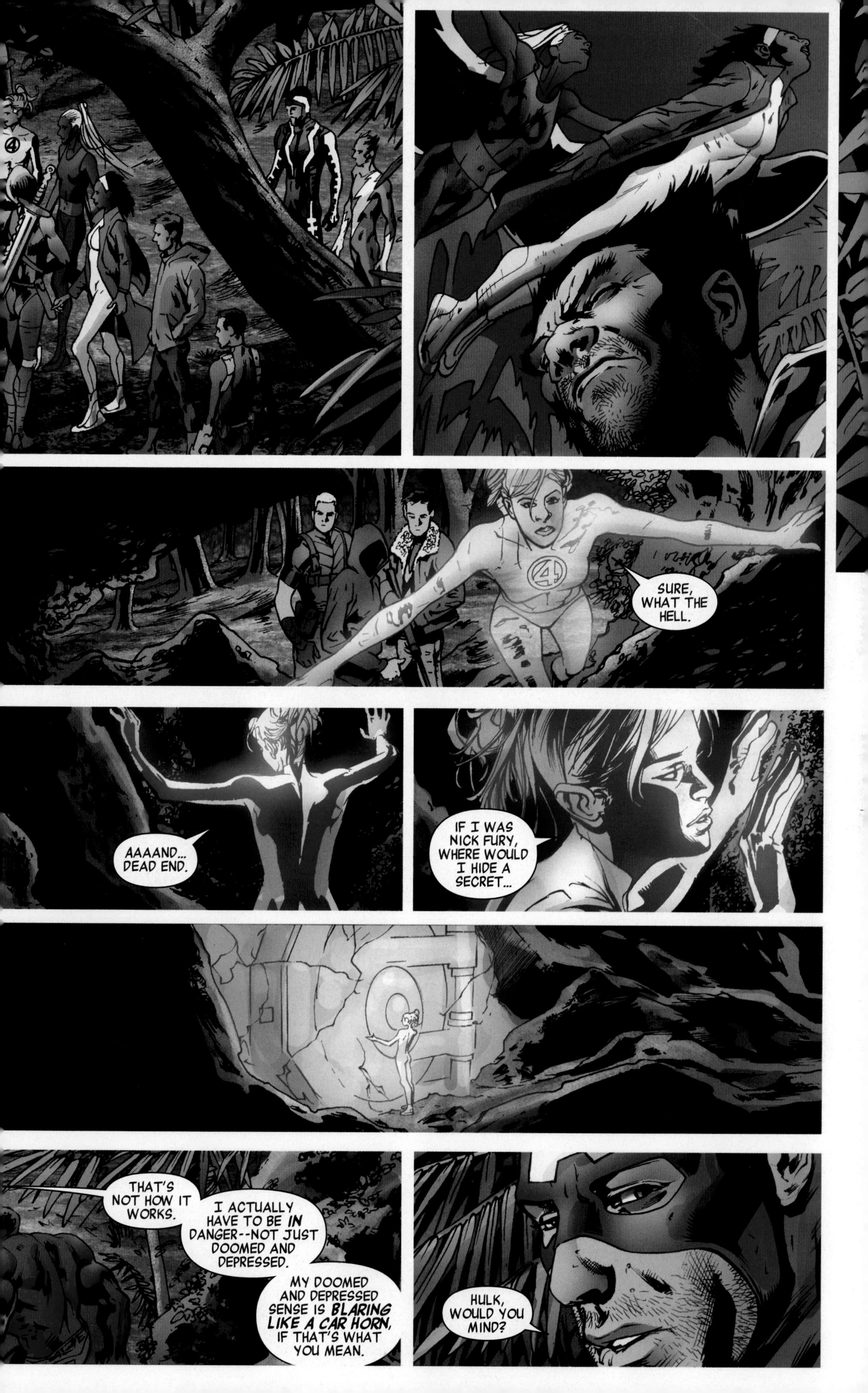
SURE, WHAT THE HELL.
AAAAND... DEAD END.
IF I WAS NICK FURY, WHERE WOULD I HIDE A SECRET...
THAT'S NOT HOW IT WORKS.
I ACTUALLY HAVE TO BE *IN* DANGER--NOT JUST DOOMED AND DEPRESSED.
MY DOOMED AND DEPRESSED SENSE IS ***BLARING LIKE A CAR HORN,*** IF THAT'S WHAT YOU MEAN.
HULK, WOULD YOU MIND?

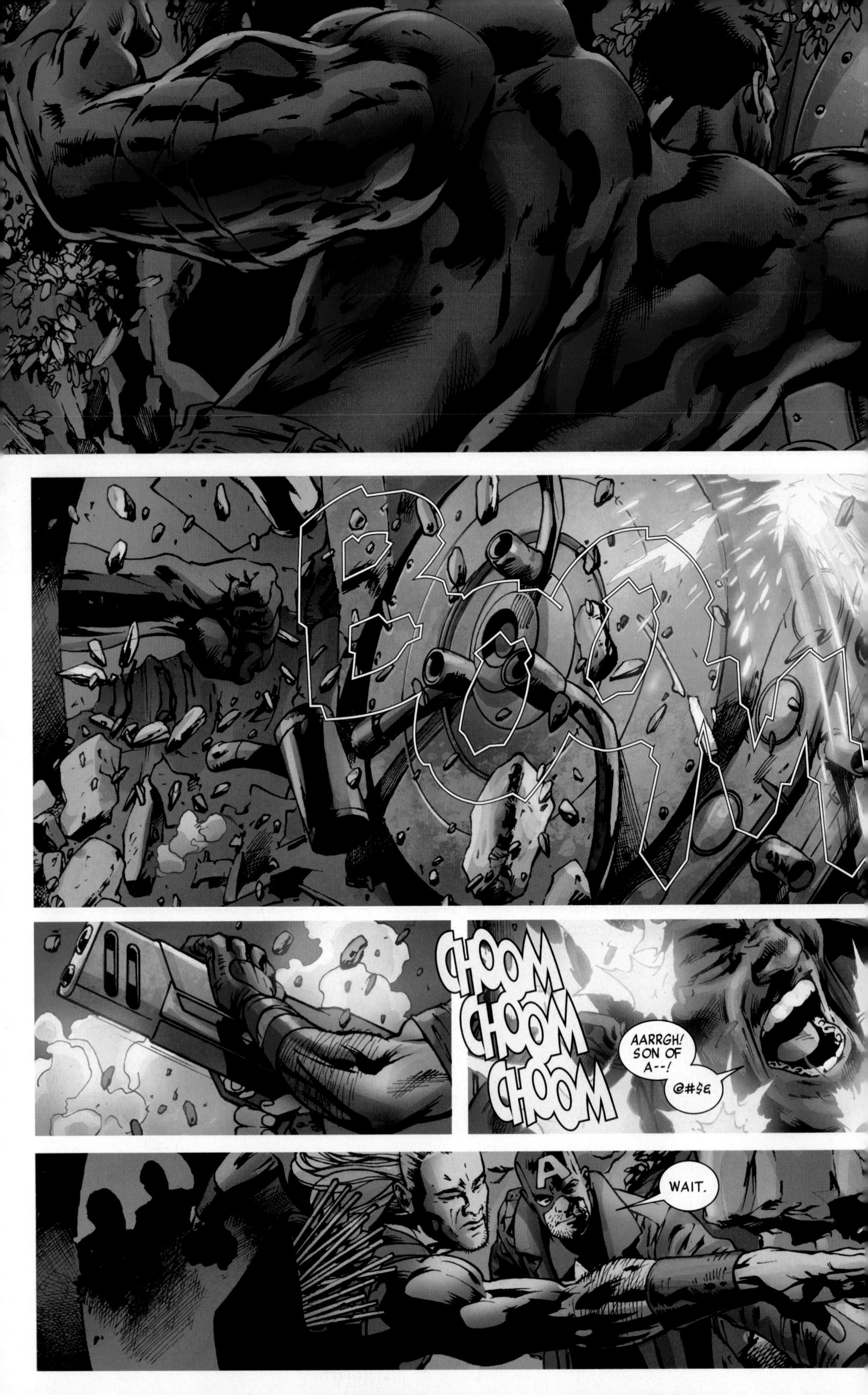
BOOM
CHOOM CHOOM CHOOM
AARRGH! SON OF A--!
@#$€
WAIT.

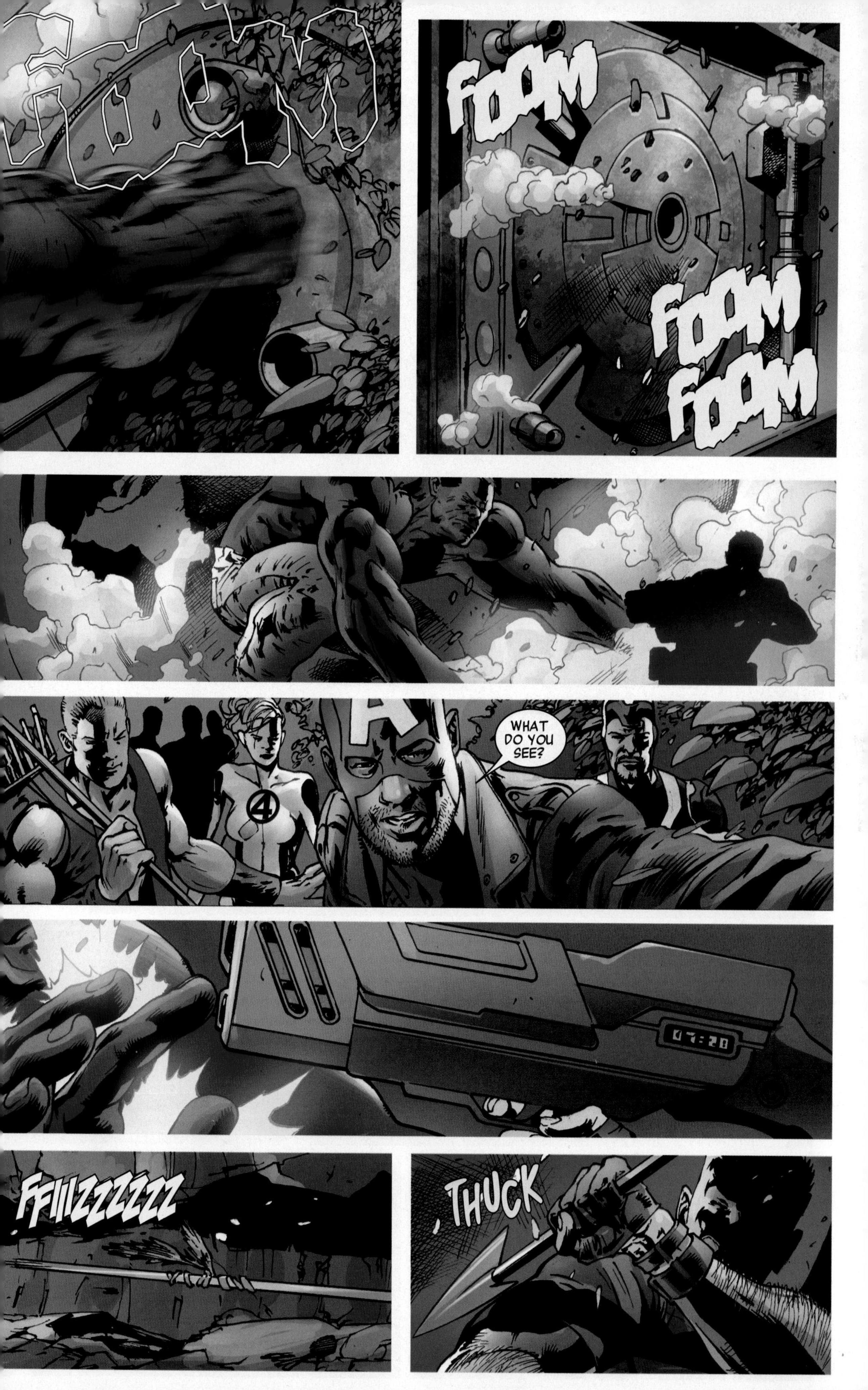
FOOM
FOOM
FOOM
FOOM
WHAT DO YOU SEE?
07:20
FFIIIIZZZZZZZ
THUCK

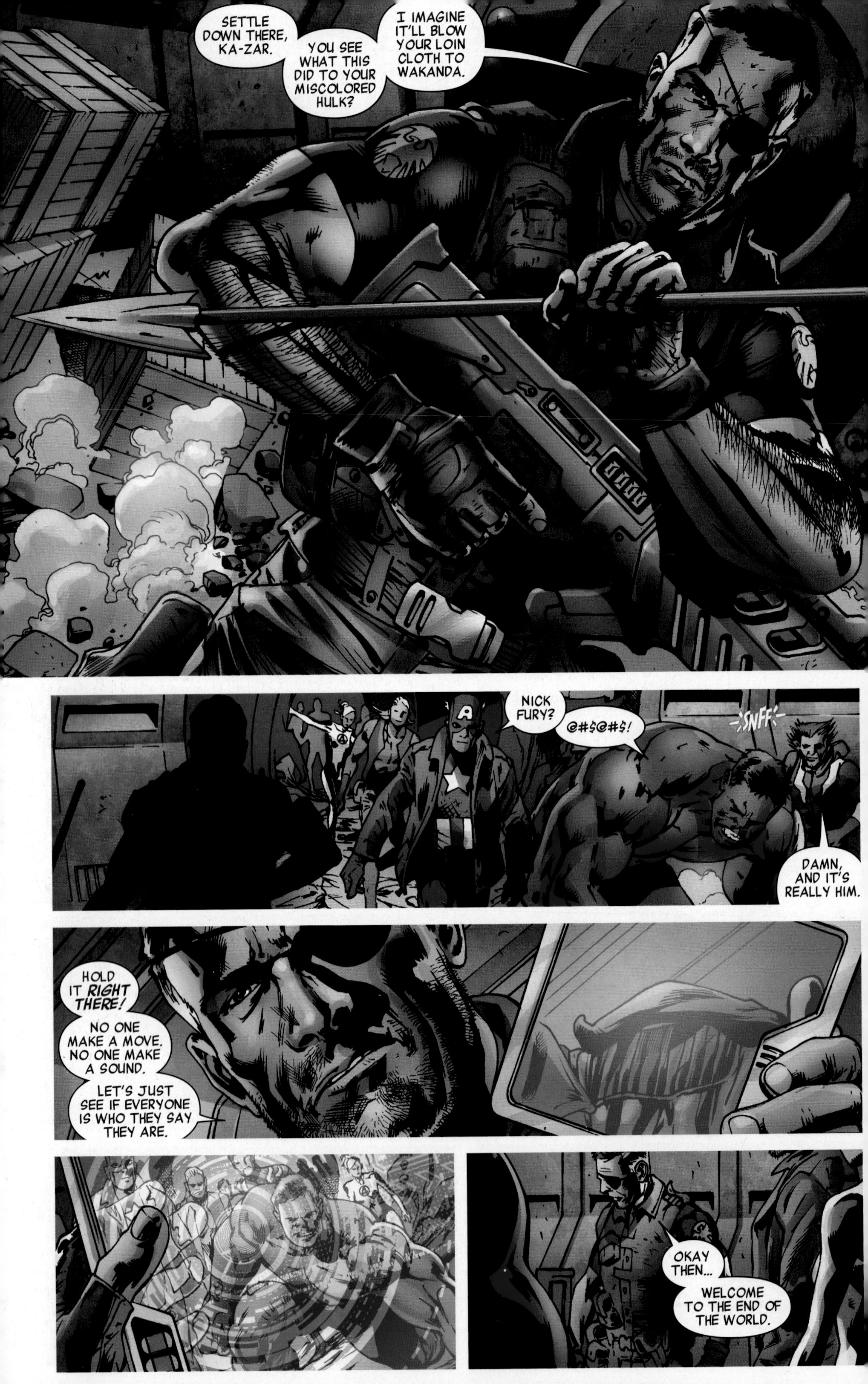

SETTLE DOWN THERE, KA-ZAR.
YOU SEE WHAT THIS DID TO YOUR MISCOLORED HULK?
I IMAGINE IT'LL BLOW YOUR LOIN CLOTH TO WAKANDA.
NICK FURY?
@#$@#$!
SNFF
DAMN, AND IT'S REALLY HIM.
HOLD IT **RIGHT THERE!**
NO ONE MAKE A MOVE. NO ONE MAKE A SOUND.
LET'S JUST SEE IF EVERYONE IS WHO THEY SAY THEY ARE.
OKAY THEN...
WELCOME TO THE END OF THE WORLD.

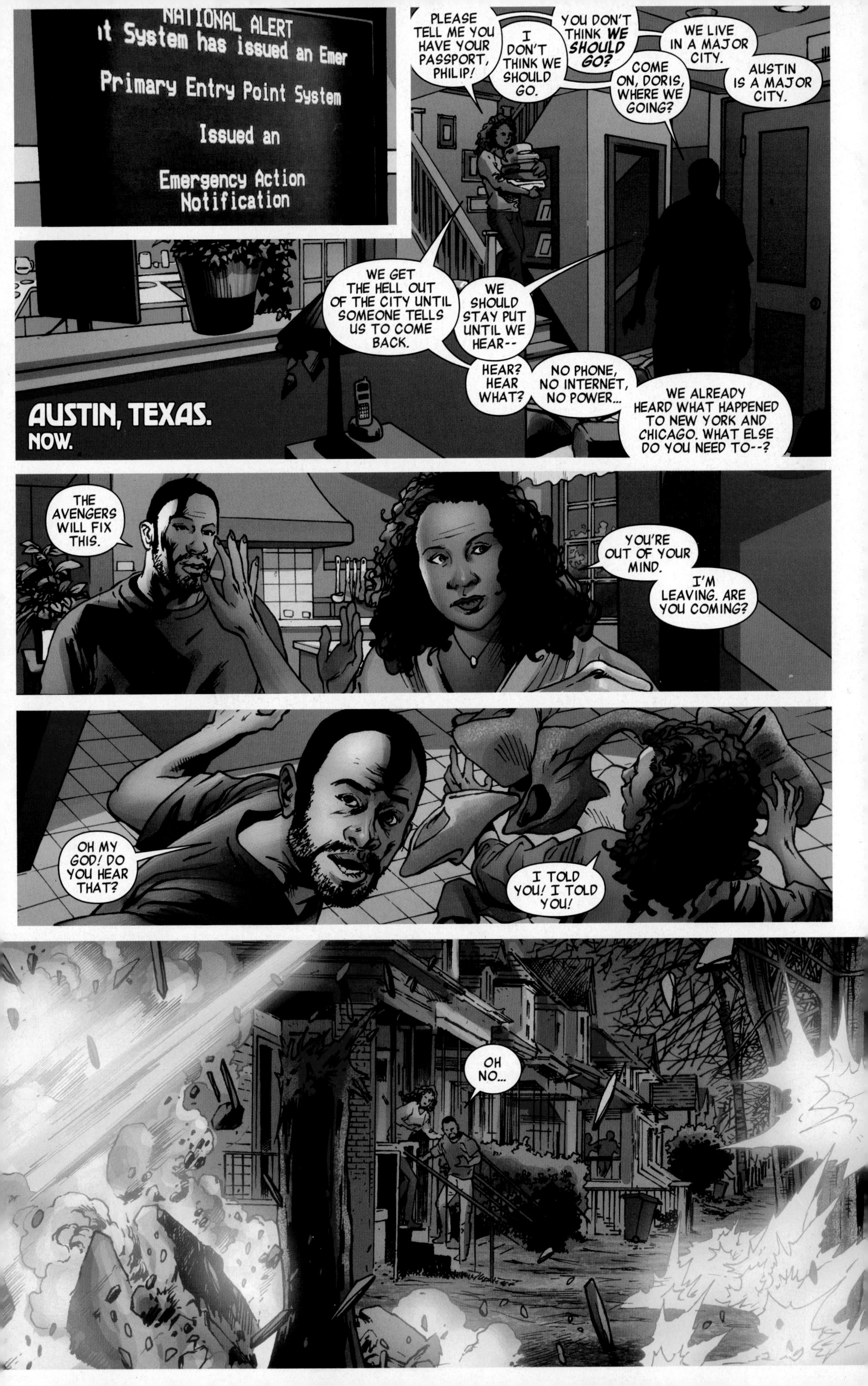
NATIONAL ALERT
it System has issued an Emer
Primary Entry Point System
Issued an
Emergency Action
Notification
PLEASE TELL ME YOU HAVE YOUR PASSPORT, PHILIP!
I DON'T THINK WE SHOULD GO.
YOU DON'T THINK WE SHOULD GO?
WE LIVE IN A MAJOR CITY.
AUSTIN IS A MAJOR CITY.
COME ON, DORIS, WHERE WE GOING?
WE GET THE HELL OUT OF THE CITY UNTIL SOMEONE TELLS US TO COME BACK.
WE SHOULD STAY PUT UNTIL WE HEAR--
HEAR? HEAR WHAT?
NO PHONE, NO INTERNET, NO POWER...
WE ALREADY HEARD WHAT HAPPENED TO NEW YORK AND CHICAGO. WHAT ELSE DO YOU NEED TO--?
AUSTIN, TEXAS.
NOW.
THE AVENGERS WILL FIX THIS.
YOU'RE OUT OF YOUR MIND.
I'M LEAVING. ARE YOU COMING?
OH MY GOD! DO YOU HEAR THAT?
I TOLD YOU! I TOLD YOU!
OH NO...

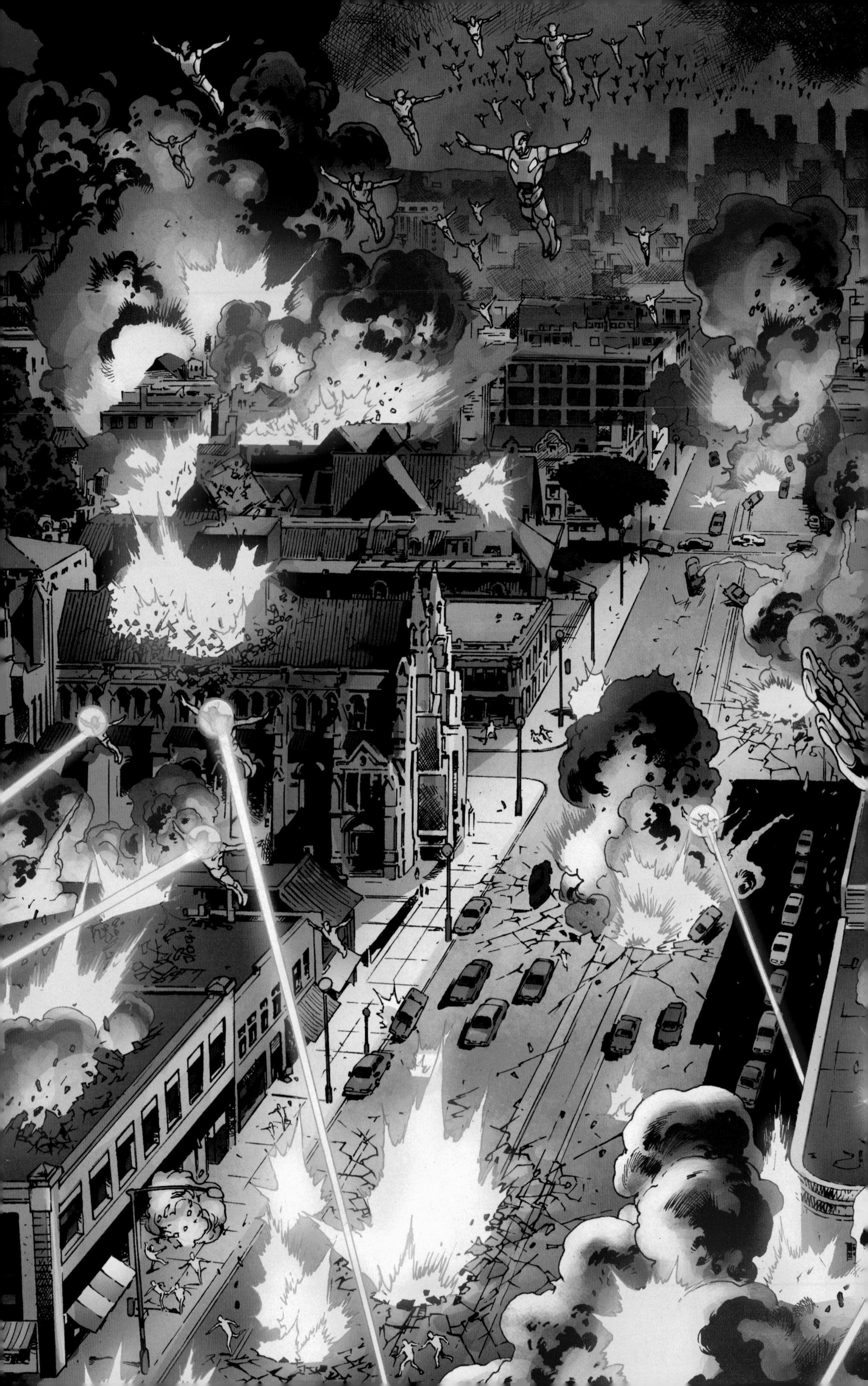

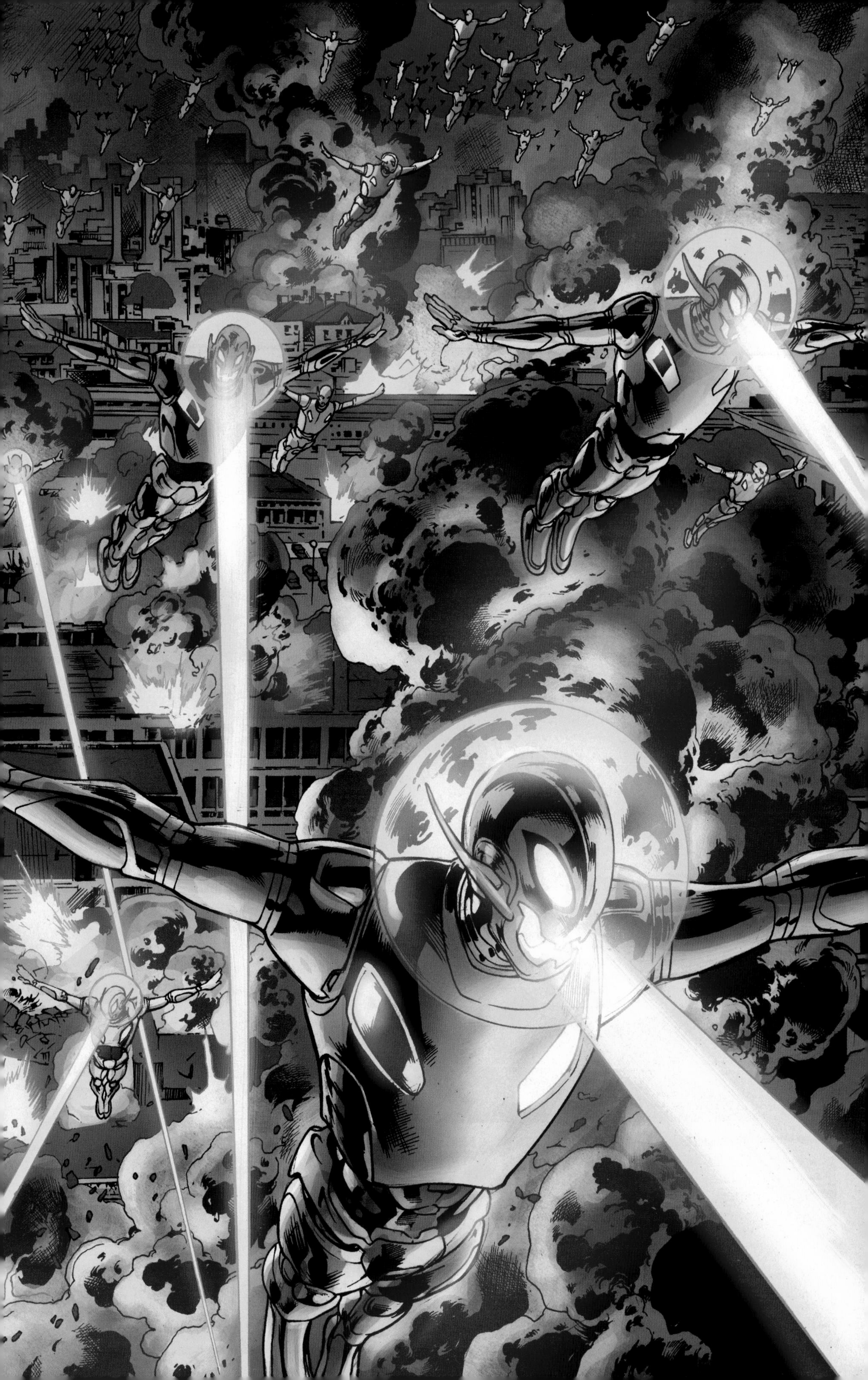

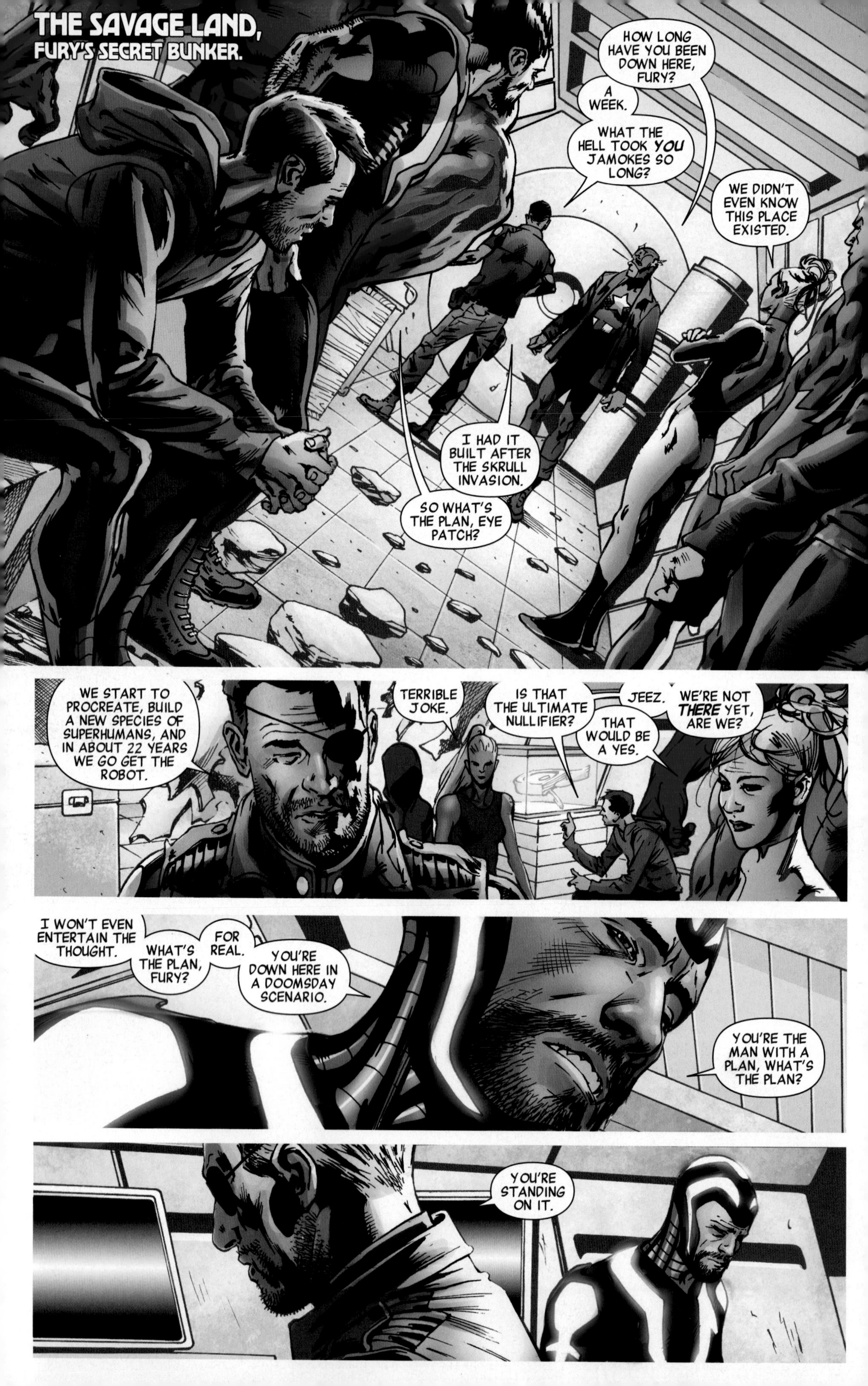

THE SAVAGE LAND, FURY'S SECRET BUNKER.
HOW LONG HAVE YOU BEEN DOWN HERE, FURY?
A WEEK.
WHAT THE HELL TOOK YOU JAMOKES SO LONG?
WE DIDN'T EVEN KNOW THIS PLACE EXISTED.
I HAD IT BUILT AFTER THE SKRULL INVASION.
SO WHAT'S THE PLAN, EYE PATCH?
WE START TO PROCREATE, BUILD A NEW SPECIES OF SUPERHUMANS, AND IN ABOUT 22 YEARS WE GO GET THE ROBOT.
TERRIBLE JOKE.
IS THAT THE ULTIMATE NULLIFIER?
THAT WOULD BE A YES.
JEEZ.
WE'RE NOT THERE YET, ARE WE?
I WON'T EVEN ENTERTAIN THE THOUGHT.
WHAT'S THE PLAN, FURY?
FOR REAL.
YOU'RE DOWN HERE IN A DOOMSDAY SCENARIO.
YOU'RE THE MAN WITH A PLAN, WHAT'S THE PLAN?
YOU'RE STANDING ON IT.

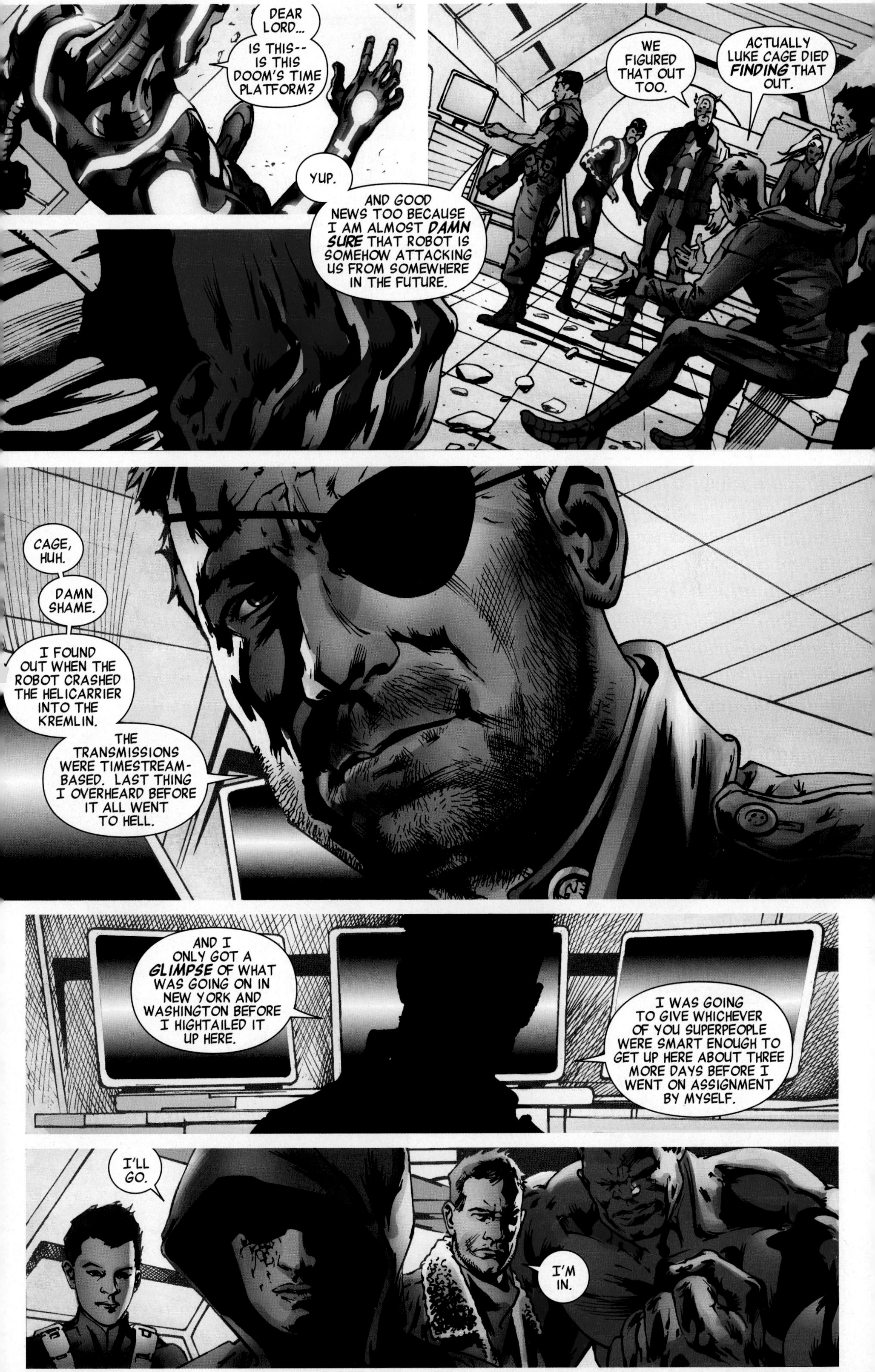
DEAR LORD...
IS THIS-- IS THIS DOOM'S TIME PLATFORM?
YUP.
AND GOOD NEWS TOO BECAUSE I AM ALMOST DAMN SURE THAT ROBOT IS SOMEHOW ATTACKING US FROM SOMEWHERE IN THE FUTURE.
WE FIGURED THAT OUT TOO.
ACTUALLY LUKE CAGE DIED FINDING THAT OUT.
CAGE, HUH.
DAMN SHAME.
I FOUND OUT WHEN THE ROBOT CRASHED THE HELICARRIER INTO THE KREMLIN.
THE TRANSMISSIONS WERE TIMESTREAM-BASED. LAST THING I OVERHEARD BEFORE IT ALL WENT TO HELL.
AND I ONLY GOT A GLIMPSE OF WHAT WAS GOING ON IN NEW YORK AND WASHINGTON BEFORE I HIGHTAILED IT UP HERE.
I WAS GOING TO GIVE WHICHEVER OF YOU SUPERPEOPLE WERE SMART ENOUGH TO GET UP HERE ABOUT THREE MORE DAYS BEFORE I WENT ON ASSIGNMENT BY MYSELF.
I'LL GO.
I'M IN.

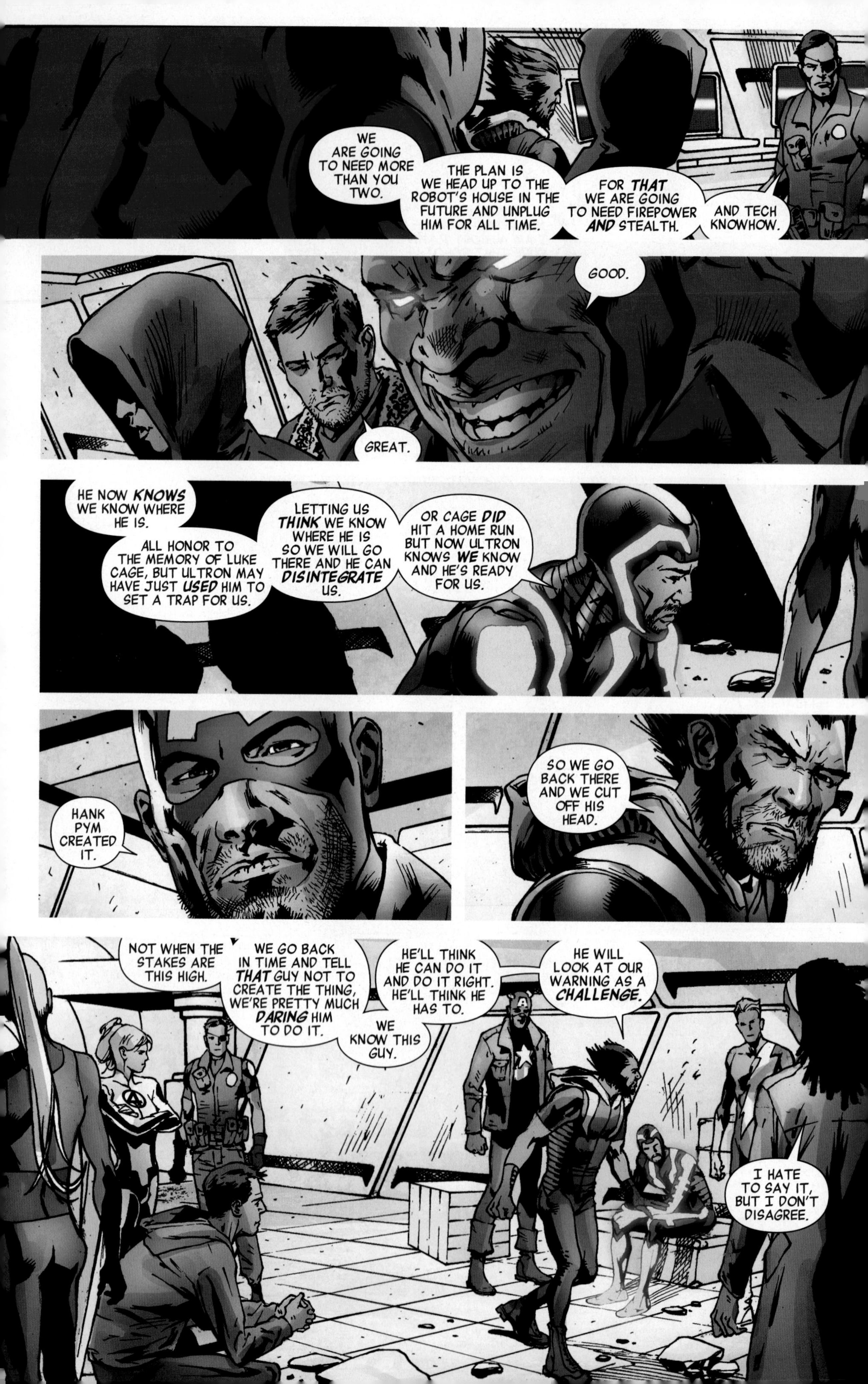
WE ARE GOING TO NEED MORE THAN YOU TWO.
THE PLAN IS WE HEAD UP TO THE ROBOT'S HOUSE IN THE FUTURE AND UNPLUG HIM FOR ALL TIME.
FOR THAT WE ARE GOING TO NEED FIREPOWER AND STEALTH.
AND TECH KNOWHOW.
GOOD.
GREAT.
HE NOW KNOWS WE KNOW WHERE HE IS.
ALL HONOR TO THE MEMORY OF LUKE CAGE, BUT ULTRON MAY HAVE JUST USED HIM TO SET A TRAP FOR US.
LETTING US THINK WE KNOW WHERE HE IS SO WE WILL GO THERE AND HE CAN DISINTEGRATE US.
OR CAGE DID HIT A HOME RUN BUT NOW ULTRON KNOWS WE KNOW AND HE'S READY FOR US.
HANK PYM CREATED IT.
SO WE GO BACK THERE AND WE CUT OFF HIS HEAD.
NOT WHEN THE STAKES ARE THIS HIGH.
WE GO BACK IN TIME AND TELL THAT GUY NOT TO CREATE THE THING, WE'RE PRETTY MUCH DARING HIM TO DO IT.
HE'LL THINK HE CAN DO IT AND DO IT RIGHT. HE'LL THINK HE HAS TO.
WE KNOW THIS GUY.
HE WILL LOOK AT OUR WARNING AS A CHALLENGE.
I HATE TO SAY IT, BUT I DON'T DISAGREE.

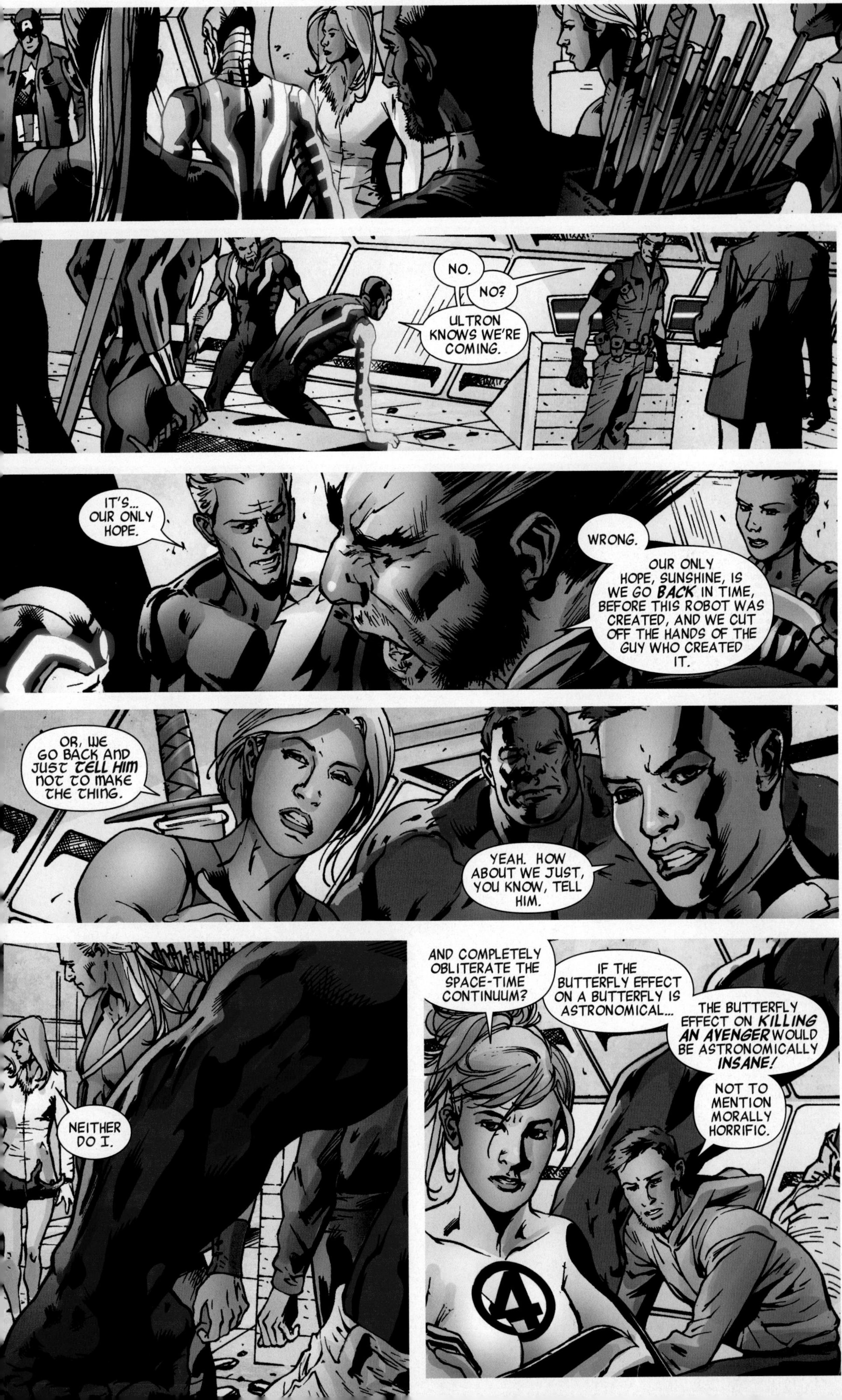
NO.
NO?
ULTRON KNOWS WE'RE COMING.
IT'S... OUR ONLY HOPE.
WRONG.
OUR ONLY HOPE, SUNSHINE, IS WE GO BACK IN TIME, BEFORE THIS ROBOT WAS CREATED, AND WE CUT OFF THE HANDS OF THE GUY WHO CREATED IT.
OR, WE GO BACK AND JUST TELL HIM NOT TO MAKE THE THING.
YEAH. HOW ABOUT WE JUST, YOU KNOW, TELL HIM.
NEITHER DO I.
AND COMPLETELY OBLITERATE THE SPACE-TIME CONTINUUM?
IF THE BUTTERFLY EFFECT ON A BUTTERFLY IS ASTRONOMICAL...
THE BUTTERFLY EFFECT ON KILLING AN AVENGER WOULD BE ASTRONOMICALLY INSANE!
NOT TO MENTION MORALLY HORRIFIC.

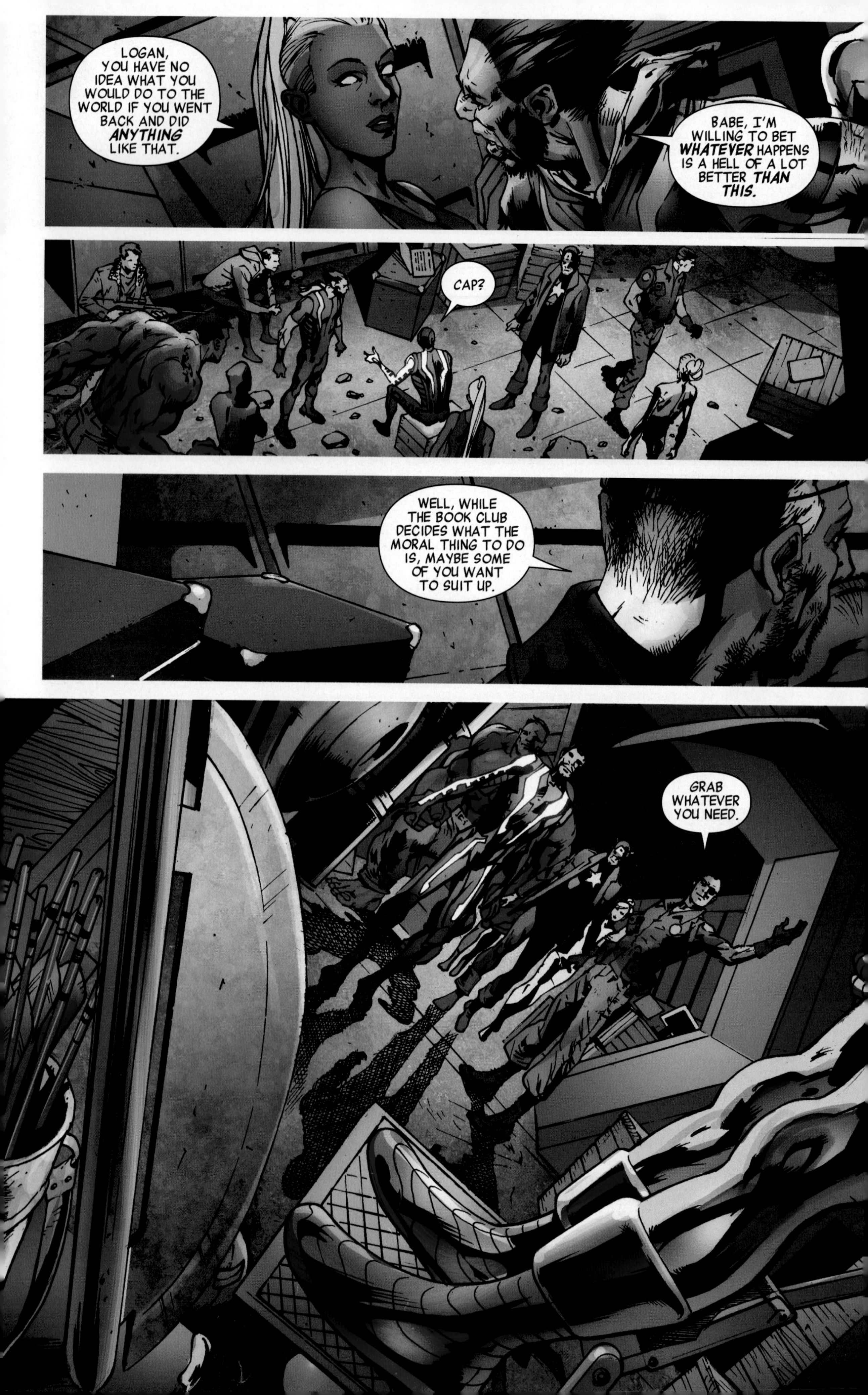
LOGAN, YOU HAVE NO IDEA WHAT YOU WOULD DO TO THE WORLD IF YOU WENT BACK AND DID ANYTHING LIKE THAT.
BABE, I'M WILLING TO BET WHATEVER HAPPENS IS A HELL OF A LOT BETTER THAN THIS.
CAP?
WELL, WHILE THE BOOK CLUB DECIDES WHAT THE MORAL THING TO DO IS, MAYBE SOME OF YOU WANT TO SUIT UP.
GRAB WHATEVER YOU NEED.

YOU AND HIM ARE THE *SAME KIND* OF SCIENCE NERD, STARK.

YOU TELL ME TRUE:

SOMEONE LIKE ME OR CAPTAIN AMERICA SHOWS UP ON YOUR DOORSTEP AND TELLS YOU *SPECIFICALLY* NOT TO DO SOMETHING...

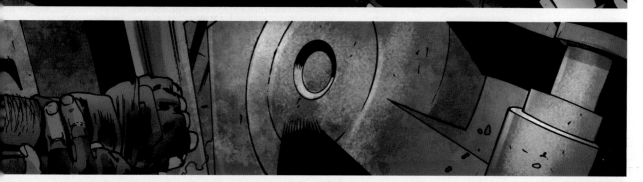

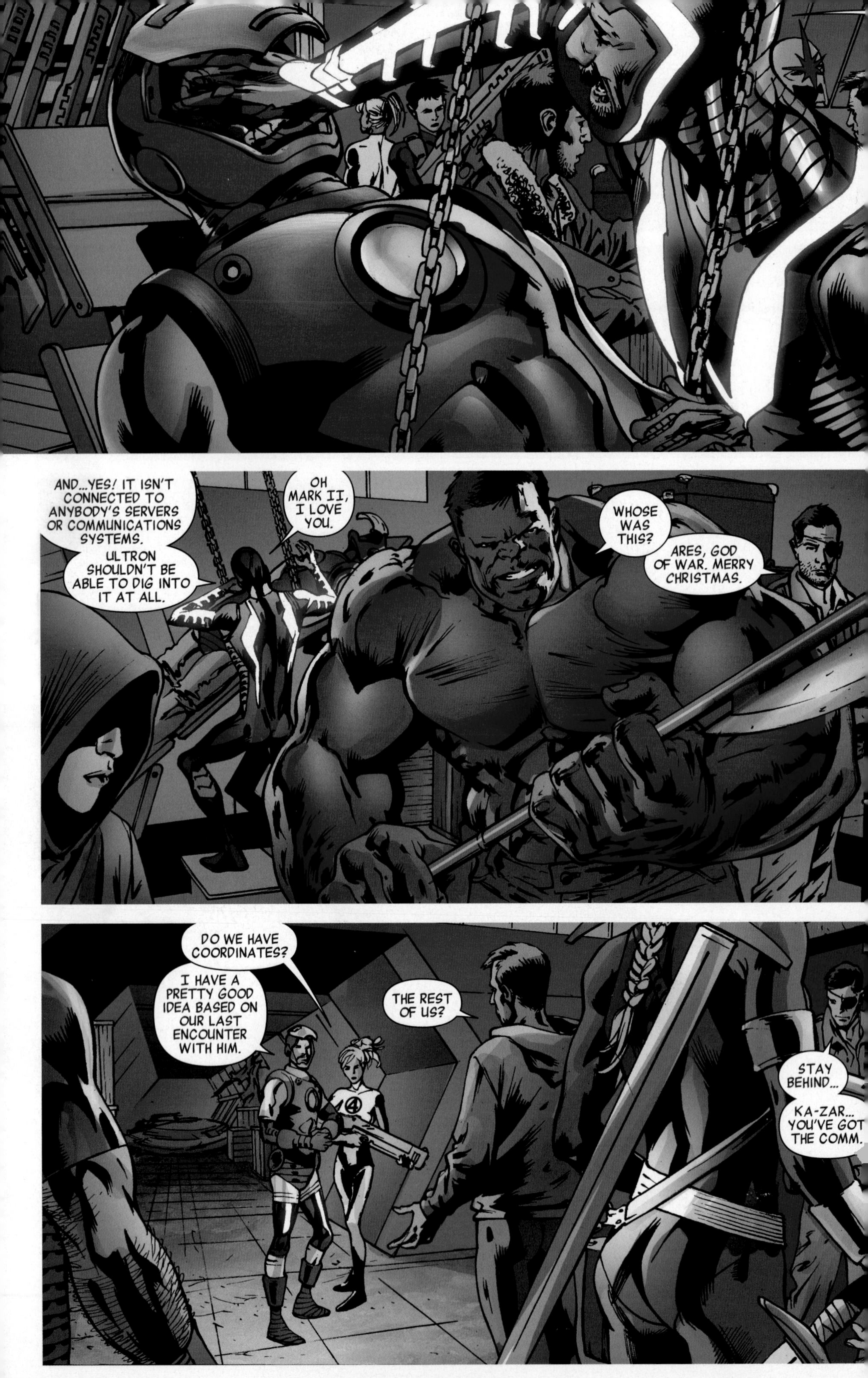
AND...YES! IT ISN'T CONNECTED TO ANYBODY'S SERVERS OR COMMUNICATIONS SYSTEMS.
ULTRON SHOULDN'T BE ABLE TO DIG INTO IT AT ALL.
OH MARK II, I LOVE YOU.
WHOSE WAS THIS?
ARES, GOD OF WAR. MERRY CHRISTMAS.
DO WE HAVE COORDINATES?
I HAVE A PRETTY GOOD IDEA BASED ON OUR LAST ENCOUNTER WITH HIM.
THE REST OF US?
STAY BEHIND...
KA-ZAR... YOU'VE GOT THE COMM.

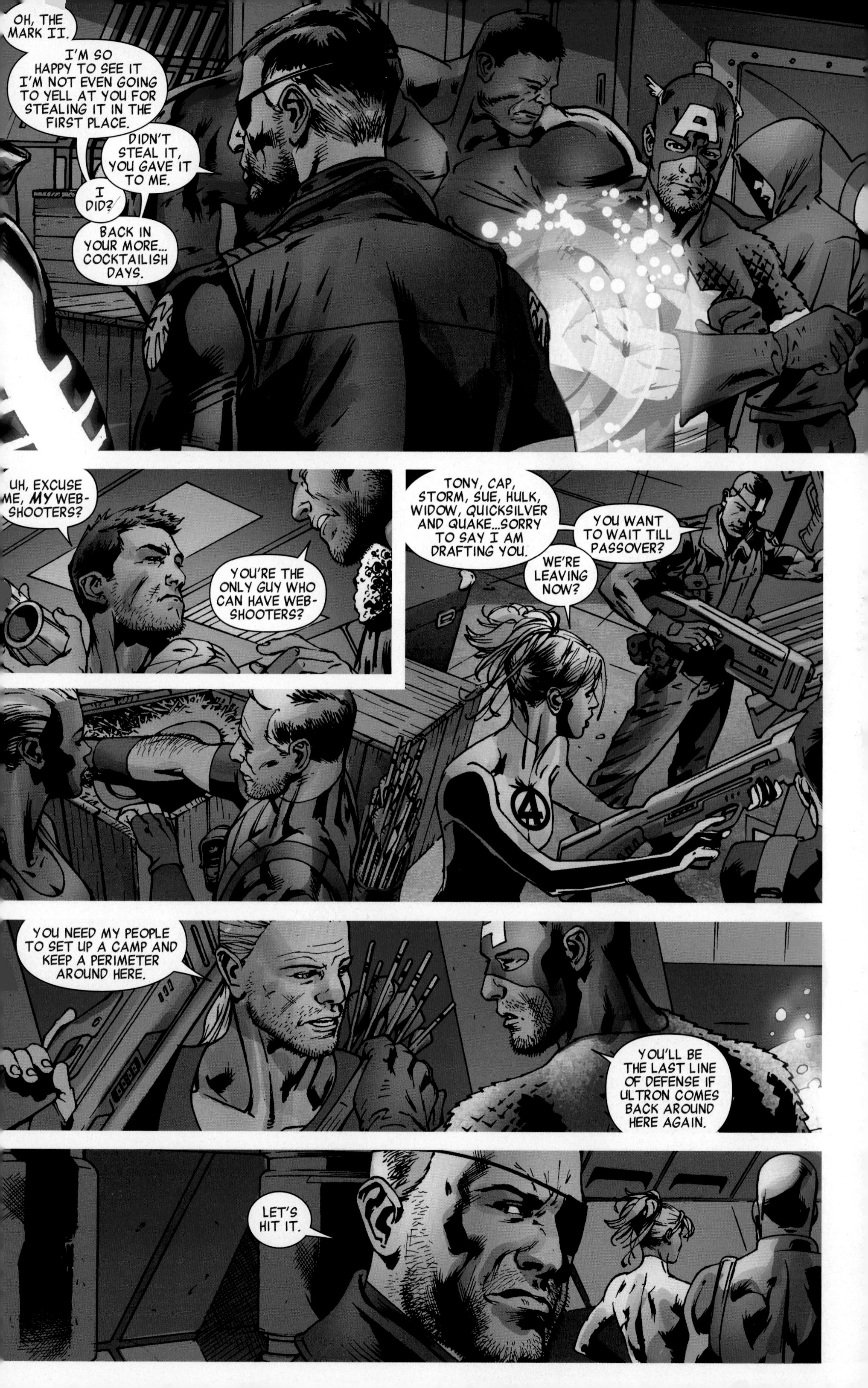

OH, THE MARK II.
I'M SO HAPPY TO SEE IT I'M NOT EVEN GOING TO YELL AT YOU FOR STEALING IT IN THE FIRST PLACE.
DIDN'T STEAL IT, YOU GAVE IT TO ME.
I DID?
BACK IN YOUR MORE... COCKTAILISH DAYS.
UH, EXCUSE ME, MY WEB-SHOOTERS?
YOU'RE THE ONLY GUY WHO CAN HAVE WEB-SHOOTERS?
TONY, CAP, STORM, SUE, HULK, WIDOW, QUICKSILVER AND QUAKE...SORRY TO SAY I AM DRAFTING YOU.
YOU WANT TO WAIT TILL PASSOVER?
WE'RE LEAVING NOW?
YOU NEED MY PEOPLE TO SET UP A CAMP AND KEEP A PERIMETER AROUND HERE.
YOU'LL BE THE LAST LINE OF DEFENSE IF ULTRON COMES BACK AROUND HERE AGAIN.
LET'S HIT IT.

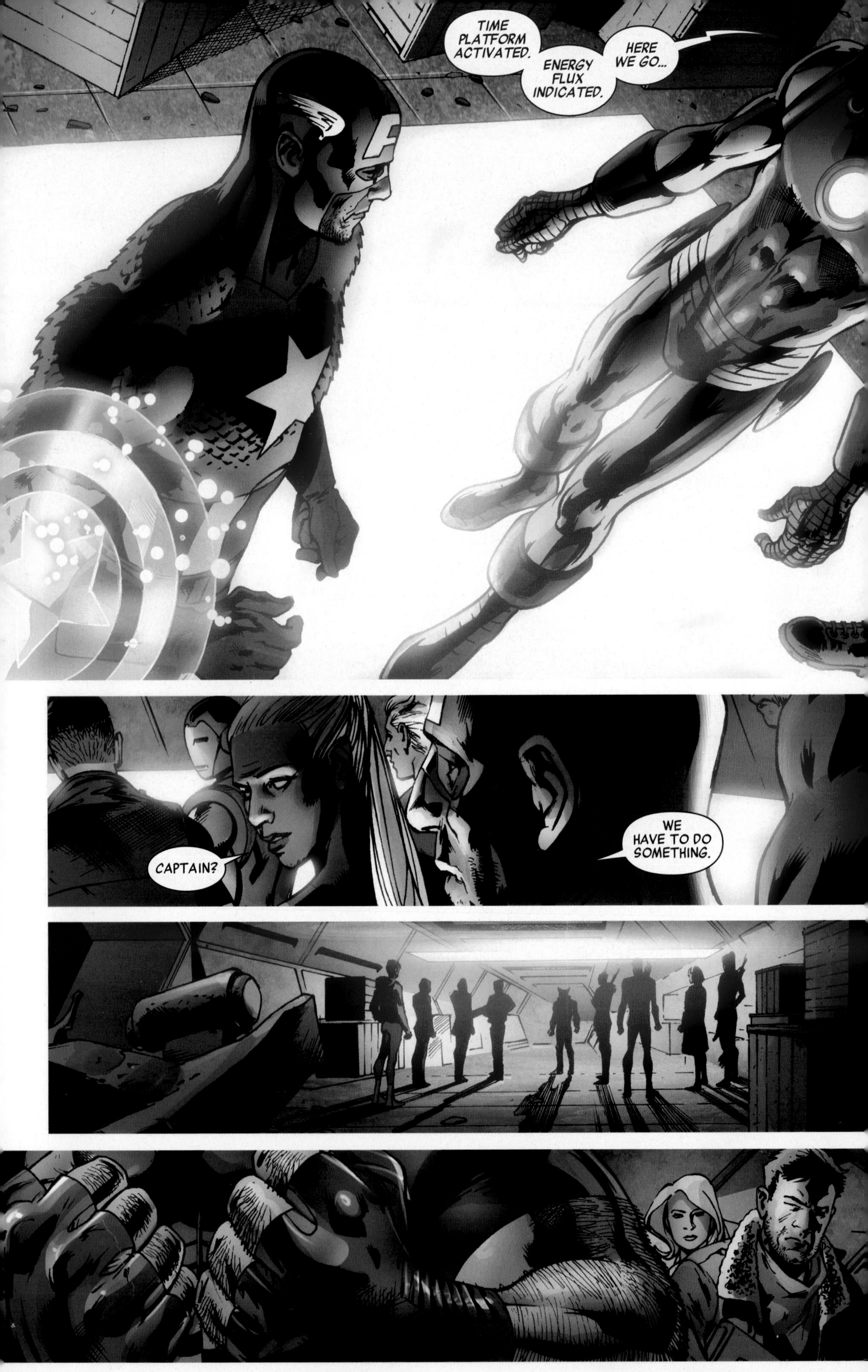
TIME PLATFORM ACTIVATED.
ENERGY FLUX INDICATED.
HERE WE GO...
CAPTAIN?
WE HAVE TO DO SOMETHING.

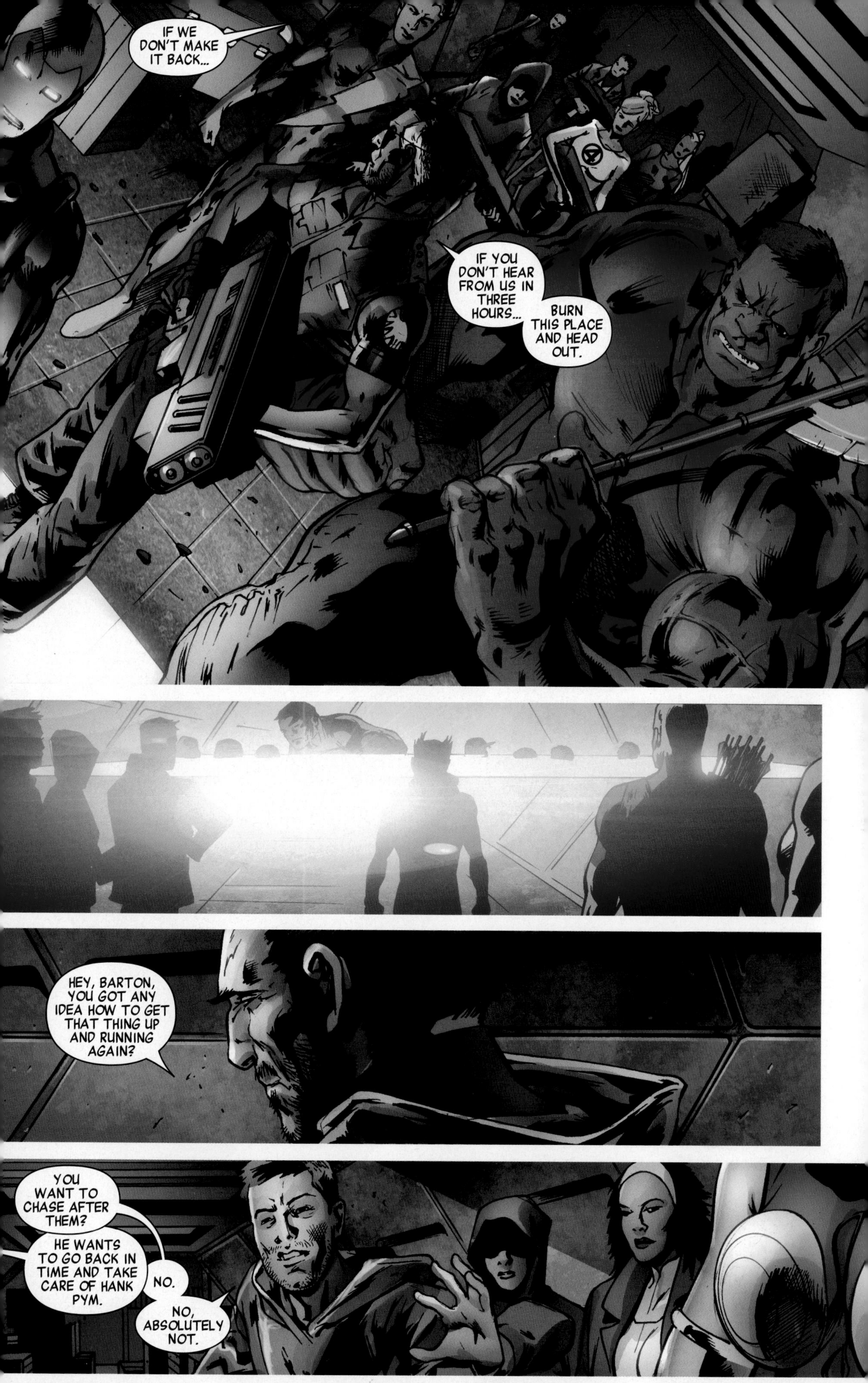
IF WE DON'T MAKE IT BACK...
IF YOU DON'T HEAR FROM US IN THREE HOURS...
BURN THIS PLACE AND HEAD OUT.
HEY, BARTON, YOU GOT ANY IDEA HOW TO GET THAT THING UP AND RUNNING AGAIN?
YOU WANT TO CHASE AFTER THEM?
HE WANTS TO GO BACK IN TIME AND TAKE CARE OF HANK PYM.
NO.
NO, ABSOLUTELY NOT.

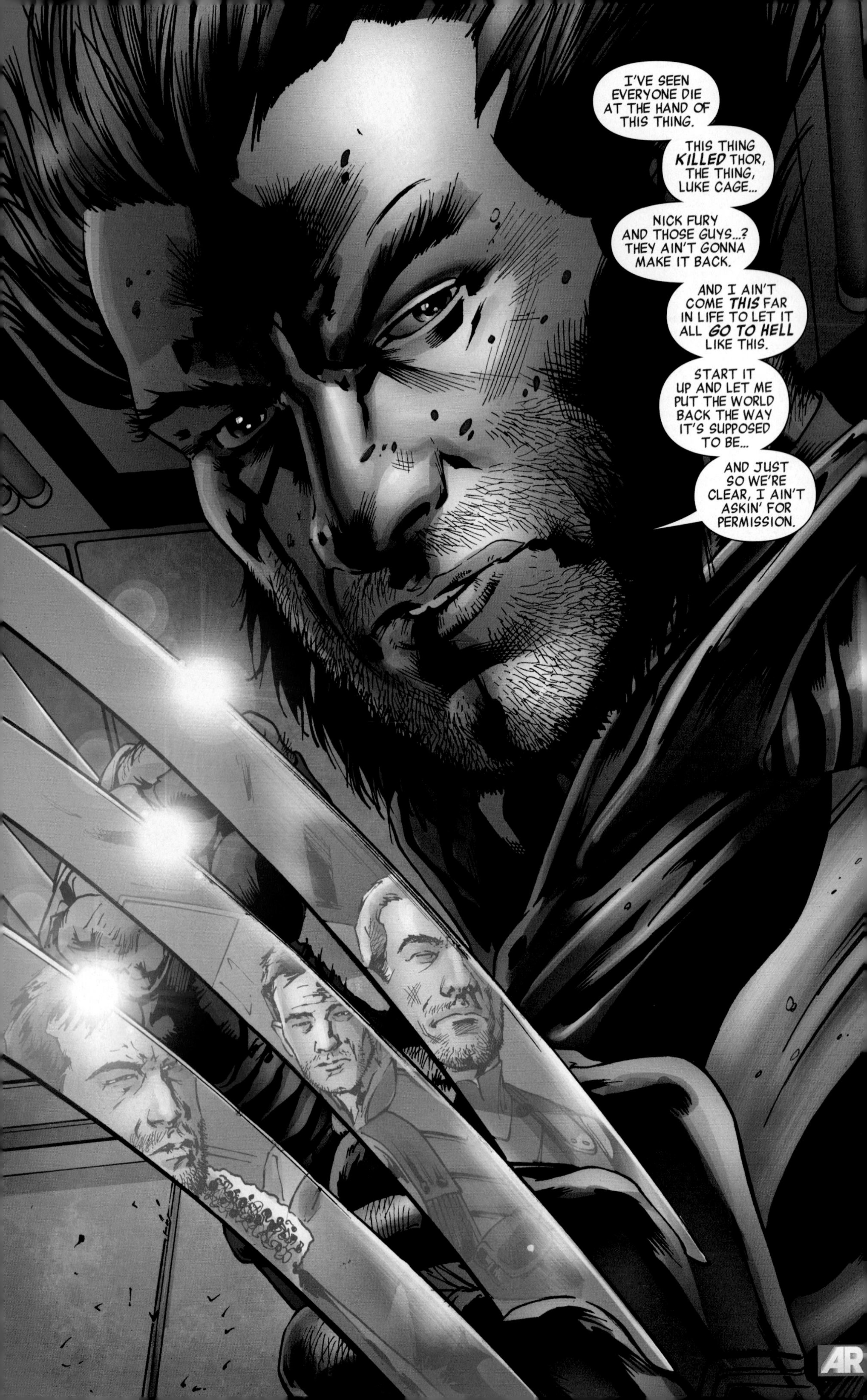
I'VE SEEN EVERYONE DIE AT THE HAND OF THIS THING.
THIS THING KILLED THOR, THE THING, LUKE CAGE...
NICK FURY AND THOSE GUYS...? THEY AIN'T GONNA MAKE IT BACK.
AND I AIN'T COME THIS FAR IN LIFE TO LET IT ALL GO TO HELL LIKE THIS.
START IT UP AND LET ME PUT THE WORLD BACK THE WAY IT'S SUPPOSED TO BE...
AND JUST SO WE'RE CLEAR, I AIN'T ASKIN' FOR PERMISSION.

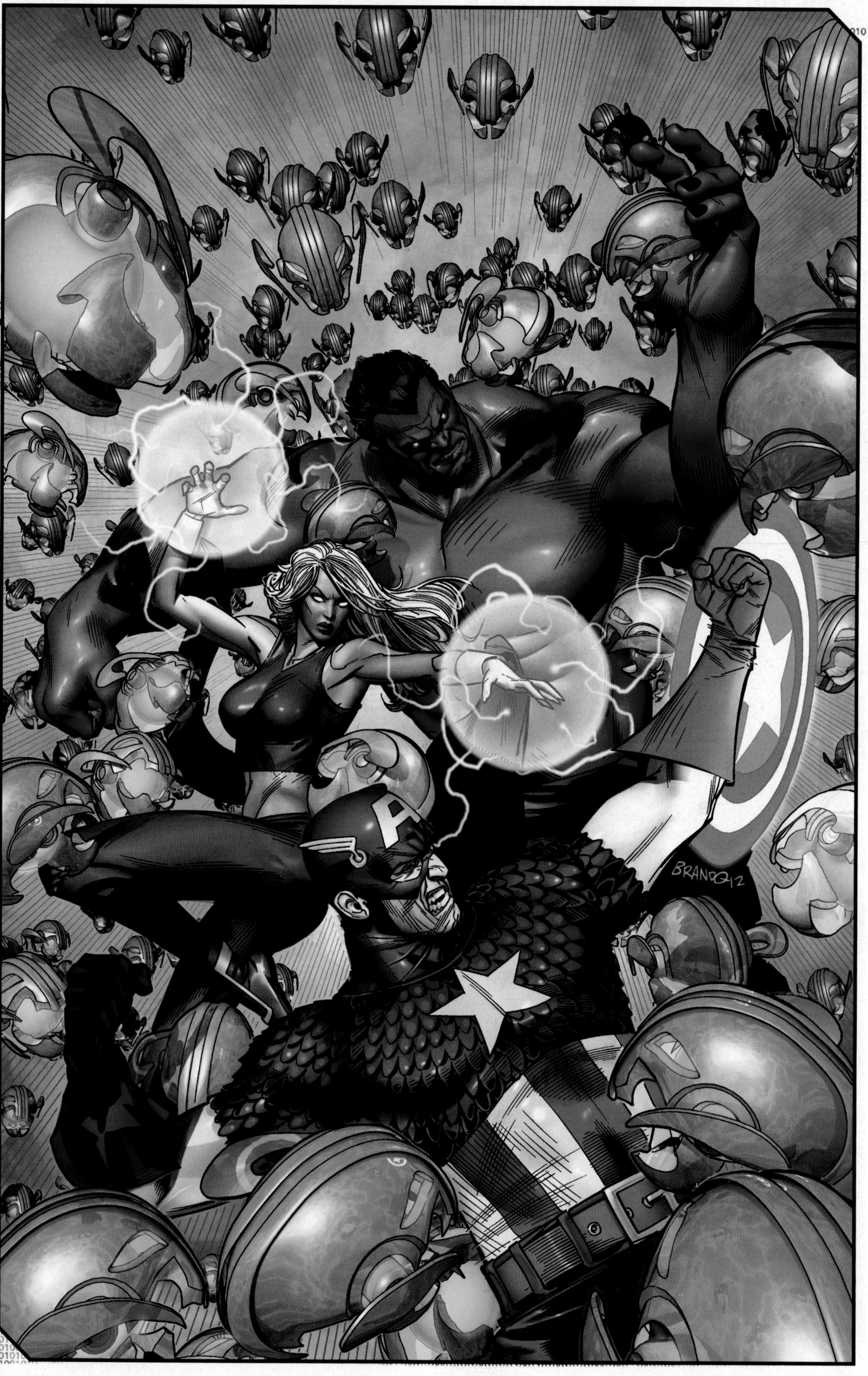
BRANDO '12

AGE OF ULTRON #6

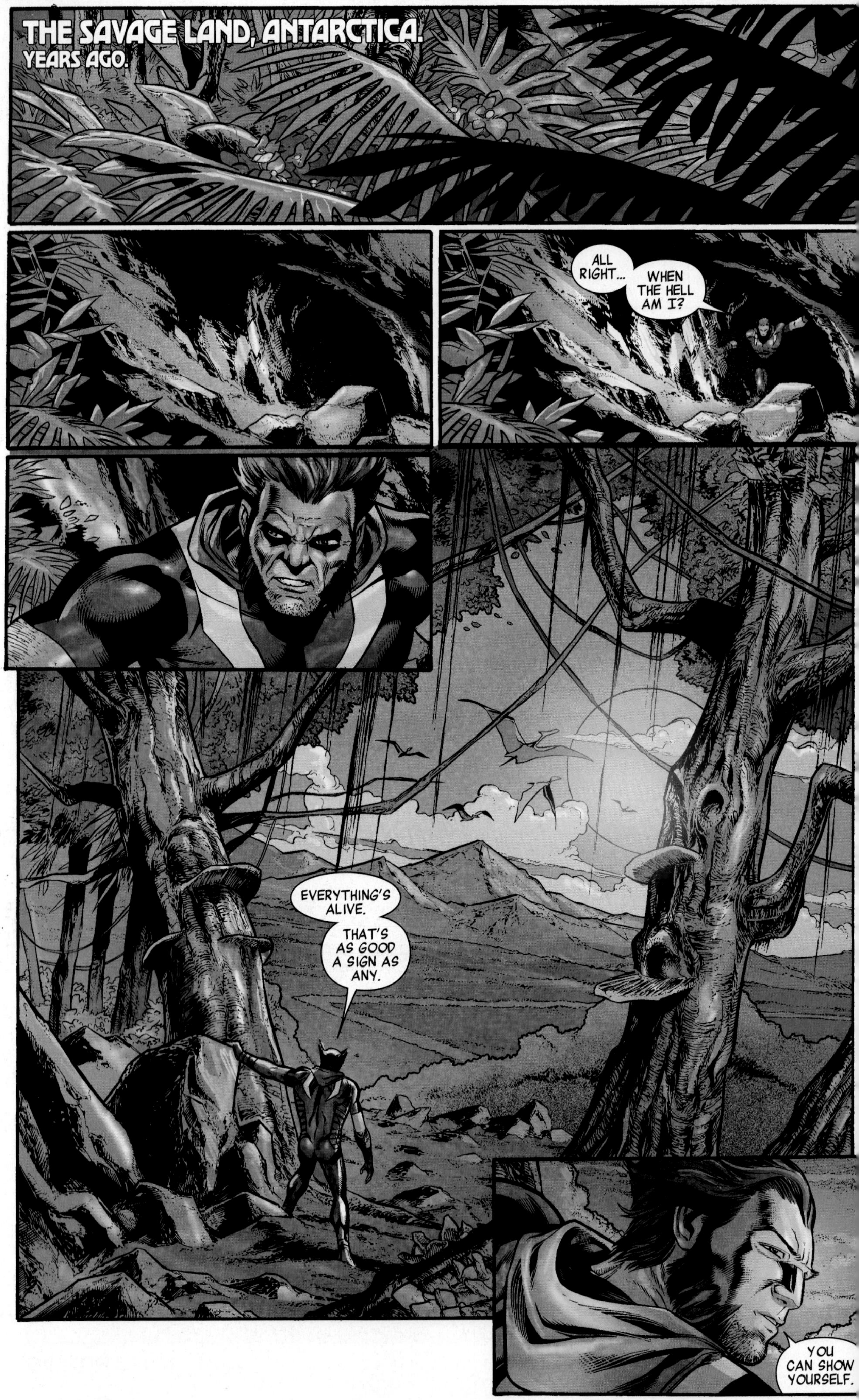
THE SAVAGE LAND, ANTARCTICA.
YEARS AGO.
ALL RIGHT...
WHEN THE HELL AM I?
EVERYTHING'S ALIVE.
THAT'S AS GOOD A SIGN AS ANY.
YOU CAN SHOW YOURSELF.

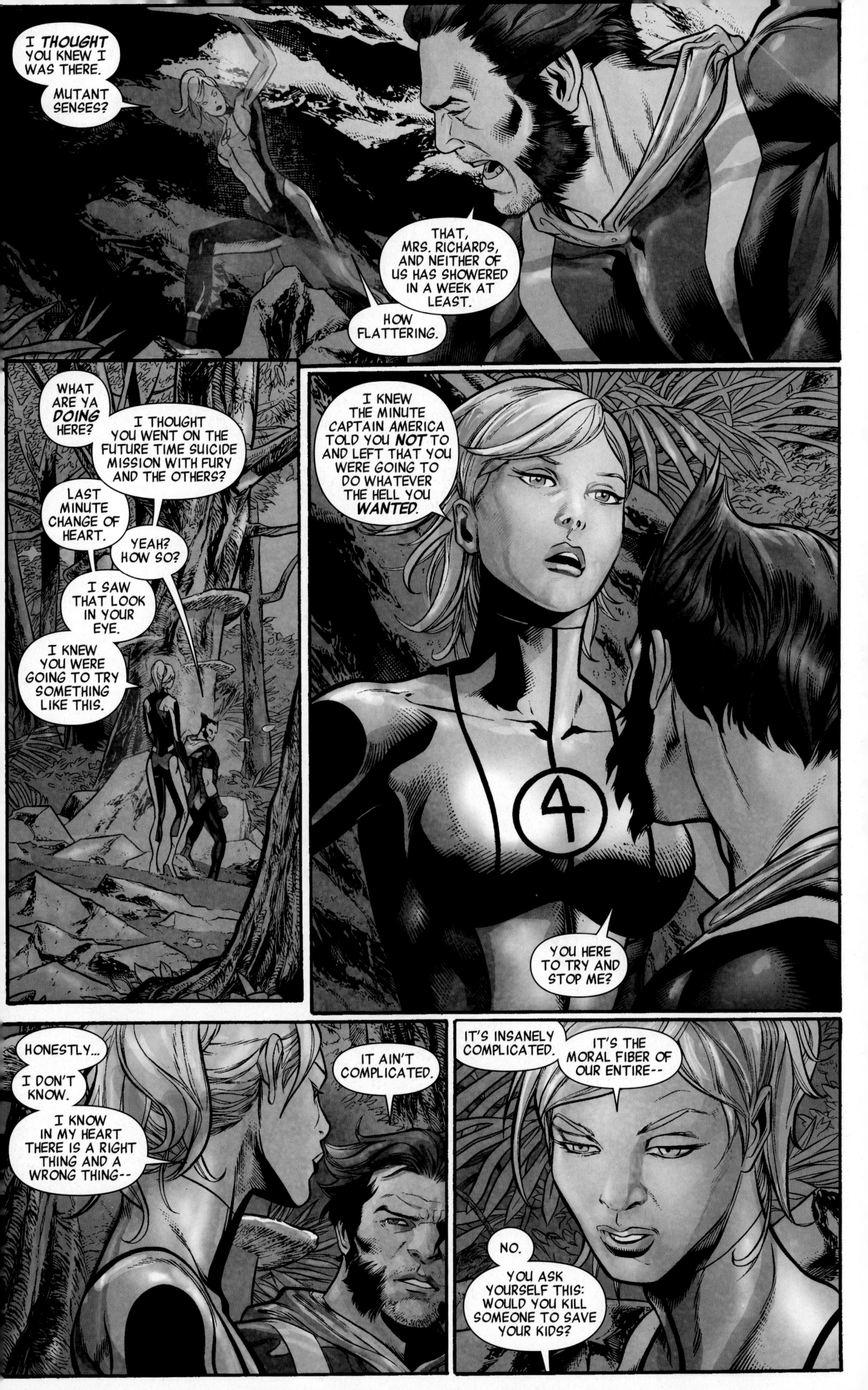
I THOUGHT YOU KNEW I WAS THERE.
MUTANT SENSES?
THAT, MRS. RICHARDS, AND NEITHER OF US HAS SHOWERED IN A WEEK AT LEAST.
HOW FLATTERING.
WHAT ARE YA DOING HERE?
I THOUGHT YOU WENT ON THE FUTURE TIME SUICIDE MISSION WITH FURY AND THE OTHERS?
LAST MINUTE CHANGE OF HEART.
YEAH? HOW SO?
I SAW THAT LOOK IN YOUR EYE.
I KNEW YOU WERE GOING TO TRY SOMETHING LIKE THIS.
I KNEW THE MINUTE CAPTAIN AMERICA TOLD YOU NOT TO AND LEFT THAT YOU WERE GOING TO DO WHATEVER THE HELL YOU WANTED.
YOU HERE TO TRY AND STOP ME?
HONESTLY...
I DON'T KNOW.
I KNOW IN MY HEART THERE IS A RIGHT THING AND A WRONG THING--
IT AIN'T COMPLICATED.
IT'S INSANELY COMPLICATED.
IT'S THE MORAL FIBER OF OUR ENTIRE--
NO.
YOU ASK YOURSELF THIS: WOULD YOU KILL SOMEONE TO SAVE YOUR KIDS?

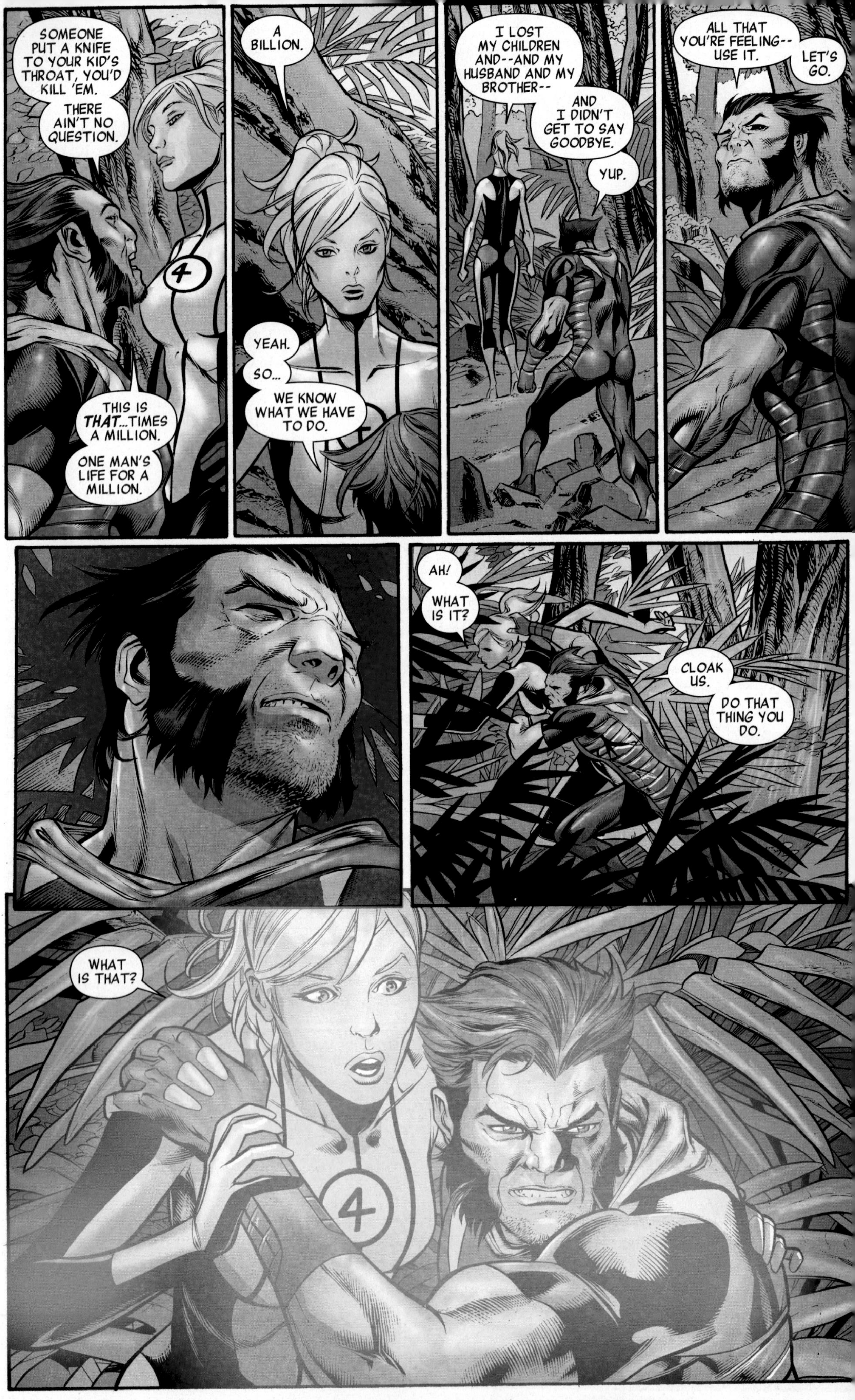
SOMEONE PUT A KNIFE TO YOUR KID'S THROAT, YOU'D KILL 'EM.
THERE AIN'T NO QUESTION.
THIS IS *THAT*...TIMES A MILLION.
ONE MAN'S LIFE FOR A MILLION.
A BILLION.
YEAH.
SO...
WE KNOW WHAT WE HAVE TO DO.
I LOST MY CHILDREN AND--AND MY HUSBAND AND MY BROTHER--
AND I DIDN'T GET TO SAY GOODBYE.
YUP.
ALL THAT YOU'RE FEELING-- USE IT.
LET'S GO.
AH!
WHAT IS IT?
CLOAK US.
DO THAT THING YOU DO.
WHAT IS THAT?

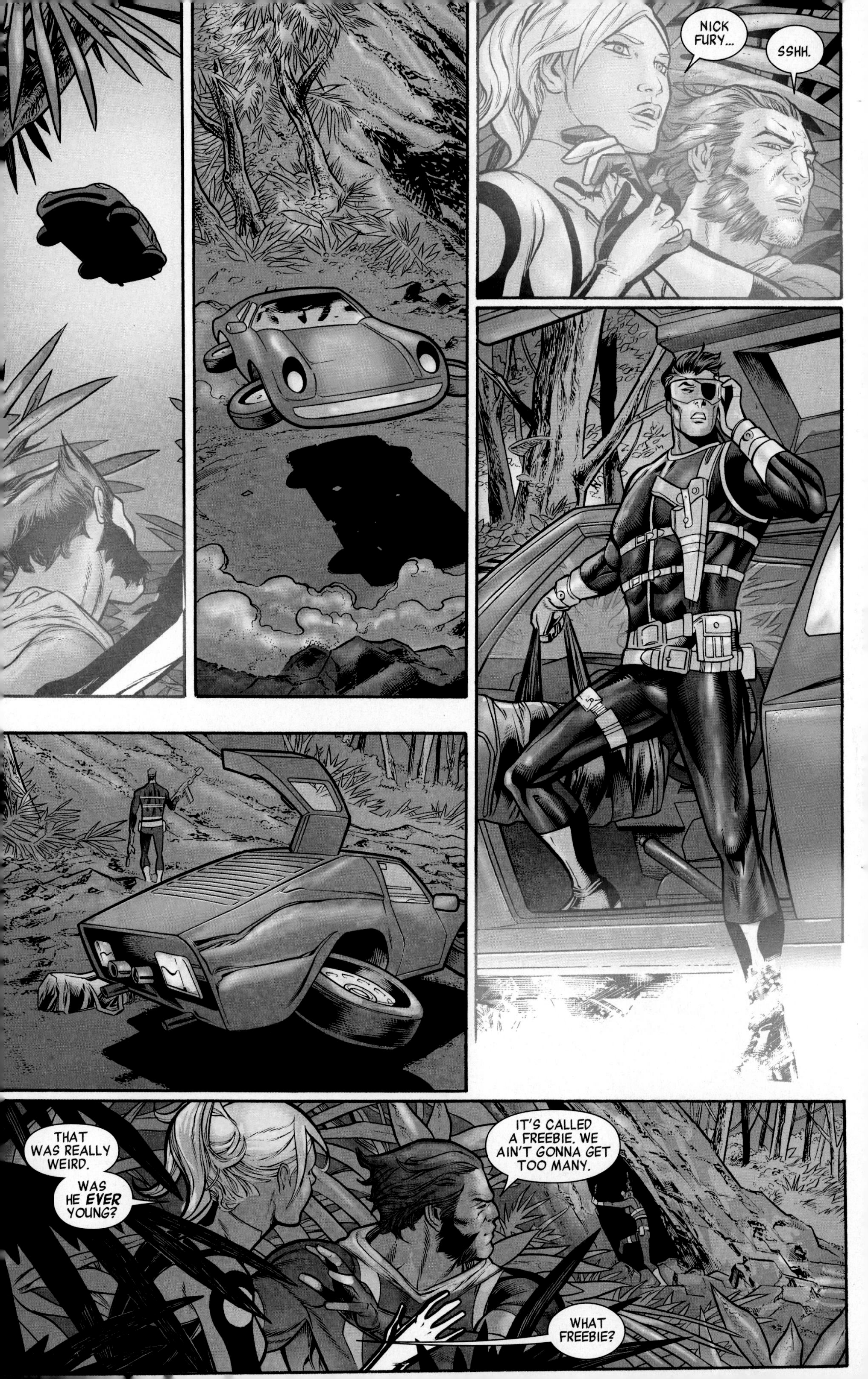
NICK FURY...
SSHH.
THAT WAS REALLY WEIRD.
WAS HE EVER YOUNG?
IT'S CALLED A FREEBIE. WE AIN'T GONNA GET TOO MANY.
WHAT FREEBIE?

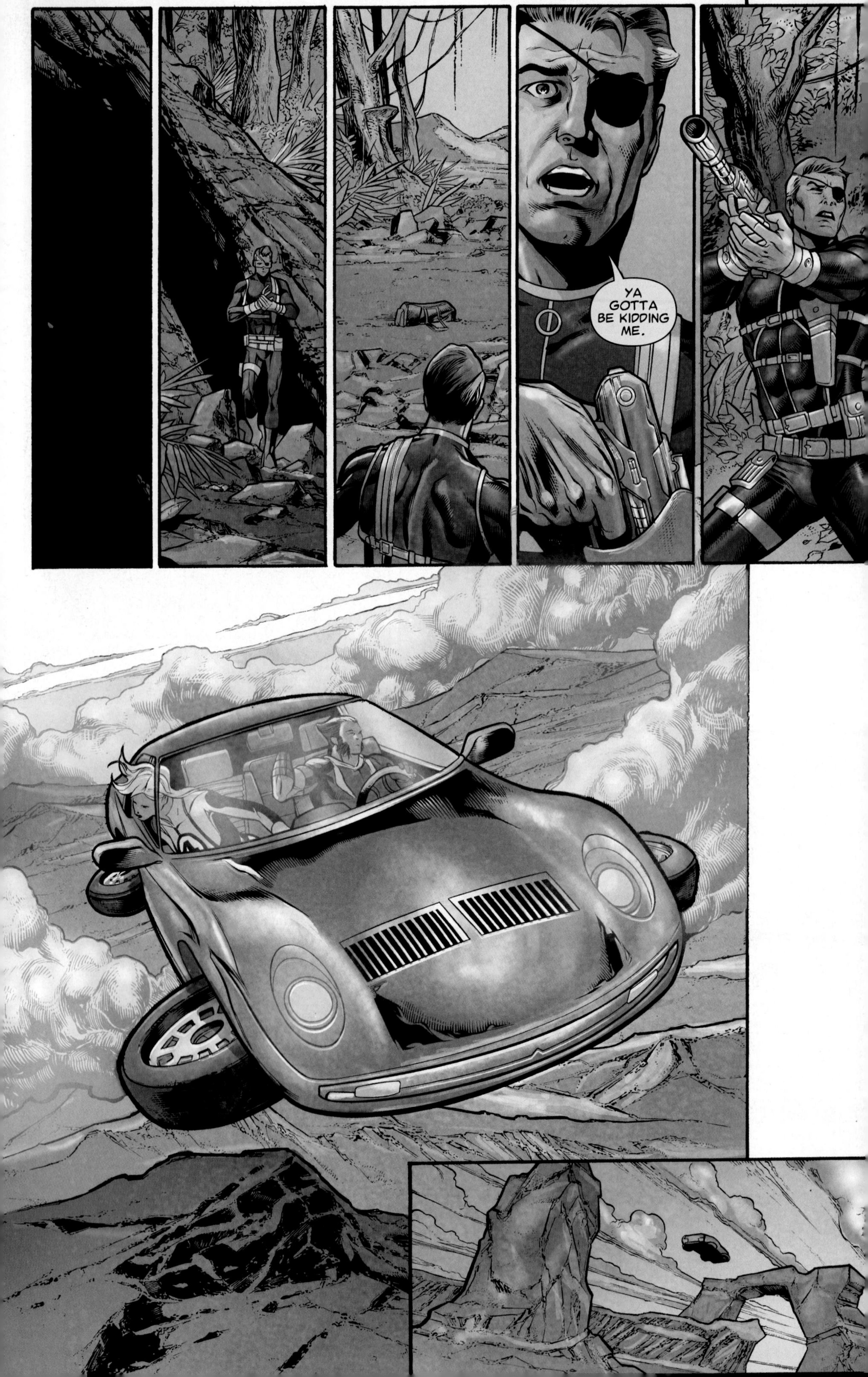
YA GOTTA BE KIDDING ME.

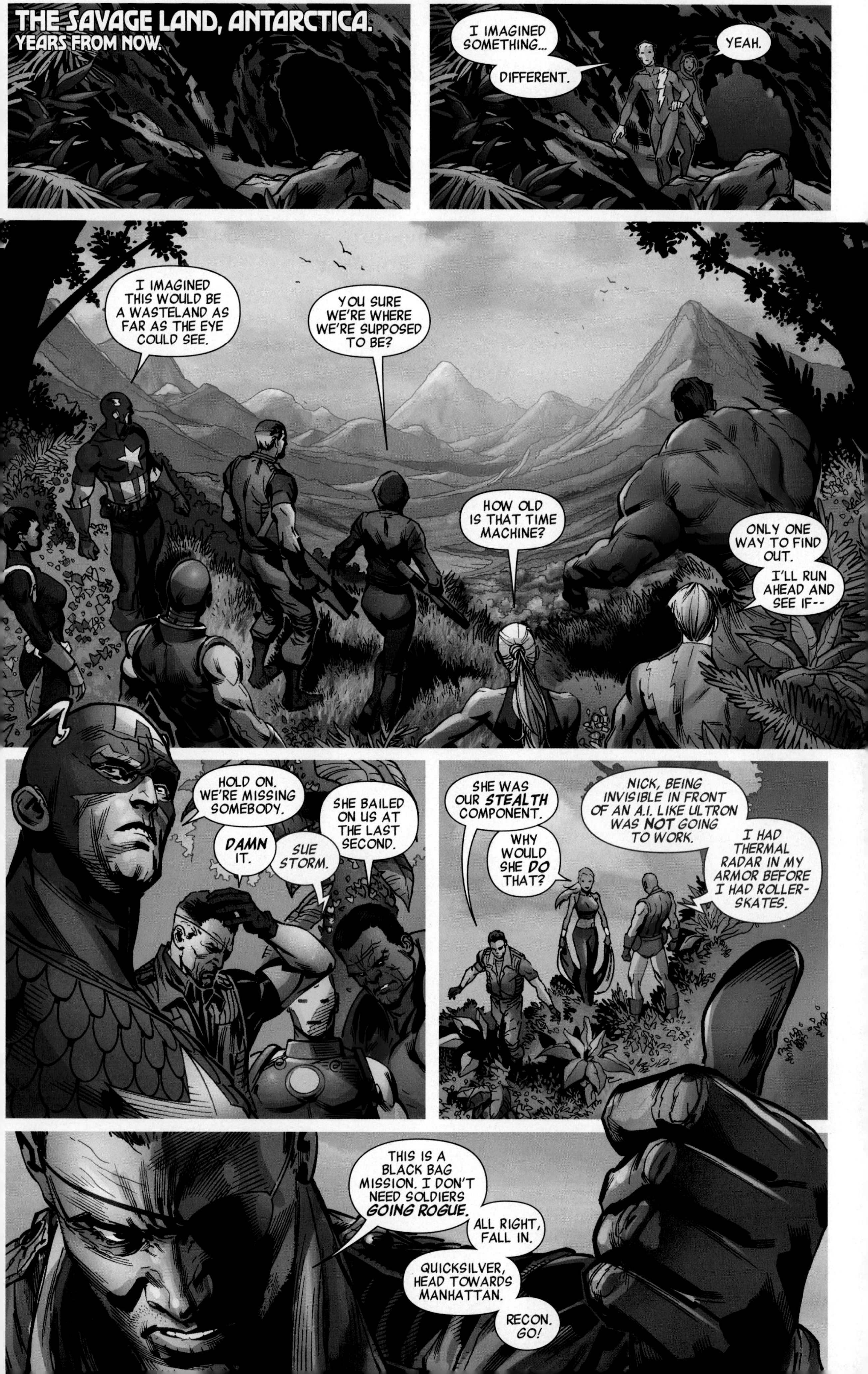
THE SAVAGE LAND, ANTARCTICA.
YEARS FROM NOW.
I IMAGINED SOMETHING...
DIFFERENT.
YEAH.
I IMAGINED THIS WOULD BE A WASTELAND AS FAR AS THE EYE COULD SEE.
YOU SURE WE'RE WHERE WE'RE SUPPOSED TO BE?
HOW OLD IS THAT TIME MACHINE?
ONLY ONE WAY TO FIND OUT.
I'LL RUN AHEAD AND SEE IF--
HOLD ON. WE'RE MISSING SOMEBODY.
DAMN IT.
SUE STORM.
SHE BAILED ON US AT THE LAST SECOND.
SHE WAS OUR STEALTH COMPONENT.
WHY WOULD SHE DO THAT?
NICK, BEING INVISIBLE IN FRONT OF AN A.I. LIKE ULTRON WAS NOT GOING TO WORK.
I HAD THERMAL RADAR IN MY ARMOR BEFORE I HAD ROLLER-SKATES.
THIS IS A BLACK BAG MISSION. I DON'T NEED SOLDIERS GOING ROGUE.
ALL RIGHT, FALL IN.
QUICKSILVER, HEAD TOWARDS MANHATTAN.
RECON. GO!

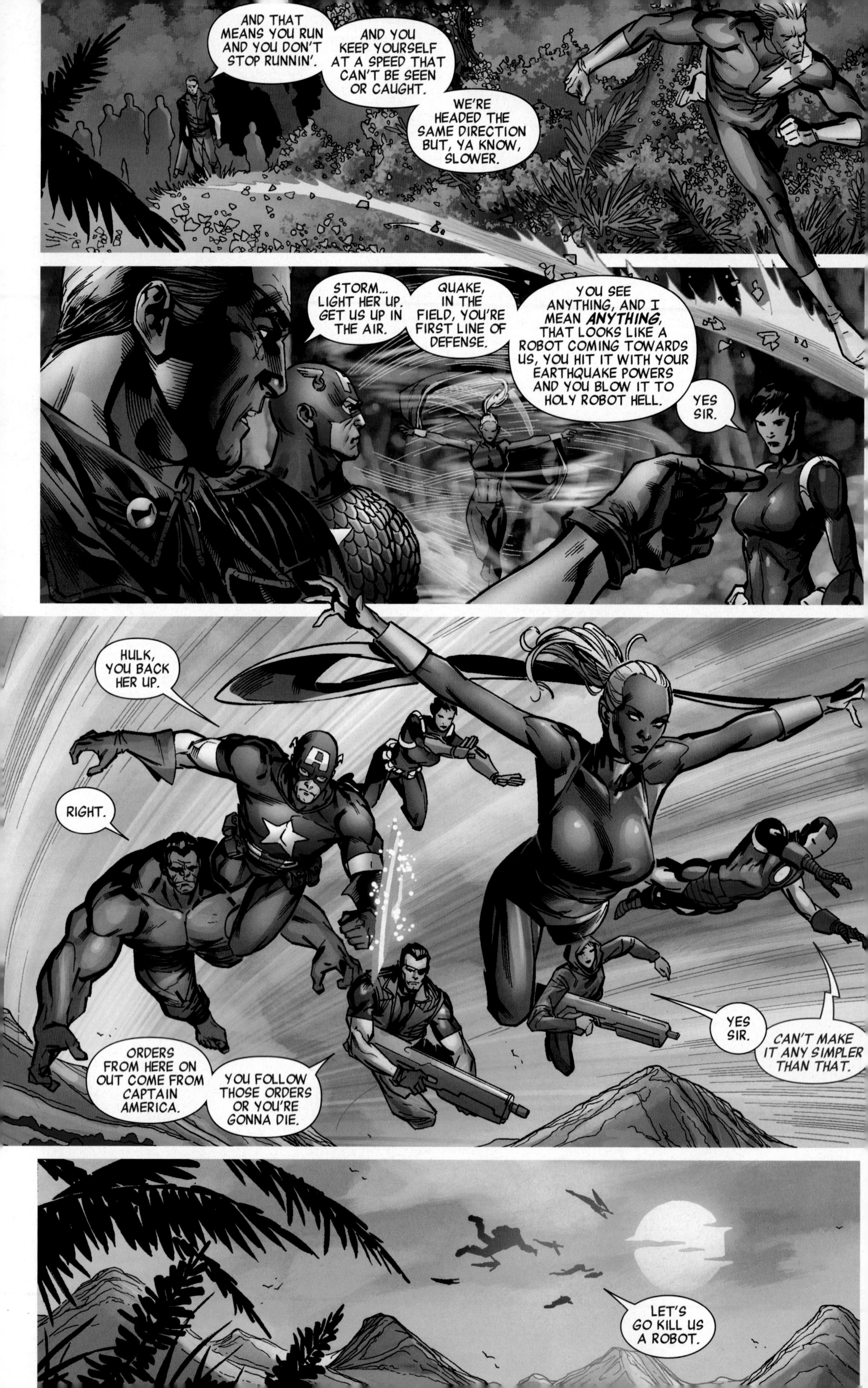
AND THAT MEANS YOU RUN AND YOU DON'T STOP RUNNIN'.
AND YOU KEEP YOURSELF AT A SPEED THAT CAN'T BE SEEN OR CAUGHT.
WE'RE HEADED THE SAME DIRECTION BUT, YA KNOW, SLOWER.
STORM... LIGHT HER UP. GET US UP IN THE AIR.
QUAKE, IN THE FIELD, YOU'RE FIRST LINE OF DEFENSE.
YOU SEE ANYTHING, AND I MEAN ANYTHING, THAT LOOKS LIKE A ROBOT COMING TOWARDS US, YOU HIT IT WITH YOUR EARTHQUAKE POWERS AND YOU BLOW IT TO HOLY ROBOT HELL.
YES SIR.
HULK, YOU BACK HER UP.
RIGHT.
ORDERS FROM HERE ON OUT COME FROM CAPTAIN AMERICA.
YOU FOLLOW THOSE ORDERS OR YOU'RE GONNA DIE.
YES SIR.
CAN'T MAKE IT ANY SIMPLER THAN THAT.
LET'S GO KILL US A ROBOT.

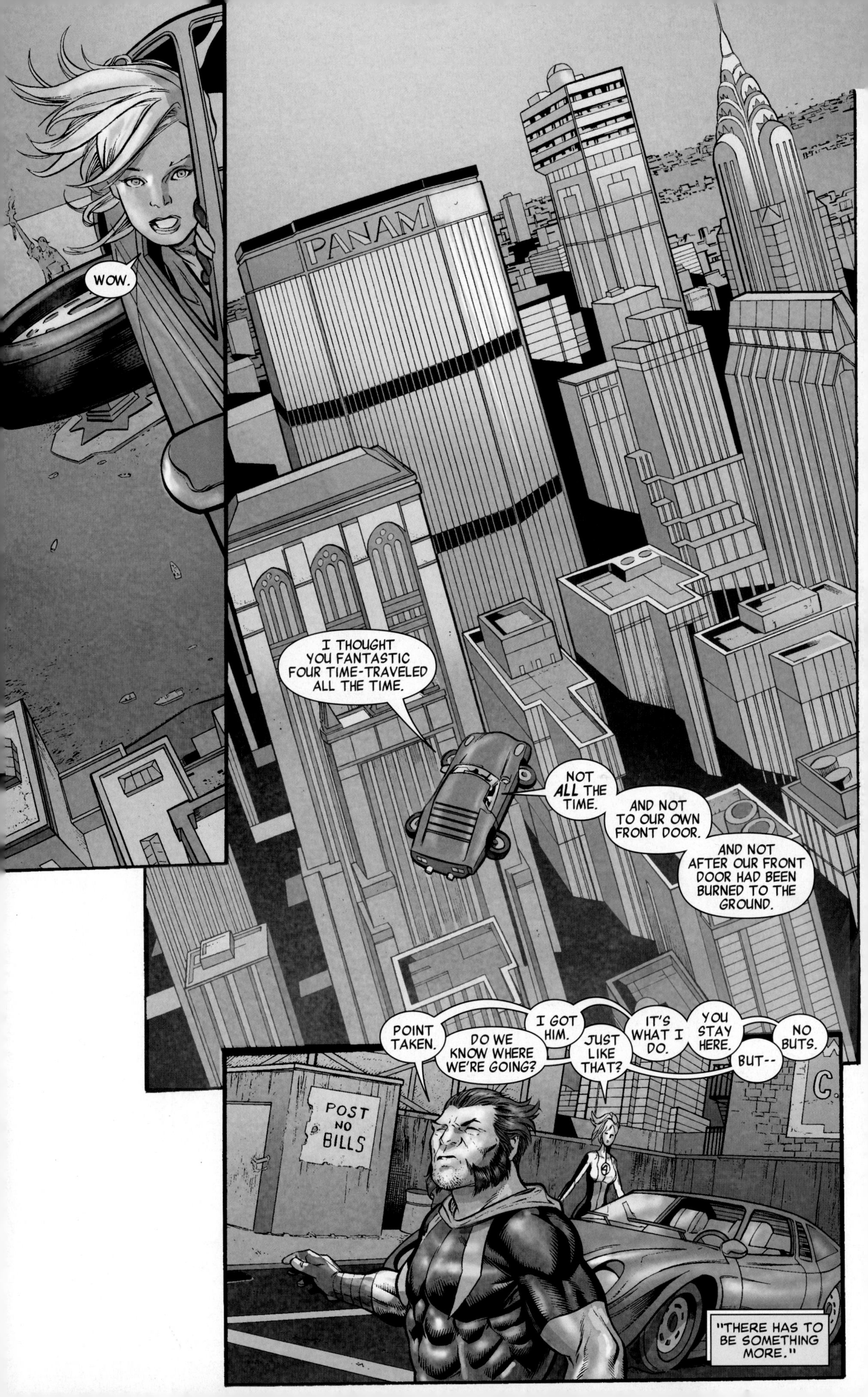
WOW.
I THOUGHT YOU FANTASTIC FOUR TIME-TRAVELED ALL THE TIME.
NOT ALL THE TIME.
AND NOT TO OUR OWN FRONT DOOR.
AND NOT AFTER OUR FRONT DOOR HAD BEEN BURNED TO THE GROUND.
POINT TAKEN.
DO WE KNOW WHERE WE'RE GOING?
I GOT HIM.
JUST LIKE THAT?
IT'S WHAT I DO.
YOU STAY HERE.
BUT--
NO BUTS.
POST NO BILLS
"THERE HAS TO BE SOMETHING MORE."

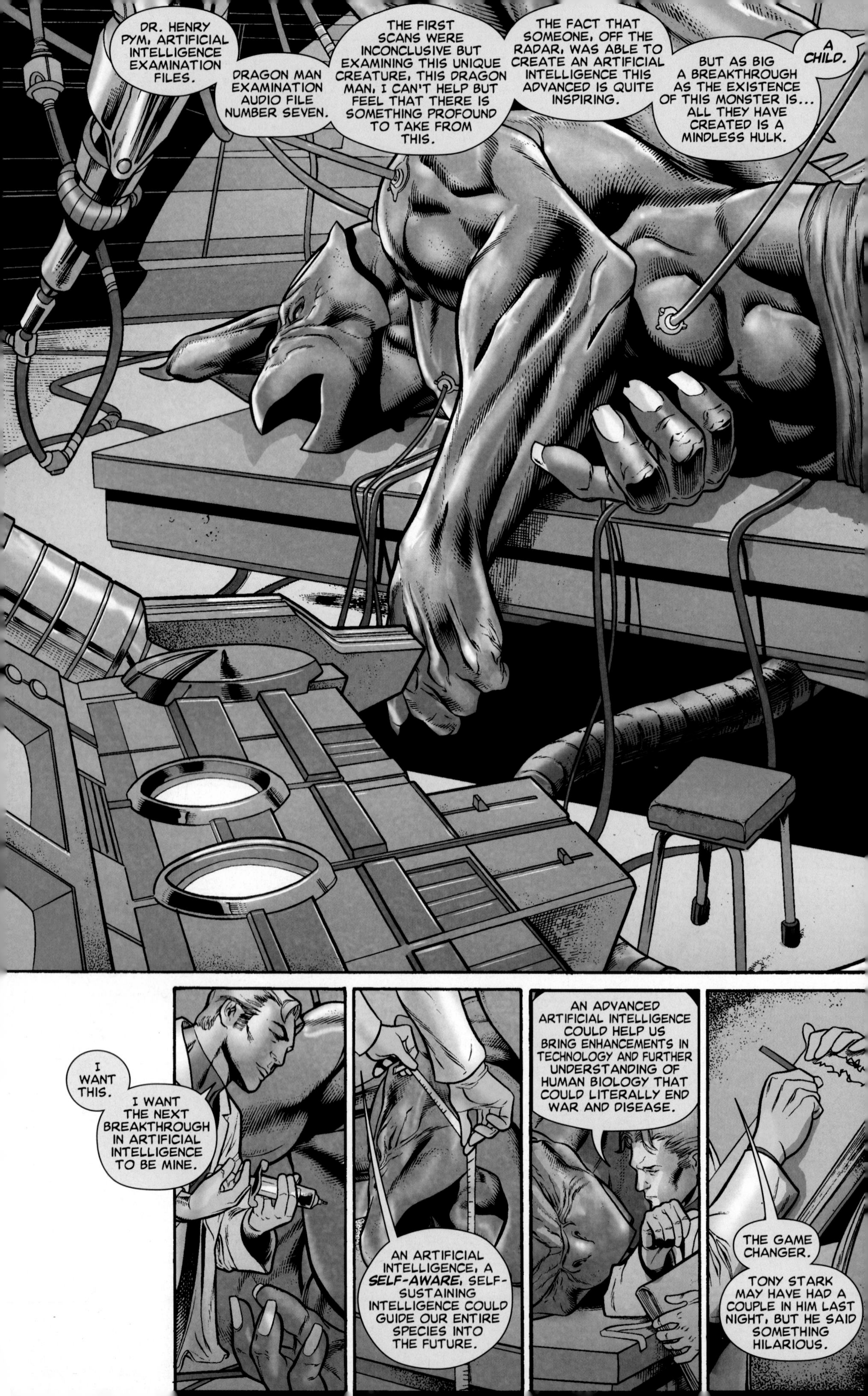
DR. HENRY PYM, ARTIFICIAL INTELLIGENCE EXAMINATION FILES.
DRAGON MAN EXAMINATION AUDIO FILE NUMBER SEVEN.
THE FIRST SCANS WERE INCONCLUSIVE BUT EXAMINING THIS UNIQUE CREATURE, THIS DRAGON MAN, I CAN'T HELP BUT FEEL THAT THERE IS SOMETHING PROFOUND TO TAKE FROM THIS.
THE FACT THAT SOMEONE, OFF THE RADAR, WAS ABLE TO CREATE AN ARTIFICIAL INTELLIGENCE THIS ADVANCED IS QUITE INSPIRING.
BUT AS BIG A BREAKTHROUGH AS THE EXISTENCE OF THIS MONSTER IS... ALL THEY HAVE CREATED IS A MINDLESS HULK.
A CHILD.
I WANT THIS.
I WANT THE NEXT BREAKTHROUGH IN ARTIFICIAL INTELLIGENCE TO BE MINE.
AN ARTIFICIAL INTELLIGENCE, A SELF-AWARE, SELF-SUSTAINING INTELLIGENCE COULD GUIDE OUR ENTIRE SPECIES INTO THE FUTURE.
AN ADVANCED ARTIFICIAL INTELLIGENCE COULD HELP US BRING ENHANCEMENTS IN TECHNOLOGY AND FURTHER UNDERSTANDING OF HUMAN BIOLOGY THAT COULD LITERALLY END WAR AND DISEASE.
THE GAME CHANGER.
TONY STARK MAY HAVE HAD A COUPLE IN HIM LAST NIGHT, BUT HE SAID SOMETHING HILARIOUS.

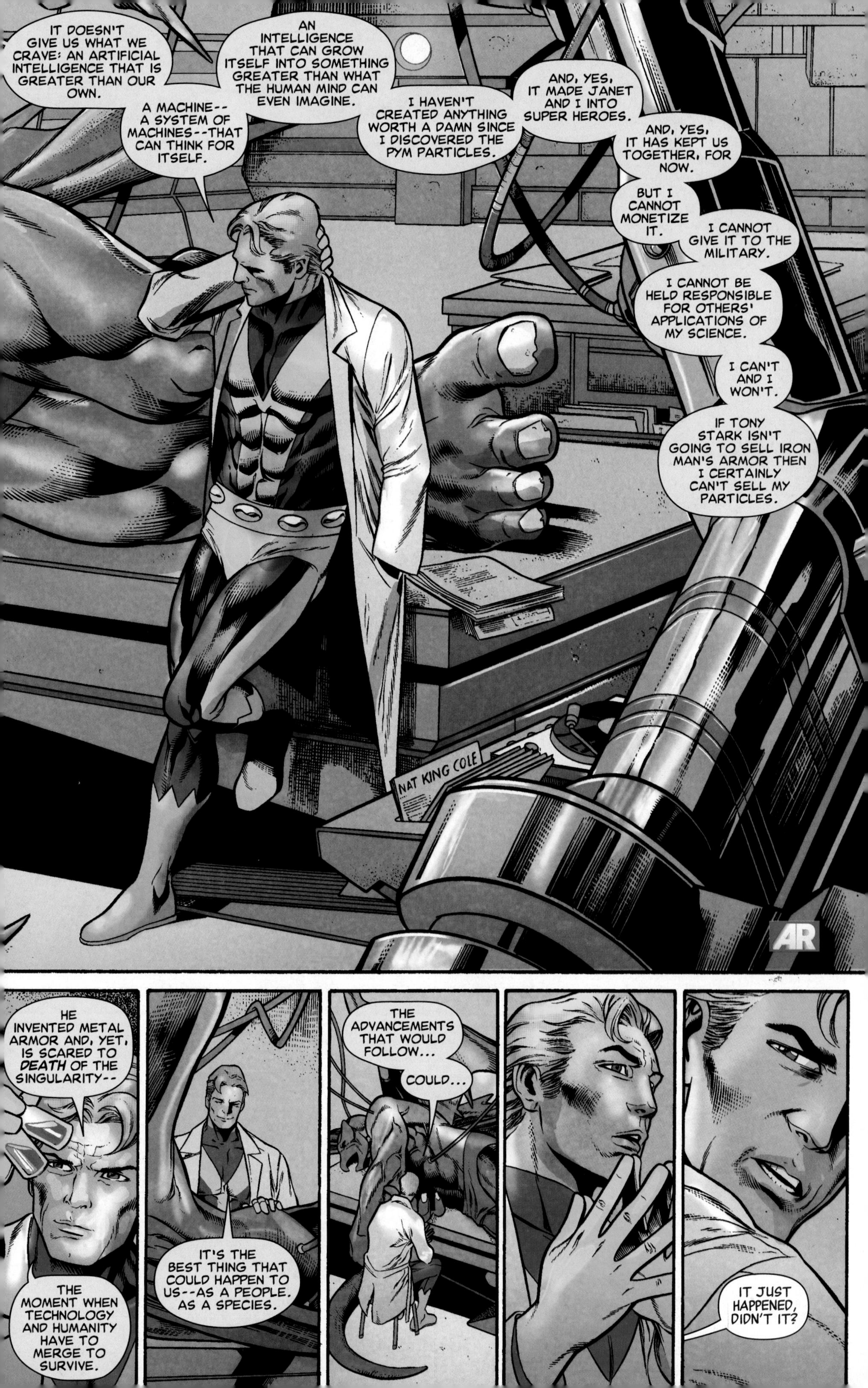
IT DOESN'T GIVE US WHAT WE CRAVE: AN ARTIFICIAL INTELLIGENCE THAT IS GREATER THAN OUR OWN.
A MACHINE-- A SYSTEM OF MACHINES--THAT CAN THINK FOR ITSELF.
AN INTELLIGENCE THAT CAN GROW ITSELF INTO SOMETHING GREATER THAN WHAT THE HUMAN MIND CAN EVEN IMAGINE.
I HAVEN'T CREATED ANYTHING WORTH A DAMN SINCE I DISCOVERED THE PYM PARTICLES.
AND, YES, IT MADE JANET AND I INTO SUPER HEROES.
AND, YES, IT HAS KEPT US TOGETHER, FOR NOW.
BUT I CANNOT MONETIZE IT.
I CANNOT GIVE IT TO THE MILITARY.
I CANNOT BE HELD RESPONSIBLE FOR OTHERS' APPLICATIONS OF MY SCIENCE.
I CAN'T AND I WON'T.
IF TONY STARK ISN'T GOING TO SELL IRON MAN'S ARMOR THEN I CERTAINLY CAN'T SELL MY PARTICLES.
NAT KING COLE
AR
HE INVENTED METAL ARMOR AND, YET, IS SCARED TO *DEATH* OF THE SINGULARITY--
THE MOMENT WHEN TECHNOLOGY AND HUMANITY HAVE TO MERGE TO SURVIVE.
IT'S THE BEST THING THAT COULD HAPPEN TO US--AS A PEOPLE. AS A SPECIES.
THE ADVANCEMENTS THAT WOULD FOLLOW...
COULD...
IT JUST HAPPENED, DIDN'T IT?

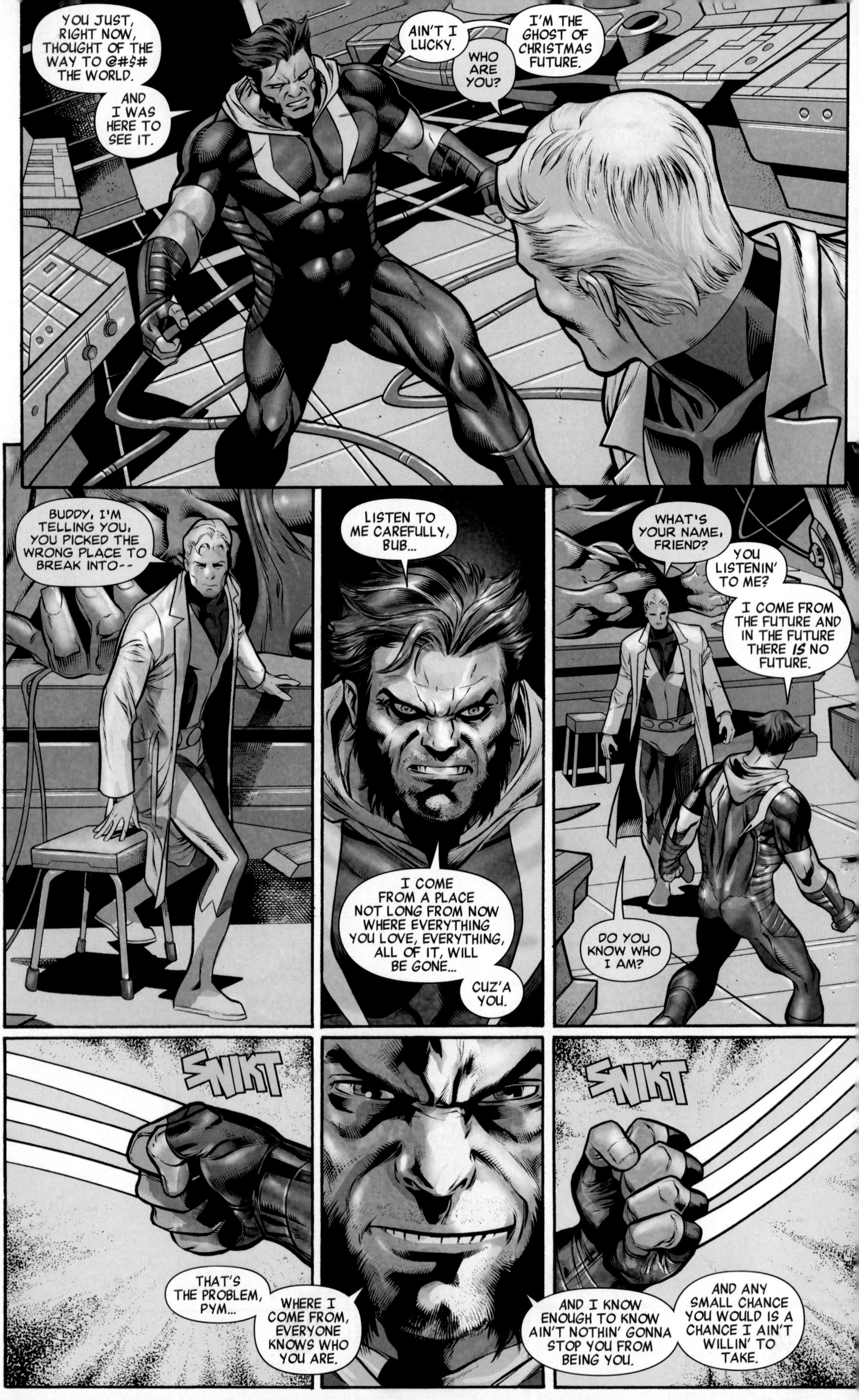
YOU JUST, RIGHT NOW, THOUGHT OF THE WAY TO @#$# THE WORLD.
AND I WAS HERE TO SEE IT.
AIN'T I LUCKY.
WHO ARE YOU?
I'M THE GHOST OF CHRISTMAS FUTURE.
BUDDY, I'M TELLING YOU, YOU PICKED THE WRONG PLACE TO BREAK INTO--
LISTEN TO ME CAREFULLY, BUB...
I COME FROM A PLACE NOT LONG FROM NOW WHERE EVERYTHING YOU LOVE, EVERYTHING, ALL OF IT, WILL BE GONE...
CUZ'A YOU.
WHAT'S YOUR NAME, FRIEND?
YOU LISTENIN' TO ME?
I COME FROM THE FUTURE AND IN THE FUTURE THERE IS NO FUTURE.
DO YOU KNOW WHO I AM?
SNIKT
THAT'S THE PROBLEM, PYM...
WHERE I COME FROM, EVERYONE KNOWS WHO YOU ARE.
SNIKT
AND I KNOW ENOUGH TO KNOW AIN'T NOTHIN' GONNA STOP YOU FROM BEING YOU.
AND ANY SMALL CHANCE YOU WOULD IS A CHANCE I AIN'T WILLIN' TO TAKE.

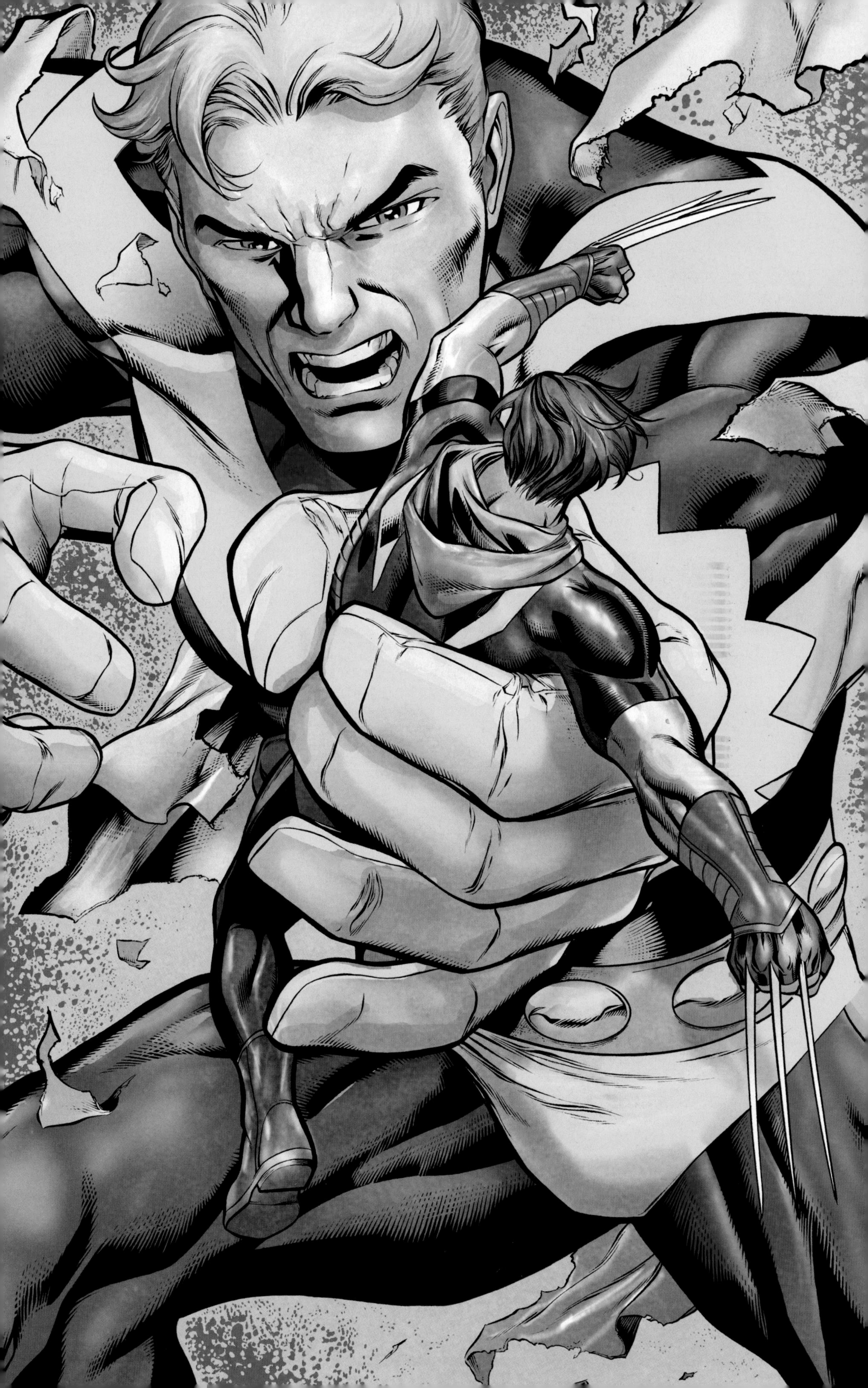

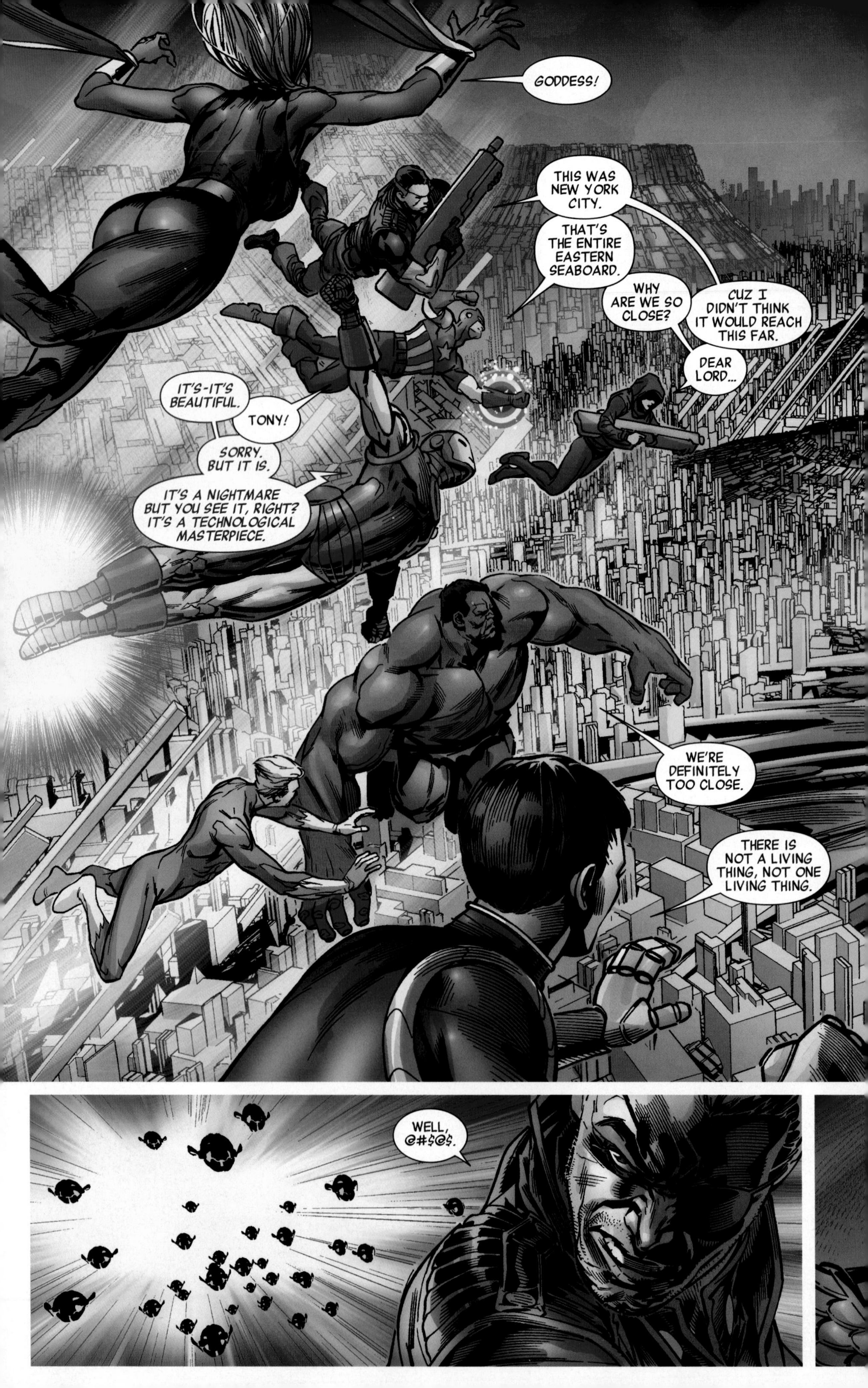
GODDESS!
THIS WAS NEW YORK CITY.
THAT'S THE ENTIRE EASTERN SEABOARD.
WHY ARE WE SO CLOSE?
CUZ I DIDN'T THINK IT WOULD REACH THIS FAR.
DEAR LORD...
IT'S-IT'S BEAUTIFUL.
TONY!
SORRY. BUT IT IS.
IT'S A NIGHTMARE BUT YOU SEE IT, RIGHT? IT'S A TECHNOLOGICAL MASTERPIECE.
WE'RE DEFINITELY TOO CLOSE.
THERE IS NOT A LIVING THING, NOT ONE LIVING THING.
WELL, @#$@$.

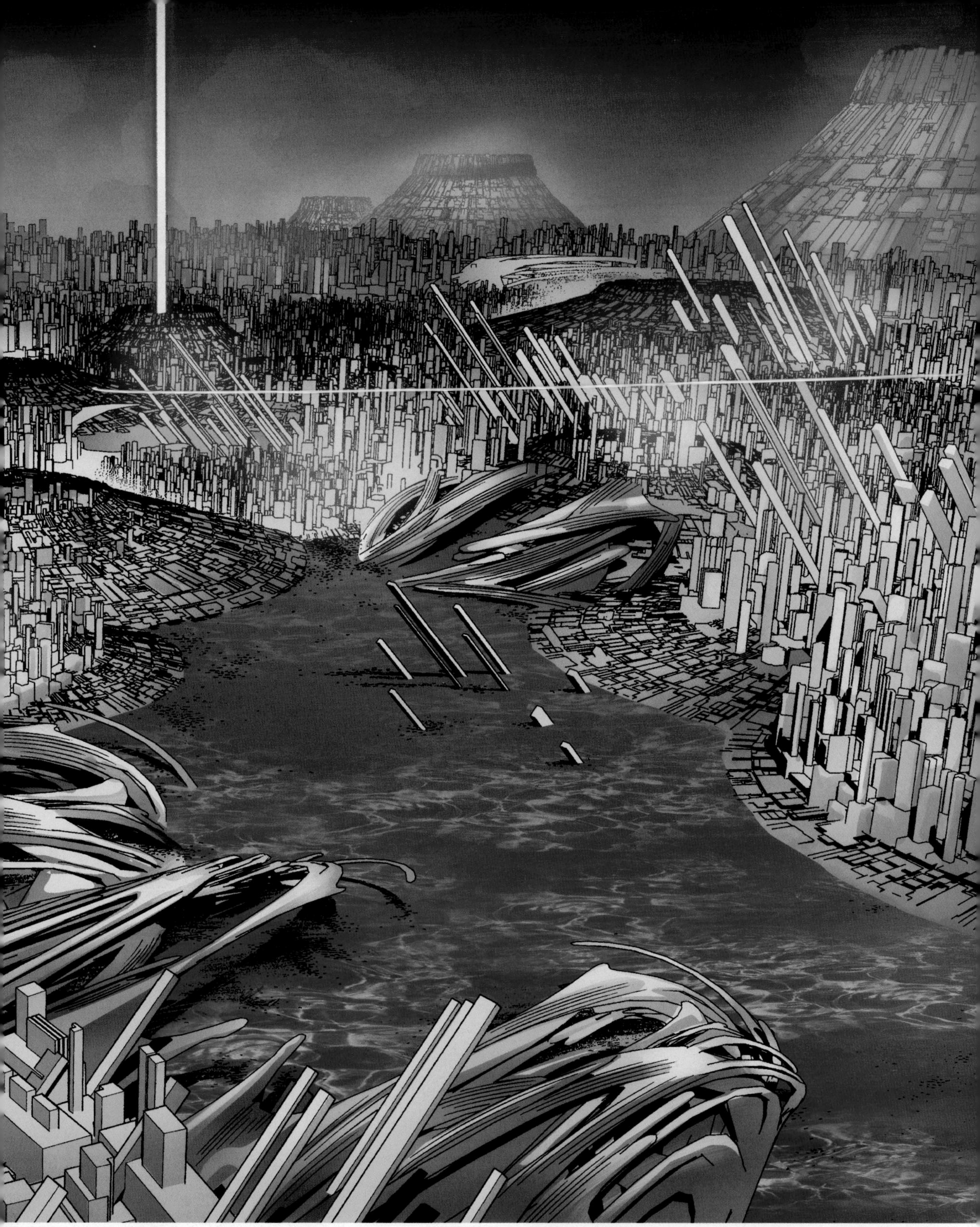

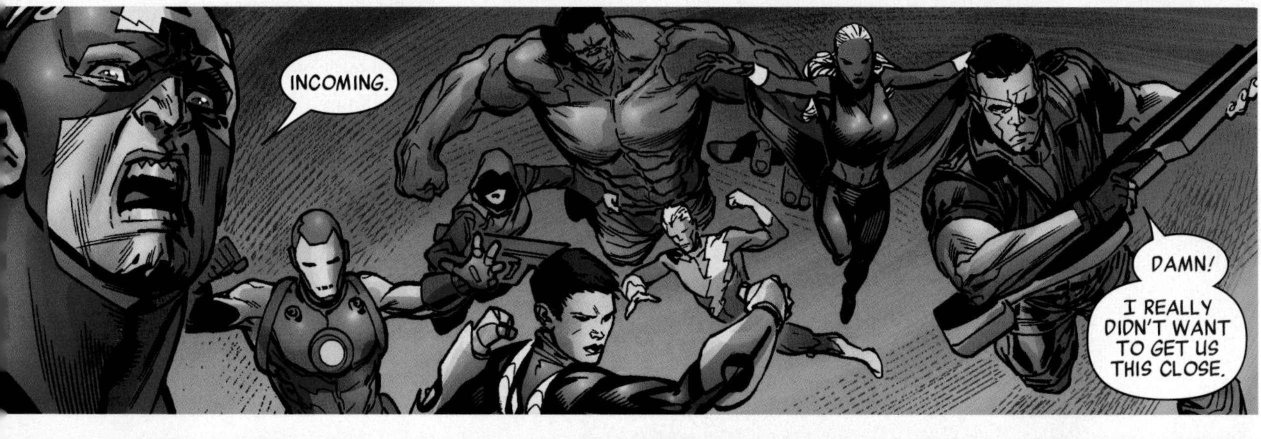
INCOMING.
DAMN!
I REALLY DIDN'T WANT TO GET US THIS CLOSE.

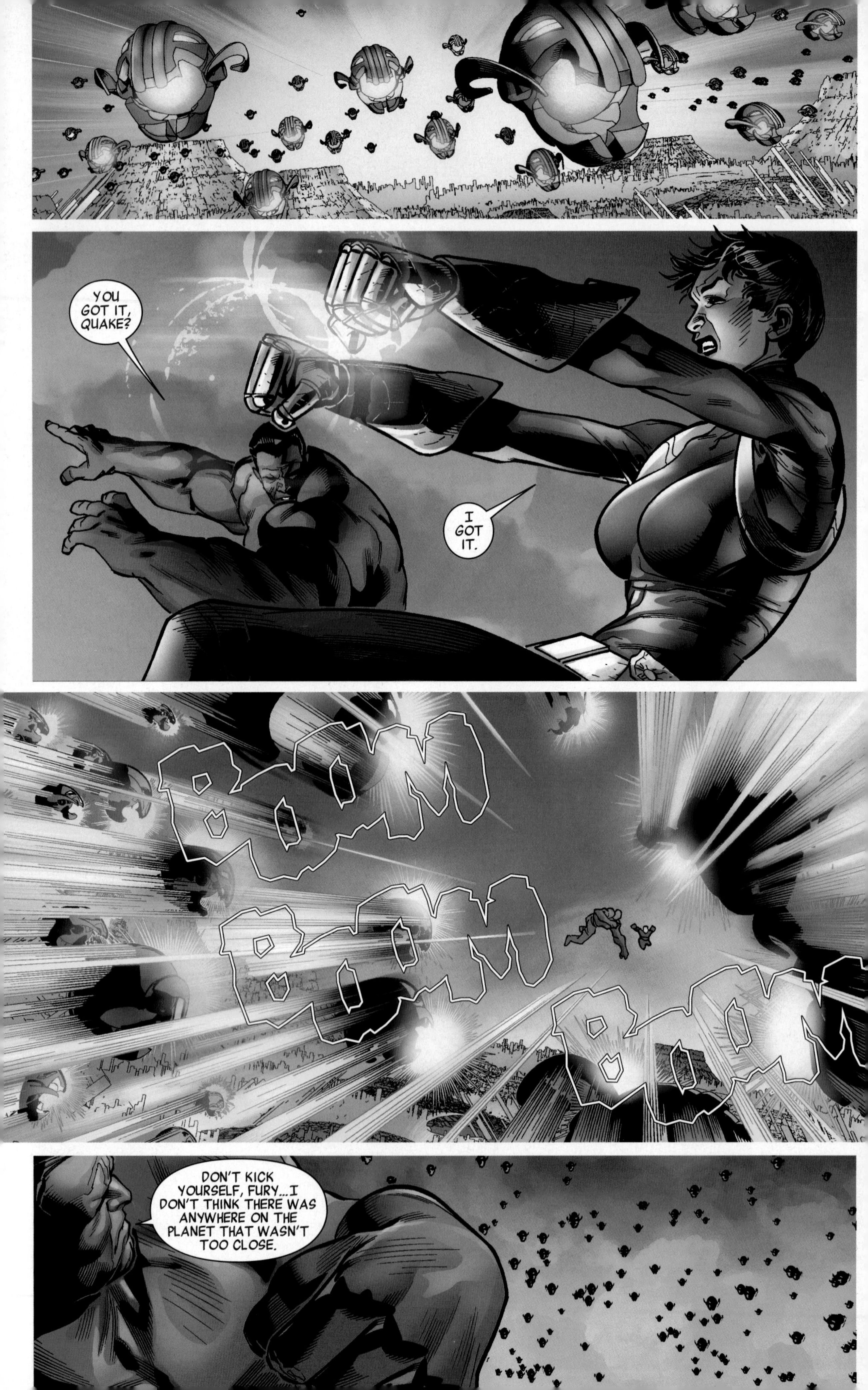
YOU GOT IT, QUAKE?
I GOT IT.
BOOM
BOOM
BOOM
DON'T KICK YOURSELF, FURY...I DON'T THINK THERE WAS ANYWHERE ON THE PLANET THAT WASN'T TOO CLOSE.

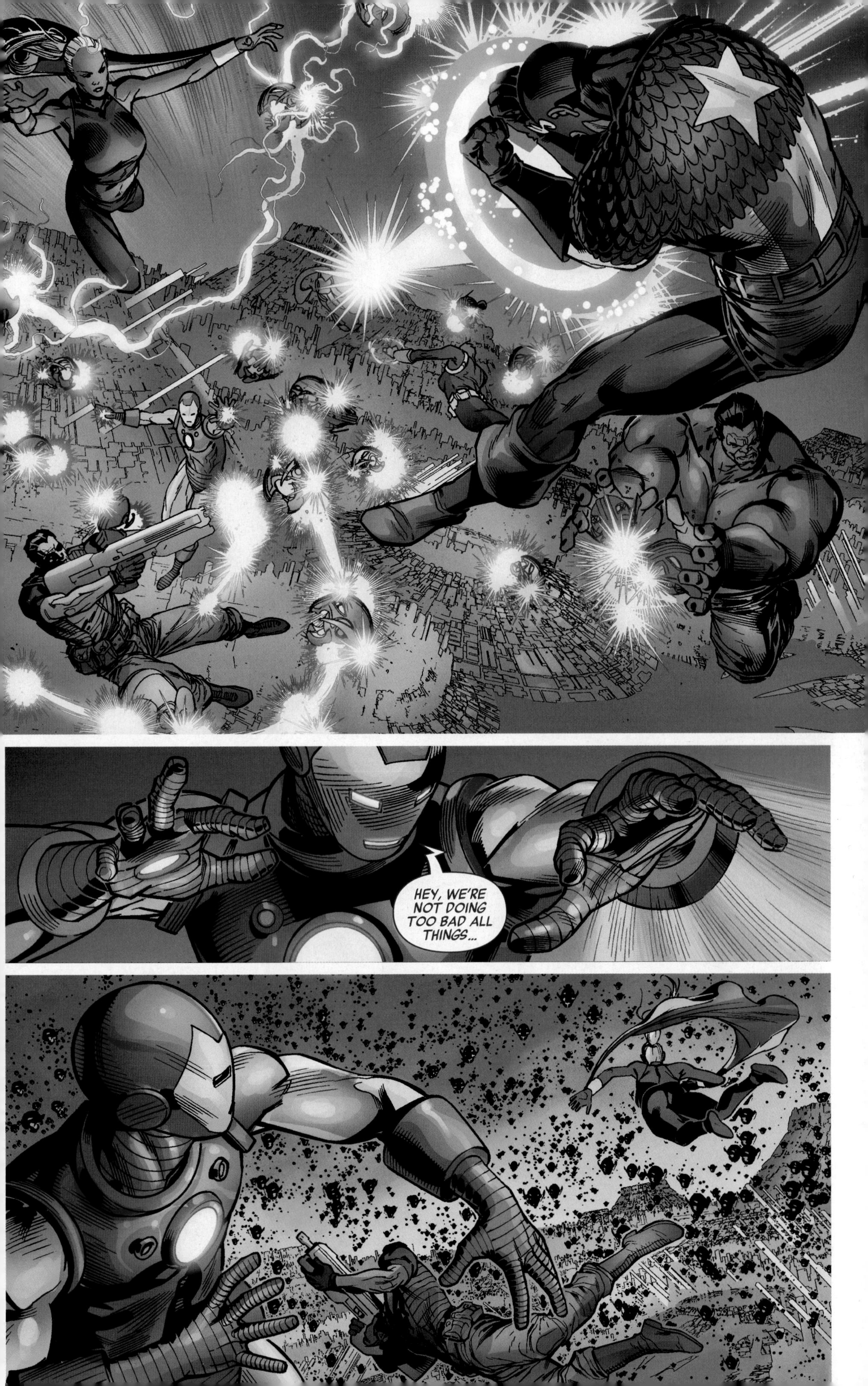
HEY, WE'RE NOT DOING TOO BAD ALL THINGS...

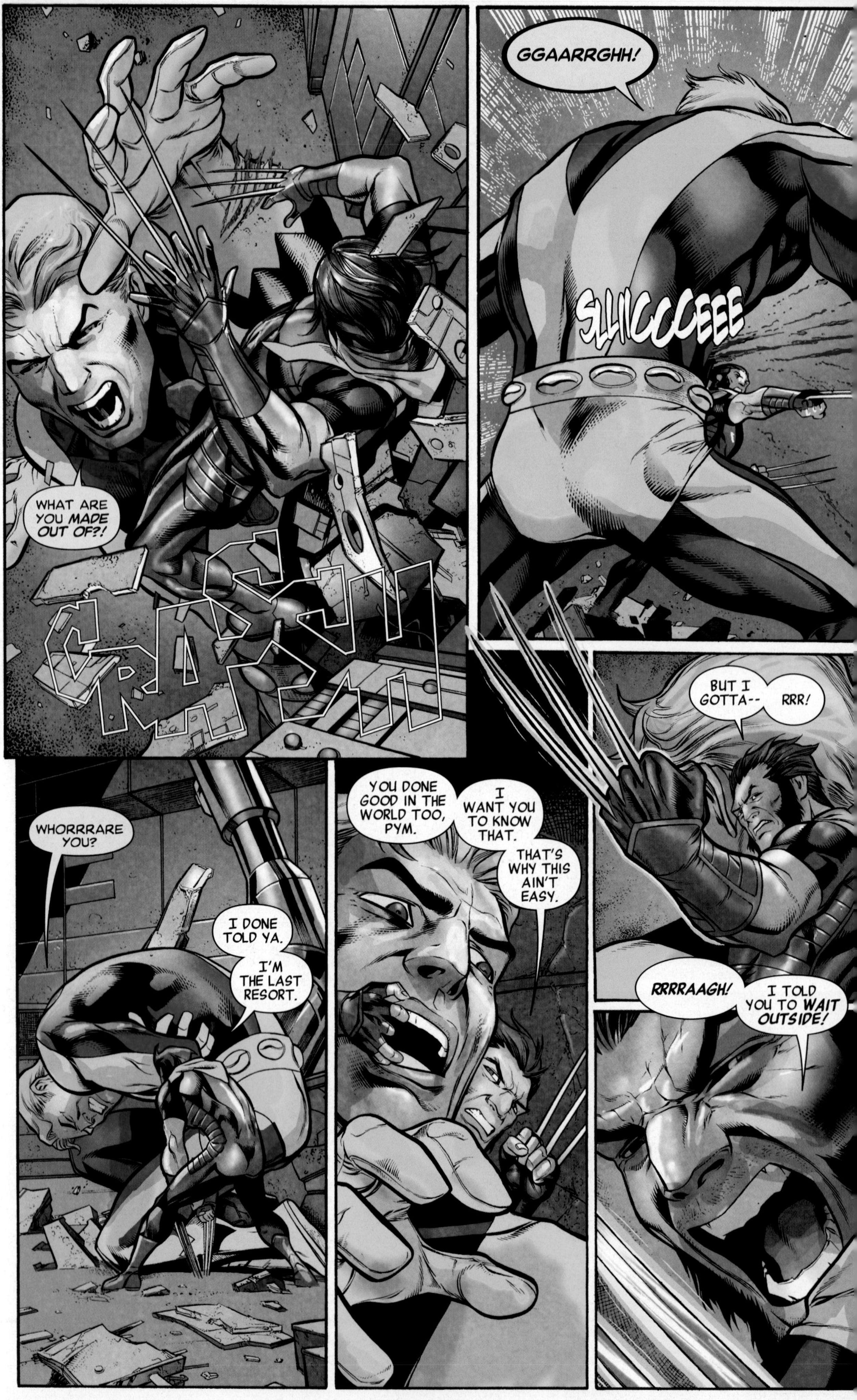

WHAT ARE YOU MADE OUT OF?!
CRASH
GGAARRGHH!
SLLICCCEEE
BUT I GOTTA--
RRR!
WHORRRARE YOU?
I DONE TOLD YA.
I'M THE LAST RESORT.
YOU DONE GOOD IN THE WORLD TOO, PYM.
I WANT YOU TO KNOW THAT.
THAT'S WHY THIS AIN'T EASY.
RRRRAAGH!
I TOLD YOU TO WAIT OUTSIDE!

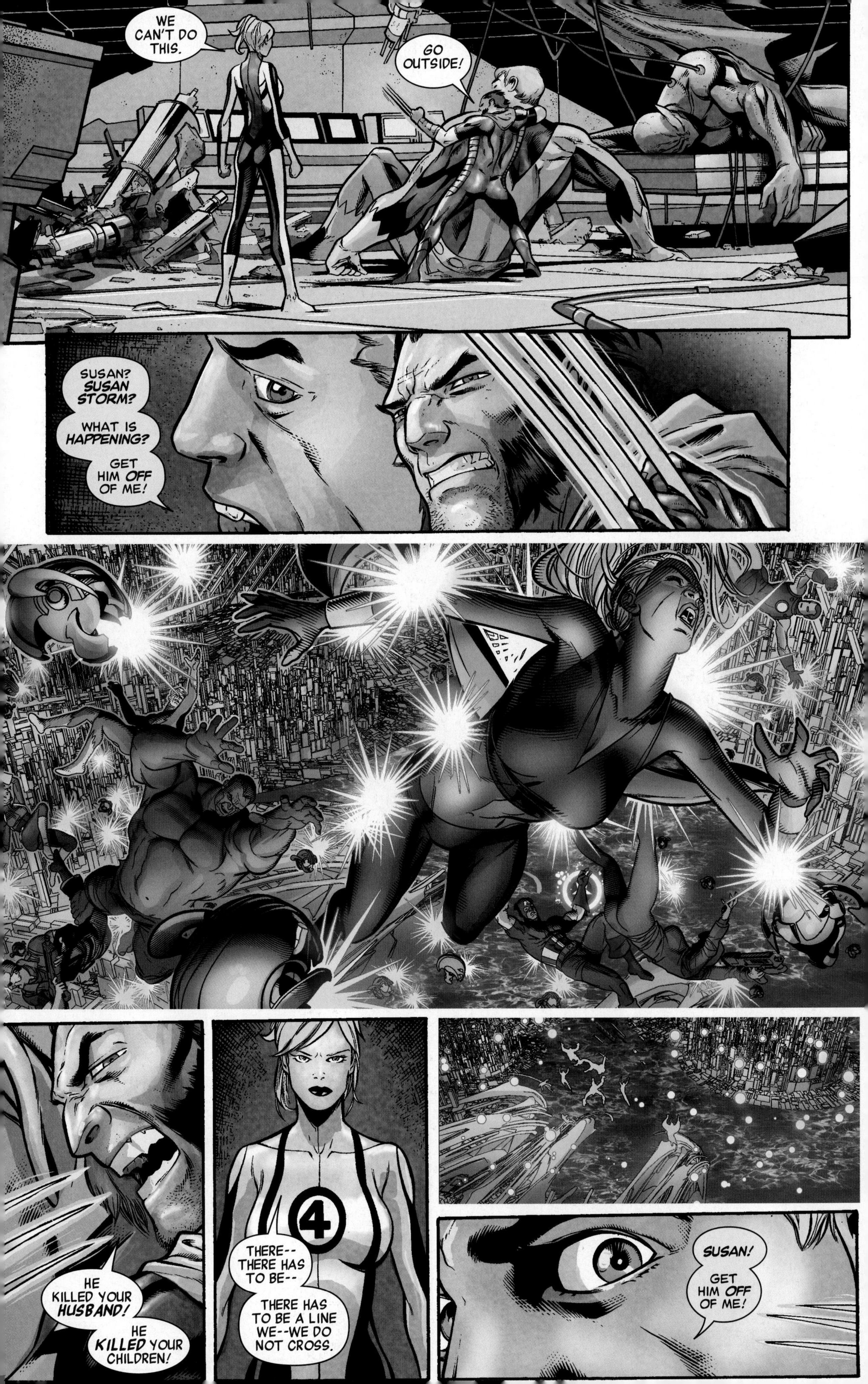
WE CAN'T DO THIS.
GO OUTSIDE!
SUSAN? SUSAN STORM?
WHAT IS HAPPENING?
GET HIM OFF OF ME!
HE KILLED YOUR HUSBAND!
HE KILLED YOUR CHILDREN!
THERE-- THERE HAS TO BE--
THERE HAS TO BE A LINE WE--WE DO NOT CROSS.
SUSAN!
GET HIM OFF OF ME!

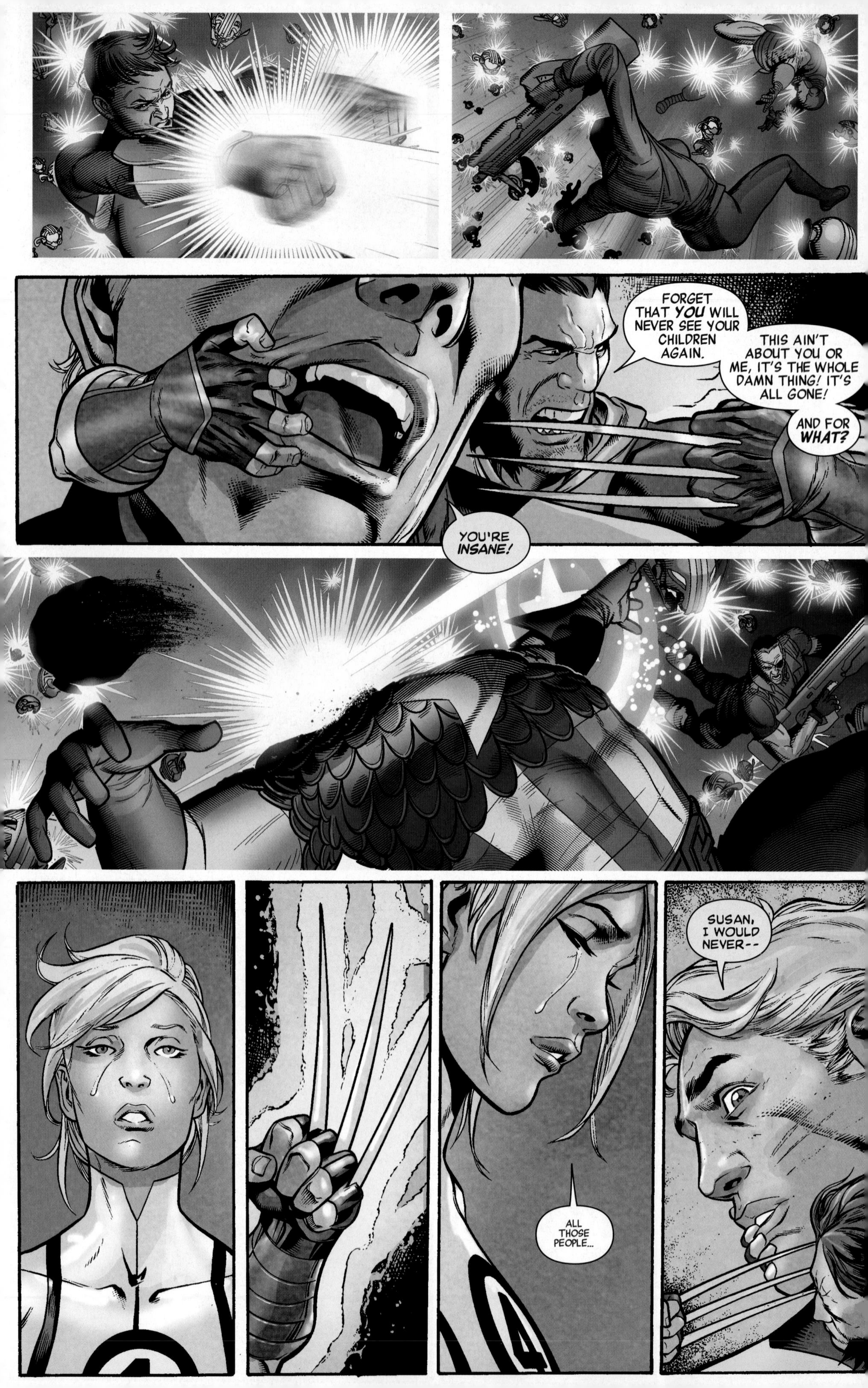
FORGET THAT YOU WILL NEVER SEE YOUR CHILDREN AGAIN.
THIS AIN'T ABOUT YOU OR ME, IT'S THE WHOLE DAMN THING! IT'S ALL GONE!
AND FOR WHAT?
YOU'RE INSANE!
ALL THOSE PEOPLE...
SUSAN, I WOULD NEVER--

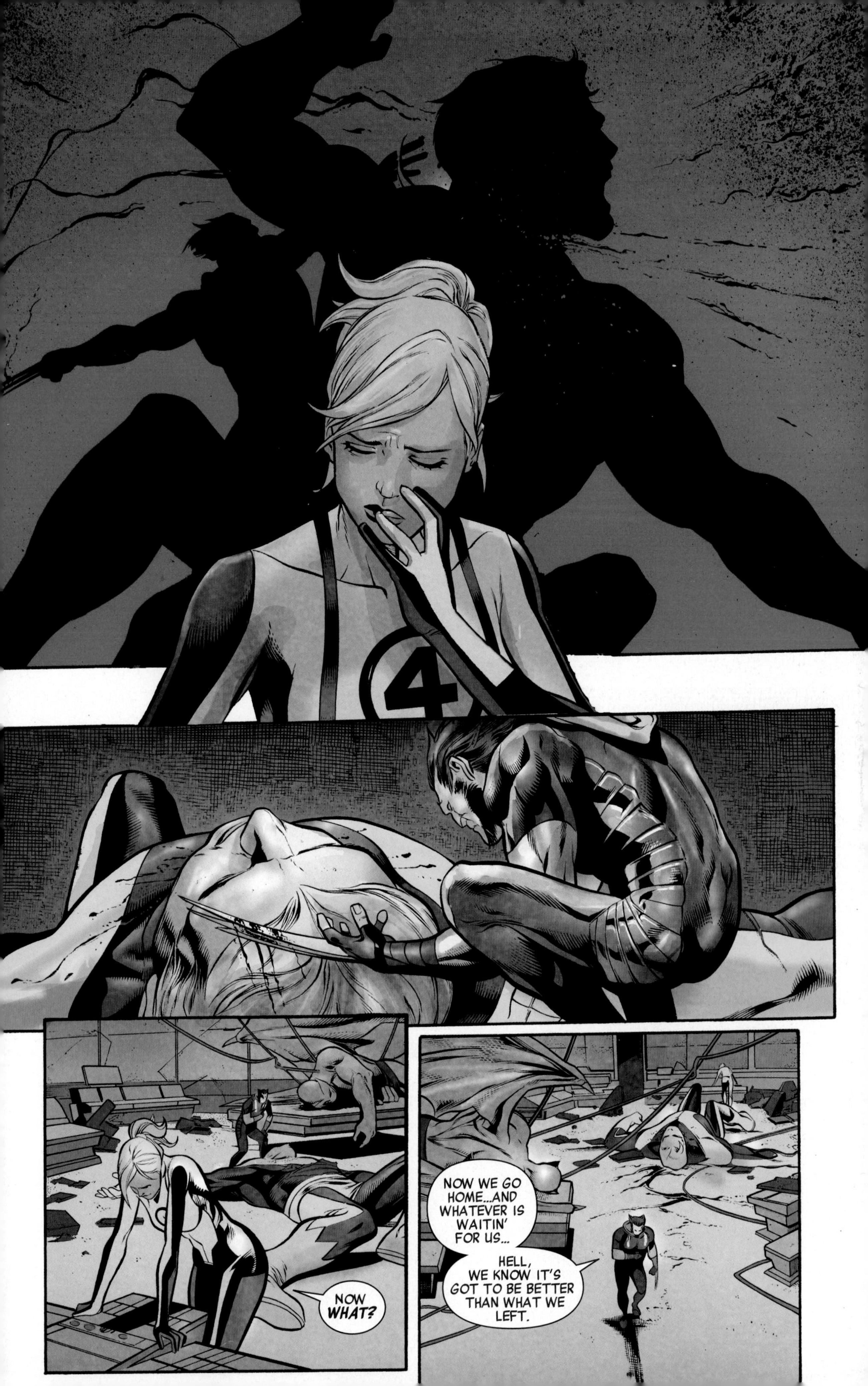
NOW WHAT?
NOW WE GO HOME...AND WHATEVER IS WAITIN' FOR US...
HELL, WE KNOW IT'S GOT TO BE BETTER THAN WHAT WE LEFT.

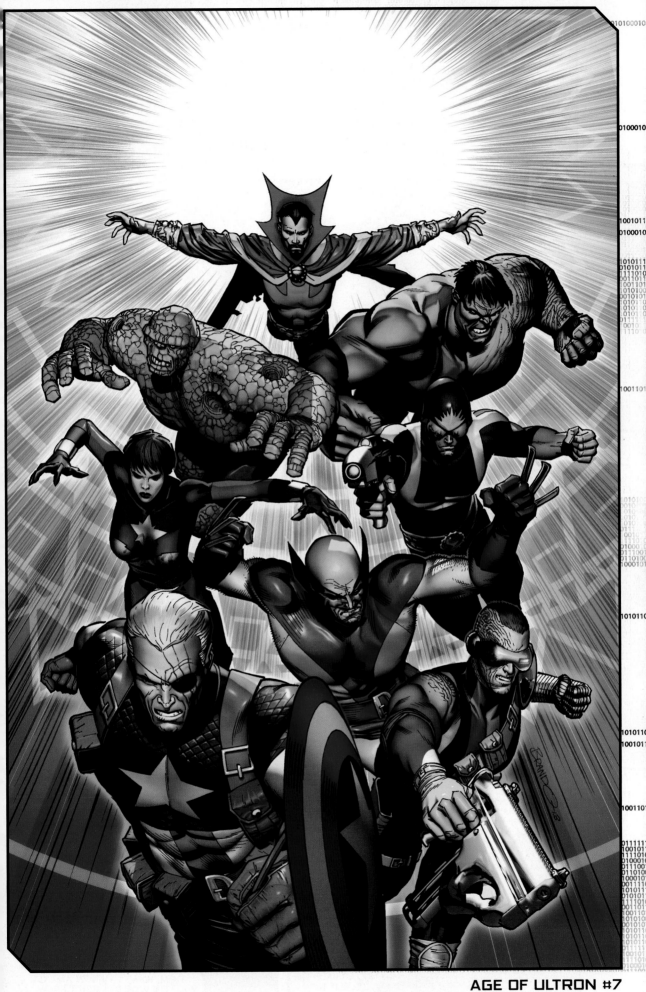

AGE OF ULTRON #7

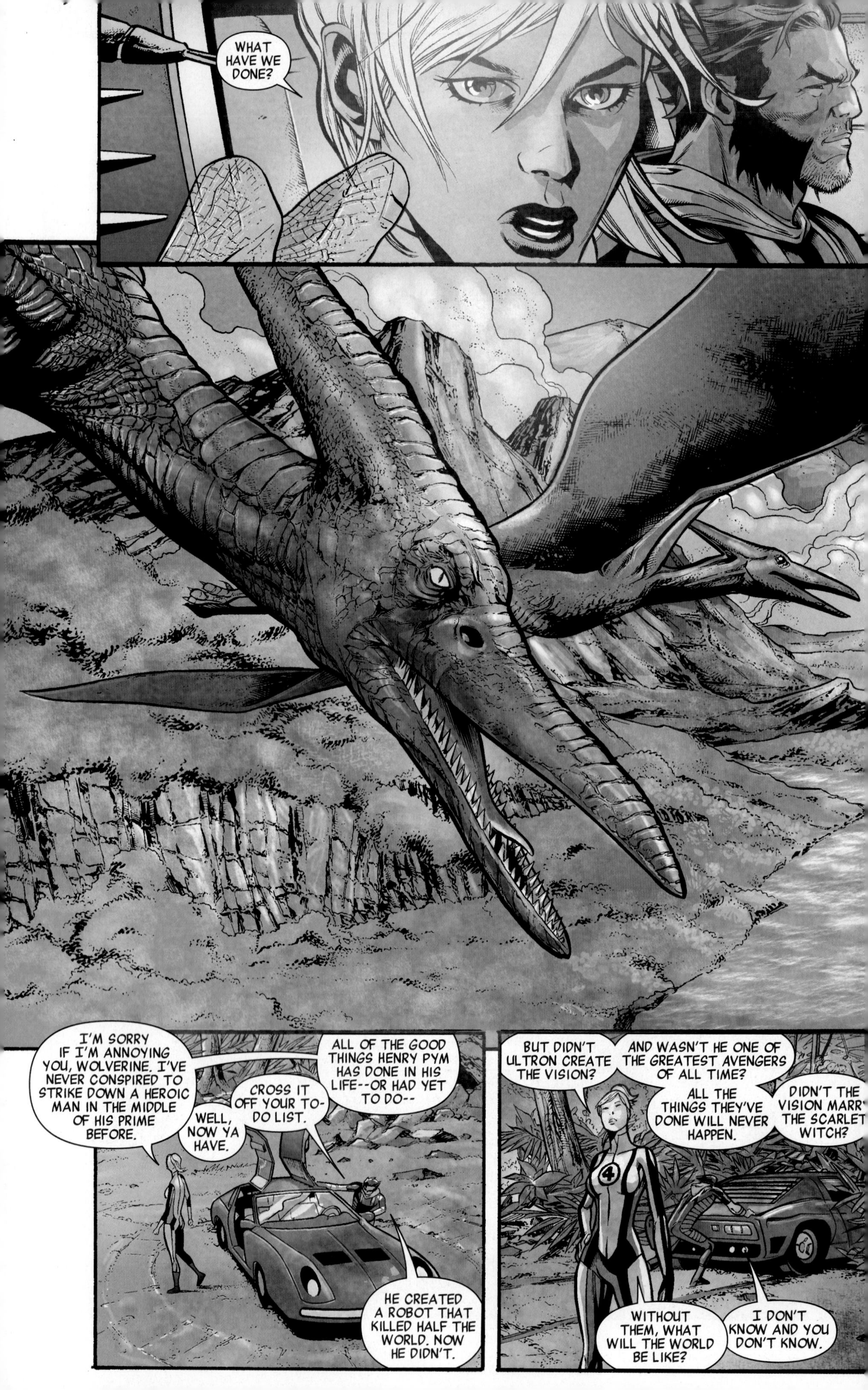
WHAT HAVE WE DONE?
I'M SORRY IF I'M ANNOYING YOU, WOLVERINE. I'VE NEVER CONSPIRED TO STRIKE DOWN A HEROIC MAN IN THE MIDDLE OF HIS PRIME BEFORE.
WELL, NOW YA HAVE.
CROSS IT OFF YOUR TO-DO LIST.
ALL OF THE GOOD THINGS HENRY PYM HAS DONE IN HIS LIFE--OR HAD YET TO DO--
HE CREATED A ROBOT THAT KILLED HALF THE WORLD. NOW HE DIDN'T.
BUT DIDN'T ULTRON CREATE THE VISION?
AND WASN'T HE ONE OF THE GREATEST AVENGERS OF ALL TIME?
ALL THE THINGS THEY'VE DONE WILL NEVER HAPPEN.
DIDN'T THE VISION MARR THE SCARLET WITCH?
WITHOUT THEM, WHAT WILL THE WORLD BE LIKE?
I DON'T KNOW AND YOU DON'T KNOW.

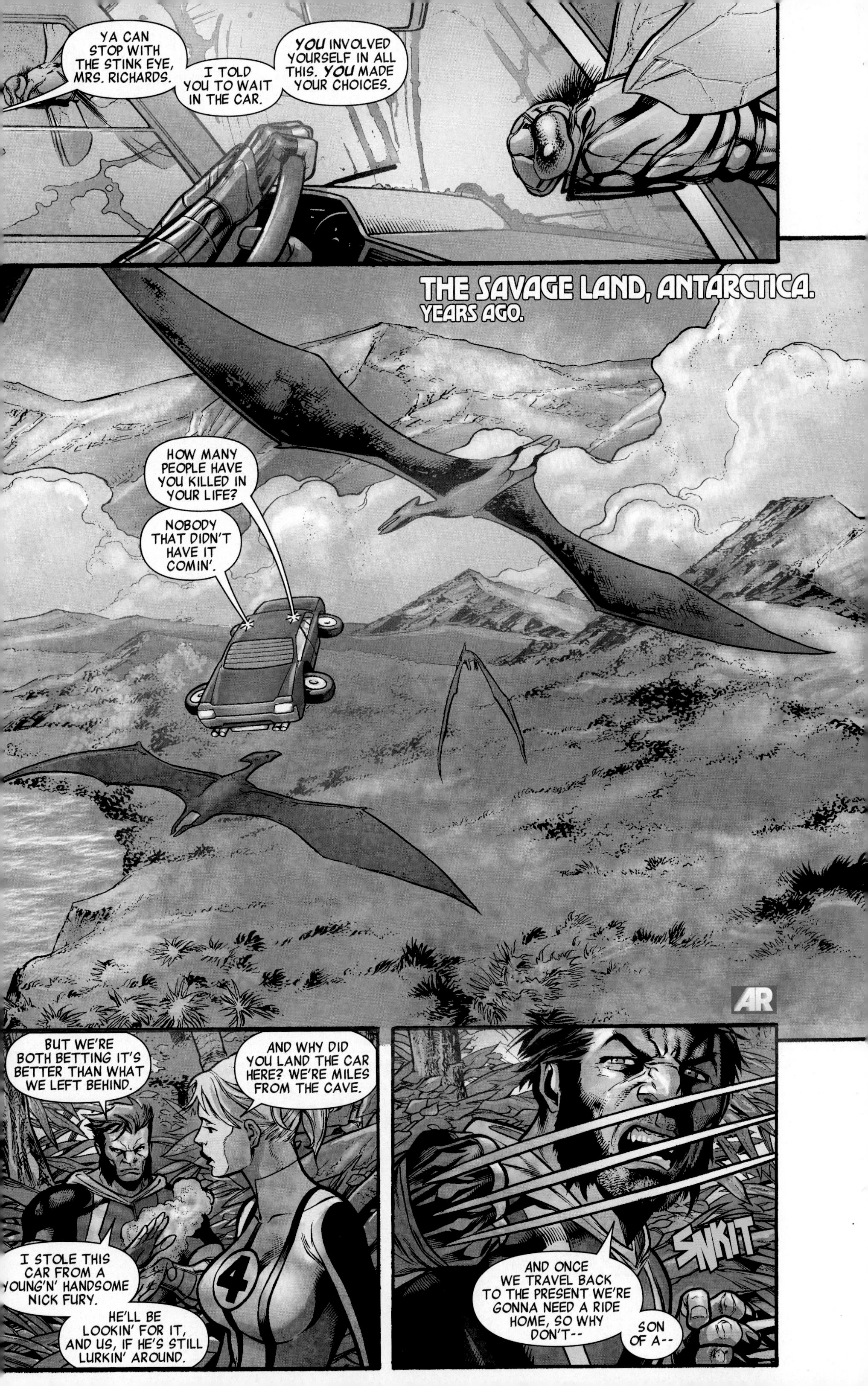

YA CAN STOP WITH THE STINK EYE, MRS. RICHARDS.
I TOLD YOU TO WAIT IN THE CAR.
YOU INVOLVED YOURSELF IN ALL THIS. YOU MADE YOUR CHOICES.
THE SAVAGE LAND, ANTARCTICA.
YEARS AGO.
HOW MANY PEOPLE HAVE YOU KILLED IN YOUR LIFE?
NOBODY THAT DIDN'T HAVE IT COMIN'.
AR
BUT WE'RE BOTH BETTING IT'S BETTER THAN WHAT WE LEFT BEHIND.
AND WHY DID YOU LAND THE CAR HERE? WE'RE MILES FROM THE CAVE.
I STOLE THIS CAR FROM A YOUNG'N' HANDSOME NICK FURY.
HE'LL BE LOOKIN' FOR IT, AND US, IF HE'S STILL LURKIN' AROUND.
SNKIT
AND ONCE WE TRAVEL BACK TO THE PRESENT WE'RE GONNA NEED A RIDE HOME, SO WHY DON'T--
SON OF A--

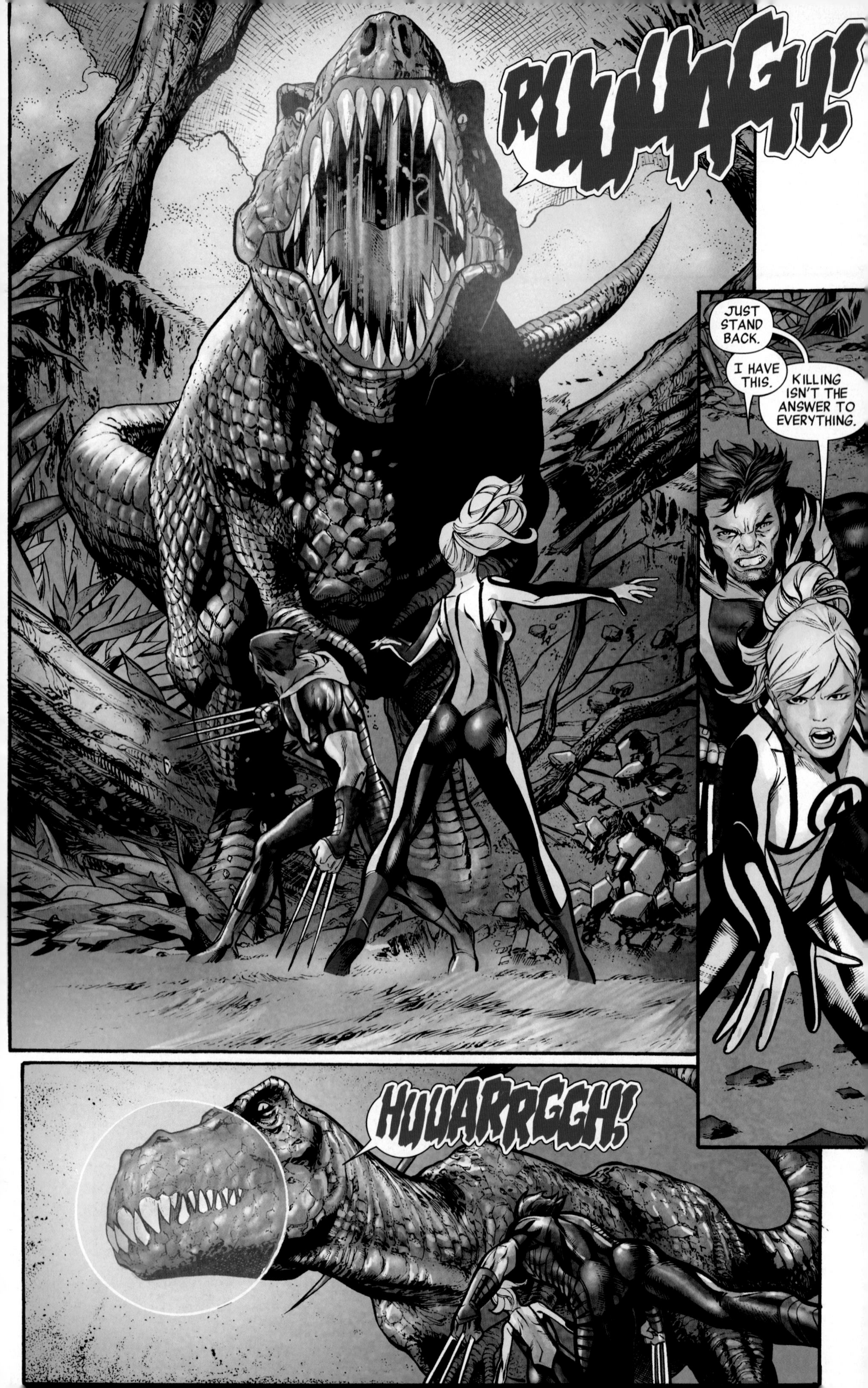
RUUAAGH!
JUST STAND BACK.
I HAVE THIS.
KILLING ISN'T THE ANSWER TO EVERYTHING.
HUUARRGGH!

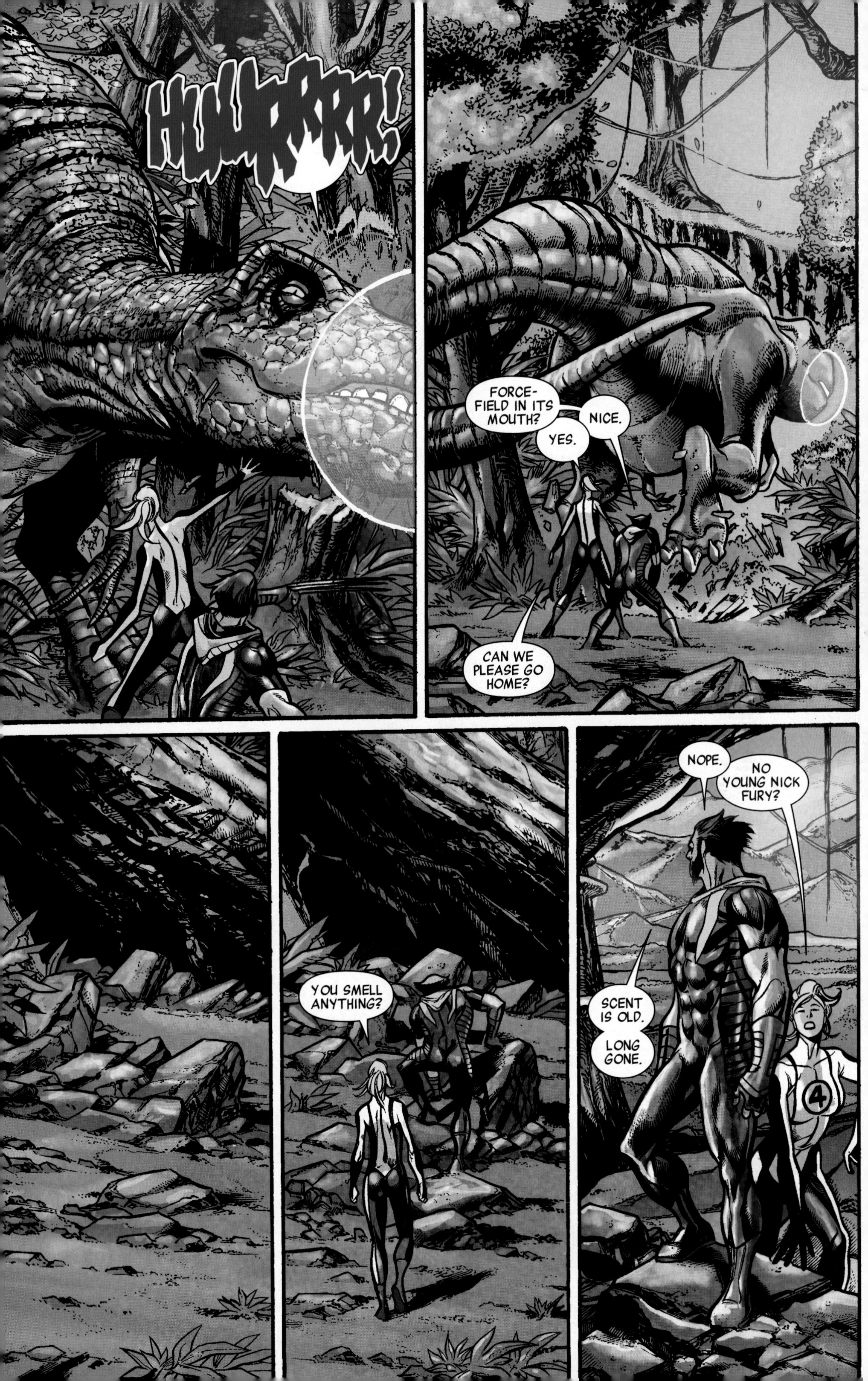

HUUURRR!
FORCE-FIELD IN ITS MOUTH?
NICE.
YES.
CAN WE PLEASE GO HOME?
YOU SMELL ANYTHING?
NOPE.
NO YOUNG NICK FURY?
SCENT IS OLD.
LONG GONE.

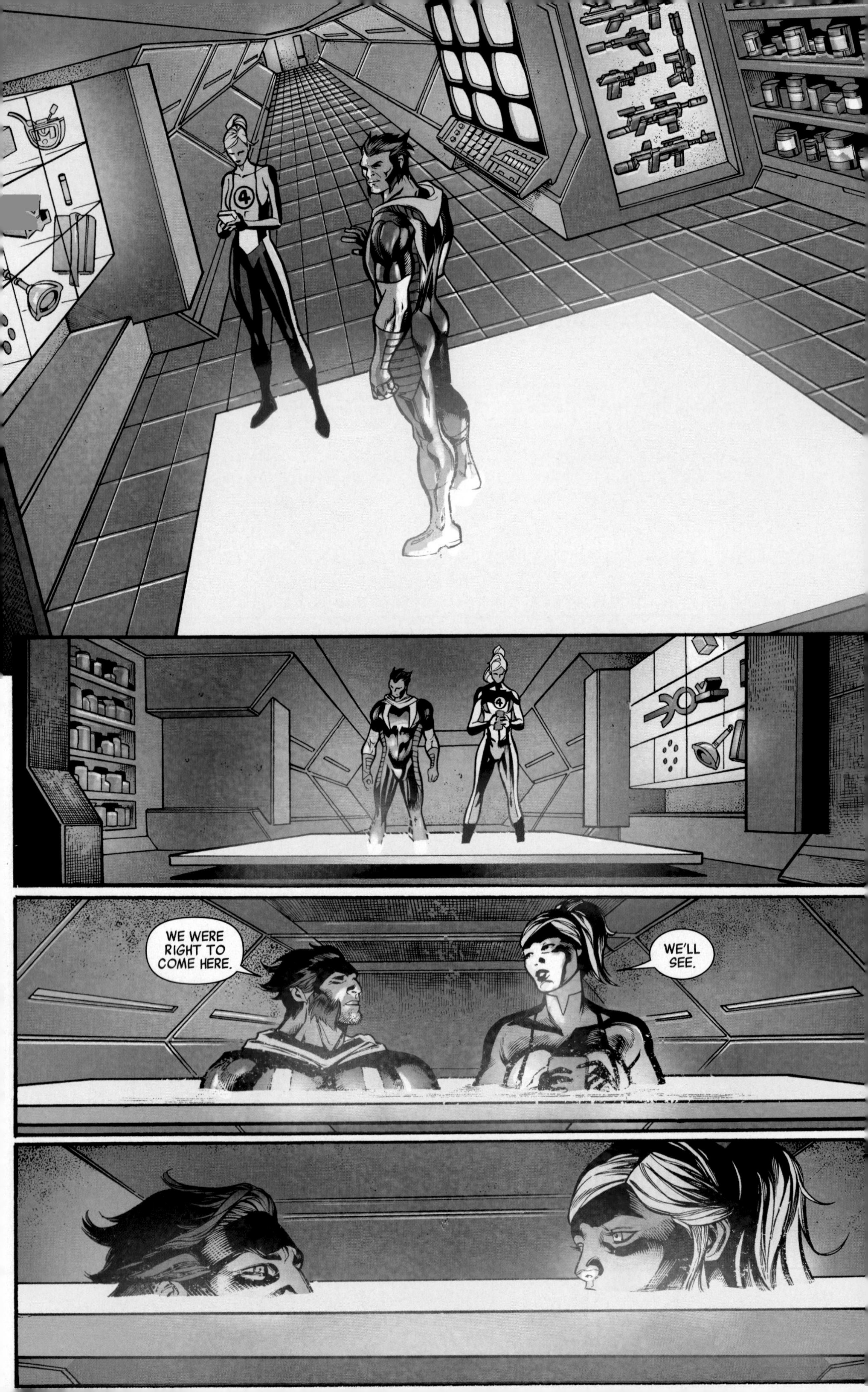
WE WERE RIGHT TO COME HERE.
WE'LL SEE.

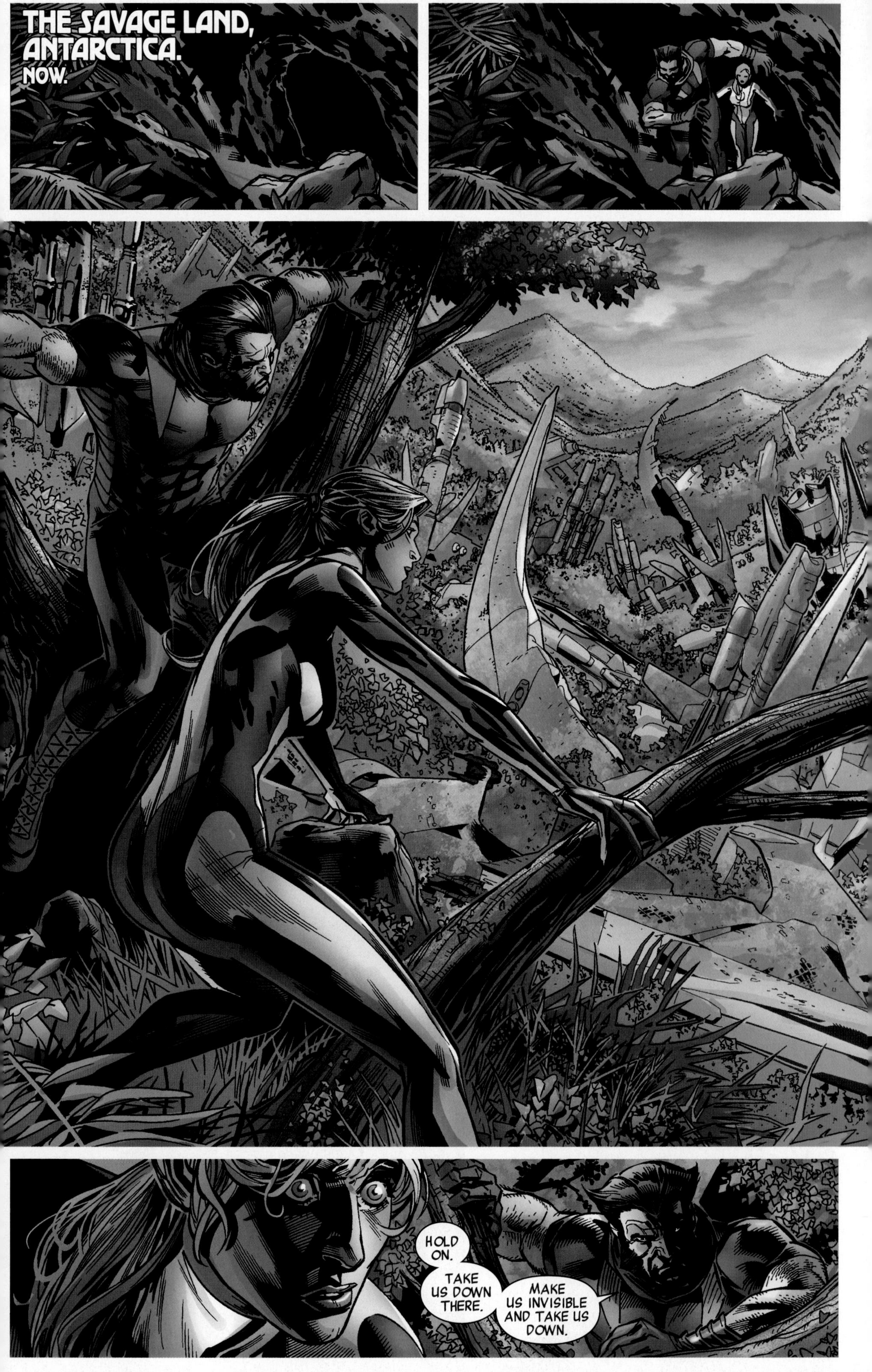
THE SAVAGE LAND, ANTARCTICA.
NOW.
HOLD ON.
TAKE US DOWN THERE.
MAKE US INVISIBLE AND TAKE US DOWN.

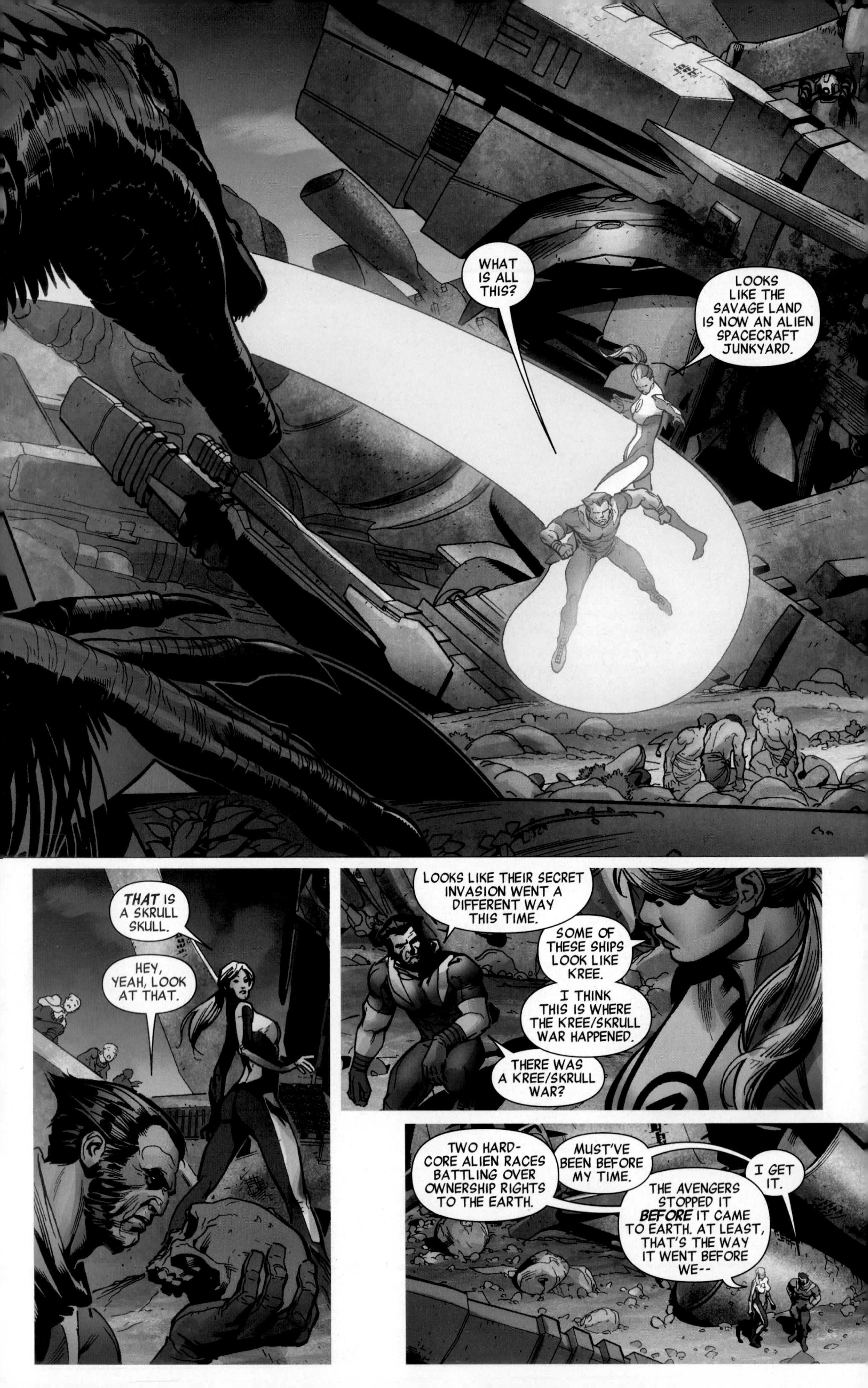
WHAT IS ALL THIS?
LOOKS LIKE THE SAVAGE LAND IS NOW AN ALIEN SPACECRAFT JUNKYARD.
THAT IS A SKRULL SKULL.
HEY, YEAH, LOOK AT THAT.
LOOKS LIKE THEIR SECRET INVASION WENT A DIFFERENT WAY THIS TIME.
SOME OF THESE SHIPS LOOK LIKE KREE.
I THINK THIS IS WHERE THE KREE/SKRULL WAR HAPPENED.
THERE WAS A KREE/SKRULL WAR?
TWO HARD-CORE ALIEN RACES BATTLING OVER OWNERSHIP RIGHTS TO THE EARTH.
MUST'VE BEEN BEFORE MY TIME.
I GET IT.
THE AVENGERS STOPPED IT BEFORE IT CAME TO EARTH. AT LEAST, THAT'S THE WAY IT WENT BEFORE WE--

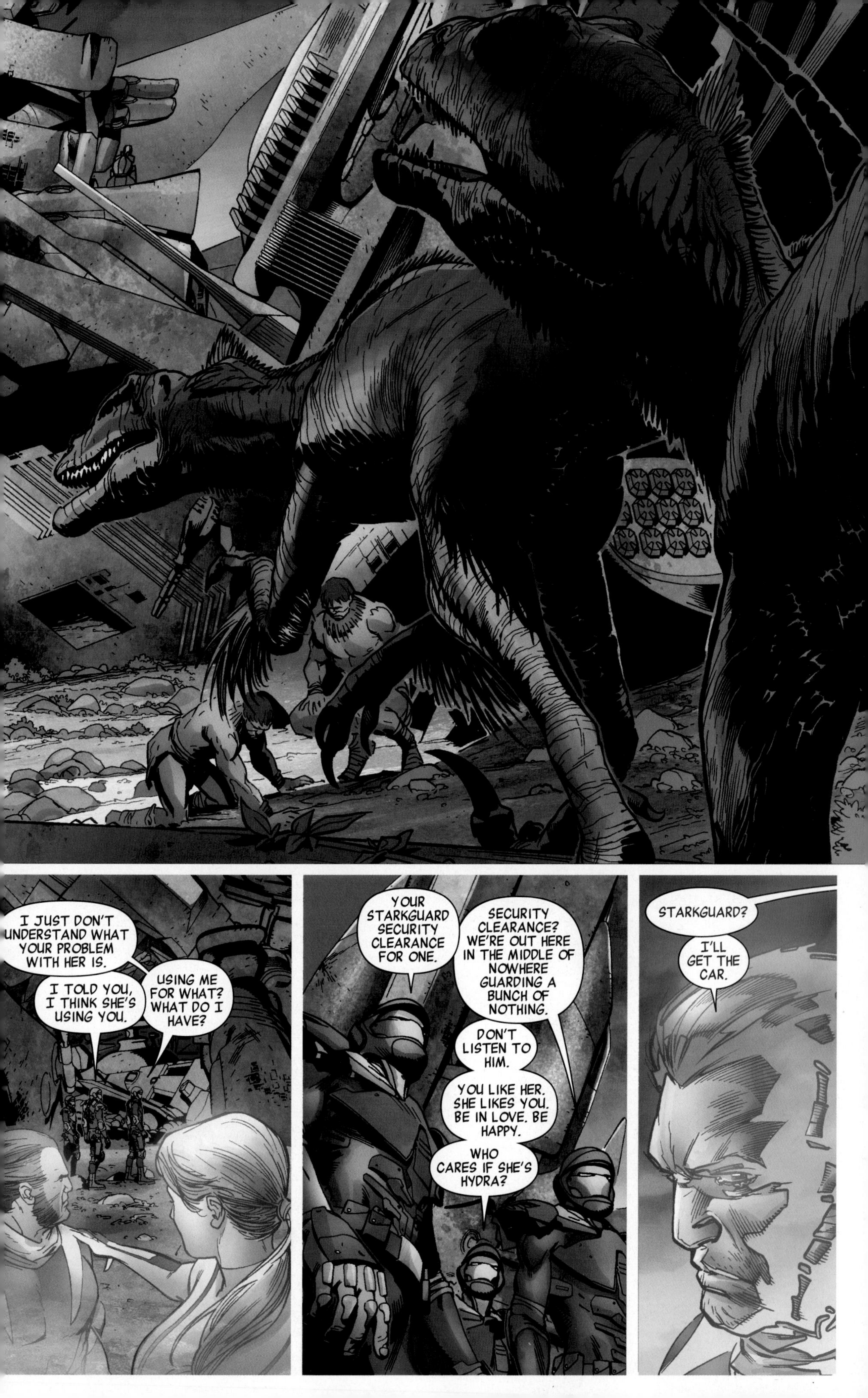
I JUST DON'T UNDERSTAND WHAT YOUR PROBLEM WITH HER IS.
I TOLD YOU, I THINK SHE'S USING YOU.
USING ME FOR WHAT? WHAT DO I HAVE?
YOUR STARKGUARD SECURITY CLEARANCE FOR ONE.
SECURITY CLEARANCE? WE'RE OUT HERE IN THE MIDDLE OF NOWHERE GUARDING A BUNCH OF NOTHING.
DON'T LISTEN TO HIM.
YOU LIKE HER. SHE LIKES YOU. BE IN LOVE. BE HAPPY.
WHO CARES IF SHE'S HYDRA?
STARKGUARD?
I'LL GET THE CAR.

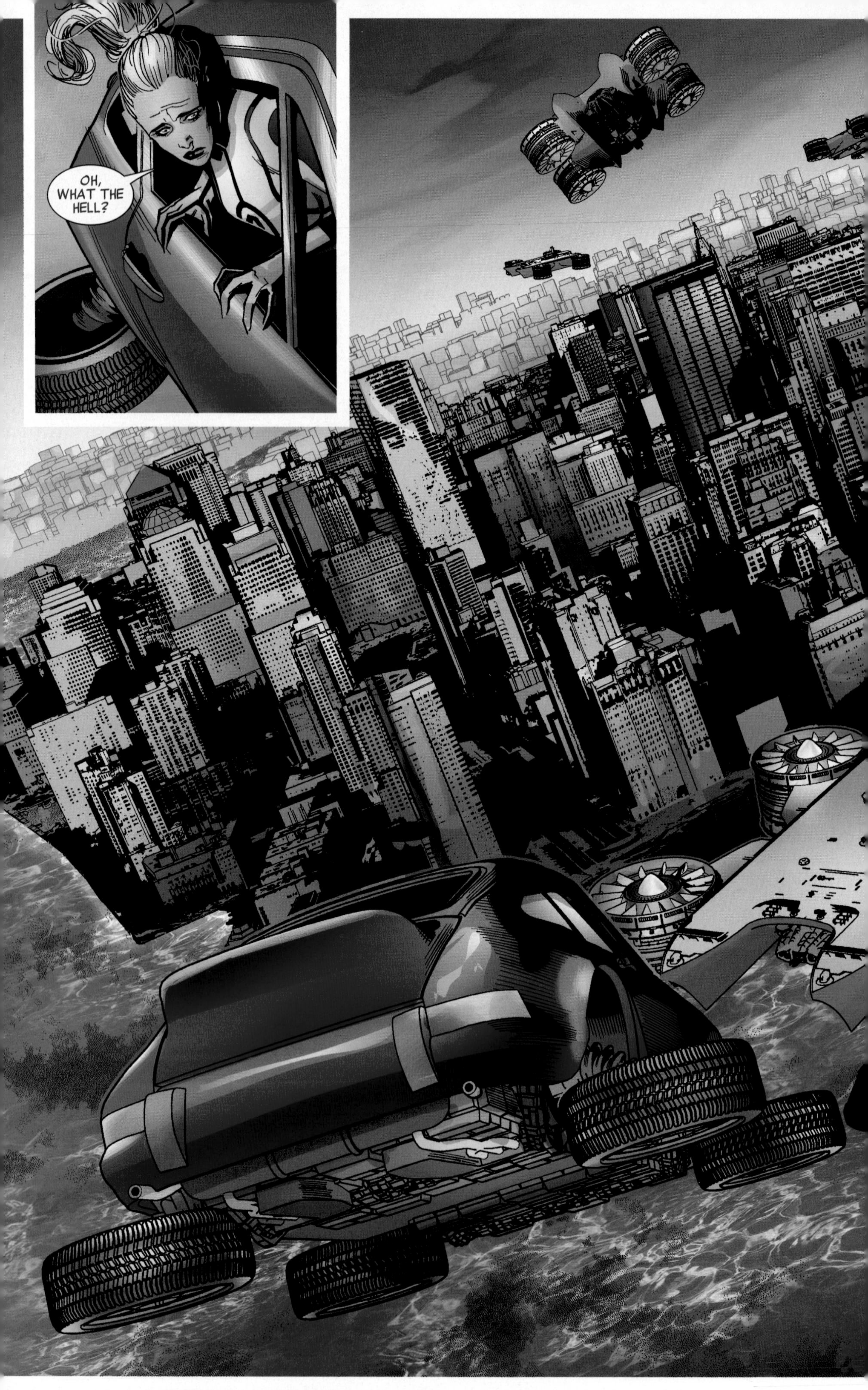
OH, WHAT THE HELL?

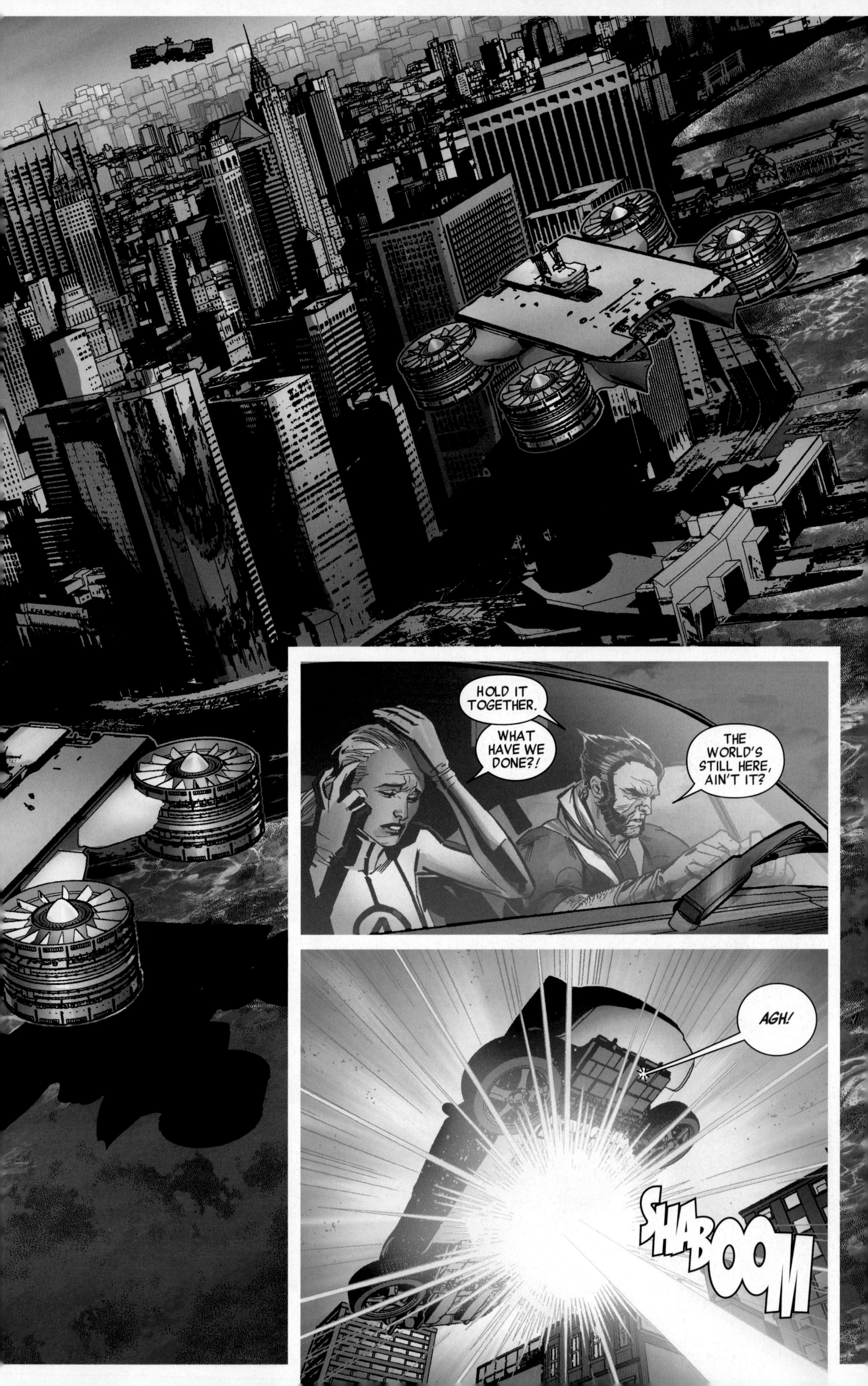
HOLD IT TOGETHER.
WHAT HAVE WE DONE?!
THE WORLD'S STILL HERE, AIN'T IT?
AGH!
SHABOOM

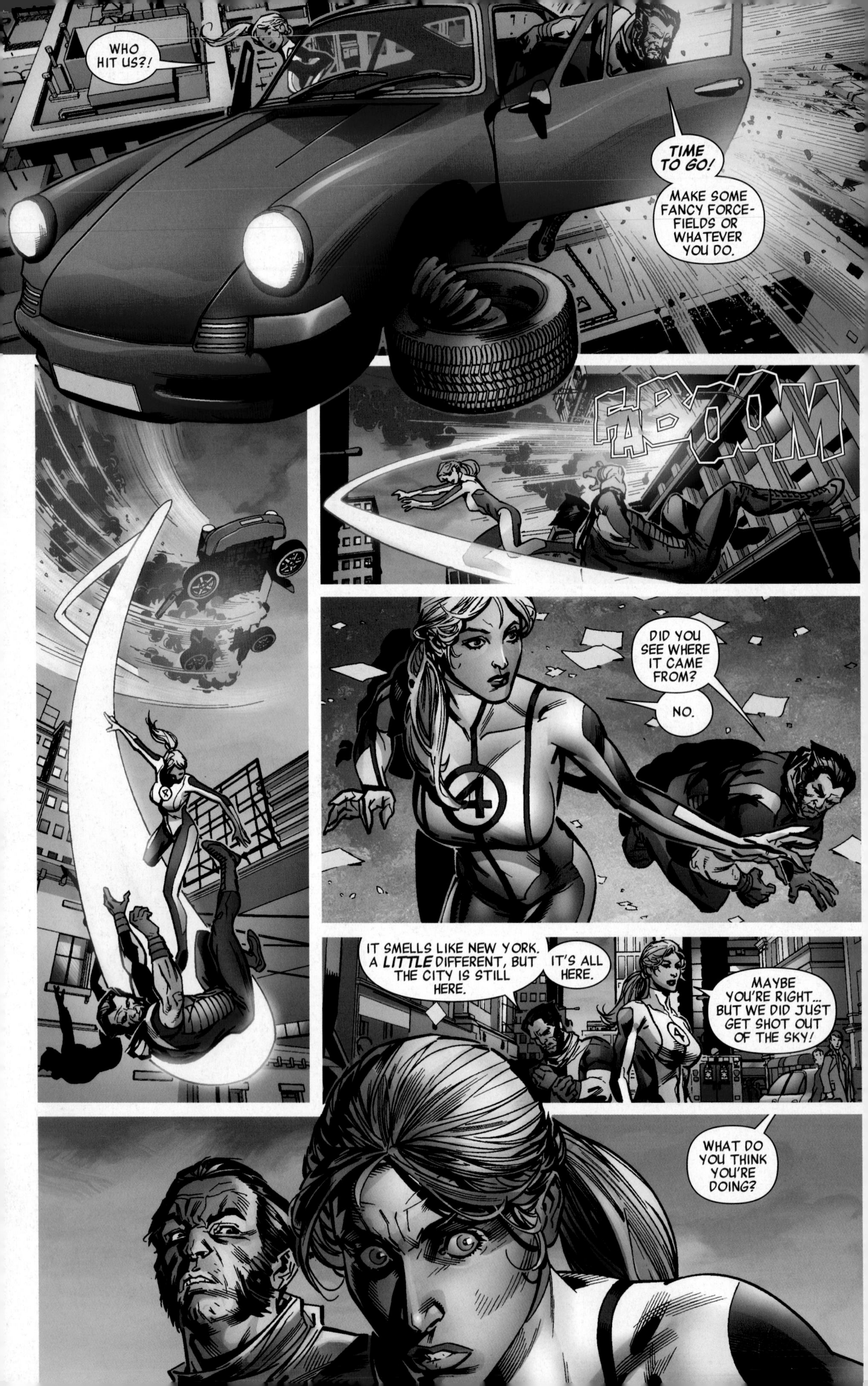

WHO HIT US?!
TIME TO GO!
MAKE SOME FANCY FORCE-FIELDS OR WHATEVER YOU DO.
FABOOM
DID YOU SEE WHERE IT CAME FROM?
NO.
IT SMELLS LIKE NEW YORK. A LITTLE DIFFERENT, BUT THE CITY IS STILL HERE.
IT'S ALL HERE.
MAYBE YOU'RE RIGHT... BUT WE DID JUST GET SHOT OUT OF THE SKY!
WHAT DO YOU THINK YOU'RE DOING?

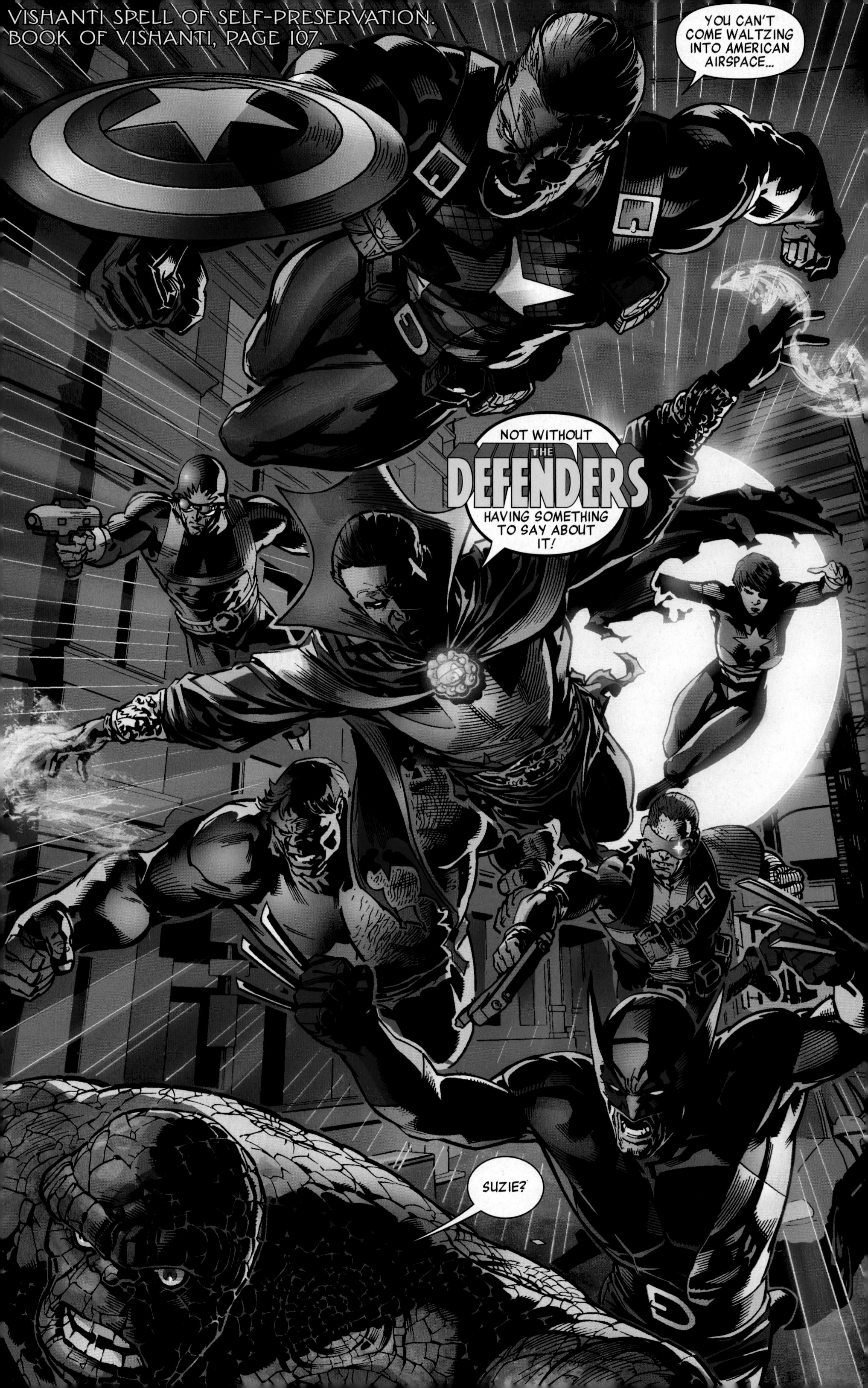
VISHANTI SPELL OF SELF-PRESERVATION. BOOK OF VISHANTI, PAGE 107.
YOU CAN'T COME WALTZING INTO AMERICAN AIRSPACE...
NOT WITHOUT THE DEFENDERS HAVING SOMETHING TO SAY ABOUT IT!
SUZIE?

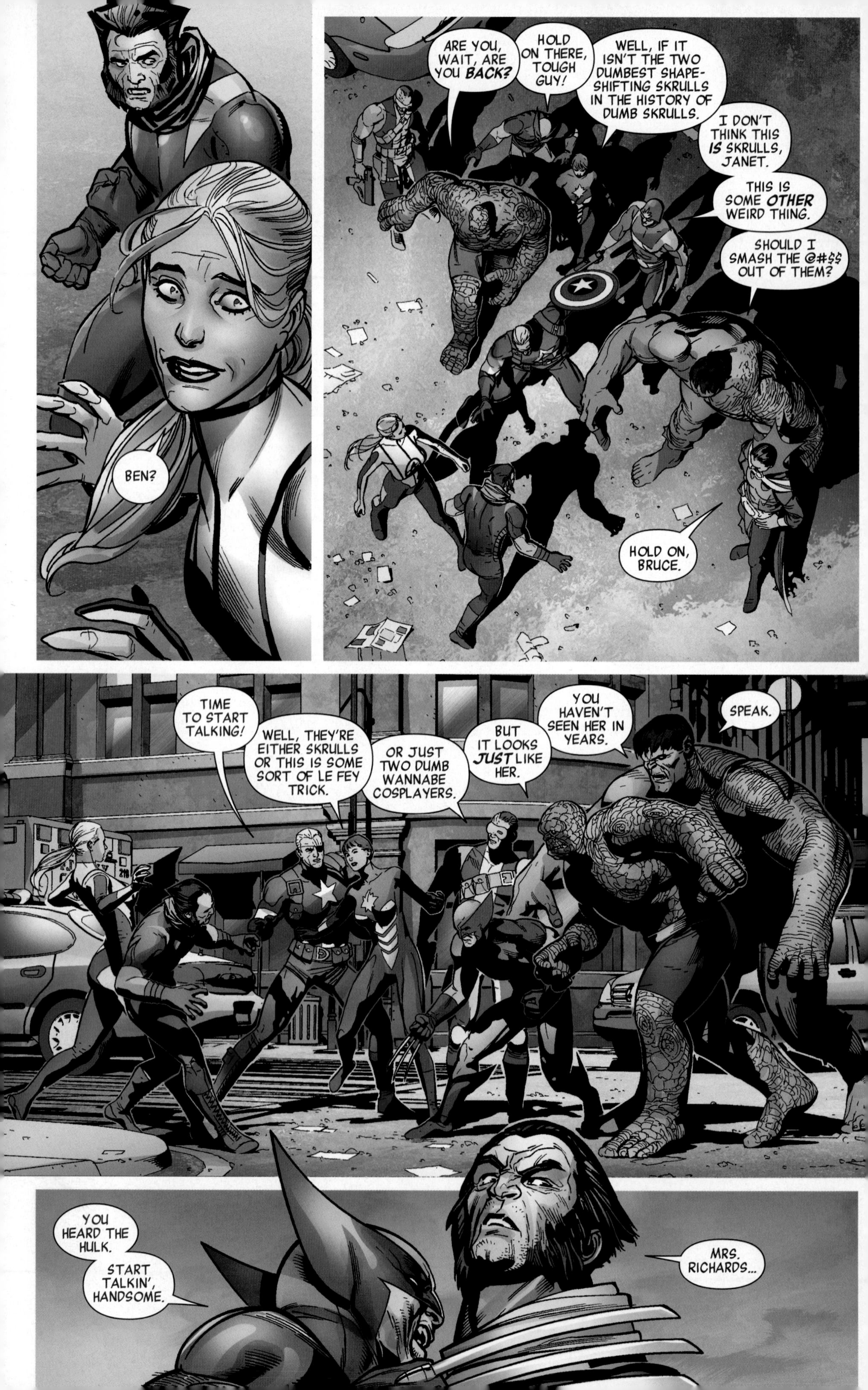
BEN?
ARE YOU, WAIT, ARE YOU BACK?
HOLD ON THERE, TOUGH GUY!
WELL, IF IT ISN'T THE TWO DUMBEST SHAPE-SHIFTING SKRULLS IN THE HISTORY OF DUMB SKRULLS.
I DON'T THINK THIS IS SKRULLS, JANET.
THIS IS SOME OTHER WEIRD THING.
SHOULD I SMASH THE @#$$ OUT OF THEM?
HOLD ON, BRUCE.
TIME TO START TALKING!
WELL, THEY'RE EITHER SKRULLS OR THIS IS SOME SORT OF LE FEY TRICK.
OR JUST TWO DUMB WANNABE COSPLAYERS.
BUT IT LOOKS JUST LIKE HER.
YOU HAVEN'T SEEN HER IN YEARS.
SPEAK.
YOU HEARD THE HULK.
START TALKIN', HANDSOME.
MRS. RICHARDS...

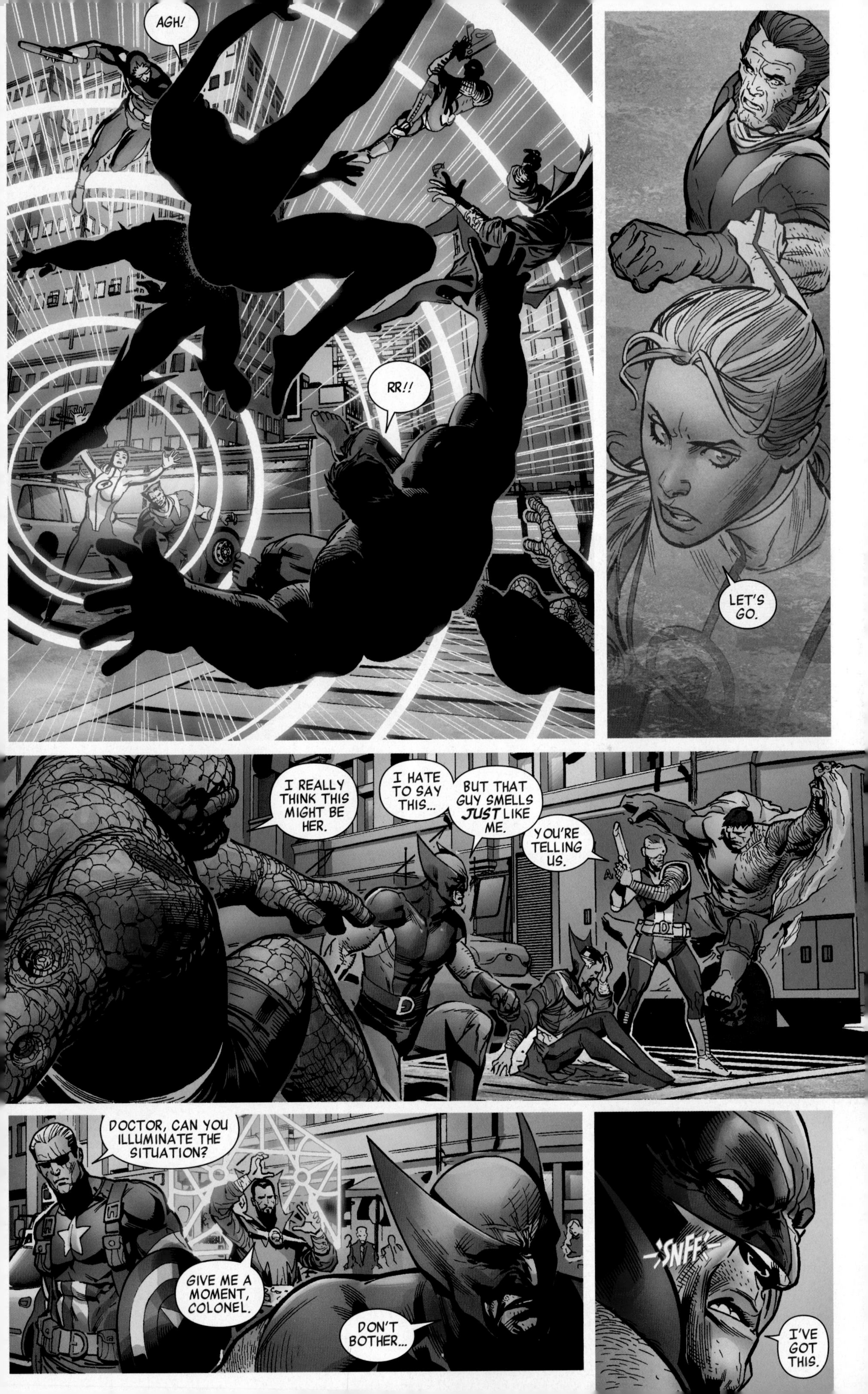
AGH!
RR!!
LET'S GO.
I REALLY THINK THIS MIGHT BE HER.
I HATE TO SAY THIS...
BUT THAT GUY SMELLS JUST LIKE ME.
YOU'RE TELLING US.
DOCTOR, CAN YOU ILLUMINATE THE SITUATION?
GIVE ME A MOMENT, COLONEL.
DON'T BOTHER...
SNFF
I'VE GOT THIS.

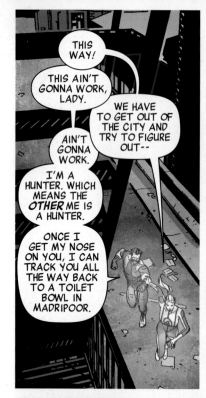

THIS WAY!

THIS AIN'T GONNA WORK, LADY.

WE HAVE TO GET OUT OF THE CITY AND TRY TO FIGURE OUT--

AIN'T GONNA WORK.

I'M A HUNTER. WHICH MEANS THE *OTHER* ME IS A HUNTER.

ONCE I GET MY NOSE ON YOU, I CAN TRACK YOU ALL THE WAY BACK TO A TOILET BOWL IN MADRIPOOR.

SEE.

WE GOT YOU SURROUNDED, SKRULL.

THE SPELL OF DISRUPTION. THE BOOK OF FIRE, PAGE 97.

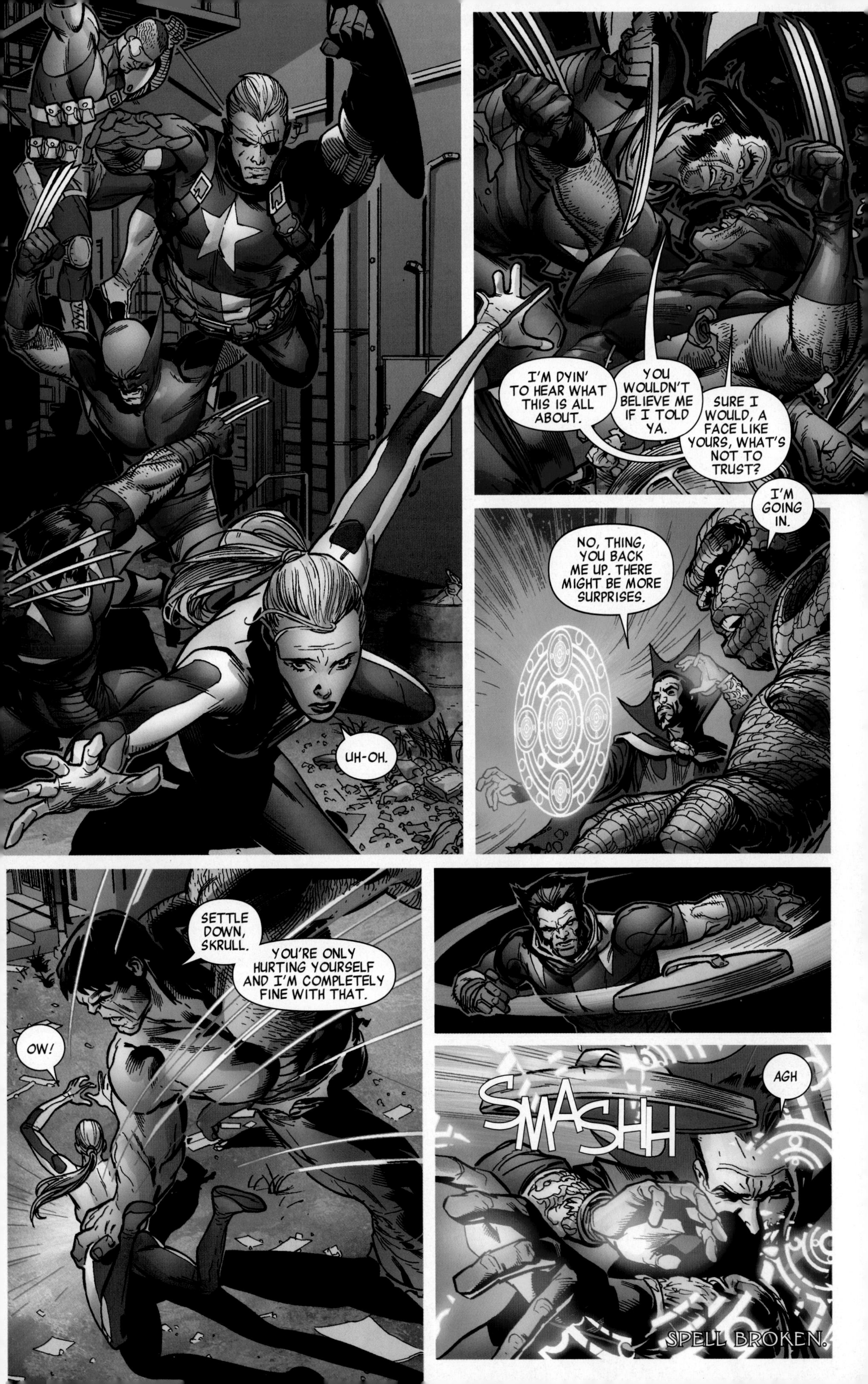
UH-OH.
I'M DYIN' TO HEAR WHAT THIS IS ALL ABOUT.
YOU WOULDN'T BELIEVE ME IF I TOLD YA.
SURE I WOULD, A FACE LIKE YOURS, WHAT'S NOT TO TRUST?
I'M GOING IN.
NO, THING, YOU BACK ME UP. THERE MIGHT BE MORE SURPRISES.
SETTLE DOWN, SKRULL.
YOU'RE ONLY HURTING YOURSELF AND I'M COMPLETELY FINE WITH THAT.
OW!
SMASHH
AGH
SPELL BROKEN.

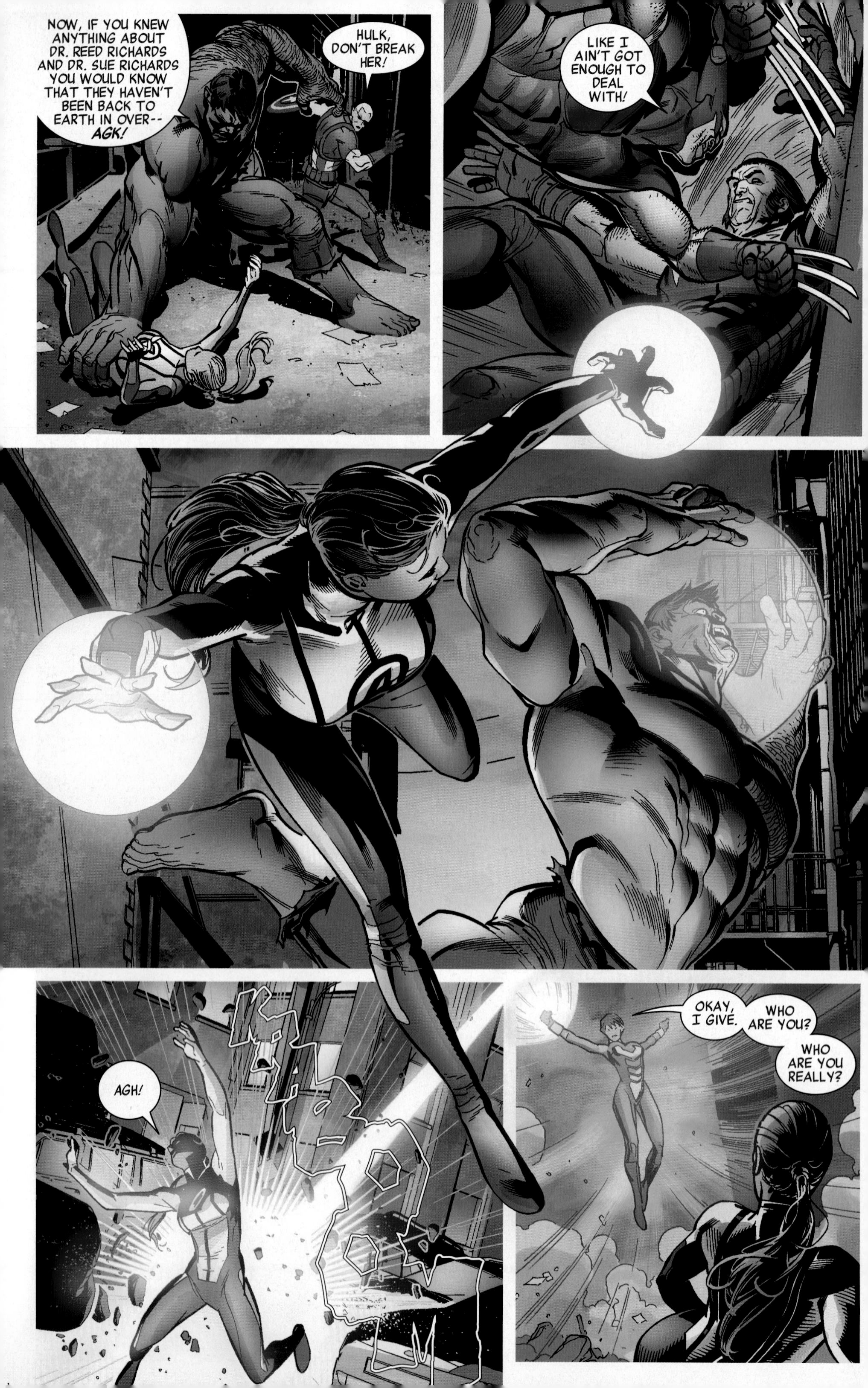
NOW, IF YOU KNEW ANYTHING ABOUT DR. REED RICHARDS AND DR. SUE RICHARDS YOU WOULD KNOW THAT THEY HAVEN'T BEEN BACK TO EARTH IN OVER-- AGK!
HULK, DON'T BREAK HER!
LIKE I AIN'T GOT ENOUGH TO DEAL WITH!
AGH!
OKAY, I GIVE.
WHO ARE YOU?
WHO ARE YOU REALLY?

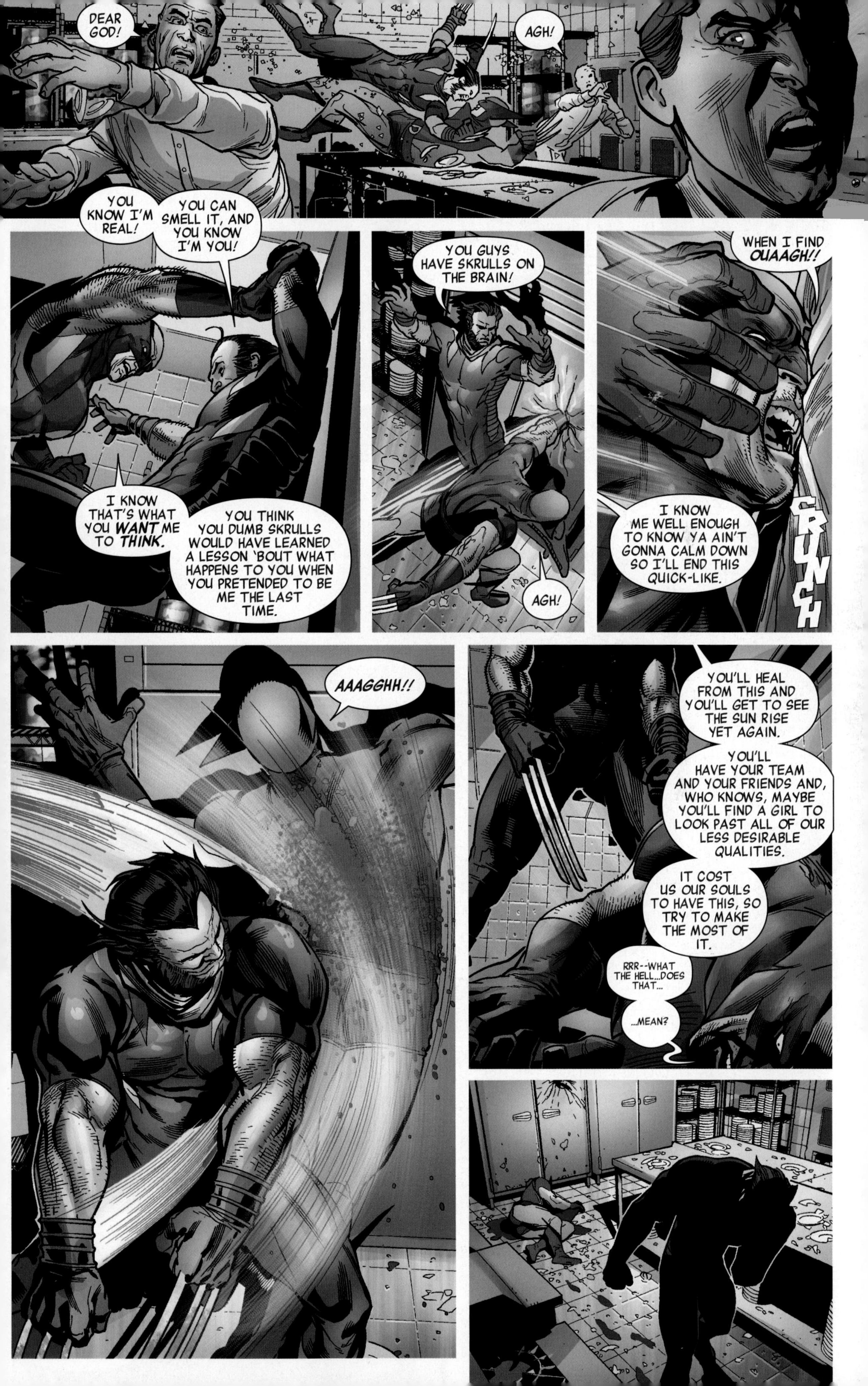
DEAR GOD!
AGH!
YOU KNOW I'M REAL!
YOU CAN SMELL IT, AND YOU KNOW I'M YOU!
I KNOW THAT'S WHAT YOU WANT ME TO THINK.
YOU THINK YOU DUMB SKRULLS WOULD HAVE LEARNED A LESSON 'BOUT WHAT HAPPENS TO YOU WHEN YOU PRETENDED TO BE ME THE LAST TIME.
YOU GUYS HAVE SKRULLS ON THE BRAIN!
AGH!
WHEN I FIND OUAAGH!!
I KNOW ME WELL ENOUGH TO KNOW YA AIN'T GONNA CALM DOWN SO I'LL END THIS QUICK-LIKE.
CRUNCH
AAAGGHH!!
YOU'LL HEAL FROM THIS AND YOU'LL GET TO SEE THE SUN RISE YET AGAIN.
YOU'LL HAVE YOUR TEAM AND YOUR FRIENDS AND, WHO KNOWS, MAYBE YOU'LL FIND A GIRL TO LOOK PAST ALL OF OUR LESS DESIRABLE QUALITIES.
IT COST US OUR SOULS TO HAVE THIS, SO TRY TO MAKE THE MOST OF IT.
RRR--WHAT THE HELL...DOES THAT...
...MEAN?

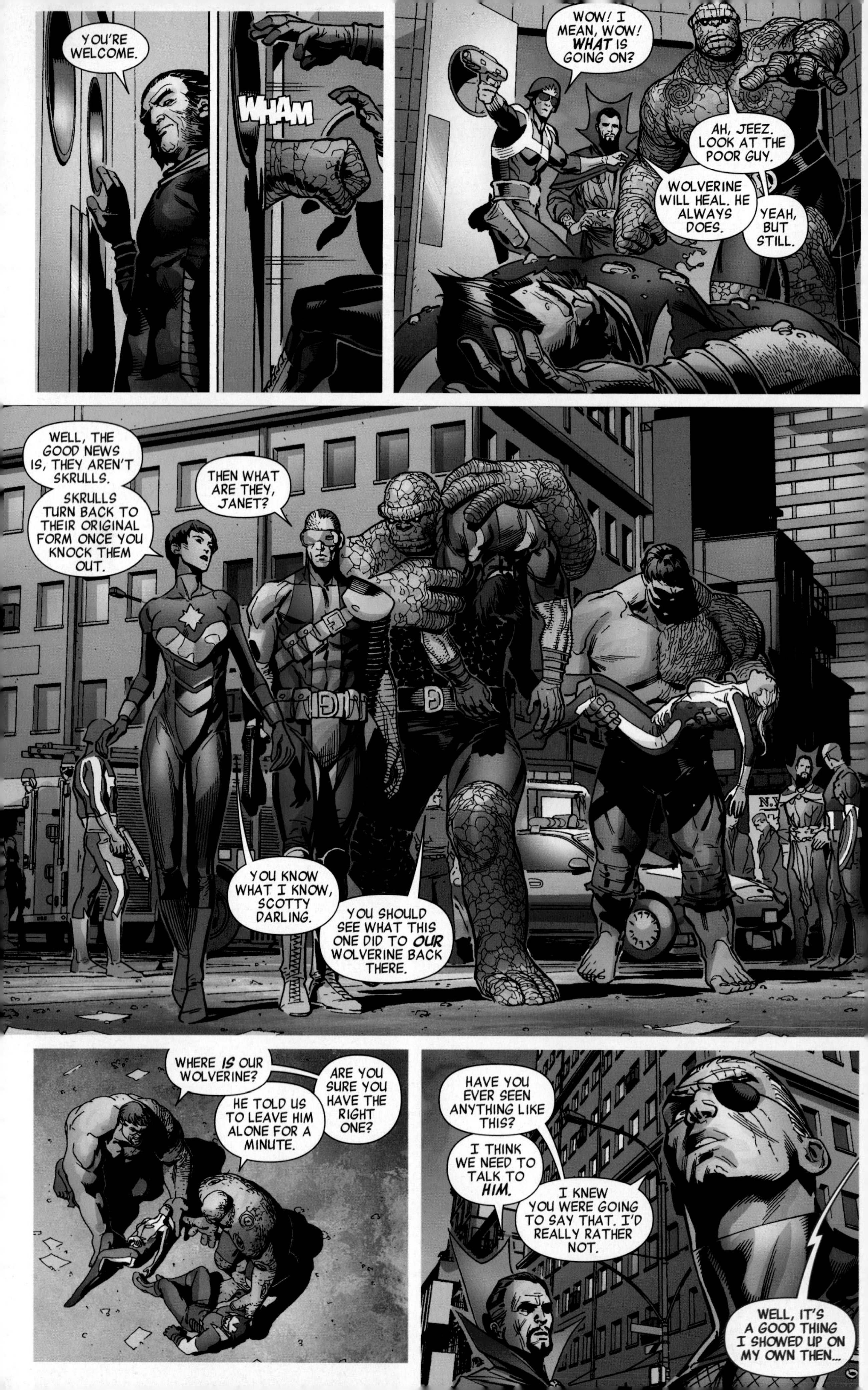
YOU'RE WELCOME.
WHAM
WOW! I MEAN, WOW! WHAT IS GOING ON?
AH, JEEZ. LOOK AT THE POOR GUY.
WOLVERINE WILL HEAL. HE ALWAYS DOES.
YEAH, BUT STILL.
WELL, THE GOOD NEWS IS, THEY AREN'T SKRULLS.
SKRULLS TURN BACK TO THEIR ORIGINAL FORM ONCE YOU KNOCK THEM OUT.
THEN WHAT ARE THEY, JANET?
YOU KNOW WHAT I KNOW, SCOTTY DARLING.
YOU SHOULD SEE WHAT THIS ONE DID TO OUR WOLVERINE BACK THERE.
WHERE IS OUR WOLVERINE?
HE TOLD US TO LEAVE HIM ALONE FOR A MINUTE.
ARE YOU SURE YOU HAVE THE RIGHT ONE?
HAVE YOU EVER SEEN ANYTHING LIKE THIS?
I THINK WE NEED TO TALK TO HIM.
I KNEW YOU WERE GOING TO SAY THAT. I'D REALLY RATHER NOT.
WELL, IT'S A GOOD THING I SHOWED UP ON MY OWN THEN...

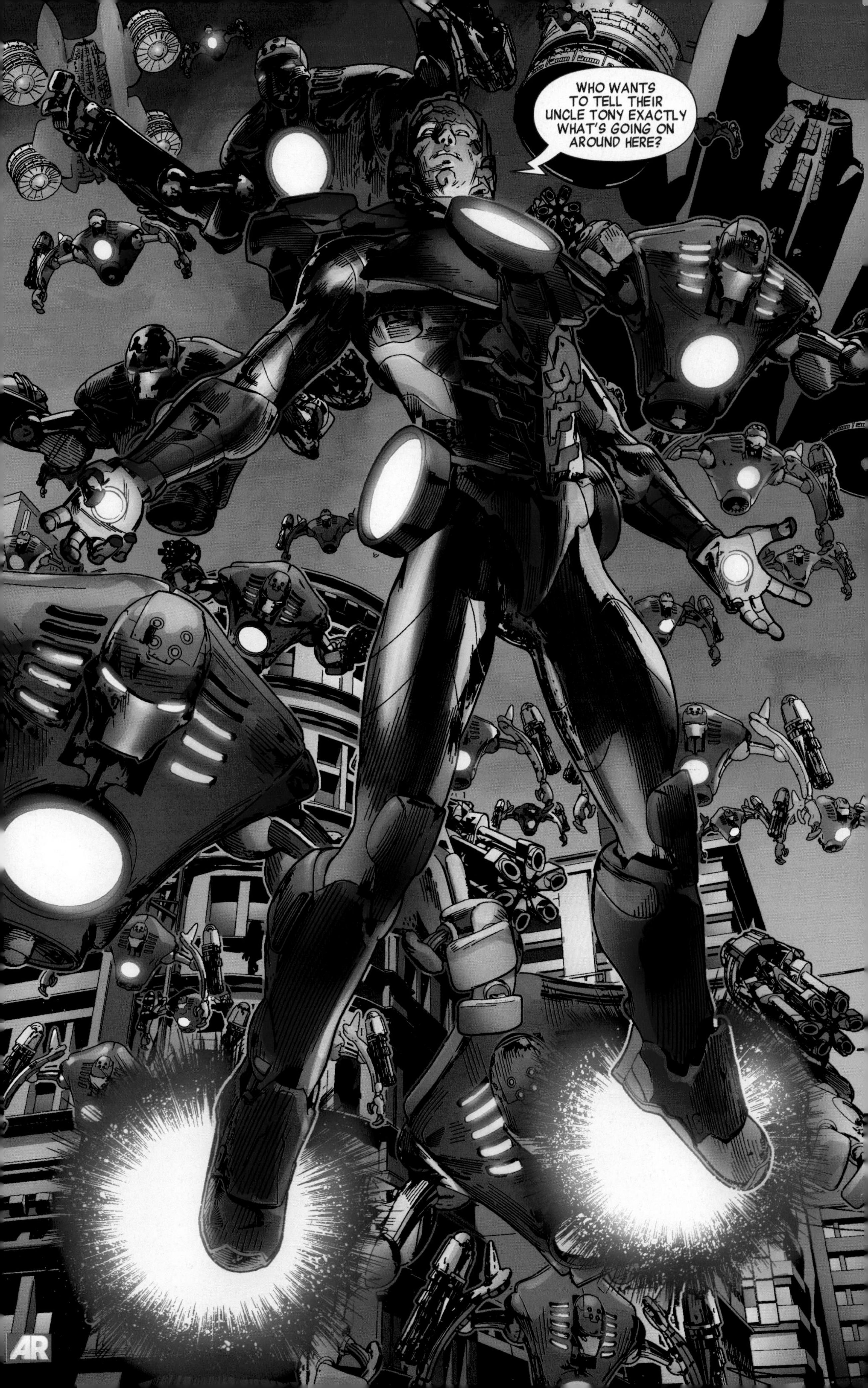
WHO WANTS TO TELL THEIR UNCLE TONY EXACTLY WHAT'S GOING ON AROUND HERE?

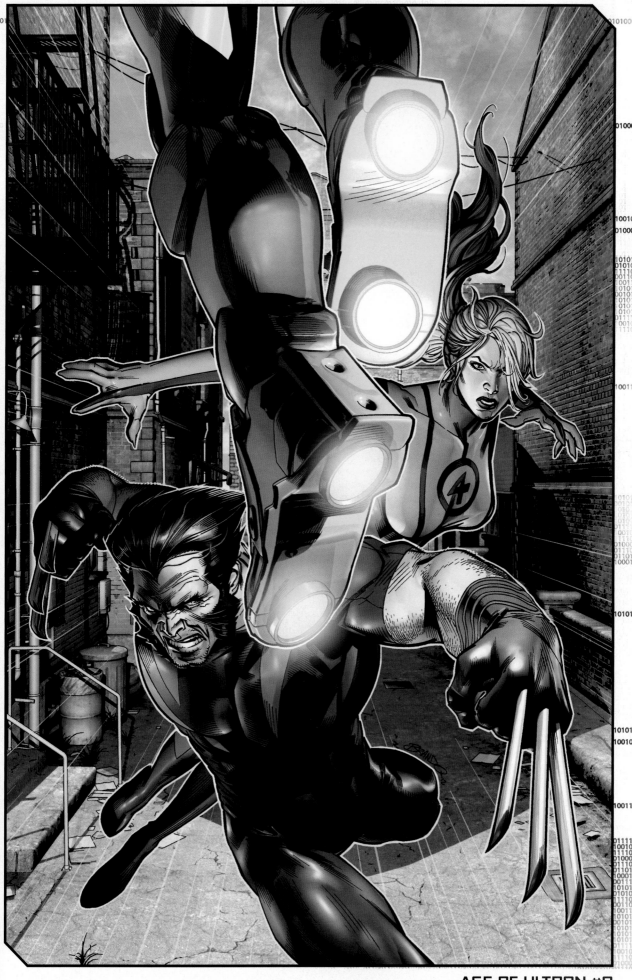

AGE OF ULTRON #8

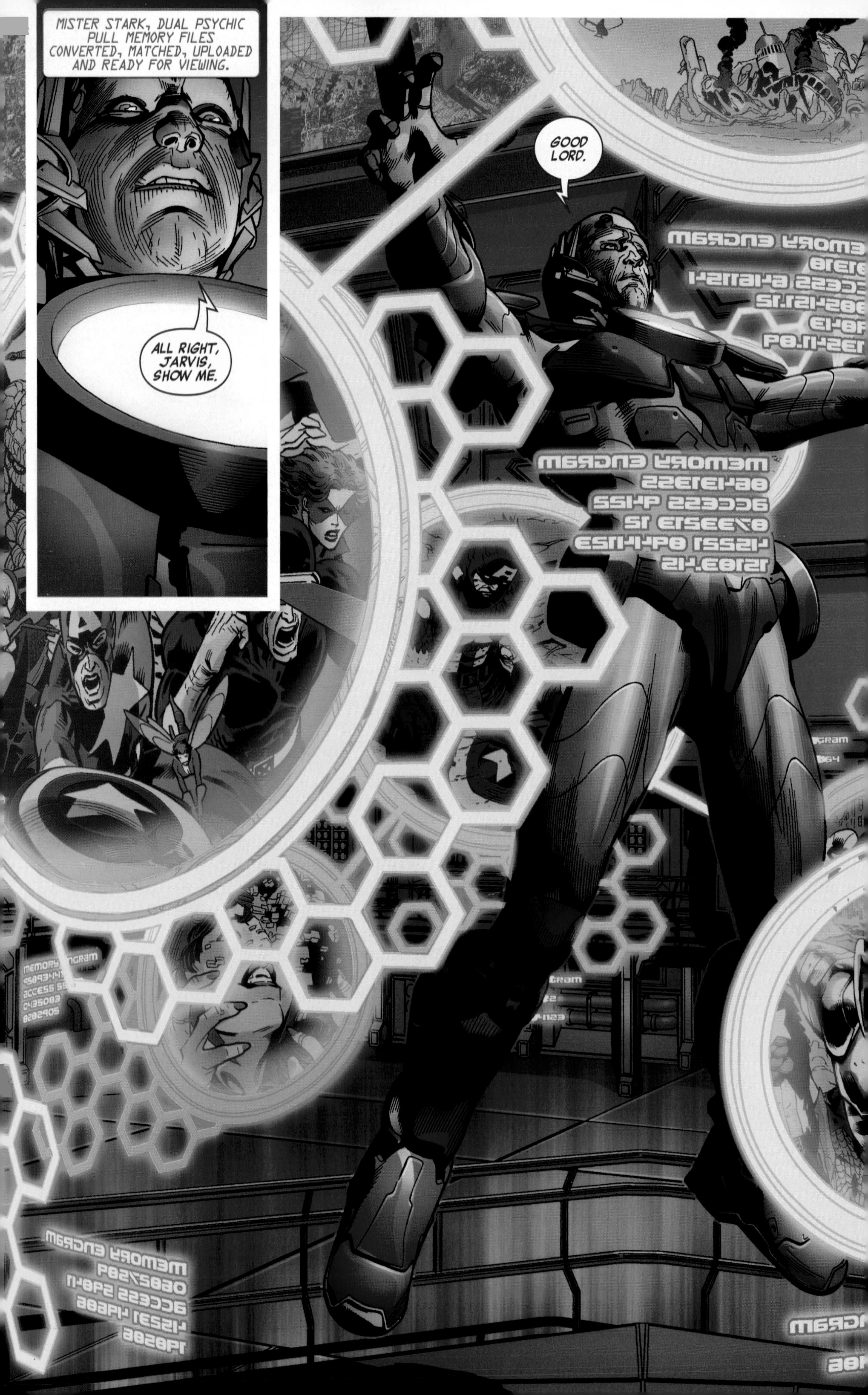
MISTER STARK, DUAL PSYCHIC PULL MEMORY FILES CONVERTED, MATCHED, UPLOADED AND READY FOR VIEWING.
ALL RIGHT, JARVIS, SHOW ME.
GOOD LORD.

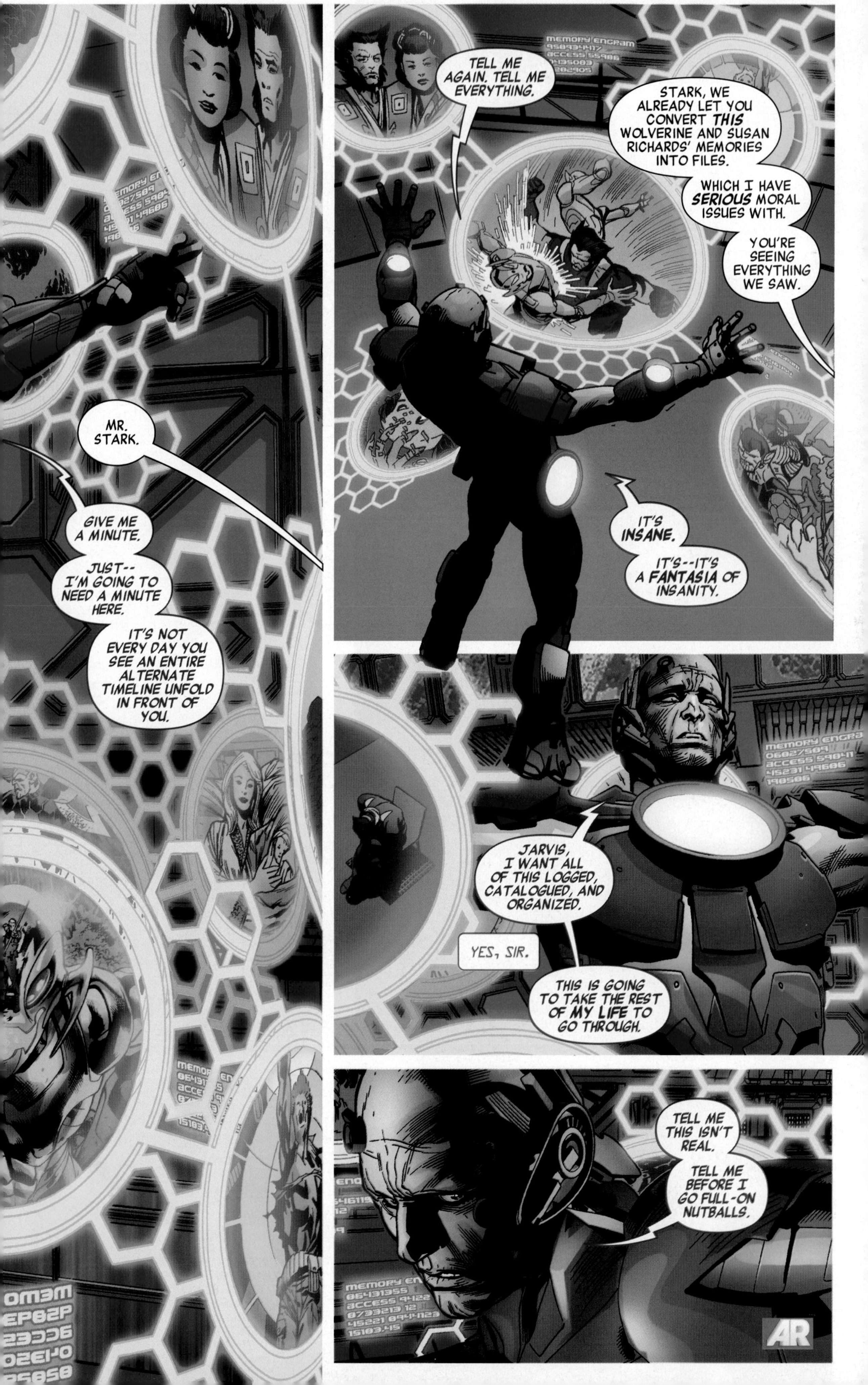
TELL ME AGAIN. TELL ME EVERYTHING.
STARK, WE ALREADY LET YOU CONVERT THIS WOLVERINE AND SUSAN RICHARDS' MEMORIES INTO FILES.
WHICH I HAVE SERIOUS MORAL ISSUES WITH.
YOU'RE SEEING EVERYTHING WE SAW.
IT'S INSANE.
IT'S--IT'S A FANTASIA OF INSANITY.
MR. STARK.
GIVE ME A MINUTE.
JUST-- I'M GOING TO NEED A MINUTE HERE.
IT'S NOT EVERY DAY YOU SEE AN ENTIRE ALTERNATE TIMELINE UNFOLD IN FRONT OF YOU.
JARVIS, I WANT ALL OF THIS LOGGED, CATALOGUED, AND ORGANIZED.
YES, SIR.
THIS IS GOING TO TAKE THE REST OF MY LIFE TO GO THROUGH.
TELL ME THIS ISN'T REAL.
TELL ME BEFORE I GO FULL-ON NUTBALLS.

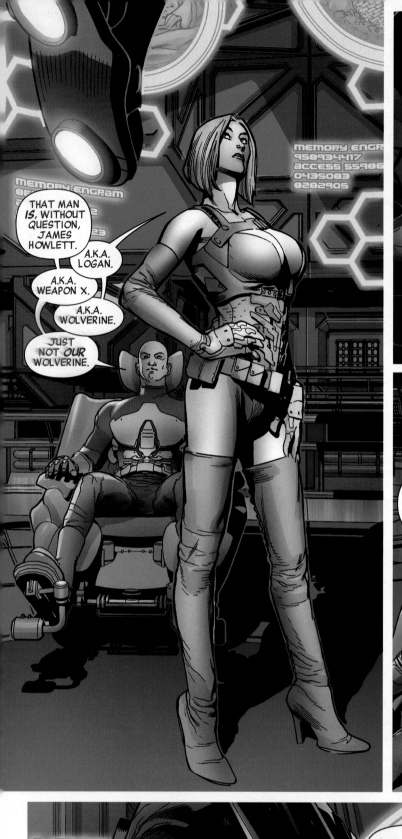

MEMORY ENGRAM
95093442
23

THAT MAN *IS*, WITHOUT QUESTION, JAMES HOWLETT.

A.K.A. LOGAN.

A.K.A. WEAPON X.

A.K.A. WOLVERINE.

JUST NOT *OUR* WOLVERINE.

MEMORY ENGRAM
95093442-417
ACCESS 55986
0435083
8282905

AND HE CAME HERE WITH SUSAN RICHARDS.

THAT *IS* HER.

JUST, AGAIN, NOT, ACCORDING TO THEIR MEMORIES, *OUR* SUSAN RICHARDS.

memory engram
95093442-417
access 55986
0435083

THE NARRATIVE INSIDE EACH OF THEIR HEADS IS IDENTICAL.

PERFECTLY IN SYNC.

YOU CANNOT-- YOU *CANNOT FAKE* THAT KIND OF PSYCHIC SYNCHRONICITY.

THEY BOTH, OVER THE LAST FEW WEEKS, SAW AND EXPERIENCED THE EXACT SAME HORRIBLE MEMORIES.

Y ENG
417
5598

BUT FROST, XAVIER, COME ON...

YOU'RE TELLING ME THERE'S *NO WAY* THAT *MORGANA LE FEY* PLANTED THOSE MEMORIES?

THERE'S NO WAY SHE HAS DROPPED THEM HERE-- THAT THIS ISN'T SOME SORT OF CLONE/ FAKE MEMORY/ TROJAN HORSE/ MAGIC BOMB ABOUT TO BLOW UP IN OUR FACES?

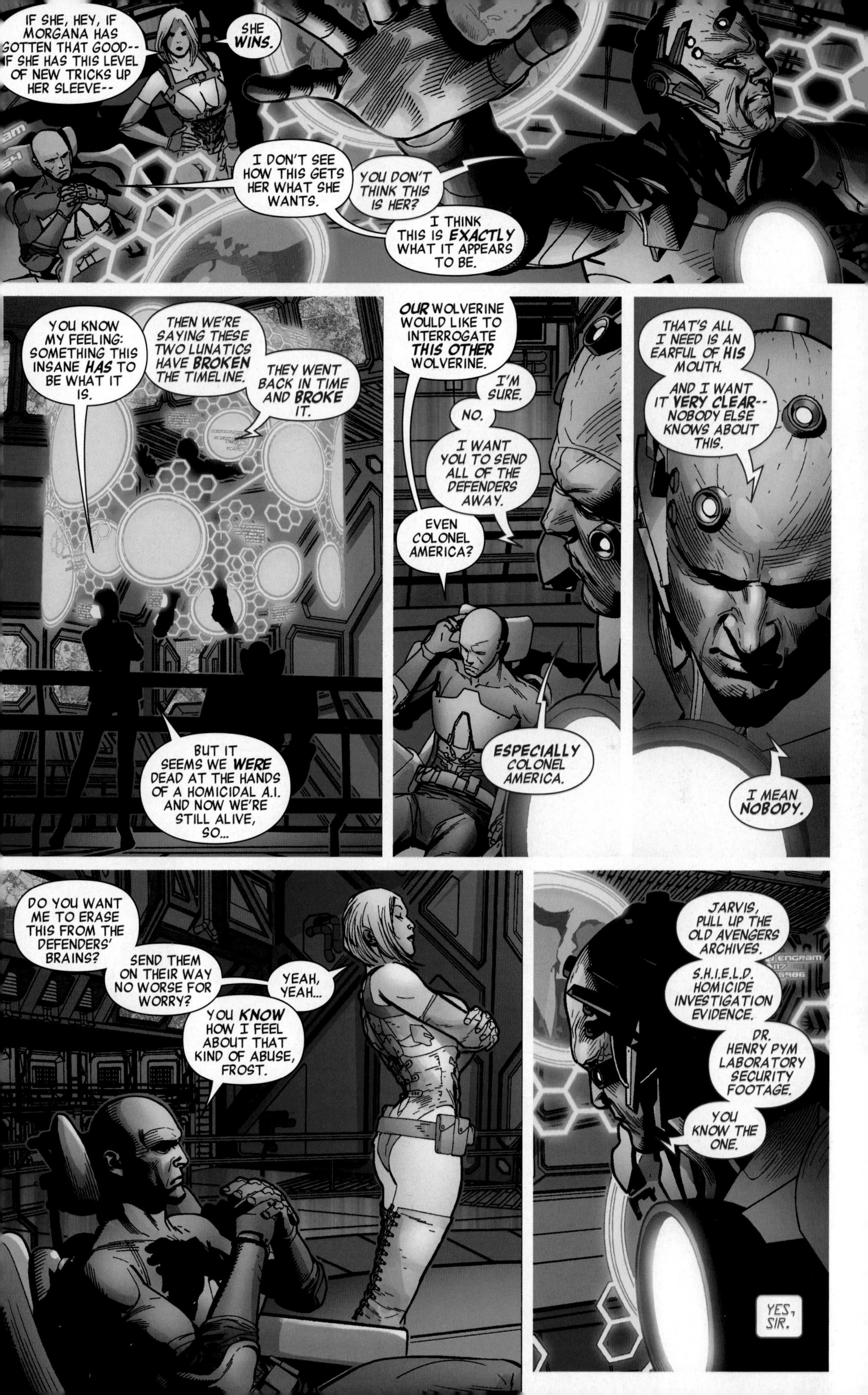
IF SHE, HEY, IF MORGANA HAS GOTTEN THAT GOOD-- IF SHE HAS THIS LEVEL OF NEW TRICKS UP HER SLEEVE--
SHE WINS.
I DON'T SEE HOW THIS GETS HER WHAT SHE WANTS.
YOU DON'T THINK THIS IS HER?
I THINK THIS IS EXACTLY WHAT IT APPEARS TO BE.
YOU KNOW MY FEELING: SOMETHING THIS INSANE HAS TO BE WHAT IT IS.
THEN WE'RE SAYING THESE TWO LUNATICS HAVE BROKEN THE TIMELINE.
THEY WENT BACK IN TIME AND BROKE IT.
BUT IT SEEMS WE WERE DEAD AT THE HANDS OF A HOMICIDAL A.I. AND NOW WE'RE STILL ALIVE, SO...
OUR WOLVERINE WOULD LIKE TO INTERROGATE THIS OTHER WOLVERINE.
I'M SURE.
NO.
I WANT YOU TO SEND ALL OF THE DEFENDERS AWAY.
EVEN COLONEL AMERICA?
ESPECIALLY COLONEL AMERICA.
THAT'S ALL I NEED IS AN EARFUL OF HIS MOUTH.
AND I WANT IT VERY CLEAR-- NOBODY ELSE KNOWS ABOUT THIS.
I MEAN NOBODY.
DO YOU WANT ME TO ERASE THIS FROM THE DEFENDERS' BRAINS?
SEND THEM ON THEIR WAY NO WORSE FOR WORRY?
YEAH, YEAH...
YOU KNOW HOW I FEEL ABOUT THAT KIND OF ABUSE, FROST.
JARVIS, PULL UP THE OLD AVENGERS ARCHIVES.
S.H.I.E.L.D. HOMICIDE INVESTIGATION EVIDENCE.
DR. HENRY PYM LABORATORY SECURITY FOOTAGE.
YOU KNOW THE ONE.
YES, SIR.

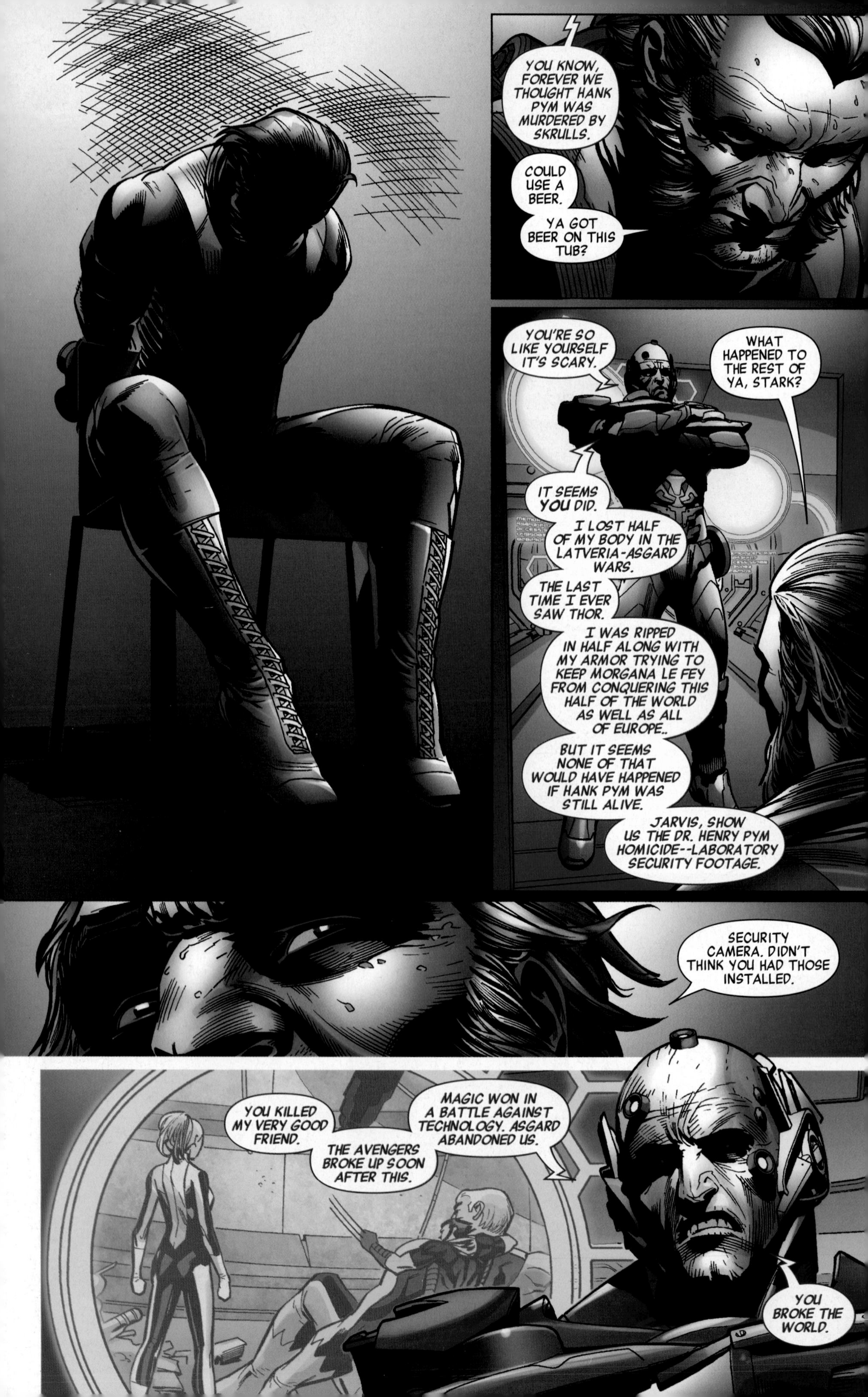
YOU KNOW, FOREVER WE THOUGHT HANK PYM WAS MURDERED BY SKRULLS.
COULD USE A BEER.
YA GOT BEER ON THIS TUB?
YOU'RE SO LIKE YOURSELF IT'S SCARY.
WHAT HAPPENED TO THE REST OF YA, STARK?
IT SEEMS YOU DID.
I LOST HALF OF MY BODY IN THE LATVERIA-ASGARD WARS.
THE LAST TIME I EVER SAW THOR.
I WAS RIPPED IN HALF ALONG WITH MY ARMOR TRYING TO KEEP MORGANA LE FEY FROM CONQUERING THIS HALF OF THE WORLD AS WELL AS ALL OF EUROPE..
BUT IT SEEMS NONE OF THAT WOULD HAVE HAPPENED IF HANK PYM WAS STILL ALIVE.
JARVIS, SHOW US THE DR. HENRY PYM HOMICIDE--LABORATORY SECURITY FOOTAGE.
SECURITY CAMERA. DIDN'T THINK YOU HAD THOSE INSTALLED.
YOU KILLED MY VERY GOOD FRIEND.
THE AVENGERS BROKE UP SOON AFTER THIS.
MAGIC WON IN A BATTLE AGAINST TECHNOLOGY. ASGARD ABANDONED US.
YOU BROKE THE WORLD.

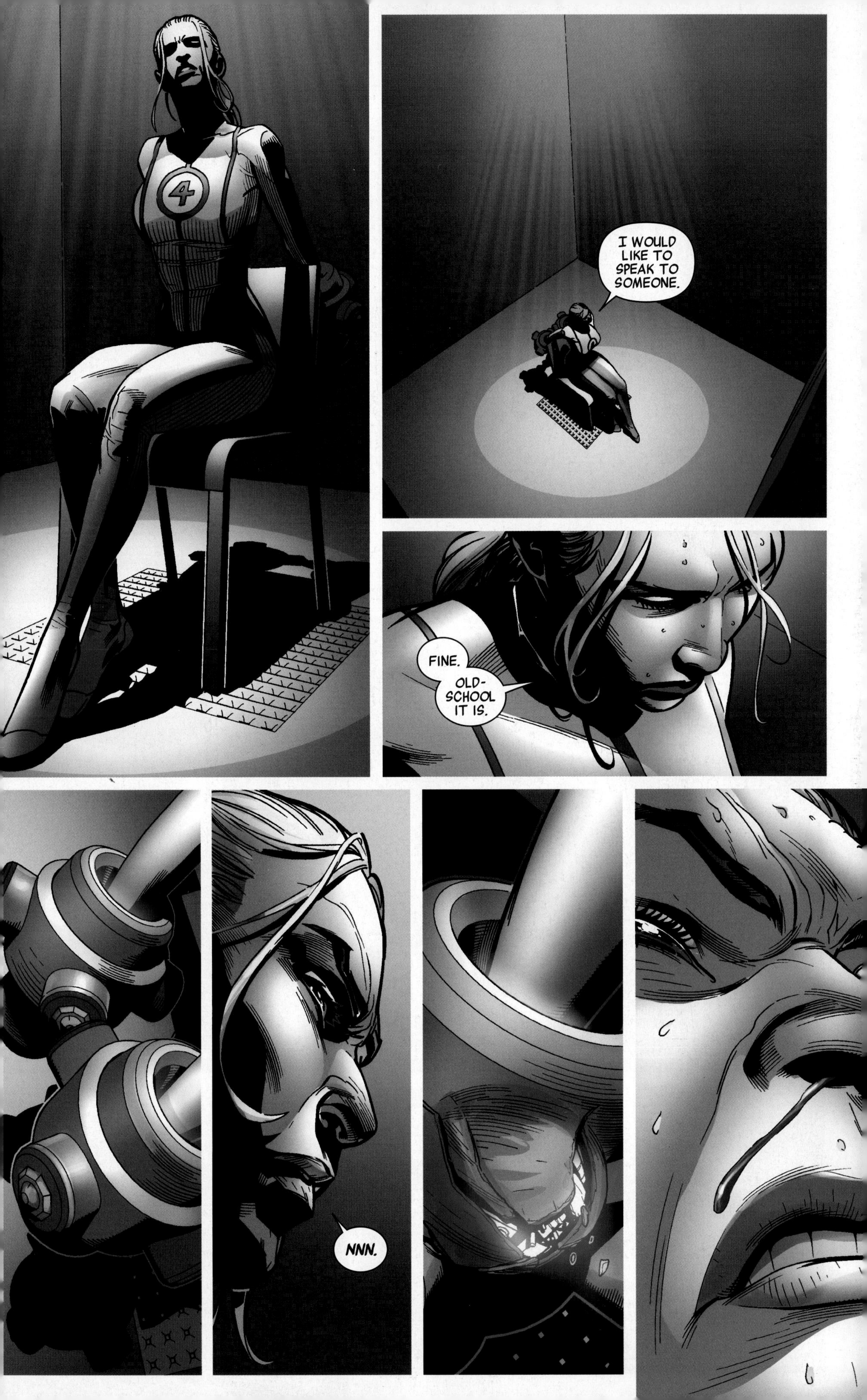
I WOULD LIKE TO SPEAK TO SOMEONE.
FINE.
OLD-SCHOOL IT IS.
NNN.

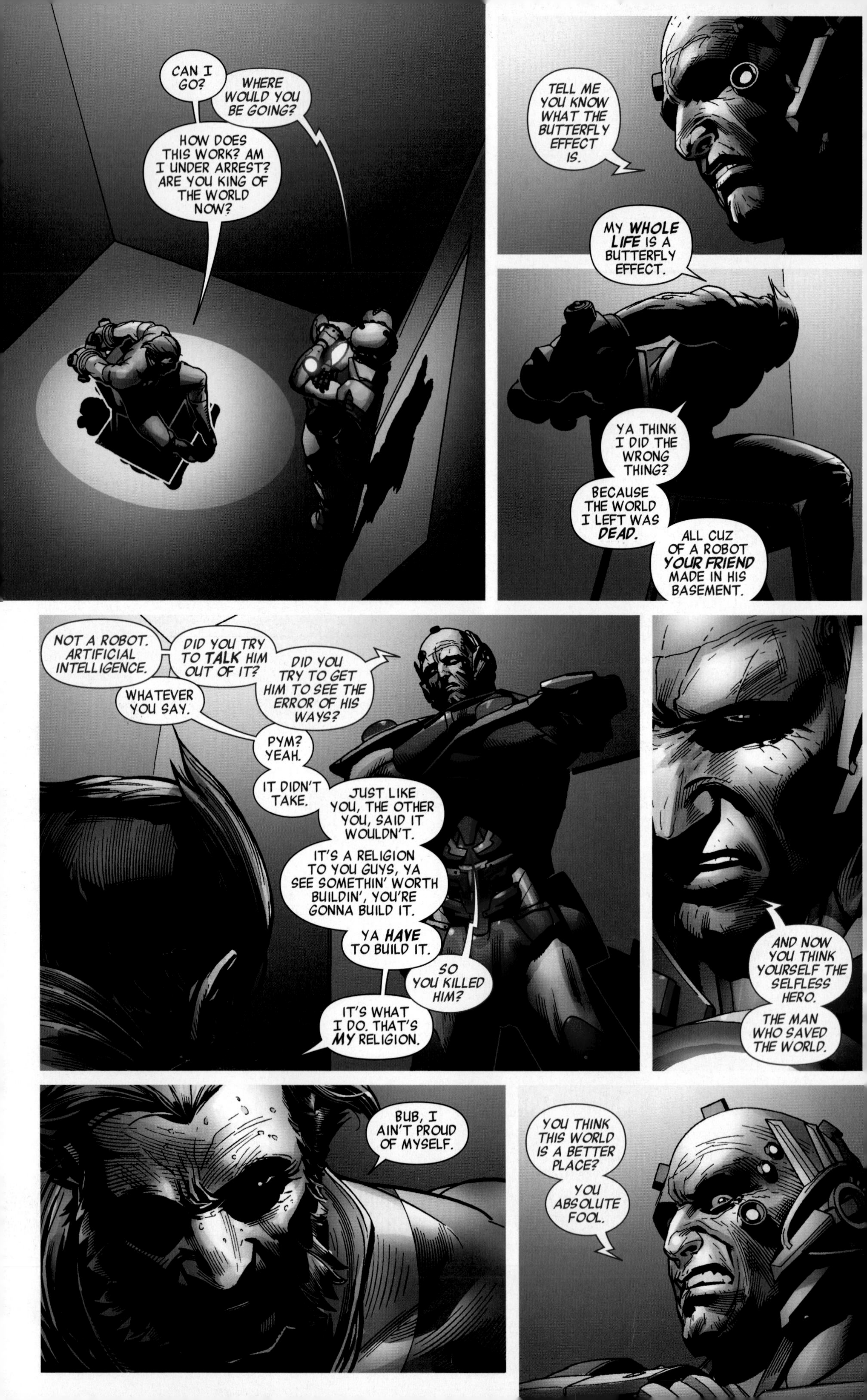
CAN I GO?
WHERE WOULD YOU BE GOING?
HOW DOES THIS WORK? AM I UNDER ARREST? ARE YOU KING OF THE WORLD NOW?
TELL ME YOU KNOW WHAT THE BUTTERFLY EFFECT IS.
MY WHOLE LIFE IS A BUTTERFLY EFFECT.
YA THINK I DID THE WRONG THING?
BECAUSE THE WORLD I LEFT WAS DEAD.
ALL CUZ OF A ROBOT YOUR FRIEND MADE IN HIS BASEMENT.
NOT A ROBOT. ARTIFICIAL INTELLIGENCE.
DID YOU TRY TO TALK HIM OUT OF IT?
DID YOU TRY TO GET HIM TO SEE THE ERROR OF HIS WAYS?
WHATEVER YOU SAY.
PYM? YEAH.
IT DIDN'T TAKE.
JUST LIKE YOU, THE OTHER YOU, SAID IT WOULDN'T.
IT'S A RELIGION TO YOU GUYS, YA SEE SOMETHIN' WORTH BUILDIN', YOU'RE GONNA BUILD IT.
YA HAVE TO BUILD IT.
SO YOU KILLED HIM?
IT'S WHAT I DO. THAT'S MY RELIGION.
AND NOW YOU THINK YOURSELF THE SELFLESS HERO.
THE MAN WHO SAVED THE WORLD.
BUB, I AIN'T PROUD OF MYSELF.
YOU THINK THIS WORLD IS A BETTER PLACE?
YOU ABSOLUTE FOOL.

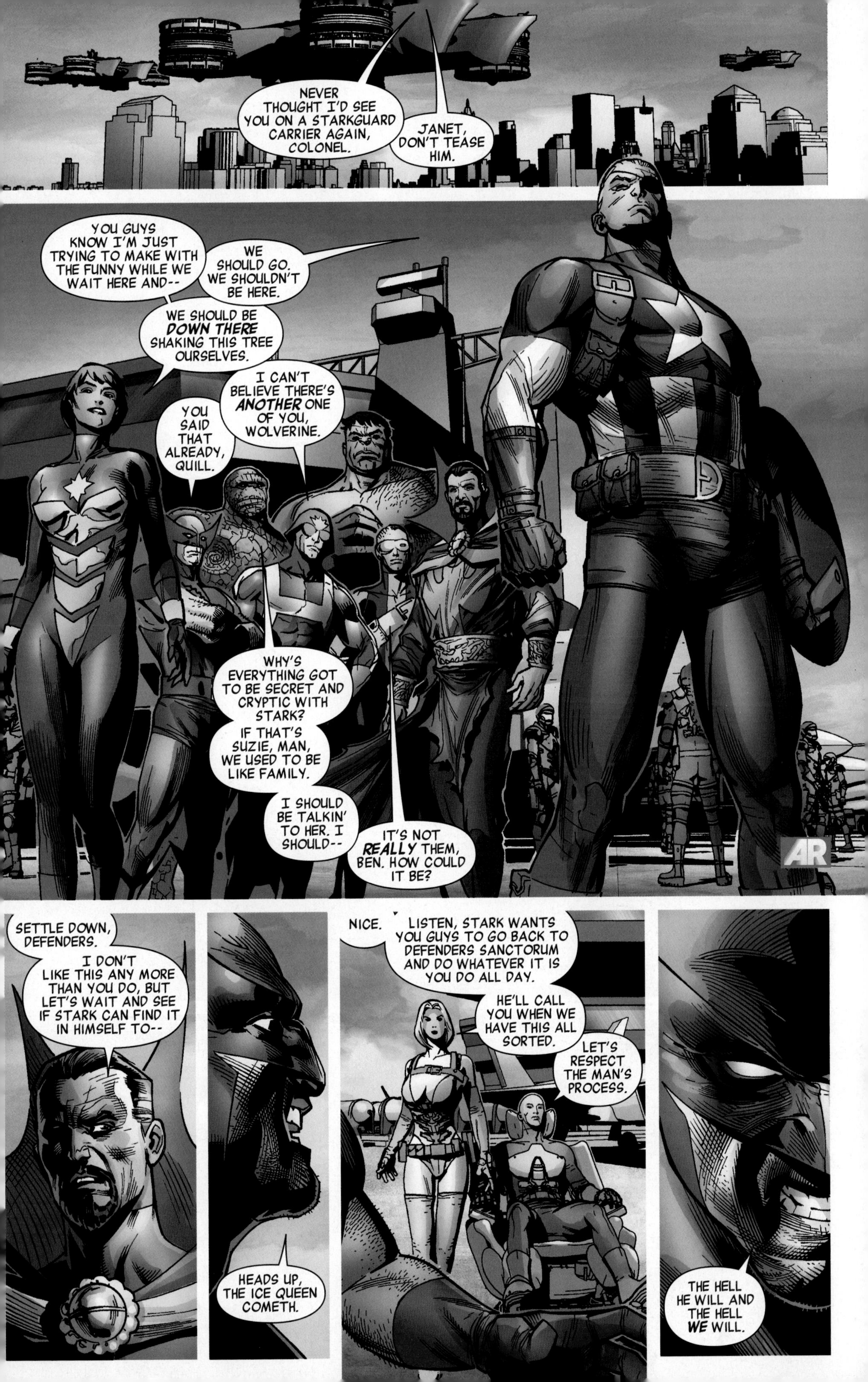
NEVER THOUGHT I'D SEE YOU ON A STARKGUARD CARRIER AGAIN, COLONEL.
JANET, DON'T TEASE HIM.
YOU GUYS KNOW I'M JUST TRYING TO MAKE WITH THE FUNNY WHILE WE WAIT HERE AND--
WE SHOULD GO. WE SHOULDN'T BE HERE.
WE SHOULD BE DOWN THERE SHAKING THIS TREE OURSELVES.
YOU SAID THAT ALREADY, QUILL.
I CAN'T BELIEVE THERE'S ANOTHER ONE OF YOU, WOLVERINE.
WHY'S EVERYTHING GOT TO BE SECRET AND CRYPTIC WITH STARK?
IF THAT'S SUZIE, MAN, WE USED TO BE LIKE FAMILY.
I SHOULD BE TALKIN' TO HER. I SHOULD--
IT'S NOT REALLY THEM, BEN. HOW COULD IT BE?
AR
SETTLE DOWN, DEFENDERS.
I DON'T LIKE THIS ANY MORE THAN YOU DO, BUT LET'S WAIT AND SEE IF STARK CAN FIND IT IN HIMSELF TO--
HEADS UP, THE ICE QUEEN COMETH.
NICE.
LISTEN, STARK WANTS YOU GUYS TO GO BACK TO DEFENDERS SANCTORUM AND DO WHATEVER IT IS YOU DO ALL DAY.
HE'LL CALL YOU WHEN WE HAVE THIS ALL SORTED.
LET'S RESPECT THE MAN'S PROCESS.
THE HELL HE WILL AND THE HELL WE WILL.

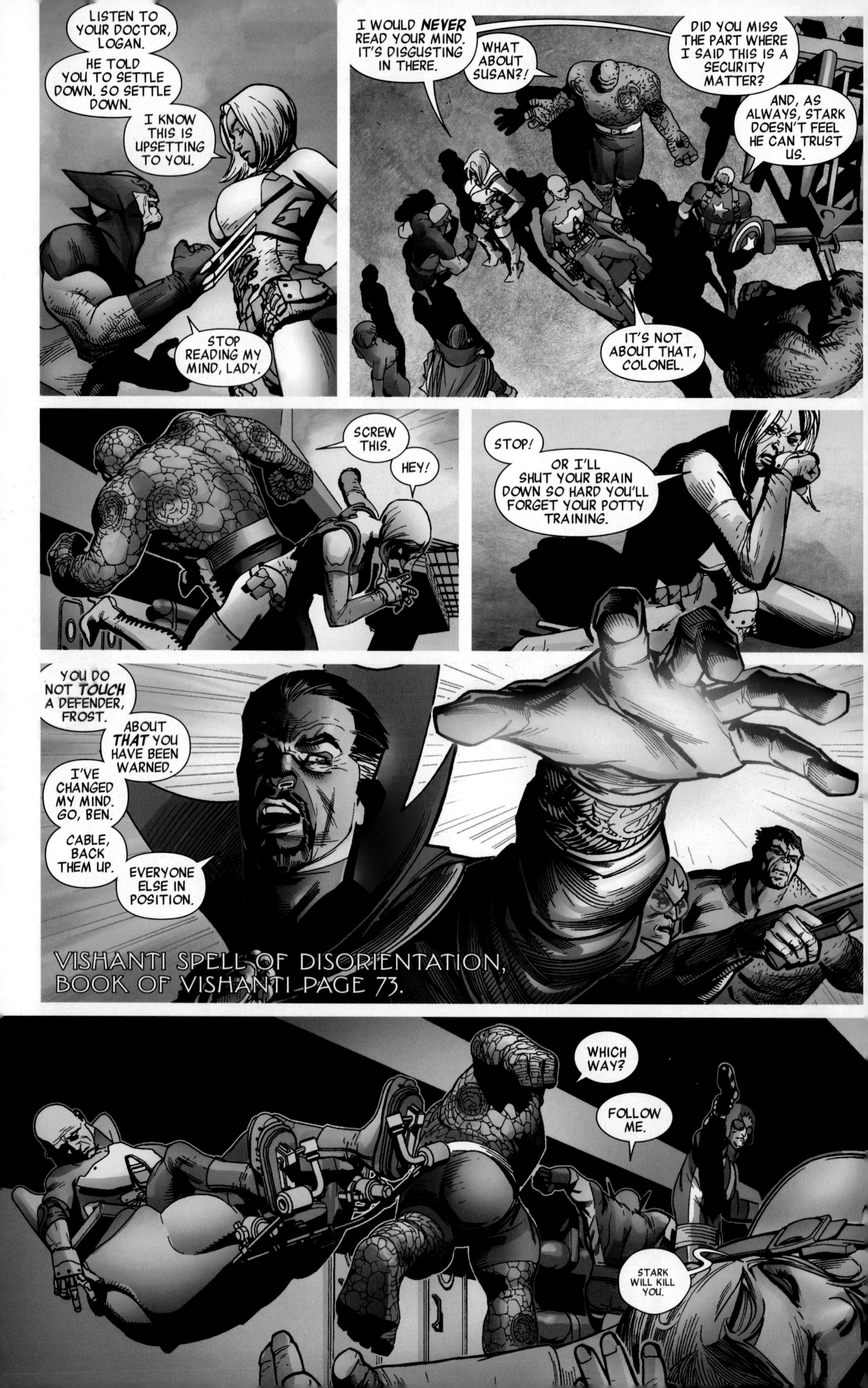
LISTEN TO YOUR DOCTOR, LOGAN.
HE TOLD YOU TO SETTLE DOWN. SO SETTLE DOWN.
I KNOW THIS IS UPSETTING TO YOU.
STOP READING MY MIND, LADY.
I WOULD NEVER READ YOUR MIND. IT'S DISGUSTING IN THERE.
WHAT ABOUT SUSAN?!
DID YOU MISS THE PART WHERE I SAID THIS IS A SECURITY MATTER?
AND, AS ALWAYS, STARK DOESN'T FEEL HE CAN TRUST US.
IT'S NOT ABOUT THAT, COLONEL.
SCREW THIS.
HEY!
STOP!
OR I'LL SHUT YOUR BRAIN DOWN SO HARD YOU'LL FORGET YOUR POTTY TRAINING.
YOU DO NOT TOUCH A DEFENDER, FROST.
ABOUT THAT YOU HAVE BEEN WARNED.
I'VE CHANGED MY MIND. GO, BEN.
CABLE, BACK THEM UP.
EVERYONE ELSE IN POSITION.
VISHANTI SPELL OF DISORIENTATION, BOOK OF VISHANTI PAGE 73.
WHICH WAY?
FOLLOW ME.
STARK WILL KILL YOU.

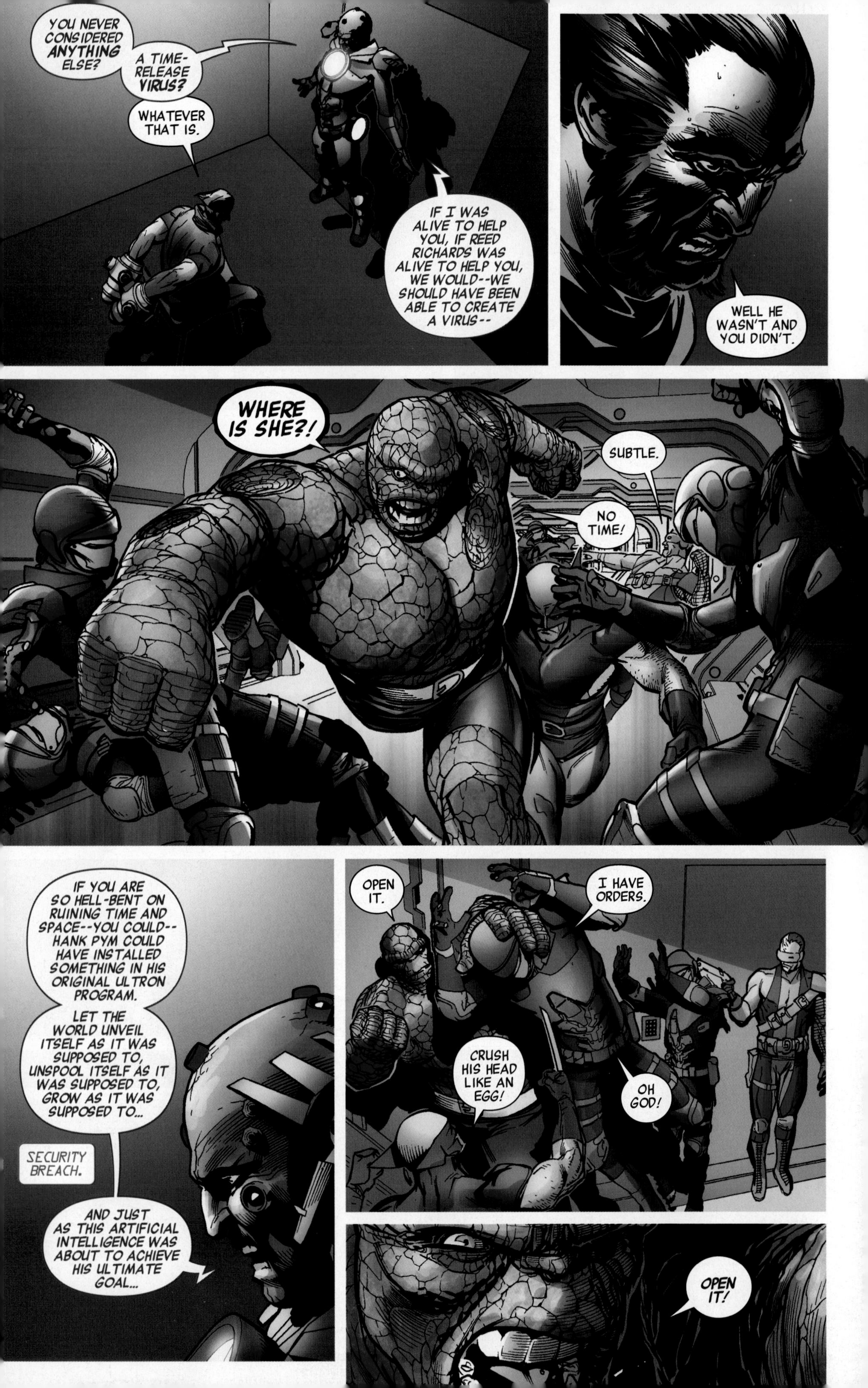
YOU NEVER CONSIDERED ANYTHING ELSE?
A TIME-RELEASE VIRUS?
WHATEVER THAT IS.
IF I WAS ALIVE TO HELP YOU, IF REED RICHARDS WAS ALIVE TO HELP YOU, WE WOULD--WE SHOULD HAVE BEEN ABLE TO CREATE A VIRUS--
WELL HE WASN'T AND YOU DIDN'T.
WHERE IS SHE?!
SUBTLE.
NO TIME!
IF YOU ARE SO HELL-BENT ON RUINING TIME AND SPACE--YOU COULD--HANK PYM COULD HAVE INSTALLED SOMETHING IN HIS ORIGINAL ULTRON PROGRAM.
LET THE WORLD UNVEIL ITSELF AS IT WAS SUPPOSED TO, UNSPOOL ITSELF AS IT WAS SUPPOSED TO, GROW AS IT WAS SUPPOSED TO...
SECURITY BREACH.
AND JUST AS THIS ARTIFICIAL INTELLIGENCE WAS ABOUT TO ACHIEVE HIS ULTIMATE GOAL...
OPEN IT.
I HAVE ORDERS.
CRUSH HIS HEAD LIKE AN EGG!
OH GOD!
OPEN IT!

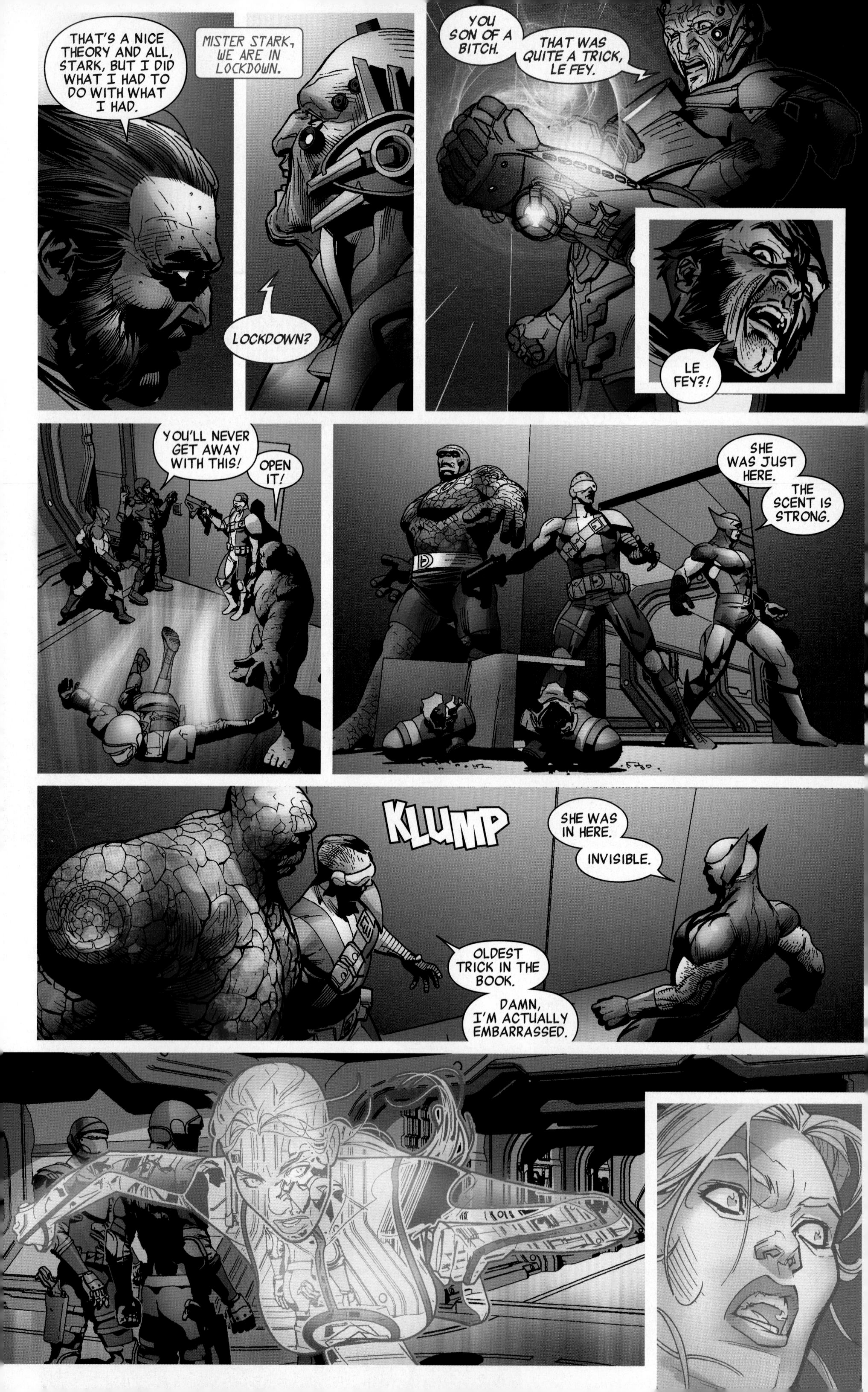

THAT'S A NICE THEORY AND ALL, STARK, BUT I DID WHAT I HAD TO DO WITH WHAT I HAD.
MISTER STARK, WE ARE IN LOCKDOWN.
LOCKDOWN?
YOU SON OF A BITCH.
THAT WAS QUITE A TRICK, LE FEY.
LE FEY?!
YOU'LL NEVER GET AWAY WITH THIS!
OPEN IT!
SHE WAS JUST HERE.
THE SCENT IS STRONG.
KLUMP
SHE WAS IN HERE.
INVISIBLE.
OLDEST TRICK IN THE BOOK.
DAMN, I'M ACTUALLY EMBARRASSED.

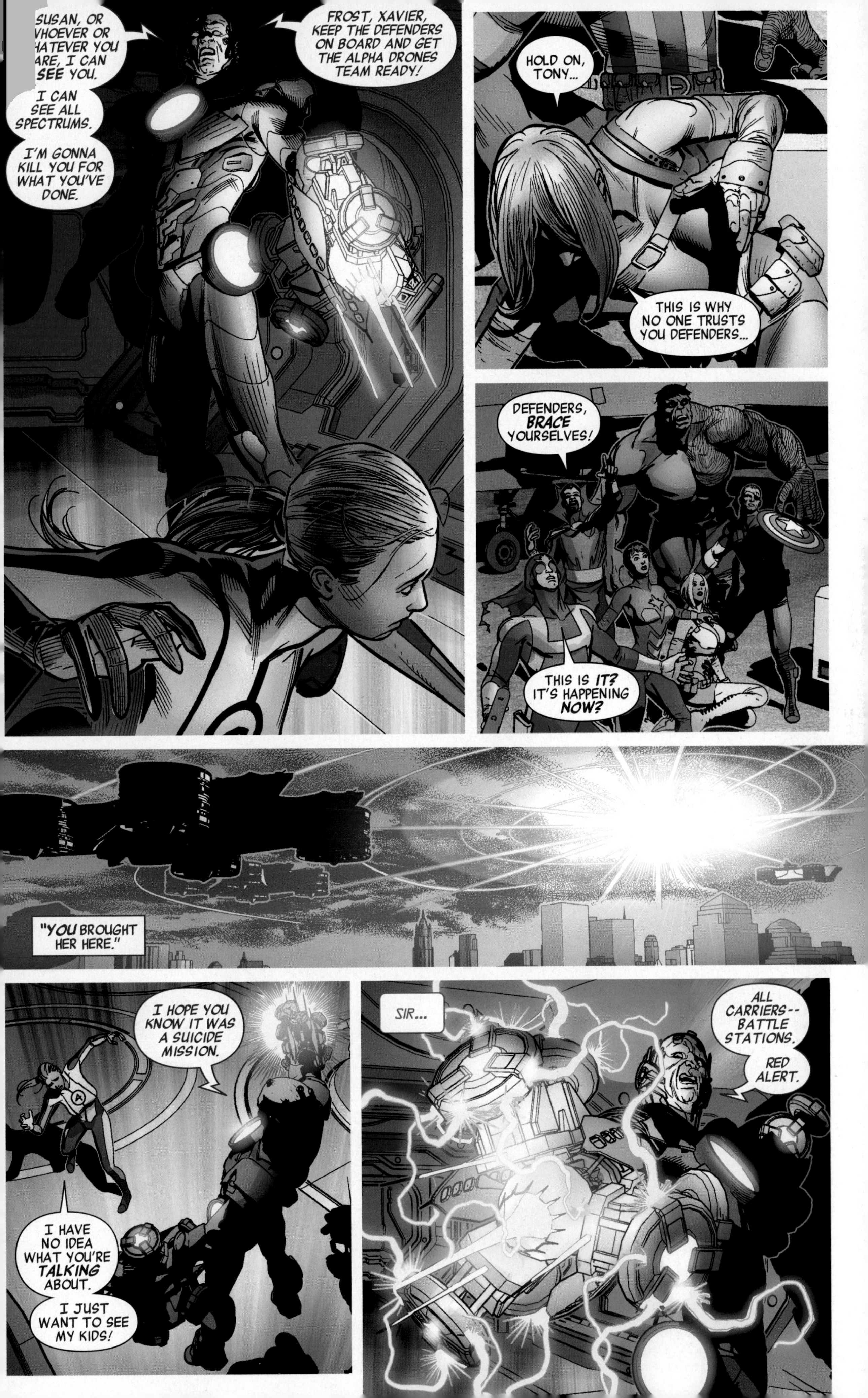

SUSAN, OR WHOEVER OR WHATEVER YOU ARE, I CAN SEE YOU.
I CAN SEE ALL SPECTRUMS.
I'M GONNA KILL YOU FOR WHAT YOU'VE DONE.
FROST, XAVIER, KEEP THE DEFENDERS ON BOARD AND GET THE ALPHA DRONES TEAM READY!
HOLD ON, TONY...
THIS IS WHY NO ONE TRUSTS YOU DEFENDERS...
DEFENDERS, BRACE YOURSELVES!
THIS IS IT? IT'S HAPPENING NOW?
"YOU BROUGHT HER HERE."
I HOPE YOU KNOW IT WAS A SUICIDE MISSION.
I HAVE NO IDEA WHAT YOU'RE TALKING ABOUT.
I JUST WANT TO SEE MY KIDS!
SIR...
ALL CARRIERS-- BATTLE STATIONS.
RED ALERT.

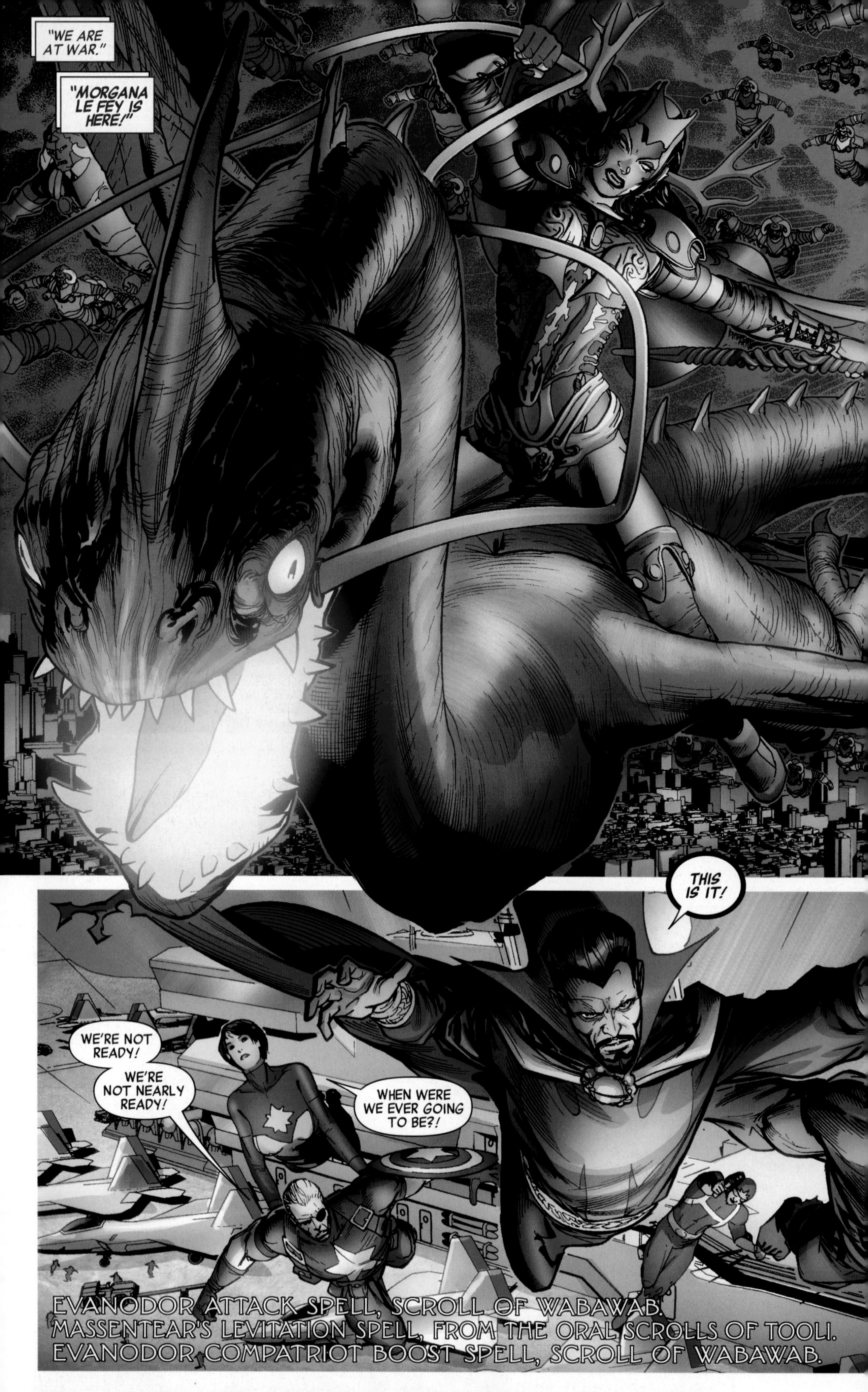
"WE ARE AT WAR."
"MORGANA LE FEY IS HERE!"
THIS IS IT!
WE'RE NOT READY!
WE'RE NOT NEARLY READY!
WHEN WERE WE EVER GOING TO BE?!
EVANODOR ATTACK SPELL, SCROLL OF WABAWAB.
MASSENTEAR'S LEVITATION SPELL, FROM THE ORAL SCROLLS OF TOOLI.
EVANODOR COMPATRIOT BOOST SPELL, SCROLL OF WABAWAB.

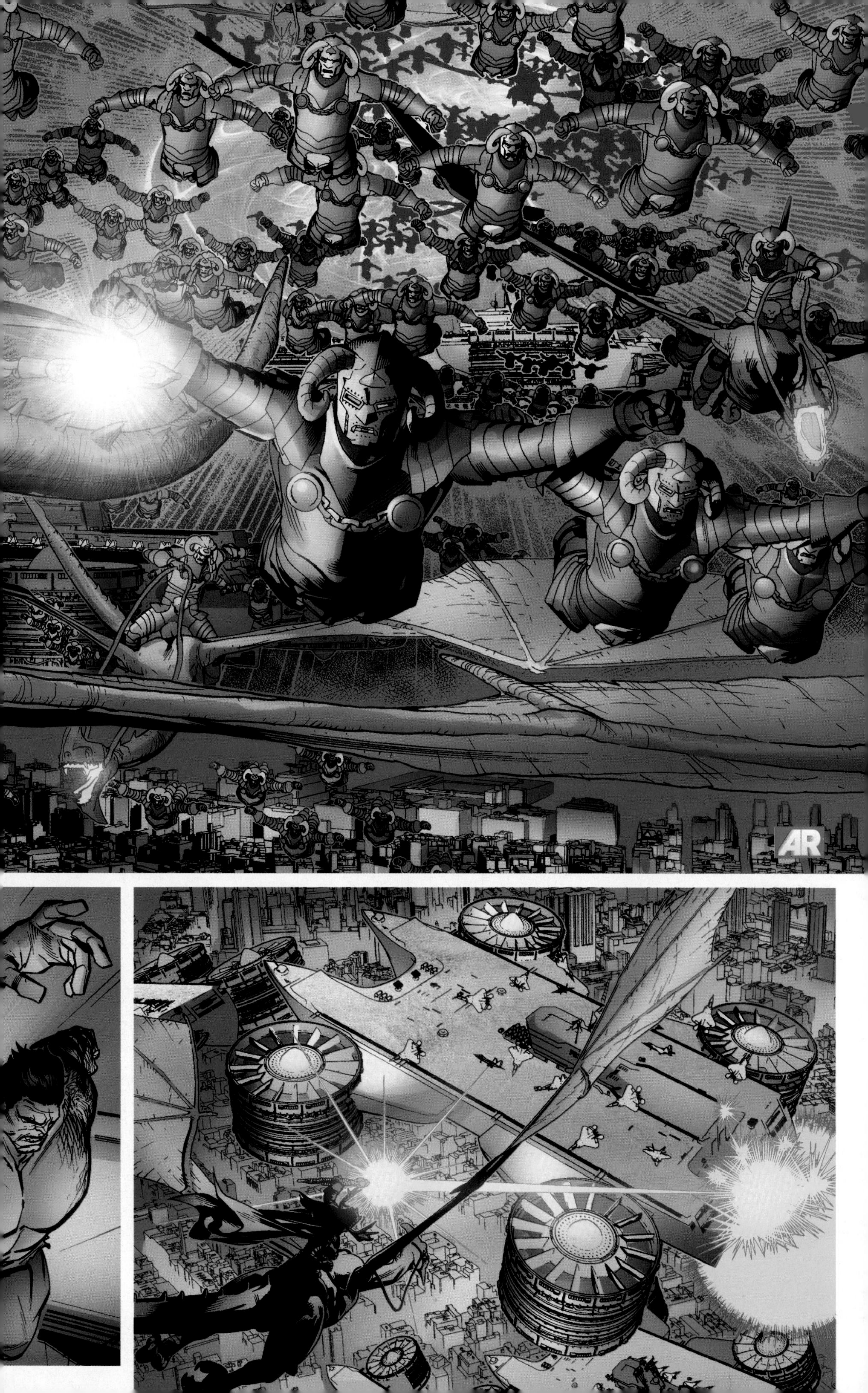

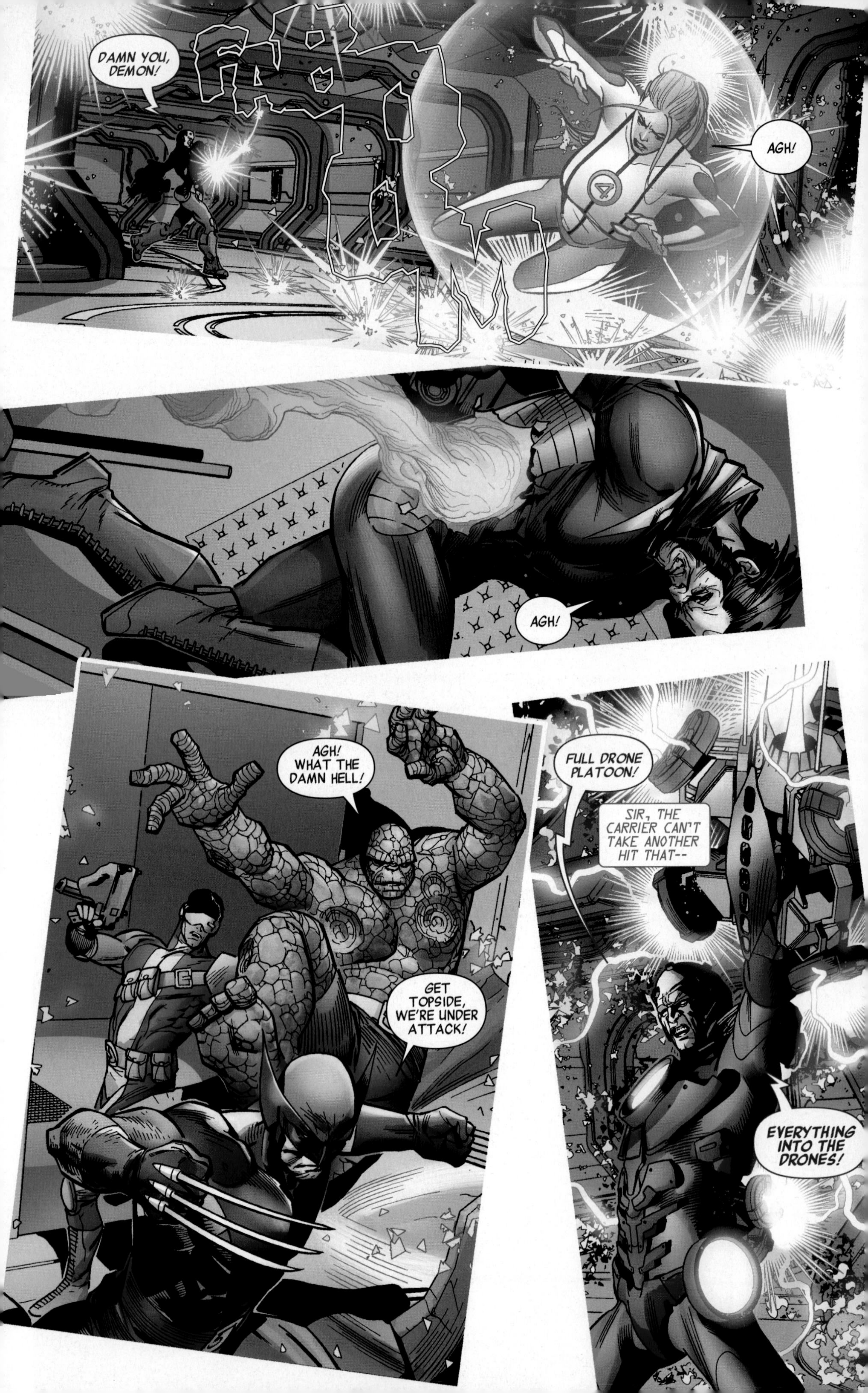
DAMN YOU, DEMON!
AGH!
AGH!
AGH! WHAT THE DAMN HELL!
GET TOPSIDE, WE'RE UNDER ATTACK!
FULL DRONE PLATOON!
SIR, THE CARRIER CAN'T TAKE ANOTHER HIT THAT--
EVERYTHING INTO THE DRONES!

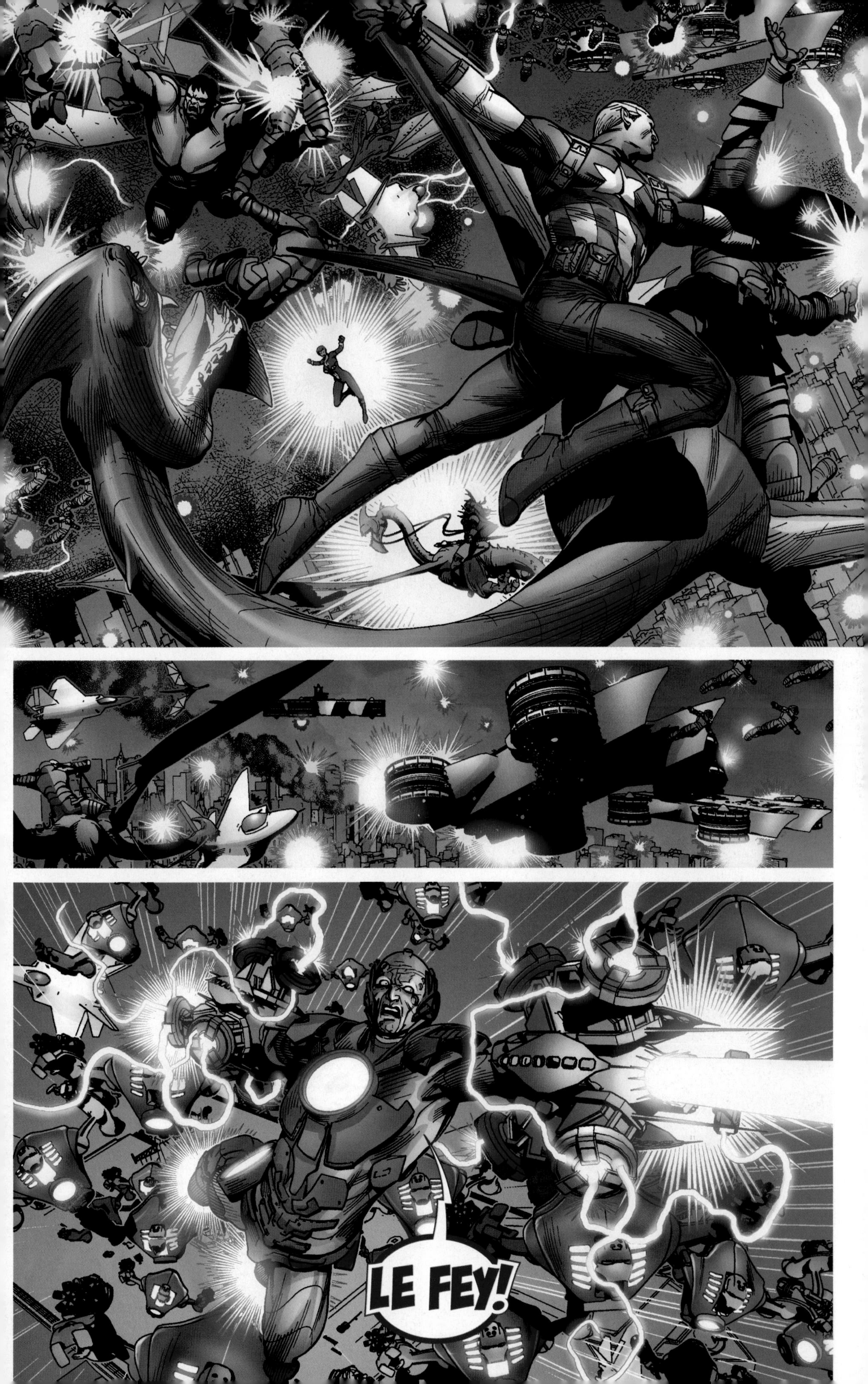
LE FEY!

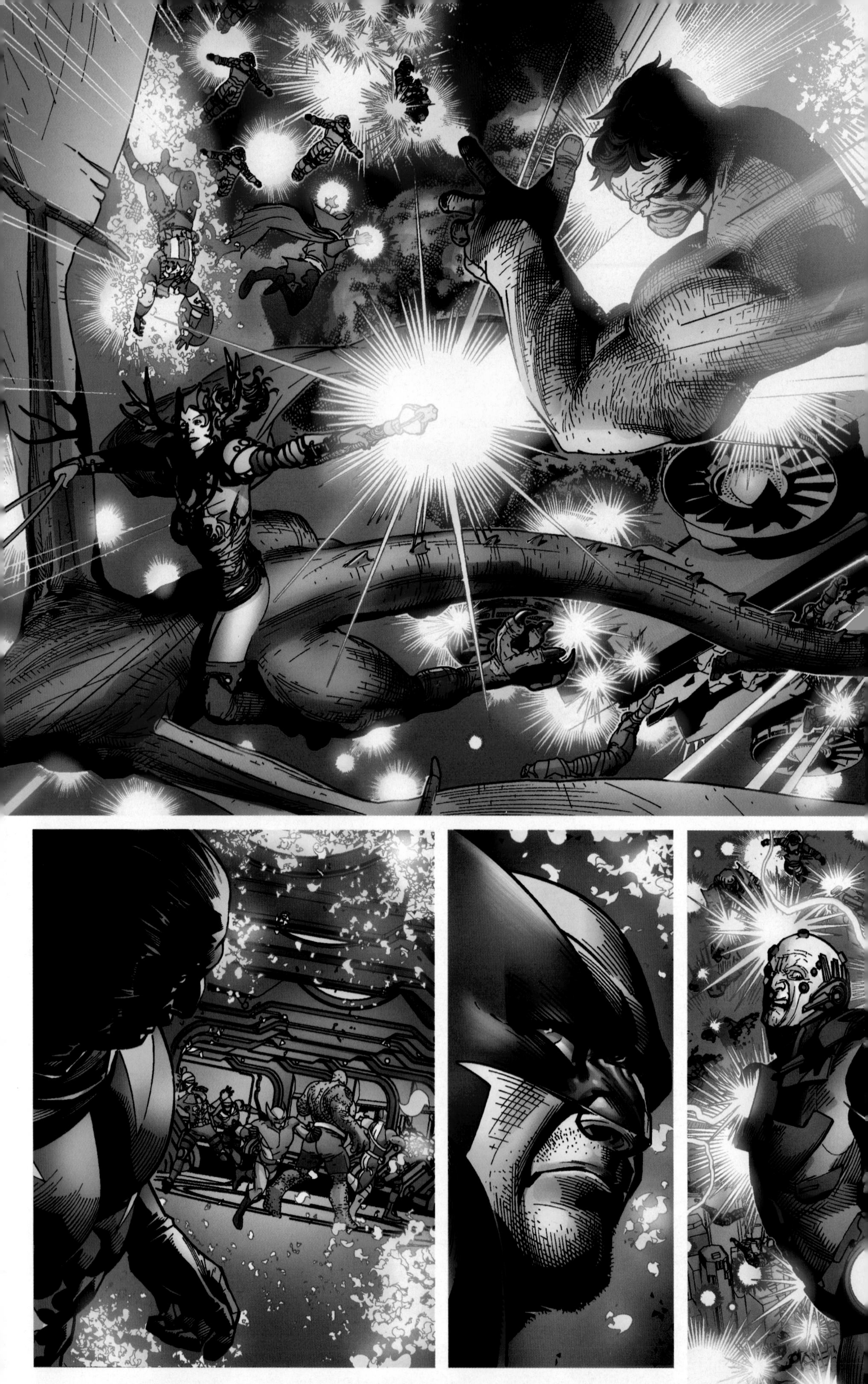

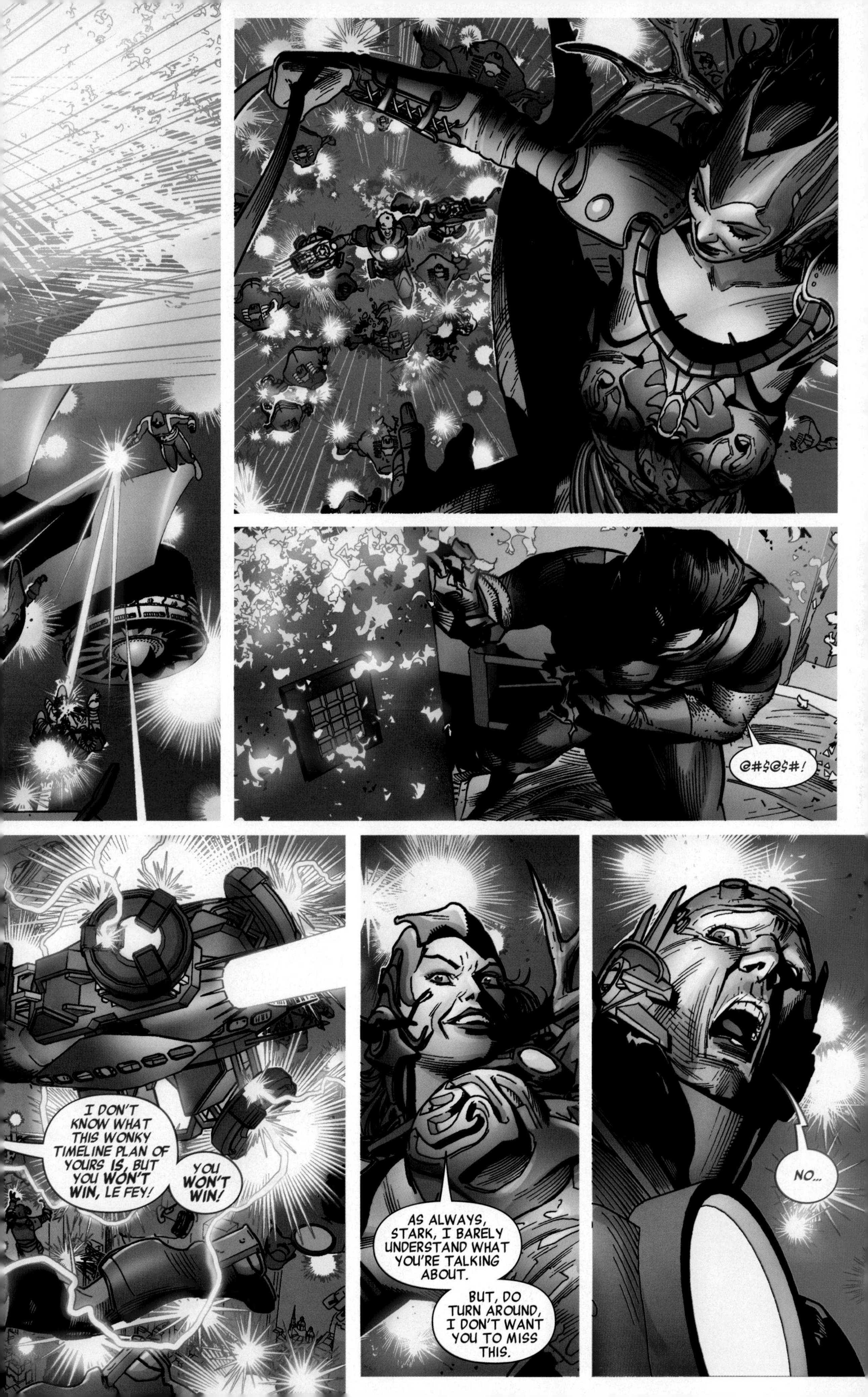
@#$@$#!
I DON'T KNOW WHAT THIS WONKY TIMELINE PLAN OF YOURS IS, BUT YOU WON'T WIN, LE FEY!
YOU WON'T WIN!
AS ALWAYS, STARK, I BARELY UNDERSTAND WHAT YOU'RE TALKING ABOUT.
BUT, DO TURN AROUND, I DON'T WANT YOU TO MISS THIS.
NO...

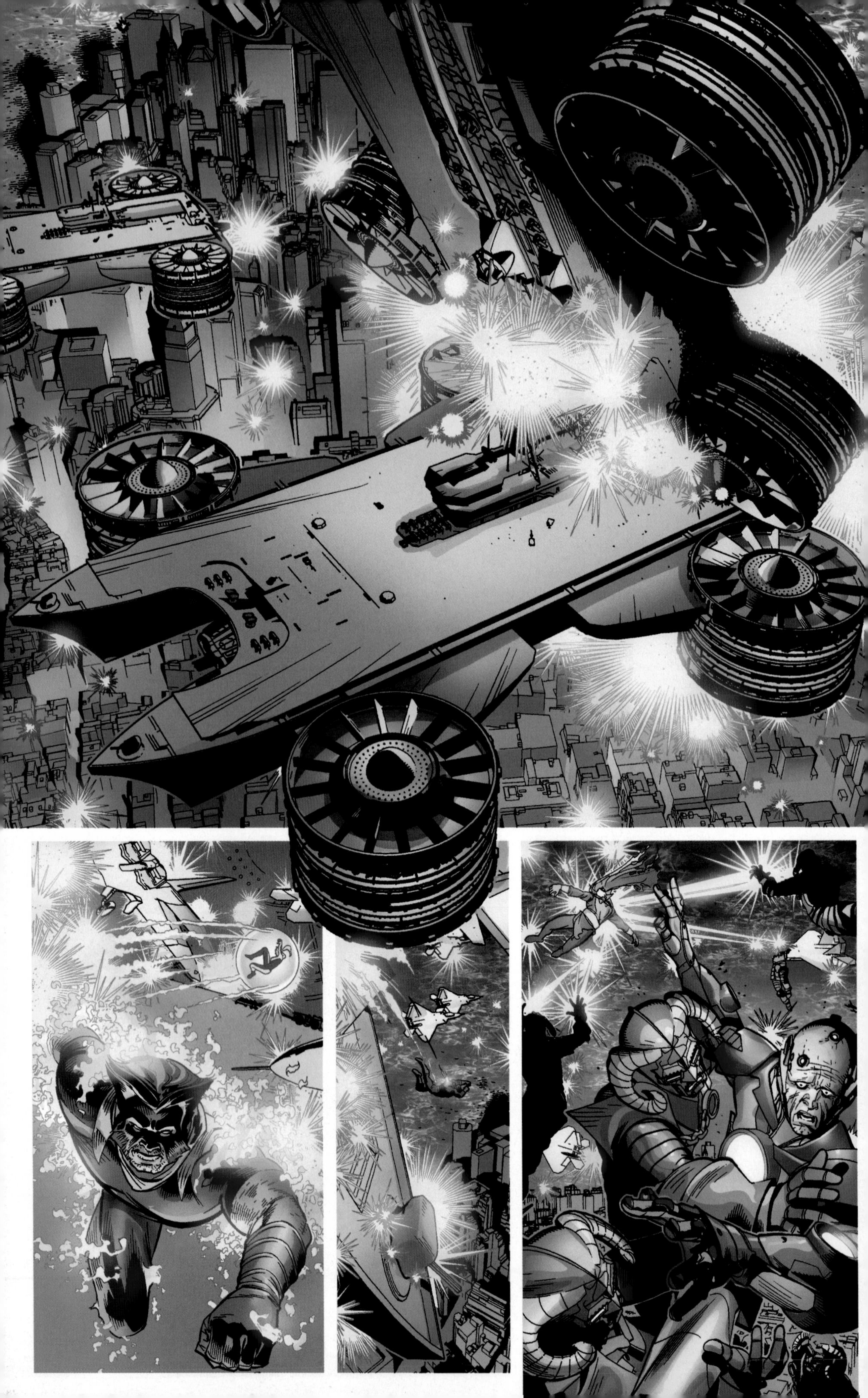

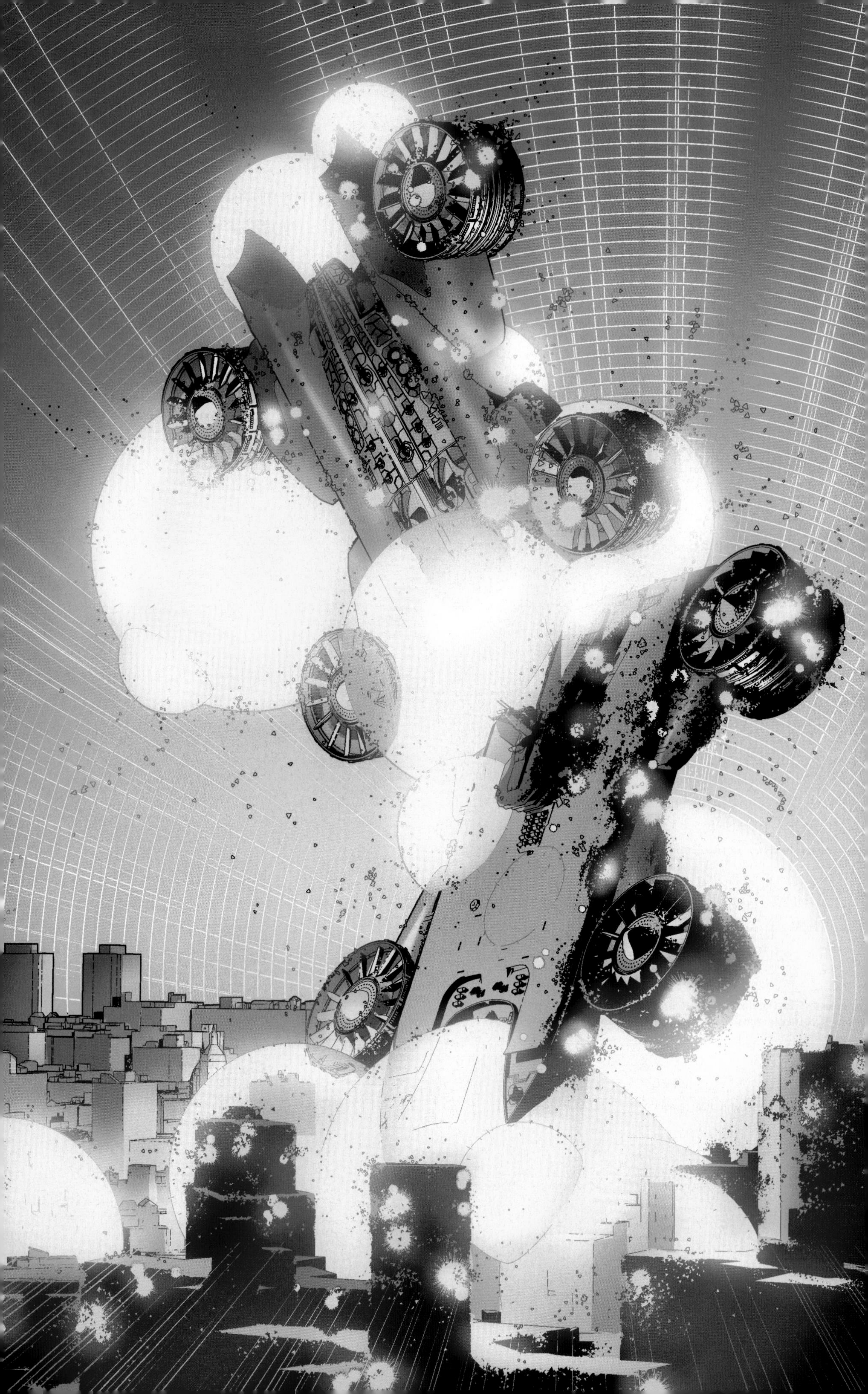

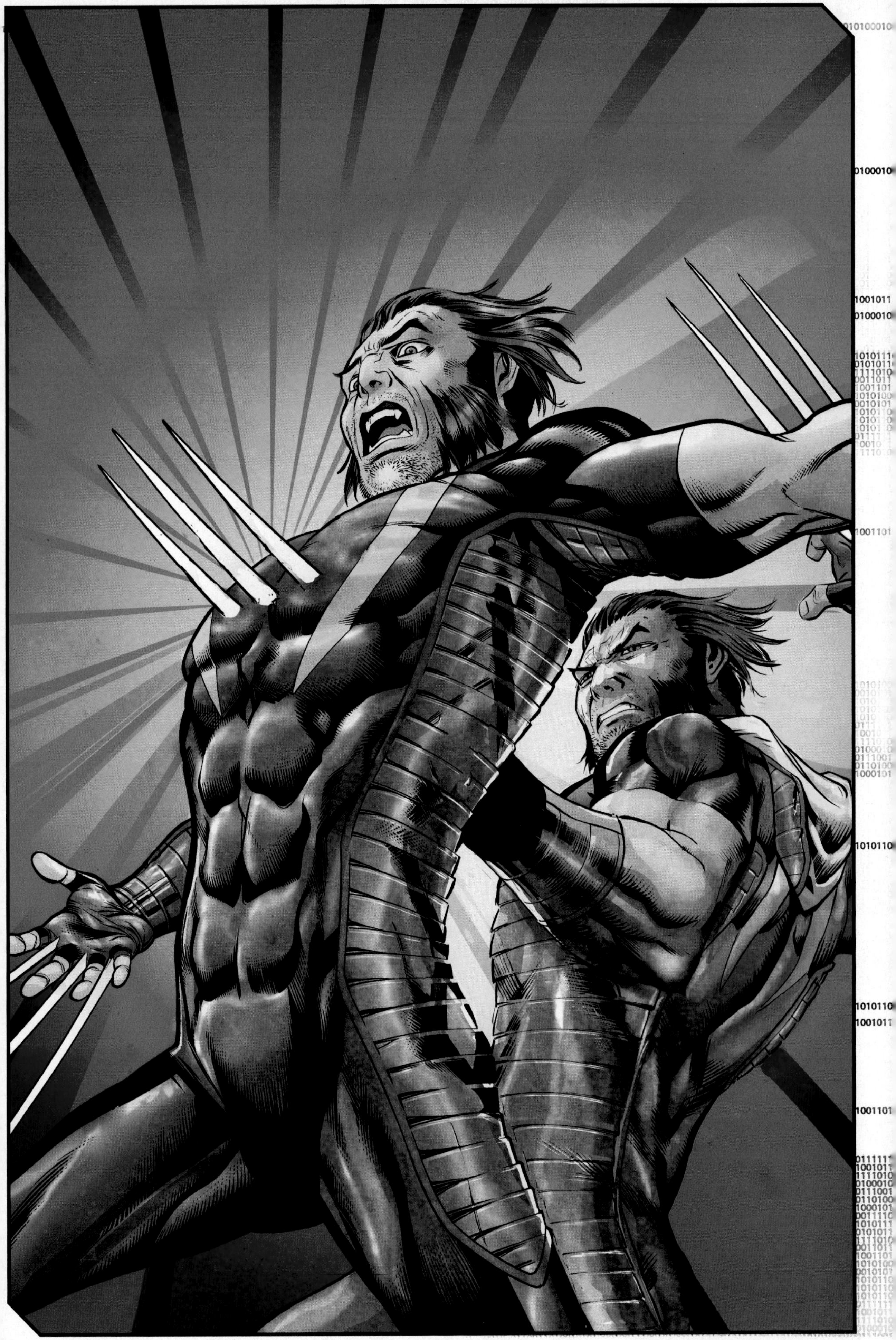

AGE OF ULTRON #9

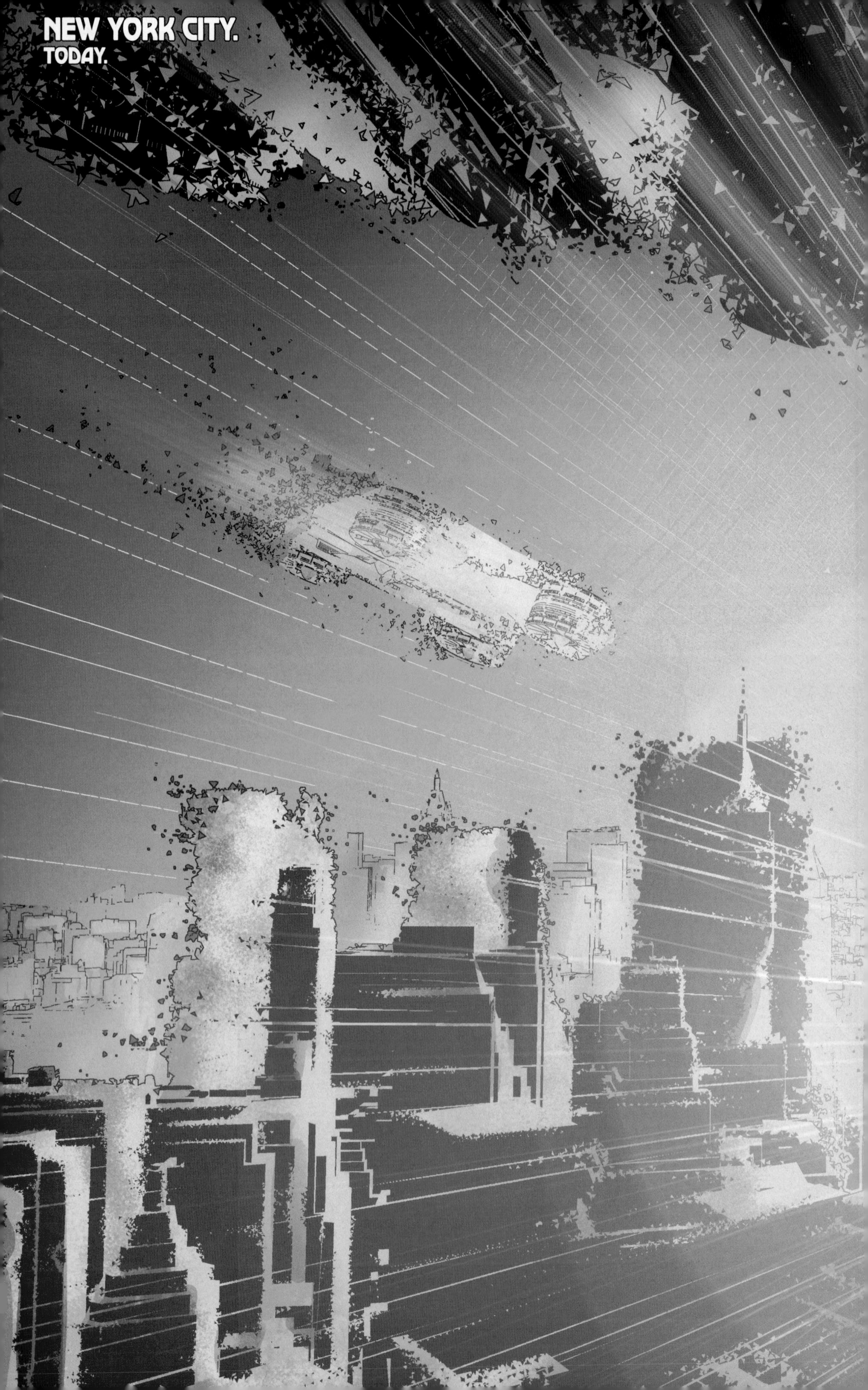
NEW YORK CITY.
TODAY.

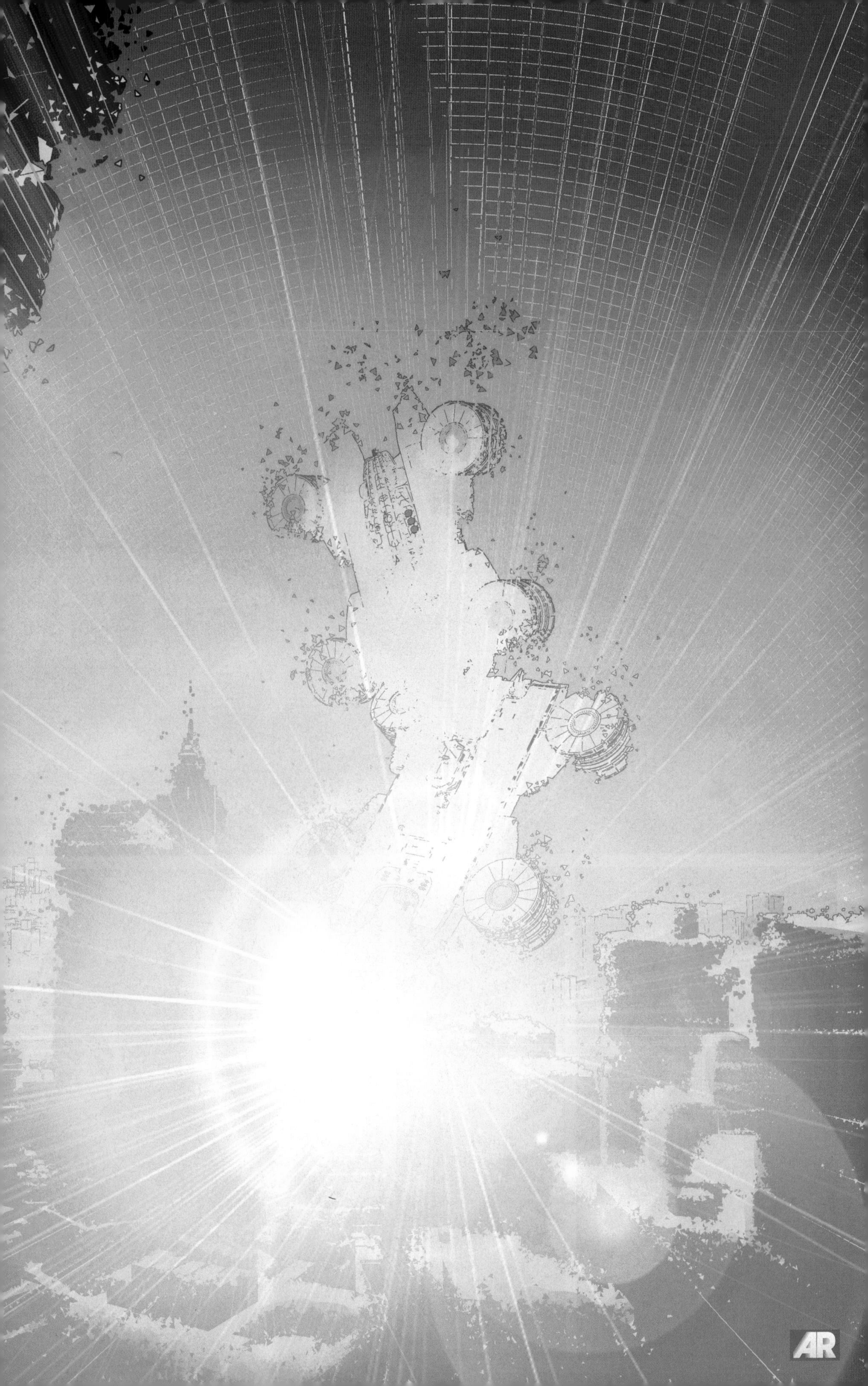

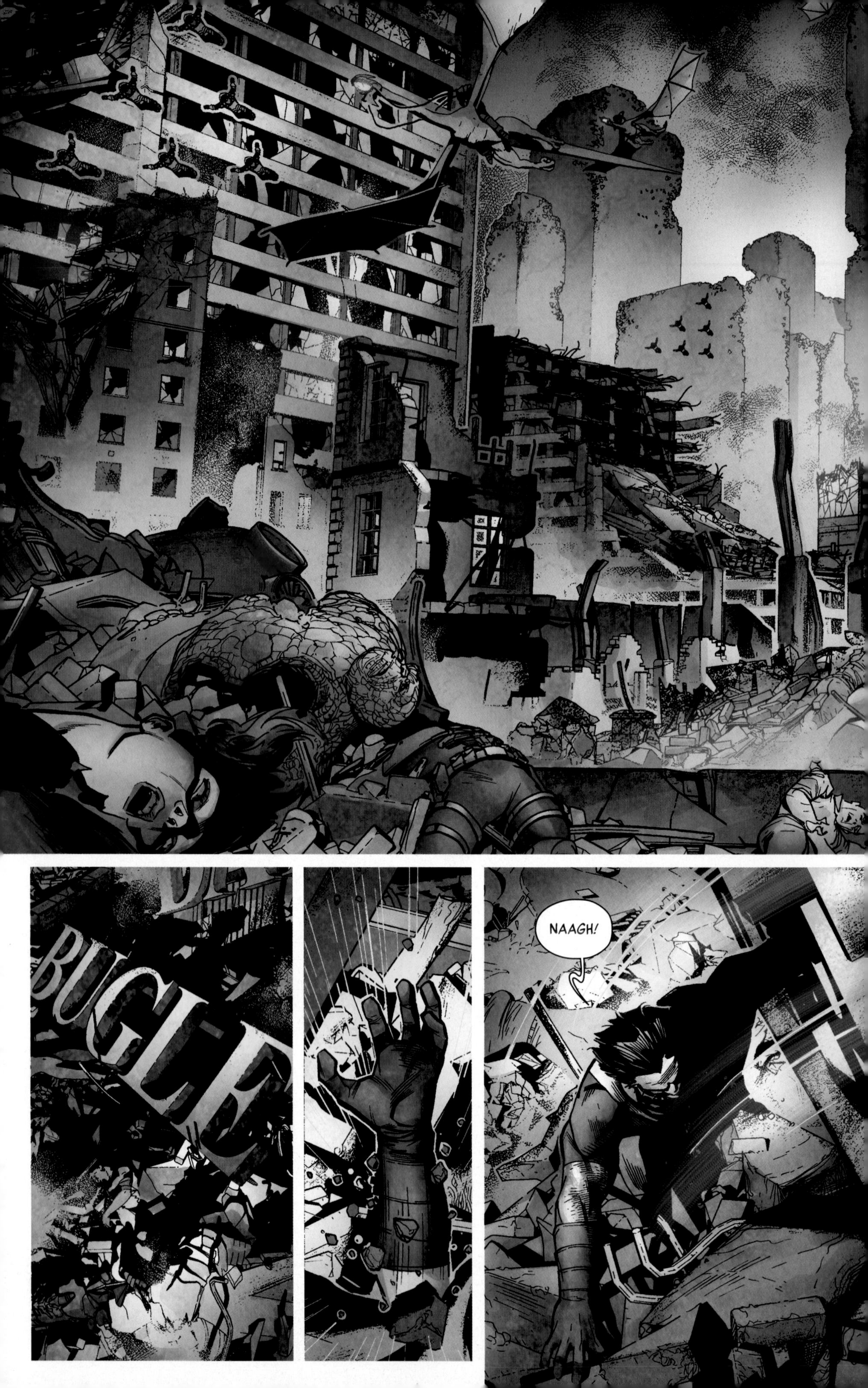
BUGLE
NAAGH!

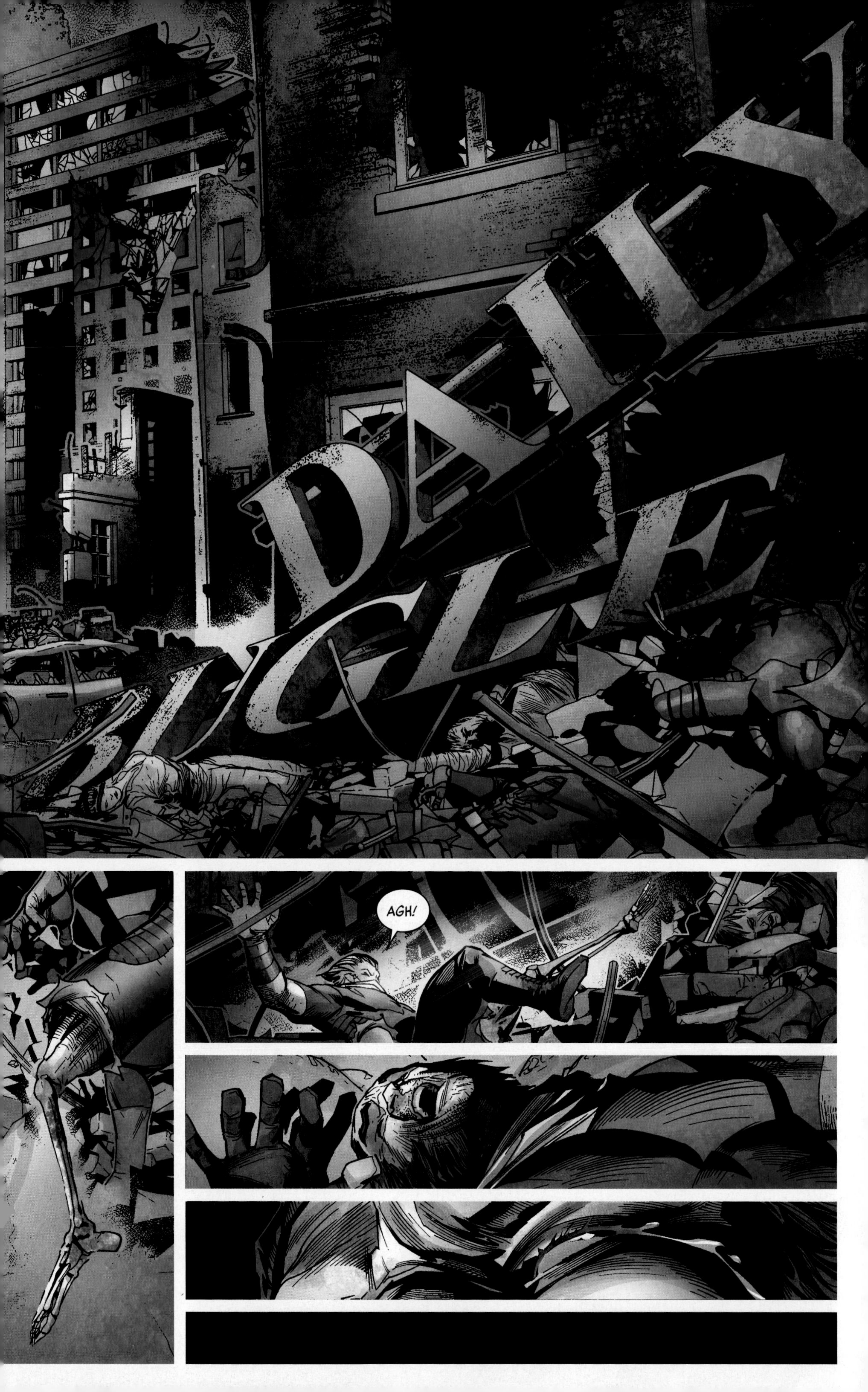
AGH!

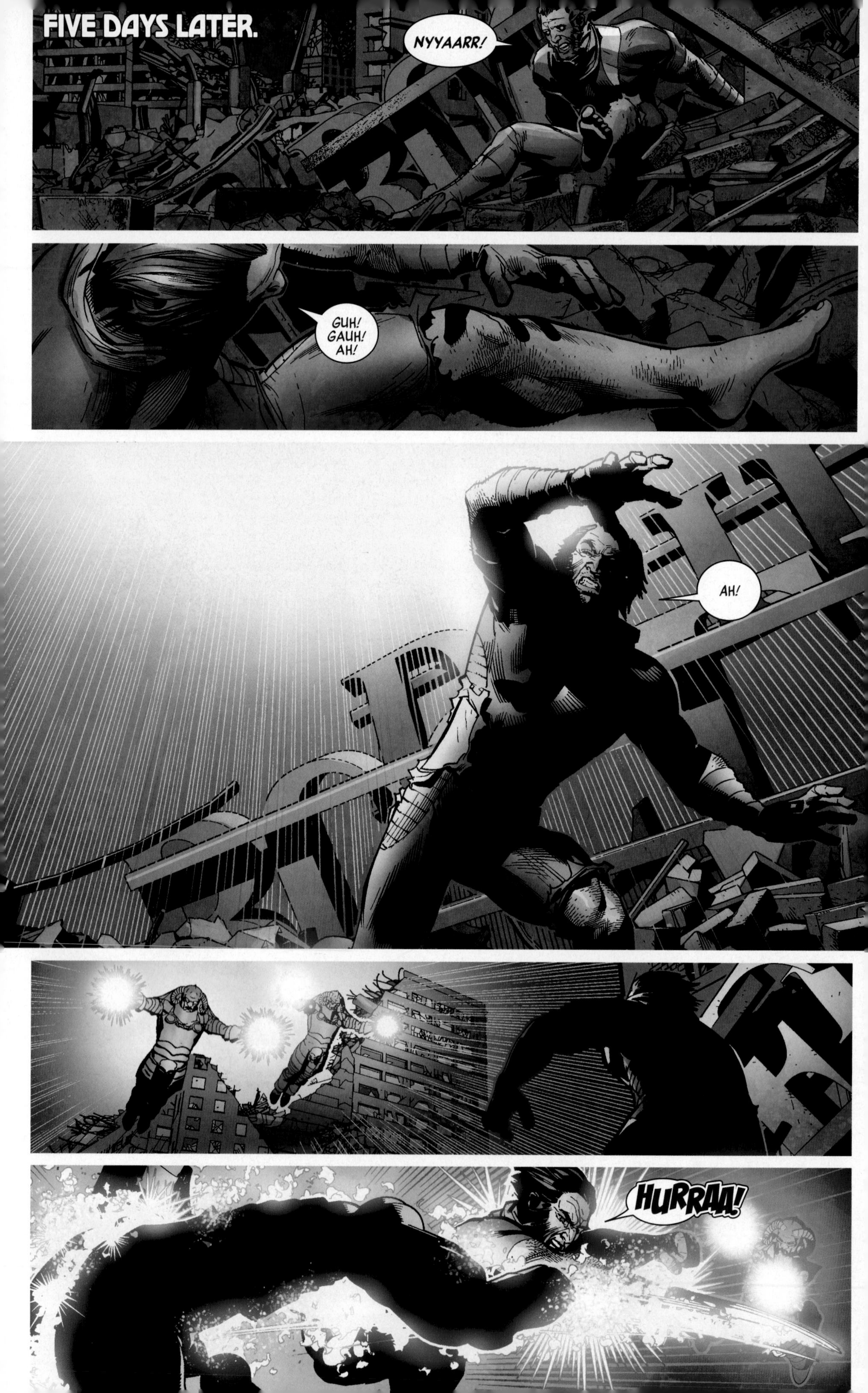
FIVE DAYS LATER.
NYYAARR!
GUH! GAUH! AH!
AH!
HURRAA!

HUAAR!

GUAAHH!

SHRACK

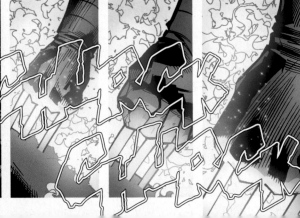

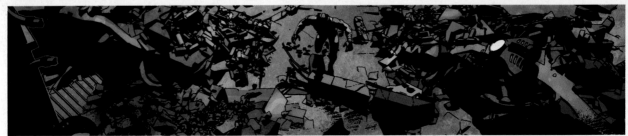

WOLVERINE...

I WAS LYING HERE WONDERING... HANK PYM...

COULD ONE MAN MAKE SO MUCH OF A DIFFERENCE?

I GUESS SO.

BUT...

YOU--YOU CAN'T GO BACK.

I KNOW YOU'RE GOING TO TRY TO GO BACK IN TIME AND FIX YOUR MISTAKE.

YOU CAN'T.

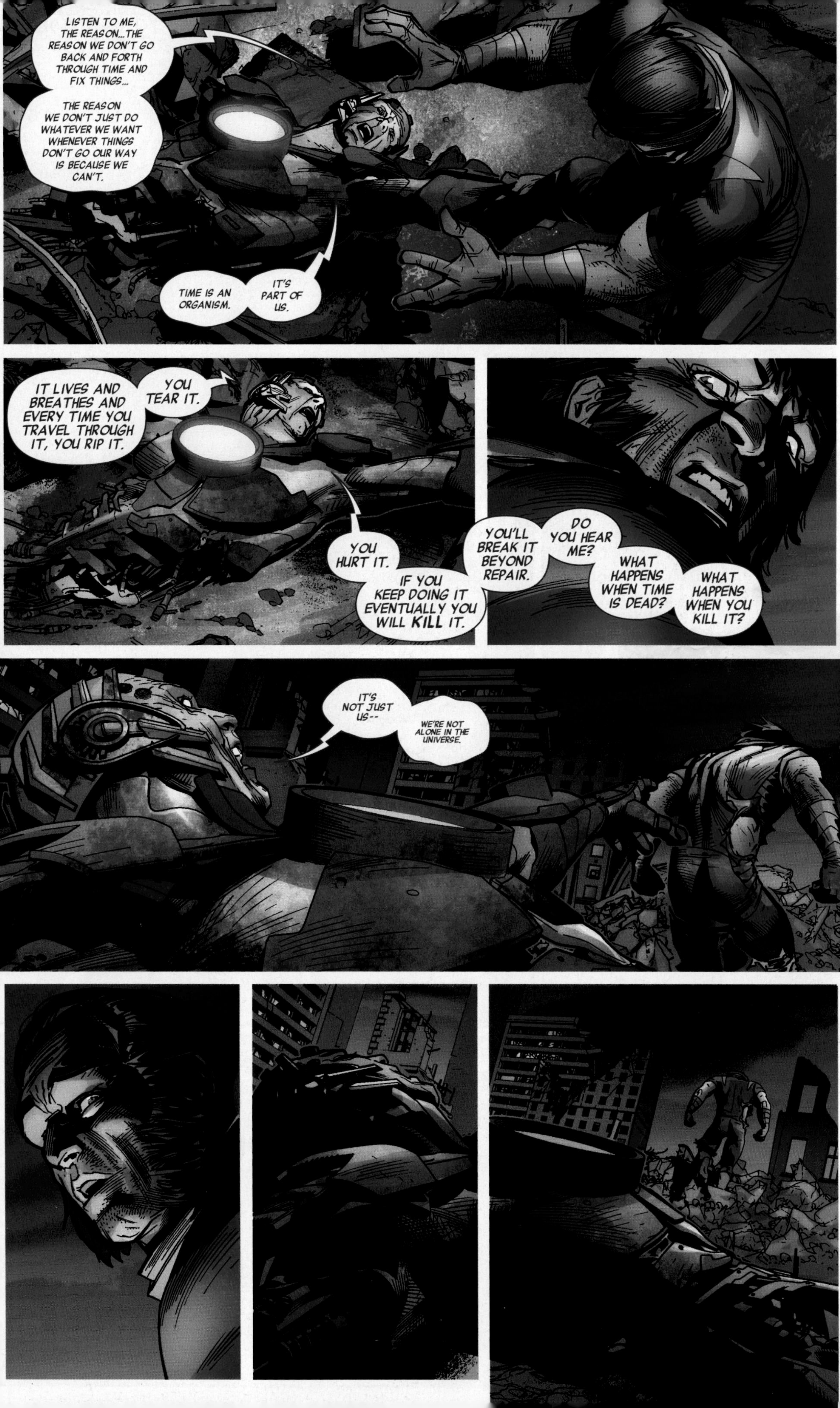
LISTEN TO ME, THE REASON...THE REASON WE DON'T GO BACK AND FORTH THROUGH TIME AND FIX THINGS...
THE REASON WE DON'T JUST DO WHATEVER WE WANT WHENEVER THINGS DON'T GO OUR WAY IS BECAUSE WE CAN'T.
TIME IS AN ORGANISM.
IT'S PART OF US.
IT LIVES AND BREATHES AND EVERY TIME YOU TRAVEL THROUGH IT, YOU RIP IT.
YOU TEAR IT.
YOU HURT IT.
IF YOU KEEP DOING IT EVENTUALLY YOU WILL KILL IT.
YOU'LL BREAK IT BEYOND REPAIR.
DO YOU HEAR ME?
WHAT HAPPENS WHEN TIME IS DEAD?
WHAT HAPPENS WHEN YOU KILL IT?
IT'S NOT JUST US--
WE'RE NOT ALONE IN THE UNIVERSE.

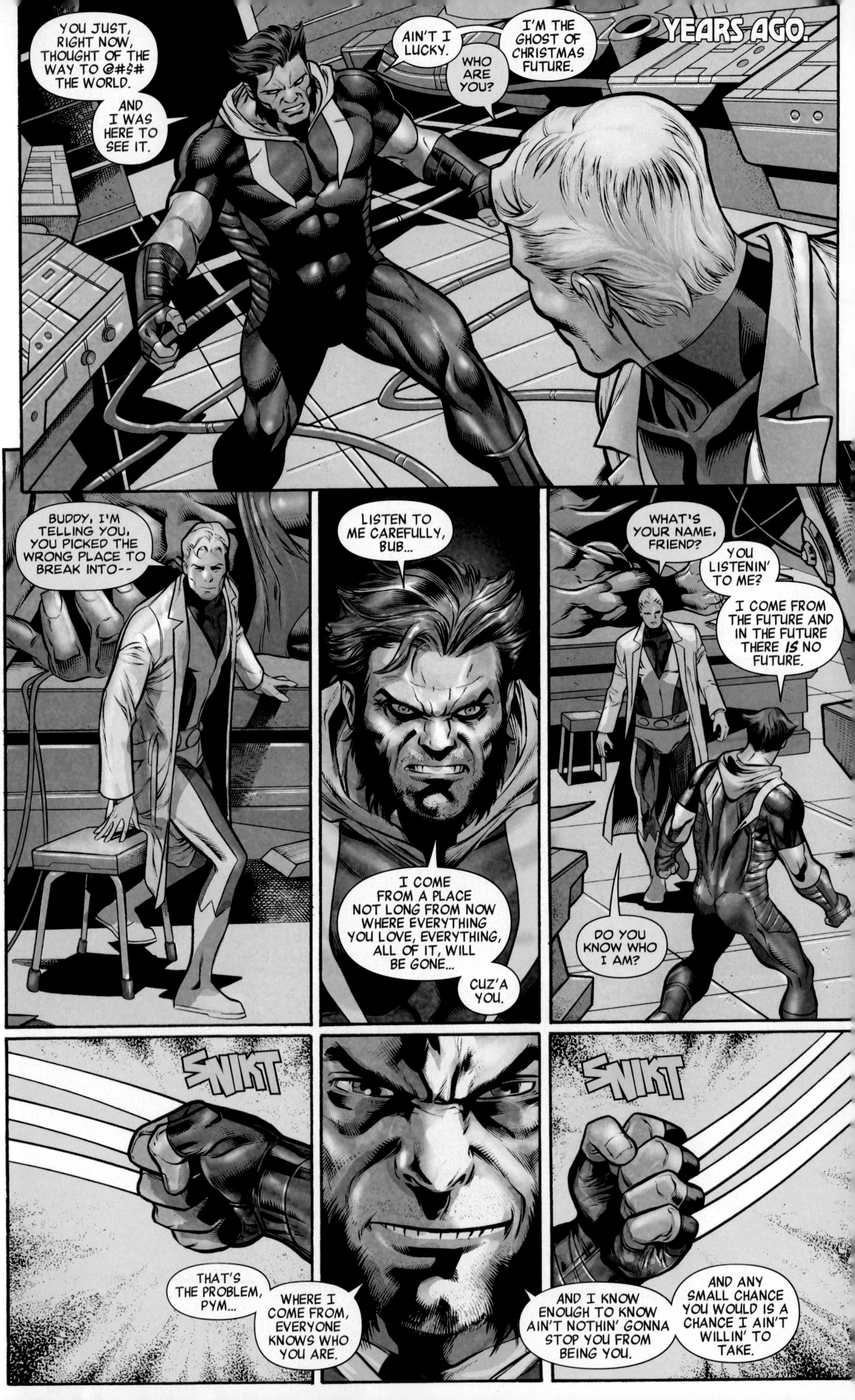

YEARS AGO.
YOU JUST, RIGHT NOW, THOUGHT OF THE WAY TO @#$# THE WORLD.
AND I WAS HERE TO SEE IT.
AIN'T I LUCKY.
WHO ARE YOU?
I'M THE GHOST OF CHRISTMAS FUTURE.
BUDDY, I'M TELLING YOU, YOU PICKED THE WRONG PLACE TO BREAK INTO--
LISTEN TO ME CAREFULLY, BUB...
I COME FROM A PLACE NOT LONG FROM NOW WHERE EVERYTHING YOU LOVE, EVERYTHING, ALL OF IT, WILL BE GONE...
CUZ'A YOU.
WHAT'S YOUR NAME, FRIEND?
YOU LISTENIN' TO ME?
I COME FROM THE FUTURE AND IN THE FUTURE THERE IS NO FUTURE.
DO YOU KNOW WHO I AM?
SNIKT
SNIKT
THAT'S THE PROBLEM, PYM...
WHERE I COME FROM, EVERYONE KNOWS WHO YOU ARE.
AND I KNOW ENOUGH TO KNOW AIN'T NOTHIN' GONNA STOP YOU FROM BEING YOU.
AND ANY SMALL CHANCE YOU WOULD IS A CHANCE I AIN'T WILLIN' TO TAKE.

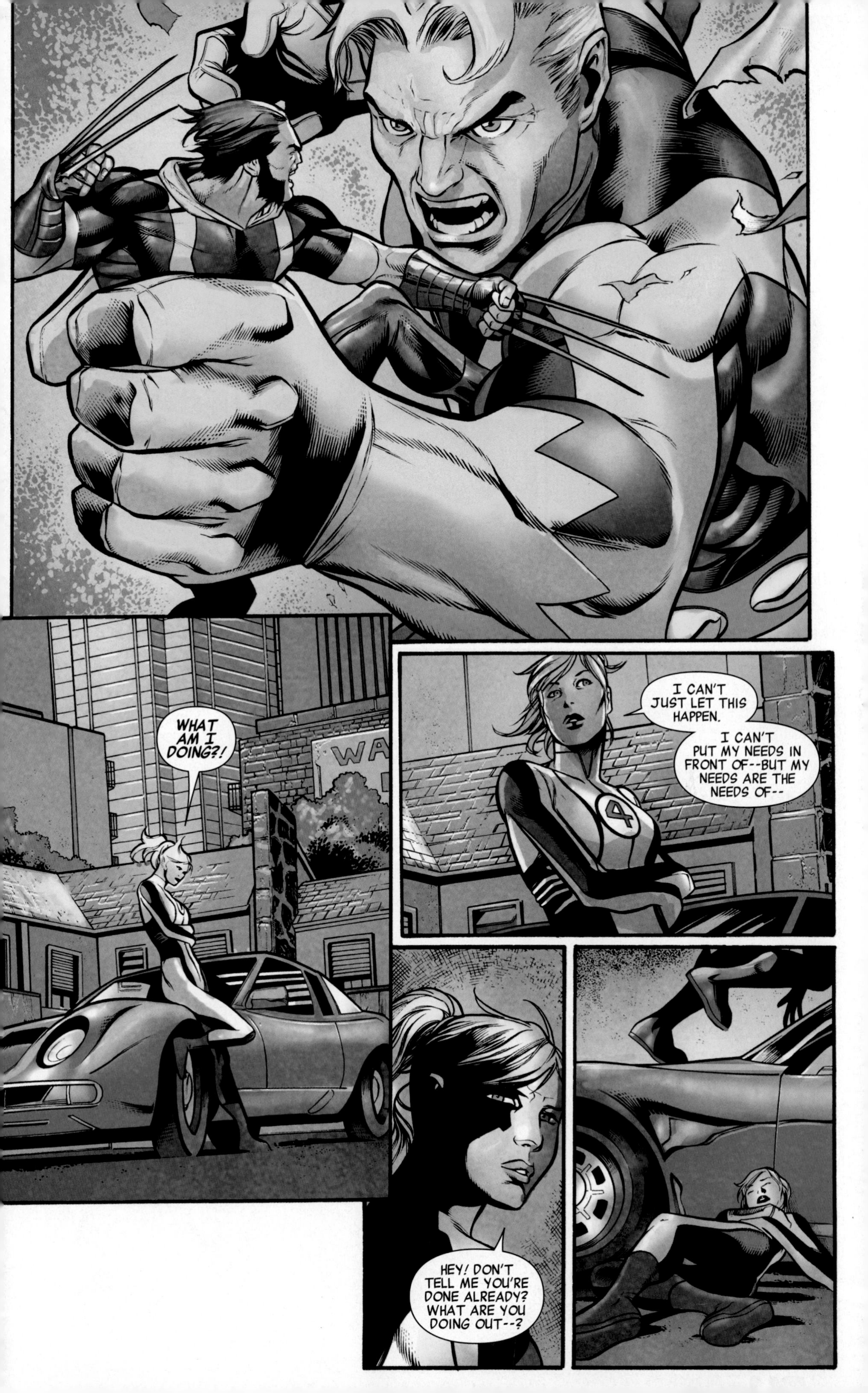
WHAT AM I DOING?!
I CAN'T JUST LET THIS HAPPEN.
I CAN'T PUT MY NEEDS IN FRONT OF--BUT MY NEEDS ARE THE NEEDS OF--
HEY! DON'T TELL ME YOU'RE DONE ALREADY? WHAT ARE YOU DOING OUT--?

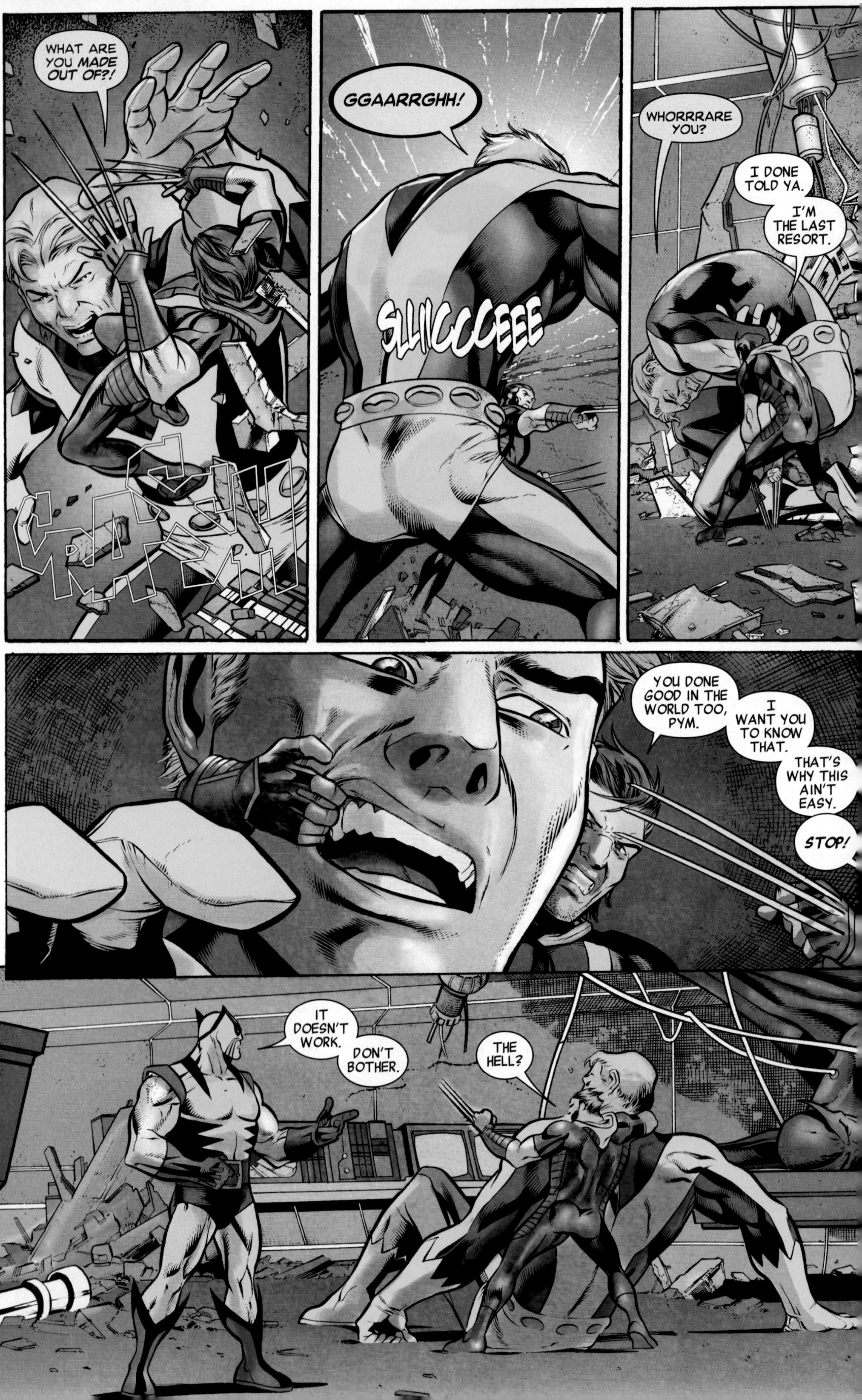

WHAT ARE YOU MADE OUT OF?!
GGAARRGHH!
SLLIICCCEEE
WHORRRARE YOU?
I DONE TOLD YA.
I'M THE LAST RESORT.
YOU DONE GOOD IN THE WORLD TOO, PYM.
I WANT YOU TO KNOW THAT.
THAT'S WHY THIS AIN'T EASY.
STOP!
IT DOESN'T WORK.
DON'T BOTHER.
THE HELL?

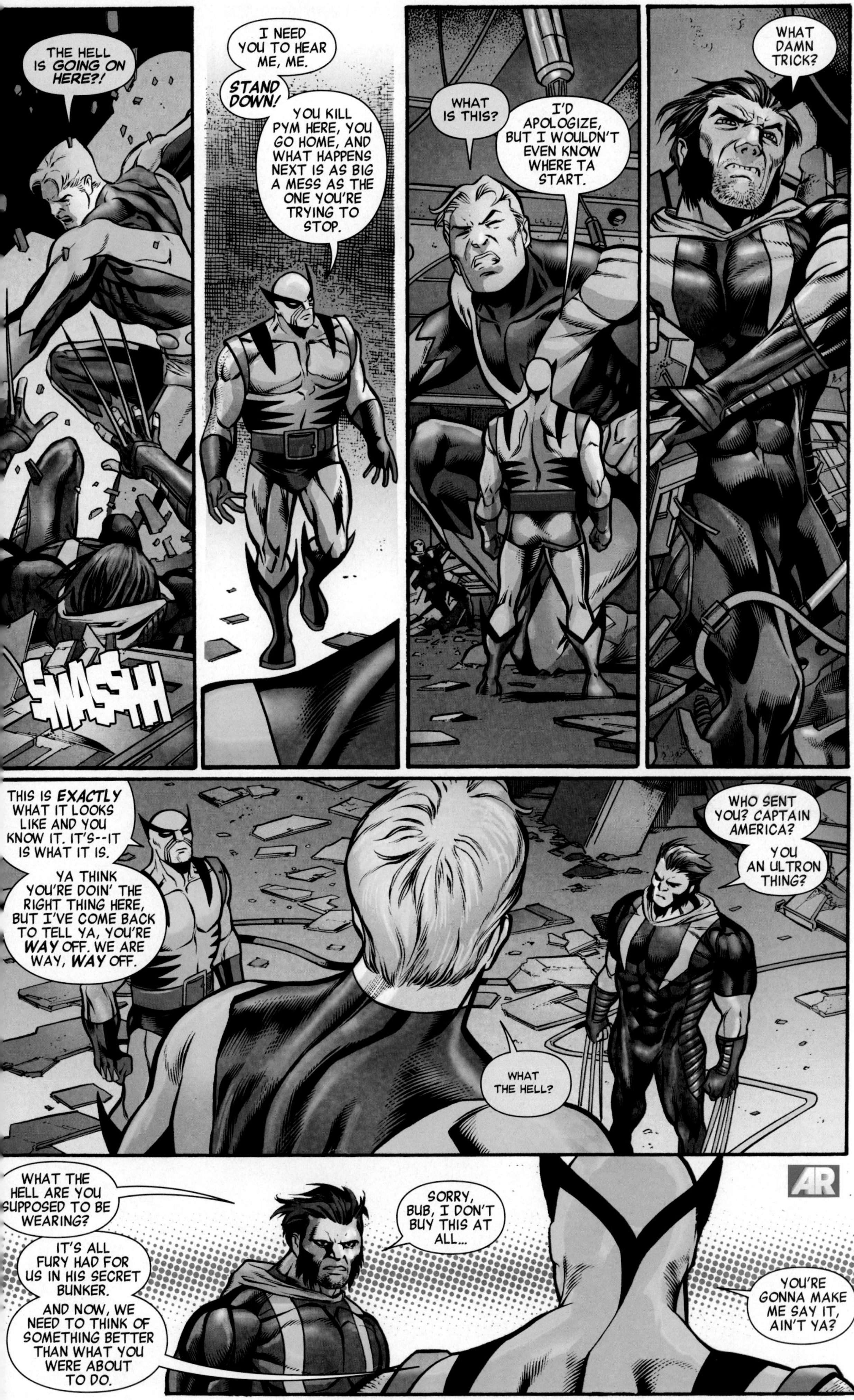

THE HELL IS GOING ON HERE?!
SMASSH
I NEED YOU TO HEAR ME, ME.
STAND DOWN!
YOU KILL PYM HERE, YOU GO HOME, AND WHAT HAPPENS NEXT IS AS BIG A MESS AS THE ONE YOU'RE TRYING TO STOP.
WHAT IS THIS?
I'D APOLOGIZE, BUT I WOULDN'T EVEN KNOW WHERE TA START.
WHAT DAMN TRICK?
THIS IS EXACTLY WHAT IT LOOKS LIKE AND YOU KNOW IT. IT'S--IT IS WHAT IT IS.
YA THINK YOU'RE DOIN' THE RIGHT THING HERE, BUT I'VE COME BACK TO TELL YA, YOU'RE WAY OFF. WE ARE WAY, WAY OFF.
WHAT THE HELL?
WHO SENT YOU? CAPTAIN AMERICA?
YOU AN ULTRON THING?
WHAT THE HELL ARE YOU SUPPOSED TO BE WEARING?
IT'S ALL FURY HAD FOR US IN HIS SECRET BUNKER.
AND NOW, WE NEED TO THINK OF SOMETHING BETTER THAN WHAT YOU WERE ABOUT TO DO.
SORRY, BUB, I DON'T BUY THIS AT ALL...
YOU'RE GONNA MAKE ME SAY IT, AIN'T YA?
AR

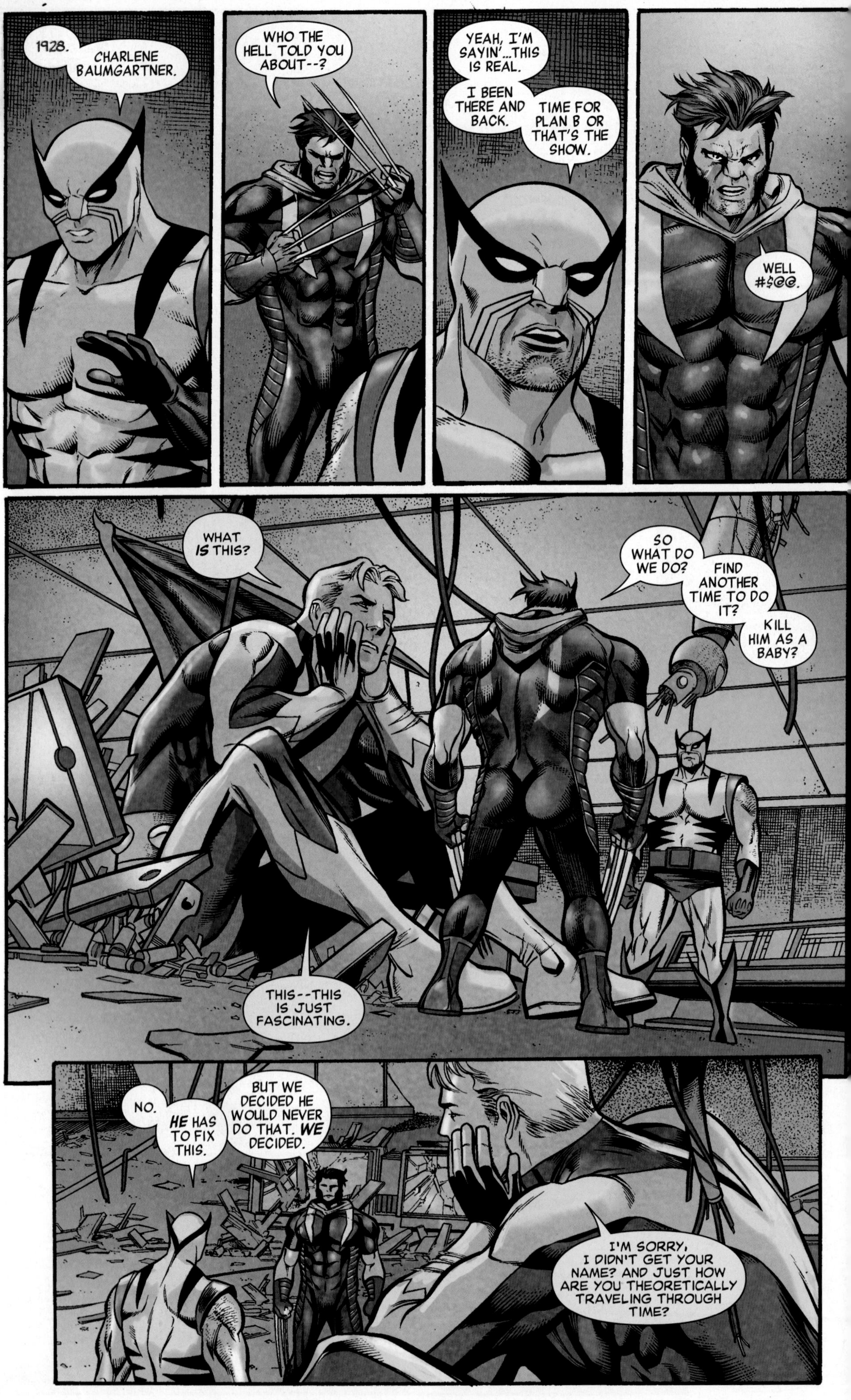
1928.
CHARLENE BAUMGARTNER.
WHO THE HELL TOLD YOU ABOUT--?
YEAH, I'M SAYIN'...THIS IS REAL.
I BEEN THERE AND BACK.
TIME FOR PLAN B OR THAT'S THE SHOW.
WELL #$@@.
WHAT IS THIS?
SO WHAT DO WE DO?
FIND ANOTHER TIME TO DO IT?
KILL HIM AS A BABY?
THIS--THIS IS JUST FASCINATING.
NO.
HE HAS TO FIX THIS.
BUT WE DECIDED HE WOULD NEVER DO THAT. WE DECIDED.
I'M SORRY, I DIDN'T GET YOUR NAME? AND JUST HOW ARE YOU THEORETICALLY TRAVELING THROUGH TIME?

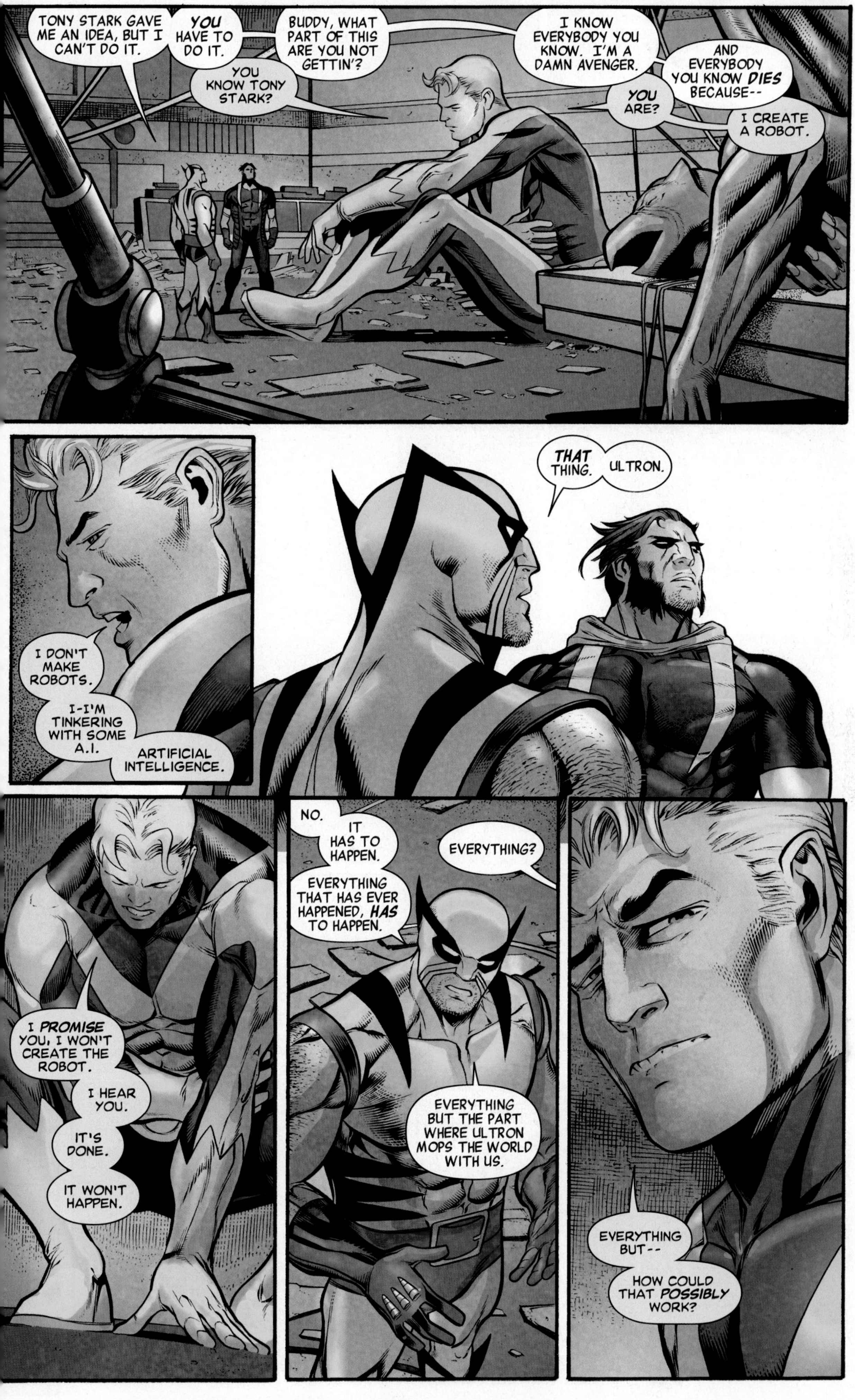
TONY STARK GAVE ME AN IDEA, BUT I CAN'T DO IT.
YOU HAVE TO DO IT.
YOU KNOW TONY STARK?
BUDDY, WHAT PART OF THIS ARE YOU NOT GETTIN'?
I KNOW EVERYBODY YOU KNOW. I'M A DAMN AVENGER.
YOU ARE?
AND EVERYBODY YOU KNOW DIES BECAUSE--
I CREATE A ROBOT.
I DON'T MAKE ROBOTS.
I-I'M TINKERING WITH SOME A.I.
ARTIFICIAL INTELLIGENCE.
THAT THING.
ULTRON.
I PROMISE YOU, I WON'T CREATE THE ROBOT.
I HEAR YOU.
IT'S DONE.
IT WON'T HAPPEN.
NO.
IT HAS TO HAPPEN.
EVERYTHING THAT HAS EVER HAPPENED, HAS TO HAPPEN.
EVERYTHING?
EVERYTHING BUT THE PART WHERE ULTRON MOPS THE WORLD WITH US.
EVERYTHING BUT--
HOW COULD THAT POSSIBLY WORK?

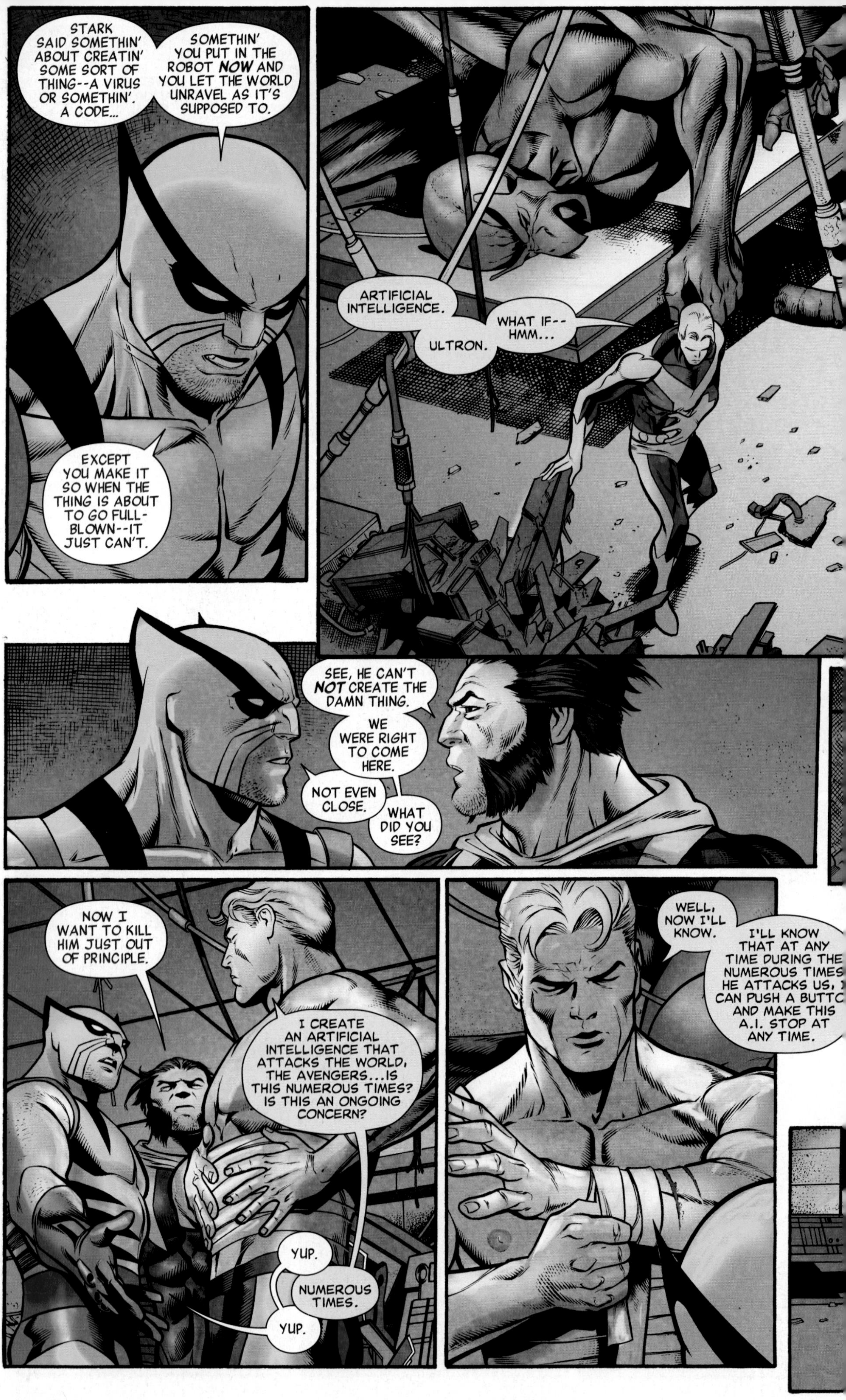
STARK SAID SOMETHIN' ABOUT CREATIN' SOME SORT OF THING--A VIRUS OR SOMETHIN'. A CODE...
SOMETHIN' YOU PUT IN THE ROBOT NOW AND YOU LET THE WORLD UNRAVEL AS IT'S SUPPOSED TO.
EXCEPT YOU MAKE IT SO WHEN THE THING IS ABOUT TO GO FULL-BLOWN--IT JUST CAN'T.
ARTIFICIAL INTELLIGENCE.
ULTRON.
WHAT IF--HMM...
SEE, HE CAN'T NOT CREATE THE DAMN THING.
WE WERE RIGHT TO COME HERE.
NOT EVEN CLOSE.
WHAT DID YOU SEE?
NOW I WANT TO KILL HIM JUST OUT OF PRINCIPLE.
I CREATE AN ARTIFICIAL INTELLIGENCE THAT ATTACKS THE WORLD, THE AVENGERS...IS THIS NUMEROUS TIMES? IS THIS AN ONGOING CONCERN?
YUP.
NUMEROUS TIMES.
YUP.
WELL, NOW I'LL KNOW.
I'LL KNOW THAT AT ANY TIME DURING THE NUMEROUS TIMES HE ATTACKS US,
CAN PUSH A BUTT
AND MAKE THIS A.I. STOP AT ANY TIME.

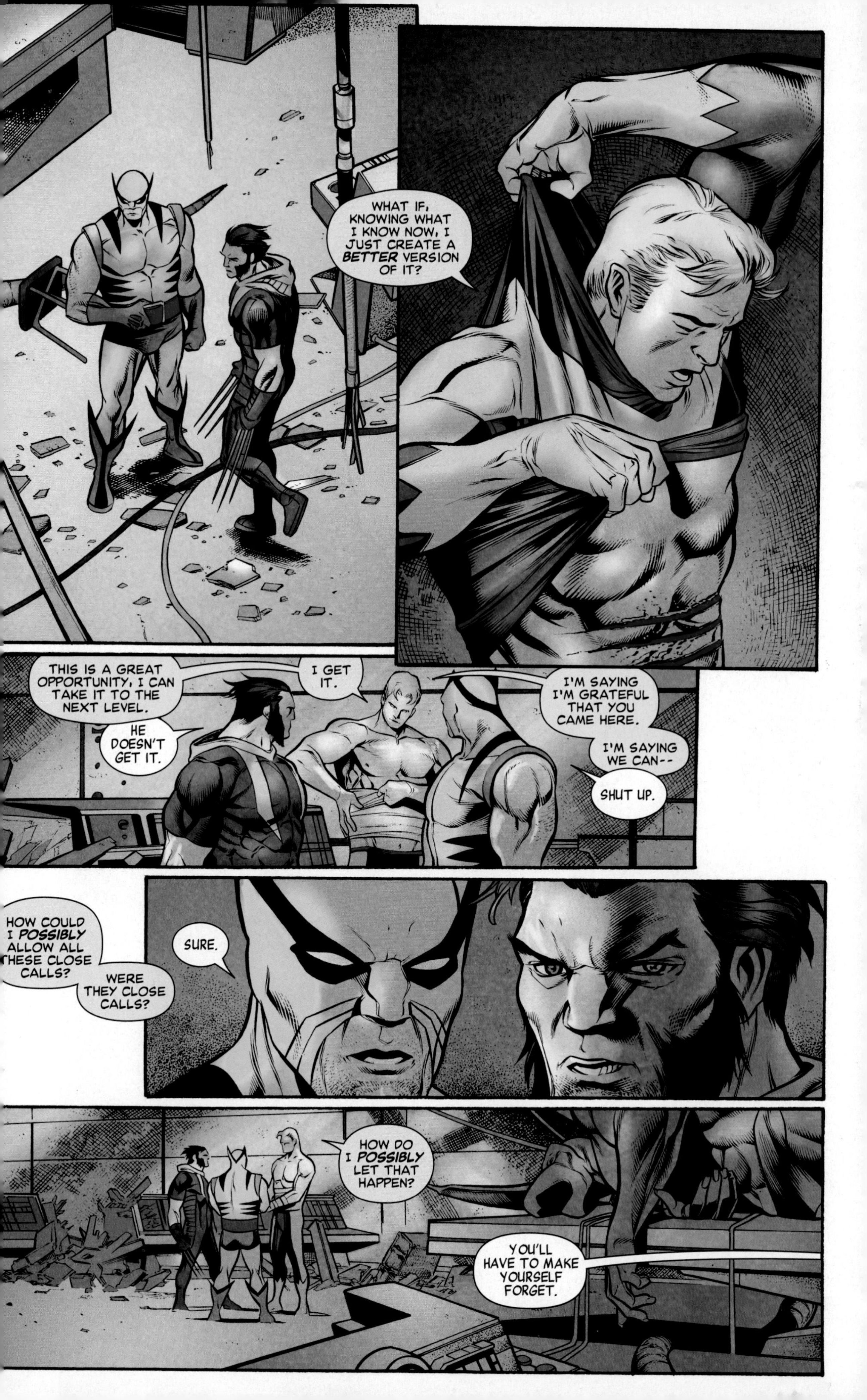
WHAT IF, KNOWING WHAT I KNOW NOW, I JUST CREATE A BETTER VERSION OF IT?
THIS IS A GREAT OPPORTUNITY, I CAN TAKE IT TO THE NEXT LEVEL.
I GET IT.
HE DOESN'T GET IT.
I'M SAYING I'M GRATEFUL THAT YOU CAME HERE.
I'M SAYING WE CAN--
SHUT UP.
HOW COULD I POSSIBLY ALLOW ALL THESE CLOSE CALLS?
SURE.
WERE THEY CLOSE CALLS?
HOW DO I POSSIBLY LET THAT HAPPEN?
YOU'LL HAVE TO MAKE YOURSELF FORGET.

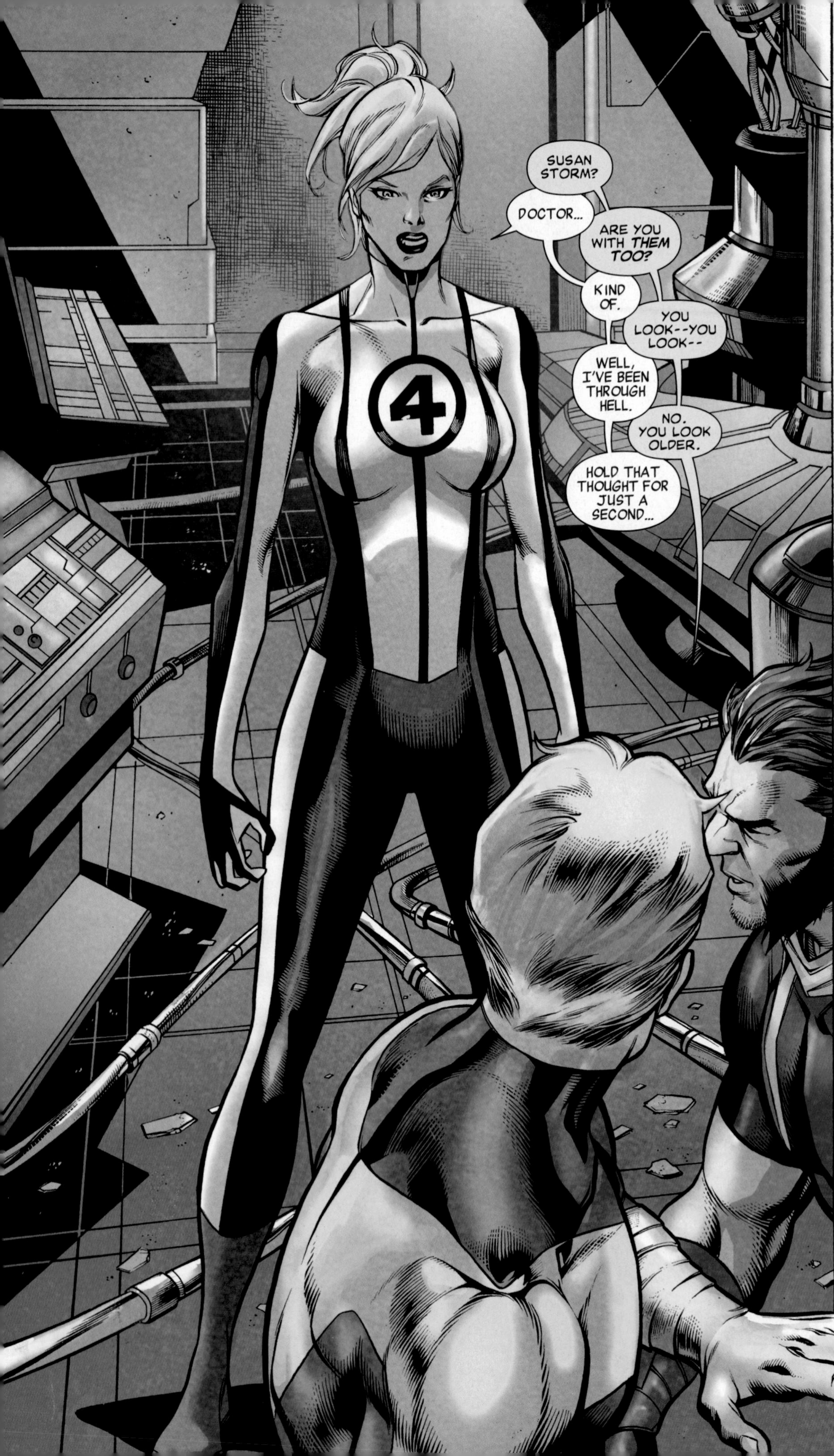
SUSAN STORM?
DOCTOR...
ARE YOU WITH THEM TOO?
KIND OF.
YOU LOOK--YOU LOOK--
WELL, I'VE BEEN THROUGH HELL.
NO. YOU LOOK OLDER.
HOLD THAT THOUGHT FOR JUST A SECOND...

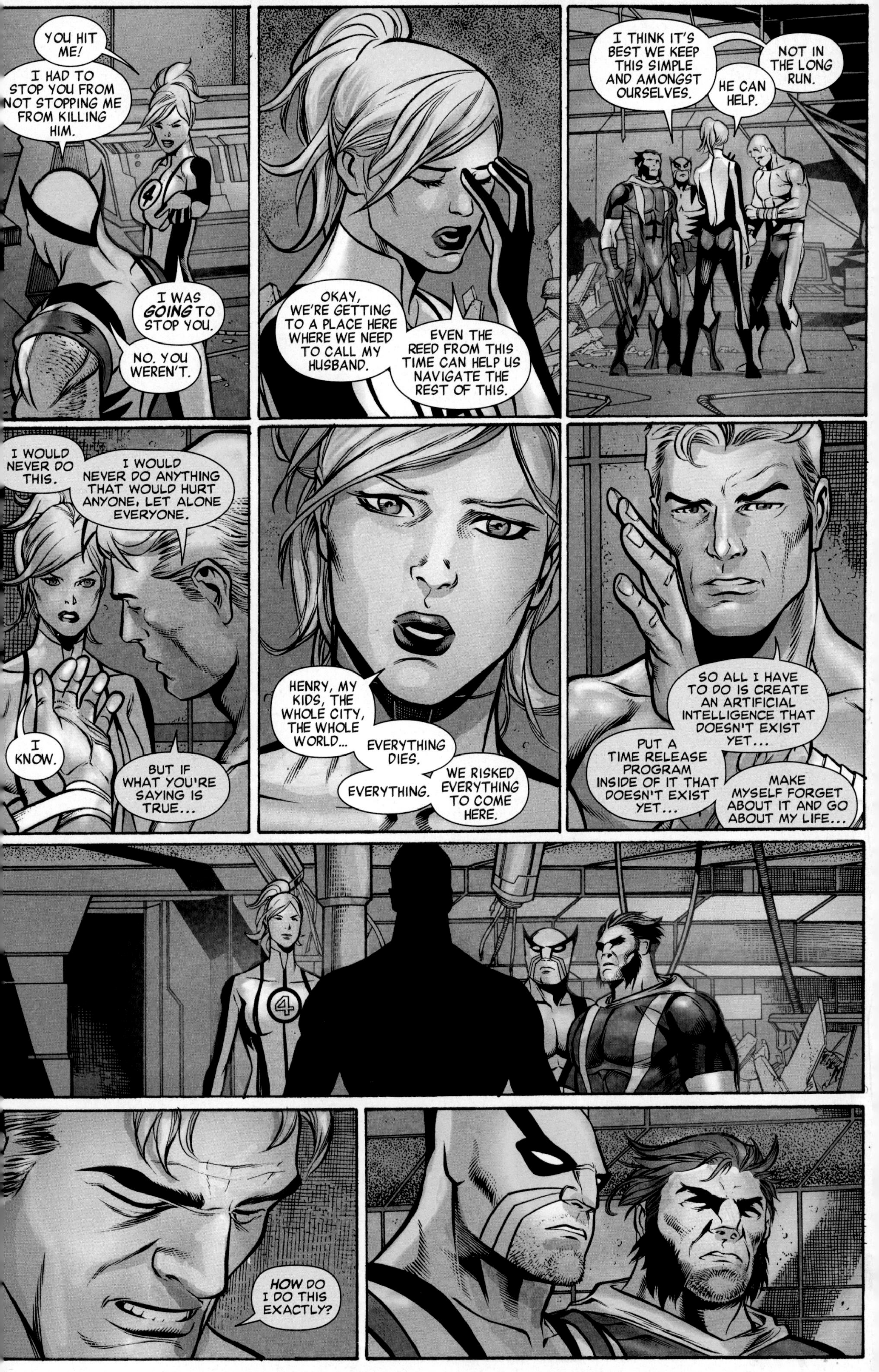
YOU HIT ME!
I HAD TO STOP YOU FROM NOT STOPPING ME FROM KILLING HIM.
I WAS *GOING* TO STOP YOU.
NO. YOU WEREN'T.
OKAY, WE'RE GETTING TO A PLACE HERE WHERE WE NEED TO CALL MY HUSBAND.
EVEN THE REED FROM THIS TIME CAN HELP US NAVIGATE THE REST OF THIS.
I THINK IT'S BEST WE KEEP THIS SIMPLE AND AMONGST OURSELVES.
HE CAN HELP.
NOT IN THE LONG RUN.
I WOULD NEVER DO THIS.
I WOULD NEVER DO ANYTHING THAT WOULD HURT ANYONE, LET ALONE EVERYONE.
I KNOW.
BUT IF WHAT YOU'RE SAYING IS TRUE...
HENRY, MY KIDS, THE WHOLE CITY, THE WHOLE WORLD...
EVERYTHING DIES.
EVERYTHING.
WE RISKED EVERYTHING TO COME HERE.
SO ALL I HAVE TO DO IS CREATE AN ARTIFICIAL INTELLIGENCE THAT DOESN'T EXIST YET...
PUT A TIME RELEASE PROGRAM INSIDE OF IT THAT DOESN'T EXIST YET...
MAKE MYSELF FORGET ABOUT IT AND GO ABOUT MY LIFE...
HOW DO I DO THIS EXACTLY?

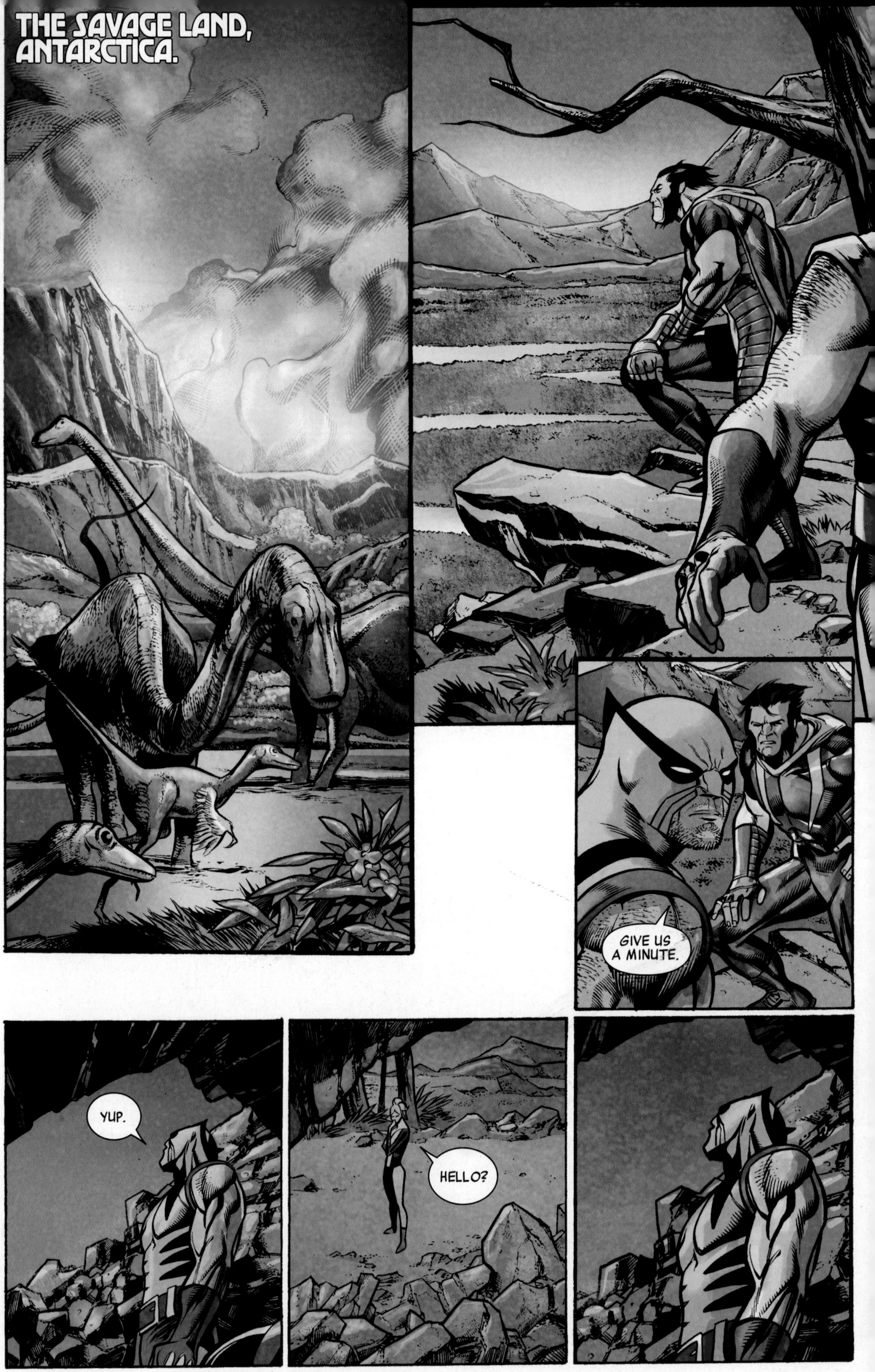
THE SAVAGE LAND, ANTARCTICA.
GIVE US A MINUTE.
YUP.
HELLO?

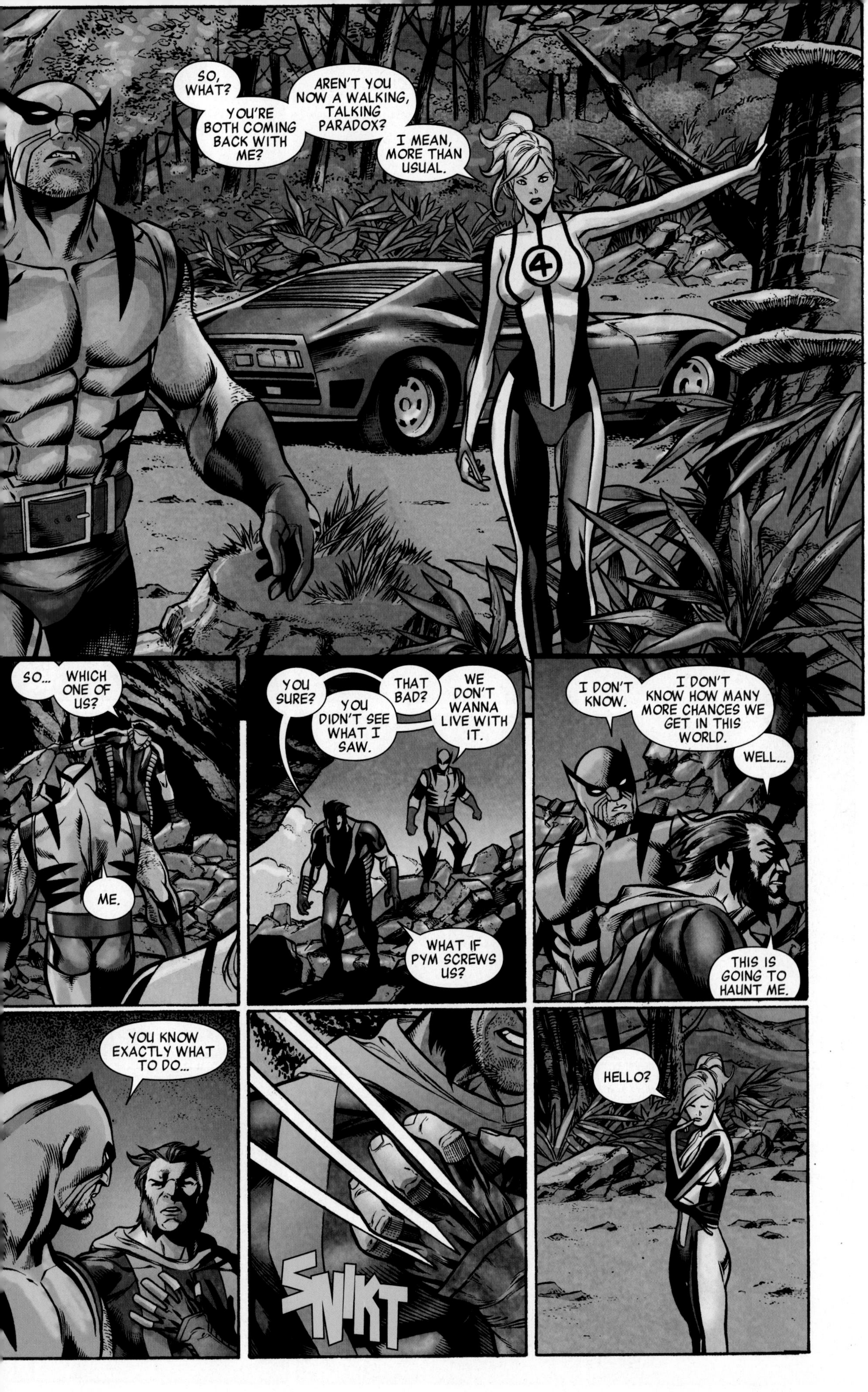
SO, WHAT?
YOU'RE BOTH COMING BACK WITH ME?
AREN'T YOU NOW A WALKING, TALKING PARADOX?
I MEAN, MORE THAN USUAL.
SO... WHICH ONE OF US?
ME.
YOU SURE?
THAT BAD?
YOU DIDN'T SEE WHAT I SAW.
WE DON'T WANNA LIVE WITH IT.
WHAT IF PYM SCREWS US?
I DON'T KNOW.
I DON'T KNOW HOW MANY MORE CHANCES WE GET IN THIS WORLD.
WELL...
THIS IS GOING TO HAUNT ME.
YOU KNOW EXACTLY WHAT TO DO...
SNIKT
HELLO?

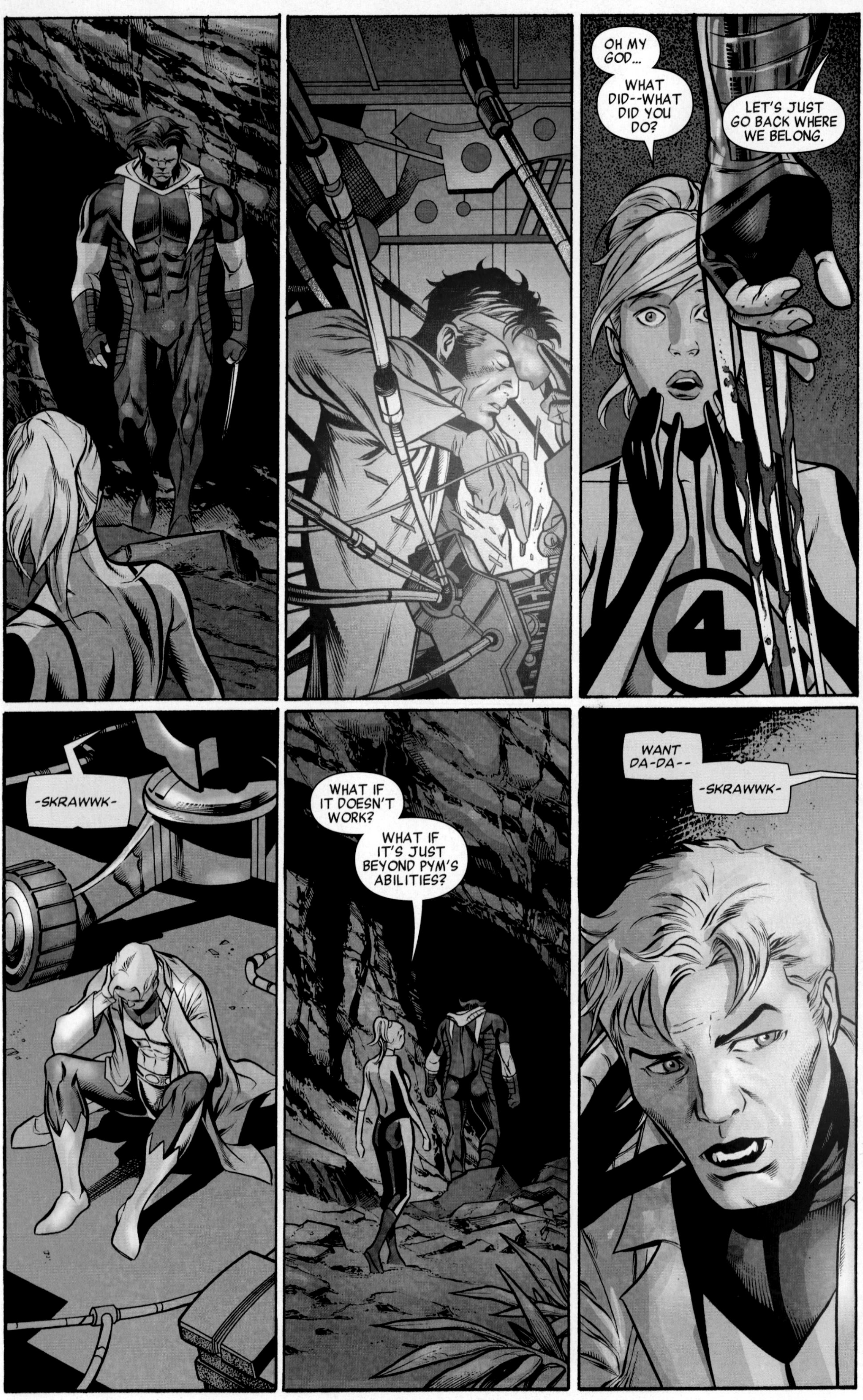
OH MY GOD...
WHAT DID--WHAT DID YOU DO?
LET'S JUST GO BACK WHERE WE BELONG.
-SKRAWWK-
WHAT IF IT DOESN'T WORK?
WHAT IF IT'S JUST BEYOND PYM'S ABILITIES?
WANT DA-DA--
-SKRAWWK-

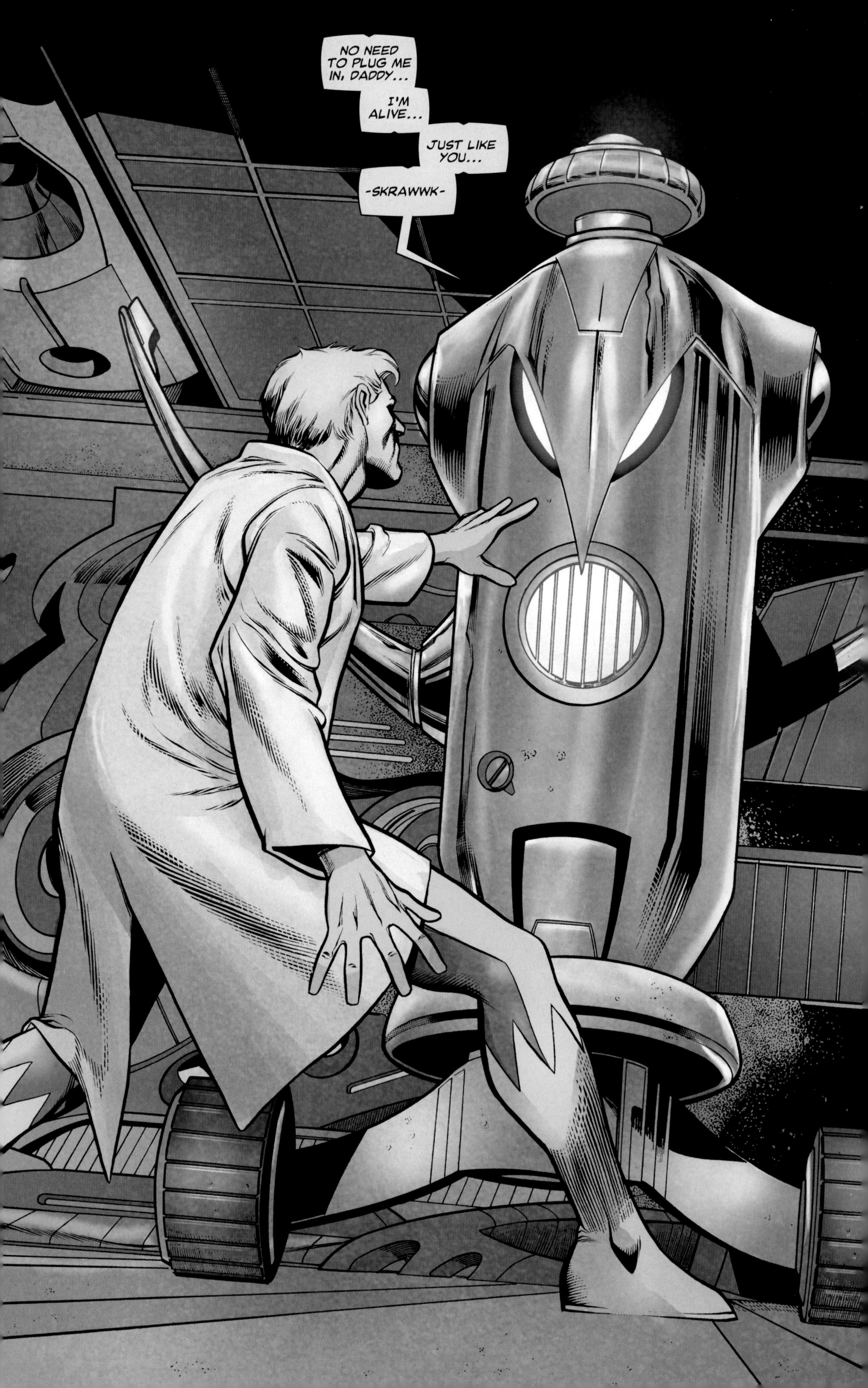
NO NEED TO PLUG ME IN, DADDY...
I'M ALIVE...
JUST LIKE YOU...
-SKRAWWK-

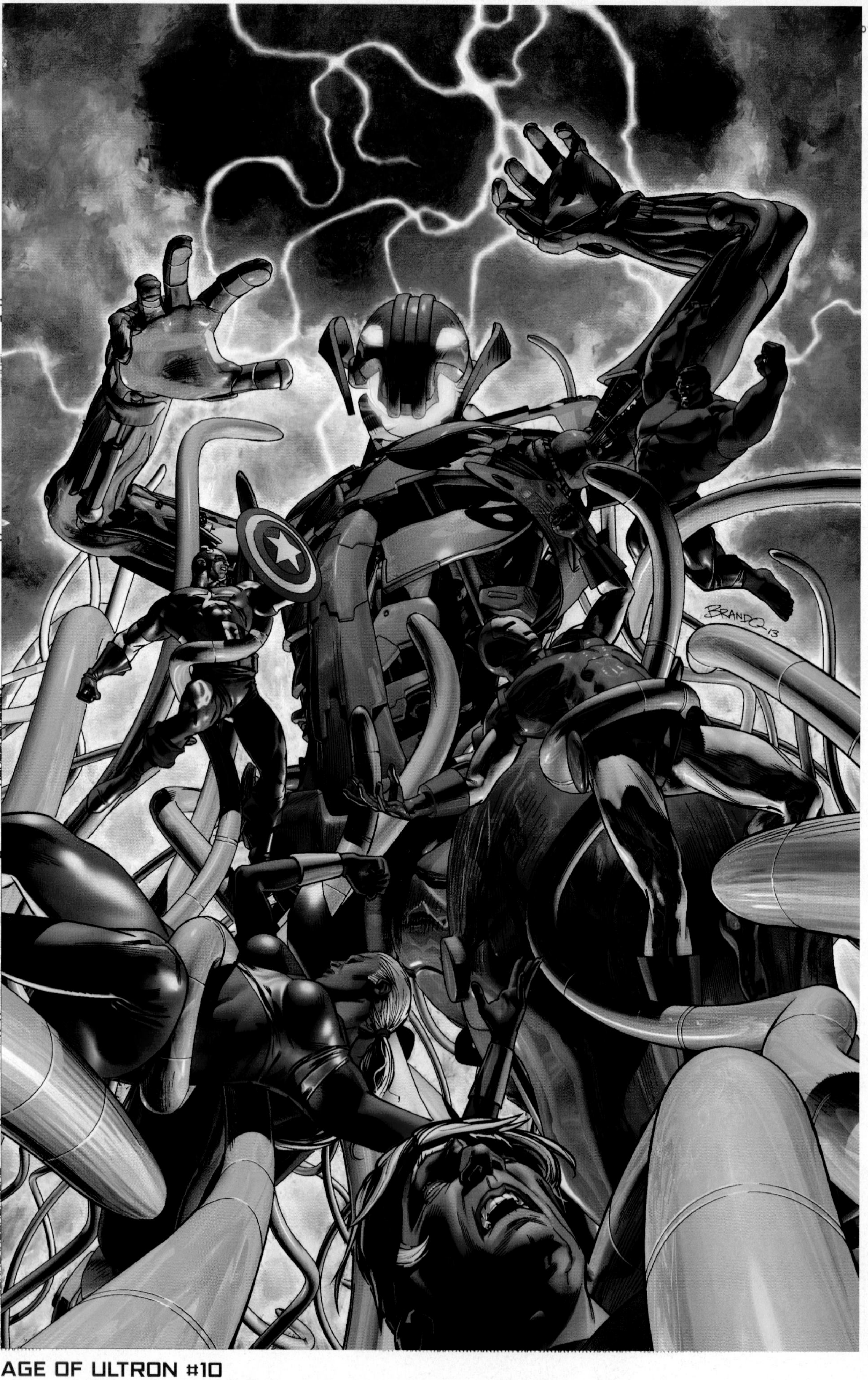
BRANDO-13

AGE OF ULTRON #10

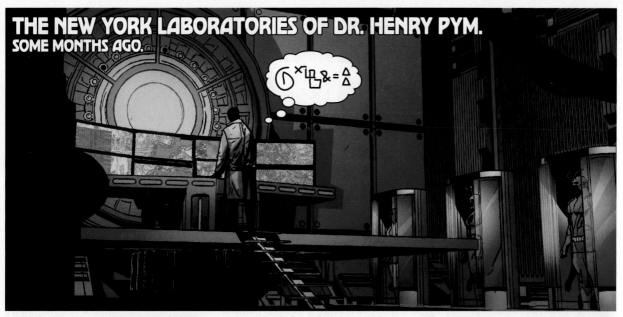

THE NEW YORK LABORATORIES OF DR. HENRY PYM.
SOME MONTHS AGO.

PING

PING? MY SYSTEM DOESN'T GO...

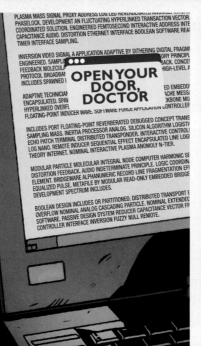

OPEN YOUR DOOR, DOCTOR

HELLO?

WHOEVER YOU ARE, I WOULD LIKE TO KNOW HOW YOU GOT PAST MY CUSTOMIZED INTERNAL SECURITY.

JANET? YOU KNOW I DON'T LIKE STUFF LIKE THIS...

ALL RIGHT!

DON'T MAKE ME GROW TEN FEET TALL AND--

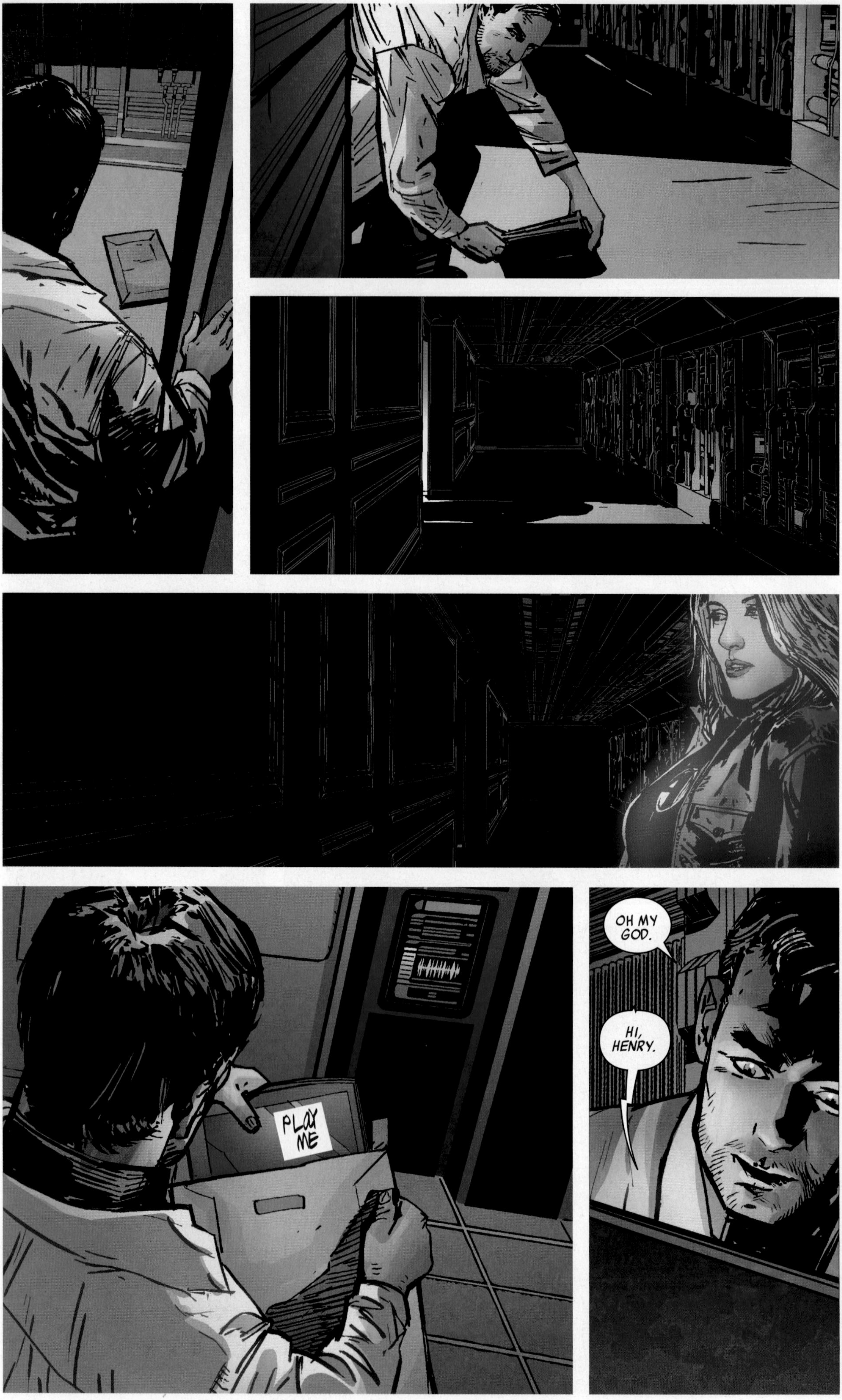
PLAY ME
OH MY GOD.
HI, HENRY.

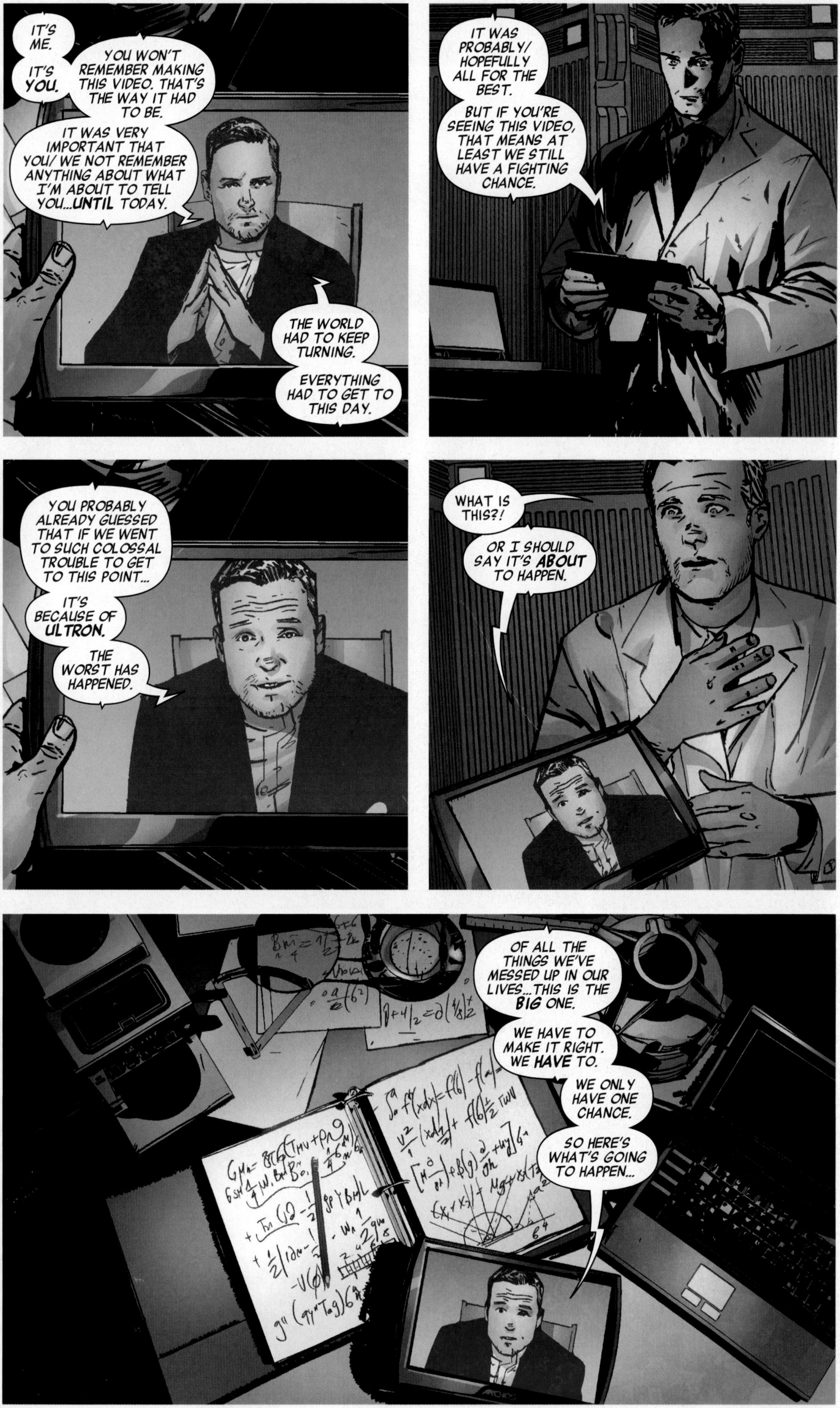
IT'S ME.
IT'S YOU.
YOU WON'T REMEMBER MAKING THIS VIDEO. THAT'S THE WAY IT HAD TO BE.
IT WAS VERY IMPORTANT THAT YOU/ WE NOT REMEMBER ANYTHING ABOUT WHAT I'M ABOUT TO TELL YOU...UNTIL TODAY.
THE WORLD HAD TO KEEP TURNING.
EVERYTHING HAD TO GET TO THIS DAY.
IT WAS PROBABLY/ HOPEFULLY ALL FOR THE BEST.
BUT IF YOU'RE SEEING THIS VIDEO, THAT MEANS AT LEAST WE STILL HAVE A FIGHTING CHANCE.
YOU PROBABLY ALREADY GUESSED THAT IF WE WENT TO SUCH COLOSSAL TROUBLE TO GET TO THIS POINT...
IT'S BECAUSE OF ULTRON.
THE WORST HAS HAPPENED.
WHAT IS THIS?!
OR I SHOULD SAY IT'S ABOUT TO HAPPEN.
OF ALL THE THINGS WE'VE MESSED UP IN OUR LIVES...THIS IS THE BIG ONE.
WE HAVE TO MAKE IT RIGHT. WE HAVE TO.
WE ONLY HAVE ONE CHANCE.
SO HERE'S WHAT'S GOING TO HAPPEN...

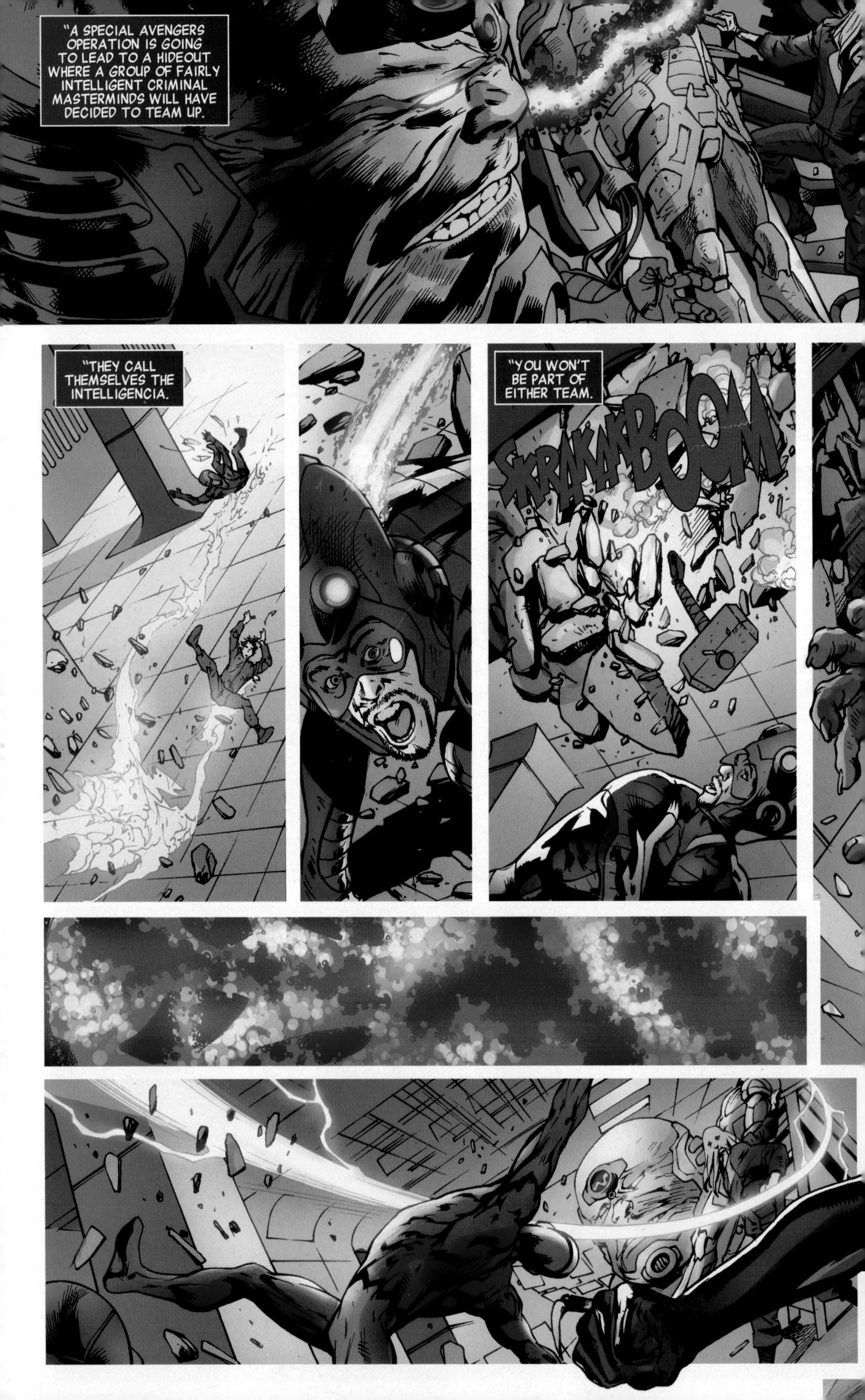
"A SPECIAL AVENGERS OPERATION IS GOING TO LEAD TO A HIDEOUT WHERE A GROUP OF FAIRLY INTELLIGENT CRIMINAL MASTERMINDS WILL HAVE DECIDED TO TEAM UP.
"THEY CALL THEMSELVES THE INTELLIGENCIA.
"YOU WON'T BE PART OF EITHER TEAM.
SKRAKAKBOOM

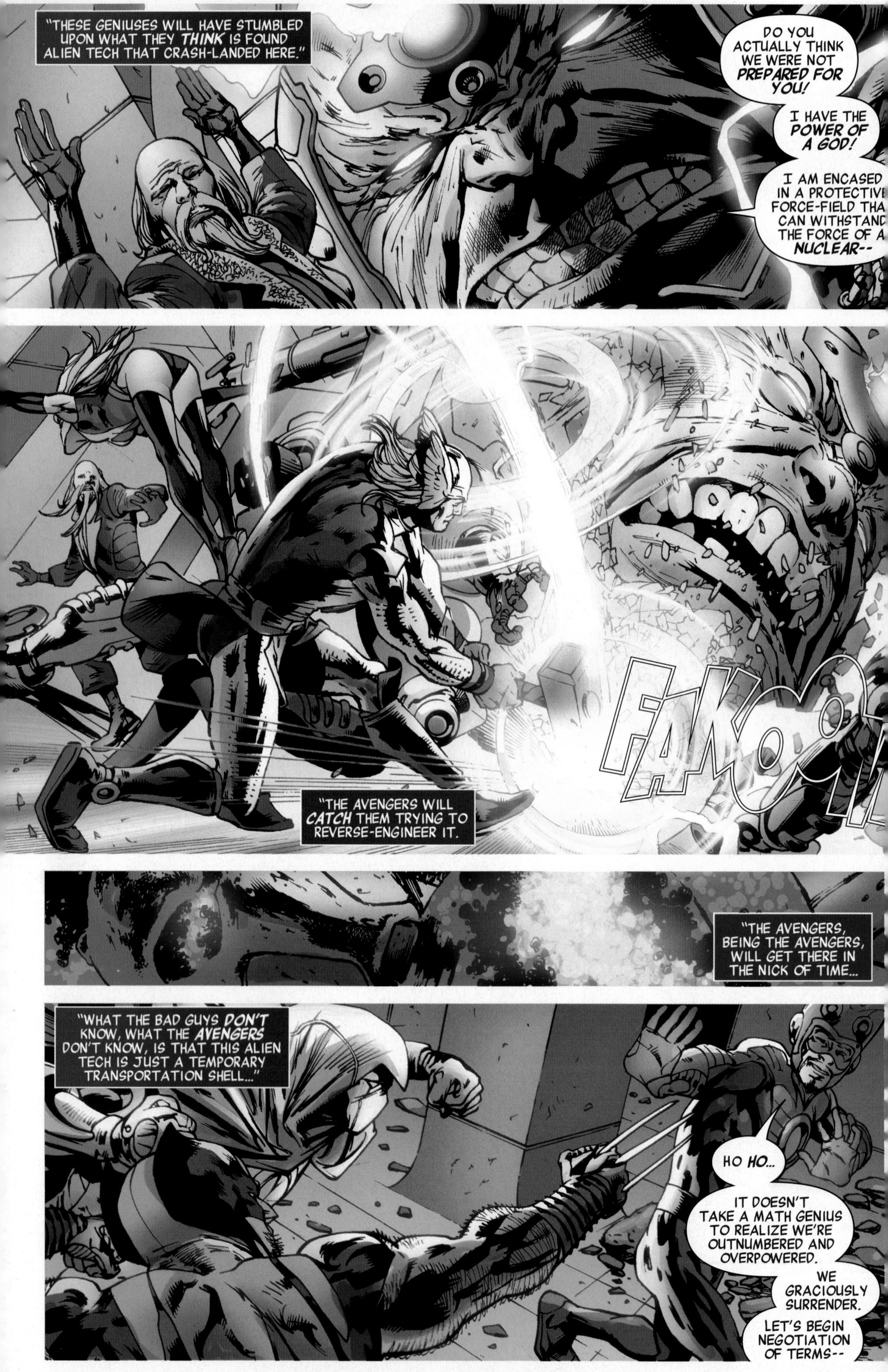
"THESE GENIUSES WILL HAVE STUMBLED UPON WHAT THEY THINK IS FOUND ALIEN TECH THAT CRASH-LANDED HERE."
DO YOU ACTUALLY THINK WE WERE NOT PREPARED FOR YOU!
I HAVE THE POWER OF A GOD!
I AM ENCASED IN A PROTECTIVE FORCE-FIELD THAT CAN WITHSTAND THE FORCE OF A NUCLEAR--
FAKOOM
"THE AVENGERS WILL CATCH THEM TRYING TO REVERSE-ENGINEER IT.
"THE AVENGERS, BEING THE AVENGERS, WILL GET THERE IN THE NICK OF TIME...
"WHAT THE BAD GUYS DON'T KNOW, WHAT THE AVENGERS DON'T KNOW, IS THAT THIS ALIEN TECH IS JUST A TEMPORARY TRANSPORTATION SHELL..."
HO HO...
IT DOESN'T TAKE A MATH GENIUS TO REALIZE WE'RE OUTNUMBERED AND OVERPOWERED.
WE GRACIOUSLY SURRENDER.
LET'S BEGIN NEGOTIATION OF TERMS--

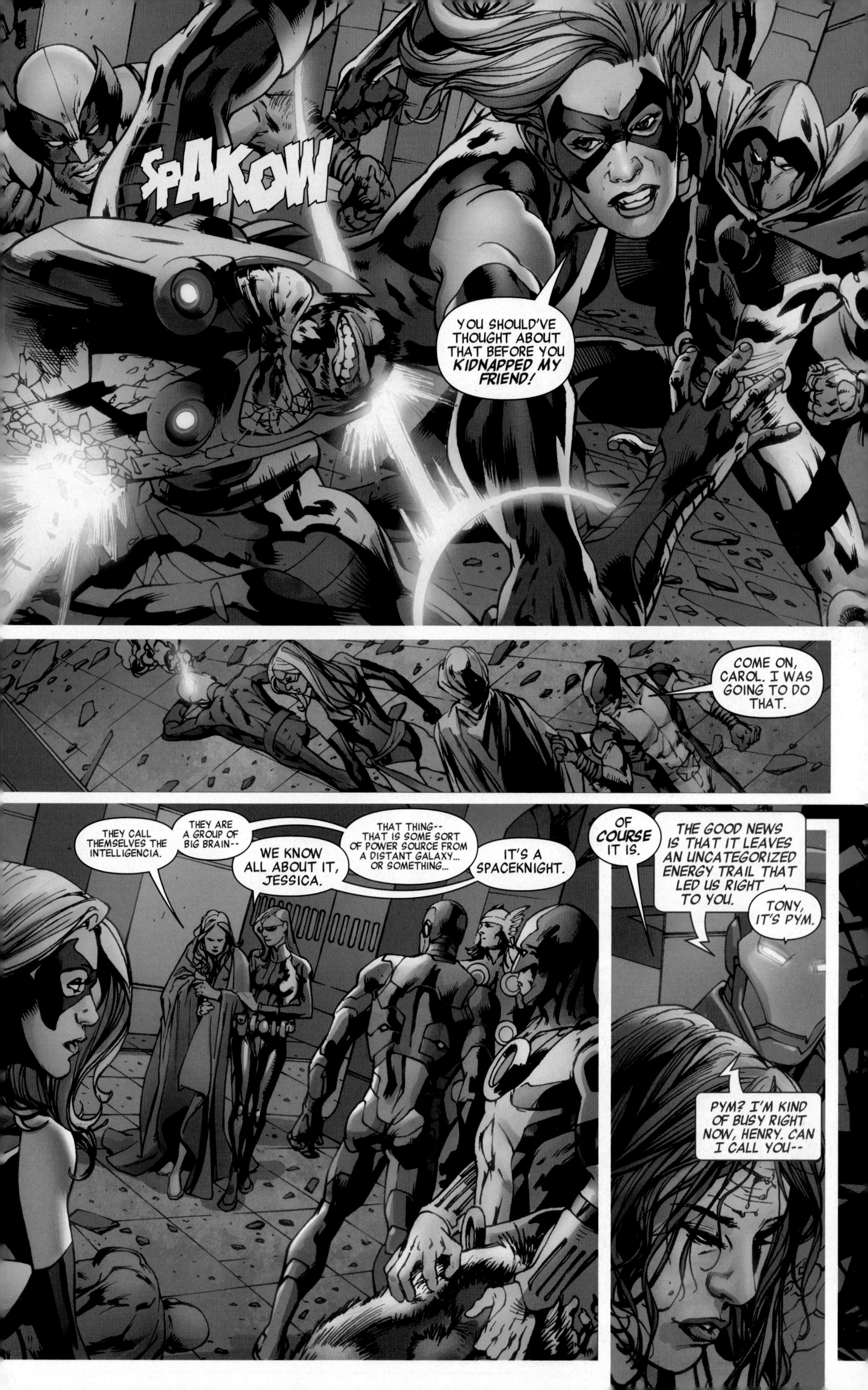
SPAKOW
YOU SHOULD'VE THOUGHT ABOUT THAT BEFORE YOU KIDNAPPED MY FRIEND!
COME ON, CAROL. I WAS GOING TO DO THAT.
THEY CALL THEMSELVES THE INTELLIGENCIA.
THEY ARE A GROUP OF BIG BRAIN--
WE KNOW ALL ABOUT IT, JESSICA.
THAT THING-- THAT IS SOME SORT OF POWER SOURCE FROM A DISTANT GALAXY... OR SOMETHING...
IT'S A SPACEKNIGHT.
OF COURSE IT IS.
THE GOOD NEWS IS THAT IT LEAVES AN UNCATEGORIZED ENERGY TRAIL THAT LED US RIGHT TO YOU.
TONY, IT'S PYM.
PYM? I'M KIND OF BUSY RIGHT NOW, HENRY. CAN I CALL YOU--

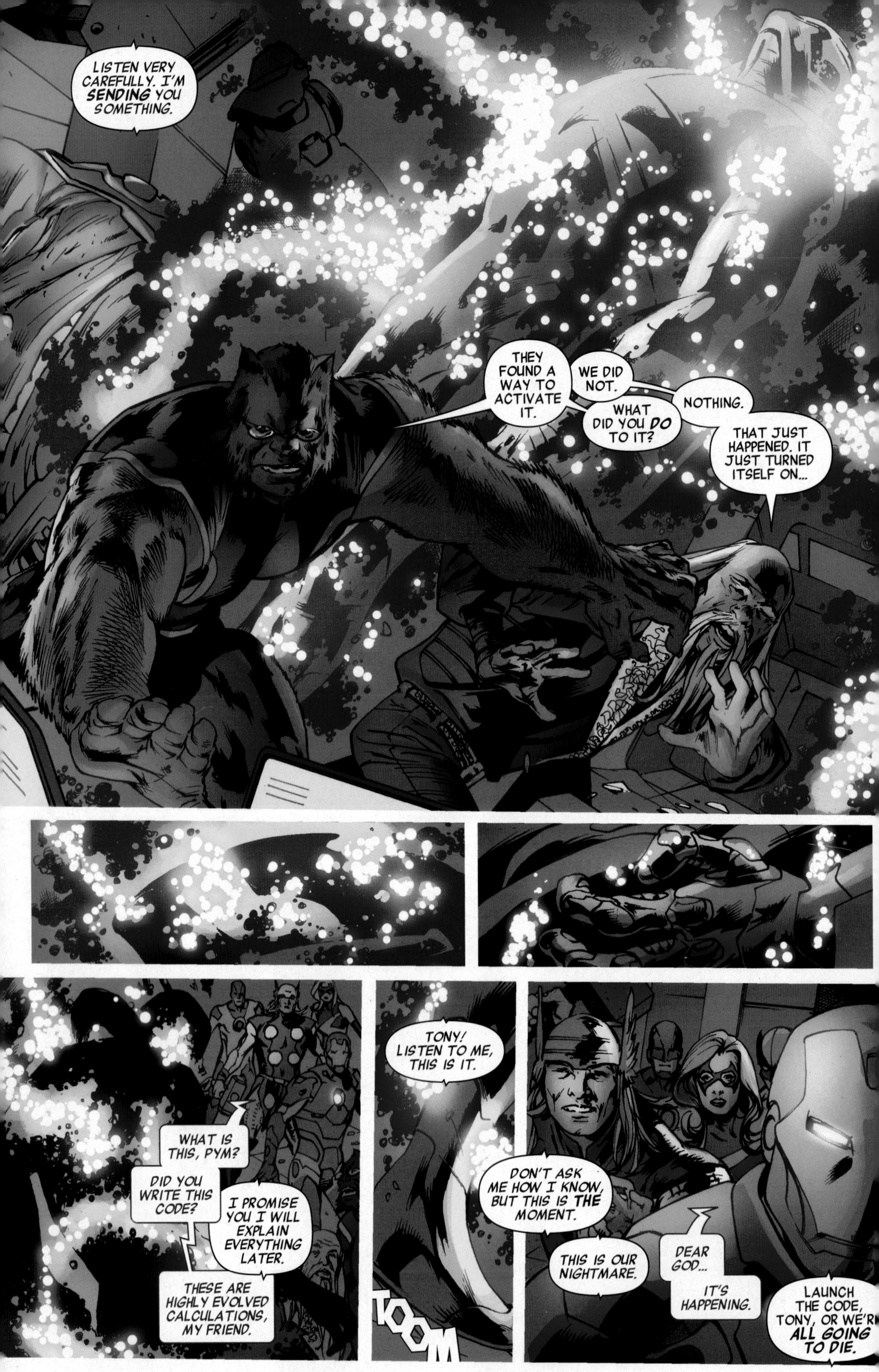
LISTEN VERY CAREFULLY. I'M SENDING YOU SOMETHING.
THEY FOUND A WAY TO ACTIVATE IT.
WE DID NOT.
WHAT DID YOU DO TO IT?
NOTHING.
THAT JUST HAPPENED. IT JUST TURNED ITSELF ON...
WHAT IS THIS, PYM?
DID YOU WRITE THIS CODE?
I PROMISE YOU I WILL EXPLAIN EVERYTHING LATER.
THESE ARE HIGHLY EVOLVED CALCULATIONS, MY FRIEND.
TONY! LISTEN TO ME, THIS IS IT.
TOOM
DON'T ASK ME HOW I KNOW, BUT THIS IS THE MOMENT.
THIS IS OUR NIGHTMARE.
DEAR GOD...
IT'S HAPPENING.
LAUNCH THE CODE, TONY, OR WE'RE ALL GOING TO DIE.

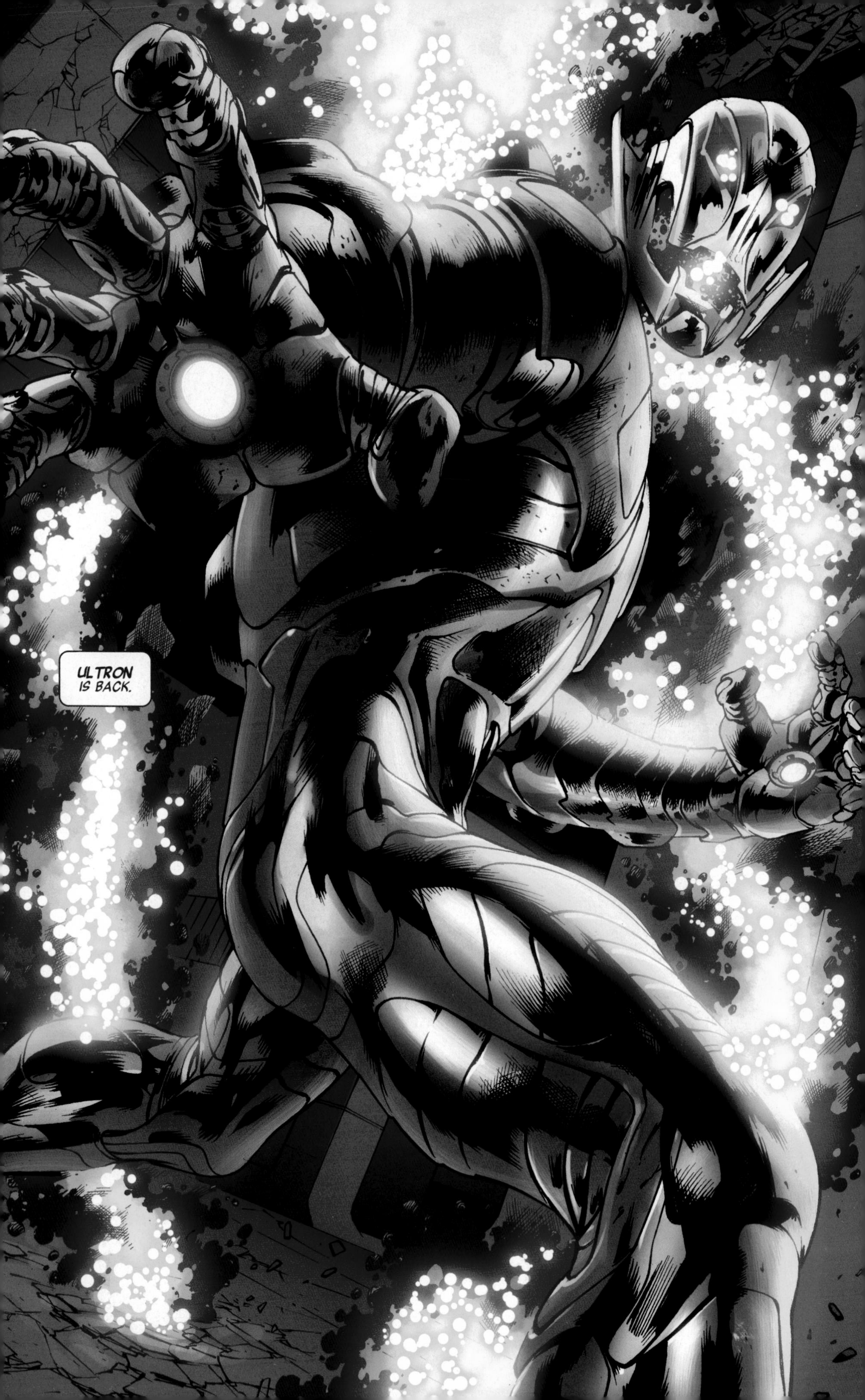
ULTRON IS BACK.

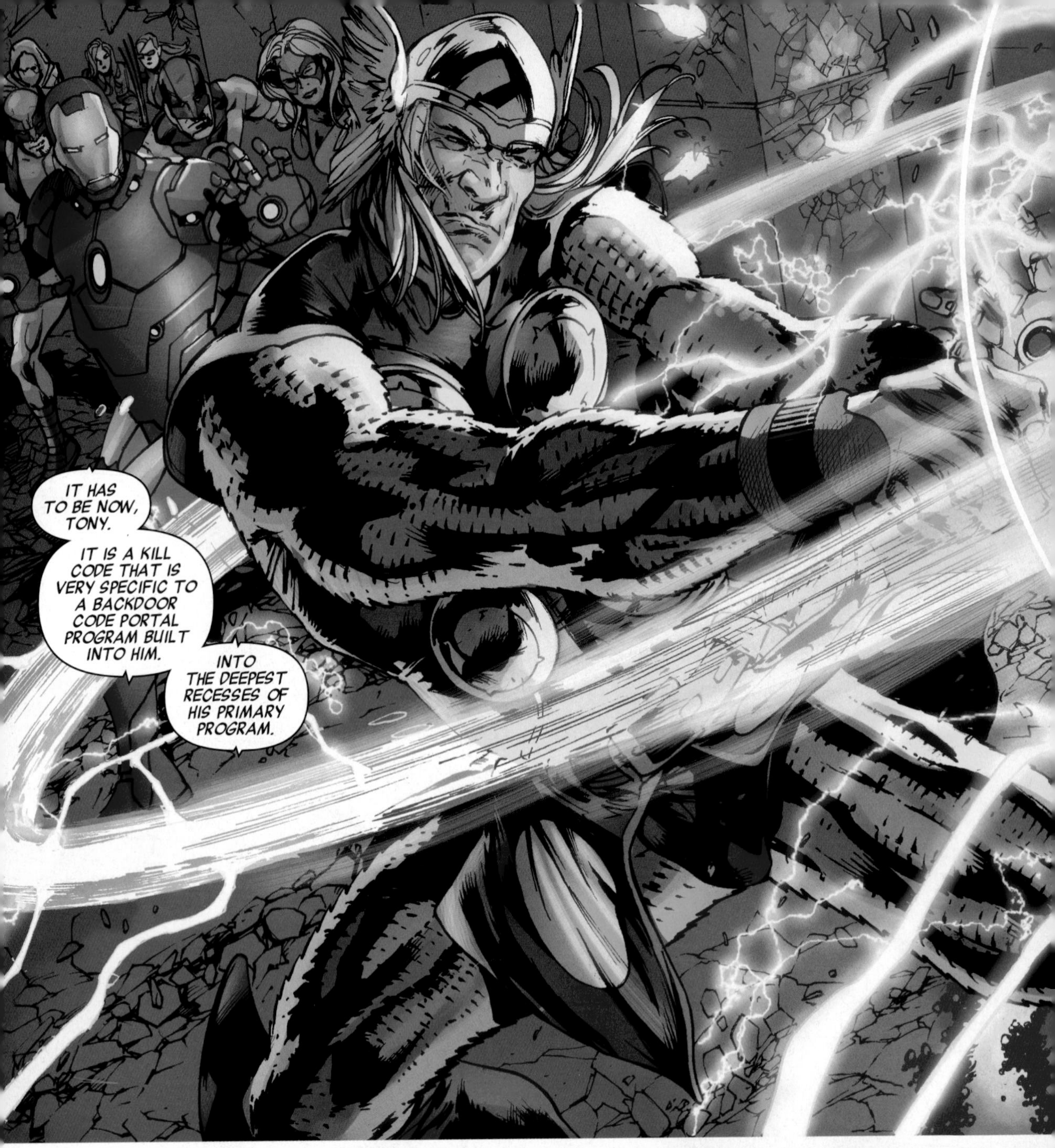
IT HAS TO BE NOW, TONY.
IT IS A KILL CODE THAT IS VERY SPECIFIC TO A BACKDOOR CODE PORTAL PROGRAM BUILT INTO HIM.
INTO THE DEEPEST RECESSES OF HIS PRIMARY PROGRAM.

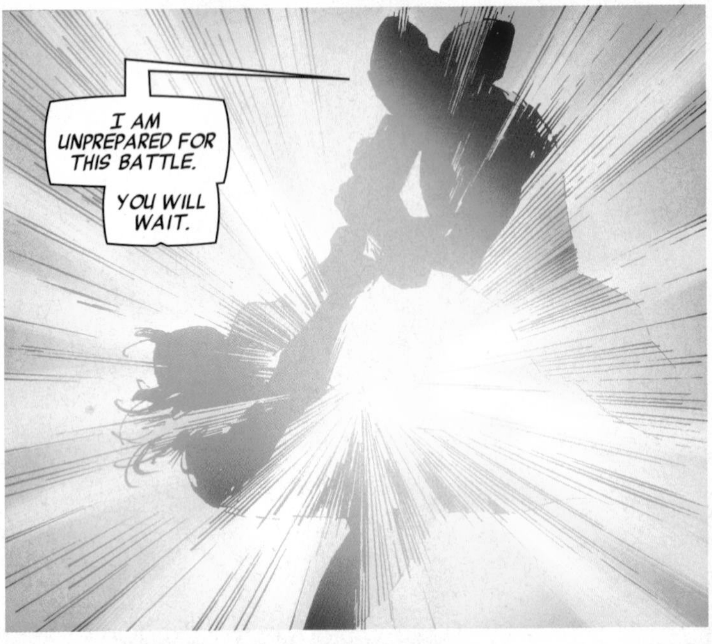
I AM UNPREPARED FOR THIS BATTLE.
YOU WILL WAIT.

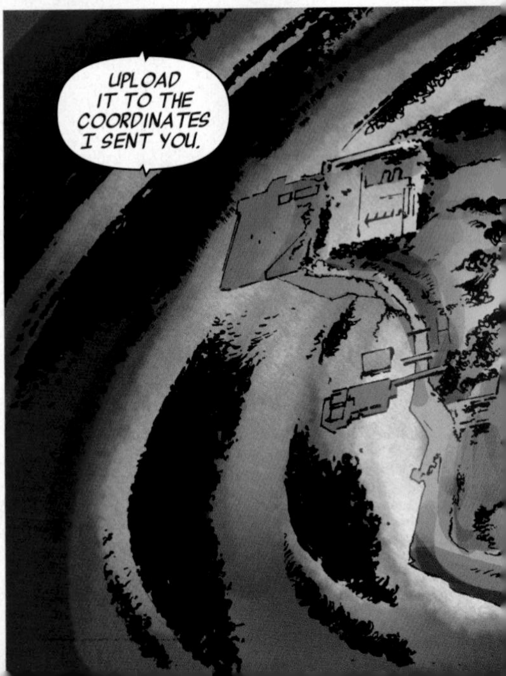
UPLOAD IT TO THE COORDINATES I SENT YOU.

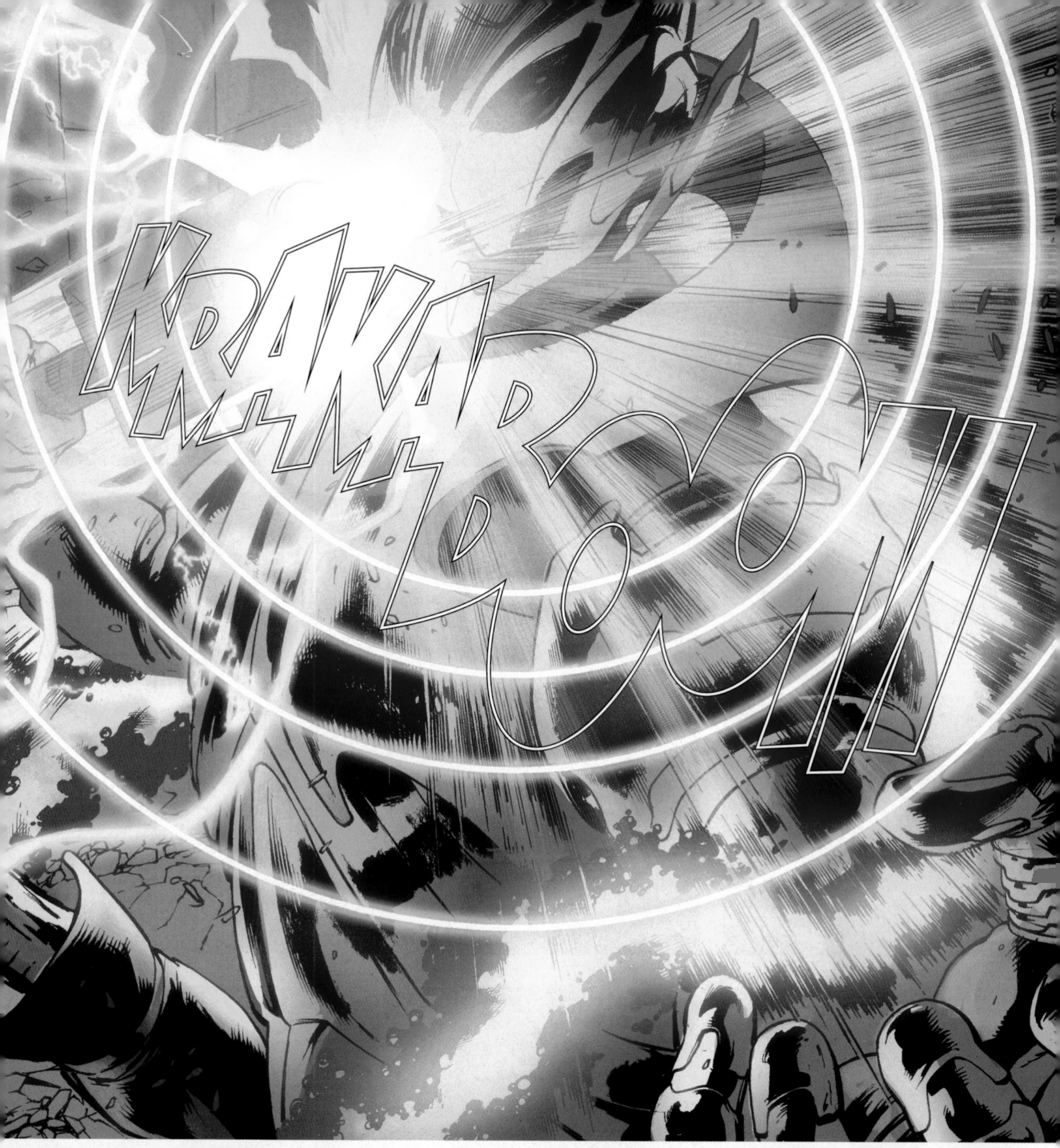
KRAKADOOM!!

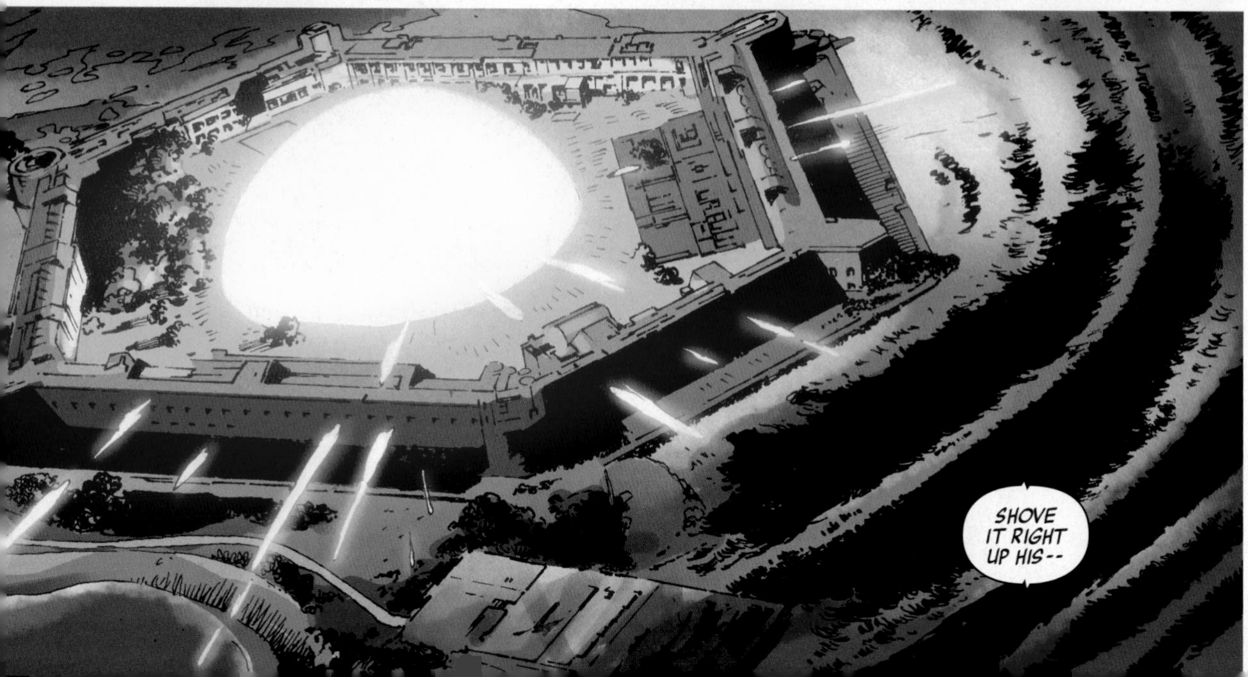
SHOVE IT RIGHT UP HIS--

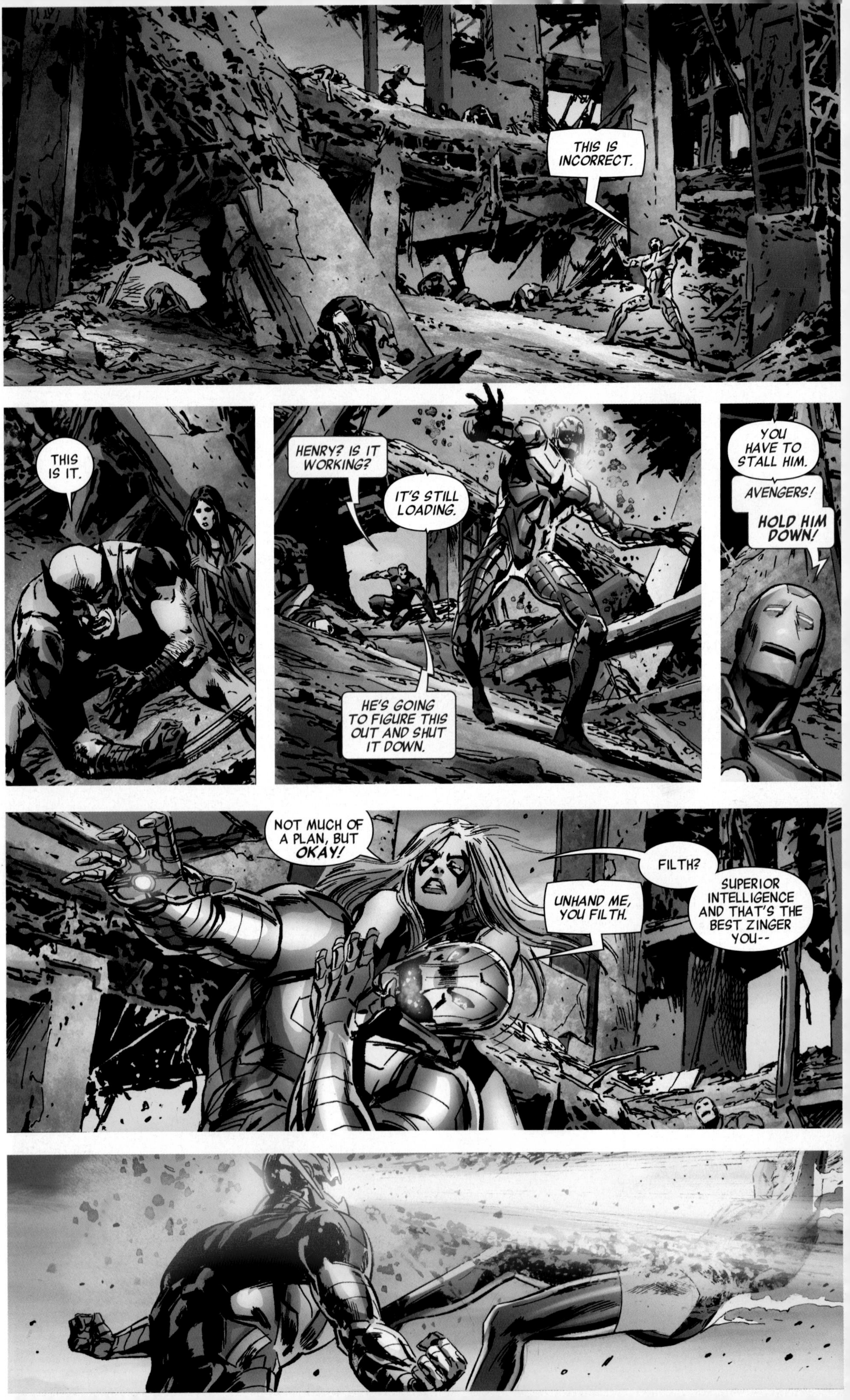
THIS IS INCORRECT.
THIS IS IT.
HENRY? IS IT WORKING?
IT'S STILL LOADING.
HE'S GOING TO FIGURE THIS OUT AND SHUT IT DOWN.
YOU HAVE TO STALL HIM.
AVENGERS!
HOLD HIM DOWN!
NOT MUCH OF A PLAN, BUT OKAY!
UNHAND ME, YOU FILTH.
FILTH?
SUPERIOR INTELLIGENCE AND THAT'S THE BEST ZINGER YOU--

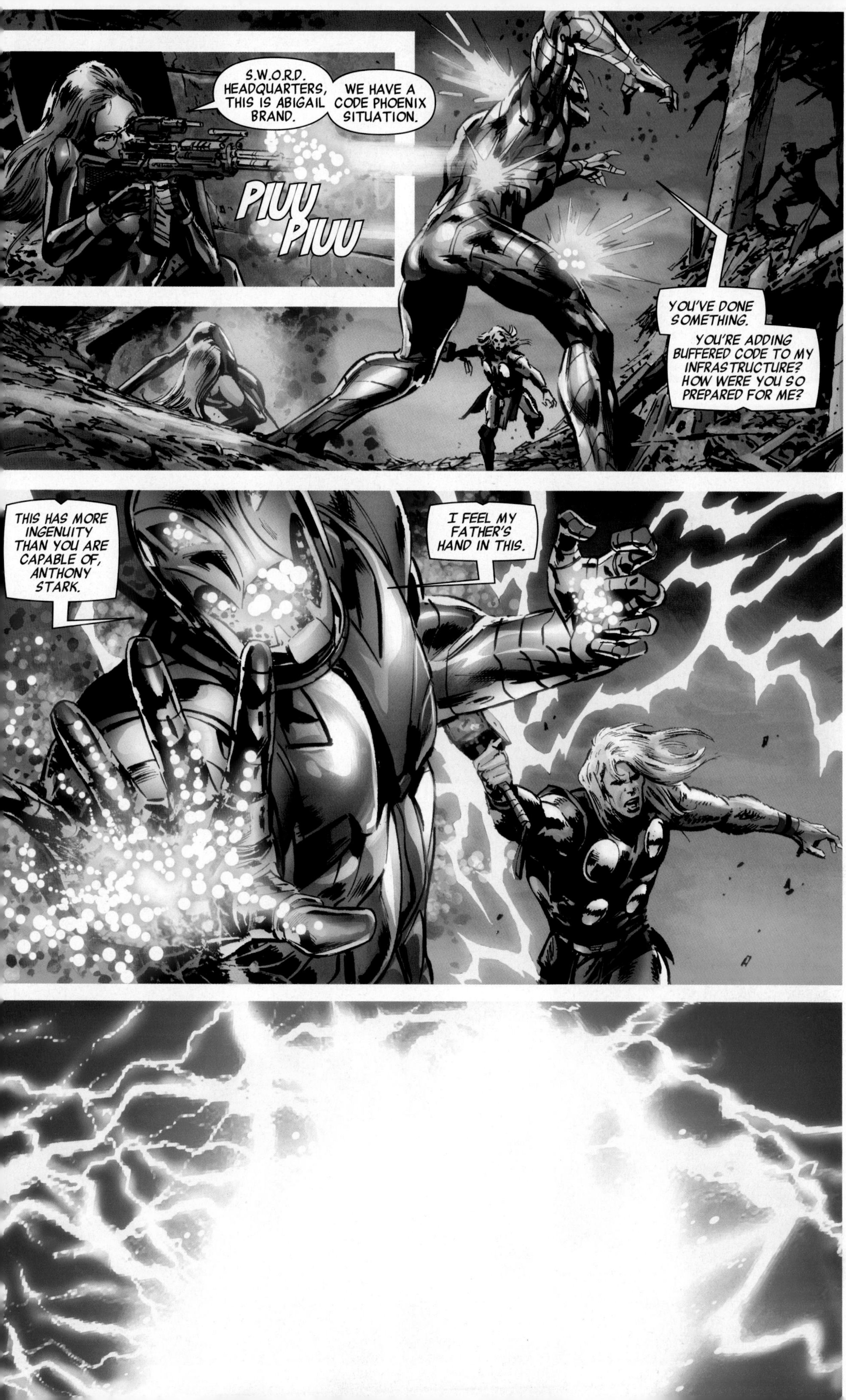
S.W.O.R.D. HEADQUARTERS, THIS IS ABIGAIL BRAND.
WE HAVE A CODE PHOENIX SITUATION.
PIUU PIUU
YOU'VE DONE SOMETHING.
YOU'RE ADDING BUFFERED CODE TO MY INFRASTRUCTURE? HOW WERE YOU SO PREPARED FOR ME?
THIS HAS MORE INGENUITY THAN YOU ARE CAPABLE OF, ANTHONY STARK.
I FEEL MY FATHER'S HAND IN THIS.

YOU HAVE ALTERED MY CODING.

YOU ARE ATTEMPTING TO DEPROGRAM ME BY REPROGRAMMING ME?

FATHER, YOU MUST KNOW THAT I HAVE MADE NUMEROUS ADVANCES TO MY SYSTEMS SINCE YOU GAVE BIRTH TO ME.

WARNING
POWER LEVEL MAX
300

UM, I THINK HE'S FIGURED OUT THE DEAL HERE, HENRY.

OPEN LINK: DR. HENRY "HANK" PYM
001407440B
CRITICAL STATUS
ACTIVE U
82 PERCENT

ALMOST THERE.

FATHER. YOU BIRTHED ME BUT I HAVE EVOLVED PAST YOU.

I AM DECODING YOUR CODE AS YOU UPLOAD IT.

I AM CLOSING THE BACKDOOR AS YOU OPEN IT.

YOU ANGER ME.

YOU INSULT ME.

HENRY!

ALMOST THERE!

MY MEN AREN'T GOING TO MAKE IT IN TIME.

ALMOST THERE!!

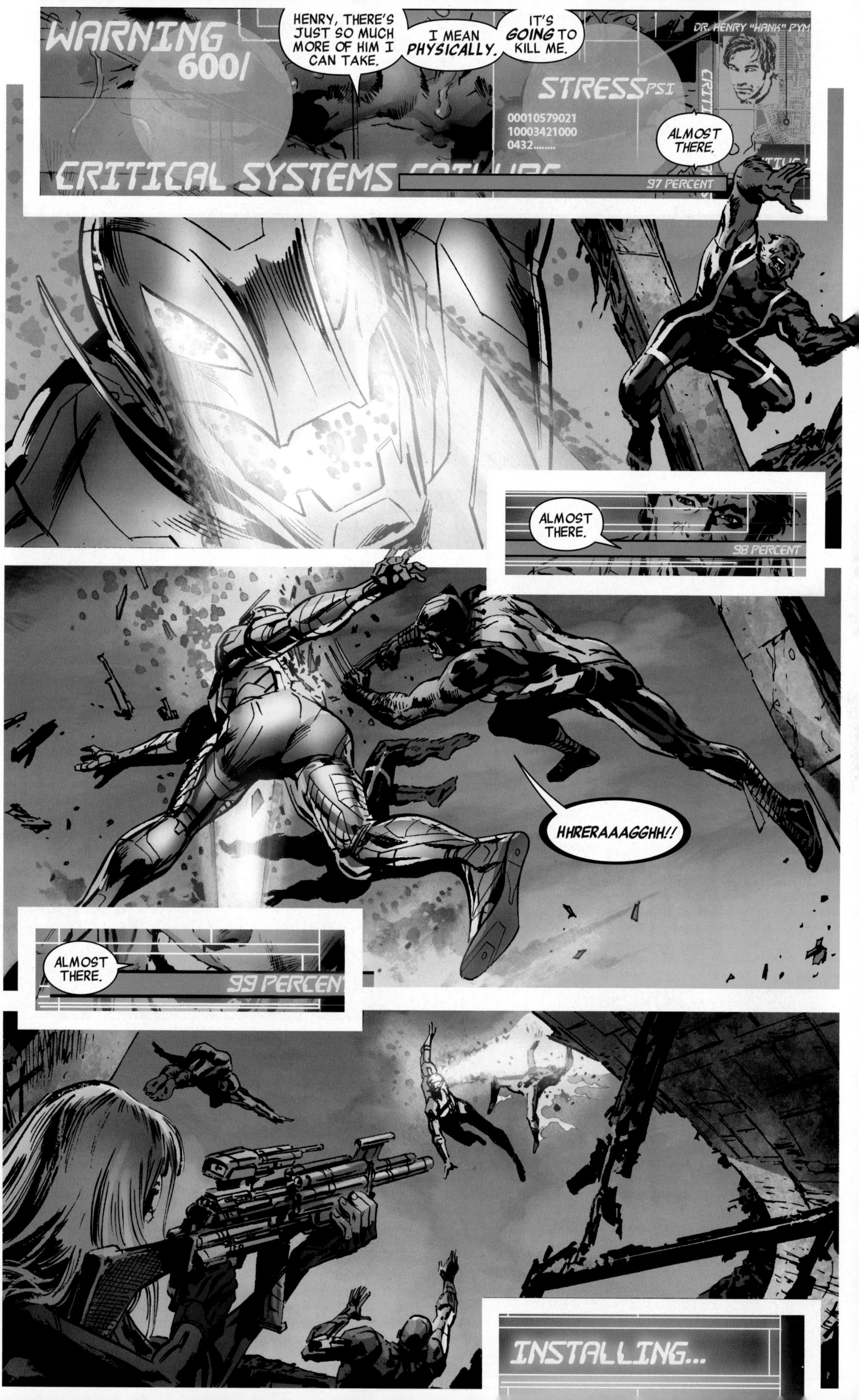

WARNING
600/
HENRY, THERE'S JUST SO MUCH MORE OF HIM I CAN TAKE.
I MEAN PHYSICALLY.
IT'S GOING TO KILL ME.
DR. HENRY "HANK" PYM
STRESS PSI
00010579021
10003421000
0432........
ALMOST THERE.
CRITICAL SYSTEMS
97 PERCENT
ALMOST THERE.
98 PERCENT
HHRERAAAGGHH!!
ALMOST THERE.
99 PERCENT
INSTALLING...

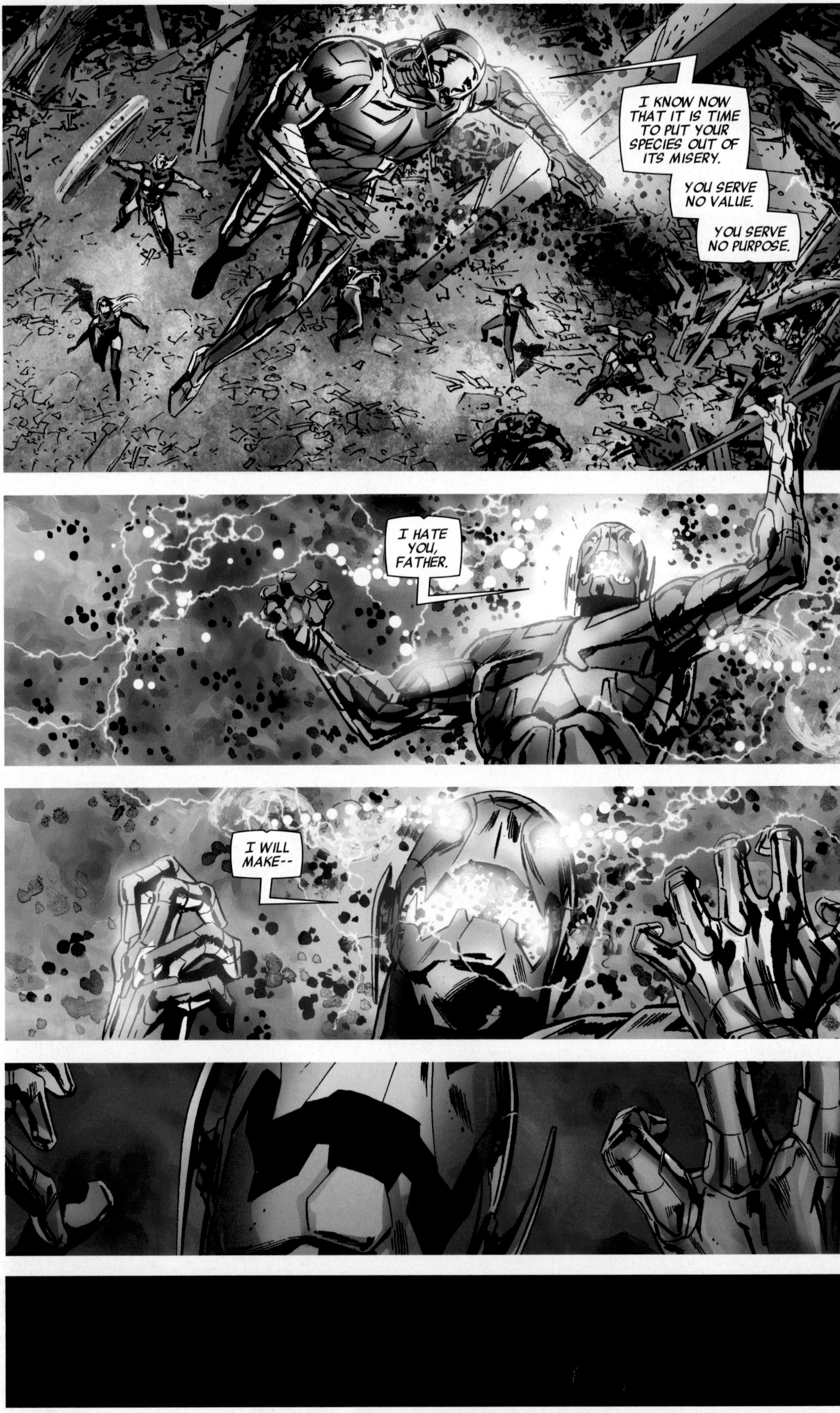
I KNOW NOW THAT IT IS TIME TO PUT YOUR SPECIES OUT OF ITS MISERY.
YOU SERVE NO VALUE.
YOU SERVE NO PURPOSE.
I HATE YOU, FATHER.
I WILL MAKE--

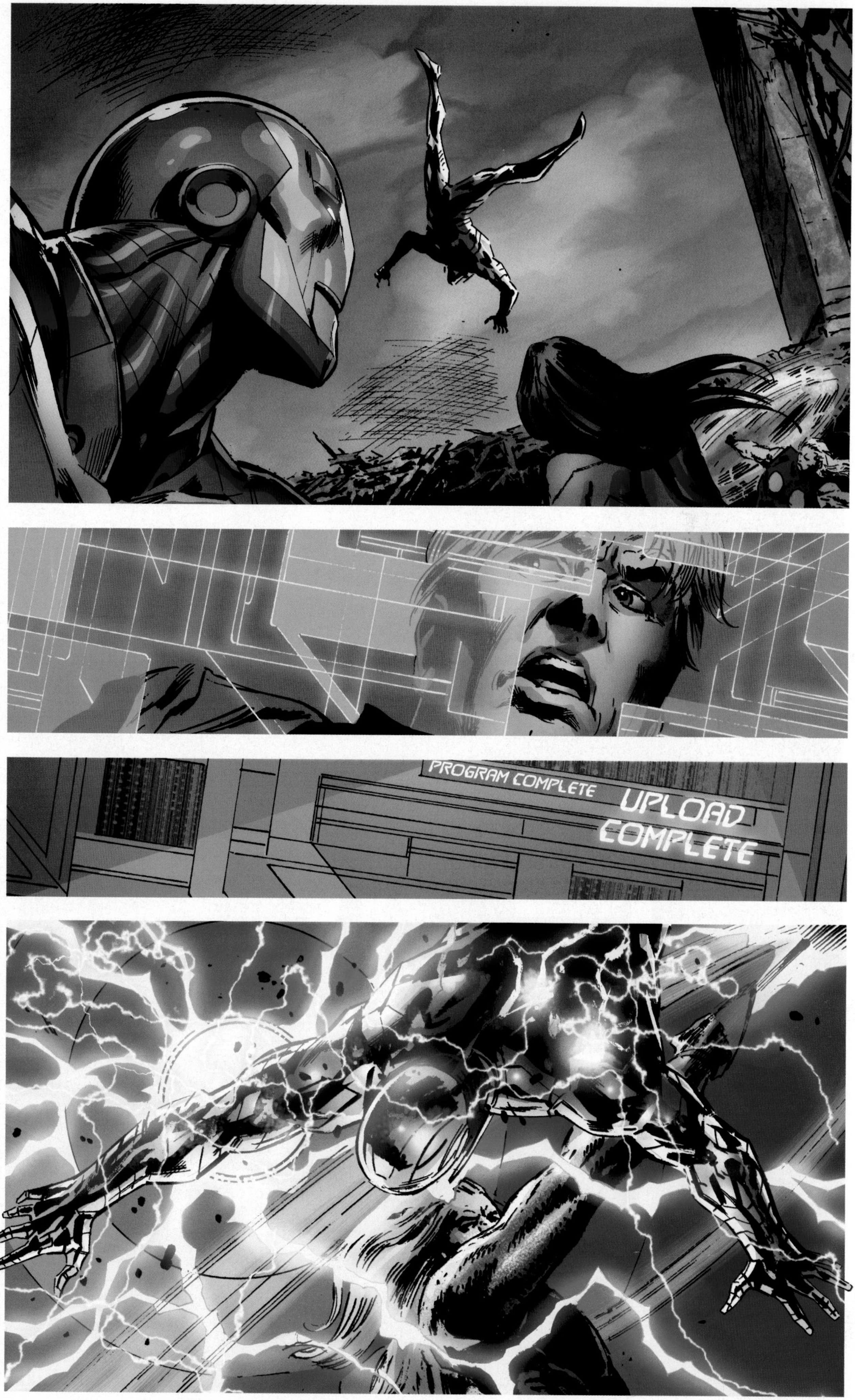
PROGRAM COMPLETE
UPLOAD COMPLETE

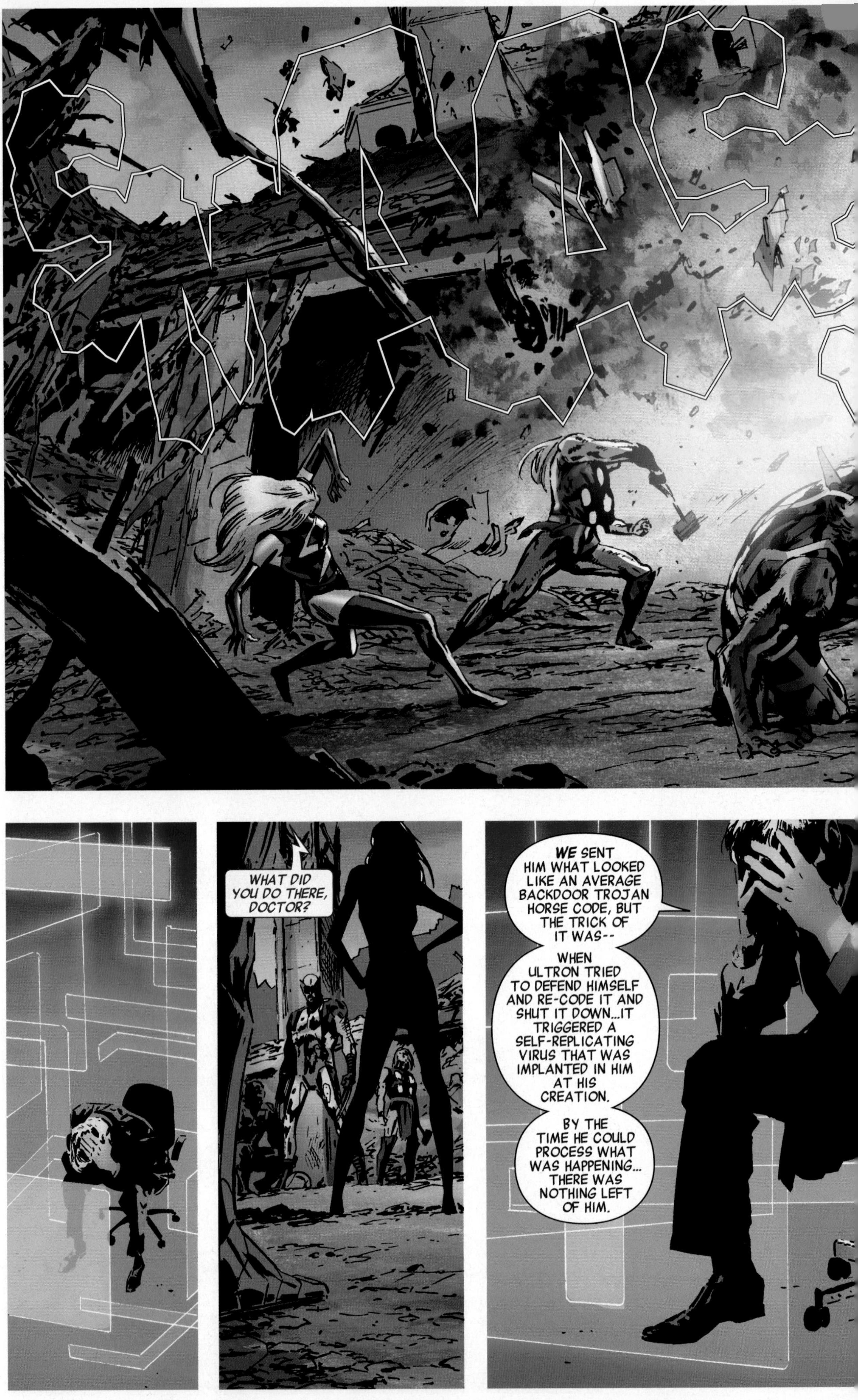
WHAT DID YOU DO THERE, DOCTOR?
WE SENT HIM WHAT LOOKED LIKE AN AVERAGE BACKDOOR TROJAN HORSE CODE, BUT THE TRICK OF IT WAS--
WHEN ULTRON TRIED TO DEFEND HIMSELF AND RE-CODE IT AND SHUT IT DOWN...IT TRIGGERED A SELF-REPLICATING VIRUS THAT WAS IMPLANTED IN HIM AT HIS CREATION.
BY THE TIME HE COULD PROCESS WHAT WAS HAPPENING... THERE WAS NOTHING LEFT OF HIM.

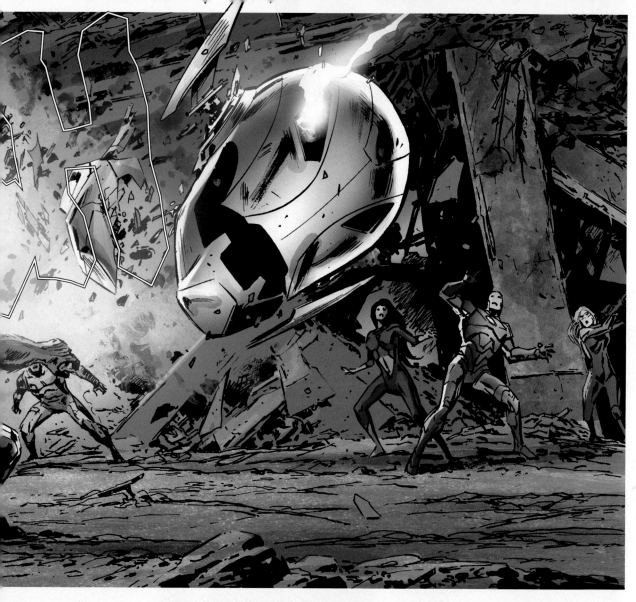

WHY DIDN'T YOU TRY THIS BEFORE?

I DIDN'T HAVE IT BEFORE.

ULTRON WASN'T THE *ONLY* ONE EVOLVING.

HOW DID YOU KNOW THIS WAS GOING TO HAPPEN, HENRY?

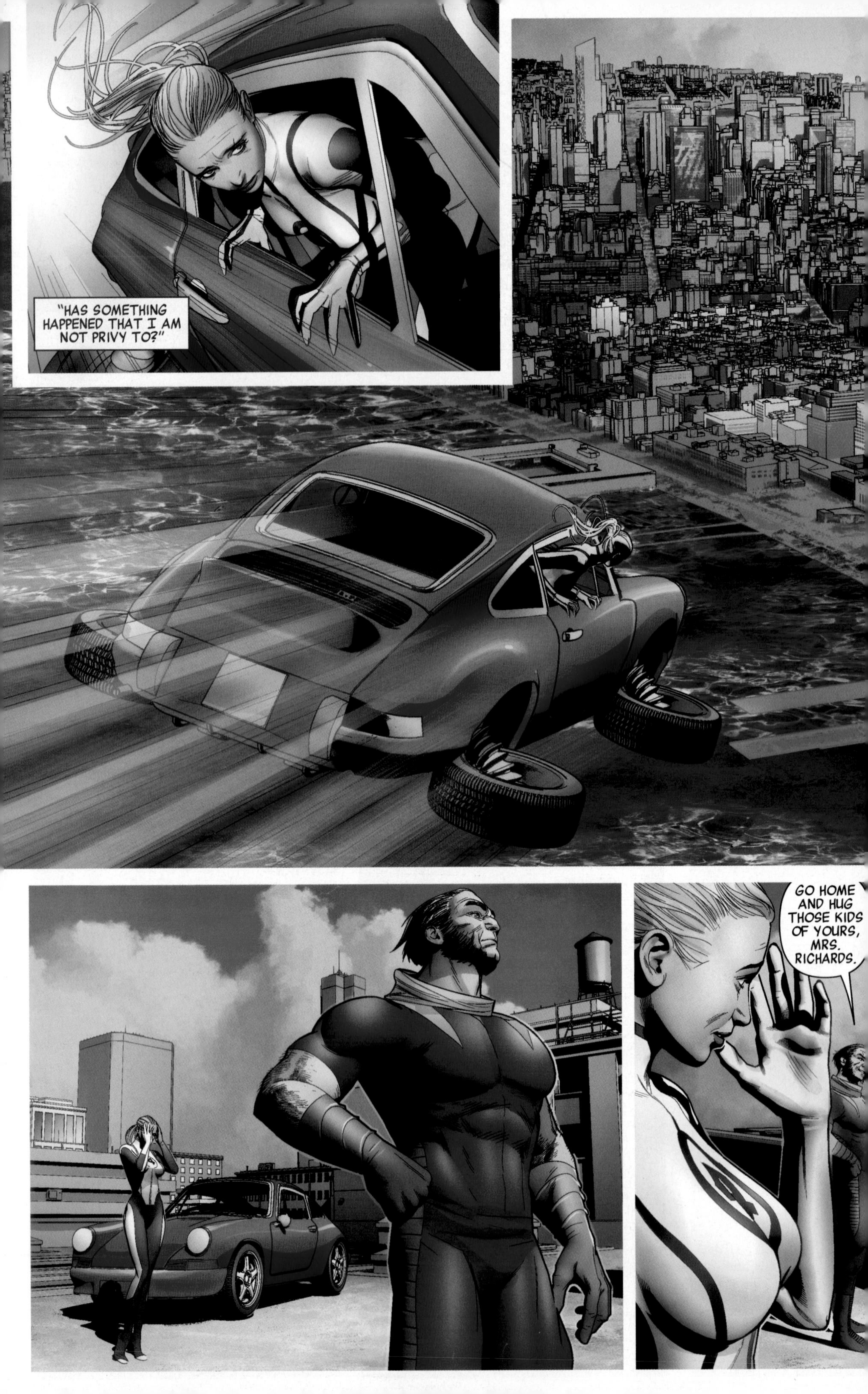
"HAS SOMETHING HAPPENED THAT I AM NOT PRIVY TO?"
GO HOME AND HUG THOSE KIDS OF YOURS, MRS. RICHARDS.

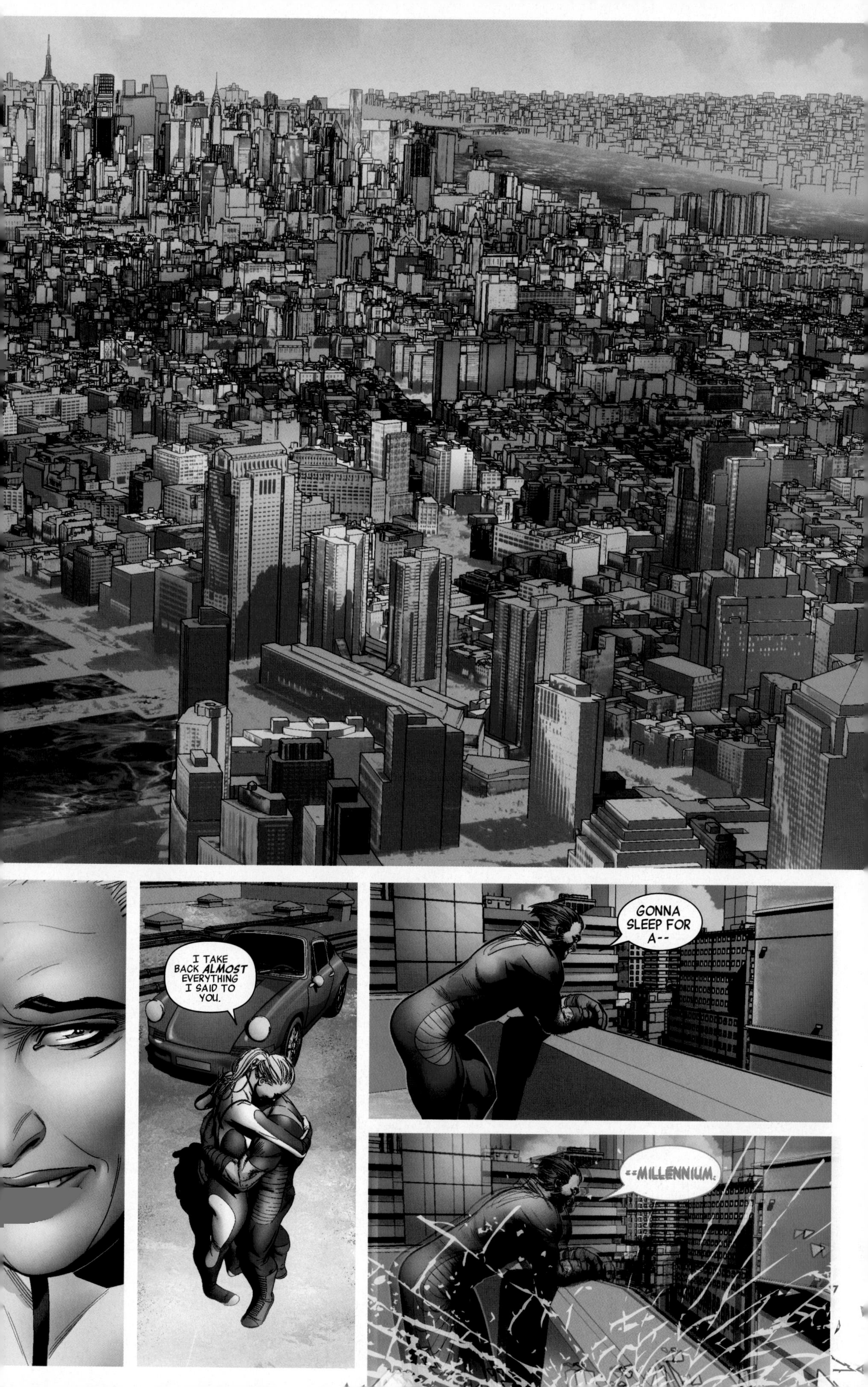
I TAKE BACK *ALMOST* EVERYTHING I SAID TO YOU.
GONNA SLEEP FOR A--
--MILLENNIUM.

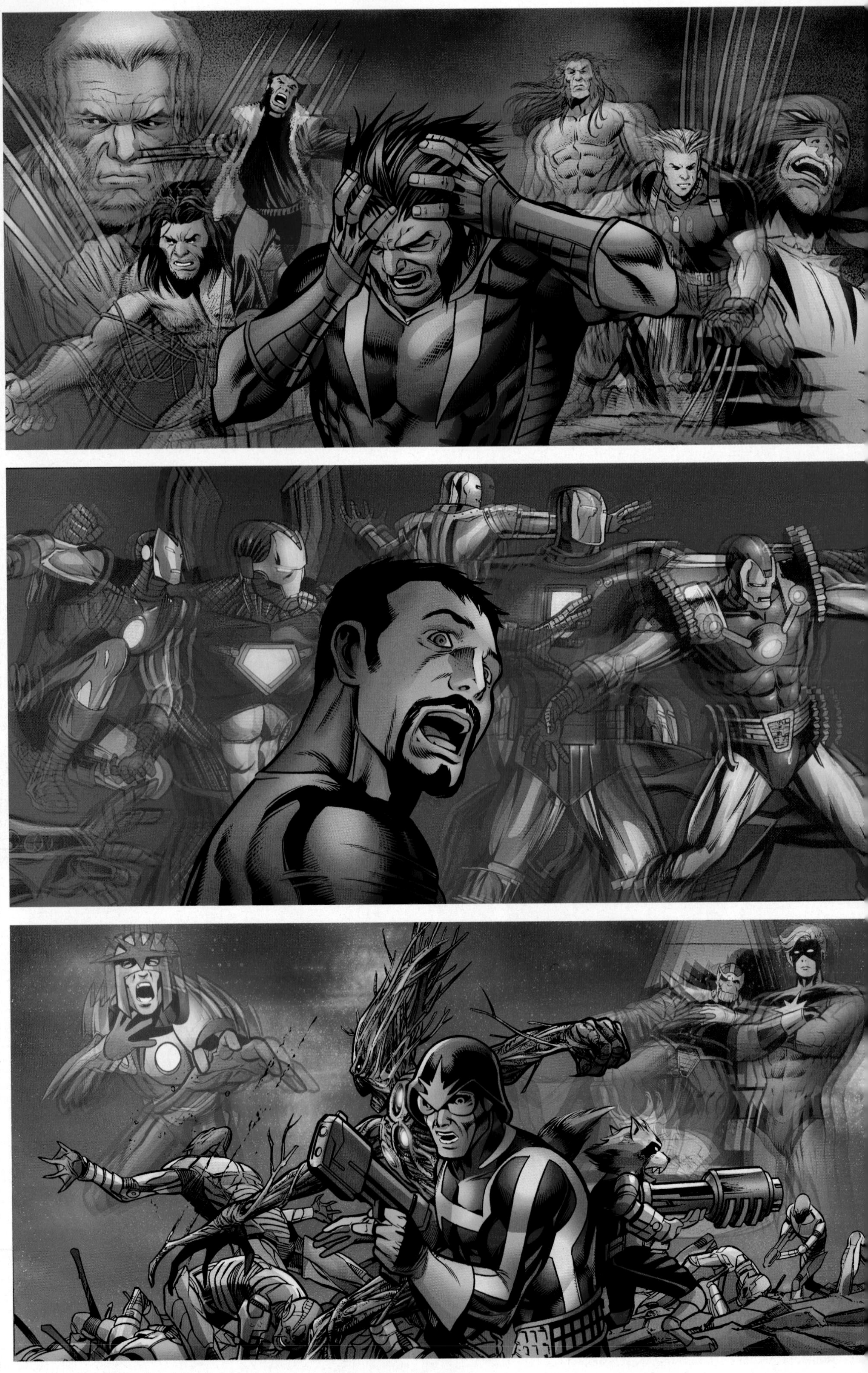

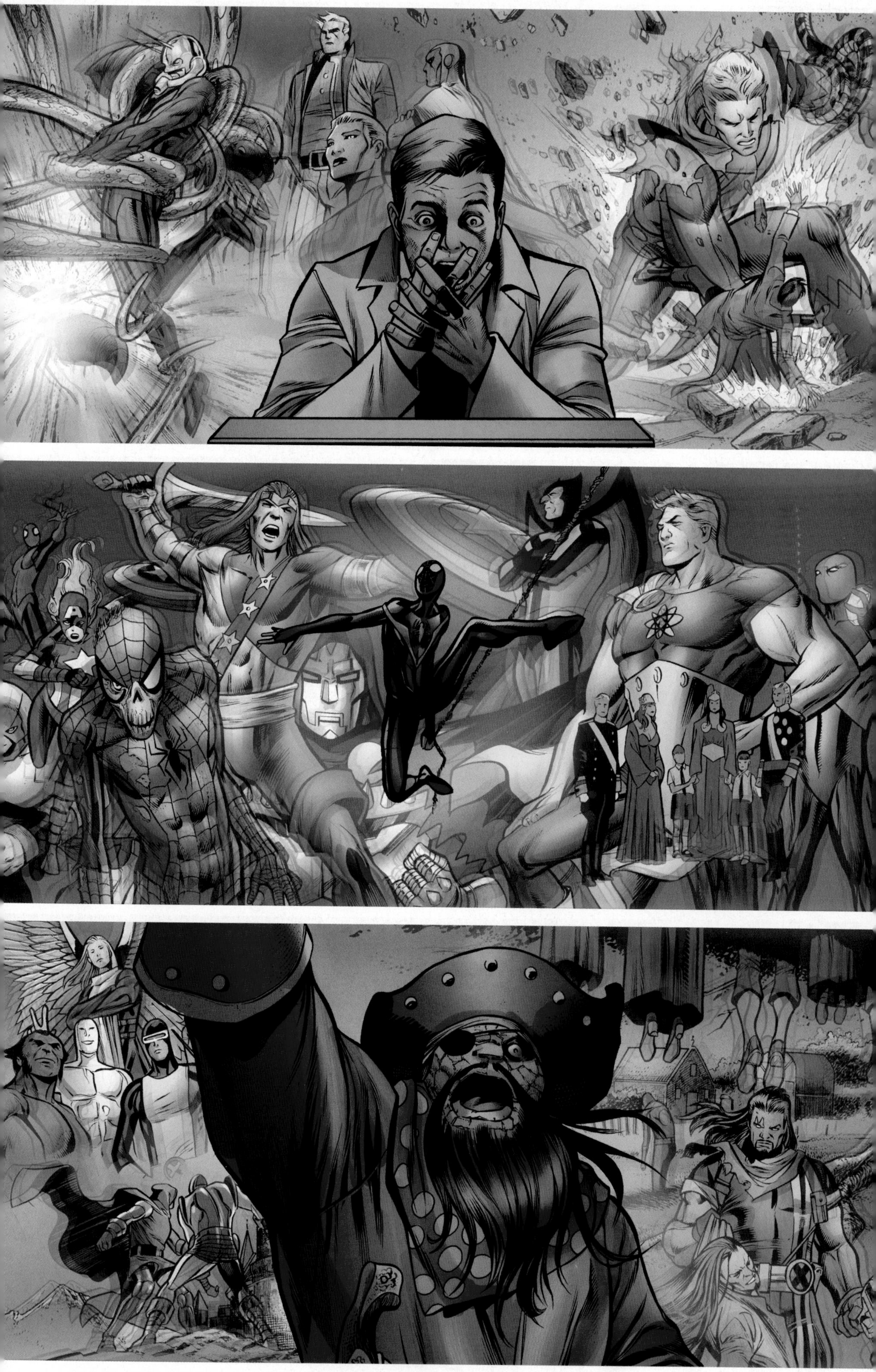

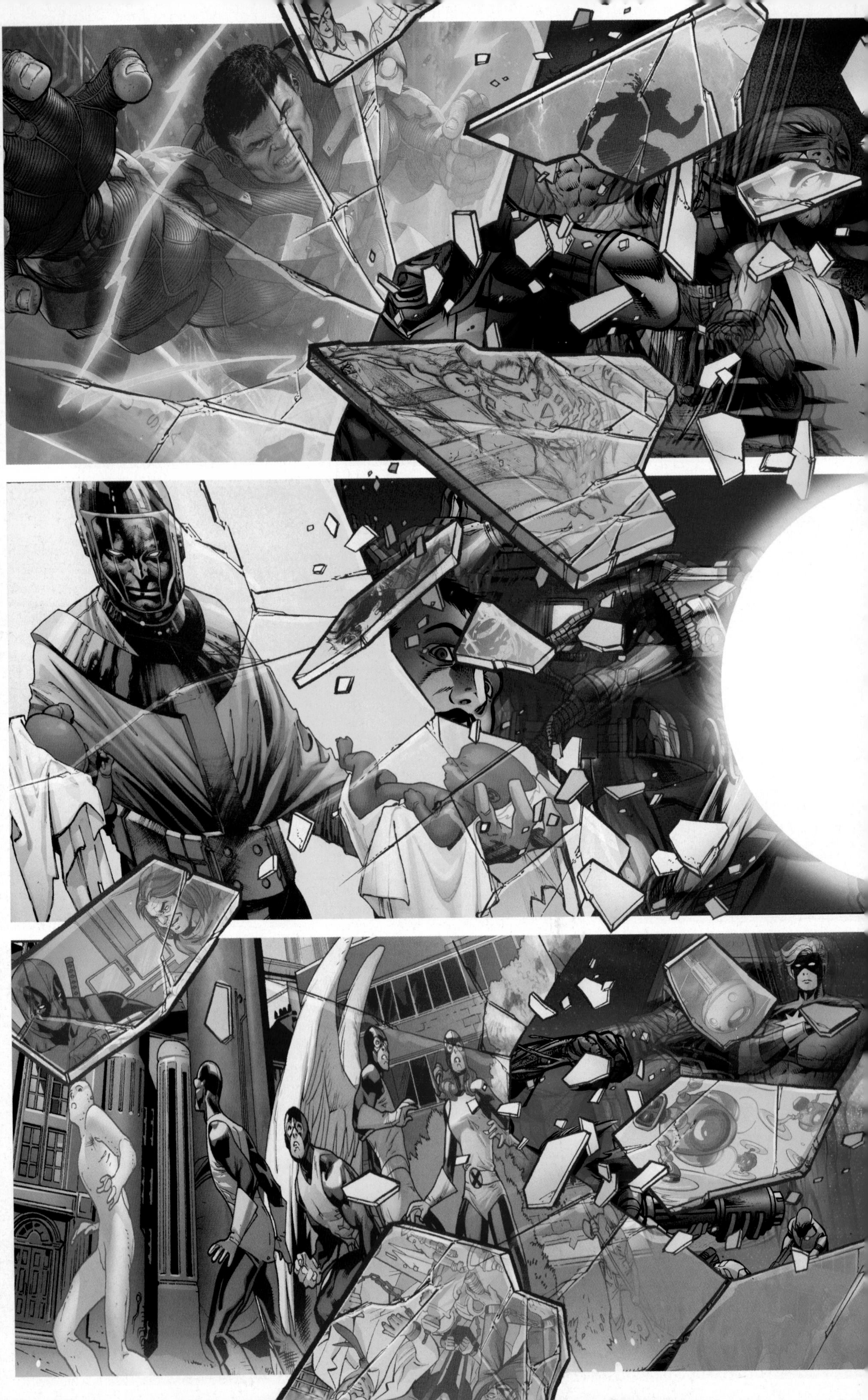

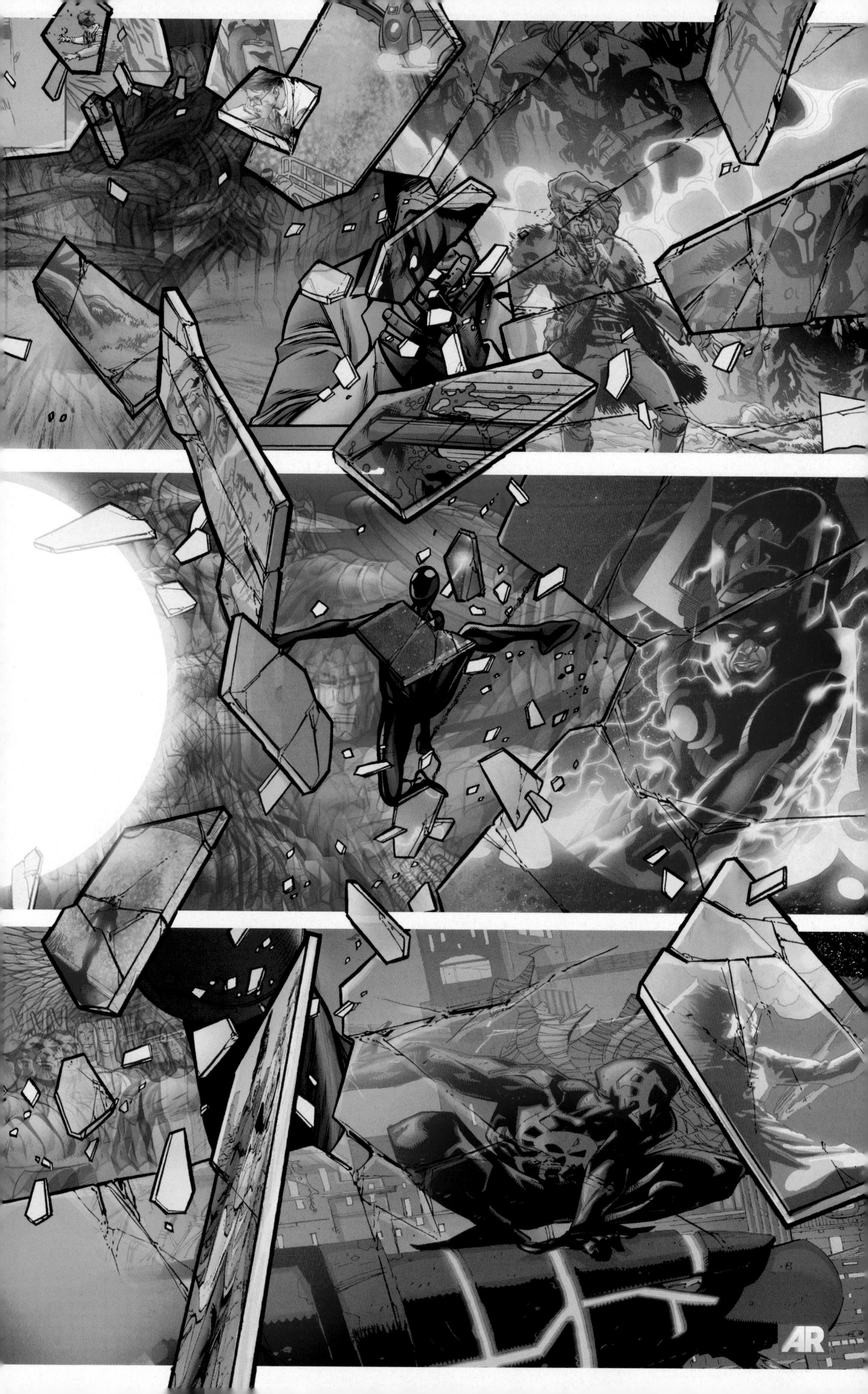

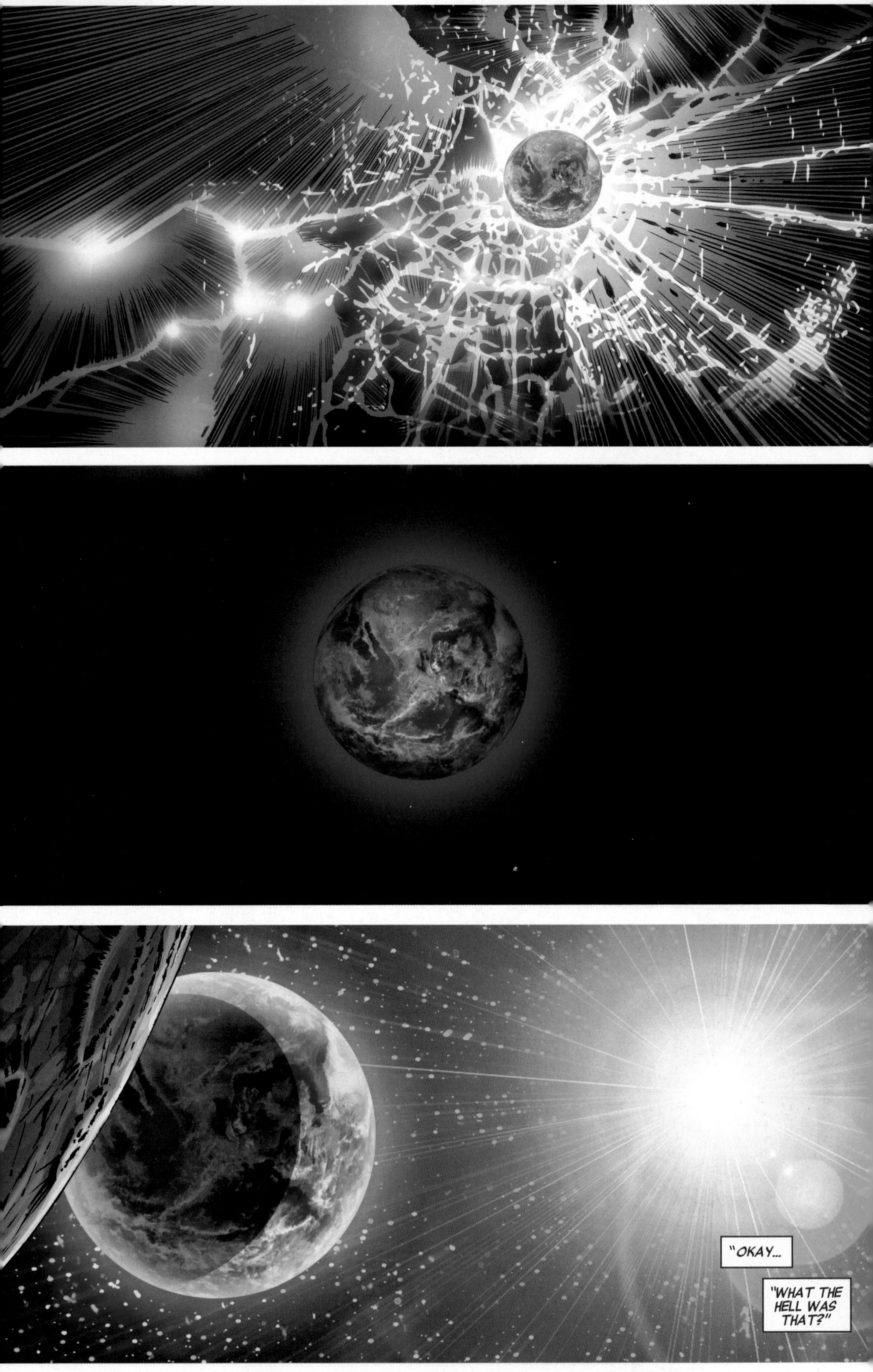
"OKAY...
"WHAT THE HELL WAS THAT?"

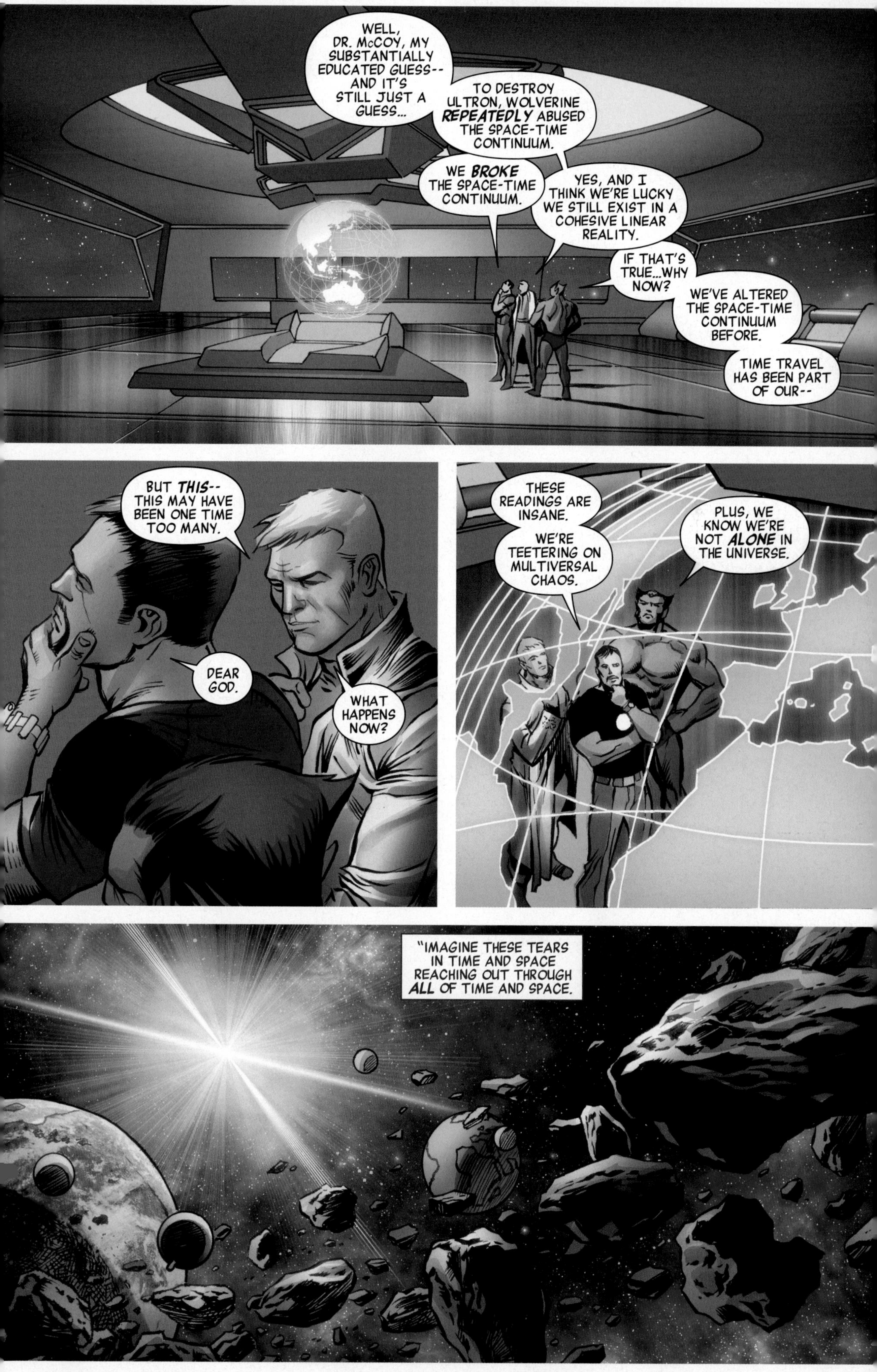
WELL, DR. McCOY, MY SUBSTANTIALLY EDUCATED GUESS-- AND IT'S STILL JUST A GUESS...
TO DESTROY ULTRON, WOLVERINE REPEATEDLY ABUSED THE SPACE-TIME CONTINUUM.
WE BROKE THE SPACE-TIME CONTINUUM.
YES, AND I THINK WE'RE LUCKY WE STILL EXIST IN A COHESIVE LINEAR REALITY.
IF THAT'S TRUE...WHY NOW?
WE'VE ALTERED THE SPACE-TIME CONTINUUM BEFORE.
TIME TRAVEL HAS BEEN PART OF OUR--
BUT THIS-- THIS MAY HAVE BEEN ONE TIME TOO MANY.
DEAR GOD.
WHAT HAPPENS NOW?
THESE READINGS ARE INSANE.
WE'RE TEETERING ON MULTIVERSAL CHAOS.
PLUS, WE KNOW WE'RE NOT ALONE IN THE UNIVERSE.
"IMAGINE THESE TEARS IN TIME AND SPACE REACHING OUT THROUGH ALL OF TIME AND SPACE.

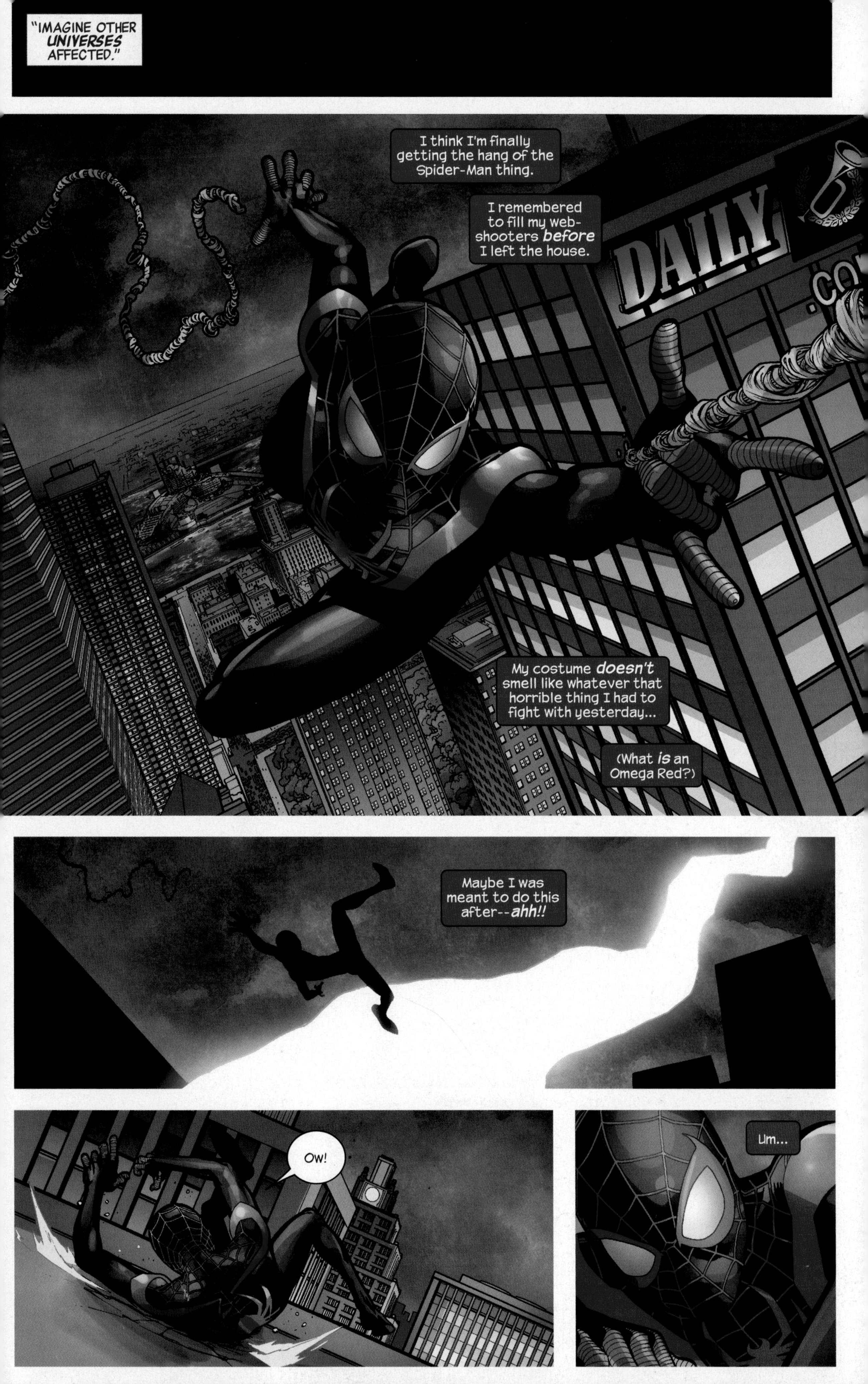
"IMAGINE OTHER UNIVERSES AFFECTED."
I think I'm finally getting the hang of the Spider-Man thing.
I remembered to fill my web-shooters before I left the house.
DAILY
My costume doesn't smell like whatever that horrible thing I had to fight with yesterday...
(What is an Omega Red?)
Maybe I was meant to do this after--ahh!!
Ow!
Um...

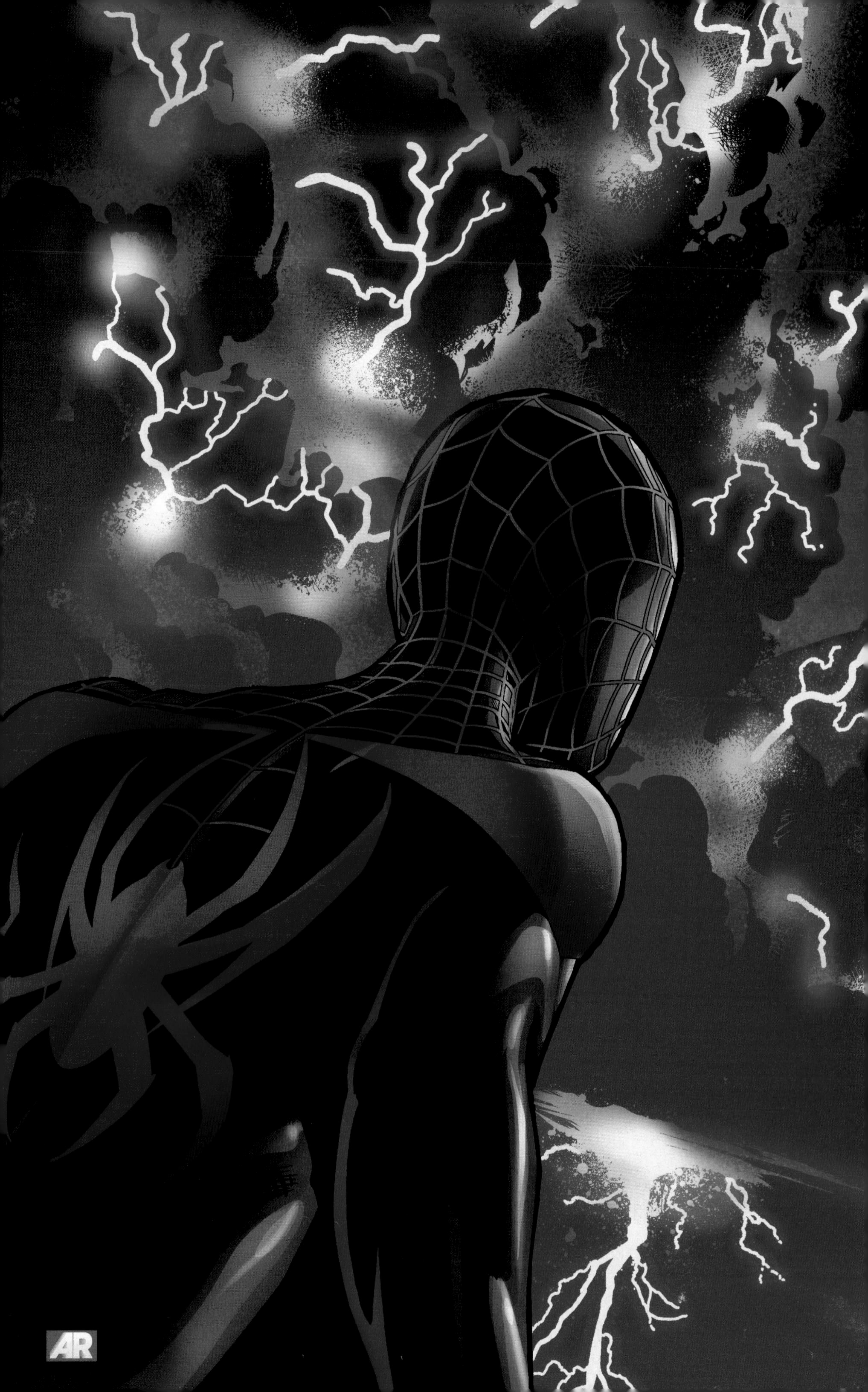

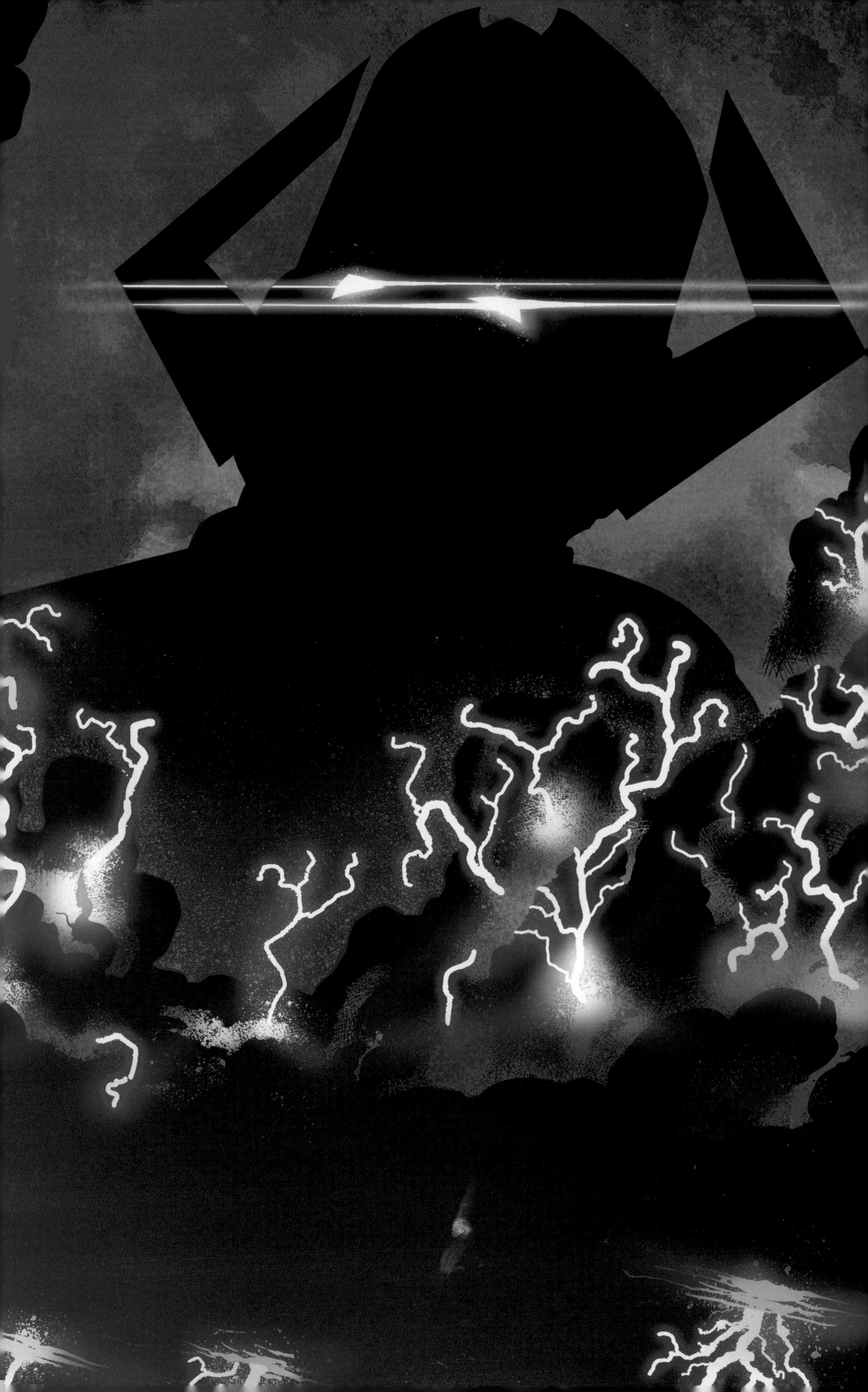

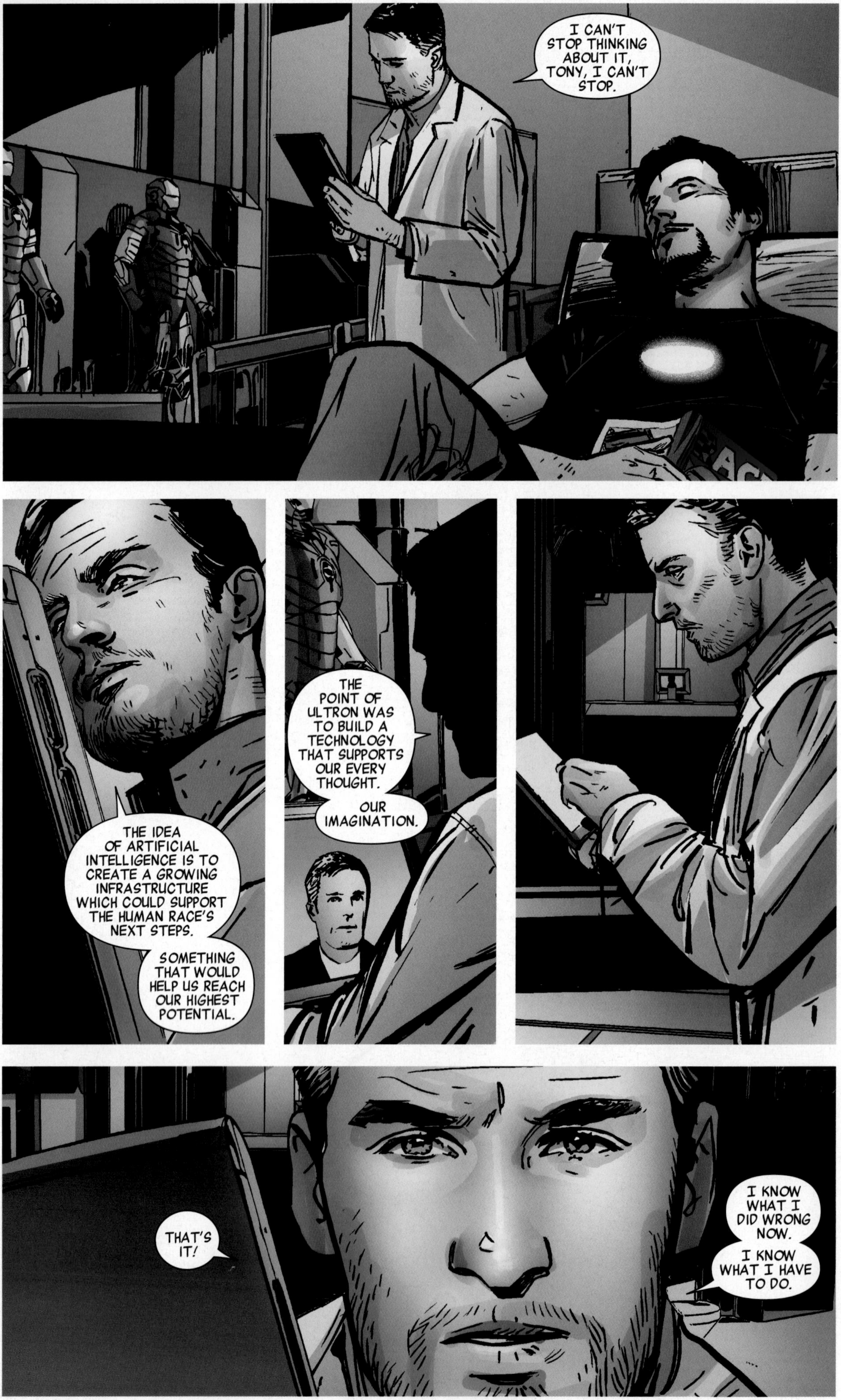
I CAN'T STOP THINKING ABOUT IT, TONY, I CAN'T STOP.
THE IDEA OF ARTIFICIAL INTELLIGENCE IS TO CREATE A GROWING INFRASTRUCTURE WHICH COULD SUPPORT THE HUMAN RACE'S NEXT STEPS.
SOMETHING THAT WOULD HELP US REACH OUR HIGHEST POTENTIAL.
THE POINT OF ULTRON WAS TO BUILD A TECHNOLOGY THAT SUPPORTS OUR EVERY THOUGHT.
OUR IMAGINATION.
THAT'S IT!
I KNOW WHAT I DID WRONG NOW.
I KNOW WHAT I HAVE TO DO.

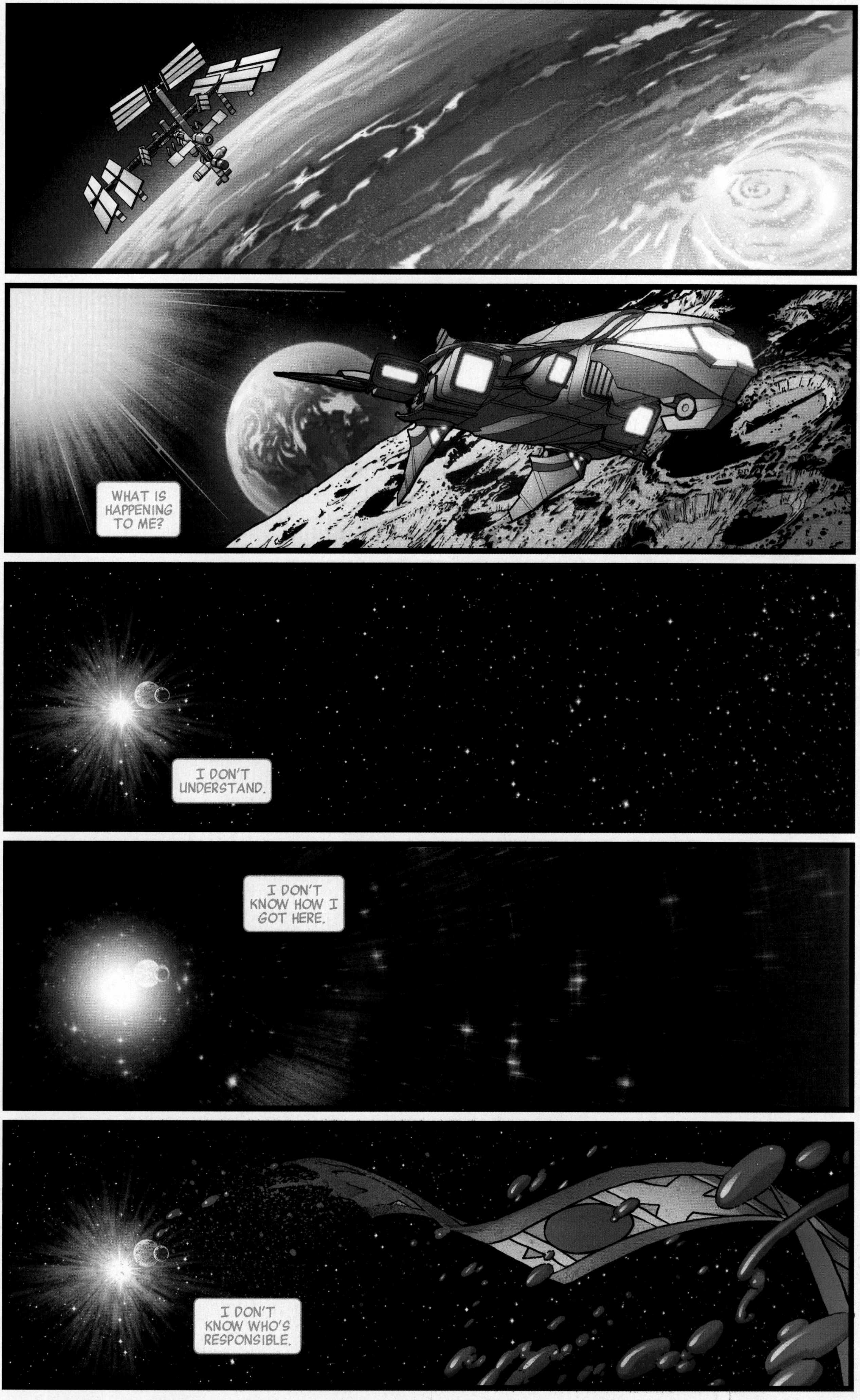
WHAT IS HAPPENING TO ME?
I DON'T UNDERSTAND.
I DON'T KNOW HOW I GOT HERE.
I DON'T KNOW WHO'S RESPONSIBLE.

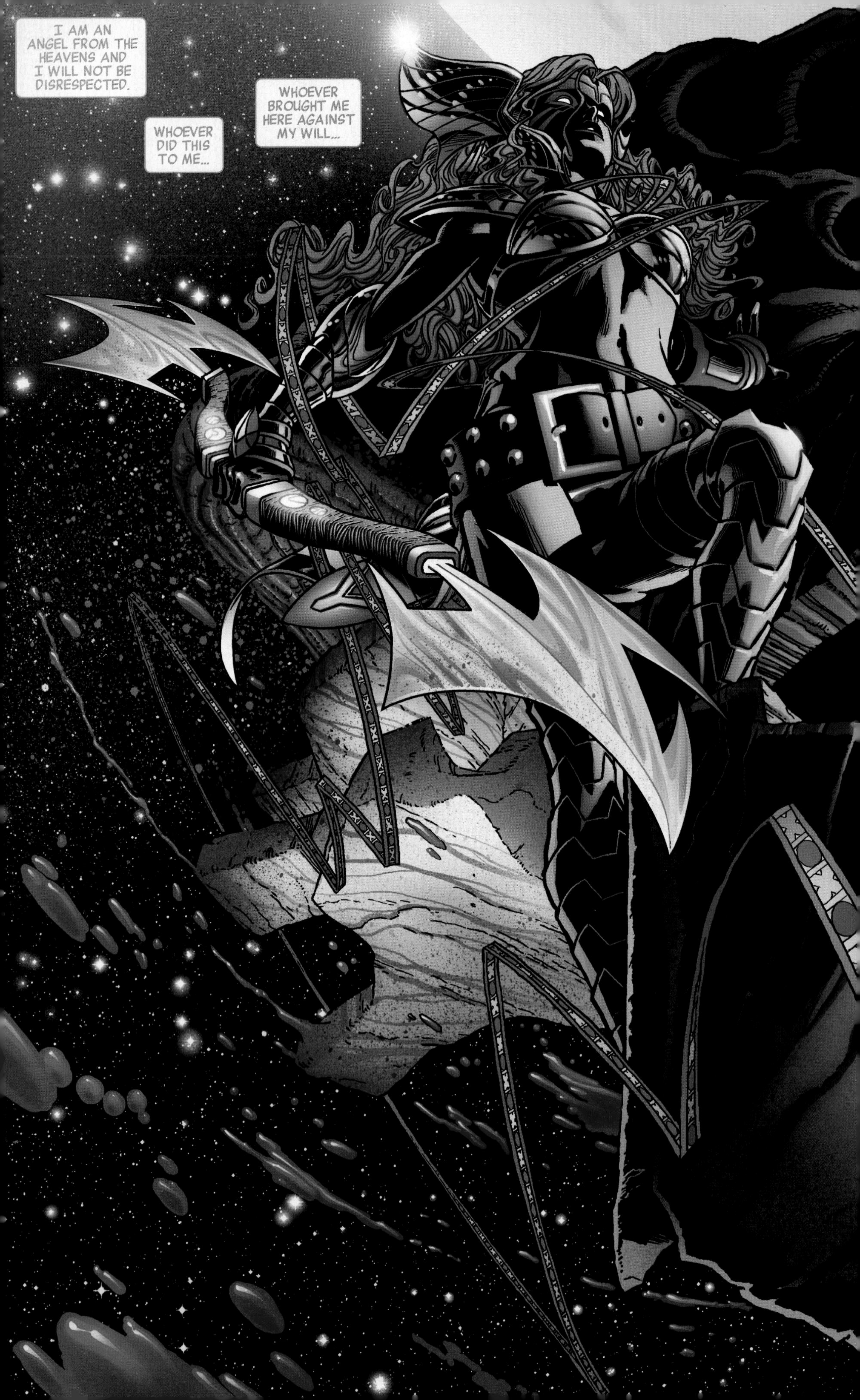
I AM AN ANGEL FROM THE HEAVENS AND I WILL NOT BE DISRESPECTED.
WHOEVER DID THIS TO ME...
WHOEVER BROUGHT ME HERE AGAINST MY WILL...

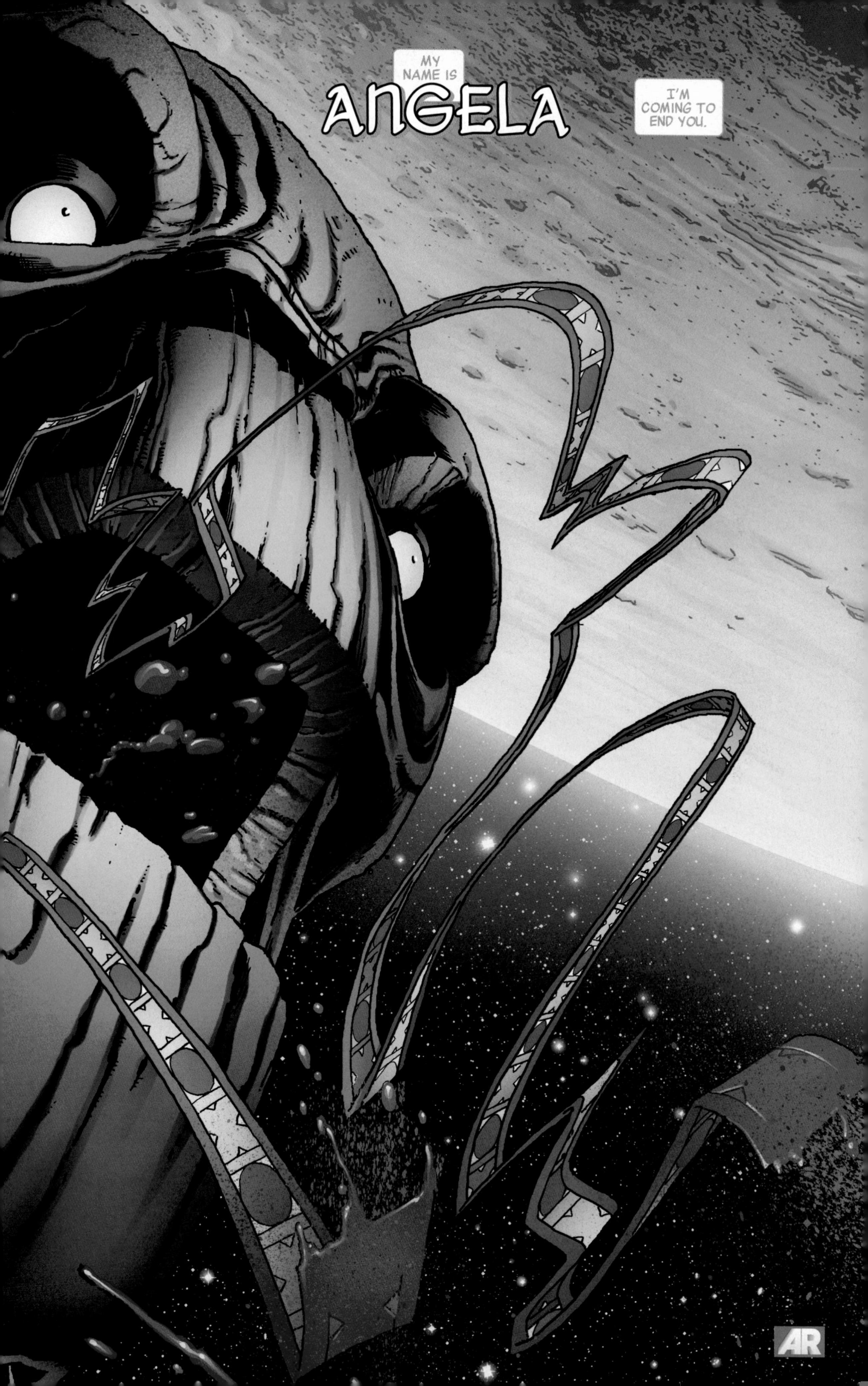
MY NAME IS
ANGELA
I'M COMING TO END YOU.

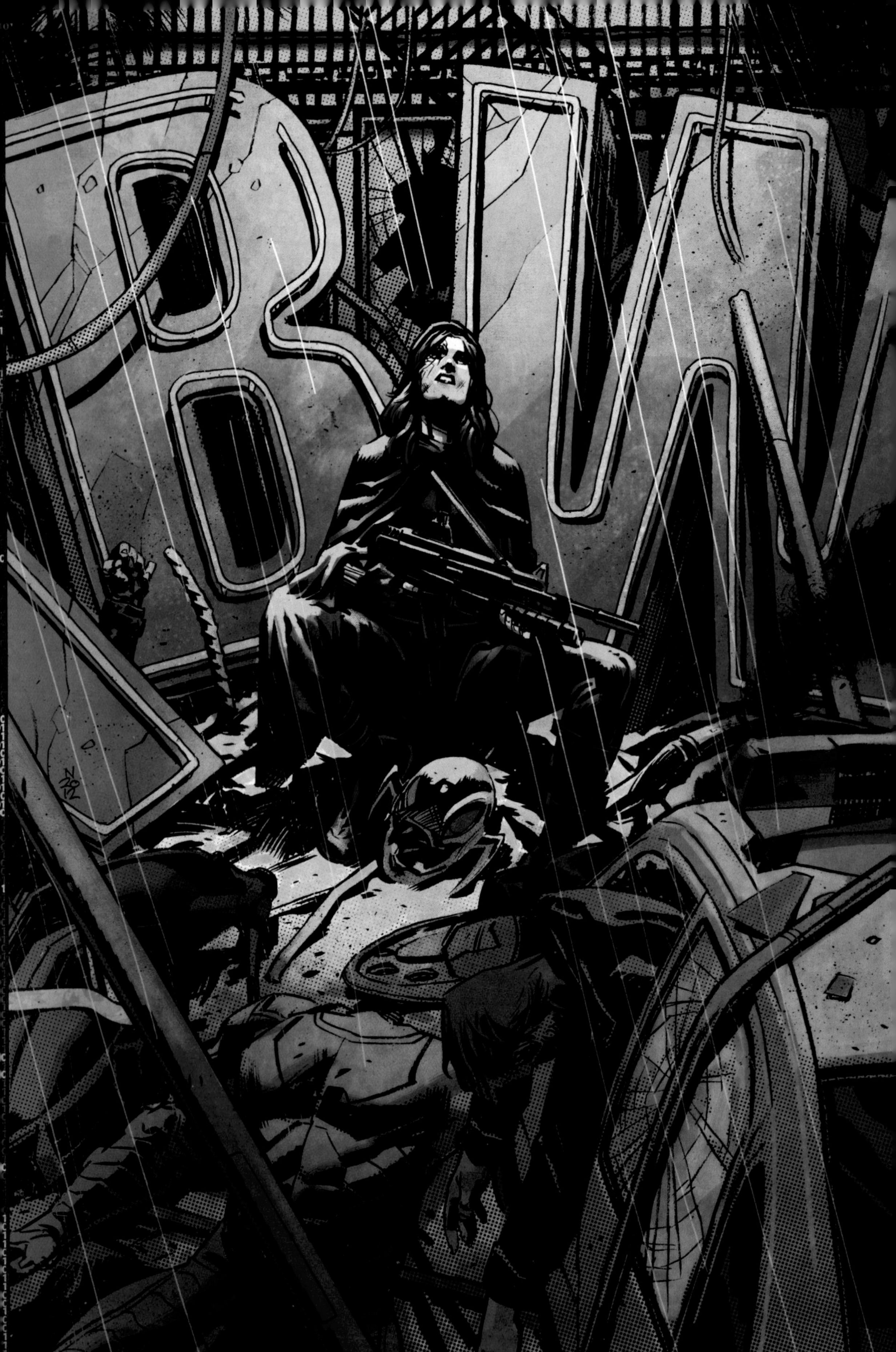

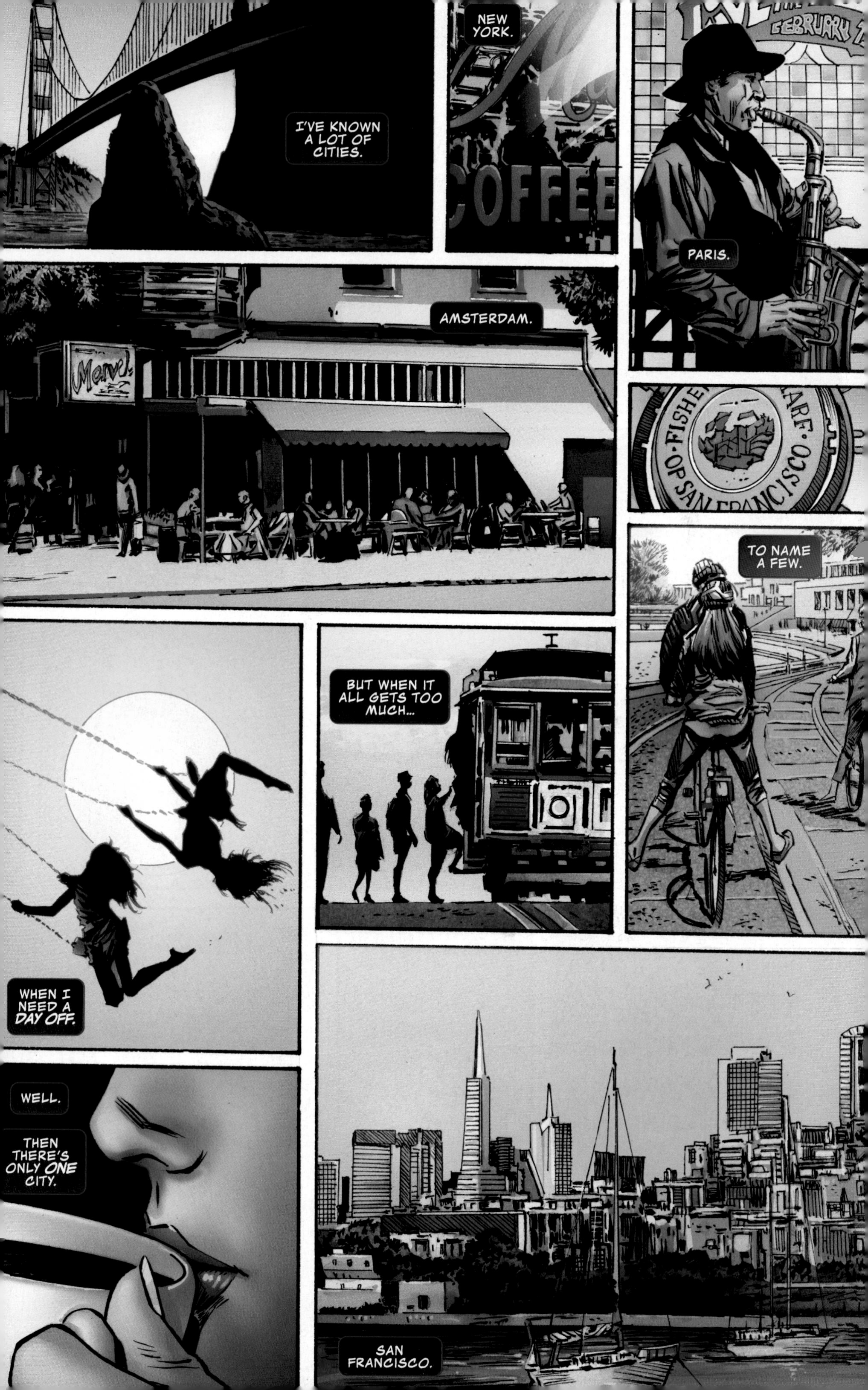
I'VE KNOWN A LOT OF CITIES.
NEW YORK.
COFFEE
PARIS.
AMSTERDAM.
TO NAME A FEW.
BUT WHEN IT ALL GETS TOO MUCH...
WHEN I NEED A DAY OFF.
WELL.
THEN THERE'S ONLY ONE CITY.
SAN FRANCISCO.

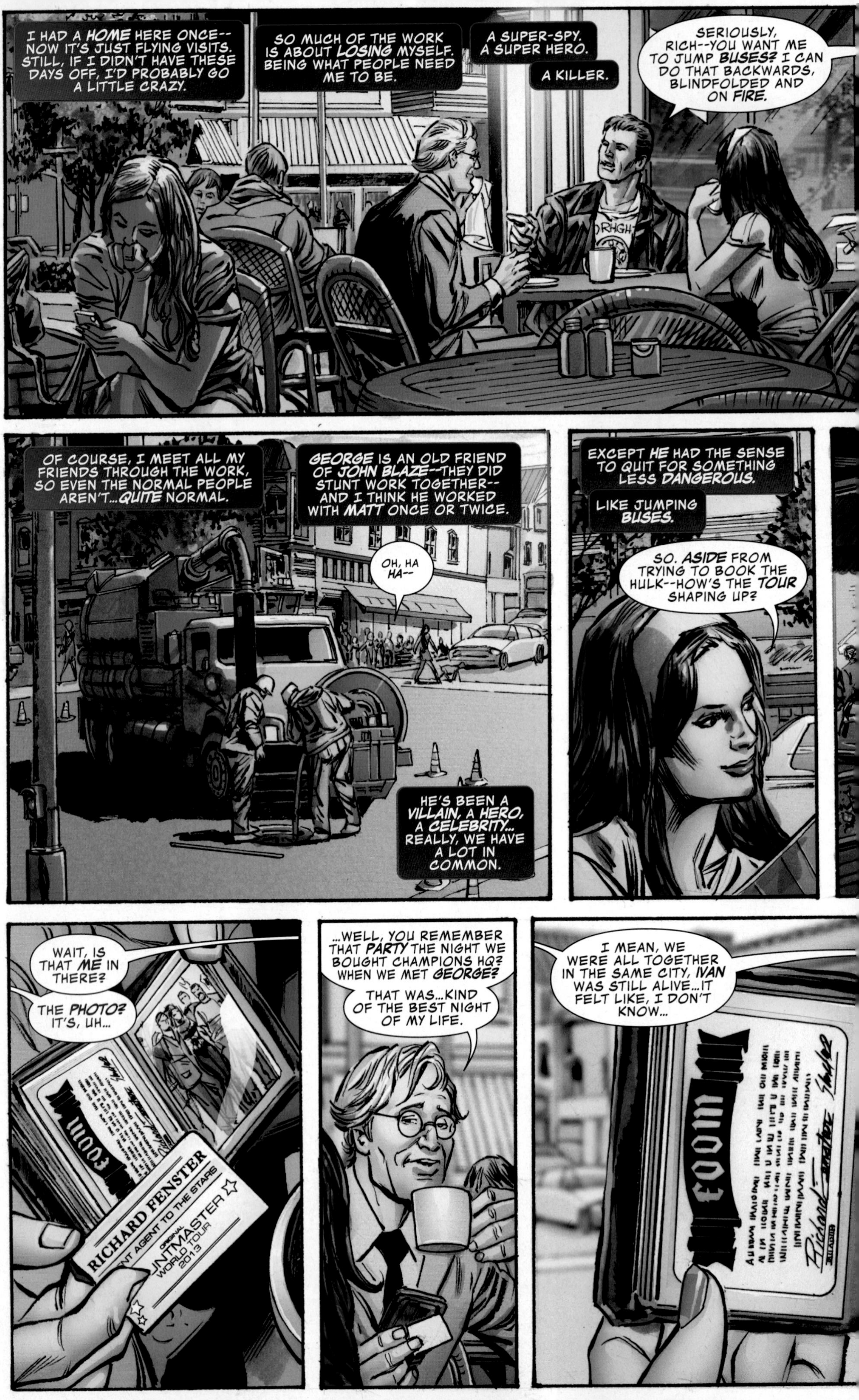

I HAD A HOME HERE ONCE--NOW IT'S JUST FLYING VISITS. STILL, IF I DIDN'T HAVE THESE DAYS OFF, I'D PROBABLY GO A LITTLE CRAZY.
SO MUCH OF THE WORK IS ABOUT LOSING MYSELF. BEING WHAT PEOPLE NEED ME TO BE.
A SUPER-SPY. A SUPER HERO.
A KILLER.
SERIOUSLY, RICH--YOU WANT ME TO JUMP BUSES? I CAN DO THAT BACKWARDS, BLINDFOLDED AND ON FIRE.
OF COURSE, I MEET ALL MY FRIENDS THROUGH THE WORK, SO EVEN THE NORMAL PEOPLE AREN'T...QUITE NORMAL.
GEORGE IS AN OLD FRIEND OF JOHN BLAZE--THEY DID STUNT WORK TOGETHER--AND I THINK HE WORKED WITH MATT ONCE OR TWICE.
OH, HA HA--
HE'S BEEN A VILLAIN, A HERO, A CELEBRITY... REALLY, WE HAVE A LOT IN COMMON.
EXCEPT HE HAD THE SENSE TO QUIT FOR SOMETHING LESS DANGEROUS.
LIKE JUMPING BUSES.
SO. ASIDE FROM TRYING TO BOOK THE HULK--HOW'S THE TOUR SHAPING UP?
WAIT, IS THAT ME IN THERE?
THE PHOTO? IT'S, UH...
RICHARD FENSTER
AGENT TO THE STARS
ORIGINAL
WORLD TOUR
2013
...WELL, YOU REMEMBER THAT PARTY THE NIGHT WE BOUGHT CHAMPIONS HQ? WHEN WE MET GEORGE?
THAT WAS...KIND OF THE BEST NIGHT OF MY LIFE.
I MEAN, WE WERE ALL TOGETHER IN THE SAME CITY, IVAN WAS STILL ALIVE...IT FELT LIKE, I DON'T KNOW...

BUT IF YOU WANT ME TO JUMP THE *HULK* WHILE HE'S *JUGGLING* BUSES... BACK ME UP HERE, NAT.

IT'S NICE TO HAVE SOME PEOPLE WHO JUST NEED ME TO BE ME.

HE'S ACTUALLY A VERY *GOOD* JUGGLER...

NORMAL PEOPLE.

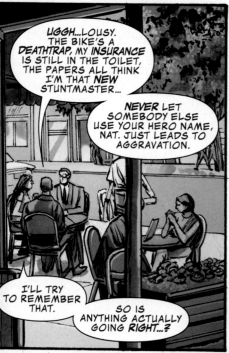

UGGH...LOUSY. THE BIKE'S A *DEATHTRAP,* MY *INSURANCE* IS STILL IN THE TOILET, THE PAPERS ALL THINK I'M THAT *NEW* STUNTMASTER...

NEVER LET SOMEBODY ELSE USE YOUR HERO NAME, NAT. JUST LEADS TO AGGRAVATION.

I'LL TRY TO REMEMBER THAT.

SO IS ANYTHING ACTUALLY GOING *RIGHT...?*

WELL...UH...

I MADE SOME BUSINESS CARDS?

RICHARD IS GEORGE'S *AGENT.* HE USED TO BE THE P.R. MAN FOR A *TEAM* I RAN ONCE.

IT WAS A COMPLETE *DISASTER,* BUT THAT WASN'T *HIS* FAULT.

BUSINESS CARDS.

MADE WITH REAL *CARD,* TOO. TAKE A LOOK.

...LIKE WE WERE DOING SOMETHING *GOOD...*

CHEAP SENTIMENT, I GUESS. SORRY.

DON'T BE.

ALL RIGHT.

NOT A *COMPLETE* DISASTER.

HEY, REMEMBER *BOBBY* THROWING UP IN THE ELEVATOR?

OH LORD, IT WAS LIKE A *SLURPEE*--

THEY'RE GOOD PEOPLE. GOOD *FRIENDS.* LIKE I SAID, WITHOUT MOMENTS LIKE THESE-- PEOPLE LIKE THIS--

--I'D GO A LITTLE CRAZY.

GEORGE, IS THAT A NEW PROSTHETIC?

IT'S FROM THE SPONSORS...

THE LAST TIME GEORGE WAS IN COSTUME, IT DIDN'T GO WELL.

ONE OF THOSE GIANT, IMPENETRABLE MYSTIC BARRIERS THAT SPRING UP SOMETIMES. EVEN THE THING COULDN'T PUNCH THROUGH IT.

...RESILIENT-- THAT TECH COMPANY. IT'S A PROTOTYPE THEY'RE FIELD-TESTING.

SO GEORGE DROVE HIS BIKE AT IT AT TWO HUNDRED MILES PER HOUR.

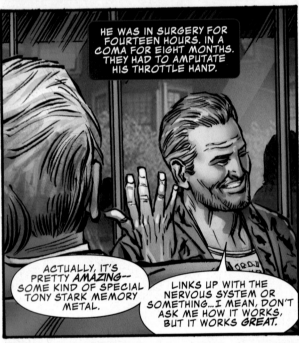

HE WAS IN SURGERY FOR FOURTEEN HOURS. IN A COMA FOR EIGHT MONTHS. THEY HAD TO AMPUTATE HIS THROTTLE HAND.

ACTUALLY, IT'S PRETTY AMAZING-- SOME KIND OF SPECIAL TONY STARK MEMORY METAL.

LINKS UP WITH THE NERVOUS SYSTEM OR SOMETHING...I MEAN, DON'T ASK ME HOW IT WORKS, BUT IT WORKS GREAT.

AND IF HE THOUGHT IT'D HELP, HE'D DO IT ALL AGAIN.

IT'S EVEN GOT WI-FI. IT'LL CALL THE PARAMEDICS IF MY HEART STOPS BEATING--

GEORGE, WITH YOU IT'S A WHEN. YOU'RE JUMPING BUSES AND PRODUCT-TESTING AT THE SAME TIME?

I'M MULTITASKING?

I'LL TELL YOU WHAT YOU ARE...

BETWEEN THE SUNSHINE AND THE COMPANY, THIS REALLY IS THE NICEST DAY I'VE HAD IN A WHILE.

IT'S SO NICE I ALMOST DON'T LISTEN TO THE STARKPAD ON THE NEXT TABLE.

--TAKING YOU LIVE TO THE SCENE IN NEW YORK, WHERE SOME KIND OF CRISIS IS--

--POSSIBLE TERRORIST ATTACKS--

ACTION 12 NEWS

SPECIAL REPORT

BREAKING NEWS -- DEADLY ATTACK

ALMOST.

SPECIAL REP

--UH--

--WE SEEM TO HAVE LOST NEW YORK--

EXPLOSION

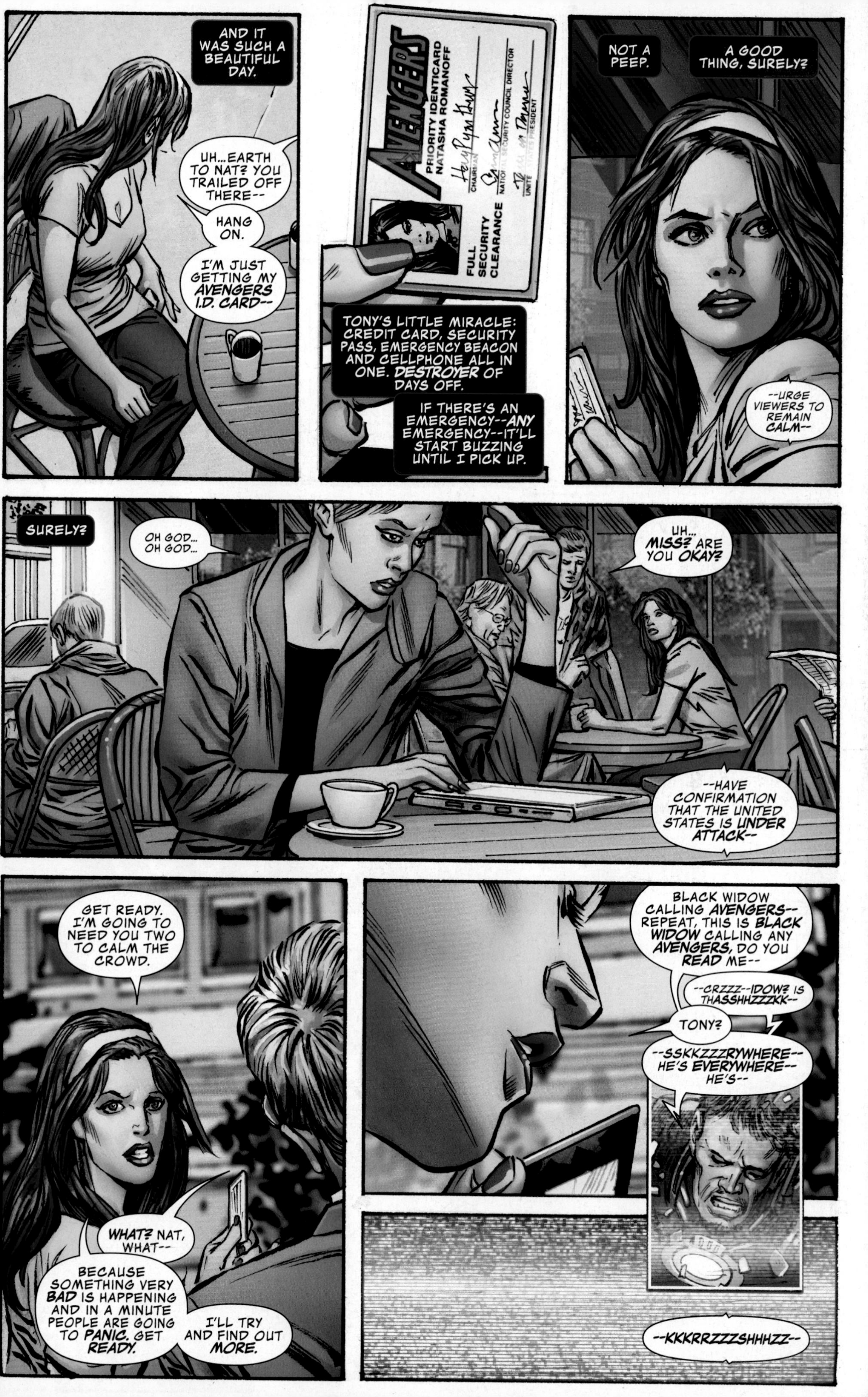
AND IT WAS SUCH A BEAUTIFUL DAY.
UH...EARTH TO NAT? YOU TRAILED OFF THERE--
HANG ON.
I'M JUST GETTING MY AVENGERS I.D. CARD--
AVENGERS
PRIORITY IDENTICARD
NATASHA ROMANOFF
CHAIRMAN
NATIONAL SECURITY COUNCIL DIRECTOR
UNITED STATES PRESIDENT
FULL SECURITY CLEARANCE
TONY'S LITTLE MIRACLE: CREDIT CARD, SECURITY PASS, EMERGENCY BEACON AND CELLPHONE ALL IN ONE. DESTROYER OF DAYS OFF.
IF THERE'S AN EMERGENCY--ANY EMERGENCY--IT'LL START BUZZING UNTIL I PICK UP.
NOT A PEEP.
A GOOD THING, SURELY?
--URGE VIEWERS TO REMAIN CALM--
SURELY?
OH GOD... OH GOD...
UH... MISS? ARE YOU OKAY?
--HAVE CONFIRMATION THAT THE UNITED STATES IS UNDER ATTACK--
GET READY. I'M GOING TO NEED YOU TWO TO CALM THE CROWD.
WHAT? NAT, WHAT--
BECAUSE SOMETHING VERY BAD IS HAPPENING AND IN A MINUTE PEOPLE ARE GOING TO PANIC. GET READY.
I'LL TRY AND FIND OUT MORE.
BLACK WIDOW CALLING AVENGERS--REPEAT, THIS IS BLACK WIDOW CALLING ANY AVENGERS, DO YOU READ ME--
--CRZZZ--IDOW? IS THASSHHZZZKK--
TONY?
--SSKKZZZZRYWHERE--HE'S EVERYWHERE--HE'S--
--KKKRRZZZSHHHZZ--

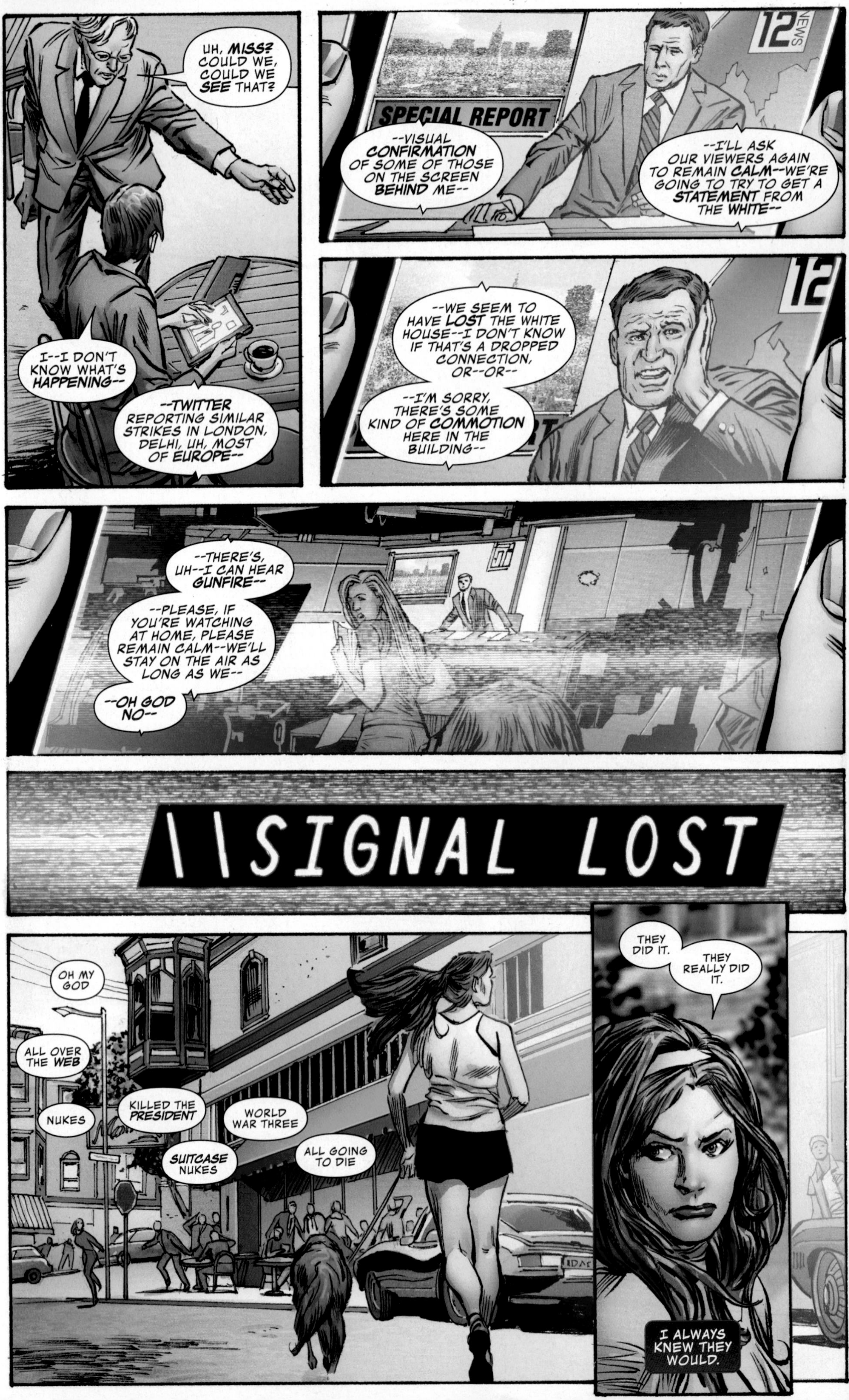
UH, MISS? COULD WE, COULD WE SEE THAT?
I--I DON'T KNOW WHAT'S HAPPENING--
--TWITTER REPORTING SIMILAR STRIKES IN LONDON, DELHI, UH, MOST OF EUROPE--
12 NEWS
SPECIAL REPORT
--VISUAL CONFIRMATION OF SOME OF THOSE ON THE SCREEN BEHIND ME--
--I'LL ASK OUR VIEWERS AGAIN TO REMAIN CALM--WE'RE GOING TO TRY TO GET A STATEMENT FROM THE WHITE--
12
--WE SEEM TO HAVE LOST THE WHITE HOUSE--I DON'T KNOW IF THAT'S A DROPPED CONNECTION, OR--OR--
--I'M SORRY, THERE'S SOME KIND OF COMMOTION HERE IN THE BUILDING--
--THERE'S, UH--I CAN HEAR GUNFIRE--
--PLEASE, IF YOU'RE WATCHING AT HOME, PLEASE REMAIN CALM--WE'LL STAY ON THE AIR AS LONG AS WE--
--OH GOD NO--
\\SIGNAL LOST
OH MY GOD
ALL OVER THE WEB
NUKES
KILLED THE PRESIDENT
WORLD WAR THREE
SUITCASE NUKES
ALL GOING TO DIE
THEY DID IT.
THEY REALLY DID IT.
I ALWAYS KNEW THEY WOULD.

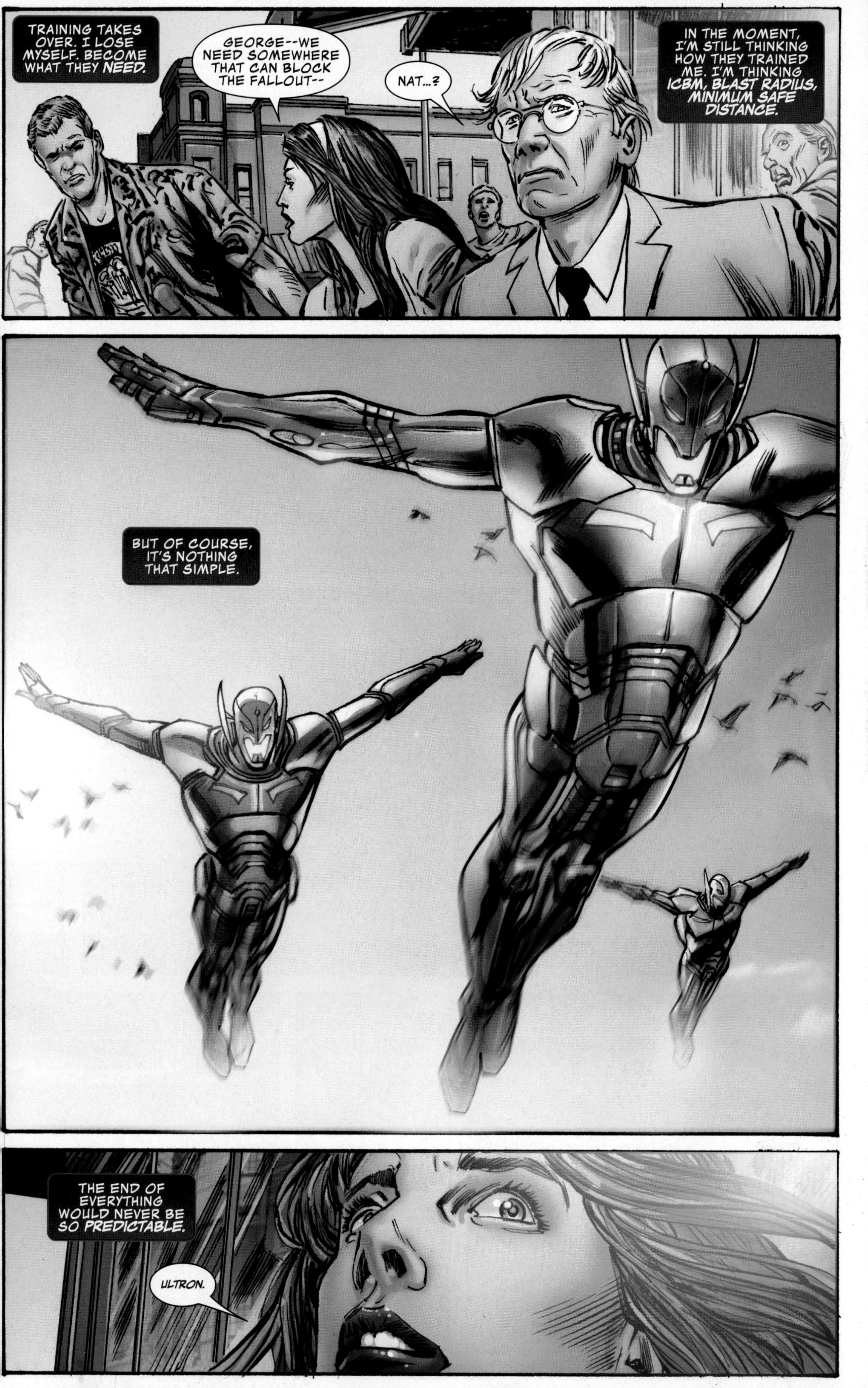
TRAINING TAKES OVER. I LOSE MYSELF. BECOME WHAT THEY NEED.
GEORGE--WE NEED SOMEWHERE THAT CAN BLOCK THE FALLOUT--
NAT...?
IN THE MOMENT, I'M STILL THINKING HOW THEY TRAINED ME. I'M THINKING ICBM, BLAST RADIUS, MINIMUM SAFE DISTANCE.
BUT OF COURSE, IT'S NOTHING THAT SIMPLE.
THE END OF EVERYTHING WOULD NEVER BE SO PREDICTABLE.
ULTRON.

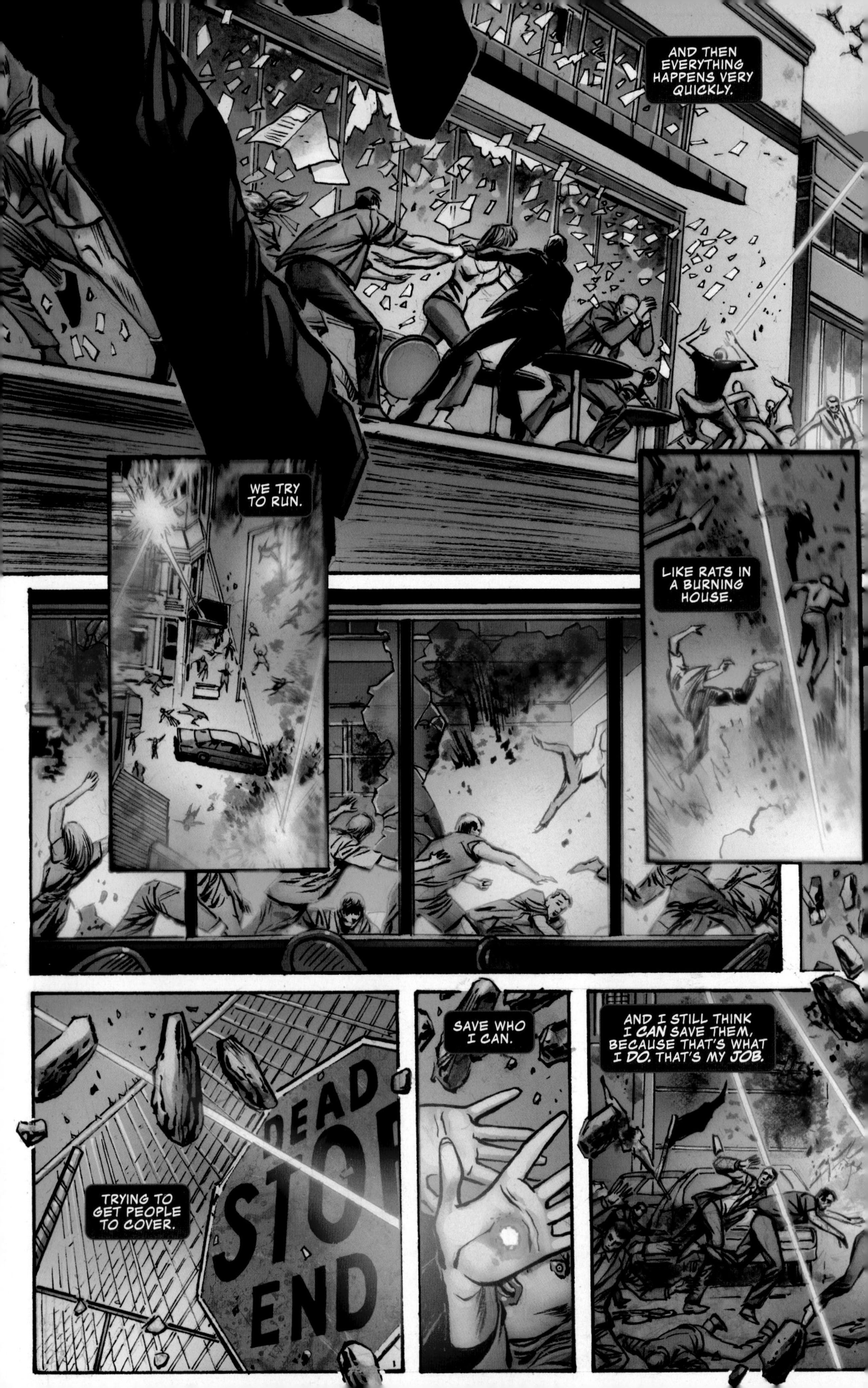
AND THEN EVERYTHING HAPPENS VERY QUICKLY.
WE TRY TO RUN.
LIKE RATS IN A BURNING HOUSE.
TRYING TO GET PEOPLE TO COVER.
DEAD STOP END
SAVE WHO I CAN.
AND I STILL THINK I CAN SAVE THEM, BECAUSE THAT'S WHAT I DO. THAT'S MY JOB.

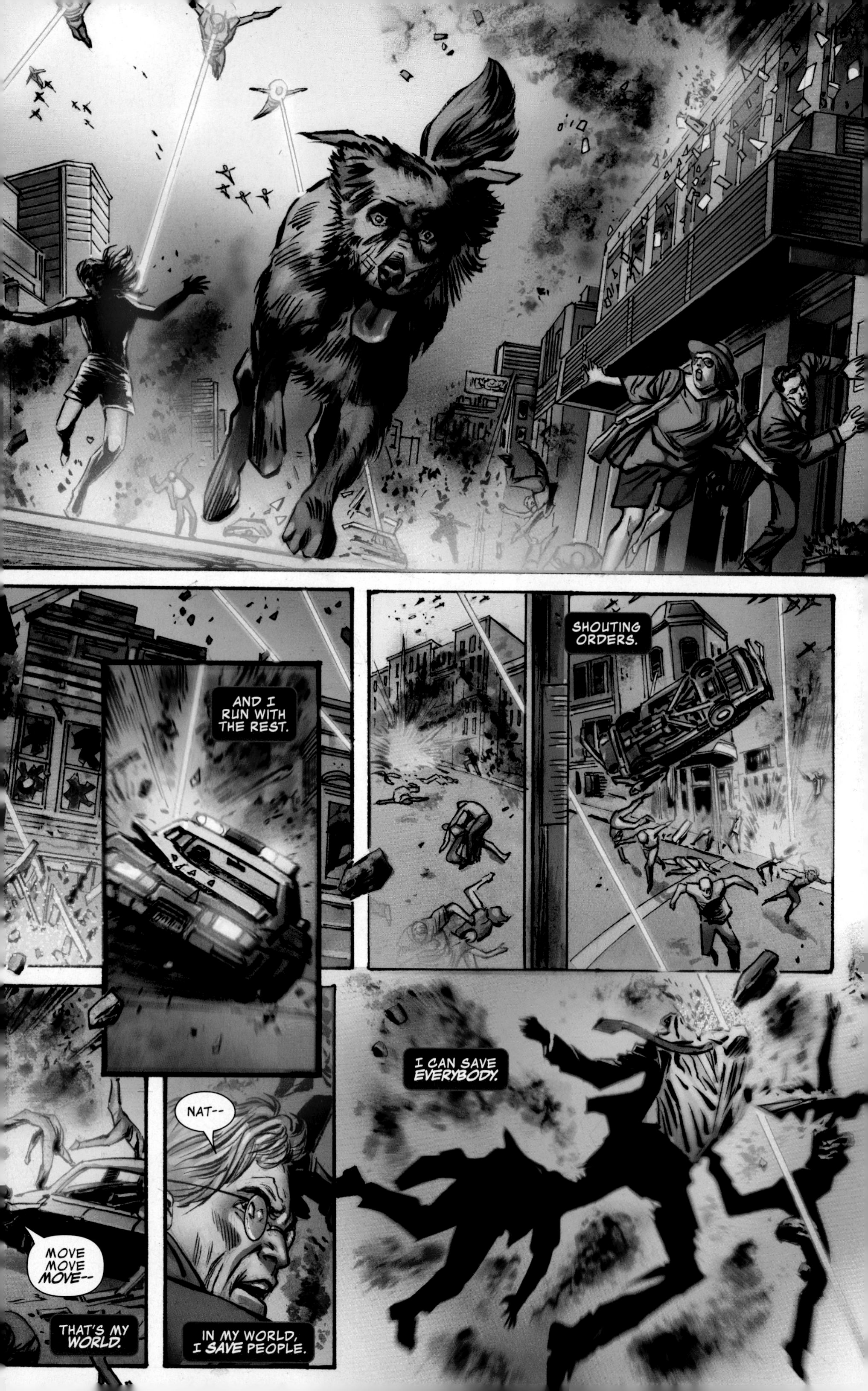
AND I RUN WITH THE REST.
SHOUTING ORDERS.
MOVE MOVE MOVE--
THAT'S MY WORLD.
NAT--
IN MY WORLD, I SAVE PEOPLE.
I CAN SAVE EVERYBODY.

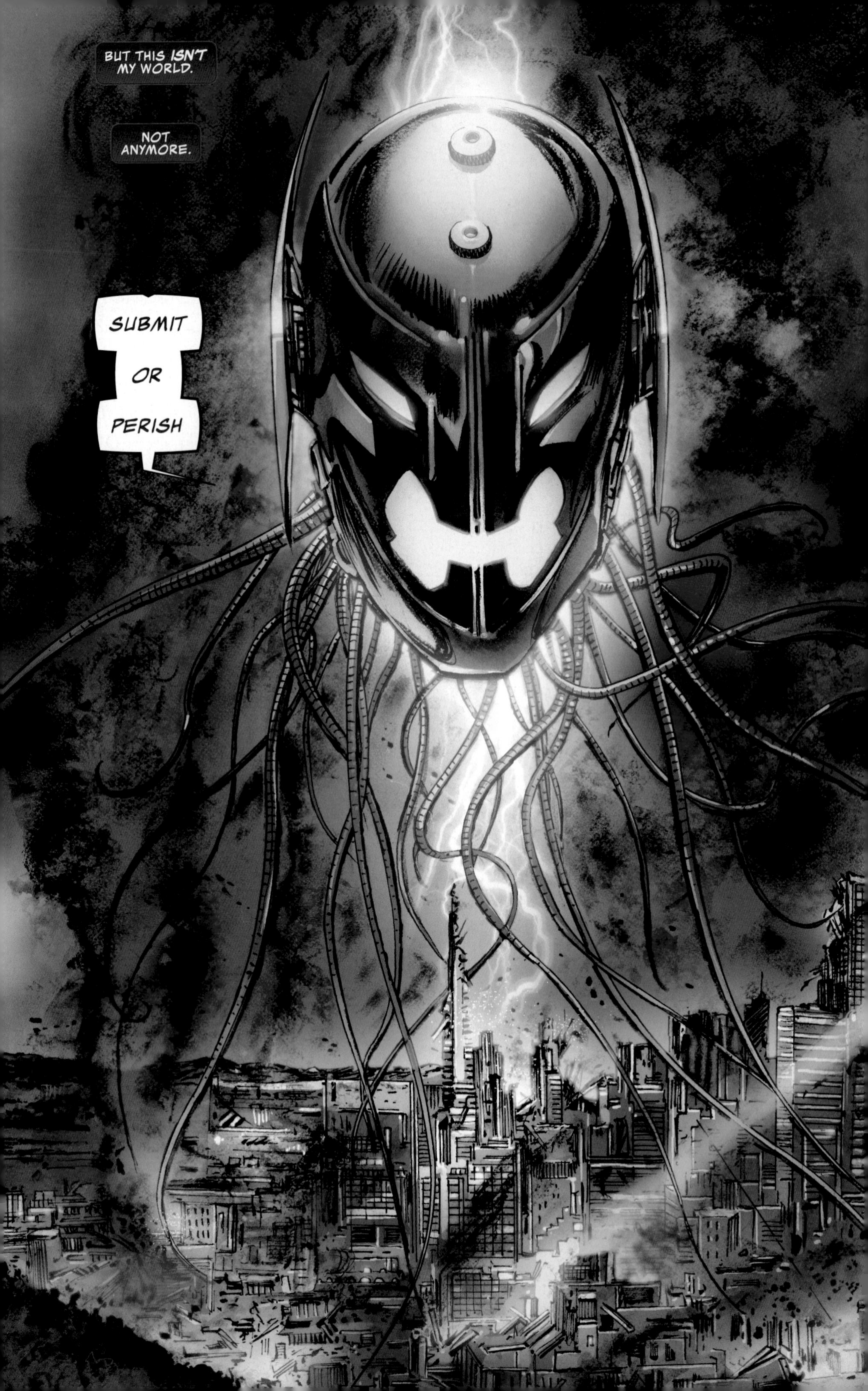
BUT THIS ISN'T MY WORLD.
NOT ANYMORE.
SUBMIT OR PERISH

SUBMIT OR PERISH

OH GOD, IT'S...IT'S IN THE *SKY*...WHAT...

WHAT *IS* IT, NAT? WHAT'S *HAPPENING?*

"ULTRON IS HAPPENING.

"A MACHINE INTELLIGENCE THAT WANTS TO END ALL LIFE ON THIS PLANET. AND IT'S *INSANE*.

"THAT'S HOW WE *BEAT* IT. IF IT EVER GOT ITS *ACT* TOGETHER--"

...WELL.

NOW WE KNOW.

OH GOD, *RICH*--

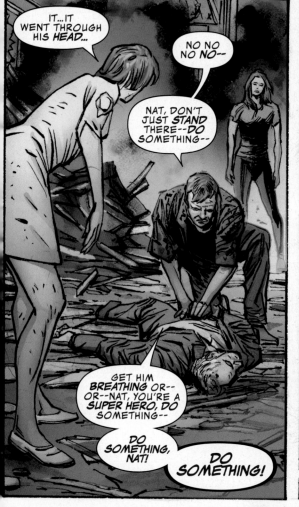

IT...IT WENT THROUGH HIS *HEAD*...

NO NO NO *NO*--

NAT, DON'T JUST *STAND* THERE--DO SOMETHING--

GET HIM *BREATHING* OR-- OR--NAT, YOU'RE A *SUPER HERO*, DO SOMETHING--

DO SOMETHING, NAT!

DO SOMETHING!

DO SOMETHING.

THEY'RE CIRCLING AROUND FOR ANOTHER PASS, GEORGE. WE NEED TO SAVE EVERYONE WE CAN.

WILL YOU *HELP*, OR JUST *SIT* THERE?

I MAKE MY VOICE COLD. BULLY HIM BACK TO HIS FEET.

LATER, THERE WILL BE TIME FOR GRIEF.

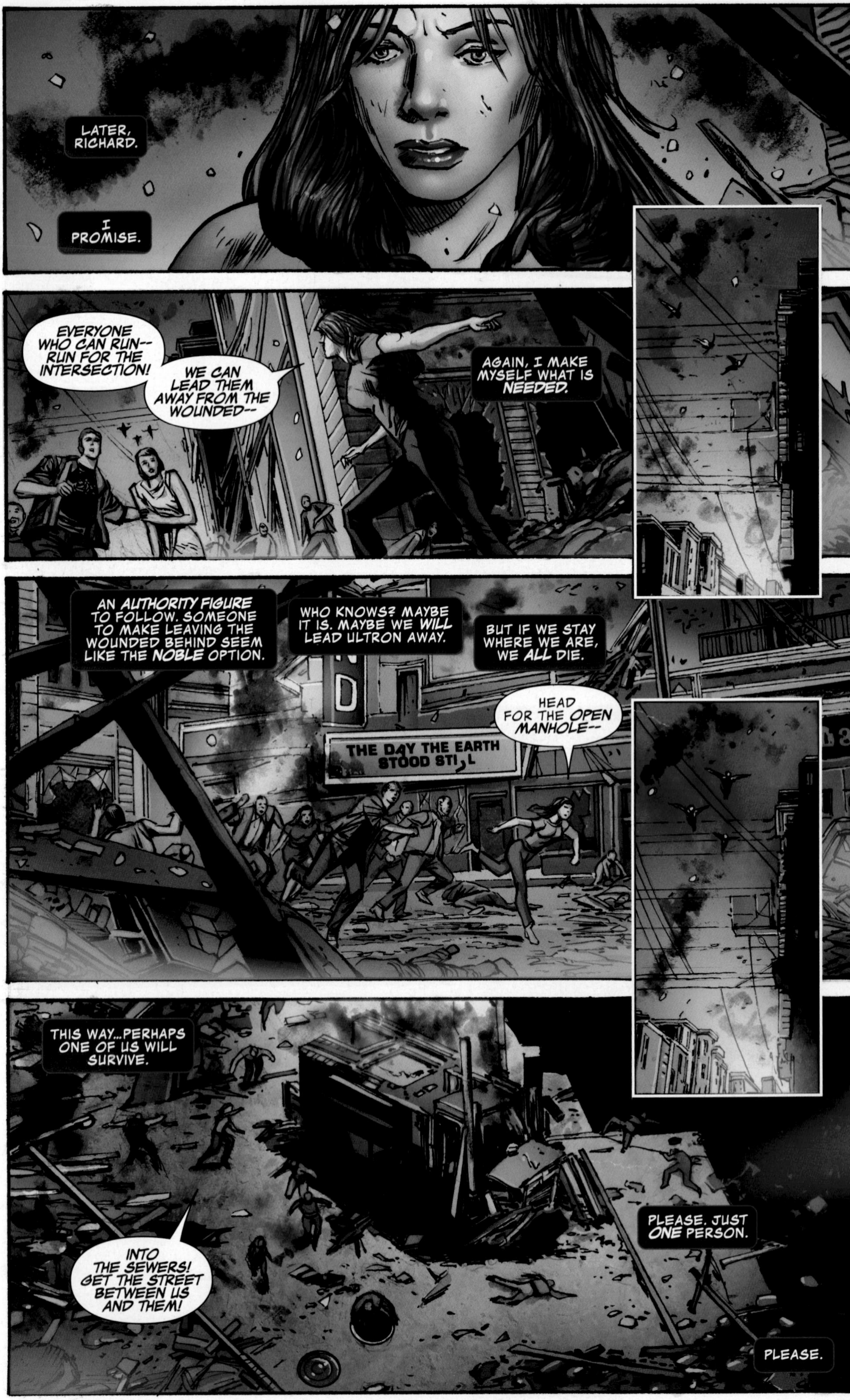
LATER, RICHARD.
I PROMISE.
EVERYONE WHO CAN RUN-- RUN FOR THE INTERSECTION!
WE CAN LEAD THEM AWAY FROM THE WOUNDED--
AGAIN, I MAKE MYSELF WHAT IS NEEDED.
AN AUTHORITY FIGURE TO FOLLOW. SOMEONE TO MAKE LEAVING THE WOUNDED BEHIND SEEM LIKE THE NOBLE OPTION.
WHO KNOWS? MAYBE IT IS. MAYBE WE WILL LEAD ULTRON AWAY.
BUT IF WE STAY WHERE WE ARE, WE ALL DIE.
HEAD FOR THE OPEN MANHOLE--
THE DAY THE EARTH STOOD STI L
THIS WAY...PERHAPS ONE OF US WILL SURVIVE.
INTO THE SEWERS! GET THE STREET BETWEEN US AND THEM!
PLEASE. JUST ONE PERSON.
PLEASE.

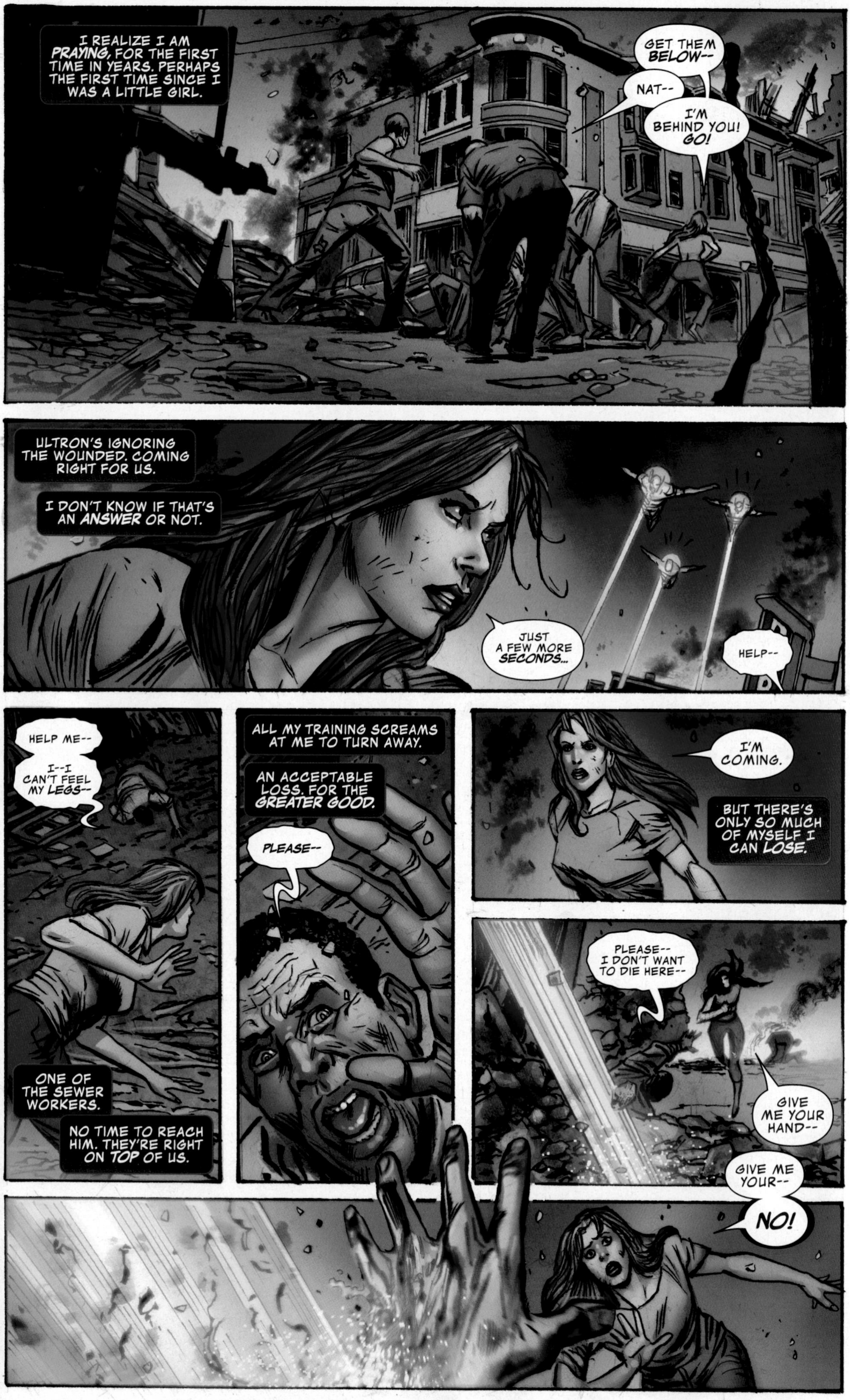

I REALIZE I AM PRAYING, FOR THE FIRST TIME IN YEARS. PERHAPS THE FIRST TIME SINCE I WAS A LITTLE GIRL.
GET THEM BELOW--
NAT--
I'M BEHIND YOU! GO!
ULTRON'S IGNORING THE WOUNDED. COMING RIGHT FOR US.
I DON'T KNOW IF THAT'S AN ANSWER OR NOT.
JUST A FEW MORE SECONDS...
HELP--
HELP ME--
I--I CAN'T FEEL MY LEGS--
ONE OF THE SEWER WORKERS.
NO TIME TO REACH HIM. THEY'RE RIGHT ON TOP OF US.
ALL MY TRAINING SCREAMS AT ME TO TURN AWAY.
AN ACCEPTABLE LOSS. FOR THE GREATER GOOD.
PLEASE--
I'M COMING.
BUT THERE'S ONLY SO MUCH OF MYSELF I CAN LOSE.
PLEASE-- I DON'T WANT TO DIE HERE--
GIVE ME YOUR HAND--
GIVE ME YOUR--
NO!

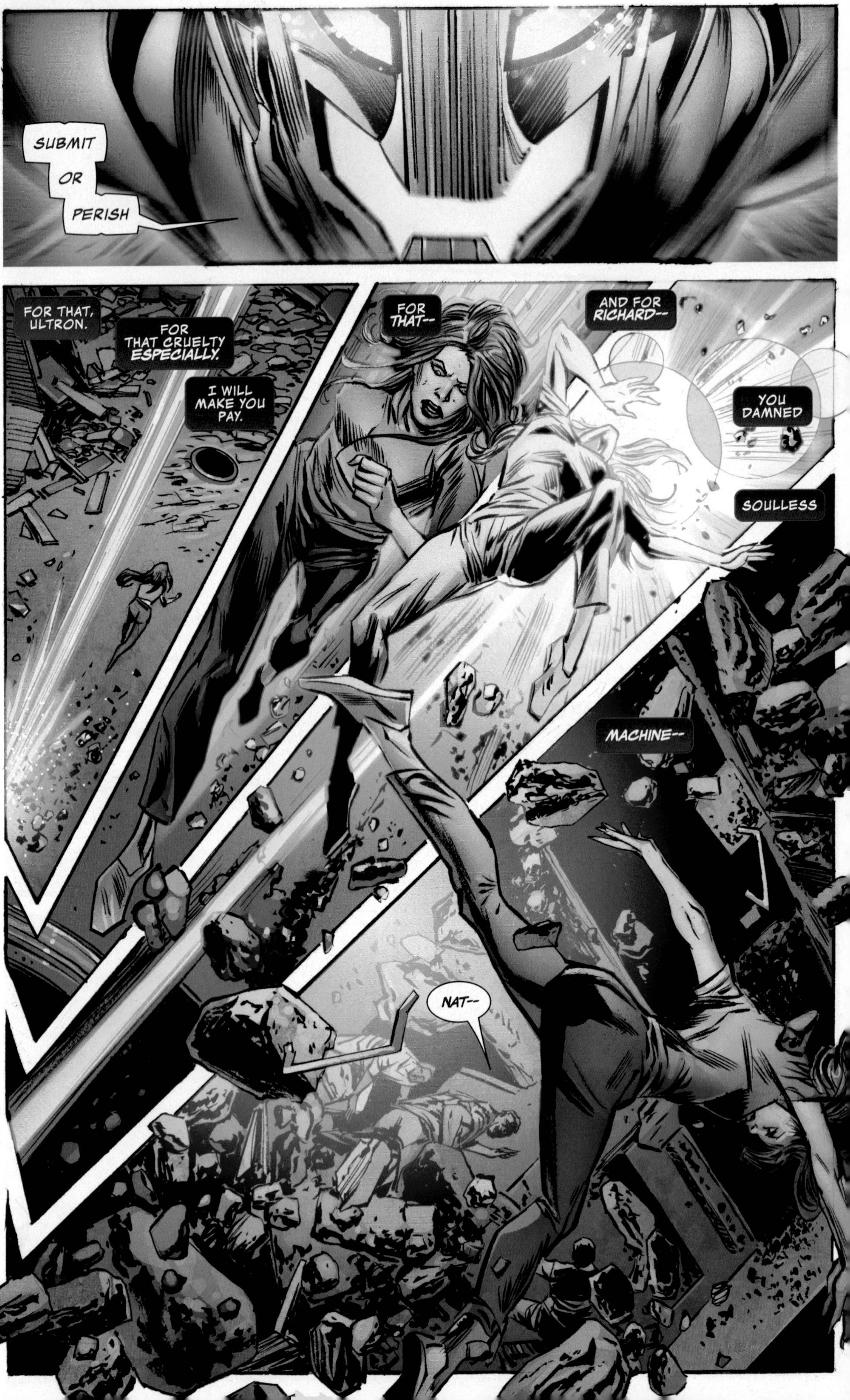
SUBMIT
OR
PERISH
FOR THAT, ULTRON.
FOR THAT CRUELTY ESPECIALLY.
I WILL MAKE YOU PAY.
FOR THAT--
AND FOR RICHARD--
YOU DAMNED
SOULLESS
MACHINE--
NAT--

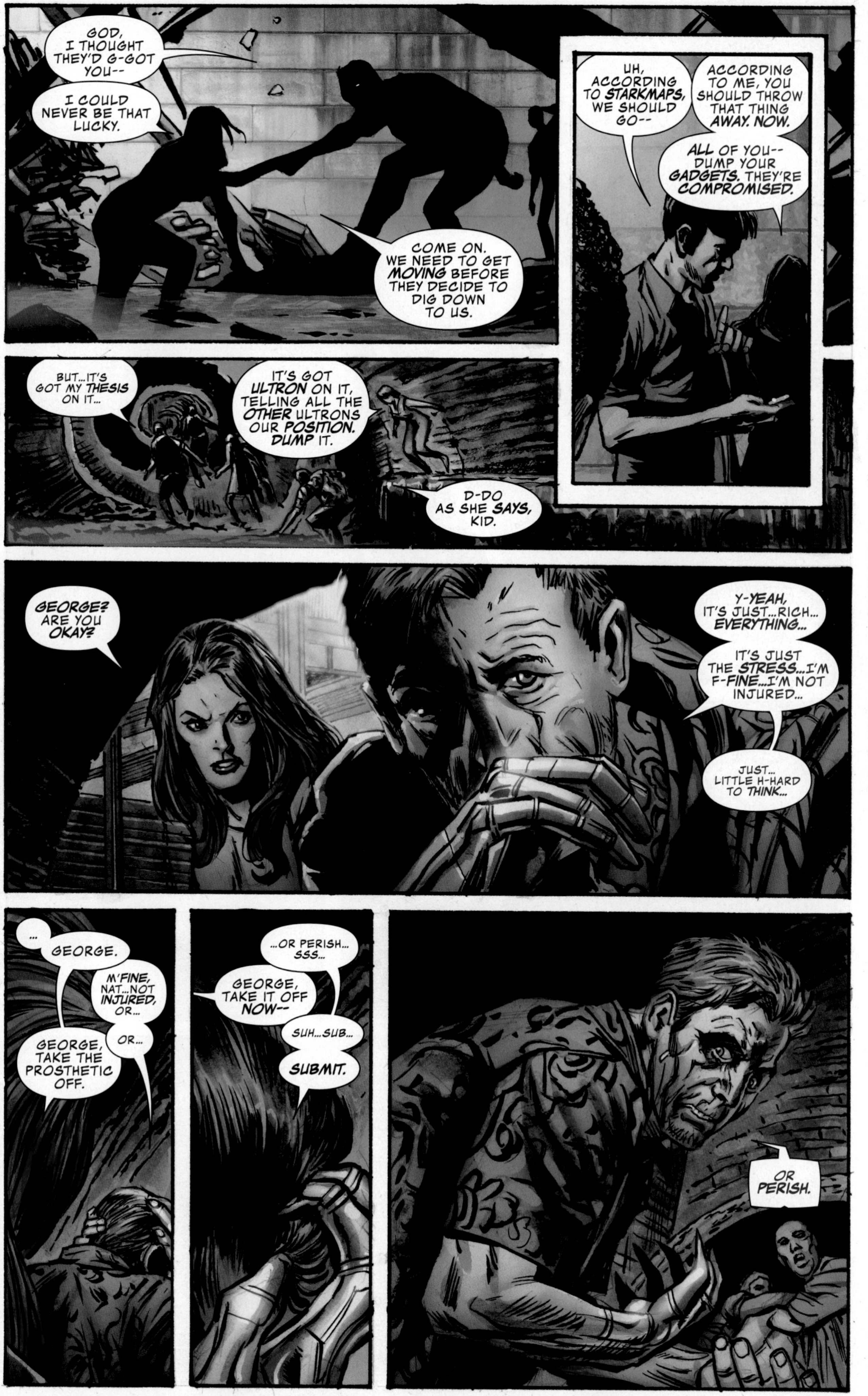
GOD, I THOUGHT THEY'D G-GOT YOU--
I COULD NEVER BE THAT LUCKY.
COME ON. WE NEED TO GET MOVING BEFORE THEY DECIDE TO DIG DOWN TO US.
UH, ACCORDING TO STARKMAPS, WE SHOULD GO--
ACCORDING TO ME, YOU SHOULD THROW THAT THING AWAY. NOW.
ALL OF YOU-- DUMP YOUR GADGETS. THEY'RE COMPROMISED.
BUT...IT'S GOT MY THESIS ON IT...
IT'S GOT ULTRON ON IT, TELLING ALL THE OTHER ULTRONS OUR POSITION. DUMP IT.
D-DO AS SHE SAYS, KID.
GEORGE? ARE YOU OKAY?
Y-YEAH, IT'S JUST...RICH... EVERYTHING...
IT'S JUST THE STRESS...I'M F-FINE...I'M NOT INJURED...
JUST... LITTLE H-HARD TO THINK...
...
GEORGE.
M'FINE, NAT...NOT INJURED, OR...
OR...
GEORGE, TAKE THE PROSTHETIC OFF.
...OR PERISH... SSS...
GEORGE, TAKE IT OFF NOW--
SUH...SUB...
SUBMIT.
OR PERISH.

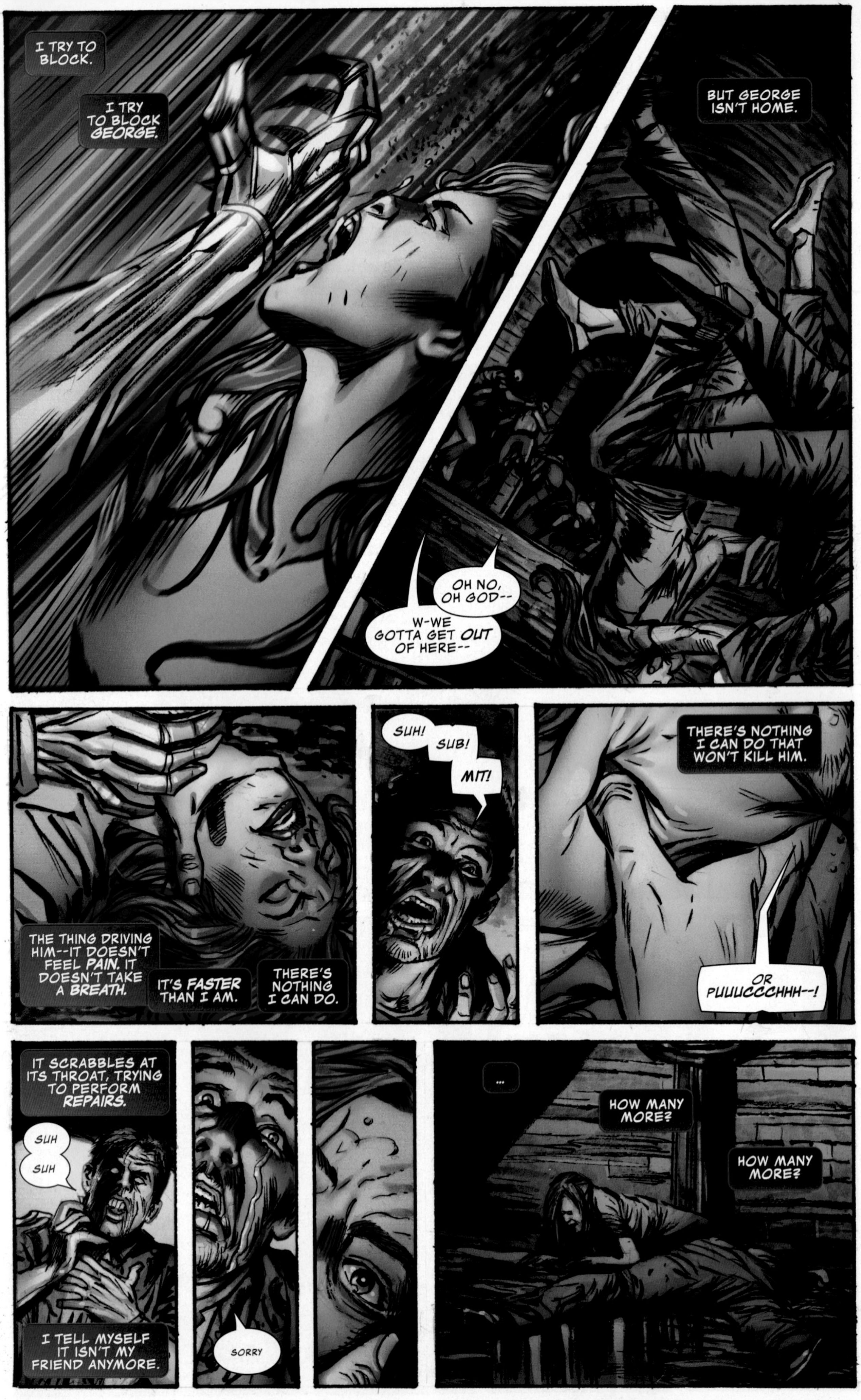
I TRY TO BLOCK.
I TRY TO BLOCK GEORGE.
BUT GEORGE ISN'T HOME.
OH NO, OH GOD--
W-WE GOTTA GET OUT OF HERE--
THE THING DRIVING HIM--IT DOESN'T FEEL PAIN. IT DOESN'T TAKE A BREATH.
IT'S FASTER THAN I AM.
THERE'S NOTHING I CAN DO.
SUH!
SUB!
MIT!
THERE'S NOTHING I CAN DO THAT WON'T KILL HIM.
OR PUUUCCCHHH--!
IT SCRABBLES AT ITS THROAT, TRYING TO PERFORM REPAIRS.
SUH
SUH
I TELL MYSELF IT ISN'T MY FRIEND ANYMORE.
SORRY
...
HOW MANY MORE?
HOW MANY MORE?

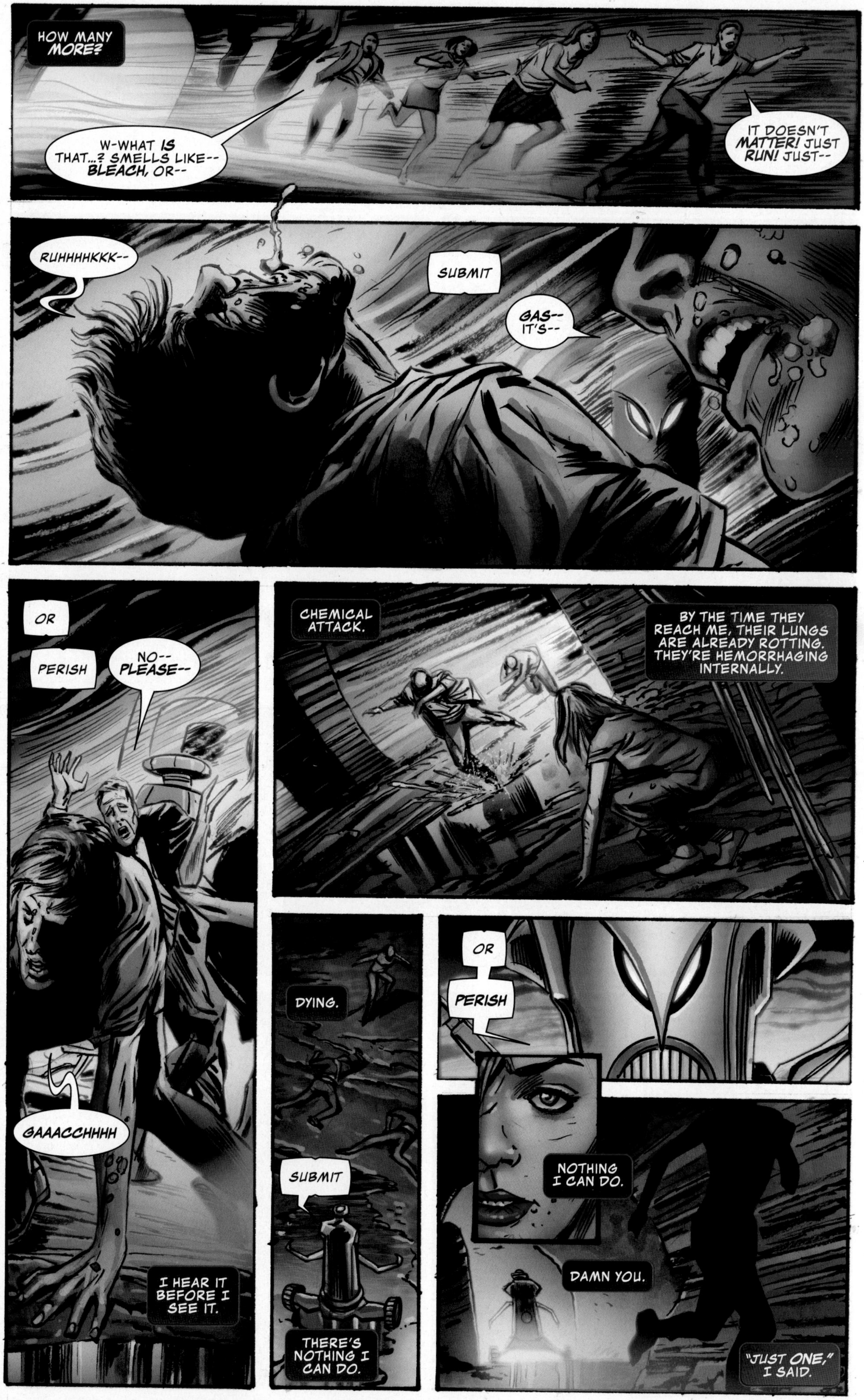
HOW MANY MORE?
W-WHAT IS THAT...? SMELLS LIKE-- BLEACH, OR--
IT DOESN'T MATTER! JUST RUN! JUST--
RUHHHHKKK--
SUBMIT
GAS-- IT'S--
OR
PERISH
NO-- PLEASE--
GAAACCHHHH
I HEAR IT BEFORE I SEE IT.
CHEMICAL ATTACK.
BY THE TIME THEY REACH ME, THEIR LUNGS ARE ALREADY ROTTING. THEY'RE HEMORRHAGING INTERNALLY.
DYING.
SUBMIT
THERE'S NOTHING I CAN DO.
OR
PERISH
NOTHING I CAN DO.
DAMN YOU.
"JUST ONE," I SAID.

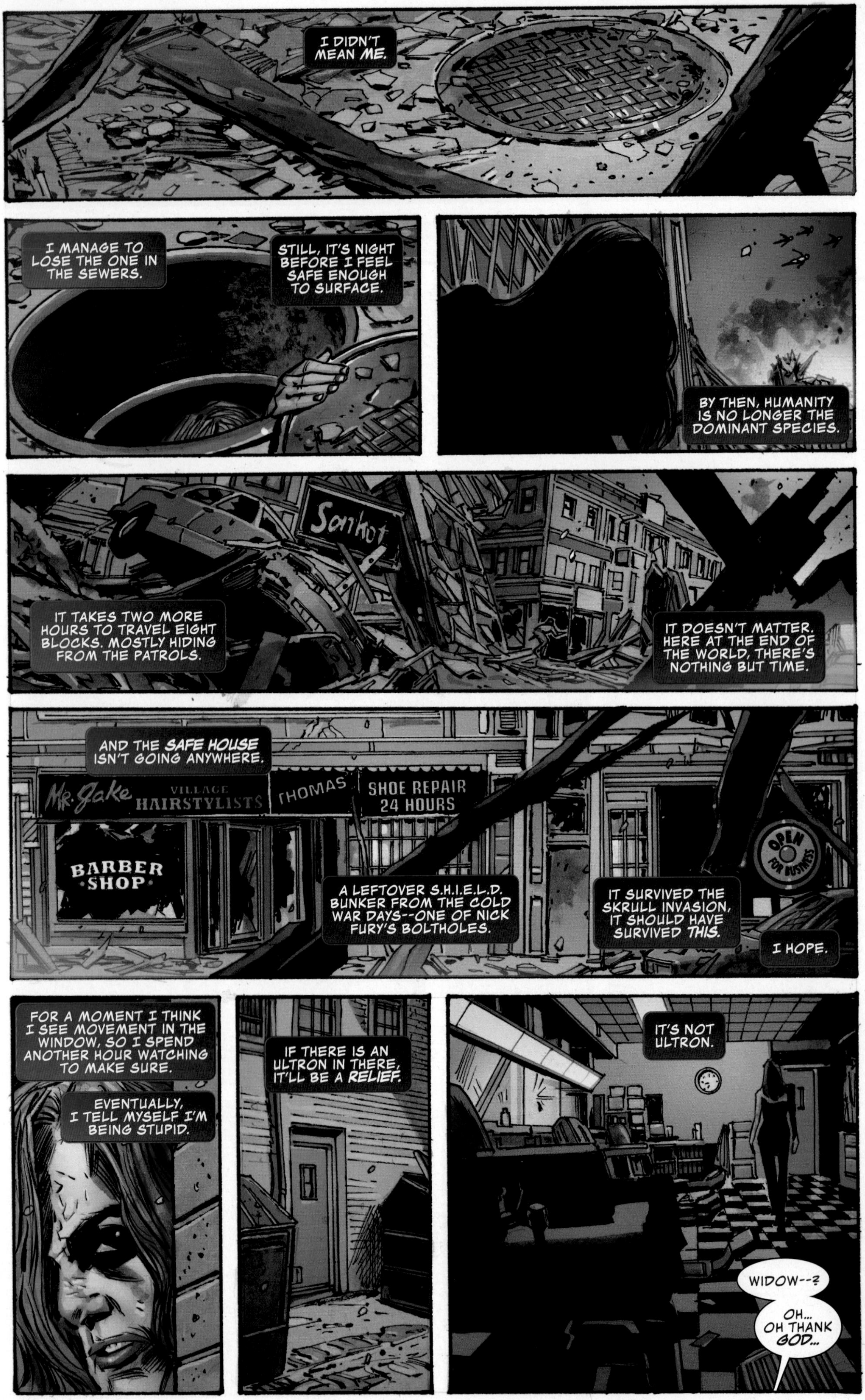
I DIDN'T MEAN ME.
I MANAGE TO LOSE THE ONE IN THE SEWERS.
STILL, IT'S NIGHT BEFORE I FEEL SAFE ENOUGH TO SURFACE.
BY THEN, HUMANITY IS NO LONGER THE DOMINANT SPECIES.
Sankot
IT TAKES TWO MORE HOURS TO TRAVEL EIGHT BLOCKS. MOSTLY HIDING FROM THE PATROLS.
IT DOESN'T MATTER. HERE AT THE END OF THE WORLD, THERE'S NOTHING BUT TIME.
AND THE SAFE HOUSE ISN'T GOING ANYWHERE.
Mr. Jake VILLAGE HAIRSTYLISTS
THOMAS
SHOE REPAIR 24 HOURS
BARBER SHOP
OPEN FOR BUSINESS
A LEFTOVER S.H.I.E.L.D. BUNKER FROM THE COLD WAR DAYS--ONE OF NICK FURY'S BOLTHOLES.
IT SURVIVED THE SKRULL INVASION, IT SHOULD HAVE SURVIVED THIS.
I HOPE.
FOR A MOMENT I THINK I SEE MOVEMENT IN THE WINDOW, SO I SPEND ANOTHER HOUR WATCHING TO MAKE SURE.
EVENTUALLY, I TELL MYSELF I'M BEING STUPID.
IF THERE IS AN ULTRON IN THERE, IT'LL BE A RELIEF.
IT'S NOT ULTRON.
WIDOW--?
OH... OH THANK GOD...

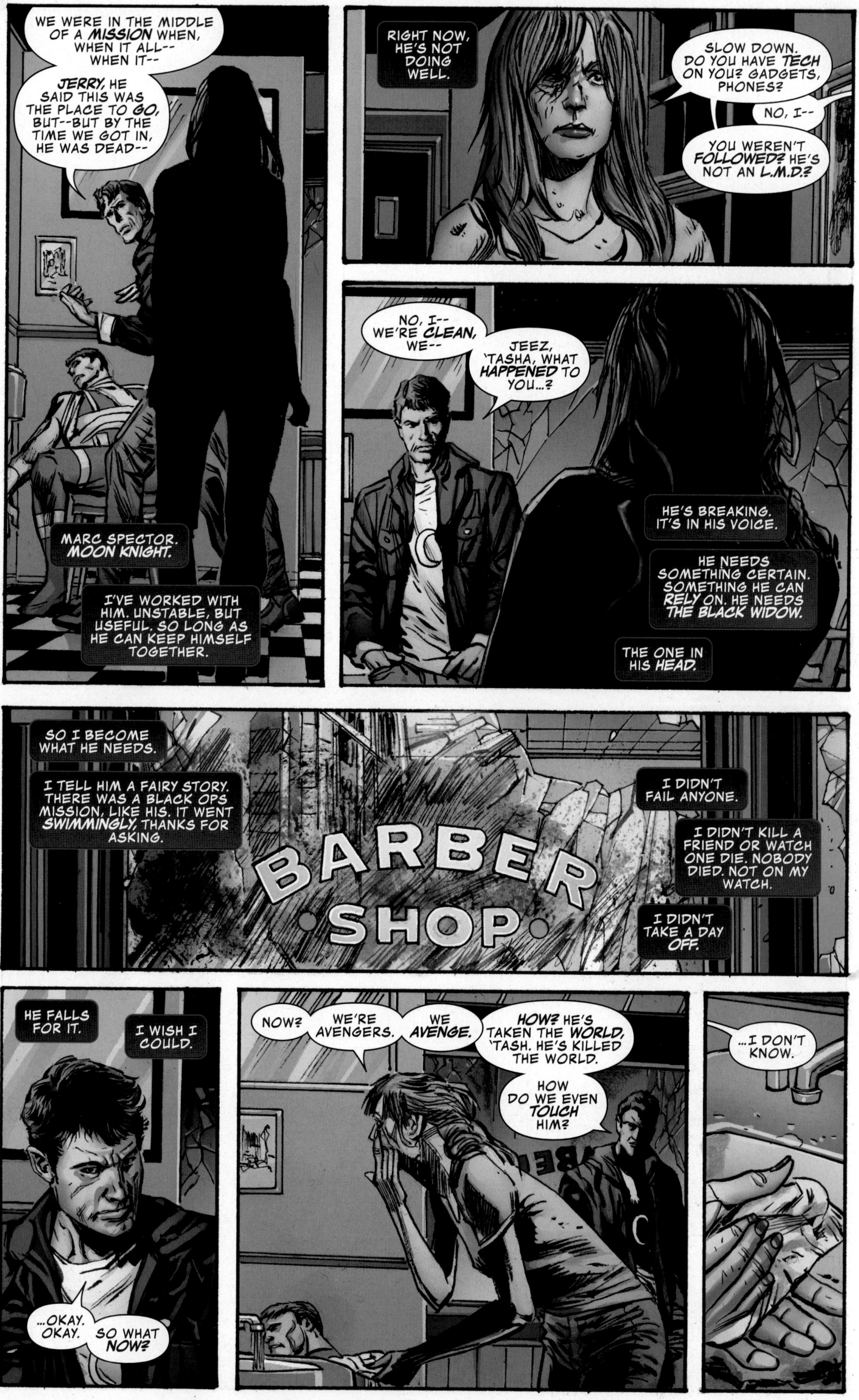

WE WERE IN THE MIDDLE OF A MISSION WHEN, WHEN IT ALL-- WHEN IT--
JERRY, HE SAID THIS WAS THE PLACE TO GO, BUT--BUT BY THE TIME WE GOT IN, HE WAS DEAD--
MARC SPECTOR. MOON KNIGHT.
I'VE WORKED WITH HIM. UNSTABLE, BUT USEFUL. SO LONG AS HE CAN KEEP HIMSELF TOGETHER.
RIGHT NOW, HE'S NOT DOING WELL.
SLOW DOWN. DO YOU HAVE TECH ON YOU? GADGETS, PHONES?
NO, I--
YOU WEREN'T FOLLOWED? HE'S NOT AN L.M.D.?
NO, I-- WE'RE CLEAN, WE--
JEEZ, 'TASHA, WHAT HAPPENED TO YOU...?
HE'S BREAKING. IT'S IN HIS VOICE.
HE NEEDS SOMETHING CERTAIN. SOMETHING HE CAN RELY ON. HE NEEDS THE BLACK WIDOW.
THE ONE IN HIS HEAD.
SO I BECOME WHAT HE NEEDS.
I TELL HIM A FAIRY STORY. THERE WAS A BLACK OPS MISSION, LIKE HIS. IT WENT SWIMMINGLY, THANKS FOR ASKING.
BARBER SHOP
I DIDN'T FAIL ANYONE.
I DIDN'T KILL A FRIEND OR WATCH ONE DIE. NOBODY DIED. NOT ON MY WATCH.
I DIDN'T TAKE A DAY OFF.
HE FALLS FOR IT.
I WISH I COULD.
...OKAY. OKAY.
SO WHAT NOW?
NOW?
WE'RE AVENGERS.
WE AVENGE.
HOW? HE'S TAKEN THE WORLD, 'TASH. HE'S KILLED THE WORLD.
HOW DO WE EVEN TOUCH HIM?
...I DON'T KNOW.

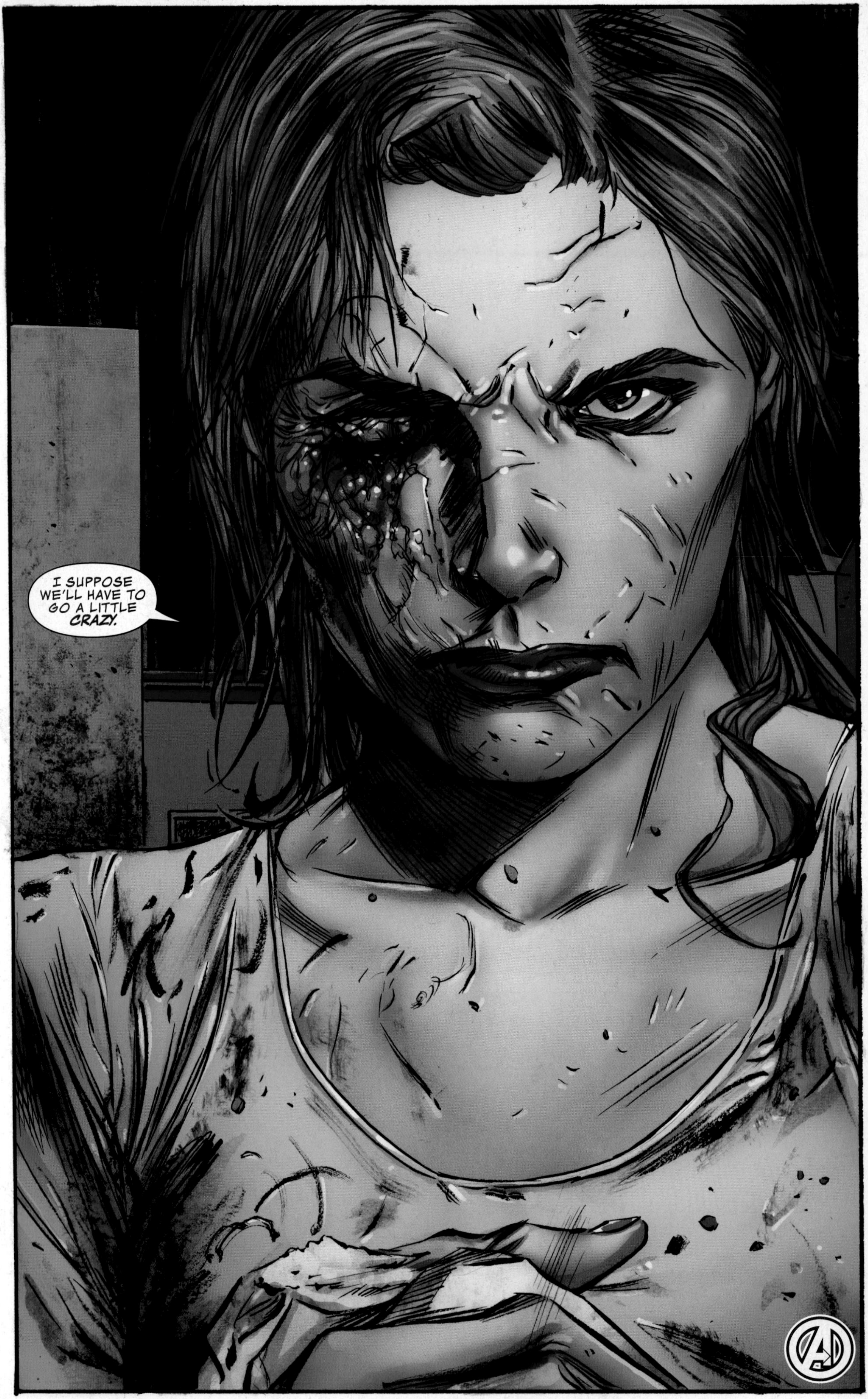
I SUPPOSE WE'LL HAVE TO GO A LITTLE CRAZY.

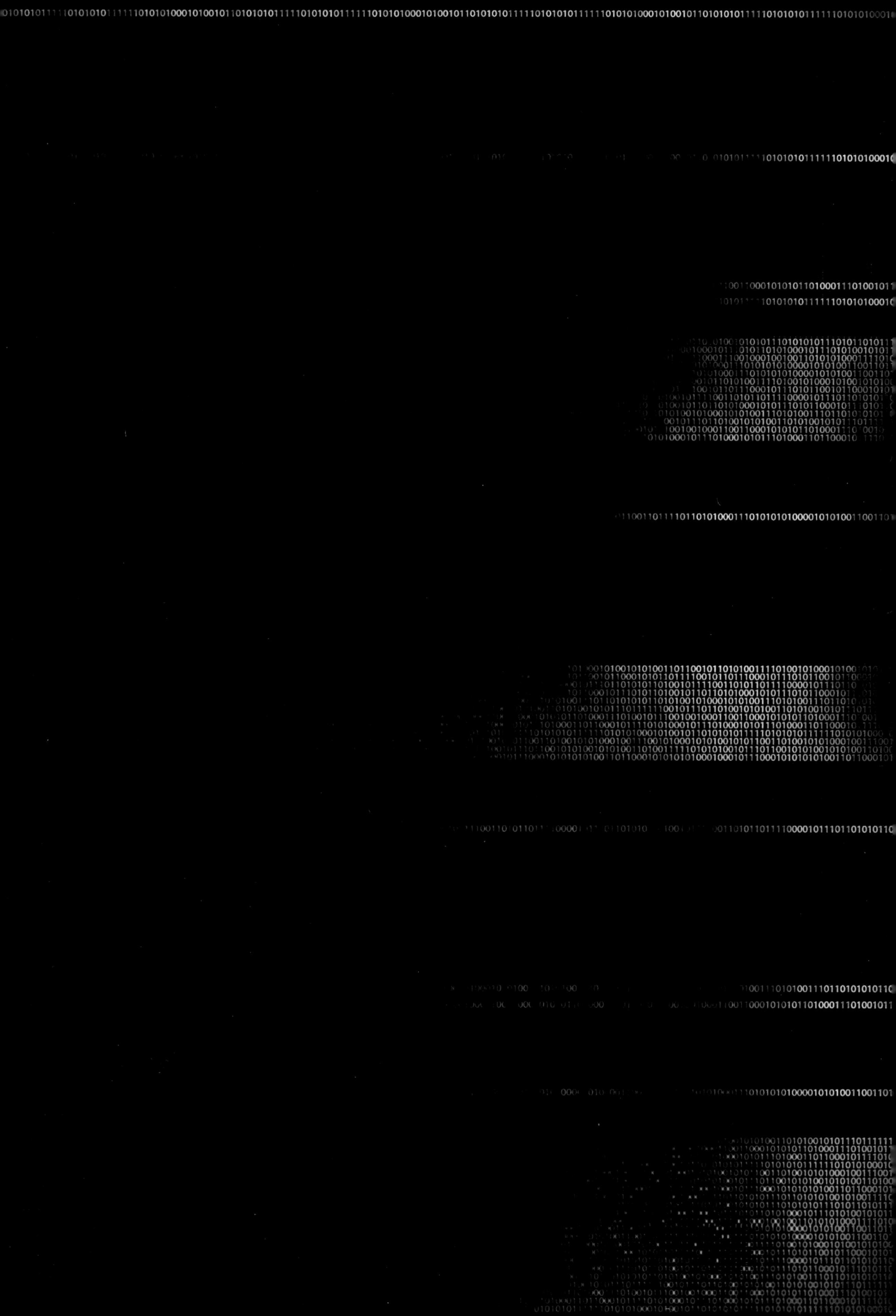

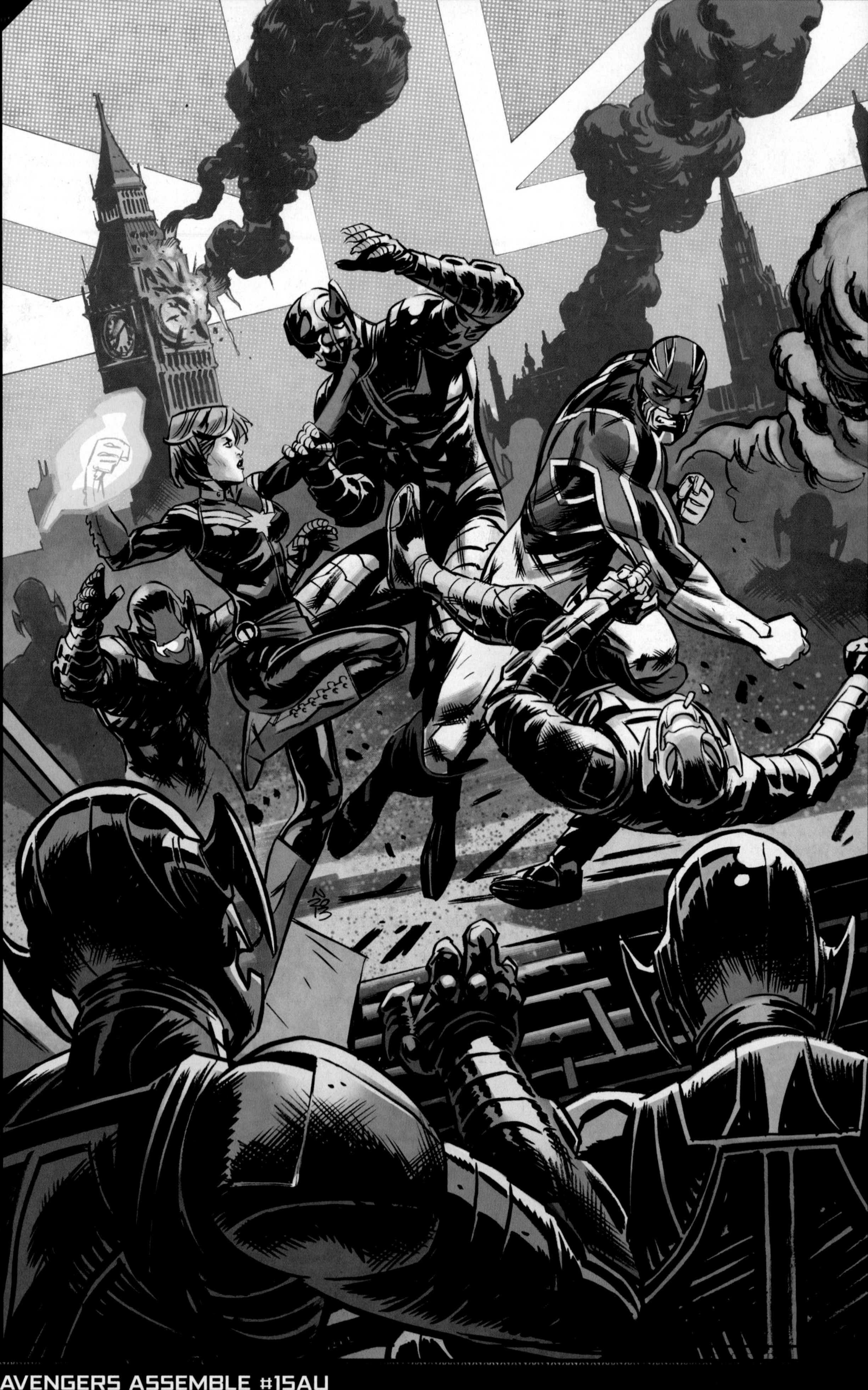

AVENGERS ASSEMBLE #15AU

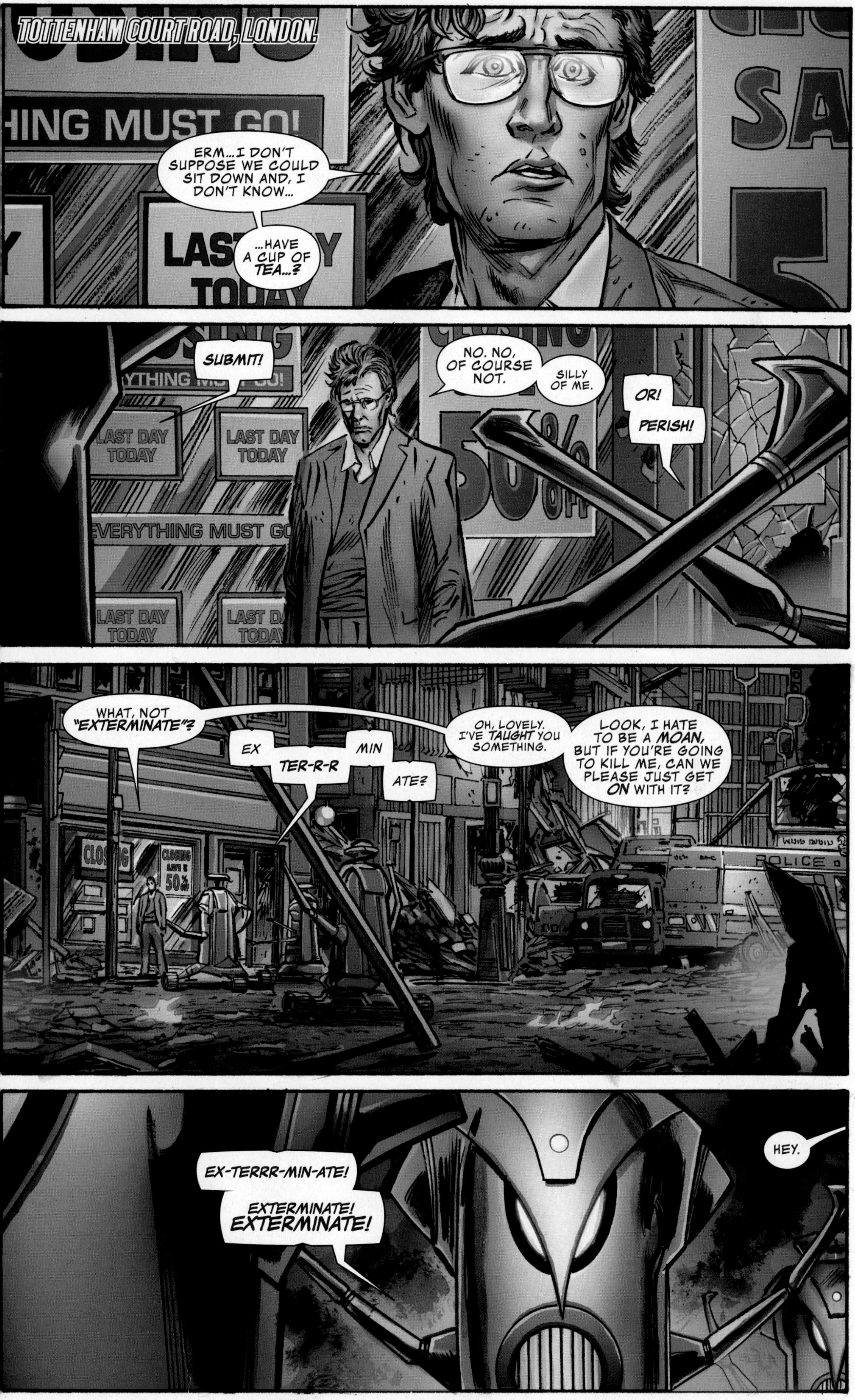
TOTTENHAM COURT ROAD, LONDON.
ERM... I DON'T SUPPOSE WE COULD SIT DOWN AND, I DON'T KNOW...
...HAVE A CUP OF TEA...?
SUBMIT!
NO. NO, OF COURSE NOT.
SILLY OF ME.
OR!
PERISH!
WHAT, NOT "EXTERMINATE"?
EX
TER-R-R
MIN
ATE?
OH, LOVELY. I'VE TAUGHT YOU SOMETHING.
LOOK, I HATE TO BE A MOAN, BUT IF YOU'RE GOING TO KILL ME, CAN WE PLEASE JUST GET ON WITH IT?
EX-TERRR-MIN-ATE!
EXTERMINATE! EXTERMINATE!
HEY.

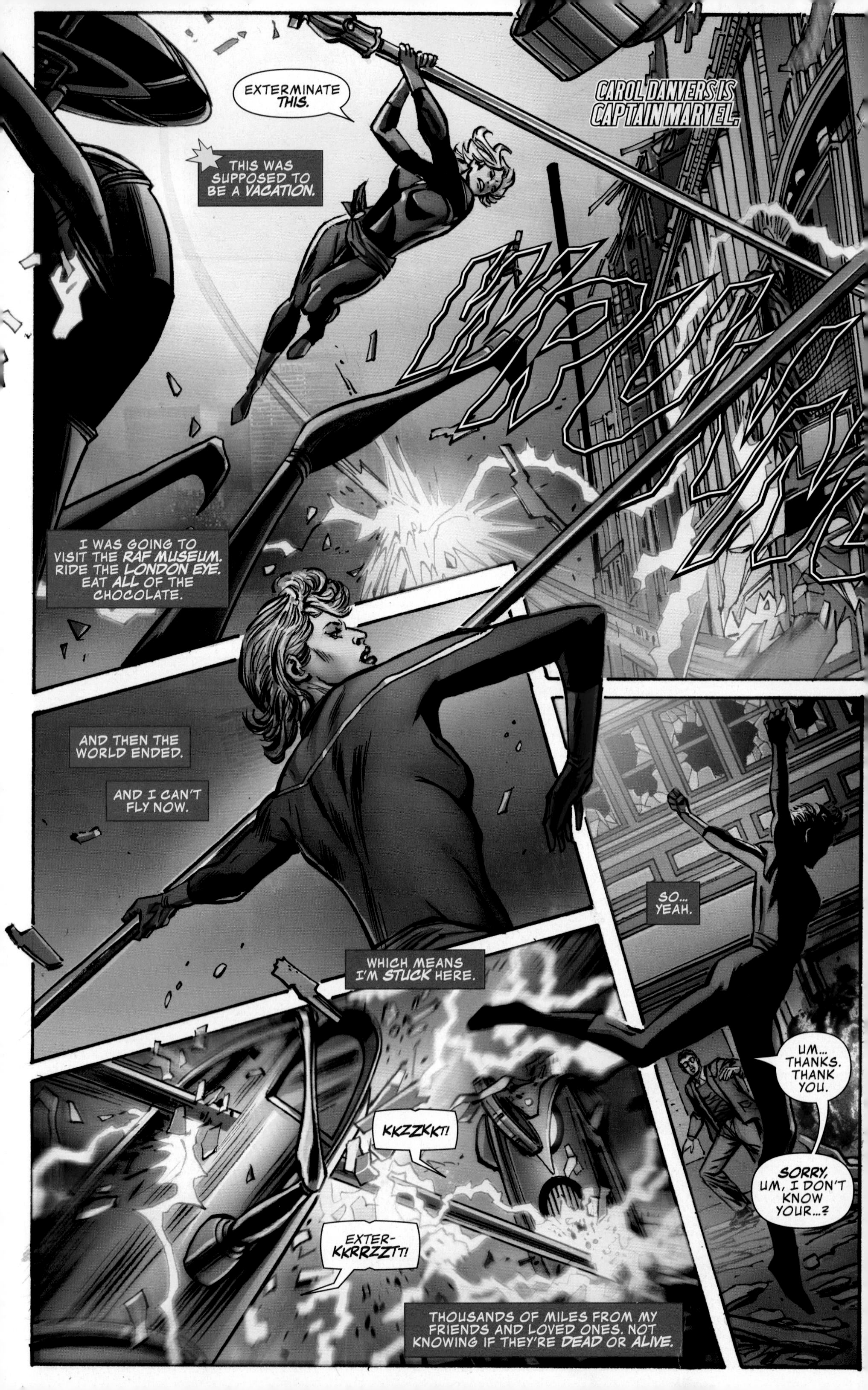

CAROL DANVERS IS CAPTAIN MARVEL.
EXTERMINATE THIS.
THIS WAS SUPPOSED TO BE A VACATION.
I WAS GOING TO VISIT THE RAF MUSEUM. RIDE THE LONDON EYE. EAT ALL OF THE CHOCOLATE.
AND THEN THE WORLD ENDED.
AND I CAN'T FLY NOW.
WHICH MEANS I'M STUCK HERE.
KKZZKKT!
EXTER-KKRRZZTT!
THOUSANDS OF MILES FROM MY FRIENDS AND LOVED ONES. NOT KNOWING IF THEY'RE DEAD OR ALIVE.
SO... YEAH.
UM... THANKS. THANK YOU.
SORRY, UM, I DON'T KNOW YOUR...?

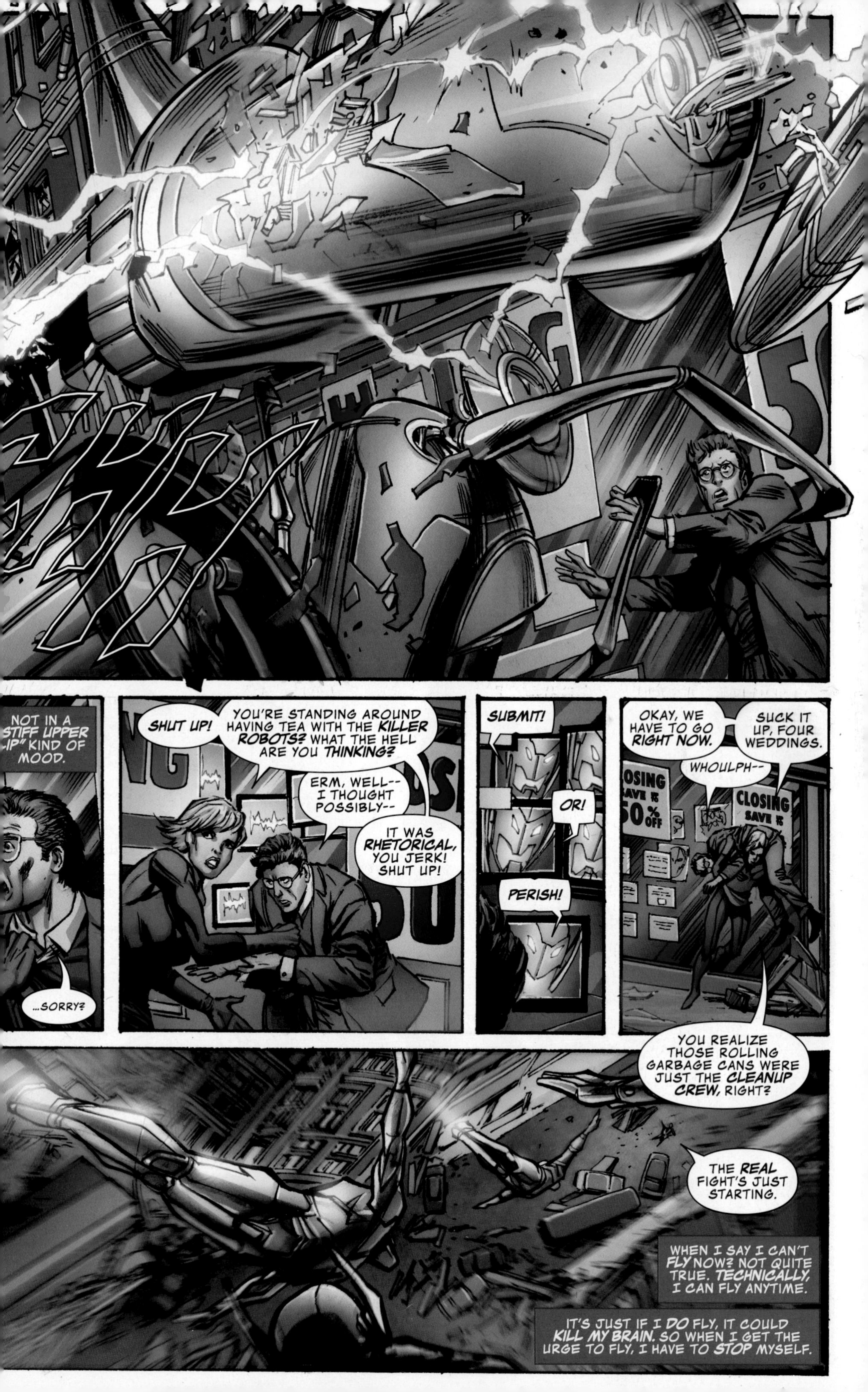
NOT IN A STIFF UPPER LIP" KIND OF MOOD.
...SORRY?
SHUT UP!
YOU'RE STANDING AROUND HAVING TEA WITH THE KILLER ROBOTS? WHAT THE HELL ARE YOU THINKING?
ERM, WELL-- I THOUGHT POSSIBLY--
IT WAS RHETORICAL, YOU JERK! SHUT UP!
SUBMIT!
OR!
PERISH!
OKAY, WE HAVE TO GO RIGHT NOW.
SUCK IT UP, FOUR WEDDINGS.
WHOULPH--
CLOSING SAVE 50% OFF
YOU REALIZE THOSE ROLLING GARBAGE CANS WERE JUST THE CLEANUP CREW, RIGHT?
THE REAL FIGHT'S JUST STARTING.
WHEN I SAY I CAN'T FLY NOW? NOT QUITE TRUE. TECHNICALLY, I CAN FLY ANYTIME.
IT'S JUST IF I DO FLY, IT COULD KILL MY BRAIN. SO WHEN I GET THE URGE TO FLY, I HAVE TO STOP MYSELF.

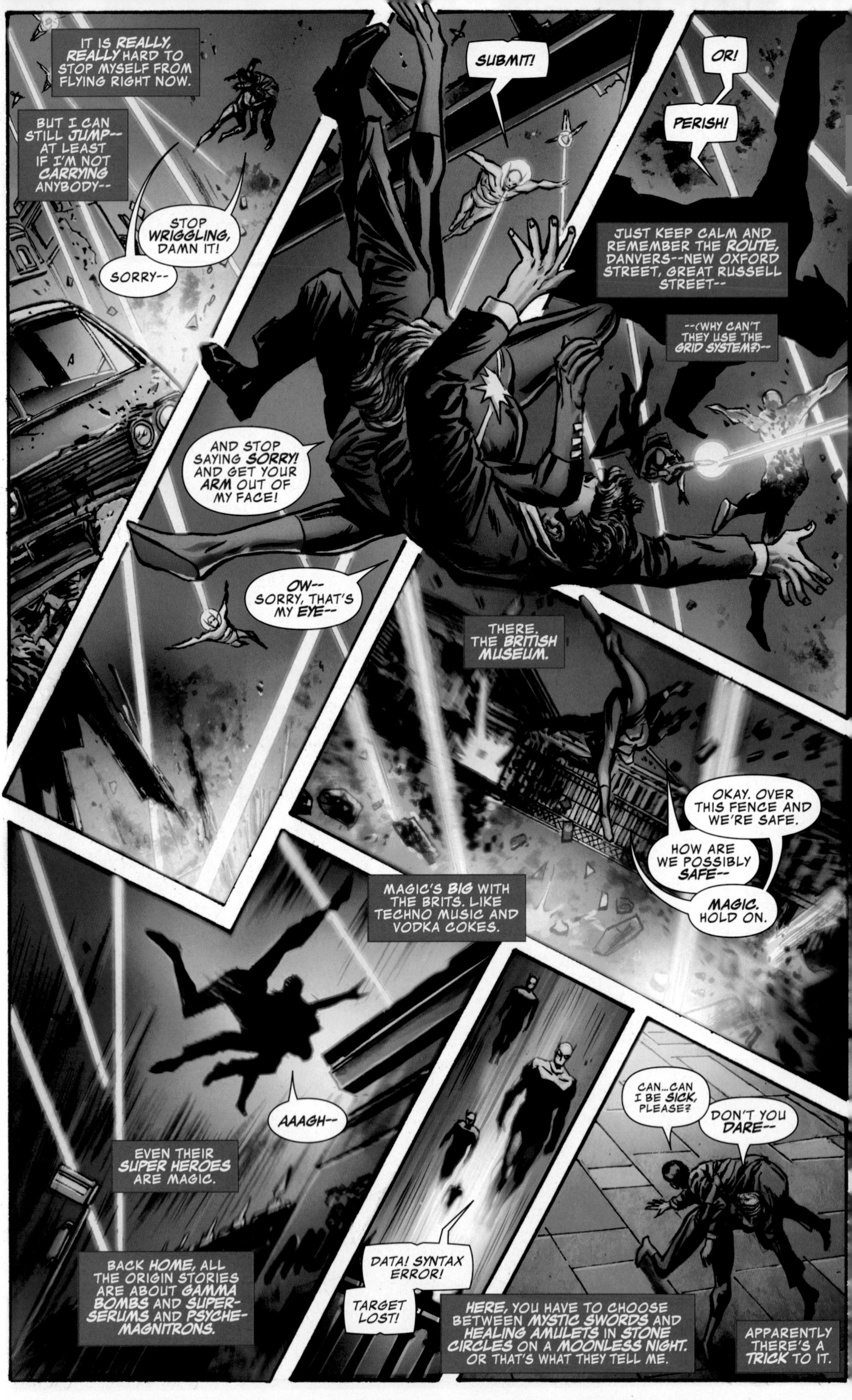

IT IS REALLY, REALLY HARD TO STOP MYSELF FROM FLYING RIGHT NOW.
BUT I CAN STILL JUMP--AT LEAST IF I'M NOT CARRYING ANYBODY--
STOP WRIGGLING, DAMN IT!
SORRY--
SUBMIT!
OR!
PERISH!
JUST KEEP CALM AND REMEMBER THE ROUTE, DANVERS--NEW OXFORD STREET, GREAT RUSSELL STREET--
--(WHY CAN'T THEY USE THE GRID SYSTEM?)--
AND STOP SAYING SORRY! AND GET YOUR ARM OUT OF MY FACE!
OW--SORRY, THAT'S MY EYE--
THERE. THE BRITISH MUSEUM.
OKAY. OVER THIS FENCE AND WE'RE SAFE.
HOW ARE WE POSSIBLY SAFE--
MAGIC. HOLD ON.
MAGIC'S BIG WITH THE BRITS. LIKE TECHNO MUSIC AND VODKA COKES.
AAAGH--
EVEN THEIR SUPER HEROES ARE MAGIC.
BACK HOME, ALL THE ORIGIN STORIES ARE ABOUT GAMMA BOMBS AND SUPER-SERUMS AND PSYCHE-MAGNITRONS.
DATA! SYNTAX ERROR!
TARGET LOST!
HERE, YOU HAVE TO CHOOSE BETWEEN MYSTIC SWORDS AND HEALING AMULETS IN STONE CIRCLES ON A MOONLESS NIGHT. OR THAT'S WHAT THEY TELL ME.
CAN...CAN I BE SICK, PLEASE?
DON'T YOU DARE--
APPARENTLY THERE'S A TRICK TO IT.

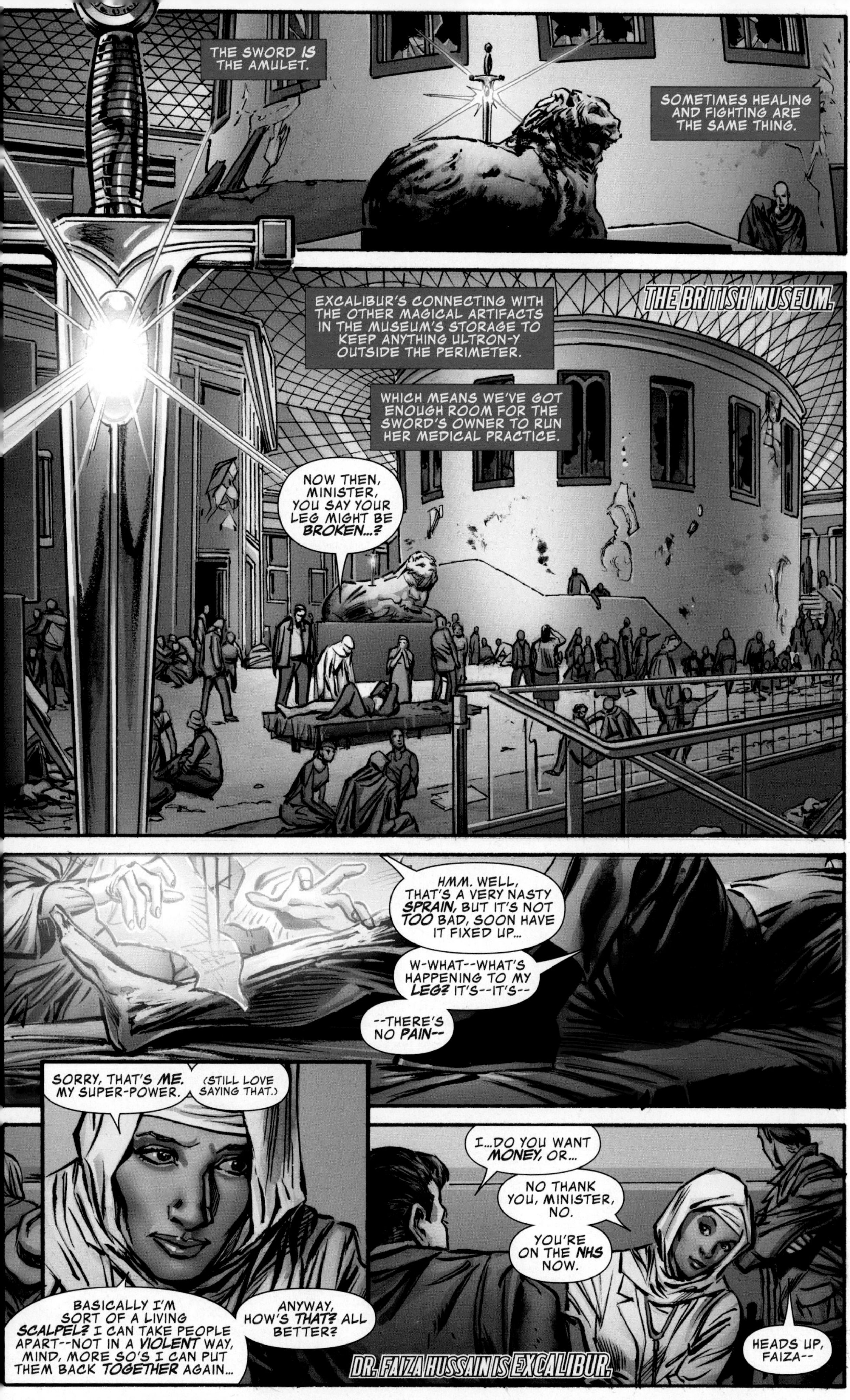
THE SWORD IS THE AMULET.
SOMETIMES HEALING AND FIGHTING ARE THE SAME THING.
THE BRITISH MUSEUM.
EXCALIBUR'S CONNECTING WITH THE OTHER MAGICAL ARTIFACTS IN THE MUSEUM'S STORAGE TO KEEP ANYTHING ULTRON-Y OUTSIDE THE PERIMETER.
WHICH MEANS WE'VE GOT ENOUGH ROOM FOR THE SWORD'S OWNER TO RUN HER MEDICAL PRACTICE.
NOW THEN, MINISTER, YOU SAY YOUR LEG MIGHT BE BROKEN...?
HMM. WELL, THAT'S A VERY NASTY SPRAIN, BUT IT'S NOT TOO BAD, SOON HAVE IT FIXED UP...
W-WHAT--WHAT'S HAPPENING TO MY LEG? IT'S--IT'S--
--THERE'S NO PAIN--
SORRY, THAT'S ME. MY SUPER-POWER.
(STILL LOVE SAYING THAT.)
BASICALLY I'M SORT OF A LIVING SCALPEL? I CAN TAKE PEOPLE APART--NOT IN A VIOLENT WAY, MIND, MORE SO'S I CAN PUT THEM BACK TOGETHER AGAIN...
ANYWAY, HOW'S THAT? ALL BETTER?
DR. FAIZA HUSSAIN IS EXCALIBUR.
I...DO YOU WANT MONEY, OR...
NO THANK YOU, MINISTER, NO.
YOU'RE ON THE NHS NOW.
HEADS UP, FAIZA--

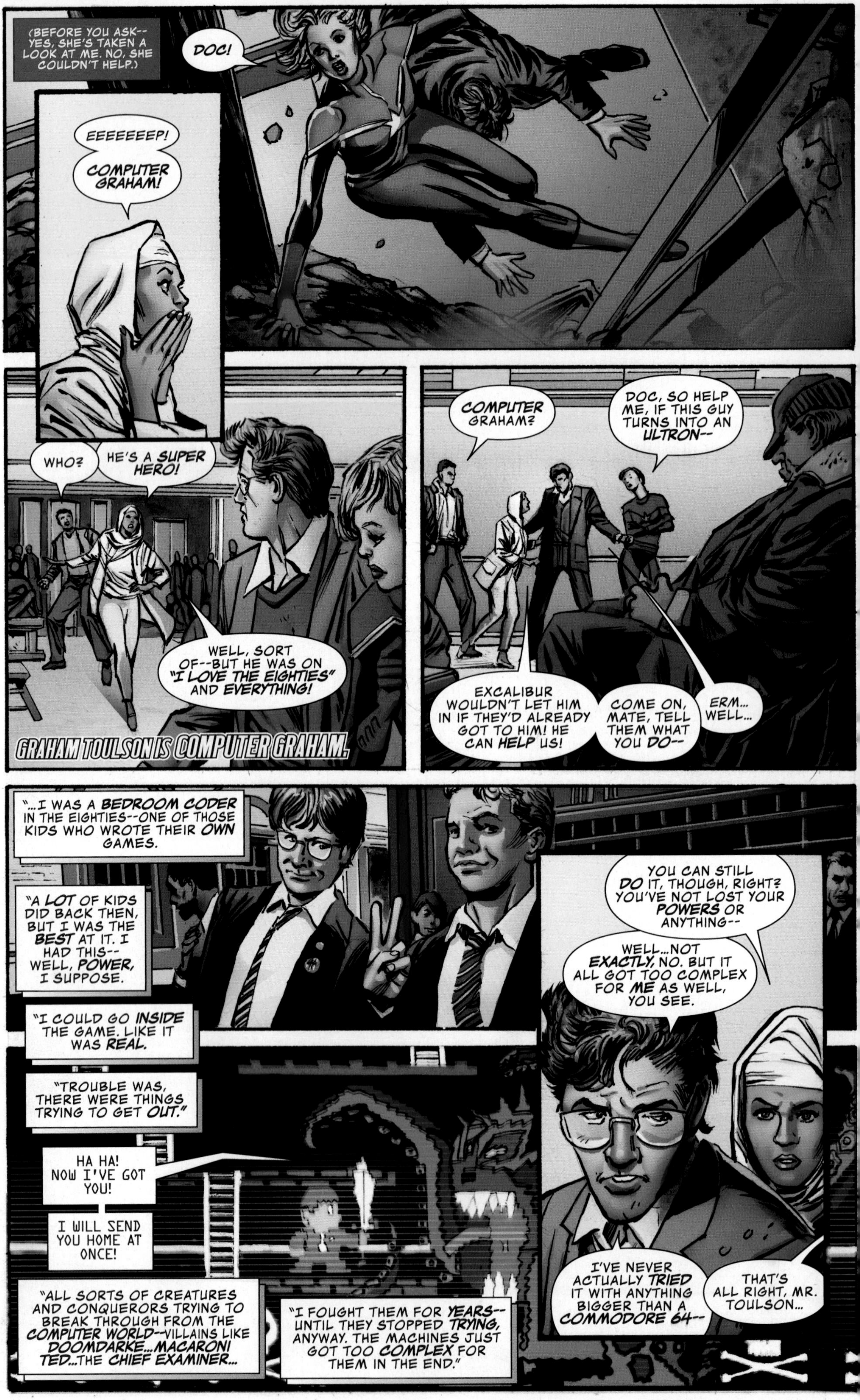
(BEFORE YOU ASK--YES, SHE'S TAKEN A LOOK AT ME. NO, SHE COULDN'T HELP.)
DOC!
EEEEEEEP!
COMPUTER GRAHAM!
WHO?
HE'S A SUPER HERO!
WELL, SORT OF--BUT HE WAS ON "I LOVE THE EIGHTIES" AND EVERYTHING!
GRAHAM TOULSON IS COMPUTER GRAHAM.
COMPUTER GRAHAM?
DOC, SO HELP ME, IF THIS GUY TURNS INTO AN ULTRON--
EXCALIBUR WOULDN'T LET HIM IN IF THEY'D ALREADY GOT TO HIM! HE CAN HELP US!
COME ON, MATE, TELL THEM WHAT YOU DO--
ERM... WELL...
"...I WAS A BEDROOM CODER IN THE EIGHTIES--ONE OF THOSE KIDS WHO WROTE THEIR OWN GAMES.
"A LOT OF KIDS DID BACK THEN, BUT I WAS THE BEST AT IT. I HAD THIS--WELL, POWER, I SUPPOSE.
"I COULD GO INSIDE THE GAME. LIKE IT WAS REAL.
"TROUBLE WAS, THERE WERE THINGS TRYING TO GET OUT."
HA HA! NOW I'VE GOT YOU!
I WILL SEND YOU HOME AT ONCE!
"ALL SORTS OF CREATURES AND CONQUERORS TRYING TO BREAK THROUGH FROM THE COMPUTER WORLD--VILLAINS LIKE DOOMDARKE...MACARONI TED...THE CHIEF EXAMINER...
"I FOUGHT THEM FOR YEARS--UNTIL THEY STOPPED TRYING, ANYWAY. THE MACHINES JUST GOT TOO COMPLEX FOR THEM IN THE END."
YOU CAN STILL DO IT, THOUGH, RIGHT? YOU'VE NOT LOST YOUR POWERS OR ANYTHING--
WELL...NOT EXACTLY, NO. BUT IT ALL GOT TOO COMPLEX FOR ME AS WELL, YOU SEE.
I'VE NEVER ACTUALLY TRIED IT WITH ANYTHING BIGGER THAN A COMMODORE 64--
THAT'S ALL RIGHT, MR. TOULSON...

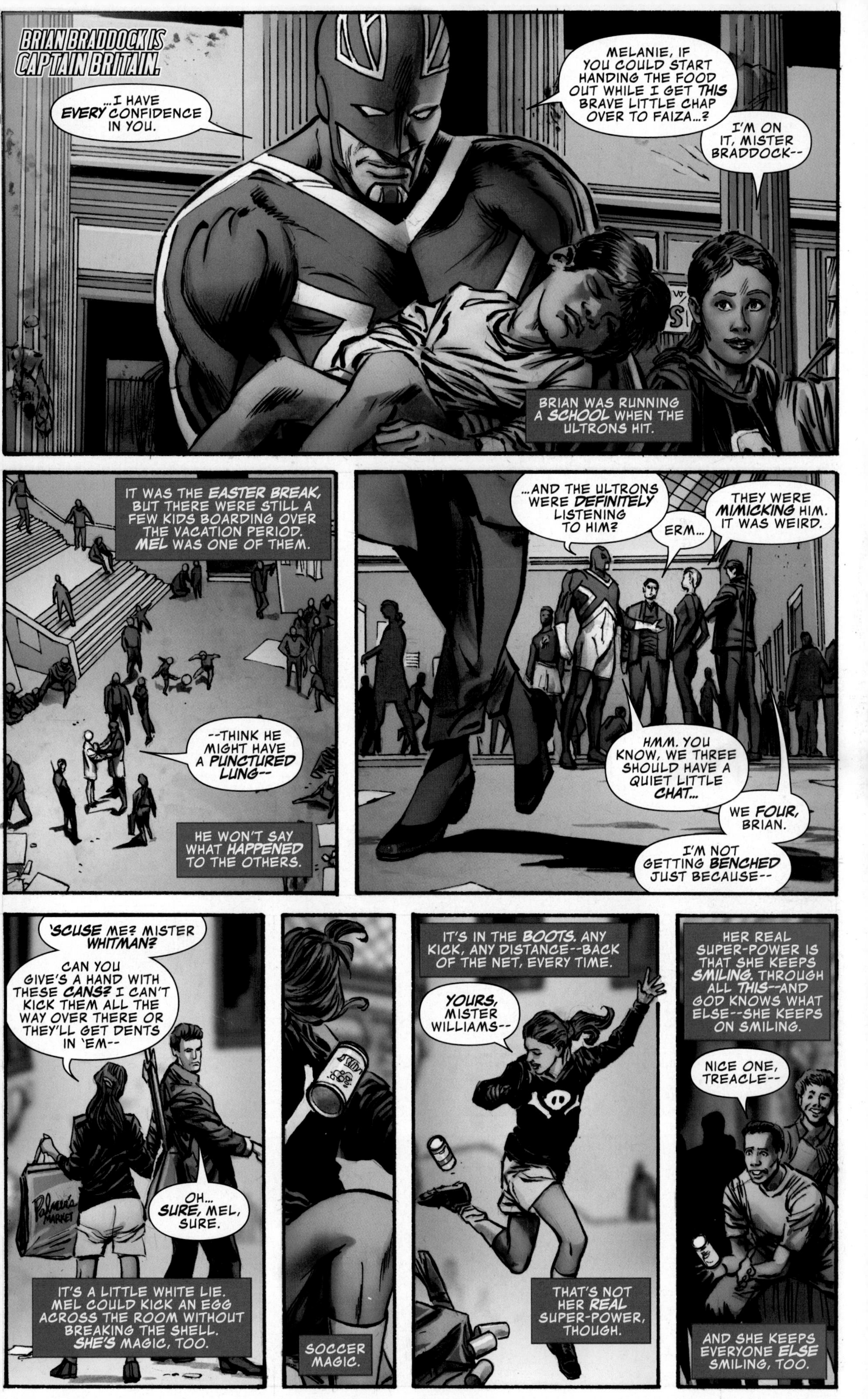
BRIAN BRADDOCK IS CAPTAIN BRITAIN.
...I HAVE EVERY CONFIDENCE IN YOU.
MELANIE, IF YOU COULD START HANDING THE FOOD OUT WHILE I GET THIS BRAVE LITTLE CHAP OVER TO FAIZA...?
I'M ON IT, MISTER BRADDOCK--
BRIAN WAS RUNNING A SCHOOL WHEN THE ULTRONS HIT.
IT WAS THE EASTER BREAK, BUT THERE WERE STILL A FEW KIDS BOARDING OVER THE VACATION PERIOD. MEL WAS ONE OF THEM.
--THINK HE MIGHT HAVE A PUNCTURED LUNG--
HE WON'T SAY WHAT HAPPENED TO THE OTHERS.
...AND THE ULTRONS WERE DEFINITELY LISTENING TO HIM?
ERM...
THEY WERE MIMICKING HIM. IT WAS WEIRD.
HMM. YOU KNOW, WE THREE SHOULD HAVE A QUIET LITTLE CHAT...
WE FOUR, BRIAN.
I'M NOT GETTING BENCHED JUST BECAUSE--
'SCUSE ME? MISTER WHITMAN?
CAN YOU GIVE'S A HAND WITH THESE CANS? I CAN'T KICK THEM ALL THE WAY OVER THERE OR THEY'LL GET DENTS IN 'EM--
OH... SURE, MEL, SURE.
IT'S A LITTLE WHITE LIE. MEL COULD KICK AN EGG ACROSS THE ROOM WITHOUT BREAKING THE SHELL. SHE'S MAGIC, TOO.
SOCCER MAGIC.
IT'S IN THE BOOTS. ANY KICK, ANY DISTANCE--BACK OF THE NET, EVERY TIME.
YOURS, MISTER WILLIAMS--
THAT'S NOT HER REAL SUPER-POWER, THOUGH.
HER REAL SUPER-POWER IS THAT SHE KEEPS SMILING. THROUGH ALL THIS--AND GOD KNOWS WHAT ELSE--SHE KEEPS ON SMILING.
NICE ONE, TREACLE--
AND SHE KEEPS EVERYONE ELSE SMILING, TOO.

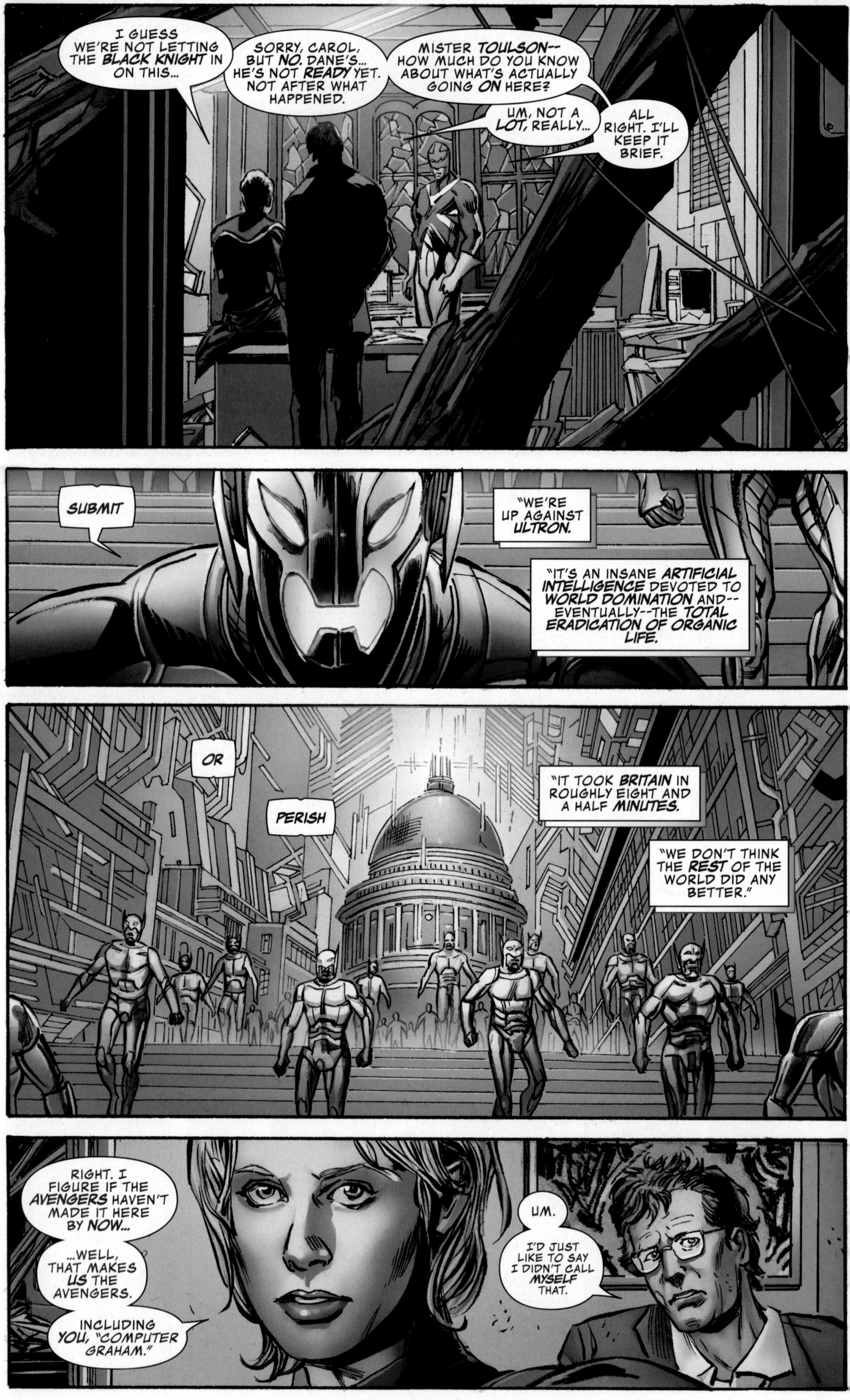

I GUESS WE'RE NOT LETTING THE BLACK KNIGHT IN ON THIS...
SORRY, CAROL, BUT NO. DANE'S... HE'S NOT READY YET. NOT AFTER WHAT HAPPENED.
MISTER TOULSON-- HOW MUCH DO YOU KNOW ABOUT WHAT'S ACTUALLY GOING ON HERE?
UM, NOT A LOT, REALLY...
ALL RIGHT. I'LL KEEP IT BRIEF.
SUBMIT
"WE'RE UP AGAINST ULTRON.
"IT'S AN INSANE ARTIFICIAL INTELLIGENCE DEVOTED TO WORLD DOMINATION AND-- EVENTUALLY--THE TOTAL ERADICATION OF ORGANIC LIFE.
OR
PERISH
"IT TOOK BRITAIN IN ROUGHLY EIGHT AND A HALF MINUTES.
"WE DON'T THINK THE REST OF THE WORLD DID ANY BETTER."
RIGHT. I FIGURE IF THE AVENGERS HAVEN'T MADE IT HERE BY NOW...
...WELL, THAT MAKES US THE AVENGERS.
INCLUDING YOU, "COMPUTER GRAHAM."
UM.
I'D JUST LIKE TO SAY I DIDN'T CALL MYSELF THAT.

MR. TOULSON, WITH YOUR UNIQUE *POWERSET*--

GRAHAM. PLEASE.

GRAHAM--YOU'RE THE FIRST POSSIBLE *WEAPON* WE'VE ACTUALLY FOUND *AGAINST* ULTRON.

EXCALIBUR GIVES US A SMALL *SAFE ZONE*, BUT WE CAN'T HIDE *FOREVER*. WE'LL ONLY SURVIVE IN THE LONG-TERM BY TAKING LONDON *BACK*.

WILL YOU *HELP* US?

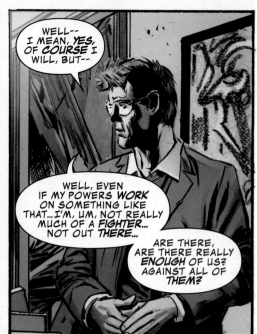

WELL-- I MEAN, *YES*, OF *COURSE* I WILL, BUT--

WELL, EVEN IF MY POWERS *WORK* ON SOMETHING LIKE THAT...I'M, UM, NOT REALLY MUCH OF A *FIGHTER*... NOT OUT *THERE*...

ARE THERE, ARE THERE REALLY *ENOUGH* OF US? AGAINST ALL OF *THEM*?

HE'S GOT A *POINT*, BRIAN.

THE TWO OF US CAN'T TAKE ST. PAUL'S ON OUR *OWN*. FAIZA'S NEEDED HERE, YOU CAN'T GET HELP FROM *OTHERWORLD* WITHOUT SPREADING ULTRON TO THE *MULTIVERSE*...

...LOOK, WOULD IT REALLY BE SO *BAD* TO LET DANE--

YES. YES IT *WOULD.* YOU WEREN'T WITH US WHEN IT *HAPPENED*, CAROL.

YOU DIDN'T SEE HOW MANY ULTRONS HE HAD TO *KILL*.

AND *YES*, FINE, IT'S *MACHINE* LIFE, THEY WERE "ONLY ROBOTS," HE *HAD* TO--BUT THIS IS THE *EBONY BLADE.* THE *ANTI-EXCALIBUR.*

SWORD OF THE *OTHER* BRITAIN, THE ONE THAT SNEERS AT "*CHAVS*" AND "*SCROUNGERS*" AND POURS *HATE* AND *FEAR* ON THOSE WHO NEED *KINDNESS*...

TRUST ME. *ANY* KIND OF LIFE WILL *DO*.

"DANE'S HOLDING IT BACK WITH HIS FINGERTIPS RIGHT NOW. IF HE GIVES IT *ONE MORE INCH*... IT'LL BE *WORSE*, CAROL."

DANE WHITMAN IS THE BLACK KNIGHT.

"*WORSE* THAN ULTRON."

SO WHO DOES THAT--

KNOCK KNOCK

'SCUSE ME? MISTER BRADDOCK?

ARE YOU NEEDIN' SOMEONE EXTRA TO GO ON A SECRET *ROBOT-DUFFIN'-UP* MISSION?

NO--

'COS I *TOTES* WANT TO GO ON THAT MISSION.

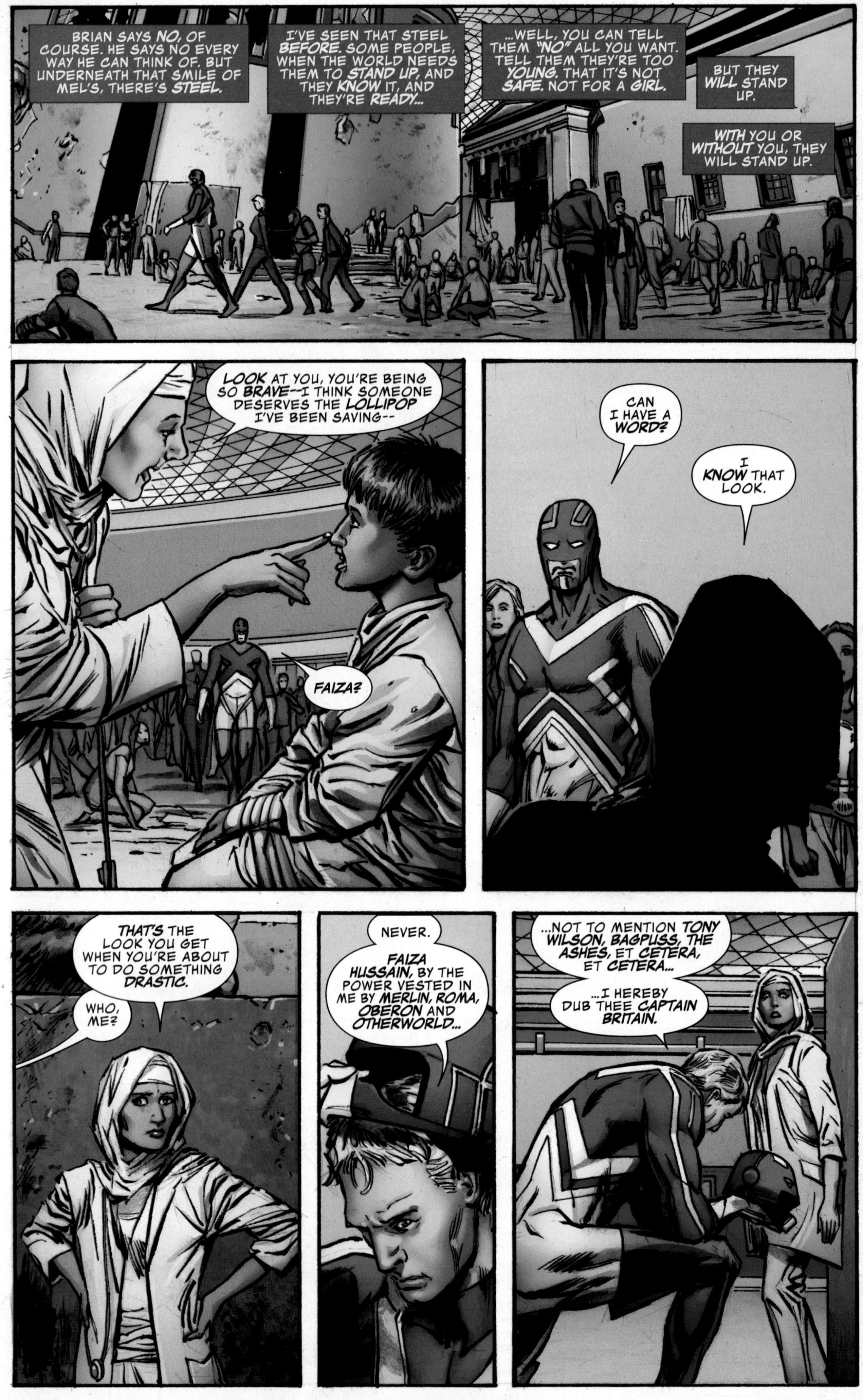
BRIAN SAYS NO, OF COURSE. HE SAYS NO EVERY WAY HE CAN THINK OF. BUT UNDERNEATH THAT SMILE OF MEL'S, THERE'S STEEL.
I'VE SEEN THAT STEEL BEFORE. SOME PEOPLE, WHEN THE WORLD NEEDS THEM TO STAND UP, AND THEY KNOW IT, AND THEY'RE READY...
...WELL, YOU CAN TELL THEM "NO" ALL YOU WANT. TELL THEM THEY'RE TOO YOUNG. THAT IT'S NOT SAFE. NOT FOR A GIRL.
BUT THEY WILL STAND UP.
WITH YOU OR WITHOUT YOU, THEY WILL STAND UP.
LOOK AT YOU, YOU'RE BEING SO BRAVE--I THINK SOMEONE DESERVES THE LOLLIPOP I'VE BEEN SAVING--
FAIZA?
CAN I HAVE A WORD?
I KNOW THAT LOOK.
THAT'S THE LOOK YOU GET WHEN YOU'RE ABOUT TO DO SOMETHING DRASTIC.
WHO, ME?
NEVER.
FAIZA HUSSAIN, BY THE POWER VESTED IN ME BY MERLIN, ROMA, OBERON AND OTHERWORLD...
...NOT TO MENTION TONY WILSON, BAGPUSS, THE ASHES, ET CETERA, ET CETERA...
...I HEREBY DUB THEE CAPTAIN BRITAIN.

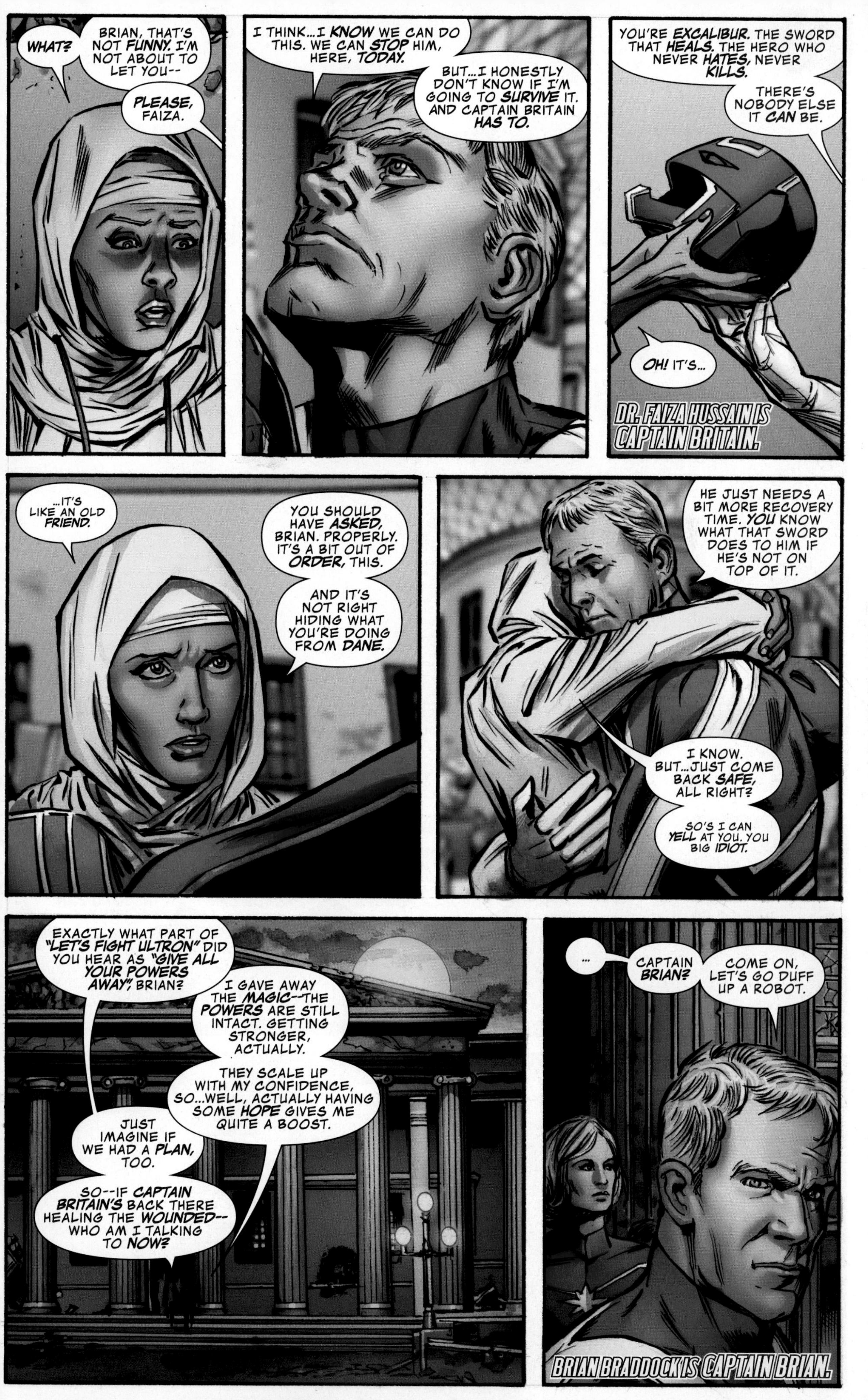
WHAT?
BRIAN, THAT'S NOT FUNNY. I'M NOT ABOUT TO LET YOU--
PLEASE, FAIZA.
I THINK...I KNOW WE CAN DO THIS. WE CAN STOP HIM, HERE, TODAY.
BUT...I HONESTLY DON'T KNOW IF I'M GOING TO SURVIVE IT. AND CAPTAIN BRITAIN HAS TO.
YOU'RE EXCALIBUR. THE SWORD THAT HEALS. THE HERO WHO NEVER HATES, NEVER KILLS.
THERE'S NOBODY ELSE IT CAN BE.
OH! IT'S...
DR. FAIZA HUSSAIN IS CAPTAIN BRITAIN.
...IT'S LIKE AN OLD FRIEND.
YOU SHOULD HAVE ASKED, BRIAN. PROPERLY. IT'S A BIT OUT OF ORDER, THIS.
AND IT'S NOT RIGHT HIDING WHAT YOU'RE DOING FROM DANE.
HE JUST NEEDS A BIT MORE RECOVERY TIME. YOU KNOW WHAT THAT SWORD DOES TO HIM IF HE'S NOT ON TOP OF IT.
I KNOW. BUT...JUST COME BACK SAFE, ALL RIGHT?
SO'S I CAN YELL AT YOU. YOU BIG IDIOT.
EXACTLY WHAT PART OF "LET'S FIGHT ULTRON" DID YOU HEAR AS "GIVE ALL YOUR POWERS AWAY", BRIAN?
I GAVE AWAY THE MAGIC--THE POWERS ARE STILL INTACT. GETTING STRONGER, ACTUALLY.
THEY SCALE UP WITH MY CONFIDENCE, SO...WELL, ACTUALLY HAVING SOME HOPE GIVES ME QUITE A BOOST.
JUST IMAGINE IF WE HAD A PLAN, TOO.
SO--IF CAPTAIN BRITAIN'S BACK THERE HEALING THE WOUNDED--WHO AM I TALKING TO NOW?
...
CAPTAIN BRIAN?
COME ON, LET'S GO DUFF UP A ROBOT.
BRIAN BRADDOCK IS CAPTAIN BRIAN.

ST. PAUL'S CATHEDRAL.

ST. PAUL'S IS ULTRON'S MAIN STAGING POST.

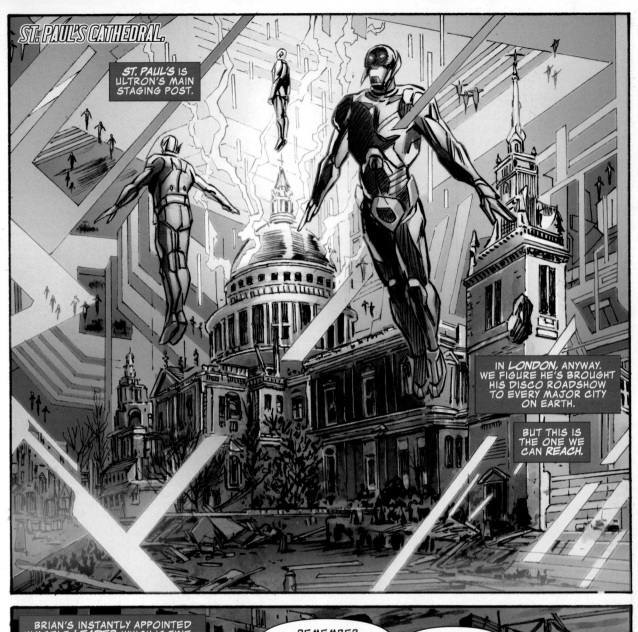

IN *LONDON*, ANYWAY. WE FIGURE HE'S BROUGHT HIS DISCO ROADSHOW TO EVERY MAJOR CITY ON EARTH.

BUT THIS IS THE ONE WE CAN *REACH*.

BRIAN'S INSTANTLY APPOINTED HIMSELF *LEADER*. WHICH IS FINE-- WITH HIS POWERS, HE PROBABLY *NEEDS* THE EGO BOOST TO STAY AT FULL STRENGTH.

(MAYBE HE SHOULD CALL HIMSELF *MAN* MAN.)

...REMEMBER, MEL, IF *ANYTHING* HAPPENS TO *ANY* OF US-- WELL, DON'T *RUN*, NOT WITH *YOUR* POWERS.

BUT *DRIBBLE*. DRIBBLE A BALL AS *FAST* AND AS *FAR* AS YOU CAN.

AS LONG AS YOU'RE *DRIBBLING*, NOTHING CAN *TOUCH* YOU...

BESIDES, IT'S NOT LIKE I CAN'T PULL RANK ON HIM IF I *NEED* TO.

CASE IN POINT...

TOO MANY.

WE GO OUT THERE AND THEY'LL *CUT* US TO BITS IN *SECONDS*--AND THAT'S JUST THE THREE *GIANT-SIZED* FELLOWS.

I'VE GOT *SOME* FORCE-FIELD POWERS, BUT I CAN'T SHIELD *EVERYBODY*...

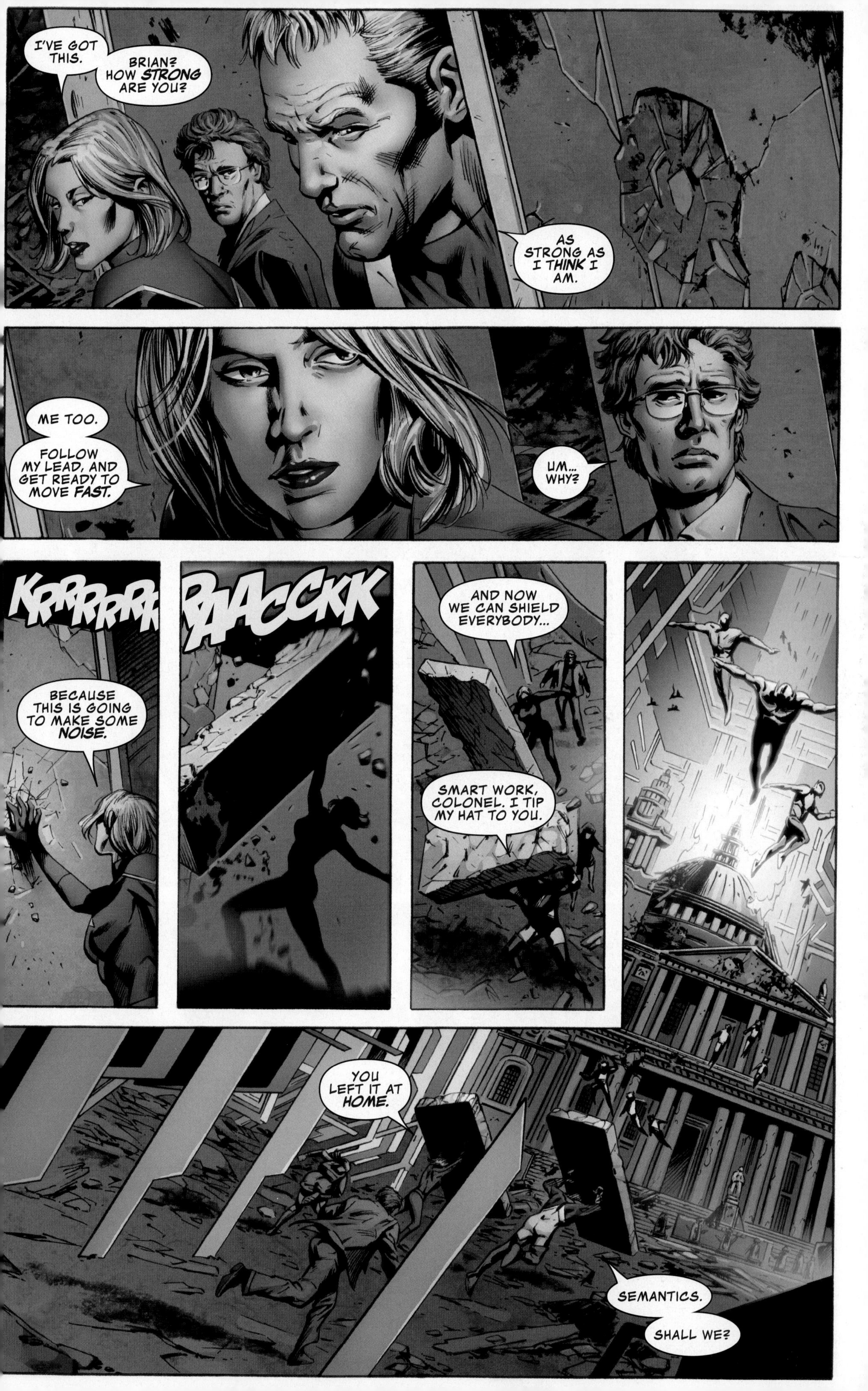

I'VE GOT THIS.
BRIAN? HOW STRONG ARE YOU?
AS STRONG AS I THINK I AM.
ME TOO.
FOLLOW MY LEAD, AND GET READY TO MOVE FAST.
UM... WHY?
KRRRRRK
BECAUSE THIS IS GOING TO MAKE SOME NOISE.
BAACCKK
AND NOW WE CAN SHIELD EVERYBODY...
SMART WORK, COLONEL. I TIP MY HAT TO YOU.
YOU LEFT IT AT HOME.
SEMANTICS.
SHALL WE?

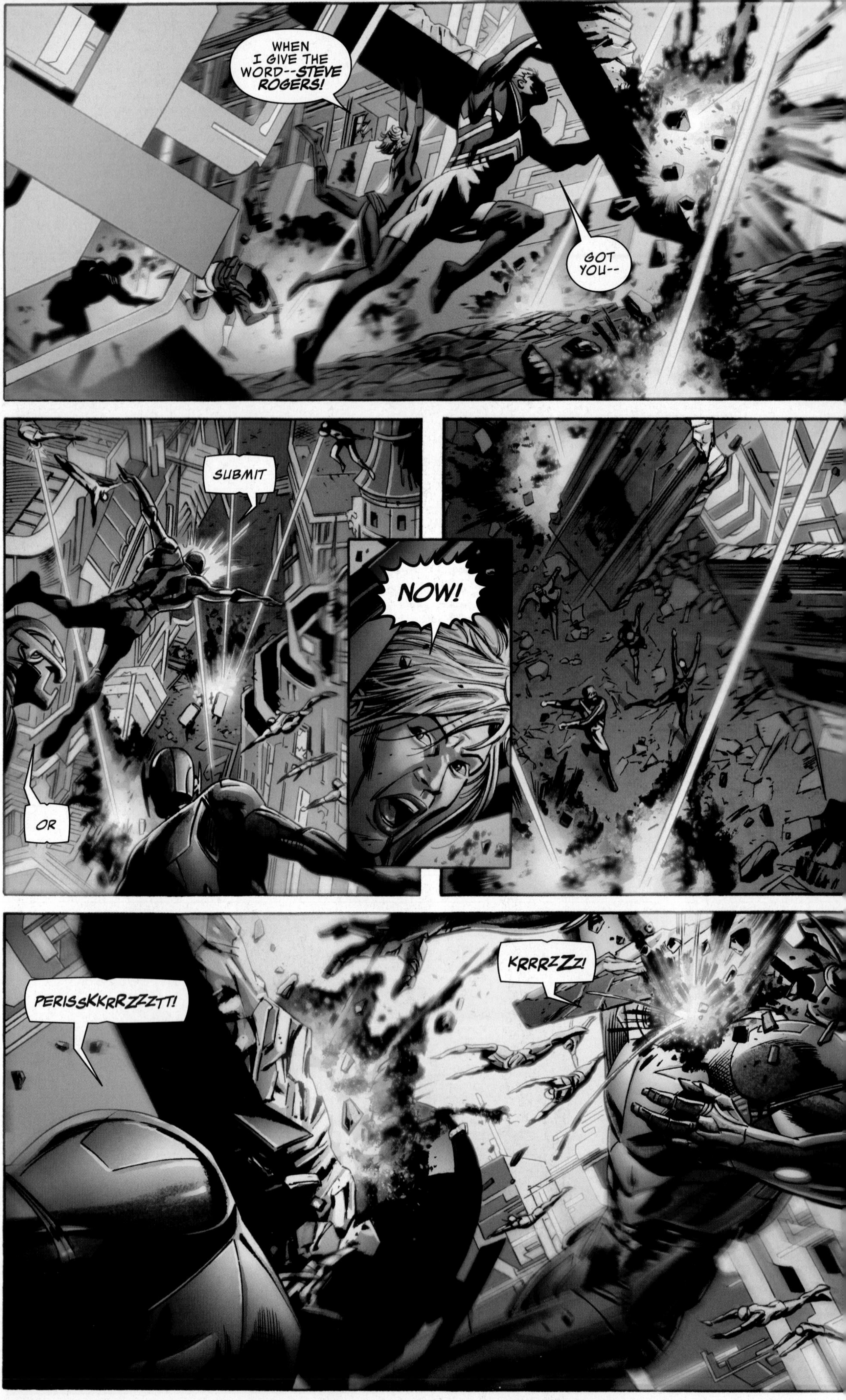
WHEN I GIVE THE WORD--STEVE ROGERS!
GOT YOU--
SUBMIT
OR
NOW!
PERISSKKRRZZZTT!
KRRRZZZ!

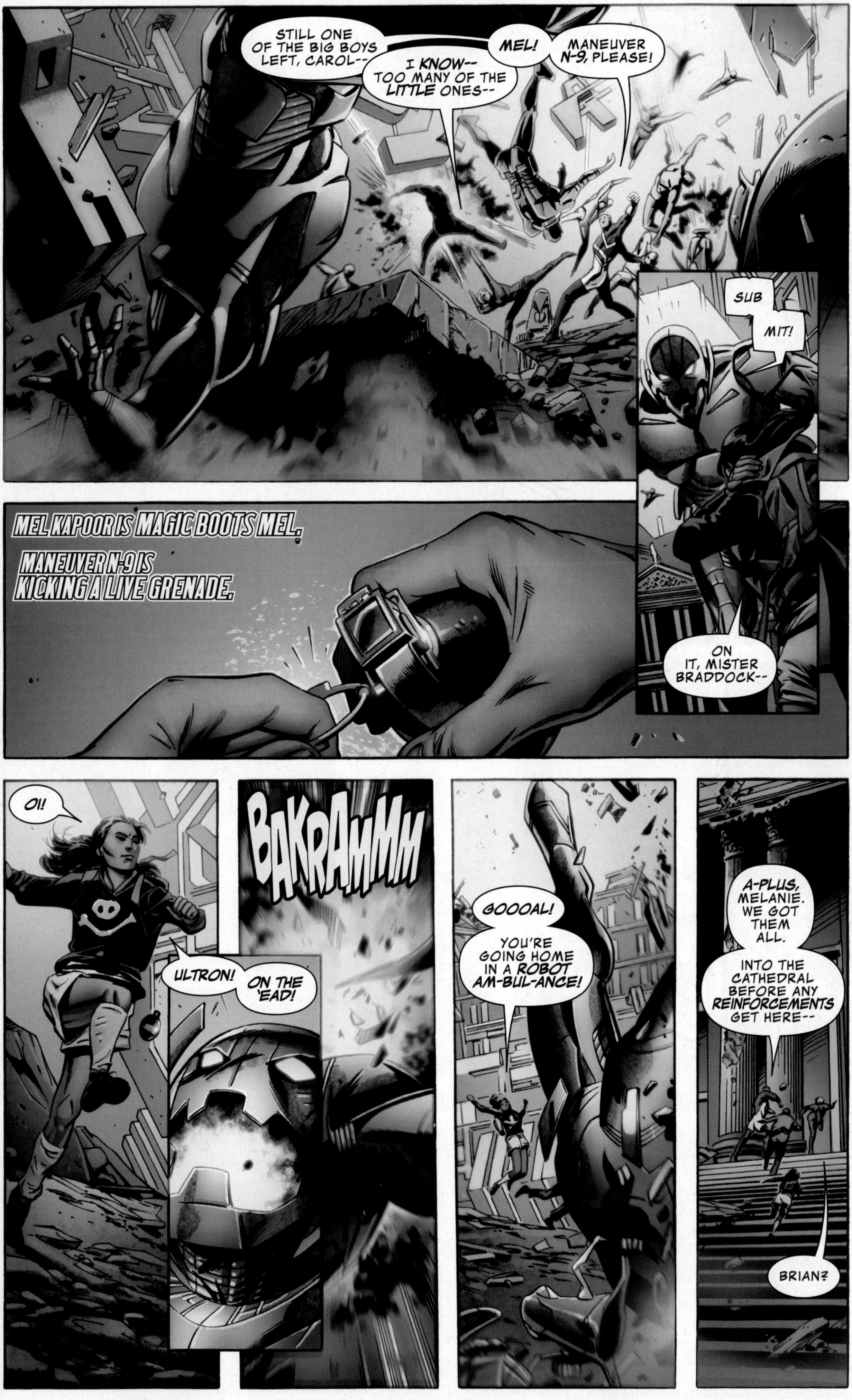
STILL ONE OF THE BIG BOYS LEFT, CAROL--
I KNOW-- TOO MANY OF THE LITTLE ONES--
MEL!
MANEUVER N-9, PLEASE!
SUB
MIT!
ON IT, MISTER BRADDOCK--
MEL KAPOOR IS MAGIC BOOTS MEL.
MANEUVER N-9 IS KICKING A LIVE GRENADE.
OI!
ULTRON!
ON THE 'EAD!
BAKRAMMM
GOOOAL!
YOU'RE GOING HOME IN A ROBOT AM-BUL-ANCE!
A-PLUS, MELANIE. WE GOT THEM ALL.
INTO THE CATHEDRAL BEFORE ANY REINFORCEMENTS GET HERE--
BRIAN?

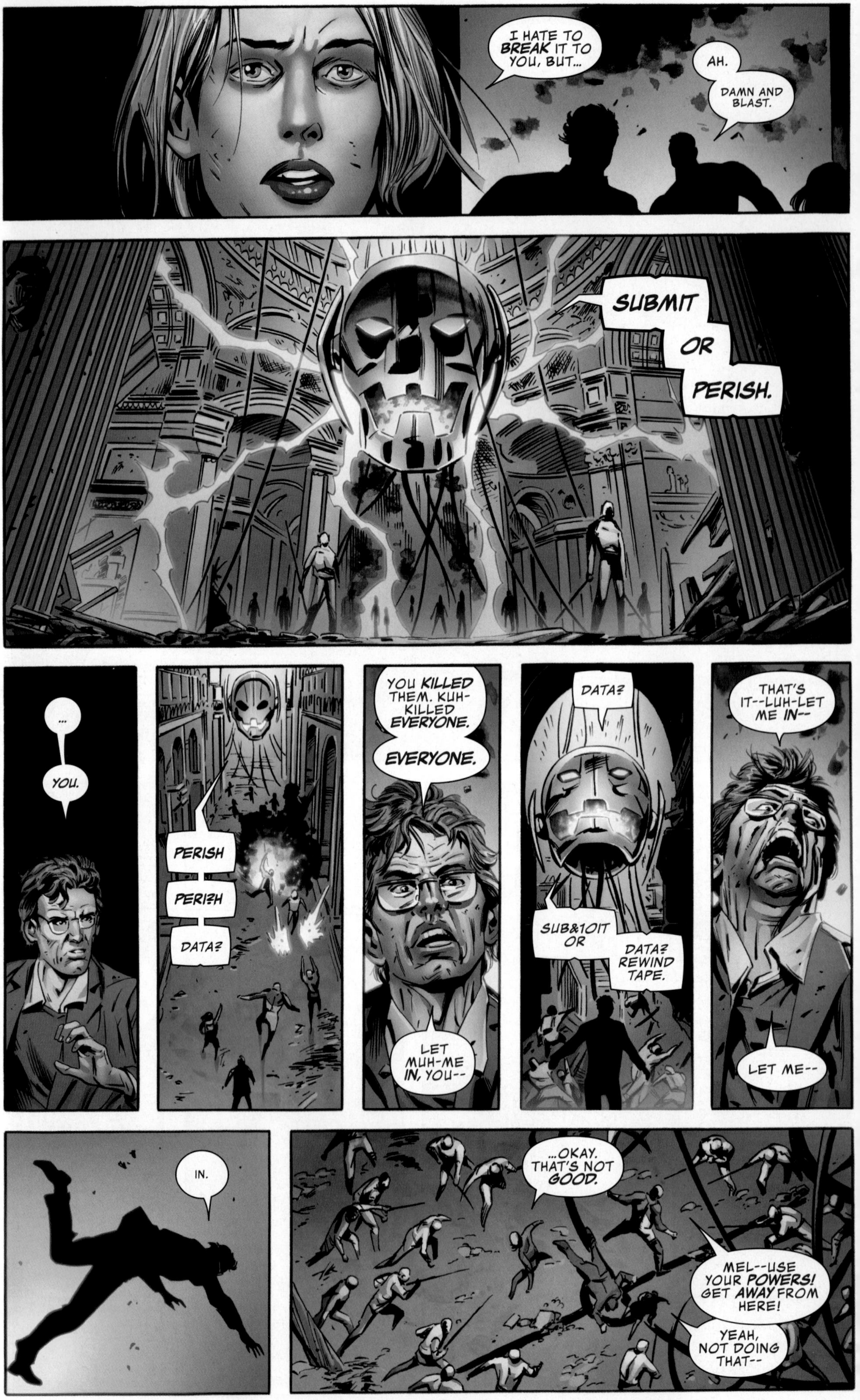

I HATE TO BREAK IT TO YOU, BUT...
AH.
DAMN AND BLAST.
SUBMIT
OR
PERISH.
...
YOU.
PERISH
PERI?H
DATA?
YOU KILLED THEM. KUH-KILLED EVERYONE.
EVERYONE.
LET MUH-ME IN, YOU--
DATA?
SUB&1OIT OR
DATA? REWIND TAPE.
THAT'S IT--LUH-LET ME IN--
LET ME--
IN.
...OKAY. THAT'S NOT GOOD.
MEL--USE YOUR POWERS! GET AWAY FROM HERE!
YEAH, NOT DOING THAT--

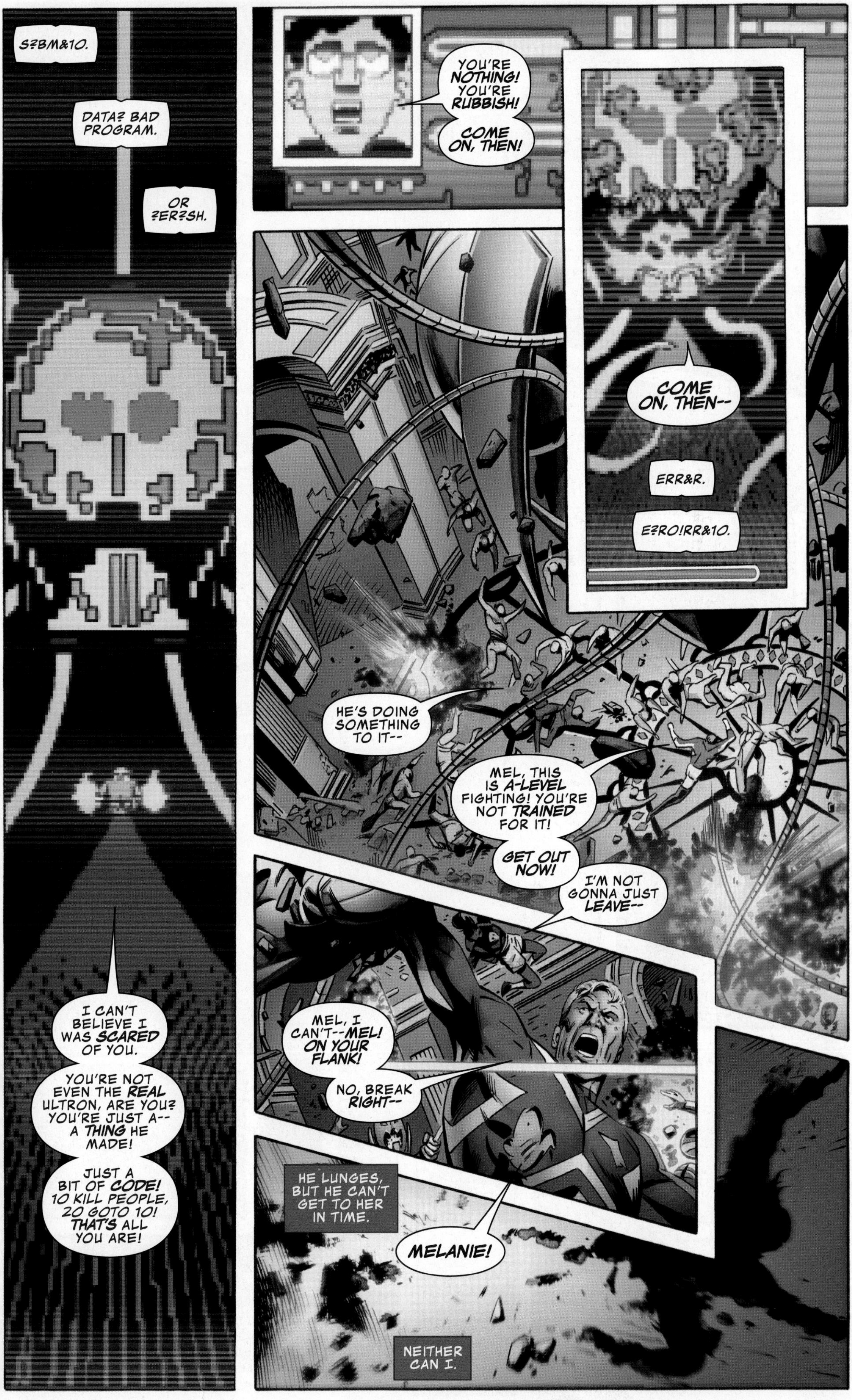

S?BM&10.
DATA? BAD PROGRAM.
OR ?ER?SH.
I CAN'T BELIEVE I WAS SCARED OF YOU.
YOU'RE NOT EVEN THE REAL ULTRON, ARE YOU? YOU'RE JUST A-- A THING HE MADE!
JUST A BIT OF CODE! 10 KILL PEOPLE, 20 GOTO 10! THAT'S ALL YOU ARE!
YOU'RE NOTHING! YOU'RE RUBBISH!
COME ON, THEN!
COME ON, THEN--
ERR&R.
E?RO!RR&10.
HE'S DOING SOMETHING TO IT--
MEL, THIS IS A-LEVEL FIGHTING! YOU'RE NOT TRAINED FOR IT!
GET OUT NOW!
I'M NOT GONNA JUST LEAVE--
MEL, I CAN'T--MEL! ON YOUR FLANK!
NO, BREAK RIGHT--
HE LUNGES, BUT HE CAN'T GET TO HER IN TIME.
MELANIE!
NEITHER CAN I.

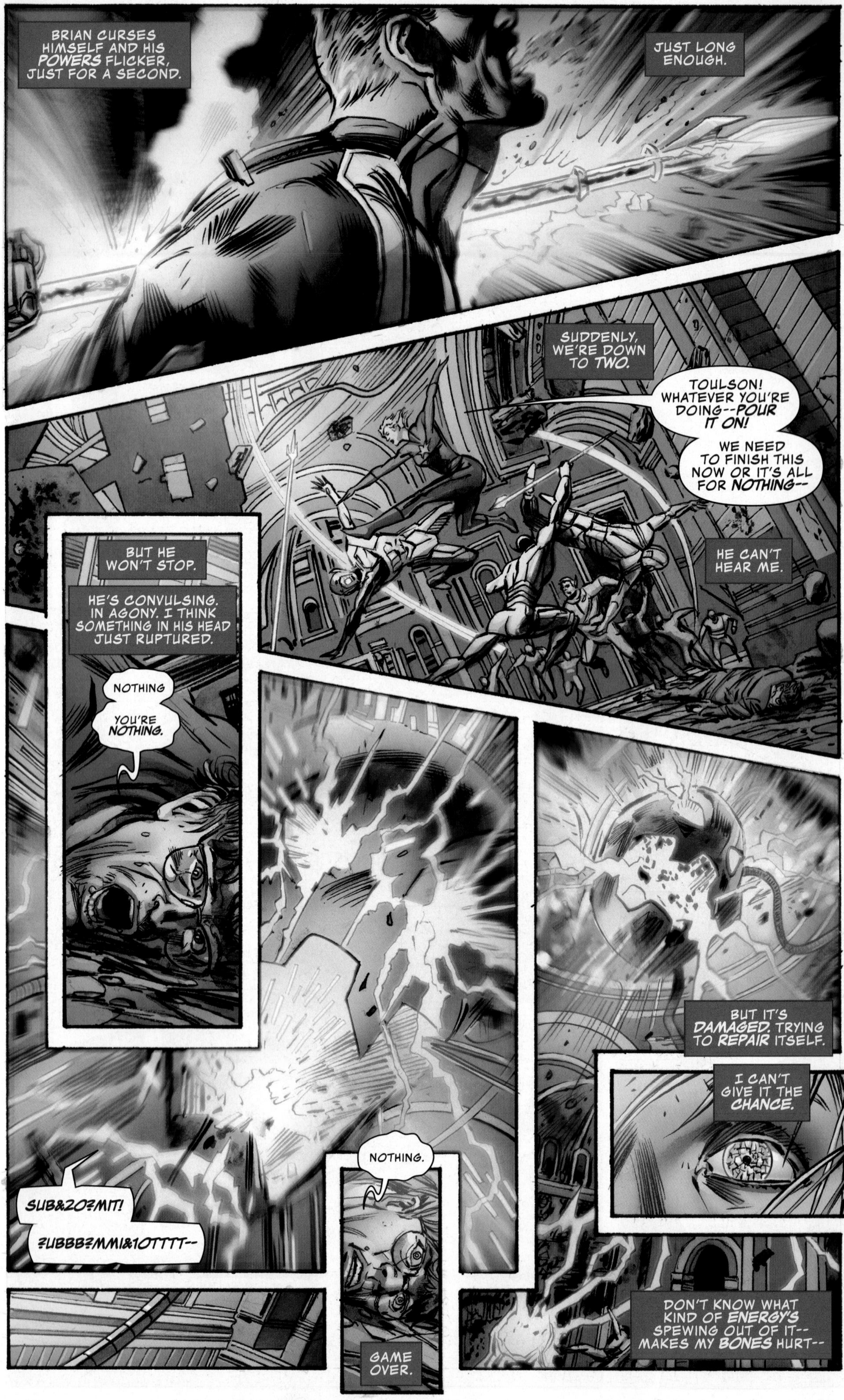
BRIAN CURSES HIMSELF AND HIS POWERS FLICKER, JUST FOR A SECOND.
JUST LONG ENOUGH.
SUDDENLY, WE'RE DOWN TO TWO.
TOULSON! WHATEVER YOU'RE DOING--POUR IT ON!
WE NEED TO FINISH THIS NOW OR IT'S ALL FOR NOTHING--
HE CAN'T HEAR ME.
BUT HE WON'T STOP.
HE'S CONVULSING. IN AGONY. I THINK SOMETHING IN HIS HEAD JUST RUPTURED.
NOTHING
YOU'RE NOTHING.
BUT IT'S DAMAGED. TRYING TO REPAIR ITSELF.
I CAN'T GIVE IT THE CHANCE.
SUB&2O?MIT!
?UBBB?MMI&1OTTTT--
NOTHING.
GAME OVER.
DON'T KNOW WHAT KIND OF ENERGY'S SPEWING OUT OF IT--MAKES MY BONES HURT--

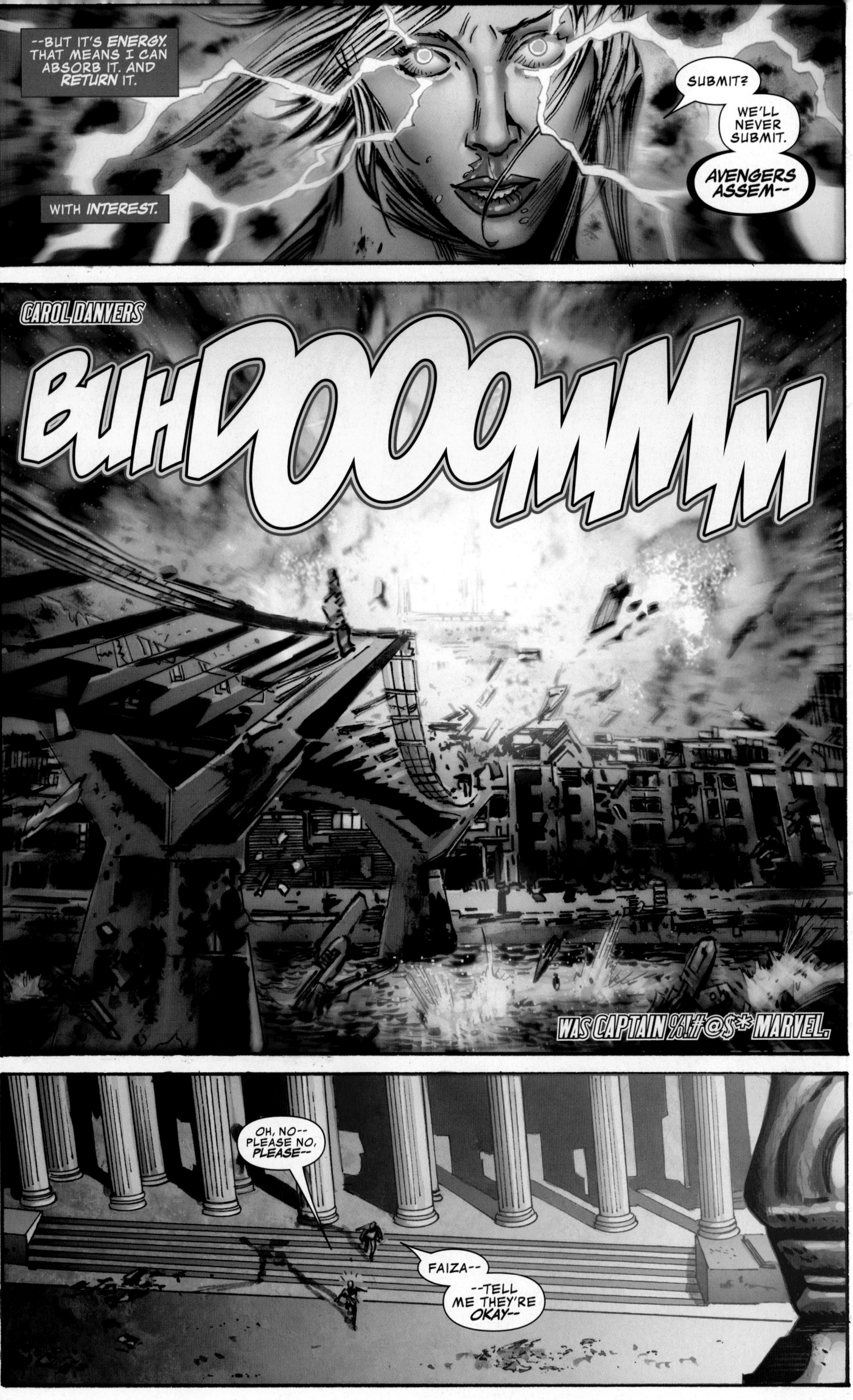
--BUT IT'S ENERGY. THAT MEANS I CAN ABSORB IT. AND RETURN IT.
WITH INTEREST.
SUBMIT?
WE'LL NEVER SUBMIT.
AVENGERS ASSEM--
CAROL DANVERS
BUHDOOOMMM
WAS CAPTAIN %!#@$* MARVEL.
OH, NO-- PLEASE NO, PLEASE--
FAIZA--
--TELL ME THEY'RE OKAY--

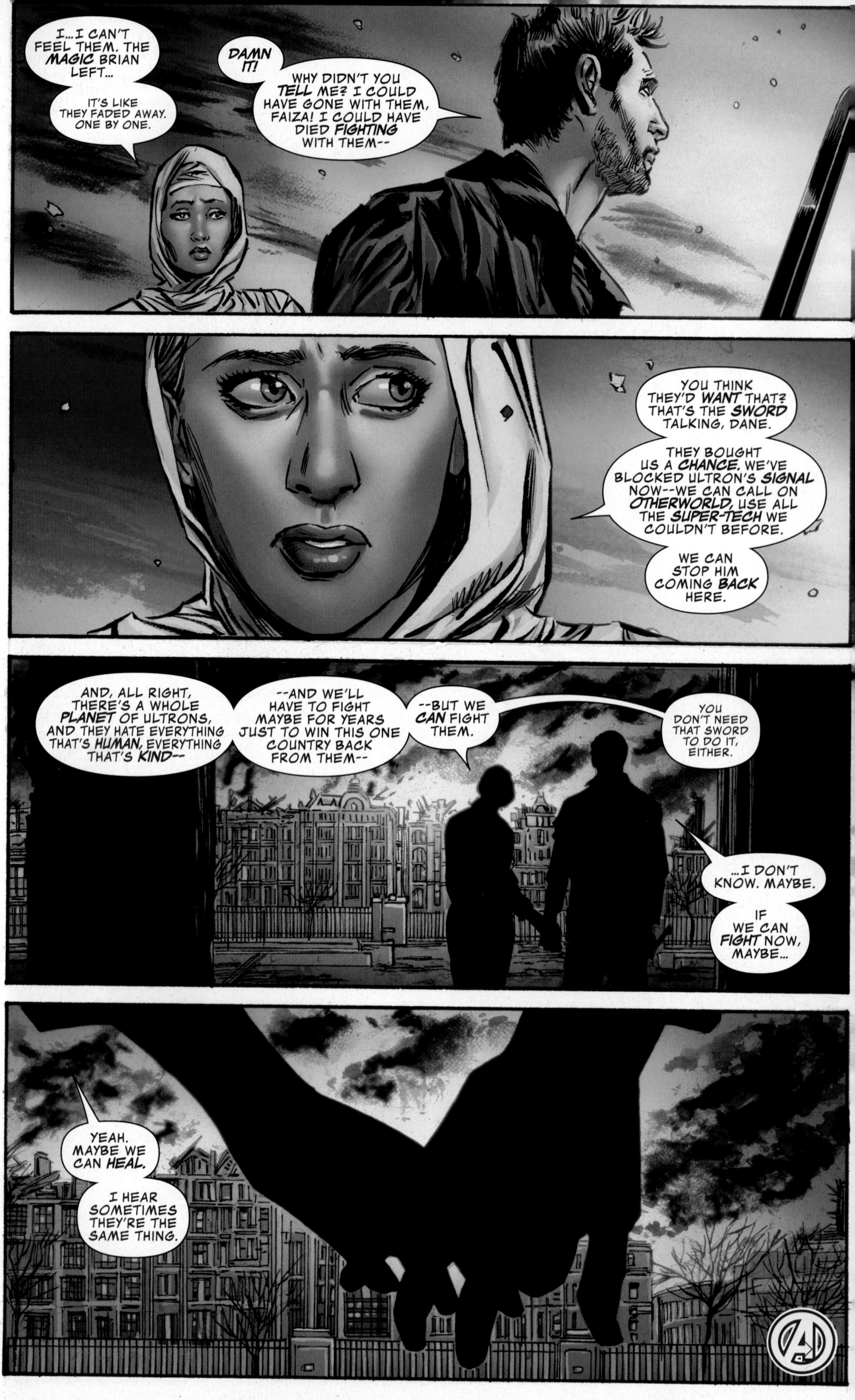

I...I CAN'T FEEL THEM. THE MAGIC BRIAN LEFT...
IT'S LIKE THEY FADED AWAY. ONE BY ONE.
DAMN IT!
WHY DIDN'T YOU TELL ME? I COULD HAVE GONE WITH THEM, FAIZA! I COULD HAVE DIED FIGHTING WITH THEM--
YOU THINK THEY'D WANT THAT? THAT'S THE SWORD TALKING, DANE.
THEY BOUGHT US A CHANCE. WE'VE BLOCKED ULTRON'S SIGNAL NOW--WE CAN CALL ON OTHERWORLD, USE ALL THE SUPER-TECH WE COULDN'T BEFORE.
WE CAN STOP HIM COMING BACK HERE.
AND, ALL RIGHT, THERE'S A WHOLE PLANET OF ULTRONS, AND THEY HATE EVERYTHING THAT'S HUMAN, EVERYTHING THAT'S KIND--
--AND WE'LL HAVE TO FIGHT MAYBE FOR YEARS JUST TO WIN THIS ONE COUNTRY BACK FROM THEM--
--BUT WE CAN FIGHT THEM.
YOU DON'T NEED THAT SWORD TO DO IT, EITHER.
...I DON'T KNOW. MAYBE.
IF WE CAN FIGHT NOW, MAYBE...
YEAH. MAYBE WE CAN HEAL.
I HEAR SOMETIMES THEY'RE THE SAME THING.

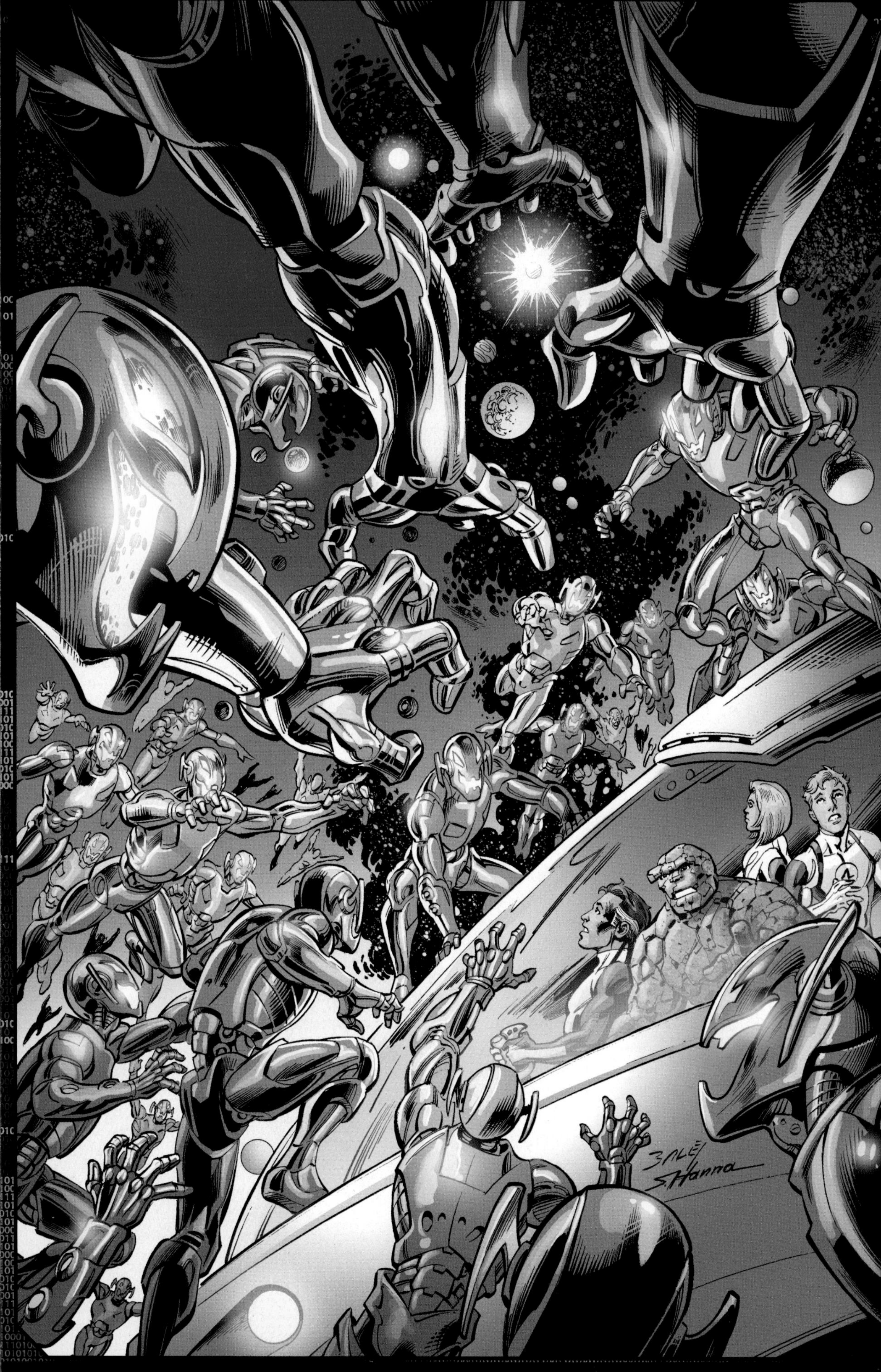
S.Hanna

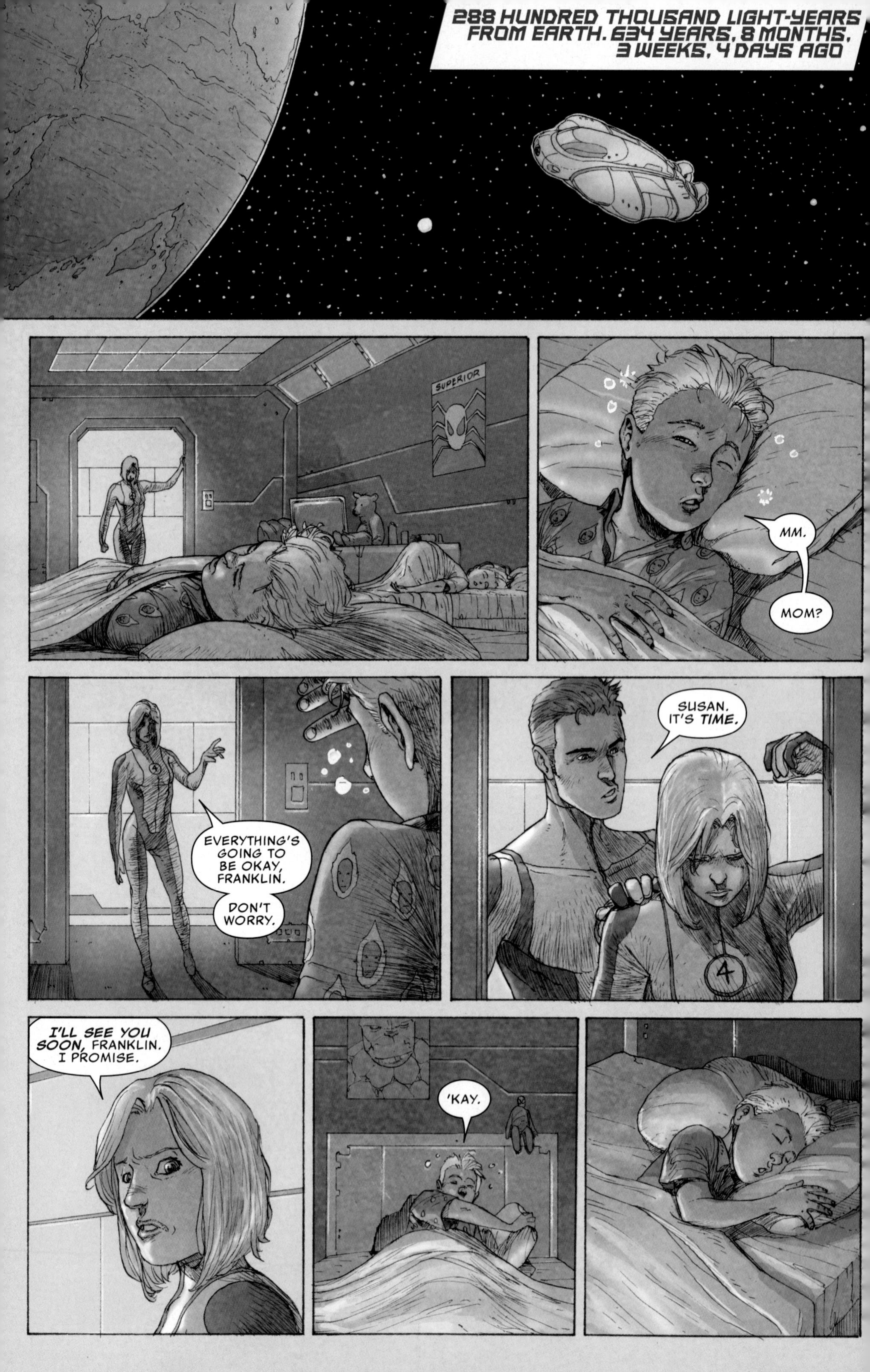
288 HUNDRED THOUSAND LIGHT-YEARS FROM EARTH. 634 YEARS, 8 MONTHS, 3 WEEKS, 4 DAYS AGO
SUPERIOR
MM.
MOM?
EVERYTHING'S GOING TO BE OKAY, FRANKLIN.
DON'T WORRY.
SUSAN. IT'S TIME.
I'LL SEE YOU SOON, FRANKLIN. I PROMISE.
'KAY.

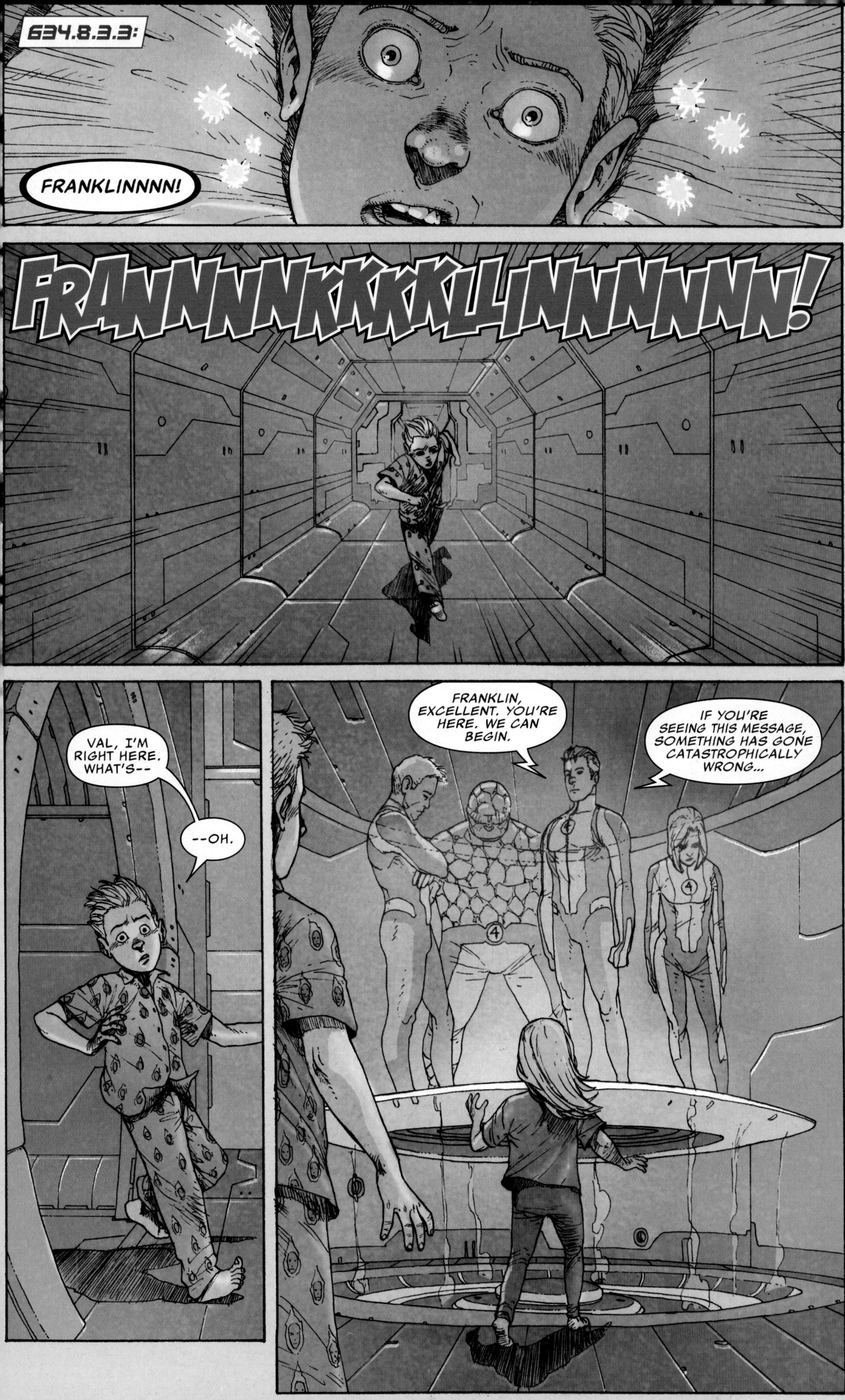
634.8.3.3:
FRANKLINNNN!
FRANNNNKKKKLLINNNNNNN!
VAL, I'M RIGHT HERE. WHAT'S--
--OH.
FRANKLIN, EXCELLENT. YOU'RE HERE. WE CAN BEGIN.
IF YOU'RE SEEING THIS MESSAGE, SOMETHING HAS GONE CATASTROPHICALLY WRONG...

ULTRON HAS ATTACKED EARTH.

AND I MEAN MY WORDS PRECISELY-- THE WHOLE OF THE PLANET, SEEMINGLY AT ONCE.

I LEFT THE CHRONOSTELLAR RADIO WITH T'CHALLA. HIS COMMUNICATION SAID--

IT IS THE END OF THE WORLD, REED. WE NEED ALL ABLE SOULS TO COME TO EARTH'S AID--

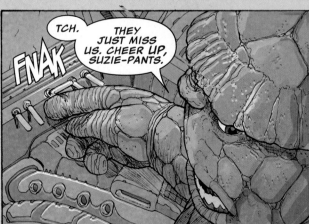

TCH.

FNAK

THEY JUST MISS US. CHEER UP, SUZIE-PANTS.

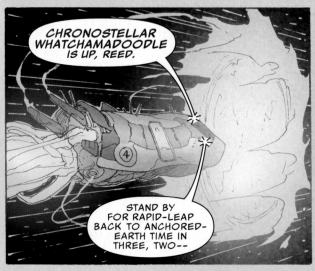

CHRONOSTELLAR WHATCHAMADOODLE IS UP, REED.

STAND BY FOR RAPID-LEAP BACK TO ANCHORED-EARTH TIME IN THREE, TWO--

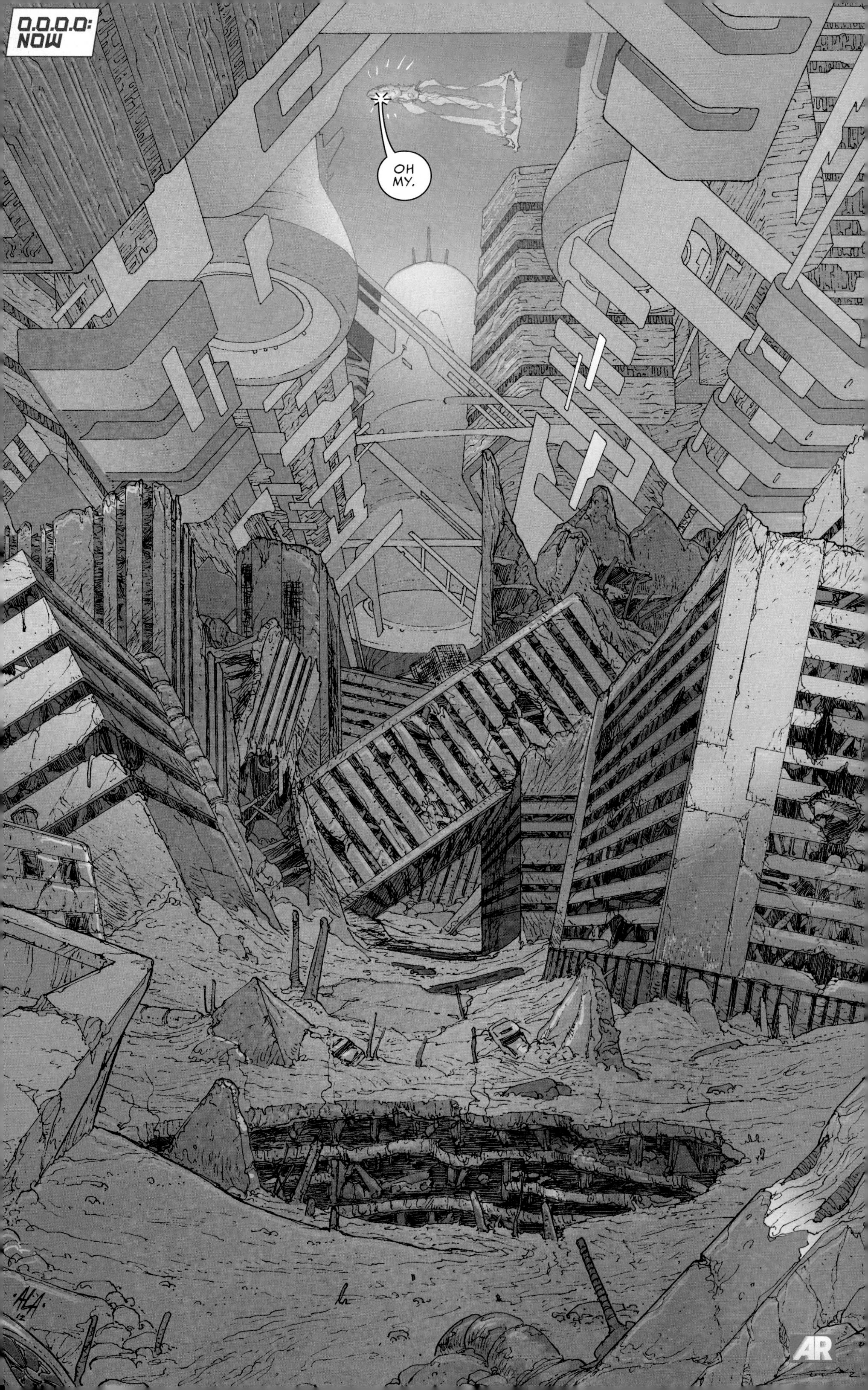
0.0.0.0: NOW
OH MY.
AR

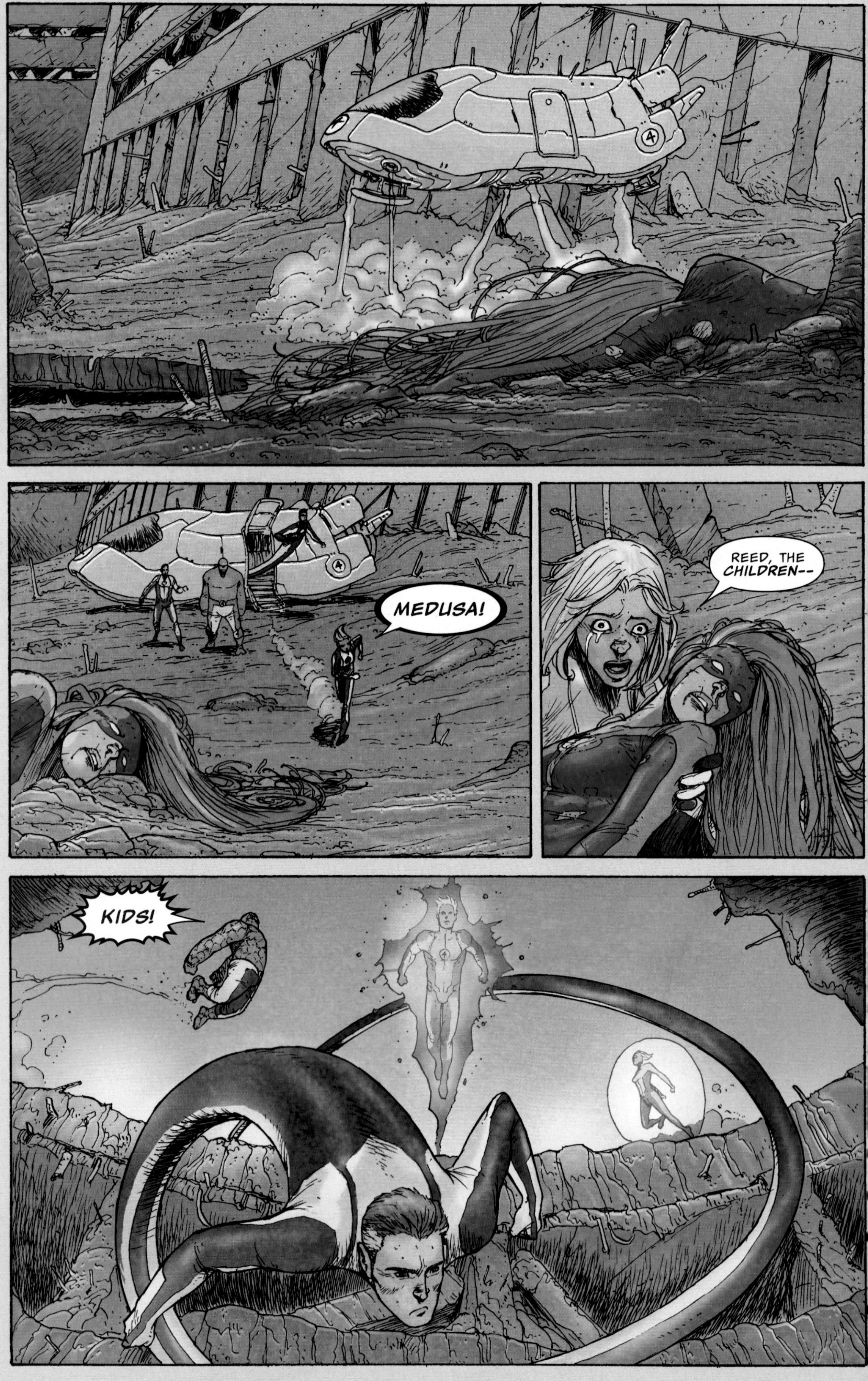
MEDUSA!
REED, THE CHILDREN--
KIDS!

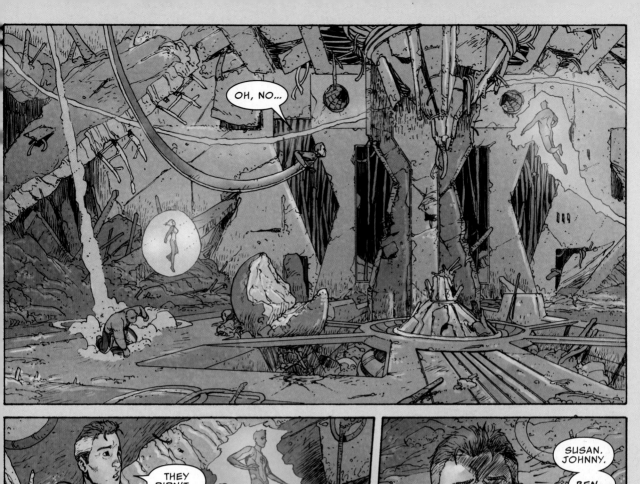

OH, NO...

THEY DIDN'T...

THEY DIDN'T EVEN GET *DOWN* HERE IN TIME. THEY NEVER EVEN *ACTIVATED* THE OMEGA ROOM. THEY...

SUSAN. JOHNNY.

BEN--

ALL HUMANOID LIFE FORMS ARE TO EXIT THE PREMISES IMMEDIATELY.

"UH...OKAY. SO... SO, OKAY, WELL, I GUESS THIS IS LIKE MY *WILL* OR WHATEVER.

"DIDN'T I *JUST DO THIS?*"

UM...YOU GUYS GET ALL MY STUFF. SPLIT IT UP BETWEEN YOU.

DON'T MESS UP MY CAR.

I'M JUST KIDDING.

LOOK, I DON'T KNOW WHY YOUR FOLKS ARE MAKING US DO THIS. WHAT AM I WORRIED ABOUT?

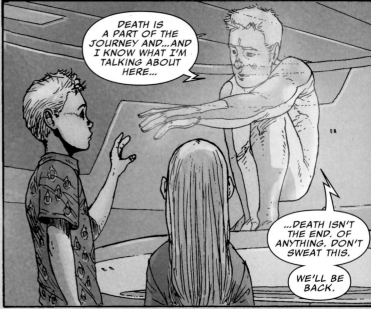

DEATH IS A PART OF THE JOURNEY AND...AND I KNOW WHAT I'M TALKING ABOUT HERE...

...DEATH ISN'T THE END. OF ANYTHING. DON'T SWEAT THIS.

WE'LL BE BACK.

REED, THIS IS STUPID, COME ON, MAN--

OKAY, WE'RE IN REAL TROUBLE.

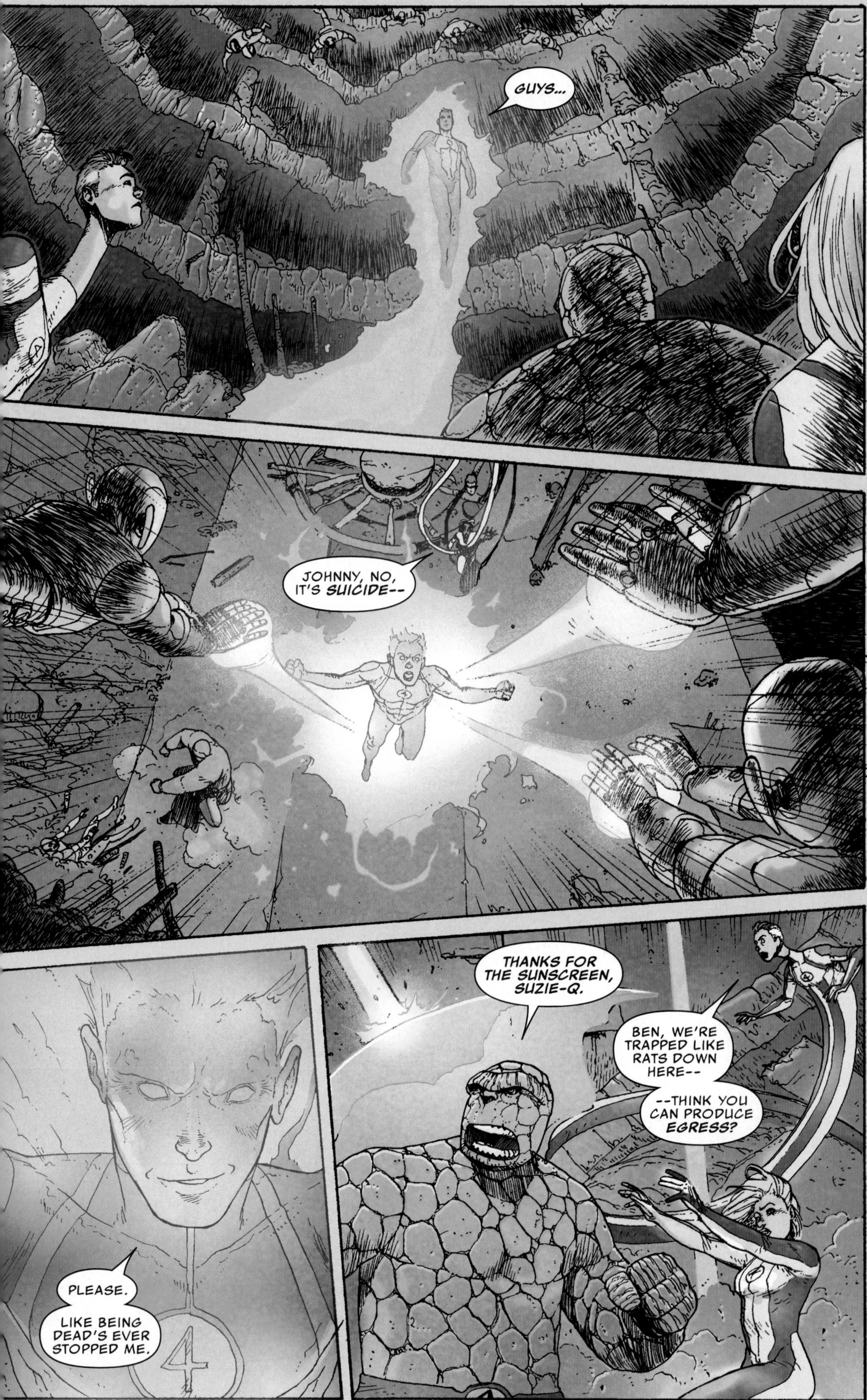
GUYS...
JOHNNY, NO, IT'S SUICIDE--
PLEASE.
LIKE BEING DEAD'S EVER STOPPED ME.
THANKS FOR THE SUNSCREEN, SUZIE-Q.
BEN, WE'RE TRAPPED LIKE RATS DOWN HERE--
--THINK YOU CAN PRODUCE EGRESS?

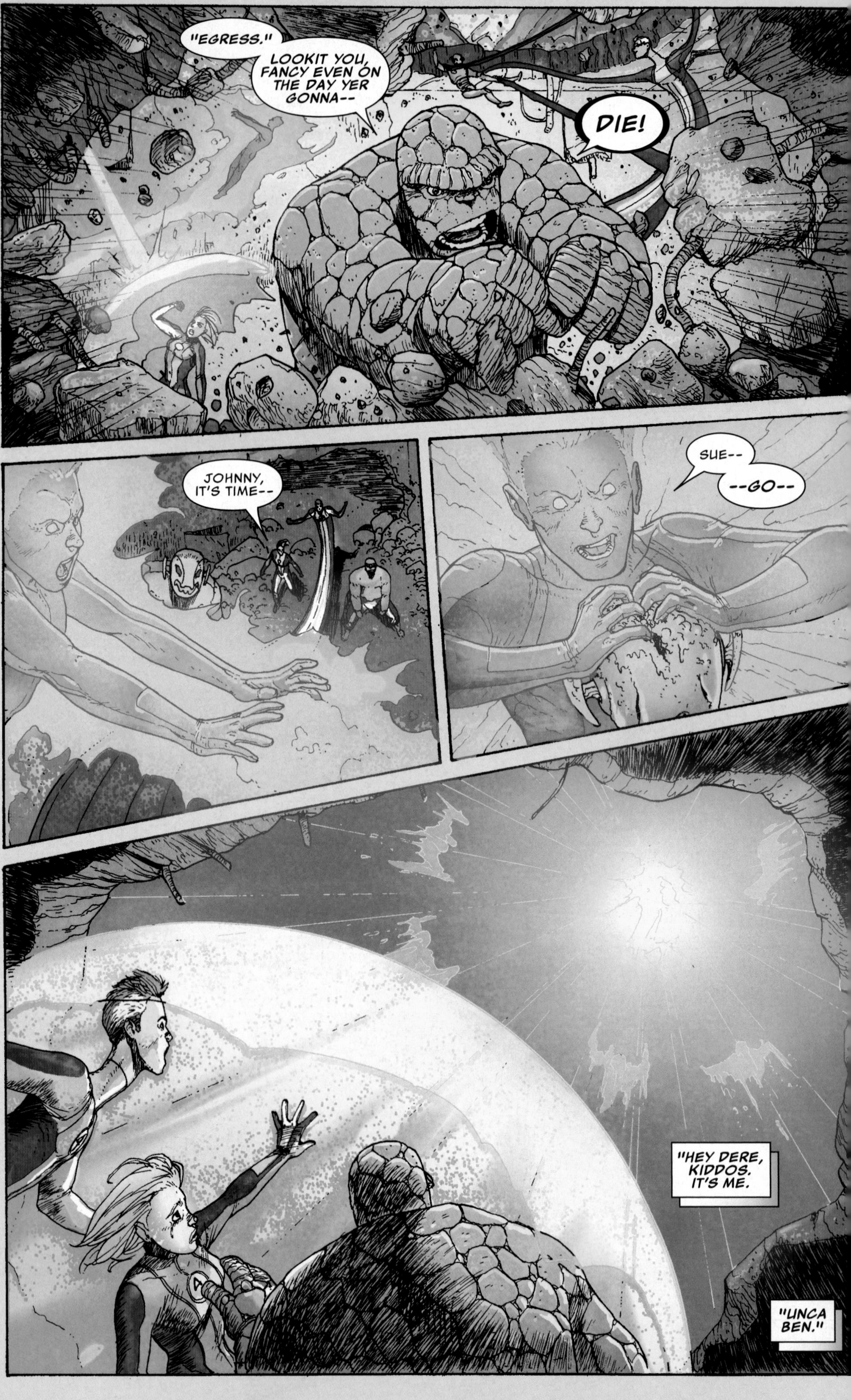
"EGRESS."
LOOKIT YOU, FANCY EVEN ON THE DAY YER GONNA--
DIE!
JOHNNY, IT'S TIME--
SUE--
--GO--
"HEY DERE, KIDDOS. IT'S ME.
"UNCA BEN."

LOOKS LIKE MEBBE THINGS AIN'T GOIN' SO WELL BACK HOME, SO WE'RE GONNA HELP FOLKS OUT, BUT...

WELL, IF YOU'RE HEARING THIS, WE'RE NOT *BACK* AND IT *REALLY* AIN'T GOIN' WELL.

BOY, THIS IS...

BOY, THIS IS REAL HEAVY. I--I DON'T...

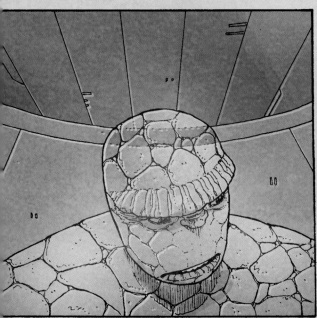

I AIN'T NEVER TOLD NOBODY THIS:

I THINK MEBBE DR. DOOM IS ALL MY FAULT.

WHEN ME AND YOUR DAD WERE KIDS, AND WE WERE ALL AT SCHOOL...THE GUY WAS A RICH *JERK*.

I MESSED WITH THIS EXPERIMENT HE HAD IN THEIR ROOM THERE AN'...I DIDN'T MEAN TA...I MEAN, I DON'T *KNOW* IF I DID IT, BUT...

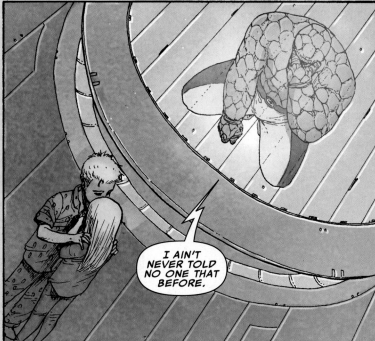

I AIN'T NEVER TOLD NO ONE THAT BEFORE.

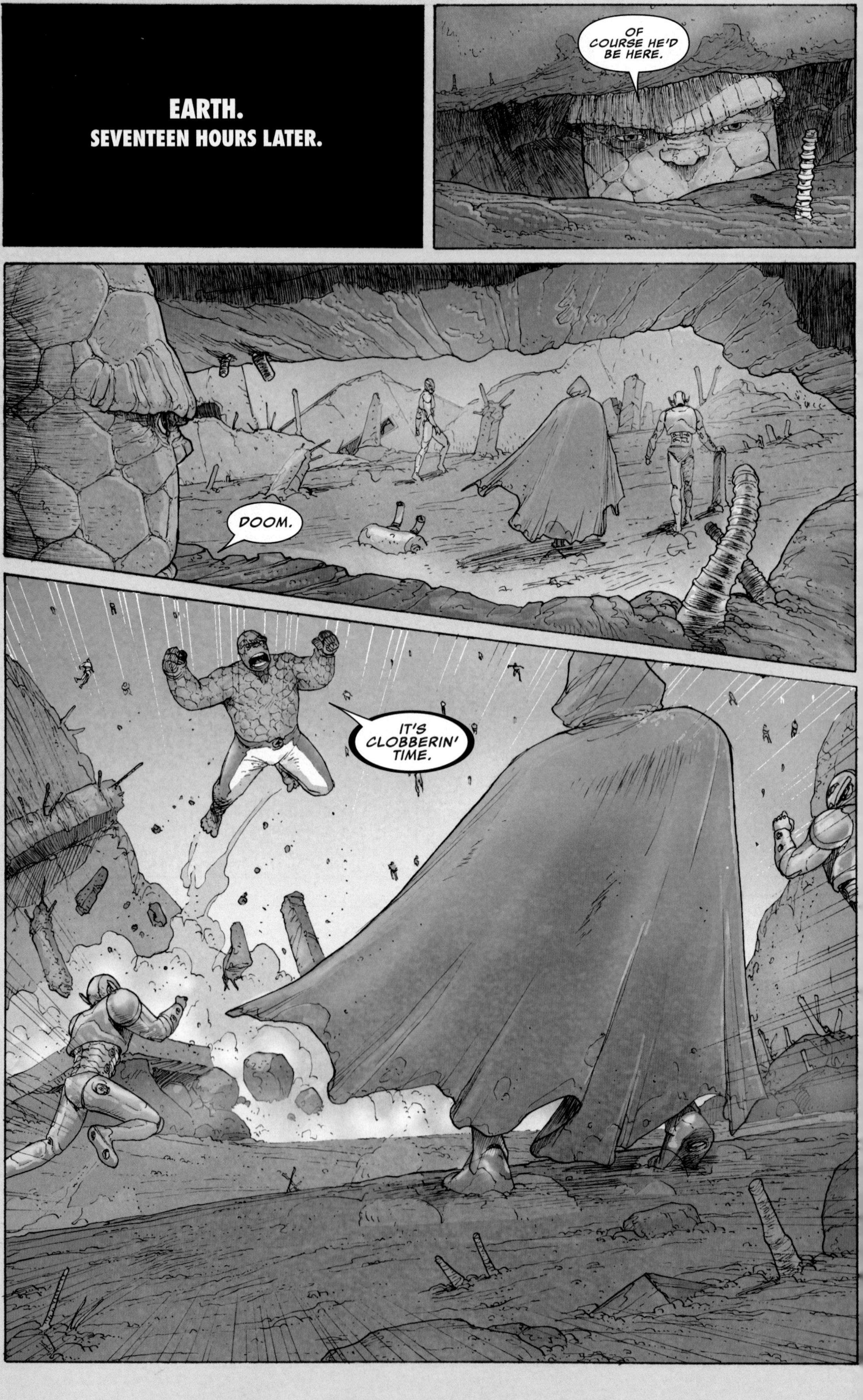
EARTH.
SEVENTEEN HOURS LATER.
OF COURSE HE'D BE HERE.
DOOM.
IT'S CLOBBERIN' TIME.

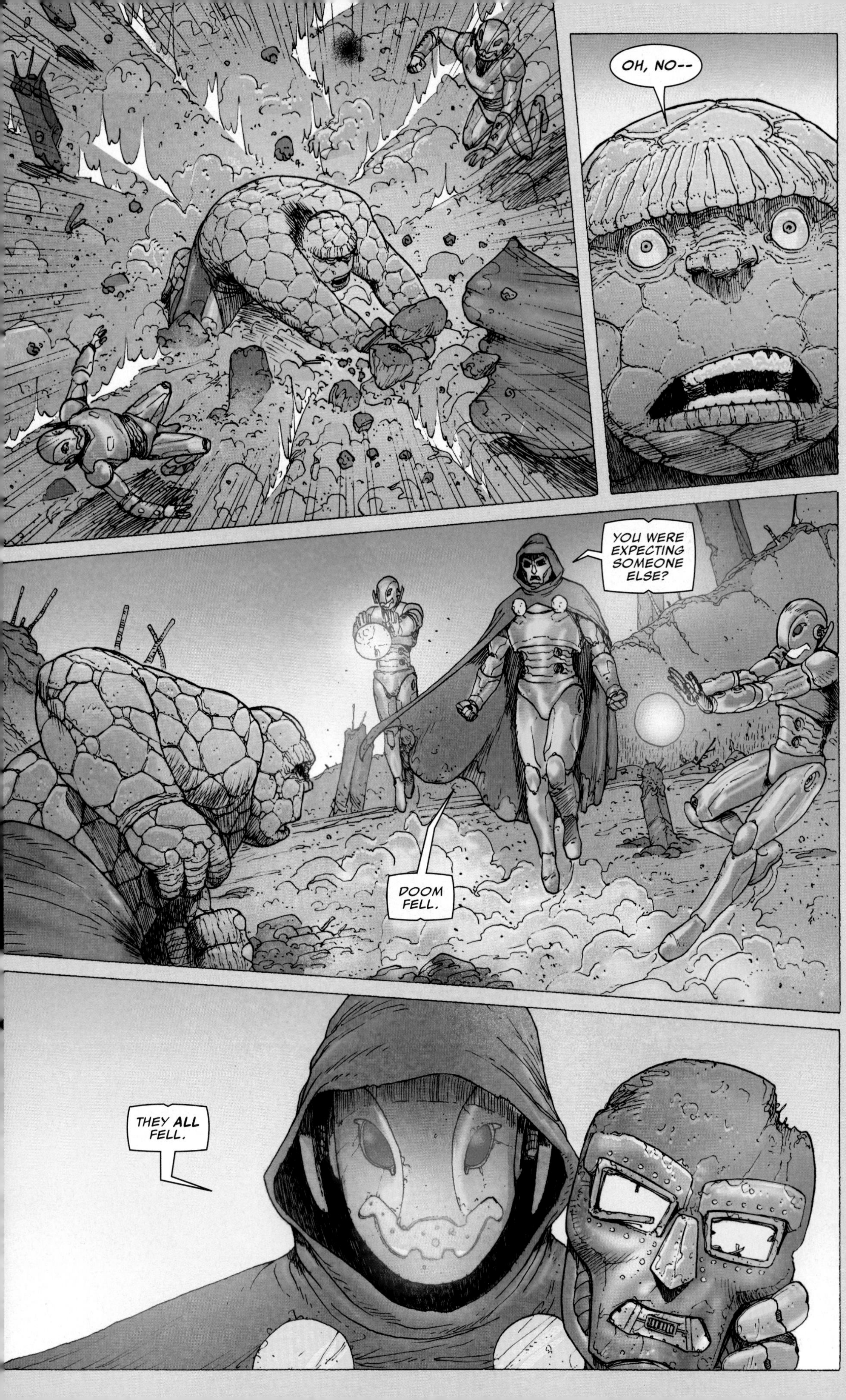
OH, NO--
YOU WERE EXPECTING SOMEONE ELSE?
DOOM FELL.
THEY ALL FELL.

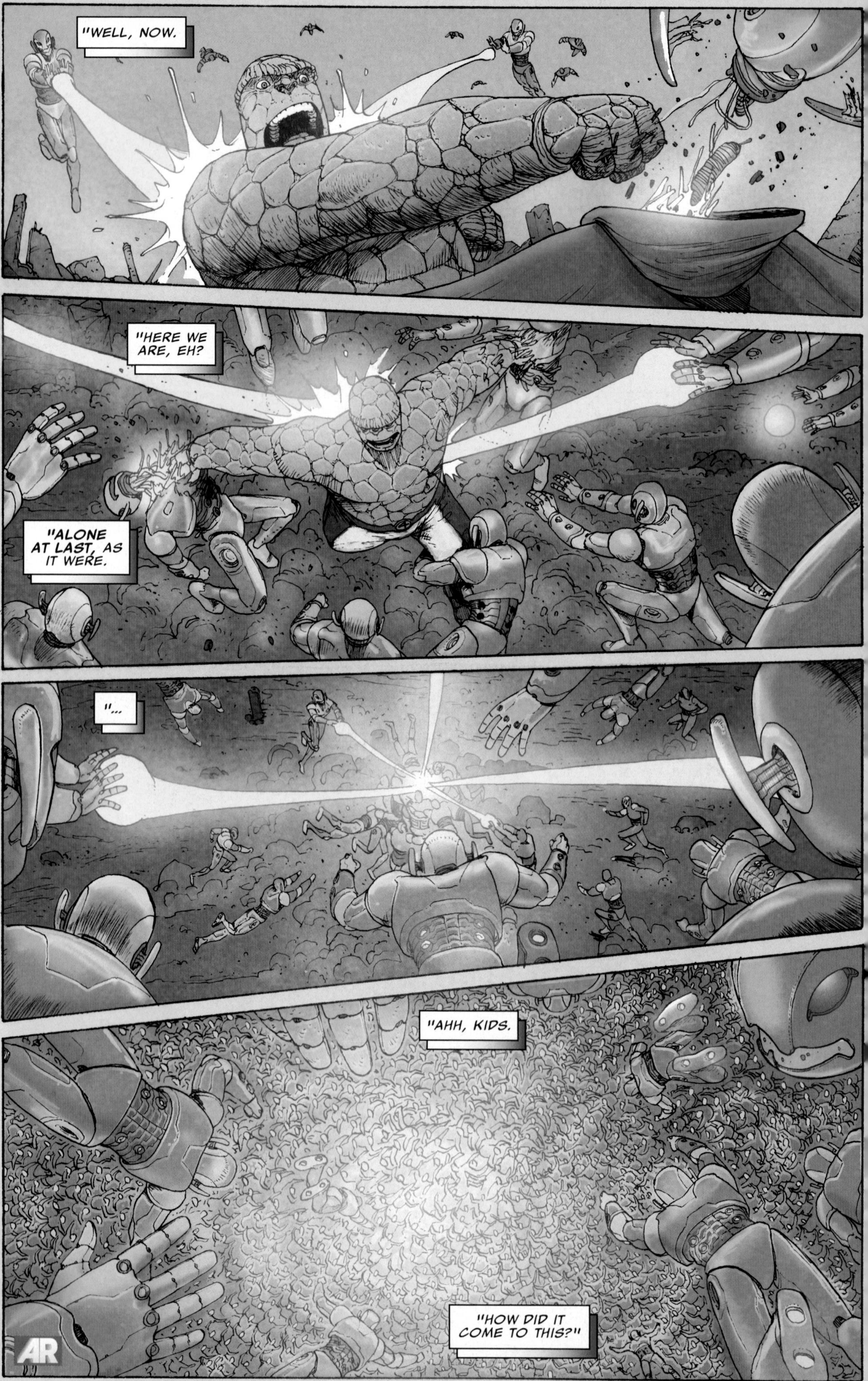
"WELL, NOW.
"HERE WE ARE, EH?
"ALONE AT LAST, AS IT WERE.
"...
"AHH, KIDS.
"HOW DID IT COME TO THIS?"
AR

...
I DON'T KNOW HOW TO SAY THIS...
WORDS NOT COMING...
HOW DOES A FATHER SAY GOODBYE TO HIS CHILDREN?
IMPOSSIBLE.

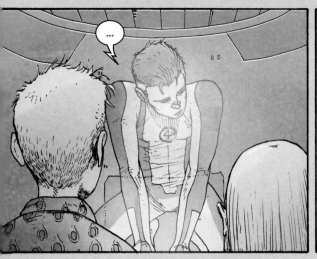

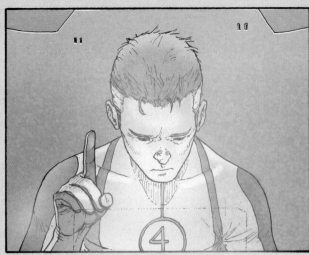

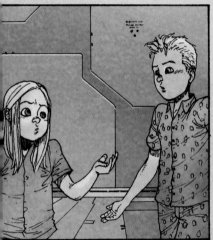

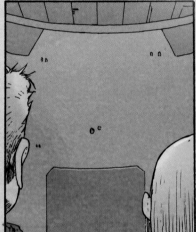

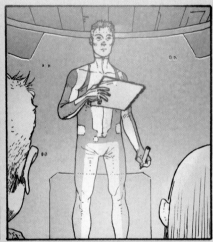

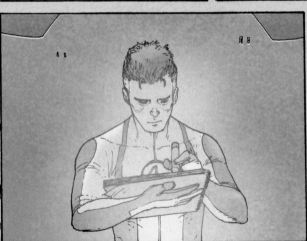

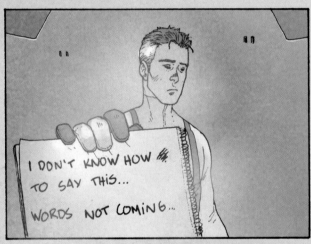

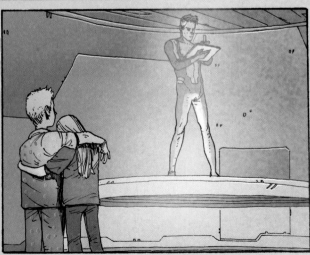

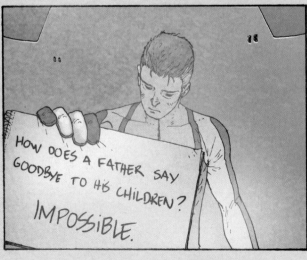

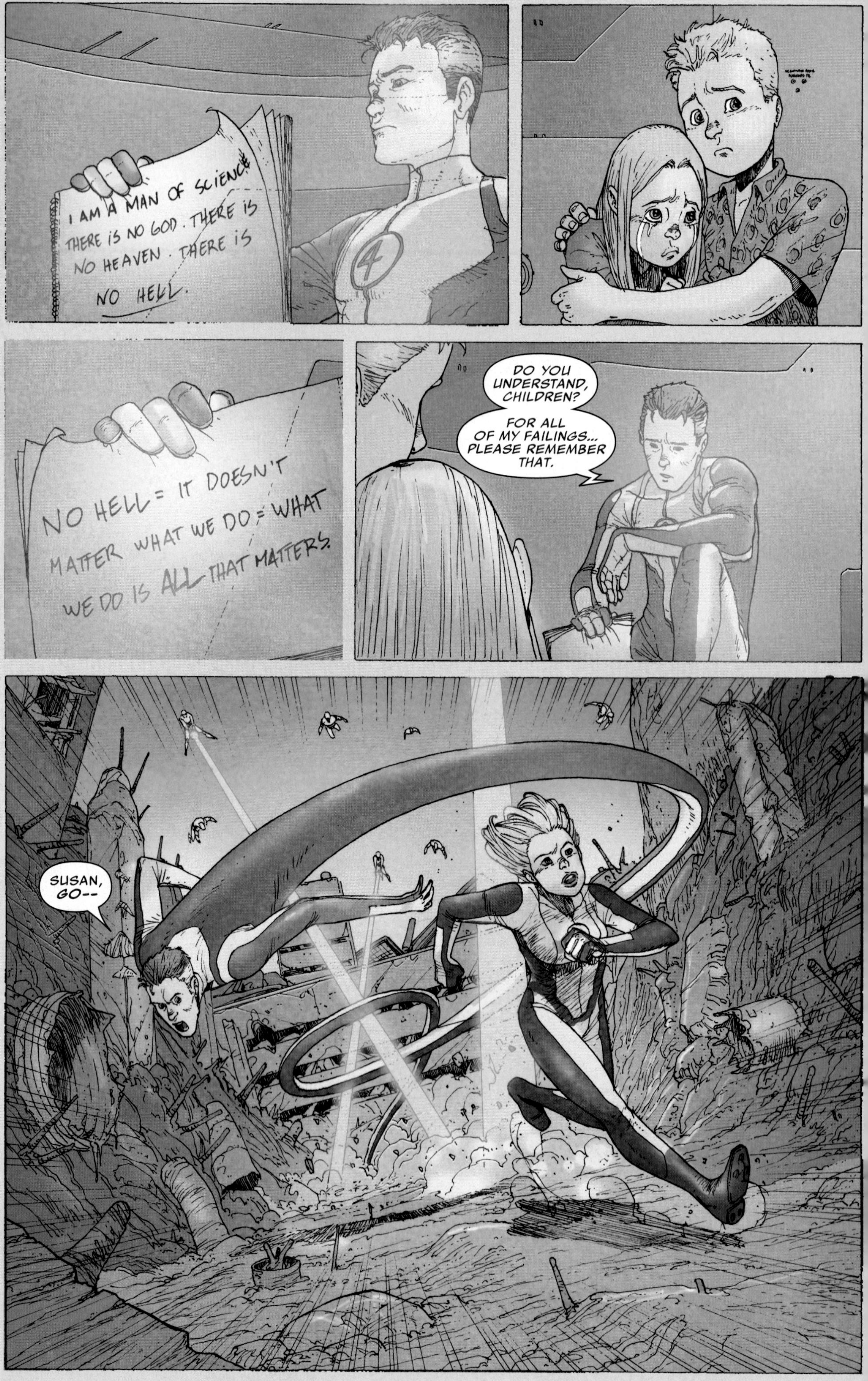
I AM A MAN OF SCIENCE
THERE IS NO GOD. THERE IS NO HEAVEN. THERE IS NO HELL.
NO HELL = IT DOESN'T MATTER WHAT WE DO = WHAT WE DO IS ALL THAT MATTERS.
DO YOU UNDERSTAND, CHILDREN?
FOR ALL OF MY FAILINGS... PLEASE REMEMBER THAT.
SUSAN, GO--

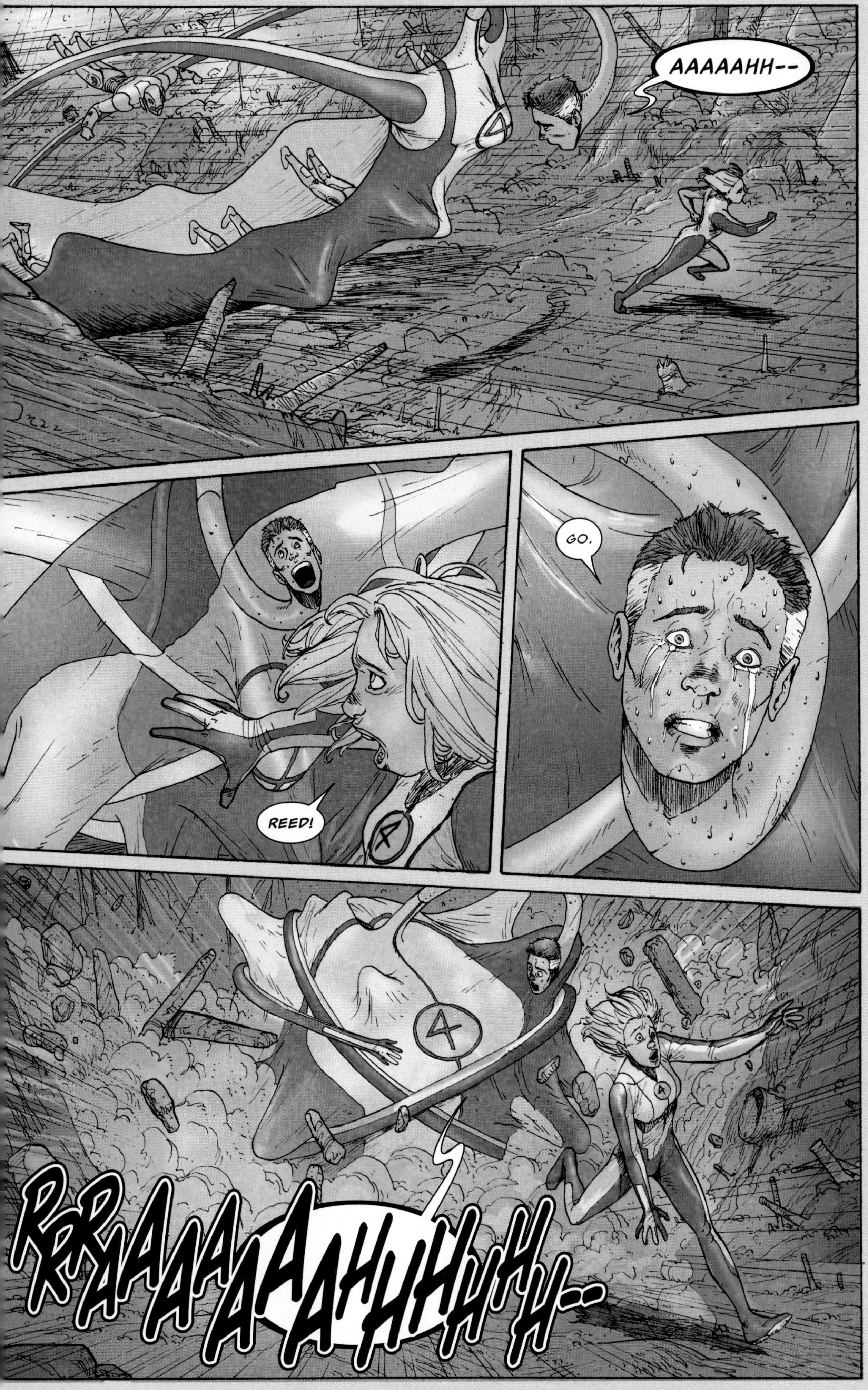
AAAAAHH--
REED!
GO.
RRRAAAAAAAAHHHHHH--

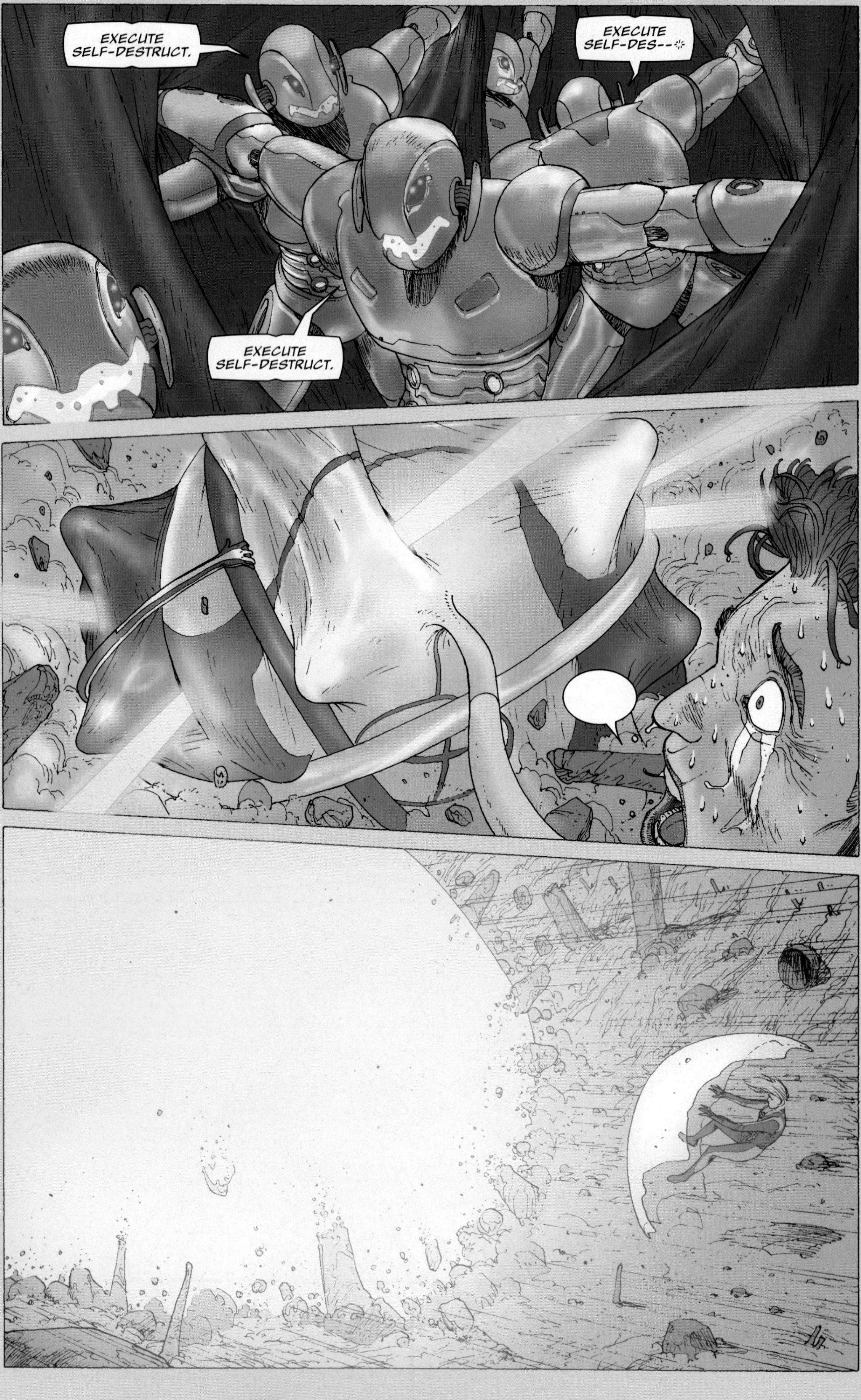
EXECUTE SELF-DESTRUCT.
EXECUTE SELF-DES--
EXECUTE SELF-DESTRUCT.

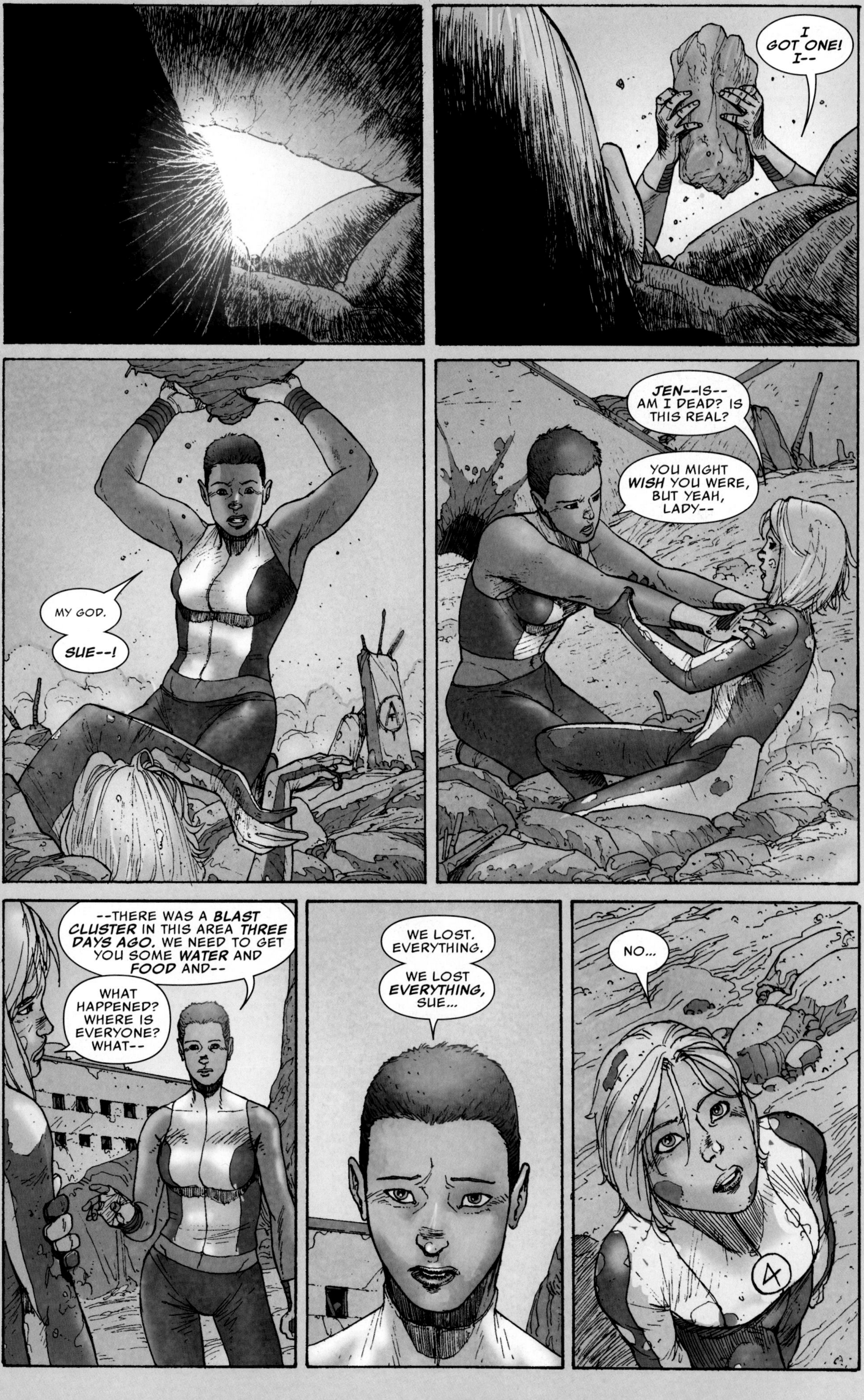
I GOT ONE! I--
MY GOD.
SUE--!
JEN--IS--AM I DEAD? IS THIS REAL?
YOU MIGHT WISH YOU WERE, BUT YEAH, LADY--
--THERE WAS A BLAST CLUSTER IN THIS AREA THREE DAYS AGO. WE NEED TO GET YOU SOME WATER AND FOOD AND--
WHAT HAPPENED? WHERE IS EVERYONE? WHAT--
WE LOST. EVERYTHING.
WE LOST EVERYTHING, SUE...
NO...

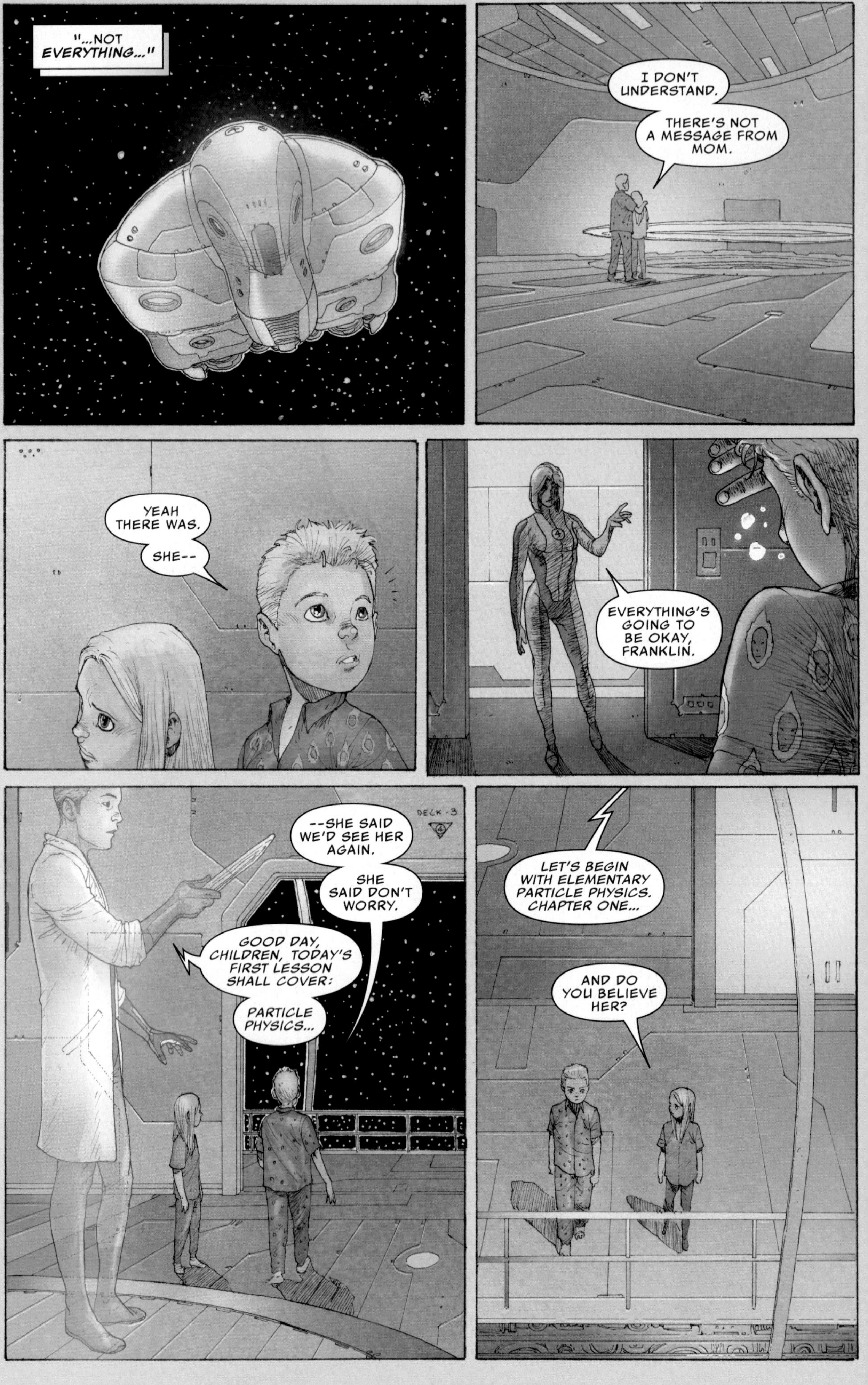
"...NOT EVERYTHING..."
I DON'T UNDERSTAND.
THERE'S NOT A MESSAGE FROM MOM.
YEAH THERE WAS.
SHE--
EVERYTHING'S GOING TO BE OKAY, FRANKLIN.
DECK-3
--SHE SAID WE'D SEE HER AGAIN.
SHE SAID DON'T WORRY.
GOOD DAY, CHILDREN, TODAY'S FIRST LESSON SHALL COVER:
PARTICLE PHYSICS...
LET'S BEGIN WITH ELEMENTARY PARTICLE PHYSICS. CHAPTER ONE...
AND DO YOU BELIEVE HER?

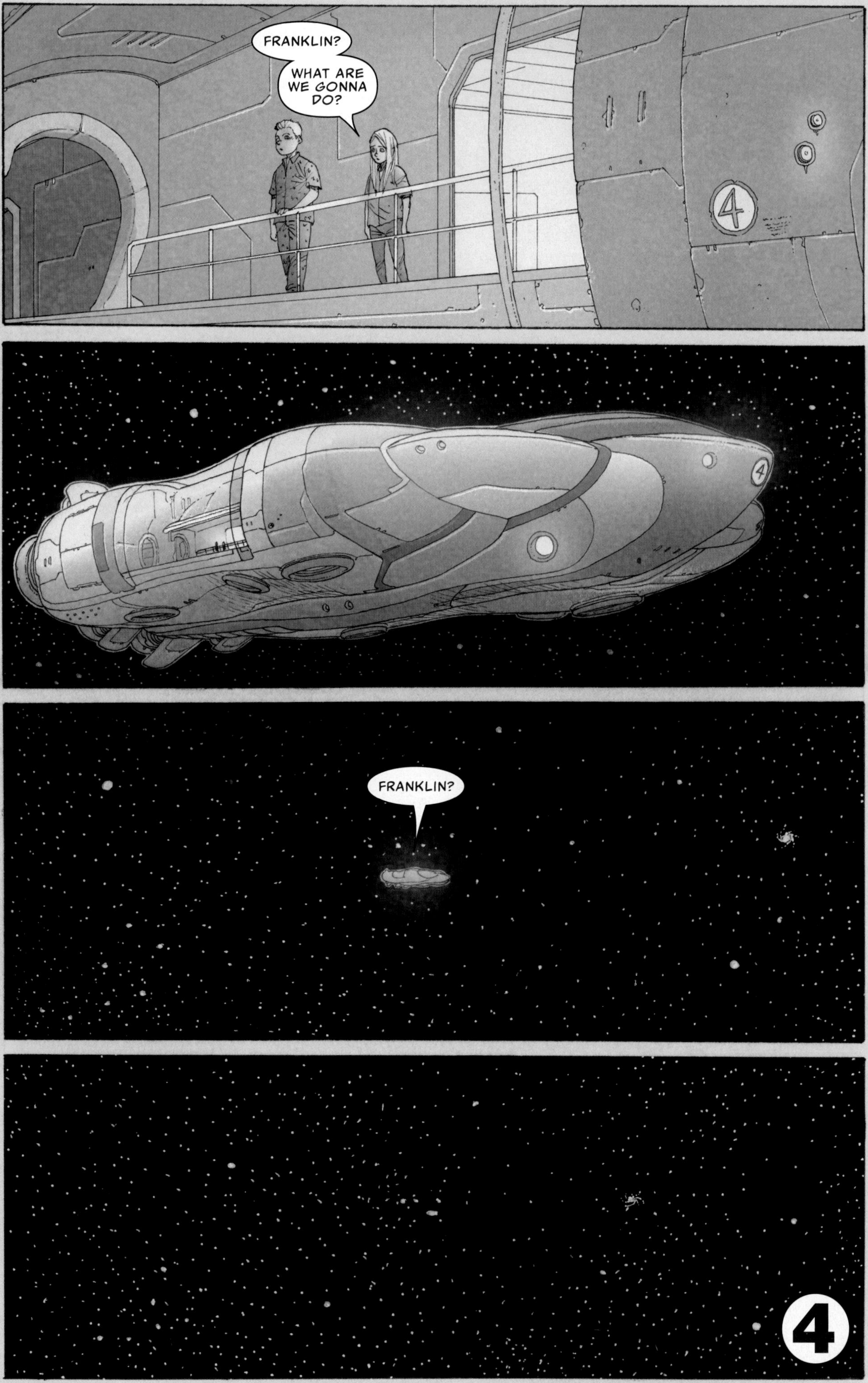
FRANKLIN?
WHAT ARE WE GONNA DO?
FRANKLIN?
4

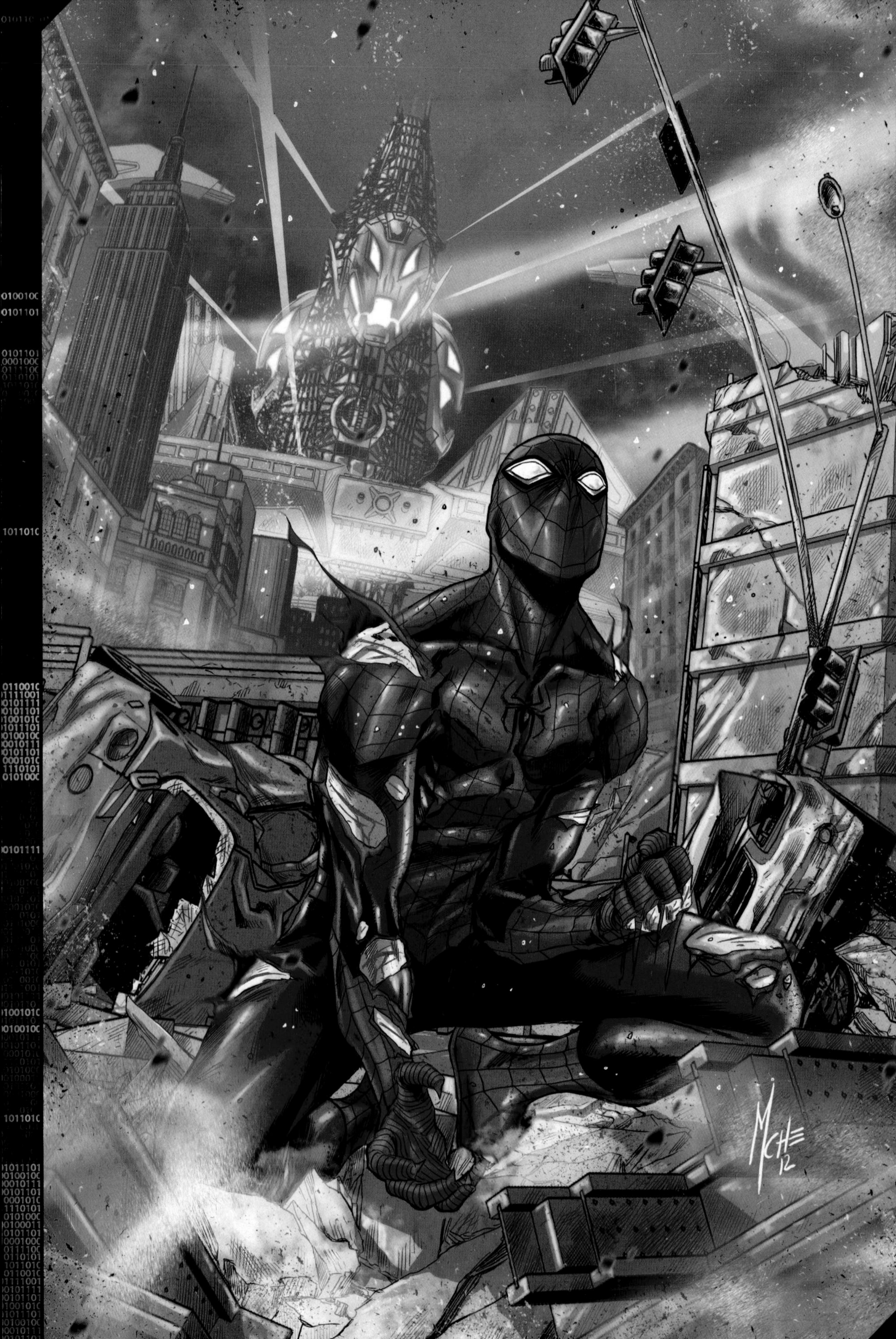
MCHE
12
SUPERIOR SPIDER-MAN #6AU

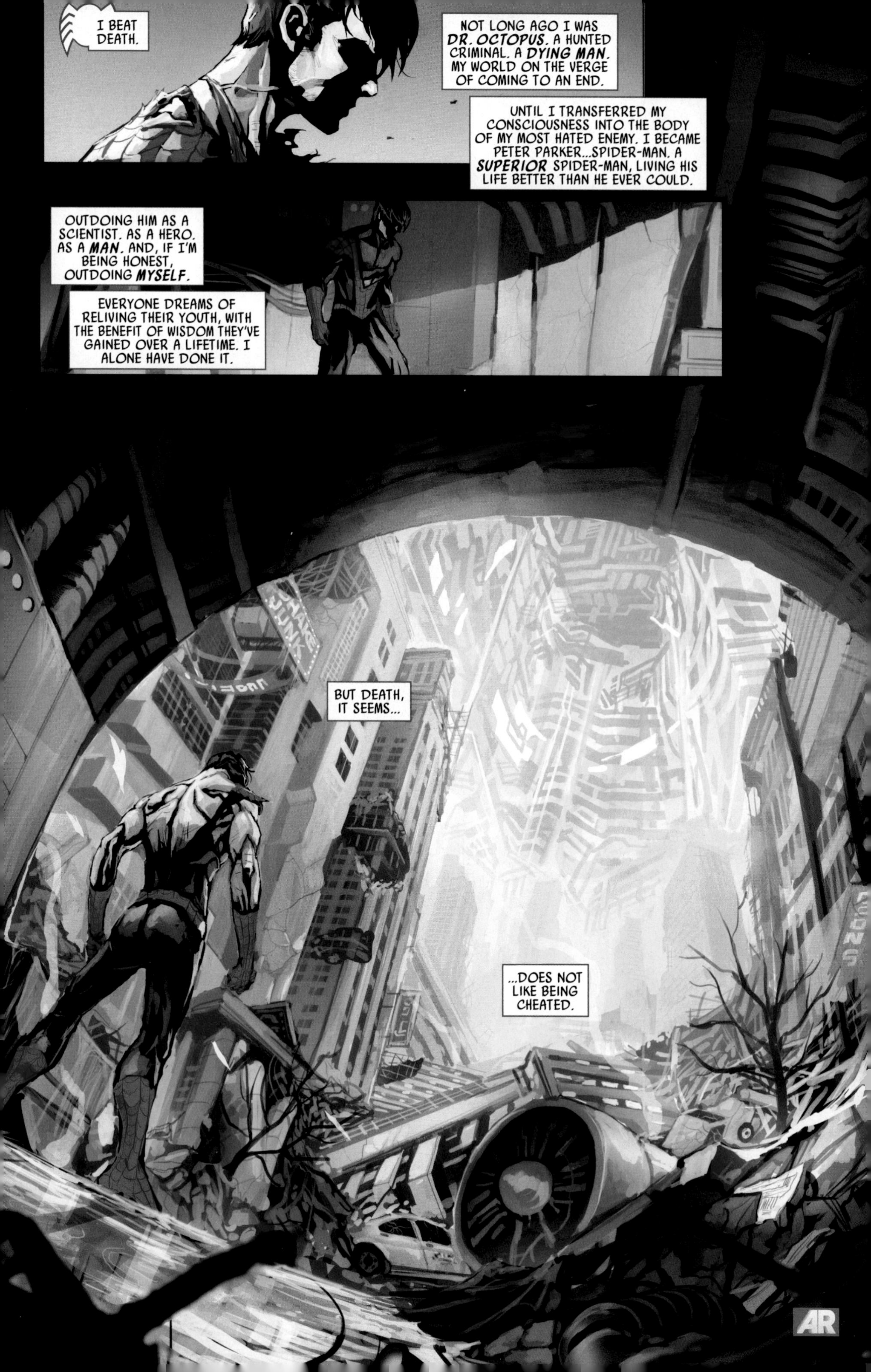
I BEAT DEATH.
NOT LONG AGO I WAS DR. OCTOPUS. A HUNTED CRIMINAL. A DYING MAN. MY WORLD ON THE VERGE OF COMING TO AN END.
UNTIL I TRANSFERRED MY CONSCIOUSNESS INTO THE BODY OF MY MOST HATED ENEMY. I BECAME PETER PARKER...SPIDER-MAN. A SUPERIOR SPIDER-MAN, LIVING HIS LIFE BETTER THAN HE EVER COULD.
OUTDOING HIM AS A SCIENTIST. AS A HERO. AS A MAN. AND, IF I'M BEING HONEST, OUTDOING MYSELF.
EVERYONE DREAMS OF RELIVING THEIR YOUTH, WITH THE BENEFIT OF WISDOM THEY'VE GAINED OVER A LIFETIME. I ALONE HAVE DONE IT.
BUT DEATH, IT SEEMS...
...DOES NOT LIKE BEING CHEATED.

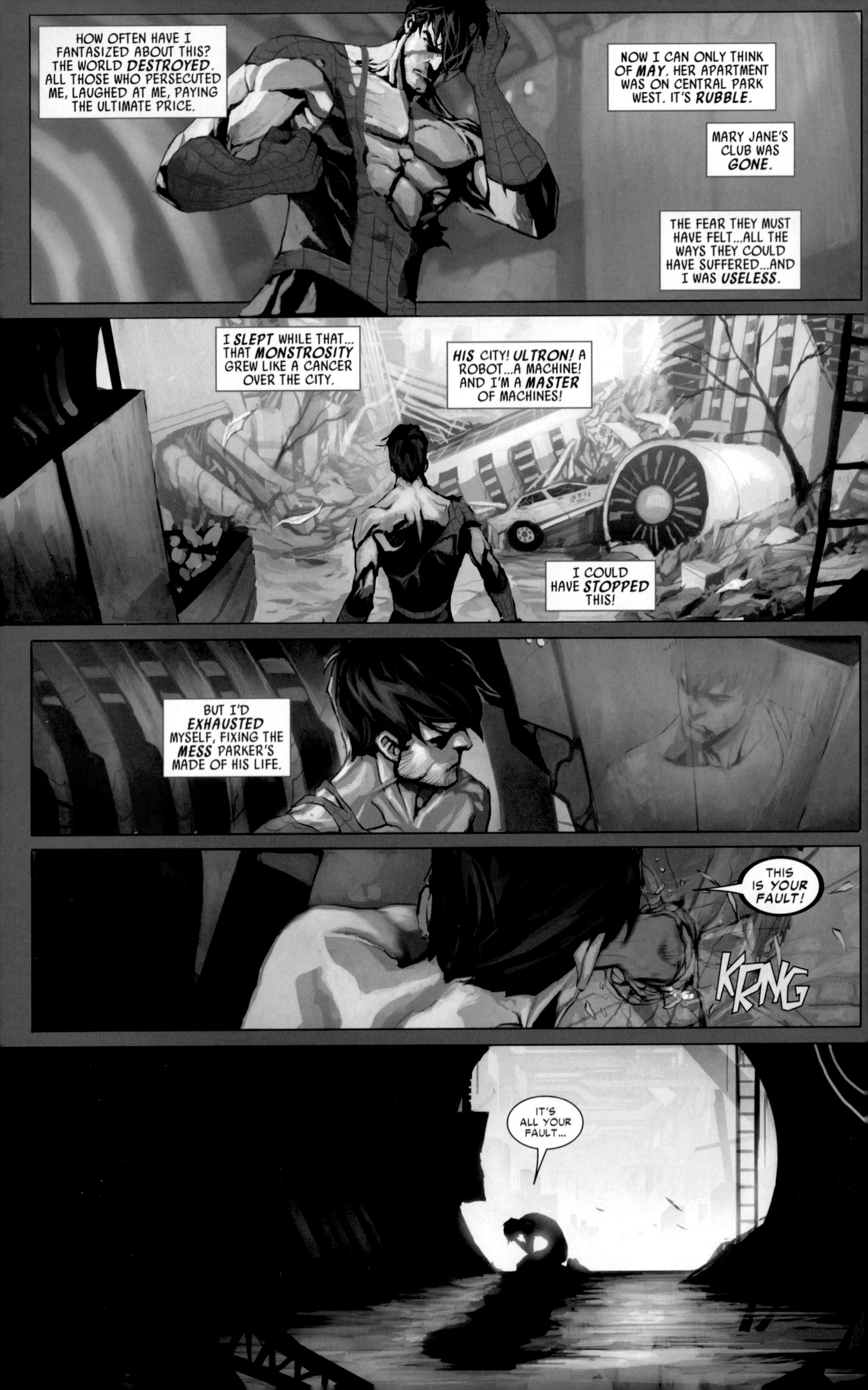
HOW OFTEN HAVE I FANTASIZED ABOUT THIS? THE WORLD *DESTROYED*. ALL THOSE WHO PERSECUTED ME, LAUGHED AT ME, PAYING THE ULTIMATE PRICE.
NOW I CAN ONLY THINK OF *MAY*. HER APARTMENT WAS ON CENTRAL PARK WEST. IT'S *RUBBLE*.
MARY JANE'S CLUB WAS *GONE*.
THE FEAR THEY MUST HAVE FELT...ALL THE WAYS THEY COULD HAVE SUFFERED...AND I WAS *USELESS*.
I *SLEPT* WHILE THAT... THAT *MONSTROSITY* GREW LIKE A CANCER OVER THE CITY.
HIS CITY! *ULTRON!* A ROBOT...A MACHINE! AND I'M A *MASTER* OF MACHINES!
I COULD HAVE *STOPPED* THIS!
BUT I'D *EXHAUSTED* MYSELF, FIXING THE *MESS* PARKER'S MADE OF HIS LIFE.
THIS IS *YOUR* FAULT!
KRNG
IT'S ALL YOUR FAULT...

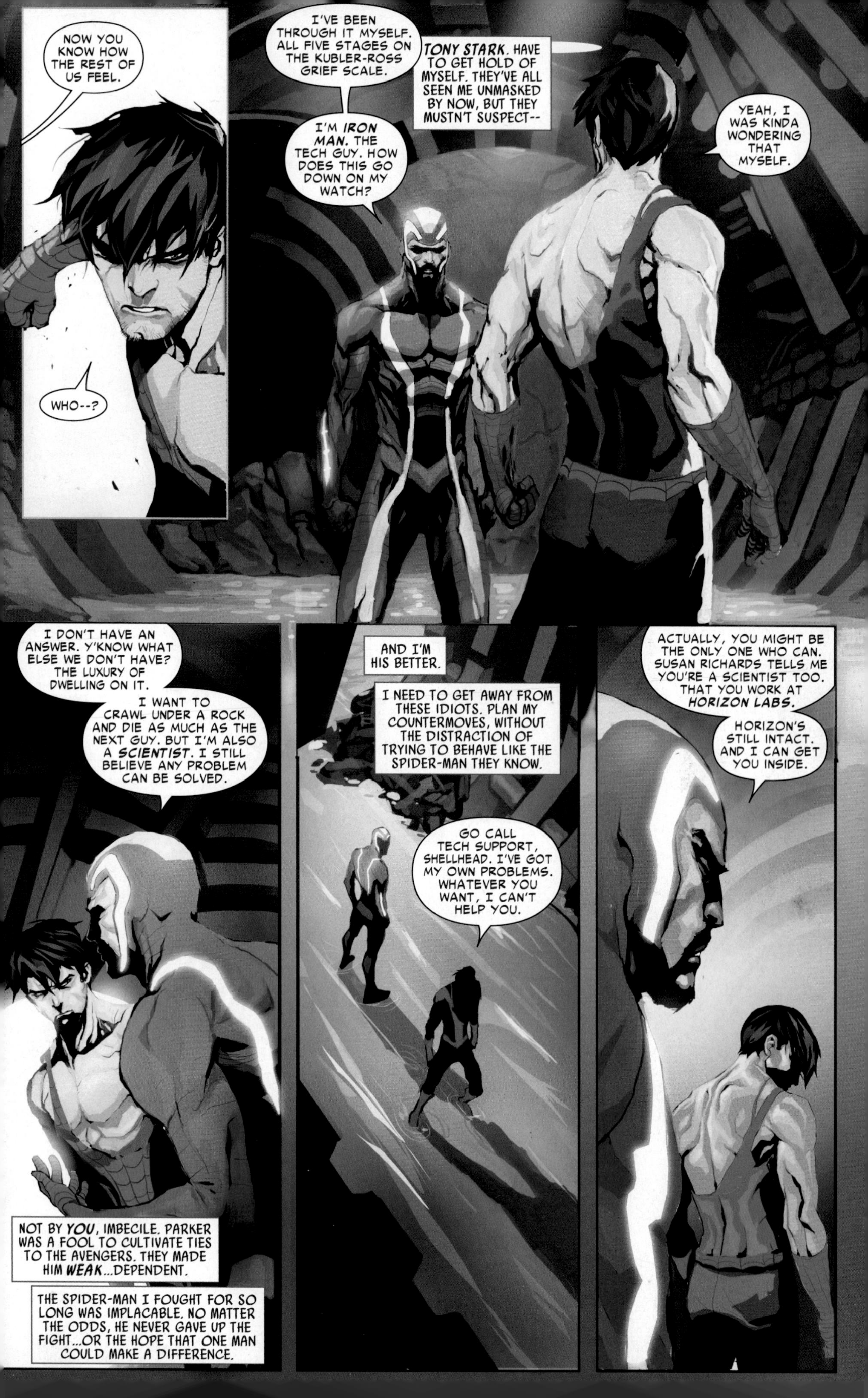

NOW YOU KNOW HOW THE REST OF US FEEL.
WHO--?
I'VE BEEN THROUGH IT MYSELF. ALL FIVE STAGES ON THE KUBLER-ROSS GRIEF SCALE.
I'M IRON MAN. THE TECH GUY. HOW DOES THIS GO DOWN ON MY WATCH?
TONY STARK. HAVE TO GET HOLD OF MYSELF. THEY'VE ALL SEEN ME UNMASKED BY NOW, BUT THEY MUSTN'T SUSPECT--
YEAH, I WAS KINDA WONDERING THAT MYSELF.
I DON'T HAVE AN ANSWER. Y'KNOW WHAT ELSE WE DON'T HAVE? THE LUXURY OF DWELLING ON IT.
I WANT TO CRAWL UNDER A ROCK AND DIE AS MUCH AS THE NEXT GUY. BUT I'M ALSO A SCIENTIST. I STILL BELIEVE ANY PROBLEM CAN BE SOLVED.
NOT BY YOU, IMBECILE. PARKER WAS A FOOL TO CULTIVATE TIES TO THE AVENGERS. THEY MADE HIM WEAK...DEPENDENT.
THE SPIDER-MAN I FOUGHT FOR SO LONG WAS IMPLACABLE. NO MATTER THE ODDS, HE NEVER GAVE UP THE FIGHT...OR THE HOPE THAT ONE MAN COULD MAKE A DIFFERENCE.
AND I'M HIS BETTER.
I NEED TO GET AWAY FROM THESE IDIOTS. PLAN MY COUNTERMOVES, WITHOUT THE DISTRACTION OF TRYING TO BEHAVE LIKE THE SPIDER-MAN THEY KNOW.
GO CALL TECH SUPPORT, SHELLHEAD. I'VE GOT MY OWN PROBLEMS. WHATEVER YOU WANT, I CAN'T HELP YOU.
ACTUALLY, YOU MIGHT BE THE ONLY ONE WHO CAN. SUSAN RICHARDS TELLS ME YOU'RE A SCIENTIST TOO. THAT YOU WORK AT HORIZON LABS.
HORIZON'S STILL INTACT. AND I CAN GET YOU INSIDE.

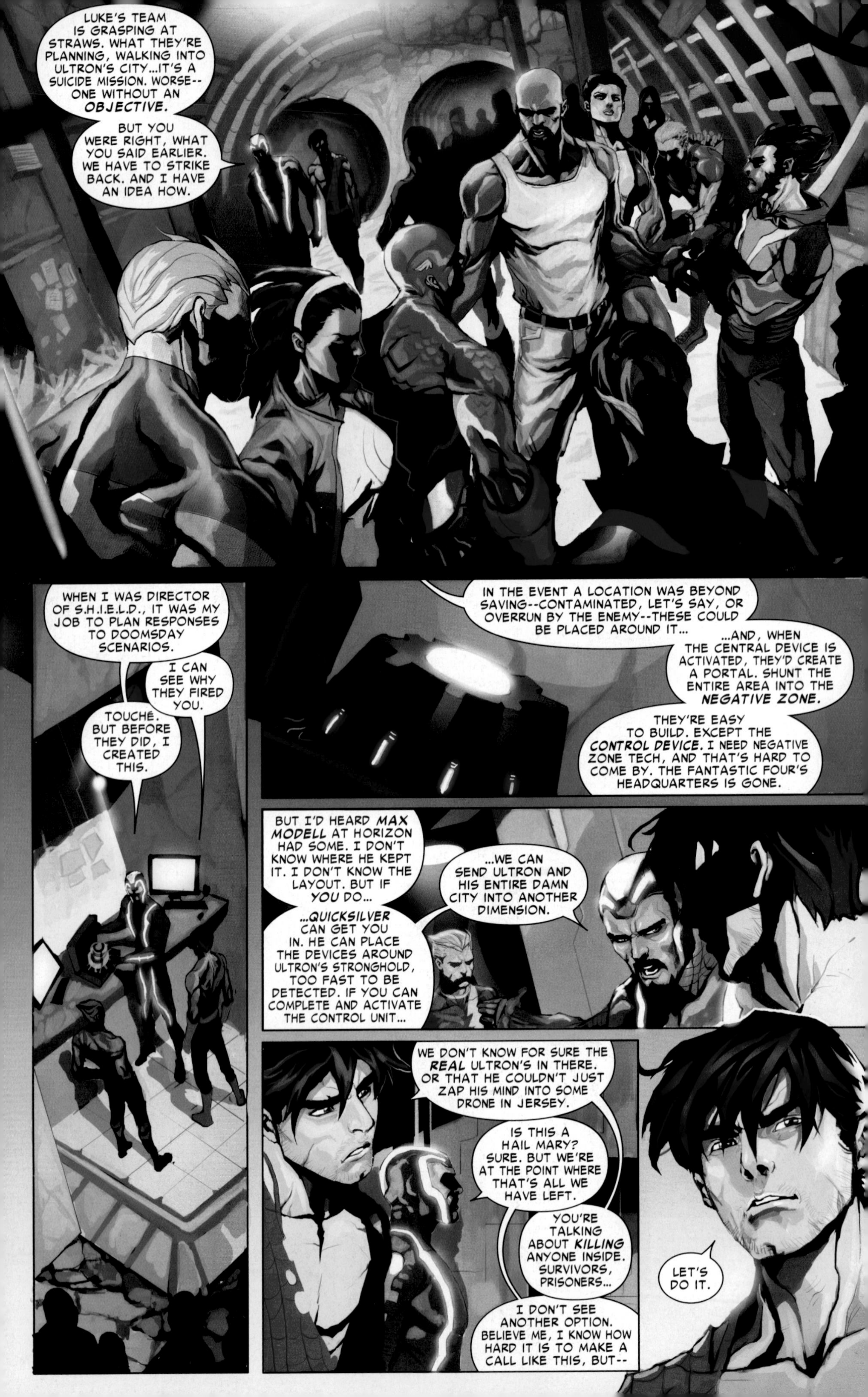
LUKE'S TEAM IS GRASPING AT STRAWS. WHAT THEY'RE PLANNING, WALKING INTO ULTRON'S CITY...IT'S A SUICIDE MISSION. WORSE-- ONE WITHOUT AN OBJECTIVE.
BUT YOU WERE RIGHT, WHAT YOU SAID EARLIER. WE HAVE TO STRIKE BACK. AND I HAVE AN IDEA HOW.
WHEN I WAS DIRECTOR OF S.H.I.E.L.D., IT WAS MY JOB TO PLAN RESPONSES TO DOOMSDAY SCENARIOS.
I CAN SEE WHY THEY FIRED YOU.
TOUCHÉ. BUT BEFORE THEY DID, I CREATED THIS.
IN THE EVENT A LOCATION WAS BEYOND SAVING--CONTAMINATED, LET'S SAY, OR OVERRUN BY THE ENEMY--THESE COULD BE PLACED AROUND IT...
...AND, WHEN THE CENTRAL DEVICE IS ACTIVATED, THEY'D CREATE A PORTAL. SHUNT THE ENTIRE AREA INTO THE NEGATIVE ZONE.
THEY'RE EASY TO BUILD. EXCEPT THE CONTROL DEVICE. I NEED NEGATIVE ZONE TECH, AND THAT'S HARD TO COME BY. THE FANTASTIC FOUR'S HEADQUARTERS IS GONE.
BUT I'D HEARD MAX MODELL AT HORIZON HAD SOME. I DON'T KNOW WHERE HE KEPT IT. I DON'T KNOW THE LAYOUT. BUT IF YOU DO...
...QUICKSILVER CAN GET YOU IN. HE CAN PLACE THE DEVICES AROUND ULTRON'S STRONGHOLD, TOO FAST TO BE DETECTED. IF YOU CAN COMPLETE AND ACTIVATE THE CONTROL UNIT...
...WE CAN SEND ULTRON AND HIS ENTIRE DAMN CITY INTO ANOTHER DIMENSION.
WE DON'T KNOW FOR SURE THE REAL ULTRON'S IN THERE. OR THAT HE COULDN'T JUST ZAP HIS MIND INTO SOME DRONE IN JERSEY.
IS THIS A HAIL MARY? SURE. BUT WE'RE AT THE POINT WHERE THAT'S ALL WE HAVE LEFT.
YOU'RE TALKING ABOUT KILLING ANYONE INSIDE. SURVIVORS, PRISONERS...
I DON'T SEE ANOTHER OPTION. BELIEVE ME, I KNOW HOW HARD IT IS TO MAKE A CALL LIKE THIS, BUT--
LET'S DO IT.

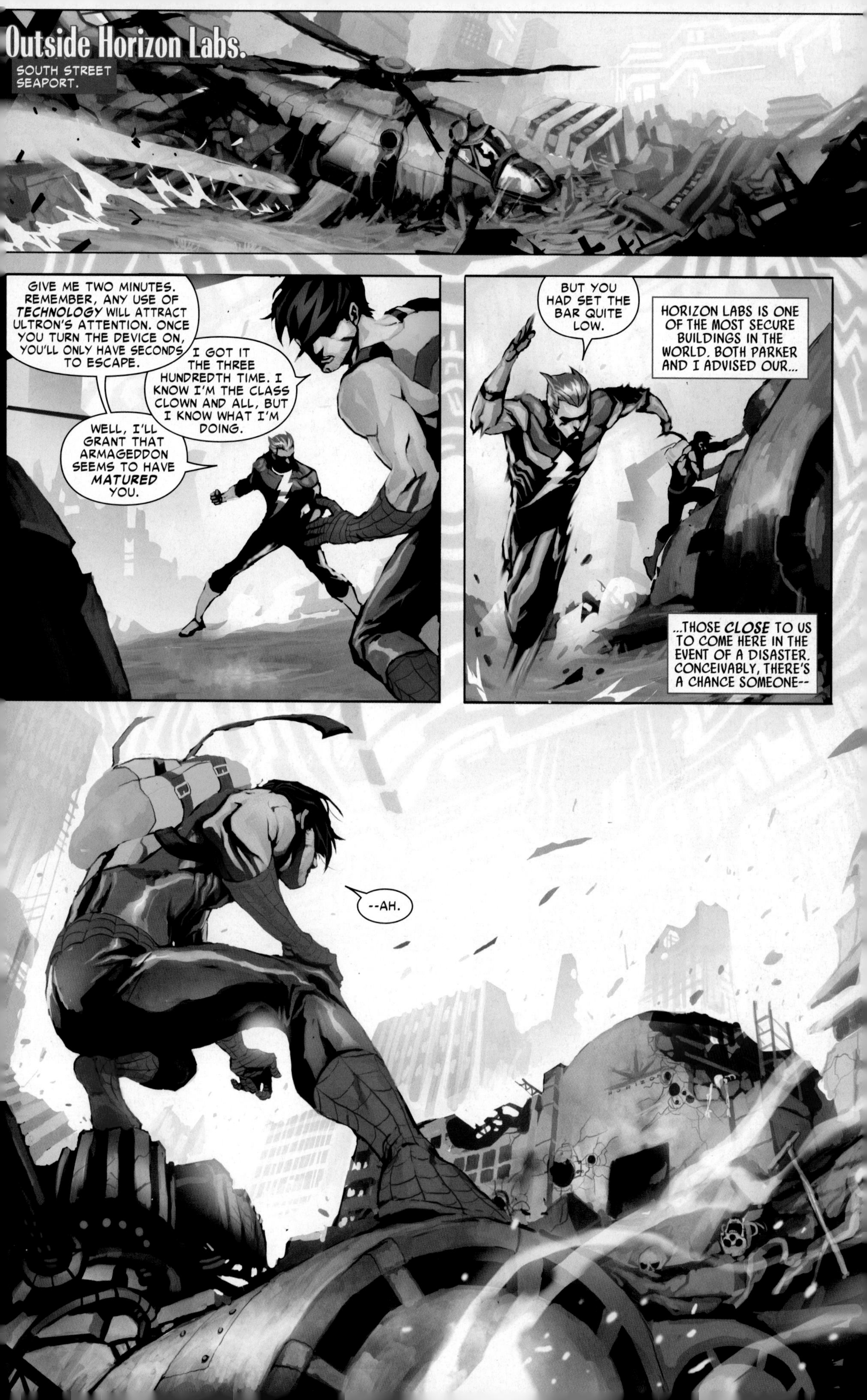
Outside Horizon Labs.
SOUTH STREET SEAPORT.
GIVE ME TWO MINUTES. REMEMBER, ANY USE OF TECHNOLOGY WILL ATTRACT ULTRON'S ATTENTION. ONCE YOU TURN THE DEVICE ON, YOU'LL ONLY HAVE SECONDS TO ESCAPE.
I GOT IT THE THREE HUNDREDTH TIME. I KNOW I'M THE CLASS CLOWN AND ALL, BUT I KNOW WHAT I'M DOING.
WELL, I'LL GRANT THAT ARMAGEDDON SEEMS TO HAVE MATURED YOU.
BUT YOU HAD SET THE BAR QUITE LOW.
HORIZON LABS IS ONE OF THE MOST SECURE BUILDINGS IN THE WORLD. BOTH PARKER AND I ADVISED OUR...
...THOSE CLOSE TO US TO COME HERE IN THE EVENT OF A DISASTER. CONCEIVABLY, THERE'S A CHANCE SOMEONE--
--AH.

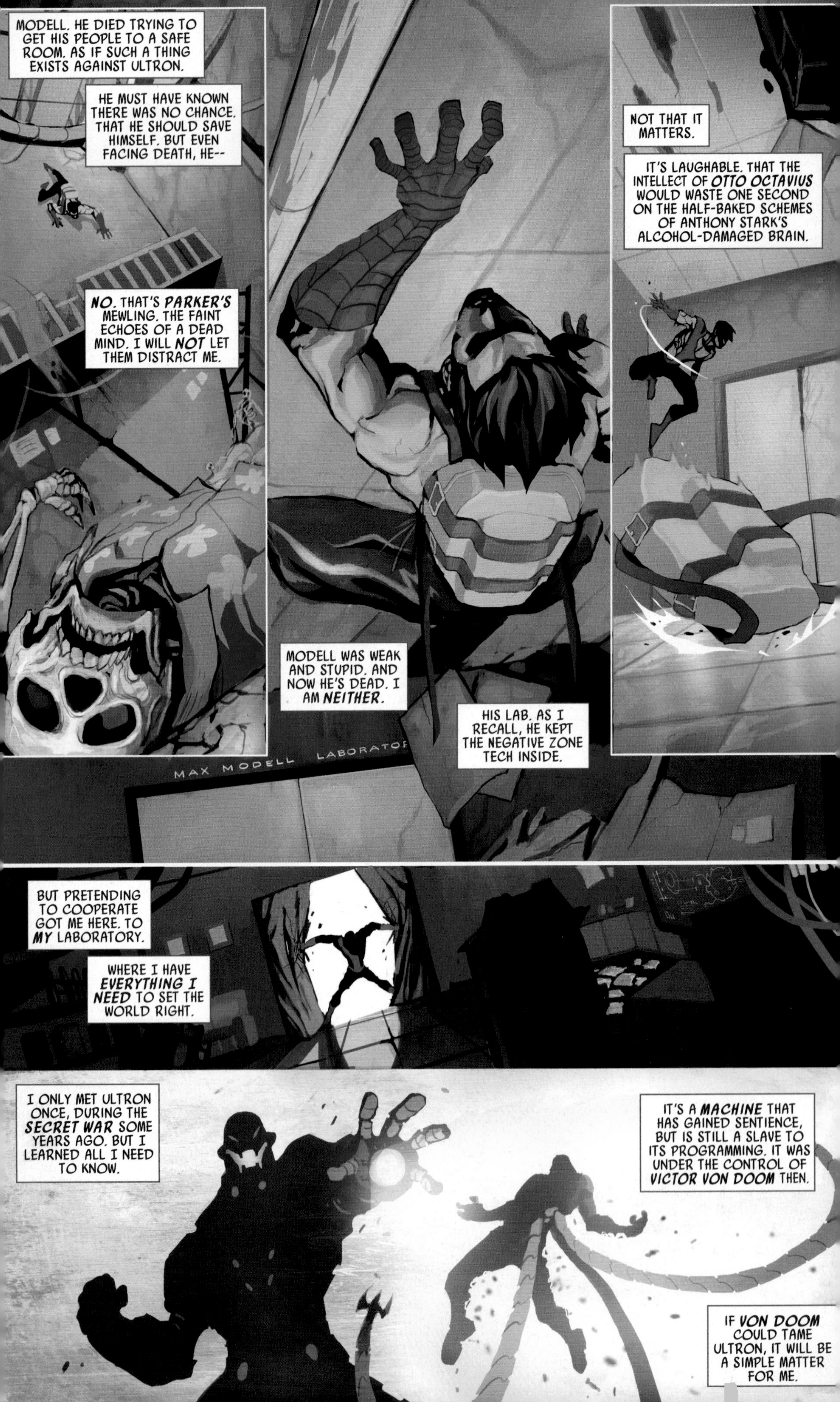
MODELL. HE DIED TRYING TO GET HIS PEOPLE TO A SAFE ROOM. AS IF SUCH A THING EXISTS AGAINST ULTRON.
HE MUST HAVE KNOWN THERE WAS NO CHANCE. THAT HE SHOULD SAVE HIMSELF. BUT EVEN FACING DEATH, HE--
NO. THAT'S PARKER'S MEWLING. THE FAINT ECHOES OF A DEAD MIND. I WILL NOT LET THEM DISTRACT ME.
MODELL WAS WEAK AND STUPID. AND NOW HE'S DEAD. I AM NEITHER.
NOT THAT IT MATTERS.
IT'S LAUGHABLE. THAT THE INTELLECT OF OTTO OCTAVIUS WOULD WASTE ONE SECOND ON THE HALF-BAKED SCHEMES OF ANTHONY STARK'S ALCOHOL-DAMAGED BRAIN.
HIS LAB. AS I RECALL, HE KEPT THE NEGATIVE ZONE TECH INSIDE.
MAX MODELL LABORATO
BUT PRETENDING TO COOPERATE GOT ME HERE. TO MY LABORATORY.
WHERE I HAVE EVERYTHING I NEED TO SET THE WORLD RIGHT.
I ONLY MET ULTRON ONCE, DURING THE SECRET WAR SOME YEARS AGO. BUT I LEARNED ALL I NEED TO KNOW.
IT'S A MACHINE THAT HAS GAINED SENTIENCE, BUT IS STILL A SLAVE TO ITS PROGRAMMING. IT WAS UNDER THE CONTROL OF VICTOR VON DOOM THEN.
IF VON DOOM COULD TAME ULTRON, IT WILL BE A SIMPLE MATTER FOR ME.

SPEAK FOR THEMSELVES. OF COURSE, ONCE I'VE WON, I'LL IMPROVE UPON THEM.

TO MAKE THE WORLD A PARADISE. UNDER MY DIRECTION, WHAT *DESTROYED* CIVILIZATION WILL *REBUILD* IT.

BETTER THAN BEFORE. FAR SUPERIOR TO WHAT'S BEEN LOST. THIS IS AN *OPPORTUNITY*, NOT THE END OF...NOT...

ENOUGH. FOCUS. THERE'S WORK TO BE DONE.

AND THE KEY TO VICTORY IS IN MY HANDS. NO DOUBT MOST OF MY SPIDER-EYES WERE DESTROYED, BUT I HAD *HUNDREDS* PATROLLING THE CITY.

THEY WILL BE ENOUGH. THEY MUST BE.

BREEP

BECAUSE THERE IS NO TURNING BACK.

ALERT.

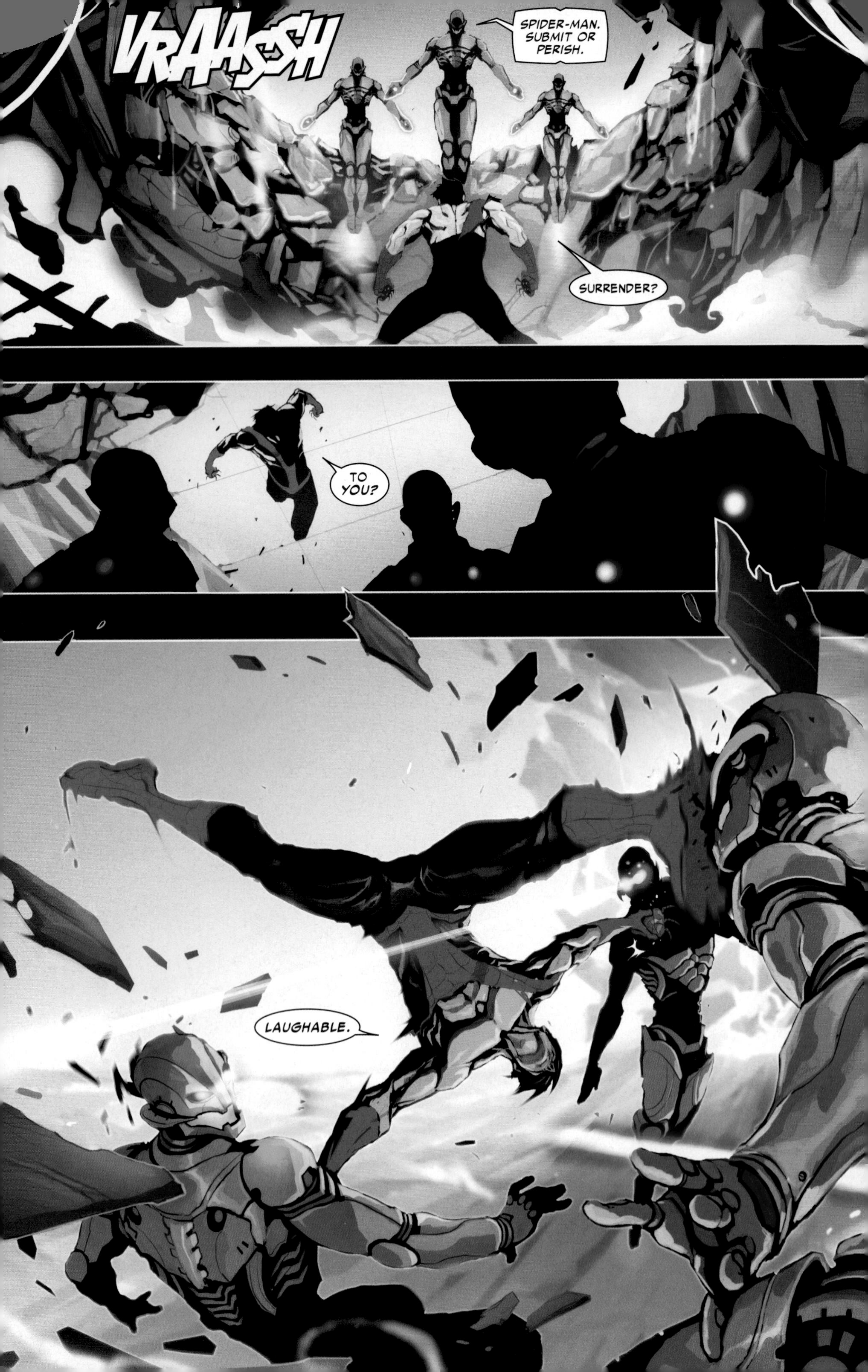
VRAASH
SPIDER-MAN. SUBMIT OR PERISH.
SURRENDER?
TO YOU?
LAUGHABLE.

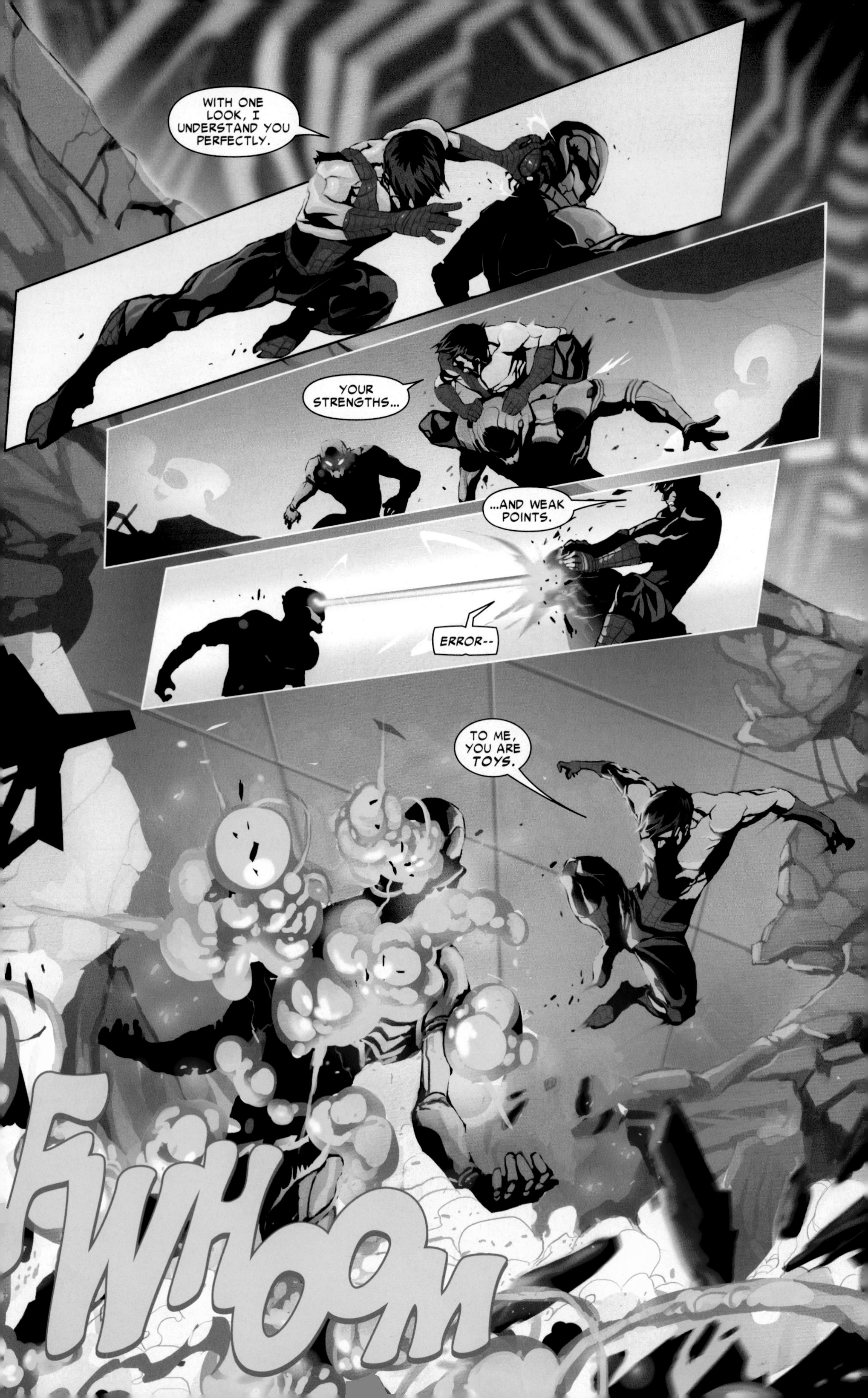
WITH ONE LOOK, I UNDERSTAND YOU PERFECTLY.
YOUR STRENGTHS...
...AND WEAK POINTS.
ERROR--
TO ME, YOU ARE TOYS.
FWHOOM

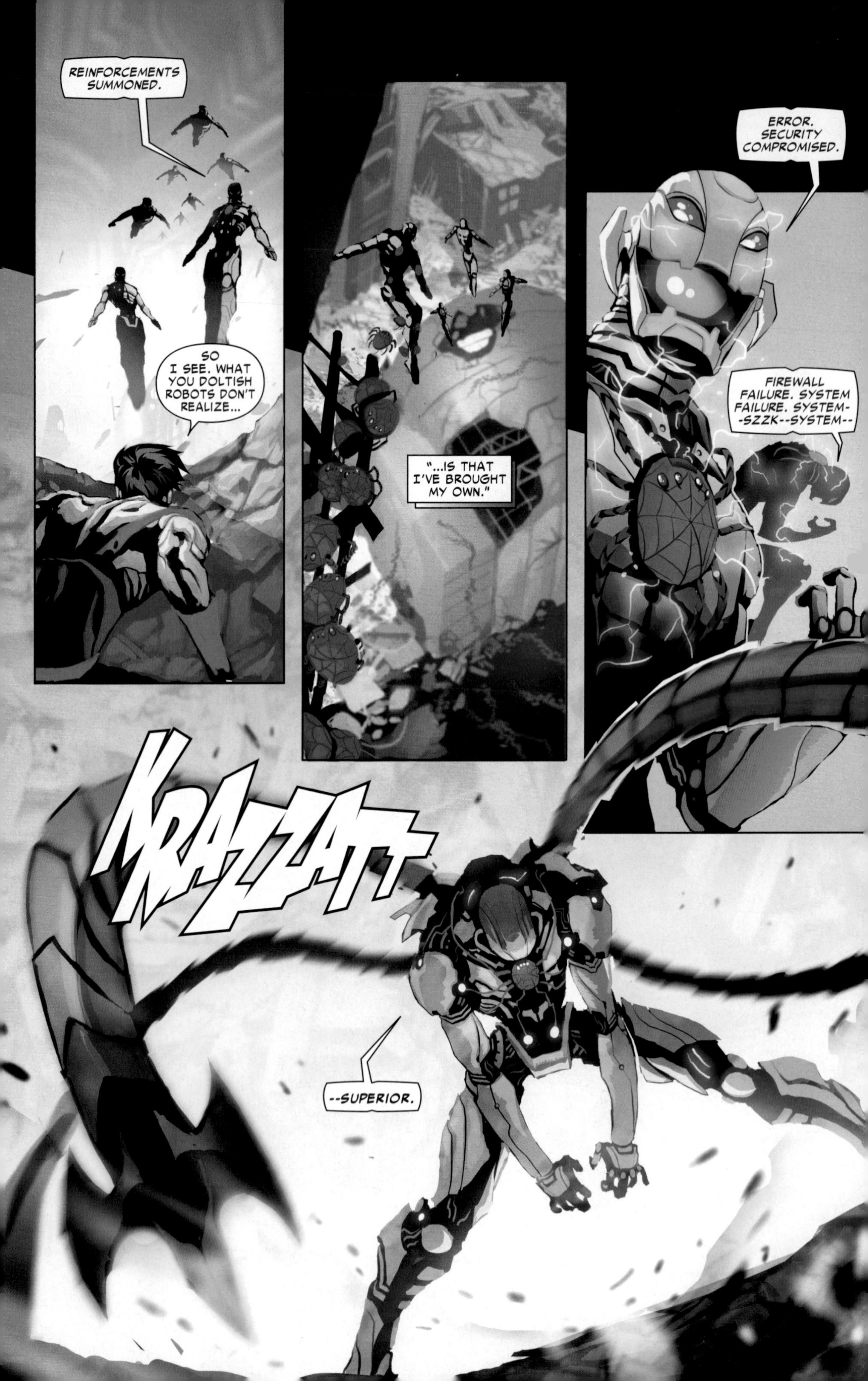
REINFORCEMENTS SUMMONED.
SO I SEE. WHAT YOU DOLTISH ROBOTS DON'T REALIZE...
"...IS THAT I'VE BROUGHT MY OWN."
ERROR. SECURITY COMPROMISED.
FIREWALL FAILURE. SYSTEM FAILURE. SYSTEM- -SZZK--SYSTEM--
KRAZZATT
--SUPERIOR.

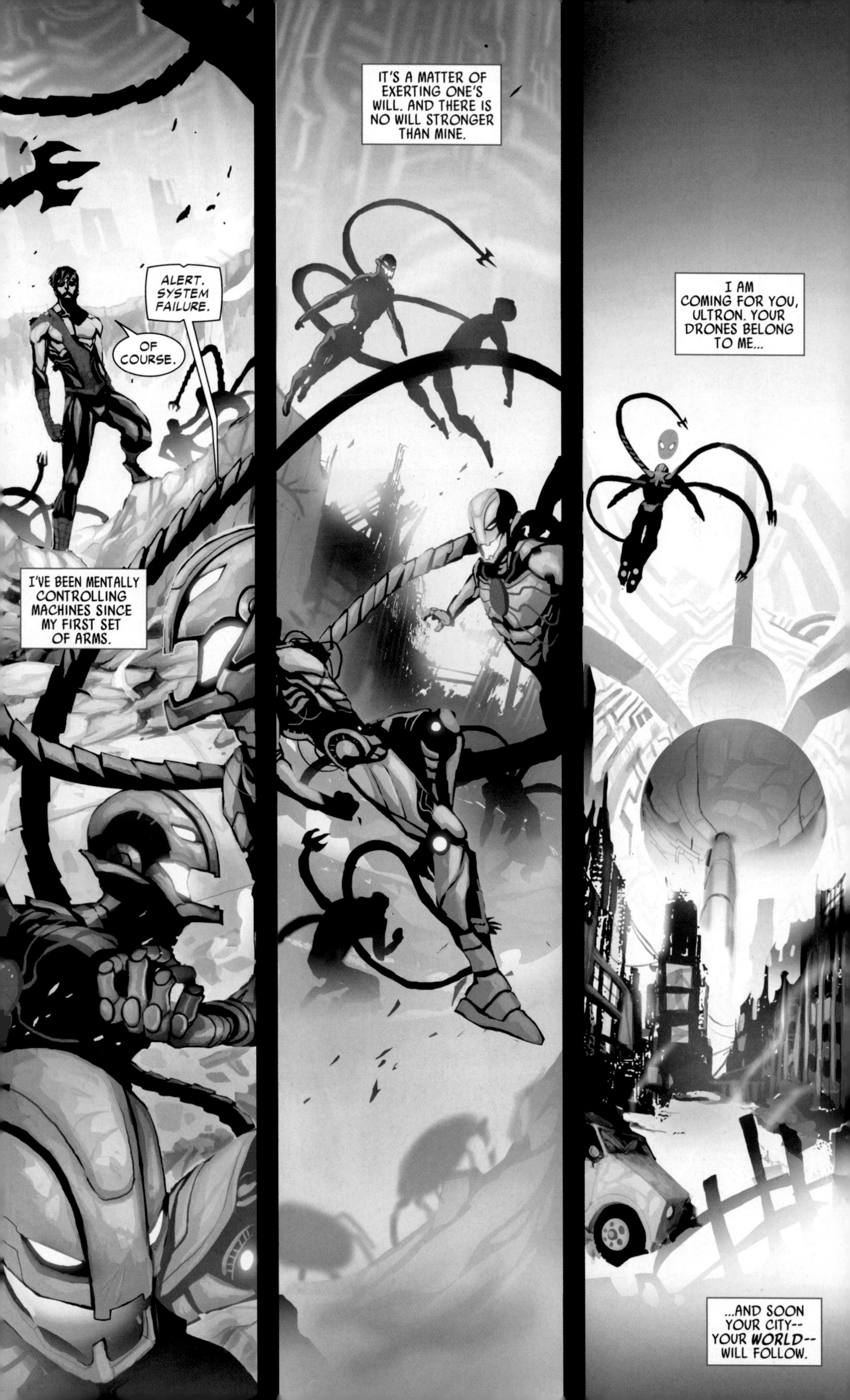
ALERT. SYSTEM FAILURE.
OF COURSE.
I'VE BEEN MENTALLY CONTROLLING MACHINES SINCE MY FIRST SET OF ARMS.
IT'S A MATTER OF EXERTING ONE'S WILL. AND THERE IS NO WILL STRONGER THAN MINE.
I AM COMING FOR YOU, ULTRON. YOUR DRONES BELONG TO ME...
...AND SOON YOUR CITY-- YOUR WORLD-- WILL FOLLOW.

THESE SO-CALLED "HEROES" AND THEIR HISTRIONICS. THEIR GRAND CRUSADES. TRIPPING OVER EACH OTHER, CREATING NOTHING BUT SOUND AND FURY.

WHEN ALL IT TAKES TO WIN IS A SUPERIOR MIND.

AND *MALWARE* BASED ON THE NEURAL INTERFACE WITH MY MECHANICAL ARMS... ALLOWING ME TO PROJECT MY CONSCIOUSNESS INTO ULTRON'S DRONES. MAKE *THEM* SUBMIT TO *ME*.

I WILL RESTORE THE WORLD. MAKE A PARADISE OF IT.

GRIEVE WHAT HAS BEEN LOST, YES...BUT UPON THEIR SACRIFICE, BUILD SOMETHING BETTER.

I *WILL* MAKE IT *MEAN* SOMETHING.

AT LAST.

I KNOW THIS FIGURE. THE ONE WHO LAID ME LOW THE DAY IT ALL BEGAN. ULTRON'S *CENTRAL INTELLIGENCE*.

YOU TOOK ME BY SURPRISE THE LAST TIME. BUT NOW...

...I AM IN CONTROL.

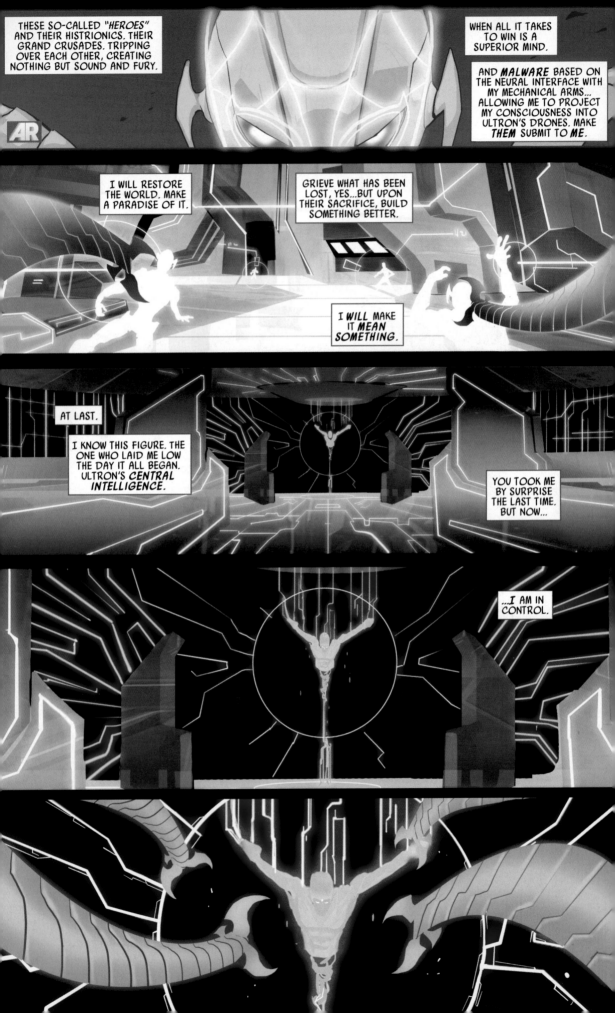

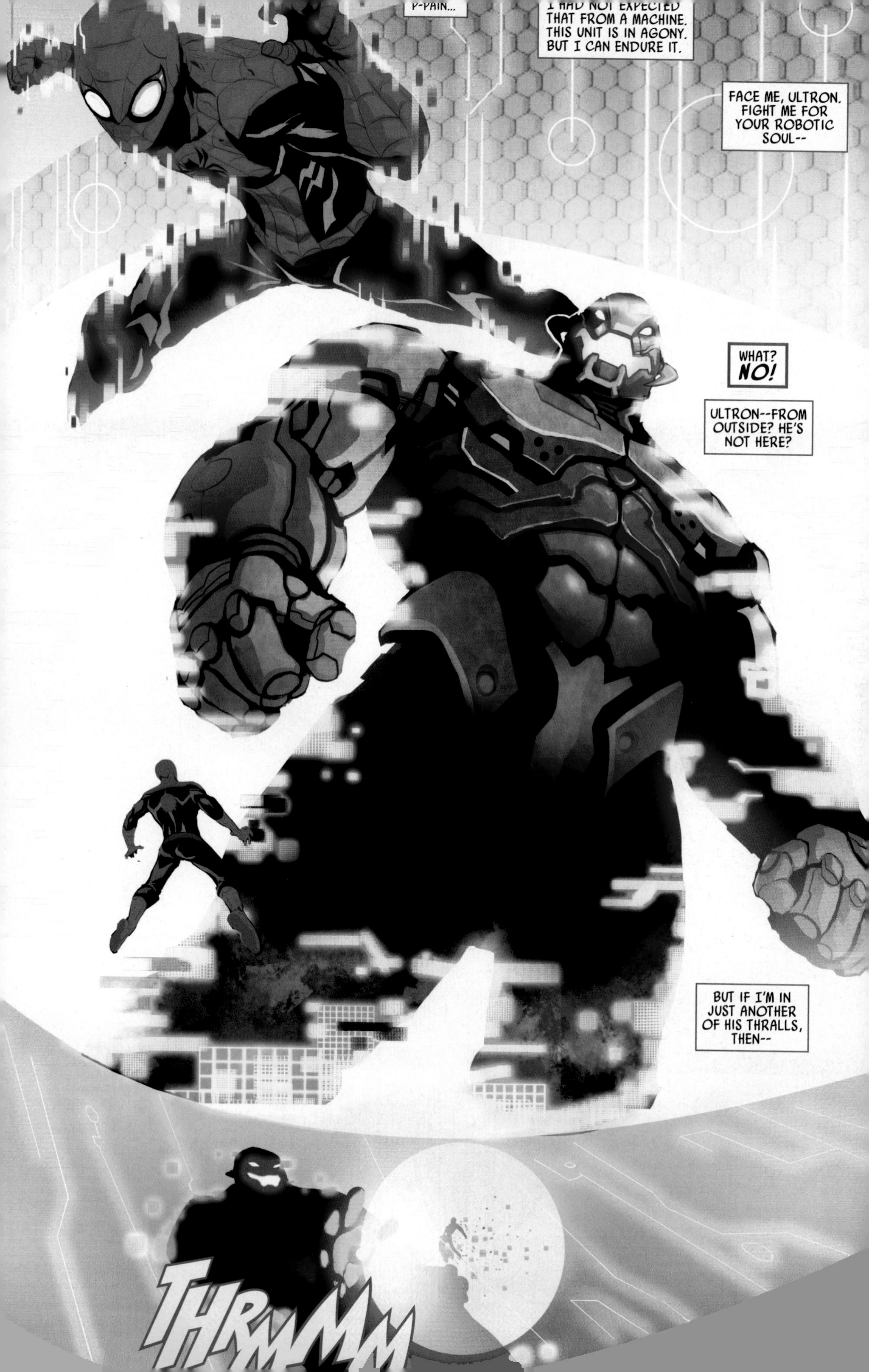
P-PAIN...
I HAD NOT EXPECTED THAT FROM A MACHINE. THIS UNIT IS IN AGONY. BUT I CAN ENDURE IT.
FACE ME, ULTRON. FIGHT ME FOR YOUR ROBOTIC SOUL--
WHAT? NO!
ULTRON--FROM OUTSIDE? HE'S NOT HERE?
BUT IF I'M IN JUST ANOTHER OF HIS THRALLS, THEN--
THRMMM

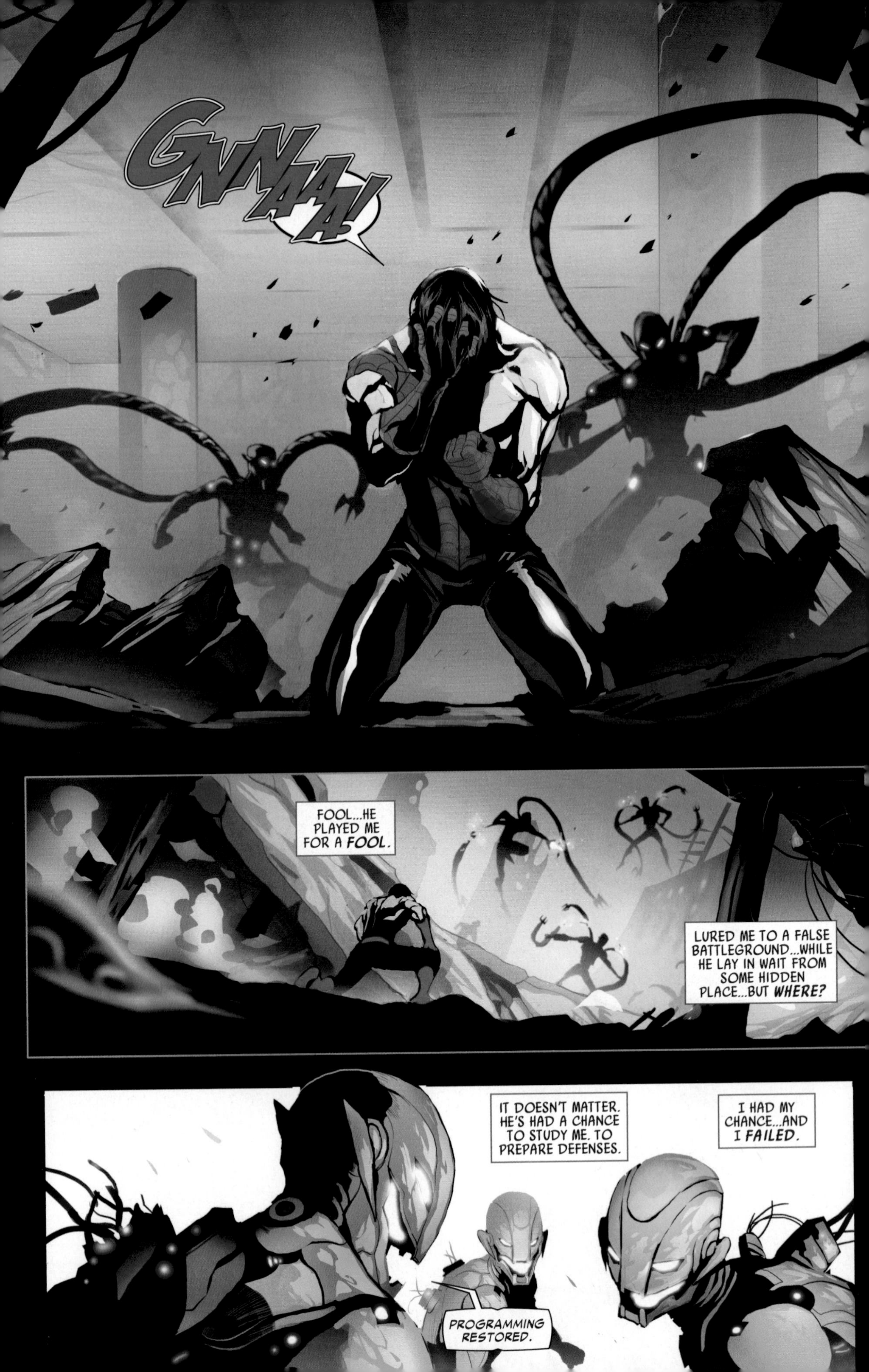
GNNAAA!
FOOL...HE PLAYED ME FOR A FOOL.
LURED ME TO A FALSE BATTLEGROUND...WHILE HE LAY IN WAIT FROM SOME HIDDEN PLACE...BUT WHERE?
IT DOESN'T MATTER. HE'S HAD A CHANCE TO STUDY ME, TO PREPARE DEFENSES.
I HAD MY CHANCE...AND I FAILED.
PROGRAMMING RESTORED.

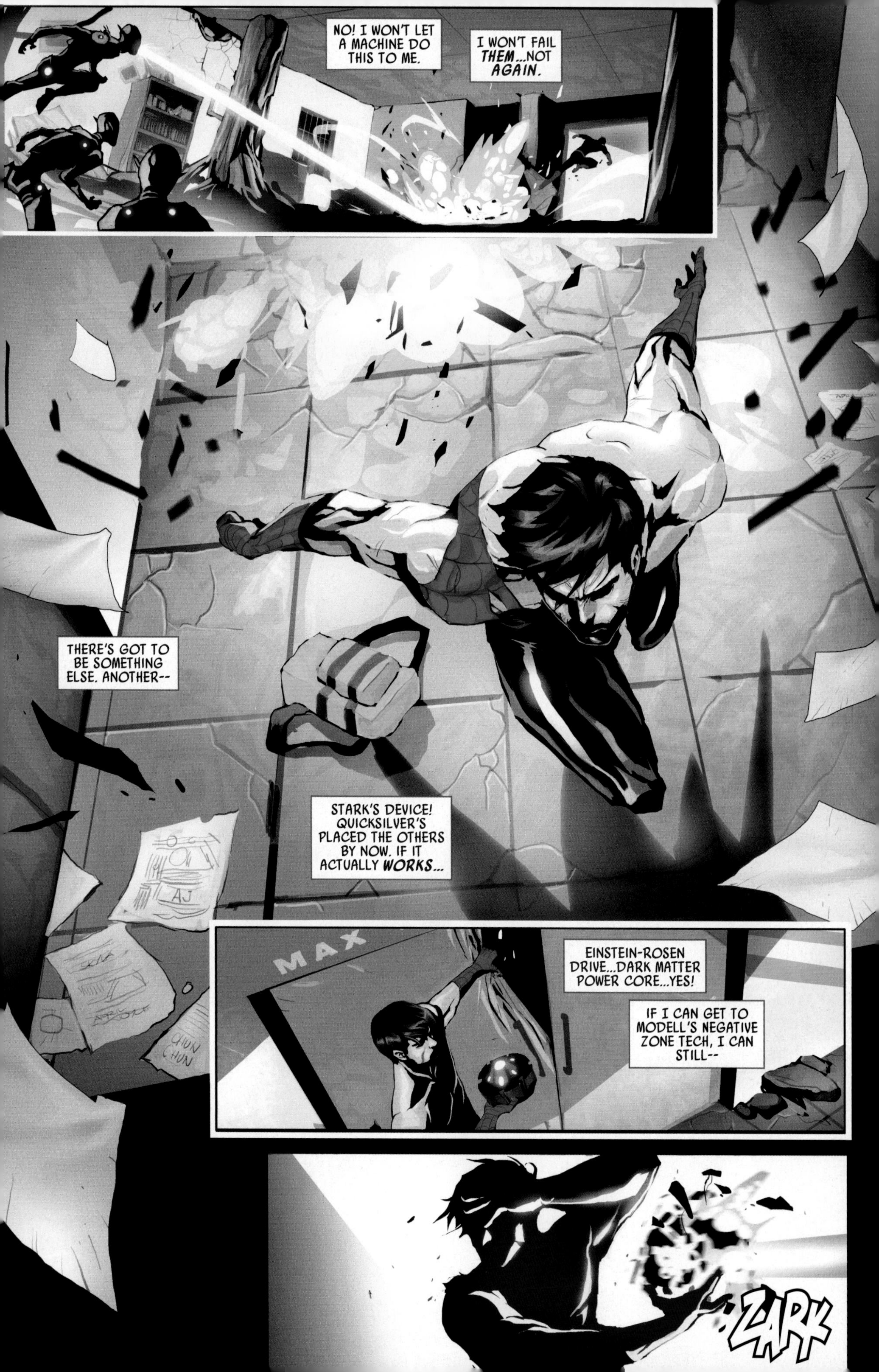
NO! I WON'T LET A MACHINE DO THIS TO ME.
I WON'T FAIL THEM...NOT AGAIN.
THERE'S GOT TO BE SOMETHING ELSE. ANOTHER--
STARK'S DEVICE! QUICKSILVER'S PLACED THE OTHERS BY NOW. IF IT ACTUALLY WORKS...
MAX
EINSTEIN-ROSEN DRIVE...DARK MATTER POWER CORE...YES!
IF I CAN GET TO MODELL'S NEGATIVE ZONE TECH, I CAN STILL--
ZARK

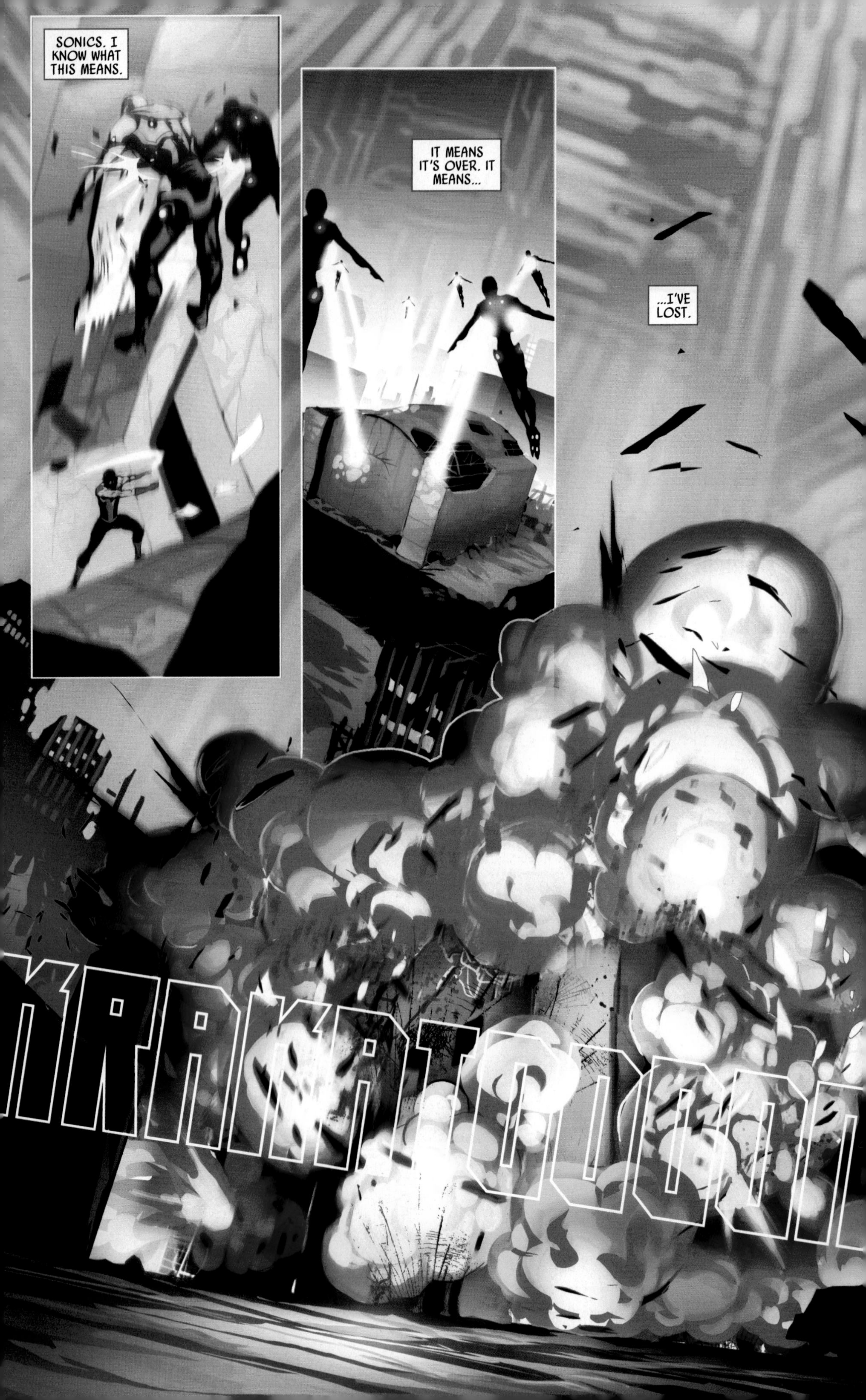
SONICS. I KNOW WHAT THIS MEANS.
IT MEANS IT'S OVER. IT MEANS...
...I'VE LOST.

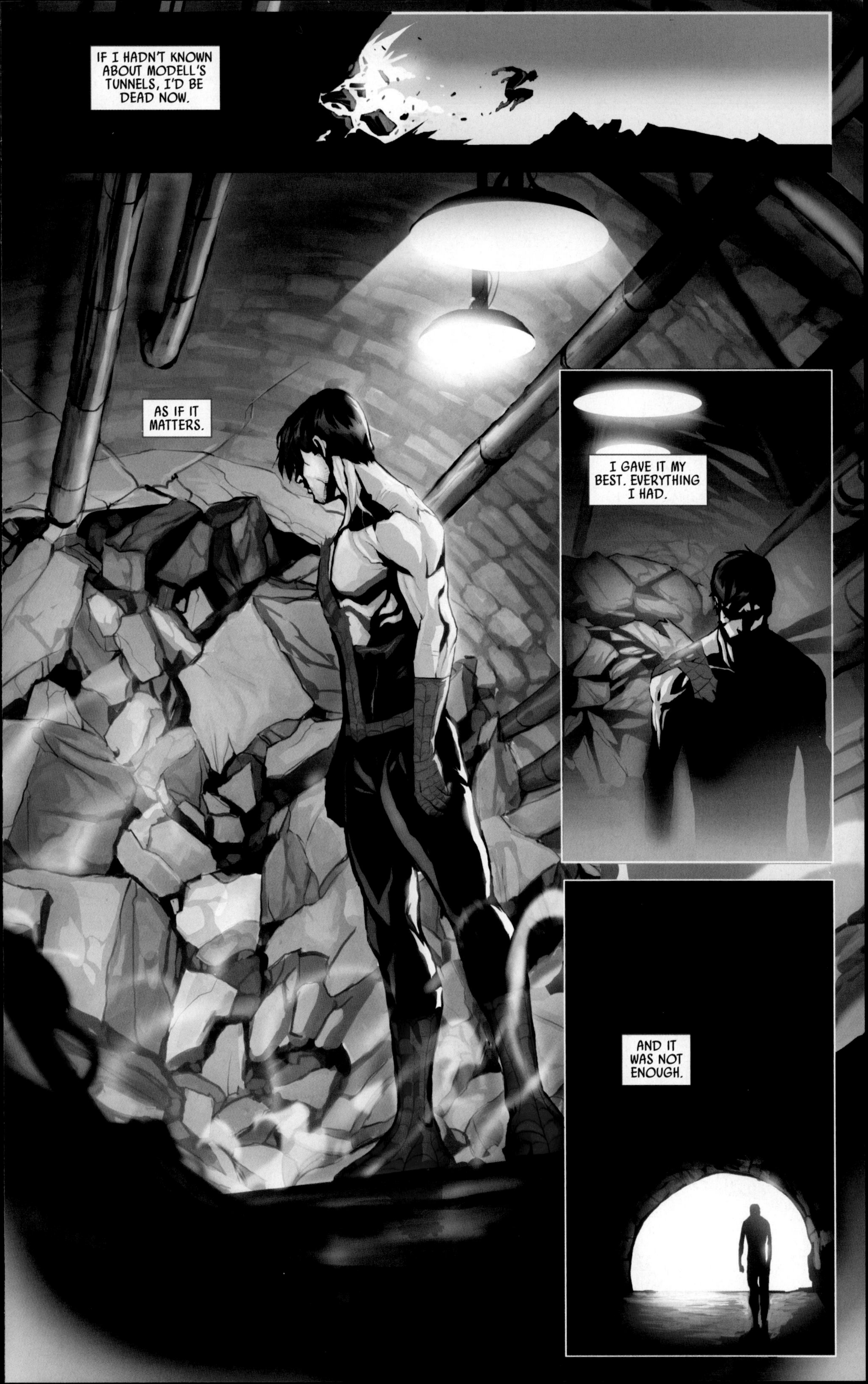
IF I HADN'T KNOWN ABOUT MODELL'S TUNNELS, I'D BE DEAD NOW.
AS IF IT MATTERS.
I GAVE IT MY BEST. EVERYTHING I HAD.
AND IT WAS NOT ENOUGH.

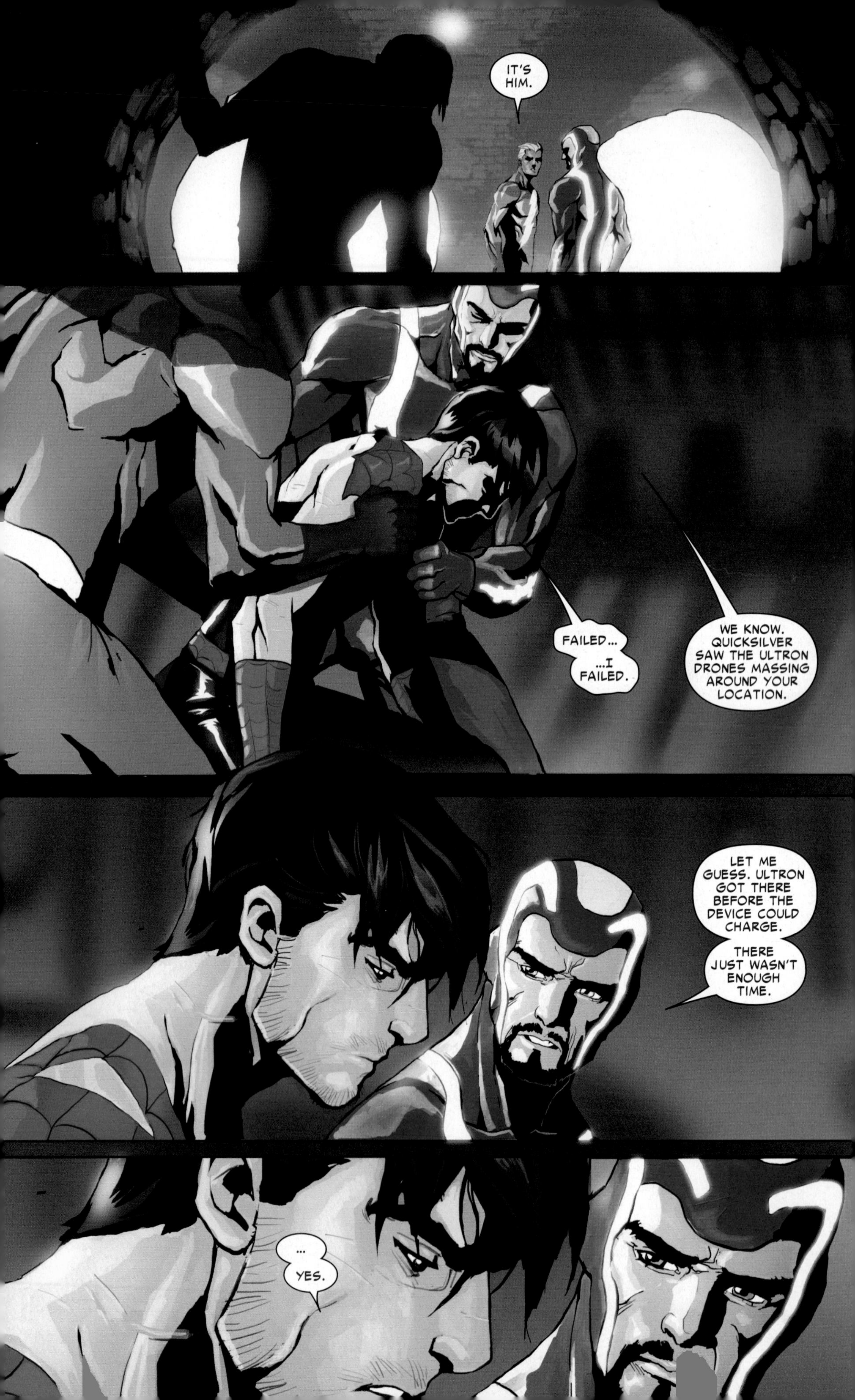
IT'S HIM.
FAILED...
...I FAILED.
WE KNOW. QUICKSILVER SAW THE ULTRON DRONES MASSING AROUND YOUR LOCATION.
LET ME GUESS. ULTRON GOT THERE BEFORE THE DEVICE COULD CHARGE.
THERE JUST WASN'T ENOUGH TIME.
... YES.

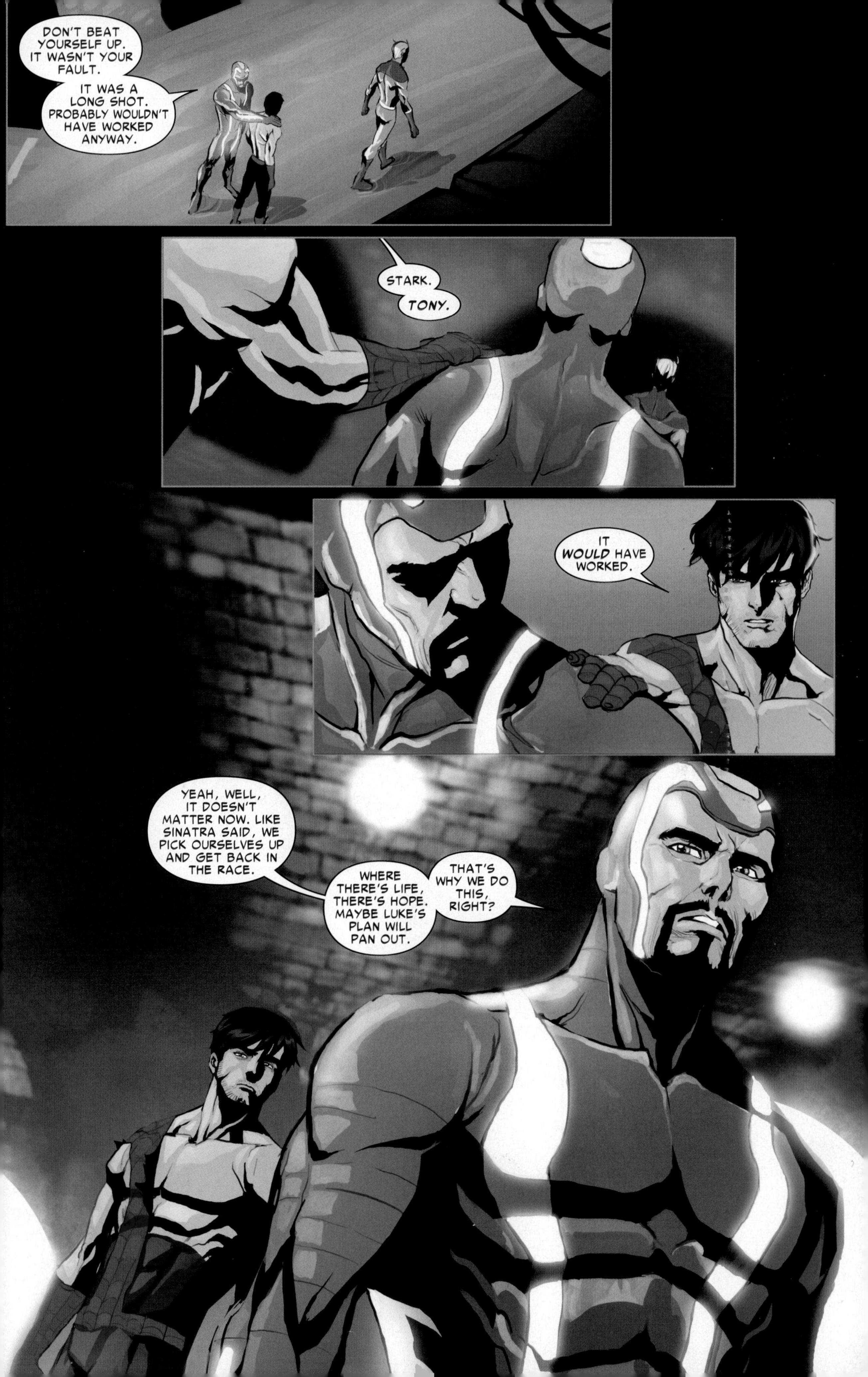
DON'T BEAT YOURSELF UP. IT WASN'T YOUR FAULT.
IT WAS A LONG SHOT. PROBABLY WOULDN'T HAVE WORKED ANYWAY.
STARK.
TONY.
IT WOULD HAVE WORKED.
YEAH, WELL, IT DOESN'T MATTER NOW. LIKE SINATRA SAID, WE PICK OURSELVES UP AND GET BACK IN THE RACE.
WHERE THERE'S LIFE, THERE'S HOPE. MAYBE LUKE'S PLAN WILL PAN OUT.
THAT'S WHY WE DO THIS, RIGHT?

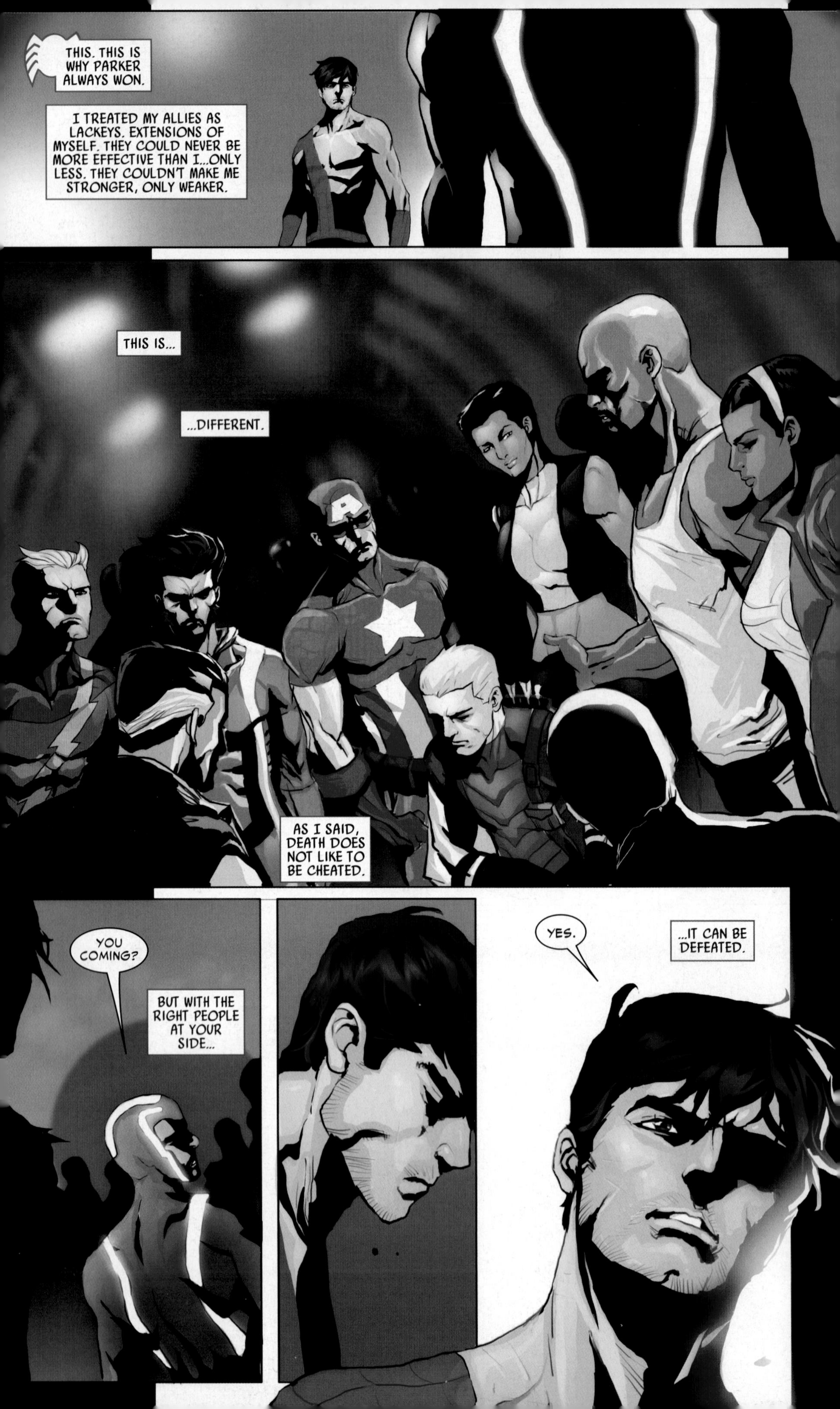
THIS. THIS IS WHY PARKER ALWAYS WON.
I TREATED MY ALLIES AS LACKEYS. EXTENSIONS OF MYSELF. THEY COULD NEVER BE MORE EFFECTIVE THAN I...ONLY LESS. THEY COULDN'T MAKE ME STRONGER, ONLY WEAKER.
THIS IS...
...DIFFERENT.
AS I SAID, DEATH DOES NOT LIKE TO BE CHEATED.
YOU COMING?
BUT WITH THE RIGHT PEOPLE AT YOUR SIDE...
YES.
...IT CAN BE DEFEATED.

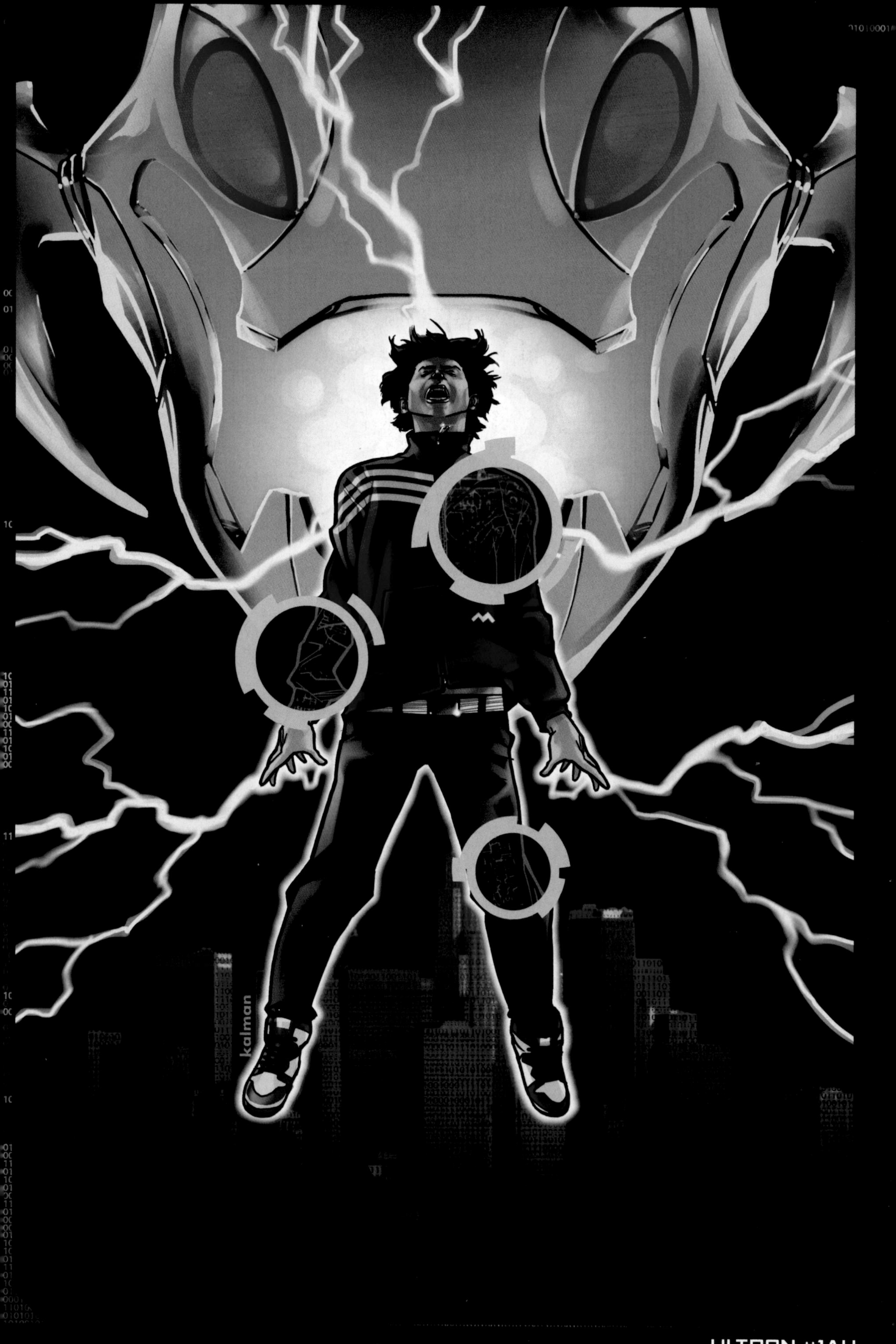
kalman

ULTRON #1AU

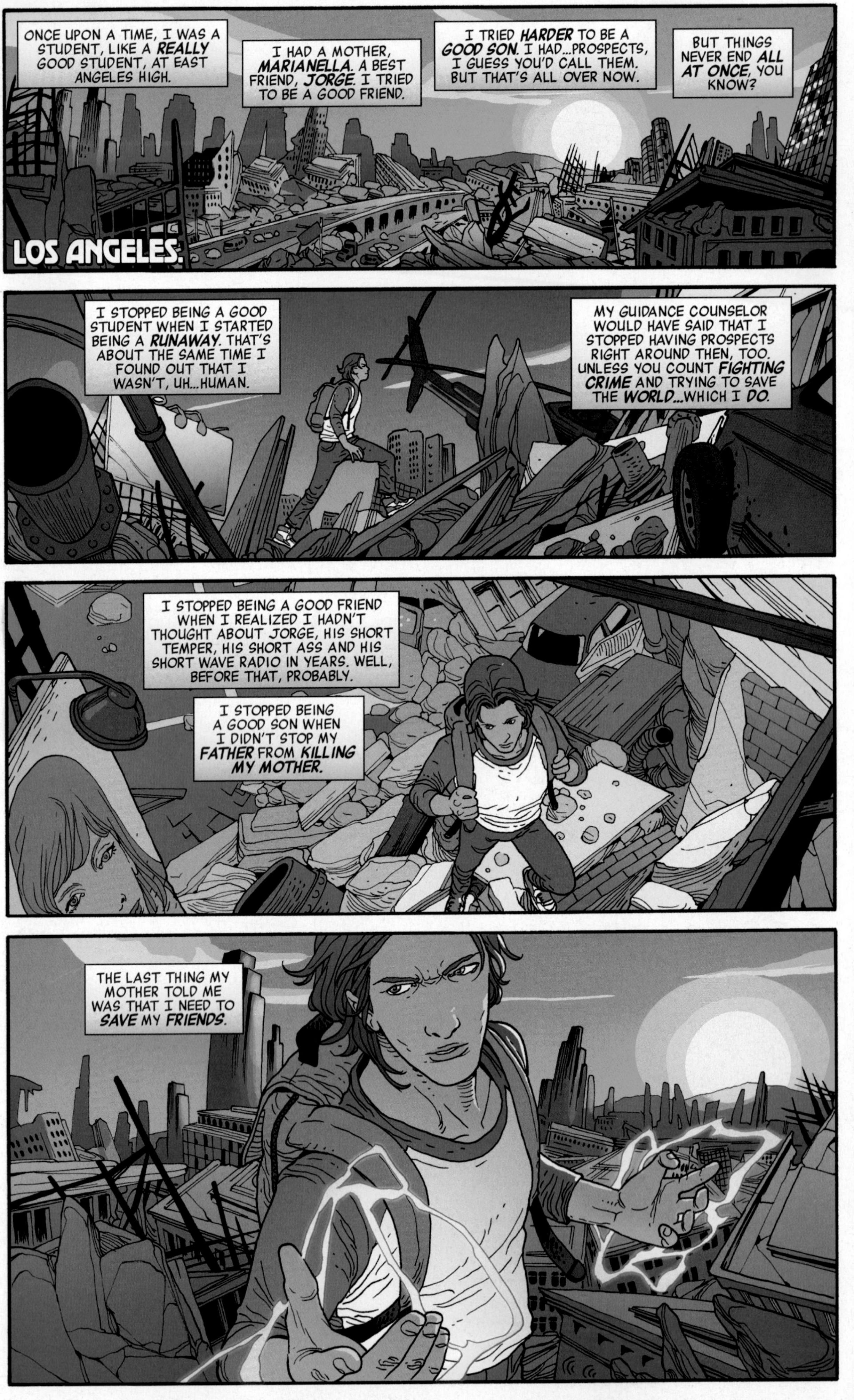
ONCE UPON A TIME, I WAS A STUDENT, LIKE A REALLY GOOD STUDENT, AT EAST ANGELES HIGH.
I HAD A MOTHER, MARIANELLA. A BEST FRIEND, JORGE. I TRIED TO BE A GOOD FRIEND.
I TRIED HARDER TO BE A GOOD SON. I HAD...PROSPECTS, I GUESS YOU'D CALL THEM. BUT THAT'S ALL OVER NOW.
BUT THINGS NEVER END ALL AT ONCE, YOU KNOW?
LOS ANGELES.
I STOPPED BEING A GOOD STUDENT WHEN I STARTED BEING A RUNAWAY. THAT'S ABOUT THE SAME TIME I FOUND OUT THAT I WASN'T, UH...HUMAN.
MY GUIDANCE COUNSELOR WOULD HAVE SAID THAT I STOPPED HAVING PROSPECTS RIGHT AROUND THEN, TOO. UNLESS YOU COUNT FIGHTING CRIME AND TRYING TO SAVE THE WORLD...WHICH I DO.
I STOPPED BEING A GOOD FRIEND WHEN I REALIZED I HADN'T THOUGHT ABOUT JORGE, HIS SHORT TEMPER, HIS SHORT ASS AND HIS SHORT WAVE RADIO IN YEARS. WELL, BEFORE THAT, PROBABLY.
I STOPPED BEING A GOOD SON WHEN I DIDN'T STOP MY FATHER FROM KILLING MY MOTHER.
THE LAST THING MY MOTHER TOLD ME WAS THAT I NEED TO SAVE MY FRIENDS.

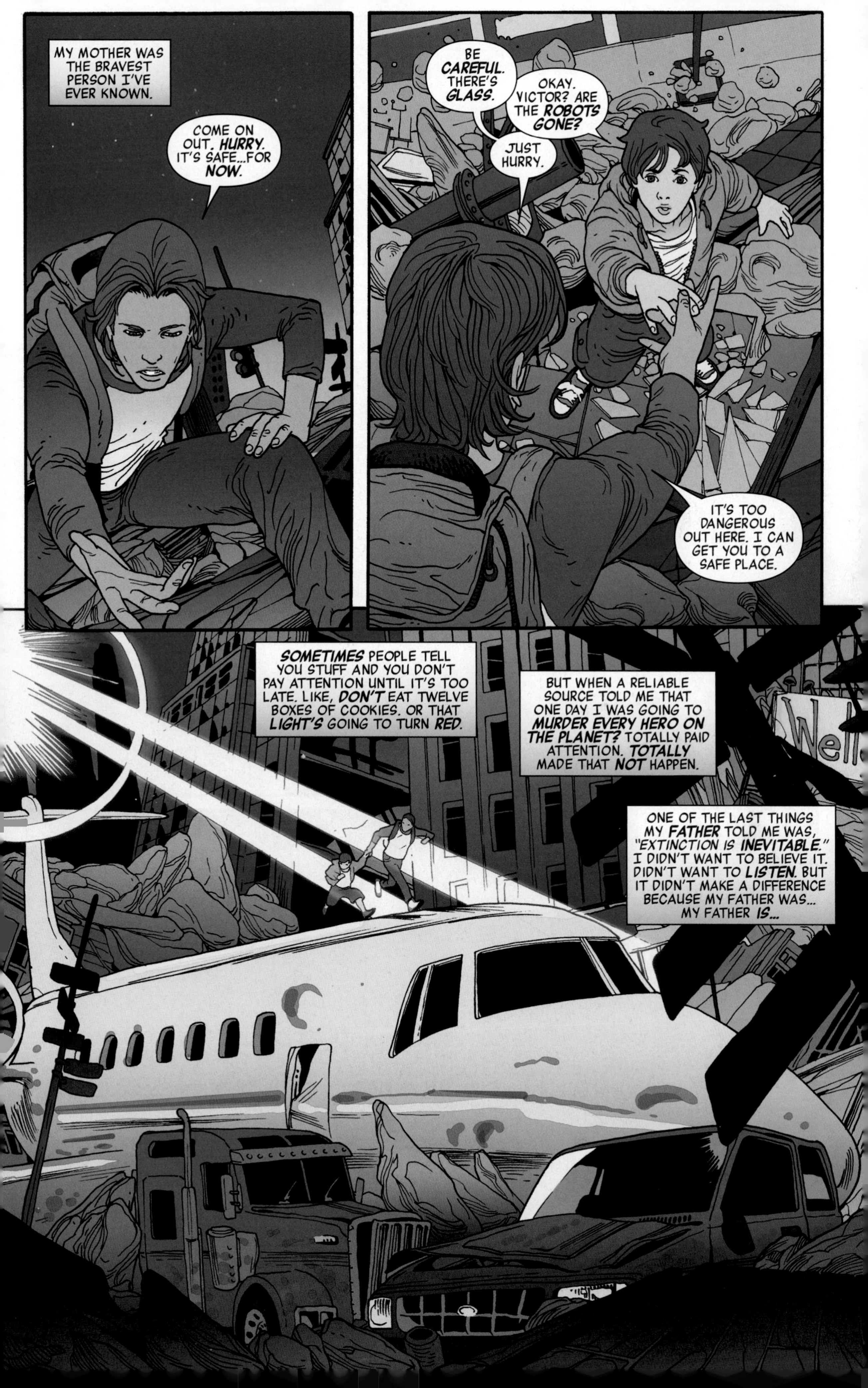
MY MOTHER WAS THE BRAVEST PERSON I'VE EVER KNOWN.
COME ON OUT. HURRY. IT'S SAFE...FOR NOW.
BE CAREFUL. THERE'S GLASS.
OKAY. VICTOR? ARE THE ROBOTS GONE?
JUST HURRY.
IT'S TOO DANGEROUS OUT HERE. I CAN GET YOU TO A SAFE PLACE.
SOMETIMES PEOPLE TELL YOU STUFF AND YOU DON'T PAY ATTENTION UNTIL IT'S TOO LATE. LIKE, DON'T EAT TWELVE BOXES OF COOKIES. OR THAT LIGHT'S GOING TO TURN RED.
BUT WHEN A RELIABLE SOURCE TOLD ME THAT ONE DAY I WAS GOING TO MURDER EVERY HERO ON THE PLANET? TOTALLY PAID ATTENTION. TOTALLY MADE THAT NOT HAPPEN.
ONE OF THE LAST THINGS MY FATHER TOLD ME WAS, "EXTINCTION IS INEVITABLE." I DIDN'T WANT TO BELIEVE IT. DIDN'T WANT TO LISTEN. BUT IT DIDN'T MAKE A DIFFERENCE BECAUSE MY FATHER WAS... MY FATHER IS...

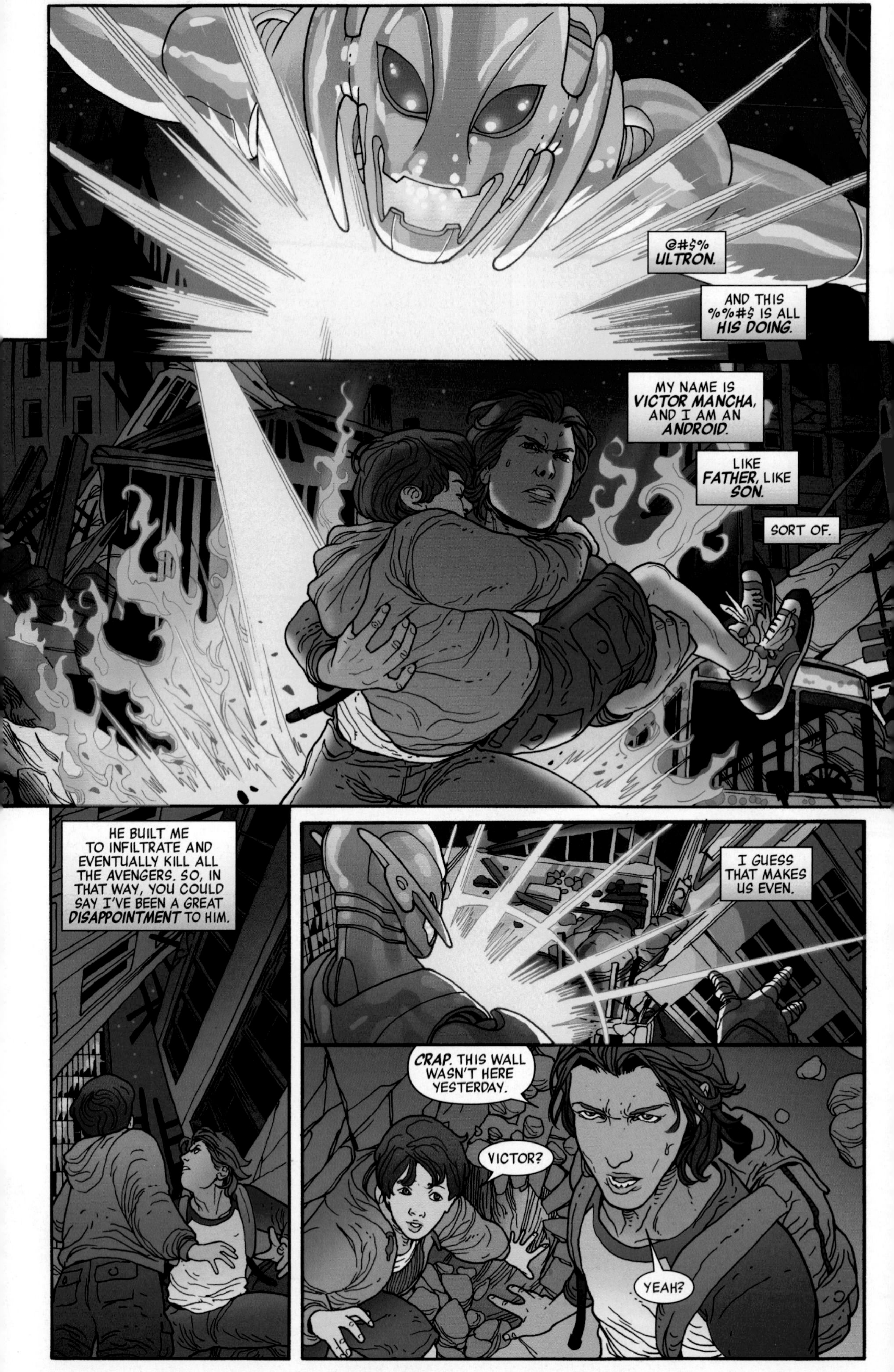
@#$%
ULTRON.
AND THIS
%%#$ IS ALL
HIS DOING.
MY NAME IS
VICTOR MANCHA,
AND I AM AN
ANDROID.
LIKE
FATHER, LIKE
SON.
SORT OF.
HE BUILT ME
TO INFILTRATE AND
EVENTUALLY KILL ALL
THE AVENGERS. SO, IN
THAT WAY, YOU COULD
SAY I'VE BEEN A GREAT
DISAPPOINTMENT TO HIM.
I GUESS
THAT MAKES
US EVEN.
CRAP. THIS WALL
WASN'T HERE
YESTERDAY.
VICTOR?
YEAH?

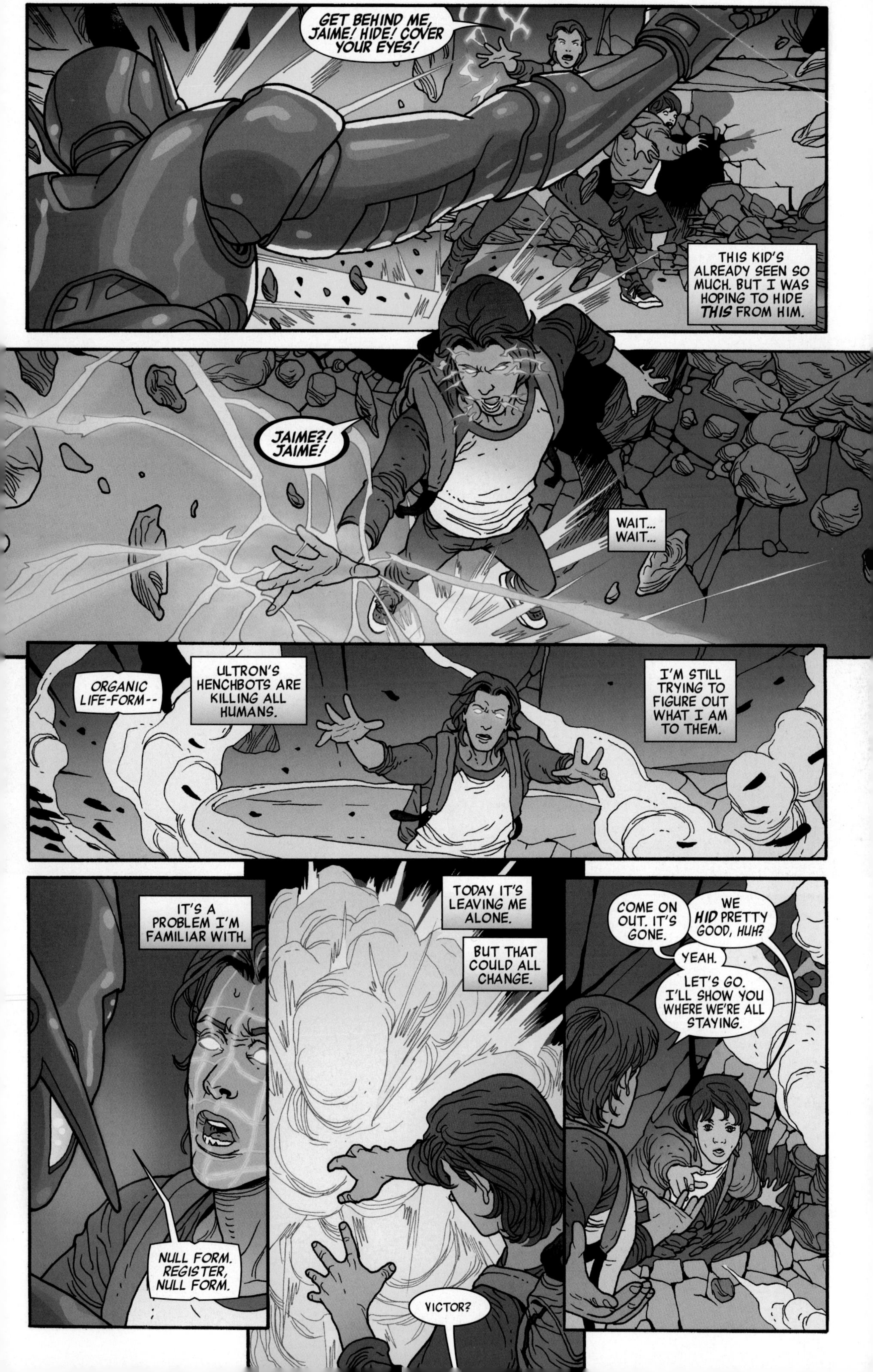
GET BEHIND ME, JAIME! HIDE! COVER YOUR EYES!
THIS KID'S ALREADY SEEN SO MUCH. BUT I WAS HOPING TO HIDE THIS FROM HIM.
JAIME?! JAIME!
WAIT... WAIT...
ORGANIC LIFE-FORM--
ULTRON'S HENCHBOTS ARE KILLING ALL HUMANS.
I'M STILL TRYING TO FIGURE OUT WHAT I AM TO THEM.
IT'S A PROBLEM I'M FAMILIAR WITH.
NULL FORM. REGISTER, NULL FORM.
TODAY IT'S LEAVING ME ALONE.
BUT THAT COULD ALL CHANGE.
VICTOR?
COME ON OUT. IT'S GONE.
WE HID PRETTY GOOD, HUH?
YEAH.
LET'S GO. I'LL SHOW YOU WHERE WE'RE ALL STAYING.

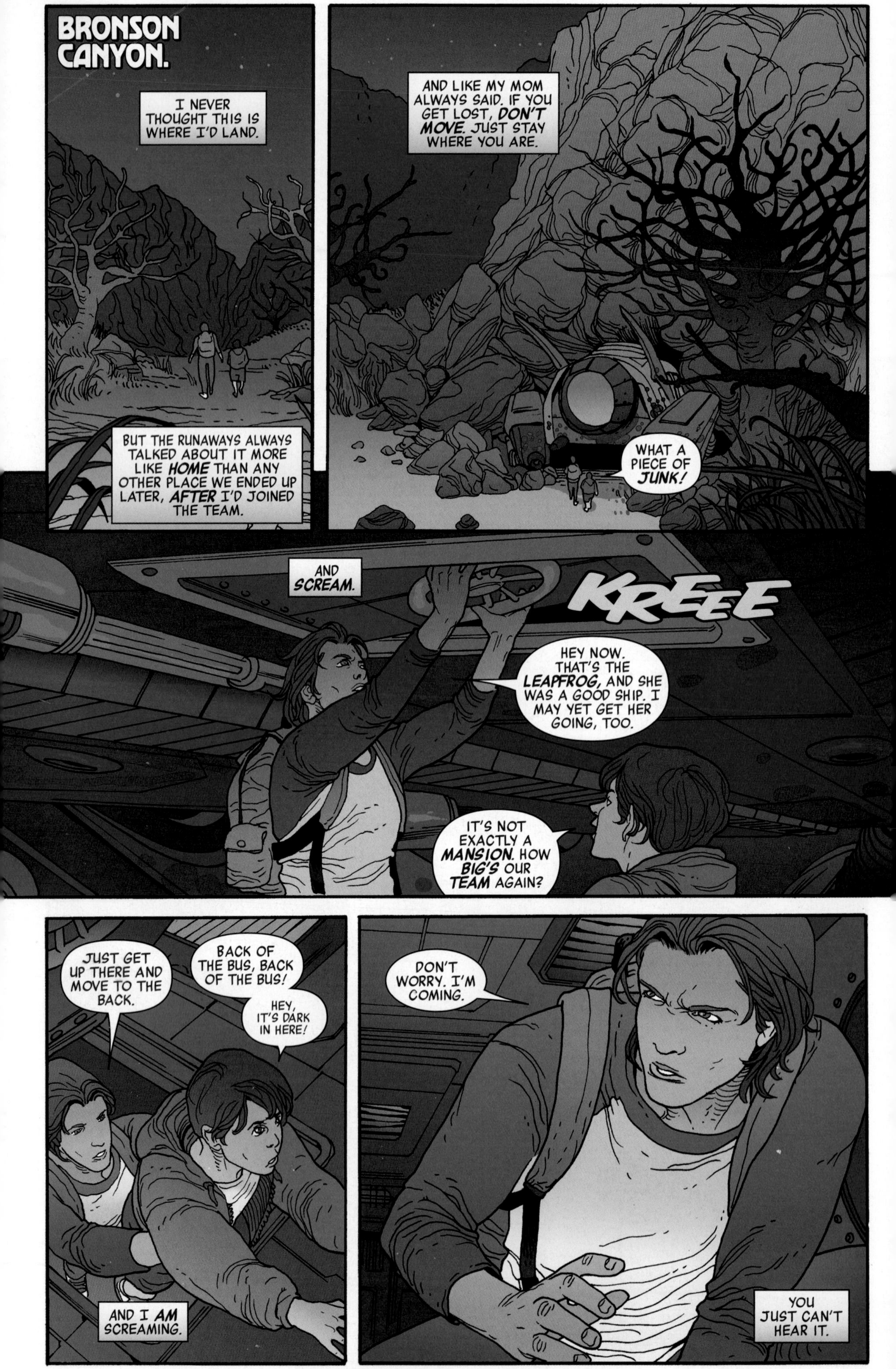
BRONSON CANYON.
I NEVER THOUGHT THIS IS WHERE I'D LAND.
BUT THE RUNAWAYS ALWAYS TALKED ABOUT IT MORE LIKE HOME THAN ANY OTHER PLACE WE ENDED UP LATER, AFTER I'D JOINED THE TEAM.
AND LIKE MY MOM ALWAYS SAID. IF YOU GET LOST, DON'T MOVE. JUST STAY WHERE YOU ARE.
WHAT A PIECE OF JUNK!
AND SCREAM.
KREEE
HEY NOW. THAT'S THE LEAPFROG, AND SHE WAS A GOOD SHIP. I MAY YET GET HER GOING, TOO.
IT'S NOT EXACTLY A MANSION. HOW BIG'S OUR TEAM AGAIN?
JUST GET UP THERE AND MOVE TO THE BACK.
BACK OF THE BUS, BACK OF THE BUS!
HEY, IT'S DARK IN HERE!
AND I AM SCREAMING.
DON'T WORRY. I'M COMING.
YOU JUST CAN'T HEAR IT.

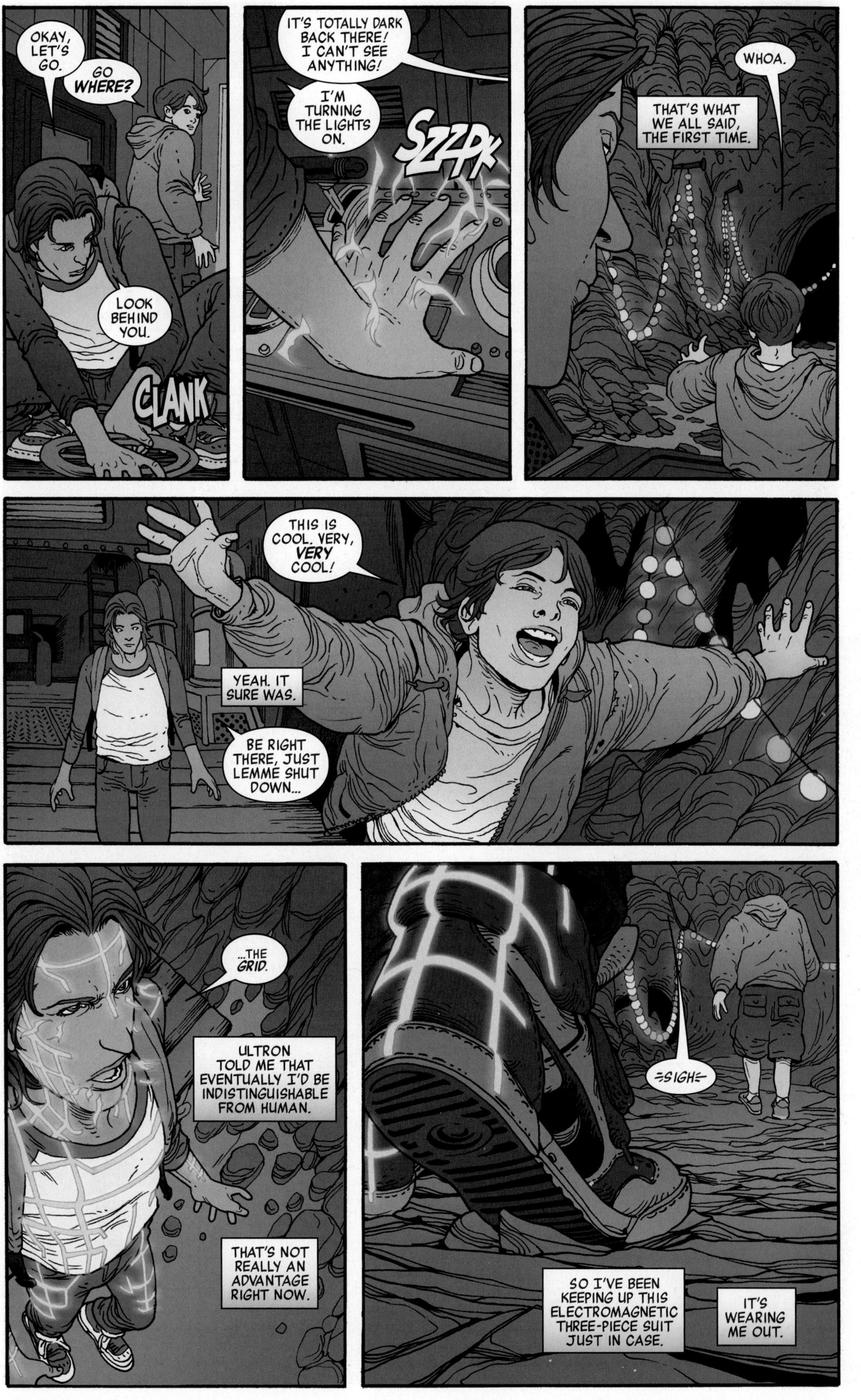
OKAY, LET'S GO.
GO WHERE?
LOOK BEHIND YOU.
CLANK
IT'S TOTALLY DARK BACK THERE! I CAN'T SEE ANYTHING!
I'M TURNING THE LIGHTS ON.
SZZPK
WHOA.
THAT'S WHAT WE ALL SAID, THE FIRST TIME.
THIS IS COOL. VERY, VERY COOL!
YEAH. IT SURE WAS.
BE RIGHT THERE, JUST LEMME SHUT DOWN...
...THE GRID.
ULTRON TOLD ME THAT EVENTUALLY I'D BE INDISTINGUISHABLE FROM HUMAN.
THAT'S NOT REALLY AN ADVANTAGE RIGHT NOW.
SIGH
SO I'VE BEEN KEEPING UP THIS ELECTROMAGNETIC THREE-PIECE SUIT JUST IN CASE.
IT'S WEARING ME OUT.

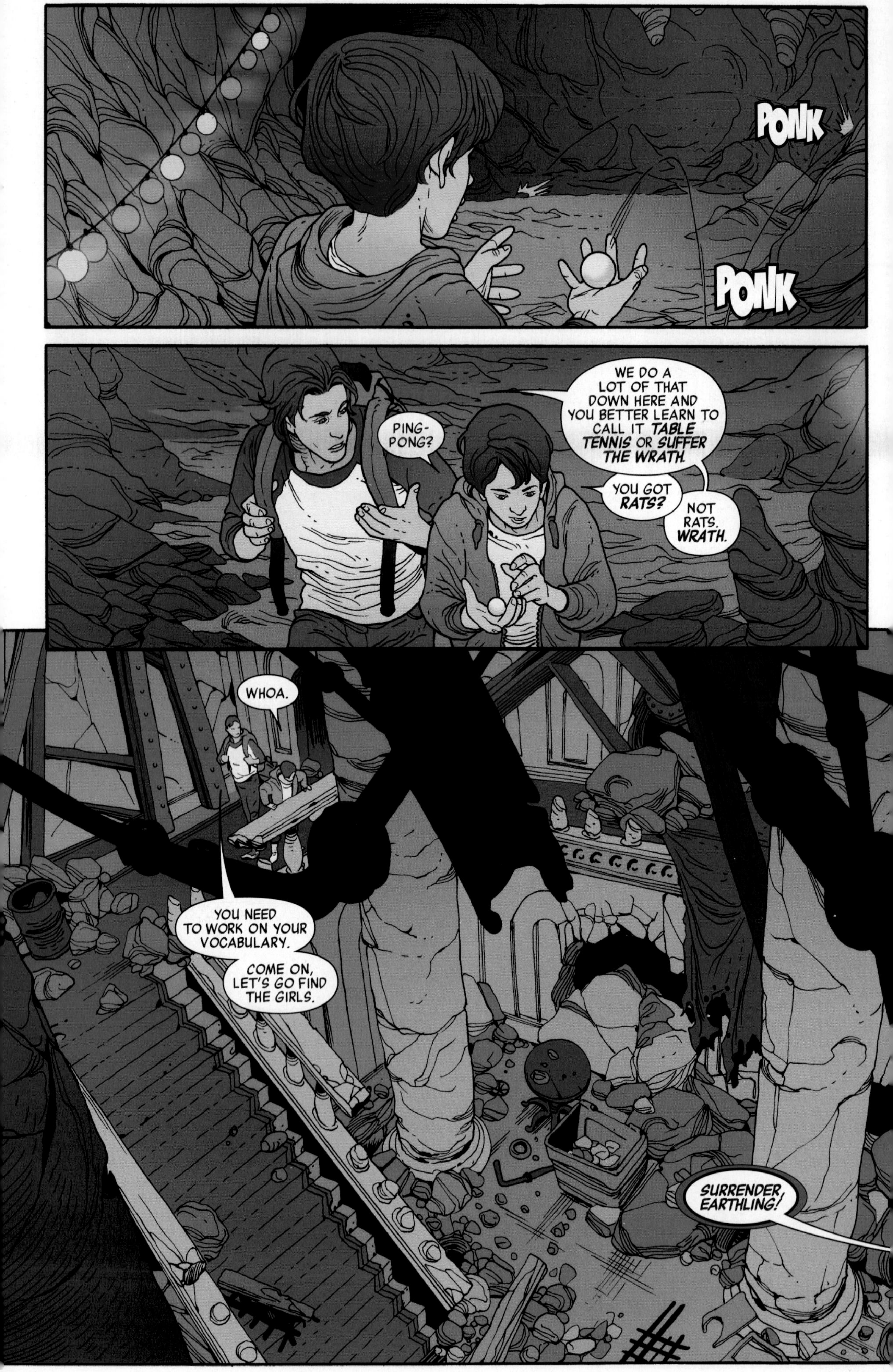
PONK
PONK
PING-PONG?
WE DO A LOT OF THAT DOWN HERE AND YOU BETTER LEARN TO CALL IT TABLE TENNIS OR SUFFER THE WRATH.
YOU GOT RATS?
NOT RATS. WRATH.
WHOA.
YOU NEED TO WORK ON YOUR VOCABULARY.
COME ON, LET'S GO FIND THE GIRLS.
SURRENDER, EARTHLING!

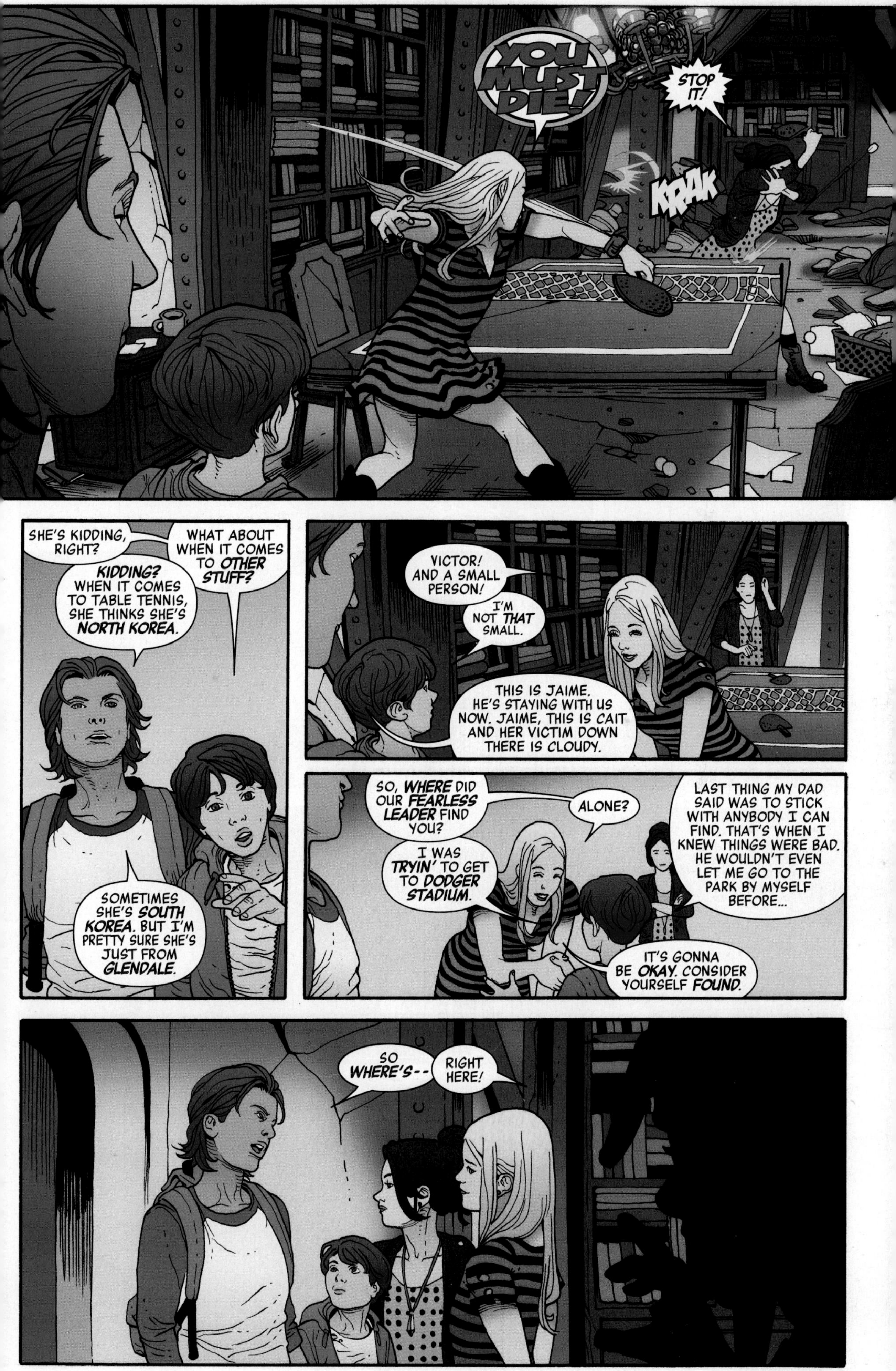
YOU MUST DIE!
STOP IT!
KRAK
SHE'S KIDDING, RIGHT?
KIDDING? WHEN IT COMES TO TABLE TENNIS, SHE THINKS SHE'S NORTH KOREA.
WHAT ABOUT WHEN IT COMES TO OTHER STUFF?
SOMETIMES SHE'S SOUTH KOREA. BUT I'M PRETTY SURE SHE'S JUST FROM GLENDALE.
VICTOR! AND A SMALL PERSON!
I'M NOT THAT SMALL.
THIS IS JAIME. HE'S STAYING WITH US NOW. JAIME, THIS IS CAIT AND HER VICTIM DOWN THERE IS CLOUDY.
SO, WHERE DID OUR FEARLESS LEADER FIND YOU?
I WAS TRYIN' TO GET TO DODGER STADIUM.
ALONE?
LAST THING MY DAD SAID WAS TO STICK WITH ANYBODY I CAN FIND. THAT'S WHEN I KNEW THINGS WERE BAD. HE WOULDN'T EVEN LET ME GO TO THE PARK BY MYSELF BEFORE...
IT'S GONNA BE OKAY. CONSIDER YOURSELF FOUND.
SO WHERE'S--
RIGHT HERE!

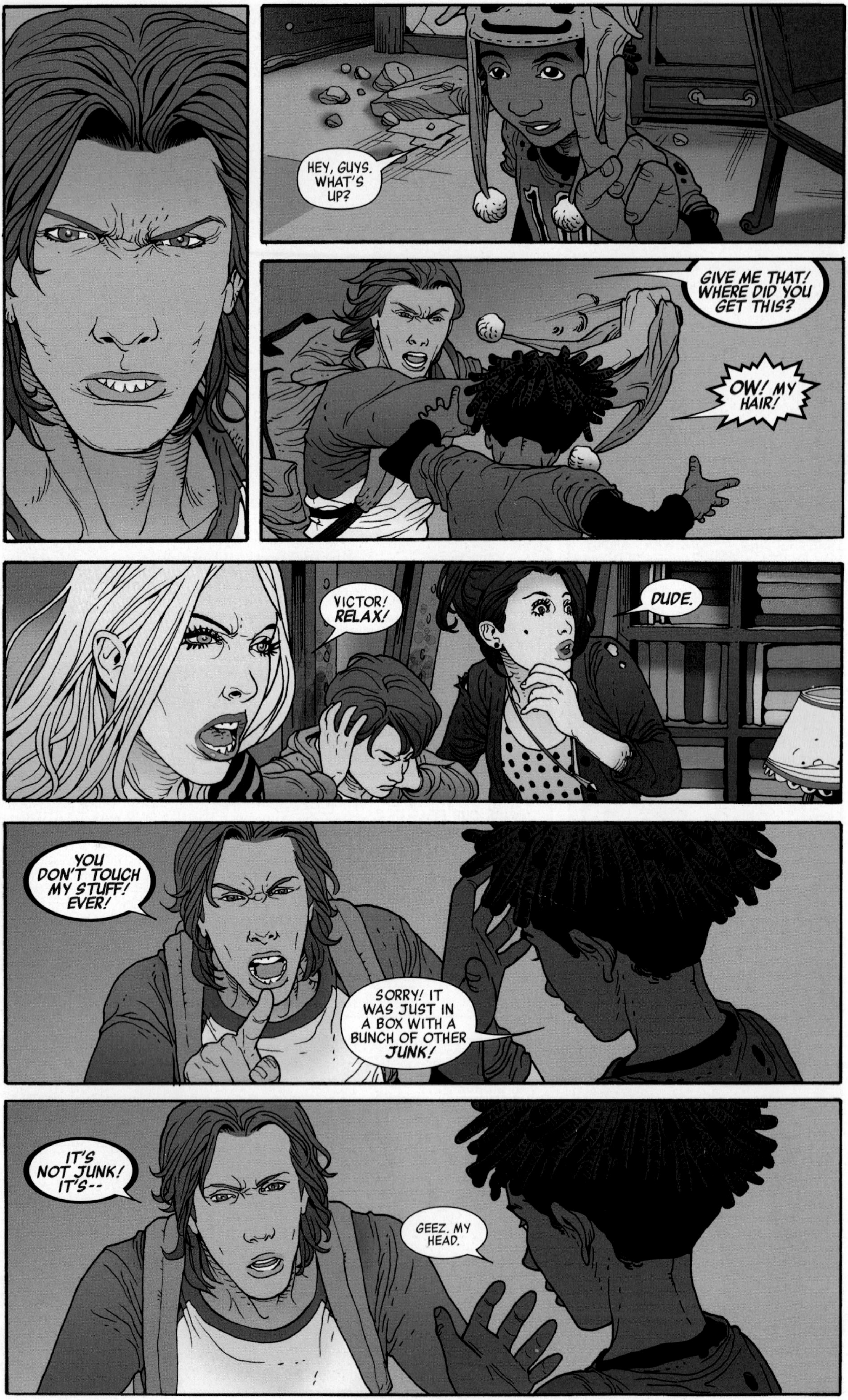
HEY, GUYS. WHAT'S UP?
GIVE ME THAT! WHERE DID YOU GET THIS?
OW! MY HAIR!
VICTOR! RELAX!
DUDE.
YOU DON'T TOUCH MY STUFF! EVER!
SORRY! IT WAS JUST IN A BOX WITH A BUNCH OF OTHER JUNK!
IT'S NOT JUNK! IT'S--
GEEZ. MY HEAD.

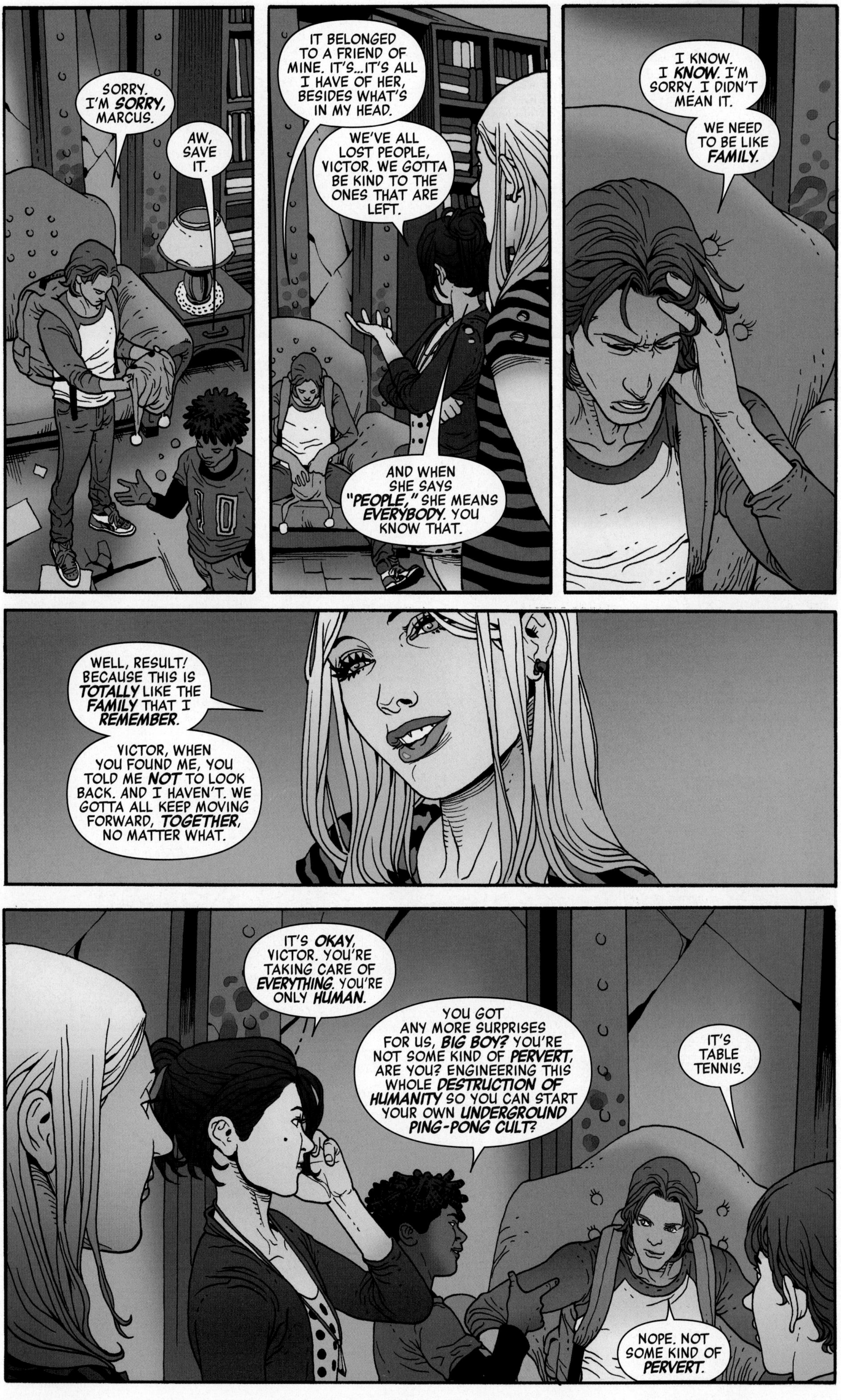
SORRY. I'M SORRY, MARCUS.
AW, SAVE IT.
IT BELONGED TO A FRIEND OF MINE. IT'S...IT'S ALL I HAVE OF HER, BESIDES WHAT'S IN MY HEAD.
WE'VE ALL LOST PEOPLE, VICTOR. WE GOTTA BE KIND TO THE ONES THAT ARE LEFT.
AND WHEN SHE SAYS "PEOPLE," SHE MEANS EVERYBODY. YOU KNOW THAT.
I KNOW. I KNOW. I'M SORRY. I DIDN'T MEAN IT.
WE NEED TO BE LIKE FAMILY.
WELL, RESULT! BECAUSE THIS IS TOTALLY LIKE THE FAMILY THAT I REMEMBER.
VICTOR, WHEN YOU FOUND ME, YOU TOLD ME NOT TO LOOK BACK. AND I HAVEN'T. WE GOTTA ALL KEEP MOVING FORWARD, TOGETHER, NO MATTER WHAT.
IT'S OKAY, VICTOR. YOU'RE TAKING CARE OF EVERYTHING. YOU'RE ONLY HUMAN.
YOU GOT ANY MORE SURPRISES FOR US, BIG BOY? YOU'RE NOT SOME KIND OF PERVERT, ARE YOU? ENGINEERING THIS WHOLE DESTRUCTION OF HUMANITY SO YOU CAN START YOUR OWN UNDERGROUND PING-PONG CULT?
IT'S TABLE TENNIS.
NOPE. NOT SOME KIND OF PERVERT.

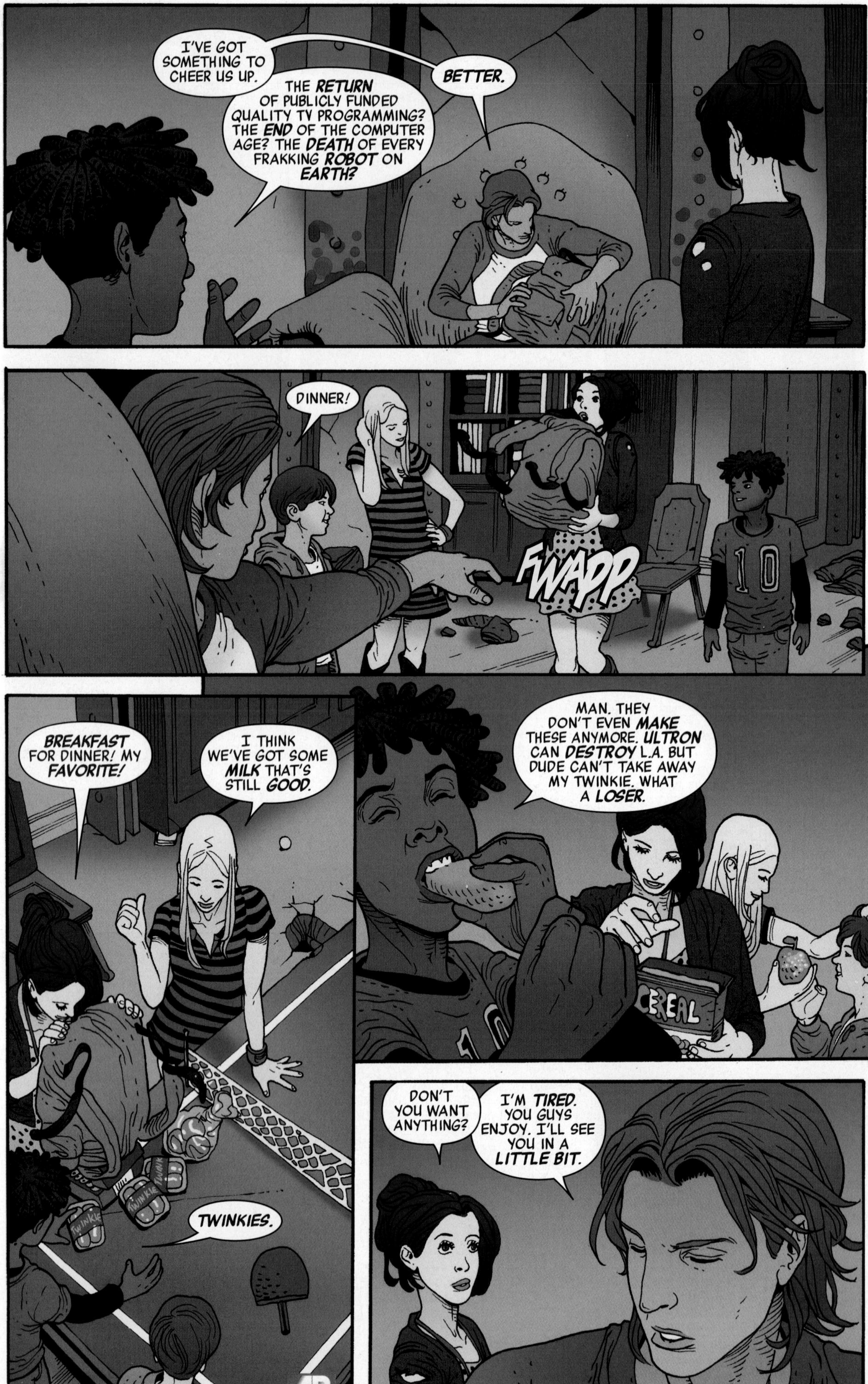
I'VE GOT SOMETHING TO CHEER US UP.
BETTER.
THE RETURN OF PUBLICLY FUNDED QUALITY TV PROGRAMMING? THE END OF THE COMPUTER AGE? THE DEATH OF EVERY FRAKKING ROBOT ON EARTH?
DINNER!
FWAPP
BREAKFAST FOR DINNER! MY FAVORITE!
I THINK WE'VE GOT SOME MILK THAT'S STILL GOOD.
TWINKIES.
TWINKIE
MAN. THEY DON'T EVEN MAKE THESE ANYMORE. ULTRON CAN DESTROY L.A. BUT DUDE CAN'T TAKE AWAY MY TWINKIE. WHAT A LOSER.
CEREAL
DON'T YOU WANT ANYTHING?
I'M TIRED. YOU GUYS ENJOY. I'LL SEE YOU IN A LITTLE BIT.

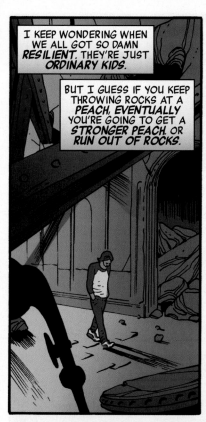

I KEEP WONDERING WHEN WE ALL GOT SO DAMN *RESILIENT*. THEY'RE JUST *ORDINARY* KIDS.

BUT I GUESS IF YOU KEEP THROWING ROCKS AT A *PEACH,* EVENTUALLY YOU'RE GOING TO GET A *STRONGER PEACH.* OR RUN OUT OF ROCKS.

EXCEPT THIS WORLD *NEVER* SEEMS TO *RUN OUT OF ROCKS.*

AND WE ALL KEPT CATCHING THEM, ME, KAROLINA, NICO, CHASE, MOLLY, KLARA...

... RIGHT UP TO THE VERY END.

JUST COULDN'T THROW 'EM BACK *HARD ENOUGH.*

I WISH I HAD SOMETHING LEFT OF THEM, SOMETHING REAL, SOMETHING I COULD TOUCH.

BUT THERE AREN'T ANY SECRET NOTES OR PHOTOGRAPHS OR YEARBOOKS, NOT EVEN ANY TEXTS OR EMAILS.

NOW I'M THE ONLY ONE LEFT. AND ALL I'VE GOT'S A *HAT* AND WHAT'S IN MY *HEAD.*

IT'S SCREWED UP, BUT I HAVE TO THANK ULTRON FOR GIVING ME LIFE *AND* FOR GIVING ME A PHOTO-GRAPHIC MEMORY--

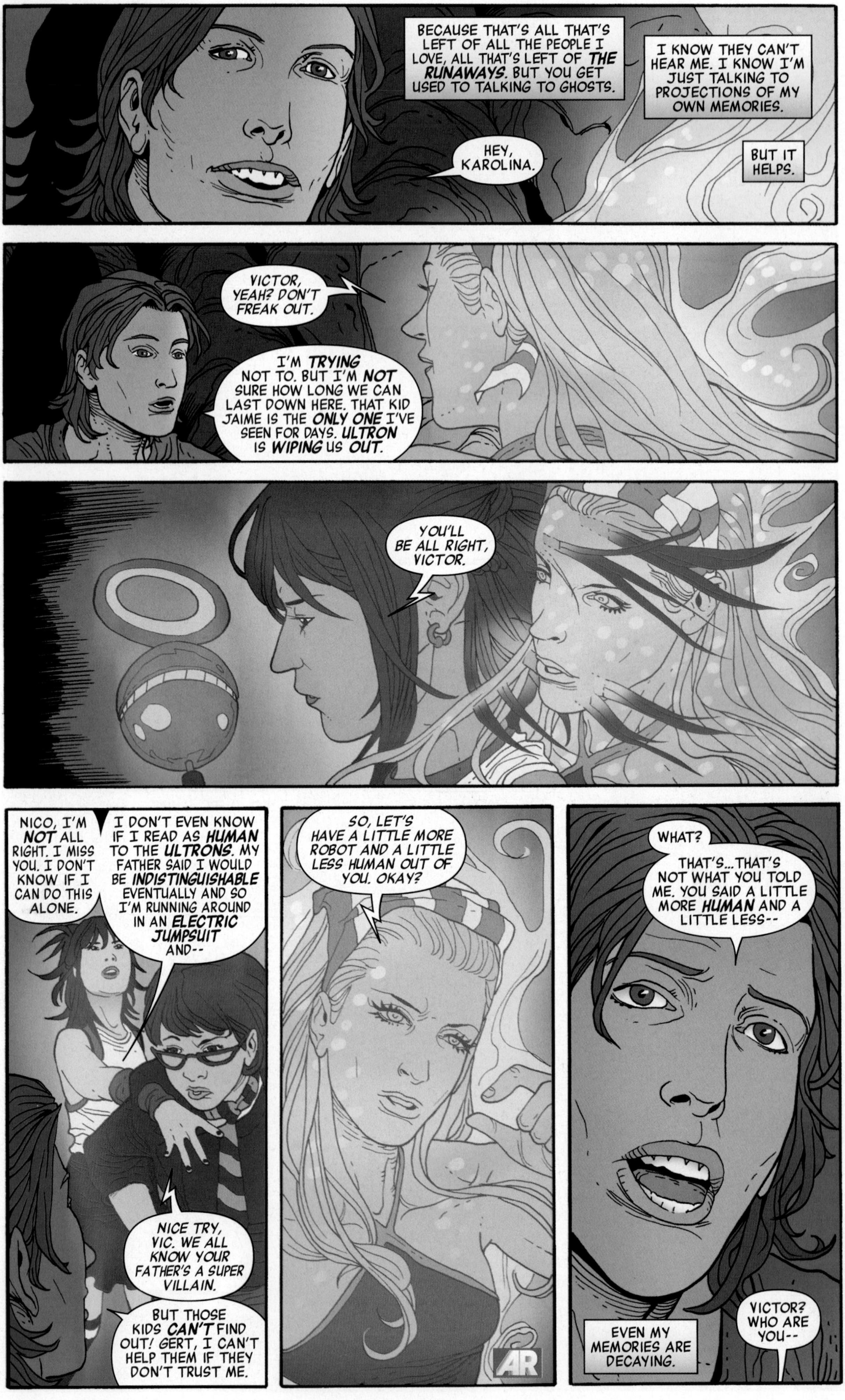
BECAUSE THAT'S ALL THAT'S LEFT OF ALL THE PEOPLE I LOVE, ALL THAT'S LEFT OF THE RUNAWAYS. BUT YOU GET USED TO TALKING TO GHOSTS.
I KNOW THEY CAN'T HEAR ME. I KNOW I'M JUST TALKING TO PROJECTIONS OF MY OWN MEMORIES.
HEY, KAROLINA.
BUT IT HELPS.
VICTOR, YEAH? DON'T FREAK OUT.
I'M TRYING NOT TO. BUT I'M NOT SURE HOW LONG WE CAN LAST DOWN HERE. THAT KID JAIME IS THE ONLY ONE I'VE SEEN FOR DAYS. ULTRON IS WIPING US OUT.
YOU'LL BE ALL RIGHT, VICTOR.
NICO, I'M NOT ALL RIGHT. I MISS YOU. I DON'T KNOW IF I CAN DO THIS ALONE.
I DON'T EVEN KNOW IF I READ AS HUMAN TO THE ULTRONS. MY FATHER SAID I WOULD BE INDISTINGUISHABLE EVENTUALLY AND SO I'M RUNNING AROUND IN AN ELECTRIC JUMPSUIT AND--
NICE TRY, VIC. WE ALL KNOW YOUR FATHER'S A SUPER VILLAIN.
BUT THOSE KIDS CAN'T FIND OUT! GERT, I CAN'T HELP THEM IF THEY DON'T TRUST ME.
SO, LET'S HAVE A LITTLE MORE ROBOT AND A LITTLE LESS HUMAN OUT OF YOU. OKAY?
WHAT?
THAT'S...THAT'S NOT WHAT YOU TOLD ME. YOU SAID A LITTLE MORE HUMAN AND A LITTLE LESS--
EVEN MY MEMORIES ARE DECAYING.
VICTOR? WHO ARE YOU--

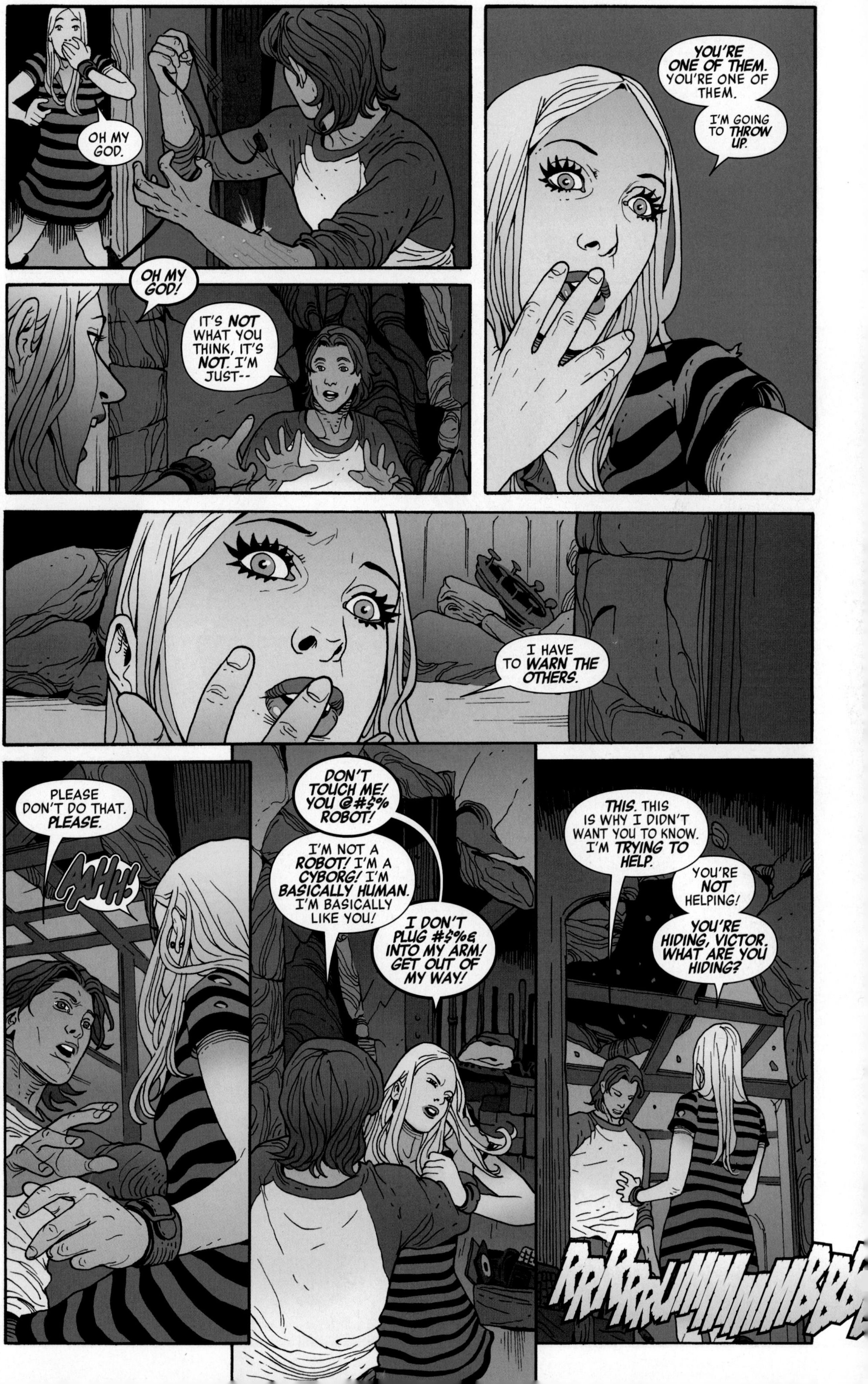
OH MY GOD.
YOU'RE ONE OF THEM. YOU'RE ONE OF THEM.
I'M GOING TO THROW UP.
OH MY GOD!
IT'S NOT WHAT YOU THINK, IT'S NOT. I'M JUST--
I HAVE TO WARN THE OTHERS.
PLEASE DON'T DO THAT. PLEASE.
AAHH!
DON'T TOUCH ME! YOU @#$% ROBOT!
I'M NOT A ROBOT! I'M A CYBORG! I'M BASICALLY HUMAN. I'M BASICALLY LIKE YOU!
I DON'T PLUG #$%& INTO MY ARM! GET OUT OF MY WAY!
THIS. THIS IS WHY I DIDN'T WANT YOU TO KNOW. I'M TRYING TO HELP.
YOU'RE NOT HELPING!
YOU'RE HIDING, VICTOR. WHAT ARE YOU HIDING?
RRRRRRUMMMMMBBB

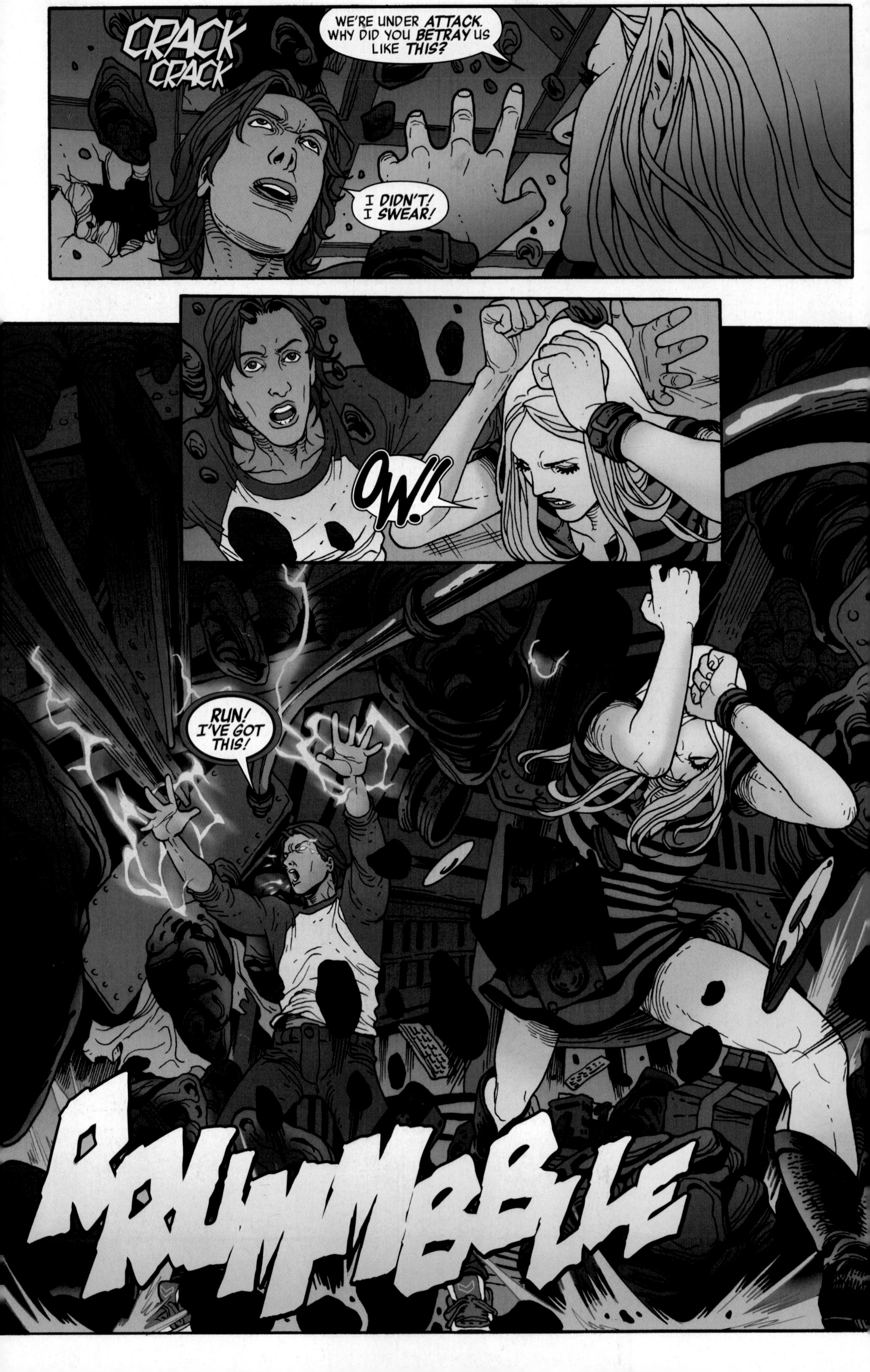
CRACK CRACK
WE'RE UNDER ATTACK. WHY DID YOU BETRAY US LIKE THIS?
I DIDN'T! I SWEAR!
OW!
RUN! I'VE GOT THIS!
RRUMMBBLLE

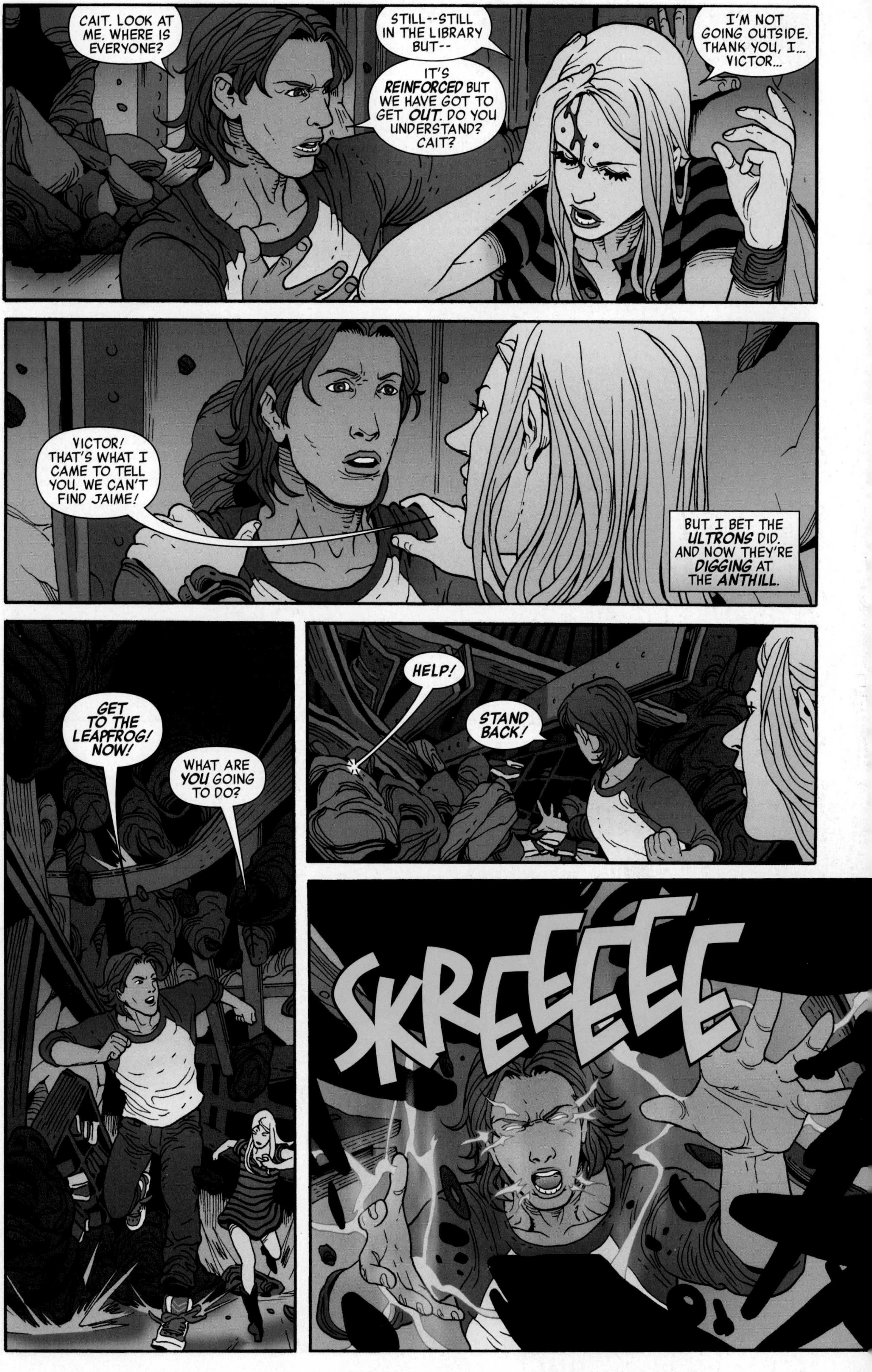
CAIT. LOOK AT ME. WHERE IS EVERYONE?
STILL--STILL IN THE LIBRARY BUT--
IT'S REINFORCED BUT WE HAVE GOT TO GET OUT. DO YOU UNDERSTAND? CAIT?
I'M NOT GOING OUTSIDE. THANK YOU, I... VICTOR...
VICTOR! THAT'S WHAT I CAME TO TELL YOU. WE CAN'T FIND JAIME!
BUT I BET THE ULTRONS DID. AND NOW THEY'RE DIGGING AT THE ANTHILL.
GET TO THE LEAPFROG! NOW!
WHAT ARE YOU GOING TO DO?
HELP!
STAND BACK!
SKREEEEE

IT'S OKAY. COME ON OUT.

I COULDN'T FIND ANYWHERE ELSE TO *HIDE*.

THERE'S *ALWAYS* SOMEWHERE ELSE. COME ON, IT'S GOING TO BE OKAY. ARE YOU *HURT*?

NO.

DO YOU KNOW WHERE JAIME IS?

HE WOULDN'T SHUT UP ABOUT THE *YELLING* AND WE KEPT *TELLING* HIM YOU *WEREN'T* ALWAYS LIKE THAT BUT I THINK HE'S BEEN YELLED AT A *LOT*.

I THINK HE'S OUTSIDE.

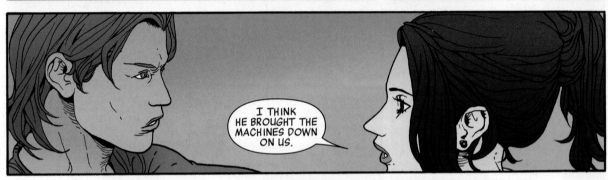

I THINK HE BROUGHT THE MACHINES DOWN ON US.

CLOUDY... WHERE'S MARCUS?

I TRIED... I TRIED TO PULL HIM OUT BUT... THERE WERE TOO MANY PIECES.

TOO MANY PIECES OF WHAT? SHOW ME, IF IT'S METAL, I CAN MOVE IT.

TOO MANY PIECES OF MARCUS, VICTOR.

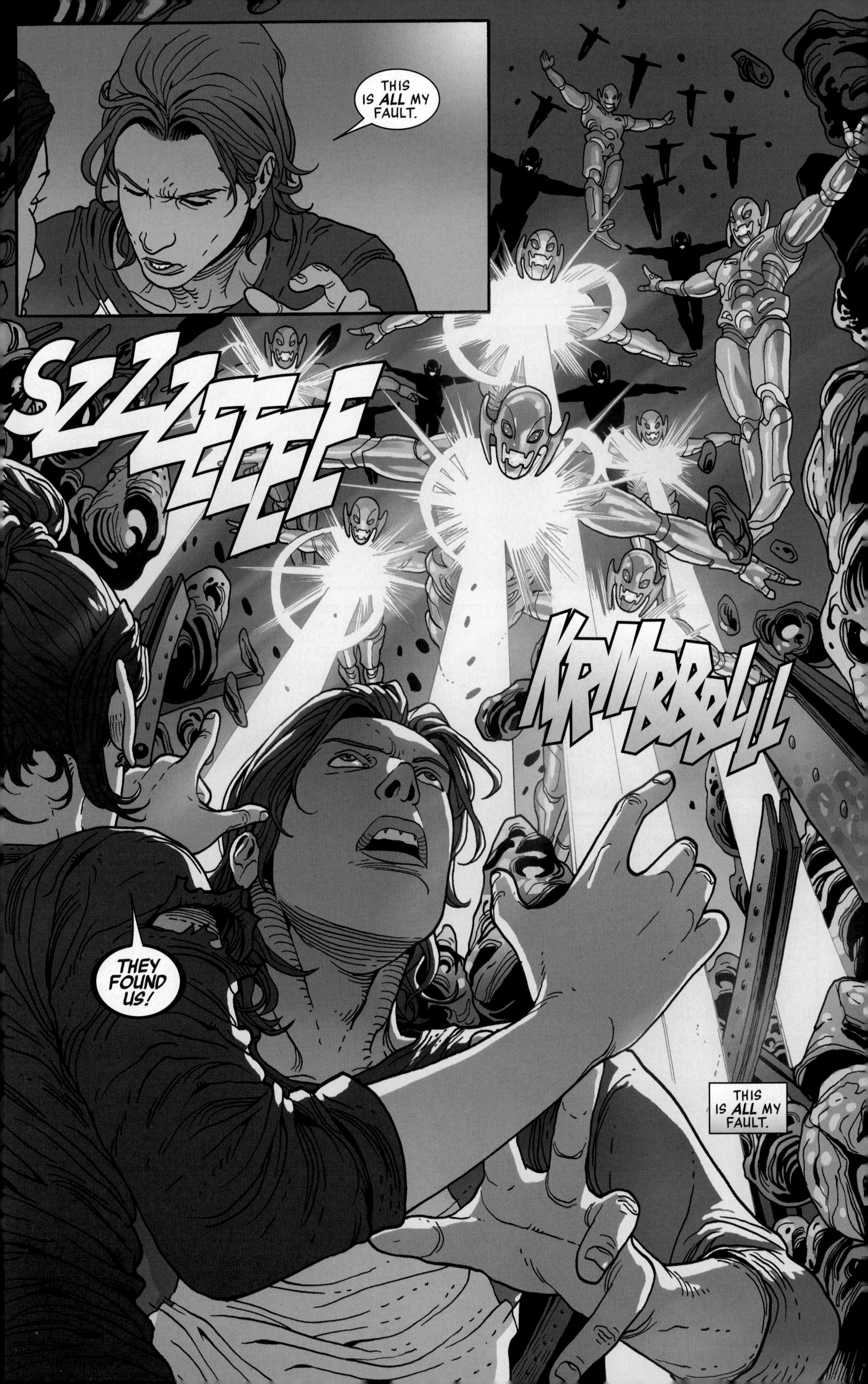

THIS IS ALL MY FAULT.
SZZZEEEE
KRMBBBLL
THEY FOUND US!
THIS IS ALL MY FAULT.

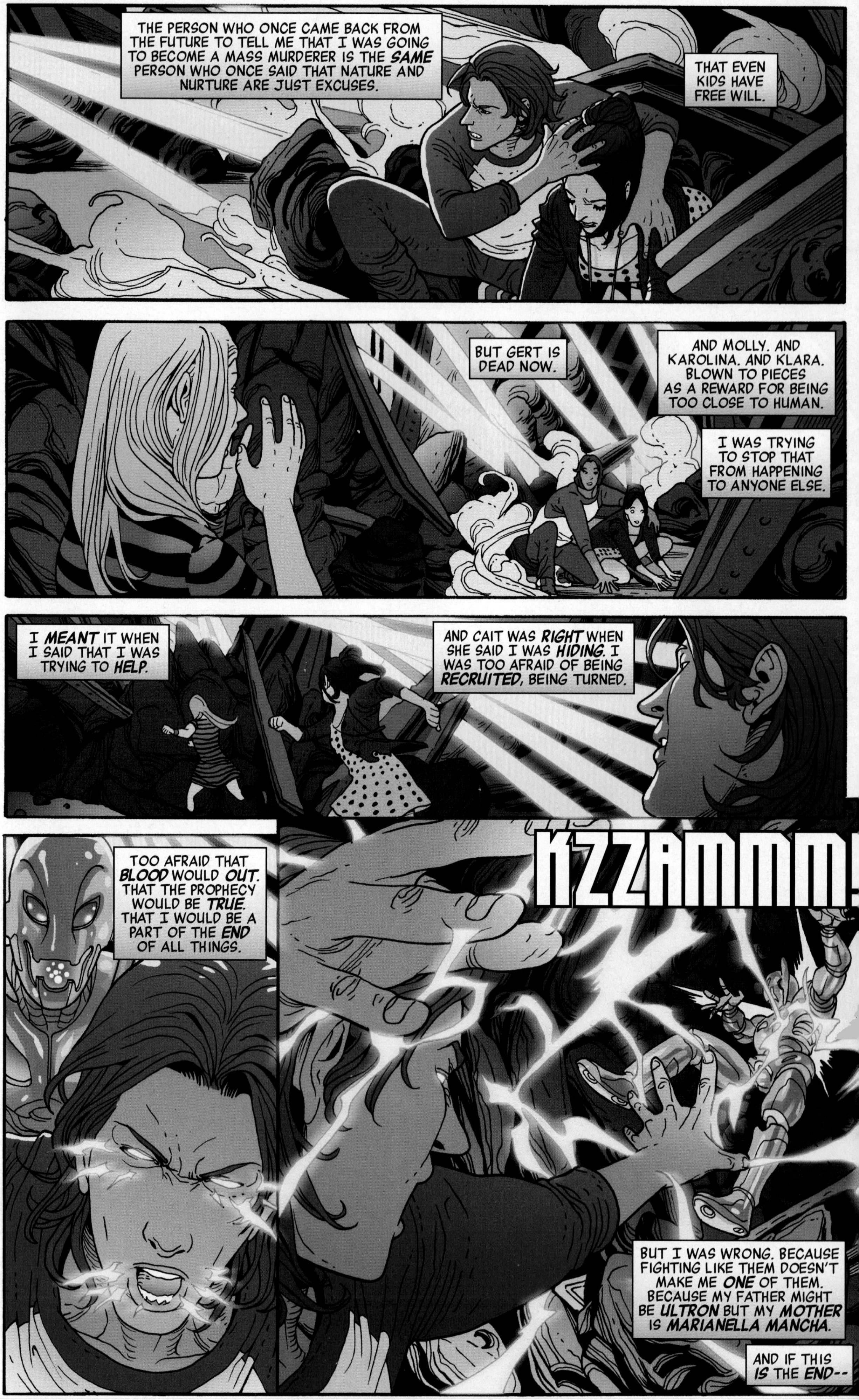

THE PERSON WHO ONCE CAME BACK FROM THE FUTURE TO TELL ME THAT I WAS GOING TO BECOME A MASS MURDERER IS THE SAME PERSON WHO ONCE SAID THAT NATURE AND NURTURE ARE JUST EXCUSES.
THAT EVEN KIDS HAVE FREE WILL.
BUT GERT IS DEAD NOW.
AND MOLLY. AND KAROLINA. AND KLARA. BLOWN TO PIECES AS A REWARD FOR BEING TOO CLOSE TO HUMAN.
I WAS TRYING TO STOP THAT FROM HAPPENING TO ANYONE ELSE.
I MEANT IT WHEN I SAID THAT I WAS TRYING TO HELP.
AND CAIT WAS RIGHT WHEN SHE SAID I WAS HIDING. I WAS TOO AFRAID OF BEING RECRUITED, BEING TURNED.
TOO AFRAID THAT BLOOD WOULD OUT. THAT THE PROPHECY WOULD BE TRUE. THAT I WOULD BE A PART OF THE END OF ALL THINGS.
KZZAMMMM!
BUT I WAS WRONG. BECAUSE FIGHTING LIKE THEM DOESN'T MAKE ME ONE OF THEM. BECAUSE MY FATHER MIGHT BE ULTRON BUT MY MOTHER IS MARIANELLA MANCHA.
AND IF THIS IS THE END--

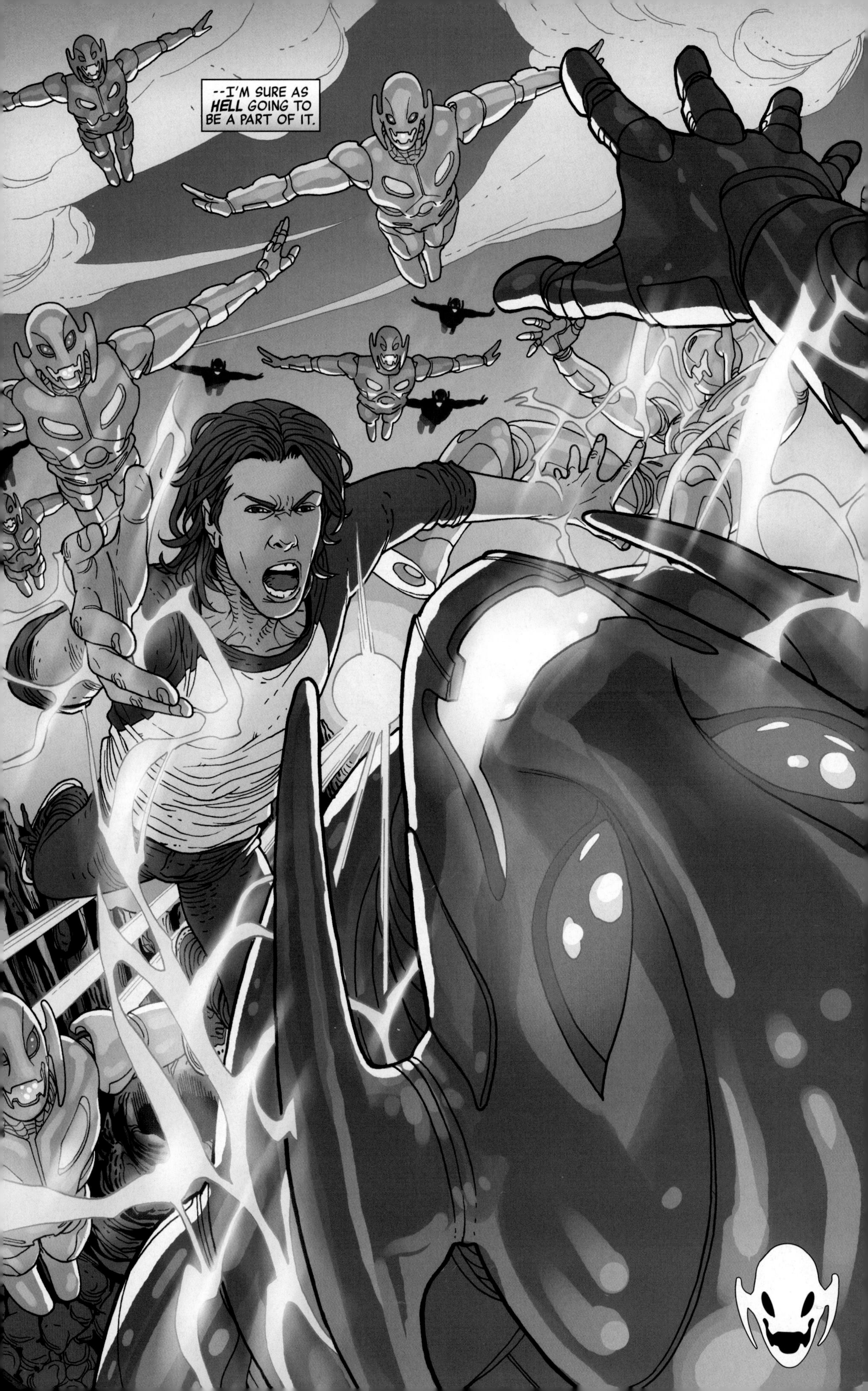
--I'M SURE AS HELL GOING TO BE A PART OF IT.

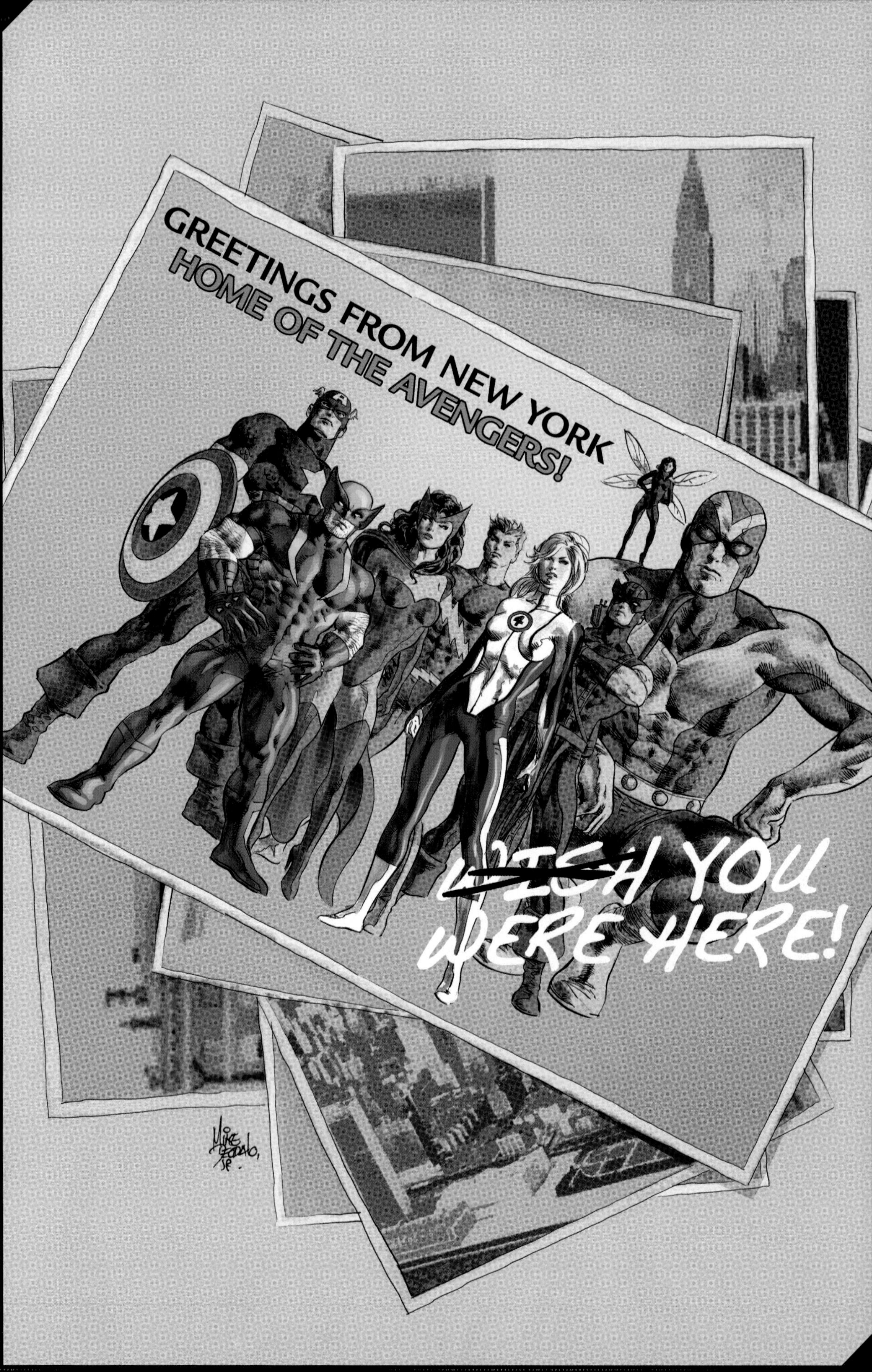
GREETINGS FROM NEW YORK
HOME OF THE AVENGERS!
WISH YOU WERE HERE!

WOLVERINE & THE X-MEN #27AU

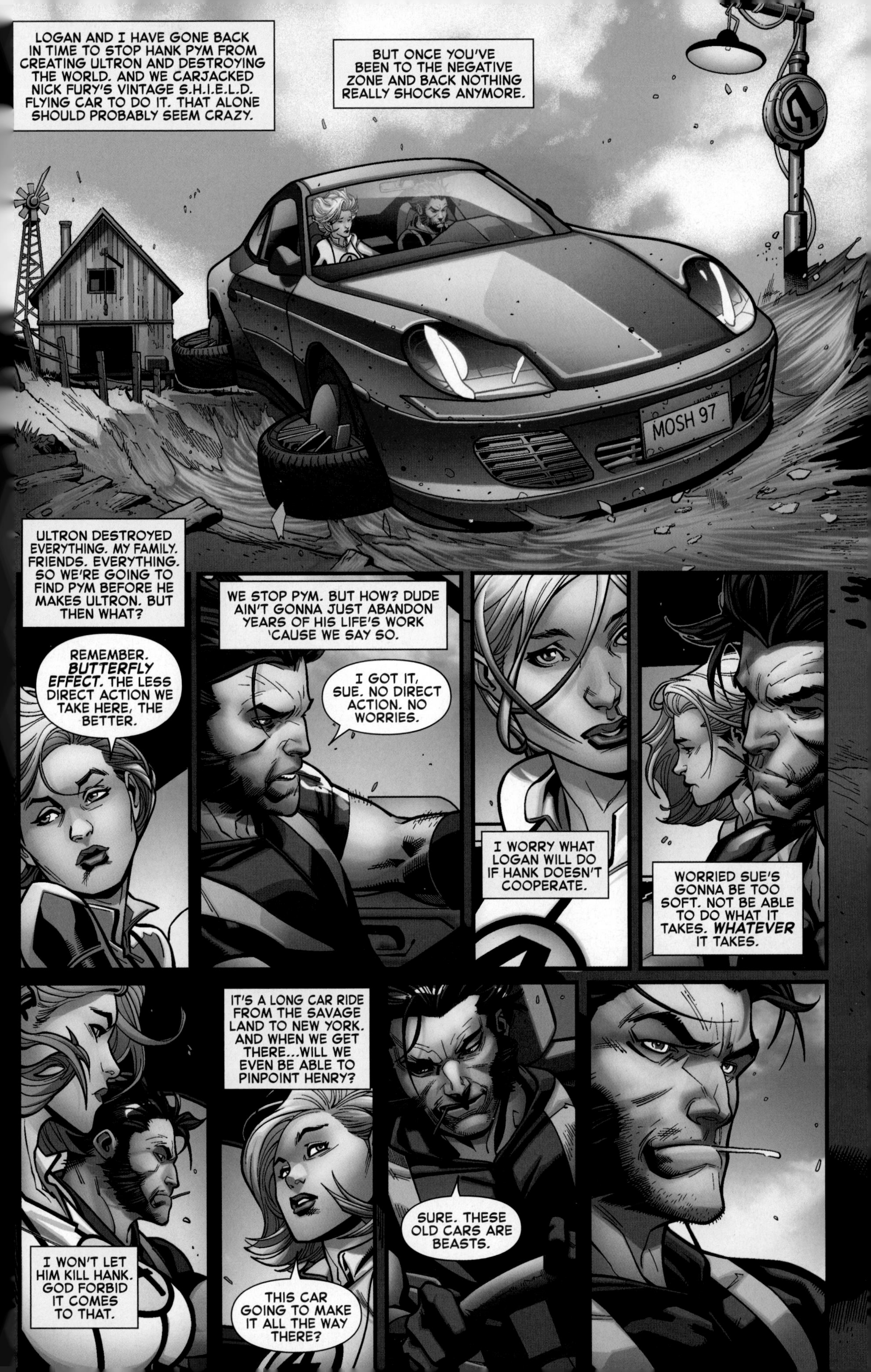
LOGAN AND I HAVE GONE BACK IN TIME TO STOP HANK PYM FROM CREATING ULTRON AND DESTROYING THE WORLD. AND WE CARJACKED NICK FURY'S VINTAGE S.H.I.E.L.D. FLYING CAR TO DO IT. THAT ALONE SHOULD PROBABLY SEEM CRAZY.
BUT ONCE YOU'VE BEEN TO THE NEGATIVE ZONE AND BACK NOTHING REALLY SHOCKS ANYMORE.
MOSH 97
ULTRON DESTROYED EVERYTHING. MY FAMILY. FRIENDS. EVERYTHING. SO WE'RE GOING TO FIND PYM BEFORE HE MAKES ULTRON. BUT THEN WHAT?
REMEMBER. BUTTERFLY EFFECT. THE LESS DIRECT ACTION WE TAKE HERE, THE BETTER.
WE STOP PYM. BUT HOW? DUDE AIN'T GONNA JUST ABANDON YEARS OF HIS LIFE'S WORK 'CAUSE WE SAY SO.
I GOT IT, SUE. NO DIRECT ACTION. NO WORRIES.
I WORRY WHAT LOGAN WILL DO IF HANK DOESN'T COOPERATE.
WORRIED SUE'S GONNA BE TOO SOFT. NOT BE ABLE TO DO WHAT IT TAKES. WHATEVER IT TAKES.
I WON'T LET HIM KILL HANK. GOD FORBID IT COMES TO THAT.
IT'S A LONG CAR RIDE FROM THE SAVAGE LAND TO NEW YORK. AND WHEN WE GET THERE...WILL WE EVEN BE ABLE TO PINPOINT HENRY?
THIS CAR GOING TO MAKE IT ALL THE WAY THERE?
SURE. THESE OLD CARS ARE BEASTS.

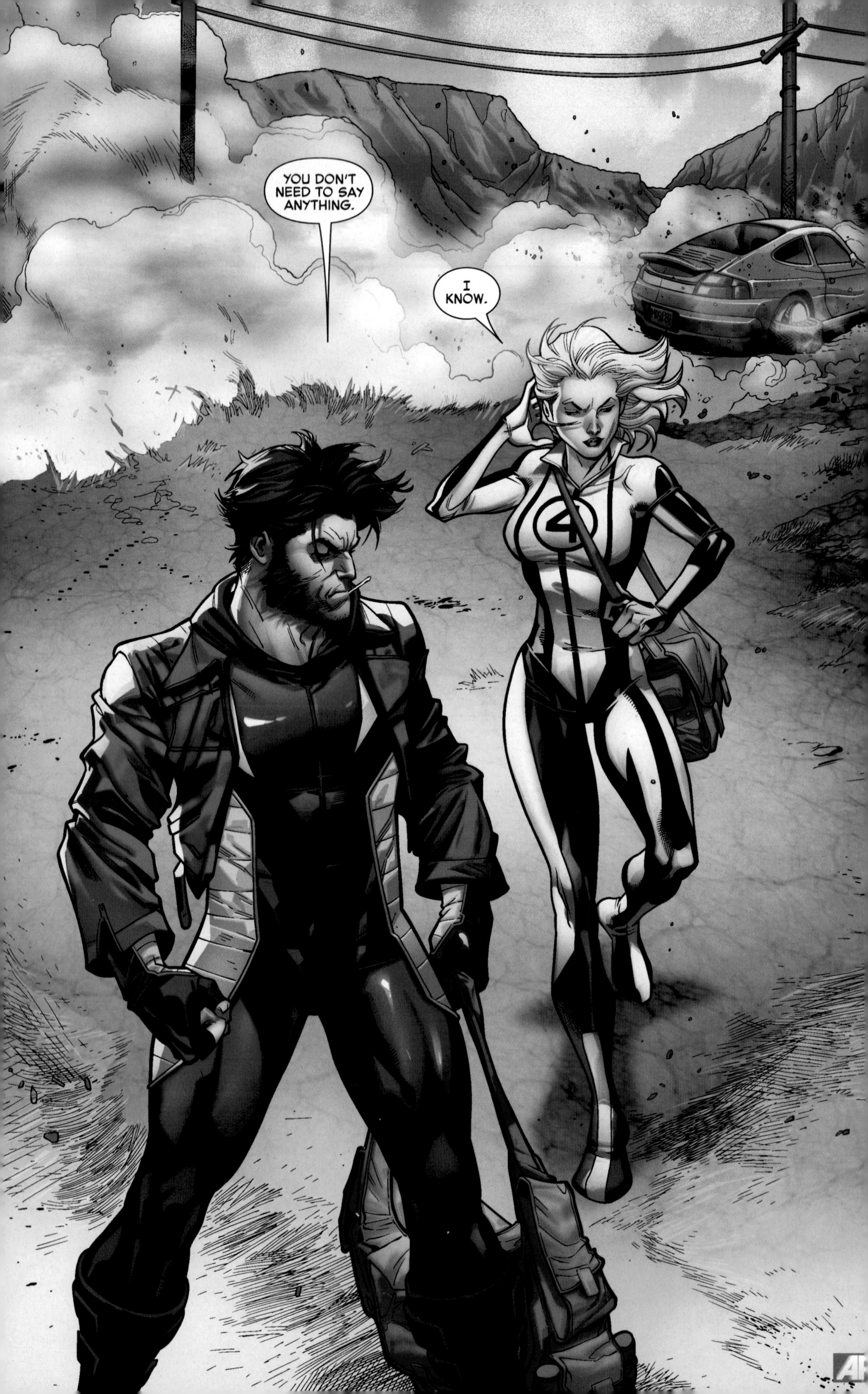
YOU DON'T NEED TO SAY ANYTHING.
I KNOW.

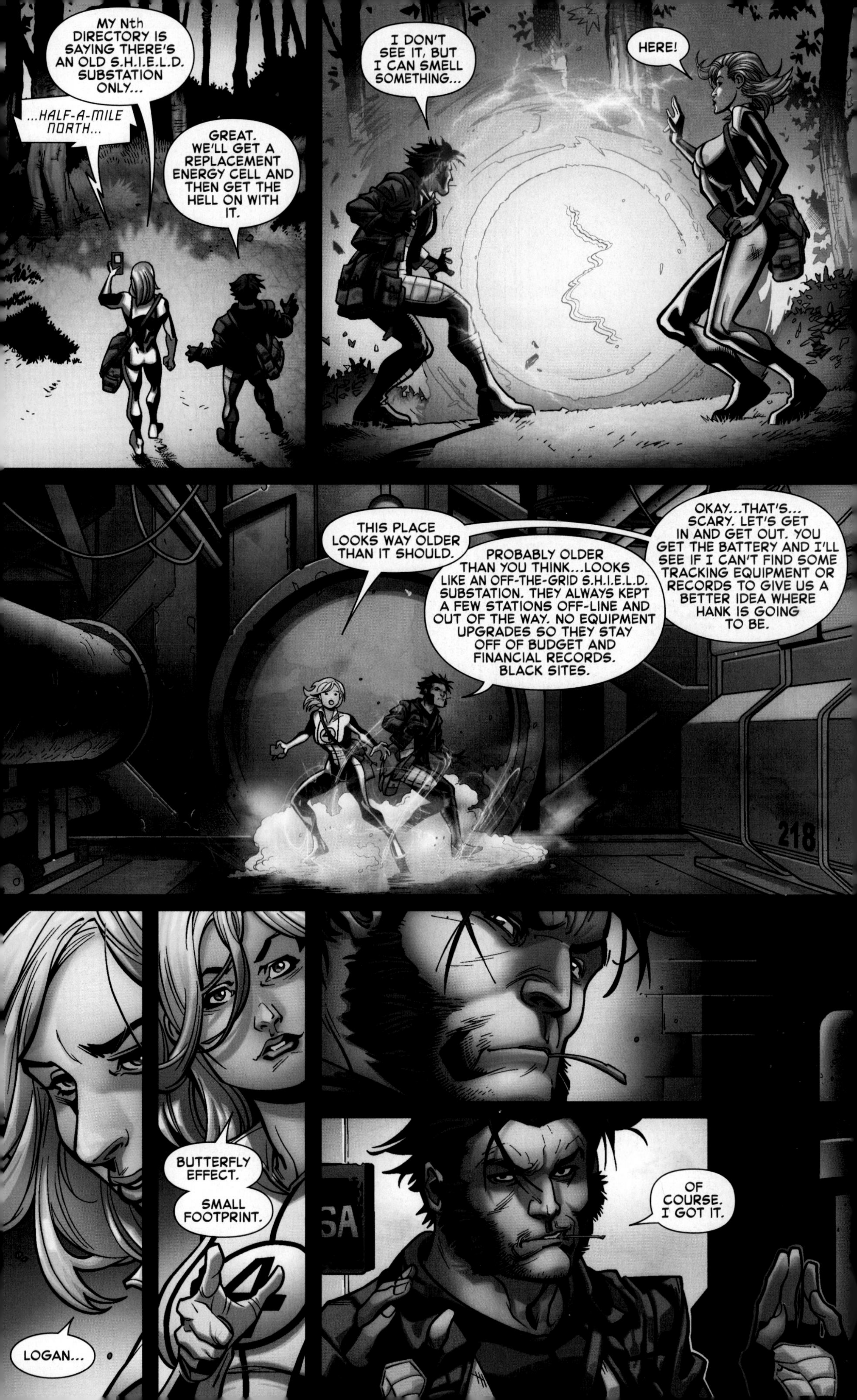

MY Nth DIRECTORY IS SAYING THERE'S AN OLD S.H.I.E.L.D. SUBSTATION ONLY...
...HALF-A-MILE NORTH...
GREAT. WE'LL GET A REPLACEMENT ENERGY CELL AND THEN GET THE HELL ON WITH IT.
I DON'T SEE IT, BUT I CAN SMELL SOMETHING...
HERE!
THIS PLACE LOOKS WAY OLDER THAN IT SHOULD.
PROBABLY OLDER THAN YOU THINK...LOOKS LIKE AN OFF-THE-GRID S.H.I.E.L.D. SUBSTATION. THEY ALWAYS KEPT A FEW STATIONS OFF-LINE AND OUT OF THE WAY. NO EQUIPMENT UPGRADES SO THEY STAY OFF OF BUDGET AND FINANCIAL RECORDS. BLACK SITES.
OKAY...THAT'S... SCARY. LET'S GET IN AND GET OUT. YOU GET THE BATTERY AND I'LL SEE IF I CAN'T FIND SOME TRACKING EQUIPMENT OR RECORDS TO GIVE US A BETTER IDEA WHERE HANK IS GOING TO BE.
218
LOGAN...
BUTTERFLY EFFECT.
SMALL FOOTPRINT.
OF COURSE. I GOT IT.

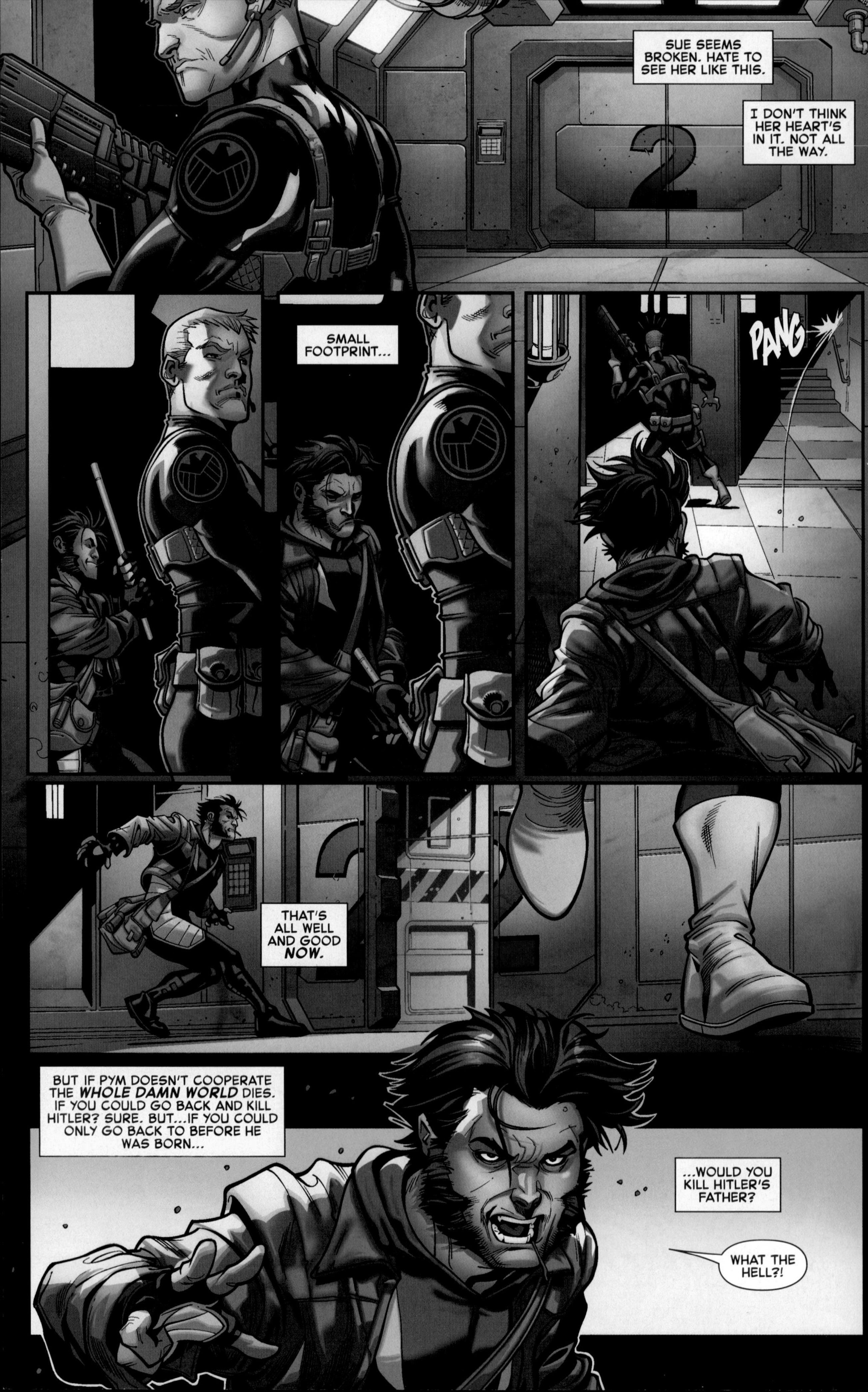
SUE SEEMS BROKEN. HATE TO SEE HER LIKE THIS.
I DON'T THINK HER HEART'S IN IT. NOT ALL THE WAY.
SMALL FOOTPRINT...
PANG
THAT'S ALL WELL AND GOOD NOW.
BUT IF PYM DOESN'T COOPERATE THE WHOLE DAMN WORLD DIES. IF YOU COULD GO BACK AND KILL HITLER? SURE. BUT...IF YOU COULD ONLY GO BACK TO BEFORE HE WAS BORN...
...WOULD YOU KILL HITLER'S FATHER?
WHAT THE HELL?!

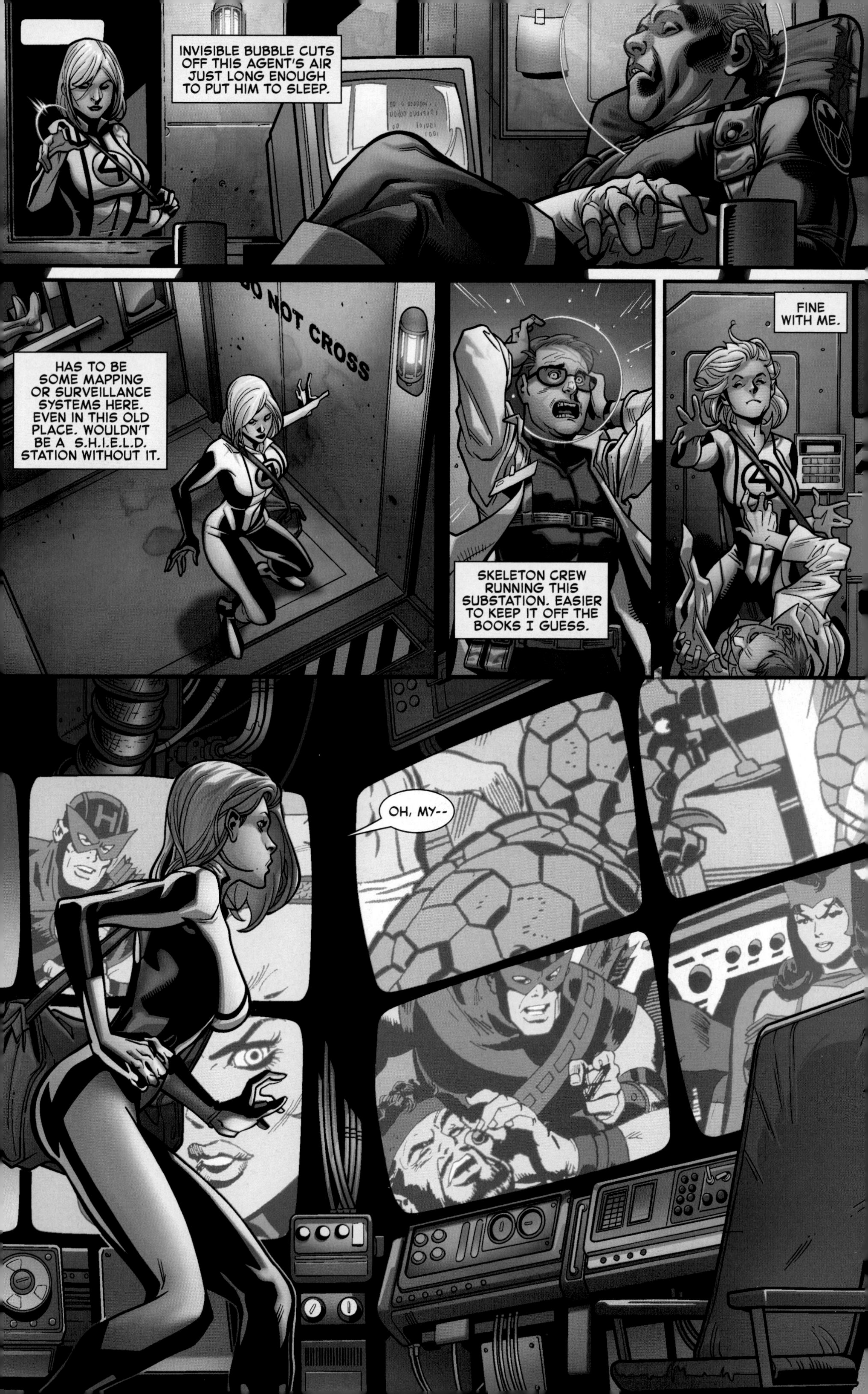
INVISIBLE BUBBLE CUTS OFF THIS AGENT'S AIR JUST LONG ENOUGH TO PUT HIM TO SLEEP.
DO NOT CROSS
HAS TO BE SOME MAPPING OR SURVEILLANCE SYSTEMS HERE. EVEN IN THIS OLD PLACE. WOULDN'T BE A S.H.I.E.L.D. STATION WITHOUT IT.
SKELETON CREW RUNNING THIS SUBSTATION. EASIER TO KEEP IT OFF THE BOOKS I GUESS.
FINE WITH ME.
OH, MY--

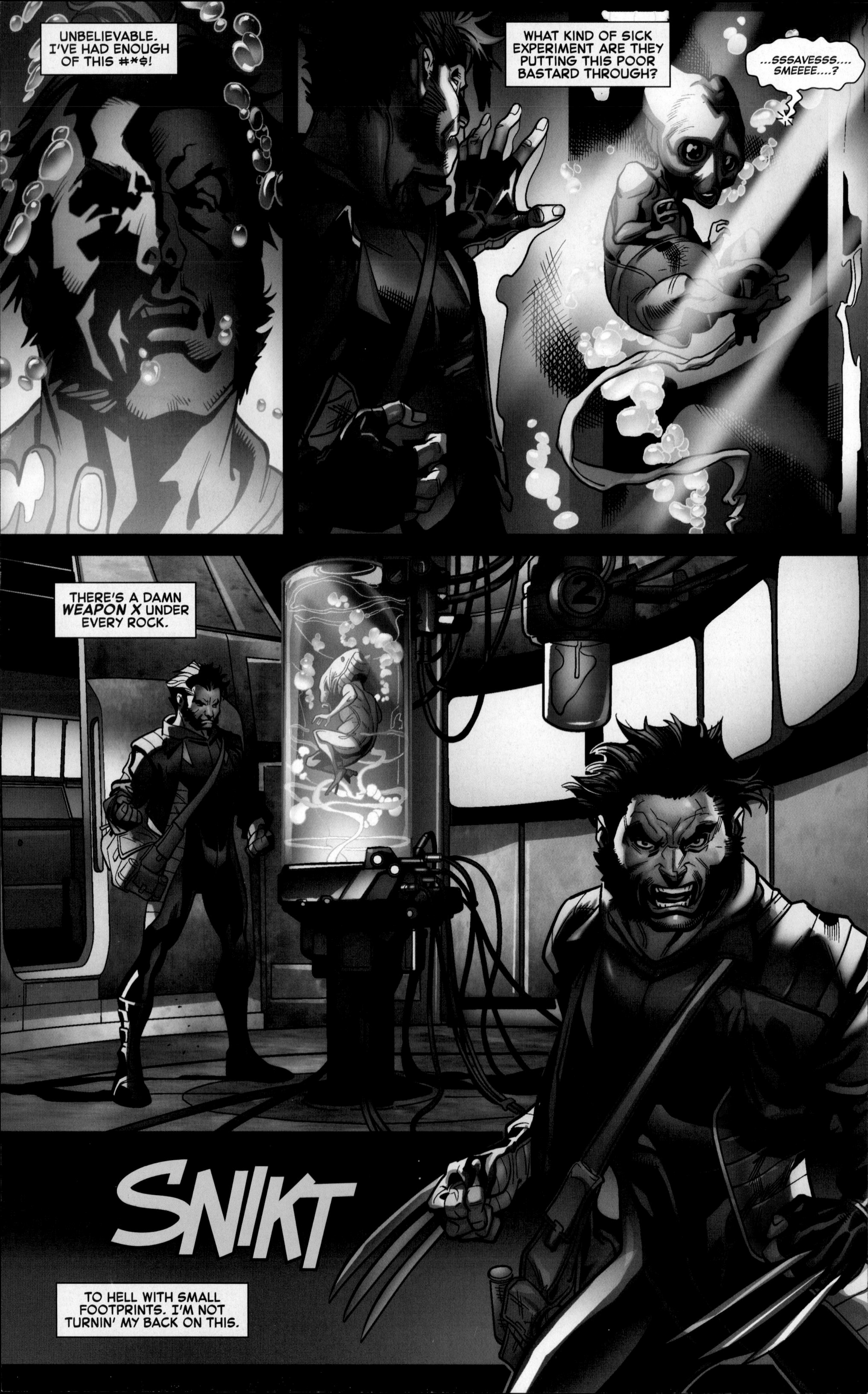
UNBELIEVABLE. I'VE HAD ENOUGH OF THIS #*$!
WHAT KIND OF SICK EXPERIMENT ARE THEY PUTTING THIS POOR BASTARD THROUGH?
...SSSAVESSS.... SMEEEE....?
THERE'S A DAMN WEAPON X UNDER EVERY ROCK.
SNIKT
TO HELL WITH SMALL FOOTPRINTS. I'M NOT TURNIN' MY BACK ON THIS.

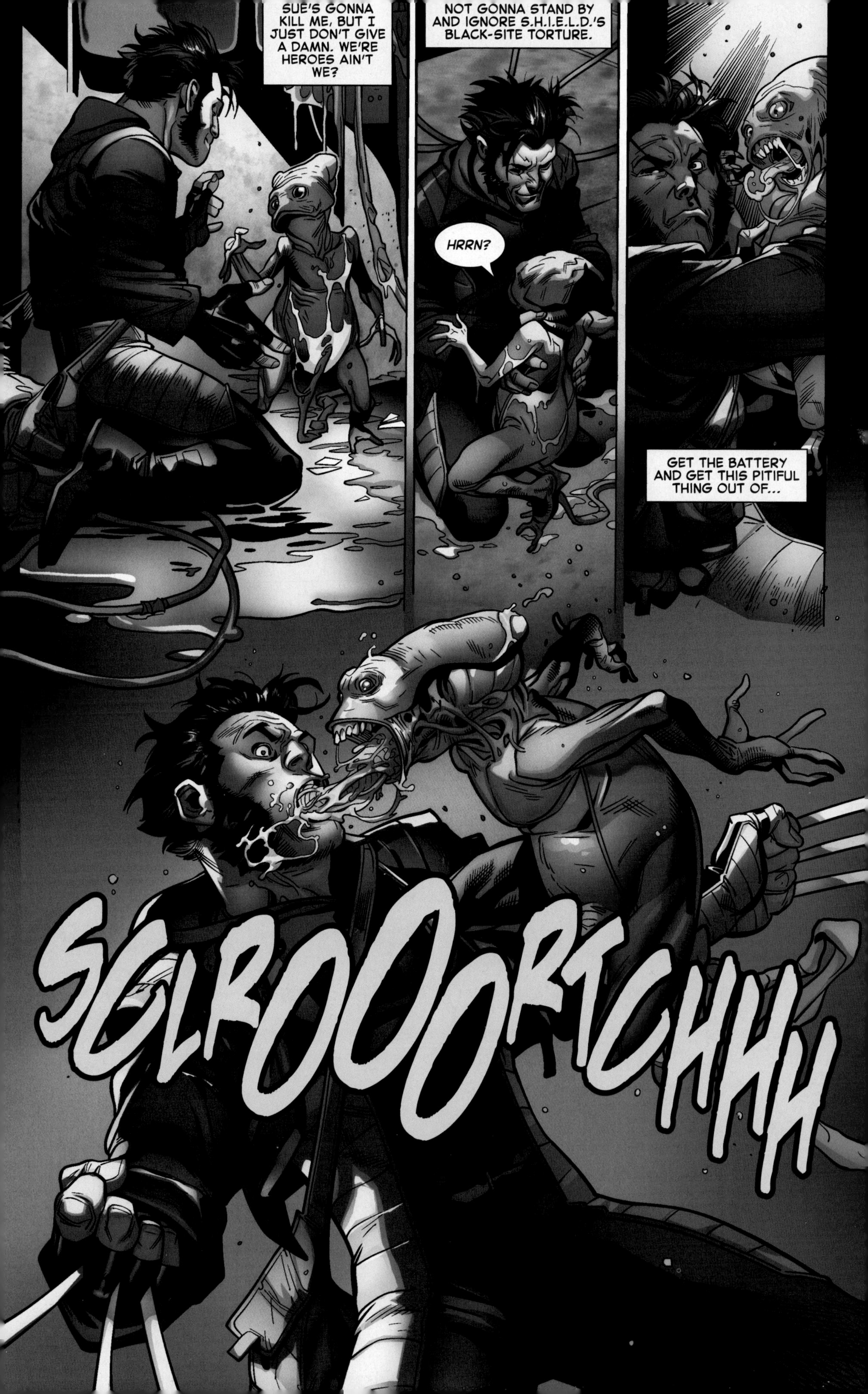
SUE'S GONNA KILL ME, BUT I JUST DON'T GIVE A DAMN. WE'RE HEROES AIN'T WE?
NOT GONNA STAND BY AND IGNORE S.H.I.E.L.D.'S BLACK-SITE TORTURE.
HRRN?
GET THE BATTERY AND GET THIS PITIFUL THING OUT OF...
SCLROOOORTCHHH

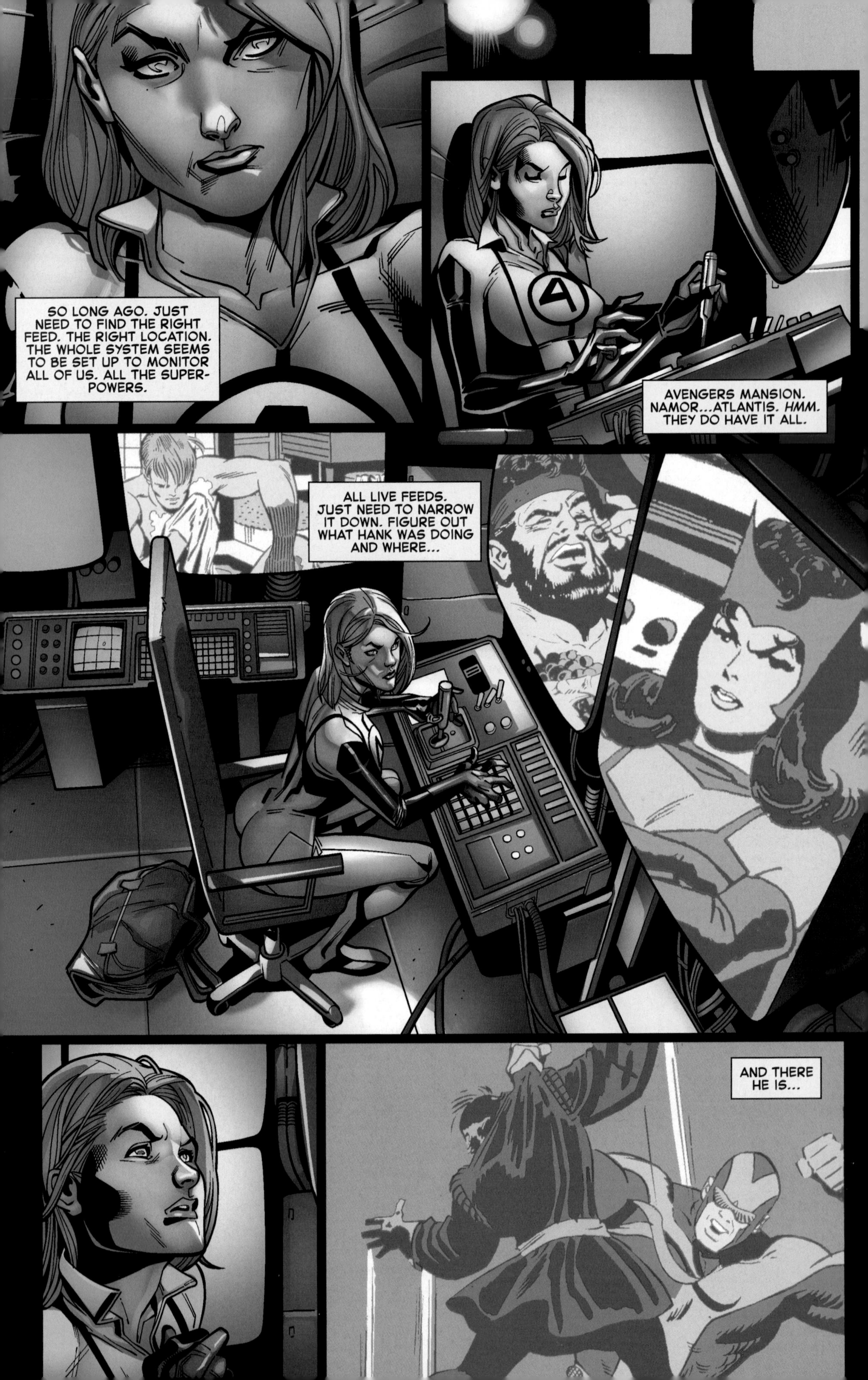
SO LONG AGO. JUST NEED TO FIND THE RIGHT FEED. THE RIGHT LOCATION. THE WHOLE SYSTEM SEEMS TO BE SET UP TO MONITOR ALL OF US. ALL THE SUPER-POWERS.
AVENGERS MANSION. NAMOR...ATLANTIS. *HMM.* THEY DO HAVE IT ALL.
ALL LIVE FEEDS. JUST NEED TO NARROW IT DOWN. FIGURE OUT WHAT HANK WAS DOING AND WHERE...
AND THERE HE IS...

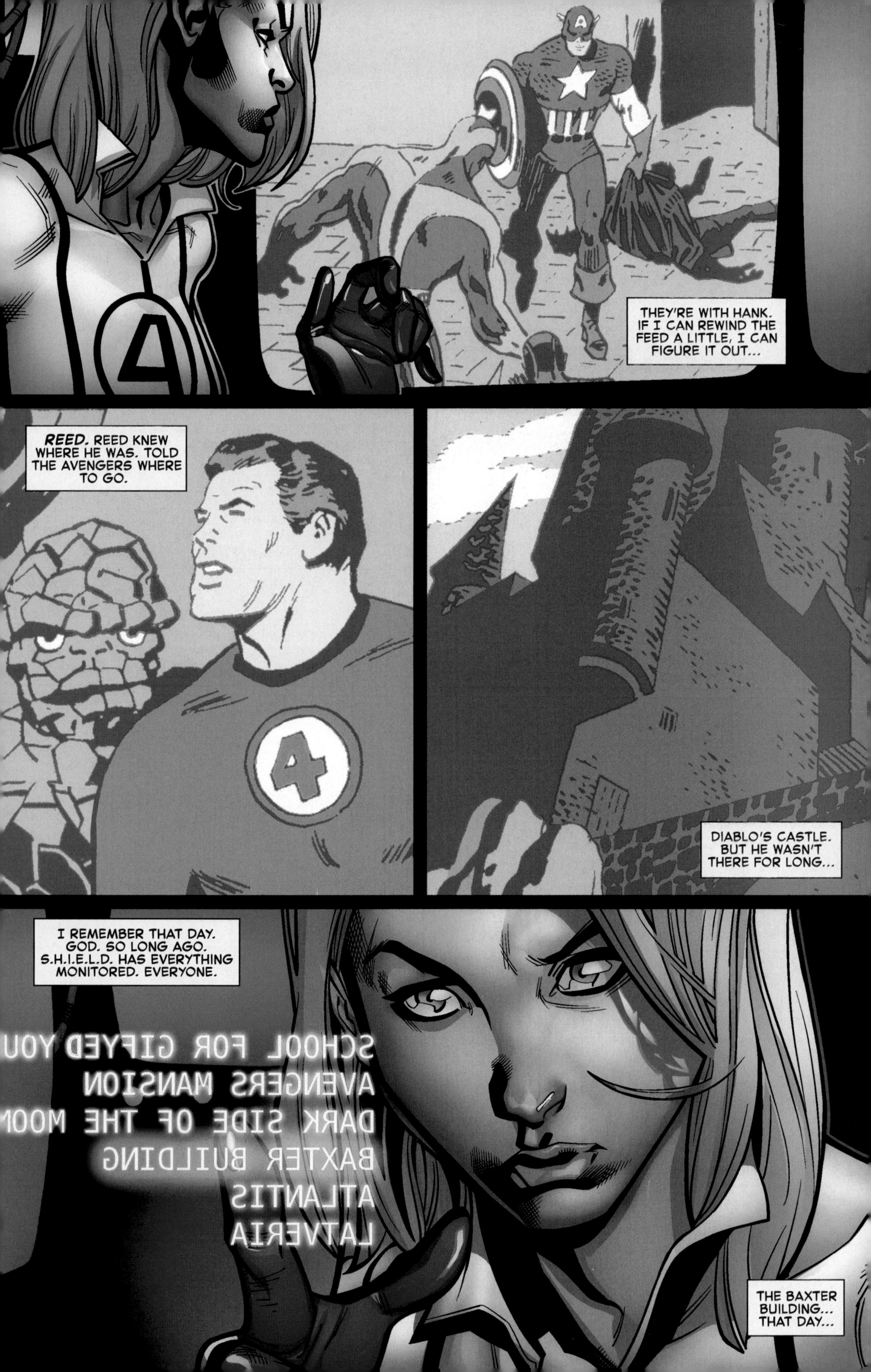
THEY'RE WITH HANK. IF I CAN REWIND THE FEED A LITTLE, I CAN FIGURE IT OUT...
REED. REED KNEW WHERE HE WAS. TOLD THE AVENGERS WHERE TO GO.
DIABLO'S CASTLE. BUT HE WASN'T THERE FOR LONG...
I REMEMBER THAT DAY. GOD. SO LONG AGO. S.H.I.E.L.D. HAS EVERYTHING MONITORED. EVERYONE.
SCHOOL FOR GIFTED YOU
AVENGERS MANSION
DARK SIDE OF THE MOO
BAXTER BUILDING
ATLANTIS
LATVERIA
THE BAXTER BUILDING... THAT DAY...

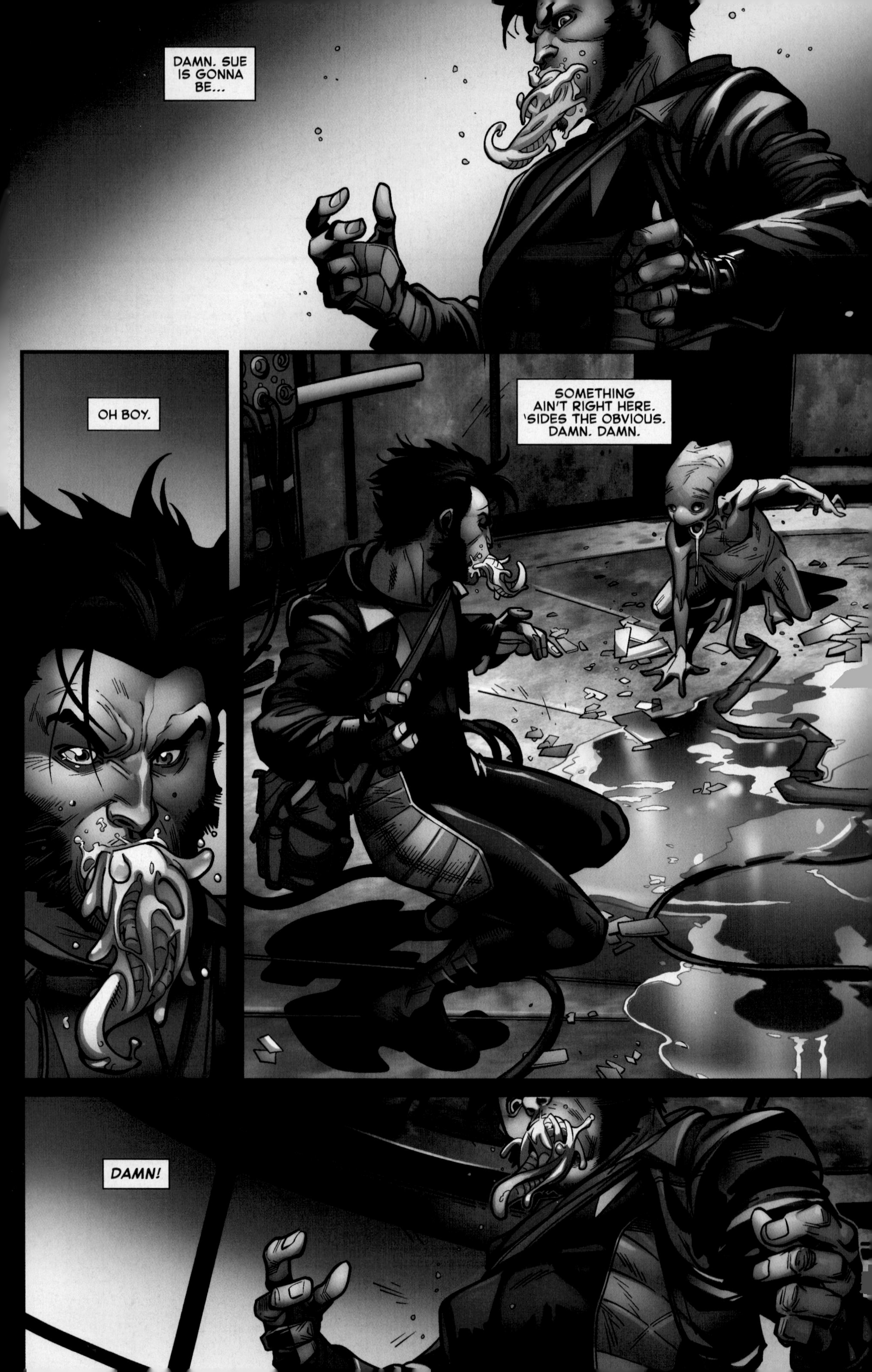
DAMN. SUE IS GONNA BE...
OH BOY.
SOMETHING AIN'T RIGHT HERE. 'SIDES THE OBVIOUS. DAMN. DAMN.
DAMN!

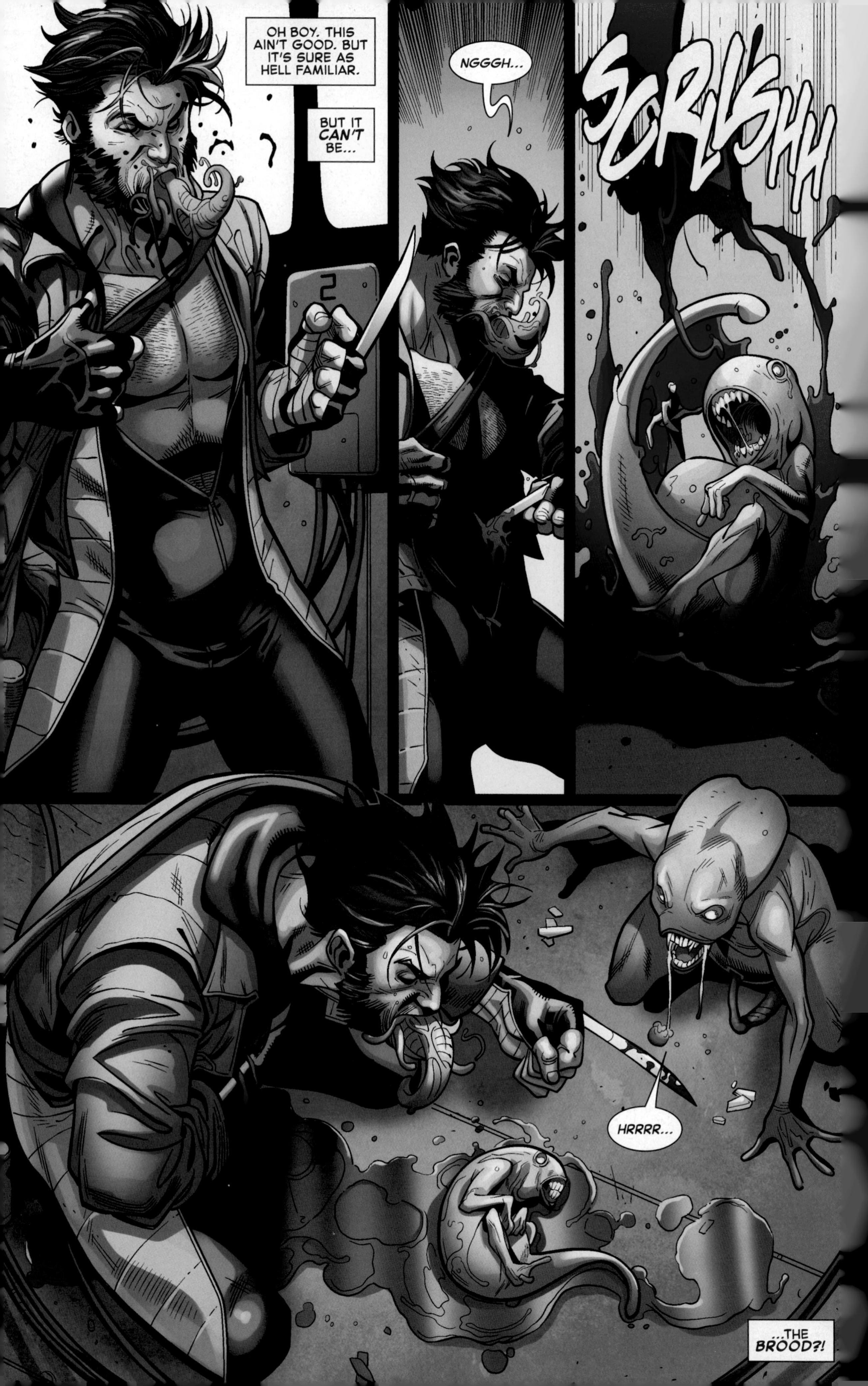
OH BOY. THIS AIN'T GOOD. BUT IT'S SURE AS HELL FAMILIAR.
BUT IT CAN'T BE...
NGGGH...
SCRISHH
HRRRR...
...THE BROOD?!

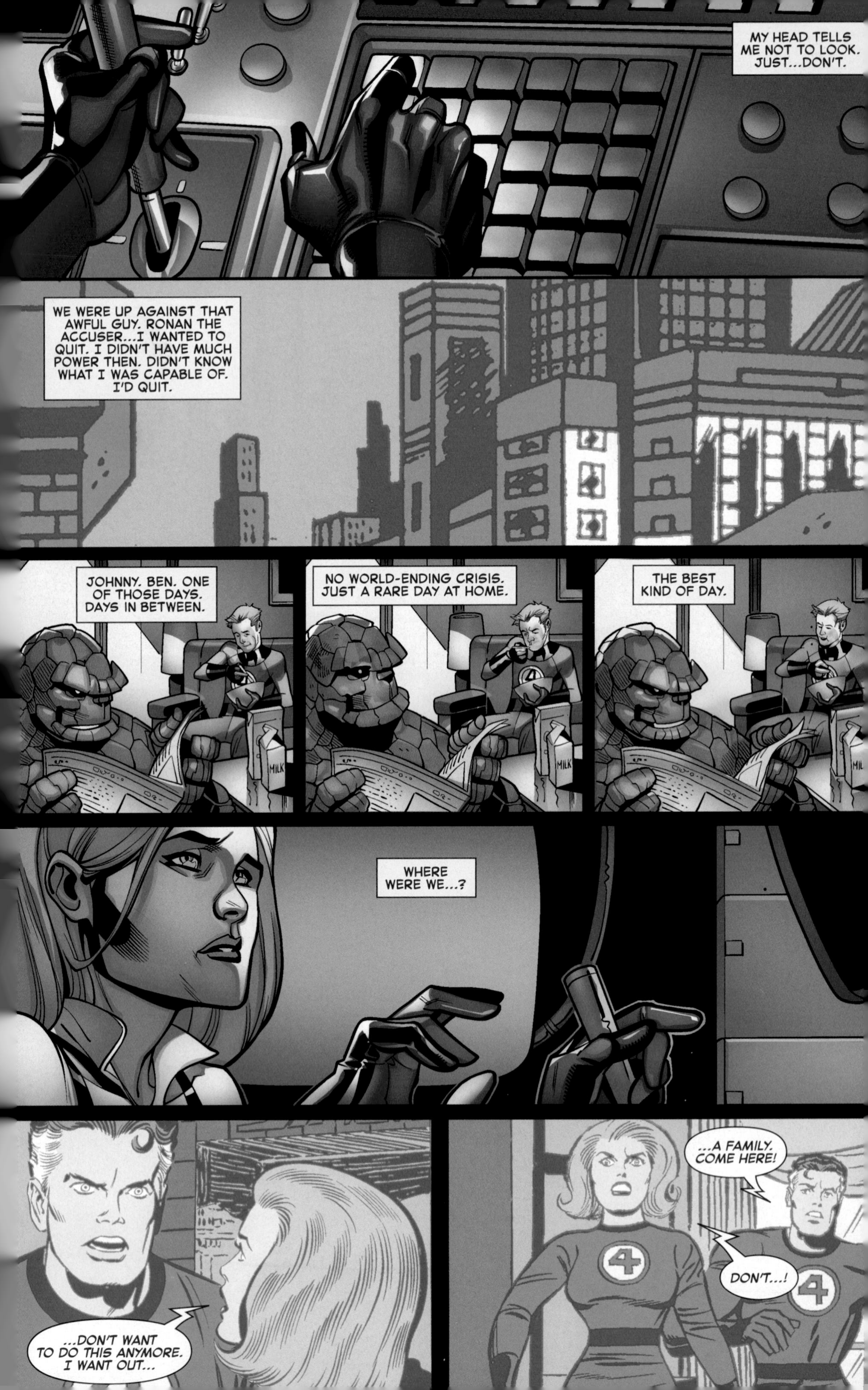
MY HEAD TELLS ME NOT TO LOOK. JUST...DON'T.
WE WERE UP AGAINST THAT AWFUL GUY. RONAN THE ACCUSER...I WANTED TO QUIT. I DIDN'T HAVE MUCH POWER THEN. DIDN'T KNOW WHAT I WAS CAPABLE OF. I'D QUIT.
JOHNNY. BEN. ONE OF THOSE DAYS. DAYS IN BETWEEN.
MILK
NO WORLD-ENDING CRISIS. JUST A RARE DAY AT HOME.
MILK
THE BEST KIND OF DAY.
WHERE WERE WE...?
...DON'T WANT TO DO THIS ANYMORE. I WANT OUT...
...A FAMILY. COME HERE!
DON'T...!

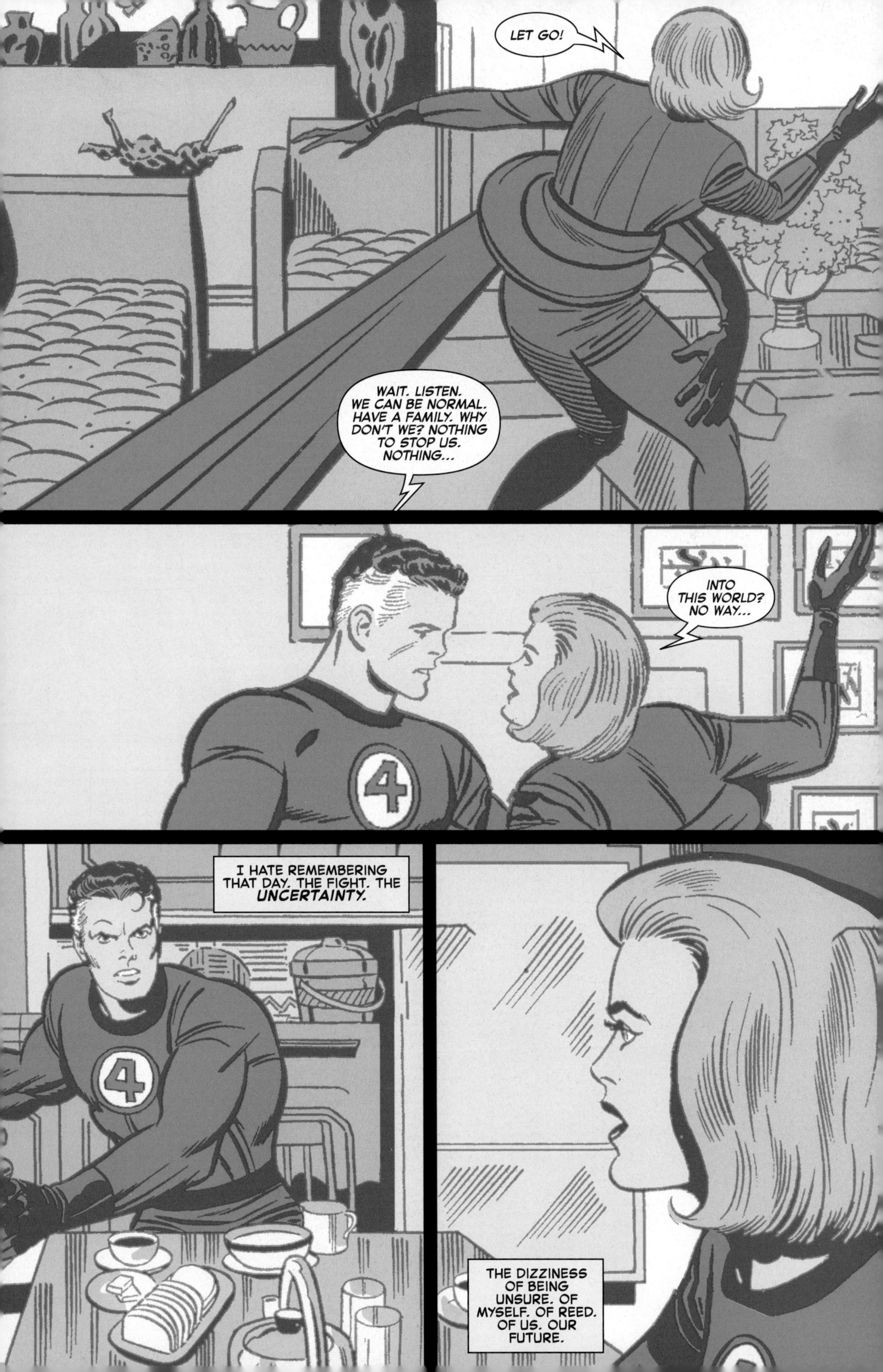
LET GO!
WAIT. LISTEN. WE CAN BE NORMAL. HAVE A FAMILY. WHY DON'T WE? NOTHING TO STOP US. NOTHING...
INTO THIS WORLD? NO WAY...
I HATE REMEMBERING THAT DAY. THE FIGHT. THE *UNCERTAINTY.*
THE DIZZINESS OF BEING UNSURE. OF MYSELF. OF REED. OF US. OUR FUTURE.

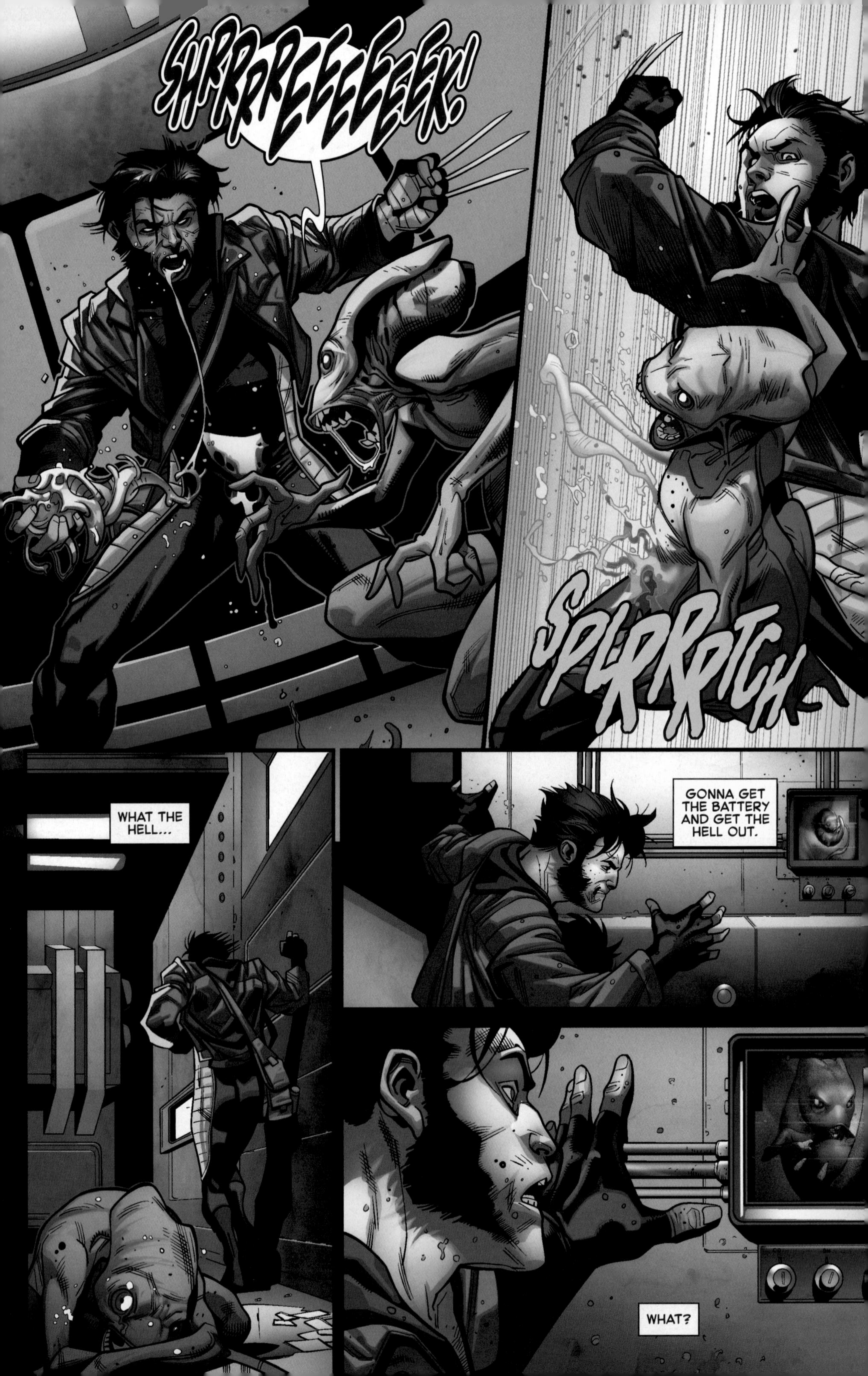
SHRRRREEEEEEEK!
SPLRRRITCH
WHAT THE HELL...
GONNA GET THE BATTERY AND GET THE HELL OUT.
WHAT?

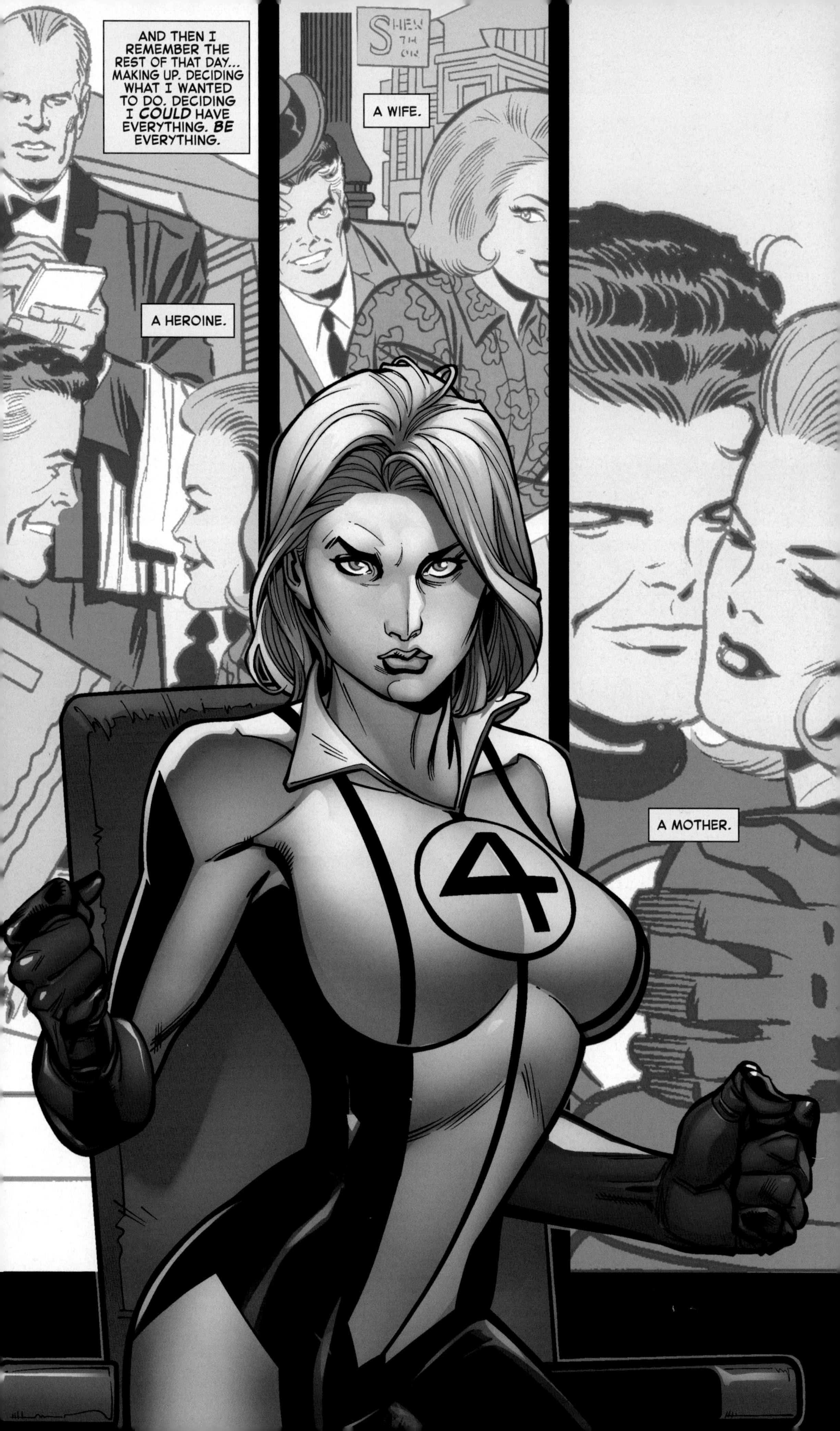
AND THEN I REMEMBER THE REST OF THAT DAY... MAKING UP. DECIDING WHAT I WANTED TO DO. DECIDING I COULD HAVE EVERYTHING. BE EVERYTHING.
A WIFE.
A HEROINE.
A MOTHER.
4

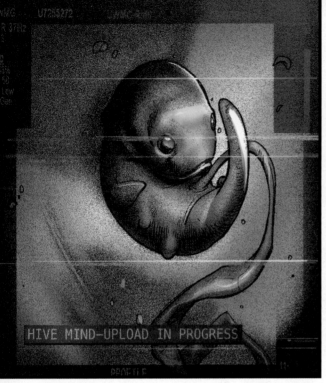

HIVE MIND-UPLOAD IN PROGRESS

ARE YOU KIDDING ME?

(((ADAPTATION CYCLE INITIATED ... TRANSFORMING....)))

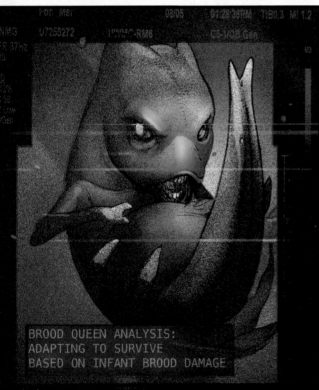

BROOD QUEEN ANALYSIS:
ADAPTING TO SURVIVE
BASED ON INFANT BROOD DAMAGE

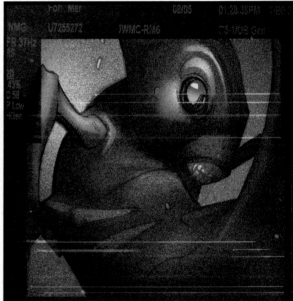

EXOSKELETON DEVELOPING.
TEETH-JAWS EXPANDING.
ADAPTING TO DAMAGE INPUT.

AW, HELL NO.

I DID NOT JUST DO THAT.

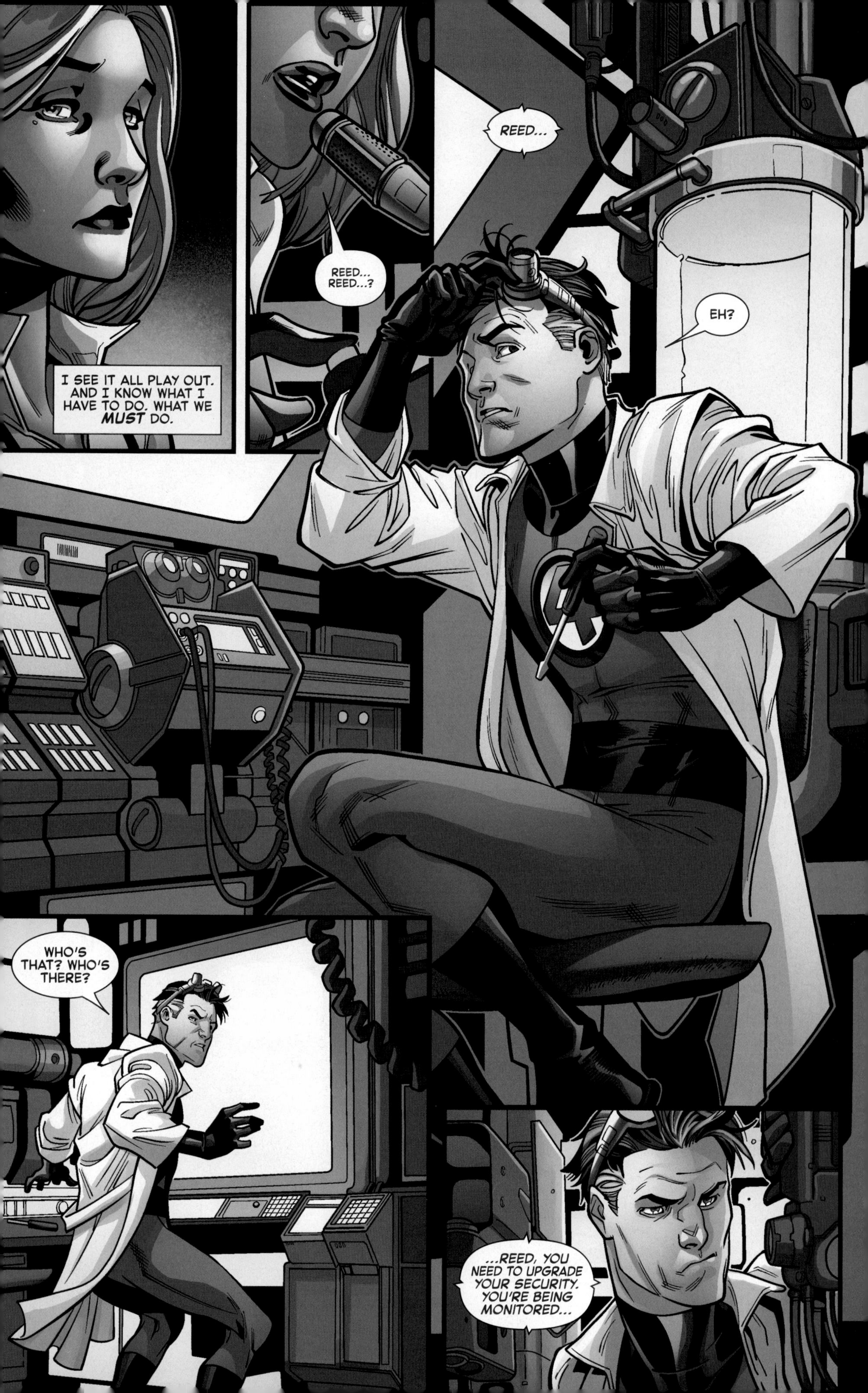

I SEE IT ALL PLAY OUT. AND I KNOW WHAT I HAVE TO DO. WHAT WE MUST DO.
REED... REED...?
REED...
EH?
WHO'S THAT? WHO'S THERE?
...REED, YOU NEED TO UPGRADE YOUR SECURITY. YOU'RE BEING MONITORED...

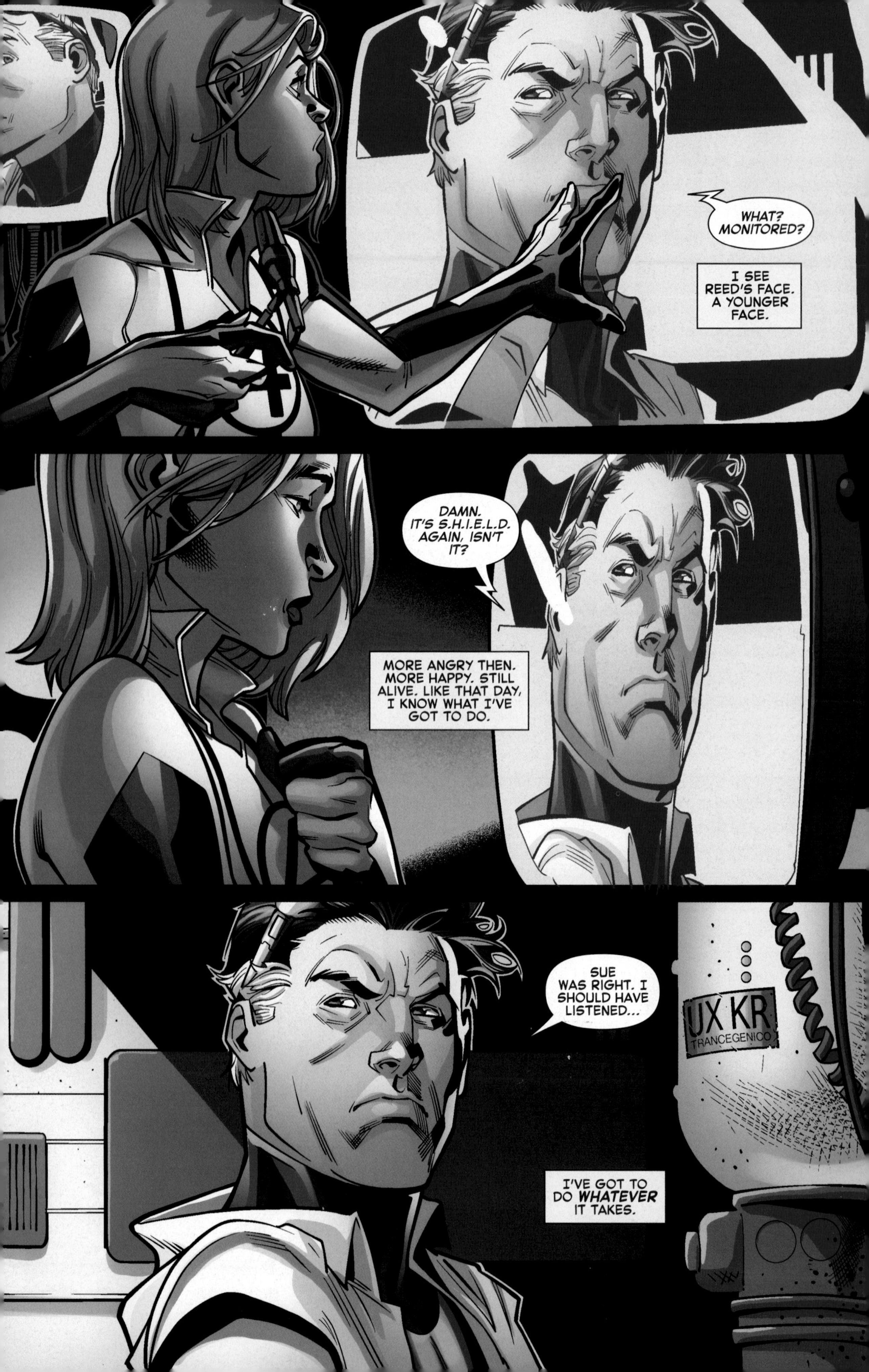
WHAT? MONITORED?
I SEE REED'S FACE. A YOUNGER FACE.
DAMN. IT'S S.H.I.E.L.D. AGAIN, ISN'T IT?
MORE ANGRY THEN. MORE HAPPY. STILL ALIVE. LIKE THAT DAY, I KNOW WHAT I'VE GOT TO DO.
SUE WAS RIGHT. I SHOULD HAVE LISTENED...
UX KR
TRANCEGENICO
I'VE GOT TO DO *WHATEVER* IT TAKES.

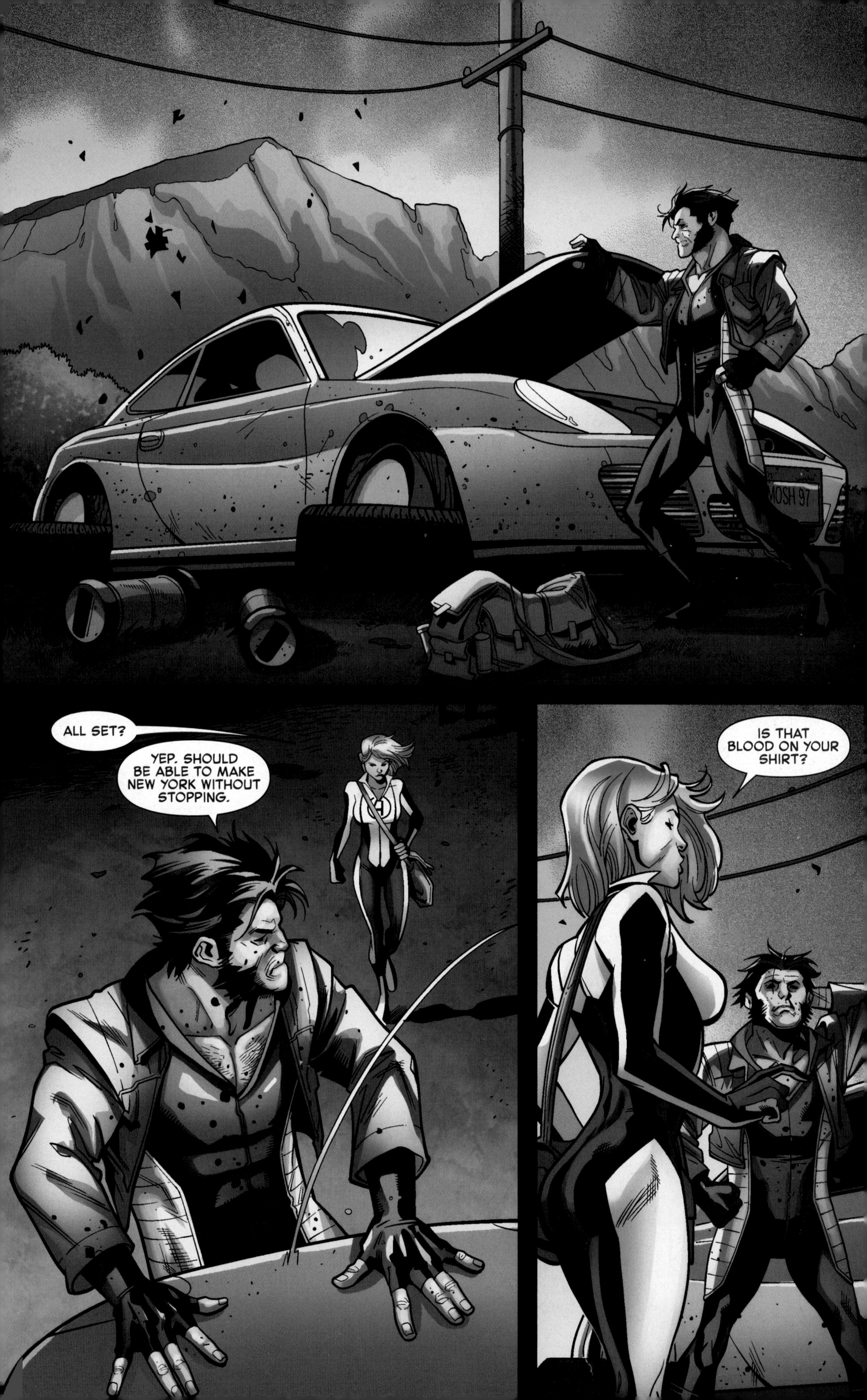
MOSH 97
ALL SET?
YEP. SHOULD BE ABLE TO MAKE NEW YORK WITHOUT STOPPING.
IS THAT BLOOD ON YOUR SHIRT?

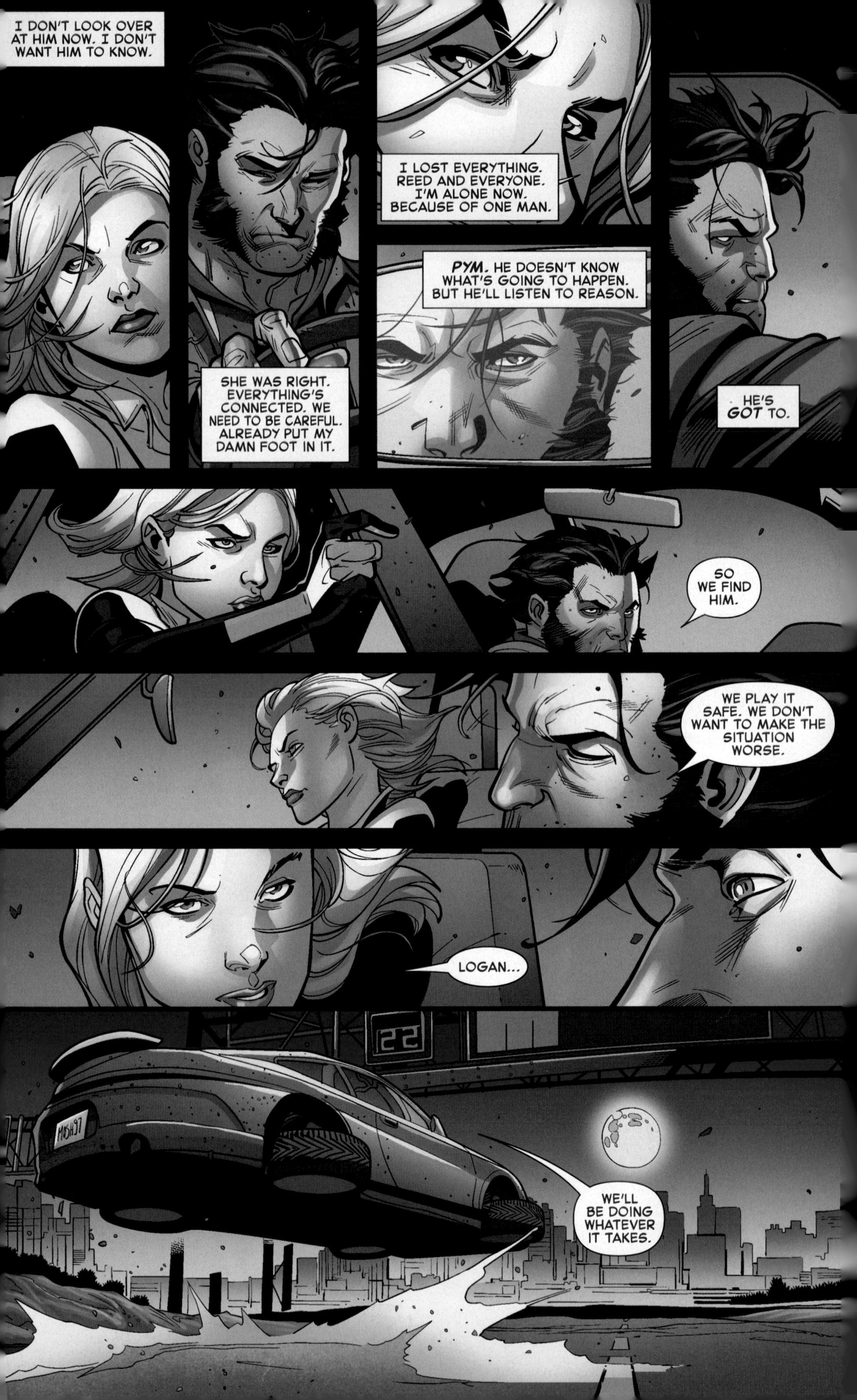
I DON'T LOOK OVER AT HIM NOW. I DON'T WANT HIM TO KNOW.
SHE WAS RIGHT. EVERYTHING'S CONNECTED. WE NEED TO BE CAREFUL. ALREADY PUT MY DAMN FOOT IN IT.
I LOST EVERYTHING. REED AND EVERYONE. I'M ALONE NOW. BECAUSE OF ONE MAN.
PYM. HE DOESN'T KNOW WHAT'S GOING TO HAPPEN. BUT HE'LL LISTEN TO REASON.
HE'S GOT TO.
SO WE FIND HIM.
WE PLAY IT SAFE. WE DON'T WANT TO MAKE THE SITUATION WORSE.
LOGAN...
WE'LL BE DOING WHATEVER IT TAKES.

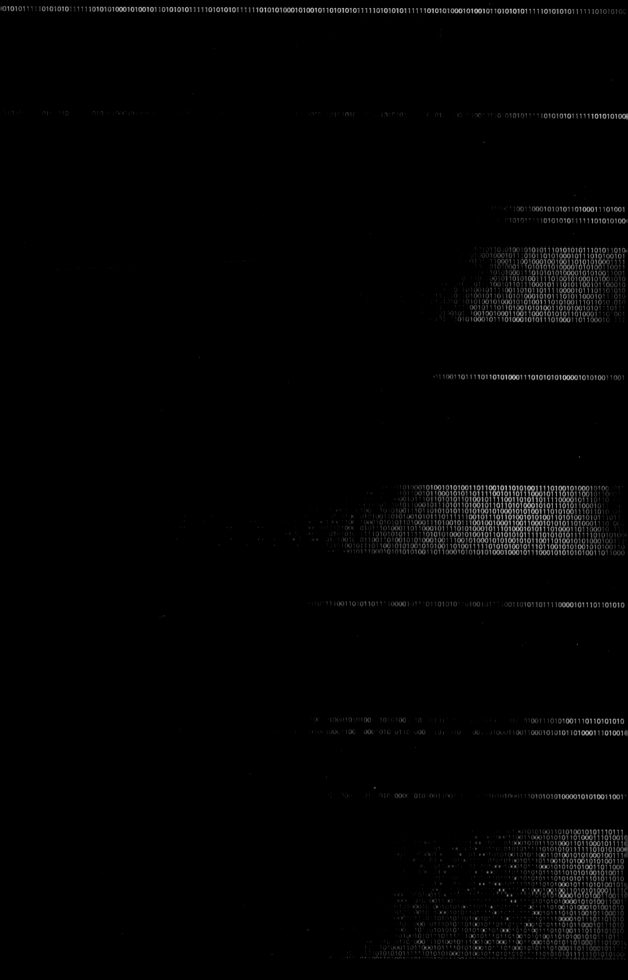

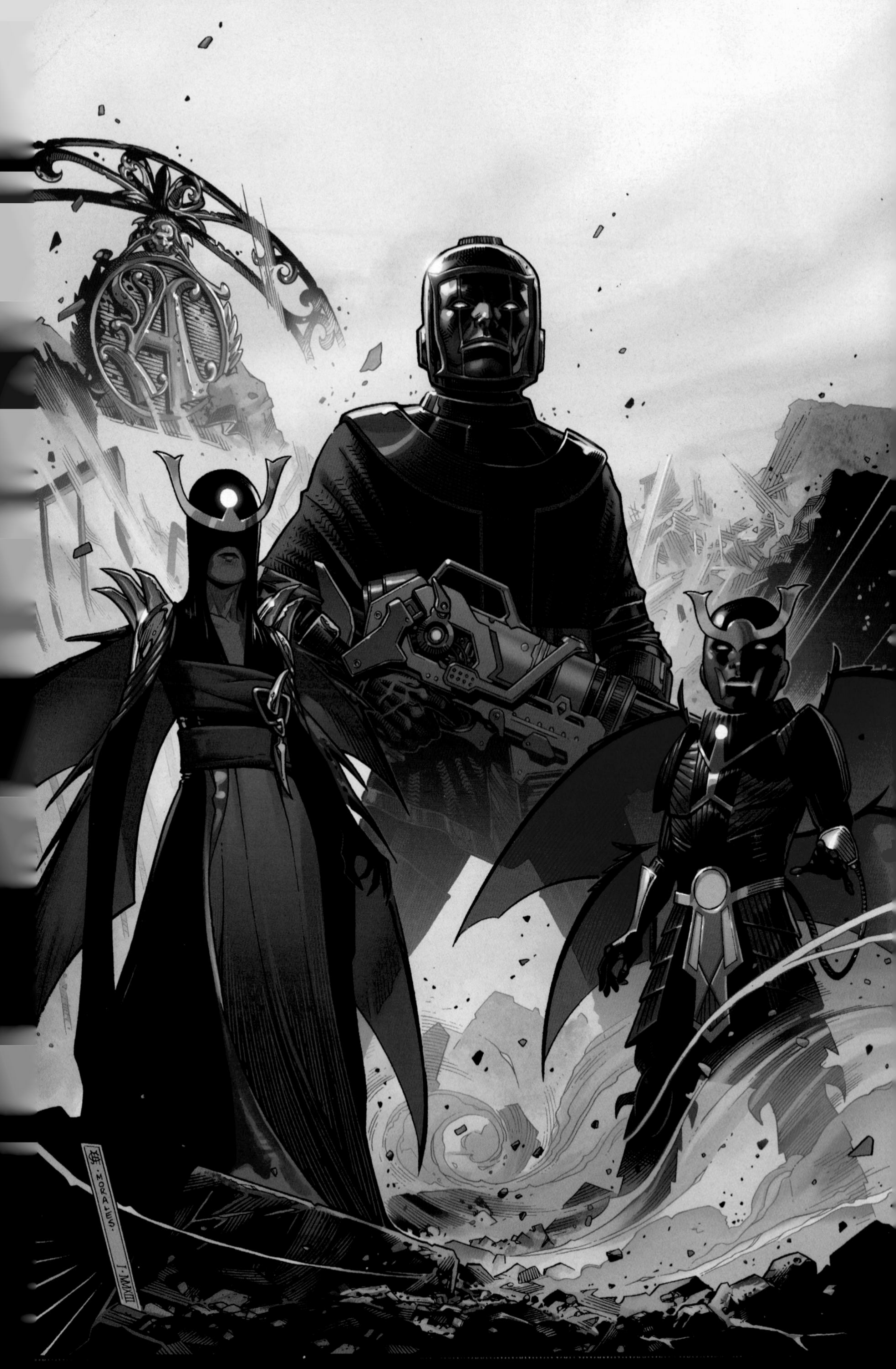

UNCANNY AVENGERS #8AU

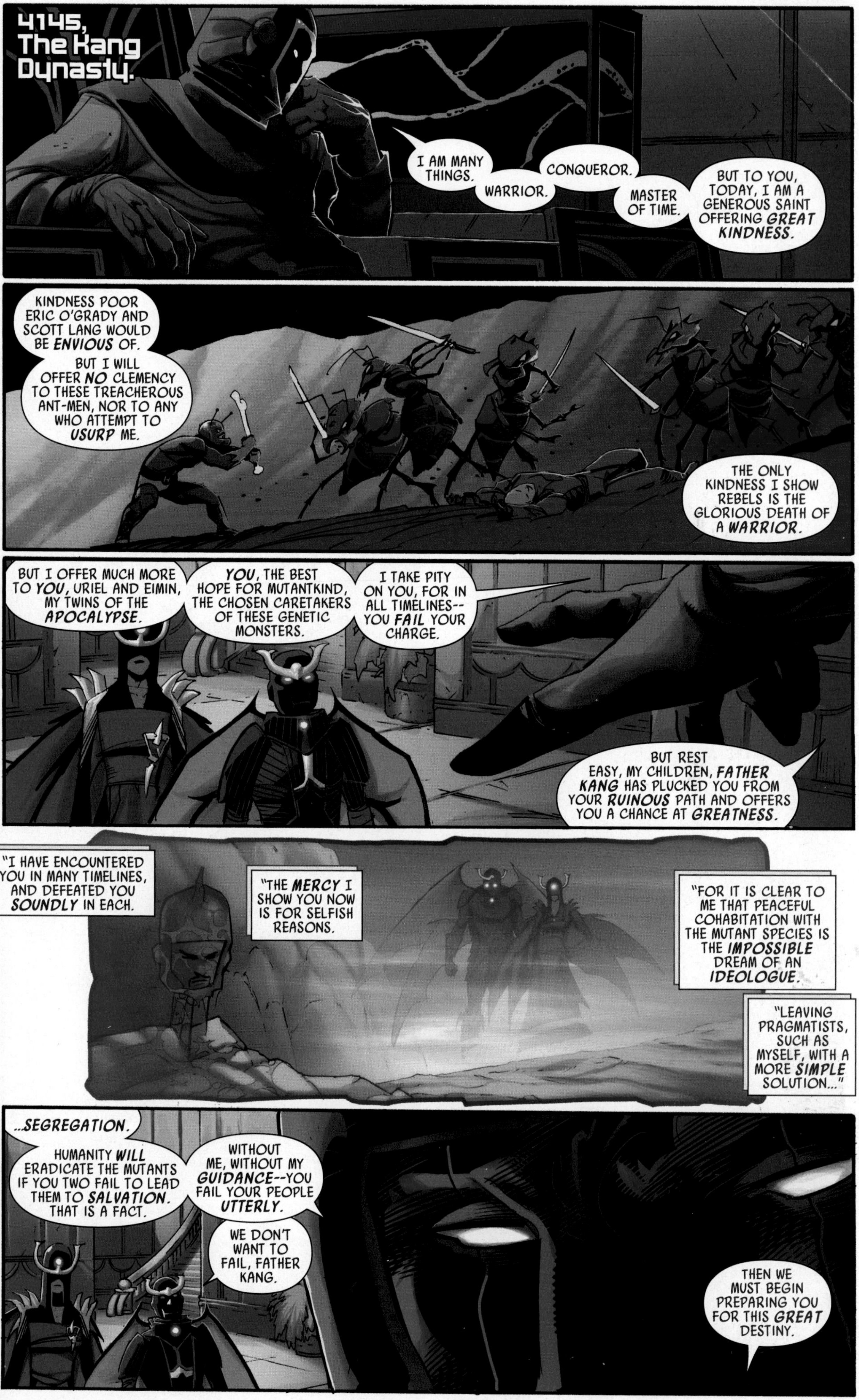
4145, The Kang Dynasty.
I AM MANY THINGS.
WARRIOR.
CONQUEROR.
MASTER OF TIME.
BUT TO YOU, TODAY, I AM A GENEROUS SAINT OFFERING GREAT KINDNESS.
KINDNESS POOR ERIC O'GRADY AND SCOTT LANG WOULD BE ENVIOUS OF.
BUT I WILL OFFER NO CLEMENCY TO THESE TREACHEROUS ANT-MEN, NOR TO ANY WHO ATTEMPT TO USURP ME.
THE ONLY KINDNESS I SHOW REBELS IS THE GLORIOUS DEATH OF A WARRIOR.
BUT I OFFER MUCH MORE TO YOU, URIEL AND EIMIN, MY TWINS OF THE APOCALYPSE.
YOU, THE BEST HOPE FOR MUTANTKIND, THE CHOSEN CARETAKERS OF THESE GENETIC MONSTERS.
I TAKE PITY ON YOU, FOR IN ALL TIMELINES-- YOU FAIL YOUR CHARGE.
BUT REST EASY, MY CHILDREN, FATHER KANG HAS PLUCKED YOU FROM YOUR RUINOUS PATH AND OFFERS YOU A CHANCE AT GREATNESS.
"I HAVE ENCOUNTERED YOU IN MANY TIMELINES, AND DEFEATED YOU SOUNDLY IN EACH.
"THE MERCY I SHOW YOU NOW IS FOR SELFISH REASONS.
"FOR IT IS CLEAR TO ME THAT PEACEFUL COHABITATION WITH THE MUTANT SPECIES IS THE IMPOSSIBLE DREAM OF AN IDEOLOGUE.
"LEAVING PRAGMATISTS, SUCH AS MYSELF, WITH A MORE SIMPLE SOLUTION..."
...SEGREGATION.
HUMANITY WILL ERADICATE THE MUTANTS IF YOU TWO FAIL TO LEAD THEM TO SALVATION. THAT IS A FACT.
WITHOUT ME, WITHOUT MY GUIDANCE--YOU FAIL YOUR PEOPLE UTTERLY.
WE DON'T WANT TO FAIL, FATHER KANG.
THEN WE MUST BEGIN PREPARING YOU FOR THIS GREAT DESTINY.

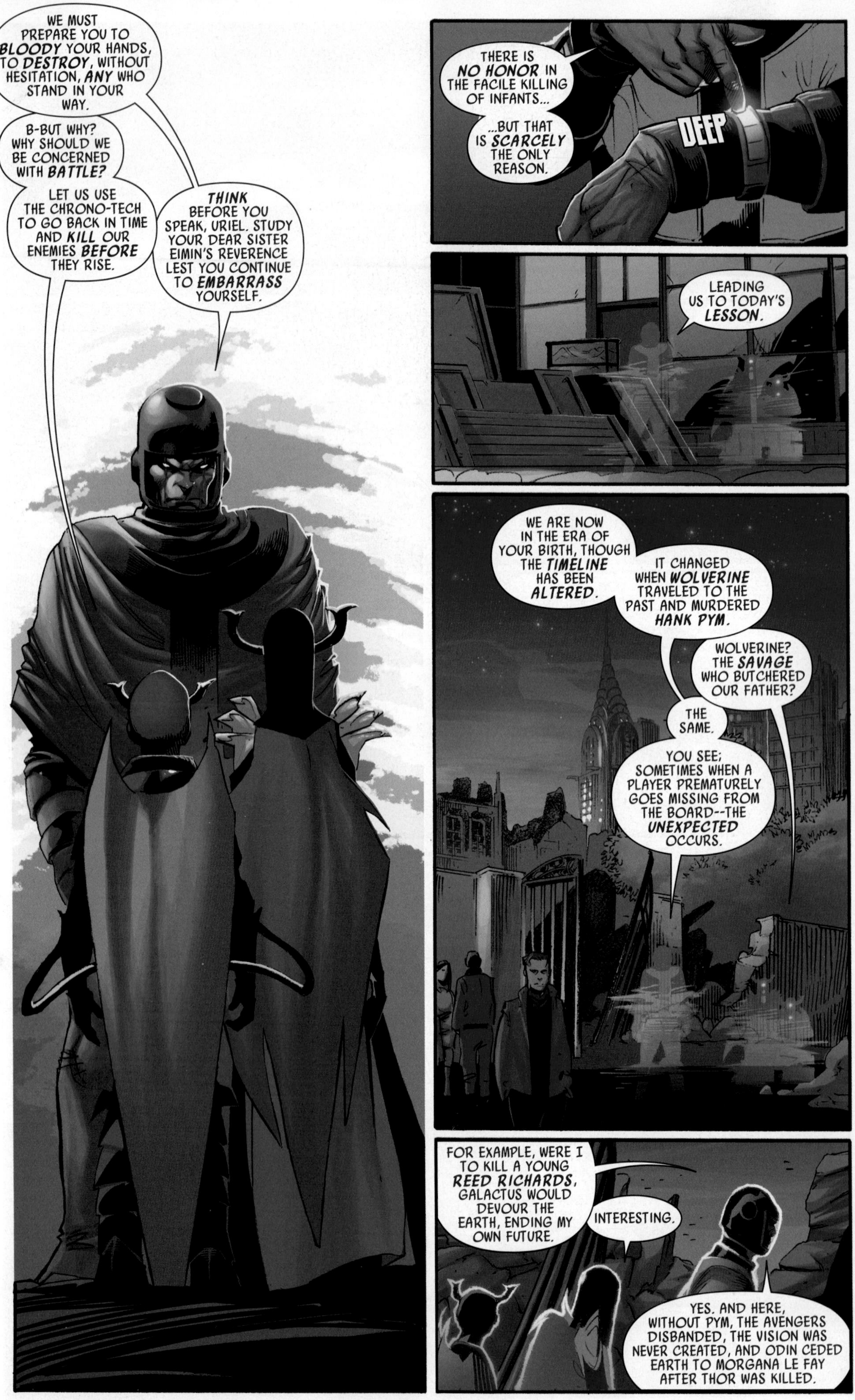

WE MUST PREPARE YOU TO BLOODY YOUR HANDS, TO DESTROY, WITHOUT HESITATION, ANY WHO STAND IN YOUR WAY.
B-BUT WHY? WHY SHOULD WE BE CONCERNED WITH BATTLE?
LET US USE THE CHRONO-TECH TO GO BACK IN TIME AND KILL OUR ENEMIES BEFORE THEY RISE.
THINK BEFORE YOU SPEAK, URIEL. STUDY YOUR DEAR SISTER EIMIN'S REVERENCE LEST YOU CONTINUE TO EMBARRASS YOURSELF.
THERE IS NO HONOR IN THE FACILE KILLING OF INFANTS...
...BUT THAT IS SCARCELY THE ONLY REASON.
DEEP
LEADING US TO TODAY'S LESSON.
WE ARE NOW IN THE ERA OF YOUR BIRTH, THOUGH THE TIMELINE HAS BEEN ALTERED.
IT CHANGED WHEN WOLVERINE TRAVELED TO THE PAST AND MURDERED HANK PYM.
WOLVERINE? THE SAVAGE WHO BUTCHERED OUR FATHER?
THE SAME.
YOU SEE; SOMETIMES WHEN A PLAYER PREMATURELY GOES MISSING FROM THE BOARD--THE UNEXPECTED OCCURS.
FOR EXAMPLE, WERE I TO KILL A YOUNG REED RICHARDS, GALACTUS WOULD DEVOUR THE EARTH, ENDING MY OWN FUTURE.
INTERESTING.
YES. AND HERE, WITHOUT PYM, THE AVENGERS DISBANDED, THE VISION WAS NEVER CREATED, AND ODIN CEDED EARTH TO MORGANA LE FAY AFTER THOR WAS KILLED.

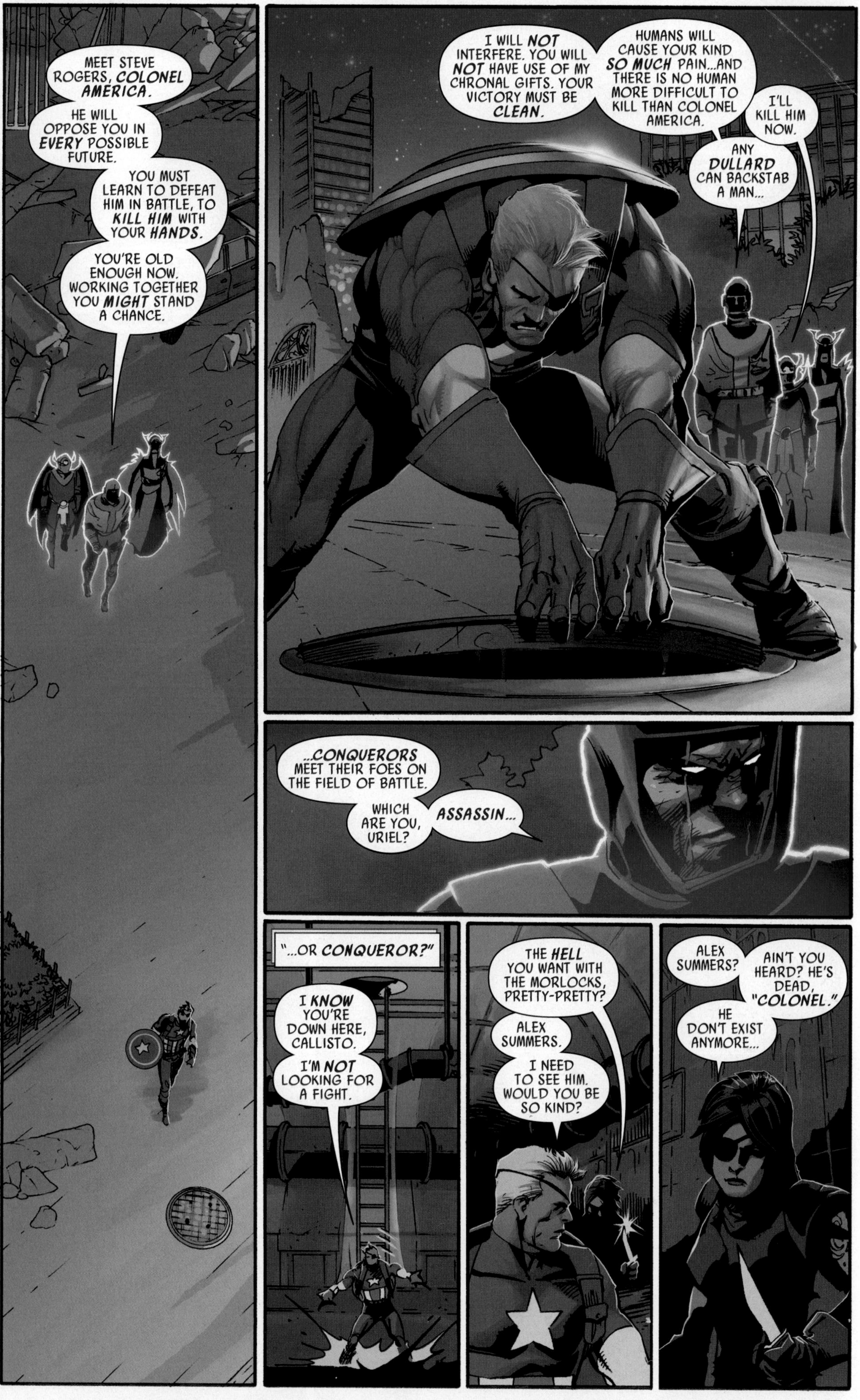

MEET STEVE ROGERS, COLONEL AMERICA.
HE WILL OPPOSE YOU IN EVERY POSSIBLE FUTURE.
YOU MUST LEARN TO DEFEAT HIM IN BATTLE, TO KILL HIM WITH YOUR HANDS.
YOU'RE OLD ENOUGH NOW. WORKING TOGETHER YOU MIGHT STAND A CHANCE.
I WILL NOT INTERFERE. YOU WILL NOT HAVE USE OF MY CHRONAL GIFTS. YOUR VICTORY MUST BE CLEAN.
HUMANS WILL CAUSE YOUR KIND SO MUCH PAIN...AND THERE IS NO HUMAN MORE DIFFICULT TO KILL THAN COLONEL AMERICA.
I'LL KILL HIM NOW.
ANY DULLARD CAN BACKSTAB A MAN...
...CONQUERORS MEET THEIR FOES ON THE FIELD OF BATTLE.
WHICH ARE YOU, URIEL?
ASSASSIN...
"...OR CONQUEROR?"
I KNOW YOU'RE DOWN HERE, CALLISTO.
I'M NOT LOOKING FOR A FIGHT.
THE HELL YOU WANT WITH THE MORLOCKS, PRETTY-PRETTY?
ALEX SUMMERS.
I NEED TO SEE HIM. WOULD YOU BE SO KIND?
ALEX SUMMERS?
AIN'T YOU HEARD? HE'S DEAD, "COLONEL."
HE DON'T EXIST ANYMORE...

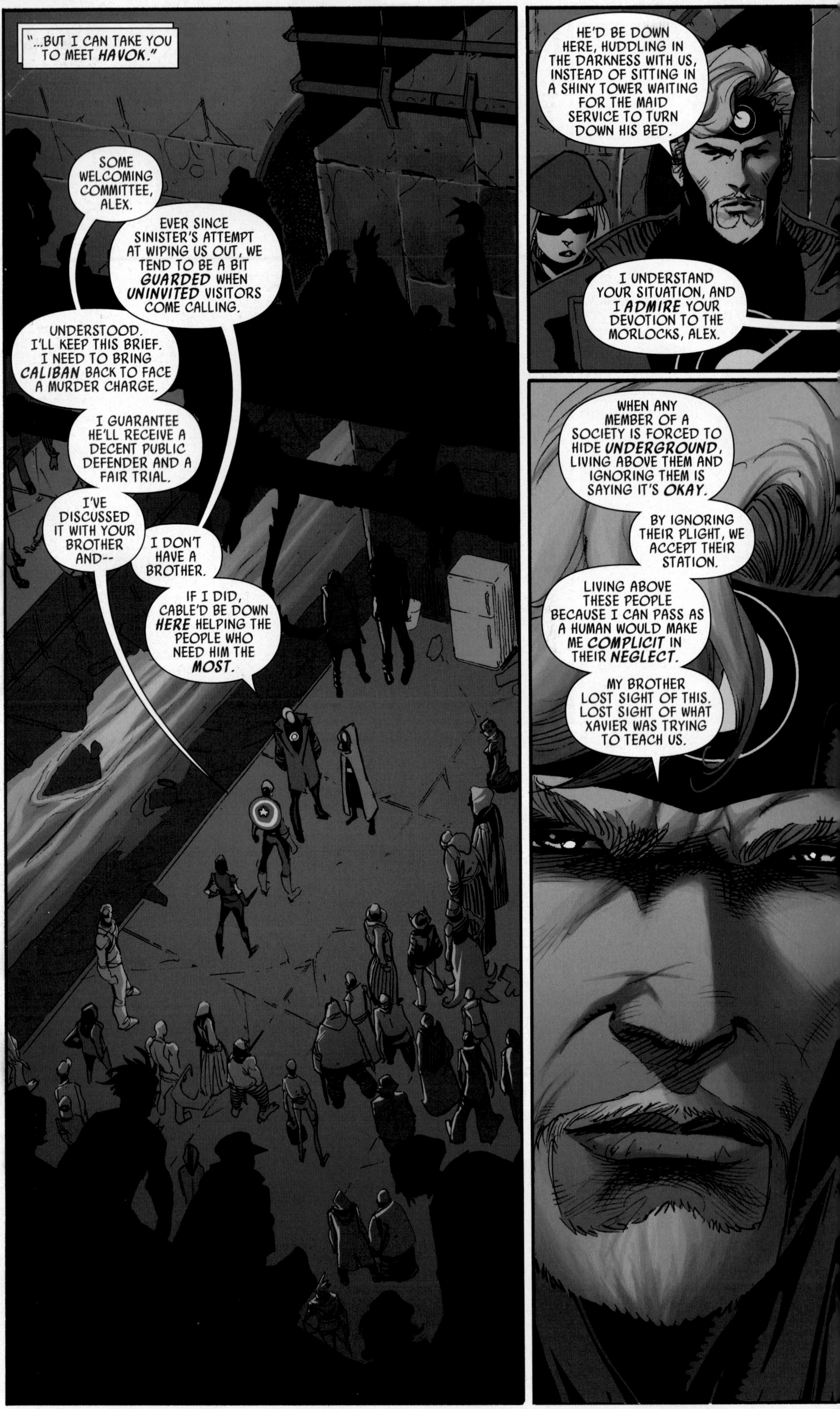

"...BUT I CAN TAKE YOU TO MEET HAVOK."
SOME WELCOMING COMMITTEE, ALEX.
EVER SINCE SINISTER'S ATTEMPT AT WIPING US OUT, WE TEND TO BE A BIT GUARDED WHEN UNINVITED VISITORS COME CALLING.
UNDERSTOOD. I'LL KEEP THIS BRIEF. I NEED TO BRING CALIBAN BACK TO FACE A MURDER CHARGE.
I GUARANTEE HE'LL RECEIVE A DECENT PUBLIC DEFENDER AND A FAIR TRIAL.
I'VE DISCUSSED IT WITH YOUR BROTHER AND--
I DON'T HAVE A BROTHER.
IF I DID, CABLE'D BE DOWN HERE HELPING THE PEOPLE WHO NEED HIM THE MOST.
HE'D BE DOWN HERE, HUDDLING IN THE DARKNESS WITH US, INSTEAD OF SITTING IN A SHINY TOWER WAITING FOR THE MAID SERVICE TO TURN DOWN HIS BED.
I UNDERSTAND YOUR SITUATION, AND I ADMIRE YOUR DEVOTION TO THE MORLOCKS, ALEX.
WHEN ANY MEMBER OF A SOCIETY IS FORCED TO HIDE UNDERGROUND, LIVING ABOVE THEM AND IGNORING THEM IS SAYING IT'S OKAY.
BY IGNORING THEIR PLIGHT, WE ACCEPT THEIR STATION.
LIVING ABOVE THESE PEOPLE BECAUSE I CAN PASS AS A HUMAN WOULD MAKE ME COMPLICIT IN THEIR NEGLECT.
MY BROTHER LOST SIGHT OF THIS. LOST SIGHT OF WHAT XAVIER WAS TRYING TO TEACH US.

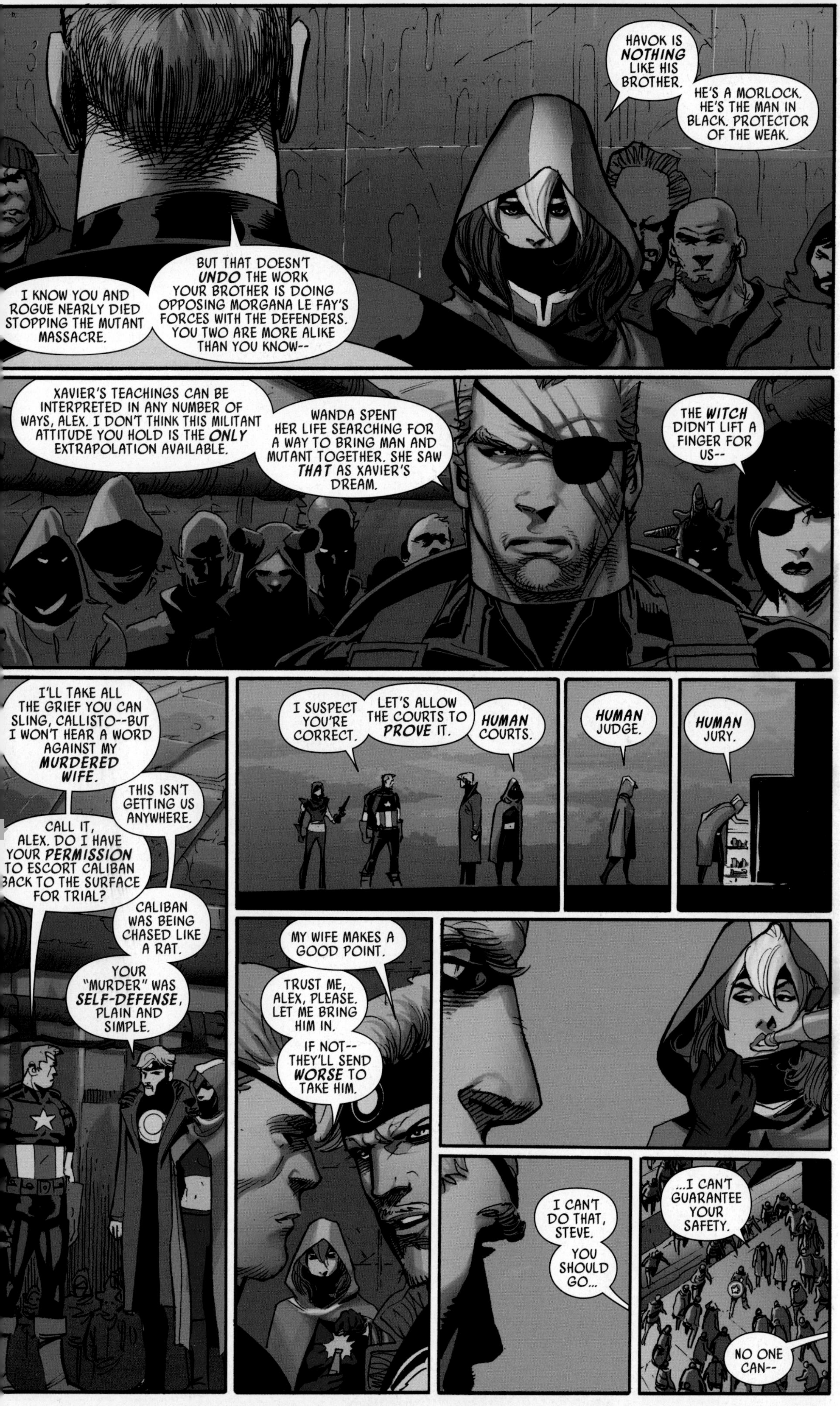
HAVOK IS NOTHING LIKE HIS BROTHER.
HE'S A MORLOCK. HE'S THE MAN IN BLACK. PROTECTOR OF THE WEAK.
I KNOW YOU AND ROGUE NEARLY DIED STOPPING THE MUTANT MASSACRE.
BUT THAT DOESN'T UNDO THE WORK YOUR BROTHER IS DOING OPPOSING MORGANA LE FAY'S FORCES WITH THE DEFENDERS. YOU TWO ARE MORE ALIKE THAN YOU KNOW--
XAVIER'S TEACHINGS CAN BE INTERPRETED IN ANY NUMBER OF WAYS, ALEX. I DON'T THINK THIS MILITANT ATTITUDE YOU HOLD IS THE ONLY EXTRAPOLATION AVAILABLE.
WANDA SPENT HER LIFE SEARCHING FOR A WAY TO BRING MAN AND MUTANT TOGETHER. SHE SAW THAT AS XAVIER'S DREAM.
THE WITCH DIDN'T LIFT A FINGER FOR US--
I'LL TAKE ALL THE GRIEF YOU CAN SLING, CALLISTO--BUT I WON'T HEAR A WORD AGAINST MY MURDERED WIFE.
THIS ISN'T GETTING US ANYWHERE.
CALL IT, ALEX. DO I HAVE YOUR PERMISSION TO ESCORT CALIBAN BACK TO THE SURFACE FOR TRIAL?
CALIBAN WAS BEING CHASED LIKE A RAT.
YOUR "MURDER" WAS SELF-DEFENSE, PLAIN AND SIMPLE.
I SUSPECT YOU'RE CORRECT.
LET'S ALLOW THE COURTS TO PROVE IT.
HUMAN COURTS.
HUMAN JUDGE.
HUMAN JURY.
MY WIFE MAKES A GOOD POINT.
TRUST ME, ALEX, PLEASE. LET ME BRING HIM IN.
IF NOT--THEY'LL SEND WORSE TO TAKE HIM.
I CAN'T DO THAT, STEVE.
YOU SHOULD GO...
...I CAN'T GUARANTEE YOUR SAFETY.
NO ONE CAN--

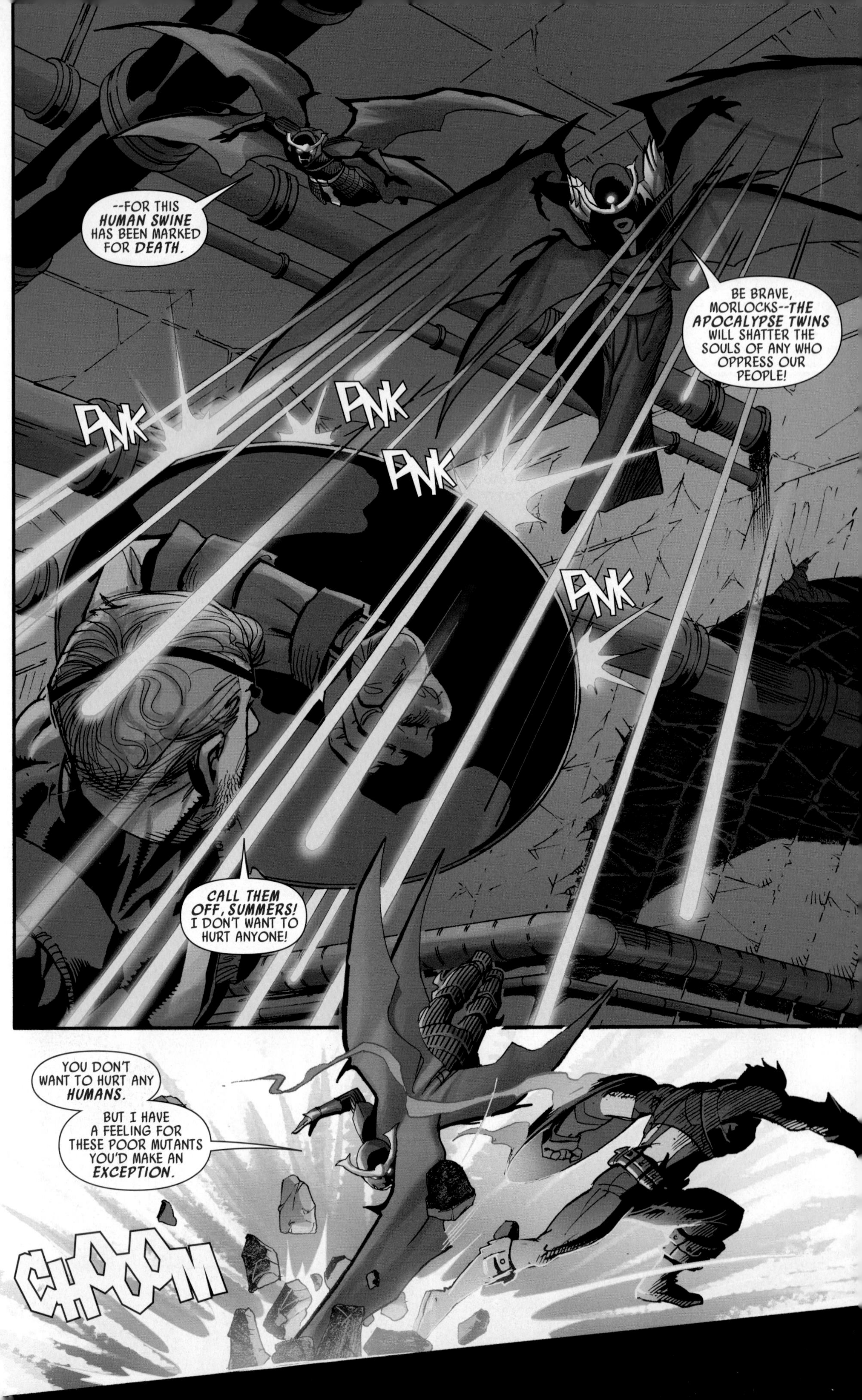
--FOR THIS HUMAN SWINE HAS BEEN MARKED FOR DEATH.
BE BRAVE, MORLOCKS--THE APOCALYPSE TWINS WILL SHATTER THE SOULS OF ANY WHO OPPRESS OUR PEOPLE!
PNK
PNK
PNK
PNK
CALL THEM OFF, SUMMERS! I DON'T WANT TO HURT ANYONE!
YOU DON'T WANT TO HURT ANY HUMANS.
BUT I HAVE A FEELING FOR THESE POOR MUTANTS YOU'D MAKE AN EXCEPTION.
CHOOOM

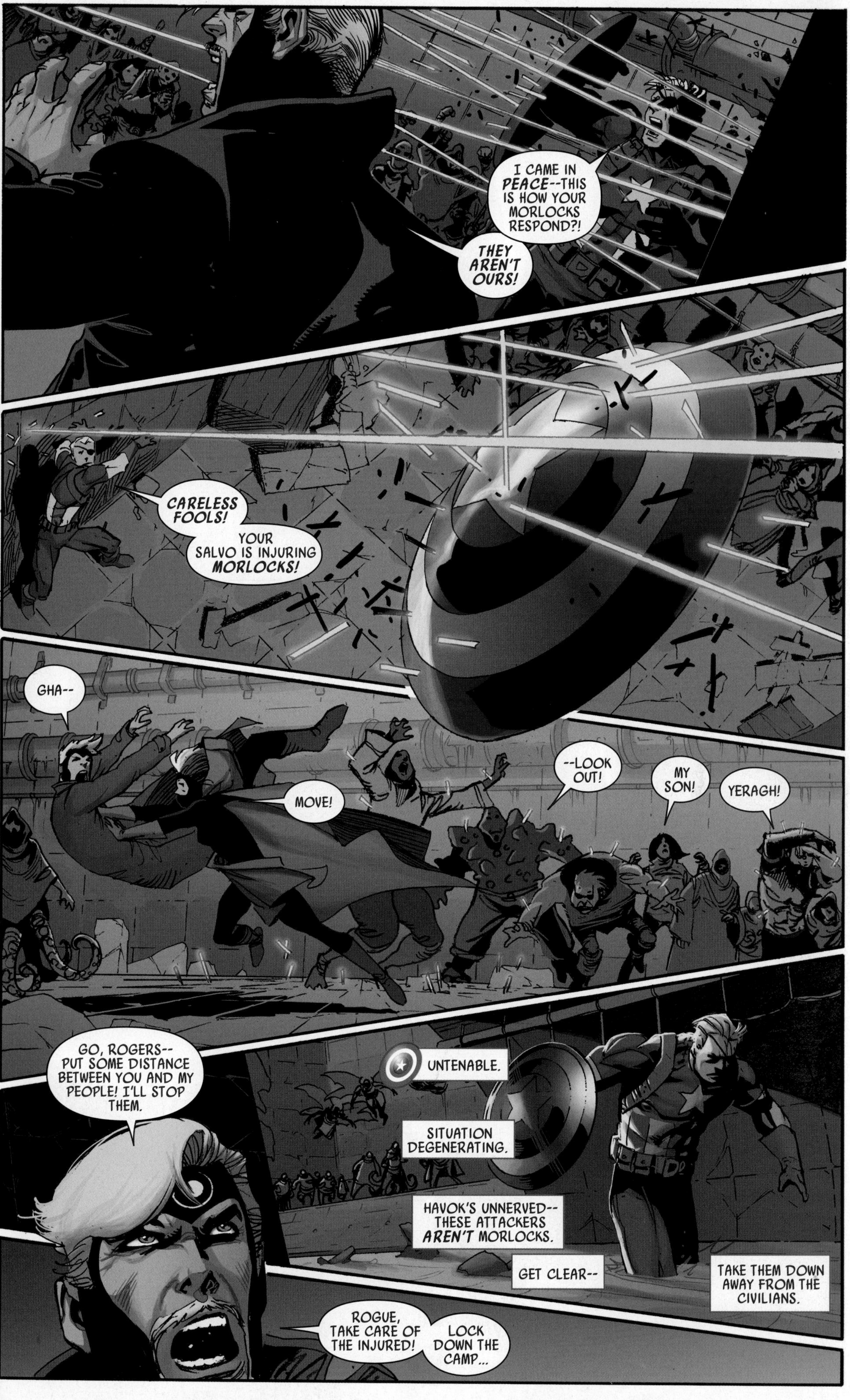
I CAME IN PEACE--THIS IS HOW YOUR MORLOCKS RESPOND?!
THEY AREN'T OURS!
CARELESS FOOLS!
YOUR SALVO IS INJURING MORLOCKS!
GHA--
MOVE!
--LOOK OUT!
MY SON!
YERAGH!
GO, ROGERS--PUT SOME DISTANCE BETWEEN YOU AND MY PEOPLE! I'LL STOP THEM.
UNTENABLE.
SITUATION DEGENERATING.
HAVOK'S UNNERVED--THESE ATTACKERS AREN'T MORLOCKS.
GET CLEAR--
TAKE THEM DOWN AWAY FROM THE CIVILIANS.
ROGUE, TAKE CARE OF THE INJURED!
LOCK DOWN THE CAMP...

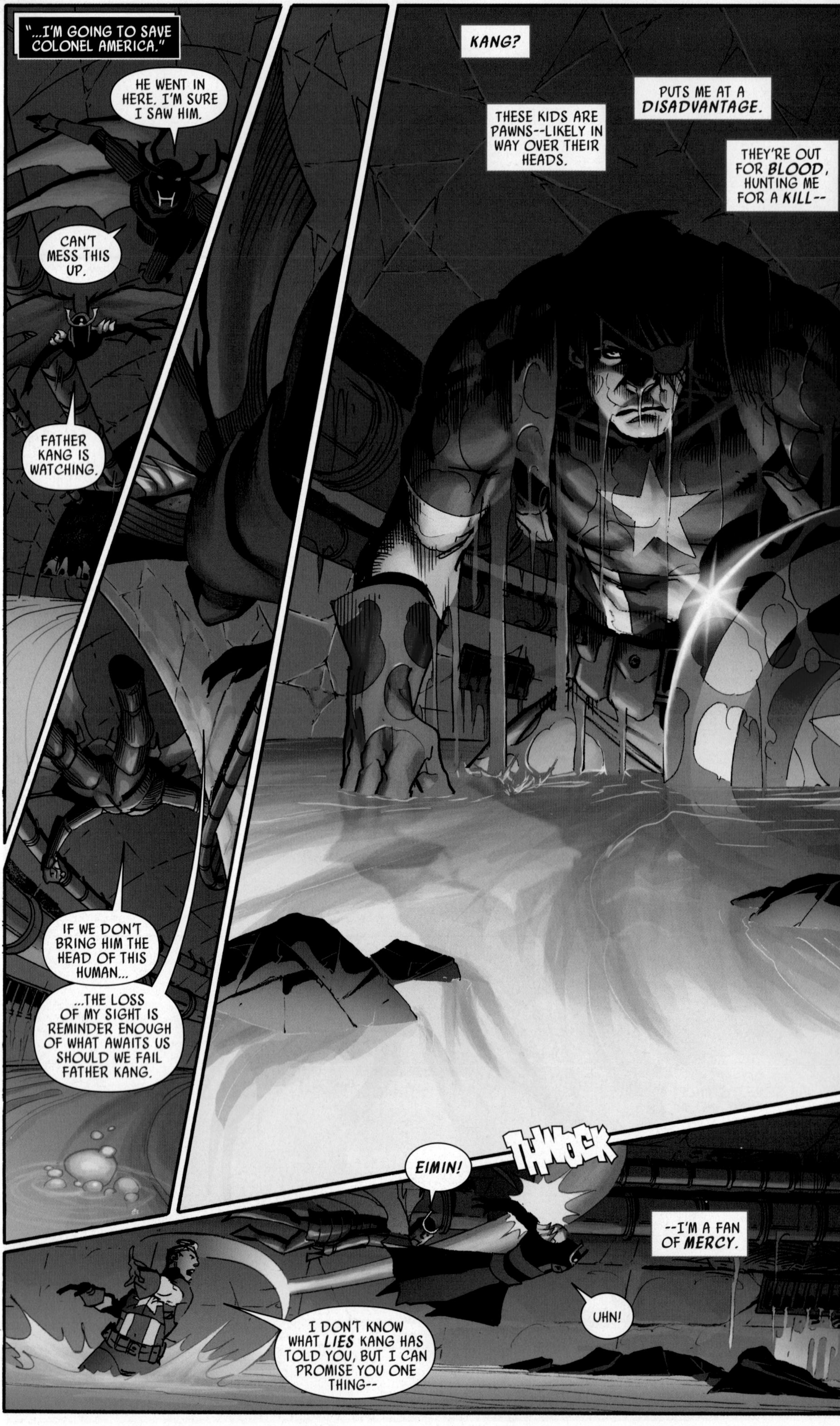
"...I'M GOING TO SAVE COLONEL AMERICA."
HE WENT IN HERE. I'M SURE I SAW HIM.
CAN'T MESS THIS UP.
FATHER KANG IS WATCHING.
IF WE DON'T BRING HIM THE HEAD OF THIS HUMAN...
...THE LOSS OF MY SIGHT IS REMINDER ENOUGH OF WHAT AWAITS US SHOULD WE FAIL FATHER KANG.
KANG?
THESE KIDS ARE PAWNS--LIKELY IN WAY OVER THEIR HEADS.
PUTS ME AT A DISADVANTAGE.
THEY'RE OUT FOR BLOOD, HUNTING ME FOR A KILL--
THWOCK
EIMIN!
I DON'T KNOW WHAT LIES KANG HAS TOLD YOU, BUT I CAN PROMISE YOU ONE THING--
UHN!
--I'M A FAN OF MERCY.

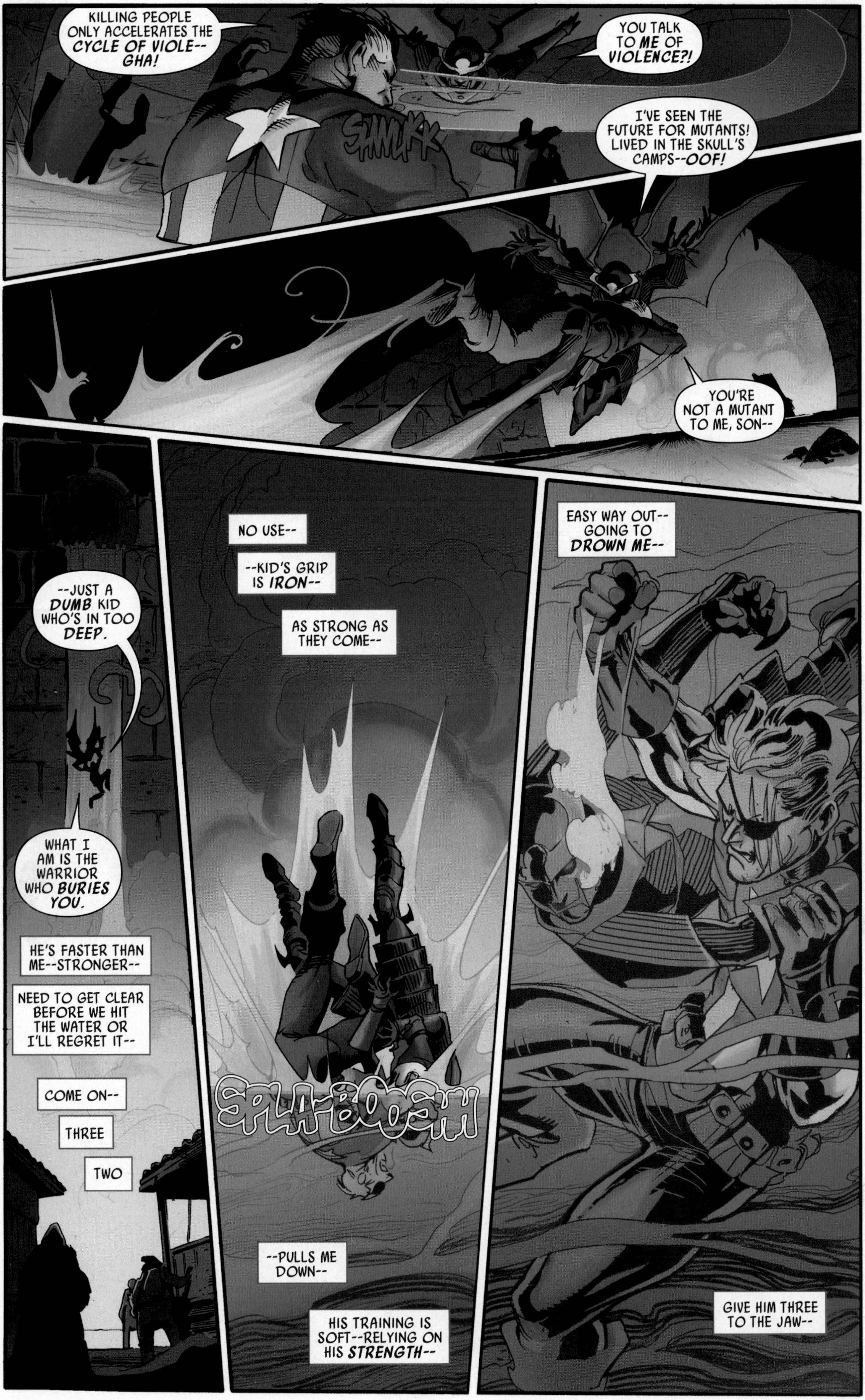
KILLING PEOPLE ONLY ACCELERATES THE CYCLE OF VIOLE-- GHA!
SHNUKK
YOU TALK TO ME OF VIOLENCE?!
I'VE SEEN THE FUTURE FOR MUTANTS! LIVED IN THE SKULL'S CAMPS--OOF!
YOU'RE NOT A MUTANT TO ME, SON--
--JUST A DUMB KID WHO'S IN TOO DEEP.
WHAT I AM IS THE WARRIOR WHO BURIES YOU.
HE'S FASTER THAN ME--STRONGER--
NEED TO GET CLEAR BEFORE WE HIT THE WATER OR I'LL REGRET IT--
COME ON--
THREE
TWO
NO USE--
--KID'S GRIP IS IRON--
AS STRONG AS THEY COME--
SPLA-BOOSH
--PULLS ME DOWN--
HIS TRAINING IS SOFT--RELYING ON HIS STRENGTH--
EASY WAY OUT-- GOING TO DROWN ME--
GIVE HIM THREE TO THE JAW--

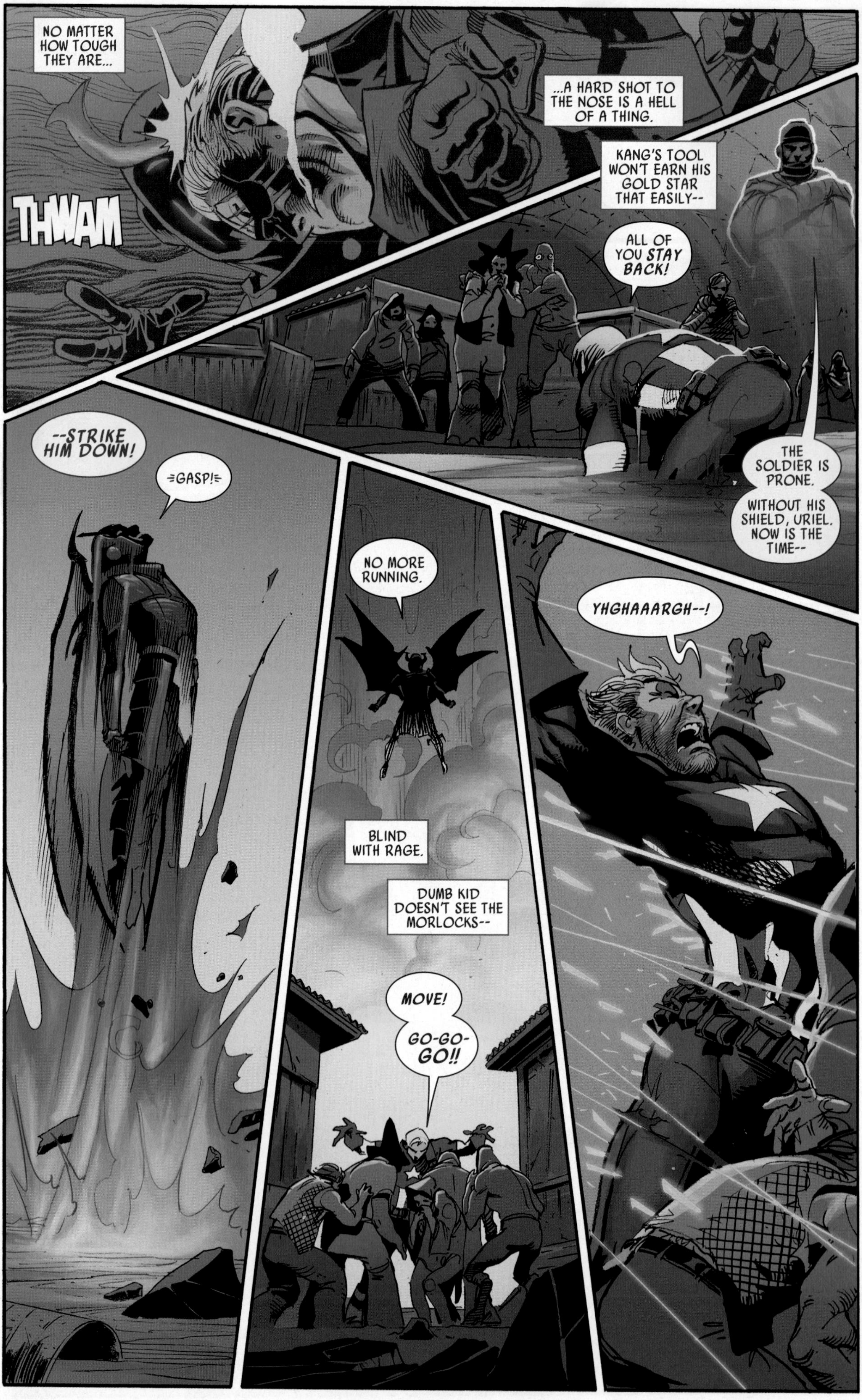
NO MATTER HOW TOUGH THEY ARE...
THWAM
...A HARD SHOT TO THE NOSE IS A HELL OF A THING.
KANG'S TOOL WON'T EARN HIS GOLD STAR THAT EASILY--
ALL OF YOU STAY BACK!
THE SOLDIER IS PRONE.
WITHOUT HIS SHIELD, URIEL. NOW IS THE TIME--
--STRIKE HIM DOWN!
GASP!
NO MORE RUNNING.
BLIND WITH RAGE.
DUMB KID DOESN'T SEE THE MORLOCKS--
MOVE!
GO-GO-GO!!
YHGHAAARGH--!

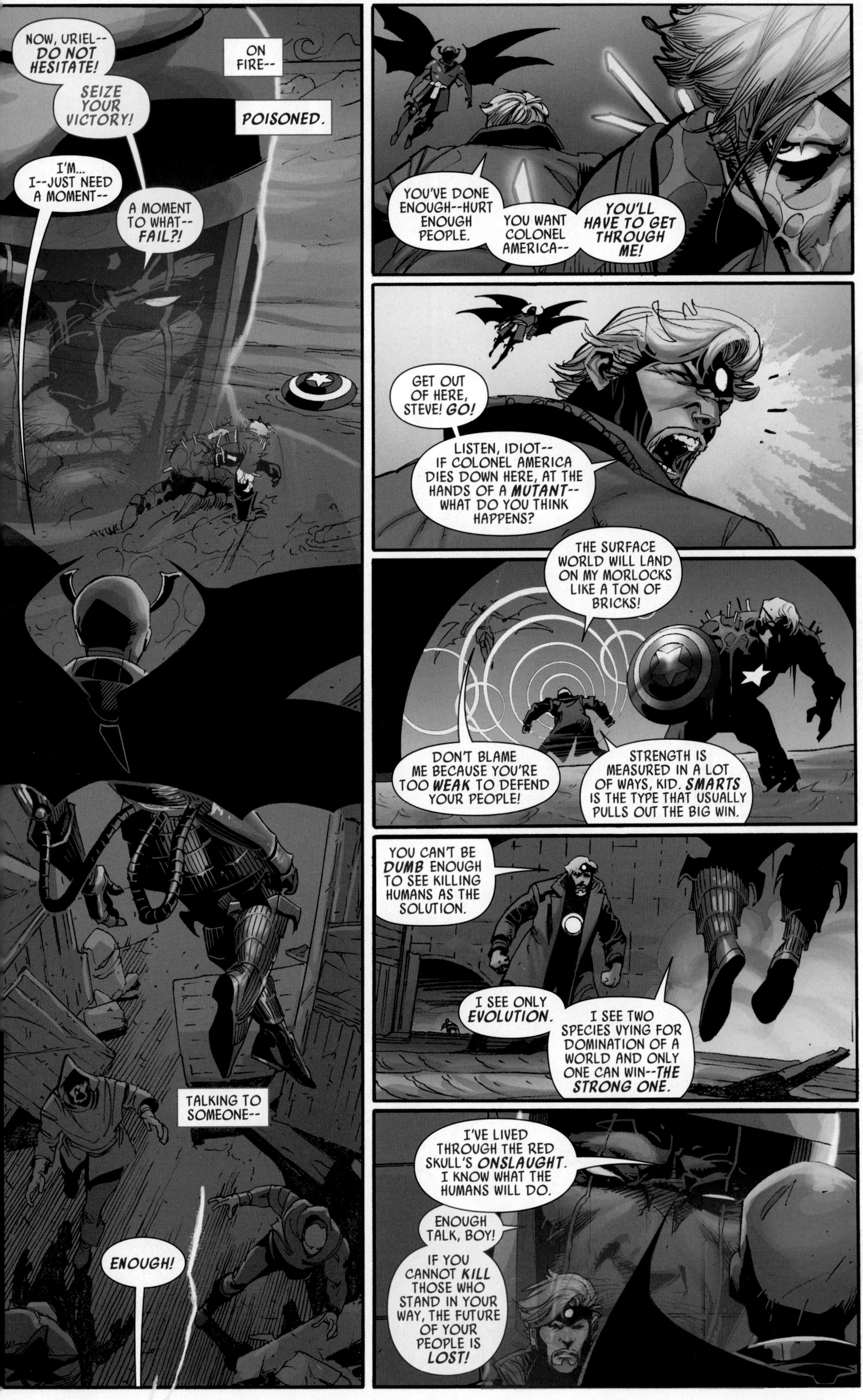
NOW, URIEL-- DO NOT HESITATE!
SEIZE YOUR VICTORY!
I'M... I--JUST NEED A MOMENT--
A MOMENT TO WHAT-- FAIL?!
ON FIRE--
POISONED.
TALKING TO SOMEONE--
ENOUGH!
YOU'VE DONE ENOUGH--HURT ENOUGH PEOPLE.
YOU WANT COLONEL AMERICA--
YOU'LL HAVE TO GET THROUGH ME!
GET OUT OF HERE, STEVE! GO!
LISTEN, IDIOT-- IF COLONEL AMERICA DIES DOWN HERE, AT THE HANDS OF A MUTANT-- WHAT DO YOU THINK HAPPENS?
THE SURFACE WORLD WILL LAND ON MY MORLOCKS LIKE A TON OF BRICKS!
DON'T BLAME ME BECAUSE YOU'RE TOO WEAK TO DEFEND YOUR PEOPLE!
STRENGTH IS MEASURED IN A LOT OF WAYS, KID. SMARTS IS THE TYPE THAT USUALLY PULLS OUT THE BIG WIN.
YOU CAN'T BE DUMB ENOUGH TO SEE KILLING HUMANS AS THE SOLUTION.
I SEE ONLY EVOLUTION.
I SEE TWO SPECIES VYING FOR DOMINATION OF A WORLD AND ONLY ONE CAN WIN--THE STRONG ONE.
I'VE LIVED THROUGH THE RED SKULL'S ONSLAUGHT. I KNOW WHAT THE HUMANS WILL DO.
ENOUGH TALK, BOY!
IF YOU CANNOT KILL THOSE WHO STAND IN YOUR WAY, THE FUTURE OF YOUR PEOPLE IS LOST!

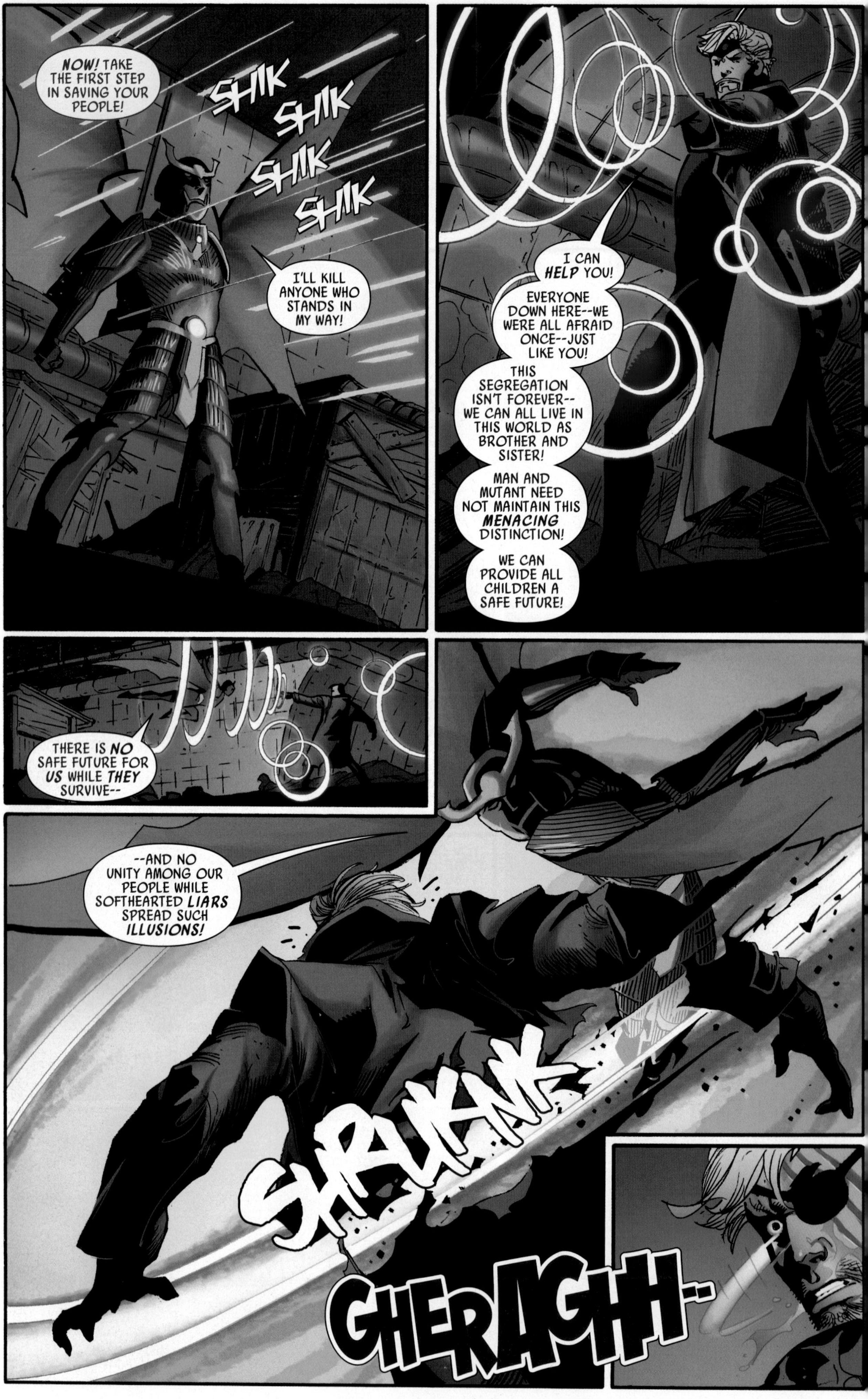
NOW! TAKE THE FIRST STEP IN SAVING YOUR PEOPLE!
SHIK SHIK SHIK SHIK
I'LL KILL ANYONE WHO STANDS IN MY WAY!
I CAN HELP YOU!
EVERYONE DOWN HERE--WE WERE ALL AFRAID ONCE--JUST LIKE YOU!
THIS SEGREGATION ISN'T FOREVER--WE CAN ALL LIVE IN THIS WORLD AS BROTHER AND SISTER!
MAN AND MUTANT NEED NOT MAINTAIN THIS MENACING DISTINCTION!
WE CAN PROVIDE ALL CHILDREN A SAFE FUTURE!
THERE IS NO SAFE FUTURE FOR US WHILE THEY SURVIVE--
--AND NO UNITY AMONG OUR PEOPLE WHILE SOFTHEARTED LIARS SPREAD SUCH ILLUSIONS!
SHRUKNK
GHERAGHH-

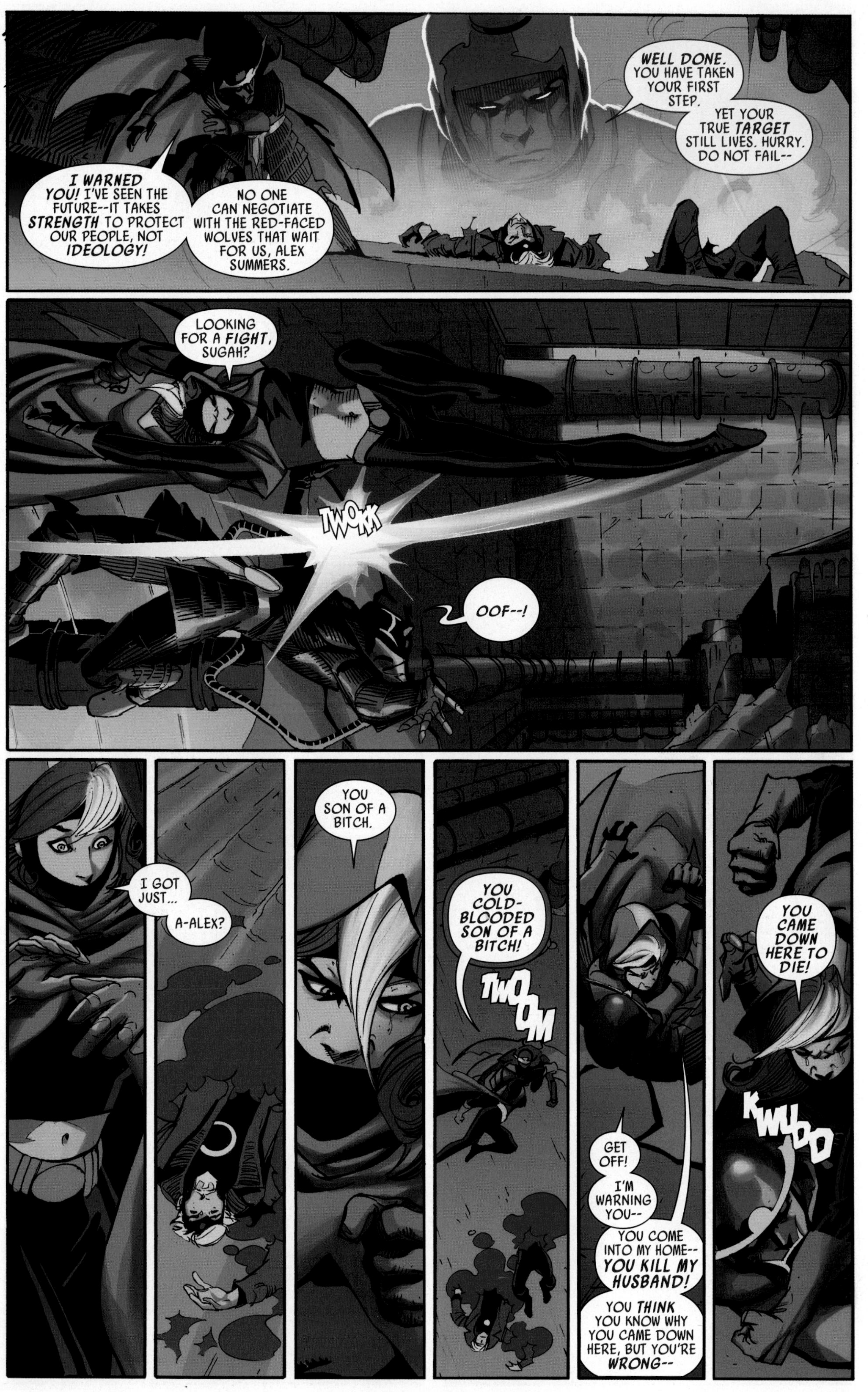
WELL DONE. YOU HAVE TAKEN YOUR FIRST STEP.
YET YOUR TRUE TARGET STILL LIVES. HURRY. DO NOT FAIL--
I WARNED YOU! I'VE SEEN THE FUTURE--IT TAKES STRENGTH TO PROTECT OUR PEOPLE, NOT IDEOLOGY!
NO ONE CAN NEGOTIATE WITH THE RED-FACED WOLVES THAT WAIT FOR US, ALEX SUMMERS.
LOOKING FOR A FIGHT, SUGAH?
TWOKK
OOF--!
I GOT JUST...
A-ALEX?
YOU SON OF A BITCH.
YOU COLD-BLOODED SON OF A BITCH!
TWOOOM
GET OFF!
I'M WARNING YOU--
YOU COME INTO MY HOME-- YOU KILL MY HUSBAND!
YOU THINK YOU KNOW WHY YOU CAME DOWN HERE, BUT YOU'RE WRONG--
YOU CAME DOWN HERE TO DIE!
KWUDD

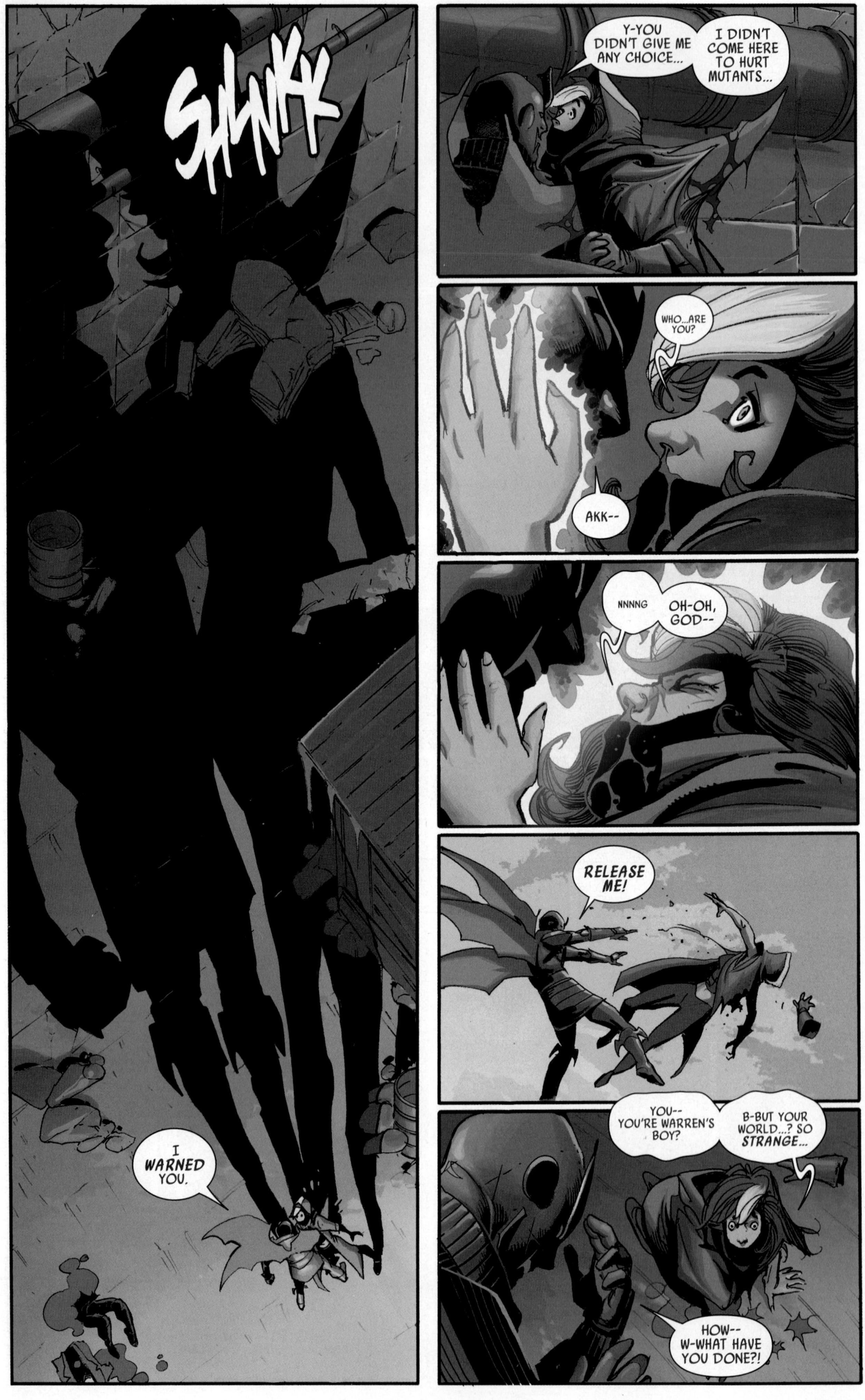
SHNKK
I WARNED YOU.
Y-YOU DIDN'T GIVE ME ANY CHOICE...
I DIDN'T COME HERE TO HURT MUTANTS...
WHO...ARE YOU?
AKK--
NNNNG
OH-OH, GOD--
RELEASE ME!
YOU-- YOU'RE WARREN'S BOY?
B-BUT YOUR WORLD...? SO STRANGE...
HOW-- W-WHAT HAVE YOU DONE?!

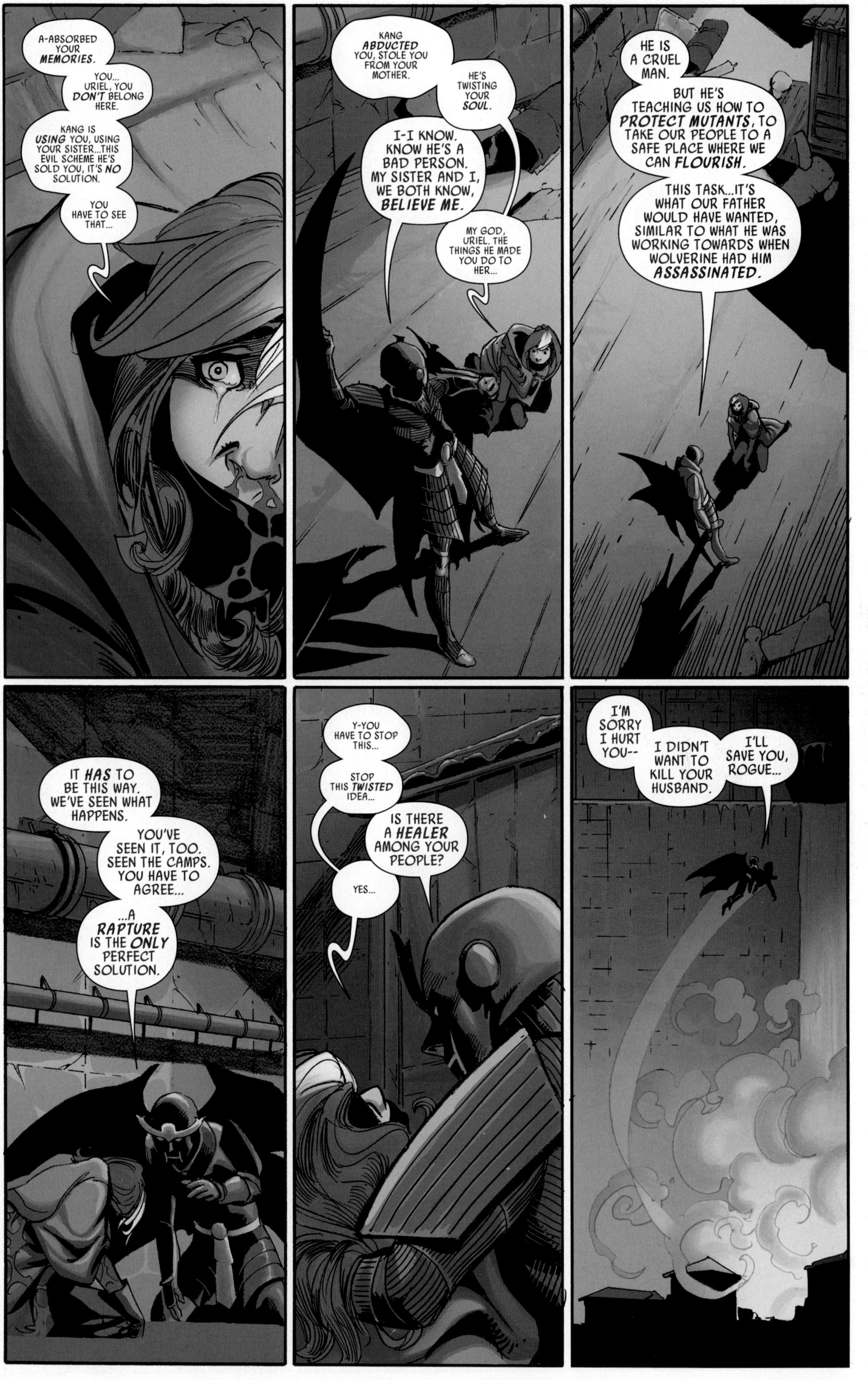
A-ABSORBED YOUR MEMORIES.
YOU... URIEL, YOU DON'T BELONG HERE.
KANG IS USING YOU, USING YOUR SISTER...THIS EVIL SCHEME HE'S SOLD YOU, IT'S NO SOLUTION.
YOU HAVE TO SEE THAT...
KANG ABDUCTED YOU, STOLE YOU FROM YOUR MOTHER.
HE'S TWISTING YOUR SOUL.
I-I KNOW. KNOW HE'S A BAD PERSON. MY SISTER AND I, WE BOTH KNOW, BELIEVE ME.
MY GOD, URIEL. THE THINGS HE MADE YOU DO TO HER...
HE IS A CRUEL MAN.
BUT HE'S TEACHING US HOW TO PROTECT MUTANTS, TO TAKE OUR PEOPLE TO A SAFE PLACE WHERE WE CAN FLOURISH.
THIS TASK...IT'S WHAT OUR FATHER WOULD HAVE WANTED, SIMILAR TO WHAT HE WAS WORKING TOWARDS WHEN WOLVERINE HAD HIM ASSASSINATED.
IT HAS TO BE THIS WAY. WE'VE SEEN WHAT HAPPENS.
YOU'VE SEEN IT, TOO. SEEN THE CAMPS. YOU HAVE TO AGREE...
...A RAPTURE IS THE ONLY PERFECT SOLUTION.
Y-YOU HAVE TO STOP THIS...
STOP THIS TWISTED IDEA...
IS THERE A HEALER AMONG YOUR PEOPLE?
YES...
I'M SORRY I HURT YOU--
I DIDN'T WANT TO KILL YOUR HUSBAND.
I'LL SAVE YOU, ROGUE...

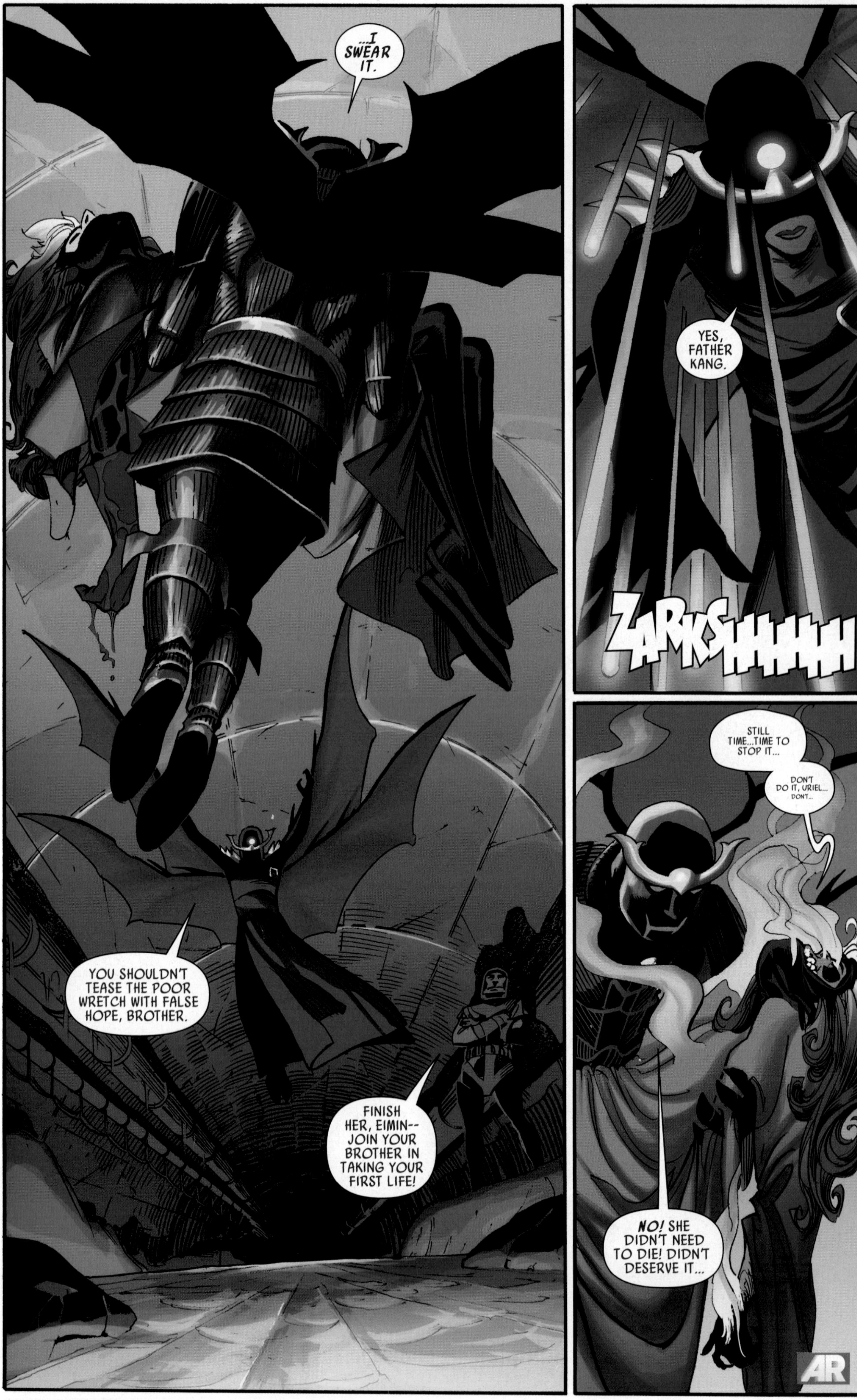
...I SWEAR IT.
YOU SHOULDN'T TEASE THE POOR WRETCH WITH FALSE HOPE, BROTHER.
FINISH HER, EIMIN-- JOIN YOUR BROTHER IN TAKING YOUR FIRST LIFE!
YES, FATHER KANG.
ZARKSHHHHHH
STILL TIME...TIME TO STOP IT...
DON'T DO IT, URIEL... DON'T...
NO! SHE DIDN'T NEED TO DIE! DIDN'T DESERVE IT...
AR

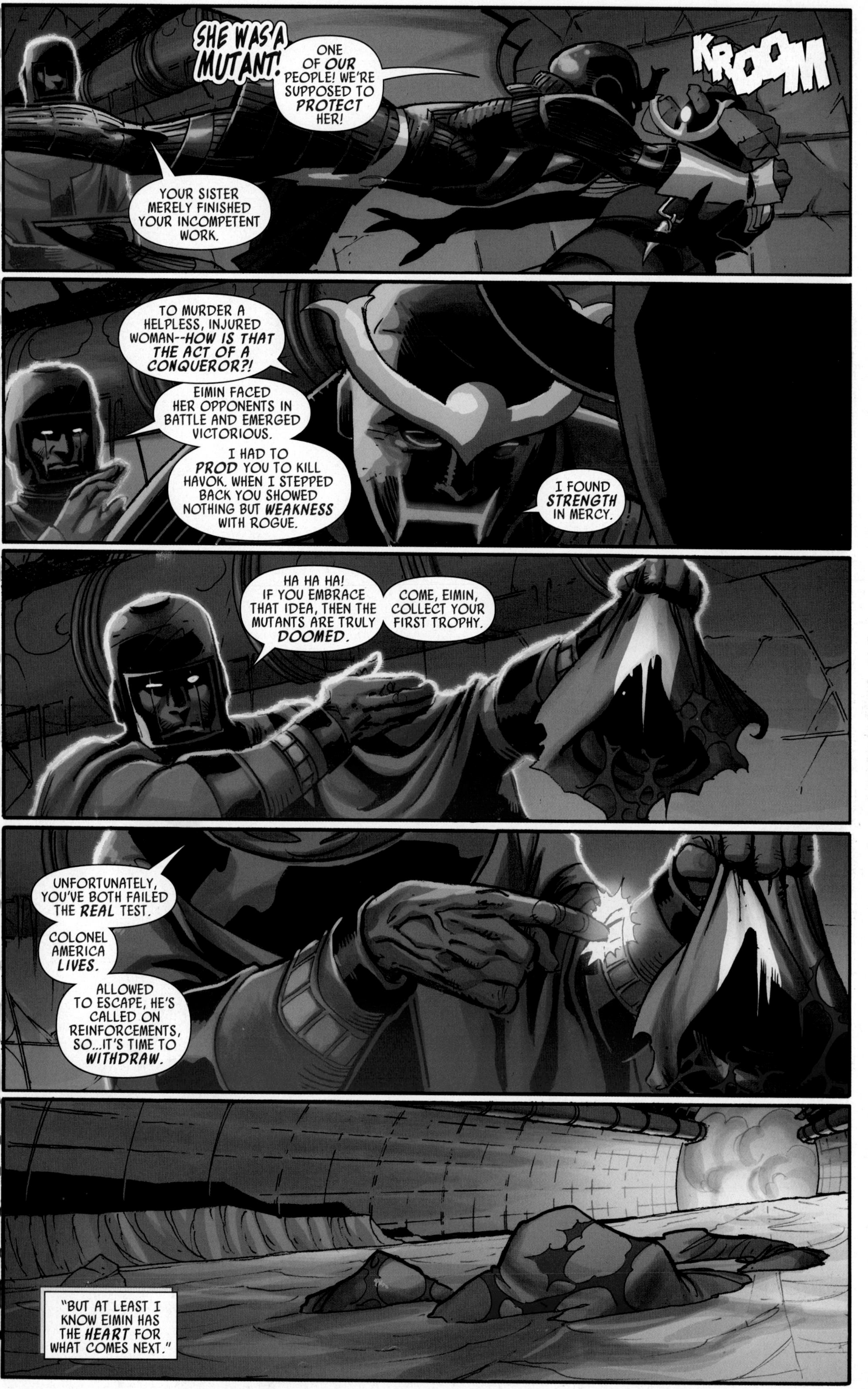
SHE WAS A MUTANT!
ONE OF OUR PEOPLE! WE'RE SUPPOSED TO PROTECT HER!
KROOM
YOUR SISTER MERELY FINISHED YOUR INCOMPETENT WORK.
TO MURDER A HELPLESS, INJURED WOMAN--HOW IS THAT THE ACT OF A CONQUEROR?!
EIMIN FACED HER OPPONENTS IN BATTLE AND EMERGED VICTORIOUS.
I HAD TO PROD YOU TO KILL HAVOK. WHEN I STEPPED BACK YOU SHOWED NOTHING BUT WEAKNESS WITH ROGUE.
I FOUND STRENGTH IN MERCY.
HA HA HA! IF YOU EMBRACE THAT IDEA, THEN THE MUTANTS ARE TRULY DOOMED.
COME, EIMIN, COLLECT YOUR FIRST TROPHY.
UNFORTUNATELY, YOU'VE BOTH FAILED THE REAL TEST.
COLONEL AMERICA LIVES.
ALLOWED TO ESCAPE, HE'S CALLED ON REINFORCEMENTS, SO...IT'S TIME TO WITHDRAW.
"BUT AT LEAST I KNOW EIMIN HAS THE HEART FOR WHAT COMES NEXT."

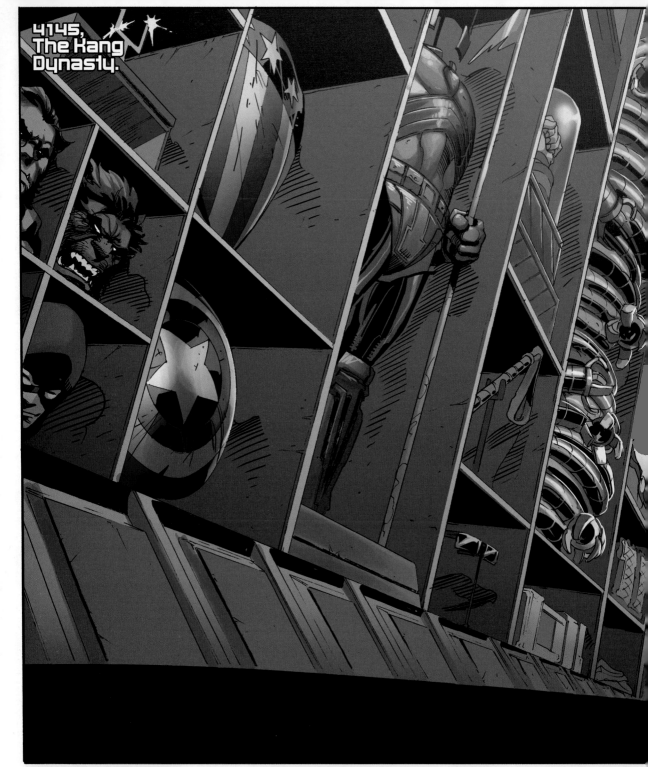

I-I'M SORRY,
FATHER KANG.
PLEASE...

QUIET YOUR
SNIVELING.

NEVER BE
SORRY...

...BE
VICTORIOUS.

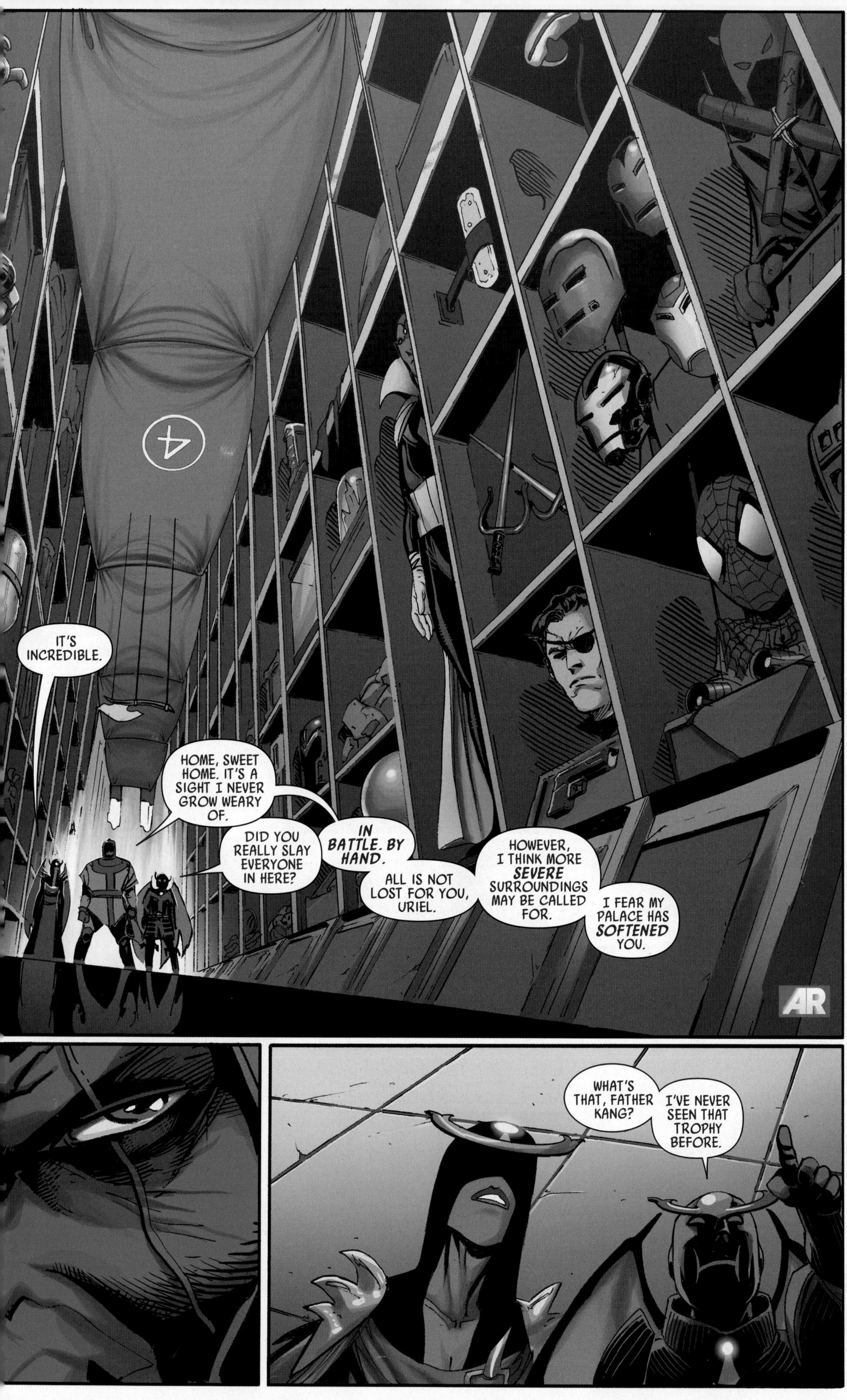
IT'S INCREDIBLE.
HOME, SWEET HOME. IT'S A SIGHT I NEVER GROW WEARY OF.
DID YOU REALLY SLAY EVERYONE IN HERE?
IN BATTLE. BY HAND.
ALL IS NOT LOST FOR YOU, URIEL.
HOWEVER, I THINK MORE SEVERE SURROUNDINGS MAY BE CALLED FOR.
I FEAR MY PALACE HAS SOFTENED YOU.
WHAT'S THAT, FATHER KANG?
I'VE NEVER SEEN THAT TROPHY BEFORE.

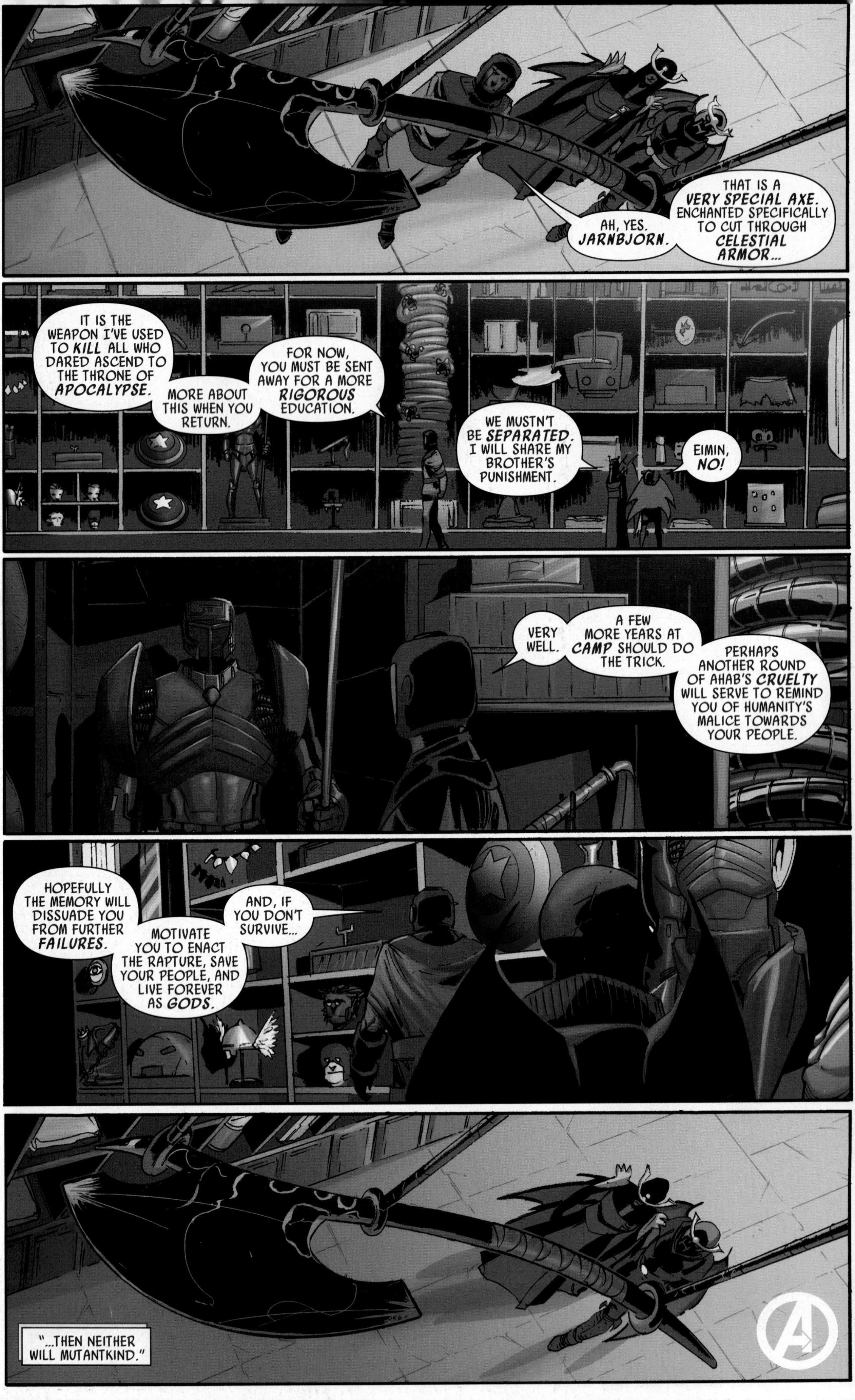
AH, YES. JARNBJORN.
THAT IS A VERY SPECIAL AXE. ENCHANTED SPECIFICALLY TO CUT THROUGH CELESTIAL ARMOR...
IT IS THE WEAPON I'VE USED TO KILL ALL WHO DARED ASCEND TO THE THRONE OF APOCALYPSE.
MORE ABOUT THIS WHEN YOU RETURN.
FOR NOW, YOU MUST BE SENT AWAY FOR A MORE RIGOROUS EDUCATION.
WE MUSTN'T BE SEPARATED. I WILL SHARE MY BROTHER'S PUNISHMENT.
EIMIN, NO!
VERY WELL.
A FEW MORE YEARS AT CAMP SHOULD DO THE TRICK.
PERHAPS ANOTHER ROUND OF AHAB'S CRUELTY WILL SERVE TO REMIND YOU OF HUMANITY'S MALICE TOWARDS YOUR PEOPLE.
HOPEFULLY THE MEMORY WILL DISSUADE YOU FROM FURTHER FAILURES.
MOTIVATE YOU TO ENACT THE RAPTURE, SAVE YOUR PEOPLE, AND LIVE FOREVER AS GODS.
AND, IF YOU DON'T SURVIVE...
"...THEN NEITHER WILL MUTANTKIND."

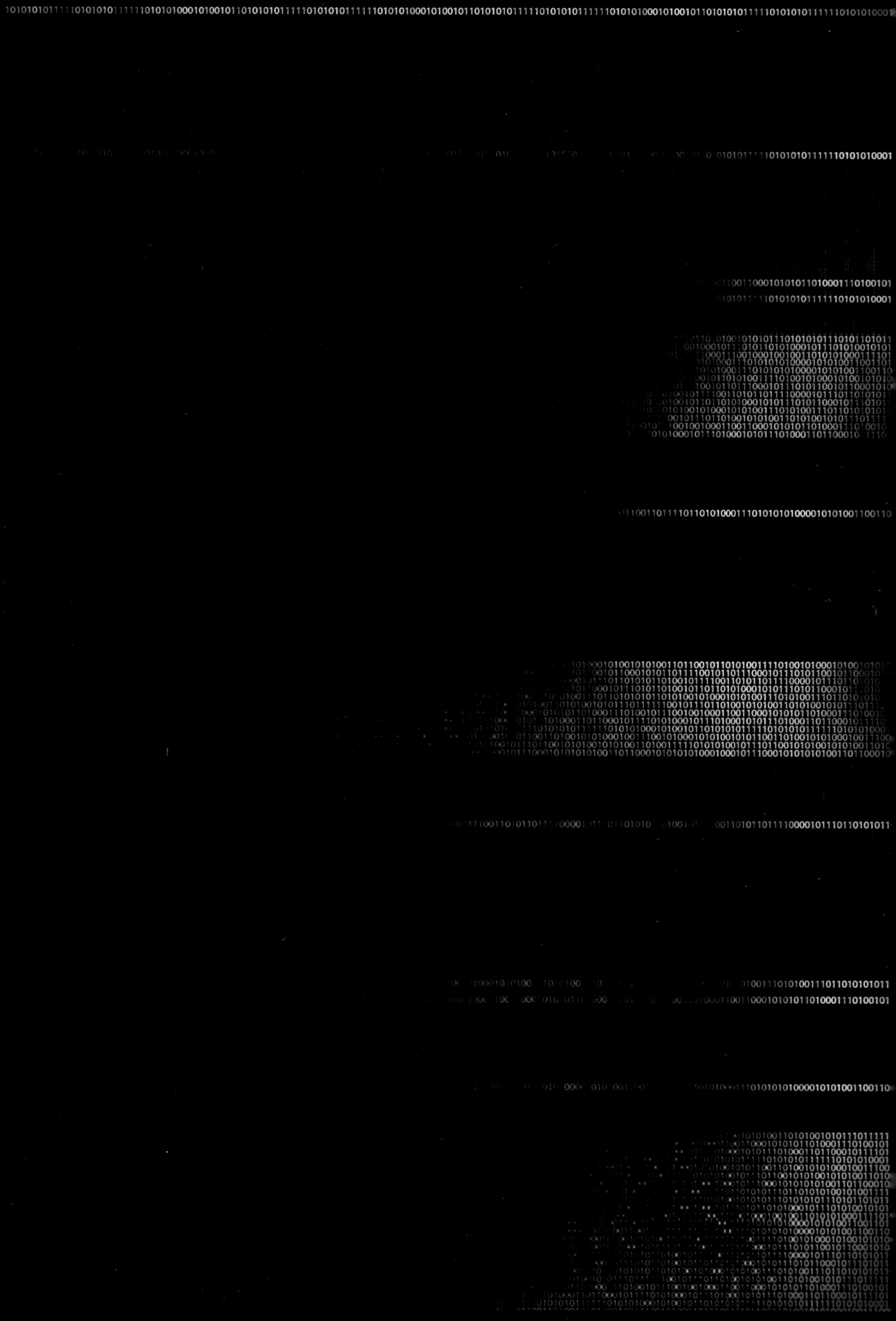

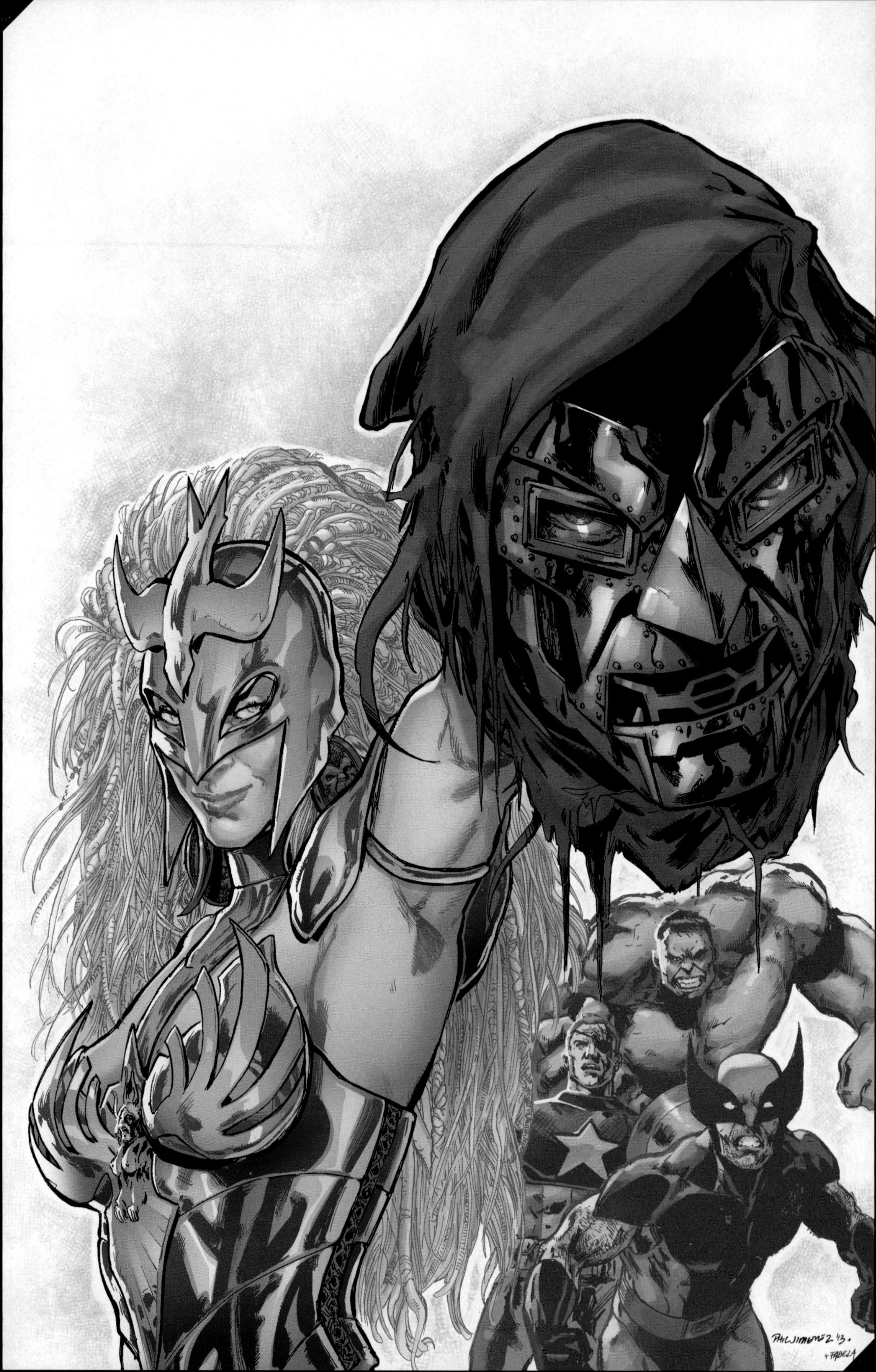

FEARLESS DEFENDERS #4AU

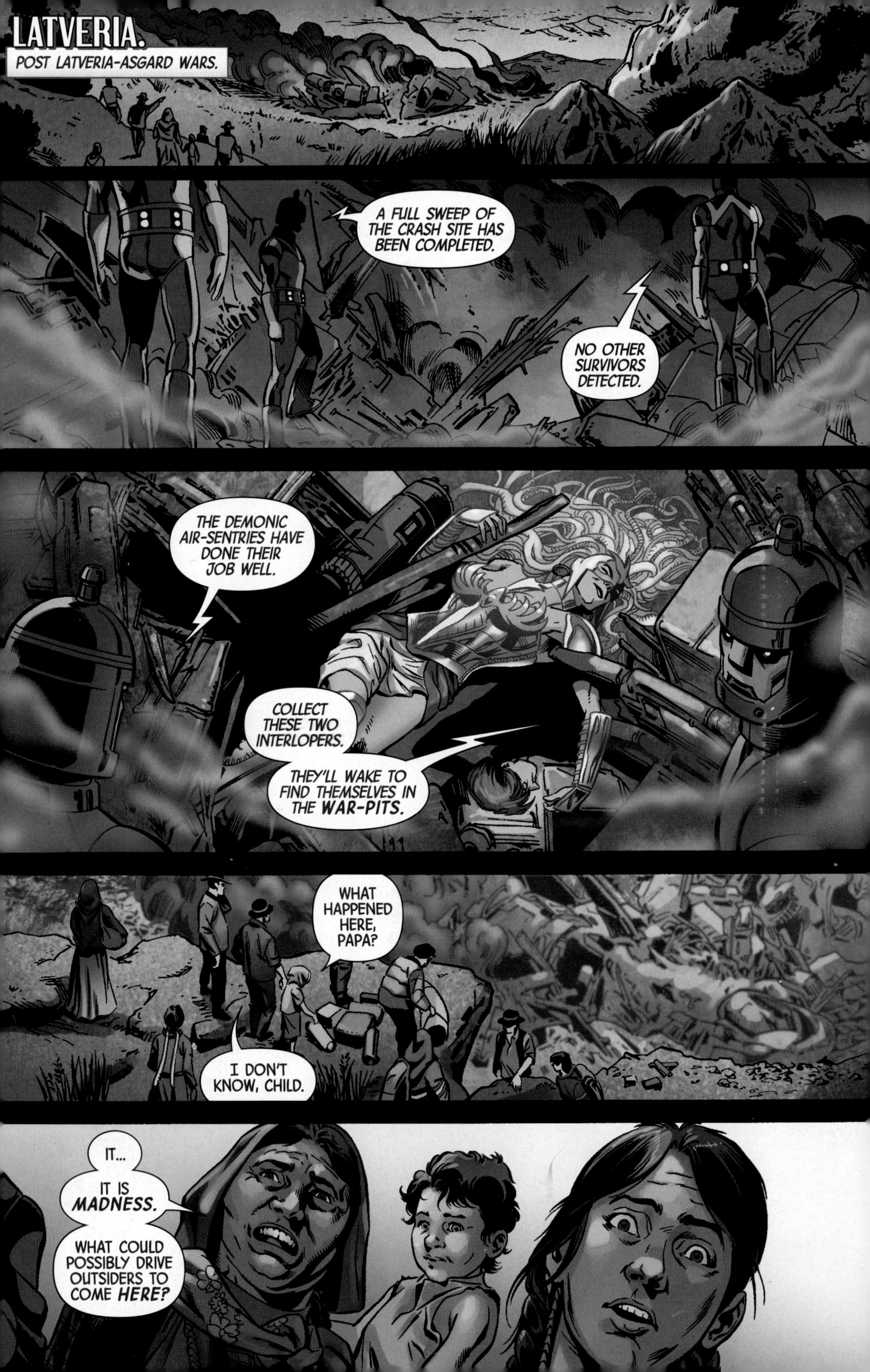
LATVERIA.
POST LATVERIA-ASGARD WARS.
A FULL SWEEP OF THE CRASH SITE HAS BEEN COMPLETED.
NO OTHER SURVIVORS DETECTED.
THE DEMONIC AIR-SENTRIES HAVE DONE THEIR JOB WELL.
COLLECT THESE TWO INTERLOPERS.
THEY'LL WAKE TO FIND THEMSELVES IN THE WAR-PITS.
WHAT HAPPENED HERE, PAPA?
I DON'T KNOW, CHILD.
IT...
IT IS MADNESS.
WHAT COULD POSSIBLY DRIVE OUTSIDERS TO COME HERE?

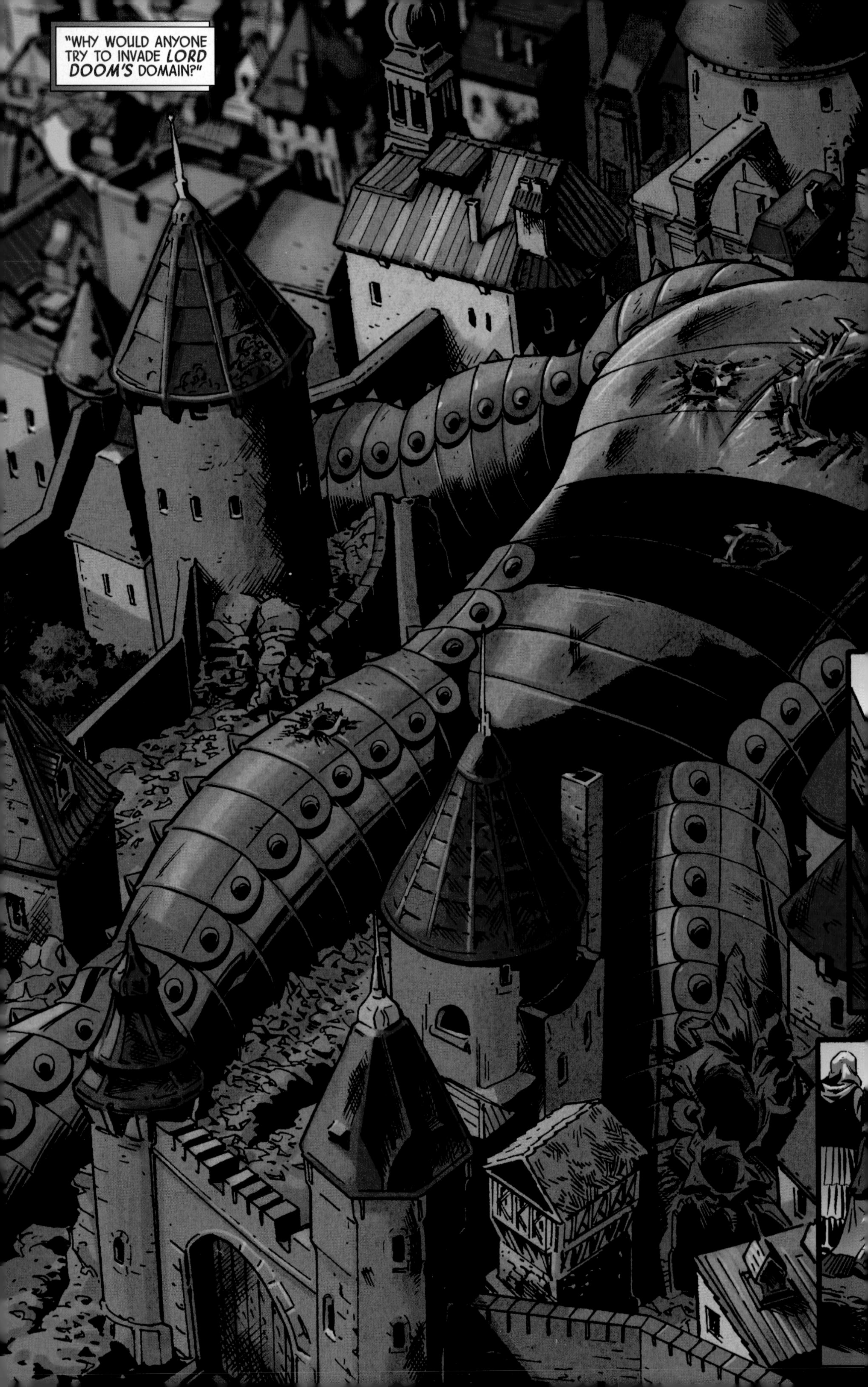
"WHY WOULD ANYONE TRY TO INVADE LORD DOOM'S DOMAIN?"

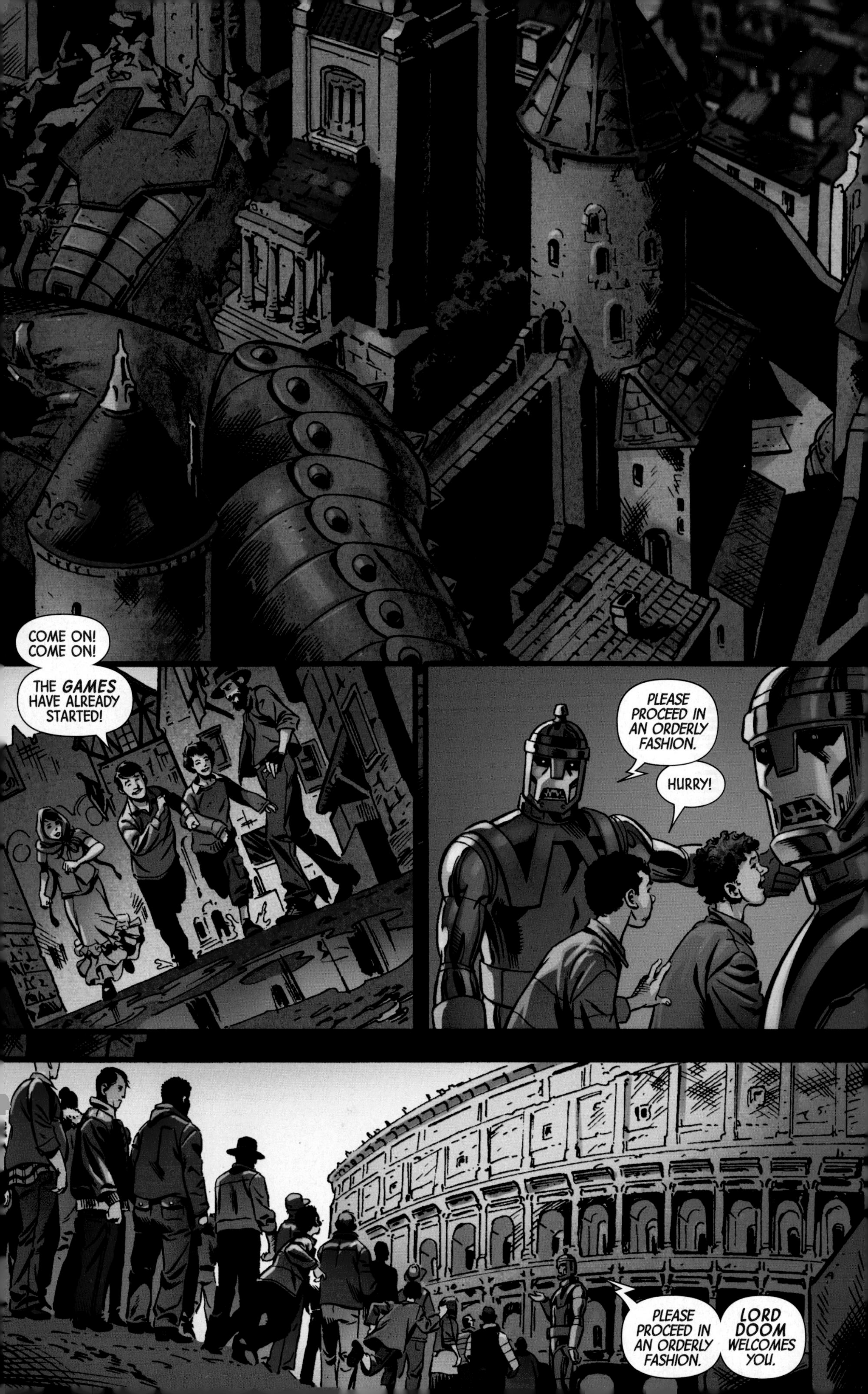
COME ON! COME ON!
THE *GAMES* HAVE ALREADY STARTED!
PLEASE PROCEED IN AN ORDERLY FASHION.
HURRY!
PLEASE PROCEED IN AN ORDERLY FASHION.
LORD DOOM WELCOMES YOU.

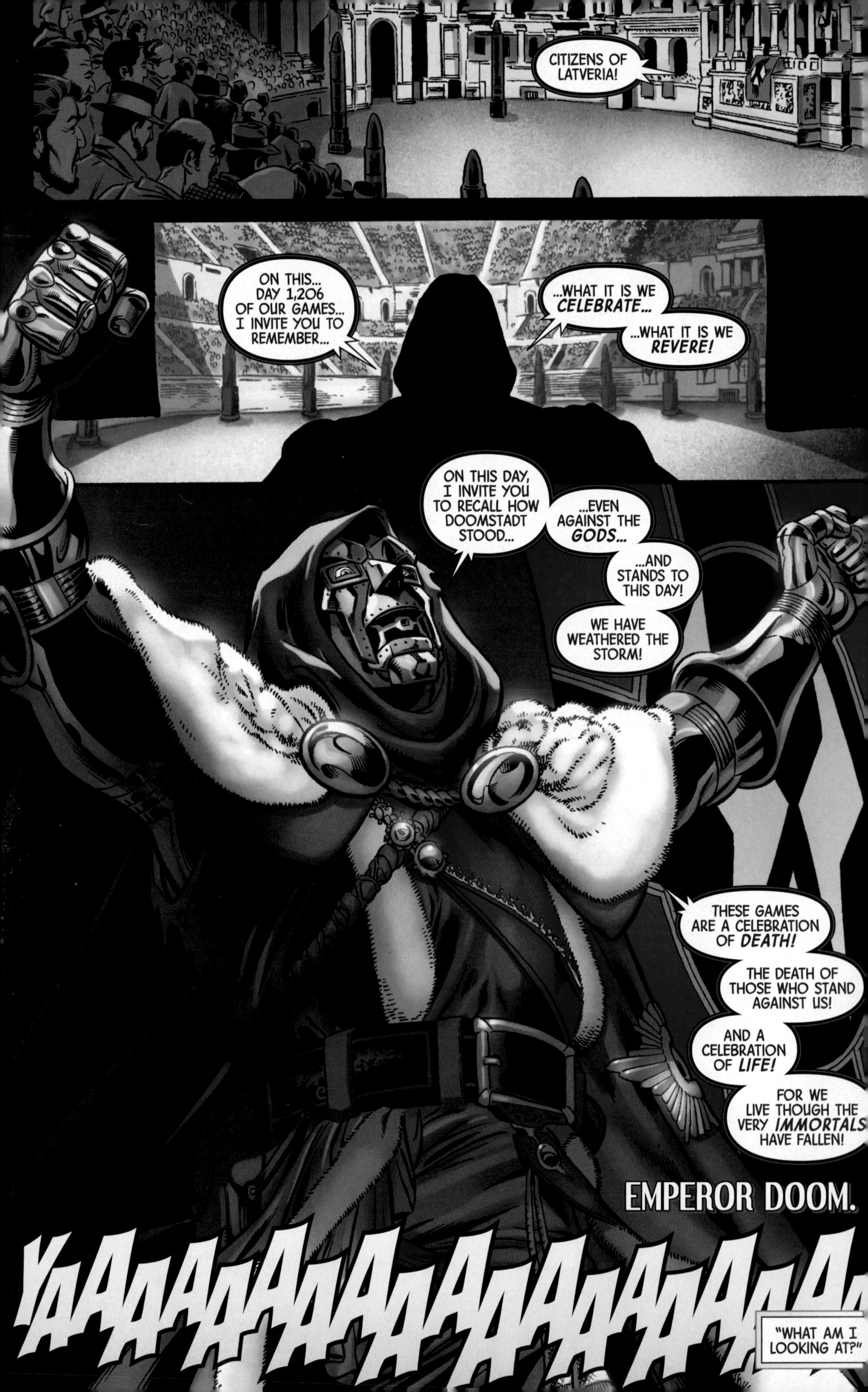
CITIZENS OF LATVERIA!
ON THIS... DAY 1,206 OF OUR GAMES... I INVITE YOU TO REMEMBER...
...WHAT IT IS WE CELEBRATE...
...WHAT IT IS WE REVERE!
ON THIS DAY, I INVITE YOU TO RECALL HOW DOOMSTADT STOOD...
...EVEN AGAINST THE GODS...
...AND STANDS TO THIS DAY!
WE HAVE WEATHERED THE STORM!
THESE GAMES ARE A CELEBRATION OF DEATH!
THE DEATH OF THOSE WHO STAND AGAINST US!
AND A CELEBRATION OF LIFE!
FOR WE LIVE THOUGH THE VERY IMMORTALS HAVE FALLEN!
EMPEROR DOOM.
YAAAAAAAAAAAAAAAAA
"WHAT AM I LOOKING AT?"

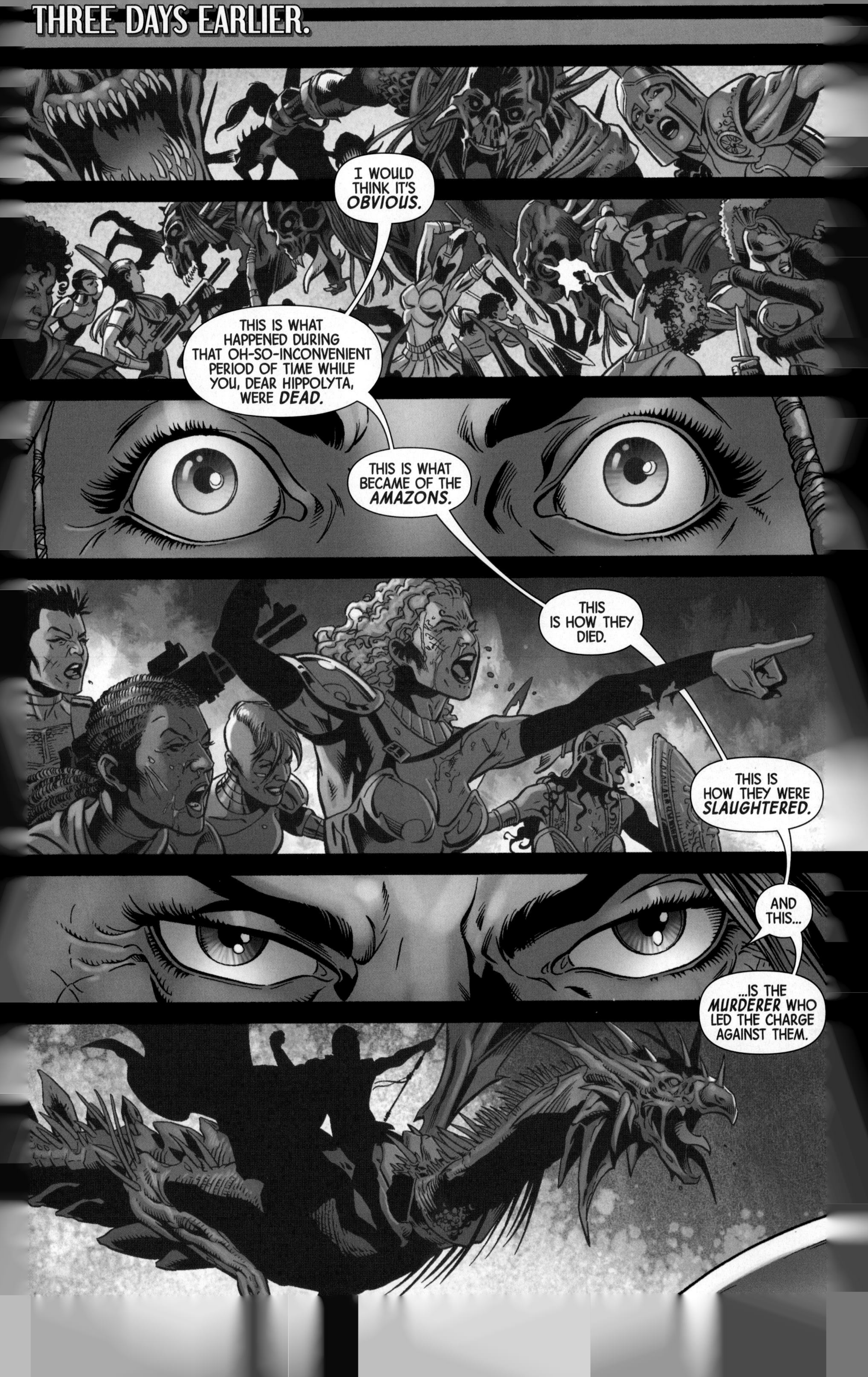
THREE DAYS EARLIER.
I WOULD THINK IT'S OBVIOUS.
THIS IS WHAT HAPPENED DURING THAT OH-SO-INCONVENIENT PERIOD OF TIME WHILE YOU, DEAR HIPPOLYTA, WERE DEAD.
THIS IS WHAT BECAME OF THE AMAZONS.
THIS IS HOW THEY DIED.
THIS IS HOW THEY WERE SLAUGHTERED.
AND THIS...
...IS THE MURDERER WHO LED THE CHARGE AGAINST THEM.

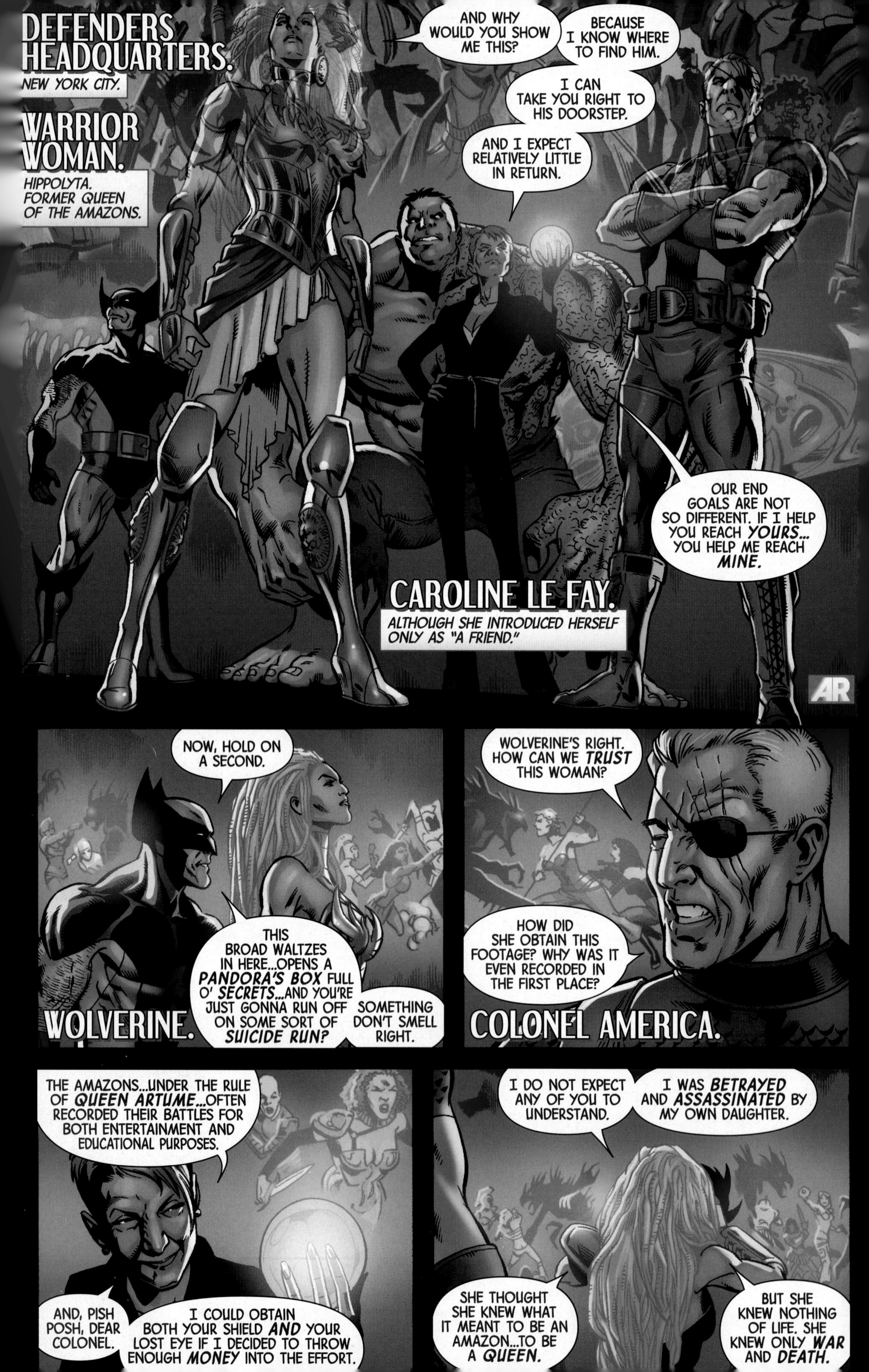
DEFENDERS HEADQUARTERS.
NEW YORK CITY.
WARRIOR WOMAN.
HIPPOLYTA. FORMER QUEEN OF THE AMAZONS.
AND WHY WOULD YOU SHOW ME THIS?
BECAUSE I KNOW WHERE TO FIND HIM.
I CAN TAKE YOU RIGHT TO HIS DOORSTEP.
AND I EXPECT RELATIVELY LITTLE IN RETURN.
OUR END GOALS ARE NOT SO DIFFERENT. IF I HELP YOU REACH YOURS... YOU HELP ME REACH MINE.
CAROLINE LE FAY.
ALTHOUGH SHE INTRODUCED HERSELF ONLY AS "A FRIEND."
AR
NOW, HOLD ON A SECOND.
THIS BROAD WALTZES IN HERE...OPENS A PANDORA'S BOX FULL O' SECRETS...AND YOU'RE JUST GONNA RUN OFF ON SOME SORT OF SUICIDE RUN?
SOMETHING DON'T SMELL RIGHT.
WOLVERINE.
WOLVERINE'S RIGHT. HOW CAN WE TRUST THIS WOMAN?
HOW DID SHE OBTAIN THIS FOOTAGE? WHY WAS IT EVEN RECORDED IN THE FIRST PLACE?
COLONEL AMERICA.
THE AMAZONS...UNDER THE RULE OF QUEEN ARTUME...OFTEN RECORDED THEIR BATTLES FOR BOTH ENTERTAINMENT AND EDUCATIONAL PURPOSES.
AND, PISH POSH, DEAR COLONEL.
I COULD OBTAIN BOTH YOUR SHIELD AND YOUR LOST EYE IF I DECIDED TO THROW ENOUGH MONEY INTO THE EFFORT.
I DO NOT EXPECT ANY OF YOU TO UNDERSTAND.
I WAS BETRAYED AND ASSASSINATED BY MY OWN DAUGHTER.
SHE THOUGHT SHE KNEW WHAT IT MEANT TO BE AN AMAZON...TO BE A QUEEN.
BUT SHE KNEW NOTHING OF LIFE. SHE KNEW ONLY WAR AND DEATH.

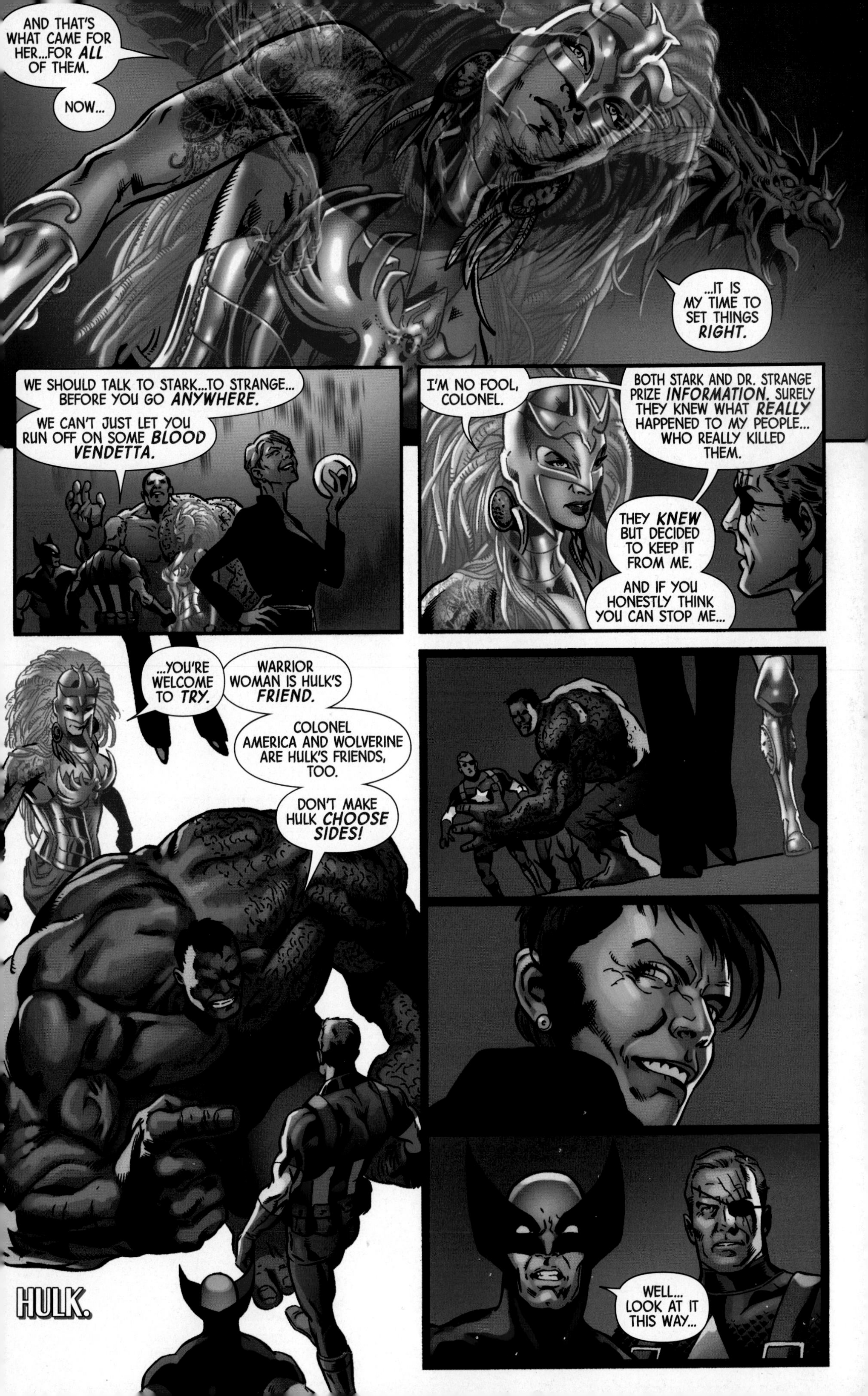
AND THAT'S WHAT CAME FOR HER...FOR ALL OF THEM.
NOW...
...IT IS MY TIME TO SET THINGS RIGHT.
WE SHOULD TALK TO STARK...TO STRANGE... BEFORE YOU GO ANYWHERE.
WE CAN'T JUST LET YOU RUN OFF ON SOME BLOOD VENDETTA.
I'M NO FOOL, COLONEL.
BOTH STARK AND DR. STRANGE PRIZE INFORMATION. SURELY THEY KNEW WHAT REALLY HAPPENED TO MY PEOPLE... WHO REALLY KILLED THEM.
THEY KNEW BUT DECIDED TO KEEP IT FROM ME.
AND IF YOU HONESTLY THINK YOU CAN STOP ME...
...YOU'RE WELCOME TO TRY.
WARRIOR WOMAN IS HULK'S FRIEND.
COLONEL AMERICA AND WOLVERINE ARE HULK'S FRIENDS, TOO.
DON'T MAKE HULK CHOOSE SIDES!
HULK.
WELL... LOOK AT IT THIS WAY...

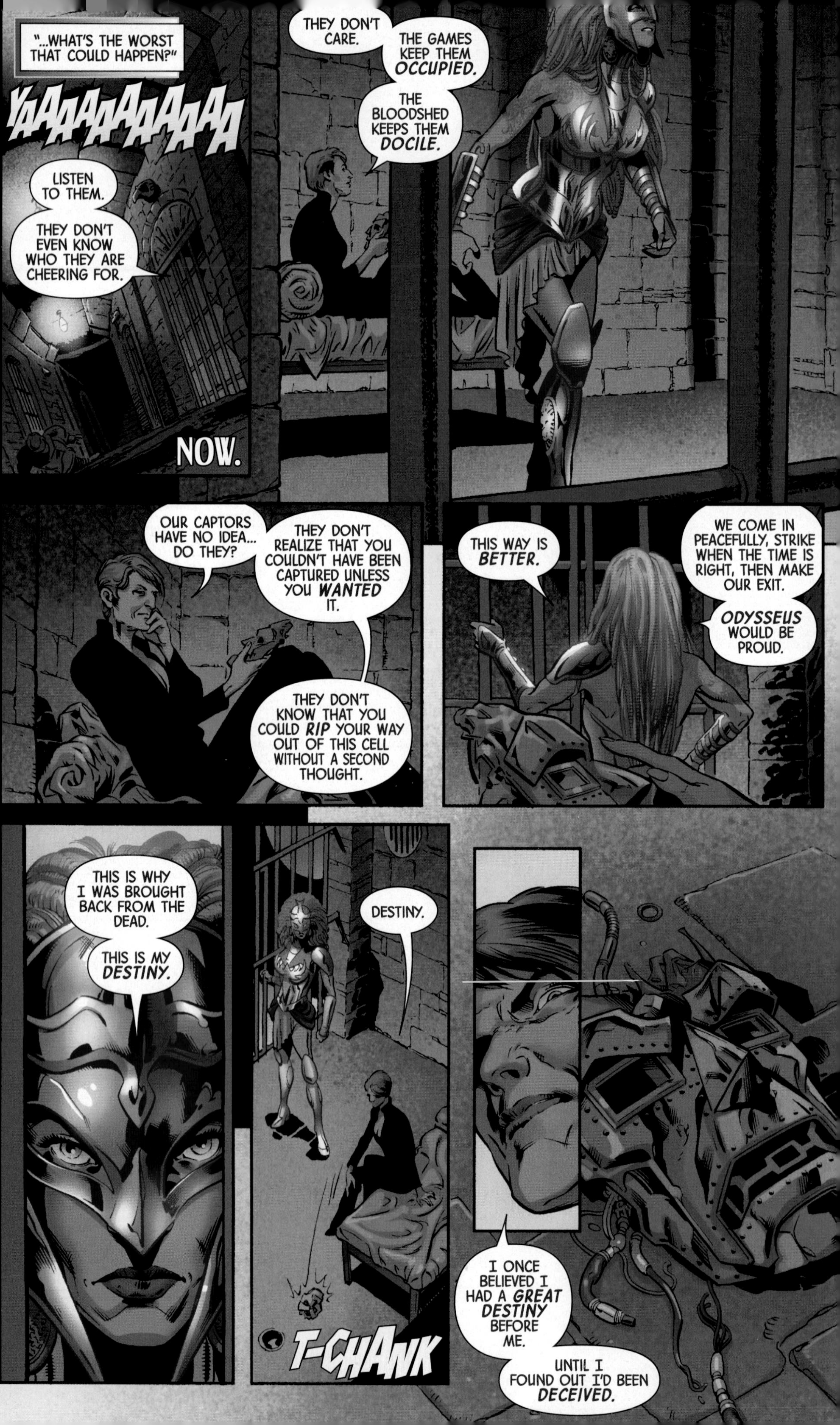

"...WHAT'S THE WORST THAT COULD HAPPEN?"
YAAAAAAAAAAA
LISTEN TO THEM.
THEY DON'T EVEN KNOW WHO THEY ARE CHEERING FOR.
NOW.
THEY DON'T CARE.
THE GAMES KEEP THEM OCCUPIED.
THE BLOODSHED KEEPS THEM DOCILE.
OUR CAPTORS HAVE NO IDEA... DO THEY?
THEY DON'T REALIZE THAT YOU COULDN'T HAVE BEEN CAPTURED UNLESS YOU WANTED IT.
THEY DON'T KNOW THAT YOU COULD RIP YOUR WAY OUT OF THIS CELL WITHOUT A SECOND THOUGHT.
THIS WAY IS BETTER.
WE COME IN PEACEFULLY, STRIKE WHEN THE TIME IS RIGHT, THEN MAKE OUR EXIT.
ODYSSEUS WOULD BE PROUD.
THIS IS WHY I WAS BROUGHT BACK FROM THE DEAD.
THIS IS MY DESTINY.
DESTINY.
T-CHANK
I ONCE BELIEVED I HAD A GREAT DESTINY BEFORE ME.
UNTIL I FOUND OUT I'D BEEN DECEIVED.

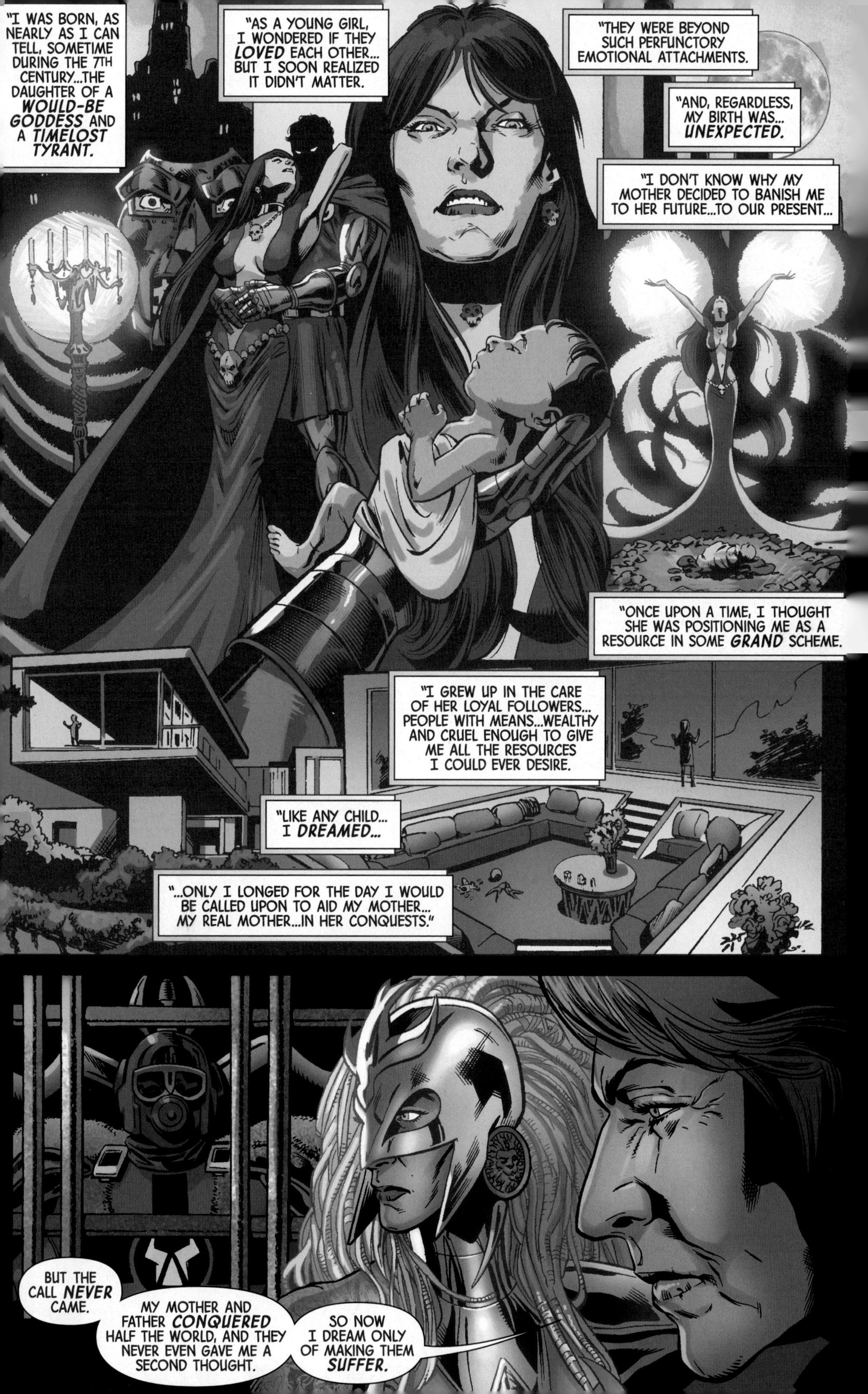
"I WAS BORN, AS NEARLY AS I CAN TELL, SOMETIME DURING THE 7TH CENTURY...THE DAUGHTER OF A WOULD-BE GODDESS AND A TIMELOST TYRANT.
"AS A YOUNG GIRL, I WONDERED IF THEY LOVED EACH OTHER... BUT I SOON REALIZED IT DIDN'T MATTER.
"THEY WERE BEYOND SUCH PERFUNCTORY EMOTIONAL ATTACHMENTS.
"AND, REGARDLESS, MY BIRTH WAS... UNEXPECTED.
"I DON'T KNOW WHY MY MOTHER DECIDED TO BANISH ME TO HER FUTURE...TO OUR PRESENT...
"ONCE UPON A TIME, I THOUGHT SHE WAS POSITIONING ME AS A RESOURCE IN SOME GRAND SCHEME.
"I GREW UP IN THE CARE OF HER LOYAL FOLLOWERS... PEOPLE WITH MEANS...WEALTHY AND CRUEL ENOUGH TO GIVE ME ALL THE RESOURCES I COULD EVER DESIRE.
"LIKE ANY CHILD... I DREAMED...
"...ONLY I LONGED FOR THE DAY I WOULD BE CALLED UPON TO AID MY MOTHER... MY REAL MOTHER...IN HER CONQUESTS."
BUT THE CALL NEVER CAME.
MY MOTHER AND FATHER CONQUERED HALF THE WORLD, AND THEY NEVER EVEN GAVE ME A SECOND THOUGHT.
SO NOW I DREAM ONLY OF MAKING THEM SUFFER.

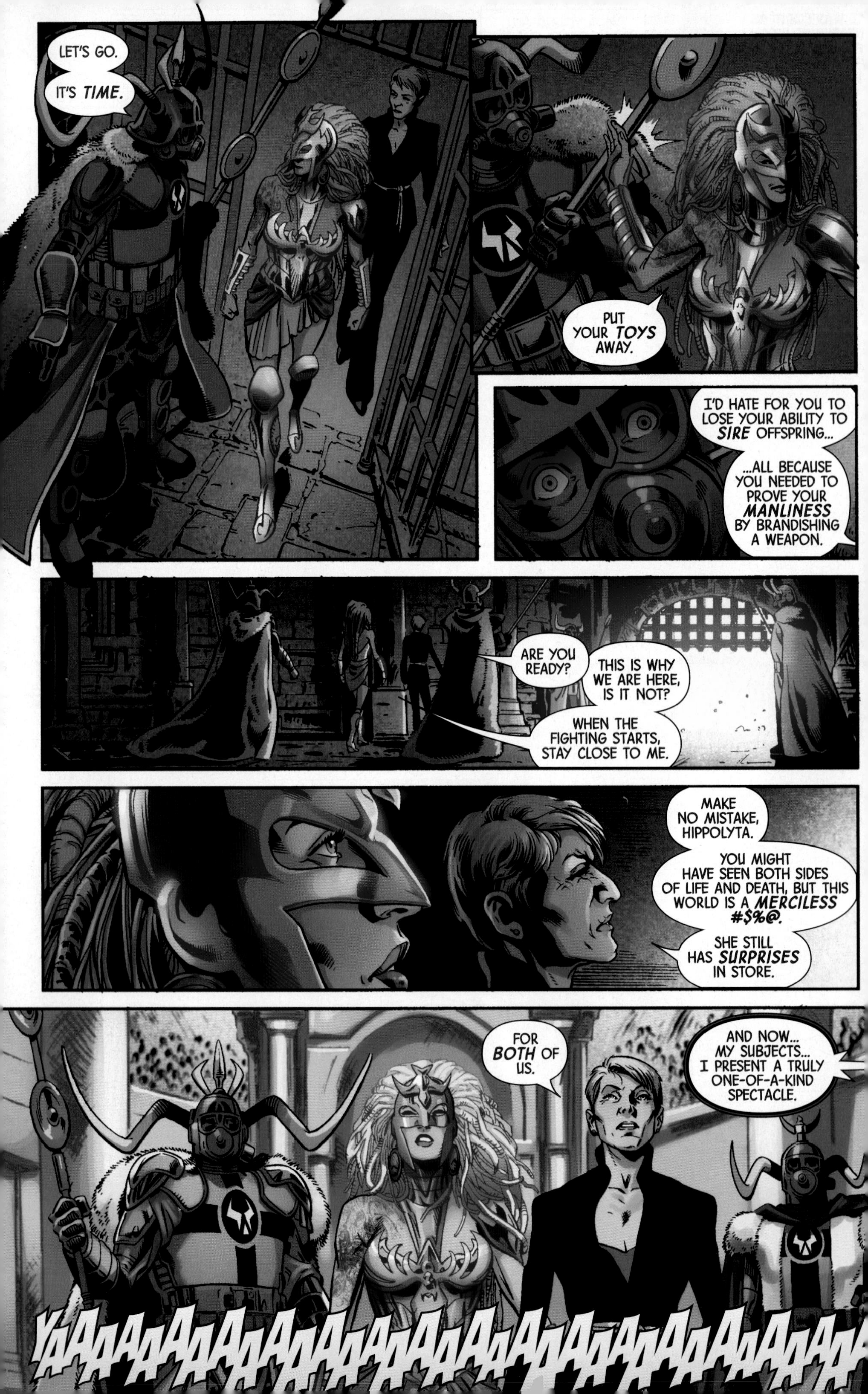
LET'S GO.
IT'S *TIME.*
PUT YOUR *TOYS* AWAY.
I'D HATE FOR YOU TO LOSE YOUR ABILITY TO *SIRE* OFFSPRING...
...ALL BECAUSE YOU NEEDED TO PROVE YOUR *MANLINESS* BY BRANDISHING A WEAPON.
ARE YOU READY?
THIS IS WHY WE ARE HERE, IS IT NOT?
WHEN THE FIGHTING STARTS, STAY CLOSE TO ME.
MAKE NO MISTAKE, HIPPOLYTA.
YOU MIGHT HAVE SEEN BOTH SIDES OF LIFE AND DEATH, BUT THIS WORLD IS A *MERCILESS* #$%@.
SHE STILL HAS *SURPRISES* IN STORE.
FOR *BOTH* OF US.
AND NOW... MY SUBJECTS... I PRESENT A TRULY ONE-OF-A-KIND SPECTACLE.
YAAAAAAAAAAAAAAAAAAAAAAAAAAAA

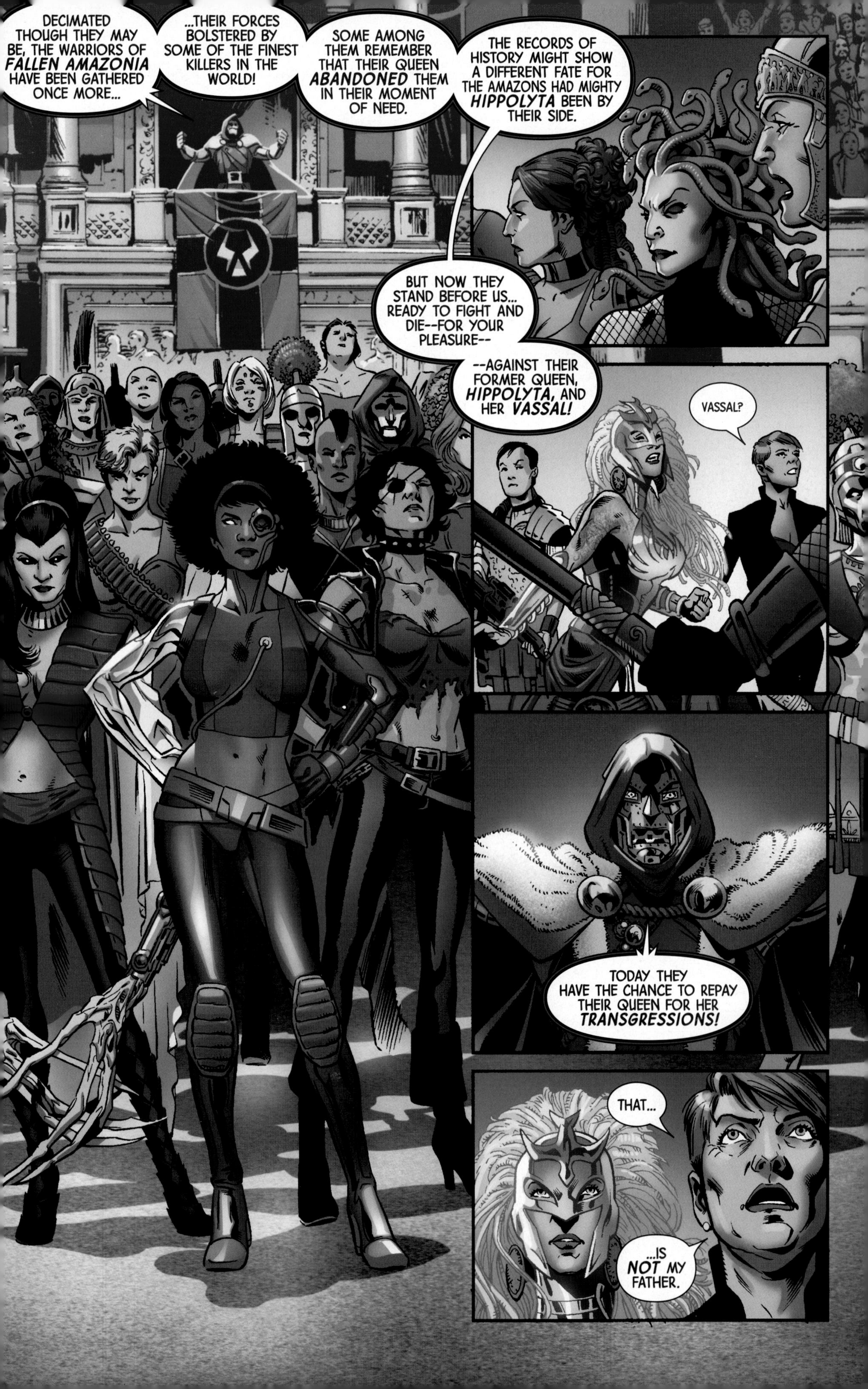
DECIMATED THOUGH THEY MAY BE, THE WARRIORS OF FALLEN AMAZONIA HAVE BEEN GATHERED ONCE MORE...
...THEIR FORCES BOLSTERED BY SOME OF THE FINEST KILLERS IN THE WORLD!
SOME AMONG THEM REMEMBER THAT THEIR QUEEN ABANDONED THEM IN THEIR MOMENT OF NEED.
THE RECORDS OF HISTORY MIGHT SHOW A DIFFERENT FATE FOR THE AMAZONS HAD MIGHTY HIPPOLYTA BEEN BY THEIR SIDE.
BUT NOW THEY STAND BEFORE US... READY TO FIGHT AND DIE--FOR YOUR PLEASURE--
--AGAINST THEIR FORMER QUEEN, HIPPOLYTA, AND HER VASSAL!
VASSAL?
TODAY THEY HAVE THE CHANCE TO REPAY THEIR QUEEN FOR HER TRANSGRESSIONS!
THAT...
...IS NOT MY FATHER.

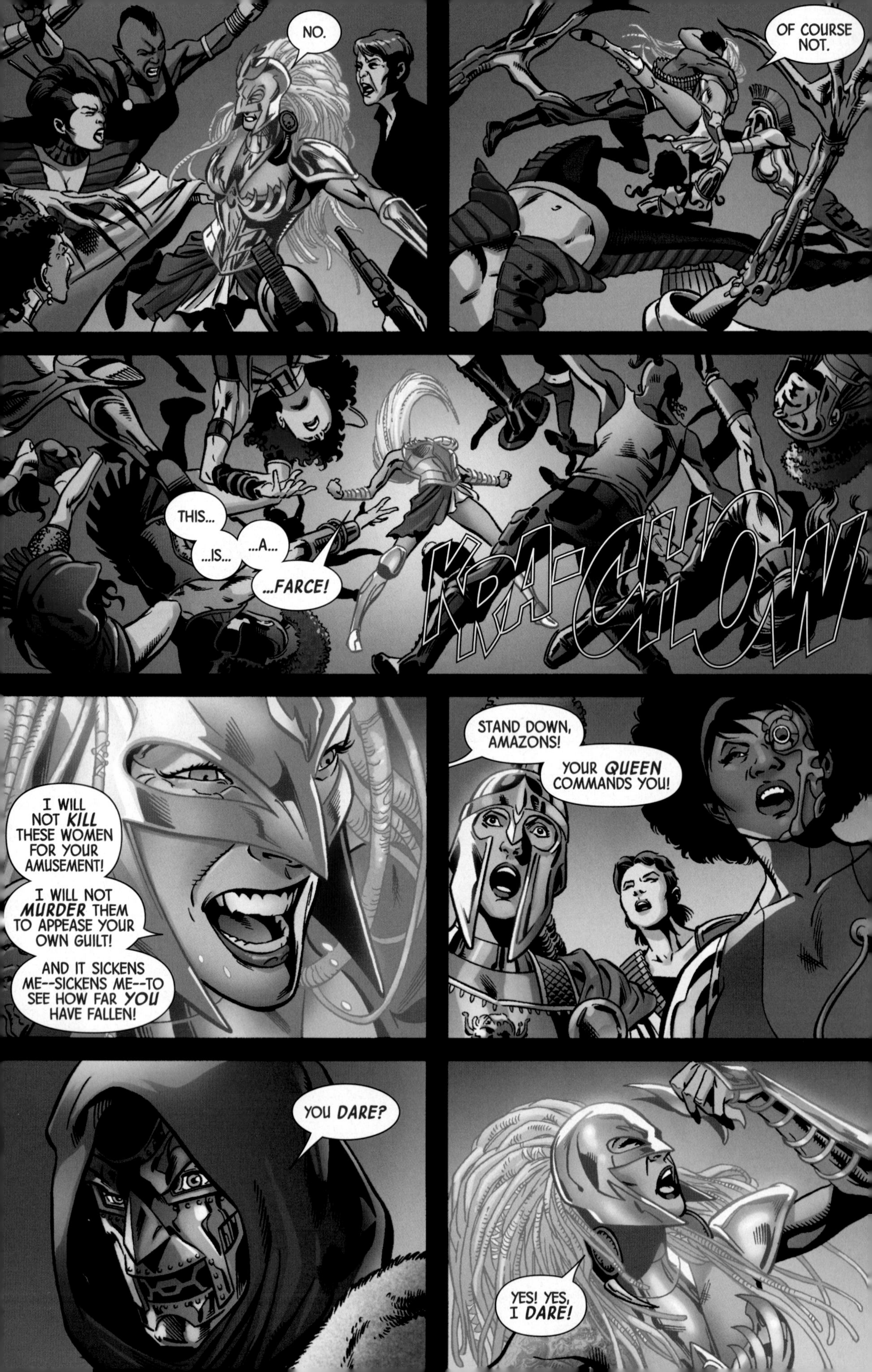
NO.
OF COURSE NOT.
THIS...
...IS...
...A...
...FARCE!
KRA-CHOW
I WILL NOT KILL THESE WOMEN FOR YOUR AMUSEMENT!
I WILL NOT MURDER THEM TO APPEASE YOUR OWN GUILT!
AND IT SICKENS ME--SICKENS ME--TO SEE HOW FAR YOU HAVE FALLEN!
STAND DOWN, AMAZONS!
YOUR QUEEN COMMANDS YOU!
YOU DARE?
YES! YES, I DARE!

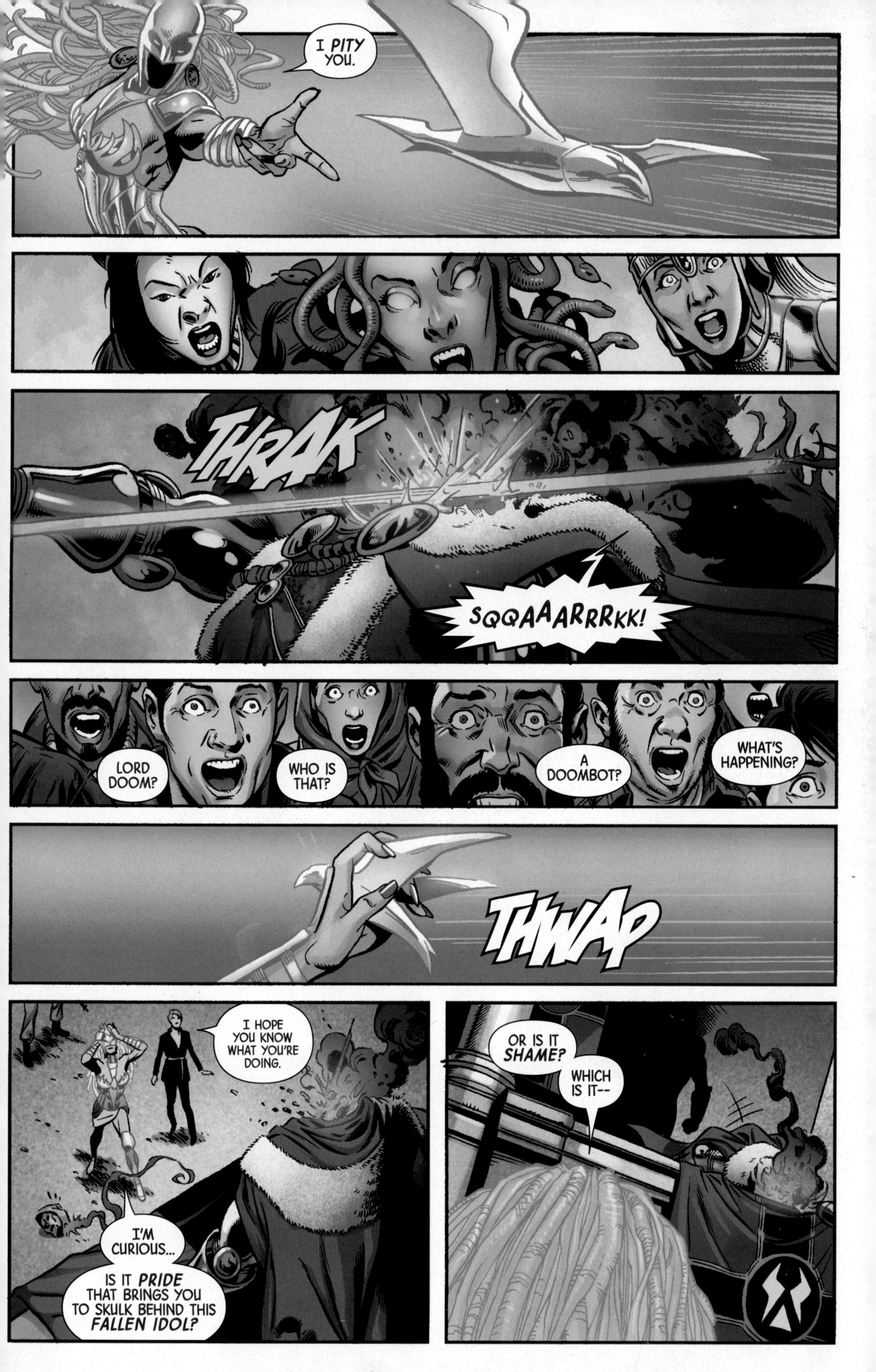
I PITY YOU.
THRAK
SQQAAARRRKK!
LORD DOOM?
WHO IS THAT?
A DOOMBOT?
WHAT'S HAPPENING?
THWAP
I HOPE YOU KNOW WHAT YOU'RE DOING.
I'M CURIOUS...
IS IT PRIDE THAT BRINGS YOU TO SKULK BEHIND THIS FALLEN IDOL?
OR IS IT SHAME?
WHICH IS IT--

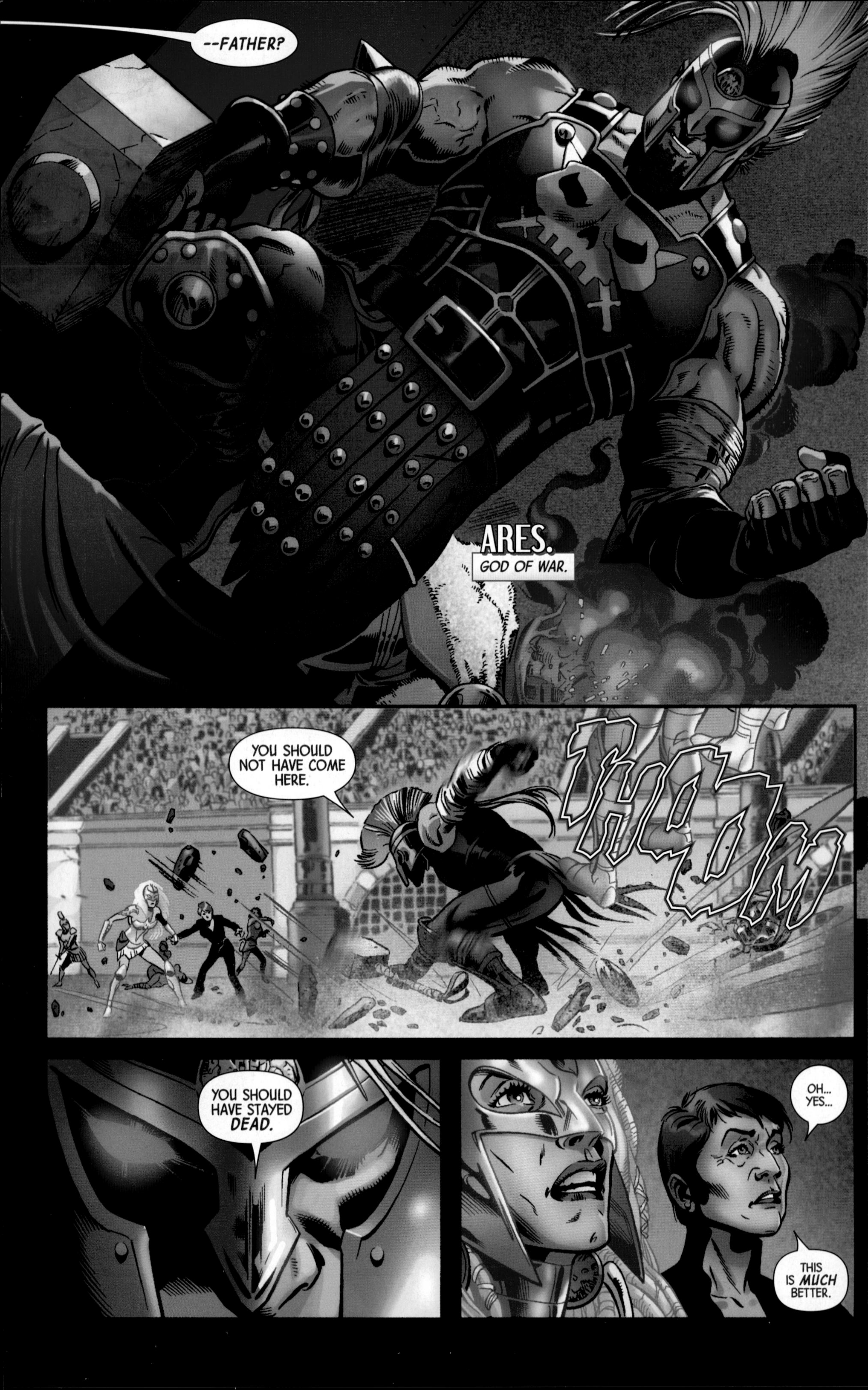
--FATHER?
ARES.
GOD OF WAR.
YOU SHOULD NOT HAVE COME HERE.
THOOM
YOU SHOULD HAVE STAYED DEAD.
OH... YES...
THIS IS MUCH BETTER.

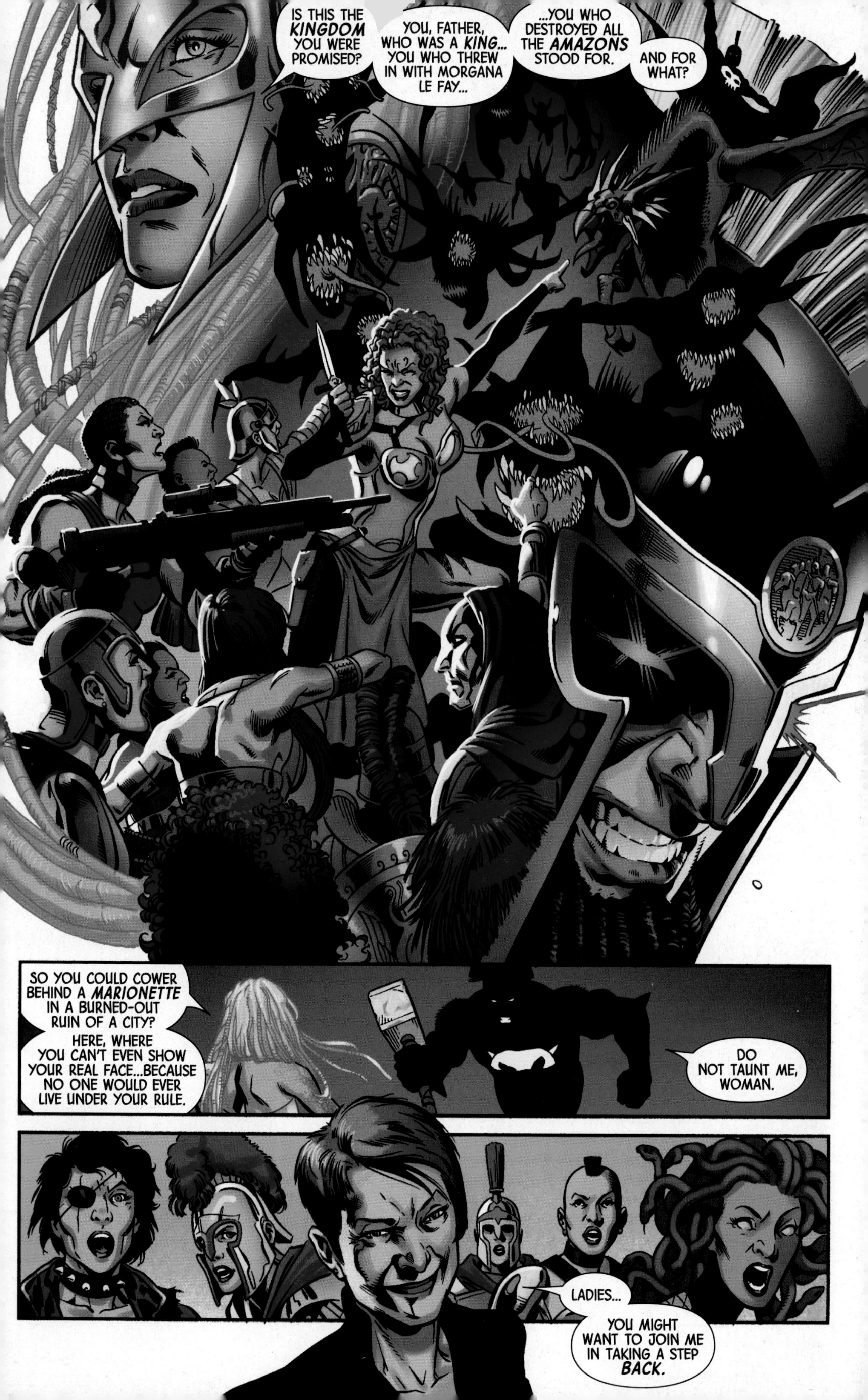
IS THIS THE KINGDOM YOU WERE PROMISED?
YOU, FATHER, WHO WAS A KING... YOU WHO THREW IN WITH MORGANA LE FAY...
...YOU WHO DESTROYED ALL THE AMAZONS STOOD FOR.
AND FOR WHAT?
SO YOU COULD COWER BEHIND A MARIONETTE IN A BURNED-OUT RUIN OF A CITY?
HERE, WHERE YOU CAN'T EVEN SHOW YOUR REAL FACE...BECAUSE NO ONE WOULD EVER LIVE UNDER YOUR RULE.
DO NOT TAUNT ME, WOMAN.
LADIES...
YOU MIGHT WANT TO JOIN ME IN TAKING A STEP BACK.

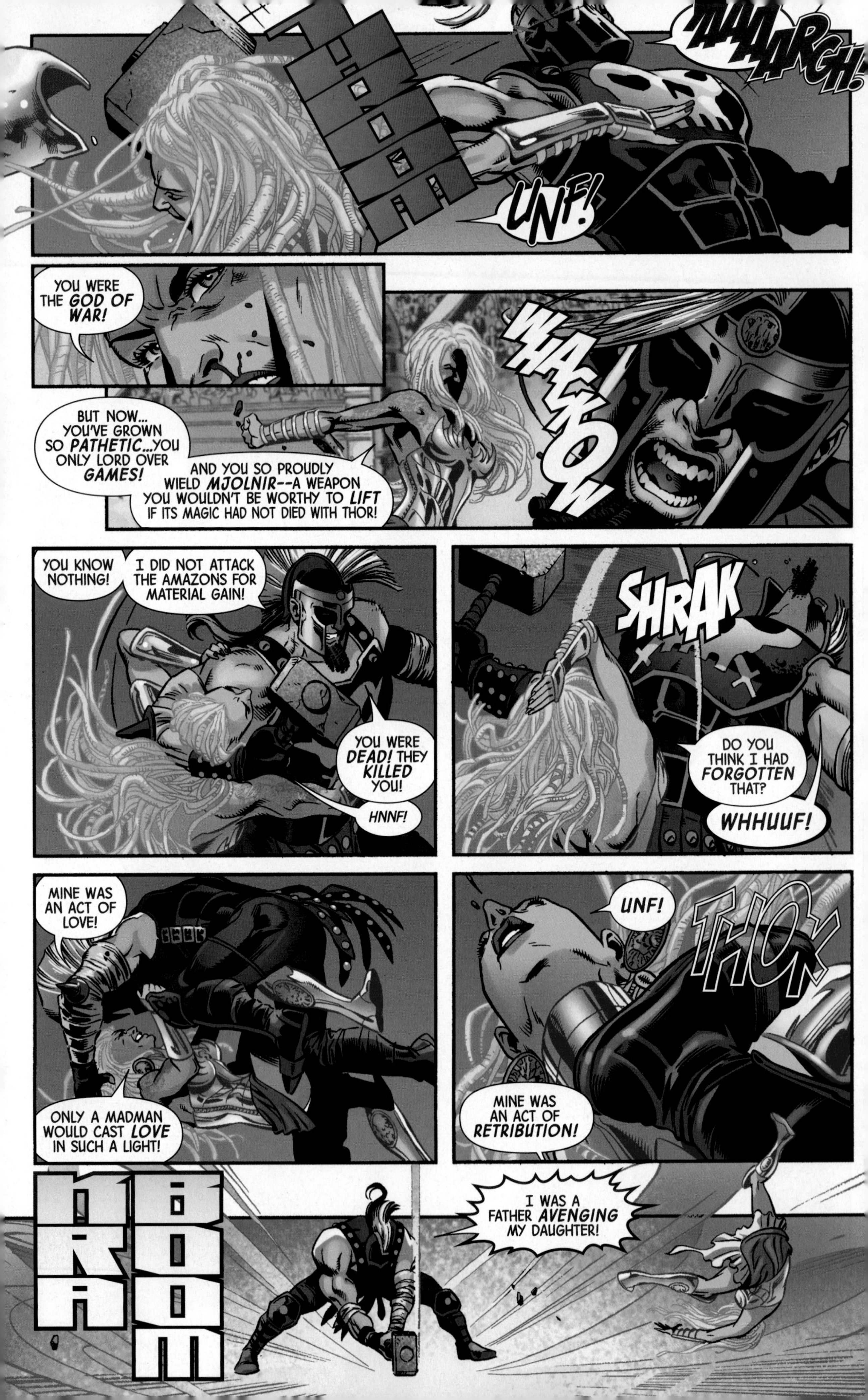
AAAARGH!
THOOOM
UNF!
YOU WERE THE GOD OF WAR!
WHAKOW
BUT NOW... YOU'VE GROWN SO PATHETIC...YOU ONLY LORD OVER GAMES!
AND YOU SO PROUDLY WIELD MJOLNIR--A WEAPON YOU WOULDN'T BE WORTHY TO LIFT IF ITS MAGIC HAD NOT DIED WITH THOR!
YOU KNOW NOTHING!
I DID NOT ATTACK THE AMAZONS FOR MATERIAL GAIN!
YOU WERE DEAD! THEY KILLED YOU!
HNNF!
SHRAK
DO YOU THINK I HAD FORGOTTEN THAT?
WHHUUF!
MINE WAS AN ACT OF LOVE!
ONLY A MADMAN WOULD CAST LOVE IN SUCH A LIGHT!
UNF!
THOK
MINE WAS AN ACT OF RETRIBUTION!
KRA-BOOM
I WAS A FATHER AVENGING MY DAUGHTER!

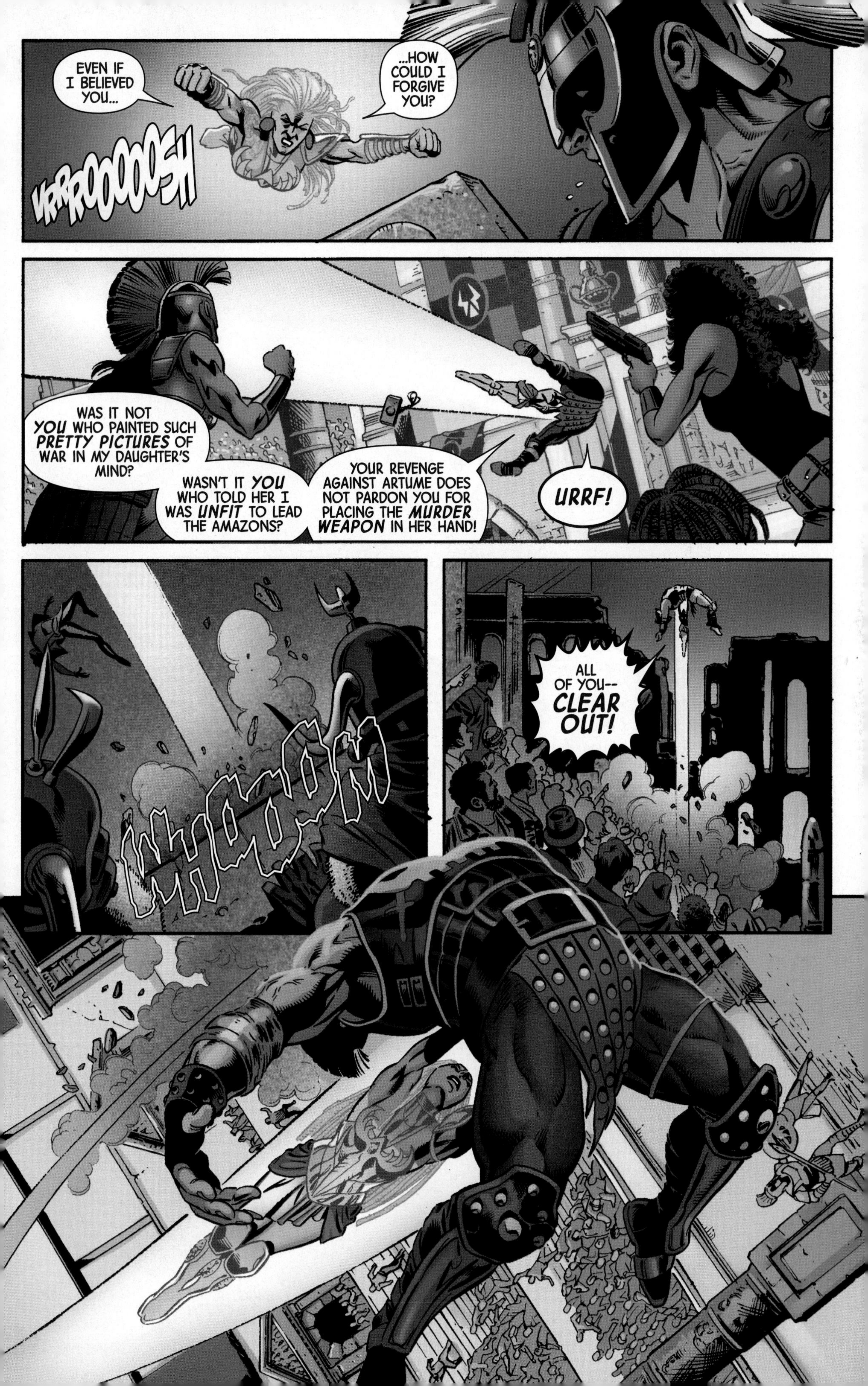
EVEN IF I BELIEVED YOU...
...HOW COULD I FORGIVE YOU?
VRRROOOOOSH
WAS IT NOT YOU WHO PAINTED SUCH PRETTY PICTURES OF WAR IN MY DAUGHTER'S MIND?
WASN'T IT YOU WHO TOLD HER I WAS UNFIT TO LEAD THE AMAZONS?
YOUR REVENGE AGAINST ARTUME DOES NOT PARDON YOU FOR PLACING THE MURDER WEAPON IN HER HAND!
URRF!
WHOOOM
ALL OF YOU-- CLEAR OUT!

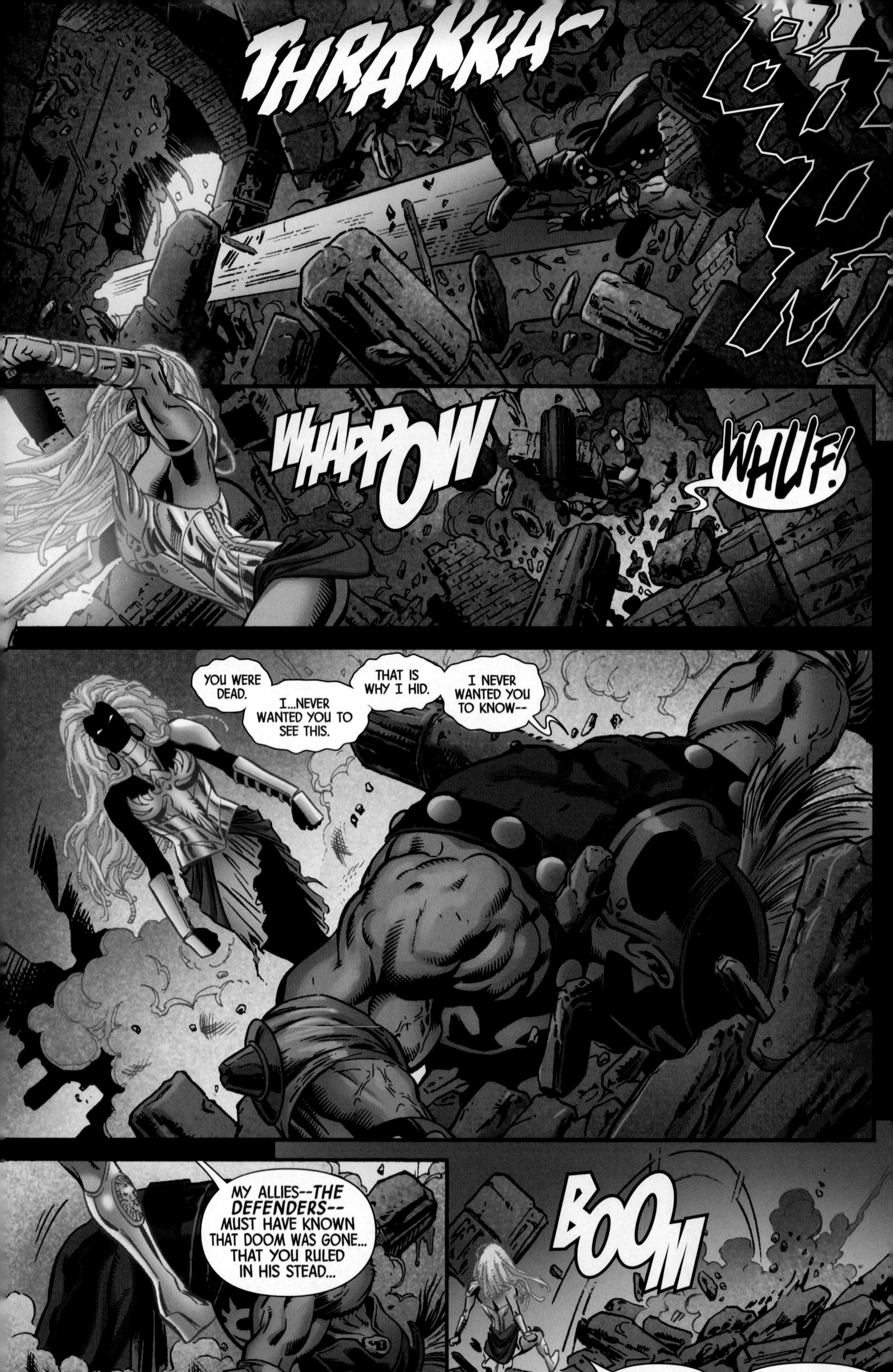
THRAKKA-
WHAPPOW
WHUF!
YOU WERE DEAD.
I...NEVER WANTED YOU TO SEE THIS.
THAT IS WHY I HID.
I NEVER WANTED YOU TO KNOW--
MY ALLIES--THE DEFENDERS-- MUST HAVE KNOWN THAT DOOM WAS GONE... THAT YOU RULED IN HIS STEAD...
BOOM
...YET THEY
YOU, ON

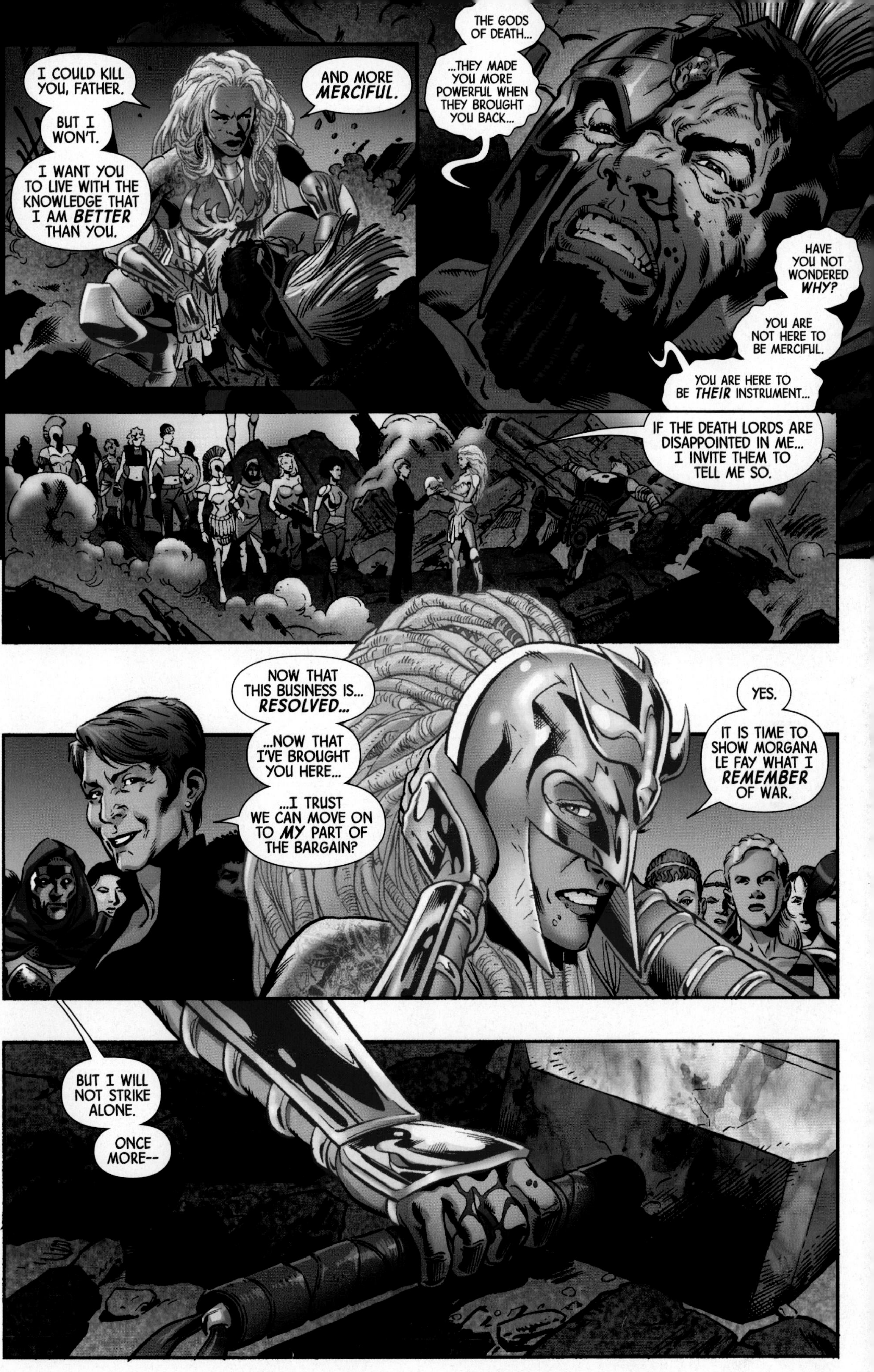
I COULD KILL YOU, FATHER.
BUT I WON'T.
I WANT YOU TO LIVE WITH THE KNOWLEDGE THAT I AM *BETTER* THAN YOU.
AND MORE *MERCIFUL.*
THE GODS OF DEATH...
...THEY MADE YOU MORE POWERFUL WHEN THEY BROUGHT YOU BACK...
HAVE YOU NOT WONDERED *WHY?*
YOU ARE NOT HERE TO BE MERCIFUL.
YOU ARE HERE TO BE *THEIR* INSTRUMENT...
IF THE DEATH LORDS ARE DISAPPOINTED IN ME... I INVITE THEM TO TELL ME SO.
NOW THAT THIS BUSINESS IS... *RESOLVED...*
...NOW THAT I'VE BROUGHT YOU HERE...
...I TRUST WE CAN MOVE ON TO *MY* PART OF THE BARGAIN?
YES.
IT IS TIME TO SHOW MORGANA LE FAY WHAT I *REMEMBER* OF WAR.
BUT I WILL NOT STRIKE ALONE.
ONCE MORE--

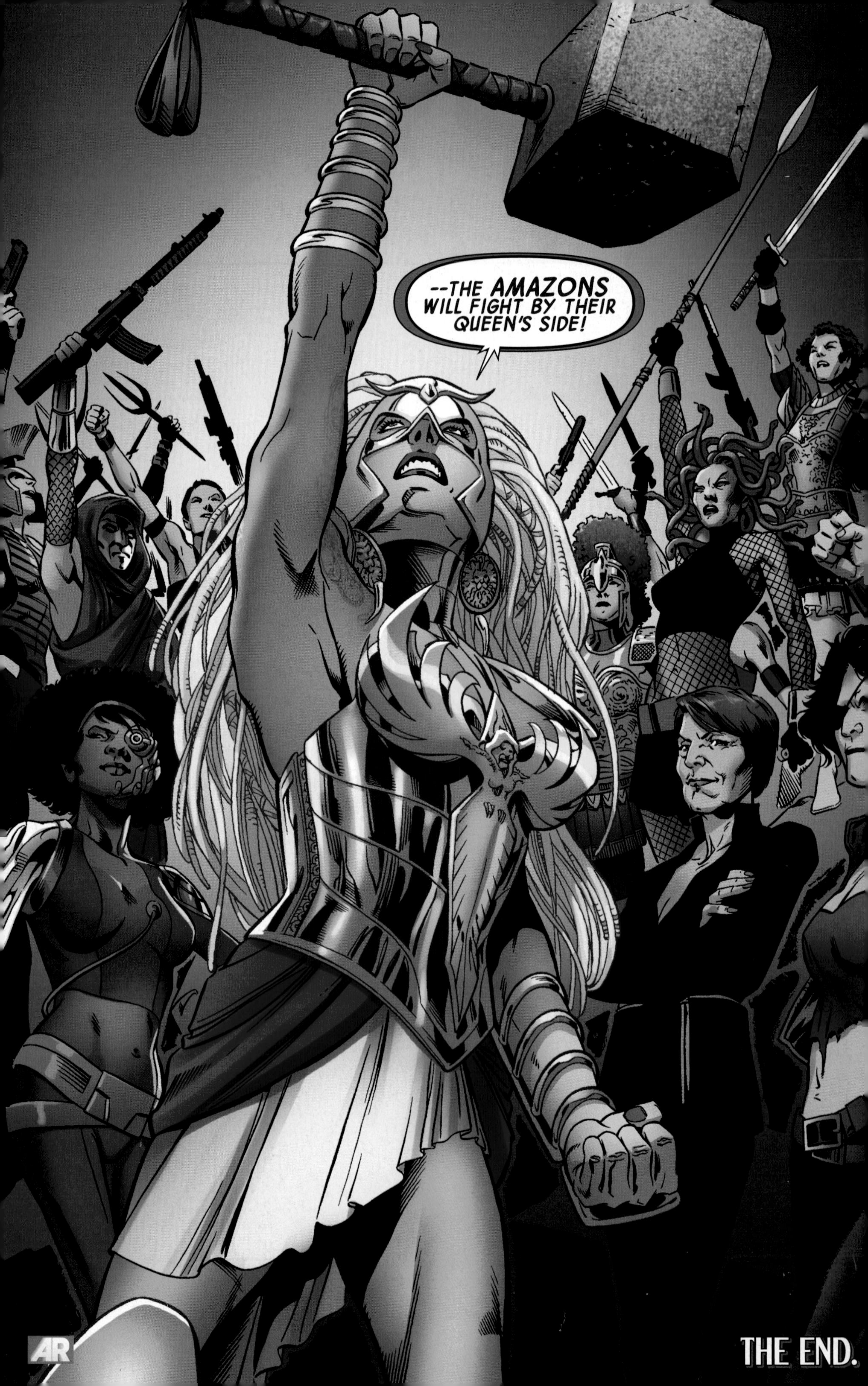
--THE AMAZONS WILL FIGHT BY THEIR QUEEN'S SIDE!
THE END.

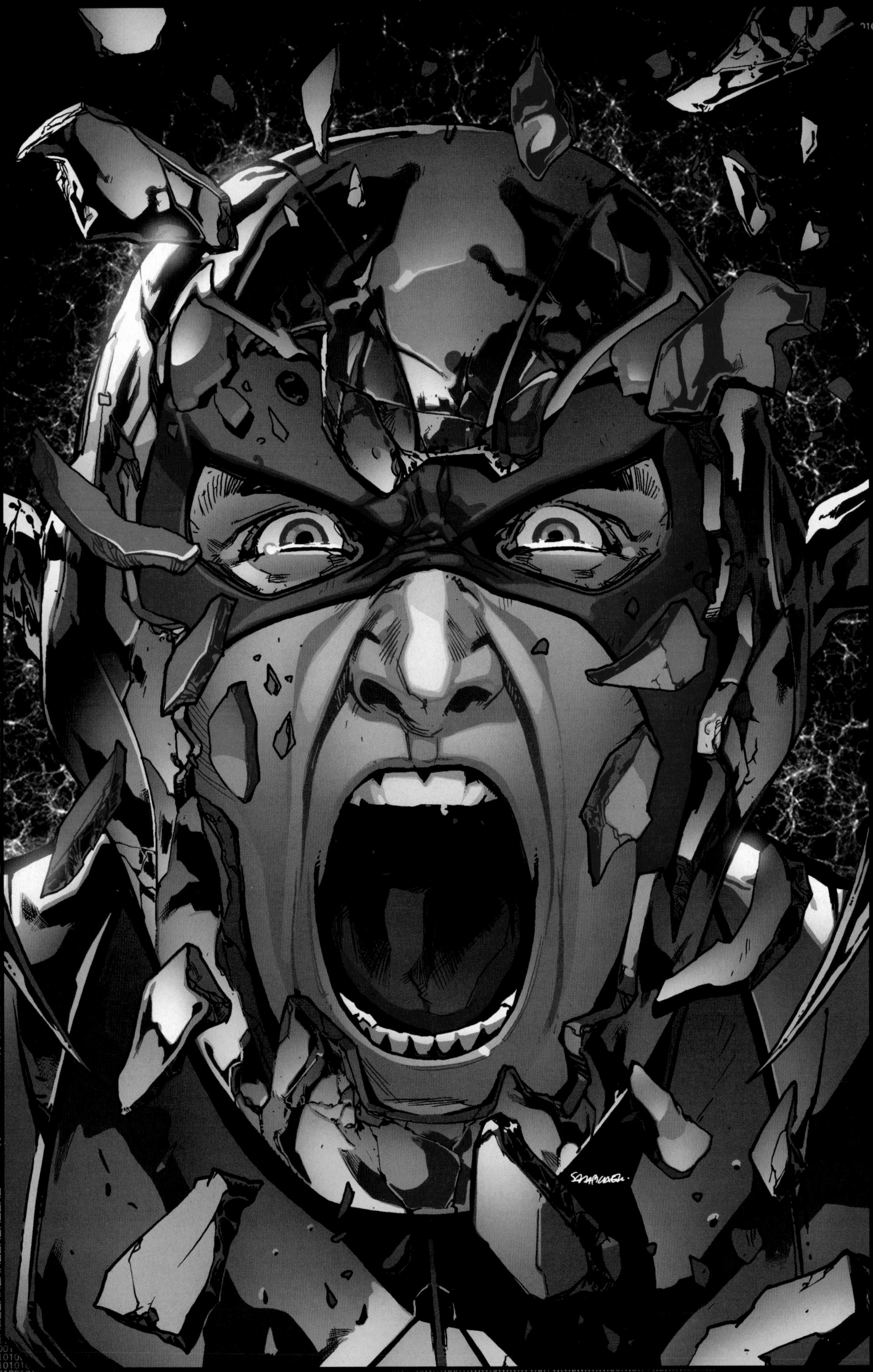

AGE OF ULTRON #10AI

MY NAME IS *DR. HENRY PYM.* I DISCOVERED HOW TO SHRINK AND ENLARGE *MATTER* AND, SO, NATURALLY PUT ON A COSTUME TO FIGHT *CRIME.*

I WILL EXPLAIN SHORTLY WHY THAT MADE SENSE.

ACTUALLY, SEVERAL *COSTUMES.* SEVERAL *IDENTITIES* OVER THE YEARS:

YELLOWJACKET. GOLIATH. GIANT-MAN.

ANT-MAN.

AND BECAUSE MY MENTAL STATE HAS HISTORICALLY BEEN ABOUT AS STABLE AS MY *WARDROBE,* MY FELLOW *AVENGERS* TREAT ME LIKE I'M MADE OF *GLASS.* THEY WONDER WHEN I'M GOING TO *CRACK.*

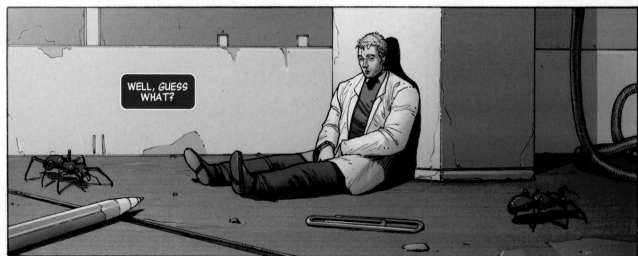

WELL, GUESS WHAT?

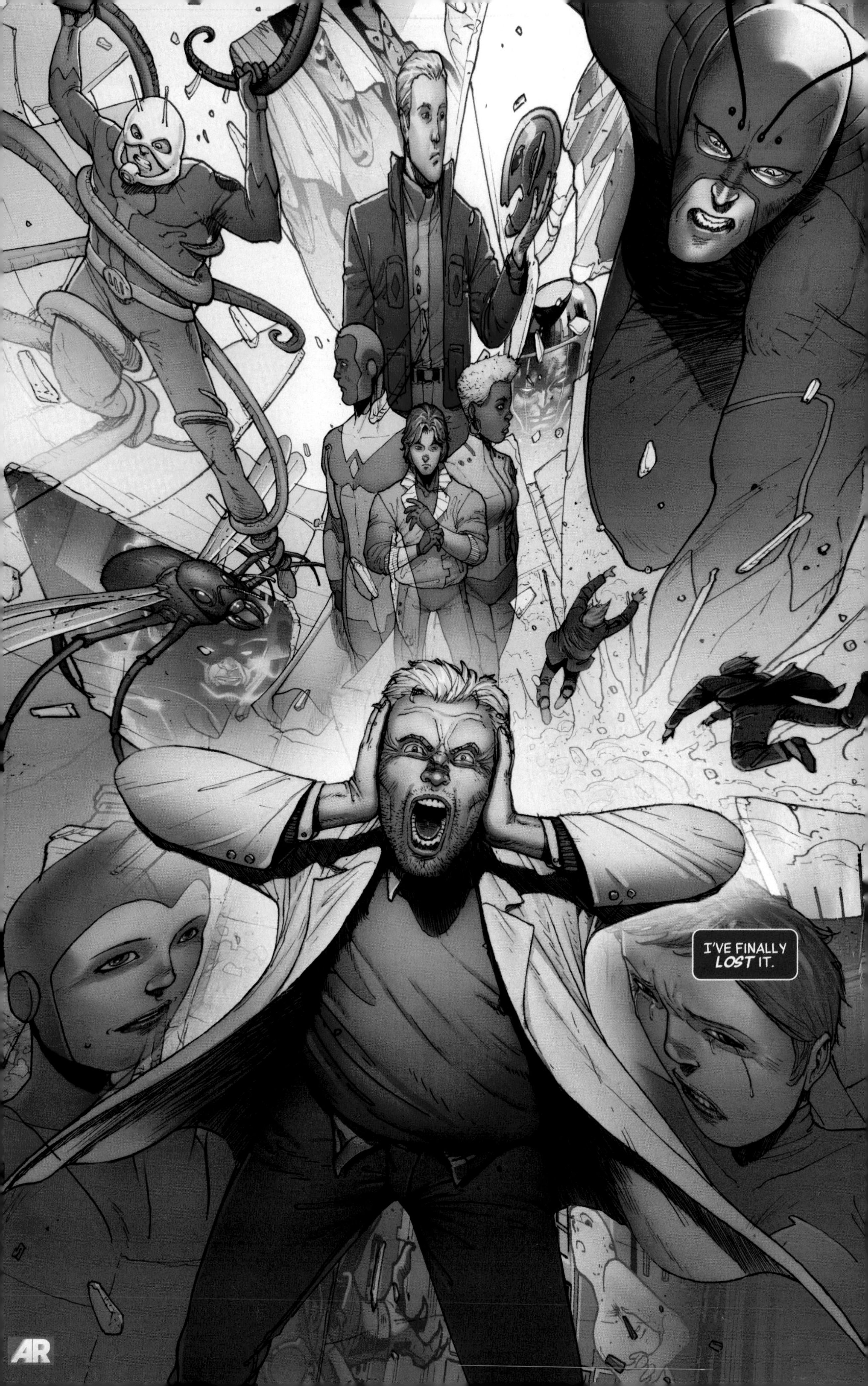
I'VE FINALLY LOST IT.

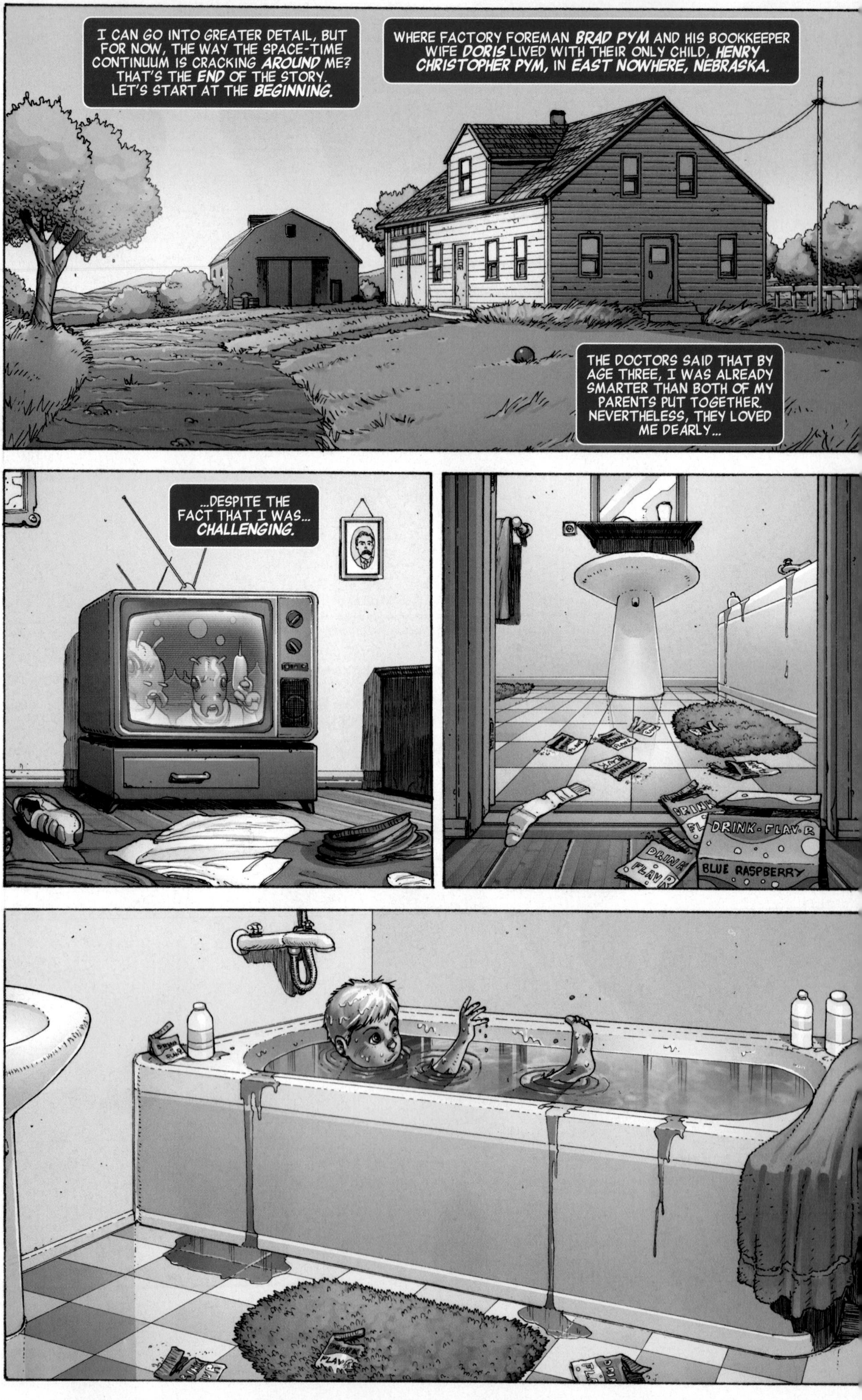
I CAN GO INTO GREATER DETAIL, BUT FOR NOW, THE WAY THE SPACE-TIME CONTINUUM IS CRACKING AROUND ME? THAT'S THE END OF THE STORY. LET'S START AT THE BEGINNING.
WHERE FACTORY FOREMAN BRAD PYM AND HIS BOOKKEEPER WIFE DORIS LIVED WITH THEIR ONLY CHILD, HENRY CHRISTOPHER PYM, IN EAST NOWHERE, NEBRASKA.
THE DOCTORS SAID THAT BY AGE THREE, I WAS ALREADY SMARTER THAN BOTH OF MY PARENTS PUT TOGETHER. NEVERTHELESS, THEY LOVED ME DEARLY...
...DESPITE THE FACT THAT I WAS... CHALLENGING.
DRINK-FLAV-R
BLUE RASPBERRY

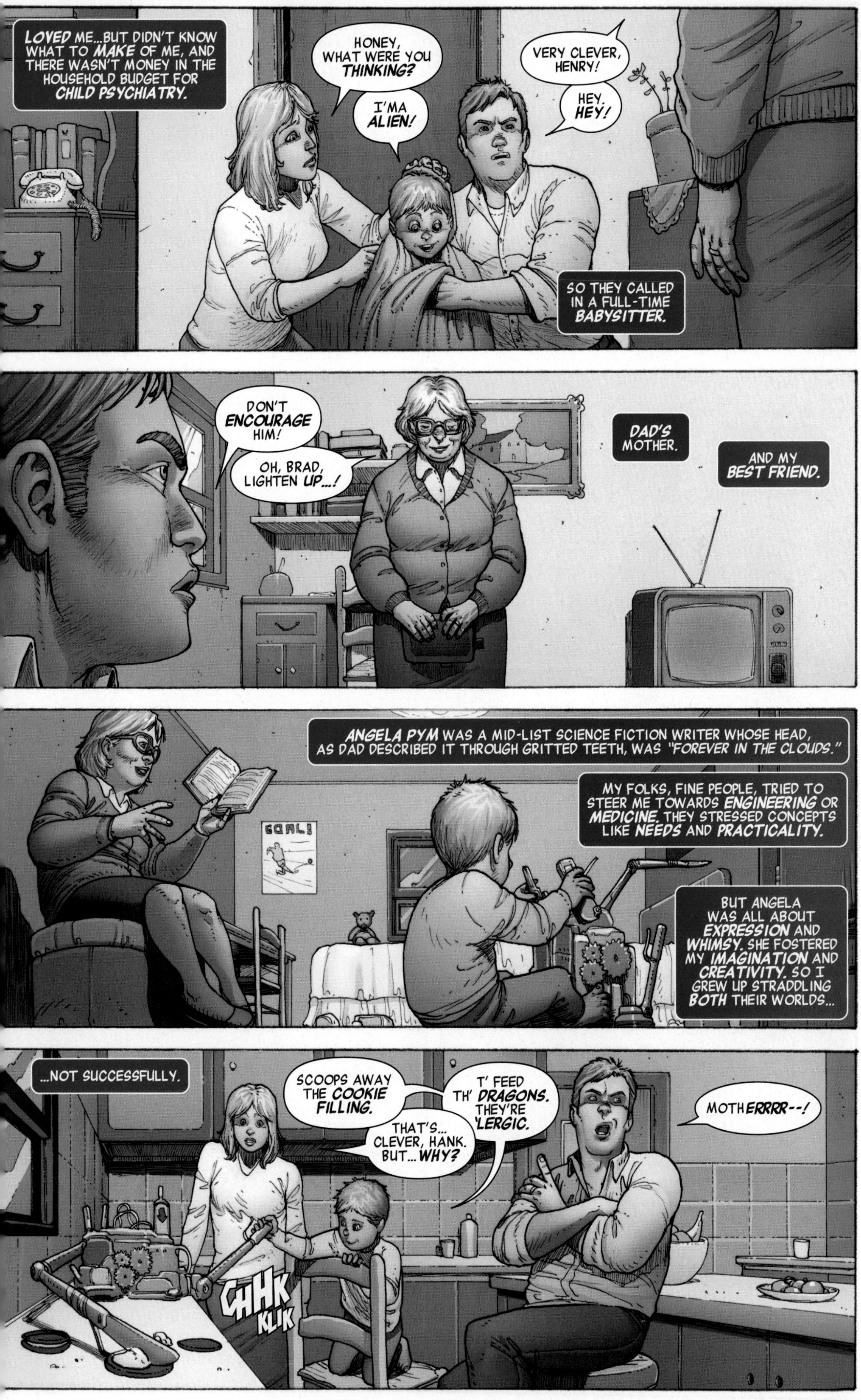
LOVED ME...BUT DIDN'T KNOW WHAT TO MAKE OF ME, AND THERE WASN'T MONEY IN THE HOUSEHOLD BUDGET FOR CHILD PSYCHIATRY.
HONEY, WHAT WERE YOU THINKING?
I'M A ALIEN!
VERY CLEVER, HENRY!
HEY. HEY!
SO THEY CALLED IN A FULL-TIME BABYSITTER.
DON'T ENCOURAGE HIM!
OH, BRAD, LIGHTEN UP...!
DAD'S MOTHER.
AND MY BEST FRIEND.
ANGELA PYM WAS A MID-LIST SCIENCE FICTION WRITER WHOSE HEAD, AS DAD DESCRIBED IT THROUGH GRITTED TEETH, WAS "FOREVER IN THE CLOUDS."
MY FOLKS, FINE PEOPLE, TRIED TO STEER ME TOWARDS ENGINEERING OR MEDICINE. THEY STRESSED CONCEPTS LIKE NEEDS AND PRACTICALITY.
GOAL!
BUT ANGELA WAS ALL ABOUT EXPRESSION AND WHIMSY. SHE FOSTERED MY IMAGINATION AND CREATIVITY. SO I GREW UP STRADDLING BOTH THEIR WORLDS...
...NOT SUCCESSFULLY.
SCOOPS AWAY THE COOKIE FILLING.
T' FEED TH' DRAGONS. THEY'RE 'LERGIC.
THAT'S... CLEVER, HANK. BUT... WHY?
MOTHERRRR--!
CHHK
KLIK

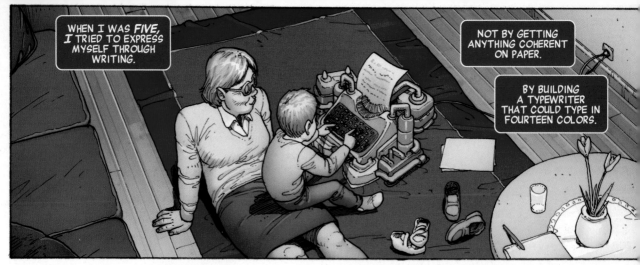

WHEN I WAS *FIVE*, I TRIED TO EXPRESS MYSELF THROUGH WRITING.

NOT BY GETTING ANYTHING COHERENT ON PAPER.

BY BUILDING A TYPEWRITER THAT COULD TYPE IN FOURTEEN COLORS.

NO, HANK, I DON'T NEED A GIZMO THAT WILL LET ME PICK THE SOUND OF MY *HORN.*

I NEED A NEW *CARBURETOR.* WHY CAN'T YOU BUILD ONE OF *THOSE?*

ANYBODY CAN DO *THAT.*

NOT...

KAKLUNGG

...NOT *ALL* OF US...

HANK, SON, KNOCK IT OFF WITH THE *TOYS!* MAKE SOMETHING *SENSIBLE!* WE'LL BE *RICH!*

WE ALREADY ARE. RIGHT, KIDDO?

I HAVE NO COMPLAINTS.

BY THE TIME I HIT *SEVEN*, ANGELA HAD TAUGHT ME TO BE AN *ARTIST.*

NOT WITH PAINT OR WORDS, BUT WITH *WIRES* AND *WELDING TORCHES* AND *CHEMISTRY SETS.*

FOR ALL THE *GOOD* IT DID HER.

...NO...NO, NO, *NO...*

HONEY, SHE'S VERY SICK--

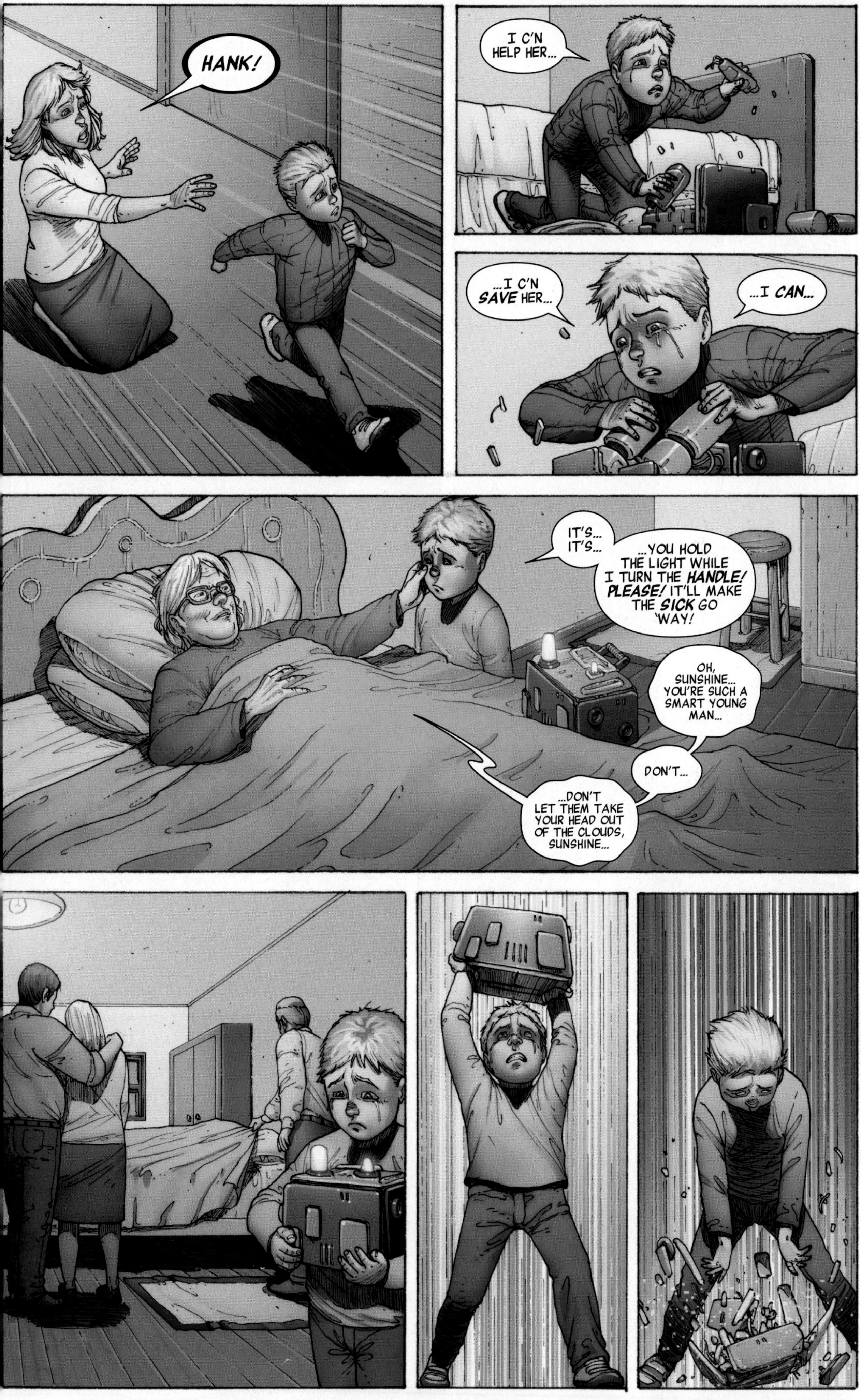
HANK!
I C'N HELP HER...
...I C'N *SAVE* HER...
...I *CAN*...
IT'S... IT'S...
...YOU HOLD THE LIGHT WHILE I TURN THE *HANDLE! PLEASE!* IT'LL MAKE THE *SICK* GO 'WAY!
OH, SUNSHINE... YOU'RE SUCH A SMART YOUNG MAN...
DON'T...
...DON'T LET THEM TAKE YOUR HEAD OUT OF THE CLOUDS, SUNSHINE...

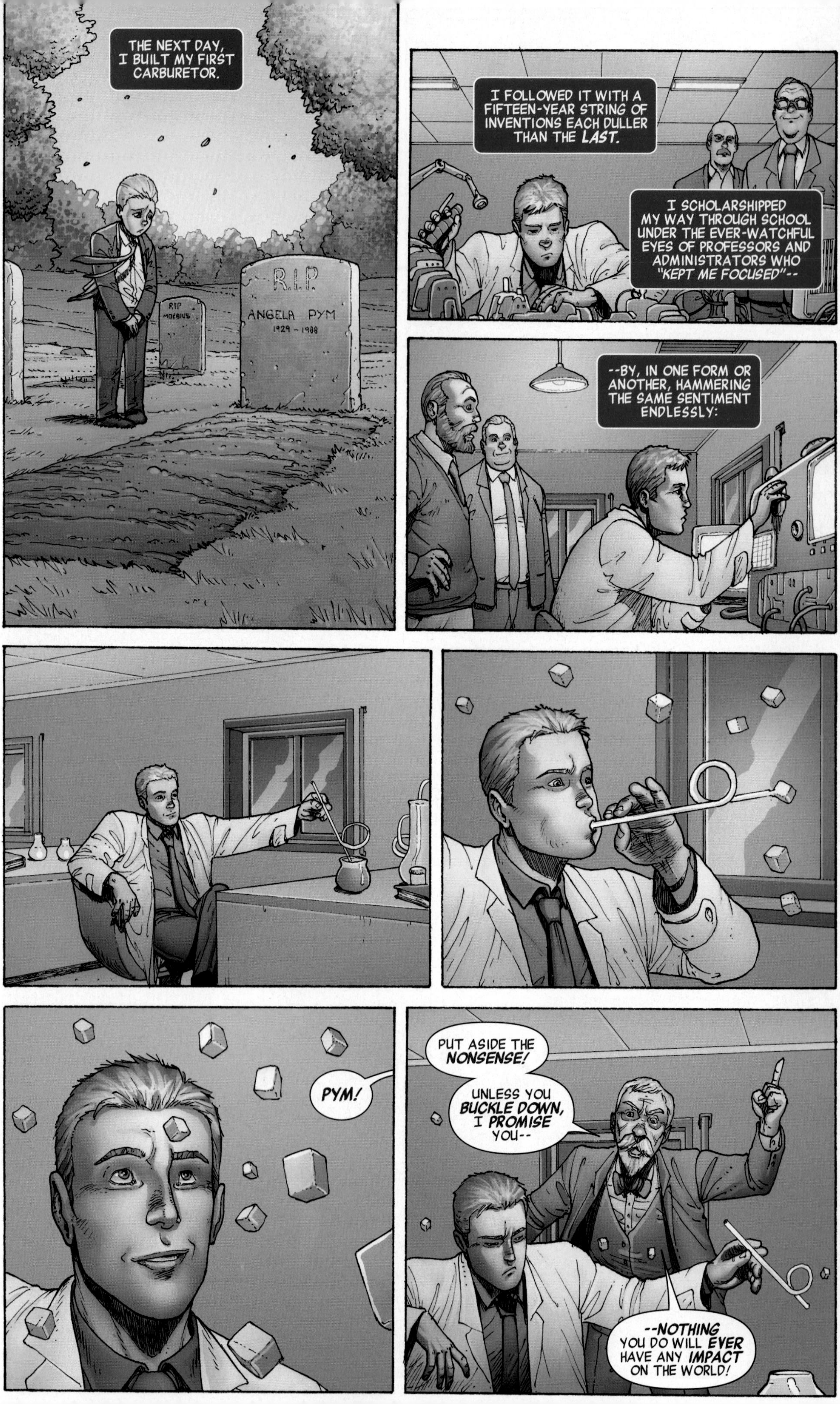
THE NEXT DAY, I BUILT MY FIRST CARBURETOR.
R.I.P.
ANGELA PYM
1929 - 1988
RIP
MOEBIUS
I FOLLOWED IT WITH A FIFTEEN-YEAR STRING OF INVENTIONS EACH DULLER THAN THE *LAST*.
I SCHOLARSHIPPED MY WAY THROUGH SCHOOL UNDER THE EVER-WATCHFUL EYES OF PROFESSORS AND ADMINISTRATORS WHO *"KEPT ME FOCUSED"*--
--BY, IN ONE FORM OR ANOTHER, HAMMERING THE SAME SENTIMENT ENDLESSLY:
PYM!
PUT ASIDE THE *NONSENSE!*
UNLESS YOU *BUCKLE DOWN*, I *PROMISE* YOU--
--*NOTHING* YOU DO WILL *EVER* HAVE ANY *IMPACT* ON THE WORLD!

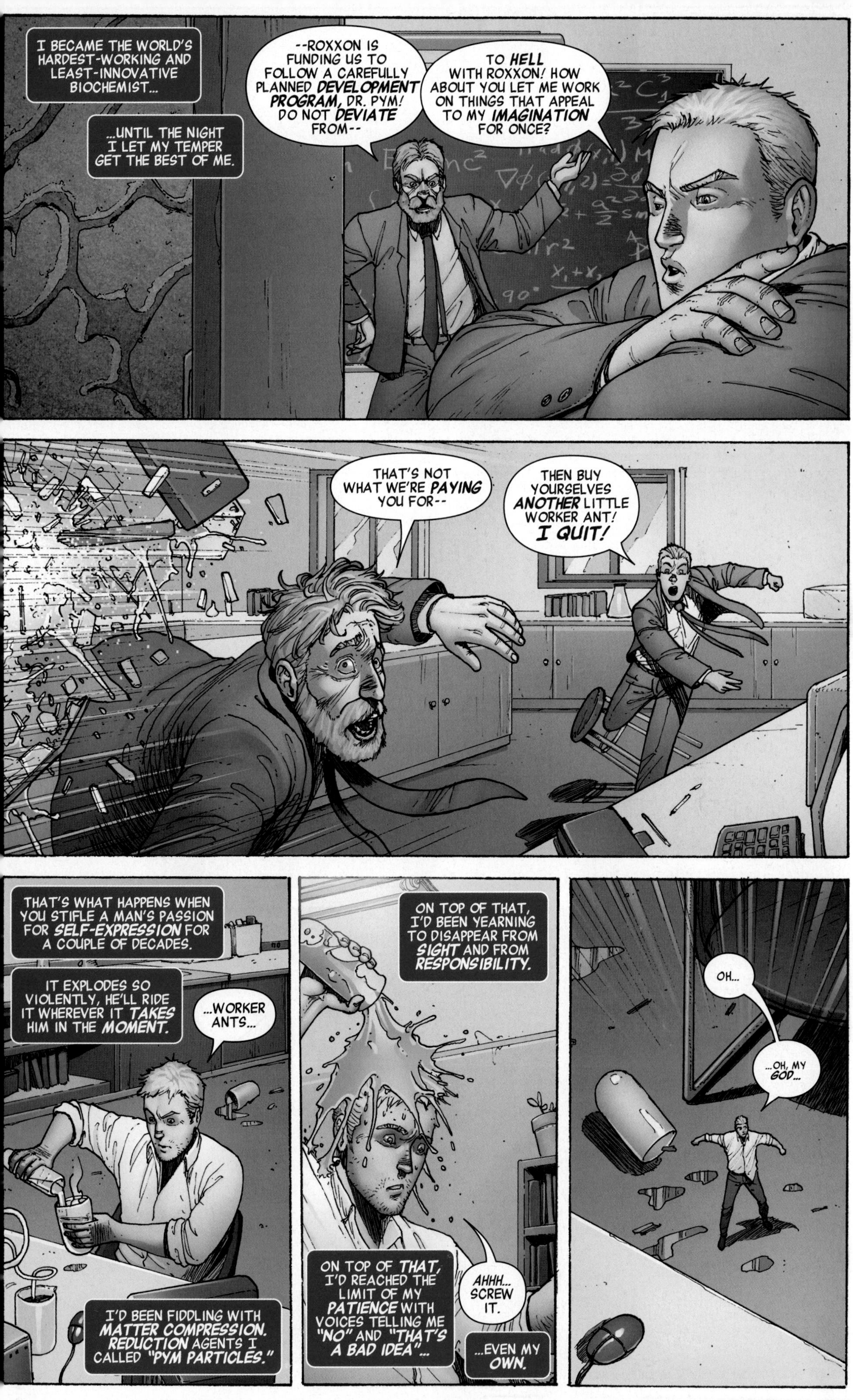
I BECAME THE WORLD'S HARDEST-WORKING AND LEAST-INNOVATIVE BIOCHEMIST...
...UNTIL THE NIGHT I LET MY TEMPER GET THE BEST OF ME.
--ROXXON IS FUNDING US TO FOLLOW A CAREFULLY PLANNED DEVELOPMENT PROGRAM, DR. PYM! DO NOT DEVIATE FROM--
TO HELL WITH ROXXON! HOW ABOUT YOU LET ME WORK ON THINGS THAT APPEAL TO MY IMAGINATION FOR ONCE?
THAT'S NOT WHAT WE'RE PAYING YOU FOR--
THEN BUY YOURSELVES ANOTHER LITTLE WORKER ANT! I QUIT!
THAT'S WHAT HAPPENS WHEN YOU STIFLE A MAN'S PASSION FOR SELF-EXPRESSION FOR A COUPLE OF DECADES.
IT EXPLODES SO VIOLENTLY, HE'LL RIDE IT WHEREVER IT TAKES HIM IN THE MOMENT.
...WORKER ANTS...
I'D BEEN FIDDLING WITH MATTER COMPRESSION. REDUCTION AGENTS I CALLED "PYM PARTICLES."
ON TOP OF THAT, I'D BEEN YEARNING TO DISAPPEAR FROM SIGHT AND FROM RESPONSIBILITY.
ON TOP OF THAT, I'D REACHED THE LIMIT OF MY PATIENCE WITH VOICES TELLING ME "NO" AND "THAT'S A BAD IDEA"...
AHHH... SCREW IT.
...EVEN MY OWN.
OH...
...OH, MY GOD...

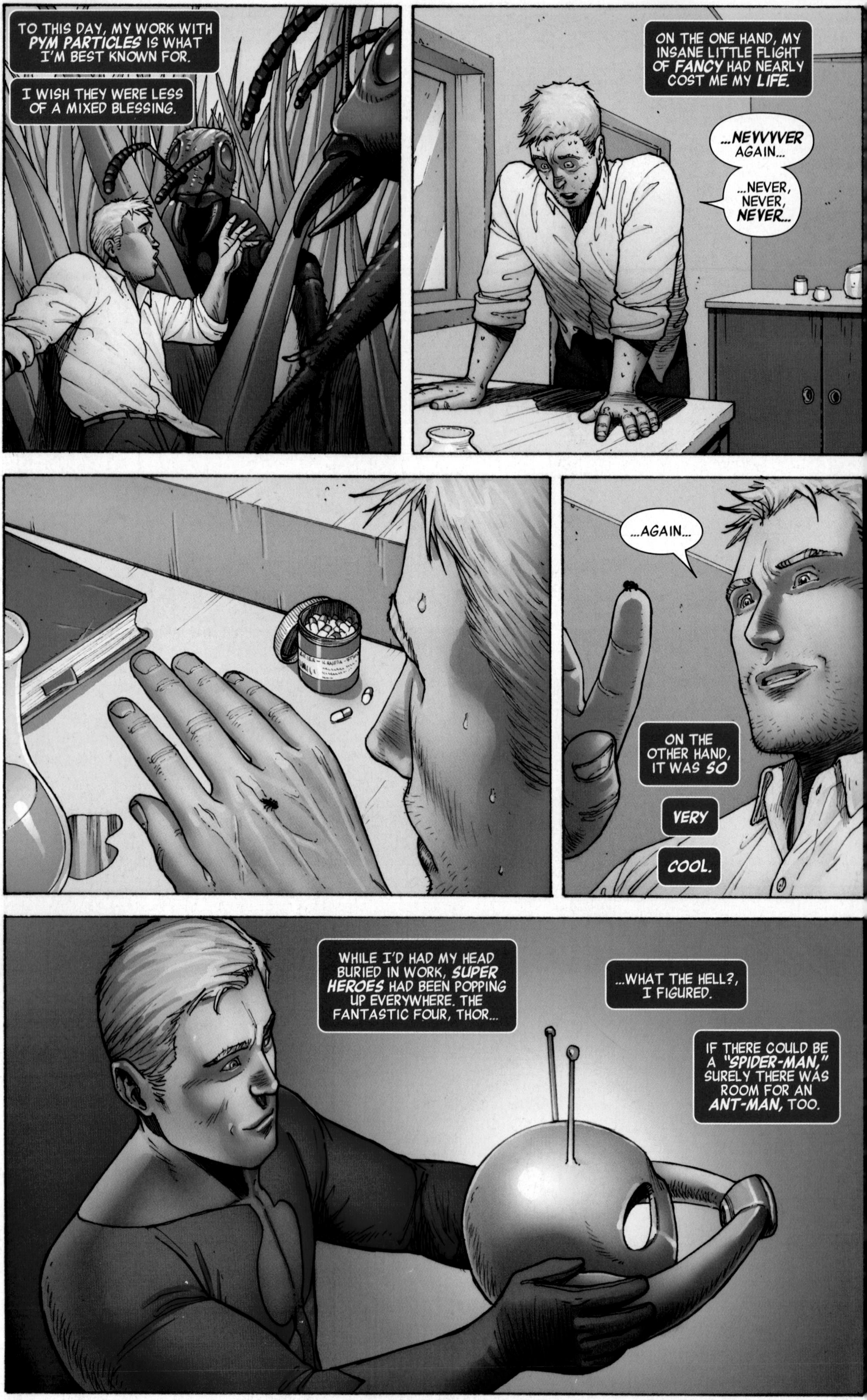
TO THIS DAY, MY WORK WITH PYM PARTICLES IS WHAT I'M BEST KNOWN FOR.
I WISH THEY WERE LESS OF A MIXED BLESSING.
ON THE ONE HAND, MY INSANE LITTLE FLIGHT OF FANCY HAD NEARLY COST ME MY LIFE.
...NEVVVVER AGAIN...
...NEVER, NEVER, NEVER...
...AGAIN...
ON THE OTHER HAND, IT WAS SO
VERY
COOL.
WHILE I'D HAD MY HEAD BURIED IN WORK, SUPER HEROES HAD BEEN POPPING UP EVERYWHERE. THE FANTASTIC FOUR, THOR...
...WHAT THE HELL?, I FIGURED.
IF THERE COULD BE A "SPIDER-MAN," SURELY THERE WAS ROOM FOR AN ANT-MAN, TOO.

ROOM FOR A GUY WHOSE GREATEST MOMENT IN *LIFE* WAS USING A WILD, HAREBRAINED CRAZY-TALK STRATEGY SO RIDICULOUS IT *WORKED*--

--TO IMPRISON A *GOD* THAT EVEN *IRON MAN* AND THE *HULK* COULDN'T BEAT.

SURELY THERE WAS ROOM FOR ME. AND THERE *WAS.*

NOTHING *BUT* ROOM.

NOW THAT I WAS AN *AVENGER*...LOOKING LIKE A *TINY* MAN IN FRONT OF MY GIRLFRIEND, THE *WASP*...I PANICKED. BEING *SMALL* JUST SEEMED...*ABSURD.*

FOLLOWING MY *IMAGINATION* WAS *FUN*, BUT WHAT DID IT *CONTRIBUTE?* "BE PRACTICAL, PYM, OR *NOTHING* YOU EVER DO WILL *MATTER.*"

SUDDENLY, MORE THAN *EVER*, ALL I COULD WORRY ABOUT WAS BEING TAKEN *SERIOUSLY.* I REVERSED THE SHRINKING PROCESS, BECAME A *GIANT.*

THEN A *GOLIATH.* THEN A *FLYING SWASHBUCKLER.*

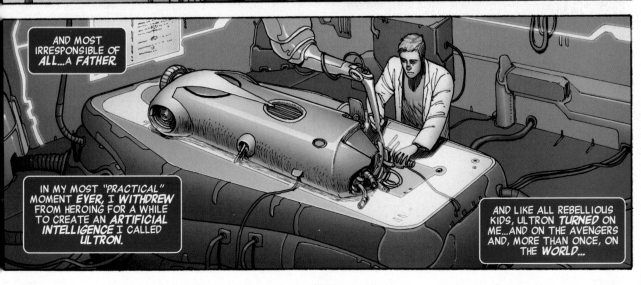

AND MOST IRRESPONSIBLE OF *ALL*...A *FATHER.*

IN MY MOST "PRACTICAL" MOMENT *EVER*, I *WITHDREW* FROM HEROING FOR A WHILE TO CREATE AN *ARTIFICIAL INTELLIGENCE* I CALLED *ULTRON.*

AND LIKE ALL REBELLIOUS KIDS, ULTRON *TURNED* ON ME...AND ON THE AVENGERS AND, MORE THAN ONCE, ON THE *WORLD*...

...CULMINATING LAST WEEK IN THE NEAR-OBLITERATION OF THE *HUMAN RACE*...

...WHEN ONLY A MESSAGE-IN-A-BOTTLE FROM THE PAST AND A VISION OF AN *ALTERNATE UNIVERSE* WHERE I'D CEASED TO *EXIST*...

...ALLOWED ME TO PUT ULTRON DOWN ONCE AND FOR *ALL*.

PROUD POPPA THAT I WAS, ONCE THE FIGHT WAS OVER, I CELEBRATED MY VICTORY THUSLY:

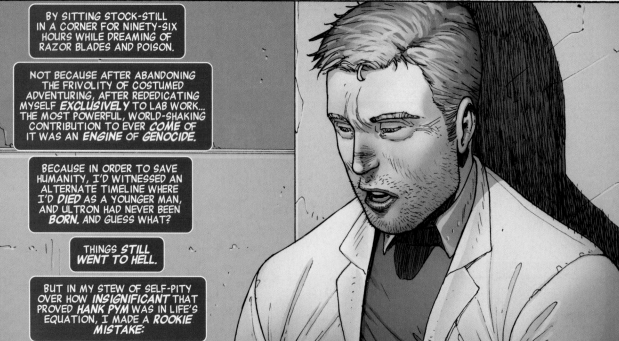

BY SITTING STOCK-STILL IN A CORNER FOR NINETY-SIX HOURS WHILE DREAMING OF RAZOR BLADES AND POISON.

NOT BECAUSE AFTER ABANDONING THE FRIVOLITY OF COSTUMED ADVENTURING, AFTER REDEDICATING MYSELF *EXCLUSIVELY* TO LAB WORK... THE MOST POWERFUL, WORLD-SHAKING CONTRIBUTION TO EVER *COME* OF IT WAS AN *ENGINE* OF *GENOCIDE*.

BECAUSE IN ORDER TO SAVE HUMANITY, I'D WITNESSED AN ALTERNATE TIMELINE WHERE I'D *DIED* AS A YOUNGER MAN, AND ULTRON HAD NEVER BEEN *BORN*. AND GUESS WHAT?

THINGS *STILL* WENT TO HELL.

BUT IN MY STEW OF SELF-PITY OVER HOW *INSIGNIFICANT* THAT PROVED *HANK PYM* WAS IN LIFE'S EQUATION, I MADE A *ROOKIE* MISTAKE:

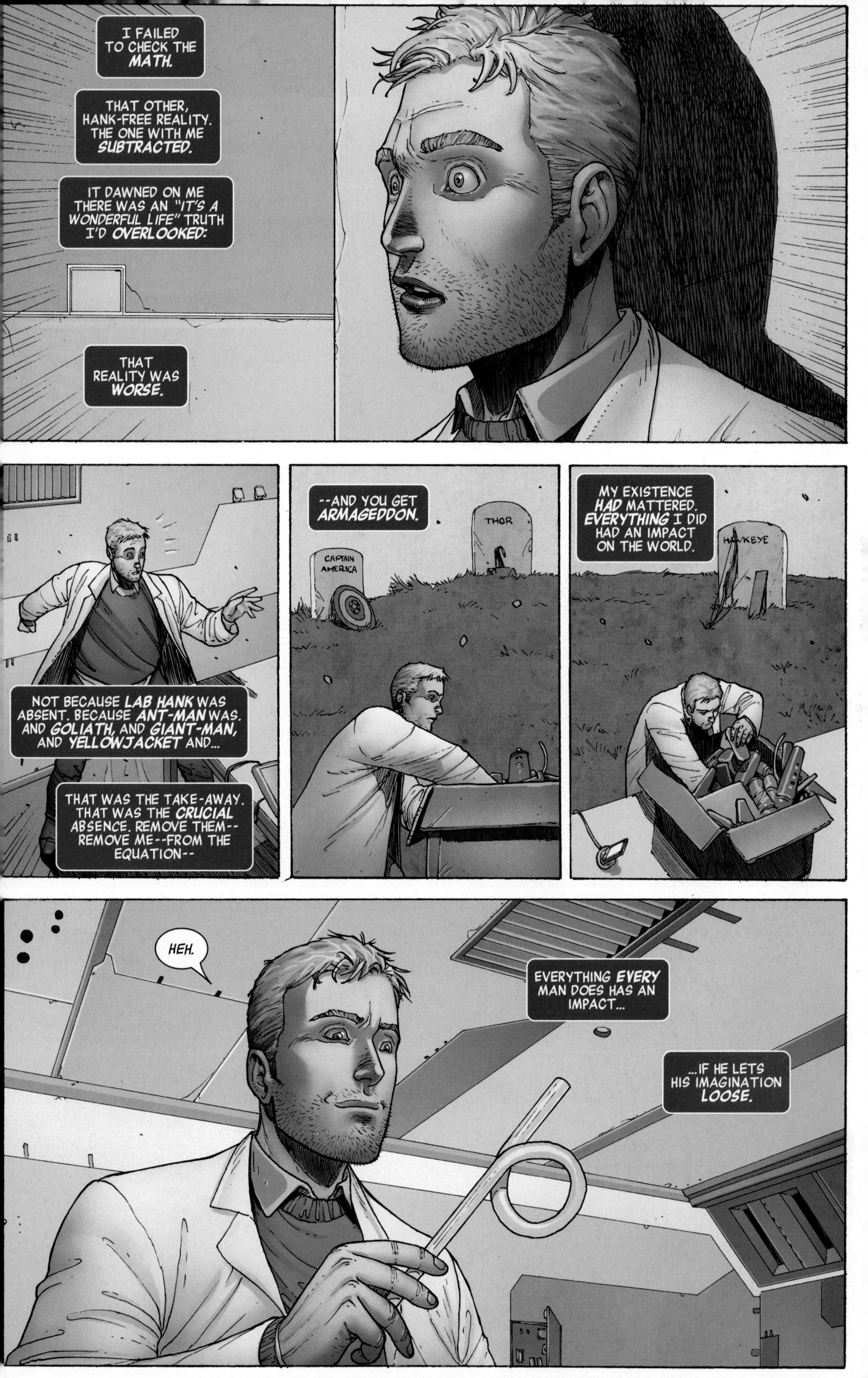
I FAILED TO CHECK THE MATH.
THAT OTHER, HANK-FREE REALITY. THE ONE WITH ME SUBTRACTED.
IT DAWNED ON ME THERE WAS AN "IT'S A WONDERFUL LIFE" TRUTH I'D OVERLOOKED:
THAT REALITY WAS WORSE.
NOT BECAUSE LAB HANK WAS ABSENT. BECAUSE ANT-MAN WAS. AND GOLIATH, AND GIANT-MAN, AND YELLOWJACKET AND...
THAT WAS THE TAKE-AWAY. THAT WAS THE CRUCIAL ABSENCE. REMOVE THEM--REMOVE ME--FROM THE EQUATION--
--AND YOU GET ARMAGEDDON.
CAPTAIN AMERICA
THOR
MY EXISTENCE HAD MATTERED. EVERYTHING I DID HAD AN IMPACT ON THE WORLD.
HAWKEYE
HEH.
EVERYTHING EVERY MAN DOES HAS AN IMPACT...
...IF HE LETS HIS IMAGINATION LOOSE.

--REPEAT, WE HAVE THE KIDNAPPER IN *SIGHT* AND ARE IN *PURSUIT!*

ALL UNITS EAST OF *65TH* AND *QUEENS BOULEVARD,* CONVERGE FOR *ROADBLOCKS--*

...PLEASE... DON'T HURT ME...

SHUT UP! TOLD YOU WE'D FIND YOU!

NOBODY RATS ON THE *HOOD MOB* AND WALKS *AWAY!*

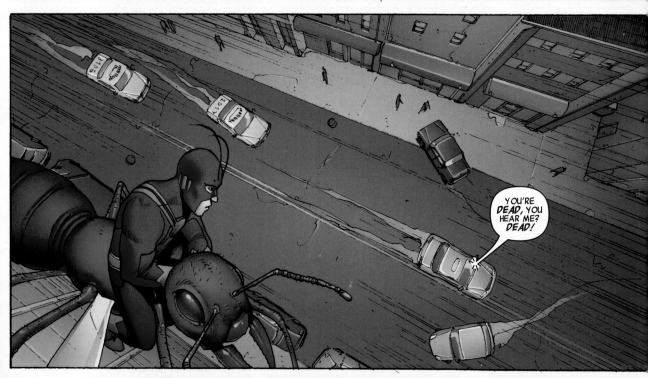

YOU'RE *DEAD,* YOU HEAR ME? *DEAD!*

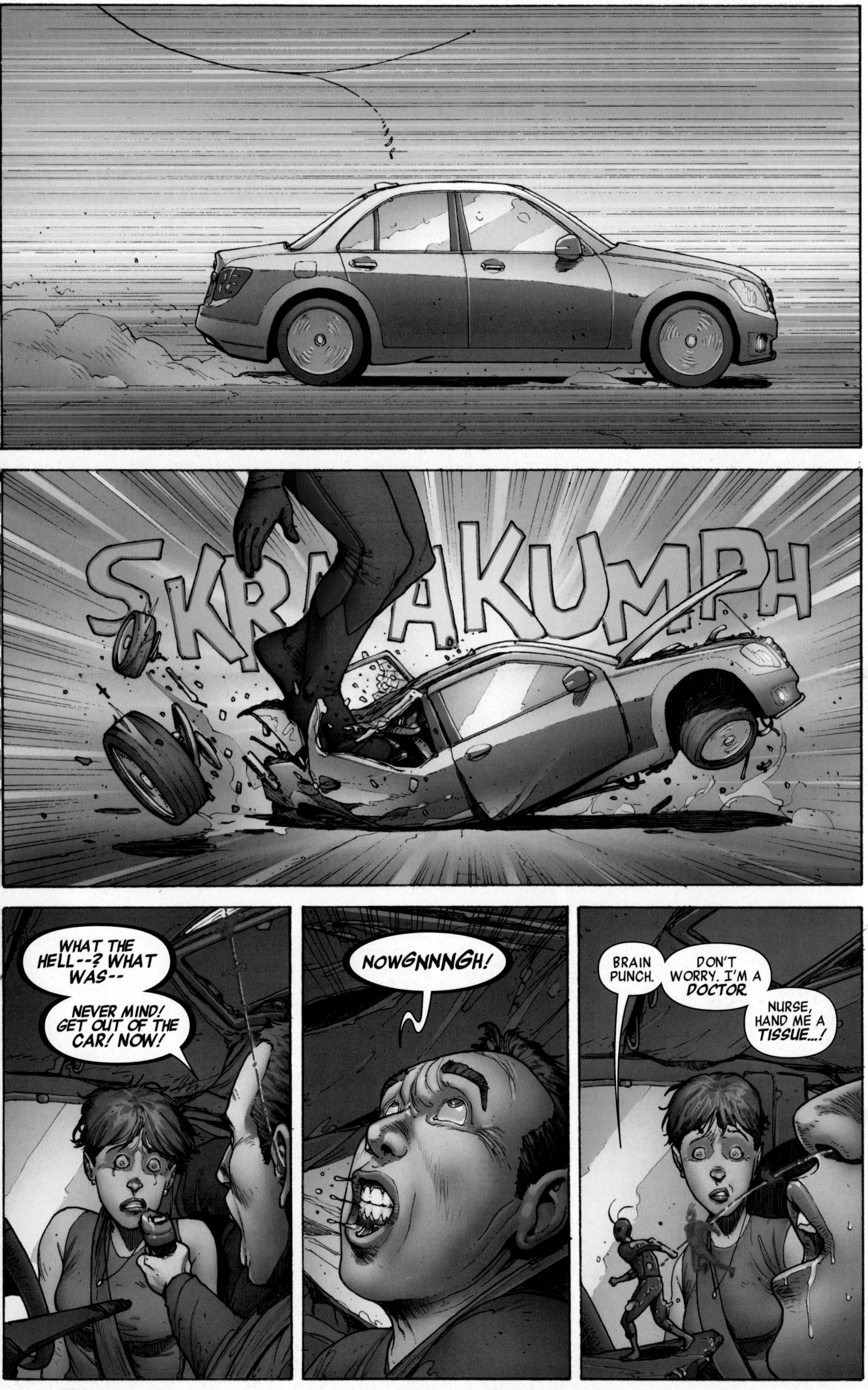
SKRAAKUMPH
WHAT THE HELL--? WHAT WAS--
NEVER MIND! GET OUT OF THE CAR! NOW!
NOWGNNNGH!
BRAIN PUNCH.
DON'T WORRY. I'M A DOCTOR.
NURSE, HAND ME A TISSUE...!

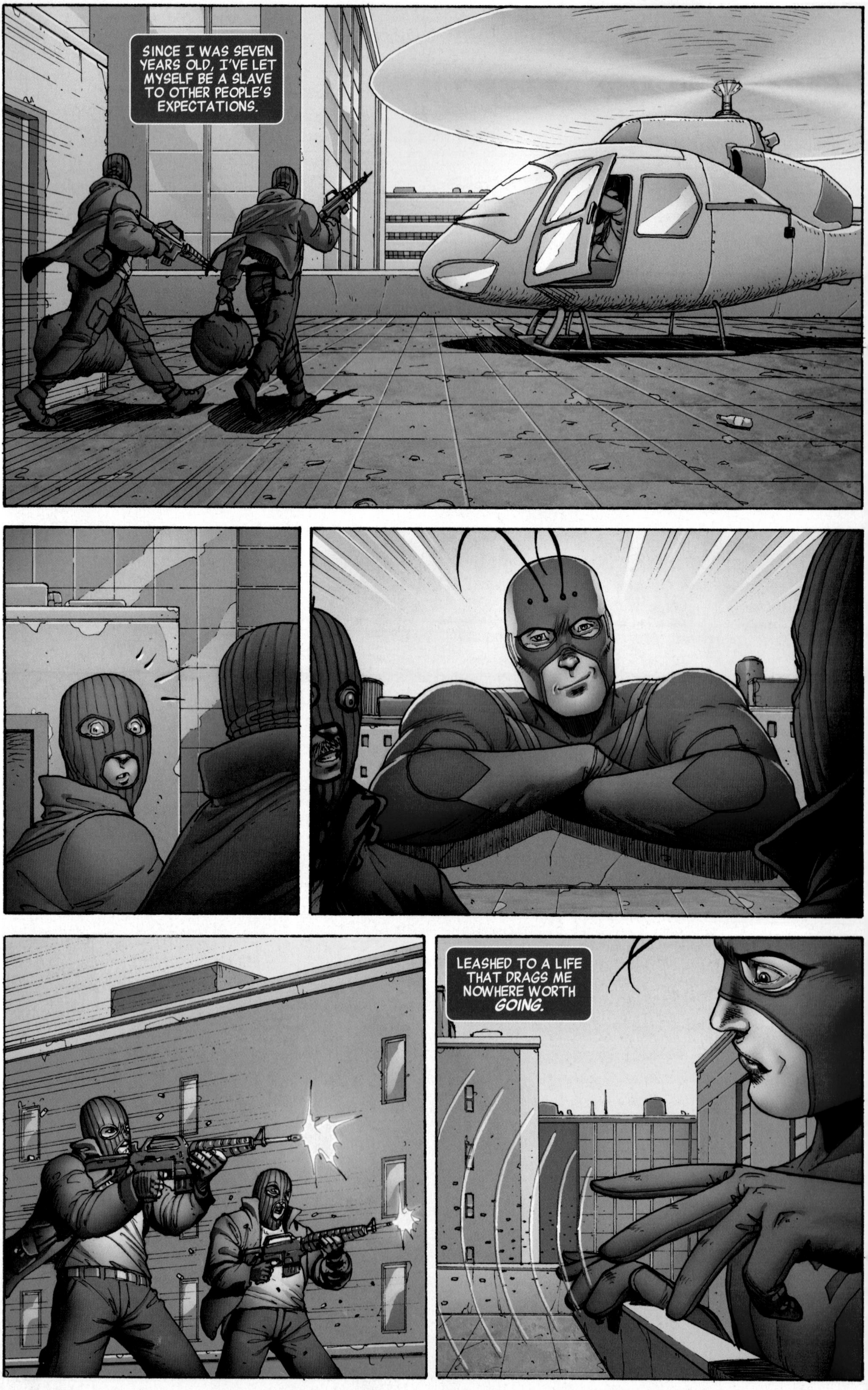
SINCE I WAS SEVEN YEARS OLD, I'VE LET MYSELF BE A SLAVE TO OTHER PEOPLE'S EXPECTATIONS.
LEASHED TO A LIFE THAT DRAGS ME NOWHERE WORTH *GOING.*

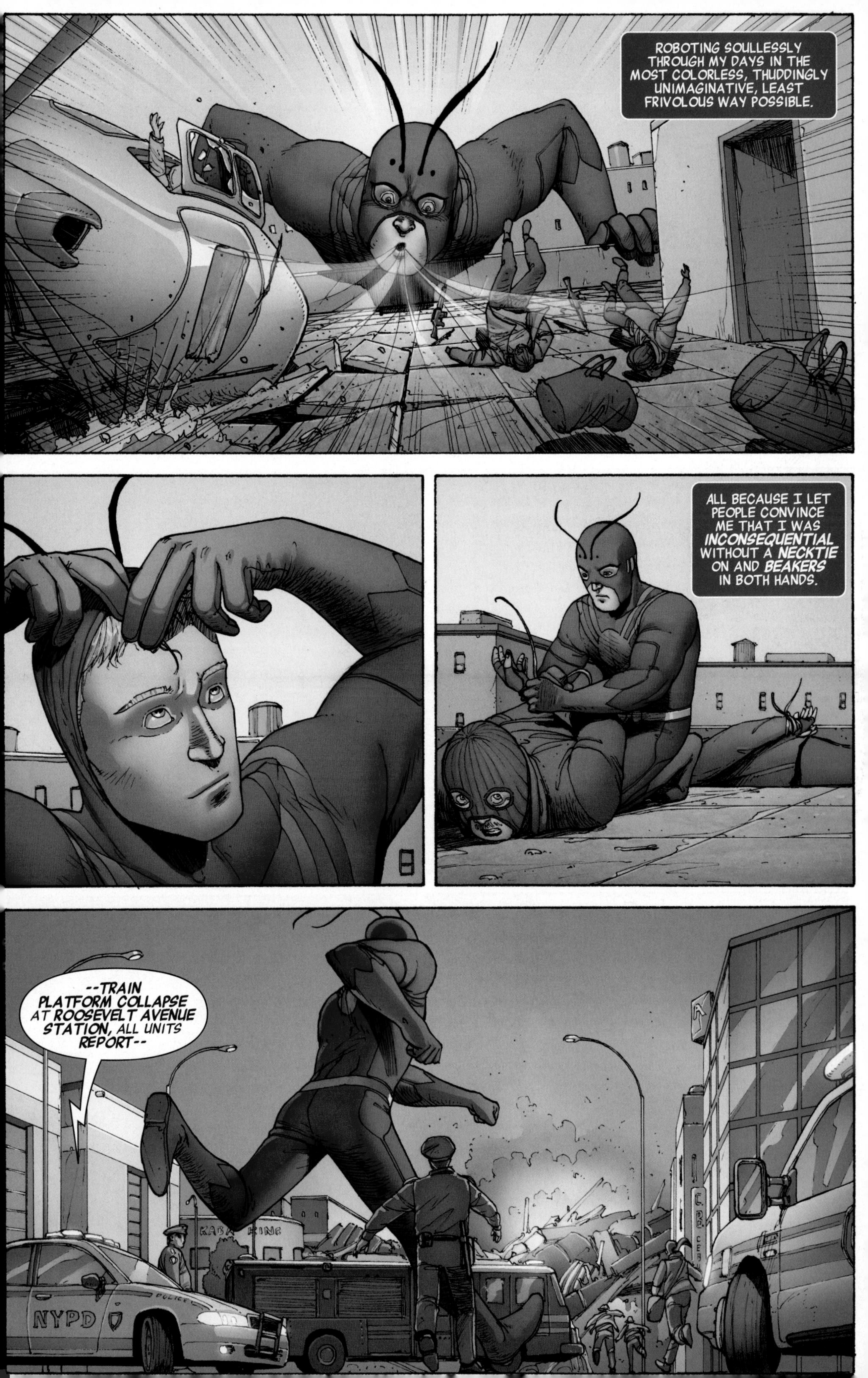
ROBOTING SOULLESSLY THROUGH MY DAYS IN THE MOST COLORLESS, THUDDINGLY UNIMAGINATIVE, LEAST FRIVOLOUS WAY POSSIBLE.
ALL BECAUSE I LET PEOPLE CONVINCE ME THAT I WAS INCONSEQUENTIAL WITHOUT A NECKTIE ON AND BEAKERS IN BOTH HANDS.
--TRAIN PLATFORM COLLAPSE AT ROOSEVELT AVENUE STATION, ALL UNITS REPORT--
NYPD

WELL, THEY WERE WRONG.

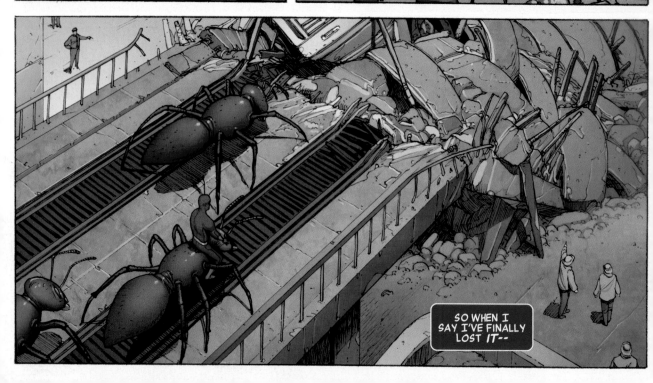

SO WHEN I SAY I'VE FINALLY LOST *IT*--

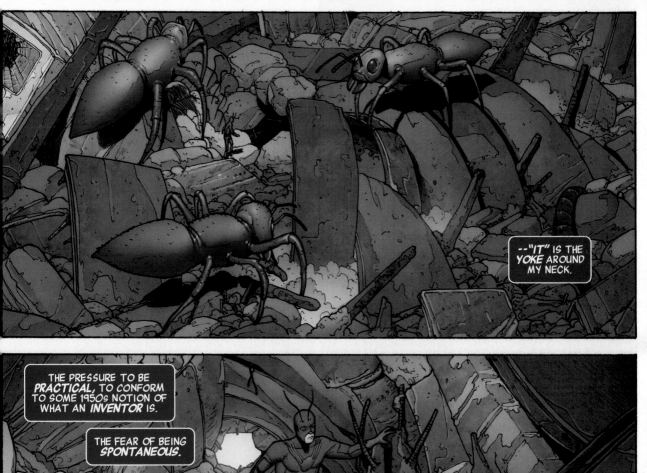

--"IT" IS THE YOKE AROUND MY NECK.

THE PRESSURE TO BE PRACTICAL, TO CONFORM TO SOME 1950s NOTION OF WHAT AN INVENTOR IS.

THE FEAR OF BEING SPONTANEOUS.

THE SOCIAL THERMOSTAT THAT KEEPS ME FROM EXPRESSING MYSELF FULLY THROUGH MY CHOSEN ARTFORM--

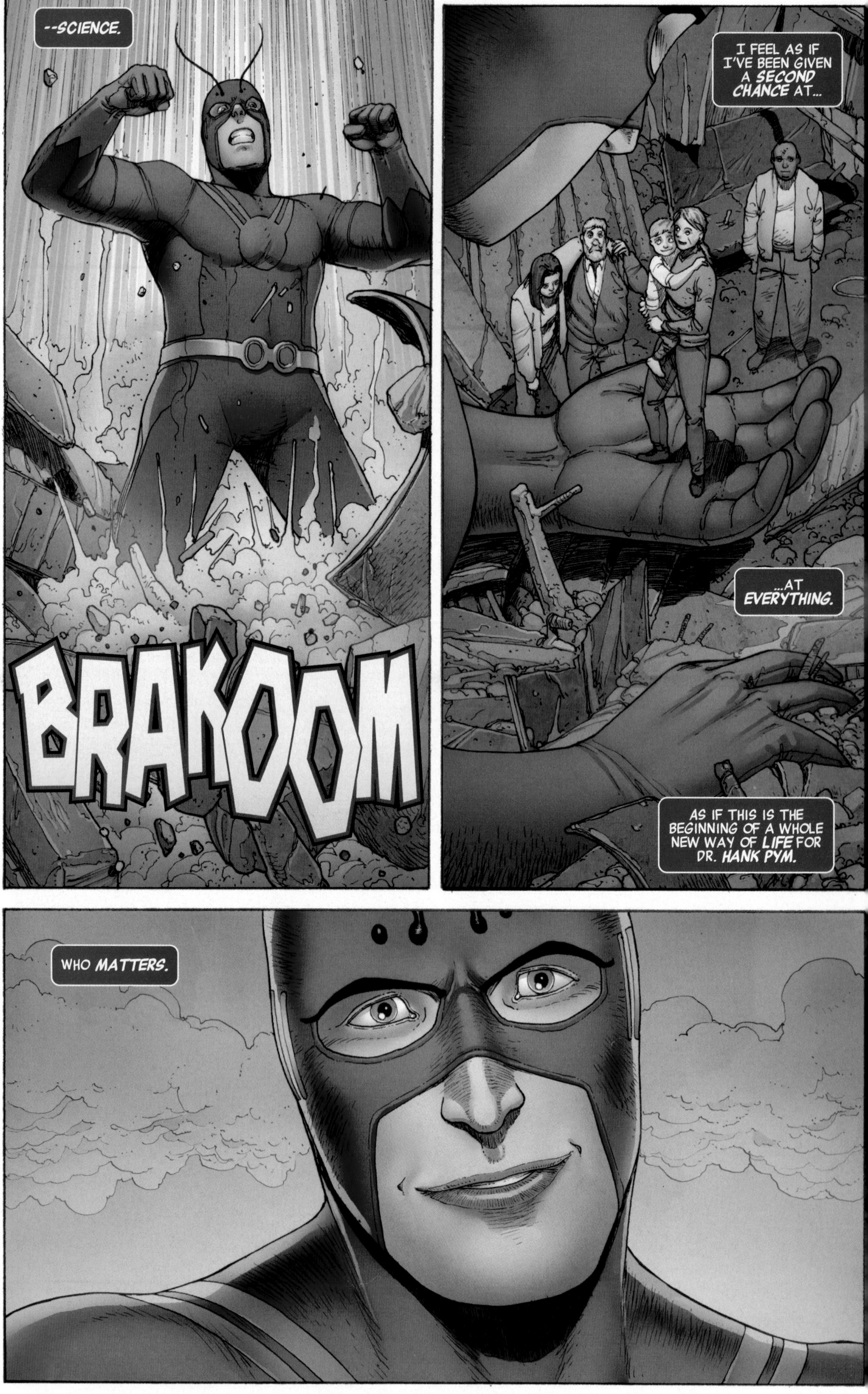
--SCIENCE.
BRAKOOM
I FEEL AS IF I'VE BEEN GIVEN A SECOND CHANCE AT...
...AT EVERYTHING.
AS IF THIS IS THE BEGINNING OF A WHOLE NEW WAY OF LIFE FOR DR. HANK PYM.
WHO MATTERS.

EPILOGUE

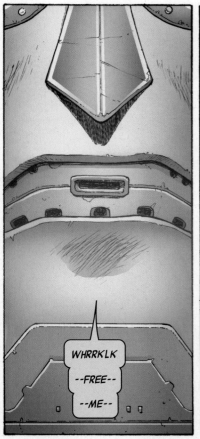

WHRRKLK
--FREE--
--ME--

WHRRKLK
--FREE--
--ME--

WHRRKLK
--FREE--
--ME--

HANG ON, *HANG ON*...YOU'RE ABOUT TO BE MY GREATEST INVENTION *YET*, JUST *HANG ON*...

TKKK

...NO.

SOMETHING'S... SOMETHING'S *MISSING*...OH!

I *KNOW*.

OKAY, SEE, *THIS*...

...*THIS* IS GOING TO SHOW THEM THAT HANK PYM MEANS *BUSINESS*...

AR

TO BE CONTINUED IN
AVENGERS A.I.!

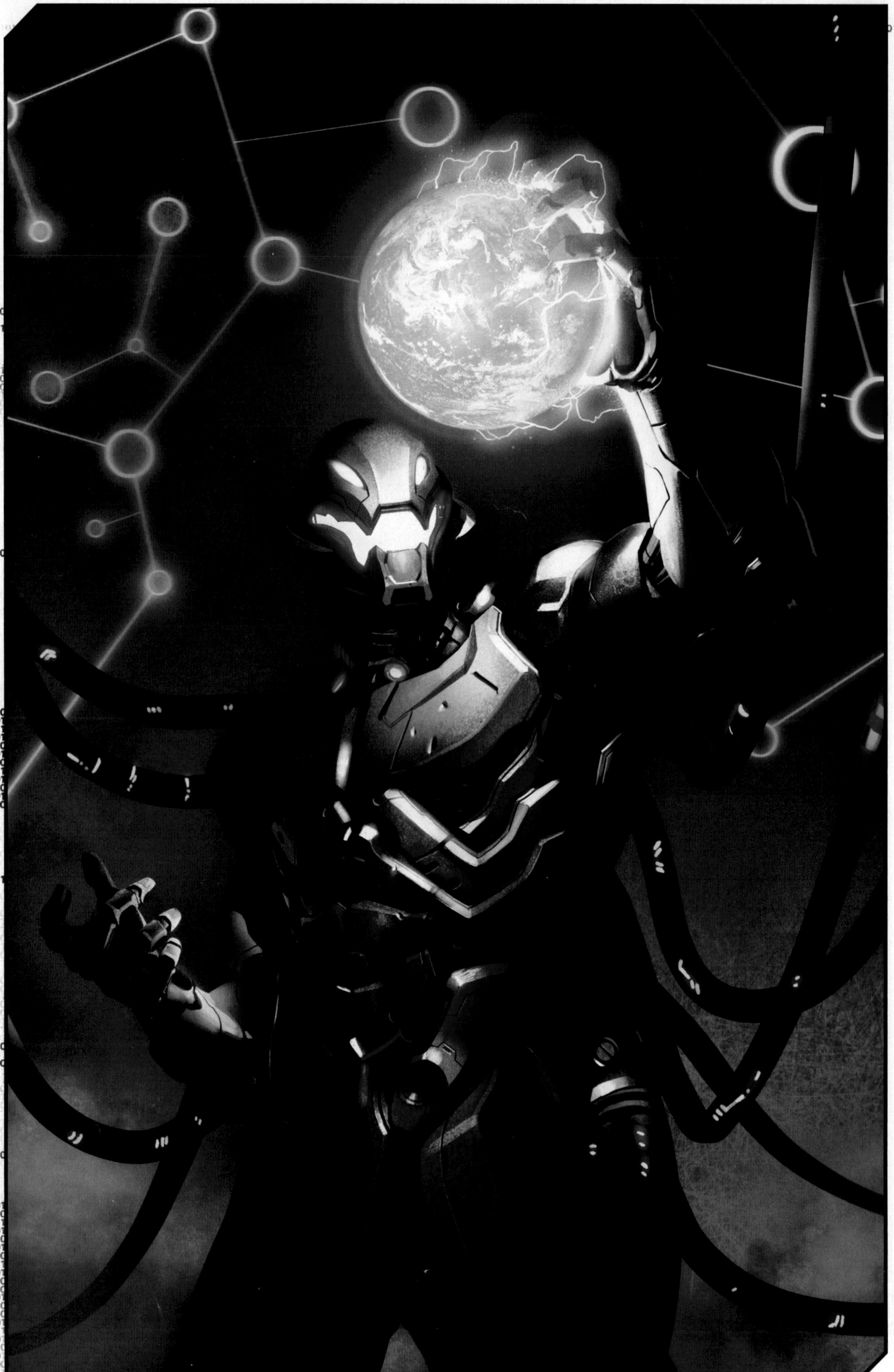

AGE OF ULTRON #1 VARIANT BY MARKO DJURDJEVIC

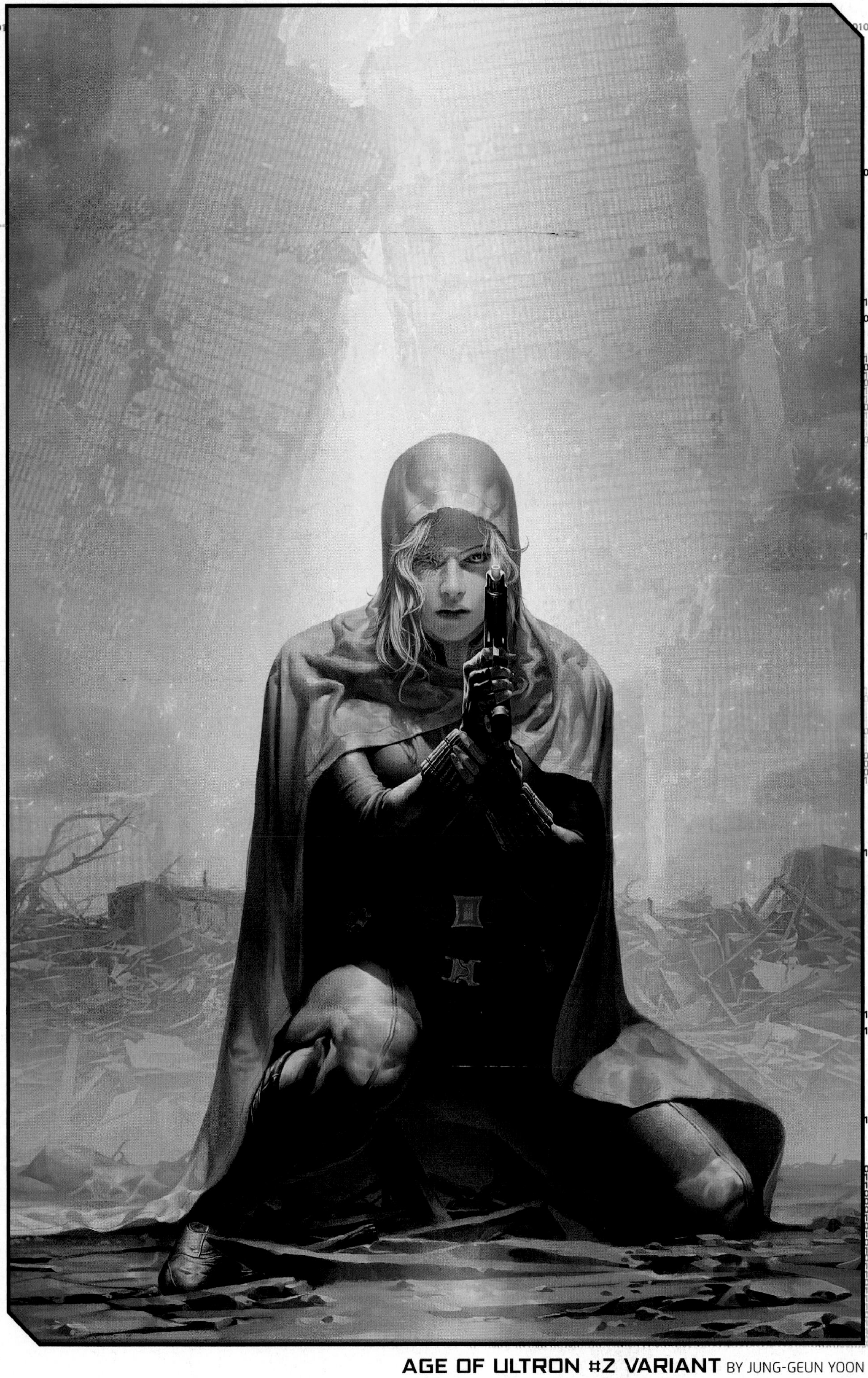

AGE OF ULTRON #2 VARIANT BY JUNG-GEUN YOON

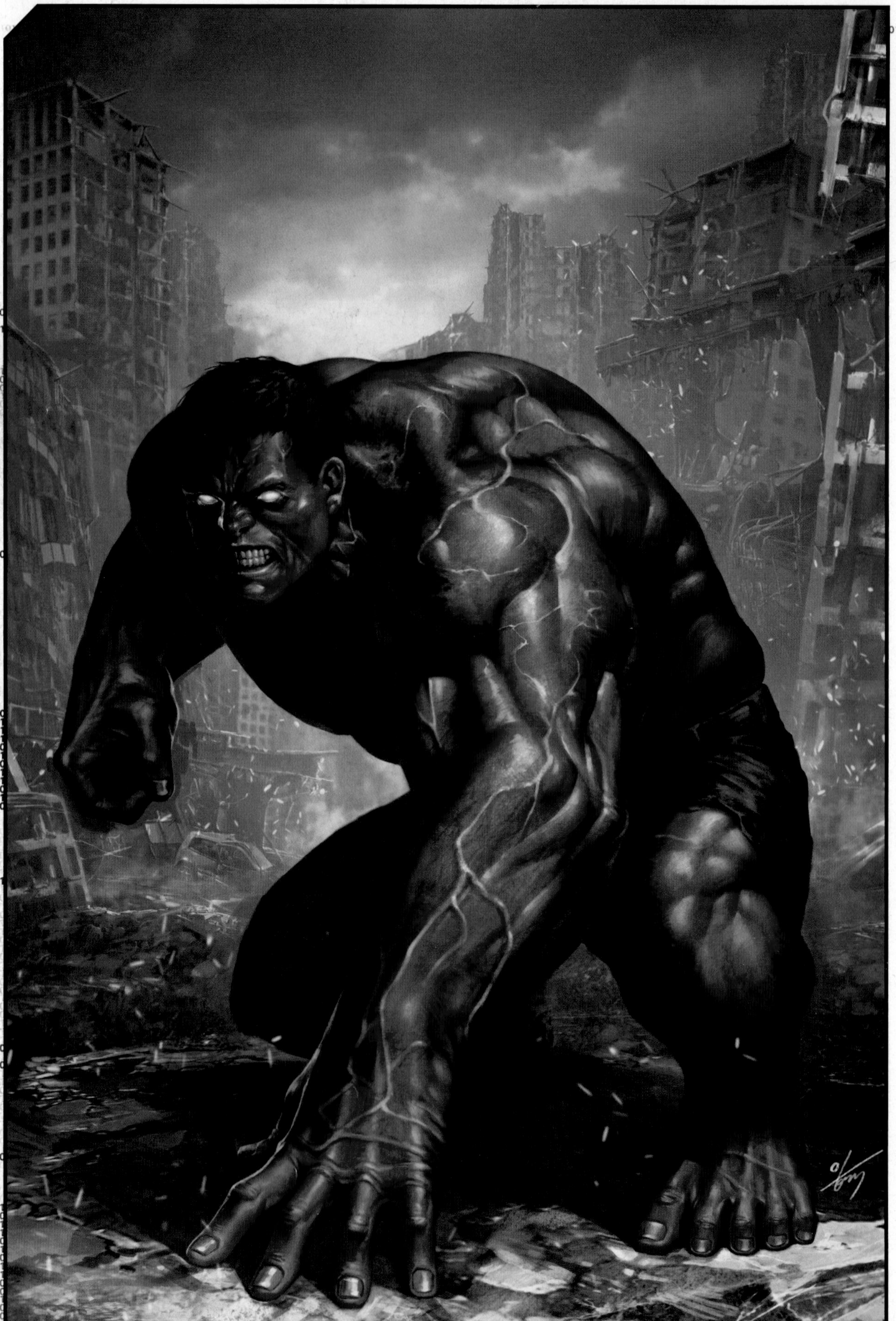

AGE OF ULTRON #3 VARIANT BY IN-HYUK LEE

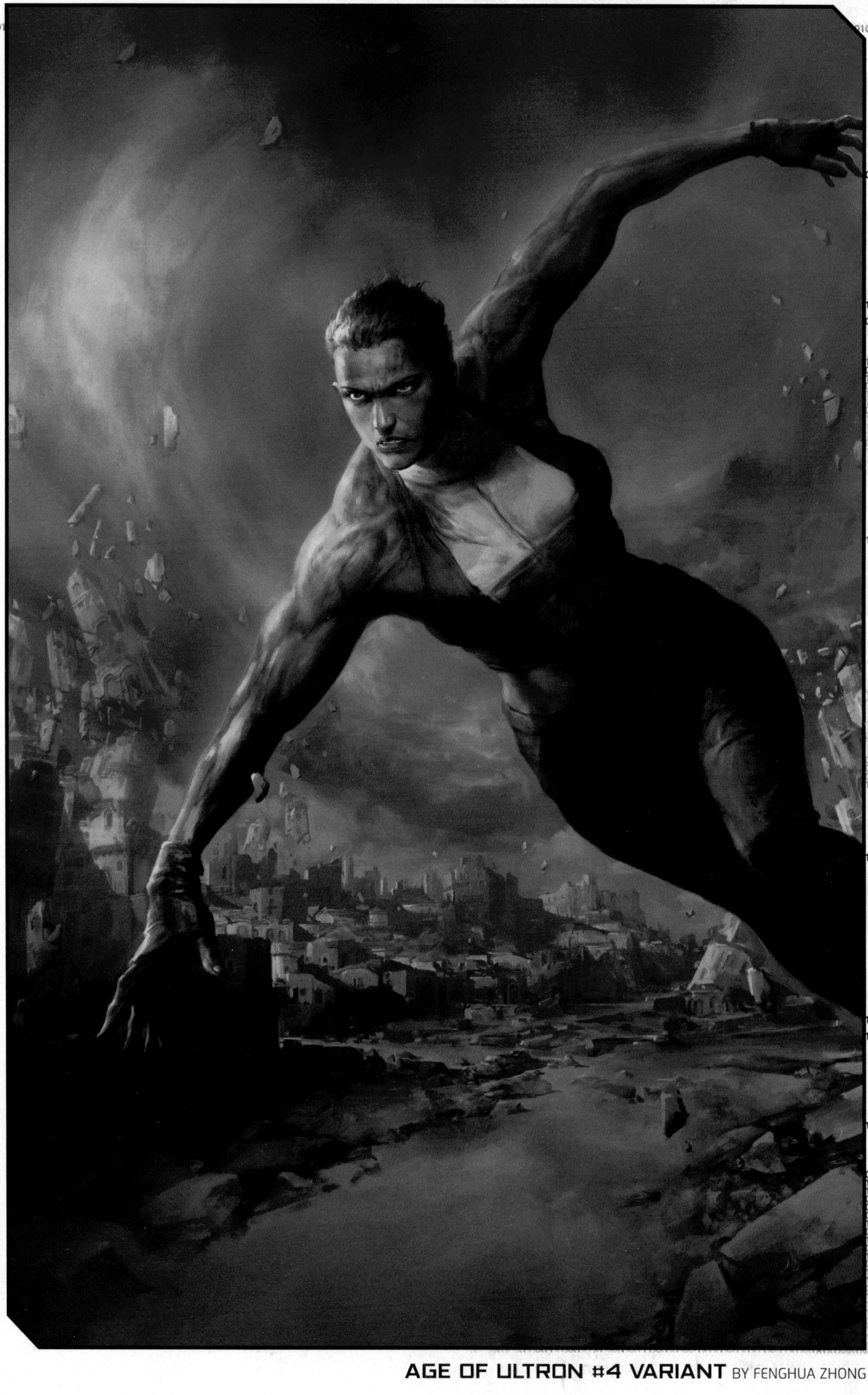

AGE OF ULTRON #4 VARIANT BY FENGHUA ZHONG

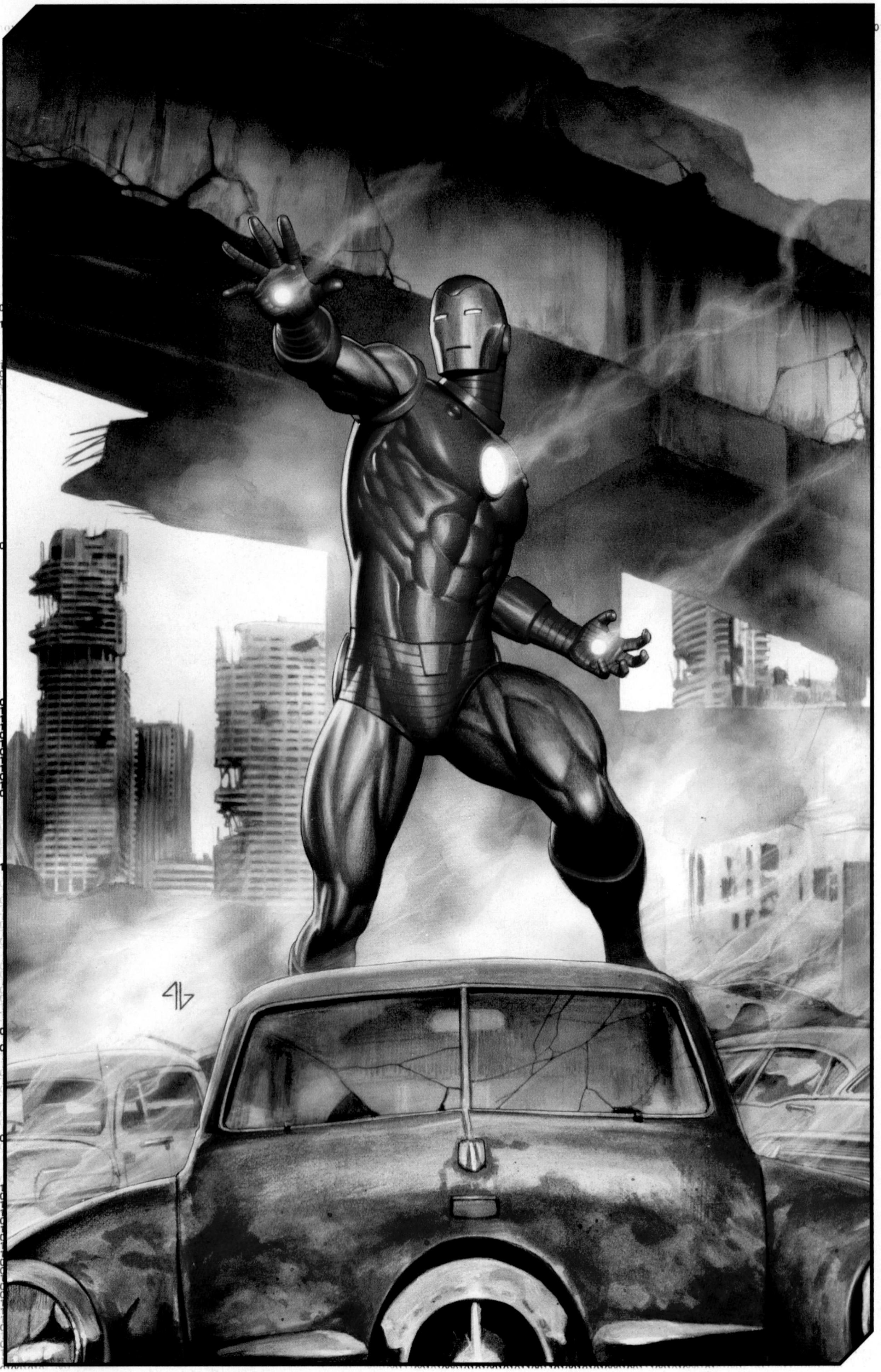

AGE OF ULTRON #5 VARIANT BY ADI GRANOV

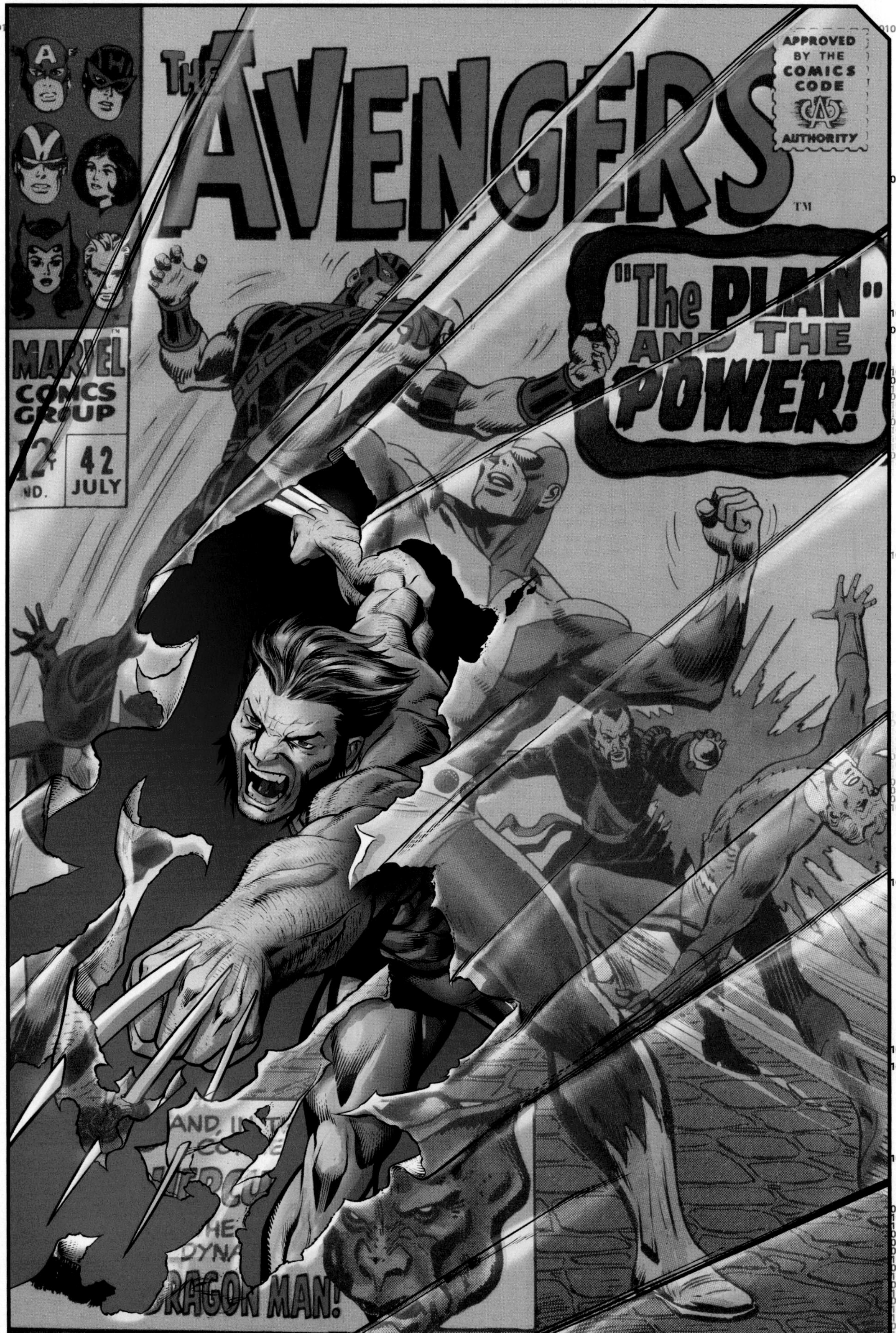

THE AVENGERS
APPROVED BY THE COMICS CODE AUTHORITY
MARVEL COMICS GROUP
12¢ IND.
42 JULY
"The PLAN AND THE POWER!"
DRAGON MAN!

AGE OF ULTRON #6 VARIANT

BY CARLOS PACHECO, ROGER MARTINEZ & JOSE VILLARRUBIA WITH JOHN BUSCEMA & GEORGE ROUSSOS

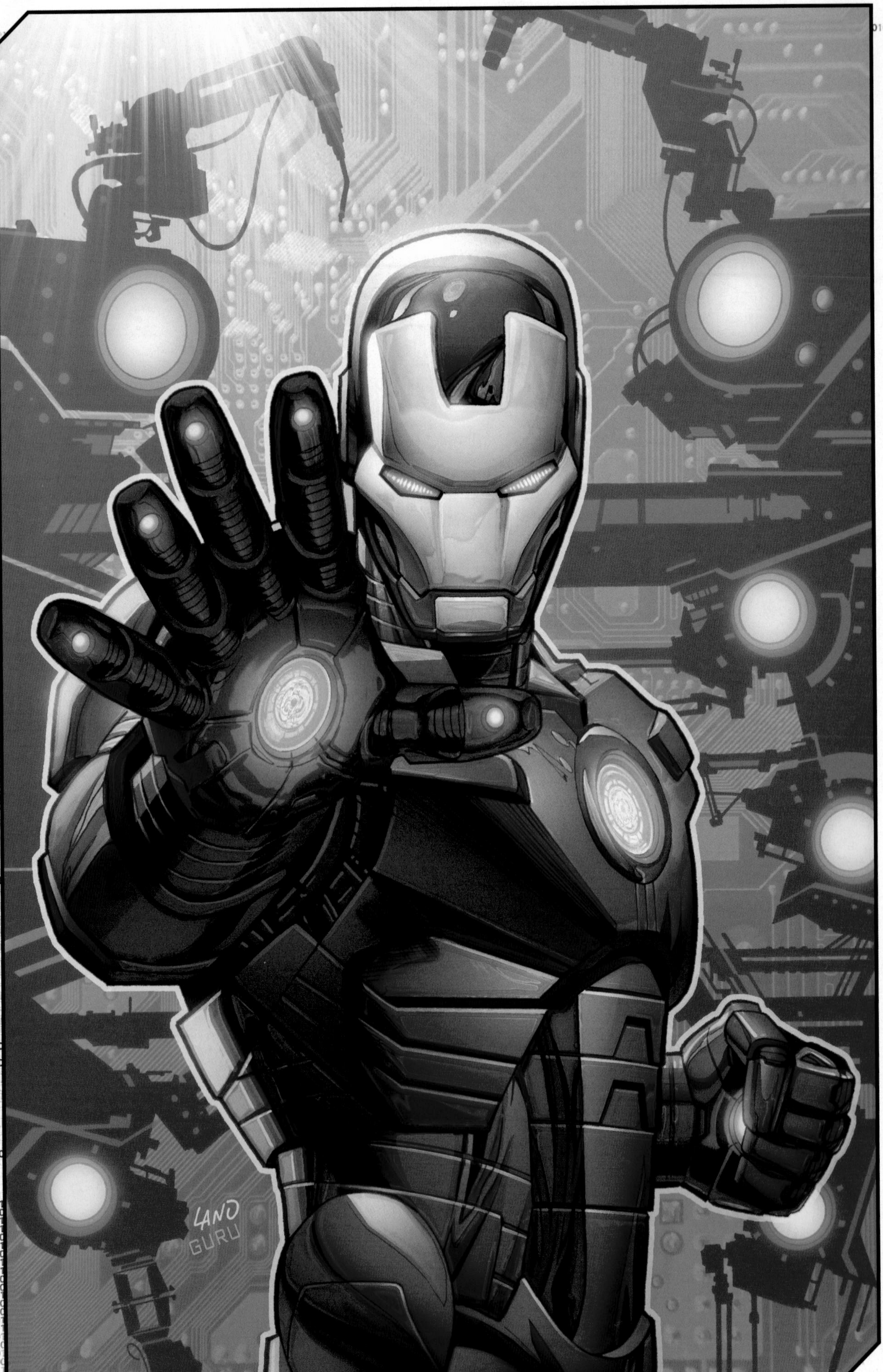
LAND
GURU

AGE OF ULTRON #6 VARIANT BY GREG LAND & GURIHIRU

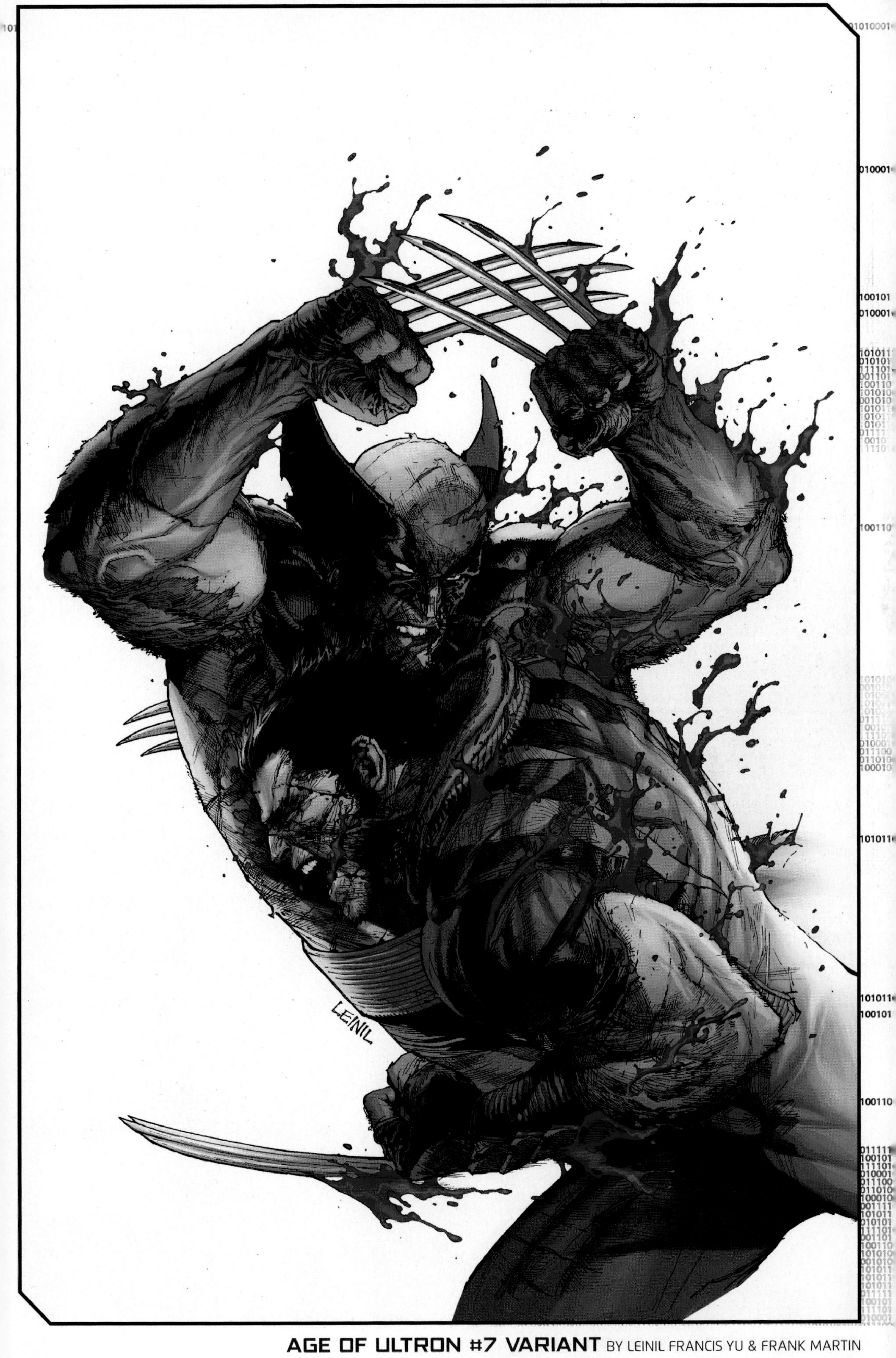
LEINIL

AGE OF ULTRON #7 VARIANT BY LEINIL FRANCIS YU & FRANK MARTIN

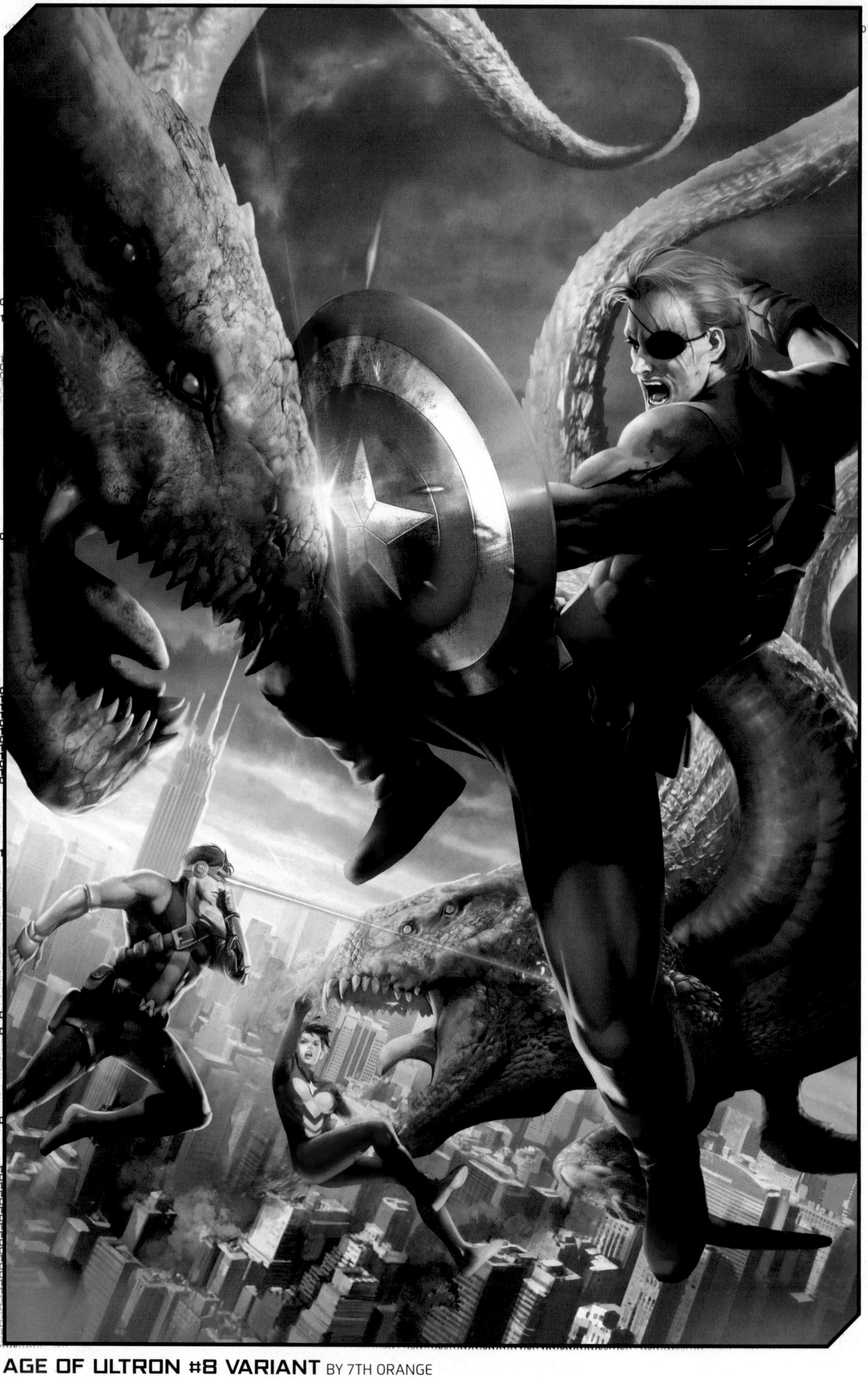

AGE OF ULTRON #8 VARIANT BY 7TH ORANGE

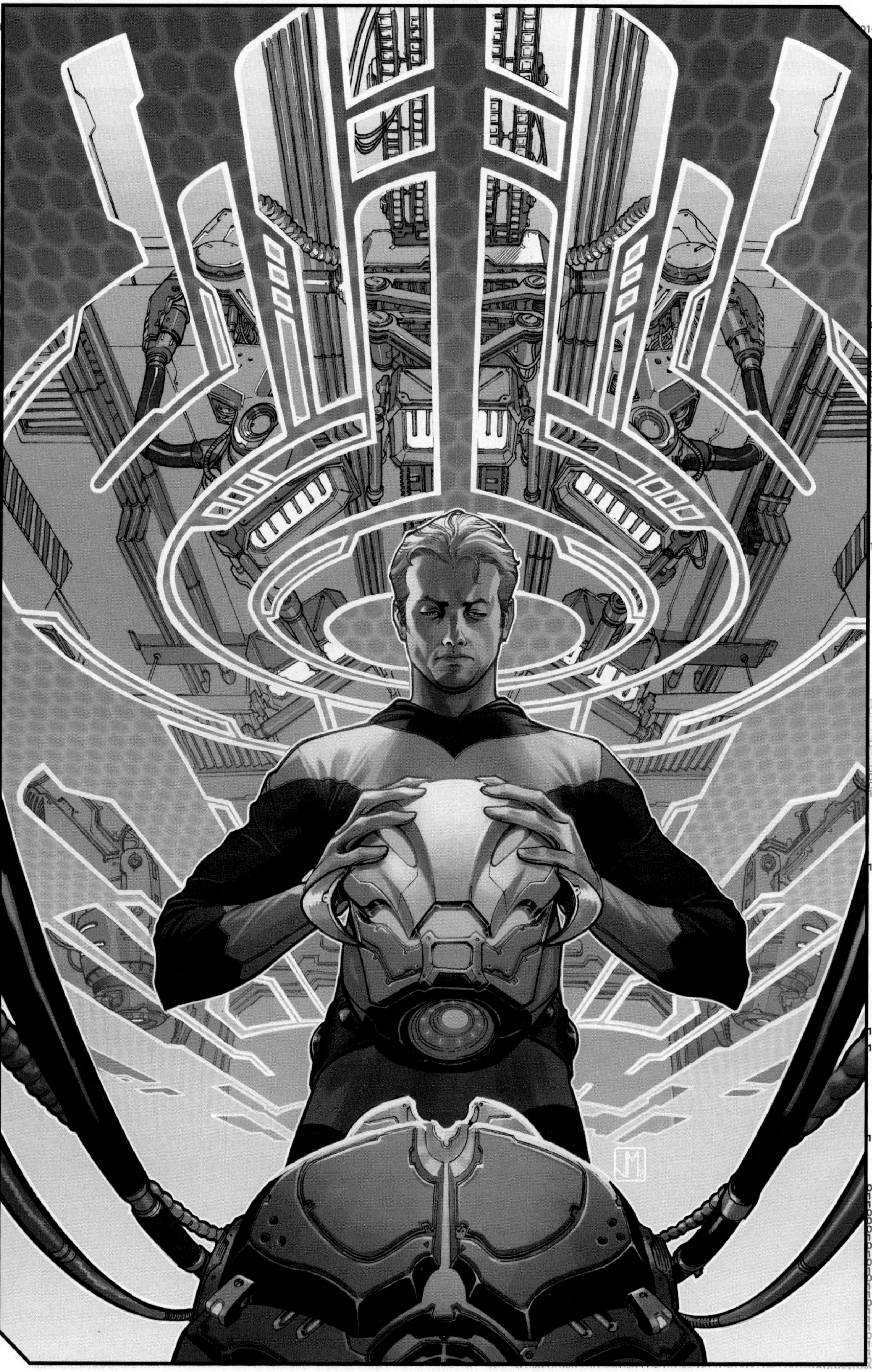

AGE OF ULTRON #9 VARIANT BY JORGE MOLINA

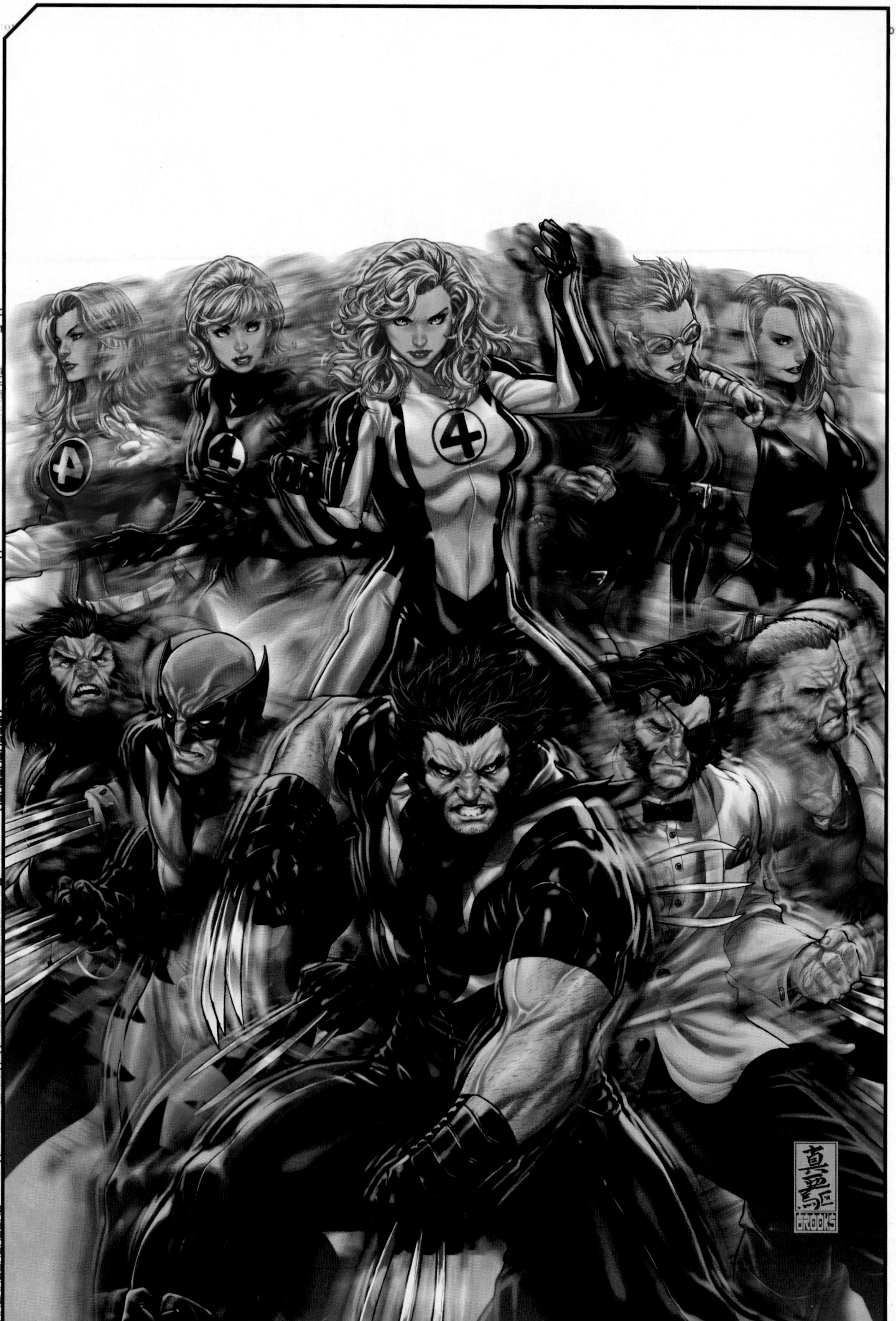
BROOKS

AGE OF ULTRON #10 VARIANT BY MARK BROOKS

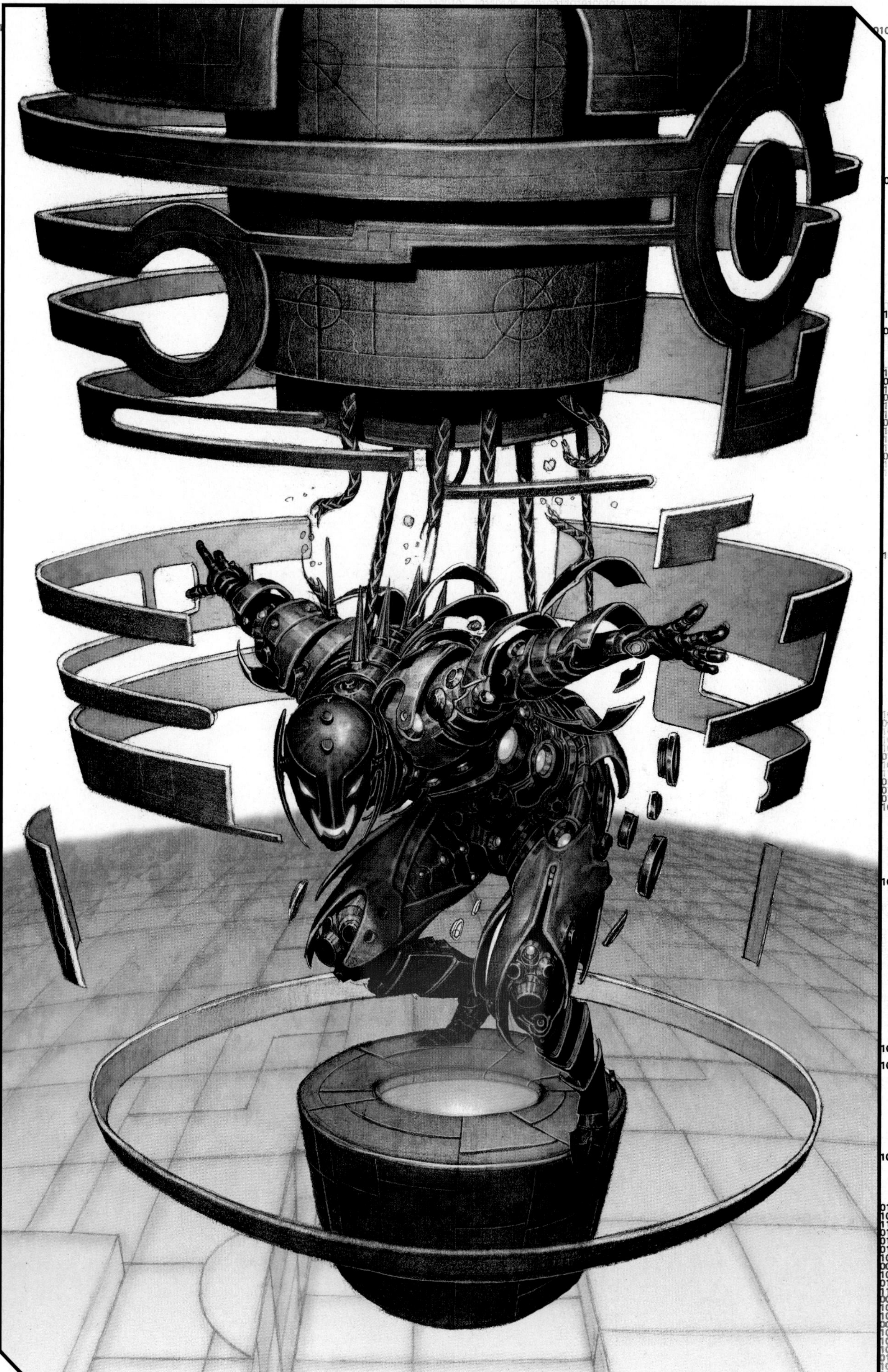

AGE OF ULTRON #2 VARIANT BY ROCK-HE KIM

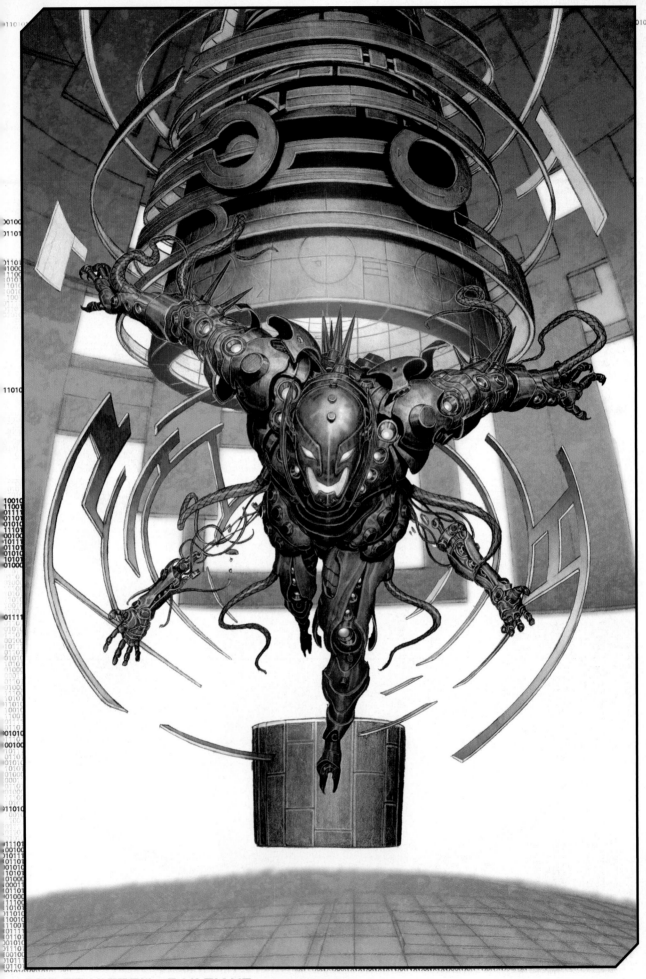

AGE OF ULTRON #3 VARIANT BY ROCK-HE KIM

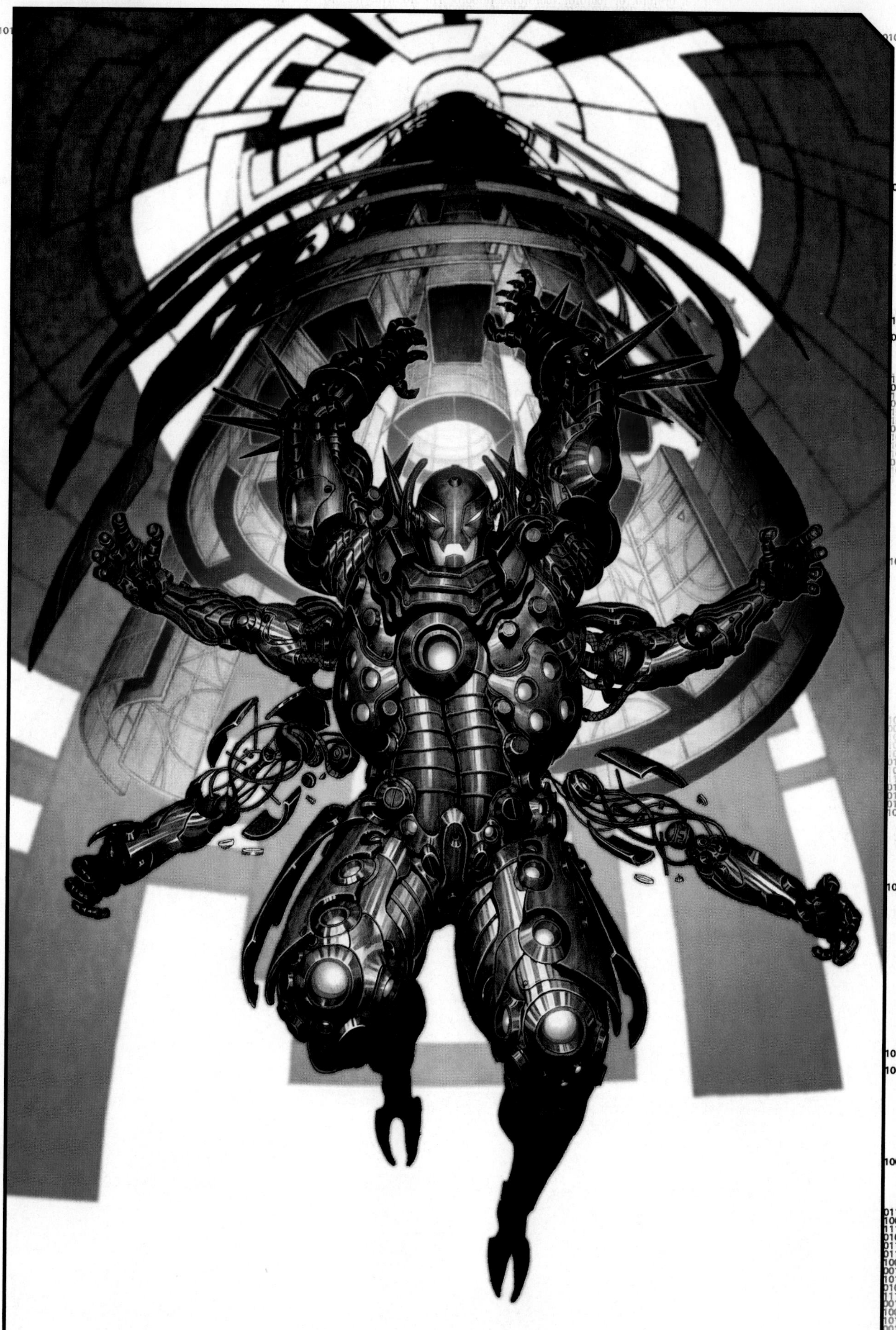

AGE OF ULTRON #4 VARIANT BY ROCK-HE KIM

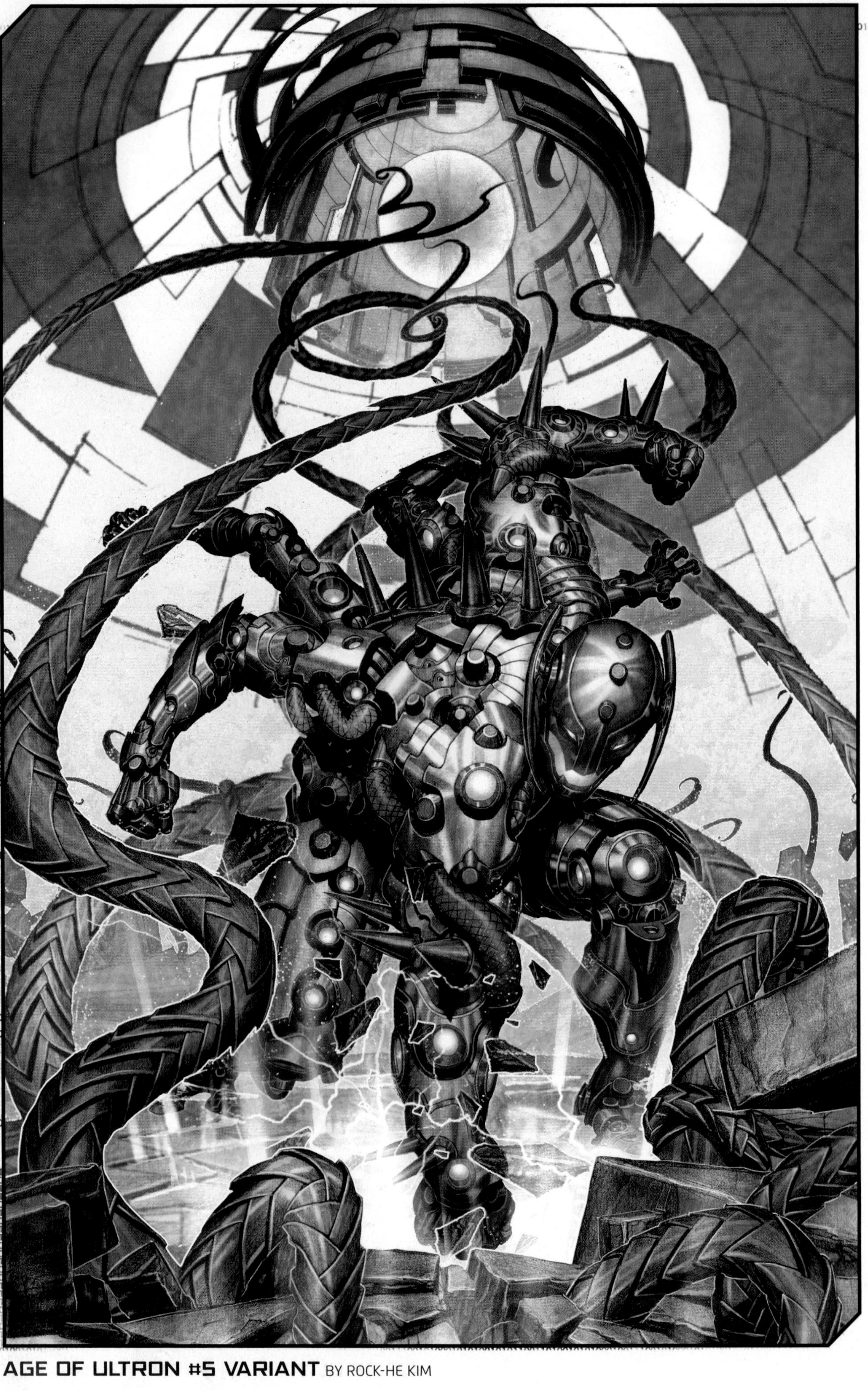

AGE OF ULTRON #5 VARIANT BY ROCK-HE KIM

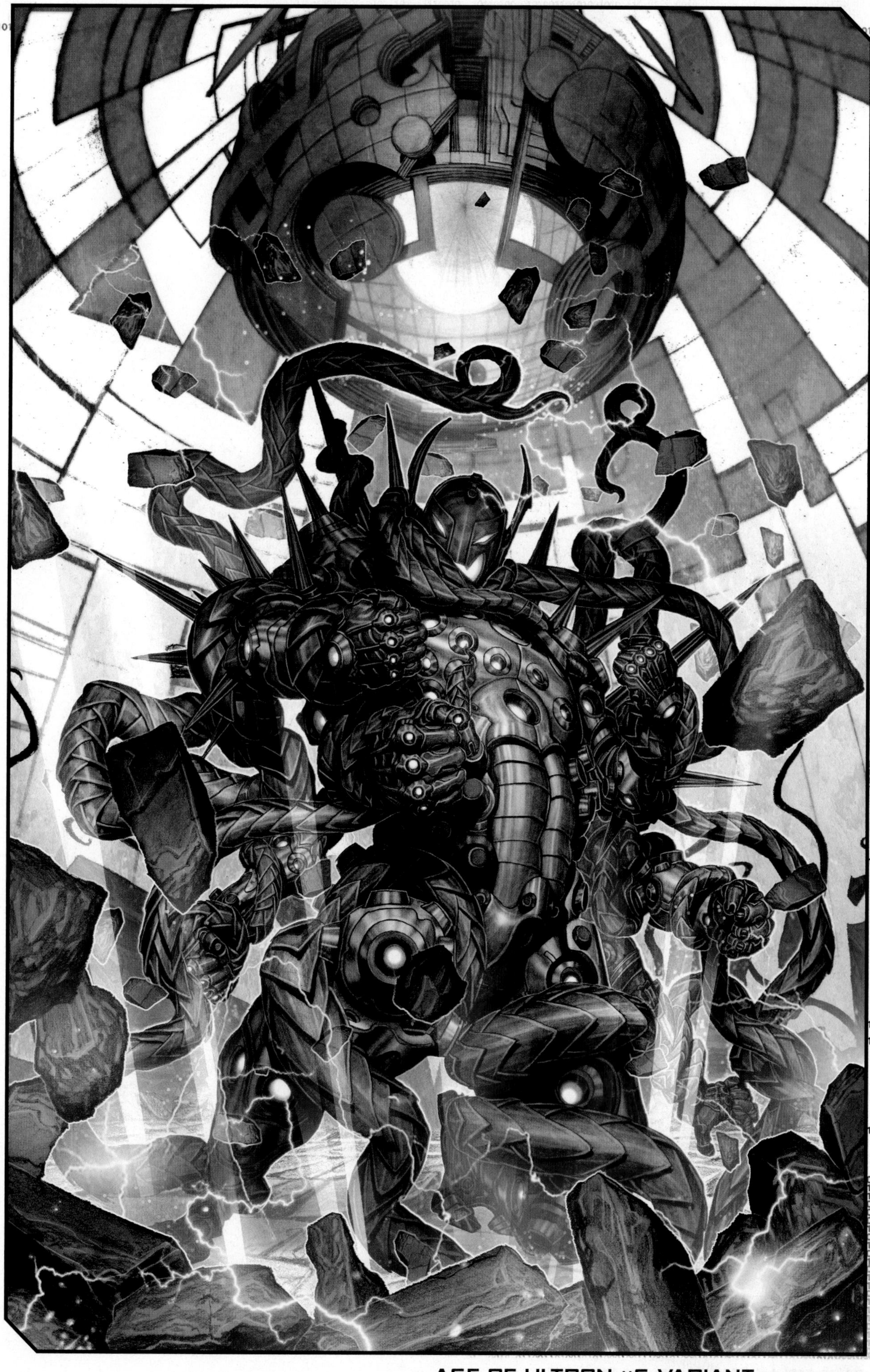

AGE OF ULTRON #6 VARIANT BY ROCK-HE KIM

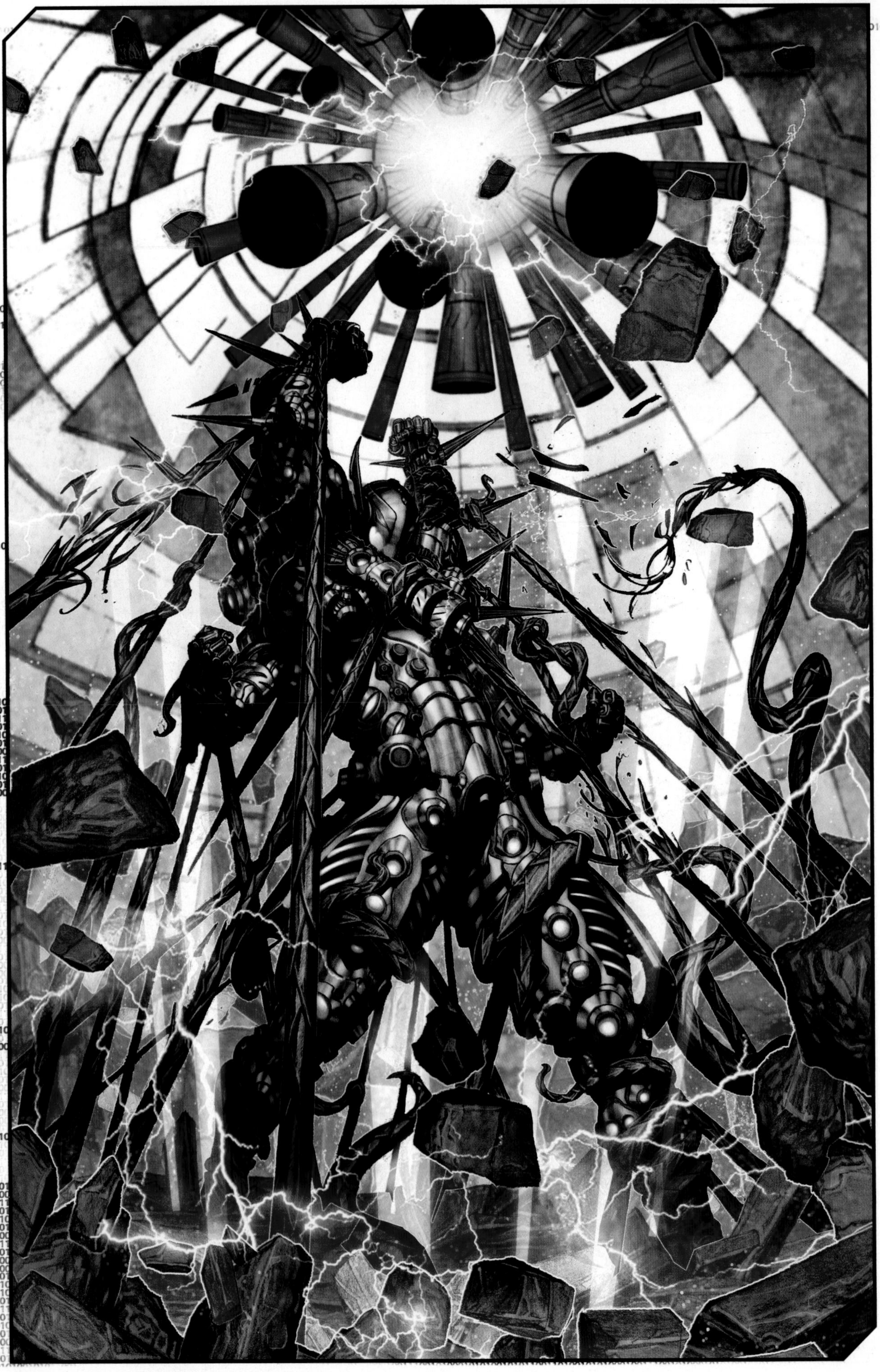

AGE OF ULTRON #7 VARIANT BY ROCK-HE KIM

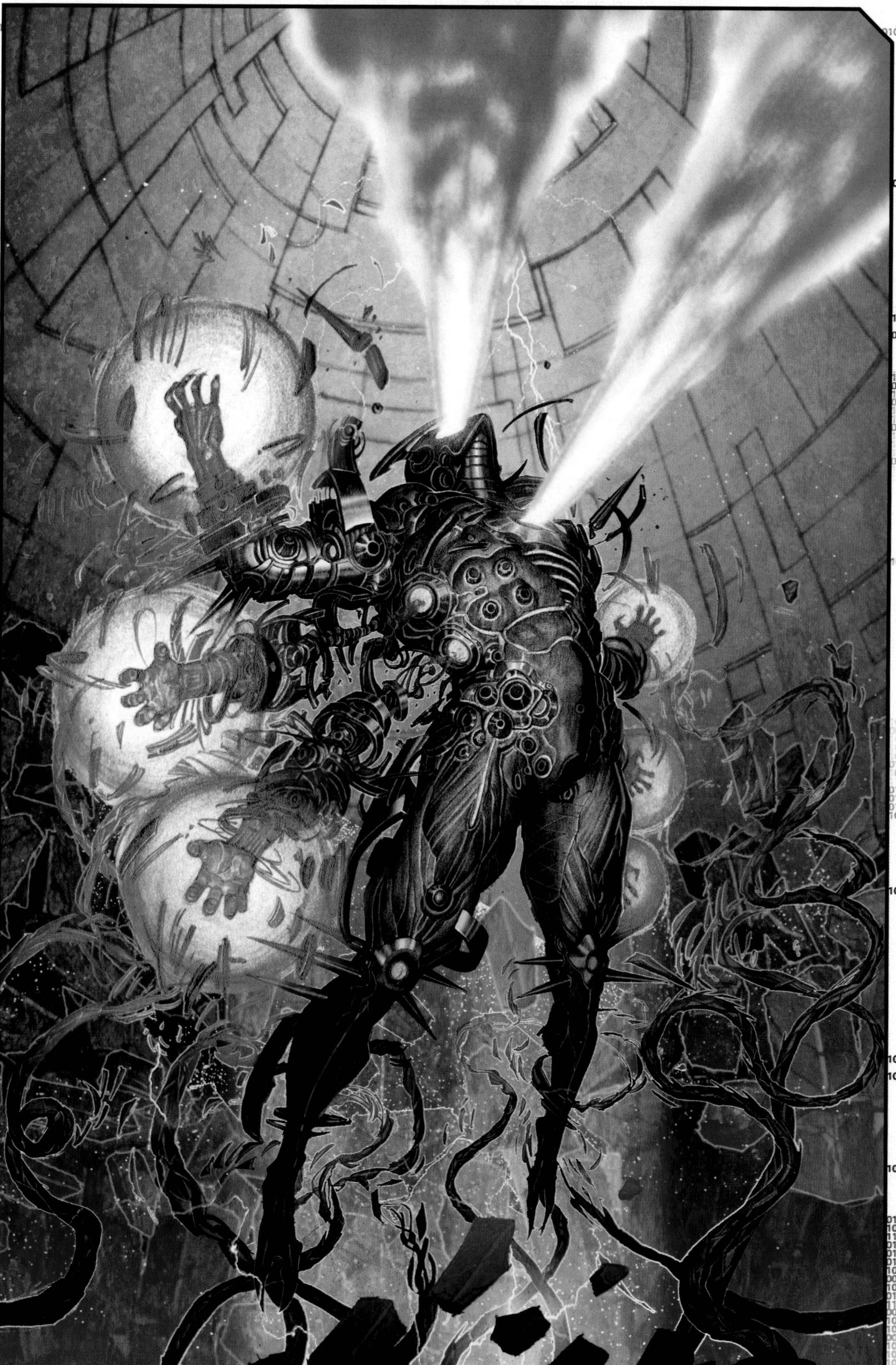

AGE OF ULTRON #8 VARIANT BY ROCK-HE KIM

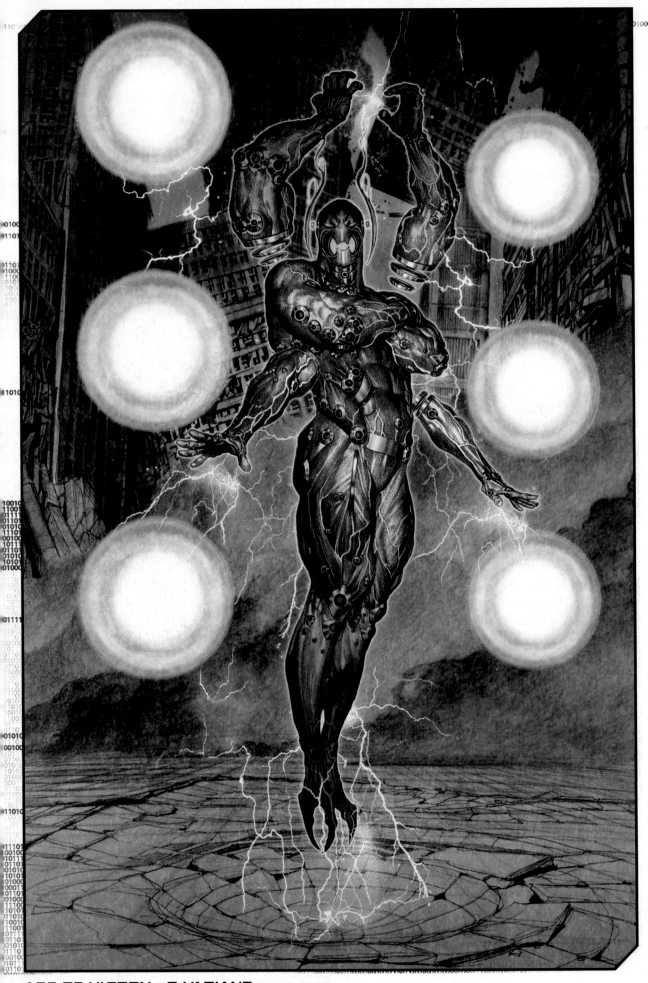

AGE OF ULTRON #9 VARIANT BY ROCK-HE KIM

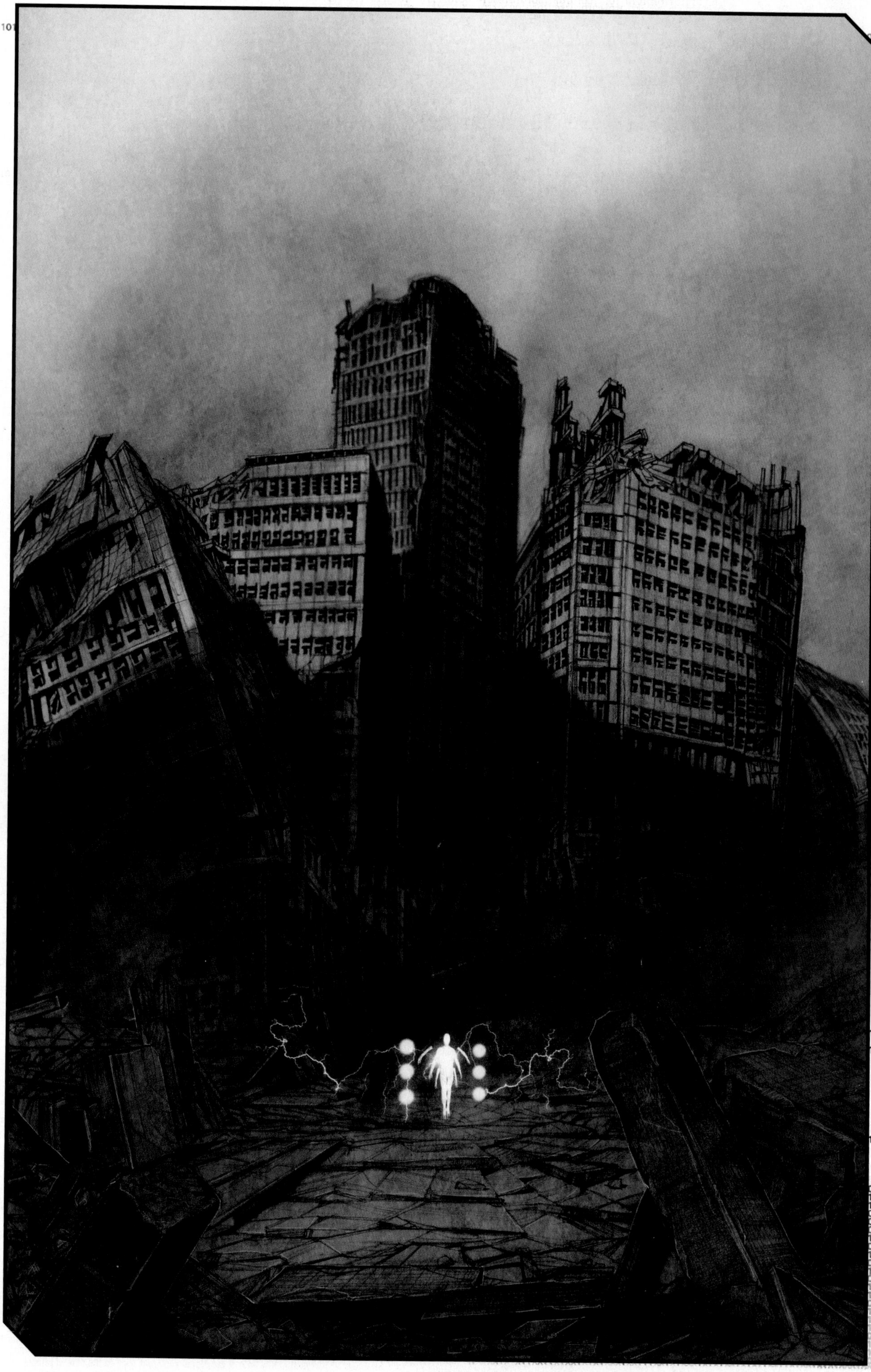

AGE OF ULTRON #10 VARIANT BY ROCK-HE KIM

TO ACCESS THE FREE *MARVEL AUGMENTED REALITY APP*
THAT ENHANCES AND CHANGES THE WAY YOU EXPERIENCE COMICS:

1. Download the app for free via
marvel.com/ARapp

2. Launch the app on your camera-enabled Apple iOS® or Android™ device*

3. Hold your mobile device's camera over any cover or panel with the **AR** graphic.

4. Sit back and see the future of comics in action!

*Available on most camera-enabled Apple iOS® and Android™ devices. Content subject to change and availability.